THE LIBRARY

OF

LITERARY CRITICISM

OF

ENGLISH AND AMERICAN AUTHORS

VOLUME V
1825 - 1854

EDITED BY CHARLES WELLS MOULTON
ASSISTED BY A CORPS OF ABLE CONTRIBUTORS

GLOUCESTER, MASS.
PETER SMITH
1959

REPRINTED 1959
BY
PETER SMITH

To

Charles Warren Stoddard, L. H. D.

INTRODUCTION.

KNOWLEDGE IS POWER

When you know a thing, to hold that you know it; and when you do not know a thing, to allow that you do not know it; this is knowledge.—CONFUCIUS, *Analects*, *bk*. i, *ch*. iv.

Knowledge comes
Of learning well retain'd, unfruitful else.
—DANTE ALIGHIERI, 1307? *Vision of Paradise, Canto* v, l. 41.

An humble knowledge of thyself is a surer way to God than a deep search after knowledge.—À KEMPIS, THOMAS, 1424? *Imitation of Christ, bk*. i, *ch*. iii.

It is only knowledge, which worne with yeares waxeth young, and when all things are cut away with the Cicle of Time, knowledge flourisheth so high that Time cannot reach it.—LYLY, JOHN, 1579, *The Anatomy of Wit, of the Education of Youth, Euphues*.

My mind, aspire to higher things:
Grow rich in that which never taketh rust.
—SIDNEY, SIR PHILIP, 1586? *Sonnet, Leave me, O Love!*

He hath never fed of the dainties that are bred in a book; he hath not eat paper, as it were; he hath not drunk ink: his intellect is not replenished; he is only an animal, only sensible in the duller parts.—SHAKESPEARE, WILLIAM, 1588–98, *Love's Labour's Lost, act* iv, *sc*. 2.

By knowledge we do learn ourselves to know
And what to man, and what to God we owe.
—SPENSER, EDMUND, 1591, *The Tears of the Muses*.

Read not to contradict and confute, nor to believe and take for granted, nor to find talk and discourse, but to weigh and consider. Some books are to be tasted, others to be swallowed, and some few to be chewed and digested; that is, some books are to be read only in parts; others to be read, but not curiously; and some few to be read wholly, and with diligence and attention.—BACON, FRANCIS LORD, 1597, *Of Studies, Essays*.

O blessed Letters! that combine in one
All ages past, and make one live with all:
By you we do confer with who are gone,
And the Dead-living unto council call!
By you the unborn shall have communion
Of what we feel and what doth us befall.
—DANIEL, SAMUEL, 1599, *Musophilus*.

Since knowledge is but sorrow's spy,
It is not safe to know.
—DAVENANT, SIR WILLIAM, 1630, *The Just Italian, Act* v, *sc*. 1.

All foreign wisdom doth amount to this,
To take all that is given, whether wealth,
Or love, or language; nothing comes amiss:
A good digestion turneth all to health.
—HERBERT, GEORGE, 1633, *Church Porch, The Temple, st*. 60.

Beside, he was a shrewd Philosopher,
And had read ev'ry text and gloss over;
Whate'er the crabbed'st author hath,
He understood b' implicit faith.
—BUTLER, SAMUEL, 1663, *Hudibras, pt*. i, *Canto* i, l. 127.

Who reads
Incessantly, and to his reading brings not
A spirit and judgment equal or superior,
(And what he brings what need he elsewhere seek?)
Uncertain and unsettled still remains,
Deep versed in books and shallow in himself,
Crude or intoxicate, collecting toys
And trifles for choice matters, worth a sponge,
As children gathering pebbles on the shore.
—MILTON, JOHN, 1671, *Paradise Regained, bk*. iv, l. 322.

Read Homer once, and you can read no more;
For all books else appear so mean, so poor;
Verse will seem prose; but still persist to read,
And Homer will be all the books you need.
—SHEFFIELD, JOHN, 1682, *Essay on Poetry*.

The improvement of the understanding is for two ends: first, for our own increase of knowledge; secondly, to enable us to deliver and make out that knowledge to others. — LOCKE, JOHN, 1704? *Some Thoughts Concerning Reading and Study.*

Whoe'er excels in what we prize,
Appears a hero in our eyes;
Each girl when pleased with what is taught,
Will have the teacher in her thought,
. . . .
A blockhead with melodious voice,
In boarding-schools may have his choice.
—SWIFT, JONATHAN, 1713, *Cadenus and Vanessa*, l. 733.

Knowledge is, indeed, that which, next to virtue, truly and essentially raises one man above another.—ADDISON, JOSEPH, 1713, *The Guardian, No.* iii.

To master John, the English maid
A horn-book gives of gingerbread;
And, that the child may learn the better,
As he can name, he eats the letter.
Proceeding thus with vast delight,
He spells and gnaws from left to right.
—PRIOR, MATTHEW, 1718, *Alma, Canto* ii, l. 463.

Delightful task! to rear the tender thought,
To teach the young idea how to shoot,
To pour the fresh instruction o'er the mind,
To breathe the enliv'ning spirit, and to fix
The generous purpose in the glowing breast.
—THOMSON, JAMES, 1728, *Spring, Seasons*, l. 1156.

'Tis greatly wise to talk with our past hours;
And ask them what report they bore to heaven;
And how they might have borne more welcome news.
—YOUNG, EDWARD, 1742, *Night Thoughts, Night* ii, l. 376.

Ah, happy hills! ah, pleasing shade!
Ah! fields belov'd in vain!
Where once my careless childhood stray'd,
A stranger yet to pain!
I feel the gales that from ye blow,
A momentary bliss bestow,
As waving fresh their gladsome wing,
My weary soul they seem to soothe,
And, redolent of joy and youth,
To breathe a second spring.
—GRAY, THOMAS, 1747, *Ode on a distant prospect of Eton College, st.* 2.

Wisdom, slow product of laborious years,
The only fruit that life's cold winter bears.
Thy sacred seeds in vain in youth we lay,
By the fierce storm of passion torn away;
Should some remain in a rich, gen'rous soil,
They long lie hid, and must be rais'd with toil;
Faintly they struggle with inclement skies,
No sooner born than the poor planter dies.
—MONTAGU, LADY MARY WORTLEY, 1755, *Written at Louvere.*

The first time I read an excellent book, it is to me just as if I had gained a new friend: when I read over a book I have perused before, it resembles the meeting with an old one.—GOLDSMITH, OLIVER, 1762, *A Citizen of the World, Letter* lxxxiii.

A desire of knowledge is the natural feeling of mankind; and every human being whose mind is not debauched, will be willing to give all that he has to get knowledge. — JOHNSON, SAMUEL, 1763, *Life by Boswell, July* 30.

The philosopher is the lover of wisdom and truth; to be a sage, is to avoid the senseless and the depraved. The philosopher therefore should live only among philosophers.—VOLTAIRE, FRANÇOIS MARIE AROUET, 1778? *A Philosophical Dictionary, sec.* 5.

Come Child of Care! to make thy soul serene,
Approach the treasures of this tranquil scene;
Survey the dome, and, as the doors unfold,
The soul's best cure, in all her cares, behold!
Where mental wealth the poor in thought may find,
And mental physic the diseased in mind;
See here the balms that passion's wounds assuage;
See coolers here, that damp the fire of rage;
Here alteratives, by slow degrees control
The chronic habits of the sickly soul;
And round the heart, and o'er the aching head,
Mild opiates here their sober influence shed.
Now bid thy soul man's busy scenes exclude,
And view composed this silent multitude:—
Silent they are—but though deprived of sound,
Here all the living languages abound;
Here all that live no more; preserved they lie,
In tombs that open to the curious eye.
—CRABBE, GEORGE, 1781, *The Library.*

Knowledge and Wisdom, far from being one,
Have oft-times no connexion. Knowledge dwells
In heads replete with thoughts of other men;
Wisdom in minds attentive to their own.
—COWPER, WILLIAM, 1785, *The Task, bk.* vi, l. 88.

Flattery's the turnpike road to Fortune's door—
Truth is a narrow lane, all full of quags
Leading to broken heads, abuse, and rags,
And workhouses,—sad refuge for the poor!—
Flattery's a Mountebank so spruce—gets riches;
Truth, a plain Simon Pure, a Quaker Preacher,
A Moral Mender, a disgusting Teacher,
That never got a sixpence by her Speeches!
—WOLCOT, JOHN (PETER PINDAR), 1785, *Lyric Odes*, ix.

Some will only read old books, as if there were no valuable truths to be discovered in modern publications: while others will only read new books, as if some valuable truths are not among the old. Some will not read a book, because they are acquainted with the author; by which the reader may be more injured than the author: others not only read the book, but would also read the man; by which the most ingenius author may be injured by the most impertinent reader.—DISRAELI, ISAAC, 1796–1818, *On Reading, Literary Character of Men of Genius.*

Deep subtle wits,
In truth, are master spirits in the world,
The brave man's courage, and the student's lore,
Are but as tools his secret ends to work,
Who hath the skill to use them.
—BAILLIE, JOANNA, 1802, *Basil, Act* ii, *sc.* 3.

Divine Philosophy! by whose pure light
We first distinguish, then pursue the right;
Thy power the breast from every error frees,
And weeds out all its vices by degrees.
— GIFFORD, WILLIAM, 1803, *Juvenal, Satire* xiii, l. 254.

What does Philosophy impart to man
But undiscover'd wonders?—Let her soar
Even to her proudest heights—to where she caught
The soul of Newton and of Socrates,
She but extends the scope of wild amaze
And admiration.
—WHITE, HENRY KIRKE, 1804, *Time*, l. 307.

Only the refined and delicate pleasures that spring from research and education can build up barriers between different ranks.—STAËL, MADAME DE, 1805, *Corinne, bk.* ix, *ch.* i.

Knowledge is not happiness, and science
But an exchange of ignorance for that
Which is another kind of ignorance.
—BYRON, LORD, 1817, *Manfred, Act* ii, *sc.* 4.

What a place to be in is an old library. It seems as though all the souls of all the writers, that have bequeathed their labours to these Bodleians, were reposing here, as in some dormitory, or middle state. I do not want to handle, to profane the leaves, their winding-sheets. I could as soon dislodge a shade. I seem to inhale learning, walking amid their foliage, and the odour of their old moth-scented coverings is fragrant as the first bloom of those sciential apples which grew amid the happy orchard.—LAMB, CHARLES, 1820, *Oxford in the Vacation, Essays of Elia.*

We enter our studies, and enjoy a society which we alone can bring together. We raise no jealousy by conversing with one in preference to another; we give no offence to the most illustrious by questioning him as long as we will, and leaving him as abruptly. Diversity of opinion raises no tumult in our presence: each interlocutor stands before us, speaks or is silent, and we adjourn or decide the business at our leisure.—LANDOR, WALTER SAVAGE, 1824, *Milton and Andrew Marvell, Imaginary Conversations.*

One truth discovered is immortal, and entitles its author to be so: for, like a new substance in nature, it cannot be destroyed. —HAZLITT, WILLIAM, 1825, *Jeremy Bentham, The Spirit of the Age.*

The first step to self-knowledge is self-distrust. Nor can we attain to any kind of knowledge, except by a like process.—HARE, J. C. AND A. W., 1827–48, *Guesses at Truth.*

No thought which ever stirred
A human breast should be untold.
—BROWNING, ROBERT, 1835, *Paracelsus, sc.* 2.

Truth, crushed to earth, shall rise again;
Th' eternal years of God are hers;
But Error, wounded, writhes in pain,
And dies among his worshippers.

—BRYANT, WILLIAM CULLEN, 1837, *The Battlefield.*

The true purpose of education is to cherish and unfold the seed of immortality already sown within us; to develop, to their fullest extent, the capacities of every kind with which the God who made us has endowed us.—JAMESON, ANNA BROWNELL, 1838, *Education, Winter Studies and Summer Rambles.*

All rests with those who read. A work or thought
Is what each makes it to himself, and may
Be full of great dark meanings, like the sea,
With shoals of life rushing.

—BAILEY, PHILIP JAMES, 1839, *Festus, Proem,* l. 307.

Where should the scholar live? In solitude, or in society? in the green stillness of the country, where he can hear the heart of Nature beat, or in the dark gray town? . . . O, they do greatly err who think that the stars are all the poetry which cities have; and therefore that the poet's only dwelling should be in sylvan solitudes, under the green roof of trees.—LONGFELLOW, HENRY WADSWORTH, 1839, *Hyperion, bk.* i, *ch.* viii.

Because the Few with signal virtue crowned,
The heights and pinnacles of human mind,
Sadder and wearier than the rest are found,
Wish not thy Soul less wise or less refined.
True that the small delights of every day
Cheer and distract the pilgrim are not theirs;
True that, though free from Passion's lawless sway,
A loftier being brings severer cares.
Yet have they special pleasures, even mirth,
By those undreamed of who have only trod
Life's valley smooth; and if the rolling earth
To their nice ear have made a painful tone,
They know, that Man does not live by Joy alone,
But by the presence of the power of God.

—MILNES, RICHARD MONCKTON, 1840, (LORD HOUGHTON), *Books.*

Knowledge is the only fountain, both of the love and the principles of human liberty.—WEBSTER, DANIEL, 1843, *Address Delivered on Bunker Hill, June* 17.

Knowledge by suffering entereth;
And Life is perfected by Death!

—BROWNING, ELIZABETH BARRETT, 1844, *A Vision of Poets, st.* 37.

Many a genius has been slow of growth. Oaks that flourish for a thousand years do not spring up into beauty like a reed.—LEWES, GEORGE HENRY, 1847, *The Spanish Drama, ch.* ii.

What a wonderful,—what an almost magical boon, a writer of great genius confers upon us, when we read him intelligently. As he proceeds from point to point in his argument or narrative, we seem to be taken up by him, and carried from hill-top to hill-top, where, through an atmosphere of light, we survey a glorious region of thought, looking freely, far and wide, above and below, and gazing in admiration upon all the beauty and grandeur of the scene.—MANN, HORACE, 1848, *Lectures on Education, Lecture* vi.

Who loves not Knowledge? Who shall rail
Against her beauty? May she mix
With men and prosper! Who shall fix
Her pillars? Let her work prevail.

—TENNYSON, ALFRED LORD, 1850, *In Memoriam, pt.* cxiv.

Knowledge alone is the being of nature,
Giving a soul to her manifold features,
Lighting through paths of the primitive darkness,
The footsteps of Truth and the vision of Song.

—TAYLOR, BAYARD, 1852, *Kilimandjaro, st.* 2.

I lock upon a library as a kind of mental chemist's shop, filled with the crystals of all forms and hues which have come from the union of individual thought with local circumstances or universal principles.—HOLMES, OLIVER WENDELL, 1860, *The Professor at the Breakfast Table, ch.* i.

The literature of any age is but the mirror of its prevalent tendencies.—PUNSHON, WILLIAM MORLEY, 1860, *Bunyan, Lectures and Sermons, p.* 123.

His classical reading is great: he can quote
Horace, Juvenal, Ovid, and Martial by
rote.
He has read Metaphysics . . . Spinoza
and Kant;
And Theology too: I have heard him descant
Upon Basil and Jerome. Antiquities, art,
He is fond of. He knows the old masters by
heart,
And his taste is refined.

—LYTTON, EDWARD ROBERT BULWER (OWEN MEREDITH), 1860, *Lucile, Canto* ii, *pt.* iv.

Letters are the fetters of language, even if they are its golden fetters. . . . Literature, therefore, whatever the etymology of the term may seem to indicate, has no essential connection with letters. And its connection even with language, which is essential, is still no more than such a connection as is created by the fact that literature consists necessarily of words. It is of thought and emotion transformed into or manifested in language that the fabric of literature is woven. But literature is not, like language, a necessary product of our humanity. Man has been nowhere found without a language: there have been and are many nations and races without a literature. A langauge is to a people a necessary of existence; a literature is only a luxury. Hence it sometimes happens that the origin of a nation's literature, and the influences which have inspired and moulded it, have been more or less distinct from the sources whence the language has taken its beginning and the inner operating spirit or external circumstances which have modified its shape and character. The literature will generally be acted upon by the language, and the language by the literature; but each may have also had fountains of its own at which the other has not drunk.—CRAIK, GEORGE L., 1861, *A Compendious History of English Literature and of the English Language, vol.* I, *pp.* 21, 22.

In science, read by preference, the newest works; in literature, the oldest. The classic literature is always modern.—LYTTON, EDWARD GEORGE BULWER LORD, 1863, *Hints on Mental Culture, Caxtoniana.*

Knowledge ordained to live! although the
fate
Of much that went before it was—to die,
And be called ignorance by such as wait
Till the next drift comes by.
O marvellous credulity of man!
If God indeed kept secret, couldst thou
know
Or follow up the mighty Artisan
Unless He willed it so?

—INGELOW, JEAN, 1863, *Honors, pt.* ii.

A library may be regarded as the solemn chamber in which a man may take counsel with all that have been wise and great and good and glorious amongst the men that have gone before him.—DAWSON, GEORGE, 1866, *Address on Opening the Birmingham Free Library, Oct.* 26.

The best that we can do for one another is to exchange our thoughts freely; and that, after all, is but little.—FROUDE, JAMES ANTHONY, 1867, *Education, Short Studies on Great Subjects.*

Two angels guide
The path of man, both aged and yet young,
As angels are, ripening through endless
years.
On one he leans; some call her Memory,
And some, Tradition; and her voice is sweet,
With deep mysterious accords: the other,
Floating above, holds down a lamp which
streams
A light divine and searching on the earth,
Compelling eyes and footsteps. Memory
yields,
Yet clings with loving check, and shines
anew
Reflecting all the rays of that bright lamp
Our angel Reason holds. We had not walked
But for Tradition; we walk evermore
To higher paths, by brightening Reason's
lamp.

—ELIOT, GEORGE, 1868, *The Spanish Gypsy, bk.* ii.

Truth is one;
And, in all lands beneath the sun,
Whoso hath eyes to see may see
The tokens of its unity.

—WHITTIER, JOHN GREENLEAF, 1870, *Miriam.*

As diamond cuts diamond, and one hone smooths a second, all the parts of intellect are whetstones to each other; and genius, which is but the result of their mutual sharpening is character too.—BARTOL, CYRUS AUGUSTUS, 1872, *Individualism, Radical Problems.*

That which we know is sweeter yet.
  Do we not love the near Earth more
Than the far Heaven? Does not Regret
  Walk with us, always, from the door
That shuts behind us, though we leave
  Not much to make us grieve?

—PIATT, SARAH M. B., 1874, *A Voyage to the Fortunate Isles.*

The literature of a nation is the embodiment of that which is most artistic and complete in its intellectual, literary life. There are many practical products of composition, records, chronicles, works of instruction, of science, and of reference, which contain the material of knowledge, the raw staple of art, but are not literature. These change with succeeding years, and reappear in altered and enlarged forms, as the progress of events and investigation determine. Many books, in each generation, are the seed which is returned to the soil as the condition of farther increase. No work is a part of national literature, in its more specific sense, till it is possessed of such merit of execution, aside from mere matter, or it were better to say in conjunction with matter, as to give it permanent value. Thought alone, the substance of wisdom merely, cannot save a work to literature. It may be rather the occasion of its speedy disappearance. More skilful laborers will swarm around the sweet morsel, let fall as it were in the highway of thought, and each bear off a portion of the unidentified product. It is some completeness, symmetry, excellence of form that gives identity, ownership to a product; and a permanent interest in its careful, exact preservation.—BASCOM, JOHN, 1874, *Philosophy of English Literature, p.* 1.

As you grow ready for it, somewhere or other you will find what is needful for you in a book or a friend, or, best of all, in your own thoughts—the eternal thought speaking in your thought. — MACDONALD, GEORGE, 1877, *The Marquis of Lossie, ch.* xlii.

Surely at last, far off, sometime, somewhere,
The veil would lift for his deep-searching
  eyes,
The road would open for his painful feet,
That should be won for which he lost the
  world,
And Death might find him conqueror of
  death.

—ARNOLD, SIR EDWIN, 1879, *Light of Asia, bk.* iv, l. 343.

To be able to write! Throughout Mr. Ogilvy's life, save when he was about one and twenty, this had seemed the great thing, and he ever approached the thought reverently, as if it were a maid of more than mortal purity. And it is, and because he knew this she let him see her face, which shall ever be hidden from those who look not for the soul, and to help him nearer to her came assistance in strange guise, the loss of loved ones, dolour unutterable. . . . Once or twice in a long life he touched her fingers, and a heavenly spark was lit, for he had risen higher than himself, and that is literature. —BARRIE, J. M., 1896, *Sentimental Tommy, chap.* xxvi.

Literature, especially poetry, may be appreciated simply as art, and without any reference to the human society in which it is produced. But in that case much of its significance and interest is lost, for everything that is written is addressed to contemporaries, and the author himself, if not entirely the product of social conditions, is at least molded by them. The historic method of study is the true one, unless in a blind study of surroundings the fact that literary productions are primarily creations of the art impulse is entirely lost sight of, in which case, indeed, the study of literature might be reduced to barren classifications of facts.—JOHNSON, CHARLES F., 1900, *Outline History of English and American Literature, p.* 5.

CONTENTS.

		PAGE.
ADAMS, HANNAH,	1755—1832	124
ADAMS, JOHN,	1735—1826	50
ADAMS, JOHN QUINCY,	1767—1848	514
ADAMS, SARAH FLOWER,	1805—1848	529
AGUILAR, GRACE,	1816—1847	504
ALISON, ARCHIBALD,	1757—1839	341
ALLSTON, WASHINGTON,	1779—1843	418
ARNOLD, THOMAS,	1795—1842	376
AUDUBON, JOHN JAMES,	1780—1851	695
BAILLIE, JOANNA,	1762—1851	689
BANIM, JOHN,	1798—1842	389
BARBAULD, ANNA LÆTITIA,	1743—1825	22
BARHAM, RICHARD HARRIS,	1788—1845	474
BARNARD, LADY ANNE,	1750—1825	28
BARTON, BERNARD,	1784—1849	594
BAYLY, THOMAS HAYNES,	1797—1839	339
BECKFORD, WILLIAM,	1759—1844	446
BEDDOES, THOMAS LOVELL,	1803—1849	584
BENTHAM, JEREMY,	1748—1832	162
BLAKE, WILLIAM,	1757—1827	56
Personal, 56; Art, 58; Poetry, 59; General, 63		
BLANCHARD, SAMUEL LAMAN,	1804—1845	480
BLESSINGTON, MARGUERITE COUNTESS OF,	1789—1849	589
BOWLES, WILLIAM LISLE,	1762—1850	658
BRAINARD, JOHN GARDINER CALKINS,	1796—1828	84
BRONTË, ANNE,	1820—1849	599
BRONTË, EMILY,	1818—1848	521
BRYDGES, SIR SAMUEL EGERTON,	1762—1837	320
BURNEY, FRANCES,	1752—1840	343
Personal, 343; Evelina, 345; Camilla, 348; Cecilia, 348; The Wanderer, 349; Diary and Letters, 349; General, 349		
CALHOUN, JOHN CALDWELL,	1782—1850	674
CAMPBELL, THOMAS,	1777—1844	433
Personal, 434; Pleasures of Hope, 438; Gertrude of Wyoming, 439; Specimens of the British Poets 440; Theodric, 441; General, 441		

PAGE.

CANNING, GEORGE, ... 1770—1827 64
CARY, HENRY FRANCIS, ... 1772—1844 455
CHALMERS, GEORGE, ... 1742—1825 29
CHALMERS, THOMAS, ... 1780—1847 489
CHANNING, WILLIAM ELLERY, ... 1780—1842 365
CLARKE, ADAM, ... 1762?—1832 184
CLAY, HENRY, ... 1777—1852 730
COBBETT, WILLIAM, ... 1762—1835 269
COLERIDGE, HARTLEY, ... 1796—1849 572
COLERIDGE, SAMUEL TAYLOR, . . . 1772—1834 205
Personal, ... 206 Christabel, ... 219 Aids to Reflection, . . 221
Poetry, ... 214 Kubla Khan, ... 220 General, ... 221
The Ancient Mariner, 217
COLERIDGE, SARA, ... 1802—1852 733
COLMAN, GEORGE (THE YOUNGER), . . 1762—1836 315
COOPER, JAMES FENIMORE, ... 1789—1851 679
CRABBE, GEORGE, ... 1754—1832 170
CUNNINGHAM, ALLAN, ... 1784—1842 382
D ARBLAY, MADAME, ... 1752—1840 343
DAVIDSON, LUCRETIA MARIA, . . . 1808—1825 26
DAVY, SIR HUMPHRY, ... 1778—1829 90
DIBDIN, THOMAS FROGNALL, ... 1776—1847 506
DISRAELI, ISAAC, ... 1766—1848 510
EDGEWORTH, MARIA, ... 1767—1849 561
Personal, ... 561 Belinda, ... 565 Helen, ... 566
Practical Education, . 564 Tales of Fashionable Life, . 566 General, ... 567
Castle Rackrent, . . 565
ELLIOTT, EBENEZER, ... 1781—1849 579
FERRIER, SUSAN EDMONSTONE, . . . 1782—1854 763
FOSTER, JOHN, ... 1770—1843 424
FRENEAU, PHILIP, ... 1752—1832 186
FRERE, JOHN HOOKHAM, ... 1769—1846 485
FULLER, SARAH MARGARET, ... 1810—1850 663
GALT, JOHN, ... 1779—1839 334
GIFFORD, WILLIAM, ... 1756—1826 31
GODWIN, WILLIAM, ... 1756—1836 292
Personal, ... 292 Caleb Williams, ... 298 Fleetwood, ... 302
Enquiry Concerning Political Justice, ... 296 St. Leon, ... 300 Mandeville, ... 302
Life of Geoffrey Chaucer, . 301 General, ... 303
GRANT, ANNE, ... 1755—1838 328
GRIFFIN, GERALD, ... 1803—1840 351
HALL, BASIL, ... 1788—1844 456
HALL, ROBERT, ... 1764—1831 108
HALLAM, ARTHUR HENRY, ... 1811—1833 197
HAMILTON, THOMAS, ... 1789—1842 394

PAGE.

HAZLITT, WILLIAM, ... 1778—1830 97
Personal, ... 97 Liber Amoris, ... 101 General, ... 102

HEBER, REGINALD, ... 1783—1826 36
HEMANS, FELICIA DOROTHEA, . . . 1793—1835 254
HILLHOUSE, JAMES ABRAHAM, . . . 1789—1841 363
HOGG, JAMES, ... 1770—1835 262
HONE, WILLIAM, ... 1780—1842 391
HOOD, THOMAS, ... 1799—1845 458
HOOK, THEODORE EDWARD, ... 1788—1841 355
IRELAND, WILLIAM HENRY, ... 1777—1835 289
IRVING, EDWARD, ... 1792—1834 245
JAY, JOHN, ... 1745—1829 94
JEFFERSON, THOMAS, ... 1743—1826 40
Personal, ... 40 Declaration of Independence, 47 General, ... 48
Statesman, ... 45

JEFFREY, FRANCIS LORD, ... 1773—1850 647
KENT, JAMES, ... 1763—1847 500
KNOX, WILLIAM, ... 1789—1825 30
LAMB, LADY CAROLINE, ... 1785—1828 81
LAMB, CHARLES, ... 1775—1834 228
Personal, ... 229 Rosamund Gray, ... 238 General, ... 239
Poetry, ... 236 Letters, ... 238

LAMB, MARY ANN, ... 1764—1847 507
LANDON, LETITIA ELIZABETH, . . . 1802—1838 322
LESLIE, SIR JOHN, ... 1766—1832 189
LOCKHART, JOHN GIBSON, ... 1794—1854 753
LYTE, HENRY FRANCIS, ... 1793—1847 499
MACKENZIE, HENRY, ... 1745—1831 112
MACKINTOSH, SIR JAMES, ... 1765—1832 177
MACLEAN, MRS. GEORGE, ... 1802—1838 322
MADISON, JAMES, ... 1751—1836 311
MAGINN, WILLIAM, ... 1793—1842 385
MALTHUS, THOMAS ROBERT, ... 1765—1834 249
MANGAN, JAMES CLARENCE, ... 1803—1849 600
MARRYAT, FREDERICK, ... 1792—1848 530
MARSHALL, JOHN, ... 1755—1835 281
MATHIAS, THOMAS JAMES, ... 1754?—1835 287
MILL, JAMES, ... 1773—1836 304
MITFORD, WILLIAM, ... 1744—1827 69
MOIR, DAVID MACBETH, ... 1798—1851 704
MONROE, JAMES, ... 1758—1831 122
MONTGOMERY, JAMES. . . . . 1771—1854 765
MOORE, THOMAS, ... 1779—1852 705

		Page.
More, Hannah,	1745—1833	190
Motherwell, William,	1797—1835	276
Murray, Lindley,	1745—1826	54
Nairne, Baroness,	1766—1845	476
North, Christopher,	1785—1854	744
O'Keeffe, John,	1747—1833	196
Oliphant, Carolina,	1766—1845	476
Opie, Amelia,	1769—1853	741
Osgood, Frances Sargent,	1812—1850	677
Ossoli, Marchioness,	1810—1850	663
Parr, Samuel,	1747—1825	17
Payne, John Howard,	1792—1852	735
Pinkney, Edward Coate,	1802—1828	85
Poe, Edgar Allan,	1809—1849	534

Personal, 535; Poetry, 546; The Bells, 550; Ulalume, 550; The Raven, 551; Tales, 552; Criticisms, 554; General, 556

Pollok, Robert,	1798—1827	72
Porter, Jane,	1776—1850	673
Praed, Winthrop Mackworth,	1802—1839	330
Robertson, Frederick William,	1816—1853	737
Roscoe, William,	1753—1831	116
Sadler, Michael Thomas,	1780—1835	286
Scott, Michael,	1789—1835	278
Scott, Sir Walter,	1771—1832	125

Personal, 126; Poetry, 135; Lay of the Last Minstrel, 138; Marmion, 139; Lady of the Lake, 140; Novels, 141; Waverley, 147; Guy Mannering, 149; The Antiquary, 149; Old Mortality, 149; Rob Roy, 150; Heart of Mid-Lothian, 151; The Bride of Lammermoor, 151; Ivanhoe, 153; Kenilworth, 154; The Pirate, 154; Fortunes of Nigel, 155; St. Ronan's Well, 156; Life of Napoleon Bonaparte, 156; Fair Maid of Perth, 157; General, 157

Shelley, Mary Wollstonecraft,	1797—1851	700
Smith, Horace,	1779—1849	597
Smith, James,	1775—1839	337
Smith, Sydney,	1771—1845	466
Sotheby, William,	1757—1833	204
Southey, Caroline Anne Bowles,	1787—1854	762
Southey, Robert,	1774—1843	395

Personal, 396; Poems, 403; Joan of Arc, 406; Thalaba the Destroyer, 407; Madoc, 407; The Curse of Kehama, 408; Roderick, 409; Wat Tyler, 409; A Vision of Judgment, 411; Life of Nelson, 411; Life of John Wesley, 412; History of the Peninsular War, 412; The Doctor, 413; Life of Cowper, 413; General, 414

Sterling, John,	1806—1844	451

PAGE.

STEWART, DUGALD, ... 1753—1828 76
Personal, ... 76 — Philosophical Essays, . 77 — First Preliminary Dissertation, ... 78 — General, ... 79

STORY, JOSEPH, ... 1779—1845 482

TALFOURD, SIR THOMAS NOON, . . . 1795—1854 759

TAYLOR, THOMAS, ... 1758—1835 290

TAYLOR, WILLIAM, ... 1765—1836 318

TENNANT, WILLIAM, ... 1784—1848 527

TRUMBULL, JOHN, ... 1750—1831 119

TURNER, SHARON, ... 1768—1847 498

WARE, HENRY, JR., ... 1794—1843 431

WEBSTER, DANIEL, ... 1782—1852 719

WEBSTER, NOAH, ... 1758—1843 427

WHITE, JOSEPH BLANCO, ... 1775—1841 359

WILBERFORCE, WILLIAM, ... 1759—1833 199

WILDE, RICHARD HENRY, ... 1789—1847 503

WILLIAMS, HELEN MARIA, ... 1762—1827 74

WILSON, JOHN, ... 1785—1854 744

WORDSWORTH, WILLIAM, ... 1770—1850 605
Personal, ... 605 — Descriptive Sketches in Verse, ... 617 — The Borderers . . . 618 — Lyrical Ballads, ... 618 — Peter Bell, ... 620 — Intimations of Immortality, 620 — The White Doe of Rylstone, 621 — The Excursion, . . . 622 — The Prelude, ... 625 — Sonnets, ... 626 — General, ... 628

YOUNG, THOMAS, ... 1773—1829 86

ENGRAVINGS.

PAGE.

ADAMS, JOHN, ... 41
Engraving by J. B. Longacre, Painting by B. Otis, after Original by Gilbert Stuart.

ADAMS, JOHN QUINCY, ... 719
Engraving by J. W. Paradise, Painting by A. B. Durand.

ARNOLD, THOMAS, ... 377
From Steel Engraving.

BECKFORD, WILLIAM, ... 447
Engraving by S. Freeman from Original by P. Savage.

BLAKE, WILLIAM, ... 293
Engraving by A. L. Dick, from a Portrait by William Blake.

CAMPBELL, THOMAS, ... 433
Engraving by J. F. E. Proudhomme, Portrait by Sir Thomas Lawrence, P. R. A.

CHALMERS, THOMAS, ... 377
Engraving by W. G. Jackman, from a daguerreotype by Claudets.

COLERIDGE, SAMUEL TAYLOR, ... 205
From the Original Painting by Peter Vandyke, now in the National Portrait Gallery, London.

COOPER, JAMES FENIMORE, ... 679
Engraving by J. C. Buttre.

DISRAELI, ISAAC, ... 447
Engraving by G. Cook, from the Original by Denning.

EDGEWORTH, MARIA, ... 191
From the Original Painting by Chappel.

FULLER, SARAH MARGARET, ... 535
Engraving by H. B. Hall, Jr.

GODWIN, WILLIAM, ... 293
From the Original Painting by Northcote.

HALL, ROBERT, ... 17
Engraving by W. Finden, Painting by N. C. Branwhite.

HEMANS, FELICIA DOROTHEA, ... 255
Engraving by Edward Smith, from a Miniature by Edward Robertson.

HOOD, THOMAS, ... 433
From Steel Engraving.

JEFFERSON, THOMAS, ... 41
Engraving by T. Johnson, Painting by Gilbert Stuart.

JEFFREY, FRANCIS, ... 647
Engraving by Sartain, from the Original by G. Hayter.

LAMB, CHARLES, ... 205
From "In the Footprints of Charles Lamb."

LANDON, LETITIA ELIZABETH, ... 255
Engraving by J. Thomson, Painting by D. Maclise.

MARRYAT, FREDERICK, ... 679
Engraving by C. Cook, Drawing by William Behnes.

MOORE, THOMAS, ... 125
Engraving from a Photogravure.

MORE, HANNAH, ... 191
Engraving by J. C. Buttrie, Painting by John Opie, R. A.

PARR, SAMUEL, ... 17
Engraving by W. Skelton, Painting by George Dawe.

POE, EDGAR ALLAN, ... 535
Engraving by F. Halpin.

SCOTT, SIR WALTER, ... 125
From the Original Painting by Sir Thomas Lawrence, P. R. A.

SOUTHEY, ROBERT, ... 395
Engraving by H. Heath, Portrait by Lane.

WEBSTER, DANIEL, ... 719
From a Portrait by Healy.

WILBERFORCE, WILLIAM, ... 87
From Painting by Sir Thomas Lawrence, P. R. A.

WILSON, JOHN, ... 647
Engraving by F. Halpin.

WORDSWORTH, WILLIAM, ... 395
Engraving by G. J. Stodart, after Lupton's Engraving of Haydon's Portrait.

YOUNG, THOMAS, ... 87
Engraving by G. R. Ward, Painting by Sir Thomas Lawrence, P. R. A.

SAMUEL PARR

Engraving by W. Skelton. Painting by George Dawe.

ROBERT HALL

Engraving by W. Finden. Painting by N. C. Branwhite.

The Library of Literary Criticism of English and American Authors

VOLUME V.

Samuel Parr
1747–1825

Born at Harrow, 26 Jan. 1747. At Harrow School, Easter 1752 to 1761. Assisted his father in business of apothecary and surgeon, 1761–64. Began to study Divinity 1764. To Emmanuel Coll., Camb., as Sizar, Oct. 1765; left Cambridge, 1766. Assistant-master at Harrow, Feb. 1767 to 1771. Ordained Deacon, Dec. 1769; Priest, 1778. M. A., Camb., 14 Dec. 1771. Failed in candidature for Head-mastership of Harrow, and started a school at Stanmore, Oct. 1771. Married (i) Jane Morsingale, Nov. 1771. Head-master of Colchester Grammar School, 1777–79; of Norwich Grammar School, 1779-85. Rector of Asterby, Lincs., 1780–83. LL. D., Camb., 1781. Perpetual Curate of Hatton, Warwickshire, 1783–89. Prebendary of Wenlock Barnes, in St. Paul's Cathedral, March 1783; removed to Hatton, 1785; took pupils there; resided there till his death. Rector of Wadenhoe, Northamptonshire, 1789. Rector of Graffham Hunts, 1802. Wife died, 9 April 1810. Married (ii) Mary Eyre, 17 Dec. 1816. Died, at Hatton, 6 March 1825. Buried in Hatton Church. *Works:* "Two Sermons preached at Norwich," 1780; "Discourse on the late Fast" (under pseud.: "Phileleutherus Norfoliciensis"), 1781; "Discourse on Education," 1786; "Præfatio ad Bellendenum de Statu," 1787; "Letter from Irenopolis to the Inhabitants of Eleutheropolis" (anon.), 1792 (2nd edn. same year); "Sequel to the Printed Paper late circulated in Warwickshire," 1792; "Remarks on the Statement of Dr. C. Combe" (anon.), 1795; "Spital Sermon," 1801; "A Sermon preached on the late Fast Day," 1804; "Fast Day Sermon," 1808; "Characters of the late Charles James Fox" (under pseud. "Philopatris Varvicensis," 2 vols.), 1809. *Posthumous:* "Letter to . . . Dr. Milner," ed. by J. Lynes, 1825; "Sermons preached on Several Occasions" (4 vols.), 1831. He *edited:* G. Bellendenus's "De Statu," 1787; "Tracts by Warburton and a Warburtonian," 1789; "Four Sermons," 1822; "Metaphysical Tracts," 1837. *Collected Works:* in 8 vols., 1828. *Life:* "Memoirs," by W. Field, 1828.—SHARP, R. FARQUHARSON, 1897, *A Dictionary of English Authors, p.* 222.

PERSONAL

Having spent an evening at Mr. Langton's with the Reverend Dr. Parr, he was much pleased with the conversation of that learned gentleman; and after he was gone, said to Mr. Langton, "Sir, I am obliged to you for having asked me this evening. Parr is a fair man. I do not know when I have had an occasion of such free controversy. It is remarkable how much of a man's life may pass without meeting with any instance of this kind of open discussion."—JOHNSON, SAMUEL, 1780, *Life by Boswell, ed. Hill, vol.* IV, *p.* 18.

Parr, Lords and Dukes came forward to command;
But who appears at Court the Doctor's friend?
His books, his riches, and his only rule
A village pulpit or a country school.
—DYER, GEORGE, 1797, *The Poet's Fate.*

Is there no one among you who can

throw a Congreve rocket among the gerunds and supines of that model of pedants, Dr. Philopatris Parr? I understand your foreign lingos too little to attempt it, but pretty things might be said upon the memorable tureen which he begged of Lord Somebody, whom he afterwards wished to prove to be mad.—SCOTT, SIR WALTER, 1809, *Letter to Mr. Ellis, Sept.* 14; *Life by Lockhart, ch.* xix.

What did Parr mean by "haughtiness and coldness?" I listened to him with admiring ignorance, and respectful silence. What more could a talker for fame have?—they don't like to be answered. It was at Payne Knight's I met him, where he gave me more Greek than I could carry away. But I certainly meant to (and *did*) treat him with the most respectful deference.—BYRON, LORD, 1818, *Letter to Thomas Moore, Sept.* 19.

In domestic life, Parr was too great a scholar, and too studious a man, to be the exact favorite of the drawing-room. All was to yield to his wishes, all was to be regulated by his habits. The ladies were obliged to bear his tobacco, or to give up his company; and at Hatton now and then, he was the tyrant of the fire-side. But he was so good humoured in his disposition, and was so easily led by kindness, that the cloud never lasted long, and the thunder was soon succeeded by sunshine and by calm. At table he has been called an Epicurean glutton. In society he has often been denominated a bear, and his moroseness, and impracticability, and severity, were the terror of many weak and effeminate spirits. It is not true that he was a glutton. He only loved a good dinner, as all healthy men with good appetites, and many studious men without them, love it. . . . His pipe was so necessary to his comfort, that he always left the table for it, and the house of the person he visited, if it was not prepared. . . . To the lady of the house, though a ceremonious Dr. Parr was sometimes a troublesome guest. When he was thwarted or attacked, or in company of those he disliked or suspected, he certainly had the power of being most exquisitely disagreeable.—JOHNSTONE, JOHN, 1828, *ed., The Works of Samuel Parr, LL.D., with Memoirs of his Life and Writings and a Selection from his Correspondence, pp.* 812, 815, 816.

It may be said with truth that never was the liturgy of the church read with more exact propriety, or with more impressive energy, than by the officiating minister of Hatton. The most careless hearer could scarcely fail to be roused to attention, and struck with awe, when, with his majestic air, his devout looks, his deep and solemn tones, he repeated such admirable prayers as the confession, the general supplication, and the general thanksgiving; or when he recited that beautiful and animated, though not wholly unexceptionable form, the litany; or when, from the communion table, he delivered the decalogue, with a voice which seemed to speak his sense of that high and holy authority, under which it was originally promulgated. — FIELD, WILLIAM, 1828, *Memoirs of the Life, Writings and Opinions of the Rev. Samuel Parr, vol.* II, *p.* 327.

In smoke the Doctor's day commenced; in smoke it closed; smoke literal and abominable to his ox and his ass, to his man-servant and his maid-servant, and to the stranger that was within his gates. But to me there seemed always to settle a smoke symbolical upon the whole sum of the Doctor's life—all that he did, and all that he tried to do. . . . His person was poor, and his features were coarse and ignoble, with an air, at the same time, of drollery, that did not sit well upon age or the gravity of his profession. Upon one feature, indeed, Dr. Parr valued himself exceedingly; this was his eye. He fancied that it was peculiarly searching and significant: he conceited, even, that it frightened people, and had a particular form of words for expressing the severe use of this basilisk function: "I *inflicted* my eye upon him," was his phrase in such cases. But the thing was all a mistake; his eye could be borne very well; there was no mischief in it.—DE QUINCEY, THOMAS, 1831–57, *Dr. Parr, Works, ed. Masson, vol.* V, *pp.* 12, 20.

"Dr. Parr," said a young student once to the old linguist,—"let's you and I write a book."—"Very well, "replied the doctor, "put in all that I know, and all that you don't know, and we'd make a big one."—WHIPPLE, EDWIN P., 1845, *Wit and Humor, Literature and Life, p.* 107.

Parr was frequently very tiresome in conversation, talking like a schoolmaster.

He had a horror of the east wind; and Tom Sheridan once kept him prisoner in the house for a fortnight by fixing the weathercock in that direction.—ROGERS, SAMUEL, 1855, *Recollections of Table-Talk, ed. Dyce, p.* 49.

With all his bitterness at his neglect, his terrible powers of satire, and his torrents of rage and verbosity, no man seems to have had more friends or to have been more widely liked personally than Parr. Even Johnson enjoyed his society, and spoke in high terms of his personal qualities apart from his learning. His correspondence, which makes two volumes of his works, shows that he was on familiar terms with a greater number of distinguished people than probably any other author in the history of English literature. Thirty or forty noblemen, many bishops, and nearly every one who held any position in the world of scholarship and learning figure in it. The charm and power of his conversation were no doubt the chief cause of this long list of friendships. DeQuincey and the next generation, who inhabited a different world from Parr's, would not, it has been said, accept the verdict of the old scholar's contemporaries on his extraordinary ability as a talker. They seem to have been too disappointed with his old-fashioned works to allow him any sort of excellence. Men like Johnson and Burke must, however, be allowed to be judges who could not have listened with admiration to the drivel which DeQuincey has reported Parr's conversation to have been made up of on the one occasion when he seems to have heard it.—ATTENBOROUGH, JOHN MAX, 1901, *Samuel Parr, The Westminster Review, vol.* 155, *p.* 64.

GENERAL

There is another *just* or *unjust* volume that makes its appearance not composed of milk and honey: the object, Bishop Hurd; the author Dr. Parr. The vehicle, like his "Bellendenus," an old carriage on new wheels. The title "Tracts by a Warburtonian." It is desperately well written; but probably not of the amusing kind to your Ladyship.—WALPOLE, HORACE, 1789, *To the Countess of Ossory; Letters, ed. Cunningham, vol.* IX, *p.* 173.

What has Dr. Parr written? A Sermon or two, rather long; a Latin Preface to Bellendenus (rather long too), consisting of a cento of Latin and Greek expressions applied to political subjects: another preface to some English tracts, and two or three English pamphlets about his own private quarrels. And this is the man to be compared with Dr. Samuel Johnson!!! —MATHIAS, THOMAS JAMES, 1794–98, *The Pursuits of Literature, Eighth ed., p.* 219.

Whoever has had the good fortune to see Dr. Parr's wig, must have observed, that while it trespasses a little on the orthodox magnitude of perukes in the anterior parts, it scorns even Episcopal limits behind, and swells out into boundless convexity of frizz, the μεγα θαυμα of barbers, and the terror of the literary world. After the manner of his wig the Doctor has constructed his sermon, giving us a discourse of no common length, and subjoining an immeasurable mass of notes, which appear to concern every learned thing, every learned man, and almost every unlearned man, since the beginning of the world.—SMITH, SYDNEY, 1802, *Dr. Parr, Edinburgh Review, Essays, p.* 1.

Of flexibility Parr's style has none; it is totally deficient in the grand secret and capital charm of first-rate composition, light and shade, intention and remission. Instead of treating common things in a common way, and reserving great efforts for great occasions, Parr's mind seems always on the stretch. *Nihil solet leniter, nihil definate, nihil explicate dicere.*—GREEN, THOMAS, 1810, *Diary of a Lover of Literature.*

The dedication of Parr ["Tracts by Warburton and a Warburtonian"] stands unparalleled for comparative criticism. It is the eruption of a volcano; it sparkles, it blazes, and scatters light and destruction. How deeply ought we to regret that this Nazarite suffered his strength to be shorn by the Delilahs of spurious fame. Never did this man, with his gifted strength, grasp the pillars of a temple, to shake its atoms over Philistines; but pleased the child-like simplicity of his mind by pulling down houses over the heads of their unlucky inhabitants. He consumed, in local and personal literary quarrels, a genius which might have made the next age his own.—DISRAELI, ISAAC, 1814, *Warburton, Quarrels of Authors.*

An excellent clergyman in his parish, an excellent schoolmaster in his school, but in his character of a wit and an author one of the most genuine feather-beds of humbug that ever filled up a corner in the world.—WILSON, JOHN (CHRISTOPHER NORTH), 1824, *Noctes Ambrosianæ, Blackwood's Magazine, vol.* 16, *p.* 243.

Of his sermons, those on education, . . . though the first he published, are among the most valuable. They will be read with interest by every parent and instructer. They present the results of long experience, the matured reflections of a wise preceptor, a lover of virtue, and a friend of youth, who, though from temperament and principle a disciplinarian of the straitest sect, believing that much goodness and learning came with the rod, was eminently skilful and kind in discerning and cherishing, in guarding and correcting the various tendencies of youth.—WARE, HENRY, 1828, *Memoirs of Dr. Parr, The Christian Examiner, vol.* 5, *p.* 476.

One word on the style of Dr. Parr. That it is stately, measured, copious, abundant in fine diction, none can deny, but we confess that we should like it better, were it less perfect, less laboured, less rhythmical. In its structure it is weakened by antithesis; in its terms it is not the mother-tongue in which we were born.—BLUNT, J. J., 1829, *Life and Writings of Dr. Parr, The Quarterly Review, vol.* 39, *p.* 308.

Dr. Parr as an author! And what, now, might happen to be the Doctor's works? For I protest upon my honour, that I never heard their names. Was ever case like this? Here is a learned doctor, whose learned friend has brought him forward as a first-rate author of his times, and yet nothing is extant of his writing, beyond an occasional preface, or a pamphlet on private squabbles. . . . Certainly the world had never before seen so great a pomp of pretension rising from so slight a ground. The delusion was absolutely unrivalled, and prevailed throughout Dr. Parr's long life. He and his friends seemed constantly to appeal to some acknowledged literary reputation, established upon foundations that could not be shaken, and notorious to all the world. Such a mistake, and in that extent, was never heard of before. Dr. Parr talked, and his friends listened, not only as giving and receiving oracles of moral wisdom, but of wisdom owned to be such by all the world; whereas, this *auctoritas* (to borrow a Roman word for its Roman sense), whether secretly due to the Doctor or not, evidently could not exist as a fact, unless according to the weight and popularity of published works, by which the world had been taught to know him and to rank him. Starting originally from the erroneous assumption, insinuated by his preposterous self-conceit, that he was Johnson redivivus, he adopted Johnson's colloquial pretentions—and that was vainglorious folly; but he also conceived that these pretensions were familiarly recognised—and that was frenzy.—DE QUINCEY, THOMAS, 1831–57, *Dr. Parr, Works, ed. Masson, vol.* V, *pp.* 51, 52.

In some points of character there is a closer analogy between Parr and Bentley, yet at the same time almost as much dissimilarity. Parr's strength lay not so much in critical skill and penetration, as in the metaphysics of language and morals. He would have been more likely to rival the "Boyle Lectures," or the "Letters of Phileleutherus Lipsiensis," than the "Epistle to Mill," or the "Dissertation on Phalaris." But both were equally arrogant and overbearing in literature and conversation; in private, good-natured, and often kind-hearted men. Both were fully possessed with the conviction that a great scholar is the greatest of men. But the different effect of their self-confidence and haughtiness on their writings is not without interest. The pride of Bentley betrayed him to negligence and haste; whatever came from him, whatever he condescended to communicate to the world, must be worthy of his high name; he could strike out, while the anxious printer waited for the proofs, notes which would set the world right on the most abstruse points. With Parr, on the other hand, nothing but what was most elaborate could be worthy of coming from so consummate a scholar; his style is swollen, as it were, with the conscious dignity of its master. Parr must not demean himself to the familiar tone of ordinary men. Even in his bitterness Parr abstains from the vulgar tongue, not from mildness of temper or courtesy of manners, but his sarcasms, not to do discredit to his page, must be as highly wrought as the rest of his style. . . . It was probably the same proud jealousy of his reputation which prevented

Parr from contributing more largely to our instruction and knowledge; for few, with such powers of understanding, notwithstanding the number and bulk of the volumes to which his works have grown, have added less to the standard stock of our literature.—BLOOMFIELD, C. J., 1831, *Bishop Monk's Life of Bentley, Quarterly Review, vol.* 46, *p.* 168.

The late Dr. Parr, whose erudition was as unexclusive as profound.—HAMILTON, SIR WILLIAM, 1839, *Metaphysical Tracts of the Eighteenth Century, Edinburgh Review, vol.* 68, *p.* 338.

A vast treasure of erudition, a treasure too often buried in the earth, too often paraded with injudicious and inelegant ostentation; but still precious, massive, and splendid.—MACAULAY, THOMAS BABINGTON, 1841, *Warren Hastings, Edinburgh Review; Critical and Historical Essays.*

He certainly was a man of learning and talent, but was as far from being a man of genius as any man of learning and talent ever was. He has not left on paper a single thought that can be called original. He has produced abundance of declamation, but declamation composed of material from other writers. An author he can scarcely be called. If we compare a page of Addison, or Locke, or Bacon, with a page of Parr, we see the difference between the productions of a writer who thinks for himself, and those of a writer who draws his supplies from the fountains of others. No man can say that he has gathered nutriment for his mind, or added to his intellectual stores, from the writings of Parr. Nor was his language more original than his matter; if he praised Burke, or abused Pitt, he delivered his praises or abuse in the phrase of Cicero or Johnson. His Preface to Bellendenus is but a cento, and his English efforts are of a similar nature. His sentences are full of sound, and sometimes of fury, but the effect is altogether disproportionate to the rage and noise.—WATSON, JOHN SELBY, 1861, *The Life of Richard Porson, p.* 300.

Parr was a man of unquestionable ability, and the oblivion that has overtaken his name is due to his having left no great work on any great subject.—MINTO, WILLIAM, 1872-80, *Manual of English Prose Literature, p.* 510.

Dr. Parr swelled with pride at the very thought of his own Life of Johnson, had he ever written it. "I once intended," he said, "to write Johnson's life; and I had read through three shelves of books to prepare myself for it. It would have been the third most learned work that has ever yet appeared. It would have come next to Bentley on the Epistles of Phalaris and Salmasius on the Hellenistic Language. Mine should have been not the droppings of Johnson's lips, but the history of his mind." It would have been so uniform in its stately ponderosity, that even the famous stamp would most certainly have been passed over in silence, which he gave that evening when he argued with Johnson about the liberty of the press. "Whilst Johnson was arguing, I observed that he stamped. Upon this I stamped. Dr. Johnson said, 'Why did you stamp, Dr. Parr?' I replied, 'Because you stamped; and I was resolved not to give you the advantage even of a stamp in the argument.'" It would have added one, or perhaps two more, to that pile of eight thick volumes in which Parr's learning has been buried past all hopes of a resurrection by the piety of his friend and executor.—HILL, GEORGE BIRKBECK, 1891, *The Centenary of Boswell, Macmillan's Magazine, vol.* 64, *p.* 37.

Parr's mannerism and his verbosity make his English writings generally unreadable. He complains on his return to Combe that his duties as a teacher and parish priest, his correspondence, and frequent consultations upon the affairs of friends, left him no leisure. He meditated lives of his old colleague Sumner, of Dr. Johnson, of Fox and of Sir W. Jones; but never got beyond the stage of collecting material. His personal remarks are pointed, though necessarily laboured; but in his general discussions the pomposity remains without the point. He was admitted a fine Latin scholar, as scholarship was understood by the schoolmaster of his day, and perhaps did not assume too much in placing himself between Porson and Charles Burney.—STEPHEN, LESLIE, 1895, *Dictionary of National Biography, vol.* XLIII, *p.* 362.

It may be said, without fear of contradiction, that of all the men who have enjoyed the highest fame in the world of English scholarship and literature not one is more faded in reputation today than Dr.

Parr. To the lover of untrodden literary paths, his works, in eight volumes quarto, containing six thousand pages, offer an ideal retreat. There is no better way into the world of the last century, with all its forgotten thoughts and figures. In his own day, Parr's name was as much on men's lips as his friend Johnson's. Now, in spite of his eight massive tomes, the doctor is only known to readers through the mention of him in Boswell, and has become, in common estimation, one of the least of that numerous class of writers who, in Southey's words draw their fame from Johnson as the mistletoe draws its life from the oak. The reason why Parr's works have thus gone the way to dusty death is not far to seek. Parr was great in two fields of knowledge, which are necessarily fenced off from nine out of ten readers—classical scholarship and metaphysics—and they are fields, besides, in which, since his day, explorations have been pushed so much further than he could carry them that his work has now little attraction even for the erudite.—ATTENBOROUGH, JOHN MAX, 1901, *Samuel Parr, The Westminster Review, vol.* 155, *p.* 54.

Anna Lætitia Barbauld

1743–1825

Born (Anna Letitia Aikin), at Kibworth Harcourt, Leicestershire, 20 June 1743. Early youth spent there. At Warrington, 1758–73. Married to Rev. Rochemont Barbauld, May 1774. Settled at Palgrave, Suffolk, and started boys' school with husband. No children; adopted a nephew, Charles Rochemont Aikin, 1776. School given up, 1785. Travelled in France and Switzerland, Sept. 1785 to June 1786. In London, 1786–87. To Hampstead, April 1787. Visit to Scotland, 1794. Removed to Stoke Newington, 1802. Husband died, 1808. She died, at Stoke Newington, 9 March 1825. *Works:* "Poems," 1773; "Miscellaneous Pieces" (with J. Aikin), 1773; "Devotional Pieces," 1775; "Hymns in Prose: for Children" (under initials: A. L. B.), 1781; "An Address to the Opposers of the Repeal of the Corporation and Test Acts" (anon.), 1790; "Epistle to W. Wilberforce," 1791; "Evenings at Home" (anon., with J. Aikin), 1792; "Remarks on Mr. G. Wakefield's Enquiry, etc.," 1792; "Civic Sermons" (anon.), 1792; "Sins of the Government, Sins of the Nation" (anon.), 1793; "The Religion of Nature" (under pseud. of "Bob Short"), 1793; "Reasons for National Penitence" (anon.), 1794; "Selections from the 'Spectator,' etc.," 1804; "Lessons for Children" (anon.), 1808; "The Female Speaker," 1811; "Eighteen Hundred and Eleven," 1812. *Posthumous:* "Works, with Memoir by L. Aikin" (2 vols.), 1825; "Hymns in Rhyme," 1838; "Memoir, Letters and Selection," ed. by G. A. Ellis, 1874. She *edited:* Akenside's "Pleasures of Imagination," 1794, and "Works," 1808; Samuel Richardson's "Correspondence," 1804; "The British Novelists" (50 vols.,) 1810; and, *translated:* Jauffret's "Travels of Rolando," 1823.—SHARP, R. FARQUHARSON, 1897, *A Dictionary of English Authors, p.* 16.

PERSONAL

Too much is expected from precocity, and too little performed. Miss Aikin was an instance of early cultivation, but in what did it terminate? In marrying a little Presbyterian parson, who keeps an infant boarding-school, so that all her employment now is

"To suckle fools, and chronicle small-beer."

She tells the children, "This is a cat, and that is a dog, with four legs and a tail; see there! you are much better than a cat or a dog, for you can speak." If I had bestowed such an education on a daughter, and had discovered that she thought of marrying such a fellow, I would have sent her to the *Congress.*—JOHNSON, SAMUEL, 1775, *Life by Boswell, ed. Hill, vol.* II, *p.* 468.

Went to Mrs. Barbauld's. She was in good spirits, but she is now the confirmed old lady. Independently of her fine understanding and literary reputation, she would be interesting. Her white locks, fair and unwrinkled skin, brilliant starched linen, and rich silk gown, make her a fit object for a painter. Her conversation is lively, her remarks judicious, and always pertinent. — ROBINSON, HENRY CRABB, 1821, *Diary, Jan.* 21.

Mind and heart formed a rare union and well balanced her character. She was governed in her views by reason, and her enthusiasm, though not wanting, was restrained by common-sense and practical judgment. Her heart was warm, full of love and sympathy for all mankind; but the expansion of her interest did not make her overlook the claims of those around her, and her duties to her own little circle. In "the little, nameless, unremembered acts of kindness and of love" she was most charming and attractive; as the author and poet she was respected and admired; but as a woman, a friend, and a relation, she was beloved and revered.—ELLIS, GRACE A., 1874, *A Memoir of Mrs. Anna Lœtitia Barbauld, vol* I, *p*. 337.

Mrs. Barbauld might have easily taken rank as the female Johnson of her day, had not circumstances, together with a natural indolence of temperament, largely associated with modesty, prevented her from making more than occasional use of her literary powers. As it is, this writer leaves behind her a body of very respectable verse and some prose of the highest excellence, with a private reputation which every writer cannot boast of, namely, the reputation of having led a God-fearing, spotless life, as a tender wife to an afflicted husband, a cheerful toiler in the shadow of trouble, a charitable critic of all her acquaintance, and a woman who died, at a very advanced age, idolised by a large family circle. The serene nobility of such a life as Mrs. Barbauld's is a refreshing thing to come across.—ROBERTSON, ERIC S., 1883, *English Poetesses, p*. 77.

To the quiet little home at Newington came many distinguished men and women. Earnest thinkers, learned men and women, clever and appreciative of the talents of others were often seen at the door, and the little parlor of Mrs. Barbauld was frequently the meeting-place of England's men of mark. Here came Mackintosh and Macaulay, Coleridge and Charles Lamb, Sir Henry Holland, Dr. Channing, the Edgeworths, Sir John Bowring, Sir James Smith. Samuel Rogers, and Joanna Baillie, with her sister Agnes, were among the old Hampstead friends. In 1815 one reads of a day at Hampstead at the Carrs, "a charming day," when Sir Walter Scott told the old lady her reading of Taylor's "Lenöre's" "Tramp, tramp, splash, splash," "made him a poet."—OLIVER, GRACE A., 1884, *ed. Tales, Poems and Essays of Mrs. Barbauld, Biographical Sketch, p*. lxxii.

Her epitaph justly says of her that she was "endowed by the Giver of all good with wit, genius, poetic talent, and a vigorous understanding;" and the readers of her works will readily allow the easy grace of her style and her lofty but not puritanical principles. Her letters, some few of which have been published since her death, show that though her life was habitually retired she greatly enjoyed society.—BRODRIBB, A. A., 1885, *Dictionary of National Biography, vol*. III, *p*. 145.

GENERAL

I have neither read her verses, nor will. As I have not your aspen conscience, I cannot forgive the heart of a woman that is party per pale blood and tenderness, that curses our clergy and feels for negroes.—WALPOLE, HORACE, 1791, *To Miss Hannah More, Sept*. 29; *Letters, ed. Cunningham, vol*. IX, *p*. 354.

The fair biographer ["Life of Richardson"] unquestionably possesses very considerable talents, and exercises her powers of writing with singular judgment and propriety. Many of her observations are acute and striking, and several of them very fine and delicate. Yet this is not, perhaps, the general character of her genius: and it must be acknowledged, that she has a tone and manner which is something formal and heavy; that she occasionally delivers trite and obvious truths with the pomp and solemnity of important discoveries, and sometimes attempts to exalt and magnify her subject by a very clumsy kind of declamation. With all those defects, however, we think the Life and Observations have so much substantial merit, that most readers will agree with us in thinking that they are worth much more than all the rest of the publication. —JEFFREY, FRANCIS LORD, 1804, *Richardson, Edinburgh Review, vol*. 5, *p*. 23.

If ever there was a writer whose wisdom is made to be useful in the time of need, it is Mrs. Barbauld. No moralist has ever more exactly touched the point of the greatest practicable purity, without being lost in exaggeration, or sinking into meanness. She has cultivated a philosophy which will raise and animate her, without refining it to that degree, when it is no longer applicable to the gross purposes of human life, and when it is too apt to evaporate in hypocrisy and ostentation. Her observations on the moral of "Clarissa" are as fine a piece of mitigated and rational stoicism as our language can boast of: and she who has so beautifully taught us the folly of inconsistent expectations and complaints, can never want practical wisdom under the sharpest calamities.—MACKINTOSH, SIR JAMES, 1808, *Letter to Mrs. John Taylor, Oct.* 10; *Memoirs, ed. Mackintosh, vol.* I, *p.* 441.

Our old acquaintance Mrs. Barbauld turned satirist! The last thing we should have expected, and now that we have seen her satire, the last thing that we could have desired. . . . Mrs. Barbauld's former works have been of some utility; her "Lessons for Children," her "Hymns in Prose," her "Selections from the Spectator," *et id genus omne*, though they display not much of either taste or talents are yet something better than harmless: but we must take the liberty of warning her to desist from satire, which indeed is satire on herself alone; and of entreating, with great earnestness, that she will not, for the sake of this ungrateful generation, put herself to the trouble of writing any more party pamphlets in verse.—SOUTHEY, ROBERT, 1812, *Mrs. Barbauld's Eighteen Hundred and Eleven, Quarterly Review, vol.* 7, *pp.* 309, 313.

The first poetess I can recollect is Mrs. Barbauld, with whose works I became acquainted before those of any other author, male or female, when I was learning to spell words of one syllable in her story-books for children. I became acquainted with her poetical works long after in Enfield's Speaker; and remember being much divided in my opinion, at that time, between her Ode to Spring and Collin's Ode to Evening. I wish I could repay my childish debt of gratitude in terms of appropriate praise. She is a very pretty poetess; and, to my fancy, strews the flowers of poetry most agreeably round the borders of religious controversy. She is a neat and pointed prose-writer. Her "Thoughts on the Inconsistency of Human Expectations" is one of the most ingenious and sensible essays in the language. —HAZLITT, WILLIAM, 1818, *Lectures on the English Poets, Lecture* viii.

Elegance and strength—qualities rarely uniting without injury to each other combine most perfectly in her style, and this rare combination, added to their classical purity, form, perhaps, the distinguishing characteristics of her writings.—EDGEWORTH, MARIA, 1825, *Letters, vol.* II, *p.* 132.

There were many striking points of resemblance between her genius and that of Addison. As prose writers, both were remarkable for uniting wit of the light and sportive kind with vividness of fancy, and a style at once rich and lively, flowing and full of idiom: both of them rather avoided the pathetic: in both, "the sentiments of rational and liberal devotion" were "blended with the speculations of philosophy and the paintings of a fine imagination:" both were admirable for "the splendour they diffused over a serious, the grace with which they touched a lighter subject." The humorous delineation of manners and characters indeed, in which Addison so conspicuously shone, was never attempted by Mrs. Barbauld:—in poetry, on the other hand, she surpassed him in all the qualities of which excellence in that style is composed. Certainly this great author could not elsewhere have found a critic so capable of entering, as it were, into the soul of his writings, culling their choicest beauties, and drawing them forth for the admiration of a world by which they had begun to be neglected.—AIKIN, LUCY, 1825, *ed., The Works of Anna Lætitia Barbauld, Memoir, vol.* I, *p.* XL.

"Early Lessons," a publication which has ever since been a standard work, and, though frequently imitated, yet remains unrivalled amidst all its competitors. . . . The cause of rational education is more indebted to her than to any individual of modern times, inasmuch as she was the leader in that reformation which has resulted in substituting the use of truth and reason for folly and fiction, in books for the nursery.—GOODRICH, S. G., 1844, *Lives of Celebrated Women, pp.* 173, 178.

She had both intellect and passion enough to match a spirit heroical.—HUNT, LEIGH, 1847, *British Poetesses; Men, Women and Books.*

Mrs. Barbauld was exceedingly clever. Her mimicry of Dr. Johnson's style was the best of all that exist. Her blank-verse "Washing Day," descriptive of the discomforts attending a mistimed visit to a rustic friend, under the affliction of a family-washing, is picturesquely circumstantiated. And her prose hymns for children have left upon my childish recollection a deep impression of solemn beauty and simplicity.—DE QUINCEY, THOMAS, 1851–52, *Infant Literature, Works, ed. Masson, vol.* I, *p.* 127, *note.*

To claim for Mrs. Barbauld the praise of purity and elevation of mind, might well appear superfluous. She is decidedly one of the most eminent female writers which England has produced; and both in prose and poetry she takes the highest rank. Her prose style is easy and graceful, alike calculated to engage the most common and the most elevated understanding. — CLEVELAND, CHARLES D., 1853, *English Literature of the Nineteenth Century, p.* 168.

Neither in her earliest or her latest works is there any manifestation of an unformed or a feeble style; all is clear, pointed, forcible, and elegant in her prose; thoughtful, imaginative, spiritual, and musical in her verse.—BALFOUR, CLARA LUCAS, 1854, *Working Women of this Century, p.* 100.

At a dinner-party where I was, Fox met Aikin. "I am greatly pleased with your 'Miscellaneous Pieces,' Mr. Aikin," said Fox (alluding to the volume written partly by Aikin, and partly by his sister Mrs. Barbauld). Aikin bowed. "I particularly admire," continued Fox, "your essay 'Against Inconsistency in our Expectations.'" "That," replied Aikin, "is my sister's!" "I like much," resumed Fox, "your essay 'On Monastic Institutions.'" "That," answered Aikin, "is also my sister's." Fox thought it best to say no more about the book.—ROGERS, SAMUEL, 1855, *Recollections of Table-Talk, ed. Dyce, p.* 81.

I still think her one of the first of writers in our language, and the best example we have of the benefits of a sound classical education to a woman.—MARTINEAU, HARRIET, 1855, *Autobiography, ed. Chapman, vol.* I, *p.* 228.

In her prose as well as her poetry she never offered her work to the public without the most perfect finish which it was possible to give it. She felt that the most self-commending and noble thought could not dispense with the added lustre of the choice and elegant language in which she carefully clothed her sentiments and opinions. As I have said, the essay "Of Inconsistency in Our Expectations" has an acknowledged and prominent rank, being thought by those whose opinions are of value to stand at the head of that class of literature.—ELLIS, GRACE A., 1874, *A Memoir of Mrs. Anna Lætitia Barbauld, vol.* I, *p.* 330.

That her writings will occupy a very high place among the authors of her time is more than can be reasonably hoped for. Her voice is "lost among the throng of louder minstrels in these latter days." Her hymns, however, will keep her name fresh as long as sacred music is a part of divine worship. . . . These lyrics show that she possessed the spirit of genuine poetry, though it sometimes insensibly slipped into prose as it took form and pressure.—QUINCY, EDMUND, 1874, *Mrs. Barbauld, The Nation, vol.* 18, *p.* 206.

The poems of Mrs. Barbauld are chiefly written in the elegant pseudo-classic style of the close of the last century. She expresses herself clearly and with grace; a certain artificiality of manner harmonises with her choice of subject. Her poetry is without deep thought or passion; but it is free from blunders of an avoidable kind. The spirit of self-criticism which prompted her to destroy all her juvenile verses, never permitted her to include with her published works any ill-considered thought or unsuccessful effort. . . . The fame of Mrs. Barbauld's hymns has outlived the rest of her work. Yet with the exception of her charming "Hymns in Prose for Little Children," they seem, to a modern reader, deficient in fervour and in religious emotion. They are pure in tone and lofty, but often singularly cold. There can be no doubt, however, of their sincerity.—ROBINSON, A. MARY F., 1880, *English Poets, ed. Ward, vol.* III, *p.* 576.

Her poetry belongs to that artificial didactic school of the eighteenth century which is so antipathetic to the present age, and must remain in oblivion until the wheel of Time brings round again its fashion. Her prose style, however, is admirable, being modelled upon our best writers; both Macaulay and Mackintosh were warm in their praise of it.—BAKER, H. BARTON, 1881, *Mrs. Barbauld, The Argosy, vol.* 31, *p.* 308.

She has left behind her at least one scrap of verse which is immortal, and much beside that is well worthy a place in the recollection of her country. . . . The delightful "Early Lessons," which is the most poetical and idyllic of all baby books. Never were words of one syllable so charmingly employed. The "Hymns in Prose," perhaps as having a somewhat higher aim, have held their place longer. But hymns in prose are a mistake, and never will be so popular as verse with children; whereas the lovely little pictures of the "Early Lessons" are never out of date. They are, among the dull pages of ordinary lesson books, like vignettes by Stothard among the common illustrations of a penny journal.—OLIPHANT, MARGARET O. W., 1882, *The Literary History of England, XVIII-XIX Century, vol.* II, *pp.* 280, 283.

It is noteworthy that few of Mrs. Barbauld's earlier productions equalled what she wrote at the very end of her life. She seems to have been one of those who ripened with age, growing wider in spirit with increasing years. Perhaps, too, she may have been influenced by the change of manners, the reaction against formalism, which was growing up as her own days were ending. Prim she may have been in manner, but she was not a formalist by nature; and even at eighty was ready to learn to submit, to accept the new gospel that Wordsworth and his disciples had given to the world, and to shake off the stiffness of early training.—RITCHIE, ANNE ISABELLA THACKERAY, 1883, *A Book of Sibyls.*

In those days we read Mrs. Barbauld's "Early Lessons" with a curiosity never gratified as to what became of Charles, who was sometimes such an idiot and sometimes such a sage. In later years Charles Barbauld, as we called him, whose real name was Charles Aikin, reappeared in Carlyle's "Life of Sterling."—HALE, EDWARD EVERETT, 1888, *Books That Have Helped Me, p.* 5.

I, of course, committed to memory, as children are wont to do, numberless hymns and poems, and I trust that they did me good; but there is nothing of this kind to which I can ascribe any specific benefit, with the exception of Mrs. Barbauld's "Hymns in Prose," which, I think, made me permanently appreciative of euphony as distinguished from poetic rhythm, and gave rise to my lifelong habit of testing by the ear the sentences that I read and write.—PEABODY, A. P., 1888, *Books That Have Helped Me, p.* 42.

Mrs. Barbauld, the author of the noble lines, "Life, we've been long together,"—the nobility of which is rather in its sentiment than in its expression—and of much tame and unimportant stuff.—SAINTSBURY, GEORGE, 1896, *A History of Nineteenth Century Literature, p.* 19.

Lucretia Maria Davidson

1808-1825

Born, Plattsburg, N. Y.: poet. She began composing verses in secret when only four years old and before she could write, using print letters, and on being discovered burned all her compositions. She learned to write when seven years old, composed her earliest preserved poem, "Epitaph on a Robin," when nine, and at twelve had read many historical and dramatic works, including Shakespeare and Goldsmith. She was sent to school when sixteen, but soon became a victim to consumption. Her preserved poems, numbering 278, were published under the title of "Amir Khan and Other Poems," 1829; in conjunction with those of her sister, Margaret Miller D., 1850, and with illustrations, 1871.—JOHNSON, ALFRED SIDNEY, *ed.*, 1890, *The Columbian Cyclopedia, vol.* VIII.

PERSONAL

She composed with great rapidity; as fast as most persons usually copy. There are several instances of four or five pieces on different subjects, and containing three or four stanzas each, written on the same day. Her thoughts flowed so rapidly, that she often expressed the wish that she had two pair of hands, that she might employ them to transcribe. When "in the vein," she would write standing, and be wholly abstracted from the company present and their conversation. But if composing a piece of some length, she wished to be entirely alone; she shut herself into her room, darkened the windows, and in summer placed her Æolian harp in the window. . . . In those pieces on which she bestowed more than ordinary pains, she was very secret; and if they were, by any accident, discovered in their unfinished state, she seldom completed them and often destroyed them. She cared little for any of her works after they were completed: some, indeed, she preserved with care for future correction, but a great proportion she destroyed: very many that are preserved, were rescued from the flames by her mother. Of a complete poem, in five cantos, called "Rodri," and composed when she was thirteen years of age, a single canto, and part of another, are all that are saved from a destruction which she supposed had obliterated every vestige of it.—MORSE, SAMUEL F. B., 1829, *Amir Khan and Other Poems, Biographical Sketch.*

Prodigious as the genius of this young creature was, still marvellous after all the abatements that may be made for precociousness and morbid development, there is something yet more captivating in her moral loveliness. Her modesty was not the infusion of another mind, not the result of cultivation, not the effect of good taste; nor was it a veil, cautiously assumed and gracefully worn; but an innate quality, that made her shrink from incense, even though the censer were sanctified by love. Her mind was like the exquisite mirror, that cannot be stained by human breath.—SEDGWICK, CATHERINE M., 1839, *Sparks's Library of American Biography, vol.* VII, *p.* 292.

In person she was exceedingly beautiful. Her forehead was high, open, and fair as infancy—her eyes large, dark, and of that soft beaming expression which shows the soul in the glance—her features were fine and symmetrical, and her complexion brilliant, especially when the least excitement moved her feelings. But the prevailing expression of her face was melancholy. Her beauty, as well as her mental endowments, made her the object of much regard; but she shrunk from observation—any particular attention always seemed to give her pain; so exquisite was her modesty. In truth, her soul was too delicate for this "cold world of storms and clouds." Her imagination never revelled in the "garishness of joy;"—a pensive, meditative mood was the natural tone of her mind. The adverse circumstances by which she was surrounded, no doubt deepened this seriousness, till it became almost morbid melancholy—but no external advantages of fortune would have given to her disposition buoyant cheerfulness.—HALE, SARAH JOSEPHA, 1852, *Woman's Record, p.* 283.

GENERAL

In our own language, except in the cases of Chatterton and Kirke White, we can call to mind no instance of so early, so ardent, and so fatal a pursuit of intellectual advancement. . . . In these poems there is enough of originality, enough of aspiration, enough of conscious energy, enough of growing power, to warrant any expectations, however sanguine, which the patron, and the friends, and parents of the deceased could have formed; nor can any person rise from the perusal of such a volume without feeling the vanity of human hopes.—SOUTHEY, ROBERT, 1829, *Remains of Lucretia Davidson, Quarterly Review, vol.* 41, *pp.* 293, 301.

"As the work of a girl of sixteen," most assuredly we do not think it ["Amir Khan"] "prodigious." In regard to it we may repeat what we said of "Lenore," —that we have seen finer poems in every respect, written by children of more immature age. It is a creditable composition; nothing beyond this. And, in so saying, we shall startle none but the brainless, and the adopters of ready-made ideas. We are convinced that we express the unuttered sentiment of every educated individual who has read the poem. Nor, having given the plain facts of the case, do we feel called upon to proffer any apology for our flat refusal to play ditto either to Miss Sedgwick, to Mr. Irving, or to Mr. Southey.—POE, EDGAR ALLAN, 1841, *Graham's Magazine, Works, ed. Stedman and Woodberry, vol.* VIII, *p.* 300.

As a poet, Lucretia Davidson possessed a depth of thought, a delicacy of expression, a tenderness of sentiment, and an appreciation of melody rarely to be met. She had a fine fancy, a quick imagination, and quiet and unobtrusive humor, and underlying all a foundation of thorough and unwavering thoughtfulness. Her writings are marked by grace, ease and refinement, and evince not only a catholic but a classical taste. Her heart as well as her mind is apparent in her compositions;

and soul, as well as intellect, permeates and gives character to her productions.—COFFIN, ROBERT BARRY (BARRY GRAY), 1870, *Poems by Lucretia Maria Davidson. Introduction, p.* viii.

The great admiration of the best critics of the time for Lucretia Maria Davidson is explained by the difference between her freshness and pensive sentiment and the affectation of the school who preceded her. . . . Whose works now seem so very commonplace.—FORD, EMILY ELLSWORTH, 1893, *Early Prose and Verse, pp.* 132, 133.

Those precocious girls, the Davidson sisters, who died when scarcely out of childhood, leaving volumes of fluent and monotonous verse, long haunted, as pathetic wraiths, the little American Parnassus. —BATES, KATHARINE LEE, 1897, *American Literature, p.* 104.

Lady Anne Barnard

1750-1825

Poetess, was born in Fifeshire, and was the daughter of the Earl of Balcarres; her maiden name being Lindsay. She became one of the minor Scottish poets of the time, whose names are only remembered by a single great poem or song, her assurance of immortality being the beautiful ballad of "Auld Robin Gray," written in early youth. —SANDERS, LLOYD C., 1887, *Celebrities of the Century, p.* 95.

PERSONAL

To entire rectitude of principle, amiability of manners, and kindliness of heart, Anne Barnard added the more substantial, and, in females, the more uncommon quality of eminent devotedness to intellectual labour. Literature had been her favourite pursuit from childhood, and even in advanced life, when her residence was the constant resort of her numerous relatives, she contrived to find leisure for occasional literary *réunions*, while her forenoons were universally occupied in mental improvement. She maintained a correspondence with several of her brilliant contemporaries, and in her more advanced years, composed an interesting narrative of family Memoirs. She was skilled in the use of the pencil, and sketched scenery with effect. In conversation she was acknowledged to excel; and her stories and anecdotes were a source of delight to her friends. She was devotedly pious, and singularly benevolent. She was liberal in sentiment, charitable to the indigent, and sparing of the feelings of others. Every circle was charmed by her presence; by her condescension she inspired the diffident; and she banished dullness by the brilliancy of her humour. Her countenance, it should be added, wore a pleasant and animated expression, and her figure was modelled with the utmost elegance of symmetry and grace.—ROGERS, CHARLES, 1855-57-70, *The Scottish Minstrel, The Songs of Scotland Subsequent to Burns, p.* 17.

AULD ROBIN GRAY

In the course of our walk he [Scott] entertained us much by an account of the origin of the beautiful song of "Auld Robin Gray." "It was written," he said, "by Lady Anne Lindsay, now Lady Anne Barnard. She happened to be at a house where she met Miss Suff Johnstone, a well known person, who played the air, and accompanied it by words of no great delicacy, whatever their antiquity might be; and Lady Anne, lamenting that no better words should belong to such a melody, immediately set to work and composed this very pathetic story. Truth, I am sorry to say, obliges me to add that it was a fiction. Robin Gray was her father's gardener, and the idea of the young lover going to sea, which would have been quite out of character here amongst the shepherds, was natural enough where she was then residing, on the coast of Fife. It was long unknown," he added, "who the author was; and indeed there was a clergyman on the coast whose conscience was so large that he took the burden of this matter upon himself, and pleaded guilty to the authorship. About two years ago I wrote to Lady Anne to know the truth—and she wrote back to say she was certainly the author, but wondered how I could have guessed it, as there was no person alive to whom she had told it. When I mentioned having heard it long ago from a common friend who was dead, she then recollected me, and wrote one of the kindest letters I ever received, saying she had till now not the smallest idea that I was the little *lame boy* she had known so many years before."—HALL, CAPTAIN BASIL, 1825, *Journal, Jan.* 8.

O lady Anne Barnard, thou that didst write the ballad of "Auld Robin Gray," which must have suffused more eyes with tears of the first water than any other ballad that ever was written, we hail, and pay thee homage, knowing thee now for the first time by thy real name! But why wast thou desirous of being only a woman of quality, when thou oughtest to have been (nature intended thee) nothing but the finest gentlewoman of thy time? And what bad example was it, that, joining with the sophistications of thy rank, did make thee so anxious to keep thy secret from the world, and ashamed to be spoken of as an authoress? Shall habit and education be so strong with those who ought to form, instead of being formed by them? Shall they render such understandings as thine insensible to the humiliation of the fancied dignity of concealment, and the poor pride of being ashamed to give pleasure? . . . The most pathetic ballad that ever was written.—HUNT, LEIGH, 1847, *British Poetesses, Men, Women and Books.*

One of the most celebrated of all the Scotch songs is "Auld Robin Gray." . . . Fine as was the old air, the more modern tune which has supplemented it, composed in 1770 by the Rev. William Leeves, Rector of Wrington, in Somersetshire, is still more accordant with the spirit of the verses. Words and music are now so perfectly combined in their sensibility, that "Auld Robin Gray" ranks in popular estimation as the very first of Scotch songs.—ROBERTSON, ERIC S., 1883, *English Poetesses, p.* 156.

A song altogether of Fife origin and authorship marks the commencement of the period of modern ballads. It will be acknowledged that "Auld Robin Gray" has few superiors, either amongst its predecessors or successors, though to call it the "King of Scottish Ballads," as Chambers does, is to raise it to a dangerous eminence, which it would not be prudent even for the most patriotic native of the "Kingdom" to claim for it.—MACKAY, ÆNEAS, 1891, *The Songs and Ballads of Fife, Blackwood's Magazine, vol.*150, *p.*344.

George Chalmers

1742-1825

Scottish antiquary, was born at Fochabers, and was educated there and at King's College, Aberdeen. Having afterwards studied law at Edinburgh, in 1763 he went to North America, where he practised as a lawyer at Baltimore till the breaking out of the war of independence. He then settled in London (1775), and was appointed clerk to the Board of Trade in 1786. Of his thirty-three works the chief is "Caledonia; an Account, Historical and Topographical, of North Britain" (vols. I–III, 1807–24). In 1888–95 it was reprinted at Paisley in 7 vols., comprising the matter prepared for the unpublished 4th vol., and furnished with a much-needed index. Among his other works are: "A Collection of Treaties between Great Britain and other Powers" (2 vols. 1790); Lives of Defoe, Paine, Ruddiman, and Mary Queen of Scotts; and editions of Allan Ramsay and Lyndsay.—PATRICK AND GROOME, *eds.*, 1898, *Chambers's Biographical Dictionary, p.* 196.

GENERAL

This gentleman is the *Atlas* of Scotch antiquaries and historians; bearing on his own shoulders whatever seems to have been collected, and with pain *separately* endured, by his predecessors; whom, neither difficulties tire nor dangers daunt: and who, in a green and vigorous old age, is yet laying the foundation of works for the enlargement of a legitimate fame, and the edification of a grateful posterity.—DIBDIN, THOMAS FROGNALL, 1824, *The Library Companion, p.* 272.

The Caledonia is to the Anglo-Saxon History what Stonehenge is to a carved front in an old cathedral. It is one of the children of Anak. In deep research the heaping together of matter, the Britannia of Camden fades away before it. A life, and a long and busy one, was almost exclusively devoted to this stupendous work: the author lived to complete it, and no more. The concluding volume is still in manuscript; and no bookseller has appeared willing to hazard the expense of giving to the world a thousand pages quarto. This is one of those cases in which literature is not its own reward; and had Chalmers lived in any land under the sun but this, his Caledonia would have been published by the government, and the learned author pensioned.—CUNNINGHAM, ALLAN, 1833, *Biographical and Critical History of the Literature of the Last Fifty Years.*

You will sometimes see the work of Chalmers referred to. It is an immense, heavy, tedious book, to explain the legal history of the different colonies of America. It should be consulted on all such points. It goes down to the revolution of 1688. But it is impossible to read it. The leaves, however, should be turned over, for curious particulars often occur, and the nature of the first settlement and original laws of each colony should be known. The last chapter, indeed, ought to be read. The right to tax the colonies became a great point of dispute. Chalmers means to show that the sovereignity of the British parliament existed over America, because the settlers, though emigrants, were still English subjects and members of the empire.—SMYTH, WILLIAM, 1840, *Lectures on Modern History, Lecture* xxxi.

The life of Chalmers is comprised in a record of the works which he compiled with indefatigable industry, and issued without a break during the last fifty years of his long life. His fame rests on one of them, the "Caledonia," which he called his standing work. The rest have been superseded by better editions, or become antiquated through his want of originality or mistaken views. Even the "Caledonia," has not stood the test of time. It is below the standard of Camden's "Britannia" or the works of Dugdale, the English antiquarian treatises which can most fairly be compared with it. Still, to have composed what is, though never completed, the fullest account of the antiquities of a nation which has specially cultivated that department of history is a merit not to be despised, and subsequent writers have borrowed from Chalmers without acknowledging their obligations. MACKAY, ÆNEAS, 1887, *Dictionary of National Biography, vol.* IX, *p.* 445.

William Knox

1789-1825

Scottish Poet, was born at Firth, parish of Lilliesleaf, Roxburghshire, 17 Aug. 1789. After receiving elementary education at Lilliesleaf and Musselburgh, he farmed without success near Langholm, Dumfriesshire, from 1812 to 1817. He "became too soon his own master," says Scott, "and plunged into dissipation and ruin." His farming career over, he returned to his native place. In 1820 his family settled in Edinburgh, and Knox became a journalist. Sir Walter Scott, Professor Wilson, and others befriended him, and Scott frequently gave him substantial pecuniary relief. His convivial habits undermined his health, and he died at Edinburgh of paralysis, 12 Nov. 1825. Besides a prose, "Visit to Dublin," and a Christmas tale, "Mariamne, or the Widower's Daughter," Knox published "The Lonely Hearth, and other Poems," 1818; "The Songs of Israel," 1824; and "The Harp of Zion," 1825. His lyrics are graceful and thoughtful. Scott thought Knox in "The Lonely Hearth" superior to Michael Bruce, and "Mortality," in "Songs of Israel," was a favourite with President Lincoln. A complete edition of Knox's poems appeared in 1847.—BAYNE, THOMAS, 1892, *Dictionary of National Biography, vol.* XXXI, *p.* 337.

PERSONAL

Talking of the *vixisse*, it may not be impertinent to notice that Knox, a young poet of considerable talent, died here a week or two since. His father was a respectable yeoman, and he himself, succeeding to good farms under the Duke of Buccleuch, became too soon his own master, and plunged into dissipation and ruin. . . . I had him, Knox, at Abbotsford, about ten years ago, but found him unfit for that sort of society. I tried to help him, but there were temptations he could never resist. He scrambled on writing for the booksellers and magazines, and living like the Otways, and Savages, and Chattertons, of former days, though I do not know that he was in extreme want. His connexion with me terminated in begging a subscription or a guinea, now and then.—SCOTT, SIR WALTER, 1825, *Diary, Dec.* 8; *Life by Lockhart, ch.* lxv.

Knox was short in stature, but handsomely formed; his complexion was fair, and his hair of a light colour. Subject to a variation of spirits in private, he was generally cheerful in society. He sang or repeated his own songs with much enthusiasm, and was keenly alive to his literary reputation. Possessing a fund of humour, he excelled in relating curious anecdotes.—ROGERS, CHARLES, 1855–57–70, *The Scottish Minstrel, The Songs of Scotland Subsequent to Burns, p.* 224.

GENERAL

His talent then showed itself in a fine strain of pensive poetry, called, I think, "The Lonely Hearth," far superior to that of Michael Bruce, whose *consumption*, by the way, has been the *life* of his verses. . . . His last works were spiritual hymns, and which he wrote very well. In his own line of society he was said to exhibit infinite humour; but all his works are grave and pensive—a style, perhaps, like Master Stephen's melancholy, affected for the nonce.—SCOTT, SIR WALTER, 1825, *Diary, Dec.* 8; *Life by Lockhart, ch.* lxv.

Knox's poetry is largely pervaded with pathetic and religious sentiment. In the preface to his "Songs of Israel" he says—"It is my sincere wish that, while I may have provided a slight gratification for the admirer of poetry, I may also have done something to raise the devotional feelings of the pious Christian." . . . As a prose writer his works are of little account, but the same cannot be said of his poetry, which possesses a richness and originality that insure for it a more lasting popularity. . . . He was keenly alive to his literary reputation, and could not but have been greatly gratified had he known that a poem of his would one day go the rounds of the American press and that of the Canadas as the production of a president of the United States.—WILSON, JAMES GRANT, 1876, *The Poets and Poetry of Scotland, vol.* II, *p.* 107.

His "Lonely Hearth," "Songs of Israel," and "Harp of Zion," displayed a talent which years afterward attracted the attention of Abraham Lincoln to what is now, through his commendation, a poem of classic excellence. In 1864, during the month of March, the artist Carpenter and the sculptor Swayne were both in Washington. The sculptor was working on a bust of Mr. Lincoln in a temporary studio in the Treasury Building. The President asked Mr. Carpenter to accompany him thither, and there, referring again to this poem by Knox, he was delighted to find that Mr. Swayne possessed a copy of the verses in print, which he had cut, several years before, from a Philadelphia paper. They had been originally given to Mr. Lincoln by a young man named Jason Duncan, and the President had recently written them from memory for the wife of Secretary Stanton, saying that he had often tried to discover the author, but in vain. Subsequently the republication of the stanzas in the New York "Evening Post" secured the identification of the poem with the name of William Knox.—DUFFIELD, SAMUEL WILLOUGHBY, 1886, *English Hymns, p.* 11.

William Gifford

1756–1826

Born, at Ashburton, April 1756. Educated at Ashburton Free School. Afterwards at work on a farm. At sea, 1767–70. To school again at Ashburton, 1770. Apprenticed to shoe-maker, 1 Jan. 1772. To school again, 1776. Matric. at Exeter Coll., Oxford, as Bible Clerk, 16 Feb. 1779; B. A., 10 Oct. 1782. Travelling tutor to son of Lord Grosvenor, 1781. Unsuccessfully prosecuted for libel in "The Baviad," 1797. Edited "Anti-Jacobin," Nov. 1797 to July 1798. Editor of "Quarterly Review," Feb. 1809 to Sept. 1824. Held posts of Commissioner of Lottery and Paymaster of Gentlemen-Pensioners. Died, in London, 31 Dec. 1826; buried in Westminster Abbey. *Works:* "Easton Chronicle" (anon.), 1789: "The Baviad" (anon.), 1791; "The Mæviad" (anon.), 1795 (two preceding pubd. together, 1797); "Epistle to Peter Pindar" (anon.), 1800; "An Examination of the strictures . . . on the translation of Juvenal," 1803. He *translated:* "Juvenal" (with *autobiography*), 1802; "Persius," 1821; and edited: Massinger's "Works," 1805; Ben Jonson's "Works," 1816; Ford's "Dramatic Works," 1827; Shirley's "Dramatic Works," 1833.—SHARP, R. FARQUHARSON, 1897, *A Dictionary of English Authors, p.* 112.

PERSONAL

The mildest man in the world till he takes a pen in his hand, but then all gall and spitefulness.—MOORE, THOMAS, 1818, *Diary, Dec.* 1; *ed. Russell, vol.* II, *p.* 230.

I hear some one say "Murrain take him, the ape!"
And so Murrain shall, in a bookseller's shape;
An evil-eyed elf, in a down-looking flurry,
Who'd fain be a coxcomb, and calls himself Murray.
Adorn thou his door, like the sign of the Shoe,
For court-understrappers to congregate to;
For Southey to come, in his dearth of invention,
And eat his own words for mock-praise and a pension;
For Croker to lurk with his spider-like limb in,
And stock his lean bag with waylaying the women;
And Jove only knows for what creatures beside
To shelter their envy and dust-liking pride,
And feed on corruption, like bats, who at nights,
In the dark take their shuffles, which they call their flights;
Be these the court-critics and vamp a Review.
And by a poor figure, and therefore a true,
For it suits with thy nature, both shoe-like and slaughterly
Be its hue leathern, and title the Quarterly,
Much misconduct; and see that the others
Misdeem, and misconstrue, like miscreant brothers;
Misquote, and misplace, and mislead, and misstate,
Misapply, misinterpret, misreckon, misdate,
Misinform, misconjecture, misargue; in short,
Miss all that is good, that ye miss not the Court.

. . . .

And finally, thou, my old soul of the tritical,
Noting, translating, high slavish, hot critical,
Quarterly-scutcheon'd, great heir to each dunce,
Be Tibbald, Cook, Arnall, and Dennis at once.

—HUNT, LEIGH, 1823, *Ultra-crepidarius; a Satire on William Gifford.*

With respect to Gifford, I have never seen him; but I know that his conversation, particularly since his health began to decline, is excessively splenetic. He is a fanatical Ministerialist, and retains even now his old hatred of the Jacobins, Della Cruscans, &c. His information on all points is prodigious, and he pours it forth very freely. I am told he dislikes all his associates—Croker, J. Murray, &c.—but I do not know how true that is. He would be a hard card to manage in a dialogue. —MAGINN, WILLIAM, 1823, *Letter to Blackwood, William Blackwood and His Sons, vol.* I, *p.* 397.

He was very valetudinary, and realized two verses, wherein he says Fortune assigned him—

—"One eye not over good,
Two sides that to their cost have stood
A ten years' hectic cough,
Aches, stitches, all the various ills
That swell the devilish doctor's bills,
And sweep poor mortals off.

But he might also justly claim as his gift, the moral qualities expressed in the next fine stanza—

——"A soul
That spurns the crowd's malign control,
A firm contempt of wrong;
Spirits above affliction's power,
And skill to soothe the lingering hour
With no inglorious song."

He was a little man, dumpled up together, and so ill made as to seem almost deformed, but with a singular expression of talent in his countenance.—SCOTT, SIR WALTER, 1827, *Diary, Jan.* 17; *Life by Lockhart, ch.* lxxiii.

I see in the papers, to-day [?], the death of Mr. Gifford—the direst, darkest enemy I ever had. We never saw each other; he hated me for my success and my principles.

Mort la bête, mort le venin,

at least *esperons!*—MORGAN, LADY SYDNEY, 1829, *Diary, Memoirs, vol.* II, *p.* 281.

He was a singularly ugly little man, of a wasping temper, and, in my opinion, much overrated both as a poet and a critic. His "Autobiography" is amusing, and there are some good lines in his "Baviad and Mæviad." But he had a self-conceit which led him to despise others in a very unjustifiable manner; and he had an idea of retaining his dominion by menaces and superciliousness. He affected almost a puritan strictness of morals in his writings; but this did not become the companion of the late Lord Grosvenor. I found him, however, courteous, communicative, and frank, when I paid him a visit.—BRYDGES, SIR SAMUEL EGERTON, 1834, *Autobiography, vol.* I, *p.* 148.

Hitherto we have seen Gifford only in his blander moods—bent on being amiable in return for the assistance cordially rendered to his studies by a stranger. But these were weaker moments—the tiger assuming the bleat of the lamb. The gall in his system lay too near the surface not to ooze through the thin layer of suavity upon the smallest provocation.—PRIOR, SIR JAMES, 1860, *Life of Edmond Malone, Editor of Shakspeare, p.* 308.

Giffard looked very aged [in 1819] his face much wrinkled, and he seemed to be in declining health; his dress was careless, and his cravat and waistcoat covered with snuff. There was an antique, philosophic cast about his head and countenance, better adapted to excite a feeling of curiosity in a stranger than the head of Sir Walter Scott; the latter seemed more a man of this world's mould.—BRAY, ANNA ELIZA, 1883, *Autobiography, ed. Kempe, p.* 147.

He must have had many literary and political acquaintances and friends; but in this year, 1824, when I knew him, sick and moribund, he appeared to be a solitary old man.—TAYLOR, SIR HENRY, 1885, *Autobiography, vol.* I, *p.* 81.

It was not merely because he was a critic that he was hated, but because he was malicious and malignant, and because he did not criticise from a literary, but from a political, point of view. That he was not alone, in this last peculiarity, this deliberate and obstinate incompetency, as we may say, was admitted by his victims, who belabored by the bludgeons of Lockhart, Maginn, and Wilson, were able before long to forgive, if they could not quite forget, those jocose blackguards, who could take as well as give hard blows; but Gifford they never forgave. They despised him for his venal pen, his sycophancy to the great, and for his low origin. That he should have been despised on account of his origin was hard; for he neither concealed it, as most men would have done, nor boasted of it, as many might have done, but acknowledged it in the frankest and manliest way. The story of his early years, as related by himself, was a melancholy, a pathetic one, and to have lived through them and risen above them, as he did, was to deserve well of the world.—STODDARD, RICHARD HENRY, 1892, *Under the Evening Lamp, p.* 91.

GENERAL

The name suggests the honourable mention of a poem lately published, under the title of "The Baviad, or an Imitation of the first Satire of Persius." . . . If this be a first production, the poet must proceed with the consciousness of genius: he has the ground work of all excellence, good sense, and a knowledge of just, and harmonious expression. — MATHIAS, THOMAS JAMES, 1794, *The Pursuits of Literature, p.* 47.

In these cold shades, beneath these shifting skies,
Where Fancy sickens, and where Genius dies;
Where few and feeble are the muse's strains,
And no fine frenzy riots in the veins,
There still are found a few to whom belong
The fire of virtue and the soul of song;
Whose kindling ardour still can wake the strings,
When learning triumphs, and when Gifford sings.
To thee the lowliest bard his tribute pays,
His little wild-flower to thy wreath conveys;
Pleased, if permitted round thy name to bloom,
To boast one effort rescued from the tomb.
While this delirious age enchanted seems
With hectic Fancy's desultory dreams;
While wearing fast away is every trace
Of Grecian vigour, and of Roman grace,
With fond delight, we yet one bard behold,
As Horace polish'd, and as Perseus bold,
Reclaim the art, assert the muse divine,
And drive obtrusive dulness from the shrine.
—CLIFFTON, WILLIAM, 1799, *Baviad and Mœviad, Preface.*

Have got through half of Gifford's "Memoirs of Ben Jonson." What a "canker'd carle" it is! Strange that a man should be able to lash himself up into such a spiteful fury, not only against the living but the dead, with whom he engages in a sort of *sciomachy* in every page. Poor dull and dead Malone is the shadow at which he thrusts in his "Jonson," as he did at poor Monck Mason, still duller and deader in his "Massinger."— MOORE, THOMAS, 1819, *Diary, Jan.* 1; *ed. Russell, vol.* II, *p.* 248.

All his notions are low, upstart, servile. He thinks it the highest honour to a poet to be patronised by a peer or by some dowager of quality. He is prouder of a court-livery than of a laurel-wreath; and is only sure of having established his claims to respectability by having sacrificed those of independence. He is a retainer to the Muses; a door-keeper to learning; a lacquey in the state. He believes that modern literature should wear the fetters of classical antiquity; that truth is to be weighed in the scales of opinion and prejudice; that power is equivalent to right; that genius is dependent on rules; that taste and refinement of language consist in *word-catching*. Many persons suppose that Mr. Gifford knows better than he pretends; and that he is shrewd, artful, and designing. But perhaps it may be nearer the mark to suppose that his dulness is guarantee for his sincerity; or that before he is the tool of the profligacy of others, he is the dupe of his own jaundiced feelings, and narrow, hoodwinked perceptions. . . . Mr. Gifford, as a satirist, is violent and abrupt. He takes obvious or physical defects, and dwells upon them with much labour and harshness of invective, but with very little wit or spirit. He expresses a great deal of anger and contempt, but you cannot tell very well why—except that he seems to be sore and out of humour. His satire is mere peevishness and spleen, or something worse—personal antipathy and rancour. We are in quite as much pain for the writer, as for the object of his resentment.—HAZLITT, WILLIAM, 1825, *The Spirit of the Age, pp.* 166, 177.

He was a man of rare attainments and many excellent qualities. His Juvenal is one of the best versions ever made of a classical author, and his satire of the Baviad and Mæviad squabashed at one blow a set of coxcombs, who might have humbugged the world long enough. As a commentator he was capital, could he but have suppressed his rancours against those who had preceded him in the task; but a misconstruction or misinterpretation, nay, the misplacing of a comma, was in Gifford's eyes a crime worthy of the most severe animadversion. The same fault of extreme severity went through his critical labours, and in general he flagellated with so little pity, that people lost their sense of the criminal's guilt in dislike of the savage pleasure which the executioner seemed to take in inflicting the punishment.—SCOTT, SIR WALTER, 1827, *Diary, Jan.* 17; *Life, by Lockhart, ch.* lxxiii.

Considered as a poet, was merely Pope, without Pope's wit and fancy; and whose satires are decidedly inferior in vigour and poignancy to the very imperfect juvenile performance of Lord Byron himself.—MACAULAY, THOMAS BABINGTON, 1830, *Moore's Life of Lord Byron, Critical and Miscellaneous Essays.*

Gifford has done a great deal for the text of Massinger, but not as much as might easily be done. His comparison of Shakspere with his contemporary dramatist is obtuse indeed.—COLERIDGE, SAMUEL TAYLOR, 1833, *Table-Talk, Apr.* 7; *ed. Ashe, p.* 206.

He was a man of extensive knowledge; was well acquainted with classic and old English lore; so learned, that he considered all other people ignorant; so wise, that he was seldom pleased with any thing; and, as he had not risen to much eminence in the world, he thought no one else was worthy to rise. He almost rivalled Jeffrey in wit, and he surpassed him in scorching sarcasm and crucifying irony. Jeffrey wrote with a sort of levity which induced men to doubt if he were sincere in his strictures: Gifford wrote with an earnest fierceness which showed the delight which he took in his calling.—CUNNINGHAM, ALLAN, 1833, *Biographical and Critical History of the Literature of the Last Fifty Years.*

Read the "Baviad" and "Mæviad," preferred the former: the subject was too much exhausted for a new satire, at least to equal in pungent effect the former one. They are, however, both extremely good, and must have fallen like a giant's arm upon the insect-like flutterings of the half-formed witlings whom they aimed to crush. But to imagine that Burns lived in comparative neglect while these apes were attracting notice by their absurdities!—MACREADY, W. C., 1834, *Diary, Sept.* 20; *Reminiscences, ed. Pollock, p.* 331.

He was fierce, dogmatic, bigoted, libellous, and unsympathizing. Whatever may have been his talents, they were exquisitely unfitted for his position—his literary judgments being contemptible, where any sense of beauty was required, and principally distinguished for malice and word-picking. The bitter and snarling spirit with which he commented on the excellence he could not appreciate; the extreme narrowness and shallowness of his taste; the labored blackguardism in which he was wont to indulge under the impression that it was satire; his detestable habit of carrying his political hatreds into literary criticism; his gross personal attacks on Hunt, Hazlitt, and others who might happen to profess less illiberal principles than his own; made him a dangerous and disagreeable adversary, and one of the worst critics of modern times.—WHIPPLE, EDWIN P., 1845, *British Critics, Essays and Reviews, vol.* II, *p.* 150.

Distinguished as a satirist, as a translator of satires, and as the editor of several of the illustrious but somewhat neglected dramatists of the Elizabethan age, his writings, admirable for sincerity, good sense, and learning, were also strongly tinged with bitterness and personality.—SHAW, THOMAS B., 1847, *Outlines of English Literature, p.* 414.

He is the only man I ever attacked, respecting whom I have felt no regret. It would be easy for me at this distance of time to own that Gifford possessed genius, had such been the case. It would have been easy for me at any time. But he had not a particle. The scourger of poetasters was himself a poetaster. When he had done with his whip, everybody had a right to take it up, and lay it over the scourger's shoulders; for though he had sense enough to discern glaring faults, he abounded in commonplaces. His satire itself, which, at its best never went beyond smartness, was full of them.—HUNT, LEIGH, 1850, *The Autobiography, vol.* I, *p.* 254.

The power wielded thirty years ago by that little arid mass of commonplace and dried venom is, to us, absolutely marvellous. The manner in which he exercised the critical profession showed, indeed, that he was perfectly skilled in his former one, especially in the adroit use of the awl. He was admirable at boring small holes; but beyond this he was nothing. If Shakespeare's works had appeared in his time, he would have treated them precisely as he treated Shelley's and Keats', unless, indeed, they had been submitted to his revision before, or dedicated to him at publication.—GILFILLAN, GEORGE, 1855, *A Third Gallery of Portraits, p.*176.

When Lord Byron began to write, the classical satirist of the day was William Gifford, our friend who did the butchering business in the *Anti-Jacobin.* He had published, in 1794 and '95, the "Baviad" and "Mæviad;" and he was now extolled by the party who had taken him up, as the censor of the age. It is pleasant to know that the satirist has generally ranked in this country as an official of some dignity; though there is a constant tendency in officiality to degenerate into beadledom. One learns something of that age, and of the difference between our times and *it*, by observing the Giffordian phenomenon; by reflecting that Gifford was a great authority; was listened to when he mauled Shelley and Keats; and was deferred to respectfully by the author of "Childe Harold" and "Don Juan." . . . Gifford was hearty in his abuse, as in his general energy, and flung his whole soul into Billingsgate with the same zeal which he had displayed when he studied algebra in the shoemaker's shop, working out "my problems with a blunted awl on pieces of leather." Hunt attacked him; Hazlitt attacked him; but I think the worst treatment he met with was from old Peter Pindar, whom he incautiously assailed in 1800, and from whom he instantly got a *douche* of savage buffoonery, which splashed him from head to foot. Those were energetic fighting-days—days when, if people hated each other, they said so in public. They gave no quarter, and expected none.—HANNAY, JAMES, 1855, *Satire and Satirists, pp.* 204, 205.

William Gifford's best title to fame was, no doubt, his edition of the "Early English Dramatists"—Ford, Massinger, Shirley, and Ben Jonson. His generous and able vindication of Jonson reflects credit both upon the critic and the poet.—WINKS, WILLIAM EDWARD, 1882, *Lives of Illustrious Shoemakers, p.* 76.

Although as a literary critic Gifford was crabbed and strangely wanting in taste, the fault was redeemed by strong common sense.—STEPHEN, LESLIE, 1890, *Dictionary of National Biography, vol.* XXI, *p.* 311.

How could a rhinoceros like Gifford have been expected to behave when what was hung in front of him for investigation and report was such an unprecedented invention of sheer phantasy and lusciousness as Keats's "Endymion?"—MASSON, DAVID, 1892, *The Story of Gifford and Keats, The Nineteenth Century, vol.* 31, *p.* 604.

Gifford was so intent on denouncing the inaccuracies of others that he frequently failed to secure accuracy himself. The hectoring tone that he chose to adopt has been generally, though not universally, discarded by later scholars. In reading the old dramatists we do not want to be distracted by editorial invectives and diatribes.—BULLEN, A. H., 1895, *ed., The Works of John Ford, Note to Preface, vol.* I.

His critical taste was none of the most delicate, but he knew nonsense when he saw it, and possessing a considerable fund of rough but genuine humour, together with the mastery of a satiric verse which stands to that of Pope in the relation of the oaken cudgel to the rapier, he turned the faculty and the weapon to such effective account in the "Baviad" and the "Mæviad," his two famous lampoons on the Della Cruscan school, as to reduce that incorporated society of idiots to its constituent atoms of individual imbecility. —TRAILL, HENRY DUFF, 1896, *Social England, vol.* V, *p.* 442.

Gifford is perhaps our capital example in English of a cast of mind which is popularly identified with that of the critic, though in truth nothing is more fatal to the attainment of the highest critical competence. It was apparently impossible for him (as it has been, and, it would seem, is for others), to regard the author whom he was criticising, the editor who had preceded him in his labours, or the adversary with whom he was carrying on a polemic, as anything but a being partly idiotic and partly villainous, who must be soundly scolded, first for having done what he did, and secondly to prevent him from doing it again. So ingrained was this habit in Gifford that he could refrain from indulging it, neither in editing the essays of his most distinguished contributors, nor in commenting on their work. . . . Yet he was a really useful influence in more ways than one. The service that he did in forcibly suppressing the Della Cruscans nuisance is even yet admitted, and there has been plentiful occasion, not always taken, for similar literary *dragonnades* since. And his work as an editor of English classics, was, blemishes of manner and temper excepted, in the main very good work.—SAINTSBURY, GEORGE, 1896, *A History of Nineteenth Century Literature.*

Gifford did not apply his personal canons of taste with more serene assurance than Jeffrey to the most original poets of his time; but he was a duller man, and with all his classic zeal lacked Roman urbanity as conspicuously as Romantic imagination. Before the end of his editorship he had committed sins of blind rancour against the new poetry and the new prose which modern criticism justly finds unpardonable, and which raised up more than one avenger with a voice more resonant than his own. . . . In the presence of almost all that was great and prophetic in the literature of his time, Gifford was purely futile or mischievous; but his bludgeon fell at times upon weeds or reptiles.—HERFORD, C. H., 1897, *The Age of Wordsworth, p.* 56.

Reginald Heber

1783-1826

Born, at Malpas, Cheshire, 21 April 1783. First education at Whitchurch Grammar School; with private tutor, 1796-1800. Matric., Brasenose Coll., Oxford, 8 Nov. 1800; Latin verse prize, 1800; Newdigate, 1803; B. A., 1804; Fellow of All Souls, 1804; English Essay, 1805; M. A., 1808. Travelled in Germany, Russia and Crimea, 1805-07. Ordained, 1807; Vicar of Hodnet, 1807-23. Married Amelia Shipley, April 1809. Contrib. to "Christian Observer" and "Quarterly Review." Prebendary of St. Asaph, 1812. Bampton Lecturer, Oxford, 1815. Preacher at Lincoln's Inn, 1822. D. D., Oxford, by diploma, 10 Feb. 1823. Bishop of Calcutta, 1823. Died, at Trichinopoly, 3 April 1826. Buried there. *Works:* "A Sense of Honour" (prize essay), 1805; "Palestine" (Newdigate poem), 1807; "Europe," 1809 (2nd edn. same year); "Poems" 1812; "The Personality and Office of the Christian Comforter" (Bampton lectures), 1816. *Posthumous:* "Hymns," edited by his wife, 1827; "Narrative of a Journey through the upper Provinces of India" (2 vols.), 1828; "Sermons preached in England," ed. by Mrs. Heber, 1829; "Sermons preached in India," ed. by Mrs. Heber, 1830; "Sermons," ed. by Sir R. H. Inglis (3 vols.), 1837; "Poetical Works," 1841. He *edited:* Jeremy Taylor's works, 1822. *Life:* by Mrs. Heber (including correspondence and some unpublished works), 1830; by G. Smith, 1895.—SHARP, R. FARQUHARSON, 1897, *A Dictionary of English Authors, p.* 130.

PERSONAL

He—this eminent divine—goes to Calcutta in the very spirit of martyrdom; he carries all those fine and consecrated talents, all that wealth of knowledge, and that power of genius, to a region where they will be comparatively little understood or appreciated. You know, perhaps, that he goes out as Bishop. Mr. Canning, who greatly loves and admires him, urges him to stay for the first vacant English bishoprick. His brother, who has a large estate, and has no heirs, is equally averse to his going; but the highest and purest motives urge him to spend and be spent in the service of his Master.—GRANT, ANNE, 1823, *Letters, Dec.* 23; *Memoir and Correspondence, ed. Grant, vol.* III, *p.* 18.

If it be sad to speak of treasures gone,
Of sainted genius called too soon away,
Of light from this world taken, while it shone
Yet kindling onward to the perfect day—
How shall our grief, if mournful these things be,
Flow forth, O thou of many gifts! for thee?
Hath not thy voice been here amongst us heard?
And that deep soul of gentleness and power,
Have we not felt its breath in every word,
Wont from thy lips, as Hermon's dew, to shower?
Yes! in our hearts thy fervent thoughts have burned—
Of heaven they were, and thither have returned.

—HEMANS, FELICIA D., 1826, *To the Memory of Heber.*

Heber's recitation, like that of all poets whom we have heard recite, was altogether untrammelled by the critical laws of elocution, which were not set at defiance, but either by the poet unknown, or forgotten; and there was a charm in his somewhat melancholy voice, that occasionally faltered, less from a feeling of the solemnity, and even grandeur of the scene, of which he was himself the conspicuous object—though that feeling did not suffuse his pale, ingenuous, and animated countenance—than from the deep-felt sanctity of his subject, comprehending the most awful mysteries of God's revelations to man. As his voice grew bolder and more sonorous in the hush, the audience felt that this was not the mere display of the skill and ingenuity of a clever youth, the accidental triumph of an accomplished versifier over his compeers in the dexterity of scholarship, which is all that can generally be truly said of such exhibitions,—but that here was a poet indeed, not only of bright promise, but of high achievement,—one whose name was already written in the roll of the Immortals. And that feeling, whatever might have been the share of the boundless enthusiasm, with which the poem was listened to, attributable to the influence of the *genius loci,* has been since sanctioned by the judgment of the world, that has placed "Palestine" at the very head of the poetry on divine subjects of this age. It is now incorporated for ever with the Poetry of England.—WILSON, JOHN (CHRISTOPHER NORTH), 1827, *Heber's Hymns, Blackwood's Magazine, vol.* 22, *p.* 619.

Learned, polished, and dignified, he was undoubtedly; yet far more conspicuously kind, humble, tolerant, and laborious—zealous for his church too, and not forgetful of his station; but remembering it more for the duties than for the honours that were attached to it, and infinitely more zealous for the religious improvement, and for the happiness, and spiritual and worldly good of his fellow-creatures, of every tongue, faith, and complexion: indulgent to all errors and infirmities—liberal, in the best and truest sense of the word—humble and conscientiously diffident of his own excellent judgment and never-failing charity—looking on all men as the children of one God, on all Christians as the redeemed of one Saviour, and on all Christian teachers as fellow-labourers, bound to help and encourage each other in their arduous and anxious task. His portion of the work, accordingly, he wrought faithfully, zealously, and well; and, devoting himself to his duty with a truly apostolical fervour, made no scruple to forego, for its sake, not merely his personal ease and comfort, but those domestic affections which were ever so much more valuable in his eyes, and in the end, we fear, consummating the sacrifice with his life.—JEFFREY, FRANCIS LORD, 1828–1844, *Bishop Heber's India, Contributions to the Edinburgh Review, vol.* IV, *p.* 296.

I read Reginald Heber's "Journal" after dinner. I spent some merry days with him at Oxford when he was writing his prize poem. He was then a gay young fellow, a wit and a satirist, and burning for literary fame. My laurels were beginning to bloom, and we were both madcaps. Who would have foretold our future lot?—SCOTT, SIR WALTER, 1829, *Journal, March* 12.

We thank Him for the great missionary pioneer, whose voice first in many parts of India proclaimed the conquests of the Gospel, and set an example for all of us that follow. We thank Him for the Christian gentleman who could, in the midst of English society, set a pattern of holiness without assumption, and kindly courtesy with true purity of word and thought. We thank Him for the scholar and divine, country clergyman and country gentleman, who, at the call of duty, gave up home and country, and rest, and ease, and society, and comfort, and culture to do the will of Him that called him, and to perfect His work. We thank Him for the pattern which, in and by this His ministering servant, he set us of manly performance of duty and entire devotion to work. And thanking Him and honouring Him who has blessed His servant with so many great and excellent gifts, and led him all his life through from strength to strength, we pray that we may each, according to his measure and in his own place, have grace to follow so good an example.—STUBBS, WILLIAM, 1887, *Sermon Preached at the Dedication of the Heber Window, St. Oswald's Malpas.*

A patriot in the most stirring period of our national history, he was of no party in the Church. A theologian of ripe scholarship and evangelic zeal, he resented alike the extremes of the so-called Calvinists, and the pelagianism of the Arminians of his day. He was for Christ; he loved and he did much to elevate the great Reformed Church which he loyally served; he worked with all good men, or wished them well in the one divinely commanded cause. His short episcopate, while he was still a young man, was the rich and fruitful outcome of such zeal, such wisdom, and such charity.—SMITH, GEORGE, 1895, *Bishop Heber, Preface, p.* vii.

HYMNS

These Hymns have been by far the most popular of his productions, and deservedly so; for in purity and elevation of sentiment, in simple pathos, and an eloquent earnestness, it would be difficult to find any thing superior to them in the range of lyric poetry. They have the home truth of Watts, but rank much higher, as literary compositions, than the Moral and Divine Songs of that great benefactor of youth; and all the devotion of Wesley or Keble, without their langour and diffuse verbosity. Heber always writes like a Christian scholar, and never finds it necessary to lower his tone on account of his subject.—MOIR, D. M., 1850–51, *Sketches of Poetical Literature of the Past Half Century.*

Dear to every section of the Christian Church are the sweet measures of the poet-bishop, Heber. . . . Some of them are odes, but all are infused with the poetic element to the highest degree. —SAUNDERS, FREDERICK, 1885, *Evenings with the Sacred Poets, p.* 386.

Bishop Reginald Heber has a sure renown in several ways. He was truly a poet, as his "Palestine" denotes. He was a dignitary of the Church of England, who employed his high office for the worthiest ends. He was a traveller, whose "Journey Through India," published in 1828, showed what fine powers of observation and reflection he possessed. He was filled with genuine missionary zeal, as his religious work and his immortal lyric, "From Greenland's icy mountains," alike testify. And, to crown all, he is one of the most graceful, spiritual and effective of English hymn-writers. — DUFFIELD, SAMUEL WILLOUGHBY, 1886, *English Hymns, p.* 335.

Some of his hymns rank with the best in English.—SAINTSBURY, GEORGE, 1896, *A History of Nineteenth Century Literature, p.* 110.

"From Greenland's Icy Mountains." This hymn was written by Heber at short notice in 1819. Dean Shipley asked him one Saturday to prepare some verses to be sung at the missionary service to be held next morning. Heber sat down and dashed off these verses, which speedily became the favourite missionary hymn of the English-speaking world.—STEAD, W.T., 1897, *Hymns that have Helped, p.*173.

GENERAL

This is another book ["A Journey Through India"] for Englishmen to be proud of. . . . Independently of its moral attraction, we are induced to think it, on the whole, the most instructive and important publication that has ever been given to the world on the actual state and condition of our Indian Empire. . . . He surveys every thing with the vigilance and delight of a cultivated and most active intellect,—with the eye of an artist, and antiquary, and a naturalist,—the feelings and judgment of an English gentleman and scholar,—the sympathies of a most humane and generous man,—and the piety, charity, and humility of a Christian.—JEFFREY, FRANCIS LORD, 1828, *Bishop Heber's Journal, Edinburgh Review, vol.* 48, *pp.* 312, 314, 318.

We wish that we could speak as highly of his sermons as we might of his character; but we cannot. We confess that we were disappointed in them; and we will venture to assert, that if they become popular, it will be because he wrote them, and not because they are of high value themselves. They are certainly much above mediocrity, and take a respectable rank among the volumes of English practical divinity; but few will ever think of placing them with the first sermons in the language. Though not absolutely unconnected in their trains of thought, yet they are greatly deficient in that clear method and arrangement which is one of the most indispensable requisites in sermon writing; and though there is a vein of good sense running through them, the mind of the intelligent reader is very seldom arrested by passages which task its attention, or set its powers at work. Diffusiveness seems to us to be the reigning characteristic of their style; and hence arise the breathless and almost endless sentences, which abound in them more than in any other sermons with which we are acquainted.—GREENWOOD, F. W. P., 1829, *Heber's Sermons, Christian Examiner, vol.* 7, *p.* 212.

As a poet he could not have supported the reputation which his "Palestine" obtained, for it was greatly above its deserts, and the character of the poem, moreover, was not hopeful; it was too nicely fitted to the taste of the age. Poetry should have its lights and shades, like painting; like music, its sink and swell, its relief and its repose. So far as the piece was intended for success in a competition for a prize, and for effect in public recitation, it was certainly judiciously done to make every line tell upon the ear. But to all such poetry the motto under one of Quarles's Emblems may be applied: *tinnit, inane est.*—SOUTHEY, ROBERT, 1830, *Letter to Henry Taylor, July* 10; *Southey's Life and Correspondence.*

The lyrical writings of Heber possess great and peculiar merits. He is the only Englishman who has in any degree approached the tone of Pindar, his translations from whom may be regarded as nearly faultless; and his hymns are among the sweetest which English literature contains, breathing a fervent devotion in the most poetical language and most melodious verse. I doubt whether there is a religious lyric so universally known in the British empire or in our own country, as the beautiful missionary piece beginning "From Greenland's icy mountains." The fragments of "Morte d'Arthur," the "Mask of Gwendolen," and the "World before the Flood," are not equal to his "Palestine," "Europe," or minor poems; but they contain elegant and powerful passages. The only thing unworthy of his reputation which I have seen is "Blue Beard," a serio-comic oriental romance, which I believe was first published after his death.—GRISWOLD, RUFUS W., 1844, *The Poets and Poetry of England in the Nineteenth Century, p.* 186.

The qualities of Heber are well understood. His poetry is of a high order. He is imaginative, glowing, and vigorous, with a skill in the management of his means unsurpassed by that of any writer of his time, but without any high degree of originality. Can there be anything in the nature of a "classical" life at war with novelty *per se?* At all events, few fine scholars, such as Heber truly was, *are* original.—POE, EDGAR ALLAN, 1849? *Marginalia, Works, eds. Stedman and Woodberry, vol.* VII, *p.* 302.

Next to his hymns, Bishop Heber is best known by the journal he kept of his visitation tour, not intended for publication, but containing so much of vivid description of scenery and manners, that it forms a valuable picture of the condition of Hindostan as it then was.—YONGE, C. M., 1871, *Pioneers and Founders, p.* 189.

If we were to say that Bishop Heber was a sort of male twin to Mrs. Hemans, we fear that the comparison would be received with little favour by many readers. So few of the poets of the time accomplished all the rites of education, and trained themselves, as ancient tradition bade, on the classic models, that it is disappointing to find, in the rare instance of a fully-qualified academical poet, an example so little remarkable as this excellent and blameless soul. In the dearth of writers properly marked with the sign-manual of the Universities, it ought to be noted that Heber gained the prize of poetry at Oxford, fulfilled all his studies there with distinction, and became a fellow of All-Souls. So much for so little! But it has never ceased to be true that poets must be born, and can not be made. . . . His poems are the utterance of the most spotless of well-regulated minds and devout spirits. It is doubtful whether the best of poets ever produced anything more widely known and popular than the "Missionary Hymn" about "Greenland's icy mountains," or that which celebrates the Star in the East of the Epiphany. So that this mild singer had his reward of the most liberal kind in the affectionate enthusiasm with which the simple-hearted religious crowd regards the writers of its sacred songs. The kind of tranquil life he led, and the boundless correspondence which proceeded from his rectory, have been put before the world on various occasions. His letters were voluminous and fluent, and always, it need hardly be said, perfect in sentiment: but they have few literary attractions.—OLIPHANT, MARGARET O. W., 1882, *The Literary History of England, XVIII-XIX Century, vol.* II, *p.* 319.

In poetical style he is our last eminent representative of Pope and Addison.—PALGRAVE, FRANCIS T., 1889, *The Treasury of Sacred Song, p.* 354, *note.*

Much of Heber's poetical work was "occasional," and for the production of "occasional" verse his qualities eminently fitted him. "Palestine" was an occasional poem, and for the purpose of its occasion was a success, though it lacks the qualities necessary to secure permanent interest. He was equal to the occasion, but the subject was too big for him. . . . His hymn, "From Greenland's Icy Mountains," written for a service at Wrexham Church, at which his father-in-law, the Dean of St. Asaph, preached on behalf of the Society for the Propagation of the Gospel, and some half dozen others, are at the full tide of their popularity, nearly a century after they were first sung, and seem as unlikely to go out of favour as they were when they first caught the ears, and gave expression to the feelings of Christian worshippers nearly a hundred years ago. In other occasional and isolated efforts Heber showed a versatility which would doubtless have served him had he cared to follow the leadings of the lighter muse.—MILES, ALFRED H., 1897, *The Poets and Poetry of the Century, Sacred, Moral and Religious Verse, p.* 51.

Thomas Jefferson

1743–1826

Born at Shadwell, Albemarle Co., Va., April 13 (N. S.), 1743; father died, 1757; entered College, March, 1760; graduated, April, 1762; admitted to bar, 1767; elected to House of Burgesses, 1769; married, January, 1772; elected to Continental Congress, March, 1775; attends Virginia Assembly, October, 1776; elected Governor of Virginia, June 1, 1779; reëlected, June 1, 1780; resigned, June 1, 1781; elected delegate to Congress, November, 1781; Mrs. Jefferson died, September, 1782; elected delegate to Congress, June, 1783; minister to France, May, 1784; appointed Secretary of State, September, 1789; leaves France, October, 1789; resigns as Secretary of State, December, 1793; elected Vice-President, November, 1796; nominated for President, May, 1800; elected President, February 17, 1801; inaugurated, March 4, 1801; Louisiana Treaty signed, May 2, 1803; Louisiana Treaty ratified, October 20, 1803; reëlected President, November, 1804; retires from Presidency, March 4, 1809; University of Virginia established, 1818; writes last letter, June 25, 1826; died, July 4, 1826.—CURTIS, WILLIAM ELEROY, 1901, *The True Thomas Jefferson, p.* 15.

PERSONAL

His powers of conversation.—It appears from his character and conduct in early life, that he possessed in a high degree the art of captivating and corrupting all sorts of people with whom he conversed.

THOMAS JEFFERSON

Engraving by T. Johnson. Painting by Gilbert Stuart.

JOHN ADAMS

Engraving by J. B. Longacre. Painting by B. Otis after Original by Gilbert Stuart.

And when he was clothed with the ensigns of royalty his power and opportunity of corrupting his subjects greatly increased. He became the standard of taste and model of imitation. His sentiments and manners became a living law to his subjects. In his familiar intercourse with all around him he undoubtedly seized those soft moments which were the most favorable to his malignant design of seduction. This he could do without departing from the dignity of his station.—EMMONS, NATHANIEL, 1801, *Jeroboam Sermon, April* 9.

We left Charlottesville on Saturday morning, the 4th of February, for Mr. Jefferson's. He lives, you know, on a mountain, which he has named Monticello, and which, perhaps you do not know, is a synonyme for Carter's mountain. The ascent of this steep, savage hill, was as pensive and slow as Satan's ascent to Paradise. . . . His house, which is of brick, two stories high in the wings, with a piazza in front of a receding centre. It is built, I suppose, in the French style. You enter, by a glass folding-door, into a hall which reminds you of Fielding's "Man of the Mountain," by the strange furniture of its walls. On one side hang the head and horns of an elk, a deer, and a buffalo; another is covered with curiosities which Lewis and Clarke found in their wild and perilous expedition. On the third, among many other striking matters, was the head of a mammoth, or, as Cuvier calls it, a mastodon, containing the only *os frontis*, Mr. Jefferson tells me, that has yet been found. On the fourth side, in odd union with a fine painting of the Repentance of Saint Peter, is an Indian map on leather, of the southern waters of the Missouri, and an Indian representation of a bloody battle, handed down in their traditions. Through this hall—or rather museum—we passed to the dining-room, and sent our letters to Mr. Jefferson, who was of course in his study. Here again we found ourselves surrounded with paintings that seemed good. We had hardly time to glance at the pictures before Mr. Jefferson entered; and if I was astonished to find Mr. Madison short and somewhat awkward, I was doubly astonished to find Mr. Jefferson, whom I had always supposed to be a small man, more than six feet high, with dignity in his appearance, and ease and graciousness in his manners. . . . The evening passed away pleasantly in general conversation, of which Mr. Jefferson was necessarily the leader. I shall probably surprise you by saying that, in conversation, he reminded me of Dr. Freeman. He has the same discursive manner and love of paradox, with the same appearance of sobriety and cool reason.—TICKNOR, GEORGE, 1815, *Letter, Feb.* 7; *Life, Letters and Journals, vol.* I, *pp.* 34, 35.

HERE LIES BURIED
THOMAS JEFFERSON,
AUTHOR OF THE DECLARATION OF AMERICAN INDEPENDENCE, OF THE STATUTE OF VIRGINIA FOR RELIGIOUS FREEDOM, AND FATHER OF THE UNIVERSITY OF VIRGINIA.

—JEFFERSON, THOMAS, 1826, *Inscription on Monument.*

The Mansion House at Monticello was built and furnished in the days of his prosperity. In its dimensions, its architecture, its arrangements and ornaments, it is such a one as became the character and fortune of the man. It stands upon an elliptic plain, formed by cutting down the apex of a mountain; and, on the west, stretching away to the north and the south, it commands a view of the Blue Ridge for a hundred and fifty miles, and brings under the eye one of the boldest and most beautiful horizons in the world; while, on the east, it presents an extent of prospect bounded only by the spherical form of the earth, in which nature seems to sleep in eternal repose, as if to form one of her finest contrasts with the rude and rolling grandeur on the west. In the wide prospect, and scattered to the north and south, are several detached mountains, which contribute to animate and diversify this enchanting landscape; and among them, to the south, Willis's Mountain, which is so interestingly depicted in his Notes. From this summit, the Philosopher was wont to enjoy that spectacle, among the sublimest of Nature's operations, the looming of the distant mountains; and to watch the motions of the planets, and the greater revolution of the celestial sphere.—WIRT, WILLIAM, 1826, *Eulogy on Adams and Jefferson in the House of Representatives, Oct.* 19.

Mr. Jefferson examined much less than he rejected. He never examined the evidences of Christianity. He rejected it as an imposture,—rejected it, not by the dictate of his own mind, but upon mere perusal of the Bible, under the influence of the infidel School of his own and the immediately preceding age,—Bolingbroke, Hume, Voltaire, Diderot, and the rest of that gang. What he meant by examination was treating the Bible like Tooke's Pantheon,—studying all the fashionable atheists of the age, and never looking into the writers in favour of Christianity. So far was Mr. Jefferson from encouraging or recommending examination into the truth of the Christian Religion, that he founded his University with a cold, professed, and systematic exclusion of all theological studies from the institution. —ADAMS, JOHN QUINCY, 1830, *Thomas Jefferson, Letter to the North American Review, Old and New, vol.* 7, *p.* 135.

Of all the tests to which Jefferson was submitted, retirement is, perhaps, the one which he supported the best. In his relations with his own political subordinates, now become his successors, not the slightest trace of jealousy, depreciation, or arrogance, no affectation of directing them, and no hesitation to be of use to them by his counsels; nothing of indifference in his reserve, nor of pedantry in his advice; kindness, a sanguine interest, and a frankness that is often highly useful; in his relations with his old adversaries, much courtesy, often even a certain tone of careless freedom, without the slightest concession to their views; accessible to everybody, even to the curious and idle, but of a presence grave enough, and at times cold enough, to discourage familiarity; a large but not ostentatious retinue, a liberal hospitality supported by a ruinous expenditure without the appearance of profusion; perfectly in his place as the recent head of a State metamorphosed into a rural philosopher; living only one year too long, that last year, when the derangement of his fortune led him to occupy the attention of his fellow-citizens too much with his own private affairs, and to detail at too great a length the services which gave him a claim upon the gratitude of the United States; such were the distinguishing features of his seclusion.—DE WITT, CORNÉLIS, 1862, *Jefferson and the American Democracy, tr. Church, p.* 308.

Mr. Jefferson's stature was commanding—six feet two-and-a-half inches in height, well formed, indicating strength, activity, and robust health; his carriage erect; step firm and elastic, which he preserved to his death; his temper, naturally strong, under perfect control; his courage cool and impassive. No one ever knew him exhibit trepidation. His moral courage of the highest order—his will firm and inflexible—it was remarked of him that he never abandoned a plan, a principle, or a friend. A bold and fearless rider, you saw at a glance, from his easy and confident seat, that he was master of his horse, which was usually the fine-blood-horse of Virginia. . . . His habits were regular and systematic. He was a miser of his time, rose always at dawn, wrote and read until breakfast, breakfasted early, and dined from three to four; . . . retired at nine, and to bed from ten to eleven. He said, in his last illness, that the sun had not caught him in bed for fifty years. He always made his own fire. He drank water but once a day, a single glass, when he returned from his ride. He ate heartily, and much vegetable food, preferring French cookery, because it made the meats more tender. He never drank ardent spirits or strong wines. Such was his aversion to ardent spirits, that when, in his last illness, his physician desired him to use brandy as an astringent, he could not induce him to take it strong enough. —RANDOLPH, SARAH N., 1871, *The Domestic Life of Thomas Jefferson, p.* 338.

He belonged neither to the first nor to the second order of human beings. He was not the discoverer of the truths he loved, nor did he promote their acceptance by any of the heroic methods. He did not always avoid the errors to which his cast of character rendered him peculiarly liable. But the sum of his merit was exceedingly great. He was an almost perfect citizen. He loved and believed in his species. Few men have ever been better educated than he, or practised more habitually the methods of an educated person. He defended the honor of the human intellect when its natural foes throughout Christendom conspired to revile, degrade, and crush it. After Washington, he was the best chief magistrate of a republic the world has ever known; and, in some material particulars, he surpassed Washington. He keenly enjoyed his existence, and made it a benefaction to his kind.—PARTON, JAMES, 1874, *Life of Thomas Jefferson, p.* 746.

At Williamsburg in 1760 he dressed in colors, powdered, carried his fine laced hat beneath his arm, bowed low, paid gallant compliments to the fair sex, and danced at every "assembly" held in the capital or the vicinity. In a word, the afterward celebrated Mr. Thomas Jefferson was a beau and "macaroni," had a strong preference apparently for all that was in conflict with his subsequent social theories, laughed, jested, made love to the little belles of the little capital, and was the very last man whom any one would have regarded as the future leader of a great political party and the writer of the Declaration of Independence.—COOKE, JOHN ESTEN, 1876, *The Writer of the Declaration, Harper's Magazine, vol.* 53, *p.* 211.

Single out with me, as you easily will at the first glance, by a presence and a stature not easily overlooked or mistaken, the young, ardent, accomplished Jefferson. He is only just thirty-three years of age. Charming in conversation, ready and full in counsel, he is "slow of tongue," like the great Lawgiver of the Israelites, for any public discussion or formal discourse. But he has brought with him the reputation of wielding what John Adams well called "a masterly pen." And grandly has he justified that reputation. Grandly has he employed that pen already, in drafting a Paper which is at this moment lying on the table, and awaiting its final signature and sanction.—WINTHROP, ROBERT C., 1876, *Centennial Oration, July* 4; *Addresses and Speeches on Various Occasions, p.* 377.

There is no doubt that Thomas Jefferson failed as a speaker simply for lack of voice. He had all the other qualifications; but his voice became guttural and inarticulate in moments of great excitement, and the consciousness of this infirmity prevented him from risking his reputation in debate.—MATHEWS, WILLIAM, 1878, *Oratory and Orators, p.* 77, *note.*

If we may take Jefferson's own word for it, he habitually studied, during his second collegiate year, fifteen hours a day, and for his only exercise ran, at twilight, a mile out of the city and back again. Long afterwards, in 1808, he wrote to a grandson a sketch of this period of his life, composed in his moral and didactic vein; in it he draws a beautiful picture of his own precocious and unnatural virtue, and is himself obliged to gaze in surprise upon one so young and yet so good amid crowding temptations. Without fully sharing in this generous admiration, we must not doubt that he was sufficiently studious and sensible, for he had a natural thirst for information and he always afterwards appeared a broadly educated man. . . . Certainly morals never became in his mind one of the exact sciences.—MORSE, JOHN T., JR., 1883, *Thomas Jefferson (American Statesmen), pp.* 6, 7.

After having served the eight years of his presidential office, Jefferson retired to this his chosen refuge, the creation of his own thought and industry, of much of his own personal handiwork, and spent yet seventeen long years in what with wise forethought and manful persistence he had indeed made "the dearest spot on earth." Under his own vine and fig-tree, in his own house and his own garden, sitting in the refreshing shade of the trees he had himself planted, plucking the flowers and fruits he had himself reared, he talked wisdom to his gray-headed neighbors and contemporaries, gave kindly instruction and admonition to inquiring youths and students, or led his joyous and romping grandchildren through their juvenile games. American annals can present few pictures of so long enjoyed and so perfect a fruition of a labor of love. Bright and alluring as it is, the picture also presents painful shadows. He plucked his own domestic roses with bleeding fingers. The wounds of a bitter partisian conflict galled him; the persecutions of visitors and letter-writers worried him; and at last a hopeless bankruptcy brought him to the humiliating knowledge that the bread he ate was no longer that of his own earning.—NICOLAY, J. G., 1887, *Thomas Jefferson's Home, The Century, vol.* 12, *p.* 653.

His "Anas"—the publication of which is to be lamented—sputter and smoke with charges and insinuations against Hamilton; and he treated Aaron Burr as his friend until Burr's power to serve or injure him was gone forever. The question asked by himself, whether the world was better for his having lived, he answers by a statement in detail of what he had done. That he should have been so embarrassed in his extreme old age as to ask the Virginia legislature for authority to dispose of his property by a lottery, is a melancholy fact; and here again he catalogues his services, truthfully perhaps, but very stoutly. Though he had not escaped the virulance of criticism, he had certainly received more than compensatory public applause during his life, and was now diligent lest "the dull, cold ear of death" should escape being soothed by it afterwards.—MORRILL, JUSTIN S., 1887, *Self-Consciousness of Noted Persons, p.* 25.

For eight years this tall, loosely built, somewhat stiff figure, in red waistcoat and yarn stockings, slippers down in the heel, and clothes that seemed too small for him, may be imagined as Senator Maclay described him, sitting on one hip, with one shoulder high above the other, talking almost without ceasing to his visitors at the White House. His skin was thin, peeling from his face on exposure to the sun, and giving it a tettered appearance. This sandy face, with hazel eyes and sunny aspects; this loose, shackling person; this rambling and often brilliant conversation, belonged to the controlling influences of American history, more necessary to the story than three-fourths of the official papers, which only hid the truth. Jefferson's personality during these eight years appeared to be the government, and impressed itself, like that of Bonaparte, although by a different process, on the mind of the nation.—ADAMS, HENRY, 1889, *History of the United States of America, vol.* I, *p.* 187.

In the spring of 1825, I visited Charlottesville, Albermarle county, Virginia, —where the State University is located—and then had an opportunity to observe Jefferson somewhat closely, but for a much shorter time than I desired. He had come to town from Monticello—which is near by—in a light covered carriage, drawn by two horses and driven by an old negro man. . . . To a youth like me it appeared something more than a mere privilege that I should be permitted to look upon the author of the Declaration of Independence, who was one of the foremost men in the country and who had reflected honor upon his and my own native State, as well as upon the nation. I scrutinized him so closely that the scene was photographed upon my mind, and memory, every now and then, has summoned him again before me. He was then two years younger than I am as I now write, but bore the marks of decrepitude—the wearing away of the vigorous energies of manhood. Notwithstanding the thoughts that crowded my youthful mind, I could not avoid observing the plainness and almost simple rusticity of his dress. His clothing was evidently home-made—probably woven upon a domestic loom—and there was nothing about either its cut or make up to indicate that it had passed through the hands of a fashionable tailor. In fact he belonged to that class of men who, disregarding the frivolities of society, devote their best faculties to other and greater objects. His shoulders were considerably stooped. He did not remove his hat, and I could observe only the face below it. I obtained a position, however, which enabled me to see his eyes with tolerable distinctness; and while they had undoubtedly lost somewhat of their brilliancy, they were still clear, penetrating, and bright. His voice was feeble and slightly tremulous, but not sufficiently so to leave the impression that it was not susceptible of distinct and clear enunciation when there was occasion for it. It appeared to me that he was careful in selecting his purchases, but he did not higgle about the prices. The merchant with whom he dealt exhibited the most marked deference to him, and when his purchases closed, took him by the arm and conducted him to his carriage, which he slowly entered with his assistance and that of the driver. The carriage then drove in the direction of Monticello, and I gazed at it until out of sight, with mingled emotions of pleasure and regret —pleasure at being permitted to see a venerable statesman of such high distinction, and regret at the fear that I should never see him again.—THOMPSON, RICHARD W., 1894, *Recollections of Sixteen Presidents, from Washington to Lincoln, vol,* I, *p.* 37.

During his whole life he was fighting the battle of the masses, yet at no period did he ever associate with them save in his own county, and then only as a great planter, or county squire; nor is there discernible in anything he did or wrote, the feeling of personal as opposed to theoretical liking for mankind. Humane, sympathetic, broad-minded he always was in his views, and actions; but in relations to his fellow-kind he seems to have had a distinct repugnance to association with *hoi polloi.* On the contrary, the chief happiness of his life was found in his intercourse with his social equals; and when his adoption of the people's cause had produced social ostracism by the society of Philadephia, so that old friends of his "crossed the street merely to avoid touching their hats to him," and in his own words, "many declined visiting me with whom I had been on terms of the greatest friendship and intimacy," he ever after, when alluding to the period, used expressions implying that he had endured the keenest suffering. With scarcely an exception, democracy the world over has fought its battles with self-made men as leaders; men near enough to the soil not to feel, or at least able to resist, the pressure of higher social forces: but Jefferson was otherwise, and the suffering this alienation and discrimination caused him is over and over again shown by his reiterated expression of hatred of the very politics to which he gave the larger part of his life.—FORD, PAUL LEICESTER, 1897, *Library of the World's Best Literature, ed. Warner, vol.* XIV, *p.* 8233.

The most striking characteristics of Jefferson were his egotism, his industry, and his comprehensive learning. He had an opinion on every subject for every comer. The only subjects on which he confessed himself deficient were geology and poetry. No problem was too abstruse for him to grasp. He seldom asked advice or assistance from others. He was an infallible oracle to half the population of the country and a dangerous demagogue to the other half, but he was universally recognized as a man of scientific as well as literary attainments. . . . Thomas Jefferson is perhaps the most picturesque character in American history. He was longer in public life; he exercised a more potent and permanent influence upon his own and succeeding generations than any other man, not excepting Washington; but his character and motives have been and always will be subjects of controversy. There is no difference of opinion as to the honesty and patriotism of Washington, Franklin, Jackson, Lincoln, or Grant; while Jefferson is still extolled by some writers as the greatest and purest of statesmen and patriots, and by others denounced as a dangerous demagogue, unsound in his principles, insincere in his utterances, and dishonest in his acts. At the same time no public man ever left so much direct testimony in his own behalf. He was the most prolific of writers. There is scarcely a question in the entire range of human inquiry which he did not discuss; and his manuscripts were intentionally preserved and carefully arranged for the instruction of posterity. He frequently changed his policy and programme, and took different views of the same subjects on different occasions, perhaps on the ancient theory that "a wise man often changes his mind,—a fool never."—CURTIS, WILLIAM ELEROY, 1901, *The True Thomas Jefferson, pp.* 346, 384.

STATESMAN

Now look, my friend, where faint the moonlight falls
On yonder dome, and, in those princely halls,—
If thou canst hate, as sure that soul must hate,
Which loves the virtuous, and reveres the great,—
If thou canst loathe and execrate with me
The poisonous drug of French philosophy,
That nauseous slaver of these frantic times,
With which false liberty dilutes her crimes,—
If thou hast got, within thy freeborn breast,
One pulse that beats more proudly than the rest,
With honest scorn for that inglorious soul,
Which creeps and winds beneath a mob's control,
Which courts the rabble's smile, the rabble's nod,
And makes, like Egypt, every beast its god,
There, in those walls—but, burning tongue, forbear!
Rank must be reverenced, even the rank that's there:
So here I pause.

—MOORE, THOMAS, 1804, *To Thomas Hume from the City of Washington, Poems Relating to America.*

After Washington and Franklin, there is no person who fills so eminent a place among the great men of America, as Jefferson. Whether we regard his important services in the revolutionary contest, or his subsequent assertion of the principles upon which the separation was undertaken,—both while he filled a subordinate station in Washington's presidency, thwarted by his colleagues, as well as at variance with his chief, and while he administered himself the government of that free and prosperous country,—no reasonable doubt can be entertained, that to his enlightened views and to the firmness of his character, it is indebted for much of that freedom and prosperity.—BROUGHAM, HENRY LORD, 1837, *Professor Tucker's Life of Jefferson, Edinburgh Review, vol.* 66, *p.* 156.

The democratic party, not the turbulent and coarse democracy of antiquity or the middle ages, but the great modern democracy, never had a more faithful or more distinguished representative than Jefferson. A warm friend of humanity, liberty, and science; trusting in their goodness as well as their rights; deeply touched by the injustice with which the mass of mankind have been treated, and the sufferings they endure, and incessantly engaged, with an admirable disinterestedness, in remedying them or preventing their recurrence; accepting power as a dangerous necessity, almost as one evil opposed to another, exerting himself, not merely to restrain, but to lower it; distrusting all display, all personal splendor, as a tendency to usurpation; a temper open, kind, indulgent, though ready to take up prejudices against, and feel irritated with the enemies of his party; a mind bold, active, ingenious, inquiring, with more penetration than forecast, but with too much good sense to push things to the extreme, and capable of employing, against a pressing danger or evil, a prudence and firmness, which would perhaps have prevented it, had they been adopted earlier or more generally. — GUIZOT, FRANÇOIS PIERRE GUILLAUME, 1840, *An Essay on the Character of Washington and his Influence on the Revolution.*

Surely, Jefferson may fairly claim the merit of being the father of the great system of *repudiation!* Was he sincere in these strange and startling paradoxes? It is difficult to answer, for he talked wildly on many subjects, and often shifted his ground. Still, there is a certain thread of consistency which runs through all his opinions, and would rather tend to show that he was in earnest. If so, his views much resembled the exaggerated notions of schoolboys—respectable, as the conceptions of young, ardent, inexperienced minds, dazzled by vague dreams of liberty and popular right—but wholly deficient in the elements which constitute the character of a statesman. And among the less worthy motives which seem to have influenced his conduct, it is impossible not to recognize a restless jealousy of those superior natures, with whom he was brought in contact, and whose gifts were so different from his own.—RIETHMÜLLER, CHRISTOPHER JAMES, 1864, *Alexander Hamilton and his Contemporaries, p.* 283.

His career shows him to have possessed many diverse qualities. He was a philosopher, and sometimes a visionary. He was also a politician and a political inventor of the most practical kind. Working in the dark, his hand was felt rather than seen. His lieutenants and agents bore the brunt of the contest, the chief, like a great commander, remaining in the rear—though not always out of the reach of a chance shot.—CHANNING, EDWARD, 1896, *The United States of America*, 1765–1865, *p.* 146.

In later years, when the very form of a State constitution became a party question, the influence of Jefferson largely dominated American thought. He stood for the rights of man as these were expressed in the Declaration of Independence, or were read into it by party interpretation. During the eighteenth century his influence fell far short of what it became after the party he was instrumental in organizing obtained possession of the national government. During the half century following his death, when in one form or another slavery and State sovereignty were national issues, and the extension of the franchise and the change from property to persons as the basis of representation were State issues, Jefferson was idealized as the political philosopher and reformer, and his ideas, as interpreted by a powerful party, were of paramount influence in many States. But his influence was always strongest in the newer parts of the country.—THORPE, FRANCIS NEWTON, 1898, *A Constitutional History of the American People*, 1776–1850, *vol.* I, *p.* 43.

Though not a hero worshipper, I am too good a partisan to question my principal; and Jefferson has been not alone my file-leader, but a guiding star in my political firmament. I am used to measure all systems, to try all causes, to determine all policies by the rules laid down in his philosophy. To me he stands out, after Washington and Franklin, the one clear figure in our early history, a perfect Doric column: wanting the brilliant levity of Hamilton; the sturdy, but narrow, spirit of Adams; sure-footed and far-seeing; not merely a statesman of the first order, but a very principal in the domain of original thinking and moral forces. The minor circumstances of his private life may interest me, but could in no wise change my perspective, because I am fixed in the belief that he was an upright and disinterested man, who considered his duty to his country before all else. Such inconsistencies as appear in his career are but proofs of this, since he never can wholly be true to his convictions, or potent for good in affairs, who does not adapt himself to the changing exigencies of the times, suiting his actions to his words, his words to his actions, according to the course of events.—WATTERSON, HENRY, 1901, *The True Thomas Jefferson by William Eleroy Curtis, Note, p.* 8.

DECLARATION OF INDEPENDENCE 1776

The merit of this paper is Mr. Jefferson's. Some changes were made in it, on the suggestion of other members of the committee, and others by Congress while it was under discussion. But none of them altered the tone, the frame, the arrangement, or the general character of the instrument. As a composition, the declaration is Mr. Jefferson's. It is the production of his mind, and the high honor of it belongs to him, clearly and absolutely. . . . To say that he performed his great work well, would be doing him injustice. To say that he did excellently well, admirably well, would be inadequate and halting praise. Let us rather say, that he so discharged the duty assigned him, that all Americans may well rejoice that the work of drawing the title-deed of their liberties devolved on his hands.—WEBSTER, DANIEL, 1826, *A Discourse in Commemoration of the Lives and Services of John Adams and Thomas Jefferson, delivered in Faneuil Hall, Boston, Aug.* 2, *pp.* 26, 27.

This trust devolved on Jefferson, and with it rests on him the imperishable renown of having penned the Declaration of Independence. To have been the instrument of expressing, in one brief, decisive act, the concentrated will and resolution of a whole family of states, of unfolding, in one all-important manifesto, the causes, the motives, and the justification of this great movement in human affairs; to have been permitted to give the impress and peculiarity of his own mind to a charter of public right, destined—or, rather, let me say, already elevated—to an importance, in the estimation of men, equal to any thing human, ever borne on parchment, or expressed in the visible signs of thought,—this is the glory of Thomas Jefferson. —EVERETT, EDWARD, 1826, *Eulogy on Adams and Jefferson, Aug.* 1, *Orations and Speeches.*

He owed this distinction to respect for the colony which he represented, to the consummate ability of the state papers which he had already written, and to that general favor which follows merit, modesty, and a sweet disposition; but the quality which specially fitted him for the task was the sympathetic character of his nature by which he was able with instinctive perception to read the soul of the nation, and having collected in himself its best thoughts and noblest feelings, to give them out in clear and bold words, mixed with so little of himself, that his country, as it went along with him, found nothing but what it recognised as its own. No man of this century had more trust in the collective reason and conscience of his fellow men, or better knew how to take their counsel; and in return he came to be a ruler over the willing in the world of opinion. . . . This immortal state paper, which for its composer, was the aurora of enduring fame, was "the genuine effusion of the soul of the country at that time," the revelation of its mind, when in its youth, its enthusiasm, its sublime confronting of danger, it rose to the highest creative powers of which man is capable.—BANCROFT, GEORGE, 1866, *History of the United States.*

A document which is alone sufficient to perpetuate the name of Thomas Jefferson, and to cover it with glory in the estimation of his countrymen. It came from his mind, clear, shapely, complete as Minerva from the brain of Jupiter, and received no essential additions or important alterations from other hands, except such slight verbal modification as added little or nothing to its essential symmetry, its force, or its perspicuity.—MACKAY, CHARLES, 1885, *The Founders of the American Republic, p.* 238.

One of the most famous documents in the muniment room of history, bespeaks the hand of the philosophic Jefferson. It opens with sweeping aphorisms about the natural rights of man at which political science now smiles, and which, as American abolitionists did not fail to point out at a later day, might seem strange when framed for slave-holding communities by a publicist who himself held slaves.—SMITH, GOLDWIN, 1893, *The United States, an Outline of Political History,* 1492–1871, *p.* 87.

The one American state paper that has reached to supreme distinction in the world, and that seems likely to last as long as American civilization lasts. . . . American confidence in the supreme intellectual merit of this all-famous document received a serious wound, some forty years ago, from the hand of Rufus Choate, when, with a courage greater than would now be required for such an act, he characterized it as made up of "glittering and sounding generalities of natural right." What the great advocate then so unhesitantly suggested, many a thoughtful American since then has at least suspected, —that this famous proclamation, as a piece of political literature, cannot stand the test of modern analysis; that it belongs to the immense class of over-praised productions; that it is, in fact, a stately patchwork of sweeping propositions of somewhat doubtful validity; that it has long imposed upon mankind by the well-known effectiveness of verbal glitter and sound; that, at the best, it is an example of florid political declamation belonging to the sophomoric period of our national life —a period which, as we flatter ourselves, we have now outgrown.—TYLER, MOSES COIT, 1897, *The Literary History of the American Revolution,* 1763–1783, *vol.* I, *p.* 498.

GENERAL

The Editor, though he cannot be insensible to the genius, the learning, the philosophic inspiration, the generous devotion to virtue, and the love of country, displayed in the writings now committed to the press, is restrained, not less by his incompetency, than by his relation to the Author, from dwelling on themes which belong to an eloquence that can do justice to the names of illustrious benefactors to their country and to their fellow men.—RANDOLPH, THOMAS JEFFERSON, 1829, *Memoir, Correspondence and Miscellanies from the Papers of Thomas Jefferson, vol.* I, *p.* 8.

Mr. Jefferson, too, is entitled to great Respect, though after the conduct of his last days, and the posthumous publication of his writings, delicacy towards him from New England is an exemplification of something more than Christian meekness and forbearance.—ADAMS, JOHN QUINCY, 1830, *Thomas Jefferson, Letter to North American Review, Old and New, vol.* 7, *p.* 137.

The inaugural address of Mr. Jefferson was as novel and extraordinary, as the simplicity of the scene which ushered it before the world. For condensation of ideas and Addisonian purity of language, it is allowed to be superior to any thing in the wide circle of political composition. In the short compass in which it is compressed, all the essential principles of free governments are stated, in detail, with the measures best calculated for their attainment and security, and an ample refutation of the adversary principles. Every word is pregnant with sentiment and reproof, and every sentence contains a text on which might be written volumes of political wisdom.—RAYNER, B. L., 1832, *Sketches of the Life, Writings and Opinions of Thomas Jefferson, p.* 404.

In the *talents,* by which individuals are commonly supposed to acquire and extend their influence, he was almost wholly deficient: he had no military taste or skill; he never spoke in public, and had no peculiar power in writing. It is said by the author of the "Familiar Letters," that he ruled the American people by "the magic of his pen." This idea appears to be erroneous. Mr. Jefferson wrote through life very little. The little he wrote consisted mostly of private letters, which never went out to the people: in his few published writings, there is no extraordinary force or charm of style. As mere literary productions, they would have attracted no attention; they produced effect not as writings, but as *acts* . . . . There was no magic in his pen. The witchcraft of which he acquired influence lay, like that of the Maréchale d' Ancre, in his *mental superiority.* — EVERETT, ALEXANDER HILL, 1834, *Origin and Character of the Old Parties, North American Review, vol.* 39, *pp.* 244, 245.

As an author, he has left no memorial that is worthy of his genius; for the public papers drawn by him are admired rather for the patriotic spirit which dictated them than for the intellectual power they exhibit. They presented no occasion for novelty of thought, or argument, or diction. His purpose was only to make a judicious and felicitous use of that which every body knew and would assent to; and this object he has eminently fulfilled. His "Notes on Virginia," though stamped with his characteristic independence of mind, are rather remarkable for the extent of his statistical knowledge, in a country and at a period when knowledge of that kind was so difficult of attainment; and his "Manual" of parliamentary practice required nothing more than care and discrimination. His diplomatic correspondence throughout shows that he possessed logical powers of the highest order; and his letters, especially those of his latter years, are written with great elegance and felicity. . . . But it is on his merits as a lawgiver and political philosopher that his claims to greatness chiefly rest: it is for these that he is to be praised or condemned by posterity; for beyond all his contemporaries has he impressed his opinions of government on the minds of the great mass of his countrymen. —TUCKER, GEORGE, 1837, *The Life of Thomas Jefferson, vol.* II, *pp.* 564, 567.

Jefferson was the Danton of the West; but his forte lay not so much in oratory as in political management. More perhaps than any other statesman of his age, he aspired to be an author, to which title the most vivacious pages of his "Notes on Virginia," conspicuously his graphic description of the passage of the Potomac through the Blue Ridge, his "Autobiography" and "Correspondence," give him a fair claim. His sketches of continental society, though bearing the mark of a somewhat superficial study of French models, and marred by eighteenth-century mannerism, are lively; and his occasional flights of fancy, as in the "Dialogue between the Head and the Heart," at least ingenious.—NICHOL, JOHN, 1880-85, *American Literature, p.* 77.

Those venomous "Anas," among the most unfortunate of all deeds of the pen. . . . How differently could we think of him were it not for this bequest which, like the cloven foot, peeps out from beneath his apparent guise of broad charity and kindliness.—MORSE, JOHN T., JR., 1883, *Thomas Jefferson* (*American Statesmen*), *p.* 327.

Jefferson was preëminently a writer. His speeches were not effective, nor was he strong in administration; but in the seclusion of his study or office, with a pen in his hand, his power and ability were unequaled. He was profoundly learned in the theory and practice of government; his writings and career show him to have been one of the broadest and most consistent democrats of any age.—HAWTHORNE, JULIAN, AND LEMMON, LEONARD, 1891, *American Literature, p.* 28.

Much of Jefferson's remarkable influence was due to his attractive style as a writer. Phrases from his letters and public documents, sometimes fervent, sometimes humorous, circulated through the land like silver coin. He wrote and he talked with warm blood coursing through his veins; and though the shaft might rankle where it was driven, it struck the mark. Vigour, liveliness, and choice felicity of expression marked his style, which was nevertheless scholarly; and while so many of his age modelled their style upon Addison and the "Spectator," sought out the sonorous and balanced their periods laboriously, admitting no word that might not be found in Johnson's dictionary, he preferred rather the figurative, and aimed to make the English vocabulary more copious. His style, like that of every master, was an image of himself, and adaptive he meant it to be to the current American age and institutions. —SCHOULER, JAMES, 1893, *Thomas Jefferson* (*Makers of America*), *p.* 245.

Jefferson was not a thorough American because of the strain of French philosophy that permeated and weakened all his thought. — WILSON, WOODROW, 1896, *Mere Literature and Other Essays, p.* 196.

If Jefferson be judged by any single piece of work, except perhaps the "Declaration of Independence," or by the general qualities of his style, he cannot in any fairness be termed a great writer. His "Notes on Virginia," his only book, may be justly said to be interesting and valuable, but cannot rank high as literature. His state papers, with the exception made above, and his official reports are excellent of their kind, but their kind is not sufficiently literary to warrant any one in holding them up as models. Even his countless letters, while fascinating to the student of his character, are rather barren of charm when read without some ulterior purpose. In short, while Jefferson was plainly the most widely cultured of our early statesmen and was thus in a real sense a man of letters, he would be little read to-day if his fame depended either upon his authorship of a masterpiece in the shape of a book or upon his possession of a powerful or charming style. We see at once that in at least two important respects Jefferson is inferior to Franklin as a writer. . . . But has not Jefferson given us a masterpiece? In a book, no; in a state paper, yes. The "Declaration of Independence," whatever may be the justice of the criticism directed against this and that clause or statement, is a true piece of literature, because ever since it was written it has been alive with emotion. . . . The man who drafted such a document knew the spirit of his own people and could express it to their satisfaction; to deny him literary power of a high order would therefore be pedantic.—TRENT, W. P., 1898, *American Prose, ed. Carpenter, pp.* 76, 77, 78.

John Adams

1735-1826

Born at Braintree (in present Quincy), Mass., Oct. 30, 1735: died at Quincy, Mass., July 4, 1826. The second President of the United States, 1797–1801. He was graduated at Harvard in 1755, studied law, took a leading part in opposing the Stamp Act, was counsel for the soldiers charged with murder in connection with the "Boston massacre" of 1770, and became a leader of the patriot party. In 1774 he was chosen a member of the Revolutionary congress of Massachusetts. He was a delegate to the first and second Continental Congresses, proposed Washington as commander-in-chief, signed the Declaration of Independence, was appointed commissioner to France in 1777 (arriving at Paris in 1778), negotiated a treaty with the Netherlands in 1782, was one of the negotiators of the treaties with Great Britain, 1782–83, negotiated a treaty with Prussia, was appointed minister to London in 1785, and was recalled in 1788. He was Federal Vice-President 1789–97, and was elected as Federal candidate for President in 1796. In 1800 he was the unsuccessful Federal candidate for President, and retired to Quincy in 1801. "Life and Works," edited by C. F. Adams (10 vols., 1850–56); life by J. Q. and C. F. Adams (1871), by J. T. Morse (1885).—SMITH, BENJAMIN E., *ed.*, 1894–97, *The Century Cyclopedia of Names, p.* 13.

PERSONAL

This day, dearest of friends, completes thirteen years since we were solemnly united in wedlock. Three years of this time we have been cruelly separated. I have, patiently as I could, endured it, with the belief that you were serving your country and rendering your fellow-creatures essential benefits. May future generations rise up and call you blessed, and the present behave worthy of the blessings you are laboring to secure to them, and I shall have less reason to regret the deprivation of my own particular felicity. Adieu, dearest of friends, adieu.—ADAMS, ABIGAIL, 1777, *Letter to John Adams, Oct.* 25; *Familiar Letters, ed. C. F. Adams, p.* 322.

It is confidently affirmed that Adams an aristocratic Lawyer in favor of British Dignities, manners and Government will be President.—AMES, NATHANIEL, 1796, *Diary, Dec.*

Mr. Adams had a great mind, quick, comprehensive, analytical, not easily satisfied save with ultimate causes, tenacious also of its treasures. His memory did not fail until he was old. With the exception of Dr. Franklin, I think of no American politician in the eighteenth century that was his intellectual superior. For though Hamilton and Jefferson, nay, Jay and Madison and Marshall surpassed him in some high qualities, yet no one of them seems to have been quite his equal on the whole. He was eminent in all the three departments of the Intellect—the Understanding, the practical power; the Imagination, the poetic power, and the Reason, the philosophic power. . . . At the age of forty he was the ablest lawyer in New England, perhaps the ablest lawyer in America. He was the most learned in historic legal lore, the most profound in the study of first principles. —PARKER, THEODORE, 1870, *Historic Americans, pp.* 200, 201.

In figure John Adams was not tall, scarcely exceeding middle height, but of a stout, well-knit frame, denoting vigor and long life, yet as he grew old, inclining more and more to corpulence. His head was large and round, with a wide forehead and expanded brows. His eye was mild and benignant, perhaps even humorous, when he was free from emotion, but when excited, it fully expressed the vehemence of the spirit that stirred within. His presence was grave and imposing, on serious occasions, but not unbending. He delighted in social conversation, in which he was sometimes tempted to what he called rodomontade. But he seldom fatigued those who heard him; for he mixed so much of natural vigor, of fancy, and of illustration with the stores of his acquired knowledge, as to keep alive their interest for a long time. His affections were warm, though not habitually demonstrated, towards his relatives. His anger, when thoroughly roused, was, for a time, extremely violent, but when it subsided, it left no trace of malevolence behind. Nobody could see him intimately without admiring the simplicity and truth which shone in his action, and standing in some awe at the reserved power of his will. It was in these moments that he impressed those around him with a sense of his greatness. Even the men employed on his farm were in the habit of citing instances, some of which have been remembered down to the present day. At times his vehemence would become so great as to make him overbearing and unjust. This was most apt to happen in cases of pretension or any kind of wrong-doing. Mr. Adams was very impatient of cant, of sciolism, or of opposition to any of his deeply-established convictions. Neither was his indignation at all graduated to the character of the individuals who might happen to excite it. It had little respect of persons, and would hold an illiterate man, or a raw boy, to as heavy a responsibility for uttering a crude heresy as the strongest thinker or the most profound scholar.—ADAMS, CHARLES FRANCIS, 1871, *The Life of John Adams, Revised and Corrected, vol.* II, *p.* 409.

In this rapid survey of the men assembled at Philadelphia a hundred years ago to-day, I began with Thomas Jefferson, of Virginia, and I end with John Adams, of Massachusetts; and no one can hesitate to admit that, under God, they were the very alpha and omega of that day's doings,—the pen and the tongue,—the masterly author, and the no less masterly advocate, of the Declaration.—WINTHROP, ROBERT C., 1876, *Centennial Oration, July* 4.

In nearly every respect John Adams was a typical New Englander of the times; at least it may be said that in no one individual did the colonial character find a more respectable or a more comprehensible development than in him, so that to understand and appreciate him is to understand and appreciate the New England of his day; and to draw him is to draw the colonists in their best form.—MORSE, JOHN T., JR., 1884, *John Adams* (*American Statesmen*), *p.* 23.

In integrity he was an ancient Roman. He had more force than play of character, and though his experience was wide, for he had been ambassador as well as statesman, more knowledge of books than of men. He was somewhat dogmatic, somewhat pedantic, and from his childhood too self-conscious and too laboriously self-trained, as his methodical diary shows.—SMITH, GOLDWIN, 1893, *The United States, an Outline of Political History,* 1492–1871, *p.* 151.

John Adams was the father of the public school, the State University, the State College, and the normal school. He realized when he inserted the educational clauses in the constitution of Massachusetts that he was departing from precedent and feared lest all would be struck out. Save in New England, the idea lay dormant until the national government began to make donations of public lands exclusively for school purposes. The State constitutions then introduced an administrative article on education. This act of the general government strengthened the national idea. In our day, the right to education, in popular estimation, ranks as a civil right.—THORPE, FRANCIS NEWTON, 1898, *A Constitutional History of the American People*, 1776–1850, *vol.* I, *p.* 74.

STATESMAN

I am persuaded, however, that he means well for his country, is always an honest man, often a wise one, but sometimes, and in some things, absolutely out of his senses.—FRANKLIN, BENJAMIN, 1783, *Letter to Congress.*

There never was, perhaps, a greater contrast between two characters than between those of the present President and his predecessor; although it is the boast and prop of the present that he treads in the steps of his predecessor. The one, cool, considerate, and cautious; the other, headlong, and kindled into flame by every spark that lights on his passions: the one, ever scrutinizing into the public opinion, and ready to follow, where he could not lead it; the other, insulting it by the most adverse sentiments and pursuits. Washington a hero in the field, yet ever weighing every danger in the Cabinet: Adams without a single pretension to the character of a soldier, a perfect Quixote as a statesman.—MADISON, JAMES, 1798, *To Thomas Jefferson, Feb.; Letters and Other Writings, vol.* II, *p.* 127.

President Adams has written a very long letter to General Varnum on our national affairs. He speaks with great approbation of the Administration, and goes the whole length with them in vindication of our national rights. I assure you, that I read his letter with the greatest delight, and regretted that for a moment I had ever doubted his patriotism. The letter would do honour to any man living. He, Mr. Gray, and Mr. John Quincy Adams, have deserved highly of their country; and I venture to predict, that when party spirit has passed away, their memories will be revered by every honest and honourable American, with the greatest enthusiasm.—STORY, JOSEPH, 1809, *Letter to Joseph White, Jr., Jan.* 14; *Life and Letters, ed. Story, vol.* I, *p.* 192.

He was an eminently honest, brave, and humane man. . . . Adams was an able and an honest man, and as he had been commissioner at Paris on the recall of Silas Deane, he was not quite unaccustomed to European ways, but he appears to have been singularly wanting in the peculiar tact and delicacy required in a diplomatist.—LECKY, WILLIAM EDWARD HARTPOLE, 1882, *A History of England in the Eighteenth Century, vol.* III, *p.* 400, *vol.* IV, *p.* 190.

Adams had been sent as ambassador to England. The choice was a most happy one. Of all the men in the service of the republic, he alone was, by nature and by experience, fitted for the place. . . . Diligent, cautious, painstaking, he was an excellent man of business and a careful observer of events. His mind was in no danger of being drawn aside to investigate the ascent of balloons, to examine the pretensions of Mesmer, or to write up pamphlets on emigration to America. He was constantly intent on matters of state, and was as familiar with public opinion in England touching American affairs as with public opinion in Holland. He had indeed given it as his belief, long before the appointment was made, that the post of Minister to England would be far from a pleasant one, and that whoever should occupy it would find himself in a thicket of briers from which he could barely expect to escape without tearing his flesh.—MCMASTER, JOHN BACH, 1883, *A History of the People of the United States from the Revolution to the Civil War, vol.* I, *p.* 233.

John Adams possessed two faculties in a degree which distinguished him among his countrymen, and made him pre-eminently serviceable in a period of revolution,—the historic imagination which develops nationality from its germ, and clear intuitions of organic constitutional law. In these faculties he has never been surpassed by any American statesman, nor equalled save by him whose name needs no mention in this presence. . . . If we now look at some of those moral characteristics which marked him as a statesman, we shall find certain race traits which he seems to have inherited immediately from his British ancestry, rather than by transmission through his colonial progenitors. He possessed the pluck, courage and bull-dog tenacity which we call English, and which all through their history has stood them in such stead in desperate civil and military encounters, often changing lost fields to fields of victory, and, on the other hand, there was no trace in his composition of the craft, cunning, or selfishness which narrow circumstances and a hundred years of contest with a treacherous and skulking foe are supposed, justly or unjustly, to have engrafted on the New England character of his day.—CHAMBERLAIN, MELLEN, 1884, *John Adams, the Statesman of the American Revolution, pp.* 4, 5.

All admit his abilities, his honesty, and his patriotism; but it is only Massachusetts that ranks him among the demi-gods. As a young man he was among the greatest, if he were not the very greatest of his country. As a man of middle age he did not attain the high standard which his youth led his contemporaries to predict. He was a respectable, a useful, a zealous public servant, and an average diplomatist, with small opportunities of distinction, which he made the most of. In later life, and when he had attained the highest summit of his ambition, and wielded, as far as a President could wield, the destinies of his country, he offended the party by whose suffrages he was elected, and never conciliated in any appreciable degree the party that had opposed him. The adopted of Federalism, he threw back the cause of the Federalists for sixty years. "Whom the gods love, die young," said the ancients. Perhaps, and most probably, if John Adams had died immediately after the Declaration of Independence, his name, next to that of Washington, might have stood highest and brightest in the long muster-roll of American worthies.—MACKAY, CHARLES, 1885, *The Founders of the American Republic, p.* 206.

The credit of having originated the measures which led to building up the United States Navy—in the face of formidable opposition—can not properly be withheld from Adams. . . . Of Adams it may be most truthfully said that not one among the most illustrious statesmen of this country was more devoted to the Cause of the American Colonies, or displayed more zeal or ability in their defense. In all the varied scenes through which he passed, his patriotism never faltered and was never called in question.—THOMPSON, RICHARD W., 1894, *Recollections of Sixteen Presidents from Washington to Lincoln, vol.* I, *pp.* 27, 34.

GENERAL

The various political works of the elder President Adams, published during his lifetime, have been long out of print, and are, for the most part, to be found only in libraries formed in the last generation. They exercised a very powerful influence over public opinion at the time when they appeared. No thorough knowledge of our constitutional history can be acquired without a careful perusal of them.—EVERETT, EDWARD, 1850, *The Works of John Adams, North American Review, vol.* 71, *p.* 408.

There are few eminent persons who have drawn so lifelike a portrait of themselves as he has done. . . . Had he never emerged from the obscurity of his first estate, and lived and died an unknown man, his Diary, unearthed a century after it was written, would have been a most interesting and valuable contribution to psychology as well as to history.—QUINCY, EDMUND, 1871, *Adams's Life of John Adams, North American Review, vol.* 113, *p.* 188.

Mr. Adams lived in an age of action, and had little time for rhetorical arts. But few of his speeches have been preserved. His letters form the most valuable part of his published works, and are among the best in our literature. Those addressed to his wife, in particular, are delightfully frank, tender, and manly.—UNDERWOOD, FRANCIS H., 1872, *A Hand-Book of English Literature, American Authors, p.* 11.

The character of Mr. Adams is clearly visible in his own papers. Ardent, vehement in support of what he believed to be right, easily roused to anger by opposition, but sincere, placable, and generous, when made conscious of having committed the slightest wrong, there is no individual of his time about whom there are so few concealments of either faults or virtues.—ADAMS, CHARLES FRANCIS, 1875, *ed., Familiar Letters of John Adams and His Wife Abigail Adams During the Revolution. p.* xxviii.

As a writer of English, John Adams in many respects surpassed all his American contemporaries; his style was crisp, pungent, and vivacious.—WILSON, JAMES GRANT, *ed.*, 1886–94, *The Presidents of the United States, p.* 59.

Like his son, John Quincy, he was an

inveterate diarist, from 1755 to 1785, and his records of some important transactions are not only valuable as history but picturesque in language. . . . Adams could turn a phrase neatly enough, and there was matter as well as manner in his phrases. . . . Adams must write, but he had no literary end in view, and spent as much honest care upon a home letter as upon a state document or a newspaper article to stir the patriots.—RICHARDSON, CHARLES F., 1887, *American Literature*, 1607-1885, *vol.* I, *pp.* 204, 205, 206.

The Puritan temperament was strongly emphasized in this son of Massachusetts, but its fearless and indomitable energy was in him addressed to politics instead of to religion. He could not be at ease either in the pulpit or at the bar; but the obvious dangers threatening his country drew him to its defence as inevitably as the magnet attracts iron. . . . As a writer, he was copious, careful and weighty. His diary, kept from 1755 to 1785, contains the record of many important events, graphically described; and his private letters show a largeness of view and a force of expression that recall the style of the historian. He was a contributor to the newspapers of the time, and was the author of several essays or pamphlets on matters of public moment.—HAWTHORNE, JULIAN, AND LEMMON, LEONARD, 1891, *American Literature*, *pp.* 29, 30.

Known in literature chiefly from the charming correspondence that passed between him and his wife during the most stirring period of our history. These letters, which have been given to the world by Charles Francis Adams, are singularly frank and tender. Besides revealing two rare personalities, and an almost ideal domestic life, they possess a literary merit of very high rank. Adams, aside from the inevitable public documents and messages incident to his position, produced several powerful pamphlets of contemporary interest, and kept a journal which is now of great value to the student of our early national life.—PATTEE, FRED LEWIS, 1896, *A History of American Literature*, *p.* 82.

Lindley Murray

1745-1826

Born, at Swatara, Pennsylvania, 22 April 1745. To school at Philadelphia, 1751. Soon afterwards removed with his parents to North Carolina. To New York, 1753. Assisted his father (a merchant) in business from 1759; but, owing to literary tastes, ran away to a school at Burlington, New Jersey. Brought back to New York; placed under a tutor, and studied law. Called to Bar, 1765. Married Hannah Dobson, 22 June 1767. Practised as lawyer in New York. In England, 1770-71. To England again, owing to failing health, 1784; settled at Holdgate, near York. Devoted remainder of life to literary and scientific pursuits. Died, at Holdgate, 16 Jan. 1826. *Works:* "The Power of Religion on the Mind" (anon.), 1787 (6th edn. same year); "Some Account of the Life . . . of Sarah Grubb" (anon.), 1792; "English Grammar," 1795 (abridged edn., by author, 1797); "English Exercises," 1797; "Key" to preceding, 1797; "English Reader," 1799; "Sequel to the English Reader,". 1800; "Introduction to the English Reader," 1801; "Lecteur Français," 1802; "First Book for Children," 1804; "English Spelling Book," 1804; "Introduction au Lecteur Français," 1807; "Biographical Sketch of Henry Tuke," 1815; "Compendium of Religious Truth and Practice," 1815; "The Duty and Benefit of a Daily Perusal of the Holy Scriptures in Families," 1817. *Posthumous:* "Memoirs," ed. by E. Frank, 1826. He *edited:* "Selection from Bishop Home's Commentary on the Psalms," 1812; "Extracts from the Writings of divers eminent Authors . . . representing the evils . . . of Stage Plays," 1799.—SHARP, R. FARQUHARSON, 1897, *A Dictionary of English Authors*, *p.* 209.

PERSONAL

In general discourse he did not talk much, nor long together, except on business or occasions which rendered it necessary; indeed, he was usually prevented by the weakness of his voice. He seldom said more than the subject required; nor, apparently, more than he intended. He never seemed to talk for the sake of self display, or self gratification. To please or edify those with whom he conversed, or to obtain from them such useful information as they were capable of affording, were his favourite objects. . . . His external manners were truly pleasing. He was affable and courteous in his address; mild, yet dignified in his demeanour. His unaffected civility and kindness readily won their way to the heart.—FRANK, ELIZABETH, 1826, *Memoirs of the Life and Writings of Lindley Murray, Continuation, pp.* 217, 228.

Murray was tall, slender, and of a ruddy complexion. In spite of bad health he was always cheerful, and his manner was conspicuously modest.—SMITH, MISS C. FELL, 1894, *Dictionary of National Biography, vol.* XXXIX, *p.* 398.

ENGLISH GRAMMAR
1795

This work is not without merit in the details and examples of English construction. But its fault even at that part is that he confounds the genius of the English language, making it periphrastic and literal, instead of elliptical and idiomatic. According to Mr. Murray, hardly any of our best writers ever wrote a word of English.—HAZLITT, WILLIAM, 1825, *The Spirit of the Age, p.* 76, *note.*

In a short time after the appearance of the work a second edition was called for. This unexpected demand, induced me to revise and enlarge the book. It soon obtained an extensive circulation. And the repeated editions through which it passed in a few years encouraged me, at length, to improve and extend it still further; and, in particular, to support, by some critical discussions the principles upon which many of its positions are founded. . . . But my views in writing and publishing were not of a pecuniary nature. My great objects were, as I before observed, to be instrumental in doing a little good to others, to youth in particular; and to give my mind a rational and salutary employment. It was, I believe, my early determination that if any profits should arise from my literary labours I would apply them, not to my own private use, but to charitable purposes, and for the benefit of others. My income was sufficient to support the expenses of my family and to allow of a little to spare; and I had not any children to provide for. There was, consequently, no inducement to warrant me in deviating from the determination I had made: and as I have hitherto adhered, I trust I shall continue faithfully to adhere, to my original views and intentions.—MURRAY, LINDLEY, 1826, *Memoirs, ed. Frank, Letter* v.

One of the most profitable school books ever issued from the press—for many years the annual sale of the "Abridgement" in England alone was from 48,000 to 50,000 copies.—CURWEN, HENRY, 1873, *A History of Booksellers, p.* 92.

He has been styled the father of English grammar, and his work, although not free from error and soon superseded, undoubtedly helped more efficiently than any contemporary manual to teach the Englishmen of his day to speak and write their language correctly. He introduced system into the study of grammar where chaos had existed before, but it is noticeable that his own style of writing frequently illustrates the defects which he warns his readers to avoid. There may have been some truth in the jest of his friend John Dalton, the chemist, "that of all the contrivances invented by human ingenuity for puzzling the brains of the young, Lindley Murray's grammar was the worst."—SMITH, MISS C. FELL, 1894, *Dictionary of National Biography, vol.* XXXIX, *p.* 398.

GENERAL

The reader who takes up the autobiography of Lindley Murray with no other previous preparation than his early schoolboy recollections of the grammar, will have a sensation as agreeable as unexpected. It is like meeting the schoolmaster after we have grown up, and finding him a pleasant courteous gentleman instead of the monster we had so often vowed to thrash on arriving at the vigor of manhood prerequisite for the achievement.—DUYCKINCK, EVERT A. AND GEORGE L., 1855-65-75, *Cyclopædia of American Literature, ed. Simons, vol.* I, *p.* 269.

No work which treats of American literature should fail to notice him whose works on English philology have been the standard educational books on both sides of the Atlantic for half a century. . . . Few authors have so wide-spread a fame as Lindley Murray, and few have had so many readers. His first publication was "the Power of Religion on the Mind,"—

a treatise of great excellence, which was very favourably received, and passed through numerous editions. His next work was his "English Grammar," which was soon followed by his "English Reader;" and it is doubtless the fact that no other school-books have ever enjoyed so wide a circulation. — CLEVELAND, CHARLES D., 1859, *A Compendium of American Literature, pp.* 84, 85.

William Blake

1757–1827

Born, in London, 28 Nov. 1757. To drawing school, 1767. Began to write verse, 1768. Apprenticed to J. Basire, engraver to Soc. of Antiquaries, 1771–78. Student in Royal Academy, 1778. Engraved for magazines and books. Married Catharine Sophia Boucher, 18 Aug. 1782. Opened printseller's shop in Broad Street, 1784. Exhibited at R. A. same year. Shop given up, 1787. At Felpham, 1800–04. Returned to London. Exhibited for last time at R. A. 1808. Died, 12 Aug. 1827. Buried at Bunhill Fields, Finsbury. *Works:* [all engraved and coloured by hand unless otherwise stated]; "Poetical Sketches" (printed), 1783; "Songs of Innocence" (with assistance of his wife), 1789; "Book of Thel," 1789; "Marriage of Heaven and Hell," 1790; "French Revolution" (printed), 1791; "Prospectus," 1793; "Gates of Paradise," 1793; "Visions of the Daughters of Albion," 1793; "America," 1793; "Europe," 1794; "The Book of Urizen," 1794; "Songs of Experience," 1794; "The Song of Los," 1795; "The Book of Ahania," 1795; "Jerusalem," 1804; "Milton," 1804; "Descriptive Catalogue" (printed), 1809. *Collected Works:* Poems, edited by R. H. Shepherd, 1868; by W. M. Rossetti (Aldine Series), 1874; Works, in facsimile of original editions, 1876. *Life:* by Gilchrist, 2nd ed. 1880.—SHARP, R. FARQUHARSON, 1897, *A Dictionary of English Authors, p.* 27.

PERSONAL

Blake is a real name, I assure you, and a most extraordinary man, if he be still living. He is the Robert Blake, whose wild designs accompany a splendid folio edition of the "Night Thoughts," which you may have seen. . . . He paints in water colours marvellous strange pictures, visions of his brain, which he asserts that he has seen. They have great merit. He has *seen* the old Welsh bards on Snowdon—he has seen the Beautifullest, the strongest, and the Ugliest Man, left alone from the Massacre of the Britons by the Romans, and has painted them from memory (I have seen his paintings), and asserts them to be as good as the figures of Raphael and Angelo, but not better, as they have precisely the same retro-visions and prophetic visions with themself (himself). The painters in oil (which he will have it that neither of them practised) he affirms to have been the ruin of art, and affirms that all the while he was engaged in his Water paintings, Titian was disturbing him, Titian the Ill Genius of Oil Painting. His Pictures—one in particular, the Canterbury Pilgrims (far above Stothard's)—have great merit, but hard, dry, yet with grace. He has written a Catalogue of them with a most spirited criticism on Chaucer, but mystical and full of Vision. . . . The man is flown, whither I know not—to Hades or a Mad House. But I must look on him as one of the most extraordinary persons of the age.—LAMB, CHARLES, 1824, *Letter to Barton, May* 15; *Letters, ed. Ainger, vol.* II, *pp.* 104, 105.

Blake is an engraver by trade, a painter and poet also, whose works have been subjects of derision to men in general, but he has a few admirers, and some of eminence have eulogized his designs. He has lived in obscurity and poverty, to which the constant hallucinations in which he lives have doomed him. I do not mean to give you a detailed account of him; a few words will serve to inform you of what class he is. He is not so much a disciple of Jacob Boehme and Swedenborg as a fellow-visionary. He lives as they did, in a world of his own, enjoying constant intercourse with the world of spirits. He receives visits from Shakespeare, Milton, Dante, Voltaire, &c., and has given me repeatedly their very words in their conversations. His paintings are copies of what he sees in his visions. His books (and his MSS. are immense in quantity) are dictations from the spirits. A man so favoured, of course, has sources of wisdom and truth peculiar to himself. I will not pretend to give you an account of his religious and philosophical opinions; they are a strange compound of Christianity, Spinozism, and Platonism.—ROBINSON, HENRY CRABB, 1826, *Letter to Miss Wordsworth, Feb.; Reminiscences, ed. Sadler, vol.* II, *p.* 38.

She [Mrs. Blake] would get up in the night, when he was under his very fierce inspirations, which were as if they would tear him asunder, while he was yielding himself to the Muse, or whatever else it could be called, sketching and writing. And so terrible a task did this seem to be, that she had to sit motionless and silent, only to stay him mentally, without moving hand or foot: this for hours, and night after night.—SMITH, JOHN THOMAS, 1845, *A Book for a Rainy Day, p.* 14.

Blake, once known, could never be forgotten. His knowledge was various and extensive, and his conversation so nervous and brilliant, that, if recorded at the time, it would now have thrown much light upon his character, and in no way lessened him in the estimation of those who knew him only by his works. In him you saw at once the Maker, the Inventor; one of the few in any age: a fitting companion for Dante. He was energy itself, and shed around him a kindling influence; an atmosphere of life, full of the ideal. To walk with him in the country was to perceive the soul of beauty through the forms of matter; and the high gloomy buildings between which, from his study window, a glimpse was caught of the Thames and the Surrey shore, assumed a kind of grandeur from the man dwelling near them. Those may laugh at this who never knew such an one as Blake; but of him it is the simple truth. He was a man without a mask; his aim single, his path straightforwards, and his wants few; so he was free, noble, and happy. His voice and manner were quiet, yet all awake with intellect. Above the tricks of littleness, or the least taint of affectation, with a natural dignity which few would have dared to affront, he was gentle and affectionate, loving to be with little children, and to talk about them.—PALMER, SAMUEL, 1855, *Letter to Alexander Gilchrist, Aug.* 23; *Life of Blake, vol.* I, *p.* 302.

Mr. Butts was no believer in Blake's "madness." Strangers to the man, and they alone, believed in that. Yet he could give *piquant* accounts for his *protégé's* extravagances. One story in particular he was fond of telling, which has been since pretty extensively retailed about town. At the end of the little garden in Hercules Buildings there was a summer-house. Mr. Butts calling one day found Mr. and Mrs. Blake sitting in this summer-house, freed from "those troublesome disguises" which have prevailed since the Fall. "*Come in!*" cried Blake; "*it's only Adam and Eve, you know!*" Husband and wife had been reciting passages from "Paradise Lost," in character, and the garden of Hercules Buildings had to represent the Garden of Eden: a little to the scandal of wondering neighbours, on more than one occasion. However, they knew sufficient of the single-minded artist not wholly to misconstrue such phenomena.—GILCHRIST, ALEXANDER, 1863, *Life of William Blake, vol.* I, *p.* 115.

He came to the desert of London town,
Grey miles long;
He wandered up and he wandered down,
Singing a quiet song,
He came to the desert of London town,
Mirk miles broad;
He wandered up and he wandered down,
Ever alone with God.
There were thousands and thousands of human kind
In this desert of brick and stone:
But some were deaf and some were blind,
And he was there alone.
At length the good hour came; he died,
As he had lived, alone:
He was not missed from the desert wide,
Perhaps he was found at the Throne.

—THOMSON, JAMES ("B. V."), 1864, *The Poems of William Blake, Biographical and Critical Studies, p.* 268.

I was much with him from 1810 to 1816, when I came abroad, and have remained in Italy ever since. I might have learned much from him. I was then a student of the Royal Academy, in the antique school, where I gained a medal, and thought more of form than anything else. I was by nature a lover of colour, and my *beau ideal* was the union of Phidias and Titian. Blake was the determined enemy of colourists, and his drawing was not very academical. His high qualities I did not prize at that time; besides, I thought him mad. I do not think so now. I never suspected him of imposture. His manner was too honest for that. He was very kind to me, though very positive in his opinion, with which I never agreed. His excellent old wife was a sincere believer in all his visions. She told me seriously one day, "I have very little of Mr. Blake's company; he is always in Paradise." She prepared his colours, and was as good as a servant. He had no other. —KIRKUP, SEYMOUR, 1870, *Letter to Lord Houghton, March* 25; *The Life of Lord Houghton, ed. Reid, vol.* II, *p.* 222.

This is the place. Even here the dauntless soul,
The unflinching hand, wrought on; till in that nook,
As on that very bed, his life partook
New birth, and passed. Yon river's dusky shoal,
Whereto the close-built coiling lanes unroll,
Faced his work-window, whence his eyes would stare,
Thought-wandering, unto nought that met them there,
But to the unfettered irreversible goal.
This cupboard, Holy of Holies, held the cloud
Of his soul writ and limned; this other one,
His true wife's charge, full oft to their abode
Yielded for daily bread the martyr's stone,
Ere yet their food might be that Bread alone,
The words now home-speech of the mouth of God.

—ROSSETTI, DANTE GABRIEL, 1881, *Five English Poets, Ballads and Sonnets.*

Now, this much is certain: that plain, commonplace, sober men, well acquainted with Blake in ordinary intercourse, saw in him one of themselves; that clever, shrewd, intelligent men thought him odd, but quite rational; and that men of high powers in art and literature, scholars, and sages of various schools, unanimously pronounced him sane. The evidence of his contemporaries is great in amount, and unvarying in substance. No one knew Blake, and thought him mad.—JOHNSON, LIONEL, 1893, *The Academy, vol.* 44, *p.* 163.

ART

My friend Mr. D'Israeli possesses the largest collection of any individual of the very extraordinary drawings of Mr. Blake; and he loves his classical friends to disport with them, beneath the lighted Argand lamp of his drawing room, while soft music is heard upon the several corridors and recesses of his enchanted staircase. Meanwhile the visitor turns over the contents of the Blakëan portefeuille. Angels, Devils, Giants, Dwarfs, Saints, Sinners, Senators, and Chimney Sweeps, cut equally conspicuous figures: and the *Concettos* at times border upon the burlesque, or the pathetic, or the mysterious. Inconceivably blest is the artist, in his visions of intellectual bliss. A sort of golden halo envelopes every object impressed upon the retina of his imagination; and (as I learn) he is at times shaking hands with Homer, or playing the pastoral pipe with Virgil. Meanwhile, shadowy beings of an unearthly form hang over his couch, and disclose to him scenes . . . such as no other Mortal hath yet conceived! Mr. Blake is himself no ordinary poet.—DIBDIN, THOMAS FROGNALL, 1824, *The Library Companion, p.* 734, *note.*

These, of any series of designs which art has produced, are the most purely elevated in their relation and sentiment. It would be long to discriminate the position they hold in this respect, and at the same time the disregard in which they may be held by some who judge of them in a material relation; while the great beauty which they possess will at once be apparent to others who can appreciate their style in its immaterial connexion. But the sum of the whole in my mind is this: that these designs reach the intellectual or infinite in an abstract significance, more entirely unmixed with inferior elements and local conventions than any others; that they are the result of high intelligence of thought, and of a progress of art through many styles and stages of different times, produced through a bright generalizing and transcendental mind.—SCOTT, DAVID, 1844, *Blair's Grave, MS. note.*

The most original, and, in truth, the only new and original version of the Scripture idea of angels which I have met with, is that of William Blake, a poet-painter, somewhat mad, as we are told, if indeed his madness were not rather "the telescope of truth," a sort of poetical *clairvoyance*, bringing the unearthly nearer to him than to others.—JAMESON, MRS. ANNA, 1848, *Sacred and Legendary Art, vol.* I, *p.* 85.

Blake, no doubt, imported into the Bible a crowd of fantastic ideas that sprang from his own fertile, impetuous brain. He went to it for a revelation of facts, and seized chiefly upon those which other men were trying their best to be rid of. He was orientalized both by the Bible and by his passion for large, swelling conceptions of life, death and immortality. By degrees he peopled his mind with a strange crowd of figures, many with biblical outlines, many also, jostling these,—variations upon a few simple themes. The elemental facts of life, as has already been said, were those which were most luminous to him and for which he found visible shapes, which were repeated constantly in his designs.—SCUDDER, HORACE E., 1880, *William Blake, Painter and Poet, Scribner's Monthly, vol.* 20, *p.* 234.

If Blake was not a great master, he had in him certain elements that go to the making of one. Often these were beyond his own control. One does not need to be a painter or a poet to see, in his extraordinary work, that he frequently was the servant rather than the master; that he was swept away, like his own Elijah, by the horses and chariot of fire, and that when, like Paul, he reached the third heaven—whether he was in the body or out of it, he could not tell. This was not so at all times. The conception and execution of his "Job" are massive, powerful, sublime, maintained throughout the series. "The Marriage of Heaven and Hell" is a wonderful, a fearlessly imaginative, production. But much of his labor with pen or pencil does not show that union of genius with method which declares the master. He does not always sit above the thunder; he is enrapt, whirled, trembling in the electric vortex of a cloud.—STEDMAN, EDMUND CLARENCE, 1881, *The Critic, vol.* I, *p.* 3.

Blake, as an artist, is a more important figure than Blake the poet; and naturally so, for the smallest good poem involves a consecutiveness and complexity of thought which are required in paintings only of a character which Blake rarely attempted. Yet, even as a painter his reputation has until lately been much exaggerated. That exhibition of his collected drawings and paintings was a great blow to the fame which had grown up from a haphazard acquaintance by his admirers with a few sketches or an illustrated poem. Here and there there was a gleam of such pure and simple genius as is often revealed in the speech of a finely-natured child amid its ordinary chatter; here and there the expression of a tender or distempered dream which was not like anything else in the spectator's experience; now and then an outline that had a look of Michael Angelo, with sometimes hints which might have formed the themes of great works, and which justified the saying of Fuseli that "Blake is damned good to steal from;" but the effect of the whole collection was dejecting and unimpressive, and did little towards confirming its creator's opinion that Titian, Reynolds, and Gainsborough were bad artists, and Blake, Barry, and Fuseli good ones.—PATMORE, COVENTRY, 1889–98, *Principle in Art, p.* 97.

In art his aim was not merely to excite and satisfy the æsthetic sense; it was to move and instruct—to elevate the soul above its mundane surroundings—to create a desire for that life of the imagination in which alone "all things exist." If that end were accomplished, all was accomplished. . . . His faculty of invention was supreme. . . . It remains for ever true that as regards what is commonly known as creative works, in that, namely, wherein the imagination reigns supreme, there have been few to equal and none to excel Blake among our English artists.—STORY, ALFRED T., 1893, *William Blake, His Life, Character and Genius, pp.* 155, 156.

POETRY

Good William Blake, the hosier's son, the prophet of Carnaby Market, Golden Square, a most poetic dreamer, an enthusiast of more than Swedenborgian calibre, and a poet of no mean order; for he anticipated Wordsworth, rivalled our old dramatists in sustained majesty and dignity, and at times vied with Shelley in nervous fire.—THORNBURY, WALTER, 1861, *British Artists from Hogarth to Turner, vol.* II, *p.* 27.

Having spoken so far of Blake's influence as a painter, I should be glad if I could point out that the simplicity and purity of his style as a lyrical poet had also exercised some sway. But, indeed, he is so far removed from ordinary apprehensions in most of his poems, or more or less in all, and they have been so little spread abroad, that it would be impossible to attribute to them any decided place among the impulses which have directed the extraordinary mass of poetry displaying power of one or another kind, which has been brought before us from his day to our own. Perhaps some infusion of his modest and genuine beauties might add a charm even to the most gifted works of our present rather redundant time.—ROSSETTI, DANTE GABRIEL, 1863, *The Life of William Blake by Alexander Gilchrist, Supplementary Chapter, vol.* I, *p.* 381.

From his childhood, Poetry walked hand in hand with Painting, and beguiled his loneliness with wild, sweet harmonies. Bred up amid the stately, measured, melodious platitudes of the eighteenth century, that Golden Age of commonplace, he struck down through them all with simple, untaught, unconscious directness, and smote the spring of ever-living waters. Such wood-notes wild as trill in Shakspeare's verse sprang from the stricken chords beneath his hand. The little singing-birds that seem almost to have leaped unbidden into life among the gross creations of those old Afreets who

"Stood around the throne of Shakspeare,
Sturdy, but unclean,"

carolled their clear, pure lays to him, and left a quivering echo. Fine, fleeting fantasies we have, a tender, heartfelt, heart-reaching pathos, laughter that might at any moment tremble into tears, eternal truths, draped in the garb of quaint and simple story, solemn fervors, subtile sympathies, and the winsomeness of little children at their play,—sometimes glowing with the deepest color, often just tinged to the pale and changing hues of a dream, but touched with such coy grace, modulated to such free, wild rhythm, suffused with such a delicate, evanishing loveliness, that they seem scarcely to be the songs of our tangible earth, but snatches from fairy-land. Often rude in form, often defective in rhyme, and not unfrequently with even graver faults than these, their ruggedness cannot hide the gleam of the sacred fire.—DODGE, MARY ABIGAIL (GAIL HAMILTON), 1864, *Pictor Ignotus, The Atlantic Monthly, vol.* 13, *p.* 436.

Confidence in future friends, and contempt of present foes, may have induced him to leave his highest achievements impalpable and obscure. Their scope is as wide and as high as heaven, but not as clear; clouds involve and rains inundate the fitful and stormy space of air through which he spreads and plies an indefatigable wing. There can be few books in the world like these; I can remember one poet only whose work seems to me the same or similar in kind; a poet as vast in aim, as daring in detail, as unlike others, as coherent to himself, as strange without and as sane within. The points of contact and sides of likeness between William Blake and Walt Whitman are so many and so grave, as to afford some ground of reason to those who preach the transition of souls or transfusion of spirits. . . . No man so poor and so obscure as Blake appeared in the eyes of his generation ever did more good works in a more noble and simple spirit. It seems that in each of these men at their birth pity and passion, and relief and redress of wrong, became incarnate and innate. That may well be said of the one which was said of the other: that "he looks like a man." And in externals and details the work of these two constantly and inevitably coheres and coincides.—SWINBURNE, ALGERNON CHARLES, 1866–68, *William Blake, A Critical Essay, pp.* 300, 301.

"All deities reside in the human breast." This should be taken as the keystone of Blake's splendid arch. It is necessary again and again to recur to this, for there are some writings of his, especially the later, where he seems to have fallen into the hands of the Nemesis that pursues mysticism, and surrendered himself to the dangerous idea that his thoughts were personal spirits. As Cicero feared that the populace might, in course of time, believe that the statues of the gods are the gods themselves, there is always a peril besetting the imagination when introduced into religious speculations that it will confuse the planes of substance and form; of which Swedenborg is the saddest example, and Blake came too near being another.—CONWAY, MONCURE D., 1868, *The Fortnightly Review, vol.* 9, *p.* 218.

We are far from intending to disparage the real merits of these verses. Imitative to the verge of plagiarism as they are, they are often so skilfully composed, and relieved by such graceful touches of fancy and sweet snatches of melody, as to confer genuine pleasure in defiance of critical analysis. Here Blake's artistic power makes itself felt, nor need we grudge him the praise that belongs to it because his panegyrists perversely claim for him honours to which he is not entitled. It was most creditable to his taste that he rejected the inferior models of contemporary poetry in favour of the great masters, but from the pother that Mr. Gilchrist and Mr. Swinburne make about it, one would suppose that he was the only one of his generation who manifested such sympathy. In fact, his was an age of poetic revival, and he did but worship at shrines newly set up by others. —HEWLETT, HENRY G., 1876, *Imperfect Genius: William Blake, Contemporary Review, vol.* 28, *p.* 765.

It is to these essays of his youth and early manhood that we must look for the true sources of his fame. The "Poetical Sketches," begun when the author was only twelve years of age, and finished when he was no more than twenty, must assuredly be reckoned among the most extraordinary examples of youthful production; and it is profoundly characteristic of the man and his particular cast of mind that many of these boyish poems are among the best that Blake at any time produced. For his was a nature that owed little to development or experience. The perfect innocence of his spirit, as it kept him safe from the taint of the world, also rendered him incapable of receiving that enlargement of sympathy and deepening of emotion which others differently constituted may gain from contact with actual life. His imagination was not of the kind that could deal with the complex problems of human passion; he retained to the end of his days the happy ignorance as well as the freshness of childhood: and it is therefore perhaps less wonderful in his case than it would be in the case of a poet of richer and more varied humanity that he should be able to display at once and in early youth the full measure of his powers. But this acknowledgment of the inherent limitation of Blake's poetic gift leads us by a natural process to a clearer recognition of its great qualities. His detachment from the ordinary currents of practical thought left to his mind an unspoiled and delightful simplicity which has perhaps never been matched in English poetry.—CARR, J. COMYNS, 1880, *The English Poets, ed. Ward, vol.* III, *p.* 598.

We do not believe that the merely intelligent beholder, capable of admiring beauty and loving poetry, but without any settled creed in art or foregone conclusion, would ever of his own accord find in Blake the wonderful genius and grandeur with which it is now usual to credit him. Here and there he produces something by a sort of accidental inspiration, as in the beautiful creation, full of heavenly joy and beauty, of the "Morning stars singing together," by which the most insensible must be moved. But it is unfortunate that his exponents should strain their demands so far as to require us to applaud in an equal degree all those weird outlines flung about the windy skies, all the crouching horrors and staring wild apparitions which mope and gibber in so many of his extraordinary pages.—OLIPHANT, MARGARET O. W., 1882, *The Literary History of England, XVIIIth-XIXth Century, vol.* II. *p.* 240.

From this lack of early discipline to some extent may be ascribed the premature development of his marvellous imaginative faculty—his somewhat powerful self-assertive spirit—and his early dalliance with the muses; for he was scarcely out of the years of infancy before he began to write verse, and one of the very loveliest lyrics in the English tongue was produced by Blake before he was fourteen years old. It is merely entitled "A Song," and runs thus—

"How sweet I roamed from field to field." . . .

Talk of inspiration!—if the boy who produced that was not inspired, then who in any age ever was? For airiness, brightness, and suggestiveness, we have only a very few such lyrics; but it is remarkable that one of those few was also produced by another "marvellous boy" at about the same age that the hosier's son was when he produced this. The poem referred to is entitled "To Helen," and its writer was Edgar Allan Poe.—SKIPSEY, JOSEPH, 1885, *William Blake (Canterbury Poets), Introductory Sketch, pp.* 10, 11.

Blake's poetry, with the exception of four or five lovely lyrics and here and there in the other pieces a startling gleam of unquestionable genius, is mere drivel. A sensible person can easily distinguish between that which he cannot understand

and that in which there is nothing to be understood.—PATMORE, COVENTRY, 1889–98, *Principle in Art, p.* 92.

If we wish to understand Blake as a poet, we must discard his Ossianic and prophetic aberrations, and read him as we would any other poet, not when he is at his worst, but when he is at his best, in his "Songs of Innocence," and "Songs of Experience," which was published five years later. Here we find a poet who differed from all his contemporaries, who had no predecessor, and has had no successor, but who was altogether unique, original and individual, primitive and elemental. The qualities which distinguish his verse at this time were simplicity and sincerity, sweetness and grace, an untutored, natural note which reminds one of the singing of a child who croons to himself in his happy moments, not knowing how happy he is, wise beyond his years, superior to time or fate. They seem never to have been written, but to have written themselves, they are so frank and joyous, so inevitable and final. —STODDARD, RICHARD HENRY, 1892, *Under the Evening Lamp, p.* 174.

Happily were they called "Songs of Innocence!" If birds and babes and little children were able to put the delights of their hearts into words and utter speech, it would, one imagines, take the form of Blake's songs; and if the young poet, unable to comprehend and translate their inarticulate lispings for himself, will but go to this man with the visionary eye, he will find in him their truest interpreter. Probably no true lover of poetry ever failed to be deeply impressed by the striking beauty of these poems. Their charm is in their childlike simplicity. Coming upon them for the first time is like chancing upon a scene of rural beauty, wherein children roam at play and call angels their parents.—STORY, ALFRED T., 1893, *William Blake, His Life, Character and Genius, p.* 85.

The poems of Blake appear the simplest in the world; they treat of the most ordinary subjects; but suddenly a deeper note, an allusion to hidden sufferings and wounds, reveals to us that we are not in the presence of a shepherd who pipes, but of a prophet who knows. The effect is grand and strange. Placed on the limit of two centuries, and on the boundary line of two periods, Blake is the first in date (but the least in genius) of that group of mysterious and symbol-loving poets, amongst whom are to be ranked Shelley, Rossetti, and Browning.—JUSSERAND, J. J., 1894, *Piers Plowman, A Contribution to the History of English Mysticism, p.* 218.

Indeed it must be owned that a singer of so faulty an ear, and a writer of so shaky a grammar as Blake, was hardly well equipped for a pioneer of literary reform. Even now a considerable amount of the little that Blake has left must be rejected by the impartial critic as neither poetry nor sense; but the high poetical quality, the exquisite charm and freshness of the residue, is not to be denied. The affinity of his highest work with that of Wordsworth's best is as striking as the resemblance of the two poets at their respective flattest is amusing. He anticipated the creator of Betty Foy, not in his noble simplicities alone, but in his irritating puerilities also. If he led the way for Wordsworth up the steep of Parnassus, he as certainly preceded him down the slope on the other side into the valley of Bathos. Blake's lack of humour seems to have been as complete as Wordsworth's, and in the elder poet there are lines of sudden descent into prose which startle us almost like a prophetic parody of the younger.—TRAILL, HENRY DUFF, 1896, *Social England, vol.* V, *p.* 445.

Blake, in spite of the extravagant claims made for him by his admirers, must be held to have been primarily an artist. If he had not been an artist his poems could hardly have survived at all. . . . Blake's poetry is, from beginning to end, childish; it has the fresh simplicity, but also the vapid deficiencies of its quality—the metre halts and is imperfect; the rhymes are forced and inaccurate, and often impress one with the sense that the exigencies of assonance are so far masters of the sense, that the word that ends a stanza is obviously not the word really wanted or intended by the author, but only approximately thrown out at it.—BENSON, ARTHUR CHRISTOPHER, 1896, *Essays, pp.* 150, 151.

The little poems in the "Songs of Innocence," on infancy and first motherhood, and on subjects like the "Lamb," are without rival in our language for simplicity, tenderness, and joy. The "Songs of

Experience" give the reverse side of the "Songs of Innocence," and they see the evil of the world as a child with a man's heart would see it—with exaggerated horror. This small but predictive work of Blake, coming where it did, between 1777 and 1794, going back to Elizabethan lyrics and forward to those of Wordsworth, is very remarkable.—BROOKE, STOPFORD A., 1896, *English Literature*, *p.* 223.

The present writer deliberately ranks him as the greatest and most delectable poet of the eighteenth century proper in England, reserving Burns as specially Scotch.—SAINTSBURY, GEORGE, 1896, *A History of Nineteenth Century Literature*, *p.* 13.

This philosophy kept him more simply a poet than any poet of his time, for it made him content to express every beautiful feeling that came into his head without troubling about its utility or chaining it to any utility. . . . When one reads Blake, it is as though the spray of an inexhaustible fountain of beauty was blown into our faces, and not merely when one reads "The Songs of Innocence," or the lyrics he wished to call "The Ideas of Good and Evil;" but when one reads those "Prophetic Works" in which he spoke confusedly and obscurely because he spoke of things for whose speaking he could find no models in the world about him. He was a symbolist who had to invent his symbols; and his counties of England, with their correspondence to tribes of Israel, and his mountains and rivers, with their correspondence to parts of a man's body, are arbitrary as some of the symbolism in the "Axël" of the symbolist Villiers de l'Isle Adam is arbitrary, while they have an incongruity that "Axël" has not. He was a man crying out for a mythology, and trying to make one because he could not find one to his hand.—YEATS, WILLIAM BUTLER, 1897, *Academy Portraits, The Academy*, *vol.* 51, *p.* 634.

He was the first poet of child life, and his work is fresh and strong with the angel music of babyhood. He never attempted complex problems, but forever gave himself to reflecting with grace and simplicity the effects of beauty which impress the untutored child.—GEORGE, ANDREW J., 1898, *From Chaucer to Arnold, Types of Literary Art*, *p.* 644.

GENERAL

His Design can ill be translated into words, and very inadequately by any engraver's copy. Of his Poems, tinged with the very same ineffable qualities, obstructed by the same technical flaws and impediments—a semi-utterance as it were, snatched from the depths of the vague and unspeakable—of these remarkable Poems, never once yet fairly placed before the reading public, specimens shall by-and-bye speak more intelligibly for themselves. Both form part in a Life and Character as new, romantic, pious—in the deepest natural sense—as they: romantic, though incident be slight; animated by the same unbroken simplicity, the same high unity of sentiment.—GILCHRIST, ALEXANDER, 1863, *Life of William Blake*, *vol.* I, *p.* 4.

During the last six years Blake has been a "fancy" with many people who had before hardly known his name; but the peculiar characteristics of his genius are such as to make him "caviare to the general." With two classes, however, he is likely to hold a high place permanently: with the mystics, as the most spiritual, intense, and imaginative of English mystics; and with artists, and true lovers of art, as painter and poet, with a genius of a curiously individual stamp, and as pure and lofty as it was original. Among modern artists, Blake forms a class by himself. With great inequalities, alike in conception and execution, his work is instinct with a spirit which distinguishes it from that of any of his predecessors or contemporaries. "William Blake, his mark," ineffaceably stamps every production of his pencil or his pen. In his highest reach of imagination he has never been surpassed; in the perfection of his technical execution at its best he is one of the great masters.—NORTON, CHARLES ELIOT, 1869, *Blake's Songs and Poetical Sketches, North American Review*, *vol.* 108, *p.* 641.

In Blake, more than most, the man is identified with the artist; the spell which the life holds over the sympathetic reader is renewed and confirmed by the poet-painter's designs and verses. The drawing may be often faulty; the syntax imperfect; yet there is a subtle simplicity, a tenderness springing equally from the heart and the imagination,—sometimes a sublimity of idea, which give the best work of Blake's youth a peculiar place of its own, high up amongst our "treasures for ever." The soul of that child-like and celestial painter Fra Angelico, might have entered into Blake (who in 1789 can have known nothing of the monastic Italian artist)—when writing this and the two following pieces for his "Songs of Innocence."—PALGRAVE, FRANCIS TURNER, 1889, *The Treasury of Sacred Song, p.* 353, *note.*

Now that there is a movement in London to form a (William) Blake Society, on the lines of the Shelley and the Browning Societies, there will probably be something of the sort here. There is nobody on the face of the earth who could better serve as the centre of a Boston craze than William Blake. He was great enough to be utterly misunderstood; he wrote a good deal that is so absolutely incomprehensible to everybody that the wayfaring man, though a fool, cannot lack abundant excuse for all sorts of new and fantastic "interpretations" of it, while there is still enough that is beautiful and sublime, and at the same time intelligible, to hold the sensible, who are the saving salt of these societies. The fact that the Boston Art Museum has just accumulated the original Blake water-colors brought over here by Mr. Quaritch is an additional fact which may be counted upon as having some weight, and I live in hope that we may next winter have the amusement of a Blake Society, with all the exquisite fooling that this implies.—BATES, ARLO, 1890, *Literary Topics in Boston, The Book Buyer, vol.* 7, *p.* 199.

Looking back through the years that have passed since his death, no more remarkable a figure in poetry or painting can be discerned.—PARKES, KINETON, 1892, *ed., The Painter-Poets, p.* 244, *note.*

His work of all kinds is surprising in its inequality. In some fragments of his verse—for instance, like the lines to "The Evening Star"—there are passages of such perfection as are not to be matched by any poet of the eighteenth century. On the other hand, much of it is unintelligible, some of it absolutely absurd. So, too, of his drawing; part is graceful, brilliant and effective; part incoherent and violent, and even grotesque. His methods, too, were equally various. Thus his "Songs of Experience" were executed in a most extraordinary manner, which he explained as the result of a direct revelation from his brother Robert, in a vision of the night. He used all kinds of pigments without oil, including metallic gold and silver, and with singular success.—HUGHES, R., 1896, *Social England, ed. Traill, vol.* v, p. 567.

George Canning
1770-1827

George Canning, an English statesman, born in London, Apr. 11, 1770, educated at Oxford, and in 1793 returned to Parliament as a supporter of Pitt, then premier. He was an under secretary of state in 1796. Pitt resigning in 1801, Canning joined the opposition against the ministry of Addington. In 1807 a ministry was formed under the Duke of Portland, and Canning became secretary of foreign affairs. In 1809 he fought a duel with his colleague, Lord Castlereagh, which led to his retirement from the ministry. In 1812 he was returned to Parliament from Liverpool, and was one of the most eloquent orators in the House. In 1822 he became secretary of foreign affairs in the ministry of Lord Liverpool, upon whose disablement, in Apr. 1827, he was made premier, forming a cabinet composed of both Tories and Whigs. Died Aug. 8, 1827.—BARNARD AND GUYOT, *eds.,* 1885, *Johnson's New General Cyclopædia, vol.* I, *p.* 168.

PERSONAL

His funeral took place at Westminster Abbey, where he was buried at the foot of Mr. Pitt's tomb, on the 16th of August. It was attended by the members of the royal family, the cabinet ministers, the foreign ambassadors, and a number of political and personal friends. The morning after his funeral the king conferred a peerage on his widow. Other no less gratifying marks of public estimation were showered upon his memory, abroad and at home—statues, medals, and monuments. But the most grateful of all was the profound and universal sorrow of the people. All jealousies and animosities were extinguished in the common grief; and Faction, herself, wept upon his grave.—BELL, ROBERT, 1846, *The Life of the Right Honorable George Canning*, p. 363.

Canning was one of whom it might be said, according to ordinary notions, that he ought to have been a nobleman. High-spirited, confident, gay, genial, chivalrous, and most accomplished—he had the attributes of nobility, as they are commonly conceived of; and a nobleman he was—for he had genius. He held high rank in Nature's peerage. But this was not distinction enough in the eyes of some of his colleagues, and the majority of their party. His father had been poor, though of gentlemanly birth; and after his father's death, his mother had become an actress. Not only was there an abiding sense of these facts in the minds of his colleagues, his party, and his opponents, but some spread a rumour, which met him from time to time in his life, that his birth was illegitimate. The same was said in the case of Mr. Huskisson; and in both cases it was false.—MARTINEAU, HARRIET, 1849–58, *A History of the Thirty Years' Peace, A. D.* 1816–1846, *vol.* I, *p.* 435.

At the early hour of his death, crowds (which subsequently amounted to between three and four thousand persons) had congregated outside the lodge at Chiswick. Sorrow, deep and universal, fell upon them when the fatal termination became known. On the day of the funeral, the whole way from Downing Street to the Abbey was lined with spectators, and the large space in front of the great western door was densely covered with people. The short duration of his illness had prevented men's minds being prepared for the worst. He had just attained the highest object of a subject's ambition, and great results were expected; but it pleased God to bring his days suddenly to an end. The hopes of millions were buried in his grave: many and bitter were the tears of those numerous friends and admirers who had come from all parts to witness the sad ceremony. The funeral was a private one; there was no choral service; the solemn silence was more impressive than the organ's peal.—STAPLETON, AUGUSTUS GRANVILLE, 1859, *George Canning and His Times*, p. 604.

No imaginative artist, fresh from studying his career, would sit down to paint this minister with the broad and deep forehead—the stern compressed lip—the deep, thoughtful, concentrated air of Napoleon Bonaparte. As little would the idea of his eloquence or ambition call to our recollection the swart and iron features—the bold and haughty dignity of Strafford. We cannot fancy in his eye the volumed depth of Richelieu's—the volcanic flash of Mirabeau's—the offended majesty of Chatham's. Sketching him from our fancy, it would be as a few still living remember him, with a visage rather marked by humour and intelligence than by meditation or sternness; with something of the petulant mingling in its expression with the proud; with much of the playful overruling the profound. His nature, in short, exhibited more of the genial fancy and the quick irritability of the poet and the speaker, than of the inflexible will of the dictator who puts his foot on a nation's neck, or the fiery passions of the tribune who rouses a people against its oppressors. Still, Mr. Canning, such as he was, will remain one of the most brilliant and striking personages in our historical annals. As a statesman, the latter passages of his life cannot be too deeply studied; as an orator, his speeches will aways be models of their kind; and as a man, there was something so graceful, so fascinating, so spirited in his bearing, that even when we condemn his faults, we cannot avoid feeling affection for his memory, and a sympathetic admiration for his genius.—BULWER, SIR HENRY LYTTON, 1867, *Historical Characters, vol.* II, *p.* 430.

On the 8th of August he passed away, in the Fox chamber, in the fifty-seventh year of his age, and only four months after attaining the pinnacle of his earthly greatness. . . . His enemies had been chiefly in Parliament; outside it he was popular in his lifetime, and deplored after his decease.—EARLE, JOHN CHARLES, 1871, *English Premiers from Sir Robert Walpole to Sir Robert Peel, vol.* II, *p.* 188.

There was a charm in his fine countenance enhancing that of his conversation, and felt by all who knew him. His voice well harmonised with these endowments—an influence itself always powerful, in private even more than in public life, surpassing that of mere beauty, and often surviving when all beauty is gone. . . . The wit of Mr. Canning was of rarer and more refined workmanship, and drew larger ornament from classical sources. The "Anti-Jacobin" shows Mr. Canning's power in its youthful exuberance. When I knew him it had been sobered, perhaps saddened, by the political contrarieties and other incidents of more advanced life, but had lost none of its refinement of irony. Less obvious than the common wit of the world, it excited thought and refined it.—HOLLAND, SIR HENRY, 1871, *Recollections of Past Life, pp.* 176, 272.

The advantage of a fine presence and of a natural delivery are great in public speaking. They came to Canning unbidden, and were even observed in boyhood. It is open to anyone to linger near that monument in Westminster Abbey, and trace the high forehead and erect figure which stands near the grave of England's great Foreign Minister, and so convince themselves of the nobility which belonged naturally to his person.—THORNTON, PERCY M., 1881, *Foreign Secretaries of the XIX Century to* 1834, *vol.* I, *p.* 226.

Some of Mr. Canning's "fads," I well remember. For instance, he knew the French language well, but nothing could induce him to pronounce it properly; he pronounced all the words as if they were English. I know not what reason he gave for this, or whether he gave any: it was his way and he would not alter it. He had also some queer ideas about spelling: he was greatly averse to the letter f, and I have seen notes to my father in which the word *fat* was spelt *phat*, and other words in a similar manner. He asserted that this was the correct method of spelling. . . . I well remember how he was attired one evening in the summer time; nankeen tights, narrowed towards the ankle, and fastened there somehow; nankeen waistcoat, blue, perhaps about a shade darker than Oxford blue; tail coat; a broad pleated cambric frill all down the shirt-front; his watch in a "fob" or little pocket in the trousers, with his chain and seals dangling.—AGNEW, MARY COURTENAY, 1896, *Lions in the Twenties, Temple Bar, vol.* 107, *p.* 112.

STATESMAN

The turning of coats so common is grown,
That no one would think to attack it;
But no case until now was so flagrantly known
Of a school-boy turning his jacket.
—FITZPATRICK, RICHARD, 1793, *On Canning's Desertion of the Whigs.*

Canning is very irritable, surprisingly so for a wit who is always giving such hard knocks. He should have put on an ass's skin before he went into Parliament.—COLERIDGE, SAMUEL TAYLOR, 1823, *Table Talk, ed. Ashe, April* 27, *p.* 26.

What first and most struck me in the House of Commons, was the extreme rarity, not only of great and eloquent speakers, but even of moderately good ones, and the number of those whose delivery was not only bad, but execrable. *Canning* was the only one who could be said to speak with a polished eloquence; and he did not then speak often, and his speeches were at that time (1812–18) too much studied.—BRYDGES, SIR SAMUEL EGERTON, 1824, *Recollections of Foreign Travel, July* 23, *vol.* I, *p.* 112.

The witty, the accomplished, the ambitious;—he who had toiled thirty years, and involved himself in the most harassing discussions, to attain this dizzy height; he who had held it for three months of intrigue and obloquy—and now a heap of dust, and that is all. He was an early and familiar friend of mine, through my intimacy with George Ellis. No man possessed a gayer and more playful wit in society; no one, since Pitt's time, had more commanding sarcasm in debate; in the House of Commons he was the terror of that specie of orators called the Yelpers. His lash fetched away both skin and flesh, and would have penetrated the hide of a rhinoceros. In his conduct as a statesman he had a great fault: he lent himself too willingly to intrigue. Thus he got into his quarrel with Lord Castlereagh, and lost credit with the country for want of openness. Thus, too, he got involved with the Queen's party to such an extent, that it fettered him upon that miserable occasion, and obliged him to butter Sir Robert Wilson with *dear friend*, and *gallant general*, and so forth. The last composition with the Whigs was a sacrifice of principle on both sides.—SCOTT, SIR WALTER, 1827, *Diary, Aug.* 10; *Life by Lockhart, ch.* lxxiv.

But his declamation, though often powerful, always beautifully ornate, never deficient in admirable diction, was certainly not of the highest class. It wanted depth; it came from the mouth, not from the heart; and it tickled or even filled the ear rather than penetrated the bosom of the listener. The orator never seemed to forget himself, and to be absorbed by his theme; he was not carried away by his passions, and he carried not his audience along with him. An actor stood before us—a first-rate one no doubt, but still an actor; and we never forgot that it was a representation we were witnessing, not a real scene.—BROUGHAM, HENRY LORD, 1839-43, *Historical Sketches of Statesmen who Flourished in the Time of George III., vol.* I, *p.* 358.

He was a man of elegant gifts, of easy fluency, capable of embellishing anything; with a nice wit, gliding swiftly over the most delicate topics; passing from topic to topic like the *raconteur* of the dinner table, touching easily on them all, letting them all go as easily, confusing you as to whether he knows nothing or knows everything. The peculiar irritation which Mr. Canning excited through life was—at least in part—owing to the natural wrath with which you hear the changing talk of the practised talker running away about all the universe; never saying anything which indicates real knowledge, never saying anything which at the very moment can be shown to be a blunder; ever on the surface, and ever ingratiating itself with the superficial. When Mr. Canning was alive, sound men of all political persuasions—the Duke of Wellington, Lord Grey—ever disliked him; you may hear old Liberals to this day declaring he was the greatest charlatan who ever lived, angry to imagine that his very ghost exists; and when you read his speeches yourself, you are at once conscious of a certain dexterous insincerity which seems to lurk in the very felicities of expression, and to be made finer with the very refinements of the phraseology.—BAGEHOT, WALTER, 1856, *On the Character of Sir Robert Peel, Works, ed. Morgan, vol.* III, *p.* 37.

At the risk of startling many of our readers, we avow our conviction that the Right Hon. George Canning has never been fairly judged or duly appreciated by his countrymen. In Europe and America, he symbolises a policy; in England, he is little better than a name. "There died the last of the rhetoricians," was the exclamation of a great northern critic and man of genius. Yet the brilliant effusions, the "purple patches," of this so-called rhetorician were underlaid and elevated by more thought and argument than would suffice to set up a host of the "practical men," who complacently repeat and dwell upon the sneer.—HAYWARD, A., 1858, *Canning's Literary Remains, Edinburgh Review, vol.* 108, *p.* 104.

The graceful, finished, well-prepared speeches of Canning, sparkling with classical quotation, happy illustration, and refined wit, were delightful to all who heard him. Sometimes, indeed, the *purpurei panni* did not well combine with the plain broadcloth of a business argument, but, on the whole, the effect was entrancing and attractive to all the young members, who cared rather to support a cause well defended than to examine the solidity of the defences themselves. Mr. Ward, himself an orator of no mean rank, said once to me, "I like what is polished and perfect—I admire Virgil, Racine, and Pitt." To such men the eloquence of Canning was irresistible.—RUSSELL, JOHN EARL, 1874, *Recollections and Suggestions*, 1813-1873, *p.* 45.

By dint of continual labor and unsparing self-correction, Canning gradually reached the perfection of his own style, the distinguishing qualities of which were rapidity, polish, and ornament.—MATHEWS, WILLIAM, 1878, *Oratory and Orators, p.* 252.

It may be well said with truth that when he was finally called to the helm, he owed that well-earned elevation to the united confidence of his sovereign and the people. Nor is it less true that his premature death a few months later was not only a cause of deep sorrow throughout his own country, but was felt as a loss by every nation capable of appreciating high qualities of mind, sound principles of conduct, and resolution to confront every kind of difficulty for the honour and welfare of his native land.—REDCLIFFE, STRATFORD DE, 1880, *George Canning, The Nineteenth Century, vol.* 7, *p.* 42.

Of Canning as an orator conflicting accounts have been handed down to us; but they all agree in this, that in what may be called literary eloquence he has had few rivals. His manner, his aspect, his voice, his elocution, the selection of his words, the beauty of his imagery, and, when the subject called for it, the closeness and clearness of his reasoning, combined to make him the foremost man in the English parliament after the death of Fox. But he does not seem to have possessed in an equal degree what Aristotle calls ἠθικὴ πίστις, that quality in virtue of which the orator impresses every one who hears him with an absolute conviction of his sincerity. Many who listened to Canning thought him only a consummate actor, nothing doubting his intellectual belief in the doctrines he was enforcing, but uncertain only whether his feelings were engaged to the extent which his language would imply.—KEBBEL, T. E., 1886, *Dictionary of National Biography, vol.* VIII, *p.* 430.

Lord Russell said that of all the orators whom he had heard the most eloquent was Plunket, the most agreeable and captivating was Canning, the most formidable as an opponent in debate was Peel. Oratory can never be really appreciated without the man, his voice and manner, the occasion and the audience There is not very much in Canning's speeches of what would commonly be called eloquence. The well-known passage in the Liverpool speech comparing England's power in peaceful repose to the man-of-war with its sails furled and its thunder sleeping, may be said almost to stand alone. There are sometimes epigrams, such as the warning to prosecute war with vigour lest a war too like peace might be followed by a peace too like war. There is humour occasionally, and there is sarcasm, which probably gained much by the delivery. But there is little thunder. Lucid, lively, and effective reasoning is the principal characteristic.—SMITH, GOLDWIN, 1897, *Canning, The Cornhill Magazine, vol.* 75, *p.* 172.

GENERAL

I can only say, that I have listened to him long, and often, with the greatest attention; I have used every exertion in my power to take a fair measure of him, and it appears to me impossible to hear him upon any arduous topic without perceiving that he is eminently deficient in those solid and serious qualities, upon which, and upon which alone, the confidence of a great country can properly repose. He sweats, and labours, and works for sense, and Mr. Ellis seems always to think it is coming, but it does not come; the machine can't draw up what is not to be found in the spring; Providence has made him a light, jesting paragraph-writing man, and that he will remain to his dying day. When he is jocular he is strong; when he is serious, he is like Sampson in a wig; any ordinary person is a match for him; a song, an ironical letter, a burlesque ode, an attack in the newspaper upon Nicoll's eye, a smart speech of twenty minutes, full of gross misrepresentations and clever turns, excellent language, a spirited manner, lucky quotation, success in provoking dull men, some half information picked up in Pall Mall in the morning: these are your friend's natural weapons; all these things he can do; here I allow him to be truly great; nay, I will be just, and go still farther—if he would confine himself to these things, and consider the facete and the playful to be the basis of his character, he would, for that species of man, be universally regarded as a person of very good understanding; call him a legislator, a reasoner, and the conductor of the affairs of a great nation, and it seems to me as absurd as if a butterfly were to teach bees to make honey.—SMITH, SYDNEY, 1808, *Peter Plymley's Letters.*

Canning was at that time [1807] at the head of foreign affairs in England. History will not form the same judgment of him as that formed by contemporaries. He had great talents, but was not a great statesman; he was one of those persons who distinguished themselves as the squires of political heroes. He was highly accomplished in the two classical languages, but without being a learned scholar. He was especially conversant with Greek writers. He had likewise poetical talent, but only for satire. . . . He joined the Society of the Anti-Jacobins, which defended everything connected with existing institutions. This society published a journal, in which the most honoured names of foreign countries were attacked in the most scandalous manner. German literature was at that time little known in England, and it was associated there with the ideas of Jacobinism and revolution. Canning then published in the "Anti-Jacobin" the most shameful pasquinade which was ever written against Germany, under the title of "Matilda Pottingen." Göttingen is described in it as the sink of all infamy; professors and students as a gang of miscreants; licentiousness, incest, and atheism as the character of the German people. Such was Canning's beginning; he was at all events useful; a sort of political

Cossack.—NIEBUHR, BERTHOLD GEORG, 1845, *History of the Period of the Revolution.*

Canning's fame is too great, and his historical position too important, to permit him to linger here, in the stiller regions of the literary world. The sudden smiling onslaught of the young statesman, fresh from the academical career which he had passed through so brilliantly, and still new to the larger sphere that had received him so early, is as interesting as it is daring and effective. We feel like spectators in a crowd when an unforeseen accident happens, and the throng closes round to see what the wonder is. It is as if in an ordinary game some agile young prince should spring in and take the bat for an innings, and send the ball high over everybody's head in a long-celebrated hit, hereafter to be talked of among the traditions of the gods. Such was Canning's appearance in our world of letters. It was the best of jokes, the most delightful, ready, and telling stroke which a chance combatant ever made. But he had no time to linger upon it or repeat it, which was all the better for its fame.—OLIPHANT, MARGARET O. W., 1882, *The Literary History of England, XVIIIth-XIXth Century, vol.* II, *p.* 42.

Canning's literary tastes remained with him through life. When he and Pitt met they were soon buried in some classic. His correspondence with Sir Walter Scott turned mainly upon bookish topics; and he had literature as much as politics in his mind in promoting the foundation of the "Quarterly Review." His political antagonism with Chateaubriand, for whom he responded at a dinner of the Literary Fund, was softened by common intellectual tastes, though, unlike Chateaubriand, he was a man of action first and a man of letters second. Like one of the most illustrious of his succesors in the Premiership, he lived in—probably he could not have lived out of—an atmosphere of contention, and the noisiest brawls with Brougham or Hobhouse were more to his mind than Fox's book under a tree. Two articles in the "Quarterly Review"—one on Gifford's "Life of Pitt" and another in ridicule of Sir John Sinclair's bullion pamphlets—form, so far as I know, together with his verses of occasion, the complete works of Canning. In contrast with his theory, and especially with his master-passion for Dryden, his style was a little over ornate—the purple patch and the tinsel are in excess.—HILL, FRANK H., 1887, *George Canning (English Worthies), p.* 222.

Canning was a remarkable man, and had he not been a statesman would have distinguished himself greatly in literature. But, as it was, the world rather underestimated his talents on account of his versatility and lightness of hand in literature. Somehow the idea of statesmanship is connected with that of seriousness, despite of Canning and Lord Palmerston.—STORY, WILLIAM WETMORE, 1890, *Conversations in a Studio, vol.* II. *p.* 543.

Had he not given himself to politics Canning could have won a high place in literature as a writer both of verse and prose. There is no doubt a lack of good-humour in the "Anti-Jacobin" lampoons; the satire is as cold as it is keen. But the writers are honest and thoroughly in earnest. Canning's victims were selected, not at the bidding of personal dislike or caprice, but as representatives of opinions which he firmly believed to be subversive of healthy morality and the national welfare. Although his scorn of wild revolutionary theories certainly carried him too far, he showed sound sense as well as robust, if somewhat narrow, patriotism in many of his antipathies. The "Anti-Jacobin" was not written by free-lances. Its contributors had a set of clearly-defined principles, and were consistent in their likings and their hatreds. Canning detested the atheism, the extreme republicanism, the cosmopolitanism and "theophilanthropy" which were then in the air, and assailed them with all his powers of sarcasm and invective.—WHYTE, WALTER, 1895, *The Poets and the Poetry of the Century, Humour, Society, Parody and Occasional Verse, ed. Miles, p.* 54.

William Mitford

1744–1827

William Mitford, born in London, Feb. 10, 1744, studied at the University of Oxford, but did not take his degree. In 1761 he succeeded to the family estate, and in 1769 became captain in the South Hampshire Militia, in which corps Gibbon, with whom he became intimate, was a major. His first work, "An Essay upon Harmony in Language, &c.," was published in 1774; the first volume of his "History of Greece" in 1784; the second in 1790, the third in 1796, the fourth in 1808, and the fifth in 1818. His "Observations on the History and Doctrine of Christianity" appeared in 1823. Mitford died Feb. 8, 1827. A memoir, by Lord Redesdale, is prefixed to the edition of the "History of Greece," published in 1829.—TOWNSEND, GEORGE H., 1870, *The Every-Day Book of Modern Literature, vol.* I, *p.* 388.

PERSONAL

Mitford, the historian of Greece, possessed, besides his learning, a wonderful variety of accomplishments. I always felt the highest respect for him. When, not long before his death, I used to meet him in the street, bent almost double, and carrying a long staff in his hand, he reminded me of a venerable pilgrim just come from Jerusalem.—ROGERS, SAMUEL, 1855, *Recollections of Table Talk, ed. Dyce, p.*137.

HISTORY OF GREECE
1784–1818

I am still devouring Mitford with unabated pleasure, and, that it may last the longer, I often consult his authorities, and am led away from him, for hours together, by the narratives of Pausanias and the charming simplicity of Herodotus.—ROMILLY, SIR SAMUEL, 1796, *Letter to M. Dumont, Aug.* 26; *Memoirs by himself, vol.* II, *p.* 56.

Looked into Mitford's History of Greece. The Athenian Democracy imparts no sort of relish for that sort of government, and justifies Aristotle in saying, 'Η Δημοκρατιαη τελενταῖα Τυραννις εστ—and of the worst sort we may add. The account of the expedition and retreat of the Ten Thousand is above measure interesting. How much more than men do the Greeks appear compared with the effeminate and pusillanimous Persians! One can hardly believe them of the same species. — GREEN, THOMAS, 1798, *Diary of a Lover of Literature, Oct.* 30.

Considered with respect, not only to the whole series of antient events which it comprises, but also to any very prominent portion to that series, Mr. Mitford's history is the best that has appeared since the days of Xenophon. By calling it the best, we mean that it is the strongest in that quality, which is the cardinal virtue, or rather the four cardinal virtues in one, of the historic composition,—*trustworthiness.* Such praise, it will instantly occur to the reader, is seldom bestowed where it is best due, without a credit-account of censure being opened at the same time; and, in fact, it is our purpose to conform to this general practice. The work before us, indeed, is one which will bear to be commended with discrimination; and its excellences, if faithfully displayed, may sustain such a contrast of shadow, as would perfectly extinguish the farthing brightness of those *novels founded on fact,* commonly called histories. . . . Upon the whole, though we think it rather unfortunate that the story of the Grecian republics should have been told by one who has so many anti-republican partialities, we think it our duty to testify that it has been more justly told by Mr. Mitford than by any preceding author; and that those who differ from him in his political conclusions, must still acknowledge their obligations to the clearness and fulness of his narrative.—BROUGHAM, HENRY LORD, 1808, *Mitford's History of Greece, Edinburgh Review, vol.* 12, *pp.* 478, 517.

His great pleasure consists in praising tyrants, abusing Plutarch, spelling oddly, and writing quaintly; and, what is strange, after all, *his* is the best modern history of Greece in any language, and he is perhaps the best of all modern historians whatsoever. Having named his sins, it is but fair to state his virtues—learning, labour, research, wrath and partiality. I call the latter virtues in a writer, because they make him write in earnest.—BYRON, LORD, 1823, *Don Juan, Canto* xii, *st.* xix, *note.*

Sentiments unfavourable to democracy are made with unhesitating confidence, and with the utmost bitterness of language. Every charge brought against a monarch, or an aristocracy, is sifted with the utmost care. If it cannot be denied, some palliating supposition is suggested, or we are at least reminded that some circumstance now unknown *may* have justified what at present appears unjustifiable. Two events are reported by the same author in the same sentence; their truth rests on the same testimony; but the one supports the darling hypothesis, and the other seems inconsistent with it. The one is taken and the other is left.—MACAULAY, THOMAS BABINGTON, 1828, *History, Edinburgh Review, Critical and Miscellaneous Essays.*

History cannot fall within a survey of elegant literature, except so far as relates to its rhetorical execution. In this particular, some writers of the age,—as Mitford and Turner, for example—have been so abominably perverse, that it would seem as if they were willing to try what degree of bad writing the public would tolerate, for the sake of the valuable matter it may contain.—PRESCOTT, WILLIAM HICKLING, 1832, *English Literature of the Nineteenth Century, North American Review, vol.* 35.

Mr. Mitford is the first who brought to the arduous task of Grecian history the extensive research, accurate inquiry, and profound reflection which characterize the scholars of recent times. . . . His great work was chiefly composed during, or shortly after, the French Revolution; and it was mainly intended to counteract the visionary ideas, in regard to the blessings of Grecian democracy, which has spread so far in the world from the magic of Athenian genius. . . . The cause of truth has been essentially aided by his exertions; and the experiences of the working of democracy in our own times have been such as to forbid a doubt as to the accuracy of the facts he has stated, whatever hesitation may be felt as to the wisdom of the expressions in which they are sometimes conveyed. . . . It may appear strange to say that there is equal truth in the monarchial history of Greece by Mitford, and in the republican by Grote; but, nevertheless, it is so. Both tell the truth, and nothing but the truth, but neither the whole truth.—ALISON, SIR ARCHIBALD, 1853–59, *History of Europe,* 1815–1852, *ch.* v.

Mitford's style is in general verbose, periodic, and heavy. There is, however, a certain animation in his narratives of striking events; and his expression sometimes receives a warm colour from the strength of his feelings as a political partisan. He is included by DeQuincey among "orthographic mutineers," eccentrics in the matter of spelling.—MINTO, WILLIAM, 1872–80, *Manual of English Prose Literature, p.* 516.

William Mitford, who, at the commencement of the nineteenth century, was the fashionable historian of Greece, in one respect resembled Gibbon. Like Gibbon, he examined for himself the entire range of Greek literature, and founded his history on original authorities. Unlike Gibbon, however, his style is unequal and occasionally bad. At his best he is pure, simple, and clear; at his worst he is involved and unintelligible. He lays himself open to the charge that he is translating Greek, instead of writing English; and his translations are so poor that a schoolboy would be punished for them. . . . In his own lifetime, indeed, his opinions increased the popularity of his work; but they insured its supercession in a later age. Thirlwall and Grote were educated under circumstances differing from those amidst which Mitford had lived. With equal ability and equal industry they embraced other views. Grote occupies the position which Mitford once filled; and a Liberal age praises and reads the liberal writer, and neglects the industrious Tory who preceded him in his task.—WALPOLE, SPENCER, 1878, *A History of England from the Conclusion of the Great War in* 1815, *vol.* I, *pp.* 342, 343.

As Grote's is the greatest Liberal history of Greece, so this is the great Tory history of the same country. Before the appearance of Thirlwall, it was the history most often consulted. In the use of terse and cogent English, Mitford was superior to his successors. He could praise tyrants and abuse liberty in a manner that was sure to interest his readers; and even his constant partialities and frequent exhibitions of anger give flavor to his narration. He hated the popular party of Athens, as he hated the Whigs of England. These characteristics give spirit to a book which, with all its labor and learning, is merely a huge party pamphlet. Though it has had much influence in England, it is no longer of any considerable importance.—ADAMS, CHARLES KENDALL, 1882, *A Manual of Historical Literature, p.* 92.

Although Mitford's hatred of democracy, whether well- or ill-founded, makes him sometimes unfair, and though his "History of Greece" contains some blunders, it is on the whole rather a pity that it should have been superseded to the extent to which it actually has been by those of Grote and Thirlwall. For it is not more prejudiced and much better written than

Grote's, while it has greater liveliness and zest than the Bishop's.—SAINTSBURY, GEORGE, 1896, *A History of Nineteenth Century Literature*, p. 215.

It was at the suggestion of his fellow officer, Gibbon, that he undertook to write the history of Greece, a task for which his qualifications were a lively idiomatic style, a sufficiency of such Greek as Oxford then dispensed, a pronounced antipathy to democratic government, and a total absence of the historical sense.—HERFORD, C. H., 1897, *The Age of Wordsworth*, p. 40.

GENERAL

Mr. Mitford was one of the many accomplished scholars that are ill used. Had he possessed the splendid powers of Landor, he would have raised a clatter on the armour of modern society such as Samson threatened to the giant Harapha. For in many respects he resembled Landor: he had much of his learning; he had the same extensive access to books and influential circles in great cities, the same gloomy disdain of popular falsehoods or commonplaces, and the same disposition to run amuck against all nations, languages and spelling-books.—DE QUINCEY, THOMAS, 1847–60, *Orthographic Mutineers, Literary Theory and Criticism; Works, ed. Masson, vol.* XI, *p.* 440, *note.*

Robert Pollok

1798–1827

Robert Pollok, the author of "The Course of Time," was born at North Muirhouse, Eaglesham, Renfrewshire, on the 19th of October, 1798. He entered Glasgow University, and also studied for five years in the Divinity Hall of the United Secession Church at Glasgow with a view to the Presbyterian Ministry. While still a student, he wrote and published anonymously a series of "Tales of the Covenanters," which became popular and reached a second edition, in issuing which he acknowledged the authorship. He commenced the poem with which his name is indissolubly associated in the month of December 1824, and completed it in July 1826. It was published in March 1827, and became immediately popular. Two months after the issue of his poem, Pollok was licensed for the Ministry. He preached, however, but four times. Symptoms of a pulmonary disease, which rapidly developed, compelled rest during the following summer, and before its close he visited London, *en route* for Italy, but was too ill to pursue his intentions. Acting on advice he went to Shirley Common, near Southampton, to winter, but died there on the 18th of September, 1827.—MILES, ALFRED H., 1897, *The Poets and Poetry of the Century, Sacred, Moral and Religious Verse*, p. 167.

THE COURSE OF TIME

1827

It is with much pleasure that I am now able to tell you that I have finished my poem. Since I wrote to you last, I have written about three thousand five hundred verses; which is considerably more than a hundred every successive day. This, you will see, was extraordinary expedition to be continued so long; and I neither can nor wish to ascribe it to anything but an extraordinary manifestation of Divine goodness. Although some nights I was on the border of fever, I rose every morning equally fresh, without one twitch of headache; and, with all the impatience of a lover, hastened to my study. Towards the end of the tenth book,—for the whole consists of ten books,—where the subject was overwhelmingly great, and where, I indeed, seemed to write from immediate inspiration, I felt the body beginning to give away. . . . I am convinced that summer is the best season for great mental exertion; because the heat promotes the circulation of the blood, the stagnation of which is the great cause of misery to cogitative men. The serenity of mind which I have possessed is astonishing. Exalted on my native mountains, and writing often on the top of the very highest of them, I proceeded, from day to day, as if I had been in a world in which there was neither sin nor sickness nor poverty.—POLLOK, ROBERT, 1826, *Letter to His Brother*.

The "Course of Time," for so young a man, was a vast achievement. The book he loved best was the Bible, and his style is often scriptural. Of our poets he had studied, we believe, but Young, Milton, and Byron. He had much to learn in composition; and, had he lived, he would have looked almost with humiliation on much that is at present eulogized by his devoted admirers. But the soul of poetry is there, though often dimly enveloped, and many passages there are, and long ones too, that heave, and hurry, and glow along in a divine enthusiasm.—WILSON, JOHN, 1832, *The Maid of Elvar, Blackwood's Magazine, vol.* 31, *p.* 984.

We doubt whether his merely poetic powers are such as to make his work interesting to any poetic mind, however religious, while to render its truths palatable to the world at large would require in its poetry the magnificence and beauty of Milton himself. It is a pity that any, in their zeal for religion, should have compared our author with him the sublimity of whose mind has not been surpassed since the times of the prophets. So far from it, as a poet Mr. Pollok is neither a Cowper nor a Young. Still, his diction, for the most part, is plain;—he has not learned the art of writing without thought, or of losing himsef in a smother of words; and when you lay down his poem, you have a definite notion of what you have been reading, whatever rank you may give it,—which is more than can be said of many a favourite of these days.—DANA, RICHARD HENRY, 1828, *Poems and Prose Writings, vol.* II, *p.* 352.

The subject is a noble one, and in the poem there are graphic conceptions and passages of beauty and tenderness; but it is disfigured by amplifications and a redundancy of moral pictures; it has no continuous interest, and in parts of it which should have been and which the author endeavoured to make the most impressive, particularly those in which he subjects himself to a comparison with Dante and Milton, he utterly failed. . . . For its popularity, however, both here and in Great Britain, it is more indebted to its theology than to its merits as a poem.—GRISWOLD, RUFUS W., 1844, *The Poets and Poetry of England in the Nineteenth Century, p.* 341.

The "Course of Time" is a very extraordinary poem: vast in its conception—vast in its plan—vast in its materials—and vast, if very far from perfect, in its achievement. The wonderful thing is, indeed, that it is such as we find it, and not that its imperfections are numerous. It has nothing at all savouring of the little or conventional in it; for he passed at once from the merely elegant and graceful.—MOIR, D. M., 1850–51, *Sketches of Poetical Literature of the Past Half Century.*

Much over-lauded on its appearance, is the immature work of a man of genius who possessed very imperfect cultivation. It is clumsy in plan, tediously dissertative, and tastelessly magniloquent: but it has passages of good and genuine poetry.—SPALDING, WILLIAM, 1852, *A History of English Literature, p.* 381.

Was exactly adapted to the level of culture in the religious classes of Scotland.—ARNOLD, THOMAS, 1868–75, *Chaucer to Wordsworth, p.* 418.

In style the work is a composite imitation of Milton, Blair, and Young. The object of the poet is to describe the spiritual life and destiny of man. The religious speculations of the author are varied with episodical pictures and narratives, illustrating the effects of virtue and vice. Many splendid passages and images are scattered through the work; but the poet is often harsh, turgid, vehement, and repulsive. His morbid fancy delights most in describing the woe and wailing of that future world of despair which his cheerful theology has graciously appropriated to the "non-elect." In design and in diction the work indicates remarkable power, which tastes, refinement, and a better creed might have more happily developed. The work attained to great popularity, and Pollok was at the time even honored with the name of "the Scotch Dante." . . . Still holds its own among very devout but not over-fastidious readers.—BROOKS, SARAH WARNER, 1890, *English Poetry and Poets, p.* 492.

Concerned with the destiny of man, the poem is conceived on a stupendous scale, which baffled the writer's artistic resources. Never absolutely feeble, it tends to prolixity and discursiveness, but is relieved by passages of sustained brilliancy.—BAYNE, THOMAS, 1896, *Dictionary of National Biography, vol.* XLVI, *p.* 70.

One of the most popular of books, passing through edition after edition until it reached that desirable phase of becoming a prize book for the diligent scholars of Sunday and other schools—than which nothing could be more advantageous, from a material point of view.—OLIPHANT, MARGARET O. W., 1897, *William Blackwood and His Sons, vol.* II, *p.* 18.

Helen Maria Williams

1762-1827

Was born, in 1762, in the north of England, and was ushered into public notice by Dr. Kippis, at the age of eighteen. Between 1782 and 1788, she published "Edwin and Eltruda," "An Ode to Peace," and other poems. In 1790 she settled in Paris, and became intimate with the most eminent of the Girondists, and, in 1794, was imprisoned, and nearly shared their fate. She escaped to Switzerland, but returned to Paris in 1796, and died there in 1827. She wrote "Julia, a Novel," "Letters from France," "Travels in Switzerland," "A Narrative of Events in France," and "A Translation of Humboldt and Bonpland's Personal Narrative."—HALE, SARAH JOSEPHA, 1852, *Woman's Record, p.* 553.

PERSONAL

He had dined that day (May 30, 1784) at Mr. Hoole's, and Miss Helen Maria Williams being expected in the evening, Mr. Hoole put into his hands her beautiful "Ode on the Peace." Johnson read it over; and when this elegant and accomplished young lady was presented to him, he took her by the hand in the most courteous manner, and repeated the finest stanza of her poem. This was the most delicate and pleasing compliment he could pay. Her respectable friend, Dr. Kippis, from whom I had this anecdote, was standing by, and was not a little gratified.—BOSWELL, JAMES, 1791-93, *Life of Samuel Johnson, ed. Hill, vol.* IV, *p.* 325.

Helen Maria Williams, in 1779, lived at Berwick. The graces of her mind were then as attractive and charming as those of her person. She had a tenderness and delicacy of soul, and was a sincere friend of all order,—moral, civil, and religious. But how frail is the best nature when it is powerfully assailed, and gradually and habitually corrupted by inhuman and impious doctrines, and by licentious and profligate examples! The incense of flattery and the intoxication of vanity contributed not a little to the fall of mental rectitude. —STOCKDALE, PERCIVAL, 1816, *Ladies' Monthly Museum, Jan.*

What and how great a contrast is exhibited between this female's first appearance on the theatre of the public, and her last fatal ending! Lively, elegant, accomplished, and agreeable, of pleasing person, simple and gentle manners, without pride, or asserting any pretensions to distinction, she received the respect and attention of many of the most considerable persons in this country, both for talent and for rank. What is she now? If she lives (and whether she does or not, few know, and nobody cares), she is a wanderer—an exile, unnoticed and unknown.—BELOE, WILLIAM, 1817, *The Sexagenarian, vol.* I, *p.* 357.

Helen Maria Williams was a very fascinating person; but not handsome. I knew her intimately in her youth, when she resided in London with her mother and sisters. They used to give very agreeable evening-parties, at which I have met many of the Scotch literati, Lord Monboddo, &c. Late in life, Helen translated into English, and very beautiful English too, Humboldt's long work, "Personal Narrative of Travels, &c."; and, I believe, nearly the whole impression still lies in Longman's warehouse.—ROGERS, SAMUEL, 1855, *Recollections of Table-Talk, ed. Dyce, p.* 50.

Among the literary celebrities of the French Revolution was Helen Maria Williams, at whose house were wont to assemble the most distinguished of the liberal writers of France, her own reputation giving considerable éclat to these meetings. She wrote some of the most beautiful hymns in our language, was a prisoner under the *reign of terror* and published a work on the French Revolution, which is full of the most touching incidents, and adorned with specimens of the ardent and pathetic poetry, the product of French genius under the excitement of those most mysterious days. A. Humboldt was much attached to her, and committed to her care the publication of some of his most elaborate works.—BOWRING, SIR JOHN, 1861-72, *Autobiographical Recollections, ed. Bowring, p.* 353.

GENERAL

Your poem ["The Slave Trade"] I have read with the highest pleasure. . . . A tempest is a favorite subject with the poets, but I do not remember anything, even in Thomson's "Winter," superior to your verses from the 347th to the 351st. Indeed, the last simile, beginning with "Fancy may dress," &c., and ending with the 350th verse, is, in my opinion, the most beautiful passage in the poem; it would do honour to the greatest names that ever graced our profession.—BURNS, ROBERT, 1789, *Letter to Miss Williams, August.*

Miss Williams possessed a strong mind, much historical acumen, and great industry, though her religious sentiments were not free from some errors of the period. As a poetess she had little more than some facility and the talent inseparable from a cultivated taste.—BETHUNE, GEORGE WASHINGTON, 1848, *The British Female Poets, p.* 138.

Helen Maria Williams was another woman of great natural abilities, with a correcter taste, though her poetry is of a still more conventional cast than Miss Seward's; yet one of her sonnets made such an impression on Wordsworth that she records with a just pride his having repeated it to her, years afterwards.—HUNT, LEIGH, AND LEE, S. ADAMS, 1866, *The Book of the Sonnet, vol.* I, *p.* 85.

Her successive volumes attest not only her life-long intellectual activity, but also her constant increase of mental power and acumen. She had a passion for politics as well as for general literature. She kept a busy, vigilant eye upon what was going on in France and in surrounding nations, and especially upon the effects of the great Revolution upon the fortunes of the European countries. Her writings pertained principally to this general subject; and with all their ardor and eloquence there is much acute observation, not a little keen wit and satire, and certain valuable material for the historian of those troublous times.—PUTNAM, A. P., 1878, *Helen Maria Williams, Unitarian Review, vol.* 10, *p.* 234.

The hymn beginning

"Whilst thee I seek, protecting Power!"

has long been a great favourite with Christians of every name. It is found in almost all the Collections, and, more than all her other publications, has kept the name of the author in remembrance.—HATFIELD, EDWIN F., 1884, *The Poets of the Church, p.* 676.

Her poems, published in 1786, during her pre-revolutionary days, are dedicated to Queen Charlotte. . . . They have little merit, but are not uninteresting for their "signs of the times": sonnets, a tale called "Edwin and Eltruda," an address to Sensibility, and so forth. But the longest, "Peru," is in the full eighteenth century couplet with no sign of innovation. The "Letters from France," which extend to eight volumes, possess, besides the interest of their subject, the advantage of a more than fair proficiency on the author's part in the formal but not ungraceful prose of her time, neither unduly Johnsonian nor in any way slipshod. But it may perhaps be conceded that, but for the interest of the subject, they would not be of much importance.—SAINTSBURY, GEORGE, 1896, *A History of Nineteenth Century Literature, p.* 30.

She adopted with enthusiasm, the principles and ideas of the revolution, and wrote of it with a fervour that amounted almost to a frenzy. She became acquainted with many of the leading Girondists, was on terms of intimacy with Madame Roland, was thrown into prison by Robespierre (from October 1793 she was in the Luxembourg), and narrowly escaped the fate of so many of her friends. Both before her arrest and after her release she freely wrote her impressions of the events which she witnessed or heard of, impressions frequently formed on very imperfect, one-sided, and garbled information, travestied by the enthusiasm of a clever, badly educated woman, and uttered with the cocksureness of ignorance. It was in the nature of things that such writings should make her many enemies; and while some of these contented themselves with denouncing her works as unscrupulous fabrications, others attacked her reputation as a woman, and accused her of carrying her love of liberty to a detestation of all constraint, legal or social. . . . Her writings are very much what might be expected from a warm-hearted and ignorant woman. The honesty with which she wrote carried conviction to many of her readers; and there can be little doubt that her works were the source of many erroneous opinions as to facts, which have been largely accepted as matters of history, instead of —as they really were, in their origin—the wilful misrepresentations of interested parties.—LAUGHTON, J. K., 1900, *Dictionary of National Biography, vol.* LXI, *p.* 404.

Dugald Stewart

1753-1828

Dugald Stewart, philosopher, born in Edinburgh, 22d November 1753, son of Matthew Stewart, studied at Edinburgh and Glasgow. He became assistant (1772) to his father, and joint-professor (1775). In 1778, in the absence of Adam Ferguson, he taught also the moral philosophy class; in 1785, appointed professor of Moral Philosophy, he included in his subjects psychology, metaphysics, logic, ethics, natural theology, politics, and political economy. In 1792 appeared vol. i. of his "Elements of the Philosophy of the Human Mind," and in 1793 "Outlines of Moral Philosophy." In 1806 he received from a Whig government a sinecure worth £600 a year. From 1810 to 1820, when Stewart resigned, Dr. Thomas Brown was conjoint professor. In 1810 Stewart published his "Philosophical Essays;" in 1814-27 vols. ii. and iii. of the "Elements;" in 1815-21 the "History of Ethical Philosophy;" and in 1828 the "Philosophy of the Active and Moral Powers." Stewart lived from 1809 at Kinneil House, Bo'ness, but died in Edinburgh, 11th June 1828. He was a conspicuous representative of the Scottish school. Sir W. Hamilton's edition of his Works (11 vols. 1854-58) comprises a Life by Prof. Veitch.—PATRICK AND GROOME, *eds.*, 1897, *Chambers's Biographical Dictionary, p.* 884.

PERSONAL

I was very much pleased with the freedom and openness of his conversation. I attend his lectures regularly. I must confess I have been rather disappointed. I never heard a single discussion of Mr. Stewart's which made up one masterly and comprehensive whole. His lectures seem to be made up of detached hints and incomplete outlines, and he almost uniformly avoids every subject which involves any difficult discussion. I have acquired from him, however, a much clearer idea than I ever had of the distinctive character of Reid's philosophy.—CHALMERS, THOMAS, 1801, *Letter to Dr. Brown, Feb.* 25; *Memoirs, ed. Hanna, vol.* I, *p.* 53.

Mr. Stewart is said to be naturally or habitually grave and reserved, but towards us he has broken through his habits or his nature, and I never conversed with any one with whom I was more at ease. He has a grave, sensible face, more like the head of Shakespear than any other head or print that I can remember. I have not heard him lecture; no woman can go to the public lectures here, and I don't choose to go in men's or boys' clothes, or in the pocket of the Irish giant, though he is here and well able to carry me. Mrs. Stewart has been for years wishing in vain for the pleasure of hearing one of her husband's lectures.—EDGEWORTH, MARIA, 1803, *Letters, vol.* I, *p.* 135.

We have had Dugald Stewart and his family here for three or four days. We spoke much of the weather and other harmless subjects. He became, however, once a little elevated; and, in the gayety of his soul, let out some opinions which will doubtless make him writhe with remorse. He went so far as to say he considered the King's recovery as very problematical.—SMITH, SYDNEY, 1811, *To Lady Holland, July* 17; *Memoir by Lady Holland.*

In short, Dugald Stewart was one of the greatest of didactic orators. Had he lived in ancient times, his memory would have descended to us as that of one of the finest of the old eloquent sages.—COCKBURN, HENRY LORD, 1830-54, *Memoirs of his Time, ch.* i.

This eminent and most amiable man was fortunate in his choice of a second wife, who was a daughter of the Hon. George Cranstoun, the sister of Lord Corehouse, and of the interesting Countess Purgstall, whose widowed isolation in Schloss Hainfeld is graphically portrayed by Captain Basil Hall. She was the habitual and confidential companion of her husband during his studies, and he never considered a piece of his composition to be finished until she had reviewed it. He himself said that though she did not probably understand the abstract points of his philosophy so well as he did himself, yet when he had once given a truth an intelligible shape, she helped him to illustrate it by a play of fancy and of feeling which could come only from a woman's mind.—CONSTABLE, A. G., 1874, *Archibald Constable and His Friends, Harper's Magazine, vol.* 48, *p.* 509.

In 1785, on the resignation of Ferguson,

he was transferred to the chair of moral philosophy, which he filled for a quarter of a century and made a notable centre of intellectual and moral influence. Young men of rank and of parts were attracted by his reputation from England, and even from the Continent and America. A very large number of men who afterwards rose to eminence in literature or in the service of the state were thus among his students. Sir Walter Scott, Jeffrey, Cockburn, Francis Horner, Sydney Smith, Lord Brougham, Dr. Thomas Brown, James Mill, Sir James Mackintosh, and Sir Archibald Alison may be mentioned among others. There is a unanimous testimony to the attractive eloquence of Stewart's lectures and the moral elevation of his teaching.—SETH, ANDREW, 1887, *Encyclopædia Britannica, Ninth ed., vol.* XXII, *p.* 575.

But if he brought no original impulse to the school, the limits of which were indeed fairly well defined, there was no one who expounded its methods with greater acceptance or success than Stewart. His argument was not always close or accurate; his style was diffuse, and his illustration sometimes lavish in its copiousness. But his range of learning, as learning was esteemed in his day, was wide. He had travelled much, and had mixed on easy and familiar terms with men of every class. He had a fund of smooth eloquence. His character, calm, benevolent, and studiously courteous, fitted him admirably to attain that unquestioned and unquestionable authority which made him potent as an oracle amongst his students, and gave to his professional prelections something of the influence of powerful pulpit ministrations. In his time, and mainly through his influence, although also through the high traditions of his predecessors, the University of Edinburgh became the resort of men of all countries. From England many of those most fitted by birth, station, and ability to influence the coming generation, thronged to the northern university as to a Mecca of learning. In his classroom many who, but a few years before, would have looked upon Scotland as a country sunk in ignorance and poverty, and alien in political ideas, sat side by side with the Scottish youth and imbibed the notions which were to form their principles throughout life.—CRAIK, SIR HENRY, 1901, *A Century of Scottish History, vol.* II, *p.* 223.

PHILOSOPHICAL ESSAYS
1810

The singular eloquence with which Mr. Stewart has contrived to adorn the most unpromising parts of his subject,—the rich lights which his imagination has every where thrown in, with such inimitable judgment and effect,—the warm glow of moral enthusiasm which he has spread over the whole of his composition,—and the tone of mildness, dignity, and animation which he has uniformly sustained, in controversy, as well as in instruction; are merits which we do not remember to have seen united in any other philosophical writer; and which might have recommended to general notice, topics far less engaging than those on which they were employed. His former work, on the "Philosophy of the Human Mind," has accordingly been more read than any other modern book on such subjects; and the volume before us, we think, is calculated to be still more popular.—JEFFREY, FRANCIS LORD, 1810-44, *Stewart's Philosophical Essays, Contributions to the Edinburgh Review, vol.* iii, *p.* 377.

We may observe in general, that all the essays which it contains are remarkable for extensive and various knowledge, elevated sentiments, and uncommon dignity and beauty of style; and that some of them also display great acuteness, originality, and profundity. The first series is chiefly adapted to those readers who are conversant in the more abstract discussions of metaphysical science; the second, while equally interesting to this class, may be read with pleasure by those who have but little relish for scholastic disputations. . . . Of all the teachers of abstract knowledge, Mr. Stewart is by far the most eloquent and attractive. Philosophy, pourtrayed by his masterly pencil, wears an aspect the most pleasing as well as sublime. That noble love of truth and science by which he is actuated, diffuses through every page an ardour and animation which can hardly fail to warm and to interest every cultivated reader. He always relieves and illustrates his subject by the happiest allusions and quotations, and decorates even the most unpromising discussions with the various colouring of his chaste and cultivated imagination. Such, indeed, are the great and engaging qualities of mind which Mr. Stewart displays, that even when there is room to question the solidity or importance of any of his conclusions, it is impossible to dissent from him but with hesitation and respect. Mr. Stewart's object in the two first essays is to refute Locke's theory of the origin of ideas, and to show its connection with the sceptical doctrines of Berkeley and Hume.—NAPIER, MACVEY, 1811, *Stewart's Philosophical Essays, Quarterly Review, vol.* 6, *p.* 20.

In the first two Dissertations of the volume bearing the title of "Philosophical Essays," he with equal boldness and acuteness grapples with the most extensive and abstruse questions of mental philosophy, and points out both the sources and the uttermost boundaries of human knowledge with a Verulamean hand.—MACKINTOSH, SIR JAMES, 1830, *Second Preliminary Dissertation, Encyclopædia Britannica.*

FIRST PRELIMINARY DISSERTATION
1815–21

I have just read Dugald Stewart's "Preliminary Dissertation." In the first place, it is totally clear of all his defects: no insane dread of misrepresentation; no discussion put off till another time, just at the moment it was expected, and would have been interesting; no unmanly timidity; less formality of style and cathedral pomp of sentence. The good it would be trite to enumerate: the love of human happiness and virtue, the ardour for the extension of knowledge, the command of fine language, happiness of illusion, varied and pleasing literature, tact, wisdom, and moderation. Without these high qualities, we all know, Stewart cannot write. —SMITH, SYDNEY, 1816, *Letter to Francis Horner, Memoirs, Letter* 121.

The high fame of Dugald Stewart has rendered it a sort of duty to vindicate from his hasty censures the memory of one still more illustrious in reputation, till the lapse of time and the fickleness of literary fashion conspired with the popularity of his assailants to magnify his defects, and meet the very name of his famous treatise with a kind of scornful ridicule. That Stewart had never read much of Grotius, or even gone over the titles of his chapters, is very manifest; and he displays a similar ignorance as to the other writers on natural law, who for more than a century afterwards, as he admits himself, exercised a great influence over the studies of Europe. I have commented upon very few, comparatively, of the slips which occur in his pages on this subject.—HALLAM, HENRY, 1837–39, *Introduction to the Literature of Europe, pt.* iii, *ch.* iv, *par.* 159.

It may seem a harsh and presumptuous deliverance, but we have no dread of its being gainsaid,—that in our higher Philosophical Literature it would be difficult to find a less adequate treatment of so great a theme. From the absence of coherence,—the absence of any trace of unity or comprehensive principle,—the Dissertation is more like the expansion of a commonplace book than an effort to contemplate the continuous flow of Human Thought. It evinces, too, an extraordinary defect of sympathy with the whole progress of speculation in modern continental Europe: Stewart manifestly knew nothing of Kant, and he did not think it necessary to take notice of Spinoza.—NICHOL, J. P., 1858, *Cyclopædia of Biography, ed. E. Rich, 2nd ed.*

I look upon it as the finest of the dissertations in the "Encyclopædia Britannica;" and this is no mean praise, when we consider the number of eminent men who have written for that work. I regard it, indeed, as, upon the whole, the best dissertation which ever appeared in a philosophical serial. As a history of modern philosophy, especially of British philosophy, it has not been superseded, and, I believe, never will be set aside. It is pre-eminent for its fine literary taste, its high moral tone, its general accuracy, its comprehensiveness of survey, and its ripeness of wisdom. When we read it, we feel as if we were breathing a pure and healthy atmosphere, and that the whole spirit of the work is cheering, as being so full of hope in the progress of knowledge. Its critical strictures are ever candid, generally mild, very often just, and always worthy of being noted and pondered. The work is particularly pleasing in the account given of those who have contributed by their literary works to diffuse a taste for metaphysical studies, such as Montaigne, Bayle, Fontenelle, and Addison. It should be admitted that the author has scarcely done justice to Grotius, and failed to fathom the depth of such minds as Leibnitz and Jonathan Edwards. I agree, moreover, with those who regret that he should ever have been tempted to enter on a criticism of Kant, whose works he knew only from translations and imperfect compends.—McCOSH, JAMES, 1875, *The Scottish Philosophy*, p. 287.

GENERAL

The sagacious, the enlightened, and the virtuous Dugald Stewart, in whose writings are united the perspicuity of Dr. Reid, the acuteness of Adam Smith, and the precision of David Hume.—PARR, SAMUEL, 1801, *Spital Sermon.*

He will be disappointed who shall expect from these pages ["Life of Robertson"] an account of the progress of Dr. Robertson's mind, or a distinct view of his mental character, farther than can be obtained in his works. We meet neither with striking anecdotes, nor discriminative touches, nor fine and descriptive sketches. We recognize in every part of the piece a great master's hand; but the painting is not historical—it is not a portrait.—BROWN, THOMAS, 1803, *Dr. Stewart's Account of Robertson, Edinburgh Review, vol.* 2, *p.* 232.

His writing on literary and moral topics is the most popular in this part of the world, but Stewart ought not to write for this part of the world, or for this age of the world; he is bound to feel more courage, possessing the art of writing as he does, which always makes such a conquest over time, to say nothing of that loftiness and sensibility which pervade his philosophy, and must insure its success for ever, if England has any pretensions to immortality.—HORNER, FRANCIS, 1805, *Memoirs and Correspondence, vol.* I, *p.* 332.

The longer I study the works of this philosopher, the more I become convinced of two things—first, that in perspicacity and comprehension of understanding he yields to several; but, secondly, that in taste, variety of acquirements, and what is of more importance, in moral dignity of mind, he has no rival that I know of. Every liberal opinion has at all times found in him a zealous advocate. When he has come before the public he has borne himself with a carriage so meek, yet so commanding, and now, when, with unabating ardour, he is retired to devote the last remnant of his well-spent life to the great cause of human improvement, his attitude is so pensively sublime, I regard him with a reverence which I scarcely feel for any other living person. He is a man, take him for all in all, we shall not look upon his like again. There is something melancholy in the thought that the world cannot long enjoy the light of such a mind. But the cup goes round, and who so artful as to put it by.—CARLYLE, THOMAS, 1818, *Early Letters, ed. Norton, p.* 76.

Few writers rise with more grace from a plain ground work to the passages which require greater animation or embellishments. He gives to narrative, according to the precept of Bacon, the colour of the time, by a selection of happy expressions from original writers. Among the secret arts by which he diffuses elegance over his diction, may be remarked the skill which, by deepening or brightening a shade in a secondary term, by opening partial or preparatory glimpses of a thought to be afterwards unfolded, unobservedly heightens the import of a word, and gives it a new meaning, without any offense against old use.—MACKINTOSH, SIR JAMES, 1830, *Second Preliminary Dissertation, Encyclopædia Britannica.*

The name of Dugald Stewart is one of the few, which, of late years, serve to relieve in part the character of the mother country from the charge of a comparative neglect of the great sciences of intellectual and moral philosophy. His writings upon these all-important subjects, if not the most powerful, are perhaps the most engaging in form, and consequently the most attractive to the general reader, in the language. . . . The praise we allow to Stewart is the same which is usually given to the greatest philosophical writers of ancient and modern times. . . . The "Philosophical Essays" and the "Dissertations on the History of Philosophy," are among the most agreeable and valuable of our author's writings. It would carry us too far from our immediate object to pretend to comment upon the various subjects, which are rapidly touched upon in these works. It is much to be regretted that Stewart did not live to complete the plan of the Dissertations. Without, perhaps, fully realising the idea of a perfect History of Philosophy, they might, in that case, have justly been considered as the most remarkable essay towards a work of this kind, to be found in any language. The learning, displayed by our author in these Dissertations and in his other writings, is extensive, and as far as it goes, uniformly thorough and exact. He is familiar in particular with classical and French literature. He attaches, we think, rather too much importance to some continental writers of an inferior order, such as Buffier and Boscovich.—EVERETT, ALEXANDER HILL, 1830, *Stewart's Moral Philosophy, North American Review, vol.* 31, *pp.* 213, 214, 223.

Stewart, who cast a luminous glance over the philosophy of mind, and warmed the inmost recesses of metaphysical inquiry by the delicacy of taste and the glow of eloquence.—ALISON, SIR ARCHIBALD, 1833-42, *History of Europe During The Revolution, vol.* XIV, *p.* 3.

A Scotch philosopher of great repute, but, as it appears to me, of ability not quite equal to his repute. . . . Though a somewhat superficial thinker, was, at all events, a careful writer —BUCKLE, HENRY THOMAS, 1861, *History of Civilization in England, vol.* II, *pp.* 368, *note,* 382.

He propounded little that was original in philosophy; his opinions were for the most part modifications of Reid; but as an expositor of philosophical doctrines, his reputation stands deservedly high. Most of his works were composed after his retirement from the Chair of Philosophy in 1810. . . . He is the most ornate and elegant of our philosophical writers. His summaries of philosophical systems are sometimes praised as being especially perspicuous and interesting. His manner as a controversialist is peculiarly agreeable when taken in contrast to the hard-hitting and open ridicule of such controversialists as Priestley: Stewart's copious lubricated eloquence is much better fitted to conciliate oponents and win assent.—MINTO, WILLIAM, 1872-80, *Manual of English Prose Literature, p.* 512.

Dugald Stewart, the Professor of Moral Philosophy, whose works, if they have often been surpassed in depth and originality of speculation, have seldom been equalled for solid sense and polished ease of diction.—SHAIRP, JOHN CAMPBELL, 1879 *Robert Burns* (*English Men of Letters*) *p.* 44.

Stewart, in all probability the greatest philosopher of the age, did not, in spite of his ability, attain to the important position that was yielded, without opposition, to Jeremy Bentham. — OLIPHANT, MARGARET O. W., 1882, *Literary History of England, XVIII-XIX Century, vol.* III, *p.* 291.

Dugald Stewart, a man whose name was received with as much respect as Boswell's was with ridicule, in spite of the new example so lately set him by a brother Scot, treated Adam Smith, Robertson, and Reid with the old-fashioned solemnity, and instead of raising to them a memorial buried them beneath a monument.—HILL, GEORGE BIRKBECK, 1891, *The Centenary of Boswell, Macmillan's Magazine, vol.* 64, *p.* 37.

He has risen beyond the plainness, amounting almost to monotony, that had marked the previous writings of his school; and it was owing perhaps in great measure to his consummate gifts as an academic teacher that his written work was enriched by a vein of ornament and eloquence.—CRAIK, HENRY, 1895, *ed., English Prose, Introduction, vol.* IV, *p.* 4.

As an empirical observer, too, of psychological facts he showed genuine acuteness, and the exposition of Reid's ideas, in which his so-called philosophy mainly consists, were both more precise and more suggestive than the original text. But he was incapable of making any real advance upon Reid, and equally incapable of retreating decisively from the barren position which Reid, as a metaphysician, had taken up. His greatest distinction is the influence he admittedly had upon the school of Jouffroy and Cousin, which, though at bottom as barren as his own, commanded a far wider intellectual horizon.—HERFORD, C. H., 1897, *The Age of Wordsworth, p.* 4, *note.*

Stewart's influence owed so much to his personal attractiveness that its decline is not surprising. He was a transmitter of Reid's influence far more than an originator. He held, with Reid, that philosophy depended upon psychology treated as an inductive science. He expounded the doctrine "common-sense" so as to represent the "intuitionism" against which the Mills carried on their polemic. He repudiated, however, ontological argument still more emphatically than his master, and was a thorough nominalist. While thus approximating to the purely empirical school, he was the more anxious, as Mackintosh observes, to mark his disapproval of more thoroughgoing advocates.—STEPHEN, LESLIE, 1898, *Dictionary of National Biography, vol.* LIV, *p.* 285.

Lady Caroline Lamb

1785–1828

Born Nov. 13, 1785; died at Melbourne House, Whitehall, Jan. 26, 1828. An English novelist, daughter of Frederick Ponsonby, third earl of Bessborough. In 1805 she married William Lamb (afterward Lord Melbourne), from whom she was separated in 1825. She was involved in intrigues with Byron, who left her in 1813. She wrote "Glenarvon," (1816), which contained a caricature of Byron, "A New Canto" (1819), "Graham Hamilton" (1822), "Ada Reis; a Tale" (1823).—SMITH, BENJAMIN E., *ed.*, 1894–97, *The Century Cyclopedia of Names, p.* 587.

PERSONAL

If there is anything more delightful than another to witness, it is the spontaneous outbreak of a good kind heart, which, in serving and giving pleasure to others, obeys the instinctive impulse of a sanguine and genial disposition—waiting for no rule or maxim—not opening an account for value expected—doing unto others what you wish them to do unto you. This, in one word, is Lady Caroline Lamb; for if she does not always act wisely for herself, she generally acts only too well towards others.—MORGAN, SYDNEY LADY, 1818, *Diary, Aug.; Passages from My Autobiography, p.* 34.

"What do you think of Mrs. Felix Lorraine, Miss Manvers?" asked [Vivian Grey.] "Oh, I think her a very amusing woman, a very clever woman, a very—but—" "But what?" "But I can't exactly make her out." "Nor I; she is a dark riddle; and although I am a very Œdipus, I confess I have not yet unravelled it."—DISRAELI, BENJAMIN (LORD BEACONSFIELD), 1826–27, *Vivian Grey, ch.* ix.

There are many yet living who drew from the opening years of this gifted and warm-hearted being hopes which her maturity was not fated to realise. To these it will be some consolation to reflect that her end at least was what the best of us might envy, and the harshest of us approve. . . . Her character it is difficult to analyse, because, owing to the extreme susceptibility of her imagination, and the unhesitating and rapid manner in which she followed its impulses, her conduct was one perpetual kaleidoscope of change. . . . To the poor she was invariably charitable—she was more: in spite of her ordinary thoughtlessness of self, for them she had consideration as well as generosity, and delicacy no less than relief. For her friends she had a ready and active love: for her enemies no hatred: never perhaps was there a human being who had less malevolence: as all her errors hurt only herself, so against herself only were levelled her accusations and reproach. . . . Her manners, though somewhat eccentric, and apparently, not really, affected, had a fascination which it is difficult for any one who never encountered their effect to conceive.—LAMB, WILLIAM, 1828, *Literary Gazette, Feb.* 16.

Several women were in love with Byron, but none so violently as Lady Caroline Lamb. She absolutely besieged him. He showed me the first letter he received from her; in which she assured him that, if he was in any want of money, "all her jewels were at his service." They frequently had quarrels; and more than once, on coming home, I have found Lady C. walking in the garden, and waiting for me, and beg that I would reconcile them.—When she met Byron at a party, she would always, if possible, return home from it in *his* carriage, and accompanied by *him:* I recollect particularly their returning to town together from Holland House.—But such was the insanity of her passion for Byron, that sometimes, when not invited to a party where he was to be, she would wait for him in the street till it was over! One night, after a great party at Devonshire House, to which Lady Caroline had not been invited, I saw her,—yes saw her,—talking to Byron, with half of her body thrust into the carriage which he had just entered. In spite of all this absurdity, my firm belief is that there was nothing criminal against them. Byron at last was sick of her. When their intimacy was at an end, and while she was living in the country she burned, very solemnly, on a sort of funeral pile, "transcripts" of all the letters which she had received from Byron, and *a copy* of a miniature (his portrait) which he had presented to her; several girls from the neighbourhood, whom she had dressed in white garments, dancing round the pile, and singing a song which she had written for the occasion, "Burn, fire, Burn," &c.—She was mad; and her family allowed her to do whatever she chose.—ROGERS, SAMUEL, 1855, *Recollections of Table-Talk, ed. Dyce, p.* 231.

Lady Caroline Lamb was then between thirty and forty, but looked much younger than she was; thanks perhaps, to a slight rounded figure and childlike mode of wearing her hair (which was of a pale golden colour) in close curls. She had large hazel eyes, capable of much varied expression, exceedingly good teeth, a pleasant laugh, and a musical intonation of voice, despite a certain artificial drawl, habitual to what was called the Devonshire House Set. Apart from these gifts, she might be considered plain. But she had, to a surpassing degree, the attribute of charm, and never failed to please if she chose to do so. Her powers of conversation were remarkable. In one of Lord Byron's letters to her, which she showed me, he said, "You are the only woman I know who never bored me." There was, indeed, a wild originality in her talk, combining great and sudden contrasts, from deep pathos to infantine drollery: now sentimental, now shrewd, it sparkled with anecdotes of the great world, and of the eminent persons with whom she had been brought up, or been familiarly intimate; and, ten minutes after, it became gravely eloquent with religious enthusiasm, or shot off into metaphysical speculations—sometimes absurd, sometimes profound—generally suggestive and interesting. A creature of caprice, and impulse, and whim, her manner, her talk, and her character shifted their colours as rapidly as those of a chameleon. She has sent her page the round of her guests at three o'clock in the morning, with a message that she was playing the organ that stood in the staircase at Brocket, and begged the favour of their company to hear her. —LYTTON, EDWARD BULWER LORD, 1873–83, *Autobiography, Life, Letters and Literary Remains, ed., his Son, vol.* I, *p.* 328.

Lady Caroline Lamb I never saw, but from friends of mine who were well acquainted with her I have heard manifold instances of her extraordinary character and conduct. I remember my friend Mr. Harness telling me that, dancing with him one night at a great ball, she had suddenly amazed him by the challenge—"Gueth how many pairth of thtockingth I have on." (Her ladyship lisped, and her particular graciousness to Mr. Harness was the result of Lord Byron's school intimacy with and regard for him). Finding her partner quite unequal to the piece of divination proposed to him, she put forth a very pretty little foot, from which she lifted the petticoat ankle high, lisping out, "Thixth."—KEMBLE, FRANCES ANN, 1879, *Records of a Girlhood, p.* 45.

Lady Caroline Lamb possessed other qualities than those of high birth and physical beauty. Nature had endowed her with a multiplicity of gifts, any one of which would have rendered a less volatile woman distinguished. She painted in water colours, drew spirited caricatures, played the harp, composed music, wrote poems, recited odes, rode bare-backed horses, and delighted in polishing Derbyshire spar. Her conversation was as sprightly as her accomplishments were numerous; her ideas being clad in sentences that struck the ear by their quaintness of expression, and pleased the fancy by their singular wit.—MOLLOY, FITZGERALD, 1888, *William Lamb's Wife, Temple Bar, vol.* 84, *p.* 328.

Lady Caroline was a clever, generous, and impulsive woman, inordinately vain, and excitable to the verge of insanity. In person she was small and slight, with pale, golden-coloured hair, "large, hazel eyes, capable of much varied expression, exceedingly good teeth, and a musical intonation of voice." Her powers of conversation were remarkable, full of wild originality and combining great and sudden contrasts, while her manners "had a fascination which it is difficult for any who never encountered their effect to conceive." Lord Lytton has left on record a curious account of his brief and sentimental attachment to her. She is supposed to have been the original of Mrs. Felix Lorraine in "Vivian Grey," of Lady Monteagle in "Venetia," of Lady Melton in "De Lindsay," Lady Clara in "Lionel Hastings," and of Lady Bellenden in "Greville."—BARKER, G. F. RUSSELL, 1892, *Dictionary of National Biography, vol.* XXXI, *p.* 422.

GENERAL

By the way, I suppose you have seen "Glenarvon." Madame de Staël lent it me to read from Coppet last autumn. It seems to me that if the authoress had written the *truth*, and nothing but the truth—the whole truth—the romance would not only have been more *romantic*, but more entertaining. As for the likeness, the picture can't be good. I did not sit long enough.—BYRON, LORD, 1816, *Letter to Thomas Moore, Dec.* 5.

Lady Caroline Lamb was the authoress of three works of fiction, utterly worthless in a literary point of view, but which, from extrinsic circumstances, were highly popular in their day. The first, "Glenarvon," was published in 1816, and the hero was understood to "body forth" the character and sentiments of Lord Byron. It was a representation of the dangers attending a life of fashion. . . . The history of Lady Caroline Lamb is painful.—CHAMBERS, ROBERT, 1876, *Cyclopædia of English Literature, ed. Carruthers.*

While the scandal of Lord Byron's separation from his wife was still recent, the story of "Glenarvon" was announced, which uncontradicted rumour ascribed to Lady Caroline Lamb. Curiosity was on tip-toe to peep through a window so unexpectedly opened into the home of youth, beauty, and fame prematurely and mysteriously abandoned. The good and the bad, the wise and the unwise, were equally eager to read the book. All were alike disappointed. It was merely a rhapsodical tale, published before any one was aware who could have prevented its appearance, and which owed its brief celebrity to the portrait it was expected to contain of Byron as he was in social life. . . . That its perusal could have had any other effect upon Lamb than that of exciting his pity is inconceivable, and to suppose, as its erratic authoress did, that it justified to him her extravagant demeanour where the poet was concerned, is simply impossible. Whatever was blameworthy in her predilection for Byron or her manner of evincing it, it was far eclipsed by the infatuation and incoherence of "Calantha;" while the incidents of fashionable dissipation are thrown into the shade by a grotesque combination of foppery and Whiteboyism. It was not surprising that all who felt concerned for her reputation and welfare should have concurred to depreciate the notion of her again trying her hand in fiction. But "Glenarvon," in spite of its defects, had had a sort of success which makes a publisher ready to advise a second venture; and before long she was busily engaged in weaving the plot of another story, which made its appearance in due time. . . . None of her compositions attained high commendation from the critics of the day. "Glenarvon," "Graham Hamilton," and "Ada Reis" were the only novels acknowledged as the productions of her pen, though others were ascribed to her authorship. In the Annuals are to be found not a few stanzas of merit.—TORRENS, W. M., 1878, *Memoirs of the Right Honourable William, Second Viscount Melbourne, vol.* I, *pp.* 112, 113.

"Ada Reis," Lady Caroline's third, sometimes called her best, novel, happened, at all events; and a very "high fantastic" flowery performance it is, though exhibiting some power and only too much imagination. The "Good Spirit" she afterwards declared was intended for Bulwer; adding, "I fear he is not so good now."—MAYER, S. R. TOWNSHEND, 1878, *Lady Caroline Lamb, Temple Bar, vol.* 53, *p.* 187.

Except for her romantic attachment to the author of "Childe Harold," who seems not only to have impressed her feelings, but fired her imagination for literary work, the world would probably have heard little of her in the domain of letters, though her name might have survived for a generation in the circles of fashionable society. But her extraordinary infatuation for Lord Byron, and the difficulties to which it led, together with her sketches of his lordship and her confessions, have invested her personal history and her literary efforts with a singular attractiveness.—SMITH, GEORGE BARNETT, 1883, *Lady Caroline Lamb, Gentleman's Magazine, vol.* 255, *p.* 337.

John Gardiner Calkins Brainard

1796-1828

A Hartford journalist whose "Poems" were published first in 1825, and reissued as "Literary Remains" in 1832 in an enlarged edition, with Memoir by his friend Whittier. His verse was temporarily popular, but his chief claim to present remembrance is the fine poem beginning, "I saw two clouds at morning."—ADAMS, OSCAR FAY, 1897, *A Dictionary of American Authors, p.* 35.

PERSONAL

In private life, Brainard was most highly esteemed. He was fond of social intercourse; and superior powers of conversation, and a fund of cheerful humor, often rendered him the delight of the circle. His feelings were peculiarly sensitive—a circumstance which often proved a source of uneasiness to his friends. His character through life was marked at times by a shade of melancholy, and his verse is often imbued with a spirit of pleasing sadness. As an editor he seemed little better adapted to the rougher tasks of political partizanship than to the abstractions of law. Aside from a constitutional aversion to such duties as would bring him into a bold and public intercourse with his fellow men, he ever manifested a reluctance to engage in high and continued effort. Thus his taste and feelings inclined him rather to the literary than the political department of his paper, and in this character consisted its chief charm.—EVEREST, CHARLES W., 1843, *The Poets of Connecticut, p.* 261.

He was a small man, and sensitive on that score. His friends noticed the fine expression of his countenance when animated. He was negligent of his dress and somewhat abstracted. He wrote rapidly, and was ready in conversation, with playful repartee. — DUYCKINCK, EVERT A. AND GEORGE L., 1855-65-75, *Cyclopædia of American Literature, ed. Simons, vol.* I, *p.* 967.

GENERAL

Niagara marks an epoch in my history. Its thunders will always rise in my recollection when sublimity is mentioned. I have said, and like to say little about it, because I find all words which *I* can use utterly inadequate to convey my ideas. I have seen many drawings and read many descriptions of Niagara, but nothing produces any thing like the true impression, except a little *morceau* of poetry you once sent me, and the description by Howison in a back volume of Blackwood. — ALEXANDER, JAMES W., 1825, *Familiar Letters, May* 28.

He seldom aims at more than he can accomplish; the chief misfortune with him is, that he should be contented sometimes to accomplish so little, and this little in so imperfect a manner. That he possesses much of the genuine spirit and power of poetry, no one can doubt, who reads some of the pieces in this volume, yet there are others, which, if not absolutely below mediocrity, would never be suspected as coming from a soil that had been watered with Castalian dews. They might pass off very well as exercises in rhyme of an incipient poet, the first efforts at pluming the wing for a bolder flight, and they might hold for a day an honorable place in the corner of a gazette, but to a higher service, or more conspicuous station, they could not wisely be called. In short, if we take all the author's compositions in this volume together, nothing is more remarkable concerning them than their inequality; the high poetical beauty and strength, both in thought and language, of some parts, and the want of good taste and the extreme negligence of others. . . . The author will do wisely to forsake his humorous strain, and make poetry more of a task, and less of a pastime, than seems to have been his habit. It was a maxim with the ancients, which the moderns have never called in question, that nothing good is brought to pass without labor. No proof exists, that poets are exempt from this common fatality of the human condition. Mr. Brainard's graver pieces are much superior to his lighter and more playful, and his blank verse to his rhyme.—SPARKS, JARED, 1825, *Brainard's Poems, North American Review, vol.* 21, *pp.* 218, 224.

It ["The Tree Toad"] seems to have been hurriedly constructed, as if its author had felt ashamed of his light labor. But that in his heart there was a secret exultation over these verses for which his reason found it difficult to account, *we know;* and there is not a really imaginative man within sound of our voice to-day, who, upon perusal of this little "Tree Toad," will not admit it to be one of the truest poems ever written by Brainard.—POE, EDGAR ALLAN, 1842, *Graham's Magazine, Works, eds. Stedman and Woodberry, vol.* VIII, *p.* 271.

Brainard lacked the mental discipline and strong self-command which alone confer true power. He never could have produced a great work. His poems were nearly all written during the six years in which he edited the Mirror, and they bear marks of haste and carelessness, though some of them are very beautiful. He failed only in his humorous pieces; in all the rest his language is appropriate and pure, his diction free and harmonious, and his sentiments natural and sincere. His serious poems are characterized by deep feeling and delicate fancy; and if we had no records of his history, they would show us that he was a man of great gentleness, simplicity, and purity.—GRISWOLD, RUFUS W., 1842–46, *The Poets and Poetry of America, p.* 178.

His genius lay in the amiable walks of the *belles-lettres,* where the delicacy of his temperament, the correspondence of the sensitive mind to the weak physical frame, found its appropriate home and nourishment. His country needed results of this kind more than it did law or politics; and in his short life Brainard honored his native land. His genius is a flower plucked from the banks of the river which he loved, and preserved for posterity. — DUYCKINCK, EVERT A. AND GEORGE L., 1855–65–75, *Cyclopædia of American Literature, ed. Simons, vol.* I, *p.* 966.

Another crude Connecticut poet, J. G. C. Brainard, was writing hasty lines similarly lacking in greatness but similarly marked by occasional genuineness. Now the sea-bird was his theme. . . . Again, he wrote of some local stream, or of the autumn woods he well knew. . . . Less true and more bombastic was Brainard's once famous extemporization on Niagara, which he never saw. — RICHARDSON, CHARLES F., 1888, *American Literature,* 1607–1885, *vol.* II, *pp.* 31, 32.

An early friend of Whittier,—died young, leaving a few pieces which show that his lyrical gift was spontaneous and genuine, but had received little cultivation.—BEERS, HENRY A., 1895, *Initial Studies in American Letters, p.* 182.

Edward Coate Pinkney

1802–1828

Edward Coate Pinkney was born in London in October, 1802, while his father was there as United States Commissioner under the Jay treaty. He was educated at St. Mary's College, Baltimore, and entered the navy as a midshipman. But at the age of twenty-two he resigned his commission, and studied law. In 1826 he accepted a professorship in the University of Maryland, and in 1827 the editorship of the "Marylander," a political journal. Ill health soon compelled him to resign the latter, and he died on the 11th of April, 1828. His only volume was "Rodolph, and other Poems," published anonymously in Baltimore in 1825. It is included in Morris and Willis's "Mirror Library," with a biographical sketch by William Leggett.—JOHNSON, ROSSITER, 1875, *Little Classics, Authors, p.* 199.

PERSONAL

I knew Pinkney slightly. He was a very handsome man, punctilious to a fault, wayward, and Byronic, chivalrous and enthusiastic. . . . I have always thought him the most original of our Poets.—THOMAS, F. W., 1841, *Letter to Griswold, Passages from the Correspondence and other Papers of Rufus W. Griswold, p.* 97.

GENERAL

Rich in beauties of a peculiar nature, ["Poems"] and not surpassed by productions of a similar character in the English language.— LEGGETT, WILLIAM, 1827, *The Mirror.*

"Rodolph" is his longest work. It was first published, anonymously, soon after he left the navy, and was probably written while he was in the Mediterranean. . . . There is no novelty in the story, and not much can be said for its morality. . . . It has more faults than Pinkney's other works; in many passages it is obscure; its beauty is marred by the use of obsolete words; and the author seems to delight in drawing his comparisons from the least known portions of ancient literature. Some of his lighter pieces are very beautiful. "A Health," "The Picture-Song," and "A Serenade," have not often been equalled. . . . Pinkney's is the first instance in this country in which we have to lament the prostitution of true poetical genius to unworthy purposes. Pervading much that he wrote there is a selfish melancholy and sullen pride; dissatisfaction with the present, and doubts in regard to the future life.—GRISWOLD, RUFUS W., 1842-46, *The Poets and Poetry of America, pp.* 231, 232.

The poem just cited ["A Health"] is especially beautiful; but the poetic elevation which it induces we must refer chiefly to our sympathy in the poet's enthusiasm. We pardon his hyperboles for the evident earnestness with which they are uttered. —POE, EDGAR ALLAN, 1850, *The Poetic Principle, Works, vol.* VI, *p.* 18.

The small volume of poems, sufficiently large to preserve his memory with all generous appreciators of true poetry as a writer of exquisite taste and susceptibility, appeared in Baltimore in 1825. It contained "Rodolph, a Fragment," which had previously been printed anonymously for the author's friends. It is a powerful sketch of a broken life of passion and remorse, of a husband slain by the lover of his wife, of her early death in a convent, and of the paramour's wanderings and wild mental anticipations. Though a fragment, wanting in fulness of design and the last polish of execution, it is a poem of power and mark. There is an occasional inner music in the lines, demonstrative of the true poet. The imagery is happy and original, evidently derived from objects which the writer had seen in the impressible youth of his voyages in the navy.—DUYCKINCK, EVERT A. AND GEORGE L., 1855-65-75, *Cyclopædia of American Literature, ed. Simons, vol.* II, *p.* 147.

Trilled his airy love-lyrics like a descendant of some seventeenth-century cavalier.—PANCOAST, HENRY S., 1898, *An Introduction to American Literature. p.* 155.

Thomas Young

1773-1829

Physicist, born of Quaker parentage at Milverton, Somerset, studied medicine at London, Edinburgh, Göttingen, and Cambridge, and started as doctor in London in 1800, but devoted himself to scientific research, and in 1801 became professor of Natural Philosophy to the Royal Institution. His "Lectures" (1807) expounded the doctrine of interference, which established the undulatory theory of light. He was secretary to the Royal Society, and did valuable work in insurance, hæmodynamics, and Egyptology.—PATRICK AND GROOME, *eds.*, 1897, *Chambers's Biographical Dictionary, p.* 991.

PERSONAL

Dined at the Athenæum. Hudson Gurney asked me to dine with him. He was low spirited. His friend, Dr. Young, is dying. Gurney speaks of him as a very great man, the most learned physician and greatest mathematician of his age, and the first discoverer of the clue to the Egyptian hieroglyphics. Calling on him a few days ago, Gurney found him busy about his Egyptian Dictionary, though very ill. He is aware of his state, but that makes him most anxious to finish his work. "I would not," he said to Gurney, "live a single idle day."—ROBINSON, HENRY CRABB, 1829, *Diary, April* 29.

Dr. Young was a man, in all the relations of life, upright, kind-hearted, blameless. His domestic virtues were as exemplary as his talents were great. He was entirely free from either envy or jealousy, and the assistance which he gave to others engaged in the same lines of research with himself, was constant and unbounded. His morality through life had been pure, though unostentatious. His religious sentiments were by himself stated to be liberal, though orthodox. He had extensively studied the Scriptures, of which the precepts were deeply impressed upon his mind from his earliest years; and he evidenced the faith which he professed, in an unbending course of usefulness and rectitude.—GURNEY, HUDSON, 1831, *Memoir of the Life of Thomas Young.*

THOMAS YOUNG

Engraving by G. R. Ward. Painting by Sir Thomas Lawrence, P. R. A.

WILLIAM WILBERFORCE

From Painting by Sir Thomas Lawrence, P. R. A.

SACRED TO THE MEMORY OF
THOMAS YOUNG, M. D.,
FELLOW AND FOREIGN SECRETARY OF THE ROYAL SOCIETY,
MEMBER OF THE NATIONAL INSTITUTE OF FRANCE:
A MAN ALIKE EMINENT
IN ALMOST EVERY DEPARTMENT OF HUMAN LEARNING.
PATIENT OF UNINTERMITTED LABOUR,
ENDOWED WITH THE FACULTY OF INTUITIVE PERCEPTION,
WHO, BRINGING AN EQUAL MASTERY
TO THE MOST ABSTRUSE INVESTIGATIONS
OF LETTERS AND OF SCIENCE,
FIRST ESTABLISHED THE UNDULATORY THEORY OF LIGHT,
AND FIRST PENETRATED THE OBSCURITY
WHICH HAD VEILED FOR AGES
THE HIEROGLYPHICS OF EGYPT.
endeared to his friends by his domestic virtues,
honoured by the world for his unrivalled acquirements,
he died in the hopes of the resurrection of the just.

Born at Milverton, in Somersetshire,
June 13th, 1773;
Died in Park Square, London, May 10th, 1829,
In the 56th year of his age.
—GURNEY, HUDSON, *Inscription under Chantrey's Medallion, Westminster Abbey.*

I have not dwelt too long on the task imposed on me, if I have brought out, as I wished to do, the importance and novelty of the admirable law of interferences. Young is now placed before your eyes as one of the most illustrious men of science in whom England may justly take pride. Your thoughts, anticipating my words, may perhaps receive already, in the recital of the just honours shown to the author of so beautiful a discovery, the peroration of this historical notice. These anticipations, I regret to say, will not be realized. The death of Young has in his own country created very little sensation. The doors of Westminster Abbey, so easily accessible to titled mediocrity, remained shut upon a man of genius, who was not even a baronet. It was in the village of Farnborough, in the modest tomb of the family of his wife, that the remains of Thomas Young were deposited. The indifference of the English nation for those scientific labours which ought to add so much to its glory, is a rare anomaly, of which it would be curious to trace the causes. I should be wanting in frankness, I should be the panegyrist, not the historian, if I did not avow, that in general Young did not sufficiently accommodate himself to the capacity of his readers; that the greater part of the writings for which the sciences are indebted to him, are justly chargeable with a certain obscurity.—ARAGO, FRANÇOIS, 1832, *Thomas Young, Biographies of Distinguished Scientific Men, vol.* II, *p.* 340.

Although Westminster Abbey does not hold his dust, Dean Buckland allowed Young's devoted widow to place within its famous walls a profile medallion of him executed by Chantrey, and beneath it a slab containing an inscription written by his life-long friend Hudson Gurney. When we consider the grandeur of his genius, the multifarious greatness of his works, the simplicity and sublimity of his character, we are amazed at the indifference of mankind, which has suffered his name to rest in comparative obscurity.—MILBURN, WILLIAM HENRY, 1890, *Thomas Young, Harper's Magazine, vol.* 80, *p.* 679.

GENERAL

Such is the beautiful theory of Fresnel and Young; for we must not, in our regard for one great name, forget the justice which is due to the other; and to separate them and assign to each his share would be as impracticable as invidious, so intimately are they blended together throughout every part of this system,—early, acute, and pregnant suggestion characterizing the one, and maturity of thought, fullness of systematic development and decisive experimental illustration equally distinguishing the other.—HERSCHEL, SIR JOHN, 1827, *Peacock's Life of Young, p.* 397.

At the mention of Dr. Young's name the historian must pause. None of our countrymen has approached more nearly the character of the celebrated Dr. Brook Taylor. Possessing the same ingenuity, extensive learning, varied accomplishments, and profound science, he combined likewise a concise, hard, and sometimes obscure, mode of stating his reasonings and calculations.—LESLIE, SIR JOHN, 1853, *Fifth Preliminary Dissertation, Encyclopædia Britannica, Eighth ed.*

It may safely be affirmed that no philologer ever before made such a discovery in science as the law of interference, and that no natural philosopher ever made such a step in the interpretation of a lost tongue as the formation (up to a certain point) of an Egyptian alphabet. We cannot close this imperfect sketch of one of the greatest ornaments of our age and nation, without adding that in private life Dr. Young was exemplary, endued with warm affections, philosophic moderation, and high moral and religious principles. . . . Dr. Young's philosophical character approached in many important particulars to that of Newton. With much of the inventive fire of Davy and of the reasoning sagacity of Wollaston, he combined an amount of acquired learning, and a versatility in its application, far superior to both.—FORBES, J. D., 1853, *Sixth Preliminary Dissertation, Encyclopædia Britannica, Eighth ed.*

Young's own style of writing, if not idiomatic, was singularly pure: he had studied very carefully the principles of grammar, and one of his earliest essays in the Leptologist was in illustration of them: his sentences are usually short: he chooses the most simple words which will express his meaning: he rarely attempts to form carefully balanced periods, and never resorts to figurative expressions when those which are direct and immediate will answer his purpose: he was as little disposed to admire and imitate the poetical prose of Schiller in history as of Davy in philosophy, and was apt to regard them both as almost equally misplaced. . . . If we refer to his other scientific works, embracing so wide a range of subjects, and some of them—more especially his essays on the tides and the cohesion of fluids—so remarkable for the boldness and originality of their treatment, we shall find that they were rarely read and never appreciated by his contemporaries, and even now are neither sufficiently known nor adequately valued: whilst if justice was awarded more promptly and in more liberal measure by his own countrymen to his hieroglyphical labours, these also were singularly unfortunate, as far as concerned the general diffusion of his fame, by coming into collision with adverse claims which were most unfairly and unscrupulously urged in his own age, and not much less so by some distinguished writers in very recent times. The great variety also of his titles to commemoration as a classical scholar and archæologist, a medical writer, an optician, a mathematician, or a physical philosopher, increases the difficulty of judging his relative rank amongst men of celebrity, whether they were his contemporaries or not: for the position which he might not venture to claim in virtue of his contributions to any single department of human knowledge, might be readily conceded to him when his combined labours were taken into consideration.—PEACOCK, GEORGE, 1855, *Life of Thomas Young, pp.* 467, 472.

There is, perhaps, no name contemporary with that of Dr. Young, which will hold a higher place in the annals of British science and literature. In the various fields of natural philosophy, medicine, and archæology, he acquired a high reputation; and if he had devoted all his faculties to any one of these departments of knowledge, he would doubtless have attained to a still higher place in the temple of science. At an early period of his life Dr. Young was an accurate classical scholar. He was perfectly familiar with the principal languages of Europe. He was well versed in mathematics, and almost every department of natural philosophy and natural history. His knowledge of medicine and anatomy was profound, and he possessed a very unusual share of those personal and ornamental accomplishments which are so highly valued in the intercourse of society.—BREWSTER, SIR DAVID, 1855, *Dr. Peacock's Life of Dr. Thomas Young, North British Review, vol.* 23, *p*, 481.

The most clear-thinking and far-seeing mechanical philosopher of the nineteenth century, and one of its most accomplished and profound scholars. . . . Some of the merits of his works have already been mentioned; but it may be added that they are remarkable above all for their highly philosophical spirit, and in particular by the constancy with which they keep in view the distinction between *beings* and *actions*,—a distinction so often lost sight of in crude theories of physics.—RANKINE, W. J. M., 1866, *Imperial Dictionary of Universal Biography, vol.* VI, *p.* 1409.

He was, in short, one of those rare phenomena that disturb from time to time the speculations of theorists upon the limited range of the human intellect.—HART,

JOHN S., 1872, *A Manual of English Literature, p.* 563.

Young lectured for two years at the Royal Institution, and he afterwards threw the lectures into a permanent form in a quarto volume of 750 pages, with 40 plates, and nearly 600 figures and maps. He also produced at the same time a second volume of the same magnitude, embracing his optical and other memoirs, and a most elaborate classed catalogue of works and papers, accompanied by notes, extracts, and calculations. For this colossal work Young was to receive 1,000*l.* His publisher however became bankrupt, and he never touched the money. His lectures constitute a monument of Young's power almost equal to that of his original memoirs. They are replete with profound reflections and suggestions. In his eighth lecture, on "Collision," the term *energy*, now in such constant use, was first introduced and defined. By it he was able to avoid, and enable us to avoid, the confusion which had crept into scientific literature by the incautious employment of the word *force*. Further, the theory now known as the Young-Helmholtz theory, which refers all the sensations of colour to three primary sensations—red, green, and violet—was clearly enunciated by Young in his thirty-seventh lecture, on "Physical Optics." His views of the nature of heat were original and correct. . . . Young's essay on the "Cohesion of Fluids" is to be ranked amongst the most important and difficult of his labours. —TYNDALL, JOHN, 1886, *New Fragments, pp.* 277, 278.

May be styled, without exaggeration, the most learned, profound, variously accomplished scholar and man of science that has appeared in our age—perhaps in any age. . . . As a physician, a linguist, an archæologist, a mathematician, scholar, and philosopher in their most difficult and abstruse investigations, Thomas Young has added to almost every department of human knowledge that which will be remembered to after-times.—MILBURN, WILLIAM HENRY, 1890, *Thomas Young, Harper's Magazine, vol.* 80, *pp.* 670, 679.

The remarkable fact that Young, of whom Helmholtz says (Vorträge und Reden, vol. i, p. 279) that he came a generation too soon, remained scientifically unrecognised and popularly almost unknown to his countrymen, has been explained by his unfortunate manner of expression and the peculiar channels through which his labours were announced to the world. His frequently unintelligible style, his obscure and inelegant mathematics, the habitual incognito which he preserved, his modesty in replying to attacks, and his general want of method in enunciating his ideas, contrast very markedly with the writings of some of his rivals, especially in France, where the qualities of style, method, and elegance were highly developed, and where recognised organs existed for the publication of works of genius. The historian of thought, however, must not omit to state that several great names contributed, by the authority they commanded, to oppose Young's claims to originality and renown.—MERZ, JOHN THEODORE, 1896, *A History of European Thought in the Nineteenth Century, vol.* I.

Young has been justly called "the founder of physiological optics." He was the first to prove conclusively that the accommodation of the eye for vision at different distances was due to change of curvature of the crystalline lens. His opinion that the lens itself was muscular has, however, not been confirmed by more recent work. His memoir "On the Mechanism of the Eye" contained the first description and measurement of astigmatism, and a table of optical constants of the eye in close agreement with modern determinations. He first explained colour sensation as due to the presence in the retina of structures which respond to the three colours, red, green, and violet respectively, and colour blindness as due to the inability of one or more of these structures to respond normally to stimulus. Young's theory has been supported and extended by Helmholtz; and although a rival theory due to Hering is regarded with favour by many physiologists, there are phenomena unfavourable to the theory. Of other contributions connected with his profession two of the most noteworthy are the Croonian lecture to the Royal Society "On the Functions of the Heart and Arteries," in which the laws regulating the flow of blood through the body are clearly stated, and its predecessor, "Hydraulic Investigations," on which it depends.—LEES, C. H., 1900, *Dictionary of National Biography, vol.* LXIII, *p.* 395.

Sir Humphry Davy

1778-1829

Born at Penzance, Cornwall, England, Dec. 17, 1778; died at Geneva, May 29, 1829. A celebrated English chemist. He was the son of a woodcarver at Penzance, studied at the Penzance grammar-school, and finished his education under the Rev. Dr. Cardew at Truro. In 1795 he was apprenticed to John Bingham Borlase, a prominent surgeon at Penzance. He was appointed an assistant in the laboratory of Beddoe's Pneumatic Institution at Bristol in 1798; became assistant lecturer in chemistry at the Royal Institution, London, in 1801; was promoted professor in 1802; was made director of the laboratory in 1805; discovered the decomposition of the fixed alkalis in 1807; was knighted in 1812; resigned his professorship at the Royal Institution in 1813; invented the safety-lamp in 1815; was created a baronet in 1818; and was elected as president of the Royal Society in 1820. His chief works are "Elements of Chemical Philosophy" (1812), and "Elements of Agricultural Chemistry" (1813).—SMITH, BENJAMIN E., *ed.*, 1894-97, *The Century Cyclopedia of Names, p.* 312.

PERSONAL

I have been once to the Royal Institution, and heard Davy lecture on animal substances to a mixed and large assembly of both sexes to the number, perhaps, of three hundred or more. It is a curious scene; the reflections it excites are of an ambiguous nature; for the prospect of possible good is mingled with the observation of much actual folly. The audience is assembled by the influence of fashion merely; and fashion and chemistry form a very incongruous union. At the same time, it is a trophy to the sciences; one great advance is made towards the association of female with masculine minds in the pursuit of useful knowledge; and another domain of pleasing and liberal inquiry is included within the range of polished conversation. Davy's style of lecturing is much in favour of himself, though not, perhaps, entirely suited to the place; it has rather a little awkwardness, but it is that air which bespeaks real modesty and good sense; he is only awkward because he cannot condescend to assume that theatrical quackery of manner, which might have a more imposing effect. This was my impression from his lecture. I have since (April 2nd) met Davy in company, and was much pleased with him; a great softness and propriety of manner, which might be cultivated into elegance; his physiognomy struck me as being superior to what the science of chemistry, on its present plan, can afford exercise for; I fancied to discover in it the lineaments of poetical feeling.—HORNER, FRANCIS, 1802, *Journal; Memoirs and Correspondence, vol.* I, *p.* 182.

I breakfasted this morning with Sir Humphry Davy, of whom we have heard so much in America. He is now about thirty-three, but with all the freshness and bloom of five-and-twenty, and one of the handsomest men I have seen in England. He has a great deal of vivacity,—talks rapidly, though with great precision,—and is so much interested in conversation, that his excitement amounts to nervous impatience, and keeps him in constant motion. He has just returned from Italy, and delights to talk of it,—thinks it, next to England, the finest country in the world, and the society of Rome surpassed only by that of London, and says he should not die contented without going there again. It seemed singular that his taste in this should be so acute, when his professional eminence is in a province so different and remote; but I was much more surprised when I found that the first chemist of his time was a professed angler; and that he thinks, if he were obliged to renounce fishing or philosophy, that he should find the struggle of his choice pretty severe.—TICKNOR, GEORGE, 1815, *Journal, June* 13; *Life, Letters and Journals, vol.* I, *p.* 57.

After having introduced your safety lamp into general use in all the collieries under my direction, where inflammable air prevails, and after using them daily in every variety of explosive mixture, for upwards of three months, I feel the highest possible gratification in stating to you that they have answered to my entire satisfaction. The safety of the lamps is so easily proved by taking them into any part of a mine charged with fire-damp, and all the explosive gradations of that dangerous element are so easily and satisfactorily ascertained by their application, as to strike the minds of the most prejudiced with the strongest conviction of their high utility; and our colliers have adopted them with the greatest eagerness. Besides the facilities afforded by this invention to the working of coal mines abounding in fire-damp, it has enabled the directors and superintendents to ascertain, with the utmost precision and expedition, both the presence, the quantity, and the correct situation of the gas. Instead of creeping inch by inch with a candle, as is usual, along the galleries of a mine suspected to contain fire-damp, in order to ascertain its presence, we walk firmly in with the safe lamps, and with the utmost confidence prove the actual state of the mine. By observing attentively the several appearances upon the flame of the lamp, in an examination of this kind, the cause of accidents which have happened to the most experienced and cautious miners is completely developed; and this has been, in a great measure, matter of mere conjecture.—BUDDLE, JOHN, 1816, *Report of Superintendent of Walls End Colliery, June* 1.

Dr. Paris gave us the history of Sir Humphry Davy. His father, a carver of wooden chimney-pieces: Davy put apprentice to an apothecary; sent away because he blew the apothecary's garret window out with a clyster pipe that he had charged with gas. Davy's discovery of the decomposition of alkalis ought, he said, to immortalise him. Had broached the theory a year before, and people cavilled at it; but, at last, he applied it to this great discovery.—MOORE, THOMAS, 1828, *Diary, Feb.* 15; *Memoirs, Journal and Correspondence, ed. Russell, vol.* V, *p.* 263.

Hic jacet
HUMPHRY DAVY
Eques Magnæ Britanniæ Baronetus
Olim Regiæ Societ. Londin Præses
Summus Arcanorum Naturæ Indagator
Natus Penzantiæ Cornubiensum XVII
Decemb. MDCCLXXVIII.
Obiit Genevæ Helvetiorum XXIX Mai
MDCCCXXIX

—INSCRIPTION ON MONUMENT, 1829, *Plain Palais Cemetery, Geneva.*

A long discussion after breakfast about the necessity of one's husband being clever. Ma foi je n'en vois pas la nécessité. People don't want to be entertaining each other all day long; *very* clever men don't grow on every bush, and *middling* clever men don't amount to anything. I think I should like to have married Sir Humphry Davy.—KEMBLE, FRANCES ANN, 1832, *Records of a Girlood, p.* 498.

He was of middle stature, about five feet seven inches high; but appeared shorter, perhaps from the just proportions and symmetry of his make. His hands and feet were small, and his bones in general small; but his muscles were comparatively large, especially of the lower extremities, in consequence of which he was well adapted for those exercises and sports of the field and river in which he delighted. He could walk well and bear fatigue for a long time; his arms and shoulders were, he used to say, less able than his legs; yet their strength was perfectly adequate to the management of the salmon rod, and the laborious amusement of salmon fishing; and there were few anglers who could throw the fly further on the water, or with greater steadiness and delicate precision; and he was quick in the use of his gun, and amongst good shots a very tolerable one, especially in that kind of shooting which requires an active hand and eye, as snipe shooting. . . . His neck was rather long and slender: his head was rather small, its surface smooth and rounded, without any striking protuberances; the occipital part was small, the forehead ample and elevated, and very beautifully rising, wide and gently arched. His face was oval and rather small; but, owing to the expansion of forehead, not apparently so. His features were not perfectly regular; the nose aquiline, and broad at its base; the mouth rather large, the under lip prominent and full; the teeth not large, but irregular; his eyes were light hazel, and well formed; his hair and eyebrows were also light brown; the latter were scanty, the former abundant, and very fine and glossy, with a tendency to curl. I remember once a gentleman speaking to me about it, and expressing his admiration of its quality, very much in the manner he might use in speaking of a lady's hair. His skin was delicate, and his complexion fair, with a good deal of colour. His countenance was very expressive, and responsive to the feelings of his mind; and when these were agreeable, it was eminently pleasing, I might say beautiful, for his smile was so; and his eyes were wonderfully bright, and seemed almost to emit a soft light when animated. His voice was full-toned and melodious, with something in it which impressed his hearers, and made it remembered. . . . His temperament was what is commonly called the sanguine, in which there is a tendency to excess of sensibility and irritability, and of vital action, combined with corresponding activity of mind, and a certain warmth and impetuosity of temper.—DAVY, JOHN, 1836, *Memoirs of the Life of Sir Humphry Davy, vol.* II, *pp.* 385, 386, 388.

I was much struck with the intellectual character of his face. His eye was piercing, and when not engaged in converse, was remarkably introverted, amounting to absence, as though his mind had been pursuing some severe trains of thought scarcely to be interrupted by external objects; and, from the first interview also, his ingenuousness impressed me as much as his mental superiority.—COTTLE, AMOS, 1837, *Reminiscences of Coleridge and Southey, p.* 198.

Of all eminent persons whom I have ever seen even by a casual glimpse—was the most agreeable to know on the terms of a slight acquaintance. . . . I must say that nowhere, before or since, have I seen a man who had so felicitously caught the fascinating tone of high-bred urbanity which distinguishes the best part of the British nobility. . . . Davy was not a favorite with Coleridge; and yet Coleridge, who grasped the whole philosophy of Chemistry perhaps better than any man except Schelling, admired him, and praised him much; and often he went so far as to say that he might have been a great poet, which perhaps few people will be disposed to think, from the specimens he has left in the Bristol Anthology. . . . Davy was then supposed to be making a fortune by some manufactory of gunpowder, from which he drew a large share of profit, not for capital contributed, or not for that originally, but for chemical secrets communicated. Soon afterwards, he married a widow with a very large income (as much as £4000 a year by common report); was made a baronet; was crowned with the laureateship of science, viz., the President's chair in the London Royal Society; withdrew in consequence from further lecturing in kid gloves of any color; drank moderately, as a man of elegant tastes, of the cup of human enjoyment; throve into a prosperous leader of a circle; sickened; travelled for health, unavailingly for himself, not altogether for others; died; and left a name which, from the necessity of things, must grow fainter in its impression under each revolving sun, but which, at one time, was by much the most resounding name—the most splendid in the estimate of the *laity*, if not of the *clerus* in science —which has arisen since the days of Newton.—DE QUINCEY, THOMAS, 1853, *Literary Reminiscences, vol.* I, *ch.* ii, *pp.* 39, 48, 50.

The care with which Faraday has preserved every note-book and manuscript of Davy's at the Royal Institution, the remarks regarding Davy, in his letters, the earnestness of his praise of Davy's scientific work, show that he fully acknowledged all the debt which he owed to his master. But, with all his genius, Davy was hurt by his own great success. He had very little self-control, and but little method and order. He gave Faraday every opportunity of studying the example which was set before him during the journey abroad, and during their constant intercourse in the laboratory of the Royal Institution; and Faraday has been known to say that the greatest of all his great advantages was that he had a model to teach him what he should avoid.—JONES, BENCE, 1869, *The Life and Letters of Faraday, vol.* I, *p.* 210.

Personally he was a somewhat vain and irritable man, whom early success had made haughty to his inferiors. Indeed, in the recollections of Faraday, who as a young man attended upon him in his travels, we have a rather disagreeable picture of the *savant* who had forgotten the "pit out of which he was digged." He was not very popular among his colleagues, as he was regardless of minor etiquette, and had in consequence to bear the chagrin of frequent snubs, such as the refusal of the ribbon of the bath, which he fully expected. Yet those who knew him best have attributed his haughty consciousness of superiority not so much to his arrogance as to his timidity, his dread of being patronised as a *parvenu.*—BROWN, ROBERT, 1887, *Celebrities of the Century, ed. Sanders, p.* 324.

The love of angling amounted to a passion with him; and he told Ticknor that he thought if he were obliged to renounce either fishing or philosophy he should find the struggle of his choice pretty severe. Whenever he could escape from town he would hie him to some favorite stream and spend the day in the practice of his beloved art. He was known to have posted a couple of hundred miles for the sake of a day's fishing, and to have returned contented, although he had never a rise. When confined to Albermarle Street, and chafing at his inability to get away, he would sometimes turn over the leaves of his fly-book and derive much consolation from the sight of his hackles and harles, his green-tails, dun cuts, red spinners, and all the rest of the deadly paraphernalia associated in his mind with the memories of pleasant days and exciting combats. He greatly prided himself on his skill, and his friends were often secretly amused to notice his ill-concealed chagrin when a brother-angler outvied him in the day's catch or in the narration of some piscatorial triumph. They were amused, too, at the costume which he was wont to don on such occasions—his broad-brimmed, low-crowned hat, lined with green and garnished with flies; his grey-green jacket, with a multitude of pockets for the various articles of his angling gear; his wading-boots and knee-caps—all made up an attire as original as it was picturesque. In these fishing expeditions he enjoyed some of the happiest hours of his life; at such times he threw off his cares and annoyances; he was cheerful even to hilarity, and never was his conversation more sprightly or more entertaining.—THORPE, T. E., 1896, *Humphry Davy, Poet and Philosopher, p.* 229.

GENERAL

Yet how very few are there whom I esteem and (pardon me for this seeming deviation from the language of friendship) admire equally with yourself. It is indeed, and has long been, my settled persuasion, that of all men known to me I could not justly equal any one to you, combining in one view powers of intellect, and the steady moral exertion of them to the production of direct and indirect good.—COLERIDGE, SAMUEL TAYLOR, 1807, *To Sir H. Davy, Sept.* 11; *Letters, ed. Coleridge, vol.* II, *p.* 514.

This is a book ["Salmonia"] on a very delightful subject, by a very distinguished man. But although it is occasionally rather a pleasant book than otherwise, it is not by any means worthy either of the subject or the man—the one being Angling, and the other Sir Humphry Davy. —WILSON, JOHN, 1828, *Salmonia, Blackwood's Magazine, vol.* 24, *p.* 248.

We are informed in the preface, that many months of severe and dangerous illness have been partially occupied and amused by the present treatise, when the author was incapable of attending to more useful or more serious pursuits. While we regret that the current of scientific investigation, which has led to such brilliant results, should be, for a moment, interrupted, we have here an example, and a pleasing one, that the lightest pursuits of such a man as our angler—nay, the productions of those languid hours, in which lassitude succeeds to pain, are more interesting and instructive than the exertion of the talents of others whose mind and body are in the fullest vigour—illustrating the scriptural expression that the gleaning of the grapes of Ephraim are better than the vintage of Abiezer.—SCOTT, SIR WALTER, 1828, *Salmonia, Quarterly Review, vol.* 38, *p.* 503.

Davy was imbued with the spirit, and was a master of the practice, of the inductive logic; and he has left us some of the noblest examples of the efficacy of that great instrument of human reason in the discovery of truth. He applied it not only to connect classes of facts of more limited extent and importance but to develop great and comprehensive laws, which embrace phenomena that are almost universal to the natural world. In explaining these laws, he cast upon them the illuminations of his own clear and vivid conceptions;—he felt an intense admiration of the beauty, order and harmony which are conspicuous in the perfect chemistry of Nature:—and he expressed these feelings with a force of eloquence which could issue only from a mind of the highest powers and of the finest sensibilities.—HENRY, WILLIAM, 1830? *Elements of Chemistry, Preface.*

I was by no means in the same relation

as to scientific communication with Sir Humphry Davy after I became a Fellow of the Royal Society as before that period; but whenever I have ventured to follow in the path which Sir Humphry Davy has trod, I have done so with respect and with the highest admiration of his talents; and nothing gave me more pleasure, in relation to my last published paper, the eighth series (of "Experimental Researches"), than the thought that, whilst I was helping to elucidate a still obscure branch of science, I was able to support the views advanced twenty-eight years ago, and for the first time, by our great philosopher.—FARADAY, MICHAEL, 1835, *Life and Letters, ed. Jones, vol.* I, *p.* 353.

The book ["Elements of Agricultural Chemistry"] enjoyed some little popularity; but scarcely added anything to our previous stock of knowledge. It was hailed as a grand beginning; but nearly half a century has not shown any advancement. And this deficiency may not be owing to any lack of exertion, or remissness in using and connecting the knowledge that exists on both sides; but from the impossible nature of the enjoyment that has been projected. Agriculture and chemistry are connected in the single article of manures only; the other uses are very widely different.—DONALDSON, JOHN, 1854, *Agricultural Biography.*

Of Davy, it has been said that he was born a poet and became a chemist by accident. It was indeed a happy accident which gave to the sciences a man who united so many qualifications to adorn them —great skill and promptitude in performing, varying and devising, experiments; great speculative boldness tempered by the true spirit of inductive philosophy, and united to a power of exposition both as a lecturer and a writer which has rarely been equalled, unless by the eminent chemist, who, once his pupil, has since succeeded to his office and his honours.—PEACOCK, GEORGE, 1855, *Life of Thomas Young, p.* 470.

Whoever has perused the history of his great exploits in science, with a due knowledge of the subject, has already discerned his place, highest among all the great discoverers of his time. Even he who has little acquaintance with the subjects of his labours may easily perceive how brilliant a reputation he must have enjoyed, and how justly; while he who can draw no such inference from the facts would fail to obtain any knowledge of Davy's excellence from all the panegyrics with which general description could encircle his name.—BROUGHAM, HENRY LORD, 1855, *Lives of Philosophers of the Time of George III., p.* 122.

Much has been said of Davy as a poet, and Paris somewhat hastily says that his verses "bear the stamp of lofty genius." His first production preserved bears the date 1795. It is entitled "The Sons of Genius," and is marked by the usual immaturity of youth. The poems, produced in the following years, especially those "On the Mount's Bay" and "St. Michael's Mount," are pleasingly descriptive verses, showing sensibility, but no true poetic imagination.—HUNT, ROBERT, 1888, *Dictionary of National Biography, vol.* XIV, *p.* 187.

On the whole, however, Davy is most interesting as a member of the school of scientific writers who came between those of the eighteenth century proper, and those wholly of the nineteenth—the former, men of letters whose subject was "natural philosophy," the latter, men of science who only in rare instances pay deliberate attention to literary cultivation and form. His own attention to and achievement in these were more than respectable, and he added to these good taste, and a pleasant, if rather thin, humour.—SAINTSBURY, GEORGE, 1896, *English Prose, ed. Craik, vol.* V, *p.* 156.

John Jay

1745–1829

American statesman and jurist, born in New York, was admitted to the bar in 1768. Elected to the Continental congress in 1774 and 1775, he drafted the constitution of New York state in 1777, of which he was appointed Chief-justice; was elected president of congress in 1778; and in 1779 was sent as minister to Spain. From 1782 he was one of the most influential of the peace commissioners. In 1784–89 he was Secretary for Foreign Affairs, and ere long became Chief-justice of the supreme court. In

1794 he concluded with Lord Grenville the convention known as "Jay's treaty," which, though favourable to the United States, was denounced by the Democrats as a betrayal of France. Jay was governor of New York from 1795 to 1801. There is a Life (1833) by his son, William Jay (1789–1858), a notable anti-slavery leader. See also his "Writings and Correspondence," ed. by Prof. Johnston (4 vols. 1890–93,) and Lives by Whitlock (1887) and Pellew (1890).—PATRICK AND GROOME, *eds.*, 1897, *Chambers's Biographical Dictionary, p.* 530.

PERSONAL

The venerable, the patriotic, the virtuous John Jay, died on Tuesday last, at his seat, Bedford, Westchester County, in the eighty-fourth year of his age. The Supreme Court (which is now in session) adjourned at its hour of opening, as did the other courts now sitting. This delicate mark of respect was alike honourable to the feelings of the gentlemen constituting the several courts, as reverential to the memory of the illustrious deceased.—HONE, PHILIP, 1829, *Diary, May* 19, *ed. Tuckerman, vol.* I, *p.* 10.

The general learning and ability, and especially the prudence, the mildness, and the firmness of his character, eminently fitted Mr. Jay to be the head of such a court. When the spotless ermine of the judicial robe fell on John Jay, it touched nothing less spotless than itself.—WEBSTER, DANIEL, 1831, *Speech at Public Dinner at New York, March* 10.

A distinguishing trait in Mr. Jay's character was modesty; not an affectation of inferiority to others, or a distrust of his own powers, but a total absence of all endeavour to attract admiration. He assumed no importance, claimed no deference, and boasted of no merit. Extraordinary as it may seem, a stranger might have resided with him for months together, without discovering from his conversation that he had ever been employed in the service of his country. Whenever the important scenes in which he had been engaged were alluded to, he changed the conversation as quickly as politeness would permit. It was with difficulty that even his own children could occasionally induce him to converse on these interesting topics. Yet he cheerfully took his part in general conversation, enlivening it with anecdotes, and a wit which amused without wounding. He was fond of conversing on religious subjects, and particularly on biblical criticism, but it was the expression of opinions, not of feelings, in which he indulged. He had had full experience of the pleasures and the pains of public life, and his advice to his sons was, never to accept an office, except from a conviction of duty.—JAY, WILLIAM, 1833, *The Life of John Jay, vol.* I, *p.* 462.

Jay was decidedly an able man—a man of extensive attainments and erudition—a vigorous writer, and a sound thinker. He was more—he had a healthy, temperate, and well-balanced mind—a clear, sound, and comprehensive judgment—an admirable prudence and caution. And withal he was a conscientious and a just man—just to his neighbours, as well as to his family, just to his political opponents, as well as to his friends. The caution of Jay was a quality not resulting from timidity or irresolution. Few men were capable of acting a bolder or more determined part, when occasion demanded.—VAN SANTVOORD, GEORGE, 1854, *Sketches of the Lives and Judicial Services of the Chief-Justices of the Supreme Court of the United States, p.* 86.

He was seeking reinforcement from hope, not resolution from despair. He was eminently a man of prudence and caution. He was not sagacious of the future. His watch, unlike Talleyrand, did not go faster than his neighbour's. He seldom placed himself in the van of events. No fiery, burning zeal dwelt in his bosom. But when he assumed a position, the solid ground was not more immovable. He performed his duty under all circumstances, with steadiness, resolution, and undiverted attention. But neither his opinions nor conduct were in the smallest degree the result of impulse or enthusiasm. His perceptions were strong rather than quick. He was more remarkable for logic than intuition. Thus constituted, we might naturally infer that he would embrace the views of the moderate party, rather than those of more eager and impetuous character.—FLANDERS, HENRY, 1855, *The Lives and Times of the Chief Justices of the Supreme Court of the United States, vol.* I, *p.* 50.

Governor Jay, one of our purest and

most illustrious statesmen. — IRVING, WASHINGTON, 1855-59, *Life of George Washington.*

The mind of the first chief justice was vigorous, well balanced, and governed by enlightened moral faculties: hence his judgment was exact, logical, and discriminating. His deficiencies were, perhaps, a want of imagination,—the efficient handmaid to reason,—and a lack of that humour which gives zest to the driest logic. In the correspondence and other papers emanating from his pen, we seldom find a figure of speech employed to illustrate his meaning, and discover no trace of wit to enliven his familiar discourse. His great characteristic was superior wisdom in seeing clearly the right as distinguished from the expedient, and following it firmly and patiently. He was not a full man, in the sense of Lord Bacon, his knowledge having been mainly acquired from intercourse with others: neither was it deepened by study, nor broadened by culture. He was thoroughly imbued with the spirit of truth and loyalty to duty, as was manifested in all his public positions and private relations. Without guile, he could yet hide what should be concealed; but what was revealed carried with it, to truthful men, the conviction of truth. This straightforwardness baffled the jugglery of the Spanish and French diplomats, won Oswald and Shelburne to his views, and led sturdy John Adams to exclaim, "When my confidence in Mr. Jay shall cease, I must give up the cause of confidence, and renounce it in all men."—WHITELOCK, WILLIAM, 1887, *The Life and Times of John Jay, p.* 337.

Jay's principles of conduct were so unvarying, and his actions so consistent with them and with one another, that the most careless reader of his life, if it has been fairly presented, must be already familiar with the dignified and simple character of the man. Everything he did seems to have been inspired by a keen sense of impersonal moral duty. He might for a time be uncertain as to what this duty was, but the moment it was clear to him, he acted accordingly, promptly, fearlessly, without regard to personal considerations, undeterred by the consequences to his friends or his family. It was this singleness and uprightness of purpose, and the firmness with which he adhered to it, that made Adams call him "a Roman."—PELLEW, GEORGE, 1890, *John Jay (American Statesmen), p.* 354.

GENERAL

The literary reputation of Jay is incidental to his political career, and attaches to the national state papers which he sent forth from the Continental Congress, which did much to prepare the way for American liberty, and to his contributions to the Federalist, by which he assisted in permanently securing that liberty which he was one of the first to promote. His "Address to the people of Great Britain," in 1774, called forth the admiration of Jefferson. It is marked by moral earnestness and patriotic fervor, qualities shared by his address to the inhabitants of Canada and the people of Ireland. The appeal of the Convention of the State of New York to the people in 1776, and the address of Congress to the country in 1799, meeting the financial condition of the times, and his Address to the people of the State of New York, in support of the adoption of the Constitution, are his other chief productions of this kind. He wrote five papers of the Federalist; the second, third, fourth, and fifth, on Dangers from foreign force and influence, and the sixty-fourth on the treaty-making power of the senate. He would have furnished others had he not received an injury in the interim, in his vindication of the law in the Doctors' mob of the city of New York.—DUYCKINCK, EVERT A. AND GEORGE L., 1855-65-75, *Cyclopædia of American Literature, ed. Simons, vol.* I, *p.* 273.

As Chief-Justice, both of his own State and of the United States, he impressed grand juries and all concerned with the necessity of encouraging a profound respect for law and constitutions in the new order of things, and at the outset, through his own personal dignity and integrity, gave character to our highest courts since traditionally preserved. And again, in his native State of New York, he proved himself invaluable as a member of Provincial bodies and committees in providing the sinews of war, in suppressing conspiracies, in drafting laws, in organizing the machinery of the new State, in urging, through the "Federalist" and in the New York Convention, the adoption of our common Constitution, and finally, in twice filling the office of Governor. As Congressman, diplomatist, jurist, and State leader, seeking in each sphere of action to secure substantial results without display or effect, he was pre-eminently a man for his times. Perhaps, also, as nearly as any one in our civil history, he filled the ideal of a public servant.—JOHNSTON, HENRY P., 1890, *The Correspondence and Public Papers of John Jay, Preface, vol.* I, *p.* v.

Jay, whose short and terse sentences, straightforward and clear as crystal, with scanty illustration, manifest the lucidity of his mind and the sincerity of his convictions.—WHITE, GREENOUGH, 1890, *Sketch of the Philosophy of American Literature, p.* 38.

He was the third and last of the eminent trio who contributed to the "Federalist," five of the essays in which are from his pen. Though his mind was not properly imaginative, the intensity of his sentiments sometimes gave to his compositions a quality of lofty imagery.—HAWTHORNE, JULIAN AND LEMMON, LEONARD, 1891, *American Literature, p.* 33.

William Hazlitt

1778-1830

1778, Born, April 10th, at Maidstone, Kent. 1783, taken to the United States of America by his parents. 1786, returns to England. 1793, a scholar in the Unitarian College, Hackney. 1802, an art student in Paris. 1805, publishes "Essay on the Principles of Human Action." 1806, publishes "Free Thoughts on Public Affairs." 1808, marries Miss Sarah Stoddart. 1812, lectures upon philosophy, before the Russell Institue, London. 1814, contributes to the *Edinburgh Review*. Theatrical critic of the *Morning Chronicle*. 1817, "The Round Table" published, the joint work of Leigh Hunt and himself. Publishes "Characters of Shakespeare's Plays." 1818, lectures upon the English poets, before the Surrey Institute, London. Publishes "A View of the English Stage." 1819, lectures upon the English comic writers, before the Surrey Institute, London. 1820, lectures upon the dramatic literature of the age of Elizabeth, before the Surrey Institute, London. 1822, divorced from his wife. Writes for *The Liberal*. 1823, publishes "Liber Amoris." 1824, marries Mrs. Bridgewater, a widow, and goes abroad with her. 1825, separated from his wife. Returns to England. Publishes "The Spirit of the Age." 1828, publishes the "Life of Napoleon," vols. 1 and 2. 1830, publishes the "Life of Napoleon," vols. 3 and 4, and "Conversations of James Northcote." Dies, September 18th.—MASON, EDWARD T., 1885, *ed., Personal Traits of British Authors, p.* 178.

PERSONAL

Heard Hazlitt's first lecture on the "History of English Philosophy." He seems to have no conception of the difference between a lecture and a book. What he said was sensible and excellent, but he delivered himself in a low, monotonous voice, with his eyes fixed on his MS., not once daring to look at his audience; and he read so rapidly that no one could possibly give to the matter the attention it required. . . . The cause of his reading so rapidly was, that he was told to limit himself to an hour, and what he had prepared would have taken three hours, if it had been read slowly.—ROBINSON, HENRY CRABB, 1812, *Diary, Jan.* 14, 15, *vol.* I, *p.* 236.

I found Hazlitt living in Milton's house, the very one where he dictated his "Paradise Lost," and occupying the room where, tradition says, he kept the organ on which he loved to play. I should rather say Hazlitt sat in it, for, excepting his table, three chairs, and an old picture, this enormous room was empty and *un*occupied. It was white-washed, and all over the walls he had written in pencil short scraps of brilliant thoughts and phrases, half-lines of poetry, references, etc., in the nature of a commonplace-book. His conversation was much of the same kind, generally in short sentences, quick and pointed, dealing much in allusions, and relying a good deal on them for success; as, when he said, with apparent satisfaction, that Curran was the Homer of blackguards, and afterwards, when the political state of the world came up, said of the Emperor Alexander, that "he is the Sir Charles Grandison of Europe." On the whole, he was more amusing than interesting, and his nervous manner shows that this must be his character. He is now nearly forty, and when quite young lived several years in America, chiefly in Virginia, but a little while at our Dorchester.—TICKNOR, GEORGE, 1819, *Journal; Life, Letters and Journals, vol.* I, *p.* 293.

I really believe Hazlitt to be a disinterested and suffering man, who feels public calamities as other men do private ones; and this is perpetually redeeming him in my eyes. . . . I know that Hazlitt does *pocket* up wrongs in this way, to draw them out again some day or other. He says it is the only comfort which the friends of his own cause leave him.—HUNT, LEIGH, 1821, *Correspondence, vol.* I, *p.* 166.

I stood well with him for fifteen years (the proudest of my life), and have ever spoken my full mind of him to some, to whom his panegyric must naturally be least tasteful. I never in thought swerved from him, I never betrayed him, I never slackened in my admiration of him; I was the same to him (neither better nor worse), though he could not see it, as in the days when he thought fit to trust me. At this instant, he may be preparing for me some compliment, above my deserts, as he has sprinkled many such among his admirable books, for which I rest his debtor; or, for anything I know, or can guess to the contrary, he may be about to read a lecture on my weaknesses. He is welcome to them (as he was to my humble hearth), if they can divert a spleen, or ventilate a fit of sullenness. I wish he would not quarrel with the world at the rate he does; but the reconciliation must be affected by himself, and I despair of living to see that day. But, protesting against much that he has written, and some things which he chooses to do; judging him by his conversation which I enjoyed so long, and relished so deeply; or by his books, in those places where no clouding passion intervenes—I should belie my own conscience, if I said less, than that I think W. H. to be, in his natural and healthy state, one of the wisest and finest spirits breathing. So far from being ashamed of that intimacy, which was betwixt us, it is my boast that I was able for so many years to have preserved it entire; and I think I shall go to my grave without finding or expecting to find, such another companion. —LAMB, CHARLES, 1823, *The Tombs in the Abbey.*

Poor Hazlitt! He, too, is one of the victims to the Moloch Spirit of this Time. . . . In Hazlitt, as in Byron and Burns and so many others in their degree, there lay some tone of the "eternal melodies," which he could not fashion into terrestrial music, but which uttered itself only in harsh jarrings and inarticulate cries of pain. Poor Hazlitt. There is one star less in the heavens, though a twinkling, dimmed one; while the street-lamps and horn lanterns are all burning, with their whale-oil or coal gas, as before!—CARLYLE, THOMAS, 1830, *Letter, Life by Conway, p.* 251.

Near This Spot
Rests
William Hazlitt
Born April 10th, 1778. Died Sept. 18th, 1830.
He lived to see his deepest wishes gratified
As he expressed them in his Essay
"On The Fear of Death"
viz:
"To see the downfall of the Bourbons,
And some prospect of good in mankind."
(Charles X
Was driven from France 29th July, 1830)
"To leave some sterling work to the World"
He lived to complete his "Life of Napoleon,"
His desire
That some friendly hand should
consign him to the grave, was accomplished to a limited but profound extent; on these conditions
He was ready to depart, and to have inscribed on his tomb,
Grateful and Contented.
He was
The first (unanswered) Metaphysician of the Age;
A despiser of the merely Rich and Great,
A lover of the People, Poor or Oppressed;
A hater of the Pride and Power of the Few
As opposed to the happiness of the Many.
A man of true Moral Courage
To Principles,
And a yearning for the good of Human Nature.
Who was a burning wound to an Aristocracy
That could not answer before men,
And who may confront him before their Maker.
He lived and died
The unconquered Champion
of
Truth, Liberty and Humanity
"Dubitantes opera legite."
This Stone
is raised by one whose heart
is with him in the grave.

—INSCRIPTION ON TOMB, 1830, *Cemetery of St. Anne's Church, Wardour and Dean Streets, Soho.*

In person, Mr. Hazlitt was of the middle size, with a handsome and eager countenance, worn by sickness and thought; and dark hair, which had curled stiffly over the temples, and was only of late years sprinkled with gray. His gait was slouching and awkward, and his dress neglected; but when he began to talk he could not be mistaken for a common man. In the company of persons with whom he was not familiar his bashfulness was painful; but when he became entirely at ease, and entered on a favourite topic, no one's conversation was ever more delightful. He did not talk for effect, to dazzle, or surprise, or annoy, but with the most simple and honest desire to make his view of the subject entirely apprehended by his hearer. —TALFOURD, THOMAS NOON, 1842, *Critical and Miscellaneous Writings, p.* 349.

A friend of his it was,—a friend wishing to love him, and admiring him almost to extravagance,—who told me, in illustration of the dark sinister gloom which sate forever upon Hazlitt's countenance and gestures, that involuntarily, when Hazlitt put his hand within his waistcoat (as a mere unconscious trick of habit), he himself felt a sudden recoil of fear, as from one who was searching for a hidden dagger. Like "a Moor of Malabar," as described in the "Faery Queen," at intervals Hazlitt threw up his angry eyes and dark locks, as if wishing to affront the sun, or to search the air for hostility. And the same friend, on another occasion, described the sort of feudal fidelity to his beligerent duties which in company seemed to animate Hazlitt, as though he were mounting guard on all the citadels of malignity, under some *sacramentum militare,* by the following trait,—that, if it happened to Hazlitt to be called out of the room, or to be withdrawn for a moment from the current of the general conversation by a fit of abstraction, or by a private whisper to himself from some person sitting at his elbow, always, on resuming his place as a party to what might be called the public business of the company, he looked round him with a mixed air of suspicion and defiance, such as seemed to challenge everybody by some stern adjuration into revealing whether, during his own absence or inattention, anything had been said demanding condign punishment at his hands. "Has any man uttered or presumed to insinuate," he seemed to insist upon knowing, "during this *interregnum,* things that I ought to proceed against as treasonable to the interests which I defend?"—DE QUINCEY, THOMAS, 1845–59, *Gilfillan's Literary Portraits.*

On knocking at the door [No. 19 York Street, Westminster], it was, after a long interval, opened by a sufficiently "neat-handed" domestic. The outer door led immediately from the street (down a step) into an empty apartment, indicating an uninhabited house, and I supposed I had mistaken the number; but on asking for the object of my search, I was shown to a door, which opened (a step from the ground) on to a ladder-like staircase, bare like the rest, which led to a dark, bare landing-place and thence to a large square wainscoted apartment. The great curtainless windows of this room looked upon some dingy trees; the whole of the wall over and about the chimney-piece was entirely covered, up to the ceiling, by names written in pencil, of all sizes and characters, and in all directions, commemorative of visits of curiosity "to the home of Pindarus" (John Milton). There was, near to the empty fireplace a table with breakfast things upon it (though it was two o'clock in the afternoon). Three chairs and a sofa were standing *about* the room, and one unbound book lay on the mantlepiece. At the table sat Hazlitt, and on the sofa, a lady whom I found to be his wife. —PATMORE, PETER GEORGE, 1854, *My Friends and Acquaintances, vol.* II, *p.*261.

Mr. Hazlitt's life was particularly an intellectual one. . . . His personal and moral infirmities were the result of several combining circumstances; and his life displayed a continual conflict between a magnificent intellect and morbid, miserly physical influences. . . . On his behalf, if any new plea were capable of being urged, it would be this: that his irrepressible love of truth, and abhorrence of disguise in any shape or under any circumstances, have been the means of laying bare before us much that other men would have shrunk instinctively from divulging. We are bound to recollect that he has opened his whole heart to us; and allowances are to be made for that confessed addiction to taking the extreme view, and sailing over-closely to the wind.—HAZLITT, W. CAREW, 1867, *Memoirs of William Hazlitt, vol.* I, *Preface, pp.* vii, xiii.

Hazlitt was of the middle size, with eager, expressive eyes; near which his black hair, sprinkled sparely with gray, curled round in a wiry, resolute manner. His gray eyes, not remarkable in color, expanded into great expression when occasion demanded it. Being very shy, however, they often evaded your steadfast look. They never (as has been asserted by some one) had a sinister expression; but they sometimes flamed with indignant glances, when their owner was moved to anger; like the eyes of other angry men. At home, his style of dress (or undress) was perhaps slovenly, because there was no one to please; but he always presented a very clean and neat appearance when he went abroad. His mode of walking was loose, weak and unsteady; although his arms displayed strength, which he used to put forth when he played at rackets with Martin Burney and others. — PROCTER, BRYAN WALLER, 1874? *Recollections of Men of Letters, p.* 179.

I do not propose to write even a sketch of Hazlitt's life, for apart from its matrimonial infelicities, it was uneventful. What interest it had was literary, for except when he labored under the delusion that he was a painter, a delusion which Thackeray shared when young, he was a man of letters, and nothing else. His inclination was towards metaphysics, his forte was criticism. He was an admirable critic, though rather intolerant to the moderns, and the most brilliant and eloquent essayist that ever committed his thoughts to paper. A vein of autobiography runs through his writings, which is not the least of their charms. We share his tastes, his sympathies, his prejudices even, and are inspired by a warm personal feeling. We do not love him, as we do Lamb, but we respect him as the profounder thinker. His life was a warfare, and his death, which occurred in his fifty-third year, was a release. His last words were, "Well, I've had a happy life."—STODDARD, RICHARD HENRY, 1875, *ed., Personal Recollections of Lamb, Hazlitt and Others, Preface, p.* xx.

Under that straightforward, hard-hitting, direct-telling manner of his, both in writing and speaking, Hazlitt had a depth of gentleness—even tenderness—of feeling on certain subjects; manly friendship, womanly sympathy, touched him to the core; and any token of either would bring a sudden expression into his eyes very beautiful as well as very heart-stirring to look upon. We have seen this expression more than once, and can recall its appealing charm, its wonderful irradiation of the strong features and squarely-cut, rugged under-portion of the face.—CLARKE, CHARLES COWDEN, 1878, *Recollections of Writers, p.* 63.

I did not like Hazlitt: nobody did. He was out of place at the genial gatherings at Highgate; though he was often there: for genial he certainly was not. He wrote with a pen dipped in gall, and had a singularly harsh and ungentle look; seeming indeed as if his sole business in life was to seek for faults. He was a leading literary and art critic of his time; but he has left to posterity little either to guide or instruct. I recall him as a small, mean-looking, unprepossessing man; but I do not quite accept Haydon's estimate of him —"a singular compound of malice, candor, cowardice, genius, purity, vice, democracy, and conceit." Lamb said of him, that he was, "in his natural state, one of the wisest and finest spirits breathing." I prefer the portrait of DeQuincey: "He smiled upon no man!" He was a democrat, a devout admirer of the first Napoleon; and (I again quote DeQuincey) "hated even more than enemies those whom custom obliged him to call friends." His was the common lot of critics—few friends, many foes. His son, a very estimable gentleman, is one of the Judges in the Court of Bankruptcy.—HALL, S. C., 1883, *Retrospect of a Long Life, p.* 318.

Between the wet trees and the sorry steeple,
Keep, Time, in dark Soho, what once was Hazlitt,
Seeker of Truth, and finder oft of Beauty;
Beauty's a sinking light, ah, none too faithful;
But Truth, who leaves so here her spent pursuer,
Forgets not her great pawn: herself shall claim it.
Therefore sleep safe, thou dear and battling spirit,
Safe also on our earth, begetting ever
Some one love worth the ages and the nations!
Nothing falls under to thine eyes eternal.
Sleep safe in dark Soho: the stars are shining,
Titian and Wordsworth live; the People marches.

—GUINEY, LOUISE IMOGEN, 1891–93, *W. H.*, 1778–1830, *A Roadside Harp.*

He was not a safe man to confide in. He had a forked crest which he sometimes lifted.—BIRRELL, AUGUSTINE, 1892, *Res Judicatæ, p.* 224.

Our evenings at the theatres brought us frequently into companionship with that super-excellent critic, William Hazlitt, who was likewise occupied in writing theatrical notices,—those for the "Times" newspaper. It was always a treat to sit beside him, when he talked delightfully; and once, on going to his own lodging, he showed us a copy he had made of Titian's "Ippolito dei Medici," and conversed finely upon Titian's genius. Hazlitt's gift in painting was remarkable. A portrait he took of his old nurse,—a mere head,—the upper part of the face in strong shadow from an over-pending black silk bonnet edged with black lace, while the wrinkled cheeks, the lines about the mouth, with the touches of actual and reflected light, were given with such vigour, truth, as well might recall the style of the renowned Flemish master, and actually did cause a good judge of the art to say to Hazlitt,—"Where did you get that Rembrandt?"—CLARKE, MARY COWDEN, 1896, *My Long Life, p.* 89.

Like so many another fierce combatant with the pen, he was a shy, timid, and morbidly, horribly sensitive creature. But shy, self-absorbed, diffident before others, he was at bottom proud, scornful, brimming over with every form of stirring and tumultuous passion. He himself spoke of himself as "the king of good haters"—which, indeed, he was not; for your real hater doth never unpack his heart with words; and our poor Hazlitt was constantly assailing some literary or political antipathy as a little blacker than Satan, and more destructive than sin. His strong personality can be read between every line that he wrote.—O'CONNOR, T. P., 1895, *Some Old Love Stories, p.* 150.

LIBER AMORIS
1823

Hazlitt at present gives me great pain by the folly with which he is conducting himself. He has fallen in love to a pitch of insanity, with a lodging-house hussy, who will be his death. He has been to Scotland and divorced his wife, although he has a fine little boy by her; and after doing this, to marry this girl, he comes back and finds she has been making a fool of him in order to get presents, and in reality has been admitting a lover more favored. Hazlitt's torture is beyond expression; you may imagine it. The girl really excited in him a pure, devoted, and intense love. His imagination clothed her with that virtue which her affected modesty induced him to believe in, and he is really downright in love with an ideal perfection, which has no existence but in his own head! He talks of nothing else day and night. He has written down all the conversations without color, literal as they happened; he has preserved all the love-letters, many of which are equal to anything of the sort, and really affecting; and I believe, in order to ease his soul of this burden, means, with certain arrangements, to publish it as a tale of character. He will sink into idiotcy if he does not get rid of it. Poor Hazlitt! He who makes so free with the follies of his friends, is of all mortals the most open to ridicule. To hear him repeat in a solemn tone and with agitated mouth the things of love he said to her (to convince you that he made love in the true gallant way), to feel the beauty of the sentiment, and then look up and see his old, hard, weather-beaten, saturnine, metaphysical face—the very antidote of the sentiment—twitching all sorts of ways, is really enough to provoke a saint to laughter. He has a notion that women have never liked him. Since this affair he has dressed in the fashion, and keeps insinuating his improved appearance. *He springs up to show you his pantaloons!* What a being it is! His conversation is now a mixture of disappointed revenge, passionate remembrances, fiendish hopes, and melting lamentations.—HAYDON, BENJAMIN R., 1822, *Letter to Miss Mitford, Sept.* 8; *Life, Letters and Table Talk, ed. Stoddard, p.* 210.

Still, apart from its preface, the book is by no means to be regarded even as a work of fiction founded upon fact. It deals with truth. It relates, with an exaggeration due to excited feeling, rather than to the romancist's straining after effect, a very remarkable episode in the life of its author. Nor was its publication due simply to a writer's desire, born of his necessity very often, to capitalise his emotions, as it were: to throw his experiences, his sorrows and his sufferings into the marketable form of manuscript, and to dispose of that on the most favourable terms obtainable. In Hazlitt's case publicity was a medicine to his condition of mind. Owing to a train of circumstances, and to inherent mental peculiarities, his imagination had become distinctly diseased. It was a relief to him to give the history of his trials and troubles to the printing-press and the world; to deliver himself from his cares and pains in the ordinary way of literary work. . . . Little more has here been set forth than a chapter in the story of William Hazlitt's life as he has himself related it in the "New Pygmalion;" not a book upon which the reader's judgment of its author should be permanently founded, yet affording, nevertheless, a valuable clue to the character of a very remarkable man.—COOK, DUTTON, 1869, *The New Pygmalion, Gentleman's Magazine, N. S., vol.* 2, *pp.* 304, 315.

Hazlitt paints her as a vision of rarest beauty, somewhat undeveloped and soulless, but into whom, like Pygmalion, his devotion would infuse life and soul. The truth seems to be, that his statue was a vulgar young woman, accustomed to flirt with the lodgers who came under her mother's roof, and that she could no more understand the feeling with which she was regarded by a man of genius than she could have returned it if it had been comprehensible to her.— RICHARDSON, ABBY SAGE, 1882, *Old Love-Letters, p.* 173.

GENERAL

He seems pretty generally, indeed, in a state of happy intoxication—and has borrowed from his great original, not indeed the force and brilliancy of his fancy, but something of its playfulness, and a large share of his apparent joyousness and self-indulgence in its exercise. It is evidently a great pleasure to him to be fully possessed with the beauties of his author, and to follow the impulse of his unrestrained eagerness to impress them upon his readers.—JEFFREY, FRANCIS LORD, 1817, *Hazlitt on Shakespeare, Edinburgh Review, vol.* 28, *p.* 472.

Hazlitt had damned the bigoted and the blue-stockinged; how durst the man! He is your only good damner, and if ever I am damned, I should like him to damn me.—KEATS, JOHN, 1818, *To Haydon, March* 21, *Letters.*

We are not apt to imbibe half opinions, or to express them by halves; we shall, therefore, say at once, that when Mr. Hazlitt's taste and judgment are left to themselves, we think him among the best, if not the very best, living critic on our national literature. . . . As we have not scrupled to declare that we think Mr. Hazlitt is sometimes the very best living critic, we shall venture one step farther, and add, that we think he is sometimes the very worst. One would suppose he had a personal quarrel with all living writers, good, bad, or indifferent. In fact, he seems to know little about them, and to care less. With him, to be alive is not only a fault in itself, but it includes all other possible faults. He seems to consider life as a disease, and death as your only doctor. He reverses the proverb, and thinks a dead ass is better than a living lion. In his eyes, death, like charity, "covereth a multitude of sins." In short if you want his praise, you must die for it; and when such praise is deserved, and given really *con amore*, it is almost worth dying for.—WILSON, JOHN, 1818, *Hazlitt's Lectures on English Poetry, Blackwood's Magazine, vol.* 3, *p.* 75.

Though Mr. Hazlitt frequently shows great talent and taste, he is not qualified for the task he has undertaken. In the midst of what is good in him, he mistakes so grossly, that we are led to suspect that he has often picked up his opinions as well as his words from others, and that when he fails, it is when he relies upon himself. He is in the midst of men of genius in London, where it is no hard thing with a good memory and some smartness, and no conscience about thefts, to put together such a book as this. Of his conduct in life we know nothing; nor if we did should we speak of it, unless we might fairly with praise; neither do we altogether like giving an opinion of a man's secret principles and disposition, from his writings; yet we must say that Mr. Hazlitt appears too loose in the one, and too envious and spleeny, where there is room for it, in the other, to treat with a correct understanding and a right delicacy and truth of feeling and sentiment, upon a subject like poetry which concerns all that is moral and refined and intellectual in our natures. He is much too full of himself to have a sincere love and interest for what is abstractly good and great, and more intent upon displaying his own fine parts, than spreading before his readers the excellencies of others.—DANA, RICHARD HENRY, 1819, *Hazlitt's English Poets, North American Review, vol.* 8, *p.* 320.

He (Schlegel) is like Hazlitt, in English, who *talks pimples*—a red and white corruption rising up (in little imitation of mountains upon maps), but containing nothing, and discharging nothing, except their own humours.—BYRON, LORD, 1821, *Diary, Jan.* 28.

Mr. Hazlitt's character as a writer may, we think, be not inaptly designated by a term borrowed from the vocabulary of our transatlantic brethren, which though cacophonous, is sufficiently expressive. We would venture to recommend its importation and adoption into the language of this island, foı the particular use of such persons as we have enumerated above: they must be too partial to the produce of a Republican soil, to be displeased with the application. The word to which we allude, Slangwhanger, is interpreted in the American dictionary to be "*One who makes use of political or other gabble, vulgarly called slang, that serves to amuse the rabble.*" Those who peruse the "Table Talk" will determine how far the definition answers to the case in point; they will observe also the truth of a remark often made, that the disciples of the Radical School lose no opportunity of insinuating their poison into all sorts of subjects; a drama, a novel, a poem, an essay, or a school-book, is in their hands an equally convenient vehicle.—PALGRAVE, SIR FRANCIS, 1822, *Hazlitt's Table Talk, Quarterly Review, vol.* 26, *p.* 103.

Compare Charles Lamb's exquisite criticisms on Shakspere with Hazlitt's round and round imitations of them.—COLERIDGE, SAMUEL TAYLOR, 1832, *Table-Talk, Aug.* 6, *ed. Ashe, p.* 177.

Such was the power of beauty in Hazlitt's mind; and the interfusing faculty was wanting. The spirit, indeed, was willing, but the flesh was strong; and when these contend it is not difficult to foretell which will obtain the mastery; for "the power of beauty shall sooner transform honesty from what it is into a bawd, than the power of honesty shall transform beauty into its likeness."—TALFOURD, THOMAS NOON, 1836, *Literary Remains of the Late William Hazlitt, ed. Hazlitt.*

I suspect that half which the unobservant have taken literally, he meant, secretly, in sarcasm. As Johnson in conversation, so Hazlitt in books, pushed his own theories to the extreme, partly to show his power, partly, perhaps, from contempt of the logic of his readers. He wrote rather for himself than others; and often seems to vent all his least assured and most uncertain thoughts—as if they troubled him by the doubts they inspired, and his only anxiety was to get rid of them. He had a keen sense of the Beautiful and Subtle; and what is more, he was deeply imbued with sympathies for the Humane. He ranks high amongst the social writers—his intuitive feeling was in favour of the multitude;—yet had he nothing of the demagogue in literature; he did not pander to a single vulgar passion.—LYTTON, EDWARD BULWER LORD, 1836, *Literary Remains of the Late William Hazlitt, ed. Hazlitt.*

With the exception of William Hazlitt, England has produced no Shakespearian critic of any importance. . . . His mind was as brilliant as it was deep, a combination of Diderot and Börne, full of warm enthusiasm for the Revolution, coupled with an earnest love of art, always overflowing with *verve* and *esprit!*—HEINE, HEINRICH, 1838–95, *Notes on Shakespeare Heroines, tr. Benecke, pp.* 25, 26.

An acute but somewhat bitter observer of life and manners, and satirized rather than described them. Though bold and arrogant in the expression of his opinions, and continually provoking opposition by the hardihood of his paradoxes, he does not appear to have been influenced so much by self-esteem as sensibility. He was naturally shy and despairing of his own powers, and his dogmatism was of that turbulent kind which comes from passion and self-distrust. He had little repose of mind or manner, and in his works almost always appears as if his faculties had been stung and spurred into action.—WHIPPLE, EDWIN P., 1845, *North American Review, Essays and Reviews, vol.* II, *p.* 152.

In critical disquisitions on the leading characters and works of the drama, he is not surpassed in the whole range of English literature; and what in an especial manner commands admiration in their perusal is the indication of refined taste and chastened reflection which they contain, and which are more conspicuous in detached passages than in any entire work. He appears greater when quoted than when read. Possibly, had his life been prolonged, it might have been otherwise, and some work emanated from his gifted pen which would have placed his fame on a durable foundation.—ALISON, SIR ARCHIBALD, 1853–59, *History of Europe*, 1815–52, *ch.* v.

Hazlitt was, in many respects, the most *natural* of critics. He was *born* to criticise, not in a small and captious way, but as a just, generous, although stern and rigorous judge. Nature had denied him great constructive, or dramatic, or synthetic power—the power of the highest kind of poet or philosopher. But he possessed that mixture in proper proportions of the acute and the imaginative, the profound and the brilliant, the cool and the enthusiastic, which goes to constitute the true critic. Hence his criticism is a fine compound—pleasing, on the one hand, the lover of analysis, who feels that its power can go no farther; and, on the other, the young and ardent votary of literature, who feels that Hazlitt has expressed in language what *he* only could "with the faltering tongue and the glistening eye."—GILFILLAN, GEORGE, 1855, *A Third Gallery of Portraits, p.* 176.

Everything which he observed he seemed to observe from a certain soreness of mind: he looked at people because they offended him; he had the same vivid notion of them that a man has of objects which grate on a wound in his body.—BAGEHOT, WALTER, 1856, *Shakespeare—The Man, Works, ed. Morgan, vol.* I, *p.* 278.

A brilliant and refined critic.—COLLIER, WILLIAM FRANCIS, 1861, *A History of English Literature, p.* 427.

When Hazlitt is at his best, what critic can excel him in eloquence and discrimination.—CUNNINGHAM, LT. COL. FRANCIS, 1870, *ed., The Works of Christopher Marlowe, Introduction, p.* xiii.

Among English essayists William Hazlitt is distinguished for his psychological revelations. Less companionable than Steele, less erudite than De Quincey, without Addison's classic culture and Leigh Hunt's *bonhomie,* he is more introspective than any one of these. The speculative exceeds the literary element in his equipment. To think rather than to learn was his prevalent tendency; intuition rather than acquisition was his resource. The cast of his mind, the quality of his temperament, and the nature of his experience combined to make him thoughtful, individual, and earnest; more abstract than social, more intent than discursive, more original than accomplished, he contributed ideas instead of fantasies, and vindicated opinions instead of tastes. Zest was his inspiration; that intellectual pleasure which comes from idiosyncrasies, moods, convictions, he both felt and imparted in a rare degree; he thirsted for truth; he was jealous of his independence; he was a devotee of freedom. In him the animal and intellectual were delicately fused. Few such voluminous writers have been such limited readers.—TUCKERMAN, HENRY T., 1870, *William Hazlitt, Atlantic Monthly, vol.* 25, *p.* 664.

He did not criticise in cold blood. . . . His criticisms of his contemporaries seem to us to be, taken all in all, neither more nor less just than his criticisms of departed poets, comic writers, and dramatists. In all his criticisms alike he strikes us as a man of extravagant sentiment and hyperbolical expression, widely read in philosophy and in general literature, a habitual and acute student of human character, more alive to varieties of excellence than any of his critical contemporaries, excepting De Quincey and John Wilson, and more, perhaps, than even these, alive to what may be called varieties of mood. His judgment was liable to be "deflected" by intemperate feeling, generous or splentic. His criticisms must be taken with some grains of allowance on this score before we appreciate their substantial body of sound discernment. He often puts things graphically and incisively; but his composition strikes the general taste of critics as wearing too much an appearance of effort, and straining too much at flashing effects.—MINTO, WILLIAM, 1872–80, *Manual of English Prose Literature, pp.* 538, 539.

A versatile and refined critic, rather paradoxical at times, but who always hits the mark.—SCHERR, J., 1874, *A History of English Literature, tr. M. V., p.* 288.

Hazlitt held those extreme radical opinions which, fifty years since, were upheld by many others; and the warmth of his temper led him to denounce things and systems to which he had a strong aversion.

Subject to the faults arising out of this his warm temperament, he possessed qualities worthy of affection and respect. He was a simple, unselfish man, void of all deception and pretence; and he had a clear, acute intellect, when not traversed by some temporary passion or confused by a strong prejudice. . . . He loved the worker better than the idler. He hated pretensions supported merely by rank or wealth or repute, or by the clamor of factions. And he felt love and hatred in an intense degree. But he was never dishonest. He never struck down the weak, nor trod on the prostrate. He was never treacherous, never tyrannical, never cruel. —PROCTER, BRYAN WALLER, 1874? *Recollections of Men of Letters, pp.* 168, 169.

Hazlitt's cynicism is the souring of a generous nature; and when we turn from the politician to the critic and the essayist, our admiration for his powers is less frequently jarred by annoyance at their wayward misuse. . . . Hazlitt's point of view was rather different, nor can we ascribe to him without qualification that exquisite appreciation of purely literary charm which is so rare and so often affected. Nobody, indeed, loved some authors more heartily or understood them better; his love is so hearty that he cannot preserve the true critical attitude. Instead of trying them on his palate, he swallows them greedily. His judgment of an author seems to depend upon two circumstances. He is determined in great measure by his private associations, and in part by his sympathy for the character of the writer. His interest in this last sense is, one may say, rather psychological than purely critical. . . . Hazlitt harps a good deal upon one string; but that string vibrates forcibly. His best passages are generally an accumulation of short, pithy sentences, shaped in strong feeling, and coloured by picturesque association; but repeating, rather than corroborating, each other. The last blow goes home, but each falls on the same place. He varies the phrase more than the thought; and sometimes he becomes obscure, because he is so absorbed in his own feelings that he forgets the very existence of strangers who require explanation. Read through Hazlitt, and this monotony becomes a little tiresome; but dip into him at intervals, and you will often be astonished that so vigorous a writer has not left some more enduring monument of his remarkable powers. —STEPHEN, LESLIE, 1875, *Hours in a Library, Second Series, vol.* II, *pp.* 321, 322, 343.

Hazlitt's opinions of his contemporaries were as worthless as his strong prejudices could make them.—STODDARD, RICHARD HENRY, 1876, *ed., Anecdote Biography of Percy Bysshe Shelley, Preface, p.* xx.

Occupied a considerable place among his contemporaries, though none of his works were of a kind to live. He was not a poet or a philosopher, but a literary man in the closest sense of the word, impelled by circumstances and a vehement and lively intelligence to do such work as he was capable of in this fashion, rather than constrained by a higher necessity to utter what was in him for the advantage of men. . . . Hazlitt had no philosophy and no story; he was an essayist, a critic, a commentator upon other men's works and ways, rather than an original performer. . . . In his case the proverb does not tell, which declares that a poet must be born and not made—for he is not a poet, and his chances of commanding anything more than a present audience depend upon his thorough cultivation and knowledge. Hazlitt did not possess these qualities, and his books are already as old as if they had been written a thousand years ago, instead of half a hundred.—OLIPHANT, MARGARET O. W., 1882, *Literary History of England, XVIII-XIX Century, vol.* II, *pp.* 246, 247.

There never was such an epicure of his moods as Hazlitt.—QUILLER-COUCH, A. T., 1893, *Adventures in Criticism, p.* 306.

He stood for individualism. He wrote from what was, in the highest degree for his purpose, a full mind, and with that blameless conscious superiority which a full mind must needs feel in this empty world. His whole intellectual stand is taken on the positive and concrete side of things. . . . He delivers an opinion with the air proper to a host who is master of a vineyard, and can furnish name and date to every flagon he unseals.—GUINEY, LOUISE IMOGEN, 1894, *A Little English Gallery, pp.* 235, 236.

I believe it was Hazlitt whom I read first, and he helped me to clarify and formulate my admiration of Shakespeare as no one else had yet done.—HOWELLS, WILLIAM DEAN, 1895, *My Literary Passions, p.* 120.

If not the greatest critic of his time, Hazlitt is one of the greatest; and his greatness consists in this—that he had "the courage to say as an author what he felt as a man." With Coleridge and Lamb he introduced the new method. Literary criticism had been a scratching of the surface. They turned up the soil and showed the fresh earth; and Hazlitt was not the least lusty husbandman of the three.—DAVIDSON, JOHN, 1895, *Sentences and Paragraphs, p.* 113.

In him, much more distinctly than in Hunt or Lamb, a modern spirit is apparent. Save for a certain exuberance of style, there is nothing in his essays to suggest even now the flavour of antiquity; he approached his subjects with perfect originality and freshness; his style cannot be definitely linked to any prototype; and, as critics of his own day were quick to observe, "his taste was not the creature of schools and canons, it was begotten of Enthusiasm by Thought." It is enthusiasm, indeed, that is the most obvious characteristic of the essays—and they are his best essays—which he contributed between 1820 and 1830 to the "Examiner" and other papers. . . . If not the first, he was the most influential of those who bent the essay to this purely literary purpose, and he may be regarded as standing midway between the old essayists and the new. It was a fashion in his own time, and one that has often since been followed, to insist too strongly on Hazlitt's limitations as a critic. Yet, after all has been said, his method was essentially the same as Sainte-Beuve's, and his essays cannot even now be safely neglected by students of the literary developments with which they deal. It is impossible to read them without catching something of the ardour of his own enthusiasm, and it says much for the soundness of his taste and judgment that the great majority of his criticisms emerged undistorted from the glowing crucible of his thought.—LOBBAN, J. H., 1896, *English Essays, Introduction, pp.* lv, lvi.

His fine critical powers were marred by the strain of bitterness in his nature. And the result is that his judgment on many poets, and notably the poets of his own day, too often sounds like an intelligent version of the *Edinburgh* or the *Quarterly.* Or, to speak more accurately, he betrays some tendency to return to principles which, though assuredly applied in a more generous spirit, are at bottom hardly to be distinguished from the principles of Johnson. He too has his "indispensable laws," or something very like them. He too has his bills of exclusion and his list of proscriptions. The poetry of earth, he more than suspects, is forever dead; after Milton, no claimant is admitted to anything more substantial than a courtesy title. This, no doubt, was in part due to his morose temper; but it was partly also the result of the imperfect method with which he started. The fault of his conception—and it was that which determined his method—is to be too absolute. It allows too much room to poetry in the abstract; too little to the ever-varying temperament of the individual poet.—VAUGHAN, C. E., 1896, *English Literary Criticism, Introduction, p.* lxxxiv.

Hazlitt was beyond all question a great, a very great, critic—in not a few respects our very greatest. All his work, or almost all that has much merit, is small in individual bulk, though the total is very respectable. . . . Great as Hazlitt was as a miscellaneous and Montaignesque essayist, he was greater as a literary critic. Literature was, though he coquetted with art, his first and most constant love; it was the subject on which, as far as English literature is concerned (and he knew little and is still less worth consulting about any other), he had acquired the largest and soundest knowledge; and it is that for which he had the most original and essential genius. His intense prejudices and his occasional inadequacy make themselves felt here as they do everywhere, and even here it is necessary to give the caution that Hazlitt is never to be trusted when he shows the least evidence of dislike for which he gives no reason. But to any one who has made a little progress in criticism himself, to any one who has either read for himself or is capable of reading for himself, of being guided by what is helpful and of neglecting what is not, there is no greater critic than Hazlitt in any language. He will sometimes miss—he is never perhaps so certain as his friends Lamb and Hunt were to find—exquisite in individual points. Prejudice, accidental ignorance, or other causes may sometimes invalidate his account of authors or of subjects in general. But still the four great collections of his criticism, "The Characters of Shakespeare," "The Elizabethan Dramatists," "The English Poets," and "The English Comic Writers," with not a few scattered things in his other writings, make what is on the whole the best corpus of criticism by a single writer in English on English. He is the critics' critic as Spenser is the poets' poet; that is to say, he has, errors excepted and deficiencies allowed, the greatest proportion of the strictly critical excellencies—of the qualities which make a critic—that any English writer of his craft has ever possessed.—SAINTSBURY, GEORGE, 1896, *A History of Nineteenth Century Literature, pp.* 185, 186.

The four volumes ["Life of Napoleon"] certainly abound with magnificent passages, and when we look at the amount of technical detail and the fund of information brought together from scattered sources, we can hardly fail to admire the literary workmanship and intellectual penetration which are conspicuous throughout, and the power of the book is the more impressive when we recollect that it was produced under immense disadvantages and in declining health. He had never attempted anything on the same scale before; and he happened to undertake the task when he was, physically speaking, least qualified to carry it successfully out. —HAZLITT, W. CAREW, 1897, *Four Generations of a Literary Family, vol.* I, *p.* 192.

Hazlitt's proper work was to analyse genius. During these apparently desultory years his critical power, fed by immense reading and incessant thought, steadily matured; and when, in 1814, he made his decisive entry into literature, it was with a mind not only formed but fixed. He was one of the men who do not develop through a series of phases, but after an obscure incubation suddenly emerge complete. He was fond of saying that he had done all his work in early manhood, and merely written off his mind in his books. As a critic, too, he disdained the type of intellect which improves ("an improving poet never becomes a great one"), and was peculiarly lacking in the faculty which forsees the flower in the seed. He had no vestige of Coleridge's sense for the organic; and the "sinewy texture" of his ideas stands in sharp contrast to the iridescent web of Coleridge's shifting creeds.—HERFORD, C. H., 1897, *The Age of Wordsworth, p.* 76.

He never quite disabuses our mind of the belief that he is a paid advocate; he never conquers by calm; and, upon the whole, impresses one as a man who found little worth the living for in this world, and counted upon very little in any other.—MITCHELL, DONALD G., 1897, *English Lands Letters and Kings, The Later Georges to Victoria, p.* 170.

Gracious rills from the Hazlitt watershed have flowed in all directions, fertilising a dry and thirsty land. . . . In both poetry and prose Hazlitt's preferences were frankly avowed and his dislikes outspoken. He never hesitated to say as an author what he felt as a man. He belonged to no school or coterie. His knowledge and taste for poetry was increased and purified by his friendship with Lamb; and he had felt the stimulus of Coleridge in poetry as well as in metaphysics and politics, but he remained his own man—a solitary and independent figure. He liked Blair's "Grave" and Warton's Sonnets, and he said so. Sir Philip Sidney's "Arcadia" bored him to death, and he said so. Sir Thomas Browne's strained fancifulness and jargonised speech teased him, and he said so. On the other hand, what member of the Anglican Church has so bathed the name of Jeremy Taylor in the sunshine of eloquent appreciation as he has this Jacobinical son of a Socinian preacher? . . . We know what his point of view was, and can flatter ourselves upon our ability, real or supposed, to outline his judgments upon the books, pictures, and plays of to-day. For a critic to be alive eighty years after publication of his criticisms is in itself a feat. Hazlitt can say with the Abbé, *J'ai vécu*. . . . Hazlitt was never more philosophical than when in a passion. He always gets a good thought-basis for his hatreds. . . . Hazlitt was unhappily, unlike Sir Joshua Reynolds, a vulnerable man; and if he was hit hard and below the belt, he hit back again as hard as he could, and sometimes I am afraid below the belt.—BIRRELL, AUGUSTINE, 1902, *William Hazlitt* (*English Men of Letters*), *pp.* 129, 131, 145, 147, 169.

Robert Hall

1764–1831

Baptist preacher, born at Ansty, near Leicester, was the youngest of fourteen children. At the age of fifteen he was entered at the Baptist Academy at Bristol. Proceeding to Aberdeen University in 1781, he made the intimate acquaintance of Sir James Mackintosh, with whom he read and discussed philosophy and theology. He graduated in 1785, and became second minister in the collegiate charge of Broadmead Chapel, Bristol, and classical master in the Bristol Academy, which latter post, however, he resigned in 1790. Mr. Hall at once became a popular preacher. In 1791 he succeeded the eccentric Dr. Robinson at Cambridge, where, by the force of his preaching, the influence of his reputation, and the still better influence of his persuasive life and character, he became one of the foremost divines of the day. In 1793 he published his celebrated "Apology for the Freedom of the Press," and in 1801 his eloquent sermon on "Infidelity;" "Reflections on the War" followed in 1802, and "Sentiments Proper to the Present Crisis" in 1803. In 1806 he was transferred to Leicester, and in 1825 he returned to Bristol. His argumentative treatise, "Terms of Communion," which appeared in 1810, is distinguished by logical acuteness and catholicity of sentiment.—SANDERS, LLOYD C., *ed.*, 1887, *Celebrities of the Century, p.* 529.

PERSONAL

We had among us [1782] some English dissenters, who were educated for the ecclesiastical offices of their sect. Robert Hall, now a dissenting clergyman at Cambridge, was of this number. He then displayed the same acuteness and brilliancy; the same extraordinary vigour, both of understanding and imagination, which have since distinguished him, and which would have secured to him much more of the admiration of the learned and the elegant, if he had not consecrated his genius to the far nobler office of instructing and reforming the poor. His society and conversation had a great influence on my mind. Our controversies were almost unceasing. We lived in the same house, and we were both very disputatious. — MACKINTOSH, SIR JAMES, 1805, *Autobiography, Memoirs of Mackintosh, ed., his Son, vol.* I, *p.* 13.

From the commencement of his discourse an almost breathless silence prevailed, deeply impressive and solemnizing from its singular intenseness. Not a sound was heard but that of the preacher's voice—scarcely an eye but was fixed upon him—not a countenance that he did not watch, and read, and interpret, as he surveyed them again and again with his rapid ever-excursive glance. As he advanced and increased in animation, five or six of the auditors would be seen to rise and lean forward over the front of their pews still keeping their eyes upon him. Some new or striking sentiment or expression would, in a few minutes, cause others to rise in like manner: shortly afterwards still more, and so on, until, long before the close of the sermon, it often happened that a considerable portion of the congregation were seen standing,—every eye directed to the preacher, yet now and then for a moment glancing from one to the other, thus transmitting and reciprocating thought and feeling:—Mr. Hall himself, though manifestly absorbed in his subject, conscious of the whole, receiving new animation from what he thus witnessed, reflecting it back upon those who were already alive to the inspiration, until all that were susceptible of thought and emotion seemed wound up to the utmost limit of elevation *on earth*, when he would close, and they reluctantly and slowly resume their seats.—GREGORY, OLINTHUS, 1831, *Miscellaneous Works and Remains of the Rev. Robert Hall, Memoir, p.* 37.

He displayed, in a most eminent degree, the rare excellence of a perfect conception and expression of every thought, however rapid the succession. There were no half-formed ideas, no misty semblances of meaning, no momentary lapses of intellect into an utterance at hazard, no sentences without a distinct object, and serving merely for the continuity of speaking; every sentiment had at once a palpable shape, and an appropriateness to the immediate purpose. If now and then, which was seldom, a word, or a part of a sentence, slightly failed to denote precisely the thing he intended, it was curious to observe how perfectly he was aware of it, and how he would instantly throw in an additional clause, which did signify it precisely. . . . Under that excitement, when it was the greatest, he did unconsciously acquire a corresponding elation of attitude and expression; would turn, though not with frequent change, toward the different parts of the assembly, and, as almost his only peculiarity of action, would make one step back from his position (which, however, was instantly resumed) at the last word of a climax; an action which inevitably suggested the idea of the recoil of heavy ordnance.—FOSTER, JOHN, 1831, *Mr. Hall's Character as a Preacher, Miscellaneous Works and Remains of the Rev. Robert Hall, pp.* 77, 83.

His religious character had nothing peculiar in it. He had fine taste and great eloquence, but after all was not first-rate,—that is, not equal to Jeremy Taylor or Burke. But he was *facile princeps* of all the Dissenting preachers of the day.—ROBINSON, HENRY CRABB, 1834, *Diary, Dec.* 27; *Reminiscences, ed. Sadler, vol.* II, *p.* 203.

Robert Hall did not lose his power of retort even in madness. A hypocritical condoler with his misfortunes once visited him in the mad-house, and said, in a whining tone, "What brought you here Mr. Hall?" Hall significantly touched his brow with his finger, and replied, "What'll never bring you, sir—too much brain!"—WHIPPLE, EDWIN P., 1846, *The Ludicrous Side of Life, Literature and Life, p.* 149.

There was not the semblance of parade, nothing that betrayed the least thought of being eloquent; but there was a power of thought, a grace and beauty, and yet force of expression, a facility of commanding the best language, without apparently thinking of the language at all, combined with a countenance all glowing from the fire within, which constituted a fascination that was to me perfectly irresistible.—SPRAGUE, WILLIAM B., 1855, *Visits to European Celebrities.*

His face was far from being a handsome one. Indeed, it reminded some people of an *exaggerated frog's.* But the amplitude of his forehead, the brilliance of his eye, and the strength and breadth of his chest, marked him out always from the roll of common men, and added greatly to the momentum both of his conversation and his preaching. . . . We have heard his later mode of preaching often described by eye-witnesses. He began in a low tone of voice; as he proceeded his voice rose and his rapidity increased; the two first thirds of his sermon consisted of statement or argument; when he neared the close, he commenced a strain of appeal and then, and not till then, was there any eloquence; then his stature erected itself, his voice swelled to its utmost compass, his rapidity became prodigious, and his practical questions—poured out in thick succession—seemed to sound the very souls of his audience. Next to the impressiveness of the conclusion, what struck a stranger most was the exquisite beauty and balance of his sentences; every one of which seemed quite worthy of, and ready for, the press. Sometimes, indeed, he was the tamest and most commonplace of preachers, and men left the church wondering if this were actually the illustrious man.—GILFILLAN, GEORGE, 1855, *A Third Gallery of Portraits, pp.* 80, 81.

For forty years he had no rival in the English pulpit. During this long time men of all sects and parties, men of the highest intellect and culture, the leaders of the Church, the Bar, and the Senate, sat with rapt attention under the spell of his speech. What was the secret of this attraction? Was it in his personal magnetism,—the majesty of his mien, his gestures, or the musical intonations of his voice? Or was it in his rhetorical skill, the exquisite arrangement and rhythmical flow of his periods, and the dazzling imagery in which his affluent imagination clothed his ideas? In many of these oratorical gifts he was wanting. He had a large-built, robust figure, and a countenance "formed, as if on purpose, for the most declared manifestation of power;" but all his life he was a sufferer from acute physical pains, necessitating the use of large doses of stimulants and narcotics; his voice was weak, his action heavy and ungraceful, and in all the tricks of the rhetorician, the pomp and circumstance of oratory, he was lacking altogether. His style, while it has great vigor and impressiveness, is too highly Latinized to be popular; it abounds in technical phrases and abstract forms of expression, and, except in certain highly-wrought passages, is quite devoid of pictorial embellishment! It was, apparently, in no one predominant quality that his power lay, but in the harmony and momentum in action of all his faculties,—faculties which, whether of mind or heart, have rarely been so admirably adjusted and finely proportioned in any other human being.—MATHEWS, WILLIAM, 1878, *Oratory and Orators*, *p.* 395.

The private manners of Hall were remarkably simple and unaffected; and if his method of expressing his opinions was frequently impetuous, and occasionally somewhat brusque and imperious, this was owing rather to his constitutional energy and straightforward impulsive honesty than to an overbearing and dogmatic temper. Though exercising his sarcastic powers with great unconstraint, he reserved his severity chiefly for errors which implied some kind of moral culpability, and he was always careful to be respectful to true worth even when concealed or deformed by many superficial defects, or conjoined with humble rank or weak mental capacity. In reality few were more unassuming or unselfish or more continuously actuated by feelings truly charitable and benevolent. His mental absorption led to the contraction of many minor eccentricities, one of which was a frequent obliviousness to the flight of time and a consequent inability to remember his engagements. Towards the close of his Cambridge ministry he acquired the habit of smoking, and from that time his pipe was his almost constant companion and one of his principal solaces in his bodily suffering. Indeed talk and tobacco may be said to have supplied his chief means of recreation. In his conversation the calibre and idiosyncrasies of his genius were better displayed than in any of the writings he has left us; and it is said to have exercised an even more captivating charm than did his finest orations. Its most striking characteristics were keen, biting, and original wit, and wild and daring imaginative flights.—HENDERSON, T. F., 1880, *Encyclopædia Britannica, Ninth ed., vol.* XI, *p.* 350.

So long ago as 1828, I knew the renowned Baptist minister, the Rev. Robert Hall. I heard him preach at Bristol, and more than once visited him there. Though he lived to be an old man—born in 1764, and dying in 1831—he was a sad sufferer all his life, from some internal ailment, and his eloquent sermons were often delivered while the speaker was struggling with bodily anguish. . . . I think I never heard a pulpit orator so effective as Robert Hall; yet his eloquence flowed without effort, and was totally devoid of ostentation. He impressed on all who heard him the conviction that he spoke for his Master and not for himself.—HALL, SAMUEL CARTER, 1883, *Retrospect of a Long Life*, *p.* 415.

Think of Demosthenes, and, as there is but one Demosthenes and one Robert Hall, think of Hall! It is quite certain that Hall was a far greater man than Demosthenes in the order of his mind, in his elevation of sentiment; and, in his tastes and studies, he much more nearly resembled Cicero, most perfect of pagans and nearest approximation to the Christian philosopher; but Cicero was much more of a rhetorician than either Demosthenes or Hall, aimed more at producing superficial effect, and appears to have cared more about the posing of the body and retaining an unrumpled and uncreased robe. On the other hand, we would not degrade Hall's character to the level of the Billingsgate of Demosthenes.—HOOD, E. PAXTON, 1885, *The Throne of Eloquence*, *p.* 177.

Hall's fame rests mainly on the tradition of his pulpit oratory, which fascinated many minds of a high order. His eloquence recommended evangelical religion to persons of taste. Dugald Stewart commends his writings as exhibiting "the English language in its perfection," which is certainly extravagant praise. His conversation, of which some fragments are preserved, was brilliant when his powers were roused by intellectual society.—GORDON, ALEXANDER, 1890, *Dictionary of National Biography, vol.* XXIV, *p.* 86.

GENERAL

Please to present one of each of my pamphlets to Mr. Hall. I wish I could reach the perfection of his style. I think his style the best in the English language; if he have a rival, it is Mrs. Barbauld.—COLERIDGE, SAMUEL TAYLOR, 1796, *Letter to B. Flower, April* 1; *Biographia Literaria, Biographical Supplement.*

The works of this great preacher are, in the highest sense of the term, imaginative, as distinguished not only from the didactic, but the fanciful. He possesses the "vision and faculty divine," in as high a degree as any of our writers in prose. His noblest passages do but make truth visible in the form of beauty, and "clothe upon" abstract ideas, till they become palpable in exquisite shapes. The dullest writer would not convey the same meaning in so few words, as he has done in the most sublime of his illustrations.—TALFOURD, THOMAS NOON, 1821, *On Pulpit Oratory, London Magazine, Critical and Miscellaneous Writings, p.* 231.

With no one prejudice like Johnson, he still reminds us of him—he is what Johnson would have been (if it be possible to conceive him such) had he been a whig and a dissenter. He has something of his dogmatism—something of his superstition—something of his melancholy—something of the same proneness to erect himself before man, and prostrate himself to the earth before God; a mixture of pride and of humility—of domination and self-abasement; he has much too of Johnson's love for common-sense and home-spun philosophy, combined, however, with an imagination far more vivid and excursive, for which the former qualities did not always serve as an adequate corrective. His learning is not on the same scale as his mother-wit—it is enough, however, to add stamina to his speculations, and for more perhaps he did not greatly care. His knowledge of metaphysical and deistical writers appears to have been that in which he chiefly excelled; his allusions to classical authors are few, and his quotations from them (a practice which he somewhere gives us to understand he held cheap) in general trite and unscholar-like—but he was too affluent to borrow, and too independent to be a slave to authorities.—BLUNT, J. J., 1832, *The Works of the Rev. Robert Hall, The Quarterly Review, vol.* 48, *p.* 131.

Robert Hall's might be called a *great* mind,—large in all its capacities, and wide in the extent of its sphere of perception and action. In every such mind it is easy to discern two characters, always opposing, limiting, and balancing each other. It will not narrow itself to the service of a single idea, it will not blind itself to the majesty of nature by gazing on one truth till all others disappear. It will not live in extremes,—it is not fanatical,—it refuses to submit to any narrow rule of belief or of duty,—it is conscious to itself of expanding capacities which no rule can measure, no system bound. This is greatness of mind,—such greatness had Robert Hall. Had the circumstances which surrounded him been more favorable, his mind might have expanded into as perfect and complete humanity as our age has witnessed. This was not granted him; on some sides he was undeveloped; on others limited; yet he was, and will always remain, one of the great men of our day.—CLARKE, J. F., 1833, *Robert Hall, The Christian Examiner, vol.* 15, *p.* 2.

Hall, the most distinguished ornament of the Calvinistic dissenters, has long been justly ranked with the highest of our classics. His sermons are admirable specimens of pulpit eloquence, not to be surpassed in the whole compass of British theology. Those which received the author's own *imprimatur* are vastly superior to any that are either taken from his MSS., or supplied from the notes of Short-hand Writers.—LOWNDES, WILLIAM THOMAS, 1839, *British Librarian.*

The most striking trait in the character of Hall's mind is its entire lack of striking traits,—the evenness, harmony, and breadth of its development. He never astonishes, and never disappoints. His wisdom and learning are never obstrusive, and never at fault. In argument and illustration, we trace no redundancy, and complain of no omission. His eloquence is never quickened into a torrent-like flow, but is never dry or languid. He is majestic without pretension, and sensible without dullness. The spirits all come at his bidding, and vanish when they are no longer needed. His quick wit never encroaches on his reverence, and his scorching sarcasm is kept in check by conscientious justice. . . . Hall's style is rich, but chaste,—highly rhetorical, but never gaudy. He has no sentences penned for show or sound; but solid thought always underlies his ornament and points his metaphors.—PEABODY, ANDREW PRESTON, 1847, *Robert Hall's Character and Writings, North American Review, vol.* 64, *pp.* 390, 391.

Hall is, even in print, much more of the orator; although his language with all its richness, betrays, in his published writings, symptoms of anxious elaboration. Probably there could not be cited from him any thing equal in force or originality to some passages of Foster's; but it would still more certainly be impossible to detect him indulging in feeble commonplaces.—

SPALDING, WILLIAM, 1852, *History of English Literature, p.* 393.

His command of language is sufficiently copious, though not by any means of the first order. This is perhaps due in no small measure to the course of his reading. He spent comparatively little time upon the masters of the English language. . . . Hall's diction is not suited for a popular style. Not only does it want pictorial embellishments, except in the more highly wrought passages; it is positively dry; he has a preference for heavy Latin derivatives, and for abstract forms of expression—the result, as we have said, in some measure, of his favourite studies. . . . Hall's mind had a natural craving for broad comprehensive views, and he usually states his case with great perspicuity. . . . The distinguishing excellence of Hall's style consists in general vigour and elevation of language. His astonishing popularity was probably due to the occasional bursts of splendid eloquence. —MINTO, WILLIAM, 1872–80, *Manual of English Prose Literature, pp.* 503, 504.

It is scarcely possible, however, to set him in the history of literature in a place at all proportioned to that which he occupied in his generation. The sermons which live, save in the humble habitual reading of those classes of the community who read sermons for duty and not with any critical perception—are very few, and Robert Hall's style is of a more formal description— in print—than that of the orators who have outlived their day. But the appreciation of those who heard and knew him was so thorough and enthusiastic, that its warmth still lingers with a genial glow about his name.—OLIPHANT, MARGARET O. W., 1882, *Literary History of England, XVIII-XIX Century, vol.* III, *p.* 319.

Nonconformity, rich as it was in works of philanthropy and evangelical earnestness, did not originate any new lines of Christian thought. Robert Hall was perhaps its greatest name in the first quarter of the century; in massive and brilliant intellectuality he was unequalled; and the fame of his preaching still survives; but he propagated no new ideas, nor can he be said to have been a new force in religious literature.—TULLOCH, JOHN, 1885, *Movements of Religious Thought in Britain During the Nineteenth Century, p.* 108.

Robert Hall perhaps came nearer than any of his contemporaries to the political and prophetic Milton, whom Wordsworth longed to recall.—HERFORD, C. H., 1897, *The Age of Wordsworth, p.* 30.

Henry Mackenzie

1745–1831

Henry Mackenzie was born in Edinburgh, Scotland, July 28, 1745. He was educated at the University of Edinburgh, studied law, and became attorney for the crown. In 1804 he was appointed comptroller of taxes for Scotland. In 1771 he published anonymously a novel entitled "The Man of Feeling," which at once became very popular. A young clergyman named Eccles, of Bath, laid claim to it, and to establish his claim transcribed with his own hand the entire book, making numerous corrections and interlineations. The question of authorship was settled by the formal declaration of the publishers. Mackenzie published "The Man of the World" in 1783; [1773] and afterward "Julia de Roubigné," a tale in a series of letters. In 1779–80 he edited "The Mirror," a semi-weekly modelled after Addison's "Spectator," to which he contributed forty-two papers. Among these was the "Story of La Roche," which appeared in the "Mirror" for June 19, 22, and 26, 1779. In 1785–86 he edited a similar periodical called "The Lounger," to which he contributed fifty-seven papers. Among these was an appreciative criticism on the poetry of Burns, which gave him the reputation of having first called attention to its merits. He wrote "The White Hypocrite," a comedy, which was performed at Covent Garden, London; and two tragedies, "The Spanish Father," and "The Prince of Tunis." The latter was brought out with great success in Edinburgh. Mackenzie's other works include biographies of Home and Dr. Blacklock, essays on dramatic poetry, and numerous Tory tracts. He married in 1776, and had a large family. He died in Edinburgh, January 14, 1831.—JOHNSON, ROSSITER, 1875, *Little Classics, Authors, p.* 168.

PERSONAL

A rare thing this literature, or love of fame or notoriety which accompanies it. Here is Mr. Henry Mackenzie on the very brink of human dissolution, as actively anxious about it as if the curtain must not soon be closed on that and everything else. He calls me his literary confessor; and I am sure I am glad to return the kindnesses which he showed me long since in George Square. No man is less known from his writings. You would suppose a retired, modest, somewhat affected man, with a white handkerchief, and a sign ready for every sentiment. No such thing: H. M. is alert as a contracting tailor's needle in every sort of business—a politician and a sportsman—shoots and fishes in a sort even to this day—and is the life of company with anecdotes and fun. Sometimes his daughter tells me he is in low spirits at home, but really I never see anything of it in society.—SCOTT, SIR WALTER, 1825, *Diary, Dec.* 6; *Life by Lockhart, ch.* lxv.

Henry Mackenzie's excellent conversation, agreeable family, good evening parties, and the interest attached to united age and reputation, made his house one of the pleasantest. One of the Arbitri Elegantiarum of Old Edinburgh, he survived to flourish in a new scene. . . . The title of "The Man of Feeling" adhered to him ever after the publication of that novel; and it was a good example of the difference there sometimes is between a man and his work. Strangers used to fancy that he must be a pensive sentimental Harley; whereas he was far better,—a hard-headed practical man, as full of wordly wisdom as most of his fictitious characters are devoid of it; and this without in the least impairing the affectionate softness of his heart.—COCKBURN, HENRY LORD, 1830–54, *Memorials of His Time, ch.* v.

I never saw a form and face so instinct with goodness, so attractive of affection. The tenderness poured forth in all his works seemed diffused around his person; and I defy any man that has a soul to admire the former more than he shall feel inclined at once to love the latter.—GRIFFIN, EDMUND D., 1831, *Remains.*

He lies under a plain mural tablet in the Greyfriars' Churchyard, on the north side of the terrace. He is described thereon as "an author who for no short time and in no small part supported the literary reputation of his country;" and yet the custodian of the little city cemetery, an enthusiastic lover of the spot and of its associations, said, in a regretful way, to an Amercan visitor not very long ago, that Mackenzie was entirely forgotten by the men of the present day, and that no one had asked to see his resting place in many years. Such graves as his should be pilgrim shrines.—HUTTON, LAURENCE, 1891, *Literary Landmarks of Edinburgh, p.* 29.

THE MAN OF FEELING
1771

His "Man of Feeling" is the offspring of the "Sentimental Journey" and Werter schools: it is better regulated than the first, and less frantic than the second: the hero is possessed with a passion which he has too much modesty to utter, and dies, of true love and decline, when all wish him to live. The scene in the madhouse should be learned by heart.—CUNNINGHAM, ALLAN, 1833, *Biographical and Critical History of the Literature of the Last Fifty Years.*

The tender pleasure which "The Man of Feeling" excites is wholly without alloy. Its hero is the most beautiful personification of gentleness, patience, and meek sufferings which the heart can conceive. —TALFOURD, THOMAS NOON, 1842, *London New Monthly Magazine, Critical and Miscellaneous Writings, p.* 21.

The best writer of his school is supposed to be Mackenzie, the "Man of Feeling;" but the "Man of Feeling," from which he took his title, has passed from amongst the living. It is almost as much duller than Sterne as it is more virtuous. The sickly tone of feeling is relieved by no humour, and but slightly relieved by rather feeble satire.—STEPHEN, LESLIE, 1876, *History of English Thought in the Eighteenth Century, vol.* II, *p.* 442.

The novels of Henry Mackenzie have a charm of their own, which may be largely attributed to the fact that their author was a gentleman. Whoever has read, to any extent, the works of fiction of the eighteenth century, must have observed how perpetually he was kept in low company, how rarely he met with a character who had the instincts as well as the social position of a gentleman. A tone of refined sentiment and dignity pervades "The Man of Feeling," which recalls the "Vicar of Wakefield," and introduces the reader to better company and more elevated thoughts than the novels of the time usually afford. "The Man of Feeling" is hardly a narrative. Harley, the chief character, is a sensitive, retiring man, with feelings too fine for his surroundings. The author places him in various scenes, and traces the effect which each produces upon his character. The effect of the work is agreeable, though melancholy, and the early death of Harley contemplates the delineation of a man too gentle and too sensitive to battle with life.—TUCKERMAN, BAYARD, 1882, *A History of English Prose Fiction*, p. 241.

It is so fragmentary and so sketchy that only by courtesy can it be called a novel. —SIMONDS, WILLIAM EDWARD, 1894, *An Introduction to the Study of English Fiction*, p. 56.

Written in a style alternating between the whims of Sterne and a winning plaintiveness, enjoys the distinction of being the most sentimental of all English novels. One scene of it, in which the frail hero dies from the shock he receives when a Scotch maiden of pensive face and mild hazel eyes acknowledges that she can return his love for her, deserves to be remembered.—CROSS, WILBUR L., 1899, *The Development of the English Novel*, p. 83.

The "Man of Feeling" is nothing but a study in emotion and simply describes a few scenes in the life of a hero whose facile tears are constantly evoked by accidents obviously devised for that purpose. His visit to London in search of a government appointment, his brief stay there, his disappointment and death, compose all the story; there is no character-drawing, no humour, no plot; everything that we are accustomed to look for in a work of fiction is devoured and swallowed up by this leviathan of sentimentality.—THOMSON, CLARA LINKLATER, 1900, *Samuel Richardson, A Biographical and Critical Study*, p. 268.

THE MAN OF THE WORLD
1773

The attempt to attain intricacy of plot disturbs the emotion which in the other works of the author is so harmoniously excited. A tale of sentiment should be most simple. Its whole effect depends on its keeping the tenor of its predominant feeling unbroken. Another defect in this story is, the length of time over which it spreads its narrative. . . . Still there are in this tale scenes of pathos delicious as any which, even the author himself, has drawn.—TALFOURD, THOMAS NOON, 1842, *London New Monthly Magazine, Critical and Miscellaneous Writings*, p. 21.

"The Man of the World" is a regularly-constructed novel, and is much more interesting than the desultory sketches of "The Man of Feeling," although the chief incidents are robbery, seduction, and attempted incest.—FORSYTH, WILLIAM, 1871, *The Novels and Novelists of the Eighteenth Century*, p. 311.

The "Man of the World" which followed, and which is equally fine, but much more objectionable, has a mixture of Richardson in his worst peculiarities, the hairbreadth escapes of Pamela, over and over repeated —and not always escapes: with an absence both of wit and nature which takes all possible right of existing from such detestable complications.—OLIPHANT, MARGARET O. W., 1882, *The Literary History of England, XVIII-XIX Century*, vol. I, p. 148.

JULIA DE ROUBIGNÉ
1777

I have a sneaking kindness for Mackenzie's "Julia de Roubigné"—for the deserted mansion, and straggling gilliflowers on the mouldering garden-wall; and still more for his "Man of Feeling;" not that it is better, nor so good; but at the time I read it, I sometimes thought of the heroine, Miss Walton, and of Miss —— together, and "that ligament, fine as it was, was never broken!"—HAZLITT, WILLIAM, 1826, *The Plain Speaker*, p. 318.

The accumulation of woes in "Julia de Roubigné" makes it too melancholy to read: it is more like the revelation made in confession than a fine work of fancy and feeling. It is not a difficult thing to heap woe on woe.—CUNNINGHAM, ALLAN, 1833, *Biographical and Critical History of the Literature of the Last Fifty Years*.

The real skill and subtlety he shows in painting small delicacies of feeling and etiquette are ill suited with a tragic catastrophe involving strong passions. And the device of telling the story by means of letters, with its apparatus of confidants and witnesses, lays a heavy burden of improbability upon a feeble tragedy.—RALEIGH, WALTER, 1894, *The English Novel*, p. 202.

GENERAL

To whom we owe (in my opinion) the most exquisite pathetic fictions in our language.—MACKINTOSH, SIR JAMES, 1805, *Autobiography, Memoirs of Mackintosh, ed., his Son*, vol. I, p. 21.

Few modern writers have been more fortunate than Mr. Mackenzie, in their appeals to the heart; and his fictions in the *Mirror* hold a conspicuous rank among the best efforts in pathetic composition.—DRAKE, NATHAN, 1810, *Essays Illustrative of the Rambler, Adventurer and Idler*, vol. II, p. 369.

The universal and permanent popularity of his writings entitles us to rank him amongst the most distinguished of his class. His works possess the rare and invaluable property of originality, to which all other qualities are as dust in the balance; and the sources to which he resorts to excite our interest, are rendered accessible by a path peculiarly his own. . . . The Northern Addison. . . . Variety of character he has introduced sparingly, and has seldom recourse to any peculiarity of incident, availing himself generally of those which may be considered as common property to all writers of romance. His sense of the beauties of nature, and power of describing them, are carefully kept down, to use the expression of the artist; and like the single straggling bough, which shades the face of his sleeping veteran, just introduced to relieve his principal object, but not to eclipse it.—SCOTT, SIR WALTER, 1821, *Henry Mackenzie*.

I consider old M. to be the greatest nuisance that ever infested any Magazine. His review of Galt's "Annals" was poor and worthless: that of "Adam Blair" still worse: and this of "Lights and Shadows" the most despicable and foolish of all. His remarks on "Adam Blair" did the book no good, but much harm with dull stupid people, and this wretched article cannot fail to do the same to a greater degree. I cannot express my disgust with it.—WILSON, JOHN, 1822, *Letter to W. Blackwood, William Blackwood and his Sons*, vol. I, p. 270.

Henry Mackenzie, Sir, is one of the most original in thought, and splendid in fancy, and chaste in expression, that can be found in the whole line of our worthies. He will live as long as our tongue, or longer.—WILSON, JOHN, 1822, *Noctes Ambrosianæ, Blackwood's Magazine*, vol. 11, p. 477.

The quiet and unpresuming beauties of these works depend not on the fashion of the world. They cannot be out of date till the dreams of young imagination shall vanish, and the deepest sympathies of love and hope be stilled forever. While other works are extolled, admired, and reviewed, these will be loved and wept over.—TALFOURD, THOMAS NOON, 1842, *London Monthly Magazine, Critical and New Miscellaneous Writings*.

"The Man of Feeling," published anonymously in 1771, "The Man of the World," 1773, and "Julia de Roubigné," 1777, novels after the manner of Sterne, which are still universally read, and which have much of the grace and delicacy of style as well as of the pathos of that great master, although without any of his rich and peculiar humor.—CRAIK, GEORGE L., 1861, *A Compendious History of English Literature and of the English Language*, vol. II, p. 318.

Although wedded to the following of Sterne, Mackenzie affected the moral earnestness of Richardson also, and the characters in his three principal fictions, move, meekly robed in gentle virtue, through a succession of heartrending misfortunes. There is no observation of life, no knowledge of the world, in Mackenzie's long-drawn lachrymose novels of feeling. The personal affection of Sir Walter Scott for this amiable man has done much to preserve Mackenzie's memory.—GOSSE, EDMUND, 1888, *A History of Eighteenth Century Literature*, p. 361.

"The Man of Feeling" had nothing of Sterne's subtle humour, which plays round his pathos like a lambent flame; he "resolved," like Steele, "to be sorrowful;" but he nurses his grief so carefully, and toys with it so long, that true pathos is at last insulted by the mummery. *Crambe repetita* is not an appetizing dish, and Simon Softly, and Tom Sanguine, and Mary Muslin, and Mary Plain are names that strike cruelly on the jaded ear. His characters are, indeed, for the most part anachromisms, and are as "cruel, dull and dry" as the piping swains in a third-rate pastoral.—LOBBAN, J. H., 1896, *English Essays, Introduction*, p. liii.

William Roscoe

1753-1831

William Roscoe, historian, born at Liverpool, 8th March 1753, in 1769 was articled to an attorney, and began to practice in 1774. In 1773 he published a poem, "Mount Pleasant," and in 1787-88 "Wrongs of Africa," a protest against the slave-trade. But it was his "Life of Lorenzo de'Medici" (1796) that established his literary reputation. His second great book, "Life of Leo X" (1805) like the former appeared in German, French, and Italian. He had retired from business in 1796, but in 1799 became partner in a Liverpool Bank, which involved him (1816-20) in pecuniary embarrassment. From his pen also came poems, of which the best known is the "Butterfly's Ball" (1807); an editon of Pope; and a monograph on Monandrian plants. He died 30th June 1831. See Life by his son, Henry (1833), and Espinasse's "Lancashire Worthies" (2nd series, 1877).—PATRICK AND GROOME, *eds.*, 1897, *Chambers's Biographical Dictionary, p.* 802.

PERSONAL

He is a benevolent, cheerful, gentlemanlike old man; tall, neither thin nor fat, thick gray hair. He is very like the prints you have seen of him; his bow courteous, not courtly; his manner frank and prepossessing, without pretension of any kind. He enters into conversation readily, and immediately tells something entertaining or interesting, seeming to follow the natural course of his own thoughts, or of yours, without effort. Mrs. Roscoe seems to adore her husband, and to be so fond of her children, and has such a good understanding and such a warm heart, it is impossible not to like her.—EDGEWORTH, MARIA, 1813, *Letters, vol.* I, *p.* 193.

I desired to see nobody but Mr. Roscoe, and with him I had the pleasure of passing an evening, and finally met him at dinner the last day I spent in Europe. His circumstances have changed entirely since I passed a day with him at Allerton, on my first arrival from America, four years ago. He now lives in a small house, simply and even sparely, but I was delighted to find that poverty had not chilled the warmth of his affections, or diminished his interest in the world and the studies that formerly occupied him. He spoke of his misfortunes incidentally, of the loss of his library, with a blush which was only of regret; but still he was employed in historical and critical researches, and talked of a new edition of his "Lorenzo," in which he should reply to what Sismondi has said of him in his "History of the Republics of Italy."—TICKNOR, GEORGE, 1819, *Journal; Life, Letters and Journals, vol.* I, *p.* 297.

He was advanced in life, tall, and of a form that might once have been commanding, but it was a little bowed by time—perhaps by care. He had a noble Roman style of countenance; a head that would have pleased a painter; and though some slight furrows on his brow showed that wasting thought had been busy there, yet his eye still beamed with the fire of a poetic soul. There was something in his whole appearance that indicated a being of a different order from the bustling race around him. . . . Born in a place apparently ungenial to the growth of literary talent; in the very market-place of trade; without fortune, family connections, or patronage; self-prompted, self-sustained, and almost self-taught, he has conquered every obstacle, achieved his way to eminence, and, having become one of the ornaments of the nation, has turned the whole force of his talents and influence to advance and embellish his native town. . . . He has shown how much may be done for a place in hours of leisure by one master spirit, and how completely it can give its own impress to surrounding objects. Like his own Lorenzo de'Medici, on whom he seems to have fixed his eye as on a pure model of antiquity, he has interwoven the history of his life with the history of his native town, and has made the foundations of its fame the monuments of his virtues. Wherever you go in Liverpool, you perceive traces of his footsteps in all that is elegant and liberal.—IRVING, WASHINGTON, 1819-48, *Sketch-Book, pp.* 25, 26, 28.

In his habits Mr. Roscoe was temperate, and was attentive to the regular observance of domestic arrangements. He did not rise unusually early, and the periods he devoted to study were those which remained after concluding the more serious labors of the day. He had no stated times set apart for his studies, which were often carried on in the midst of his family. He was seldom in the habit of entrenching upon the hours devoted to sleep. Even to the latest period of life he usually enjoyed undisturbed repose. Though never in the possession of robust health he very seldom suffered from severe illness, and few persons during a long life have been more exempt from pain. He was accustomed to take exercise frequently both on foot and on horseback, and felt a particular enjoyment in country occupations. He had few amusements beyond those which his usual employments afforded, or which he derived from the cultivation of his garden, and the contemplation of his prints and drawings. He took no pleasure in field sports and other similar pursuits. In his youth he had a taste for theatrical performances, but in after life he seldom entered into public amusements. From music he derived but little pleasure, although he was a great admirer of the works of Handel. To the latest period of his life Mr. Roscoe never disregarded the proprieties of dress and of manners.—ROSCOE, HENRY, 1833, *The Life of William Roscoe, vol.* II, *p.* 358.

I quite agree as to Roscoe. But mark the reason. Worth and merit of a moral kind are the main topics, and above all, his raising himself. He was a pot-boy at a very low skittle-ground when he was sixteen or seventeen! Did any one ever rise before from such a depth to be an elegant Italian scholar? If Mackintosh had been of this kind, I should have certainly said more.—BROUGHAM, HENRY LORD, 1838, *Letter to Napier, June* 8; *Selections from the Correspondence of the late Macvey Napier, ed., his Son, p.* 251.

To us there is a new scene of meditative enjoyment in our fatherland. Before we reach the sacred precincts of Westminster, or stroll along the green banks of the Avon, we shall linger with respectful and moving interest beside the monument to the memory of William Roscoe, in the churchyard of Liverpool.—TUCKERMAN, HENRY T., 1849, *Characteristics of Literature, p.* 129.

LIFE OF LORENZO DE MEDICI
1795

The complete volume has more than answered the expectations which the sample had raised. The Grecian simplicity of the style is preserved throughout; the same judicious candour reigns in every page; and, without allowing yourself that liberty of indulging your own bias towards good or against criminal characters, which over-rigid critics prohibit, your artful candour compels your readers to think with you without seeming to take a part yourself. You have shown from his own virtues, abilities, and heroic spirit, why Lorenzo deserved to have Mr. Roscoe for his biographer. . . . Several of his translations of Lorenzo are superior to the originals, and the verses more poetic.—WALPOLE, HORACE, 1795, *To Roscoe, April* 4; *Letters, ed. Cunningham, vol.* IX, *pp.* 454, 455.

You will pardon my zeal, Sir, and you may confide in my sincerity, when I declare to you, that the contents of your book far surpassed my expectation, and amply rewarded the attention with which I perused them. You have thrown the clearest and fullest light upon a period most interesting to every scholar. You have produced much that was unknown, and, to that which was known, you have given perspicuity, order, and grace. You have shown the greatest dilligence in your researches, and the purest taste in your selection; and, upon the characters and events which passed in review before your inquisitive and discriminating mind, you have united sagacity of observation, with correctness, elegance, and vigour of style.—PARR, SAMUEL, 1795, *Letter to William Roscoe, Life by Son, vol.* I, *p.* 133.

I cannot but congratulate the publick upon this great and important addition to Classical History, which I regard as a phænomenon in Literature, in every point of view. It is pleasant to consider a gentleman, not under the auspices of an university, or beneath the shelter of academick bowers, but in the practice of the law and business of great extent, and resident in a remote commercial town, (where nothing is heard of but Guinea ships, slaves, blacks, and merchandise, in the town of *Liverpool,*) investigating and describing the rise and progress of every polite art in Italy at the revival of learning with acuteness, depth, and precision; with the spirit of the poet, and the solidity of the historian. It is pleasant to consider this. For my own part, I have not terms sufficient to express my admiration of his genius and erudition, or my gratitude for the amusement and information I have received. I may add, that *the manner* in which Mr. Roscoe procured, from the libraries at Florence, and many of the various inedited manuscripts with which he has enriched the appendix to his history, was singularly curious; not from a Fellow or Traveller of the Dilettanti, but from a commercial man in the intervals of his employment. I shall not violate the dignity of the work by slight objections to some modes of expression, or to a few words, or to some *occasional sentiments* in the Historian *of a Republick*. But I recommend it to our country as a work of unquestionable genius, and of uncommon merit. It adds the name of Roscoe to the very first rank of English classical Historians.—MATHIAS, THOMAS JAMES, 1798, *The Pursuits of Literature, Eighth ed., p.* 228.

He writes in an easier style (though not without affectation) and is more decent in his narrative than Gibbon; still he is of that school, and appears to have taken him for his model, so fine a thing it seems to our present compilers of history to have no religion.—HURD, RICHARD, 1808? *Commonplace Book, ed. Kilvert, p.* 251.

The style is pure and elegant; the facts are interesting and instructive; and the moral or application is (if I may so speak) of an incomparable tendency. These facts were new to the greater part of English readers: fresh fountain heads of pleasing intelligence were explored; and a stream of knowledge flowed forth, at once bright, pure, and nourishing. I hardly know a work, of its kind, which evinces throughout a more delicate taste, exercised upon a more felicitious subject. Roscoe is *almost* the regenerator, among Englishmen, of a love of Italian literature.—DIBDIN, THOMAS FROGNALL, 1824, *The Library Companion, p.* 525.

EDITION OF POPE

1824

In the year 1824, Mr. Roscoe appeared as the editor and biographer of Pope, an office which he executed with his wonted ability, and with the zeal of a disciple. Had Pope been his own bosom friend, he could not have dilated his virtues more fondly, or touched his failings with greater tenderness. In the court of fame Roscoe was always counsel for the panel, and has pleaded in mitigation of sentence for some very desperate reputations, such as Pope Alexander VI., Lucretia Borgia, and Bonaparte. It must therefore have been a delightful employment to him to vindicate the memory of a poet whose style of excellence was highly congenial to his sympathies, whose literary merit he thought unjustly depreciated, and whose moral character had been most ungently handled. —COLERIDGE, HARTLEY, 1833, *Biographia Borealis, p.* 541.

He barely contributed a single illustrative note, his criticisms are platitudes, and his vindications of Pope a tissue of blunders. He was misled by his credulous faith in his hero, by the rashness with which he imposed his own guesses for facts, and above all by his want of penetration and research. His half-knowledge was worse than ignorance. A few of his multitudinous errors were exposed by Bowles whom he had attacked. Roscoe replied in a feeble, disingenuous pamphlet, which drew from Bowles his taunting and crushing retort, "Lessons in Criticism to William Roscoe, Esq." This ended the Pope controversy. —ELWIN, WHITWELL, 1871, *ed., The Works of Alexander Pope, Introduction, vol.* I, *p.* xxiv.

Of the disgraceful bookseller's job called "Roscoe's Pope," nothing need be said. The booksellers could not have pitched upon a worse editor. For Roscoe, though well versed in the Italian writers of the *renaissance*, knew nothing of the eighteenth century. He was not a classical scholar. And though his English style is easy and elegant, and his "Life of Pope" very pleasant reading, his command of the facts is so slight, that Roscoe's memoir of the poet is entirely superseded by Mr. Carruthers' more correct, though less elegant biography.—PATTISON, MARK, 1872–89, *Pope and His Editors, Essays, ed. Nettleship, vol.* II, *p.* 374.

GENERAL

In the present age of intellectual activity, attention is so generally bestowed on all modern languages, which are ennobled by a literature, that it is not singular an acquaintance with the Italian in particular, should be widely diffused. Great praise, however, is due to the labours of Mr. Roscoe. There can be little doubt that his elaborate biographies of the Medici, which contain as much literary criticism as historical narrative, have mainly contributed to the promotion of these studies among his countrymen. These works have of late met with much flippant criticism in some of their leading journals. In Italy they have been translated, are now cited as authorities, and have received the most encomiastic notices from several eminent scholars. These facts afford conclusive testimony of their merits.—PRESCOTT, WILLIAM HICKLING, 1824, *Italian Narrative Poetry, North American Review, vol.* 19, *p.* 340.

The poetical talents of Roscoe have been praised by no mean judges. His verses are very fair specimens of that kind of poetry the excellence of which consists less in strength of wing than in beauty of plume and lightness of movement. His song is flowing and harmonius rather than energetic.—CUNNINGHAM, ALLAN, 1833, *Biographical and Critical History of the Literature of the Last Fifty Years.*

Mr. Roscoe was simple and manly in his demeanor; but there was the feebleness of a mere *belle-lettrist,* a mere man of *virtù,* in the style of his sentiments on most subjects. Yet he was a politician, and took an ardent interest in politics, and wrote upon politics—all which are facts usually presuming some vigour of mind. And he wrote, moreover, on the popular side, and with a boldness which, in that day, when such politics were absolutely disreputable, seemed undeniably to argue great moral courage. . . . Mr. Fox (himself the very feeblest of party writers) was probably sincere in his admiration of Mr. Roscoe's pamphlets; and did seriously think him, as I know that he is described in private letters, an antagonist well matched against Burke; and *that* he afterwards became in form. The rest of the world wondered at his presumption, or at his gross miscalculation of his own peculiar powers. An eminent person, in after years (about 1815), speaking to me of Mr. Roscoe's political writings, especially those which had connected his name with Burke, declared that he always felt of him in that relation not so much as of a feeble man, but absolutely as of a *Sporus* (that was his very expression), or a man emasculated. Right or wrong in his views, he showed the most painful defect of good sense and prudence in confronting his own understanding, so plain and homely, with the Machiavelian Briareus of a hundred arms—the Titan whom he found in Burke; all the advantages of a living antagonist over a dead one could not compensate odds so fearful in original power.—DE QUINCEY, THOMAS, 1837, *Literary and Lake Reminiscences, Works, ed. Masson, vol.* II, *p.* 127.

Allow me to say that you have hardly done justice to Mackintosh, while you have done something more than justice to Roscoe. Both are good in their way, but there is an apparent fondness in the latter, and coldness in the former that will, I think, be generally perceived. I could produce passages from Mackintosh pregnant with more thought than it would be possible to find in all the volumes of Roscoe, whom you have assuredly overpraised as a literary historian.—NAPIER, MACVEY, 1838, *Letter to Lord Brougham, June* 6; *Selections from the Correspondence of the late Macvey Napier, ed., his Son, p.* 250.

He still moves with accomplished ease among the scholars and artists, and handles with critical discernment masses of new material from the Italian archives. But he is too typical an example of the highly cultured Unitarianism of his time to enter as sympathetically into religious passions and fanaticisms as he does into art and learning; and while he draws Luther with tolerable skill from the outside, Savonarola is to him somewhat as Mohammed to Voltaire.—HERFORD, C. H., 1897, *The Age of Wordsworth, p.* 41.

John Trumbull

1750–1831

A noted jurist of Hartford, famous in his day as a satirical poet. With Barlow and others he published "The Anarchiad," a series of satirical essays, and he was the author of the "Progress of Dulness"; but "Mac Fingal," a Hudibrastic poem, the first canto of which appeared in 1775, is his best title to remembrance. It bristles with sharp points of satire, and quite deserved the extensive popularity it for a time enjoyed. —ADAMS, OSCAR FAY, 1897, *A Dictionary of American Authors, p.* 389.

PERSONAL

Judge Trumbull maintained through life an honourable and upright character. The powers of satire, which formed a striking trait of his character, while they gave a pointedness and piquancy to his common conversation, he endeavored to restrain within the bounds of courteousness and kindness. As a scholar, a wit, and gentleman, he was greatly admired; and he left a name which must always sustain a conspicuous place in the early history of American letters.—EVEREST, CHARLES W., 1843, *The Poets of Connecticut*, p. 40.

Should John Trumbull cease to be remembered among us for his achievements as a grown-up man, it may be safe to say that he will still deserve some sort of renown for the prodigies he wrought while yet in his babyhood, and immediately after that brilliant epoch in his career. In the records of intellectual precocity, scarcely anything can be cited more remarkable than some of the things that are recorded of this amazing little creature at a period of life when ordinary mortals are sufficiently employed in absorbing and digesting a lacteal diet and in getting forward with their primary set of teeth.—TYLER, MOSES COIT, 1897, *The Literary History of the American Revolution*, 1763–1783, *vol.* I, *p.* 189.

PROGRESS OF DULLNESS
1772

The "Progress of Dulness" was published in 1772. It is the most finished of Trumbull's poems, and was hardly less serviceable to the cause of education than "McFingal" was to that of liberty.—GRISWOLD, RUFUS W., 1842–46, *The Poets and Poetry of America*, p. 6.

No wonder that a notable stir was made by these three satires, so fresh and ruddy with the tints of real life, so fearless in their local tone and color, so pungent with contemporary and local criticism, and coming as they did in so rapid succession from the academic solitude of that portentous young tutor. They seemed to announce the arrival of a rather uncomfortable inhabitant,—a satirist from whose glance no folly or obliquity would be likely to hide itself. And even yet, and for us, the whole work has a masterful aspect. Though far less subtle than his later and greater satire, "M'Fingal," it deals with subjects more universal and more permanent. Moreover, like all of Trumbull's work, it shows the training of the scholar, the technical precision of the literary artist. Each poem has a unity of its own, and holds up to laughter the despicable or the detestable traits of a single type of character. To all three poems an artistic unity is given, by a correlation, not only of topics, but of incidents, the latter of which just sufficiently entangle their chief personages at the end. Here, also, one finds ample facility and variety of literary allusion, unblinking observation of the follies and vices of society, an eye for every sort of personal foible, a quick sense of the ludicrous, a sure command of the vocabulary of ridicule and invective. Then, too, the genuine power of these satires was shown by evidence that could not be contradicted,—the outcry of punctured vanity with which they were greeted, —an outcry so vociferous, so sibilant, from so many quarters, as to prove how well each arrow had found its mark.—TYLER, MOSES COIT, 1897, *The Literary History of the American Revolution*, 1763–1783, *vol.* I, *p.* 220.

M'FINGAL
1782

In a poetic manner, a general account of the American contest, with a particular description of the character and manners of the times, interspersed with anecdotes, which no history could probably record or display, and, with as much impartiality as possible, satirize the follies and extravagances of my countrymen as well as of their enemies.—TRUMBULL, JOHN, 1785, *Letter to the Marquis de Chastellux*.

A poem which will live as long as "Hudibras." If I speak freely of this Piece, I can truly say, that altho' it is not equal to itself throughout (and where is the Poem that is so?) yet there are many parts of it equal to anything in that kind of Poetry that ever was written.—ADAMS, JOHN, 1785, *Letter to Trumbull, April* 28.

A Hudibrastic poem of great merit—for doggerel—rich, bold, and happy.—NEAL, JOHN, 1825, *American Writers, Blackwood's Magazine, vol.* 17, *p.* 202.

His "McFingal" owes its decadence, not to a deficiency in genuine wit and humor of the Hudibrastic school, but to the lack of picturesqueness in the story, and of all elements of permanent interest in its heroes.—PEABODY, A. P., 1856, *American Poetry, North American Review, vol.* 82, *p.* 241.

There is no contemporaneous record which supplies so vivid a representation of the manners of the age, and the habits and modes of thinking that then prevailed.—BOTTA, ANNE C. LYNCH, 1860, *Hand-Book of Universal Literature, p.* 530.

It is everywhere lauded for its thorough American spirit. . . . This once famous and still remarkable production.—NICHOL, JOHN, 1880–85, *American Literature, p.* 90.

It may still be read for its scholarship and learning.—LAWRENCE, EUGENE, 1880, *A Primer of American Literature, p.* 44.

Trumbull's "M'Fingal" is a work that will not go quite out of repute. It still speaks well for the character, wit, and facility of the staunch and acute author, and shows genuine originality although written after a model. Not even "Hudibras" more aptly seizes upon the ludicrous phases of a turbulent epoch.—STEDMAN, EDMUND CLARENCE, 1885, *Poets of America, p.* 35.

The immense popularity of the poem is unprecedented in American literary history. The first canto rapidly ran through thirty editions. Longfellow's "Evangeline" attained about the same circulation when the population of the country was thirty millions. "McFingal" was published when our population was only three millions. The poem, indeed, is to be considered as one of the forces of the Revolution, because as a satire on the Tories it penetrated into every farm-house, and sent the rustic volunteers laughing into the ranks of Washington and Greene. The vigor of mind and feeling displayed throughout the poem gives an impetus to its incidents which "Hudibras," with all its wonderful flashes of wit, comparatively lacks.—WHIPPLE, EDWIN PERCY, 1886, *American Literature and Other Papers, ed. Whittier, p.* 23.

There's no dreaming in it; there's no swashy sentiment; it does not stay to moralize; it goes on its rhythmic and satiric beat as steady and sure and effective as a patent threshing-machine. A capital thing it must have been for a town hero, or patriotic spouter, to read aloud in a tavern with the flip-maker keeping beat with his toddy-stick!—MITCHELL, DONALD G., 1897, *American Lands and Letters; The Mayflower to Rip-Van-Winkle, p.* 158.

Butler died, poor and neglected, in 1680; Trumbull was prosperously alive one hundred and fifty years later; and yet an intelligent reader might easily mistake many verses of the latter for verses of the former. Trumbull's are less clever, more decent, and doubtless distinguishable in various more profound ways; but the two poems are so much alike as to indicate in the cleverest American satirist of the closing eighteenth century, a temper essentially like that of the cleverest English satirist of a century before.—WENDELL, BARRETT, 1900, *A Literary History of America, p.* 126.

GENERAL

"McFingal," the most popular of the writings of the former of these poets, first appeared in the year 1782. This pleasant satire on the adherents of Britain in those times may be pronounced a tolerably successful imitation of the great work of Butler, though, like every other imitation of that author, it wants that varied and inexhaustible fertility of allusion which made all subjects of thought, the lightest and most abstruse parts of learning—everything in the physical and moral world, in art and nature the playthings of his wit. The work of Trumbull cannot be much praised for the purity of its diction. Yet, perhaps, great scrupulousness in this particular was not consistent with the plan of the author, and, to give the scenes of this poem their full effect, it might have been thought necessary to adopt the familiar dialect of the country and the times. We think his "Progress of Dullness" a more pleasing poem, more finished and more perfect in its kind, and, though written in the same manner, more free from the constraint and servility of imitation. The graver poems of Trumbull contain more vigorous and animated declamation.—BRYANT, WILLIAM CULLEN, 1818–84, *Early American Verse, Prose Writings, ed. Godwin, vol.* I, *p.* 49.

Paid him a thousand dollars, and a hundred copies of the work ["Poetical Works"] for the copyright. . . . It did not come up to the public expectation, or the patriotic zeal had cooled, and more than half the subscribers declined taking the work. . . . I quietly pocketed a loss of about a thousand dollars. This was my first serious adventure in patronizing American literature.—GOODRICH, S. G., 1856, *Recollections of a Lifetime, vol.* II, *pp.* 111, 112.

James Monroe

1758-1831

A native of Westmoreland county, Virginia, graduated at William and Mary College, 1776, joined the American Revolutionary army, rose to the rank of major, and acquired great distinction by his important services. After the war he studied law with Thomas Jefferson; was elected to the Legislature of Virginia, 1782, and to the National Congress, 1783, and also from 1790 to '94; served abroad as ambassador to France and also to England; Governor of Virginia, 1799—and 1802 and 1808-11; Secretary of State of the United States, 1811, of War, 1814; President of the United States, 1817-25. 1. "View of the Conduct of the Executive in the Foreign Affairs of the United States," &c., Philadelphia, 1798, 8vo.; London, 1798, 8vo. . . . 2. "A Tour of Observation through the North-Eastern and North-Western States in 1817," Philadelphia, 1818, 8vo.—ALLIBONE, S. AUSTIN, 1870, *A Critical Dictionary of English Literature, vol.* II, *p.* 1339.

PERSONAL

In his stature he is about the middle height of men, rather firmly set, with nothing further remarkable in his person, except his muscular compactness and apparent ability to endure labor. His countenance, when grave, has rather the expression of sternness and irascibility; a smile, however (and a smile is not unusual with him in a social circle), lights it up to very high advantage, and gives it a most impressive and engaging air of suavity and benevolence. His dress and personal appearance are those of a plain and modest gentleman. He is a man of soft, polite, and even assiduous attentions; but these, although they are always well-timed, judicious, and evidently the offspring of an obliging and philanthropic temper, are never performed with the striking and captivating graces of a Marlborough or a Bolingbroke. To be plain, there is often in his manner an inartificial and even an awkward simplicity, which, while it provokes the smile of a more polished person, forces him to the opinion that Mr. Monroe is a man of a most sincere and artless soul.—WIRT, WILLIAM, 1803, *Letters of a British Spy.*

The old notions of republican simplicity are fast wearing away, and the public taste becomes more and more gratified with public amusements and parade. Mr. Monroe, however, still retains his plain and gentlemanly manners, and is in every respect a very estimable man.—STORY, JOSEPH, 1818, *To Hon. Ezekiel Bacon, March* 12; *Life and Letters, vol.* I, *p.* 311.

In the midst of the festivities of the celebration of independence yesterday, the death of James Monroe was announced. He died at the house of his son-in-law, Mr. Samuel L. Gouverneur, in this city. This venerable patriot has been ill and his life despaired of for some months past, and he seems to have lingered until this time to add to the number of the Revolutionary patriots whose deaths have occurred on this memorable anniversary. — HONE, PHILIP, 1831, *Diary, July* 5; *ed. Tuckerman, vol.* I, *p.* 32.

Such, my fellow citizens, was James Monroe. Such was the man who presents the only example of one whose public life commenced with the War of Independence and is identified with all the important events of your history from that day forth for a full half-century.—ADAMS, JOHN QUINCY, 1831, *Eulogy on the Death of James Monroe, Delivered before the Corporation of Boston.*

In person Mr. Monroe was about six feet high, perhaps rather more; broad and square shouldered and raw-boned. When I knew him he was an old man (more than seventy years of age), and he looked perhaps even older than he was, his face being strongly marked with the lines of anxiety and care. His mouth was rather large, his nose of medium size and well-shaped, his forehead broad, and his eyes blue approaching gray. Altogether his face was a little rugged; and I do not suppose he was ever handsome, but in his younger days he must have been a man of fine physique, and capable of great endurance. . . . There was no grace about Mr. Monroe, either in appearance or manner. He was, in fact, rather an awkward man, and, even in his old age, a diffident one. Nevertheless, there was a calm and quiet dignity about him with which no one in his presence could fail to be impressed, and he was one of the most polite men I ever saw to all ranks and classes. It was his habit, in his ride of a morning or evening, to bow and speak to the humblest slave whom he passed as respectfully as if he had been the first gentleman in the neighborhood.—WATSON, E. R., 1883, *Recollections of James Monroe; James Monroe (American Statesmen), by Daniel C. Gilman, p.* 186.

There was nothing peculiarly striking or impressive in the personal appearance of Monroe. He was not so tall as Jefferson, but taller than Madison. His face was not so shrunken as the former's, nor so full as that of the latter. His countenance indicated the possession of the highest reflective faculties and perfect candor and sincerity—wholly without dissimulation. For these qualities he was universally esteemed, and it was impossible to observe him closely and hear him converse, without concluding that, in this respect, his reputation was well deserved. I had been always taught thus to regard him, and this estimate of him became fixed in my mind by personal observation. He was a fine specimen of what, in my boyhood, was called an "old Virginia gentleman," —sincere in manner, simple in tastes, courteous in deportment, and manly in intercourse with all.—THOMPSON, RICHARD W., 1894, *Recollections of Sixteen Presidents from Washington to Lincoln, vol.* I, *p.* 87.

GENERAL

In December, 1817, Mr. Monroe met the first Congress that was assembled under his administration. Never, since the immortalized and sainted Washington first appeared at the head of that august body, has *any* President been received with more marked tokens of sincere respect, and deserved admiration. The great counsellors of the nation reposed in him a confidence almost unlimited. . . . His first message is in the hands of all, and by all admired. It evinces a familiar knowledge of the great principles of our admirable Constitution, and of the great interests of our expanding Republic.—WALDO, S. PUTNAM, 1815, *The Tour of James Monroe, p.* 36.

His knowledge of the history and the men of our first constitutional age must have been extensive, minute, and accurate. His memory was a storehouse of valuable facts, a gallery lined with the most valuable pictures and portraits. Had he been content to write of what he knew, and part of which he was, he might have produced a work that would have been unrivalled in its kind. But it never seems to have occurred to him that he had a story to tell that could have secured for him the nation as an audience, and he allowed his real knowledge and rich experience to die with him, instead of adding them to the intellectual treasures of the world. He devoted his time and attention to the composition of a work in which a comparison was instituted between the government of the United States and the governments of the ancient republics. But when a man enters upon an elaborate political and literary work at sixty-seven, his chances of having health enough and life enough to complete it are not of an encouraging character. Mr. Monroe's treatise is a fragment. . . . We cannot express much regret that this treatise was not completed, nor do we think the world would have lost much had it been allowed to remain in manuscript. It is a literary curiosity, and nothing more—and it has not much value even as a curiosity. As the work of a practised and practical statesman, treating of the higher politics, it has a sort of attraction that is not common,—but things that are not common are not always valuable. They may be rare, and yet not rich.—HAZEWELL, C. C., 1867, *Monroe's The People are Sovereign, North American Review, vol.* 105, *pp.* 637, 638.

His numerous state papers are not remarkable in style or in thought, but his views were generally sound, the position which he took in later life on public questions was approved by the public voice, and his administration is known as the "era of good feeling." His attention does not seem to have been called in any special manner to the significance of slavery as an element of political discord, or as an evil in itself. If he foresaw, he did not foretell the great conflict. He does not seem expert in the principles of national finance, though his views are often expressed on such matters. The one idea which he represents consistently from the beginning to the end of his career is this, that America is for Americans. He resists the British sovereignty in his early youth; he insists on the importance of free navigation in the Mississippi, he negotiates the purchase of Louisiana and Florida; he gives a vigorous impulse to the prosecution of the second war with Great Britain, when neutral rights were endangered; finally he announces the "Monroe doctrine."—GILMAN, DANIEL C., 1883, *James Monroe (American Statesmen)*, *p.* 215.

Hannah Adams

1755–1832

The first woman in the United States to make a profession of literature was born in Medfield, Mass., in 1755, and died in Brookline, Mass., 15th November, 1832. Her father was a well-to-do farmer of considerable education and culture. Hannah was a delicate child, fond of reading and study. In childhood she memorized most of the poetical works of Milton, Pope, Thomson, Young and others. Her studies were varied, including Greek and Latin, in which she was instructed by the divinity students who made their home with her family. In 1772 her father lost his property, and the children were forced to provide for themselves. Hannah supported herself during the Revolutionary War by making lace and by teaching school. After the war she opened a school to prepare young men for college, in which she was very successful. Her principal work, a volume entitled "A View of Religious Opinions," appeared in 1784. The labor necessary for so great a work resulted in a serious illness that threatened her with mental derangement. That book passed through several editions in the United States and was republished in England. It is a work of great research and erudition. When the fourth edition was published, she changed the title to "A Dictionary of Religions." It was long a standard volume. Her second work, "A History of New England," appeared in 1799, and her third, "Evidences of Christianity," in 1801. Her income from these successful works was meager, as she did not understand the art of making money so well as she knew the art of making books. Her reputation extended to Europe and won her many friends, among whom was Abbé Grégoire, who was then laboring to secure the emancipation of the Jews in France. With him she corresponded, and from him she received valuable aid in preparing her "History of the Jews," which appeared in 1812. Her next book, "A Controversy with Dr. Morse," appeared in 1814, and her "Letters on the Gospels," in 1826. All her books passed through many editions. —MOULTON, CHARLES WELLS, 1893, *A Woman of the Century, eds. Willard and Livermore*, *p.* 6.

PERSONAL

Mount Auburn wants a century to hallow it, but it is beginning to soften with time a little. Many of us remember it as yet unbroken by the spade, before Miss Hannah Adams went and lay down there under the turf, *alone*,—"first tenant of Mount Auburn." The thunder-storms do not frighten the poor little woman now as they used to in those early days when I remember her among the living.—HOLMES, OLIVER WENDELL, 1881, *The Seasons, Pages from an old Volume of Life*, *p.* 167.

When the Athenæum was in Tremont Street, occupying the stuccoed building of two stories which stood on part of the land now occupied by the Probate Office, one solitary female ventured to claim the freedom of its alcoves and to endure the raising of the masculine eyebrows, provoked by the unaccustomed sight. And this "woman who dared" was the famous American authoress, Miss Hannah Adams. It was years before any sister authoress came to follow her example; but, nothing daunted, the little lady browsed among the books, content to look as singular and as much out of place as a woman of to-day would look who frequented a fashionable club designed for the exclusive accommodation of males. . . . I was well acquainted with Miss Hannah Adams, who was as intimate in my father's family as a person so modest and retiring could be anywhere. She often stayed with us at Quincy, where she was held in awe by the

THOMAS MOORE

SIR WALTER SCOTT

From the Original Painting by

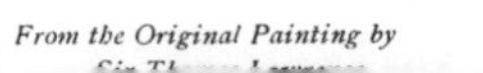

servants, from her habit of talking to herself. This seemed to them a very weird and uncanny proceeding; but our guest had penetrated a world where they could not follow her, and her lips unconsciously uttered the thoughts that it suggested. —QUINCY, JOSIAH, 1883, *Figures of the Past from the Leaves of old Journals, pp.* 328, 329.

When Hannah Adams's last book was published she was about seventy years of age. To her small apartment in Boston, friends, young and old, came to read and talk with her. They heard her repeat the poetry learned in youth; for, as she said, she could repeat "for three months together" the verses then learned, though she was "troubled continually by forgetting where she had laid a pencil or a pen." . . . Her young friends knew this when they decorated her room with flowers. Her older friends realized this when they made arrangements for her to exchange her small city room, in the last months of her life, for a home in the old Croft house at Brookline. Her love for the beautiful around her made her say almost at the close of life, "How can anybody be impatient to quit such a beautiful world?" Such testimony from one who had felt the trials and vicissitudes of a long life in a peculiarly personal manner is a precious inheritance for American women.—GOULD, ELIZABETH PORTER, 1893, *Hannah Adams, New England Magazine, vol.* 16, *p.* 369.

GENERAL

The author of this work ["Dictionary of Religions"] is in such full possession of publick regard, from the benefit conferred by her writings, and the merits of her several productions are so generally known, that we do not deem it necessary to enter into an elaborate investigation of the manner in which she has executed this new edition of a very useful book. All her works have been the fruit of great labor and extensive research. It could not be otherwise, where so many facts were to be sought among the scattered and voluminous documents, which she was obliged to examine, and where many of these facts were to be ascertained from the variant testimony, which she was compelled to adjudge or to reconcile. It was by her industry, that the history of New England was first embodied.—WILLARD, S., 1818, *Adams' Religions, North American Review, vol.* 7, *p.* 86.

Her principal work was a "View of Religions," in which she gave a comprehensive survey of the various religions of the world. The work was well received, and had an extensive circulation, but is now little known. She wrote also a "History of New England," a "History of the Jews," and "Evidences of Christianity." She was a woman of varied learning and indomitable perseverance.— HART, JOHN S., 1872, *A Manual of American Literature.*

Hannah Adams, who wrote as many religious books as if she was an orthodox Congregational minister of the day, prepared a "History of New England," which, in its way, though not an original authority, was as useful as Dr. Holmes' more ambitious work; its place in the development of woman's intellectual opportunities is obvious.—RICHARDSON, CHARLES F., 1887, *American Literature*, 1607–1885, *vol.* I, *p.* 452.

Sir Walter Scott

1771-1832.

1771—Born August 15. 1786—Began to study law. 1792—Called to the bar. 1796—Published translation of Buerger's "Ballads." 1797—Marriage. 1799—Appointed sheriff of Selkirkshire. 1799—Translated Goethe's "Goetz von Berlichingen." 1800—"The Eve of St. John: a Border Ballad." 1802—"Minstrelsy of the Scottish Border." 1804—Edited "Sir Tristrem," a Metrical Romance by Thomas of Ercildoune. 1805—"The Lay of the Last Minstrel: a Poem." 1806—Appointed Clerk of the Sessions. 1806—Edited "Memoirs," etc. 1808—"Marmion: a Tale of Flodden Field;" Edited the Works of Dryden, 18 vols., and Life; Strutt's "Queenhoo Hall: a Romance." 1809—Edited State Papers and Somers' Collection of Tracts, 1809-15. 1810—"The Lady of the Lake: a Poem;" Edited "English Minstrelsy." 1811—"The Vision of Don Roderick: a Poem." 1812—Came to live at Abbotsford. 1813—"Rokeby: a Poem;" "The Bridal of Triermain" 1814—"Waverley;" Edited

The Works of Swift, 19 vols. and Life; "The Border Antiquities,"—1814-17. 1815—"Guy Mannering;" "The Lord of the Isles: a Poem;" "The Field of Waterloo: a Poem." Edited Memoirs of the Somervilles. 1816—"The Antiquary;" "Tales of My Landlord," first series ("The Black Dwarf," "Old Mortality"). 1817—"Harold the Dauntless: a Poem." 1818—"Rob Roy;" "Tales of My Landlord," second series ("The Heart of Midlothian"). 1819—"Tales of My Landlord," third series ("The Bride of Lammermoor," "The Legend of Montrose"); "Ivanhoe." 1820—Knighted; "The Monastry;" "The Abbot." 1821—"Kenilworth;" Edited the Novelists' Library, 1821-24. 1822—"The Pirate;" "The Fortunes of Nigel;" "Halidon Hill: a Dramatic Sketch;" Much editing. 1823—"Peveril of the Peak;" "Quentin Durward." 1824—"St. Ronan's Well;" "Redgauntlet." 1825—"Tales of the Crusaders ("The Betrothed," "The Talisman"). 1826—Failure of the Ballantynes and Scott's financial distress; death of his wife; "Woodstock." 1827—"Life of Napoleon Buonaparte," 9 vols.; "Chronicles of the Canongate," first series ("The Two Drovers," "The Highland Widow," "The Surgeon's Daughter"); "Tales of a Grandfather,"—1827-30. 1828—Miscellaneous Works Collected, 6 vols.; "Chronicles of the Canongate," second series ("The Fair Maid of Perth"). 1829—"Anne of Geierstein;" "History of Scotland,"—1829-30. 1830—"Letters on Demonology and Witchcraft." 1831—Journey to Italy; "Tales of My Landlord," fourth series ("Count Robert of Paris," "Castle Dangerous"). 1832—Died September 21.—MacClintock, Porter Lander, 1900, *ed. Ivanhoe, Introduction, p.* vii.

PERSONAL

On our mentioning Mr. Scott's name the woman of the house showed us all possible civility, but her slowness was really amusing. I should suppose it is a house little frequented, for there is no appearance of an inn. Mr. Scott, who she told me was a very clever gentleman, "goes there in the fishing season;" but indeed Mr. Scott is respected everywhere: I believe that by favour of his name one might be hospitably entertained throughout all the borders of Scotland.—Wordsworth, Dorothy, 1803, *Journals, Sept.* 18, *vol.* II. *p.* 131.

Tall, and rather robust than slender, but lame in the same manner as Mr. Hayley, and in a greater measure. Neither the contour of his face, nor yet his features, are elegant; his complexion healthy, and somewhat fair, without bloom. We find the singularity of brown hair and eyelashes, with flaxen eyebrows, and a countenance open, ingenuous, and benevolent. When seriously conversing or earnestly attentive, though his eyes are rather of a lightish gray, deep thought is on their lids. He contracts his brow, and the rays of genius gleam aslant from the orbs beneath them. An upper lip too long prevents his mouth from being decidedly handsome; but the sweetest emanations of temper and heart play about it when he talks cheerfully or smiles: and in company he is much oftener gay than contemplative. His conversation is an overflowing fountain of brilliant wit, apposite allusion, and playful archness; while, on serious themes, it is nervous and eloquent; the accent decidedly Scotch, yet by no means broad.—Seward, Anna, 1807, *Letters.*

I truly rejoice in your success, and while I am entertaining in my way, a certain set of readers, for the most part, probably, of peculiar turn and habit, I can with pleasure see the effect you produce on all.—Crabbe, George, 1812, *Letter to Sir Walter Scott, Oct.* 13.

He is, indeed, the lord of the ascendant now in Edinburgh, and well deserves to be, for I look upon him to be quite as remarkable in intercourse and conversation as he is in any of his writings, even in his novels. . . . His countenance, when at rest, is dull and almost heavy, and even when in common conversation expresses only a high degree of good nature; but when he is excited, and especially when he is reciting poetry that he likes, his whole expression is changed, and his features kindle into a brightness of which there were no traces before.—Ticknor, George, 1819, *Journal, March; Life, Letters and Journals, vol.* I, *p.* 280.

He is tall and well formed, excepting one of his ankles and foot—I think the right—which is crippled, and makes him walk very lamely. He is neither fat nor thin. His face is perfectly Scotch, and though some people think it heavy, it struck me as a very agreeable one. He never could have been handsome. His forehead is very high, his nose short, his upper lip long, and the lower part of his face rather fleshy. His complexion fresh and clear, his eyes very blue, shrewd, and penetrating. I should say the predominant expression of his face is that of strong sense. His hair, which has always been very light (as well as his eyebrows and eyelashes) is now of a silvery whiteness, which makes him look somewhat older than he really is.—LESLIE, CHARLES ROBERT, 1820, *Letter to Miss Leslie, June* 28; *Autobiographical Recollections, ed. Taylor.*

My first impression was, that he was neither so large, nor so heavy in appearance as I had been led to expect by description, prints, bust, and picture. He is more lame than I expected, but not unwieldy; his countenance, even by the uncertain light in which I first saw it, pleased me much, benovelent, and full of genius without the slightest effort at expression; delightfully natural, as if he did not know he was Walter Scott or the Great Unknown of the North, as if he only thought of making others happy. . . . The impression left on my mind this night was, that Walter Scott is one of the best bred men I ever saw, with all the exquisite politeness which he knows so well how to describe, which is of no particular school or country, but which is of all countries, the politeness which arises from good and quick sense and feeling, which seems to know by instinct the characters of others, to see what will please, and put all his guests at their ease. As I sat beside him at supper, I could not believe he was a stranger, and forgot he was a great man. —EDGEWORTH, MARIA, 1823, *Letters, vol.* II, *pp.* 98, 99.

An event has just been announced which has thrown our little world into complete astonishment. Constable the bookseller has become bankrupt for a very large sum,—I cannot exactly say how much, and Sir Walter Scott is involved in this misfortune. The grief I felt on this occasion was very different indeed from the qualified sympathy with which Rochefoucault supposes us to regard the misfortunes of our friends. It was keen, deep, and by no means transient; every time I hear any allusion to him I grieve anew. I do not care about Constable personally, yet I find room for a little corner for him, for he has had by two marriages ten children. Next to our Scottish Shakspeare I lament for the kind-hearted, talented, and liberal-minded James Ballantyne. . . . A person, who to so many high endowments adds a superior portion of sound common sense, could not be quite insensible to the coming storm; but after the blast has passed over he will still be able to say, "All is lost but honour."—GRANT, ANNE, 1826, *Letters, Feb.* 23; *Memoir and Correspondence, ed. Grant, vol.* III, *pp.* 72, 73.

I do not find that he has, like most other writers of the present day, mixed up his personal feelings and history with his poetry; or that any fair and distinguished object will be so thrice fortunate as to share his laurelled immortality. We must therefore treat him like Shakspeare, whom alone he resembles—and claim him for us all.—JAMESON, ANNA BROWNELL, 1829, *The Loves of the Poets, vol.* II, *p.* 350.

Moore talked of Scott and his wonderful labor and power of composition, as well as the extent to which he has carried the art of book-making; besides writing this history of Scotland for Dr. Lardner's Encyclopædia, he is working at the prefaces for the republication of the "Waverley Novels," the "Tales of a Grandfather," and he has still found time to review Tytler, which he has done out of the scraps and chips of his other works. A little while ago he had to correct some of the proofs of the history of Scotland, and being dissatisfied with what was done, he nearly wrote it over again, and sent it up to the editor. Some time after, finding another copy of the proofs, he forgot that he had corrected them before, and he rewrote these also, and sent them up, and the editor is at this moment engaged in selecting from the two corrected copies the best parts of each. — GREVILLE, CHARLES C. F., 1829, *A Journal of the Reigns of King George IV. and King William IV., Nov.* 20, *ed. Reeve.*

I was rather agreeably surprised by his appearance, after all I had heard of its homeliness; the predominant expression of countenance, is, I think, a sort of arch good-nature, conveying a mingled impression of penetration and benevolence. — HEMANS, FELICIA DOROTHEA, 1829, *Letter, July* 13; *Memoirs, ed. Chorley, vol.* II, *p.* 32.

He is a tall man, of large but not well-filled frame. His shoulders are remarkably sloping, giving an appearance of great longitude to his neck. . . . When he walks, one knee bends under him and turns inward, making his progress very slow, and painful to the spectator. His head bald upon the crown, . . . is certainly the highest above the ears I have ever seen. . . . In court, he ordinarily appears as if asleep, or retired so far within himself that no thought or motion disturbs the placidity of the exterior surface. . . . On one occasion, his eye was turned on one of the spectators, and his countenance involuntarily became so quizzically humorous, that I really could not help laughing.—GRIFFIN, EDMUND DORR, 1831, *Remains, ed. Griffin.*

Lift up your hearts, ye Mourners! for the might
Of the whole world's good wishes with him goes;
Blessings and prayers in nobler retinue
Than sceptred king or laurell'd conqueror knows,
Follow this wondrous Potentate.
—WORDSWORTH, WILLIAM, 1831, *On the departure of Sir Walter Scott from Abbotsford for Naples.*

Mrs. Arkwright tells me that Miss Siddons, who is at Edinburgh, saw the physician who attended Walter Scott; he gives a melancholy account of his last moments. He died of a softening of the brain, and his features and countenance were so entirely changed, no one could possibly have recognised him. He had been for some time blind, and death came as a release to himself and his friends, who were worn out with watching. The anxiety to hear of him had been so great, that printed bulletins were posted all along the road from Edinburgh to Abbotsford, to prevent the crowds of people from coming to the house to inquire after him.—GREVILLE, HENRY, 1832, *Leaves from His Diary, Sept.* 29, *p.* 7.

Sir Walter was the best formed man I ever saw, and, laying his weak limb out of the question, a perfect model of a man for gigantic strength. The muscles of his arms were prodigious. I remember of one day long ago, I think it was at some national dinner in Oman's Hotel, that at a certain time of the night, a number of the young heroes differed prodigiously in regard to their various degrees of muscular strength. A general measurement took place around the shoulders and chest, and I, as a particular judge in these matters, was fixed on as the measurer and umpire. Scott, who never threw cold water on any fun, submitted to be measured with the rest. He measured most round the chest, and to their great chagrin, I was next to him, and very little short. But when I came to examine the arms! Sir Walter's had double the muscular power of mine, and very nearly so of every man's who was there. I declare, that from the elbow to the shoulder, they felt as if he had the strength of an ox.—HOGG, JAMES, 1834, *Familiar Anecdotes of Sir Walter Scott, p.* 237.

His amiable feeling, on every occasion, led him to assist and encourage all younger authors, and he seemed totally devoid of every spark of that littleness and jealousy which sometimes actuates even the most illustrious and established literati.—GELL, SIR WILLIAM, 1834, *Letter to Lady Blessington, March* 9; *Literary Life and Correspondence of the Countess of Blessington, ed. Madden, vol.* I, *ch.* xviii.

The conversation of Scott was frank, hearty, picturesque and dramatic. During the time of my visit he inclined to the comic rather than the grave, in his anecdotes and stories, and such, I was told, was his general inclination. He relished a joke, or a trait of humor in social intercourse, and laughed with right good will. He talked not for effect, nor display, but from the flow of his spirits, the stores of his memory, and the vigor of his imagination. He had a natural turn for narration, and his narratives and descriptions were without effort, yet wonderfully graphic. He placed the scene before you like a picture; he gave the dialogue with the appropriate dialect or peculiarities, and described the appearance and characters of his personages with that spirit and felicity evinced in his writings. Indeed, his conversation reminded me continually of his novels; and it seems to me, that during the whole time I was with him, he talked enough to fill volumes, and that they could not be filled more delightfully. He was as good a listener as talker, appreciating what others said, however humble might be their rank or pretensions, and was quick to testify his perception of any point in their discourse. He arrogated nothing to himself, but was perfectly unassuming and unpretending, entering with heart and soul into the business, or pleasure, or, I had almost said, folly, of the hour and the company. No one's concerns, no one's thoughts, no one's opinions, no one's tastes and pleasures seemed beneath him. He made himself so thoroughly the companion of those with whom he happened to be, that they forgot for a time his vast superiority, and only recollected and wondered, when all was over, that it was Scott with whom they had been on such familiar terms, and in whose society they had felt so perfectly at their ease. . . . I consider it one of the greatest advantages that I have derived from my literary career, that it has elevated me into genial communion with such a spirit.—IRVING, WASHINGTON, 1835, *Abbotsford, Crayon Miscellany.*

In stature, Sir Walter Scott was upwards of six feet, bulky in the upper part of the body, but never inclining in the least to what is called corpulency. His right limb was shrunk from an early period of boyhood, and required to be supported by a staff, which he carried close to the toes, the heel turning a little inwards. The other limb was perfectly sound, but the foot was too long to bring it within the description of handsome. The chest, arms, and shoulders were those of a strong man; but the frame, in its general movements, must have been enfeebled by his lameness, which was such as to give an ungainly, though not inactive appearance to the figure. The most remarkable part of Sir Walter's person was his head, which was so very tall and cylindrical as to be quite unique. The measurement of the part below the eyes was fully an inch and a half less than that above, which, both upon the old and the new systems of phrenology, must be held as a striking mark of the intellectuality of his character. —CHAMBERS, ROBERT, 1835–71, *Life of Sir Walter Scott, p.* 97.

About half-past one, P. M., on the 21st of September, 1832, Sir Walter breathed his last, in the presence of all his children. It was a beautiful day—so warm that every window was wide open—and so perfectly still that the sound of all others most delicious to his ear, the gentle ripple of the Tweed over its pebbles, was distinctly audible as we knelt around the bed, and his eldest son kissed and closed his eyes. . . . The more the details of his personal history are revealed and studied, the more powerfully will that be found to inculcate the same great lessons with his works. Where else shall we be taught better how prosperity may be extended by beneficence, and adversity be confronted by exertion? Where can we see the "follies of the wise" more strikingly rebuked, and a character more beautifully purified and exalted in the passage through affliction to death? . . . His character seems to belong to some elder and stronger period than ours; and, indeed, I cannot help likening it to the architectural fabrics of other ages, which he most delighted in, where there is such a congregation of imagery and tracery, such endless indulgence of whim and fancy, the sublime blending here with the beautiful, and there contrasted with the grotesque—half, perhaps, seen in the clear daylight, and half by rays tinged with the blazoned forms of the past—that one may be apt to get bewildered among the variety of particular impressions, and not feel either the unity of the grand design, or the height and solidness of the structure, until the docr has been closed on the labyrinth of aisles and shrines, and you survey it from a distance, but still within its shadow.—LOCKHART, JOHN GIBSON, 1836, *Memoirs of the Life of Sir Walter Scott, chs.* lxxxiii, lxxxiv.

Many people are living who had a most intimate acquaintance with him. I know no more of him than I know of Dryden or Addison, and not a tenth part so much as I know of Swift, Cowper, or Johnson. Then again, I have not, from the little that I do know of him, formed so high an opinion of his character as most people seem to entertain, and as it would be expedient for the *Edinburgh Review* to express. He seems to me to have been most carefully and successfully on his guard against the sins which most easily beset literary men. On that side he multiplied his precautions, and set double watch. Hardly any writer of note has been so free from the petty jealousies, and morbid irritabilities, of our caste. But I do not think that he kept himself equally pure from the faults of a very different kind, from the faults of a man of the world. In politics, a bitter and unscrupulous partisan; profuse and ostentatious in expense; agitated by the hopes and fears of a gambler; perpetually sacrificing the perfection of his compositions, and the durability of his fame, to his eagerness for money; writing with the slovenly haste of Dryden, in order to satisfy wants which were not, like those of Dryden, caused by circumstances beyond his control, but which were produced by his extravagant waste or rapacious speculation: this is the way in which he appears to me. I am sorry for it, for I sincerely admire the greater part of his works; but I cannot think him a high-minded man, or a man of very strict principle.—MACAULAY, THOMAS BABINGTON, 1838, *Letter to Napier, June* 26; *Life and Letters of Macaulay, ed. Trevelyan.*

No sounder piece of British manhood was put together in that eighteenth century of time. Alas! his fine Scotch face, with its shaggy honesty, sagacity and goodness, when we saw it latterly on the Edinburgh streets, was all worn with care, the joy all fled from it; ploughed deep with labour and sorrow. We shall never forget it; we shall never see it again. Adieu, Sir Walter, pride of all Scotchmen, take our proud and sad farewell.—CARLYLE, THOMAS, 1838, *Memoirs of the Life of Scott, London and Westminster Review, vol.* 28, *p.* 345.

I have, somewhere else, expressed how greatly the landlords of Scotland are indebted to Scott. It is to him that thousands of them owe not merely subsistence, but ample fortunes. In every part of the country where he has touched the earth with his magic wand, roads have run along the heretofore impassable morass, rocks have given way for men, and houses have sprung up full of the necessary "entertainment for man and horse." Steamers convey troups of summer tourists to the farthest west and north of the Scottish coast; and every lake and mountain swarms with them. On arriving at Melrose, I was greatly struck with the growth of this traffic of picturesque and romantic travel. It was twenty years since I was in that village before. Scott was then living at Abbotsford, and drew up to the inn door to take post-horses on to Kelso. While these were got out, we had a full and fair view of him as he sat, without his hat, in the carriage reading, as we ourselves were breakfasting near the window of a room just opposite. Then, there was one small inn in the place, and very few people in it; now, there were two or three; and these, beside lodging-houses, all crammed full of guests. The inn-yards stood full of traveling carriages, and servants in livery were lounging about in motley throngs. The ruins of the abbey were like a fair for people, and the intelligent and very obliging woman who shows them said, that every year the numbers increased, and, that every year, foreigners seemed to arrive from more and more distant regions. At Abbotsford it was the same.—HOWITT, WILLIAM, 1847, *Homes and Haunts of the Most Eminent British Poets, vol.* II, *p.* 210.

Abbotsford, a supremely melancholy place heretofore, will be henceforth more melancholy still. Those associations of ruined hopes and blighted prospects which cling to its picturesque beauty will now be more numerous and more striking than ever. The writings of Scott are the true monuments of his genius; while Abbotsford, on which he rested so much, will form for the future a memorial equally significant of his foibles and his misfortunes,—of bright prospects suddenly overcast, and sanguine hopes quenched in the grave forever.—MILLER, HUGH, 1847, *Essays, p.* 499.

Think of your pleasure when you read that "Ivanhoe" which was dictated in the intervals of agonizing cramp-spasms; "Bonaparte" and the "Chronicles of the Canongate," composed amid the ruins of his fortune; "Woodstock," composed while his wife was perishing in an adjoining room; the "Tales," that were written for a darling a dying grandchild, and whatever else followed amid broken health, lost riches, with the dim eyes and trembling fingers and the lone heart of old age, to pay vast debts which he had not contracted, but to which his high sense of honour and his duty as a gentleman compelled him. Truly, for him, *noblesse oblige* was not an empty word.—MACLEOD, DONALD, 1852, *Life of Sir Walter Scott, p.* 279.

No one who knew Sir Walter, will fail to remember his admirable convivial powers, or the quaint good humor, utterly *sans prétension*, by which these were animated. No sooner had he taken his place at table than by some *naif* remark, not addressed to any one in particular, he usually effected the utter demolition of "starch," and, without having once in all his life ever aimed at saying a "good thing," produced more mirth and joviality than any professional wit or punster ever could. He was so decidedly an enemy to "starch," or pretension of any kind, that it became invariably decomposed in his presence, and he cared not of what platitudes or "merry-andradas" he served himself to effect that purpose.—GILLIES, ROBERT PEARCE, 1854, *Memoirs of a Literary Veteran.*

I never saw any man who *looked* the man of genius he was, but Professor Wilson. Next to him was Sir Walter Scott. Him I first saw, in his fifty-seventh year, when I was at college in Edinburgh, and had wandered one day, in, I think, the month of June, into one of the law courts to hear Mr. Jeffrey plead. . . . I had been standing for some time in the Court of Session, in which Sir Walter Scott was one of the principal clerks, who sate at a table below the judges, when my eye fell upon an elderly man, one of those sitting at the table, wearing a rusty-looking old stuff gown. His chin rested on his left hand, and his right hung by his side with a pen in it. Without having an idea who he was, my attention was soon arrested by his lofty forehead, and a pair of eyes that seemed gazing dreamily into a distant world unseen by any one but himself. The more I looked at those eyes, the more remarkable appeared their character and expression: not bright, or penetrating, but invested with a grand, rapt, profound air. He sate motionless as a statue, apparently lost to all that was passing around him. A sudden suspicion arose within me, that I was looking on the mighty Northern novelist, who had publicly avowed himself the author of Waverly in the preceding February. To make assurance doubly sure, I asked a person standing beside me, who that was, indicating him. "Whaur d'ye come frae?" said he, looking at me rather contemptuously; "d'ye no ken that's *Sir Walter?*" Almost while this was being said, Sir Walter seemed to rouse himself from a reverie, and soon afterwards wrote rapidly on several sheets of paper, and then quitted the court, leaning on his stick, and walking very lame. —WARREN, SAMUEL, 1854, *Miscellanies, p.* 498.

We were not long in reaching Abbotsford. The house, which is more compact, and of considerably less extent than I anticipated, stands in full view from the road, and at only a short distance from it, lower down towards the river. Its aspect disappointed me; but so does everything. It is but a villa, after all; no castle, nor even a large manor-house, and very unsatisfactory when you consider it in that light. Indeed, it impressed me, not as a real house, intended for the home of human beings,—a house to die in or to be born in,—but as a plaything,—something in the same category as Horace Walpole's Strawberry Hill. The present owner seems to have found it insufficient for the actual purposes of life; for he is adding a wing, which promises to be as extensive as the original structure. . . . On the whole, there is no simple and great impression left by Abbotsford; and I felt angry and dissatisfied with myself for not feeling something which I did not and could not feel. But it is just like going to a museum, if you look into particulars; and one learns from it, too, that Scott could not have been really a wise man, nor an earnest one, nor one that grasped the truth of life; he did but play, and the play grew very sad towards its close. In a certain way, however, I understand his romances the better for having seen his house; and his house the better for having read his romances. They throw light on one another.—HAWTHORNE, NATHANIEL, 1856, *English Note-Books, vol.* II, *pp.* 46, 52.

He the first gentleman of Europe (George IV)! There is no stronger satire on the proud English society of that day than that they admire George. No thank God, we can tell of better gentlemen. . . . I will take men of my own profession of letters. I will take Walter Scott, who loved the king, and who was his sword and buckler, and championed him like that brave highlander in his own story, who fights round his craven chief. What a good gentleman! What a friendly soul, what a generous hand, what an amiable life, was that of the noble Sir Walter!—THACKERAY, WILLIAM MAKEPEACE, 1861, *George the Fourth, The Four Georges.*

Few persons who heard him speak could have doubted Scott's nationality; it could not have been said with justice that Scott

"Hung on the soft phrase of Southern tongue." His accent, on the contrary, was so broad that Mr. Harness said he sometimes could not understand him without difficulty. One day when they had been talking of "Lucia di Lammermoor," which had lately appeared, he changed the subject by observing, "Weel! I think we've a'most had enow of that chiel."—L'ESTRANGE, A. G., 1870, *The Literary Life of the Rev. William Harness.*

His traveling costume [in 1825] . . . consisted of a green cut-away coat, or rather jacket, with short skirts and brass buttons; drab trousers, vest, and gaiters; a single seal and watch-key, attached to a watered black ribbon, dangling from his fob; a loose, and not very stiff, linen collar; a black silk neck-kerchief; and a low-crowned, deep-brimmed hat. He had no gloves; and his ungloved hands, large and almost clumsy, were thickly covered with red bristles. His feet were scarcely so large as one would have expected, his height being six feet. He was muscular, but not stout; and the breadth across his chest was very great. He walked very lame, using a stout staff, with a crooked handle, even in the room; but he was active and rapid in his movements. As he stood,—just as Maclise drew him in the Fraserian sketch,—only the toes and ball of his right foot touched the ground. It appeared as if the posterior tendons had shrunk; at any rate, his heel was raised when he stood.—MACKENZIE, ROBERT SHELTON, 1871, *Sir Walter Scott, The Story of His Life, p.* 361.

Lockhart has cleverly left an impression on his readers that Scott was first a victim to the foolish schemes of these two brothers, and then of the sanguine follies of Constable, the publisher. Whereas, in truth, no sharper or keener Scotsman ever lived than the great novelist himself, nor had ever any man more trusty allies than had Scott in Constable and the Ballantynes. —CONSTABLE, A. G., 1874, *Archibald Constable and His Friends, Harper's Magazine, vol.* 48, *p.* 511.

Generous, large-hearted and magnanimous as Scott was, there was something in the days of his prosperity that fell short of what men need for their highest ideal of a strong man.—HUTTON, RICHARD HOLT, 1879, *Sir Walter Scott* (*English Men of Letters*), *p.* 175.

I remember him about that time [1821]: he used to walk up and down Princes Street, as we boys were coming from the High School, generally with some friend, and every now and then he stopped, and resting his lame leg against his stick, laughed right out at some joke of his friend's or his own: he said a good laugh was worth standing for, and besides required it for its completion. How we rejoiced when we took off our bonnets, to get a smile and a nod from him, thinking him as great as Julius Cæsar or Philopœmen, Hector or Agricola, any day.—BROWN, JOHN, 1882, *Horæ Subsecivæ, Third Series.*

The great charm of his conversation, being a man of such eminence, was its perfect simplicity, and the entire absence of vanity and love of display.—ALISON, SIR ARCHIBALD, 1883, *Some account of my Life and Writings, an Autobiography, vol.* I, *p.* 288.

I will endeavour briefly to give some idea of the impression he made on me, in this the only interview [1819], I ever had with him. He looked like a country gentleman, florid and healthy; his countenance was of a good-natured and open character, the brow very fine, and strongly marked, the eye particularly clear and bright; altogether he was a man with whom I should not have been in the least afraid to converse, had I met him in a less crowded circle.—BRAY, ANNA ELIZA, 1883, *Autobiography, ed. Kempe, p.* 146.

Passing Storr's Hall, the mind wandered back to the meeting there of Wordsworth, Southey, Coleridge, Christopher North, and greater than all, our own Walter Scott; and surely not in all the earth could a fitter spot than this have been found for their gathering. How much the world of to-day owes to the few names who spent days together here! Not often can you say of one little house, "Here had we our country's honor roofed" to so great an extent as it would be quite allowable to say in this instance. But behold the vanity of human aspirations! If there was one wish dearer than another to the greatest of these men, it was that Abbotsford should remain from generation to generation the home of his race. This very hour, while sailing on the lake, a newspaper was handed to me, and my eye caught the advertisment, "Abbotsford to let," followed by the stereotyped description, so many reception-rooms, nursery, outbuildings, and offices, suitable for a gentleman's establishment. Shade of the mighty Wizard of the North, has it come to this! Oh, the pity of it! the pity of it! Well for your fame that you built for mankind other than this stately home of your pride. It will crumble and pass utterly away long before the humble cot of Jeannie Deans shall fade from the memory of man. The time will come when the largest son of time, who wandering sang to a listening world, shall be as much forgot

"As the canoe that crossed a lonely lake
A thousand years ago."

But even the New Zealander who stands on the ruins of London Bridge will know something of Walter Scott if he knows much worth knowing. "Abbotsford to let!" This to come to us just as we were passing one of the haunts of Scott, than whom no greater Scott ever lived save one. Fortunately no such blow is possible for the memory of Burns.—CARNEGIE, ANDREW, 1883, *An American Four-in-Hand in Britain*, p. 228.

Sir,—In your biography it is recorded that you not only won the favour of all men and women; but that a domestic fowl conceived an affection for you, and that a pig, by his will, had never been severed from your company. If some Circe had repeated in my case her favourite miracle of turning mortals into swine, and had given me a choice, into that fortunate pig, blessed among his race, would I have been converted! You, almost alone among men of letters, still, like a living friend, win and charm us out of the past; and if one might call up a poet, as the scholiast tried to call Homer, from the shades, who would not, out of all the rest, demand some hours of your society? Who that ever meddled with letters, what child of the irritable race, possessed even a tithe of your simple manliness, of the heart that never knew a touch of jealousy, that envied no man his laurels, that took honour and wealth as they came, but never would have deplored them had you missed both and remained but the Border sportsman and the Border antiquary?—LANG, ANDREW, 1885, *To Sir Walter Scott, Letters to Dead Authors.*

Scott's library still remains at Abbotsford, and no one who has ever entered that embodiment of the great man's soul can ever forget it. The library, with the entire contents of the house, were restored to Scott in 1830 by his trustees and creditors, "As the best means the creditors have of expressing their very high sense of his most honourable conduct, and in grateful acknowledgment of the unparalleled and most successful exertions he has made, and continues to make for them." The library is rich in the subjects which the great author loved, such as Demonology and Witchcraft. — WHEATLEY, HENRY B., 1886, *How to Form a Library*, *p.* 52.

"Alan Fairford," "The Ariosto of the North," "A Bard of Martial Lay," "The Black Hussar of Literature," "The Border Minstrel," "A Borderer Between Two Ages," "The Caledonian Comet," "The Charmer of the World," "Colonel Grogg," "The Duke of Darnick," "Duns Scotus," "The Great Border Minstrel," "The Great Magician," "The Great Minstrel," "The Great Unknown," "A Homer of a Poet," "The Mighty Minstrel," "The Minstrel of the Border," "Our Northern Homer," "Old Peveril," "Peveril of the Peak," "The Proudest Boast of the Caledonian Muse," "Sir Tristram," "The Superlative of My Comparative," "The Wizard of the North."—FREY, ALBERT R., 1888, *Sobriquets and Nicknames, p.* 461.

It seems strange that the great-souled, great-brained author of "Waverley," whose heart was as large as his head was high, should have placed a commemoration stone over the grave of "Helen Walker, the humble individual who practised in real life the virtues with which fiction has invested the imaginary character of Jeanie Deans," and should have neglected entirely the spot where the authors of his own being were laid.—HUTTON, LAURENCE, 1891, *Literary Landmarks of Edinburgh, p.* 53.

While nothing can be found now to alter men's conception of Scott, any book about him is justified, even if it do no more than heap up superfluous testimony to the beauty of his character.—QUILLER-COUCH, A. T., 1893, *Adventures in Criticism.*

According to the distribution of Scott's brain as indicated by the outside, he should have been a conceited religious fanatic; but he was neither conceited, nor fanatical, nor over-religious. The head suggests by its height, or rather by its retreating length and narrowness, artificial compression,—not wholly a wrong suggestion for it was by compression that its peculiar shape was produced. The matter is of intense interest when we realize that only a freak of nature prevented that matchless brain from being locked within an inclosure which would have made it that of a microcephalous idiot. . . . When Dr. Charles Creighton once happened to show to a distinguished French anthropologist a skull of one of this unfortunate class, with its boat-shape formation and effaced sagittal suture, the *savant* held it up and exclaimed, "*Voilà*, Walter Scott!" Had this defect in bone-making extended to the other sutures, there would have been no Sir Walter Scott, no increase of horse-hire in the Trosachs, no Scotland of romance, and no Waverleys for the world. . . . The point of these suggestions is that vast and splendid as were Scott's gifts and achievements, he is still entitled to allowance for what Nature intended but failed to do for him through her own fault.—MUNGER, T. T., 1894, *The Head of Sir Walter Scott, Open Letters, The Century, vol.* 47, *p.* 955.

Sir Walter's daughter, Sophia, married John Lockhart, the historian. They had three children, the youngest of whom, Charlotte, married James Hope, Esq., who by act of Parliament took the name of Hope-Scott. They also had three children, the eldest of whom, Mary Monica, my hostess, was sole heiress of Abbotsford and other large estates, the other two children having died. In 1874 she married the Hon. Joseph Maxwell, a younger brother of Lord Herries, of Everingham Park, whose title and estates he will inherit, as Lord Herries has no son. Mr. Maxwell also legally took the name of Maxwell-Scott, and the first child born was named Walter Scott. Upon this auspicious occasion the Queen telegraphed with her congratulations, "He shall be knighted 'Sir Walter' when he is twenty-one." This boy is now nineteen years of age, and has six rollicksome brothers and sisters. Walter is destined for the army, Malcomb for the navy. Then follow Josephine, seventeen years old; Alice, twelve; Michael, ten; Margaret, seven; and Herbert, two.—SMITH, NINA LARRE, 1895, *A House-party at Abbottsford, The Cosmopolitan, vol.* 19, *p.* 513.

Scott's character was, in nearly every respect, one of the manliest on record. If he had lived in the times of chivalry he so dearly loved to portray, he would have worn his lady's glove in his casque and couched his lance with the bravest, seeking by deeds of prowess to distinguish himself and gain her love, after the manner of the days gone by. . . . Add to this, that in anything that affected the deeper feelings of the heart, in his tender feelings towards those near and dear to him, we have it from Lockhart, that Scott had all the sensitiveness of a maiden. Such modesty and sensitiveness, carried to excess, render a man but an indifferent wooer.—SCOTT, ADAM, 1896, *The Story of Sir Walter Scott's First Love, pp.* 52, 54.

By this time [1791] he had also become qualified for ladies' society. He had grown to be tall and strong; his figure was both powerful and graceful; his chest and arms were those of a Hercules. Though his features were not handsome, their expression was singularly varied and pleasing; his eye was bright and his complexion brilliant. It was a proud day, he said, when he found that a pretty young woman would sit out and talk to him for hours in a ballroom, where his lameness prevented him from dancing. This pretty young lady was probably Williamina, daughter of Sir John and Lady Jane Belsches, afterwards Stuart of Fettercairn near Montrose, born October 1776. She ultimately married, on 19 Jan. 1797, Sir William Forbes, bart., of Pitsligo, was mother of James David Forbes, and died 5 Dec. 1810. Scott appears to have felt for her the strongest passion of his life. Scott's father, says Lockhart, thought it right to give notice to the lady's father of the attachment. This interference, however, produced no effect upon the relations between the young people. Scott, he adds, hoped for success for "several long years." Whatever the true story of the failure, there can be no doubt that Scott was profoundly moved, and the memory of the lady inspired him when describing Matilda in "Rokeby," and probably other heroines. He refers to the passion more than once in his last journal, and he had affecting interviews with her mother in 1827.—STEPHEN, LESLIE, 1897, *Dictionary of National Biography, vol.* LI, *p.* 83.

It was a cruel disenchantment—a most

crushing blow. He left her father's house, and wandered away into a country solitude, to battle with the anguish which during two long years he was unable to quell, and which, in fact, endured more or less to the very end of his life. He said in reference to it, as we have quoted, that "the dead will feel no pain;" but still, the secret agony they have known in life ought to be sacred to us now.—SKENE, F. M. F., 1899, *Sir Walter Scott's First Love, The Century, vol.* 58, *p.* 372.

The great luminary, whose magic hand had made the spell of Scottish romance potent all over Europe, was wedded to the older views. Scott was indeed no adept in political science. His opinions were not those of any party, but exclusively his own. They were coloured by the poetry of his nature, and, while they had something of the free-lance which it was his nature to be, their very intensity of conviction, and their loyalty to old, and above all to national, traditions, gave them a halo of chivalry which puzzled and perplexed the lesser men around him. The very tenacity of his friendships, and his loyalty to the names of the past, made smaller men criticise and carp at that which they did not understand. His geniality and breadth of character prevented him from feeling any very strong sympathy with the enthusiasm of religious feeling that seemed to swathe human morality in the swaddling bands of a somewhat unctuous and obtrusive code of religious ethics.—CRAIK, SIR HENRY, 1901, *A Century of Scottish History, vol.* II, *p.* 341.

POETRY

The muse of Scott lives only in reminiscences of the old songs of Scotland; his verse is, as it were, a mosaic composed of detached fragments of romantic legend and early chivalry adapted to Scottish customs, and knit together with wondrous skill and care: just as fragmentary portions of paintings on glass out of Gothic churches are sometimes found in country houses and hermitages at the present day, neatly cemented together for the sake of picturesque effect.—SCHLEGEL, FREDERICK, 1815-59, *Lectures on the History of Literature, p.* 315.

No writer of modern times has combined so much power of imagination with such shrewdness in the observation of human character, and so much of the painter's eye in his delineation of outward objects, more particularly as regards the dresses, armour, furniture, and other decorations of past ages, insomuch that he is apt to dwell on these to the prejudice of what is more important to the general effect of his story.—CARY, HENRY FRANCIS, 1823, *Notices of Miscellaneous English Poets, Memoir, ed. Cary, vol.* II, *p.* 300.

Compared with true and great poets, our Scottish minstrel is but a "metre ballad-monger." We would rather have written one song of Burns, or a single passage in Lord Byron's "Heaven and Earth," or one of Wordsworth's "fancies and good-nights," than all his epics. . . . He is a mere narrative and descriptive poet, garrulous of the old time. The definition of his poetry is a pleasing superficiality.—HAZLITT, WILLIAM, 1825, *The Spirit of the Age.*

Great Minstrel of the Border!—WORDSWORTH, WILLIAM, 1831, *Yarrow Revisited.*

Scott is a poet truly natural and heroic. He finds his scenes in his native land, and his heroes and heroines in British history and tradition. There is an astonishing ease, vehemence and brightness in his verse; his poems are a succession of historical figures, with all the well-defined proportions of statues, but which speak and act according to the will of the poet. . . . No one, since the days of Homer, has sung with such an impetuous and burning breath the muster, the march, the onset, and all the fiery vicissitudes of battle.—CUNNINGHAM, ALLAN, 1833, *Biographical and Critical History of the Literature of the Last Fifty Years.*

To Scott, alone, of all the poets of his time, belongs the merit of comprehension. Although his works could hardly have been written in any other period than the nineteenth century, they still are remarkably free from its egotism. No writer since Shakspeare has displayed such power in the creation and delineation of character, or such freedom from idiosyncrasies and personal prejudices, in describing life and manners.—WHIPPLE, EDWIN P., 1845, *English Poets of the Nineteenth Century, Essays and Reviews, vol.* I, *p.* 303.

What did Walter Scott write without stint? a rhymed traveller's guide to Scotland. And the libraries of verses they print have this Birmingham character. How many volumes of well-bred metre we must jingle through, before we can be filled, taught, renewed!—EMERSON, RALPH WALDO, 1856-84, *English Traits, p.* 242.

The poetic style of Scott is—(it becomes necessary to say so when it is proposed to "translate Homer into the melodies of Marmion")—it is, tried by the highest standards, a bastard epic style; and that is why, out of his own powerful hands, it has had so little success. It is a less natural, and therefore a less good style, than the original ballad-style; while it shares with the ballad-style the inherent incapacity of rising into the grand style, of adequately rendering Homer.—ARNOLD, MATTHEW, 1861, *Lectures on Homer, p.* 59.

He was a poet only at rare intervals.—FRISWELL, JAMES HAIN, 1869, *Essays on English Writers, p.* 329.

No other metrical narrative in our language seem to me to possess an equal power of enchaining the attention of the reader, and carrying him on from incident to incident with such entire freedom from weariness.—BRYANT, WILLIAM CULLEN, 1872, *Orations and Addresses, p.* 390.

Walter Scott's verse is not to be sung or danced—it is to be jumped.—HOUGHTON, LORD, 1873, *Monographs Personal and Social, p.* 131.

No poet, and in this he carries on the old Scotch quality, is a finer colourist. His landscapes are painted in colour, and the colour is always true. Nearly all his natural description is Scotch, and he was the first who opened to the delight of the world the wild scenery of the Highlands and the Lowland moorland. He touched it all with a pencil so light, graceful, and true, that the very names are made romantic.—BROOKE, STOPFORD A., 1876, *English Literature (Primer), p.* 157.

Scott has always been the poet of youthful and high-hearted readers: there seems to be no reason why he should not continue indefinitely to meet their requirements, and certainly they will be considerable losers if ever, in the lapse of time and shifting of poetic models, his compositions should pass out of ready currency. He is not, and never can be, the poet of literary readers: the student and the artist remember him as a cherished enchantment of their youth, and do not recur to him. Neither the inner recesses of thought nor the high places of art thrill to his appeal. But it is highly possible for the critical tendency and estimate to be too exclusively literary; the poetry of Scott is mainly amenable to a different sort of test, and to that it responds not only adequately but triumphantly.—ROSSETTI, WILLIAM MICHAEL, 1878, *Lives of Famous Poets, p.* 233.

Scott's is almost the only poetry in the English language that not only runs in the head of average men, but heats the head in which it runs by the mere force of its hurried frankness of style. . . . No poet ever equalled Scott in the description of wild and simple scenes and the expression of wild and simple feelings.—HUTTON, RICHARD HOLT, 1879, *Sir Walter Scott (English Men of Letters), pp.* 43, 59.

Of all the poets of his time, Scott was the one who set least store by style. He worked always rapidly, often carelessly, writing whole pages, I might almost say, cantos, which do not rise above ballad ding-dong. And yet when he put forth his full strength, on a subject which really kindled him, he could rise to a dignity and elevation, truly impressive. Though the facility of the octosyllabic couplet often betrayed him into carelessness, yet there are many passages, in which he has made it the best vehicle we possess for rapid and effective narrative—perhaps also for natural description.—SHAIRP, JOHN CAMPBELL, 1881, *Modern English Poetry, Aspects of Poetry.*

Of all the names that adorn the opening of our century Scott's must be pronounced upon the whole the greatest—at once the manliest and the most original and creative. He may rank below Wordsworth and Coleridge as a poet, although he is great in poetic qualities as old as Homer, in which both are entirely wanting; but take him all in all there is no intellectual figure comparable to him in breadth and richness. He strikes the new note of the century—its larger intelligence both for nature and life—its deeper insight into the past, as well as its freer, fuller, and clearer eye for the present, with a wider, a more extended and powerful sweep than any other.—TULLOCH, JOHN, 1885, *Movements of Religious Thought in Britain During the Nineteenth Century, p.* 82.

His poetry is the poetry of action. In

imaginative power he ranks below no other poet, except Homer and Shakespeare. He delighted in war, in its movement, its pageantry, and its events; and, though lame, he was quartermaster of a volunteer corps of cavalry.—MEIKLEJOHN, J. M. D., 1887, *The English Language: Its Grammar, History and Literature, p.* 340.

What *Deus ex machina* could have come to my aid more effective than the sunny cheerfulness, strong, healthy vitality, Catholic human sympathy, deep-rooted patriotism, fine pictorial eye, and rare historic furniture of Walter Scott? To the poetry of this greatest literary Scot, whom I soon learned to associate in æsthetical bonds with the sunny sobriety of Homer and the great Greeks, I owe in no small measure that close connection with the topography and the local history of my country which appears in my poetical productions, and which, if these are destined in any smallest degree to live in the memory of my countrymen, will be the element that has most largely contributed to their vitality.—BLACKIE, JOHN STUART, 1887, *Books which have Influenced Me.*

I should be ungrateful, indeed, if I did not speak of the obligation we all were under to Scott's poems. I cannot recall the time when I could not repeat long passages of them from memory, and I may say that those passages have often been a great comfort to me since, when I have been imprisoned in my berth on an ocean steamer. Whatever else criticism may say of Scott, he is certainly the poet of boyhood and early youth. Of course, the poems led up to the novels, and by the time we were fourteen we had read all the best of them. But this is not my experience only, but that of the English-reading world.—HALE, EDWARD EVERETT, 1888, *Books that have Helped Me, p.* 7.

I got hold of Scott's poems, too, in that cabin loft, and read most of the tales which were yet unknown to me after those earlier readings of my father's. I could not say why "Harold the Dauntless" most took my fancy; the fine, strongly-flowing rhythm of the verse had a good deal to do with it, I believe. I liked these things, all of them, and in after years I liked the "Lady of the Lake" more and more, and from mere love of it got great lengths of it by heart; but I cannot say that Scott was then or ever a great passion with me.—HOWELLS, WILLIAM DEAN, 1895, *My Literary Passions, p.* 40.

Yet it seems to me impossible, on any just theory of poetry or of literature, to rank him low as a poet. He can afford to take his trial under more than one statute. To those who say that all depends on the subject, or that the handling and arrangement of the subject are, if not everything, yet something to be ranked far above mere detached beauties, he can produce not merely the first long narrative poems in English, which for more than a century had honestly enthralled and fixed popular taste, but some of the very few long narrative poems which deserve to do so. . . . In his own special divisions of the simpler lyric and of lyrical narrative he sometimes attains the exquisite, and rarely sinks below a quality which is fitted to give the poetical delight to a very large number of by no means contemptible persons. It appears to me at least, that on no sound theory of poetical criticism can Scott be ranked as a poet below Byron, who was his imitator in narrative and his inferior in lyric. But it may be admitted that this was not the opinion of most contemporaries of the two, and that, much as the poetry of Byron has sunk in critical estimation during the last half century, and slight as are the signs of its recovery, those who do not think very highly of the poetry of the pupil do not, as a rule, show much greater enthusiasm for that of the master.—SAINTSBURY, GEORGE, 1896, *A History of Nineteenth Century Literature, pp.* 74, 75.

His style was modelled at first chiefly on the Border ballads, and the word picturesque may perhaps best define it. The landscape is often rather touched-in by way of support to his figures than painted for its own sake or as the mere background of earlier days; human interests and passions, or those historical memories in which his soul delighted, in general, pervade it. . . . Scott, after Chaucer, is the one of all our non-dramatic poets who puts himself least forward; one of the few who thought little or nothing, personally, of themselves; the one who trusts most to letting his characters and scenes speak for themselves. By inevitable natural law he is indeed, of course, present in his work; but, like Homer, like Shakespeare, behind the curtain; latent in his own creation.—PALGRAVE, FRANCIS

TURNER, 1896, *Landscape in Poetry, pp.* 183, 188.

Though Scott had neither Coleridge's extraordinary musical faculty, nor his dreamy tenderness of sentiment, nor his gift of mystical imagination, there is a spirit and fire in his narrative verse, and a certain masterly breadth in his treatment of nature—as witness the noble opening to the "Lady of the Lake," "The stag at eve had drunk his fill," etc.—which must irresistibly challenge all those who scruple at bestowing the name of poetry on these splendid rhymed romances to enlarge their definitions.—TRAILL, HENRY DUFF, 1896, *Social England, vol.* V, *p.* 585.

Of the features which distinguish the poetry of Scott none, perhaps, surpass in cogency or beauty that which a heraldic view displays. Scott is pre-eminently the poet of the blazoned shield. The influence of heraldry upon his verse is evident to the least observant—throughout, passages, some of exceeding brilliancy, occur with a frequency which renders this perception keenly susceptive. Of its significance none ever enjoyed an acuter perception, or of its occult grandeur a higher comprehension. His knowledge of the theme, as his poems evidence, was indeed recondite; its entire resources—origin, mission, tradition, and laws—were at command.—PEDRICK, J. GALE, 1898, *The Heraldic Aspect of Scott's Poetical Works, Gentleman's Magazine, vol.* 285, *p.* 470.

Scott restored the Tale in Verse to literature. That achievement had an effect which far out-weighed and out-lasted his special manner, the limitations of which soon became obvious. The hot volley of short ringing lines, however telling in a recital of stirring adventure, was wanting in several qualities which had distinguished other schools of narrative verse. It was diffuse, without the leisured urbanity of Ariosto; plain, without the simplicity and reserve of Homer; old-fashioned, without the charming *naïveté* of Chaucer. Scott led the way back to romance, but his keen antiquarian taste was too much dominated by the bald manner of the medieval romancers, greatly as he surpassed them in all the dynamic qualities of story-telling. He had read the "Orlando" with delight; but on the whole the later and more splendid developments of romantic tale, whether in Italy or in England, lay beyond the range of his artistic susceptibility. The entire world of Greek letters was unknown to him. Chaucer he had naturally read; but there are curiously few signs that he loved him. Scott's achievement was to tell a tale in the semi-lyric manner of a lay; Chaucer throughout his whole later career is occupied in effacing the characteristics of the lay from his narrative style.—HERFORD, C. H., 1902, *English Tales in Verse, Introduction, p.* li.

LAY OF THE LAST MINSTREL
1805

I have been very much delighted lately in reading Walter Scott's "Lay of the Last Minstrel." I hope you have some assistance from him, if he condescends to write songs. He has the true spirit of a poet in him, and long may he flourish.—BAILLIE, JOANNA, 1805, *Letter to George Thomson, Feb.* 18; *George Thomson the Friend of Burns, ed. Hadden, p.* 153.

I began last night to read Walter Scott's "Lay of the Last Minstrel," as part of my evening readings to my children. I was extremely delighted by the poetical beauty of some passages, the Abbey of Melrose for example, and most of the prologues to the Cantos. The costume, too, is admirable. The tone is antique; and it might be read for instruction as a picture of the manners of the middle ages. Many parts are, however, tedious; and no care has been employed to make the story interesting.—MACKINTOSH, SIR JAMES, 1805, *Letter to George Philips, Sept.* 25; *Memoirs of Mackintosh, ed., his Son, vol.* I, *p.* 254.

The author, enamoured of the lofty visions of chivalry, and partial to the strains in which they were formerly embodied, seems to have employed all the resources of his genius in endeavouring to recall them to the favour and admiration of the public; and in adapting to the taste of modern readers a species of poetry which was once the delight of the courtly, but has long ceased to gladden any other eyes than those of the scholar and the antiquary. This is a romance, therefore, composed by a minstrel of the present day; or such a romance as we may suppose would have been written in modern times, if that style of composition had continued to be cultivated, and partaken consequently of the improvements which every branch of literature has received since the time of its desertion.—JEFFREY, FRANCIS LORD, 1805-44, *Contributions to the Edinburgh Review, vol.* II, *p.* 460.

It would be great affectation not to own frankly, that the Author expected some success from "The Lay of the Last Minstrel." The attempt to return to a more simple and natural style of poetry was likely to be welcomed, at a time when the public had become tired of heroic hexameters, with all the buckram and binding which belong to them of later days. But whatever might have been his expectations, whether moderate or unreasonable, the result left them far behind, for among those who smiled on the adventurous Minstrel were numbered the great names of William Pitt and Charles Fox. Neither was the extent of the sale inferior to the character of the judges who received the poem with approbation. Upwards of thirty thousand copies of the Lay were disposed of by the trade; and the Author had to perform a task difficult to human vanity, when called upon to make the necessary deductions from his own merits, in a calm attempt to account for his popularity.—SCOTT, SIR WALTER, 1830, *The Lay of the Last Minstrel, Introduction.*

The truth is that the supernatural element, so far from being an excrescence, overhangs, encompasses, and interpenetrates the human element in the story. . . . We may, if we please, call this supernatural machinery grotesque, or childish, or ridiculous, but it is absurd to speak of it as an excrescence, or otherwise than thoroughly transfused with the human interest of the story. Only a born romancer, in full imaginative sympathy with such childish or childlike superstitions, could have effected so complete a transfusion.—MINTO, WILLIAM, 1886, *ed., The Lay of the Last Minstrel, Preface, pp.*19,21.

As regards the mere telling of a tale, Scott has no equal in English literature. His power of invention and expression was extraordinary. The interest of the story is carried on in remarkably well-sustained fashion, considering the length of the poem. Scott had no power of analysing character. His character-drawing is done in a dashing scene-painting manner, with bold, broad outlines, but no subtle delineation. This is extremely suitable to the style of poem and acts as a positive help to the course of the narrative. In none of his poems does the story move more vigorously onward than in his first —"The Lay of the Last Minstrel."—M'DONNELL, A. C., 1897, *XIX Century Poetry, p.* 36.

MARMION
1808

Next view in state, proud prancing on his roan,
The golden-crested haughty Marmion,
Now forging scrolls, now foremost in the fight,
Not quite a felon, yet but half a knight,
The gibbet or the field prepared to grace;
A mighty mixture of the great and base.
And think'st thou, Scott! by vain conceit perchance,
On public taste to foist thy stale romance,
Though Murray with his Miller may combine
To yield thy muse just half-a-crown per line?
No! when the sons of song descend to trade,
Their bays are sear, their former laurels fade.
Let such forego the poet's sacred name,
Who rack their brains for lucre, not for fame.
Still for stern Mammon may they toil in vain!
And sadly gaze on gold they cannot gain!
Such be their meed, such still the just reward
Of prostituted muse and hireling bard!
For this we spurn Apollo's venal son,
And bid a long "good night to Marmion."

—BYRON, LORD, 1809, *English Bards and Scotch Reviewers.*

His modes of life, his personal feelings, are no where so detailed as in the epistles prefixed to the cantos of "Marmion." These bring us close to his side, and leading us with him through the rural and romantic scenes he loved, talk with us by the way of all the rich associations of which he was master. His dogs are with him; he surveys these dumb friends with the eye of a sportsman and a philosopher, and omits nothing in the description of them which could interest either. An old castle frowns upon the road; he bids its story live before you with all the animation of a drama and the fidelity of a chronicle. Are topics of the day introduced? He states his opinions with firmness and composure, expresses his admiration with energy, and, where he dissents from those he addresses, does so with unaffected candor and cordial benignity. Good and great man!—OSSOLI, MARGARET FULLER, 1850? *Art, Literature and the Drama, p.* 74.

"Marmion" is the greatest of his poems,

while the "Lay" is the freshest. . . . —SMITH, GOLDWIN, 1880, *The English Poets, ed. Ward, vol.* IV, *p.* 190.

Judge Scott's poetry by whatever test you will—whether it be a test of that which is peculiar to it, its glow of national feeling, its martial ardour, its swift and rugged simplicity, or whether it be a test of that which is common to it with most other poetry, its attraction for all romantic excitements, its special feeling for the pomp and circumstance of war, its love of light and colour—and tested either way, "Marmion" will remain his finest poem.—HUTTON, RICHARD HOLT, 1879, *Sir Walter Scott (English Men of Letters), p.* 59.

Skilfully as the character of Marmion has been constructed, the reader cannot help feeling that it has been put together; hence we never quite breathe in the story, as we do in the "Iliad" or the "Odyssey," the ideal atmosphere which is produced by the perfection of metrical writing. Prose alone could secure the large and unfettered liberty that historical romance requires: when Scott employs his magic powers to clothe the spirit of the Past in the language of real life the verisimilitude of his creation is complete.—COURTHOPE, WILLIAM JOHN, 1885, *The Liberal Movement in English Literature, p.* 130.

The narrative is powerful, rapid, and absorbing. There is a good deal that is second rate, parts even that are quite common-place; but there are more passages and longer passages of high merit than are to be found anywhere else in Scott's poetry. The canto on Flodden has been called "the finest battle-piece since Homer," and probably deserves the praise. "There are few men," it has been said, "who have not at some time or other thought the worse of themselves that they are not soldiers;" and no one perhaps of all who have shared this feeling has read the last canto of "Marmion" without a quickened pulse and a heightened colour. The "hurried frankness" is here exactly suited to the subject, and it rises in dignity with the greatness of the theme. —WALKER, HUGH, 1893, *Three Centuries of Scottish Literature, vol.* II, *p.* 201.

LADY OF THE LAKE
1810

I see the "Lady of the Lake" advertised. Of course it is in his old ballad style, and pretty. After all, Scott is the best of them. The end of all scribblement is to amuse, and he certainly succeeds there.—BYRON, LORD, 1810, *Letter to Mr. Hodgson, Oct.* 3.

He says Walter Scott is going to publish a new poem; I do not augur well of the title, "The Lady of the Lake." I hope this lady will not disgrace him. . . . By great good fortune, and by the good-nature of Lady Charlotte Rawdon, we had "The Lady of the Lake" to read just when the O'Beirnes were with us. A most delightful reading we had; my father, the Bishop, and Mr. Jephson reading it aloud alternately. It is a charming poem: a most interesting story, generous, finely-drawn characters, and in many parts the finest poetry. But for an old prepossession—an unconquerable prepossession —in favour of the old minstrel, I think I should prefer this to either the "Lay" or "Marmion." Our pleasure in reading it was increased by the sympathy and enthusiasm of the guests.—EDGEWORTH, MARIA, 1810, *Letters, vol.* I, *pp.* 169, 173.

With regard to diction and imagery, it is quite obvious that Mr. Scott has not aimed at writing either in a very pure or a very consistent style. He seems to have been anxious only to strike, and to be easily and universally understood; and, for this purpose, to have culled the most glittering and conspicuous expressions of the most popular authors, and to have interwoven them in splendid confusion with his own nervous diction and irregular versification. Indifferent whether he coins or borrows, and drawing with equal freedom on his memory and his imagination, he goes boldly forward, in full reliance on a never-failing abundance; and dazzles, with his richness and variety, even those who are most apt to be offended with his glare and irregularity.—JEFFREY, FRANCIS LORD, 1810–44, *Contributions to the Edinburgh Review, vol.* II, *p.* 493.

The "Lady of the Lake" was the first revelation to the world of the lovely scenery and the poetry of clan life which lay enclasped and unknown to the cultivated world in the Highlands.—SMITH, GOLDWIN, 1880, *The English Poets, ed. Ward, vol.* IV, *p.* 190.

Walter Scott is out and away the king of the romantics. "The Lady of the Lake" has no indisputable claim to be a poem beyond the inherent fitness and desirability of the tale. It is just such a story as a man would make up for himself, walking, in the best health and temper, through just such scenes as it is laid in. Hence it is that a charm dwells undefinable among these slovenly verses, as the unseen cuckoo fills the mountains with his note; hence, even after we have flung the book aside, the scenery and adventures remain present to the mind, a new and green possession, not unworthy of that beautiful name, "The Lady of the Lake," or that direct, romantic opening,—one of the most spirited and poetical in literature,—"The stag at eve had drunk his fill."—STEVENSON, ROBERT LOUIS, 1881, *Memories and Portraits.*

NOVELS

My dear Murray,—I have this moment finished the reading of 192 pages of our book—for ours it must be—and I cannot go to bed without telling you what is the strong and most favourable impression it has made upon me. If the remainder be at all equal, which it cannot fail to be from the genius displayed in what is now before me, we have been most fortunate indeed. The title is "The Tales of my Landlord; collected and reported by Jedediah Cleishbotham, Parish Clerk and Schoolmaster of Gandercleugh." There cannot be a doubt as to the splendid merit of the work. It would never have done to have higgled and protested about seeing more volumes. I have now neither doubts nor fears, and I anxiously hope you will have as little. I am so happy at the fortunate termination of all my pains and anxieties, that I cannot be in bad humour with you for not writing me two lines in answer to my two last letters.—BLACKWOOD, WILLIAM, 1816, *Letter to Murray, Aug.* 23; *William Blackwood and His Sons, vol.* I, *p.* 68.

The last series of those half novels, half romance things, called "Tales of My Landlord," are dying off apace; but if their author gets money, he will not care about the rest; having never owned his work, no celebrity can be lost, nor no venture can injure him.—PIOZZI, HESTER LYNCH, 1819, *Letter to Sir James Fellowes, March* 28; *Literary Remains, ed. Hayward, p.* 436.

The general name of these works, "the Scotch Novels," will always indicate an era in our literary history, for they add a new species to the catalogue of our native literary productions, and nothing of the same nature has been produced anywhere else. They are as valuable as history and descriptive travels for the qualities which render these valuable; while they derive a bewitching animation from the soul of poetry, and captivate the attention by the interest of romantic story. As pictures of national manners they are inestimable; as views of human nature, influenced by local circumstances, they are extremely curious; as enthusiastic appeals to the passions and the imagination, they supply a strong stimulus to these faculties; and by running the course of the story through the most touching incidents, and within sight of the grandest events, they carry the reader's sympathy perpetually with them.—SCOTT, JOHN, 1820, *London Magazine, Jan.*

Scott is certainly the most wonderful writer of the day. His novels are a new literature in themselves, and his poetry as good as any—if not better (only on an erroneous system)—and only ceased to be so popular, because the vulgar learned were tired of hearing "Aristides called the Just," and Scott the Best, and ostracised him. I like him, too, for his manliness of character, for the extreme pleasantness of his conversation, and his good nature towards myself, personally. May he prosper!—for he deserves it. I know no reading to which I fall with such alacrity as a work of W. Scott's.—BYRON, LORD, 1821, *A Journal in Italy, Jan.* 12.

It is no wonder that the public repay with lengthened applause and gratitude the pleasure they receive. He writes as fast as they can read, and he does not write himself down. He is always in the public eye, and we do not tire of him. His worst is better than any other person's best. His *back-grounds* (and his later works are little else but back-grounds capitally made out)—are more attractive than the principal figures and most complicated actions of other writers. His works (taken together) are almost like a new edition of human nature. This is indeed to be an author!—HAZLITT, WILLIAM, 1825, *The Spirit of the Age.*

We should only read what we admire, as I did in my youth, and as I now experience with Sir Walter Scott. I have just begun "Rob Roy," and will read his best novels in succession. All is great—material, import, characters, execution; and then what infinite diligence in the preparatory studies! what truth of detail in the execution! We see, too, what English history is; and what a thing it is when such an inheritance falls to the lot of a clever poet.—GOETHE, JOHANN WOLFGANG, 1831, *Conversations, ed. Eckermann, vol.* II, *p.* 364.

Scott's greatest glory, however, arises from the superior dignity to which he has raised the novel, not by its historic but its moral character, so that, instead of being obliged, as with Fielding's and Smollett's, to devour it, like Sancho Panza's cheese-cakes, in a corner as it were, it is now made to furnish a pure and delectable repast for all the members of the assembled family. In all his multifarious fictions, we remember no line, which in a moral point of view he might wish to blot. Fortunate man, who, possessed of power sufficient to affect the moral destinies of his age, has possessed also the inclination to give that power a uniformly beneficent direction! Who beside him, amid the brilliant display of genius, or the wildest frolics of wit and fancy, has never been led to compromise for a moment the interests of virtue?—PRESCOTT, WILLIAM HICKLING, 1832, *English Literature of the Nineteenth Century, North American Review, vol.* 35, *p.* 188.

When I am very ill indeed, I can read Scott's novels, and they are almost the only books I can then *read*. I cannot at such times read the Bible; my mind reflects on it, but I can't bear the open page. —COLERIDGE, SAMUEL TAYLOR, 1833, *Table-Talk, ed. Ashe, Nov.* 1, *p.* 267.

If literature had no task but that of harmlessly amusing indolent, languid men, here was the very perfection of literature; that a man, here more emphatically than ever elsewhere, might fling himself back, exclaiming, "Be mine to lie on this sofa, and read everlasting Novels of Walter Scott!" The composition, slight as it often is, usually hangs together in some measure, and *is* a composition. . . . The sick heart will find no healing here, the darkly struggling heart no guidance: the Heroic that is in all men no divine awakening voice. We say, therefore, that they do not found themselves on deep interests, but on comparatively trivial ones, not on the perennial, perhaps not even on the lasting. In fact, much of the interest of these novels results from what may be called contrasts of costume. The phraseology, fashion of arms, of dress and life, belonging to one age, is brought suddenly, with singular vividness, before the eyes of another. A great effect this; yet by the very nature of it, an altogether temporary one. Consider, brethern, shall not we too one day be antiques, and grow to have as quaint a costume as the rest?—CARLYLE, THOMAS, 1838, *Memoirs of the Life of Scott, London and Westminster Review, vol.* 28, *pp.* 334, 336.

We esteem the productions which the great novelist of Scotland has poured forth with startling speed from his rich treasury, not only as multiplying the sources of delight to thousands, but as shedding the most genial influences on the taste and feeling of the people.—TALFOURD, THOMAS NOON, 1842, *Critical and Miscellaneous Writings, p.* 24.

When I first arrived in Copenhagen, often walking about poor and forlorn, without sufficient money for a meal, I have spent the few pence I possessed to obtain from a library one of Walter Scott's novels, and, reading it, forgot hunger and cold, and felt myself rich and happy.—ANDERSEN, HANS CHRISTIAN, 1846, *Correspondence, p.* 204.

Two of Moore's contemporaries must be placed above him in any fair estimate of the authors of the first part of the nineteenth century. Byron rose as a poet above all his rivals. . . . Scott is the other wonder of this age. Picturesque, interesting, and bard-like as are his narrative poems, the pathos, humour, description, character, and, above all, the marvellous fertility, displayed in the novels, show far greater power: a whole region of the territory of Imagination is occupied by this extraordinary man, alone and unapproachable. . . . The novels of Scott will furnish entertainment to many generations; nor is there likely to be any race of men so fastidious as to require anything purer, so spoilt by excitement as to need anything more amusing, or so grave as to scorn all delight from this kind of composition.—RUSSELL, JOHN LORD, *ed.*, 1853, *Memoirs of Thomas Moore, Preface, vol.* I, *pp.* xxvi, xxvii.

On the whole, and speaking roughly,

these defects in the delineation which Scott has given us of human life are but two. He omits to give us a delineation of the soul: we have mind, manners, animation, but it is the stir of this world. We miss the consecrating power; and we miss it not only in its own peculiar sphere, —which, from the difficulty of introducing the deepest elements into a novel, would have been scarcely matter for a harsh criticism,—but in the place in which a novelist might most be expected to delineate it. There are perhaps such things as the love affairs of immortal beings, but no one would learn it from Scott. His heroes and heroines are well dressed for this world, but not for another; there is nothing even in their love which is suitable for immortality. As has been noticed, Scott also omits any delineation of the abstract side of unworldly intellect. This too might not have been so severe a reproach, considering its undramatic, unanimated nature, if it had stood alone; but taken in connection with the omission which we have just spoken of, it is most important. As the union of sense and romance makes the world of Scott so characteristically agreeable — a fascinating picture of this world in the light in which we like best to dwell on it; so the deficiency in the attenuated, striving intellect, as well as in the supernatural soul, gives to the "world" of Scott the cumbrousness and temporality—in short, the materialism which is characteristic of the world.—BAGEHOT, WALTER, 1858, *The Waverley Novels, Works, ed. Morgan, vol.* II, *p.* 235.

Scott's veneration for the past reached its highest and most shrewd and intelligent form in his Scotticism. It is a coincidence with more than the usual amount of verbal good luck in it that his name should have been Scott—generically and comprehensively *the* Scotchman. . . . Scott is greatest in his Scotticism. It is as a painter of Scottish nature and Scottish life, an interpreter of Scottish beliefs and Scottish feelings, a narrator of Scottish history, that he attains to the height of his genius. He has Scotticized European literature. He has interested the world in the little land. It had been heard of before; it had given the world some reason to be interested in it before; with, at no time, more than a million and a half of souls in it, it had spoken and acted with some emphasis in relation to the bigger nations around it. But, since Scott, the Thistle, till then a wayside weed, has had a great promotion in universal botany, and blooms, less prickly than of yore, but the identical Thistle still, in all the gardens of the world. All round the globe the little land is famous; tourists flock to it to admire its scenery, while they shoot its game; and afar off, when the kilted regiment do British work, and the pibroch shrills them to the work they do, and men, marking what they do, ask whence they come, the answer is "From the land of Scott."—MASSON, DAVID, 1859, *British Novelists and Their Styles, pp.* 169, 204.

It had become a trite remark, long before there was the reason for it that now exists, that the Waverley Novels are, even from their mere popularity, the most striking phenomenon of the age. And that popularity, unequalled as it is in extent, is perhaps more extraordinary in its permanence. It has resisted the tendency of the public, and perhaps of ourselves, much as we struggle against it, to think every subsequent work of the same author inferior to its predecessor, if it be not manifestly superior. It has resisted the satiety which might have been predicted as the necessary consequence of the frequent repetition of similar characters and situations. Above all, it has withstood *pessimum genus inimicorum laudantes.*—SENIOR, WILLIAM NASSAU, 1864, *Essays on Fiction.*

Indeed, what one novelist has been perfect in dialogue, making each person say just what he should and nothing else, but glorious Sir Walter?—DEWEY, ORVILLE, 1867, *Autobiography and Letters, p.* 298.

Scott's canvas is more thickly and variously crowded; it is inexpressibly admirable both in quantity and in quality; but in our opinion it does not betoken a genius either so wide-embracing or so deep-piercing as that of the old poet* whom the author of "Waverley" himself studied with such enthusiastic delight.—HALES, JOHN W., 1873, *Notes and Essays on Shakespeare, p.* 72.

His ease and great general power impressed me very strongly lately, when re-reading his Romances. In his unaffectedness and the apparent unconsciousness of

*Chaucer.

strength he is unequalled. There are no more spasmodic efforts in him than in Fielding. In particular subjects, and on some points, he is perhaps excelled by other writers. Thus Mrs. Inchbald is more pathetic; Miss Austen deals more effectively with ordinary domestic matters; and the narrative of Alexander Dumas carries one on more buoyantly than that of Scott. The picture of Louis XI in Notre Dame is surely superior to the portrait of the same king in "Quentin Durward," and Victor Hugo has originally more pathos and sometimes more force than Sir Walter. But I see in no other author such a combination of truth and ease and dramatic power.—PROCTER, BRYAN WALLER, 1874? *Recollections of Men of Letters*, p. 154.

My boyhood was at a period when a branch of literature, till then underrated, and indeed little worth, suddenly assumed new character and proportions. One by one, the marvellous productions of the prince of novelists startled and charmed the British public. "Guy Mannering," "The Antiquary," "Rob Roy," "Ivanhoe," and all the rest,—what sunny memories, what hours of rapt enjoyment, do the very titles still call up!—OWEN, ROBERT DALE, 1874, *Threading My Way*, p. 120.

The great merit of Walter Scott's novels is their generous and pure sentiment. There is a strain of generosity, manliness, truth, which runs through them all. They nowhere take for granted meanness; they always take for granted justice and honor.—CLARKE, JAMES FREEMAN, 1880, *Self-Culture*, p. 316.

We have all known from our childhood as among the most hale and strengthening waters in which the young soul ever bathed. They discuss no moral problems, they place us in no relation towards our fellow that can be called moral at all, they belong to that part of us which is youthful, undebating, wholly unmoral—though not immoral,—they are simply always young, always healthy, always miraculous. —LANIER, SIDNEY, 1881–83, *The English Novel*, p. 193.

People who died prior to the 7th of July, 1814, were unfortunate in one respect, if no other; for on that day was published the first of the "Waverley" romances. A world without Scott's novels in it must have been rather a lean place to live in, surely; and we can never quite estimate the dullness and vacuity of a globe which existed before that immortal story-teller was born into it. . . . Walter Scott is indeed a literature in himself. His genius throws a lustre on the art of story-telling, and renders fiction a boon to the human race. His imagination had a range of eight centuries to unfold itself in, and he roamed through them with a masterful power and beauty. No *good* reader ever outgrows Sir Walter. Once take him in your heart, and there is no parting company with him after that.—FIELDS, JAMES T., 1885, *Sir Walter Scott; Some Noted Princes, Authors, and Statesmen of our Time, ed. Parton, pp.* 222, 224.

The greatest of all novelists if quality, quantity, and originality are taken together. — SAINTSBURY, GEORGE, 1886, *Specimens of English Prose Style, p.* 281.

I began to read Scott at about eleven, and I suppose that I have not read any of the Waverley novels since I was sixteen, but I seem to remember them all. That is a grand test of a really good book: that you should remember it.—BESANT, WALTER, 1887, *Books Which Have Influenced Me, p.* 21.

As for novels, I read all of Scott's, the earlier in my early boyhood, the later as they appeared; and I have read them all twice over, some of them three or four times. They seem to me now as transcendent in their character-painting, in their dramatic power, and in the lifelikeness of their narrative, as when they were alone and unapproached.—PEABODY, A. P., 1888, *Books That Have Helped Me, p.* 44.

Never was there a more healthful and health-ministering literature than that which he gave to the world. To go back to it from Flaubert and Daudet and Tolstoï is like listening to the song of the lark after the shrieking passion of the midnight pianoforte;—nay, it is like coming out of the glare and heat and reeking vapor of a palace ball into a grove in the first light and music and breezes of the morning. It is not for nothing that so many thousands have felt toward Scott a deep personal gratitude, which few, if any other writers of English fiction have ever awakened. My own case is doubtless typical of thousands. In his novels I first came under the spell of genius in fiction, and in my reading of them the first happened to be what is usually called the least inspired—"The Monastery." But no matter, I gave it three readings, end over end, and followed it with other novels from the same source as rapidly as my dear family Puritan authorities would permit, or as often as they could be evaded.—WHITE, ANDREW D., 1889, *Walter Scott at Work, Scribner's Magazine, vol.* 5, *p.* 132.

One great charm of the Waverley Novels is the sound, healthy tone in them all. Scott regards mankind through his kindly, genial disposition. He never sneers, and there is neither mawkishness nor morbidness to be found in them. If they were not written with any exalted motive to reform society or make the world better, they have certainly given a world of pleasure to thousands of his fellowmen, and that is no small thing.—ADAM, MRS. M. L., 1891-94, *Sir Walter Scott, p.* 34.

In the beginning of any art even the most gifted worker must be crude in his methods, and we ought to keep this fact always in mind when we turn, say, from the purblind worshippers of Scott to Scott himself, and recognize that he often wrote a style cumbrous and diffuse; that he was tediously analytical where the modern novelist is dramatic, and evolved his characters by means of long-winded explanation and commentary; that, except in the case of his lower-class personages, he made them talk as seldom man and never woman talked; that he was tiresomely descriptive; that on the simplest occasions he went about half a mile to express a thought that could be uttered in ten paces across lots; and that he trusted his readers' intuitions so little that he was apt to rub in his appeals to them. He was probably right; the generation which he wrote for was duller than this; slower-witted, æsthetically untrained, and in maturity not so apprehensive of an artistic intention as the children of to-day. All this is not saying Scott was not a great man; he was a great man, and a very great novelist as compared with the novelists who went before him. He can still amuse young people, but they ought to be instructed how false and how mistaken he often is, with his mediæval ideals, his blind Jacobitism, his intense devotion to aristocracy and royalty; his acquiescence in the division of men into noble and ignoble, patrician and plebeian, sovereign and subject, as if it were the law of God; for all which, indeed, he is not to blame as he would be if he were one of our contemporaries.—HOWELLS, WILLIAM DEAN, 1891, *Criticism and Fiction, p.* 21.

Sound-hearted and true-souled Sir Walter speaks a language informed with robust health and fragrant of moral purity and sanity. We feel without going into biography that he has never deserted a wife or his children, or tried to upset the laws of marriage. He seems large, strong, safe, steadfast; and we like to have him near us. An influence like his never leaves a morbid heat in the nerve-centers, never suggests that hell has some advantages over Heaven as a high-toned summer resort. After reading "Ivanhoe" you may indulge some romantic desire for a spear, a shield, an armored horse, and plenty of muscle; but you breathe good air and feel clean.—THOMPSON, MAURICE, 1893, *The Ethics of Literary Art, p.* 76.

The steady demand for "Ivanhoe" and others of Scott's novels proves their undying charm, and it appears to be a fact that the number of those who read Scott is increasing, while the number of the readers of Dickens is diminishing.—TILLINGHAST, C. B., 1893, *Books and Readers in Public Libraries, The Forum, vol.* 16, *p.* 62.

It is late in the day, and it is no part of the purpose of this history, which reaches its goal with the publication of "Waverley," to criticise Sir Walter. Let him be praised in words taken from Carlyle's unworthy essay, wherein the name of "greatness" is refused to him because he had no express message to deliver. "Be this as it may, surely since Shakespeare's time there has been no great speaker so unconscious of an aim in speaking as Walter Scott." He saw life, and told the world what he saw. Has any writer since his time supplied it with a fuller, fairer vision? From Ivanhoe to Edie Ochiltree, from Lucy Ashton to Jeanie Deans, from the knightly achievements of the crusades to the humours of the Scottish peasantry,—this is the panorama he reveals, and he casts over it the light of his generous, gentle, and delicate nature. His very style, loose and rambling as it is, is a part of the man, and of the artistic effect he produces. The full vigour and ease with which his imagination plays on life is often suggested by his pleonasms and tautologies; the search for the single final epithet is no part of his method, for he delights in the telling, and is sorry when all is told.—RALEIGH, WALTER, 1894, *The English Novel*, p. 282.

There is much clatter of arms in his stories, much hurrying from palace to heath, from heath to dungeon; but through it all reigns the same fixed calm of characters immutable in weakness or in strength.—SCUDDER, VIDA D., 1895, *The Life of the Spirit in the Modern English Poets*, p. 24.

There are people who still read "Ivanhoe" and "The Talisman," and profess to admire them, but such persons mostly belong to the fogey species. . . . Scott is superficial. His books may suit the careless reader "lying all day long on a sofa," but they neither thrill the reader nor teach him anything new about life. They exhibit absolutely no psychological insight. They are nearly all clumsily written in a diffuse and disjointed style. Those which depend for success on their delineation of historical or quasi-historical events, are, for the most part, nothing better than "mediæval upholstery." We may, therefore, fairly assume that we are anticipating the verdict of posterity in declaring that of the once-famous Waverley Novels only some three or four will be read at all in the twentieth century.—HANNIGAN, D. F., 1895, *The Waverley Novels—after Sixty Years, The Westminster Review*, vol. 144, pp. 17, 21.

Who will pretend that Walter Scott, splendid *raconteur* though he was, represented with even a remote degree of correctness the life of the Middle Ages?—BOYESEN, H. H., 1895, *The Great Realists and the Empty Story-Tellers, The Forum*, vol. 18, p. 730.

The perennial charm of the Waverley Novels resides very largely in their healthfulness. They take us entirely out of ourselves, and absorb us in the world of incident and action. If they are not always great as works of art, they are always great in that health of mind and soul which is elemental in all true living. Men cannot be too grateful for a mass of writing so genuine in tone, so free from morbid tendencies, so true to the fundamental ethics of living. — MABIE, HAMILTON WRIGHT, 1896, *My Study Fire, Second Series*, p. 115.

The stories of Scott most likely to survive the centenary of their publication and to retain readers in the first quarter of the twentieth century are perhaps those in which he best withstands the comparison with Miss Edgeworth,—the stories in which he has recorded types of Scottish character, with its mingled humor and pathos. For mere excitement our liking is eternal: but the fashion thereof is fickle; and we prefer our romantic adventures cut this way to-day and another way to-morrow. Our interest in our fellow-man subsists unchanged forever; and we take a perennial delight in the revelation of the subtleties of human nature. It is in the "Antiquary" and in the "Heart of Midlothian" that Scott is seen at his best; and it is by creating characters like *Caleb Balderstone* and *Dugald Dalgetty* and *Wandering Willie* that he has deserved to endure.— MATTHEWS, BRANDER, 1897, *The Historical Novel, The Forum*, vol. 24, p. 83.

We may challenge the literatures of the world to produce a purer talent, or a writer who has with a more brilliant and sustained vivacity combined the novel with the romance, the tale of manners with the tale of wonder. . . . All the romances of Alexander Dumas and Victor Hugo sprang directly from him; he had inspired Fouqué in Germany, Manzoni in Italy, and Fernan Caballero in Spain. Wherever historical fiction of a picturesque and chivalrous order was produced, it bore the stamp of Walter Scott upon its margin. Nor with the decline of the imitations is it found that the original ceases to retain its hold on the interest of the English race. Walter Scott, so long a European force, has now, foiled by the victory of the school of Balzac, retired once more to the home he came from, but on British soil there is as yet no sign of any diminution of his honour or popularity. Continental criticism is bewildered at our unshaken loyalty to a writer whose art can be easily demonstrated to be obsolete in many of its characteristics. But English readers confess the perennial attractiveness of a writer whose "tone" is the most perfect in our national literature, who has left not a phrase which is morbid or petulant or base, who is the very type of that generous freedom of spirit which we are pleased to identify with the character of an English gentleman. Into the persistent admiration of Sir Walter Scott there enters something of the militant imperialism of our race.—GOSSE, EDMUND, 1897, *A Short History of Modern English Literature, pp.* 300, 302.

Though Scott founded the historical novel, enunciated its most successful theory, and is, perhaps, still the greatest historical novelist, he is not the best exponent of his own theory. Attractive as is the theory of the romantic magnetization of history, overhanging it always is the shadow of the anger of the great god Verity. Scott was almost too ingrainedly honest for his theory. There are evidences of struggle when the Scotch lawyer becomes the romantic idealist in these historical novels. In truth, the novels never really desert fact; sometimes the story almost painfully and regretfully seems to cling to fact.—STODDARD, FRANCIS HOVEY, 1900, *The Evolution of the English Novel, p.* 104.

The literary form under which Scott made the deepest impression upon the consciousness of his own generation and influenced most permanently the future literature of Europe, was prose fiction. As the creator of the historical novel and the ancestor of Kingsley, Ainsworth, Bulwer, and G. P. R. James; of Manzoni, Freytag, Hugo, Mérimée, Dumas, Alexis Tolstoi, and a host of others, at home and abroad, his example is potent yet. English fiction is directly or indirectly in his debt for "Romola," "Hypatia," "Henry Esmond," and "The Cloister and the Hearth." In several countries the historical novel had been trying for centuries to get itself born, but all its attempts had been abortive. "Waverley" is not only vastly superior to "Thaddeus of Warsaw" (1803) and "The Scottish Chiefs" (1809); it is something quite different in kind.—BEERS, HENRY A., 1901, *A History of English Romanticism in the Nineteenth Century, p.* 30.

Meanwhile, whether the novels are read or not, the novels continue to sell in endless editions. People who cannot read Shakespeare buy Shakespeare, and probably many persons who, very properly, buy Scott, cannot read him. I wish them the best of wishes,—may they have sons and daughters who can!—LANG, ANDREW, 1901, *New Work on Scott, The Critic, vol.* 38, *p.* 340.

WAVERLEY
1814

Walter Scott has no business to write novels, especially good ones. It is not fair. He has fame and profit enough as a poet, and should not be taking the bread out of the mouths of other people. I do not like him, and do not mean to like "Waverley" if I can help it, but fear I must.—AUSTEN, JANE, 1814, *Letters, vol.* II, *p.*317.

I think very highly of "Waverley," and was inclined to suspect, in reading it, that it was written by Miss Scott, of Ancram.—SMITH, SYDNEY, 1814, *To Francis Jeffrey; Letters, ed. Mrs. Austin.*

Have you read Walter Scott's "Waverley?" I have ventured to say "Walter Scott's;" though I hear he denies it, just as a young girl denies the imputation of a lover: but, if there be any belief in internal evidence, it must be his. It is his by a thousand indications,—by all the faults and all the beauties; by the unspeakable and unrecollectable names; by the vile pedantry of French, Latin, Gaelic, and Italian; by the hanging the clever hero, and marrying the stupid one; by the praise (well deserved certainly,—for when has Scotland ever such a friend?—but thrust in by his head and shoulders) of the late Lord Melville; by the sweet lyric poetry; by the perfect costume; by the excellent keeping of the picture; by the liveliness and gayety of the dialogues; and last, not least, by the entire and admirable individuality of every character in the book, high as well as low,—the life and soul which animates them all with a distinct existence, and brings them before our eyes like the portraits of Fielding and Cervantes.—MITFORD, MARY RUSSELL, 1814, *Letter to Sir William Elford, Oct.* 31.

We have this moment finished "Waverley." It was read aloud to this large family, and I wish the author could have witnessed the impression it made—the strong hold it seized of the feelings both of young and old—the admiration raised by the beautiful descriptions of nature—by the new and bold delineations of character—the perfect manner in which character is ever sustained in every change of situation from first to last, without effort, without the affectation of making the persons speak in character—the ingenuity with which each person introduced in the drama is made useful and necessary to the end—the admirable art with which the story is constructed and with which the author keeps his own secrets till the proper moment when they should be revealed, whilst in the meantime, with the skill of Shakspear, the mind is prepared by unseen degrees for all the changes of feeling and fortune, so that nothing, however extraordinary, shocks us as improbable: and the interest is kept up to the last moment. We were so possessed with the belief that the whole story and every character in it was real, that we could not endure the occasional addresses from the author to the reader. They are like Fielding: but for that reason we cannot bear them, we cannot bear that an author of such high powers, of such original genius, should for a moment stoop to imitation. This is the only thing we dislike, these are the only passages we wish omitted in the whole work: and let the unqualified manner in which I say this, and the very vehemence of my expression of this disapprobation, be a sure pledge to the author of the sincerity of all the admiration I feel for his genius.—EDGEWORTH, MARIA, 1814, *To James Ballantyne, Oct.* 23; *Letters, vol.* I, *p.* 226.

In my opinion it is the best novel that has been published these thirty years. The characters of Ebenezer Cruickshanks, mine host of the Garter, the Reverend Mr. Goukthrapple and Squire Bradwardine display a Cervantic vein of humour which has seldom been surpassed —whilst the descriptions of the gloomy caverns of the Highlands, and the delineations of the apathic Callum Beg and enterprising Vich Ian Vohr, show a richness of Scottean colouring which few have equalled.—CARLYLE, THOMAS, 1814, *Early Letters, ed. Norton, p.* 10.

When you have finished the "Fair Maid of Perth," you must at once read "Waverley," which is indeed from quite a different point of view, but which may, without hesitation, be set beside the best works that have ever been written in this world. We see that it is the same man who wrote the "Fair Maid of Perth," but that he has yet to gain the favour of the public, and therefore collects his forces so that he may not give a touch that is short of excellence. The "Fair Maid of Perth," on the other hand, is from a freer pen; the author is now sure of his public, and he proceeds more at liberty. After reading "Waverley," you will understand why Walter Scott still designates himself the author of that work; for there he showed what he could do, and he has never since written anything to surpass, or even equal, that first published novel.—GOETHE, JOHANN WOLFGANG, 1828, *Conversations, ed. Eckermann, vol.* II, *p.* 83.

"Waverley" took two or three months to win public favour, and then a perfect *furore* set in. Sloop-load after sloop-load was sent off to the London market, and on the rumoured loss of one of these vessels, half London was in despair. The interest, too, excited by public curiosity as to the author's name, was carefully fostered, and in a short time 12,000 copies were disposed of.—CURWEN, HENRY, 1873, *A History of Booksellers, p.* 127.

The sudden burst into light and publicity of a gift which had been growing through all the changes of private life, of the wonderful stream of knowledge, recollection, divination, boundless acquaintance with and affection for human nature, which had gladdened the Edinburgh streets, the Musselburgh sands, the Southland moors and river-sides, since ever Walter Scott had begun to roam among them, with his cheerful band of friends, his good stories, his kind and gentle thoughts—was received by the world with a burst of delighted recognition to which we know no parallel. We do not know, alas! what happened when the audience in the Globe Theatre made a similar discovery. Perhaps the greater gift, by its very splendour, would be less easily perceived in the dazzling of a glory hitherto unknown, and obscured it may be by jealousies of actors and their inaptitude to do justice to the wonderful poetry put into their hands. But of that we know nothing. We know, however, that there were no two opinions about "Waverley." It took the world by storm, which had had no such new sensation and no such delightful amusement for many a day. It was not only the beginning of a new and wonderful school in romance, a fresh chapter in literature, but the revelation of a region and a race unknown.—OLIPHANT, MARGARET O. W., 1890, *Royal Edinburgh, p.* 506.

GUY MANNERING
1815

We are satisfied that the time is not far distant, if it be not already arrived, when the best claim of "Guy Mannering" on the attention of its readers will be the line of the title-page, in which it is described as the work of the author of "Waverley."—GIFFORD, WILLIAM, 1816, *The Antiquary, Quarterly Review, vol.* 15, *p.* 125.

Dandie Dinmont is, beyond all question, we think, the best rustic portrait that has ever yet been exhibited to the public—the most honourable to rustics, and the most creditable to the heart, as well as the genius of the artist—the truest to nature—the most interesting and the most complete in all its lineaments.—Meg Merrilees belongs more to the department of poetry. She is most akin to the witches of Macbeth, with some traits of the antient Sybil engrafted on the coarser stock of a Gipsy of the last century. Though not absolutely in nature, however, she must be allowed to be a very imposing and emphatic personage; and to be mingled, both with the business and the scenery of the piece, with the greatest possible skill and effect.—Pleydell is a harsh caricature; and Dirk Hatteric a vulgar bandit of the German school. The lovers, too, are rather more faultless and more insipid than usual,—and all the genteel persons, indeed, not a little fatiguing. Yet there are many passages of great merit, of a gentler and less obtrusive character.—JEFFREY, FRANCIS LORD, 1817–44, *Tales of My Landlord, Contributions to the Edinburgh Review, vol.* III, *p.* 446.

There is a wide difference of opinion with regard to the relative rank of Scott's novels. Mr. Lowell once said that "The Bride of Lammermoor" was to him the most beautiful story in the language. Mr. Lang puts "Old Mortality" and "Quentin Durward" at the top of the list. But from any point of view, the popular instinct was not far astray in fastening upon "Ivanhoe" as, on the whole, the most widely acceptable of these great stories. "Kenilworth" is not far behind, but "Guy Mannering" falls below the middle of the list for the very good reason that while the first two have clear movement and cumulative dramatic interest, the latter is very defective as a story. The hero is a secondary personage.—MABIE, HAMILTON W., 1893, *The Most Popular Novels in America, The Forum, vol.* 16, *p.* 512.

THE ANTIQUARY
1816

It unites to a considerable degree the merits of "Waverley" with the faults of the "Astrologer;" and we have no hesitation in placing it, with the crowd of modern novels, below the former, and, with very few modern novels, above the latter.—GIFFORD, WILLIAM, 1816, *The Antiquary, Quarterly Review, vol.* 15, *p.* 125.

"The Antiquary" did not immediately rise into popularity (comparatively speaking), but, if we mistake not, it will stand the test of investigation with less danger from the captiousness of criticism, than almost any of its brethren.—ALLAN, GEORGE, 1835, *Life of Sir Walter Scott, p.* 304.

Perhaps of all his works, the one in which there is most of the current matter of his own mind.—CHAMBERS, ROBERT, 1835–71, *Life of Sir Walter Scott, p.* 56.

One of his most artistic works.—DENNIS, JOHN, 1890, *A Talk about Sir Walter Scott, Good Words, vol.* 31, *p.* 817.

As a novel of character, "The Antiquary" is the most remarkable of Scott's productions. Nowhere is he a more faithful observer of the turns which differing personalities take, nowhere does he give a more living picture of human beings, and this he does without aid from incident. Given the story of "Old Mortality," there are many novelists who could have written not "Old Mortality" indeed, but a good novel. A bad one, with the story of "The Antiquary," almost any novelist but Scott would have written. . . . To read the book is not certainly to have the imagination greatly quickened, but to read it—to read of Edie, of Oldbuck and his household—is to see the plain everyday world as we should not otherwise see it, till circumstances and trouble had enlarged and softened our vision.—JACK, ADOLPHUS ALFRED, 1897, *Essays on the Novel, pp.* 92, 106.

OLD MORTALITY
1816

Murray told me that Sir Walter Scott, on being taxed by him as the author of "Old Mortality," not only denied having written it, but added, "In order to convince you that I am not the author, I will review the book for you in the *Quarterly*,"—which he actually did, and Murray still has the MS. in his handwriting.—BARHAM, RICHARD HARRIS, 1833, *Life and Letters, vol.* I, *p.* 214.

Our evening's reading now is "Old Mortality." When I read that romance on its appearance, about thirty years ago, I thought it, and as it has lived in my memory I have ever since considered it, the grandest and best of all that admirable novelist's works. My recurrence to it confirms the impression it then made on me. —MACREADY, W. C., 1855, *Letter to Mrs. Pollock, March* 26; *Reminiscences, ed. Pollock, p.* 705.

When Lord Holland, whose judgment in literary matters had great weight among a certain section of the British aristocracy, was asked his opinion of the new Scotch novel, he answered, "Opinion! we did not one of us go to bed last night: nothing slept but my gout."—MACKENZIE, ROBERT SHELTON, 1871, *Sir Walter Scott: The Story of His Life, p.* 251.

Scott is the most chivalrous literary figure of this century, and the author with the widest range since Shakespeare. I think "Old Mortality" is his greatest novel.—TENNYSON, ALFRED LORD, 1890, *Comments on Various Novels, Memoir by his Son, vol.* II, *p.* 372.

Ranking foremost among the Waverley novels for variety of character sketches, stirring incidents, and infinite humour, affords also an accurate picture of the disorders and abuses under which the Scottish people suffered during the reign of the last Stuarts. . . . Lord Evandale is probably the favourite with all young readers. There is an ardour and dashing gallantry about him which, combined with his unhappy fate, renders him peculiarly attractive, while Morton's restrained and serious nature wins on us more slowly, and it is not until the close of the story that we fully realise his historic qualities.—YOUNG, GERTRUDE JULIAN, 1893, *Great Characters of Fiction, ed. Townsend, pp.* 59, 60.

Had I to choose my private favourite, it would be "Old Mortality."—LANG, ANDREW, 1897, *Library of the World's Best Literature, ed. Warner, vol.* XXII, *p.* 13002.

The novel which goes by the title of "Old Mortality" may or may not be Scott's masterpiece, but on the whole it is perhaps the one, which, if a plebiscite of literary opinion were taken, would obtain the largest following.—JACK, ADOLPHUS ALFRED, 1897, *Essays on the Novel, p.* 117.

ROB ROY
1818

This is not so good, perhaps, as some others of the family;—but it is better than any thing else; and has a charm and a spirit about it that draws us irresistibly away from our graver works of politics and science, to expatiate upon that which every body understands and agrees in; and after setting us diligently to read over again what we had scarce finished reading, leaves us no choice but to tell our readers what they all know already, and to persuade them of that of which they are most intimately convinced.—JEFFREY, FRANCIS LORD, 1818–44, *Rob Roy, Contributions to the Edinburgh Review, vol.* III, *p.* 460.

The author seems to be at home everywhere, and know every thing. His knowledge, however, has not the air of learning, amassed to be told; it is something gathered incidentally, whilst he was studying men in their pursuits, customs and amusements,—something fallen in with rather than sought. The commonest things, the lowest characters belong to the action,—it rarely stands still for the sake of description. You are in the midst of life, gaining knowledge as well as entertainment, by a process akin to actual experience and observation. Every man is in his proper situation, and suitable discourse is put into his mouth,—we have the peculiarities of his gait, the expression of his face, the tone of his voice, everything, in short, which is significant of character, or that adds to its reality;—and these are not given once for all in a formal description, but they come out in connexion with his feelings, situation or employment, and vary with them. He is allowed to unfold himself, to practise upon others, to utter fine thoughts or foolish ones, and betray all his infirmities and motives and every influence that presses on him, without the dread that he is destined for a book and therefore upon his good behaviour.—CHANNING, E. T., 1818, *Rob Roy, North American Review, vol.* 7, *p.* 150.

I acted to-night with spirit and in a

manly tone, better, perhaps, than ordinarily in the part "Rob Roy."—MACREADY, W. C., 1833, *Diary, Jan.* 22; *Reminiscences, ed. Pollock, p.* 266.

There is a peculiar fascination investing this story and its characters, and scenery that can be associated with them. Indeed, few of Scott's works have more readers, or so abound in picturesque incidents and persons, nearly all represented in romantic places, many of which can now be identified, and visited with pleasure; for this is the story of curious, old, half-haunted Osbaldistone Hall; of Glasgow Cathedral, and of the Highlands at Loch Ard; of the Scotch Robin Hood; of charming, miraculous Die Vernon; of inimitable Bailie Nichol Jarvie of the Saut Market; of that natural, calculating, conceited, semi-rascal, Andrew Fairservice; and of that wholly villainous Jesuit, Rashleigh.—HUNNEWELL, JAMES F., 1871, *The Lands of Scott, p.* 164.

HEART OF MID-LOTHIAN
1818

Our general admiration of the story of the "Heart of Mid-Lothian" does not, of course, extend to the management of all the details. The beginning, or rather the beginnings, for there are half a dozen of them, are singularly careless. The author, in his premature anxiety to get in medias res, introduces us at the point where the different interests converge; and then, instead of floating down the united streams of events, we are forced separately to ascend each of its tributary branches, like Humboldt examining the bifurcations of the Oroonoko, until we forget, in exploring their sources, the manner in which they bear on one another.—SENIOR, A. W., 1821, *Novels by the Author of Waverley, Quarterly Review, vol.* 26, *p.* 116.

During the Centenary festivities the Emperor of Brazil arrived in Edinburgh, and on the first morning of his stay he went at five o'clock in the morning, with the "Heart of Mid-Lothian" in his hand, to try and identify the localities about the region where the old Tolbooth formerly stood, described in the novel. A gentleman and lady at whose house he took luncheon assured me that the emperor had succeeded admirably in his identifications, which he declared to be due to the precision and vividness of Scott's descriptions.—CONWAY, M. D., 1872, *The Scott Centenary at Edinburgh, Harper's Magazine, vol.* 44, *p.* 337.

Last Evening I heard Jeanie Deans' Audience with Argyle, and then with the Queen. There I stop with the Book. Oh, how refreshing is the leisurely, easy, movement of the Story, with its true and well-harmonized Variety of Scene and Character! There is of course a Bore, Saddletree—as in Shakespeare, I presume to think—as in Cervantes—as in Life itself: somewhat too much of him in Scott, perhaps. But when the fuliginous and spasmodic Carlyle and Co. talk of Scott's delineating his Characters from without to within—why, he seems to have had a pretty good Staple of the inner Man of David, and Jeanie Deans, on beginning his Story.—FITZGERALD, EDWARD, 1877, *Letters to Fanny Kemble, June* 23, *ed. Wright, p.*126.

There we get his richest humour and his purest pathos, and especially that blending of the two, when the tears are close behind the smiles—as in "The Heart of Mid-Lothian" for instance—in which again he has been surpassed only by Shakespeare, and equalled, I think, only by Cervantes.—MORRIS, MOWBRAY, 1889, *Sir Walter Scott, Macmillan's Magazine, vol.* 60, *p.* 157.

It has often been said that Sir Walter Scott excelled in his feminine characters, and we must, we think, agree in this assertion and venture to assign the foremost place to this beautiful type of Lowland lassie, which he has drawn with such truth and with such a loving touch.—YOUNG, GERTRUDE JULIAN, 1893, *Great Characters of Fiction, ed. Townsend, p.* 55.

THE BRIDE OF LAMMERMOOR
1819

It is a tragedy of the highest order, and unites excellence of plot to our author's usual merits of character and description.—SENIOR, A. W., 1821, *Novels by the Author of Waverley, Quarterly Review, vol.* 26, *p.* 120.

We see, even at the very beginning of the tale, the "little cloud, no bigger than a man's hand" which gradually overshadows the whole atmosphere, and at last bursts in ruin, in madness, and in despair over the devoted heads of Ravenswood and his betrothed. The catastrophe is tremendous, crushing, complete; and even the more comic scenes (the melancholy ingenuity of poor faithful Caleb) have a sad and hopeless gaiety, which forms a dismal and appropriate relief to the profoundly tragic tone of the action. One scene in this awful tale is truly terrific—the muttered cursing of the three hideous hags at the ill-omened marriage; nor is the interview between Ravenswood and the grave-digger, or the appearance of the unhappy hero to claim his promise from Lucy Ashton, inferior. They bear the impress of our elder dramatists; they might have been conceived by Ford, by Middleton, or by the sombre genius of Webster.—SHAW, THOMAS B., 1847, *Outlines of English Literature, p.* 328.

Scott could neither have described nor even conceived the progress of jealousy in Othello. He could not have described nor even conceived that contrast between Curiace and either Horace, father or son, in which is so sublimely revealed the secret of the Roman ascendency. But, as an artist of Narrative and not of the Drama, Scott was perhaps the greater for his omissions. Let any reader bring to his recollection that passage in the grandest tragic romance our language possesses—the "Bride of Lammermoor"—in which, the night before the Master of Ravenswood vanishes from the tale, he shuts himself up in his fated tower, and all that is known of the emotions through which his soul travailed is the sound of his sleepless heavy tread upon the floor of his solitary room. What can be grander in narrative art than the suppression of all dramatic attempt to analyse emotion and reduce its expression to soliloquy?—LYTTON, EDWARD BULWER LORD, 1863–68, *Caxtoniana, Miscellaneous Prose Works, vol.* III, *p.* 473.

In some respects the best and most artistic of Scott's novels.—STEPHEN, LESLIE, 1875, *Hours in a Library, vol.* I, *p.* 79.

The most perfect, of all tragic poems in prose between the date of "Manon Lescaut" and the date of "Notre-Dame de Paris."—SWINBURNE, ALGERNON CHARLES, 1891, *The Journal of Sir Walter Scott, Fortnightly Review, vol.* 55, *p.* 689.

He calls it an "owre true tale." Never was a more unreal story written. Ravenswood is a mere stage figure, or, as Carlyle would say, a tissue of gloomy theatricalities. Then we have in Lucy Ashton another puppet; while her mother impresses us as an unnatural being, a downright monster. We may digest Lady Macbeth, but who could swallow Lady Ashton? The old Scottish servant, Caleb Balderstone, is the only lifelike person in the story. Here then we have another example of Scott's feebleness as a delineator of character.—HANNIGAN, D. F., 1895, *The Waverley Novels—after Sixty Years, The Westminster Review, vol.* 144, *p.* 20.

"No man since Æschylus could have written 'The Bride of Lammermoor'"—such are the words of Mr. Gladstone, quoted in the Life of Lord Tennyson. "The most pure and powerful of all the tragedies that Scott ever penned"—such is the deliberate criticism of Lockhart. "Scott's first approach to failure in prose"—such is the verdict of Professor Saintsbury on a book which, whatever be its merits or demerits, is unique in the position which it holds amongst the Waverley Novels. . . . He was supreme not by virtue of construction, but in the absence of it. And yet none the less it is true that in this one novel he has fulfilled, as no other novelist has ever done, and as he himself has never done elsewhere, dramatic conditions by which he was not bound, and by which it would be absurd that romance should be fettered; and that he has united in this single work the free play and variety of romance with the fundamental unity of the tragic drama. . . . That "The Bride of Lammermoor" is his greatest novel few perhaps will maintain. But surely the vast majority of critics will recognise in it, not "an approach to failure," but a combination of romance and dramatic tragedy which is absolutely unique.—CRAIK, SIR HENRY, 1897, *"The Bride of Lammermoor," Blackwood's Magazine, vol.* 162, *pp.* 853, 857.

To the merits in detail of "The Bride of Lammermoor" I never have hesitated to do justice, though I think them more sparingly found than in the case of most of the earlier novels. . . . I still maintain, for the reasons which "Maga" permitted me to give three months ago, that the tragedy of "The Bride of Lammermoor" is not "pure,"—is indeed distinctly faulty; and that, as I observed in the little book of which Sir Henry speaks so kindly, it is in its composition and general character as a novel, not indeed a failure, but Scott's first approach to one.—SAINTSBURY, GEORGE, 1897, "*The Bride of Lammermoor,*" *Blackwood's Magazine, vol.* 162, *p.* 859.

IVANHOE
1819

Never were the long-gathered stores of most extensive erudition applied to the purposes of imaginative genius with so much easy, lavish, and luxurious power; never was the illusion of fancy so complete. —WILSON, JOHN, 1819, *Ivanhoe, Blackwood's Magazine, vol.* 6, *p.* 263.

"Ivanhoe" was received throughout England with a more clamorous delight than any of the Scotch novels had been. The volumes were now for the first time of the post 8vo. form, with a finer paper than hitherto, the press-work much more elegant, and the price accordingly raised from eight shillings a volume to ten; yet the copies sold in this original shape were twelve thousand. . . . The publication of "Ivanhoe" marks the most brilliant epoch in Scott's history as the literary favorite of his contemporaries. With the novel which he next put forth the immediate sale of them began gradually to decline. —LOCKHART, JOHN GIBSON, 1836, *Memoirs of the Life of Sir Walter Scott, ch.* xlvi.

Perhaps the most favourite novel in the English language.—TROLLOPE, ANTHONY, 1879, *Thackeray* (*English Men of Letters*), *p.* 142.

We believe it is not generally known that the honor of having been the prototype and inspiration of the character of Rebecca the Jewess, in "Ivanhoe," belongs to an American lady, whose beauty and noble qualities were described to Scott by a friend. The friend was Washington Irving, and the lady Rebecca Gratz, of an honorable Jewish family of Philadelphia. —VAN RENSSELAER, GRATZ, 1882, *The Original of Rebecca in Ivanhoe, The Century, vol.* 24, *p.* 679.

"Ivanhoe" is such a very dear and old friend that no one who has ever been a boy can pretend to apply to it any stern critical tests. —LANG, ANDREW, 1895, *Ivanhoe, Border ed., Introduction.*

Tested by . . . the magic by which it evokes the past, the skill with which legend and history are used to create a poetic atmosphere . . . the masterly delineation of nationalities and professions, and representatives of every order and rank; above all its fundamental rightness, . . . tested by these qualities, "Ivanhoe" deserves its fame as one of the great romances of the world.—PERRY, BLISS, 1897, *ed. Ivanhoe* (*Longman's English Classics*), *Introduction.*

"Ivanhoe," which appeared at the end of 1819, marked a new departure. Scott was now drawing upon his reading instead of his personal experience, and the book has not the old merit of serious portraiture of real life. But its splendid audacity, its vivid presentation of mediæval life, and the dramatic vigour of the narrative, may atone for palpable anachronisms and melodramatic impossibilities. The story at once achieved the popularity which it has always enjoyed, and was more successful in England than any of the so-called "Scottish novels." It was Scott's culminating success in a book-selling sense, and marked the highest point both of his literary and his social prosperity.—STEPHEN, LESLIE, 1897, *Dictionary of National Biography, vol.* LI, *p.* 92.

"Ivanhoe" has delighted readers for full seventy years, and it delights them every whit as much to-day as it did the generation to which it first appealed.—SHORTER, CLEMENT, 1898, *Ivanhoe, Temple ed., Bibliographical Note.*

It did not seem desirable to point out in special notes the many inaccuracies and errors, grammatical and rhetorical, that may be found in "Ivanhoe." If the student is sensitive to such things he will easily discover them; and if he does not detect them he is probably destined to be a soldier, a sailor, or some such bold and active person to whom the technicalities of expression will not matter. . . . In "Ivanhoe" we breathe the sane and wholesome air of a heroic simple life—the life of objective deeds and sheer accomplishment. To the brave company that peoples our world of dreams it adds many figures, noble, bold, beautiful, gay—knights and ladies, merry-men and troubadours, pilgrim and crusader, friar and jester. It touches the past with a glow of poetry, lighting up situations, institutions, and men, making real and rich for us those things that in the technical records seem meagre and colorless. Its style gives us the refreshment of writing which, though it may not be delicately correct, is also not consciously fine nor painfully precise, but which moves buoyantly forward without strain and without weariness.—MACCLINTOCK, PORTER LANDER, 1900, *ed. Ivanhoe, Introduction, pp.* xxi, xxiii.

KENILWORTH
1821

We have just laid our hands on "Kenilworth." I saluted it with as much enthusiasm as a Catholic would a holy relic. It is now lying beside me, looking so fresh and tempting that I think I deserve some credit for having resisted it thus far.—SEDGWICK, CATHARINE M., 1821, *Life and Letters, p.* 118.

Though "Kenilworth" must rank high among his works, we think it inferior, as a whole, to his other tragedies, the "Bride of Lammermoor," the historical part of "Waverley," and the "Abbot," both in materials and in execution. Amy Robsart and Elizabeth occupy nearly the same space upon the canvas as Catherine Seyton and Mary. But almost all the points of interest, which are divided between Amy and Elizabeth, historical recollections, beauty, talents, attractive virtues and unhappy errors, exalted rank and deep misfortune, are accumulated in Mary; and we want altogether that union of the lofty and the elegant, of enthusiasm and playfulness, which enchanted us in Catherine. . . . It is a fault perhaps of the conclusion, that it is too uniformly tragical. . . . The immediate circumstances of Amy's death, as she rushes to meet, what she supposes to be, her husband's signal, almost pass the limit that divides pity from horror.—SENIOR, A. W., 1821, *Novels by the Author of Waverley, Quarterly Review, vol.* 26, *pp.* 143, 147.

"Kenilworth," however, is a flight of another wing—and rises almost, if not altogether, to the level of "Ivanhoe;" displaying, perhaps, as much power in assembling together, and distributing in striking groups, the copious historical materials of that romantic age, as the other does in eking out their scantiness by the riches of the author's imagination. —JEFFREY, FRANCIS LORD, 1822-44, *Waverley Novels, Contributions to the Edinburgh Review, vol.* III, *p.* 485.

Was particularly interested by your description of Kenilworth, round which Walter Scott's admirable novel has cast a halo of romance forever; for many who would have cared little about it as the residence of Leicester, honored for some days by the presence of Elizabeth, will remember with a thrill of interest and pity the night poor Amy Robsart passed there, and the scene between her, Leicester, and the queen, when that prince of villains, Varney, claims her as his wife. But in spite of the romantic and historical associations belonging to the place, I do not think it would have "inspired my muse." —KEMBLE, FRANCES ANN, 1827, *Letter, Records of a Girlhood, p.* 108.

I am glad you like "Kenilworth." It is certainly a splendid production, more resembling a romance than a novel, and, in my opinion, one of the most interesting works that ever emanated from the great Sir Walter's pen. I was exceedingly amused at the characteristic and naive manner in which you expressed your detestation of Varney's character—so much so, indeed, that I could not forbear laughing aloud when I perused that part of your letter. He is certainly the personification of consummate villainy; and in the delineation of his dark and profoundly artful mind, Scott exhibits a wonderful knowledge of human nature as well as surprising skill in embodying his perceptions so as to enable others to become participators in that knowledge.—BRONTË, CHARLOTTE, 1833, *Letter to Miss Ellen Nussey, Jan.* 1; *Charlotte Brontë and Her Circle, ed. Shorter, p.* 208.

I—We—have finished all Sir Walter's Scotch Novels; and I thought I would try an English one: Kenilworth—a wonderful Drama, which Theatre, Opera, and Ballet (as I once saw it represented) may well reproduce. The Scene at Greenwich, where Elizabeth "interviews" Sussex and Leicester, seemed to me as fine as what is called (I am told, wrongly) Shakespeare's Henry VIII. Of course, plenty of melodrama in most other parts:—but the Plot wonderful.—FITZGERALD, EDWARD, 1879, *Letters to Fanny Kemble, April* 25, *ed. Wright, p.*140.

THE PIRATE
1821

The "Pirate," I am afraid, has been scared and alarmed by the Beacon! It is certainly one of the least fortunate of Sir Walter Scott's productions. It seems now that he can write nothing without Meg Merrilies and Dominie Samson! One other such novel, and there's an end. But who can last forever? Who ever lasted so long.—SMITH, SYDNEY, 1821, *To Francis Jeffrey, Dec.* 30; *Letters, ed. Mrs. Austin.*

Norna is a new incarnation of Meg Merrilies, and palpably the same in the spirit. Less degraded in her habits and associates, and less lofty and pathetic in her denunciations, she reconciles fewer contradictions, and is, on the whole, inferior perhaps to her prototype; but is far above the rank of a mere imitated or borrowed character. — JEFFREY, FRANCIS LORD, 1822–44, *Waverley Novels, Contributions to the Edinburgh Review, vol.* III, *p.* 489.

I have been reading Sir Walter's "Pirate" again, and am very glad to find how much I like it—that is speaking far below the mark—I may say how I wonder and delight in it. I am rejoiced to find that this is so; and I am quite sure that it is not owing to my old prejudice, but to the intrinsic merit and beauty of the Book itself. With all its faults of detail, often mere carelessness, what a broad Shakespearian Daylight over it all, and all with no Effort, and—a lot else that one may be contented to feel without having to write an Essay about. They won't beat Sir Walter in a hurry (I mean of course his earlier, Northern, Novels,) and he was such a fine Fellow that I really don't believe any one would wish to cast him in the Shade.—FITZGERALD, EDWARD, 1871, *Letters, vol.* I, *p.* 332.

THE FORTUNES OF NIGEL
1822

It is strange how much Nigel has haunted me while reading it. In spite of all my resistance and correction of the illusion by suggesting to myself that the author may order events as he pleases, I am extremely interested by it. But I think it is partly because I consider it all as substantially true, giving the account of the manners and incidents of the day. Surely some parts absurd, as making the usurer's dry firm daughter marry the Scotch servant. Even the watchmaker forced. But some admirable strokes of nature and character. Hard on Charles I.—WILBERFORCE, WILLIAM, 1822, *Letter to J. Stephen, Aug.* 13; *Life by Sons, vol.* V, *p.* 133.

While it certainly presents us with a very brilliant, and, we believe, a very faithful sketch of the manners and habits of the time, we cannot say that it either embodies them in a very interesting story, or supplies us with any rich variety of particular characters. Except King James himself, and Richie Moniplies, there is but little individuality in the personages represented. We should perhaps add Master George Heriot; except that he is too staid and prudent a person to engage very much of our interest.—JEFFREY, FRANCIS LORD, 1822–44, *Waverley Novels, Contributions to the Edinburgh Review, vol.* III, *p.* 490.

The "Fortunes of Nigel" is perhaps behind nothing the author ever wrote, for dramatic power and masterly portraiture of character.—ALLAN, GEORGE, 1835, *Life of Sir Walter Scott, p.* 347.

It can scarcely be conceded that Scott was successful in filling out the character of the nominal hero of "The Fortunes of Nigel," who, sooth to say, is but a sorry nobleman "of the period." Neither did he make much of George Heriot, founder of the splendid institution which has perpetuated his name in Edinburgh. But King James is one of the best drawn of his numerous historical portraits. We see him in public and in private, pedantic and mean, with scarcely a thought above self. Prince Charles and the Duke of Buckingham merely pass across the stage. Moniplies, Nigel's servant, is a new edition, revised and corrected, of Andrew Fairservice, in "Rob Roy." Among the courtiers, the old Earl of Huntington is almost the only gentleman. Honest John Christie, of Paul's Wharf, who was "cursed in a fair wife," bears his wrongs with dignity. The Alsatian scenes are admirable and new; at least in prose fiction, though not in some of the old plays. For a heroine, Margaret Ramsay is far above the average; though, according to Scott's favorite practice, she dons the attire of a page for some little time.— MACKENZIE, ROBERT SHELTON, 1871, *Sir Walter Scott, The Story of His Life, p.* 335.

We are reading "Nigel," which I had not expected to care for: but so far as I got—four first Chapters—makes me long for Night to hear more. That return of Richie to his Master, and dear George Heriot's visit just after! Oh, Sir Walter is not done for yet by Austens and Eliots. If one of his Merits were not his *clear Daylight*, one thinks, there ought to be Societies to keep his Lamp trimmed as well as—Mr. Browning. — FITZGERALD, EDWARD, 1881, *Letters to Fanny Kemble, Dec., ed. Wright, p.* 220.

ST. RONAN'S WELL
1824

I have dipped in the new "Well," which was fit and proper for me to do, as all the family were plashing in it; and it is one of my duties to influence their judgments, as well as to lead their taste, if taste can be led. I differ from you and many others about this Well, and still hold to my old maxim, that "king's caff is better than ither folk's corn." We are, in the first place, startled at seeing an old friend with a new face: we have been accustomed to meet him in the familiar walks of natural feeling and character, or in the loftier scenes of courtly splendour, chivalrous manners, and romantic sentiments. The fashionables of the day, exaggerated as they are, among the idle and worthless in those haunts of idleness and dissipation called watering-places, is quite a new field, in which there is not so much for the heart as in the former, nor so much to elevate and fill the imagination as in the latter. This work is, in short, what none of the rest were, an obvious intentional satire; and we do not so readily follow him in this new and thorny walk. The story, I grant, hangs very ill together, and so do Shakspeare's; but there is character, sense, and truth, and the moral is good. In short, though the caff may abound, it is still *king's* caff.—GRANT, ANNE, 1824, *Letters, Feb.* 6; *Memoir and Correspondence, ed. Grant, vol.* III, *p.* 20.

It is strange, but only a part of the general simplicity of Scott's genius, that these revivals of earlier power were unconscious, and that the time of extreme weakness in which he wrote "St. Ronan's Well," was that in which he first asserted his own restoration. — RUSKIN, JOHN, 1880, *Fiction—Fair and Foul, The Nineteenth Century, vol.* 7, *p.* 955.

There is certainly to be said for "St. Ronan's," that, in spite of the heaviness of some of the scenes at the "hottle" and the artificial melodramatic character of some of the personages, none of Scott's stories is of more absorbing or more brilliantly diversified interest. Contradictions between contemporary popular opinion and mature critical judgment, as well as diversities of view among critics themselves, rather shake confidence in individual judgment on the vexed but not particularly wise question which is the best of Scott's novels. — MINTO, WILLIAM, 1886, *Encyclopædia Britannica, Ninth ed., vol.* XXI, *p.* 575.

LIFE OF NAPOLEON BONAPARTE
1827

You are the first person from whom I have heard a word in favor of Scott's "Napoleon," and I am really glad to hear some good of it, as I was afraid it was too probable that he *had* been bookmaking. The defect which you mention is attributable to the defect of moral force in Scott's character; invariable candour and moderation in judging men is generally accompanied by such a defect. Scott seems to be always disposed to approve of rectitude of conduct and to acquiesce in the general rules of morality, but without any instinctive or unconquerable aversion from vice—witness his friendship for Byron.—TAYLOR, SIR HENRY, 1827, *To Edward Villers, Oct.* 15; *Correspondence, ed. Dowden, p.* 19.

I am reading Walter Scott's "Napoleon," which I do with the greatest pleasure. I am as much surprised at it as at any of his works. So current, so sensible, animated, well arranged; so agreeable to take up, so difficult to put down, and, for him, so candid! there are, of course, many mistakes, but that has nothing to do with the general complexion of the work.—SMITH, SYDNEY, 1828, *To Lord Holland, July; Letters, ed. Mrs. Austin.*

It is true that the author may be reproached with great inaccuracy, and equally great partiality, but even these two defects give to his work particular value in my eyes. The success of the book, in England, was great beyond all expectation; and hence we see that Walter Scott, in this very hatred for Napoleon and the French, has been the true interpreter and representative of the English popular opinion and national feeling. His book will not be by any means a document for the history of France, but it will be one for the history of England. At all events, it is a voice which could not be wanting in this important historical process.—GOETHE, JOHANN WOLFGANG, 1830, *Conversations, ed. Eckermann, vol.* II, *p.* 213.

The paper and print of the first and

second edition, in nine volumes, brought the creditors £18,000—an amount of gain, in relation to amount of labour, unexampled in the history of literature, and which will probably have no parallel for ages to come.—CHAMBERS, ROBERT, 1835-71, *Life of Sir Walter Scott. p.* 81.

It is not a satisfactory performance. Written too near the time of which it treats to be quite impartial, it also bears in many places the marks of haste and imperfect execution. The training through which Scott had been going for the previous ten years, was not of a kind to fit him for working with perfect patience upon a theme so vast and difficult.—COLLIER, WILLIAM FRANCIS, 1861, *A History of English Literature, p.* 411.

FAIR MAID OF PERTH
1828

Walter Scott's "Fair Maid of Perth" is excellent, is it not? There is finish! there is a hand! What a firm foundation for the whole, and in particulars not a touch which does not lead to the catastrophe! Then, what details of dialogue and description, both of which are excellent. His scenes and situations are like pictures by Teniers; in the arrangement they show the summit of art, the individual figures have a speaking truth, and the execution is extended with artistical love to the minutest details, so that not a stroke is lost.—GOETHE, JOHANN WOLFGANG, 1828, *Conversations, ed. Eckermann, vol.* II, *p.* 73.

To me, one of the most remarkable figures he ever drew was that of Conachar. Nothing could be more difficult than to provoke at once pity, contempt, and sympathy for a coward. Yet he has successfully achieved this feat; and as far as I can recollect, it is the sole instance in English literature where such an attempt was ever made. More than this, he has drawn two cowards in this remarkable novel,—each quite different from the other and contrasted with eminent skill—the comic, swaggering, good-natured, fussy little coward, Oliver Proudfute, who provokes a perpetual smile; and the sullen, irritable, proud, and revengeful coward, Conachar, whom we cannot but pity, while we despise him. "The Fair Maid of Perth" was always a favorite of mine. It has perhaps more variety of interest, incident, and characters than any he ever wrote, and it never flags.—STORY, WILLIAM WETMORE, 1890, *Conversations in a Studio, vol.* I, *p.* 273.

GENERAL

The day arrived—blest be the day,
Walter the Abbot came that way! . . .
Then poured the numbers bold and free,
The ancient magic melody.
The land was charmed to list his lays;
It knew the harp of ancient days.
The Border chiefs, that lone had been
In sepulchres unhearsed and green,
Passed from their mouldy vaults away,
In armour red and stern array,
And by their moonlight halls were seen,
In visor, helm, and habergeon.
Even fairies sought our land again,
So powerful was the magic strain.

—HOGG, JAMES, 1813, *The Queen's Wake, Conclusion.*

. . . the Ariosto of the North,
Sang ladye-love and war, romance and
knightly worth.

—BYRON, LORD, 1818, *Childe Harold's Pilgrimage, canto* iv.

The broad and "high way" to fame, which he has hewn out for himself, is strewn with no thorns, and surrounded by no unseemly sights, to wound the feet, or injure the eyes, of such who choose to walk in it. No *Upas* tree sheds its poison here.—DIBDIN, THOMAS FROGNALL, 1824, *The Library Companion, p.* 739, *note.*

Thou, upon a hundred streams,
By tales of love and sorrow,
Of faithful love, undaunted truth,
Hast shed the power of Yarrow;
And streams unknown, hills yet unseen,
Wherever they invite Thee,
At parent Nature's grateful call,
With gladness must requite Thee.
A gracious welcome shall be thine,
Such looks of love and honour
As thy own Yarrow gave to me
When first I gazed upon her;
Beheld what I had feared to see,
Unwilling to surrender
Dreams treasured up from early days,
The holy and the tender.

—WORDSWORTH, WILLIAM, 1831, *Yarrow Revisited.*

Criticism on his works is now superfluous. They have taken their enduring station in the literature of the world. If the applause of foreign nations be equivalent, as it is said, to the voice of posterity, no author who ever wrote has obtained that honor in so large a measure. His novels, his poems, have been translated into every civilized language; his heroes and heroines have become household words all over the world. The painter, the sculptor, the engraver, the musician, have sought inspiration from his pages. The names of his works, or the personages introduced into them, are impressed on the man-of-war or the quadrille, the race-horse or the steamboat. The number of persons who became famous by following in their different lines, the ideas of Sir Walter, is immense, and comprehends all classes of intellect or enterprise. The tribes of imitators, whether of his verse or prose, whom he has called into existence, are countless. Many of them are persons of great abilities and unquestioned genius. Which of them will be named in competition with the master? Not one.—MAGINN, WILLIAM, 1832, *The Death of Sir Walter Scott, Fraser's Magazine, vol.* 6, *p.* 380.

The illustrious painter of Scotland seems to me to have created a false class; he has, in my opinion, confounded history and romance: the novelist has set about writing historical romances, and the historian romantic histories. . . . I refuse, therefore, to sit in judgment on any English author whose merit does not appear to me to reach that degree of superiority which it has in the eyes of his countrymen.—CHATEAUBRIAND, FRANÇOIS RENÉ, VICOMTE DE, 1837, *Sketches of English Literature, vol.* II, *pp.* 306, 307.

Scott was, in truth, master of the picturesque. He understood, better than any historian since the time of Livy, how to dispose his lights and shades so as to produce the most striking result. This property of romance he had a right to borrow. This talent is particularly observable in the animated parts of his story—in his battles, for example. No man ever painted those terrible scenes with greater effect. He had a natural relish for gunpowder; and his mettle roused, like that of the war-horse, at the sound of the trumpet. His acquaintance with military science enabled him to employ a technical phraseology, just technical enough to give a knowing air to his descriptions, without embarrassing the reader by a pedantic display of unintelligible jargon. This is a talent rare in a civilian. Nothing can be finer than many of his battle-pieces in his "Life of Bonaparte," unless, indeed, we except one or two in his "History of Scotland:" as the fight of Bannockburn, for example, in which Burns's "Scots, wha hae" seems to breathe in every line.—PRESCOTT, WILLIAM HICKLING, 1839, *Chateaubriand's English Literature, Biographical and Critical Miscellanies, p.* 284.

Close observation of nature, whether animated or inanimate, was his great characteristic; the brilliancy of fancy, the force of imagination, were directed to clothing with sparkling colours her varied creations. It is hard to say whether his genius was most conspicuous in describing the beauties of nature or delineating the passions of the heart: he was at once pictorial and dramatic. To this he owes his great success,—hence his world-wide reputation. He was first known as a poet; but, charming as his poetic conceptions were, they were ere long eclipsed by the wide-spread fame of his prose romances. The Novels of the Author of Waverley caused the poems of Walter Scott to be for a time forgotten. But time has re-established them in their celebrity; and, great as is still the fame of the Scotch novels, it is rivaled by the heart-stirring verses of "Marmion," the enduring charm of the "Lady of the Lake." . . . No man ever threw a more charming radiance over the traditions of ancient times, but none ever delineated in a nobler spirit the virtues of the present; and his discriminating eye discovered them equally under the thatch of the cottage as in the halls of the castle. It has been truly said that the influence of his writings neutralized, to a certain extent, the effect of the Reform Bill; but it is not less true that none ever contributed more powerfully to that purification without which all others are nugatory,—the reform of the human heart; and perhaps he is the only author of numerous works of fiction of whom it may with truth be said that he never wrote a line which, on death-bed, he could wish recalled.—ALISON, SIR ARCHIBALD, 1853–59, *History of Europe,* 1815–1852, *ch.* V.

Like a fair country stretching wide
With woods on woods in leafy pride
  And fields of golden grain,
And moors with purple heather glowing,
And healthful breezes bravely blowing,
  Spreads Scott his vast domain.

—BLACKIE, JOHN STUART, 1857, *Introduction to Lays and Legends of Ancient Greece.*

Now this vast and salutary change in

national opinion is directly due to Scott. Something of the kind might possibly have come with time; but he, in fact, was the man whose lot was to accomplish it. This may be regarded, on the whole, as his greatest achievement. He united the sympathies of two hostile races by the sheer force of genius. He healed the bitterness of centuries. Scott did much in idealizing, as poetry should, the common life of his contemporaries. He equally did much in rendering the past history, and the history of other countries in which Scotchmen played a conspicuous part, real to us. But it is hardly a figure of speech to say, that he created the Celtic Highlands in the eyes of the whole civilized world. If this be not first-rate power, it may be asked where we are to find it.—PALGRAVE, FRANCIS TURNER, 1866, *ed., The Poetical Works of Sir Walter Scott, Memoir, p.* xxxiii.

Walter Scott pauses on the threshold of the soul, and in the vestibule of history, selects in the Renaissance and the Middle Age only the fit and agreeable, blots out frank language, licentious sensuality, bestial ferocity. After all, his characters, to whatever age he transports them, are his neighbors, "cannie" farmers, vain lairds, gloved gentlemen, young marriageable ladies, all more or less common-place, that is, well-ordered by education and character, hundreds of miles away from the voluptuous fools of the Restoration, or the heroic brutes and fierce beasts of the Middle Age. As he has the richest supply of costumes, and the most inexhaustible talent for scenic effect, he makes his whole world get on very pleasantly, and composes tales which, in truth, have only the merit of fashion, but which yet may last a hundred years.—TAINE, H. A., 1871, *History of English Literature, tr. Van Laun, vol.* II, *bk.* iv, *ch.* i, *p.* 255.

The English claim Scott for the world; the Scotch ken him for their own. He is beloved at home, and revered abroad. We all know him intimately already from his Poems, his Tales, and his Life. There is a nobility of thought and action in his Poems which stamps him as the Poet of Chivalry. Combined with this high tone, there is minute fidelity of description, which marks careful observation and the love of Truth. There is an active principle in Scott's Novels, which, like a bracing wind, brings invigorating health and purity along with it. Where his spirit meets with kindred feeling, the reader rises a stouter-hearted man, a more genial companion, and returns to his work in life with a determination to throw greater energy into what he has to do.—LOCKHART, C. S. M., 1871, *The Centenary Memorial of Sir Walter Scott, Bart., Preface, p.* vii.

Of Walter Scott one need as little speak as of Shakespeare. He belongs to mankind, to every age and race, and he certainly must be counted as in the first line of the great creative minds of the world. His unique glory is to have definitely succeeded in the ideal reproduction of historical types, so as to preserve at once beauty, life, and truth, a task which neither Ariosto and Tasso, nor Corneille and Racine, nor Alfieri, nor Goethe and Schiller—no! nor even Shakespeare himself entirely achieved. It is true that their instrument was the more exacting one of verse, whilst Scott's was prose. But in brilliancy of conception, in wealth of character, in dramatic art, in glow and harmony of colour, Scott put forth all the powers of a master poet.—HARRISON, FREDERIC, 1879–86, *The Choice of Books and Other Literary Pieces, p.* 64.

Let the critics praise him, or let them blame. It matters not. His reputation will not wane, but will grow with time. Therefore we do well to make much of Walter Scott. He is the only Homer who has been vouchsafed to Scotland—I might almost say to modern Europe. He came at the latest hour when it was possible for a great epic minstrel to be born. And the altered conditions of the world will not admit of another.—SHAIRP, JOHN CAMPBELL, 1881, *The Homeric Spirit in Walter Scott, Aspects of Poetry.*

The delight of my youth was Scott, especially his poetry. I began with the poems, and read them so often that I almost knew them by heart before I had read a single page of the prose tales. "The Lady of the Lake" was my especial favourite, and I have no doubt that my early enthusiasm for that delightful poem implanted in me a love for beautiful lakes with romantic islands in them which had practical consequences afterwards. Even to this day these feelings are as lively in me as ever, so that nothing in the world seems to me so completely delightful as a lake if one has a sailing-boat to wander over it. Scott, too, had the same love for hills and streams that I had imbibed from nature in my youth, and in his narratives of adventure he suited my temper so exactly, that to read him was a complete satisfaction, without any drawback whatever. To a youth who becomes thoughtful Scott is insufficient, but a man who has got through most of his serious thinking may return to him again and receive from him much of the old refreshment and delight. I am still a reader of Scott, and never appreciated the qualities of "Ivanhoe" so completely as on reading that masterpiece last year. Of all authors, it is Scott who has given me the greatest sum of pleasure, and that of a very healthy kind.—HAMERTON, PHILIP GILBERT, 1887, *Books which Have Influenced Me, p.* 52.

It is one of the griefs of my old age that I know Scott by heart; but still, if I take up a volume of him, it is not laid down again for the next hour.—RUSKIN, JOHN, 1887, *Books which Have Influenced Me, p.* 45.

I find myself, as years multiply, inclined to return with most relish to Walter Scott, because of the supreme reality, out-door freshness, and simplicity of his stories. They are not disguised philosophy or disguised anything else, but they are the vivacious, adequate impressions of a mind thoroughly sincere and wholesome in its sympathy with men and things. "The Fair Maid of Perth" or "Old Mortality" brings, to one who is no longer tempted to quicken his pace by the fascination of a story, pleasant thoughts of pleasant people, and sharp resentment for wicked ones—a mixed assembly, such as has made the world, everywhere and at all times, hopeful and fearful, a land whose clouds veil but do not extinguish its sunlight.—BASCOM, JOHN, 1888, *Books that Have Helped Me, p.* 29.

His reasoning energy was locked up organically, let us say, in his marvellous imagination. And so, remembering all that Scott has left us,—those imperishable tales and romances which no subsequent successes in the British literature of fiction have superseded, and by the glamour of which his own little land of brown heath and shaggy wood, formerly of small account in the world, has become a dream and fascination for all the leisurely of all the nations,—need we cease, after all, from thinking of him in juxtaposition, due interval allowed, with England's greatest man, the whole world's greatest man, of the literary order, or abandon the habit of speaking of Sir Walter Scott as our Scottish Shakespeare?—MASSON, DAVID, 1890–92, *The Last Years of Sir Walter Scott, Edinburgh Sketches and Memories, p.* 225.

The idiosyncrasies of Scott's genius are various and delicate: his eye for color is as fine as any modern colorist's. . . . Notwithstanding his picturesque descriptions, Scott was a poor judge of the pictorial art: Abbotsford was decorated with pictures that were mere daubs.—STODDARD, ELIZABETH, 1890, *Characters of Scott, Lippincott's Magazine, vol.* 45, *p.* 728.

Lost the Homeric swing and trot,
Jingle of spur and beam of blade,
Of that moss-trooper, Walter Scott,
Riding upon his border raid,
And pricking south with all his power
To capture Shakespeare's feudal tower!
—BUCHANAN, ROBERT, 1891, *The Outcast, Canto* ii.

To him what further tribute is it possible for love or loyalty, for reverence or devotion to pay? While the language in which he wrote endures, while the human nature to which he addressed himself exists, there can be no end of the delight, the thanksgiving, and the honour with which men will salute, aloud or in silence, the utterance or the remembrance of his name.—SWINBURNE, ALGERNON CHARLES, 1891, *The Journal of Sir Walter Scott, Fortnightly Review, vol.* 55, *p.* 694.

It may safely be said that Scott is to his own country what no other writer ever has been to any country. Shakespeare no doubt may have been a greater genius than he, but Scott has done for Scotland what Shakespeare never did for England. Scotland from one end to the other is haunted with Scott's genius. The imaginary events of his novels have there almost taken the place of the actual events of history; and it is his novel rather than history that make it seem an historical country. A country small, remote, and till lately poor, with a population which recently was scarcely half that of contemporary London, and with manners and modes of thought peculiar in their severe provincialism—Scott has made it a country familiar to two hemispheres. Shakespeare may be said to go out to meet the imagination of strange readers; Scott compels the imagination of his readers to come to him among his own hills. Who when he visits Windsor thinks of Sir John Falstaff? Who when he visits Wigtonshire does not think of Guy Mannering? The Highland mountains are seen through an air enchanted and bewitched by Scott. Half the traffic on the Highland railway, if not the railway itself, is due to him; and but for him Inverness would probably be still an obscure village. One of the principal railway routes from London to Edinburgh is called by the name of one of his imaginary characters; and the historical name of a place in Lanarkshire has been cancelled and been replaced by the one which he gave in "Old Mortality." Of Hamlet it has been said that he is not *a* man but that he is man. Of Scott's characters it may be said that they are not men and women only, but a nation, and a nation in its own home.—MALLOCK, W. H., 1892, *Are Scott, Dickens and Thackeray Obsolete? The Forum, vol.* 14, *p.* 508.

In Scott the paragraphing of conversation proceeds by the modern method uniformly. His narrative and descriptive paragraphs have a certain unity always, and at times reveal a very high degree of picturesque grouping. The general straightforward coherence of his paragraphs is not to be disputed.—LEWIS, EDWIN HERBERT, 1894, *The History of the English Paragraph, p.* 126.

"Rubbish." It is a harsh word, and might well make Dean Stanley and a bygone generation of worshippers and believers in the plenary inspiration of Scott stir uneasily in their graves. It grates upon my own ear. But if it is a true word, what then? Why even then it does not matter very much, for when Time that old ravager, has done his very worst, there will be enough left of Sir Walter to carry down his name and fame to the remotest age. He cannot be ejected from his native land. Loch Katrine and Loch Leven are not exposed to criticism, and they will pull Sir Walter through.—BIRRELL, AUGUSTINE, 1894, *Essays about Men, Women and Books, p.* 197.

The defects of his prose are the more serious ones of slipshod and tawdry sentences, of clumsy and lumbering paragraphs. Where he is solemn or dignified, he rarely troubles himself with the virtues of restraint or selection; he never attempts the subtle harmony of words, or balances his style to suit with nicety the sentiments he wishes to convey. A certain amount of grandiloquence has often a quaint flavour of humour, but it is seldom so with Scott. His phrases are often rotund and ornate, but this seems to come from a careless conventionality of habit, and not from deliberate art. He pours out his words without discrimination, and frequently with an absence of all taste for style, which is perhaps akin to the insensibility of perception which his biographer admits—his obtuseness to what was disagreeable in smell or colour, his lack of musical ear, his bluntness to some of the more common tastes. He himself recognised the lack with his usual magnanimity, and neither resented its suggestion nor defended its faults. . . . The wonder is not that Scott's style had defects, but that it was not much worse. He never studied it. His mind was filled with the picturesque in scenery and in conception, and he had neither room nor leisure for more. And if the instrument was sometimes defective, no one used it with a more consummate ease. His style is best where we notice it least; and often the thrilling force and fire of genius, burning underneath, sublimes it into a certain unconscious grandeur. Nay, even this very common-placeness of Scott's style is not without its value. An artistic style must be redolent both of the writer and of his age; and the impersonality of Scott's style rather adds to, than detracts from, the perennial interest of his romance.—CRAIK, HENRY, 1896, *English Prose, vol.* v, *pp.* 9, 10.

We do not go to him for a word-craft; men of shorter imaginative range, and whose judgments wait on conventional rule, must guide us in such direction, and pose as our modellers of style. Goldsmith and Swift both may train in that company. But this master we are now considering wrote so swiftly and dashed so strongly into the current of what he had to say, that he was indifferent to methods and words, except what went to engage the reader and keep him always cognizant of his purpose. But do you say that this is the best aim of all writing? Most surely it is wise for a writer to hold attention by what arts he can: failing of this, he fails of the best half of his intent; but if he gains this by simple means, by directness, by limpid language, and no more of it than the thought calls for, and by such rhythmic and beguiling use of it as tempts the reader to follow, he is a safer exemplar than one who by force of genius can accomplish his aims by loose expressions and redundance of words.—MITCHELL, DONALD G., 1897, *English Lands Letters and Kings, The Later Georges to Victoria, p.* 74.

Another man of letters for whom Newman had a great love was Walter Scott. He delighted not only in the "Waverley Novels," but, like Mr. Ruskin, in Scott's chivalrous poetry.—DE VERE, AUBREY, 1897, *Recollections, p.* 270.

He never tried to be unlike somebody else; if he hit, as he did hit, upon great new styles of literature,—absolutely new in the case of the historical novel, revived after a long trance in the case of the verse tale,—it was from no desire to innovate, but because his genius called him. Though in ordinary ways he was very much a man of his time, he did not contort himself in any fashion by way of expressing a (then) modern spirit, a Georgian idiosyncrasy, or anything of that sort; he was content with the language of the best writers and the thoughts of the best men. He was no amateur of the topsy-turvy, and had not the very slightest desire to show how a literary head could grow beneath the shoulders. He was satisfied that his genius should flow naturally. And the consequence is that it was never checked, that it flows still for us with all its spontaneous charm, and that it will flow *in omne volubilis œvum.* — SAINTSBURY, GEORGE, 1897, *Sir Walter Scott* (*Famous Scots*).

Jeremy Bentham

1748–1832

Born, in Houndsditch, 15 Feb. 1748. Precocious ability in early years. At Westminster School, 1755–60. To Queen's Coll., Oxford, 28 June 1760; B. A., 1763; M. A., 1766. Visit to France, 1764. Called to Bar at Lincoln's Inn, 1772. Devoted himself to literary work. Visit to his brother at Zadobras, in Russia, Aug. 1785. Removed from London to Ford Abbey, near Chard, 1814. Interest in political and national affairs. Provided funds for starting the "Westminster Review," 1823. Abroad for health same year. Died, 6 June 1832. Left his body to be dissected. Skeleton preserved in University College. *Works:* Between 70 and 80 works by Bentham were published between 1775 and 1832. His "Collected Works" (11 vols.) were edited by Sir John Bowring, 1838–43. Some of the more important are: "A Fragment on Government" (anon.), 1776. "Introduction to the Principles of Morals and Legislation," 1780; "Panopticon," 1791; "Plan of Parliamentary Reform," 1817. "Codification and Public Instruction," 1817. Several of Bentham's works were translated into French by Dumont, in some cases from Bentham's unpublished *MSS. Life:* by Bowring, in 1838 edn. of Works.—SHARP, R. FARQUHARSON, 1897, *A Dictionary of English Authors, p.* 22.

PERSONAL

Our last visit was to my old and most valuable friend Jeremy Bentham, at Ford Abbey, in the neighborhood of Chard; a house which he rents, and which once belonged to Prideaux, the Attorney General of the Commonwealth. I was not a little surprized to find in what a palace my friend was lodged. The grandeur and stateliness of the buildings form as strange a contrast to his philosophy, as the number and spaciousness of the apartments, the hall, the chapel, the corridors, and the cloisters, do to the modesty and scantiness of his domestic establishment. We found him passing his time, as he has always been passing it since I have known him, which is now more than thirty years, closely applying himself for six or eight hours a day in writing upon laws and legislation, and in composing his Civil and Criminal Codes; and spending the remaining hours of every day in reading, or taking exercise by way of fitting himself for his labours, or, to use his own strangely invented phraseology, taking his antejentacular and post-prandial walks, to prepare himself for his task of codification. There is something burlesque enough in this language; but it is impossible to know Bentham, and to have witnessed his benevolence, his disinterestedness, and the zeal with which he has devoted his whole life to the service of his fellow creatures, without admiring and revering him.—ROMILLY, SIR SAMUEL, 1817, *Diary, Sept; Memoirs, ed. His Sons, vol.* III, *p.* 315.

Mr. Bentham is very much among philosophers what La Fontaine was among poets:—in general habits and in all but his professional pursuits, he is a mere child. He has lived for the last forty years in a house in Westminster, overlooking the Park, like an anchoret in his cell, reducing law to a system, and the mind of man to a machine. He scarcely ever goes out, and sees very little company. The favoured few, who have the privilege of the *entrée*, are always admitted one by one. He does not like to have witnesses to his conversation. He talks a great deal, and listens to nothing but facts. When any one calls upon him, he invites them to take a turn round his garden with him (Mr. Bentham is an economist of his time, and sets apart this portion of it to air and exercise)—and there you may see the lively old man, his mind still buoyant with thought and with the prospect of futurity, in eager conversation with some Opposition Member, some expatriated Patriot, or Transatlantic Adventurer, urging the extinction of Close Boroughs, or planning a code of laws for some "lone island in the watery waste," his walk almost amounting to a run, his tongue keeping pace with it in shrill, cluttering accents, negligent of his person, his dress, and his manner, intent only on his grand theme of UTILITY—or pausing, perhaps, for want of breath and with lack-lustre eye to point out to the stranger a stone in the wall at the end of his garden (overarched by two beautiful cotton-trees) *Inscribed to the Prince of Poets*, which marks the house where Milton formerly lived.—HAZLITT, WILLIAM, 1825, *The Spirit of the Age, p.* 4.

Mr. B. sleeps standing after dinner; fell once he says, and hurt himself on the elbows; the approaches of sleep are extremely delightful, he adds, being half asleep at the time. He sits up in bed in the morning to enjoy the approaches of sleep—not to sleep. And here it may not be amiss to describe the bed. The philosopher sleeps in a bag, and sometimes with his coat on; the bed not being made up for a month together. . . . He sleeps in his coat now—having ordered the flaps to be cut off, which are too warm for the night, and bring on the heat and itching of the skin, with which he is afflicted after dinner—the *devil* he calls it. Having drawn a line down each side of the middle-seam, with a bit of chalk, he has ordered a strip of the cloth to be cut out, and a cord to be left in, like the lacing of stays, to keep his back bone cool: D.—the mischievous dog he employed for this purpose having cut off the flaps of the coat and ripped it up in the back, now added the initials of the philosopher's name, as if to provide against his going astray,—putting them in large white letters in the very middle of the back. When I mentioned it, saying—"If you escape now, sir, you will be brought home;" instead of being offended, he laughed, said it was a foolish joke, and made the secretary rub it off. Such a figure no mortal ever saw before out of a mad-house. I cannot think of it to this day without laughing. I can see him now, it is the fourteenth of June, thermometer 76°;—There he goes with a pair of thick leather gloves on, woollen stockings rolled up over his knees outside, his coat-tail shaved away like a sailor's round-about, and stooping with his reverend rump, pushed out like that of a young chicken.—NEAL, JOHN, 1831, *Principles of Legislation; from the MS. of Jeremy Bentham, by M. Dumont, tr. Neal, Biographical Notice, pp.* 66, 81.

Personally, Mr. Bentham was like so many other great men, all simplicity and playfulness. He had that thorough amiability which arises from the warmest benevolence. He was without guile—the very antipodes of a worldly man: he who could unfold all the secrets or jurisprudence and legislation, and lay down regulations for the accurate conduct of whole nations, and resolve society and human nature into their last elements, was as simple as a child, and lived in the center of a vast capital, as far removed from actual contact with the world as if he had seated himself on the Andes. . . . He died, it seems, as he would have gone to sleep—this was sure to be the case with the calmest, pleasantest, and most innocent body that ever partook of mortal frailties. His long life passed in perfect, though far from robust, health; he was never, in all his scores of years, guilty of an excess; his fame had never been stained, for a moment, with intemperance: the old man left his body as pure as that of a child.—LYTTON, EDWARD BULWER LORD, ? 1832, *New Monthly Magazine.*

None who were present can ever forget that impressive scene. The room (the lecture-room of the Webb Street School of Anatomy) is small and circular, with no window but a central skylight, and capable of containing about three hundred persons. It was filled, with the exception of a class of medical students and some eminent members of that profession, by friends, disciples, and admirers of the diseased philosopher, comprising many men celebrated for literary talent, scientific research, and political activity. The corpse was on the table in the middle of the room, directly under the light, clothed in a night-dress, with only the head and hands exposed. There was no rigidity in the features, but an expression of placid dignity and benevolence. This was at times rendered almost vital by the reflection of the lightning playing over them; for a storm arose just as the lecturer commenced, and the profound silence in which he was listened to was broken and only broken by loud peals of thunder, which continued to roll at intervals throughout the delivery of his most appropriate and often affecting address. With the feelings which touch the heart in the contemplation of departed greatness, and in the presence of death, there mingled a sense of the power which that lifeless body seemed to be exercising in the conquest of prejudice for the public good, thus co-operating with the triumphs of the spirit by which it had been animated. It was a worthy close of the personal career of the great philanthropist and philosopher. Never did corpse of hero on the battle-field, "with his martial cloak around him," or funeral obsequies chanted by stoled and mitred priests in Gothic aisles, excite such emotions as the stern simplicity of that hour in which the principle of utility triumphed over the imagination and the heart.—FOX, W. J., 1832, *Monthly Repository, July.*

The skeleton of Bentham, dressed in the clothes which he usually wore, and with a wax face, modelled by Dr. Talrych, enclosed in a mahogany case, with folding-doors, may now be seen in the Anatomical Museum of University College Hospital, Gower Street, London.—TIMBS, JOHN, 1866, *English Eccentrics and Eccentricities, vol.* I, *p.* 182.

To
All who revere the Memory of
OUR SECOND LOCKE, JEREMY BENTHAM,
And advocate
The greatest happiness of the greatest number,
For the greatest length of time,
I inscribe these
CORN LAW RHYMES.

—ELLIOTT, EBENEZER, 1833, *Corn Law Rhymes, Dedication.*

I preserve a most agreeable recollection of that grand old face, beaming with benignity and intelligence, and occasionally with a touch of humor, which I did not expect. The portrait of him which is prefixed to the latter English editions of his "Morals and Legislation" is very like him, as I saw then, at the age of seventy-eight, six years before his death. I do not remember to have met any one of his age who seemed to have more complete possession of his faculties, bodily and mental; and this surprised me the more because I knew that, in his childhood, he had been a feeble-limbed, frail boy, precocious, indeed,—taking his degree of A. M. at eighteen,—but with little of that health of body which is sometimes spoken of as indispensable to health of mind.—OWEN, ROBERT DALE, 1874, *Threading my Way, p.* 202.

Bentham never in so many words publicly avowed himself as an atheist, but he was so in substance. His destructive criticisms of religious doctrine, in "Church-of-Englandism and its Cathechism examined," and still more his anonymous book on Natural Religion, left no residue that could be of any value. As a legislator, he had to allow a place for Religion; but he made use of the Deity, as Napoleon wished to make use of the Pope, for sanctioning whatever he himself chose, in the name of Utility, to prescribe. John Austin followed on the same track but the course was too disingenuous to suit either of the Mills. It is quite certain, however, that the whole tone of conversation in Bentham's more select circle, was atheistic.—BAIN, ALEXANDER, 1882, *James Mill, p.* 88.

Yes, it is a gratifying memory to me now—as I accounted it a high privilege then—to have looked on that great man while in life, to have beheld that nobly-molded head, that most benevolent face, in which almost childlike simplicity contended with godlike intellect, both blended in universal sympathy, while his loose gray hair streamed over his shoulders and played in the wind as he pursued his evening walk of meditation, around the very garden wherein the poet-patriot John Milton was erst accustomed to think his mighty thoughts.—HALL, SAMUEL CARTER, 1883, *Retrospect of a Long Life, from* 1815 *to* 1883, *p.* 393.

GENERAL

Read Bentham's "Panopticon" and first Appendix. All that respected the moral economy of his plan interested me greatly, but for want of plates I could not comprehend the mechanical structure. The book is (as all Bentham's are) full of original and very valuable matter. But it would possibly have had more effect if it had contained fewer novelties in substance and in language. Men are prepared to oppose when novelty is ostentatiously announced. —ROBINSON, HENRY CRABB, 1814, *Diary, July* 31; *Reminiscences, ed. Sadler, vol.* I, *p.* 279.

Mr. Bentham is long; Mr. Bentham is occasionally involved and obscure; Mr. Bentham invents new and alarming expressions; Mr. Bentham loves division and subdivision—and he loves method itself, more than its consequences. Those only, therefore, who know his originality, his knowledge, his vigour, and his boldness, will recur to the works themselves. The great mass of readers will not purchase improvement at so dear a rate; but will choose rather to become acquainted with Mr. Bentham through the medium of Reviews —after that eminent philosopher has been washed, trimmed, shaved, and forced into clean linen.—SMITH, SYDNEY, 1825, *Bentham on Fallacies, Edinburgh Review, Essays, p.* 483.

His style is unpopular, not to say unintelligible. He writes a language of his own, that *darkens knowledge.* His works have been translated into French—they ought to be translated into English. People wonder that Mr. Bentham has not been prosecuted for the boldness and severity of some of his invectives. He might wrap up high treason in one of his inextricable periods, and it would never find its way into Westminster-Hall. He is a kind of Manuscript author—he writes a cipher-hand, which the vulgar have no key to. The construction of his sentences is a curious frame-work with pegs and hooks to hang his thoughts upon, for his own use and guidance, but almost out of the reach of everybody else. It is a barbarous philosophical jargon, with all the repetitions, parentheses, formalities, uncouth nomenclature and verbiage, of law-Latin; and what makes it worse, it is not mere verbiage, but has a great deal of acuteness and meaning in it, which you would be glad to pick out if you could. In short, Mr. Bentham writes as if he was allowed but a single sentence to express his whole view of a subject in, and as if, should he omit a single circumstance or step of the argument, it would be lost to the world forever, like an estate by a flaw in the title-deeds.—HAZLITT, WILLIAM, 1825, *The Spirit of the Age, p.* 15.

Dr. Parr considered Jeremy Bentham as the wisest man of his time, whose powerful and penetrating mind had anticipated the improvements of coming ages, and who, on the all-important subject of Jurisprudence had discovered and collected knowledge, which will scarcely find its way to the great mass of human intellect, perhaps through the course of another century.—FIELD, WILLIAM, 1828, *Memoirs of the Life, Writings and Opinions of the Rev. Samuel Parr, vol.* II, *p.* 203.

One thing we see: the moral nature of man is deeper than his intellectual; things planted down into the former may grow as if for ever; the latter as a kind of drift mould produces only annuals. What is Jesus Christ's significance? *Altogether moral.* What is Jeremy Bentham's significance? Altogether intellectual, logical. I name him as the representative of a class important only for their numbers, intrinsically wearisome, almost pitiable and pitiful. Logic is their sole foundation, no other even recognised as possible; wherefore their system is a *machine* and cannot *grow* or endure; but after thrashing for a little (and doing good service that way) must thrash itself to pieces and be made fuel. Alas, poor England! stupid, purblind, pudding-eating England! Bentham with his *Mills* grinding thee out morality. —CARLYLE, THOMAS, 1830, *Journal, Sept.* 9; *Early Life by Froude, vol.* II, *p.* 72.

It cannot be denied without injustice and ingratitude, that Mr. Bentham has done more than any other writer to rouse the spirit of juridical reformation which is now gradually examining every part of law; and when further progress is facilitated by digesting the present laws, will doubtless proceed to the improvement of all. Greater praise it is given to few to earn. —MACKINTOSH, SIR JAMES, 1830, *Second Preliminary Dissertation, Encyclopædia Britannica.*

That Jeremy Bentham is a most vigorous and original thinker cannot be denied. We do not pretend to be familiar with all, or even the greater part of his works, but we have seen enough of what he has done, to be satisfied, that, like Hobbes, he may justly boast of being very little indebted to his predecessors, either for the conclusions he comes to, or for his manner of deducing and illustrating them. Whether these conclusions be discoveries or not for other people, they are so for himself. Whether it be difficult or not to establish them, in the usual way of treating such subjects, it always costs him great pains to arrive at them. He has no idea of any intellectual labor-saving contrivance—he carefully eschews the shortest distance between any two points—he hates simplicity, as if it were not the great end of all philosophers to simplify. We have seen what a jargon is used at his fireside—he adopts a similar one in his ethical and juridical speculations. His nomenclature or terminology is a study of itself—as complicated, if not quite so systematic, as that of the chemists. This wrapping up of plain matters in the mysteries of artificial language, which Hobbes detested so much, is Jeremy's great title to the admiration of the world. He is the Heracleitus of the age.—LEGARÉ, HUGH SWINTON, 1831-45, *Jeremy Bentham and the Utilitarians, Writings, ed. his Sister, vol.* II, *p.* 464.

Posterity will pronounce its calm and impartial decision, and that decision will, we firmly believe, place in the same rank with Galileo and with Locke the man who found jurisprudence a gibberish and left it a science. . . . He was, assuredly, at once a great logician and a great rhetorician. But the effect of his logic was injured by a vicious arrangement, and the effect of his rhetoric by a vicious style. His mind was vigorous, comprehensive, subtle, fertile of arguments, fertile of illustrations. But he spoke in an unknown tongue; and, that the congregation might be edified, it was necessary that some brother having the gift of interpretation should expound the invaluable jargon. His oracles were of high import, but they were traced on leaves and flung loose to the wind. So negligent was he of the arts of selection, distribution, and compression, that to persons who formed their judgment of him from his works in their undigested state, he seemed to be the least systematic of all philosophers. The truth is, that his opinions formed a system which, whether sound or unsound, is more exact, more entire, and more consistent with itself than any other.—MACAULAY, THOMAS BABINGTON, 1832, *Dumont's Recollections of Mirabeau, Edinburgh Review; Critical and Miscellaneous Essays.*

The age of law reform and the age of Jeremy Bentham are one and the same. He is the father of the most important of all the branches of Reform, the leading and ruling department of human improvement. . . . In thus assigning to Mr. Bentham, not merely the first place among Legal Philosophers, but the glory of having founded the Sect, and been the first who deserved the name, it cannot be intended to deny that other writers preceded him, who wisely and fearlessly exposed the defects of existing systems. . . . But he also excelled in the light works of fancy. An habitual despiser of eloquence, he was one of the most eloquent of men when it pleased him to write naturally, and before he had adopted that harsh style, full of involved periods and new-made words, which how accurately soever it conveyed his ideas, was almost as hard to learn as a foreign language.—BROUGHAM, HENRY LORD, 1838, *Speeches upon Questions relating to Public Rights, Duties and Interests, with Historical Introductions, and a Critical Dissertation upon the Eloquence of the Ancients.*

Bentham has been in this age and country the great questioner of things established. It is by the influence of the modes of thought with which his writings inoculated a considerable number of thinking men, that the yoke of authority has been broken, and innumerable opinions, formerly received on tradition as incontestable, are put upon their defence, and required to give an account of themselves. . . . The father of English innovation, both in doctrines and in institutions, is Bentham: he is the great *subversive*, or, in the language of continental philosophers, the great *critical*, thinker of his age and country. . . . His was an essentially practical mind. It was by practical abuses that his mind was first turned to speculation—by the abuses of the profession which was chosen for him, that of the law. . . . A place, therefore, must be assigned to Bentham among the masters of wisdom, the great teachers and permanent intellectual ornaments of the human race. . . . He was not a great philosopher, but he was a great reformer in philosophy. . . . Bentham failed in deriving light from other minds. His writings contain few traces of the accurate knowledge of any school of thinking but his own; and many proofs of his entire conviction that they could teach him nothing worth knowing. For some of the most illustrous of previous thinkers, his contempt was unmeasured.—MILL, JOHN STUART, 1838, *Bentham, Early Essays, ed. Gibbs, pp.* 329, 330, 333, 335, 345.

Seldom has a man exercised a more permanent influence on his race than Jeremy Bentham. His mind lead the leading minds of his age. Of him, Madame de Staël said —"He will give his name to the era." Happy, indeed, will it be for the world when *his* era is arrived—the era in which *the greatest happiness principle* shall be the ground-work of the laws, and the guide of the morals of mankind. Once conversing with Talleyrand, he thus expressed himself to me:—"I have known many great warriors—many great statesmen—many great authors—but only one great *genius*, and that genius is Jeremy Bentham." Talleyrand induced Napoleon to read Bentham's "Theory of Morals and Legislation." The Emperor's remark upon it was—"*That* is a book which will enlighten many libraries." It was saying more than if he had said—It will instruct many Philosophers. — BOWRING, JOHN, 1840, *Memoirs of Jeremy Bentham, Tait's Edinburgh Magazine, vol.* 7, *p.* 21.

Those who are acquainted with the chronology of Bentham's works will find in their uniformity of opinion an external argument for their truth. As he wrote a large quantity of matter almost every day, and never recurred in any shape to anything that he had previously written, it often happened that he went twice or thrice over the same ground at distant intervals; yet when these MSS.—often with an interval of twenty or thirty years between them in the dates of their composition—are confronted together, they are generally found to be so much alike, not only in the conclusions arrived at, but in the steps by which they are reached, and the very nature of the phraseology employed, that the author might be justly compared to an inductive philosopher repeating the same experiments in natural history, and obtaining, as a matter of physical certainty, the same results.—BURTON, JOHN HILL, 1842, *Memoirs of Jeremy Bentham, Westminster Review, vol.* 37, *p.* 287.

From 1820-1830 I believe the most wonderful period in our history, if we look merely at the importance of the people's *opinions*. The writings of Bentham produced a silent revolution in the *mode* of treating all political and moral subjects. The habits of thought were entirely new, and the whole body of political writers, without (for the most part) knowing whence the inspiration came, were full of a new spirit, and submitted all acts to a new test.—ROEBUCK, JOHN ARTHUR, 1849, *To Francis Place, March* 26; *Life and Letters, Autobiography, ed. Leader, p.* 217.

We cannot think that Bentham would have been more useful if, like Paley, he had adopted a notion about the will of God to help out the weakness of his Utilitarian motives. We rather consider it one of his chief merits that he utterly dispensed with any such aid; that he rejected a divine basis altogether for human society, or for the life of the individual man. That was *the* fair way of bringing the principle which he defended to a test; the only mode of ascertaining whether any society or any man has existed, does exist, or ever will exist without the confession of a Being who does not merely decree what men shall do under the terrors of punishment here or hereafter, but who *is* Righteous, who purposes to set Righteousness on the earth. The acknowledgment of such a Being lay, we believe, deep in the heart of Bentham as in the heart of Paley.—MAURICE, FREDERICK DENISON, 1862, *Moral and Metaphysical Philosophy, vol.* II, *p.* 605.

In genius was certainly superior to Beccaria, and whose influence, though perhaps not so great, was also European. —LECKY, WILLIAM EDWARD HARTPOLE, 1865, *History of the Rise and Influence of the Spirit of Rationalism in Europe, vol.* I, *ch.* iii.

The relation, indeed, of Bentham's ethical doctrines to Paley's may be expressed by saying that Bentham is Paley *minus* a belief in hell-fire. But Bentham, in another sense, is Paley *plus* a profound faith in himself, and an equally profound respect for realities.—STEPHEN, LESLIE, 1876, *History of English Thought in the Eighteenth Century, vol.* II, *p.* 125.

His system is even an important element of our current political thought; hardly a decade—though an eventful one—has elapsed since it might almost have been called a predominent element.— SIDGWICK, HENRY, 1877, *Bentham and Benthamism in Politics and Ethics.*

Bentham, at the close of the eighteenth century, was doing for jurisprudence what Adam Smith had already done for commerce. Bentham's works, however, never enjoyed the popularity of Adam Smith's, because the majority of them were not written in the clear style of the great Scotch philosopher. Bentham's earlier essays, indeed, are models of exactness of language and purity of style; but, in his later works, in his efforts to be exact he is occasionally obscure. . . . The obscurity of some of Bentham's later works probably accounts for the circumstance that, while the majority of mankind have long ago accepted most of his opinions, they have not given their originator the credit of them. Every one associates free trade with Adam Smith; but few people attribute the reform of the criminal code or the alteration of the Poor Laws to Bentham.—WALPOLE, SPENCER, 1878, *A History of England from the Conclusion of the Great War in* 1815, *vol.* I, *pp.* 334, 335.

The peculiarity of Bentham's genius lies in the fact that he perceived that legislation was an art, and brought to the art of legislation that kind of inventive talent and resource which is generally applied to the prosecution of scientific discovery, or to the improvement of mechanical inventions. . . . If he is regarded as an inventor laboring in the field of legislation for the benefit of mankind, just as a man of science seeks after discoveries which may extend the field of human knowledge, Bentham will, we are convinced, be seen in his true light, and will be acknowledged as the teacher who, beyond all others since the time of Socrates, has conceived of life as an art, and has at least pointed to the way by which the principles of legislation ought to be investigated, and to the mode in which, by the scientific amelioration of law, the amount of human happiness may be increased.—DICEY, A. V., 1878, *Bentham, The Nation, vol.* 27, *p.* 352.

Bentham's system has had the greatest influence upon the world since his time. It is sufficiently important to be considered a new departure in the world of thought; and, as such, it has received the allegiance of as devoted a band of disciples as ever surrounded any master in science or morals.—OLIPHANT, MARGARET O. W., 1882, *Literary History of England XVIII-XIX Century, vol.* III, *p.* 253.

The most hardy imagination could hardly connect Bentham, or any of his speculations, with religious thought. Great as he may have been in his own line as a legislative and legal reformer, Bentham cannot be called anything more than a sciolist in religion. He had but a feeble grasp of the subject either speculatively or historically. — TULLOCH, JOHN, 1885, *Movements of Religious Thought in Britain During the Nineteenth Century, p.* 108.

The subjects treated by Bentham are very varied. He sought to compass the whole field of ethics, jurisprudence, logic, and political economy, and to deal with points of detail as well as principles. To the last science his contributions are of small account. He did little more than apply, in his strictures on the usury laws, with courage and with happy illustrations, the principles of free trade which had been expounded by Adam Smith. His speculations on banking and currency illustrate the power these subjects have to lead astray even a singularly acute mind. To logic, though the subject of his inquiry for many years, he made no very valuable contributions; his ideas on that subject, which relate chiefly to exposition and method, will be found in his nephew's work on logic, "Outlines of a New System of Logic." His "Book on Fallacies" is a clever and brilliant refutation of popular political errors. His great work was in the field of jurisprudence and ethics, and his influence on these sciences can scarcely be overestimated. His most original and most durable works relate to law.—MACDONELL, JOHN, 1885, *Dictionary of National Biography, vol.* IV, *p.* 277.

In Bentham we reach, perhaps, the ideal —not certainly a very inviting one—of prosaic, and even acrid logic. Narrow in his conceptions, but inflexibly bold in their enunciation, with the force and vigour that come from absolute convictions, with the warmth—and that alone—which comes from hostility to what he believes to be erroneous or unsound, softened by no shadow of doubt, and illumined by no ray of imagination, Bentham yet commands respect even from those to whom his writings seem most barren of human interest. To him literary style was, so far as conscious effort went, a meaningless phrase; he is correct and lucid only from the clearness of his own views, and because he found the instrument of expression wrought to perfection by the habit of his age.—CRAIK, HENRY, 1895, *ed., English Prose, Introduction, vol.* IV, *p.* 4.

Even in handling themes of general interest Bentham, it must be owned, is literary only by accident. He cannot pretend to the sparkling elegance of Montesquieu, the careless graces of Hume, or the rhetorical pomp of Burke. His highest merit is that he is simple and vigorous. He writes like a man who has fully considered his subject and who knows exactly what he wants to say. He writes without the least endeavour to be fine. He is too much engrossed with the task of communicating his thoughts to be desirous of calling attention to his eloquence. Thus, if he had no literary graces, he had no literary affectation. By dint of devotion to his subject he comes to have a style, not a great or a beautiful style, but a style eminently characteristic of the man, adequate to his ideas and stimulating to the earnest reader.—MONTAGUE, F. C., 1895, *English Prose, ed. Craik, vol.* IV, *p.* 526.

Reminds one of a Hobbes without the literary genius.—SAINTSBURY, GEORGE, 1896, *A History of Nineteenth Century Literature, p.* 343.

To Bentham's political influence, which dates from the early years of the present century, full justice has probably never yet been done.—WHITTAKER, T., 1896, *Social England, ed. Traill, vol.* V, *p.* 415.

A clear-sighted and scrupulously veracious philosopher, abettor of the age of reason, apostle of utility, god-father of the panopticon, and donor to the English dictionary of such unimpassioned vocables as "codification" and "international." Bentham would have been glad to purify the language by purging it of those "affections of the soul" wherein Burke had found its highest glory. Yet in censuring the ordinary political usage of such a word as "innovation," it was hardly prejudice in general that he attacked, but the particular and deep-seated prejudice against novelty. The surprising vivacity of many of his own figures,—although he had the courage of his convictions, and laboured, throughout the course of a long life, to desiccate his style,—bears witness to a natural skill in the use of loaded weapons. He will pack his text with grave argument on matters ecclesiastical, and indulge himself and literature, in the notes with a pleasant description of the flesh and the spirit playing leap-frog, now one up, now the other, around the holy precincts of the Church. Lapses like these show him far enough from his own ideal of a geometric fixity in the use of words.—RALEIGH, WALTER, 1897, *Style, p.* 42.

His whole system of ethics and politics was severely utilitarian. It may indeed be compared to an arch, which has as its key-stone this principle, serving to unite his theoretical and political speculations, and to interlock them in a dogmatic whole. The new creed was soon to prove itself subversive of modes of thought and of institutions which rested only on prescription and tradition. Utility was a crucial test when rigorously applied to the Gothic irregularities of the British constitution; and Bentham was nothing if not rigorous. Exact methods of thought and reasoning were to be the sole guide of the philosophic and political inquirer. Sentiment, devotion, chivalry, appeals to the continuity of national life, all were excluded from the argument; and man was treated as if he were merely a reasoning machine, solely intent on manufacturing enjoyment by logical processes. The archaic dogmatism of the divine right of kings, the newer but equally severe dogmatism of Rousseau and the framers of the rights of man, were alike swept aside, because they lacked all proof of their utility or reality. But, as generally happens with destroyers of dogma, Bentham cleared the way for a new and formidable dogmatism, when he insisted on the undisputed sway of the principle of utility in politics. Imbued with the very one-sided and almost self-cancelling theory that man was a reasoning creature engaged in a constant pursuit after happiness, Bentham arraigned the institutions of his country at the utilitarian judgment bar.—ROSE, J. HOLLAND, 1897, *The Rise of Democracy*, p. 33.

George Crabbe

1754–1832

Born, at Aldeborough, 24 Dec. 1754. Educated at private schools at Bungay and Stowmarket. After leaving school, worked in warehouse at Slaughden; apprenticed as errand-boy to a doctor at Wickham Brook, near Bury St. Edmunds, 1768; to a surgeon at Woodbridge, 1771. Contrib. to "Wheble's Mag.," 1772. Returned to Aldeborough, 1775, to work in warehouse. Studied medicine. After a visit to London, became assistant to surgeon in Aldeborough, and afterwards set up in practice there. To London to make living by literature, April 1780. Ultimate success, mainly through assistance of Burke. Ordained Deacon, 21 Dec. 1781, as curate to Rector of Aldeborough. Ordained Priest, Aug. 1782. To Belvoir, as Chaplain to Duke of Rutland, 1782. Given degree of LL. B. by Archbishop of Canterbury, and presented (by Thurlow) with livings of Frome, St. Quentin and Evershot, Dorsetshire. Married Sarah Elmy, Dec. 1783. Accepted curacy of Stathern, 1785. Contrib. to "Annual Register," 1784. Voluminous writer, but published little. Exchanged Dorsetshire livings for Rectorship of Muston and Allington, and settled at Muston 25 Feb. 1789. Removed to Parham as curate of Sweffling and Great Glemham, 1792. Took Great Glenham Hall, 1796. Returned to Muston, Oct. 1805. Wife died, 31 Oct. 1813. Rector of Trowbridge Wiltshire, and Croxton, near Belvoir, June 1814. Visited London, 1817 and 1822. Visited Scott in Edinburgh, autumn 1822. Died, at Trowbridge, 3 Feb. 1832. Buried there. *Works:* "Inebriety" (anon.), 1775; "The Candidate," 1780; "The Library" (anon.), 1781; "The Village," 1783; "The Newspaper," 1785; "A Discourse . . . after the funeral of the Duke of Rutland," 1788; "Poems," 1807; "The Parish Register," 1807; "The Borough," 1810; "Tales," 1812; "The Variation of public opinion and feelings considered," 1817; "Tales of the Hall," 1819. *Posthumous:* "Posthumous Sermons," ed. by J. D. Hastings, 1850. *Collected Works:* with letters, and *Life* by his son George, 1834.—SHARP, R. FARQUHARSON, 1897, *A Dictionary of English Authors*, p. 68.

PERSONAL

The people with whom I live perceive my situation, and find me to be indigent and without friends. About ten days since, I was compelled to give a note for seven pounds, to avoid an arrest for about double that sum which I owe. I wrote to every friend I had, but my friends are poor likewise. . . . Having used every honest means in vain, I yesterday confessed my inability, and obtained, with much entreaty, and as the greatest favour, a week's forbearance, when I am positively told, that I must pay the money, or prepare for a prison. You will guess the purpose of so long an introduction. I appeal to you, Sir, as a good, and, let me add, a great man. I have no other pretensions to your favour than that I am an unhappy one. . . . Can you, Sir, in any degree, aid me with propriety?—Will you ask any demonstrations of my veracity? I have imposed upon myself, but I have been guilty of no other imposition. Let me, if possible, interest your compassion. I know those of rank and fortune are teased with frequent petitions, and are compelled to refuse the requests even of those whom they know to be in distress: it is, therefore, with a distant hope I ventured to solicit such favour; but you will forgive me, Sir, if you do not think proper to relieve.—CRABBE, GEORGE, 1781, *Letter to Edmund Burke, Life of Crabbe by his Son, vol.* I, *p.* 92.

Crabbe is absolutely delightful—simple as a child, but shrewd, and often good-naturedly reminding you of the best parts of his poetry. He took his wine cheerfully—far from excess; but his heart really seemed to expand; and he was full of anecdote and social feeling.—CAMPBELL, THOMAS, 1817, *To his Sister, July* 15; *Life and Letters, ed. Beattie, vol.* II, *ch.* iv.

True Bard!—and simple, as the race
Of true-born poets ever are . . .
Friend of long years! of friendship tried
Through many a bright and dark event;
In doubts, my judge—in taste, my guide—
In all, my stay and ornament!
—MOORE, THOMAS, 1832, *Verses to the Poet Crabbe's Inkstand.*

He went into Mr. Burke's room, a poor young adventurer, spurned by the opulent and rejected by the publishers, his last shilling gone, and all but his last hope with it: he came out virtually secure of almost all the good fortune that, by successive steps, afterwards fell to his lot—his genius acknowledged by one whose verdict could not be questioned—his character and manners appreciated and approved by a noble and capacious heart, whose benevolence knew no limits but its power—that of a giant in intellect, who was, in feeling, an unsophisticated child—a bright example of the close affinity between superlative talents, and the warmth of the generous affections. Mr. Crabbe had afterwards many other friends, kind, liberal, and powerful, who assisted him in his professional career; but it was one hand alone that rescued him when he was *sinking.* In reflecting upon the consequences of the letter to Burke—the happiness, the exultation, the inestimable benefits that resulted to my father,—ascribing, indeed, my own existence to that great and good man's condescension and prompt kindness—I may be pardoned for dwelling upon that interview with feelings of gratitude which I should but in vain endeavour to express.—CRABBE, GEORGE, 1834, *The Poetical Works of George Crabbe with his Letters and his Journals, Life, vol.* I, *p.* 93.

Perhaps no man of origin so very humble ever retained so few traces of it as he did, in the latter years, at least, of his long and chequered life. There was no shade of subserviency in his courtesy, or of coarseness in his hilarity; his simplicity was urbane;—the whole demeanour exactly what any one would have pronounced natural and suitable in an English clergyman of the highest class, accustomed, from youth to age, to refined society and intellectual pursuits—gentle, grave, and venerable—and only rendered more interesting by obvious unfamiliarity with some of the conventional nothings of modern town-bred usage.—LOCKHART, JOHN GIBSON, 1834, *Life of Crabbe by his Son, Quarterly Review, vol.* 50, *p.* 471.

We have tried to draw his mental, but not his physical likeness. And yet it has all along been blended with our thoughts, like the figure of one known from childhood, like the figure of our own beloved and long-lost father. We see the venerable old man, newly returned from a botanical excursion, laden with flowers and weeds (for no one knew better than he that every weed is a flower—it is the secret of his poetry), with his high narrow forehead, his grey locks, his glancing shoe-buckles, his clean dress somewhat ruffled in the woods, his mild countenance, his simple abstracted air.—GILFILLAN, GEORGE, 1847, *George Crabbe, Tait's Edinburgh Magazine, vol.* 14, *p.* 147.

Crabbe, after his literary reputation had been established, was staying for a few days at the old Hummums; but he was known to the coffee-room and to the waiters merely as "Mr. Crabbe." One forenoon, when he had gone out, a gentleman called on him, and while expressing his regret at not finding him, happened to let drop the information that Mr. Crabbe was the celebrated poet. The next time that Crabbe entered the coffee-room he was perfectly astonished at the sensation which he caused; the company were all eagerness to look at him, the waiters all officiousness to serve him.—ROGERS, SAMUEL, 1855, *Recollections of Table-Talk, ed. Dyce.*

Crabbe, when I first saw him, was an old gentleman, with white hair, and the mildest possible manner. He gave no indication of the vigor and shrewdness which he put forth in his verse. I remember that Moore was at Rogers' house one morning when Crabbe was breakfasting there, and when they were engaged to dine at some nobleman's house. Moore cautioned him, in the morning, to stand up and be manly. "For God's sake, Crabbe," said he, "don't be so *very* grateful when we go to Z—'s house to-night."—PROCTER, BRYAN WALLER, 1874? *Recollections of Men of Letters, p.* 152.

He was stern only in verse. His was the gentle, kindly nature of one who loving

God loved man, and all the creatures God has made. His early struggles, less for fame than the bare means of existence, may surely furnish a lesson, and, in their result, an encouragement, to those who labor for either through difficulties it might seem impossible to overcome.—HALL, SAMUEL CARTER, 1883, *Retrospect of a Long Life*, p. 315.

His preaching attracted large congregations. He was a clergyman of the old-fashioned school, a good friend to the poor, for whose benefit he still practised medicine, and a preacher of good home-spun morality. But he was indifferent to theological speculations, suspicious of excessive zeal, contemptuous towards "enthusiasts," and heartily opposed to Wesleyans, evangelicals, and other troublesome innovators.—STEPHEN, LESLIE, 1887, *Dictionary of National Biography, vol.* XII, *p.* 429.

GENERAL

I have sent you back Mr. Crabbe's poem, which I read with great delight. It is original, vigorous, and elegant. The alterations which I have made I do not require him to adopt, for my lines are, perhaps, not often better [than] his own; but he may take mine and his own together, and perhaps between them produce something better than either. He is not to think his copy wantonly defaced; a wet sponge will wash all the red lines away, and leave the pages clean. His Dedication will be least liked: it were better to contract it into a short sprightly address. I do not doubt of Mr. Crabbe's success.—JOHNSON, SAMUEL, 1783, *To Sir Joshua Reynolds, March* 4; *Letters, ed. Hill, vol.* II, *p.* 287.

Truth will sometimes lend her noblest fires,
And decorate the verse herself inspires:
This fact in Virtue's name let Crabbe attest;
Though Nature's sternest painter, yet the best.

—BYRON, LORD, 1809, *English Bards and Scotch Reviewers.*

I must not conclude without thanking you very gratefully for the pleasure I received in reading your extracts from Crabbe's "Borough;" some of which, particularly the "Convict's Dream," leave far behind all that any other living poet has written.—HORNER, FRANCIS, 1810, *Letter to Francis Jeffrey, July* 16; *Memoirs and Correspondence, vol.* II, *p.* 26.

It is very pleasing to perceive, that, in his best passages, Mr. Crabbe is, practically at least, a convert to the good old principle of paying some regard to fancy and taste in poetry. In these passages he works expressly for the imagination; not perhaps awakening its loftiest exertions, yet studiously courting its assistance, and conciliating its good will. He now accommodates himself to the more delicate sympathies of our nature, and flatters our prejudices by attaching to his pictures agreeable and interesting associations. Thus it is that, for his best success, he is indebted to something more than ungarnished reality. He is the Paladin, who on the day of decisive combat, laid aside his mortal arms, and took only the magic lance.—GIFFORD, WILLIAM, 1810, *Crabbe's Borough, Quarterly Review, vol.* 4, *p.* 295.

Crabbe, asking questions concerning Greek hovels.

—HUNT, LEIGH, 1811, *The Feast of the Poets.*

Crabbe, the first of living poets.—BYRON, LORD, 1819, *Observations upon an Article in Blackwood's Magazine.*

Original, terse, vigorous, and popular. He is the Hogarth of modern bards: or rather, I should say, if he display Hogarth's power of *conception*, his pictures are finished with the point and brilliancy of *Teniers.* Every body reads, because every body understands, his poems: but the subjects are too frequently painful, by being too true to nature.—DIBDIN, THOMAS FROGNALL, 1824, *The Library Companion, p.* 742, *note.*

Crabbe with all his defects stands immeasurably above Wordsworth as the Poet of the Poor.—WILSON, JOHN, 1825, *Blackwood's Magazine, Sep.*

He not only deals in incessant matters of fact, but in matters of fact of the most familiar, the least animating, and the most unpleasant kind; but he relies for the effect of novelty on the microscopic minuteness with which he dissects the most trivial objects—and for the interest he excites, on the unshrinking determination with which he handles the most painful. His poetry has an official and professional air. He is called in to cases of difficult births, of fractured limbs, or breaches of the peace; and makes out a parochial list of accidents and offenses.

He takes the most trite, the most gross and obvious and revolting part of nature, for the subject of his elaborate descriptions; but it is Nature still, and Nature is a great and mighty Goddess! . . . Mr. Crabbe is one of the most popular and admired of our living authors. That he is so, can be accounted for on no other principle than the strong ties that bind us to the world about us, and our involuntary yearnings after whatever in any manner powerfully and directly reminds us of it. —HAZLITT, WILLIAM, 1825, *The Spirit of the Age*, p. 239.

Crabbe, whose dark gold is richer than it seems.
—ELLIOTT, EBENEZER, 1829, *The Village Patriarch, bk.* iv.

That incomparable passage in Crabbe's "Borough," which has made many a rough and cynical reader cry like a child.—MACAULAY, THOMAS BABINGTON, 1830, *Mr. Robert Mongomery's Poems, Critical and Miscellaneous Essays.*

Crabbe is a cold and remorseless dissector, who pauses with the streaming knife in his hands, to explain how strongly the blood is tainted, what a gangrene is in the liver, how completely the sources of health are corrupted, and that the subject is a bad one. . . . Deliver us from Crabbe in the hour of depression! Pictures of moral, and mental, and bodily degradation, are frequent through all his works; he is one of Job's chief comforters to the people. — CUNNINGHAM, ALLAN, 1833, *Biographical and Critical History of Literature of the Last Fifty Years.*

I think Crabbe and Southey are something alike; but Crabbe's poems are founded on observation and real life—Southey's on fancy and books. In facility they are equal, though Crabbe's English is of course not upon a level with Southey's, which is next door to faultless. But in Crabbe there is an absolute defect of the high imagination; he gives me little or no pleasure: yet, no doubt, he has much power of a certain kind, and it is good to cultivate, even at some pains, a catholic taste in literature. I read all sorts of books with some pleasure, except modern sermons and treatises on political economy.—COLERIDGE, SAMUEL TAYLOR, 1834, *Table-Talk, ed. Ashe, March* 5, *p.* 276.

Crabbe is inventive; but most of the characters he draws are the reverse of poetical. There is nothing poetical in the description of a poor-house and its inhabitants.—BRYDGES, SIR SAMUEL EGERTON, 1834, *Autobiography, vol.* I, *p.* 307.

I take no pleasure in Crabbe's unpoetical representations of human life. And though no one can dispute that he had a powerful pen, and could truthfully portray what he saw, yet he had an eye only for the sad realities of life. As Mrs. Barbauld said to me many years ago, "I shall never be tired of Goldsmith's 'Deserted Village,'—I shall never look again into Crabbe's 'Village.'" Indeed, this impression is so strong, that I have never read his later works, and know little about them.—ROBINSON, HENRY CRABB, 1835, *Diary, Dec.* 29; *Reminiscences, ed. Sadler, vol.* II, *p.* 219.

The sun getting very strong, we halted the chair in a shady corner, just within the verge of his verdant arcade around the court-wall; and breathing the coolness of the spot, he [Scott] said, "Read me some amusing thing—read me a bit of Crabbe." I brought out the first volume of his old favorite that I could lay hand on, and turned to what I remembered as one of his most favourite passages in it—the description of the arrival of the Players in the "Borough." He listened with great interest, and also, as I soon perceived, with great curiosity. Every now and then he exclaimed, "Capital—excellent—very good—Crabbe has lost nothing"—and we were too well satisfied that he considered himself as hearing a new production, when, chuckling over one couplet, he said—"Better and better—but how will poor Terry endure these cuts?" I went on with the poet's terrible sarcasms upon theatrical life, and he listened eagerly, muttering, "Honest Dan!" "Dan won't like this." At length I reached those lines—

Sad happy race! soon raised and soon depressed,
Your days all passed in jeopardy and jest;
Poor without prudence, with afflictions vain,
Not warned by misery, nor enriched by gain.

"Shut the book," said Sir Walter—"I can't stand more of this—it will touch Terry to the very quick."—LOCKHART, JOHN GIBSON, 1836, *Life of Sir Walter Scott, ch.* lxxxiii.

I have given a larger space to Crabbe in

this republication than to any of his contemporary poets; not merely because I think more highly of him than of most of them, but also because I fancy that he has had less justice done him. The nature of his subjects was not such as to attract either imitators or admirers, from among the ambitious or fanciful lovers of poetry; or, consequently, to set him at the head of a School, or let him surround himself with the zealots of a Sect: And it must also be admitted, that his claims to distinction depend fully as much on his great powers of observation, his skill in touching the deeper sympathies of our nature, and his power of inculcating, by their means, the most impressive lessons of humanity, as on any fine play of fancy, or grace and beauty in his delineations. I have great faith, however, in the intrinsic worth and ultimate success of those more substantial attributes; and have, accordingly, the strongest impression that the citations I have here given from Crabbe will strike more, and sink deeper into the minds of readers to whom they are new (or by whom they may have been partially forgotten), than any I have been able to present from other writers.—JEFFREY, FRANCIS LORD, 1844, *Crabbe's Poems, Contributions to the Edinburgh Review, vol.* III, *p.* 3, *note.*

Seriously, we hope that much of Crabbe's writing will every year become less and less readable, and less and less easily understood; till, in the milder day, men shall have difficulty in believing that such physical, mental, and moral degradation, as he describes, ever existed in Britain; and till, in future Encyclopædias, his name be found recorded as a powerful but barbarous writer, writing in a barbarous age.—GILFILLAN, GEORGE, 1847, *George Crabbe, Tait's Edinburgh Magazine, vol.* 14, *p.* 147.

George Crabbe was not merely a poet, but the poet who had the sagacity to see into the real state of things, and the heart to do his duty—the great marks of the true poet, who is necessarily a true and feeling man. To him popular education, popular freedom, popular advance into knowledge and power, owe a debt which futurity will gratefully acknowledge, but no time can cancel.—HOWITT, WILLIAM, 1847, *Homes and Haunts of the Most Eminent British Poets, vol.* II, *p.* 13.

I have said that Crabbe was the least imaginative of poets. He has *no* imagination in the commonly received sense of the term; there is nothing of creation in his works; nay, I dare affirm, in opposition to that refined critic, Sir James Mackintosh, that there was no touch of an idealizing tendency in his mind; yet he is a poet; he is so through his calm but deep and steady sympathy with all that is human; he is so by his distinguished power of observation; he is so by his graphic skill. No literature boasts an author more individual than Crabbe.—OSSOLI, MARGARET FULLER, 1850? *Art, Literature and the Drama, p.* 76.

If originality, if the striking out a new path, constitutes one of the highest claims to poetical excellence, few are entitled to stand in the same rank with Crabbe. Indeed, it would be difficult to point to any prototype, either as regards his style or his subjects. The nearest approach I have met with to his sententiousness, is in the old, quaint, pointed satires of Dr. Donne; and something of his graphic truth and elaborate minuteness of description may be found in the verse of Chaucer, more especially "The Canterbury Pilgrims." But Crabbe added much—very much—which is unequivocally his own, and which acknowledges no borrowed lustre.—MOIR, D, M., 1850–51, *Sketches of the Poetical Literature of the Past Half-Century, p.* 40.

I am awfully sleepy and stupid, or should try to say something about the only book I have read for a long while back—Crabbe, whose poems were known to me long ago, but not at all familiarly till now. I fancy one might read him much oftener and much later than Wordsworth—than almost any one.—ROSSETTI, DANTE GABRIEL, 1855, *Letters to William Allingham, ed. Hill, p.* 102.

It is difficult to find a single passage, not too long for quotation, which will convey any tolerable notion of the power and beauty of Crabbe's poetry, where so much of the effect lies in the conduct of the narrative—in the minute and prolonged but wonderfully skillful as well as truthful pursuit and exposition of the course and viscissitude of passions and circumstances. —CRAIK, GEORGE L., 1861, *A Compendious History of English Literature and of the English Language, vol.* II, *p.* 513.

Crabbe adds particular to particular,

scattering rather than deepening the impression of reality, and making us feel as if every man were a species by himself.—LOWELL, JAMES RUSSELL, 1871, *Chaucer, My Study Windows, p.* 284.

Mrs. Wister quite mistook the aim of my Query about Crabbe: I asked if he were read in America for the very reason that he is not read in England. And in the October *Cornhill* is an Article upon him (I hope not by Leslie Stephen), so ignorant and self-sufficient that I am more wroth than ever. The old story of "Pope in worsted stockings"—why I could cite whole Paragraphs of as fine texture as Molière—incapable of Epigram, the Jackanapes says of "our excellent Crabbe"—why I could find fifty of the very best Epigrams in five minutes. But now do you care for him? "Honour bright?" as Sheridan used to say. I don't think I ever knew a Woman who did like C., except my Mother. What makes People (this stupid Reviewer among them) talk of worsted Stockings is because of having read only his earlier works: when he himself talked of his Muse as

"Muse of the Mad, the Foolish, and the Poor,"

the Borough: Parish Register, etc. But it is his Tales of the Hall which discover him in silk Stockings; the Subjects, the Scenery, the Actors, of a more Comedy kind: with, I say, Paragraphs, and Pages, of fine Molière style—only too often defaced by carelessness, disproportion, and "longueurs" intolerable. I shall leave my Edition of Tales of the Hall, made legible by the help of Scissors and Gum, with a word or two of Prose to bridge over pages of stupid Verse. I don't wish to try and supersede the Original, but, by the Abstract, to get People to read the whole, and so learn (as in Clarissa) how to get it all under command. I even wish that some one in America would undertake to publish—in whole, or part by part—my "Readings in Crabbe," viz., Tales of the Hall: but no one would let me do the one thing I can do.—FITZGERALD, EDWARD, 1874, *Letter, Nov.* 17; *Letters to Fanny Kemble, ed. Wright, p.* 55.

Though Crabbe occupies so marked a place in the history of English poetry, he has not met in our own generation with all the attention which he deserves. . . . As an observer and painter of the individual truths of nature no poet has ever approached him.—COURTHOPE, WILLIAM JOHN, 1880, *English Poets, ed. Ward, vol.* III, *p.* 584.

He liked Crabbe much, and thought that there was great force in his homely tragic stories. "He has a world of his own. There is a 'tramp, tramp, tramp,' a merciless sledge-hammer thud about his lines which suits his subjects." And in speaking of him he would cite Byron's "Nature's sternest painter yet the best."—TENNYSON, LORD ALFRED, 1883, *Some Criticisms on Poets, Memoirs by his Son, vol.* II, *p.* 287.

Lord Holland had not quite left the eighteenth century behind him. He preferred Dryden to Shakespeare and Crabbe to Wordsworth. It is difficult to conceive that, even in the eighteenth century, such estimates could have been common—though Wordsworth used to designate that century as "the dark age"—but they did not seem to excite surprise at Holland House. Crabbe, I think, had been personally known there; but I doubt whether, in that society, personal association went for much in the estimate of values. On Crabbe's death, Lord Melbourne rubbed his hands and took a view of it which was more than consolatory: "I am so glad when one of these fellows dies, because then one has his works complete on one's shelf and there is an end of him."—TAYLOR, SIR HENRY, 1885, *Autobiography, vol.* II. *p.* 116.

One who owns the unrivalled distinction of having been the favourite poet of the three greatest intellectual factors of the age (scientific men excepted),—Lord Byron, Sir Walter Scott, and Cardinal Newman.—BIRRELL, AUGUSTINE, 1887, *Obiter Dicta, Second Series, p.* 184.

The "Village" was intended as an antithesis to Goldsmith's idyllic sentimentalism. Crabbe's realism, preceding even Cowper and anticipating Wordsworth, was the first important indication of one characteristic movement in the contemporary school of poetry. His clumsy style and want of sympathy with the new world isolated him as a writer, as he was a recluse in his life. But the force and fidelity of his descriptions of the scenery of his native place and of the characteristics of the rural population give abiding interest to his work. His pathos is genuine and deep, and to some judgments his later works atone for the diminution in tragic interest by their gentleness and simple humour. Scott and Wordsworth had some of his poetry by heart. Scott, like Fox, had Crabbe read to him in his last illness (Lockhart, ch. lxxxiii). Wordsworth said that the poems would last as long as anything written in verse since their first appearance (note to "Village," bk. i. in Collected Works). Miss Austen said that she could fancy being Mrs. Crabbe. Jeffrey reviewed him admiringly, and in later years E. FitzGerald, the translator of "Omar Khayyám," wrote (1882) an admiring preface to a selection in which he says that Lord Tennyson appreciates them equally with himself. Cardinal Newman speaks of the "extreme delight" with which he read "Tales of the Hall," on their appearance.—STEPHEN, LESLIE, 1887, *Dictionary of National Biography, vol.* XII, *p.* 430.

He certainly succeeds in conveying his own tone of feeling to his reader—that Nature is uninteresting and has nothing in common with man. His eye for Nature was as poor as his ear for music. And we have reason to be thankful that the same wisdom which caused him to lay aside his flute, on finding that after many a painful hour he could not even master "Over the Water to Charlie," caused him also to refrain from inflicting more natural descriptions, than were necessary on his readers. . . . It is not wonderful then that Crabbe should be neglected when he has none of our three staples of existence to offer us—no treasures of nature-drawing, no psychological research, and no beauty of language.—RAE, W. F., 1887, *Crabbe, Temple Bar, vol.* 80, *pp.* 328, 329.

The question has been sometimes asked whether Crabbe was either a great poet or a great writer. If he was the first he was the second. . . . He has left behind him a body of poetry, which, whether we regard the delineation of manners, the knowledge of character, the strength of passion, or the beauty of description combined in it, need not shrink from comparison with works of which the fame is much more widely extended. Dryden, Pope, Goldsmith, Johnson, to say nothing of the later poets, each, no doubt, excelled Crabbe in some of these particulars; but they are not united to the same extent in any one of them. This distinction does not necessarily make him either so delightful a companion, or so great a poet, as those that I have named. But it qualifies him to take rank with the best of them as a Great Writer.—KEBBEL, T. E., 1888, *Life of George Crabbe* (*Great Writers*), *pp.* 102, 150.

Crabbe's description is perhaps the most nakedly realistic of any in English poetry; but it is an uncommonly good one. Realism has a narrow compass, and Crabbe's powers were confined strictly within it; but he had the best virtues of a realist. His physical vision—his sight of what presents itself to the eye—was almost perfect; he saw every object, and saw it as it was.—WOODBERRY, GEORGE EDWARD, 1890, *Studies in Letters and Life, p.* 36.

Wherefore send me Crabbe. 'Twere a pleasant leap from the Pisces to Cancer. . . . People talk about Crabbe, but they don't read him. Urge them to do so: likely enough you will only get them to read your article, but that will do them a lot of good; and it certainly will do me good, old Crabbian though I profess myself.—BROWN, THOMAS EDWARD, 1893, *To S. T. Irwin, Feb.* 26; *Letters, ed. Irwin, vol.* I, *p.* 171.

We must think of him, I believe, as a good, honest-minded, well-meaning man; dull, I dare say as a preacher; diffuse, meandering, homely and lumbering as a poet; yet touching with raw and lively colors the griefs of England's country-poor; and with a realism that is hard to match, painting the flight of petrels and of the curlew, and the great sea waves that gather and roll and break along his lines. —MITCHELL, DONALD G., 1895, *English Lands Letters and Kings, Queen Anne and the Georges, p.* 238.

With the exactness of a Dutch painter he is apt to spoil his pictures with vulgar detail, and mar his descriptions with prosaic and commonplace allusions. But, allowing for these defects there remains a large body of powerful poetry which occupies a place of its own in English literature. Crabbe was pre-eminently the poet of the poor. In early life he had lived among them and mingled with their joys and sorrows, and as he grew older, whether in the capacity of a surgeon's assistant, or in the discharge of a clergyman's duty, he must have often witnessed the extremities of sin and suffering which he afterwards so vividly described.—MILES, ALFRED H., 1895, *The Poets of the Century, Crabbe to Coleridge, p.* 14.

Nature with him is seen in her bare simplicity—austere often, sometimes ugly in her nakedness.—PALGRAVE, FRANCIS TURNER, 1896, *Landscape in Poetry, p.* 203.

Crabbe has none of the Grace of the new dispensation, if he has some glimpses of its Law. He sails so close to the wind of poetry that he is sometimes merely prosaic and often nearly so. His conception of life is anti-idealist almost to pessimism, and he has no fancy. The "jewels five words long" are not his: indeed there clung to him a certain obscurity of expression which Johnson is said to have good-naturedly smoothed out in his first work to some extent, but from which he never got quite free. . . . No writer of his time had an influence which so made for truth pure and simple, yet not untouched by the necessary "disprosing" processes of art. For Crabbe is not a mere realist; and who so considers him as such has not apprehended him. But he was a realist to this extent, that he always went to the model and never to the pattern-drawing on the Academy walls. And that was what his time needed. His general characteristics are extremely uniform: even the external shape and internal subject-matter of his poems are almost confined to the shape and matter of the verse-tale. He need not, and indeed cannot, in a book like this, be dealt with at much length. But he is a very great writer, and a most important figure at this turning-point of English literature.—SAINTSBURY, GEORGE, 1896, *A History of Nineteenth Century Literature, pp.* 8, 9.

It is superfluous to say that a writer who has been so lauded by the greatest poet, the most ardent orator, the most honored novelist, and the most refined letter-writer of England in a century must himself have possessed extraordinary qualities. Yet it remains true that Crabbe is not read, is not even likely to be much read for many years to come; and the reason of this is perfectly simple: his excellencies lie in a direction apart from the trend of modern thought and sentiment, while his faults are such as most strongly repel modern taste. . . . To me personally there is no tedium, but only endless delight, in these mated rhymes which seem to pervade and harmonize the whole rhythm. And withal they help to create the artisic illusion, that wonderful atmosphere, I may call it, which envelops Crabbe's world. No one, not even the most skeptical of Crabbe's genius, can deny that he has succeeded in giving to his work a tone or atmosphere peculiarly and consistently his own.—MORE, PAUL ELMER, 1901, *A Plea for Crabbe, Atlantic Monthly, vol.* 88, *p.* 851.

Sir James Mackintosh

1765-1832.

Born, at Aldourie, Loch Ness, 24 Oct. 1765. At school at Fortrose, 1775-80; at King's Coll., Aberdeen, Oct. 1780 to Oct. 1784. To Edinburgh, to study Medicine. To London, 1788. Married Catherine Stuart, 18 Feb. 1789. Visit to Brussels, 1790. Contrib. to "The Oracle," 1790; to "Monthly Review," 1795-96. Called to Bar at Lincoln's Inn, 1795. Wife died, 8 April 1797. Married Catherine Allen, 10 April 1798. Lectured on Philosophy at Lincoln's Inn, 1799 and 1800. Appointed Recorder of Bombay, 1803. Knighted, same year. Arrived in Bombay, May 1804. Founded Literary Society of Bombay, 1805. Judge in Vice-Admirality Court, Bombay, 1806. Returned to England, owing to ill-health, April 1812. M. P. for Nairn, 1813-19. Lived near Aylesbury, 1813-1818. Prof. of Law and General Politics at Haileybury College, Feb. 1818 to 1824. Settled at Mardocks, near Ware. M. P. for Knaresborough, 1819-32. Contrib. "History of England," vols. I.-III., and "Life of Sir Thomas More" to "Cabinet Cyclopædia," 1830; "Ethical Philosophy" to "Encyclopædia Britannica," 1830. Commissioner of Board of Control, Nov. 1831. Died, in London, 30 May 1832. Buried at Hampstead. *Works:* "Disputatio . . . de Actione Musculari," 1787; "Vindiciæ Gallicæ," 1791; "Discourse on the Study of the Law of Nature and Nations," 1799; "Speech in defence of Peltier," 1803; "Plan of a Comparative Vocabulary of Indian Languages," 1806; "Speech. . . . on the Bill for disfranchising the Borough of East Retford," 1828; "Dissertation on the Progress of Ethical Philosophy" (priv. ptd.), 1830; "Speech . . . on the . . . Bill to amend the Representation of the People" 1831. *Posthumous:* "History of the Revolution in England in 1688," 1834; "Tracts and Speeches" (priv. ptd.), 1840. He *edited:* Rev. R. Hall's "Works," 1832, etc. *Collected Works:* in 3 vols., 1846. *Life:* by R. J. Mackintosh, 1836.—SHARP, R. FARQUHARSON, 1897, *A Dictionary of English Authors, p.* 180.

PERSONAL

Though thou'rt like Judas, an apostate black,
In the resemblance one thing thou dost lack;
When he had gotten his ill-purchas'd pelf,
He went away, and wisely hang'd himself:
This thou may'st do at last; yet much I doubt
If thou hast any bowels to gush out!

—LAMB, CHARLES, 1801, *To Sir James Mackintosh.*

Nothing has pleased me more in London than the conversation of Mackintosh. I never saw so theoretical a head which contained so much practical understanding. He has lived much among various men, with great observation, and has always tried his profound moral speculations by the experience of life. He has not contracted in the world a lazy contempt for theorists, nor in the closet a peevish impatience of that grossness and corruptibility of mankind which are ever marring the schemes of secluded benevolence. He does not wish for the *best* in politics or morals, but for the best which can be attained; and what that is he seems to know well.—SMITH, SYDNEY, 1801, *To Francis Jeffrey, July; Letters of Sydney Smith, ed. Mrs. Austin.*

I confess the more I see of this wonderful man, the more I am led to believe that modern times have not degenerated from the genius of antiquity, and there is an amiable simplicity, natural to great minds, in M.'s dispositions, which commands esteem as well as admiration.—CAMPBELL, THOMAS, 1802, *To Dr. Currie, April* 13; *Life and Letters, ed. Beattie, vol.* I, *p.* 364.

He has been an intellectual master to me, and has enlarged my prospects into the wide regions of moral speculation, more than any other tutor I have ever had in the art of thinking; I cannot even except Dugald Stewart, to whom I once thought I owed more than I could ever receive from another. Had Mackintosh remained in England, I should have possessed ten years hence, powers and views which are now beyond my reach. I never left his conversation, but I felt a mixed consciousness, as it were, of inferiority and capability; and I have now and then flattered myself with this feeling, as if it promised that I might make something of myself.—HORNER, FRANCIS, 1804, *Letter to William Erskine, Feb.* 4; *Memoirs and Correspondence, vol.* I, *p.* 257.

Mackintosh, who is a rare instance of the union of very transcendent talent and great good-nature.—BYRON, LORD, 1813, *Journals, Nov.* 30.

Sir James Mackintosh is a little too precise, a little too much made up in his manners and conversation, but is at the same time very exact, definite, and logical in what he says, and, I am satisfied, seldom has occasion to regret a mistake or an error, where a matter of principle or reasoning is concerned, though, as he is a little given to affect universal learning, he may sometimes make a mistake in matters of fact. As a part of a considerable literary society, however, he discourses most eloquent music, and in private, where I also saw him several times, he is mild, gentle, and entertaining. But he is seen to greatest advantage, and in all his strength, only in serious discussion, to which he brings great disciplined acuteness and a fluent eloquence, which few may venture to oppose, and which still fewer can effectually resist.—TICKNOR, GEORGE, 1819, *Journal; Life, Letters and Journals, vol.* I, *p.* 265.

Sir James Mackintosh is the king of the men of talent. He is a most elegant converser. How well I remember his giving breakfast to me and Sir Humphry Davy, at that time an unknown young man, and our having a very spirited talk about Locke and Newton, and so forth! When Davy was gone, Mackintosh said to me, "That's a very extraordinary young man; but he is gone wrong on some points." But Davy was, at that time at least, a man of genius; and I doubt if Mackintosh ever heartily appreciated an eminently original man. He is uncommonly powerful in his own line; but it is not the line of a first-rate man. After all his fluency and brilliant erudition, you can rarely carry off anything worth preserving. You might not improperly write on his forehead, "Warehouse to let!" He always dealt too much in generalities for a lawyer. He is deficient in power in applying his principles to the points in debate. I remember Robert Smith had much more logical ability; but Smith aimed at conquest by any gladiatorial shift; whereas Mackintosh was uniformly candid in argument. I am speaking now from old recollections.—COLERIDGE, SAMUEL TAYLOR, 1823, *Table-Talk, ed. Ashe, Apr.* 27, *p.* 25.

He spoke *the truth, the whole truth, and nothing but the truth;* but the House of Commons (we dare aver it) is not the place where the truth, the whole truth, and nothing but the truth can be spoken with safety or with advantage. . . . There wanted unity of purpose, impetuosity of feeling to break through the phalanx of hostile and inveterate prejudice arrayed against him. He gave a handle to his enemies; threw stumbling-blocks in the way of his friends. He raised so many objections for the sake of answering them, proposed so many doubts for the sake of solving them, and made so many concessions where none were demanded, that his reasoning had the effect of neutralizing itself; it became a mere exercise of the understanding without zest or spirit left in it; and the provident engineer who was to shatter in pieces the strong-holds of corruption and oppression, by a well-directed and unsparing discharge of artillery, seemed to have brought not only his own cannon-balls, but his own wool-packs along with him to ward off the threatened mischief.—HAZLITT, WILLIAM, 1825, *The Spirit of the Age, pp.* 138, 139.

Whatever was valuable in the compositions of Sir James Mackintosh, was the ripe fruit of study and of meditation. It was the same with his conversation. In his most familiar talk there was no wildness, no inconsistency, no amusing nonsense, no exaggeration for the sake of momentary effect. His mind was a vast magazine, admirably arranged; everything was there, and everything was in its place. His judgments on men, on sects, on books, had been often and carefully tested and weighed, and had then been committed, each to its proper receptacle, in the most capacious and accurately constructed memory that any human being ever possessed. It would have been strange indeed, if you had asked for anything that was not to be found in that immense storehouse. The article which you required was not only there. It was ready. It was in its own proper compartment. In a moment it was brought down, unpacked, and displayed. If those who enjoyed the privilege—for privilege indeed it was—of listening to Sir James Mackintosh, had been disposed to find some fault in his conversation, they might perhaps have observed that he yielded too little to the impulse of the moment. He seemed to be recollecting, not creating. He never appeared to catch a sudden glimpse of a subject in a new light. You never saw his opinions in the making, —still rude, still inconsistent, and requiring to be fashioned by thought and discussion. They came forth, like the pillars of that temple in which no sound of axes or hammers was heard, finished, rounded, and exactly suited to their places.—MACAULAY, THOMAS BABINGTON, 1834, *Mackintosh's History of the Revolution in England in* 1688, *Critical and Miscellaneous Essays.*

His range of study and speculation was nearly as large as that of Bacon; and there were, in fact, but few branches of learning with which he was not familiar. But in any attempt at delineating his intellectual character, it is necessary to bear in mind, that his mastery was in mental philosophy, not merely in its recondite or metaphysical departments, but in its still more important application to conduct and affairs, and in their higher branches of politics and legislation, which derive their proofs and principles from history, and give authority to its lessons in return. Upon all these subjects, he was probably the most learned man of his age; and in maturing and digesting his views of them, I am persuaded that there have been few, in any age, who ever brought a more powerful and disciplined understanding to bear with so much candour, caution, and modesty, upon so large a collection of materials.—JEFFREY, FRANCIS LORD, 1835, *Letter to Robert James Mackintosh, March* 16; *Memoirs of Mackintosh, ed., his Son, vol.* II, *p.* 492.

If we might venture to conclude, that in these pages have also been revealed more abiding endowments, and such as death does not cancel;—sympathy with the triumph of truth, and justice, and liberty, and with whatever is loftiest and noblest in our nature; active devotion, through a life of labour, disappointment, some sorrow, and much sickness, to the interests of his kind, whether in struggling for their liberty, or in the still higher vocation of teaching them worthily to enjoy it; a political career, in troubled times, which, on retrospect, certainly offered no action, and probably no word, directed against an enemy, which need be recalled; an admiration of excellence in others so pure, as to be one of the principal sources of his own enjoyment, joined to an unaffected humility in estimating his own merits; warm affections, quick sensibility, and generous confidence; religious sentiments, such as might be embodied in his own confessions, "that there was nothing in this world *so* right as to cultivate and exercise kindness—the most certainly evangelical of all doctrines—THE principle of Jesus Christ," and which led him to look forward with ardent hope, and humble faith, to the day when tears shall be "wiped from all eyes:"—if these, or any of them shall have been made duly manifest, then will the labour of the present work have been amply rewarded, and its object not wholly unattained.—MACKINTOSH, ROBERT JAMES, 1836, *Memoirs of the Life of Sir James Mackintosh, vol.* II, *p.* 508.

Porson disliked Mackintosh; they differed in politics, and their reading had little in common.—MALTBY, WILLIAM, 1854, *Porsoniana.*

Mackintosh told me that he had received in his youth comparatively little instruction,—whatever learning he possessed he owed to himself. He had a prodigious memory, and could repeat by heart more of Cicero than you would easily believe. His knowledge of Greek was slender. I never met a man with a fuller mind than Mackintosh,—such readiness on all subjects, such a talker!—ROGERS, SAMUEL, 1855, *Recollections of Table-Talk, ed. Dyce.*

Sir James Mackintosh had a very Parson-Adams-like forgetfulness of common things and lesser proprieties, which was very amusing. On his arrival at Bombay, there being no house ready for his reception, the Governor offered his garden-house for the temporary accommodation of Sir James and his family, who were so comfortable in their quarters, that they forgot to quit, month after month, till a year had elapsed, when the Governor took forcible possession of his own property. Again, Sir James and his Lady, on requesting to inspect the seat of Lord Melville, in Perthshire, were invited to stay two or three days, which were protracted to as many months, till every species of hint was thrown away upon them.—TIMBS, JOHN, 1860, *A Century of Anecdote, p.* 210.

No man doing so little ever went through a long life, continually creating the belief that he would ultimately do so much. A want of earnestness, a want of passion, a want of genius, prevented him from playing a great part amongst men during his day, and from leaving any of those monuments behind him which command the attention of posterity. A love of knowledge, an acute and capacious intelligence, an early and noble ambition, led him into literary and active life, and furnished him with materials and at moments with the energy by which success in both is obtained. An amiable disposition, a lively flow of spirits, an extraordinary and various stock of information made his society agreeable to the most distinguished persons of his age, and induced them, encouraged by some occasional displays of power, to consider his abilities to be greater than they really were.—BULWER, SIR HENRY LYTTON, 1867, *Historical Characters, vol.* II, *p.* 93.

I saw much afterwards of Madame de Staël at her own house in Argyll Street, in those literary and political circles which she gathered round her, and where she declaimed or argued with all who could meet her with her own weapons and in her own language. Sir J. Mackintosh was the most frequent and expert of these intellectual combatants: and it was the combat most congenial to his own tastes. In some points there was a certain intellectual likeness between them; such as the power of putting an argument into its most pithy shape—what may be called a *wit of speech*, apart from that gift of *humour*, to which neither of them could lay much claim.—HOLLAND, SIR HENRY, 1871, *Recollections of Past Life, p.* 112.

The great Whig leader was grandly eloquent—at times; but it seemed as hard to rouse him to exertion as it would have been to move the half-torpid sloth. His exordiums were sluggish; not so his perorations. He spoke, however, like a machine, that, once set moving, will go on doing its allotted work effectually to the end. He would sway backward and forward, as if his head were too heavy for his body. Those who remember him before his actual decay will recall him as altogether Scottish in manner and mind: his accent retained the smack of early training. Lacking grace and dignity, the spirit of earnestness that pervaded his speeches almost supplied the places of both. . . . Mackintosh was usually sluggish—often as much so as his proverbially sleepy neighbor, Charles Grant—afterwards Lord Glenelg; but when suddenly excited, he poured forth a torrent of eloquence, majestic in its wrath; when indignation roused him, it was generally an instant outburst—at least in his latter days. It would not seem exaggeration, to those who remember him in his decadence, to liken it to a volcanic fire.—HALL, SAMUEL CARTER, 1883, *Retrospect of a Long Life, pp.* 119, 120.

GENERAL

Read Mackintosh's "Vindiciæ Gallicæ." His style and manner, in this piece, are magnificent, but uniformly cumbrous, and occasionally warm. He has infinitely improved both in his "Preliminary Discourse," though some of the ponderosity still remains. There can hardly be a more express and full contradiction than in two passages,—p. 265 of the "Vindiciæ" and p. 49 of the "Discourse."—GREEN, THOMAS, 1799, *Diary of a Lover of Literature, Apr.* 29.

As an author, Sir James Mackintosh may claim the foremost rank among those who pride themselves on artificial ornaments and acquired learning, or who write what may be termed a *composite* style. His "Vindiciæ Galliciæ" is a work of great labour, great ingenuity, great brilliancy, and great vigour. It is little too antithetical in the structure of its periods, too dogmatical in the announcement of its opinions. Sir James has, we believe, rejected something of the *false brilliant* of the one, as he has retracted some of the abrupt extravagance of the other. We apprehend, however, that our author is not one of those who draw from their own resources and accumulated feelings, or who improve with age. He belongs to a class (common in Scotland and elsewhere) who get up school-exercises on any given subject in a masterly manner at twenty, and who at forty are either where they were—or retrograde, if they are men of sense and modesty. . . . All his ideas may be said to be given preconceptions. They do not arise, as it were, out of the subject, or out of one another at the moment, and therefore do not flow naturally and gracefully from one another. They have been laid down before hand in a sort of formal division or frame work of the understanding; and the connexion between the premises and the conclusion, between one branch of a subject and another, is made out in a bungling and unsatisfactory manner. There is no principle of fusion in the work; he strikes after the iron is cold, and there is want of malleability in the style.—HAZLITT, WILLIAM, 1825, *The Spirit of the Age, pp.* 145, 146.

The present work ["Ethical Philosophy"] is distinguished by a similar affluence of rare learning, acute and delicate discrimination of thought, great force of argument, and singular candor and urbanity in the discussion of systems, which are at war with the opinions of the author himself, and which it is his purpose pointedly to condemn. We cannot say so much of the style of Sir James Mackintosh, as the expression of philosophical reasoning. It is elaborate to excess; but too visibly elaborate to be perfectly agreeable: and in many instances, his love of condensation betrays him into obscurity. In those passages which contain a long train of reasoning, the transition from one step to another, is usually far from being evident; and the enunciation of the propositions upon which he depends, as well as of the conclusions at which he arrives, is presented in such abstract terms, that we are often uncertain, whether we have rightly apprehended his meaning. We miss the variety and playfulness of illustration, which make the style of Hume so attractive, and which will always give him the rank of a most entertaining as well as acute writer on subjects of abstract speculation. Neither do we find any resemblance to the full and graceful flow of transparent diction, by which Dugald Stewart is quite as favorably distinguished as by the variety of his learning and the soundness of his understanding. With these abatements, which we could not in conscience omit, we regard Sir James Mackintosh as entitled to a high rank among the philosophical writers of the present and the last age, who have given an imperishable charm to the fruits of deep speculation, and erected a splendid monument to their names, in the history of English literature.—RIPLEY, GEORGE, 1833, *Sir James Mackintosh's Ethical Philosophy, Christian Examiner, vol.* 13, *p.* 311.

In these memorials of Sir James Mackintosh, we trace throughout the workings of a powerful and unclouded intellect, nourished by wholesome learning, raised and instructed by fearless though reverent questionings of the sages of other times (which is the permitted Necromancy of the wise), exercised by free discussion with the most distinguished among the living, and made acquainted with its own strength and weakness, not only by a constant intercourse with other powerful minds, but by mixing, with energy and deliberation, in practical business and affairs; and here pouring itself out in a delightful miscellany of elegant criticism, original speculation, and profound practical suggestions on politics, religion, history, and all the greater and the lesser duties, the arts and the elegances of life—all expressed with a beautiful clearness and tempered dignity—breathing the purest spirit of good-will to mankind—and brightened not merely by an ardent hope, but an assured faith in their constant advancement in freedom, intelligence, and virtue.—JEFFREY, FRANCIS LORD, 1835–1844, *Sir James Mackintosh, Contributions to the Edinburgh Review, vol.* IV, *p.* 522.

As a writer, he will ever be highly esteemed by a chosen few—but he is, we fear we must admit, not likely to sustain an *extensive* popularity with posterity.—CROKER, JOHN WILSON, 1835, *Life of Sir James Mackintosh, Quarterly Review, vol.* 54, *p.* 291.

I must now, however, mention to you the three octavo volumes on English History that were drawn up by Sir James Mackintosh, for Dr. Lardner. There is little pretension in the appearance of these volumes: do not be deceived by this circumstance; they are full of weighty matter, and are everywhere marked by paragraphs of comprehensive thought and sound philosophy, political and moral; they are well worthy their distinguished author. The sentences are now and then overcharged with reflection, so as to become obscure, particularly in the first volume. But do not be deterred by a fault that too naturally resulted from the richly stored and highly metaphysical mind of this valuable writer.—SMYTH, WILLIAM, 1839, *Lectures on Modern History, vol.* I, *p.* 132.

We do not think his works are fair and full exponents of his nature; and his reputation was always justly greater for what he was, than for what he performed, valuable as were most of his performances.—WHIPPLE, EDWIN P., 1845, *North American Review, Essays and Reviews, vol.* II, *p.* 143.

He is full of information and suggestion upon every topic which he treats. Few men have so much combined the power of judging wisely from a stationary position with the power of changing that station under changing circumstances in the age or in the subject. He moves slowly, or with velocity, as he moves amongst breakers, or amongst open seas. And upon every theme which he treats, in proportion as it rises in importance, the reader is sure of finding displayed the accomplishments of a scholar, the philosophic resources of a very original thinker, the elegance of a rhetorician, and the large sagacity of a statesman, controlled by the most sceptical caution of a lawyer.—DE QUINCEY, THOMAS, 1846–59, *Glance at the Works of Mackintosh, Works, ed. Masson, vol.* VIII, *p.* 156.

Much he learned—thought much—collected much treasure; but the greater part of it was buried with him. Many a prize, hung on high in the intellectual firmament, he could discern with eyes carefully purged from the films of ignorance and grossness; he could discern the steps even by which he might have mounted to the possession of any one which he had resolutely chosen and perseveringly sought—but this he did not. And though many a pillar and many a stone remain to tell where he dwelt and how he strove, we seek in vain for the temple of perfect workmanship with which Nature meant so skillful an architect should have adorned her Earth.—OSSOLI, MARGARET FULLER, 1850? *Art, Literature and the Drama, p.* 59.

Mackintosh has been already discussed in these pages as a senator; but his merits as an essayist, and as one of the original contributors to the *Edinburgh Review*, are too considerable to render any apology necessary for again making him the subject of discussion. His mind was essentially philosophical; his soul was imbued with principle, his memory stored with knowledge. He was fitted to have been a great teacher of men, rather than their powerful ruler. These characteristics are strongly apparent in his writings; and the English language cannot present a more perfect example of philosophical disquisition than some of his political essays, particularly that on Parliamentary Reform, exhibit.—ALISON, SIR ARCHIBALD, 1853–59, *History of Europe*, 1815–1852, *ch.* v.

If he had only had the courage to devote himself to what he knew to be his forte, but which could not bring him immediate fame; had he read systematically, instead of discursively, and made himself as well acquainted with the higher forms of the Greek and German philosophy, as he did with the later forms and of British philosophy,—he might have ranked with the highest thinkers of his age. As it is he has left us little that will endure beyond these able and candid sketches of ethical writers.—MCCOSH, JAMES, 1874, *The Scottish Philosophy, p.* 359.

In one sense Mackintosh can hardly be regarded as an historian; in another sense he is the most philosophic historian that ever lived. He accomplished so little that his fame rests on a small basis; but the little which he accomplished is remarkable for so much knowledge, research, and discrimination, that his studies deserve especial attention.—WALPOLE, SPENCER, 1878, *A History of England from the Conclusion of the Great War in* 1815, *vol.* I, *p.* 344.

His style is elegant and carefully wrought, but somewhat languid and wanting in pith and power.—NICOLL, HENRY, J., 1882, *Landmarks of English Literature, p.* 342.

This ["Vindiciæ Gallicæ"] should be read in connection with Burke's essay. Its purpose is sufficiently indicated by its title. Perhaps Mackintosh was the only man at the time in England who by his literary skill and his political sympathy was qualified to review the work and break the force of its great influence. Through the whole essay there runs a strong current of liberal thought, which gives to it a constant value. As a presentation of the view opposed to that of Burke, it has had no superior, and, perhaps, has never been equalled. Its appearance in England raised the author at once to a position of supreme influence among the members of the Whig party.—ADAMS, CHARLES KENDALL, 1882, *A Manual of Historical Literature, p.* 364.

Mackintosh's historical writings, though tending to discourse rather than narrative, show reading and a judicial temper, but have been superseded by later books. The "Dissertation upon Ethical Philosophy" is perfunctory, except in regard to the English moralists since Hobbes, and greatly wanting in clearness and precision. It is intended to be eclectic, accepting Hume's doctrine of utility as the "criterion" of morals, and Butler's doctrine of the supremacy of the conscience, while the formation of the conscience is explained by Hartley's doctrine of association. In substance it seems to be a modification of utilitarianism, and suggests some important amendments in the theory. James Mill, however, attacked it with excessive severity in his "Fragment on Mackintosh," 1835, and exposed much looseness of thought and language.—STEPHEN, LESLIE, 1893, *Dictionary of National Biography, vol.* XXXV, *p.* 177.

The "Dissertation" is not faultless either in matter or style. The position of Kant for example, could hardly be properly understood from it; nor do we learn much when we are told that the system of Hobbes was like a "palace of ice gradually undermined by the central warmth of human feeling, before it was thawed into muddy water by the sunshine of true philosophy." Mackintosh could use the language of common life when he chose. The question whether a simple representative legislature is better than a constitution of mutal control, is (he says in the *Vind. Gall.*) simply the question "whether the vigilance of the master, or the squabbles of the servants, are the best security for faithful service." A little more of this plainness of speech would have enhanced the value of his writings; but formed habits were too strong for him.—BONAR, JAMES, 1895, *English Prose, ed. Craik, vol.* IV, *p.* 589.

To pass from Burke to Mackintosh is to make the descent from genius to talent with more suddenness, not to say violence, than one would naturally prefer. Yet Mackintosh is perhaps the only other prose writer who can be even mentioned in the period overshadowed by Gibbon and Burke; for Robertson, though an historian of merit, can hardly be said as a prose writer to be anything more than an echo of his English models. Mackintosh has undoubtedly more individuality. The "Vindiciæ Gallicæ" can still be read with pleasure; and did it not everywhere challenge a disastrous comparison with the monumental work to which it is the very inadequate answer, it would win more admiration than it does. As it is, one cannot help reading it with a feeling that with all its more than respectable merit it is thoroughly characteristic of that universal genius whom partial friends regarded as an Admirable Crichton and posterity has clean forgotten.—TRAILL, HENRY DUFF, 1896, *Social England, vol.* v, *p.* 452.

His range of acquirements was most wide—too wide and too unceasing for the persistency which goes with great single achievements. His histories are fragments. His speeches are misplaced treatises; his treatises are epitomes of didactic systems. When we weigh his known worth, his keenness of intellect, his sound judgment, his wealth of language, his love for thoroughness—which led him to remotest sources of information—his amazing power in coloquial discourse, we are astonished at the little store of good things he has left.—MITCHELL, DONALD G., 1897, *English Lands Letters and Kings, The Later Georges to Victoria, p.* 105.

There has been a certain tendency, both in his own time and since, to regard Mackintosh as a sort of philosopher thrown away. If he was so, he would probably have made his mark rather in the history of philosophy than in philosophy itself, for there are no signs in him of much original depth. But he wrote very well, and was a sound and on the whole a fair critic.—SAINTSBURY, GEORGE, 1896, *A History of Nineteenth Century Literature, p.* 345.

In James Mackintosh the school of Stewart stepped from its academic seclusion into the world of politics and law, only to betray more obviously its academic quality; its capacity for learned and luminous exposition of principles, but not for the philosophy that shapes lives and transforms states.—HERFORD, C. H., 1897, *The Age of Wordsworth, p.* 20.

Adam Clarke

1762?–1832.

A Wesleyan divine, distinguished for his varied learning, was born at Moybeg, in the north of Ireland, in 1760 or 1762. After receiving a very limited education he was apprenticed to a linen manufacturer, but, finding the employment uncongenial, he soon abandoned it, and devoted himself to study. . . . In 1782 he entered on the duties of the ministry, being appointed by Wesley to the Bradford (Wiltshire) circuit. His popularity as a preacher was very great, and his influence in the denomination is indicated by the fact that he was three times chosen to be president of the Conference. He served twice on the London circuit, the second period being extended considerably longer than the rule allowed, at the special request of the British and Foreign Bible Society, who had employed him in the preparation of their Arabic Bible. He had found time during his itinerancy for diligent study of Hebrew and other Oriental languages, undertaken chiefly with the view of qualifying himself for the great work of his life, his "Commentary on the Holy Scriptures," the first volume of which appeared in 1810, and the eighth and last in 1826. It is a work of much learning and ability, and it still possesses some value, though it is in great part superseded by the results of later scholarship. Dr. Clarke's other literary works were very numerous. In 1802 he published a "Bibliographical Dictionary" in six volumes, to which he afterwards added a supplement. He was selected by the Record's Commission to edit Rymer's "Fœdera," a task for which he was not well qualified, and which he did not complete. He also wrote "Memoirs of the Wesley Family" (1823), and edited a large number of religious works. He died of cholera in London on the 16th August, 1832. His Miscellaneous Works have been published in a collected form in 13 vols., and a Life by J. B. B. Clarke appeared in 1833.—BAYNES, THOMAS SPENCER, *ed.*, 1877, *Encyclopædia Britannica, Ninth ed., vol.* v, *p.* 707.

PERSONAL

In personal appearance there was nothing particularly remarkable in my Father: he was about five feet nine inches high, and in the latter years of his life had a tendency to a full habit of body; his frame was one of considerable strength, his limbs straight and well-proportioned, and his person unbowed to the last hour of his life. His features were characteristic of the benevolence of his mind; his smile inspired a confidence which the kindness of his manner confirmed; and no one could feel distrustful in the presence of his cheerful frankness, nor fail to do reverence to a dignity resulting from piety and wisdom, rendered more venerable by his grey hairs. His personal habits were those of unintermitted industry, unincumbered by busy haste, and directed by the exactest order; what he had to do was performed at once and to the best of his power, his mind never giving way to that sort of hesitating examination of a difficulty or duty which only discourages from its conquest or performance, without affording any additional power or wisdom to undertake the task. I never once saw my father idle: even in his relaxations his mind was occupied either in contriving and affording entertainment for others, or else in deriving healthful pleasure to himself. . . . A tolerably correct estimate of my Father's diligence in *preaching* may be formed from the following statement:—from the year 1784 to 1785, he preached 568 sermons, independently of lectures, expositions, etc.; and from 1782 to 1808, he preached no less than 6,615 sermons, also exclusive of exhortations, etc. During his abode in London, for three years, commencing 1795, he walked more than 7,000 miles, merely on journeys to preach in the city and its neighborhood, not reckoning his walking on other private and public business.—CLARKE, J. B. B., 1833, *An Account of the Infancy, Religious and Literary Life of Adam Clarke, pp.* 626, 628.

In the midst of incessant toils as an evangelist, he acquired an amount of erudition which is truly surprising, and which made him one of the foremost scholars of his time. In addition to the classics and Hebrew, Dr. Clarke was familiar with the Syriac and Chaldee languages, with Persian, Arabic, and Sanscrit, and had some knowledge of Ethiopic and Coptic, together with Anglo-Saxon, French, and German. Besides these, he had studied nearly all the natural sciences, and was well read in general literature. Do our young readers ask, with amazement, How could this possibly be done by one so actively engaged? We reply, Adam Clarke knew the value of time, and emphatically he "redeemed" it—redeemed it from sleep, idle gossip, and frivolous pursuits. Like Doddridge, he was an *early* student, rising at four or five o'clock, and giving the first morning hours to study and meditation.—GROSER, WILLIAM H., 1871, *Men Worth Imitating, p.* 145.

He conveyed little idea of a man who labored by lamp-light; but rather that of one whose work was done, at all seasons, in the open air. In the pulpit he had only the eloquence that proceeds from perseverance and convincing zeal. It is something to have known a man who was the associate and friend as well as one of the chosen missionaries of John Wesley. Dr. Clarke loved much to speak of his knowledge of that great man, who, in 1782, had laid his hand on the head of the young neophyte, and dedicated him to the ministry: and when the subject of this brief notice died, his mortal remains were interred in the burial-ground of the Methodists in the City Road, close beside those of the Gamaliel at whose feet he had sat. —HALL, SAMUEL CARTER, 1883, *Retrospect of a Long Life, p.* 415.

GENERAL

The literary world in general, and biblical students in particular, are greatly indebted to Dr. Clarke for the light he has thrown on many very difficult passages.—HORNE, THOMAS HARTWELL, 1818–39, *A Manual of Biblical Bibliography.*

It ["Commentary"] displays much learning and vast reading. It dwells frequently on minute points of comparatively small importance, and touches some other points very lightly. . . . The doctrines of Arminius appeared in it, but are not offensively urged; and those who cannot afford to purchase many books, will find in the stores of Dr. Clarke's "Commentary" valuable assistance for the understanding of the Bible.—ORME, WILLIAM, 1824, *Bibliotheca Biblica.*

There is much valuable matter in it

["Commentary"]. Light is sometimes thrown on difficult passages; but he is too fond of innovations, and justifying generally condemned characters, and has both eccentric and exceptionable passages; yet he often makes good practical remarks.—BICKERSTETH, EDWARD, 1844, *The Christian Student.*

One hardly likes to close this sketch of the Methodist leaders without at least a passing notice of the most learned of them all, Dr. Adam Clarke.—OVERTON, JOHN HENRY, 1886, *The Evangelical Revival in the Eighteenth Century, p.* 43.

The literary power and capacity of investigation evinced by Clarke bore fruit in two ways. As a theological writer he produced many works of ability, including English translations and new editions of other men's books.—BLAIKIE, WILLIAM GARDEN, 1887, *Dictionary of National Biography, vol.* X, *p.* 413.

Philip Freneau

1752–1832.

A journalist of New York city who, during the Revolution, produced much patriotic verse that was very effective as well as popular, though none of it is marked by any high degree of excellence. "Poems of Philip Freneau, written chiefly during the Late War" (1786); "Poems Written between the Years 1768 and 1794"; "Poems Written and Published during the American Revolution"; "Collection of Poems on American Affairs." Among his prose writings are, "The Philosopher of the Forest"; "Essays by Robert Slender."—ADAMS, OSCAR FAY, 1897, *A Dictionary of American Authors, p.* 138.

PERSONAL

On the eighteenth of December, 1832, an old man, sprightly and vigorous under the weight of nearly eighty-one years, started, just as the evening was coming on, to walk from the village of Monmouth, in New Jersey, to his home in the open country, a distance of about two miles. At that home, a paternal estate of a thousand acres, this man had passed, at intervals, many years of his long life—filled as it had been with manifold employments on land and sea. He was still a fine specimen of active and manly old age; in person somewhat below the ordinary height, but muscular and compact; his face pensive in expression and with a careworn look; his dark gray eyes sunken deep in their sockets, but sending out gleams and flashes of fire when aroused in talk; his hair once abundant and beautiful, now thinned and bleached by time; stooping a little as he walked; to those who knew him, accustomed to give delight by a conversation abounding in anecdotes of the great age of the American Revolution. On the evening just referred to, he had started alone on his walk towards his home, but the night passed away without his arrival there; and the next morning his lifeless body was found in a swampy meadow, into which, as it seemed, he must have wandered,—missing his way in the darkness, and in his exhaustion and bewilderment surrendering at last to death. That dead old man was Philip Freneau, incomparably the bitterest and the most unrelenting, and, in some respects the most powerful, of the satirical poets belonging to the insurgent side of the Revolution.—TYLER, MOSES COIT, 1897, *The Literary History of the American Revolution,* 1763–1783, *vol.* I, *p.* 171.

Extremely hospitable, Freneau always warmly welcomed his friends at Mount Pleasant, where he devoted his declining years to reading and answering his numerous correspondents, and in occasionally penning an article for the press. He always retained his original frankness in expressing himself, but it was softened down considerably as he advanced in years. In fact it was his pen, as some author has said, more than his heart that was so acrimonious in his early years; no personal malice ever rested in his mind, and he was ever ready to pardon those who had injured him. Even his adversaries, some of whom he had treated pretty roughly with his pen in early days, in later times claimed him as a friend. In his friendships he was ardent and sincere, and they were usually life-long. — AUSTIN, MARY S., 1901, *Philip Freneau the Poet of the Revolution, p.* 202.

GENERAL

Philip Freneau was the most distinguished poet of our revolutionary time. He was a voluminous writer, and many of his compositions are intrinsically worthless, or, relating to persons and events now forgotten, are no longer interesting; but enough remain to show that he had more genius and more enthusiasm than any other bard whose powers were called into action during the great struggle for liberty.—GRISWOLD, RUFUS W., 1842-46, *The Poets and Poetry of America, p.* 1.

He wrote many songs and ballads in a patriotic and historical vein, which attracted and somewhat reflected the feelings of his contemporaries, and were not destitue of merit. Their success was owing, in part, to the immediate interest of the subjects, and in part to musical versification and pathetic sentiment. One of his Indian ballads has survived the general neglect to which more artistic skill and deeper significance in poetry have banished the mass of his verses; to the curious in the metrical writings, however, they yet afford a characteristic illustration of the taste and spirit of the times.—TUCKERMAN, HENRY T., 1852, *A Sketch of American Literature.*

The poems of Philip Freneau represent his times, the war of wit and verse no less than of sword and stratagem of the Revolution; and he superadds to this material a humorous, homely simplicity peculiarly his own, in which he paints the life of village rustics, with their local manners fresh about them, of days when tavern delights were to be freely spoken of, before temperance societies and Maine laws were thought of; when men went to prison at the summons of inexorable creditors, and when Connecticut deacons rushed out of meeting to arrest and waylay the passing Sunday traveller. When these humors of the day were exhausted, and the impulses of patriotism were gratified in song, when he had paid his respects to Rivington and Hugh Gaine, he solaced himself with higher themes, in the version of an ode of Horace, a visionary meditation on the antiquities of America, or a sentimental effusion on the loves of Sappho. These show the fine tact and delicate handling of Freneau, who deserves much more consideration in this respect from critics than he has ever received. — DUYCKINCK, EVERT A. AND GEORGE L., 1855-65-75, *Cyclopædia of American Literature, ed. Simons, vol.* I.

The headlong mass of his verse far exceeded his powers to keep it up to the highest standard of that age, far less to escape the anathemas of our own when every graduate can make fair jingle on moon or glacier, on love or war. Nine-tenths of his patriotic hymns, of his odes valedictory, worshipful, or comminative, are such as are consigned to the corners of weekly newspapers. Some half dozen pieces, however, remain to prove that Philip Freneau was a poet.—NICHOL, JOHN, 1880-85, *American Literature, p.* 94.

Freneau was a genius in his way, and had brilliant instincts. Some of his poetry sprung from the intense flame of oppression, and as a poet he blew it to a white heat. He was possessed of an impetuous flow of song for freedom, and his wit was pungent and stinging. That he used this with effect can be readily seen by any person who reads his supposed interview with King George and Fox. Then take his exquisite dirge of the heroes of Eutaw Springs, his odes like "Benedict Arnold's Departure;" some parts of them unrivalled. His works show that he imitated in some degree both Gray and Shelley.—MURRAY, JAMES D., 1883, *Lecture Before the Long Island Historical Society.*

Perhaps the most versatile of our early writers of verse was Philip Freneau, a man of French extraction, possessing the talents of a ready writer, and endowed with that brightness and elasticity of mind which makes even shallowness of thought and emotion pleasing.—WHIPPLE, EDWIN PERCY, 1886, *American Literature and Other Papers, ed. Whittier, p.* 22.

Philip Freneau is talked about, but is not read. His name is known, in a vague way, as that of "the Poet of the Revolution;" and those unfamiliar with his voluminous verse are ready to believe that he was a patriot, a wit, and a successful lyrist. . . . Freneau's masterpiece, which seems to me the best poem written in America before 1800, is "The House of Night, a Vision," in one hundred and thirty-six four-line stanzas, which appeared in his 1786 collection. Its occasional faults of expression and versification are manifest, but in thought and execution, notwithstanding the influence of Gray, it is surprisingly original and strong, distinctly anticipating some of the methods of Coleridge, Poe, and the English pre-Raphaelite poets, none of whom, probably, ever read a line of it. To those who enjoy a literary "find," and like to read and praise a bit of bizarre genius unknown to the multitude, I confidently commend "The House of Night."—RICHARDSON, CHARLES F., 1888, *American Literature*, 1607–1885, *vol.* II, *pp.* 13, 15.

"Wild-Honeysuckle"—the first stammer of poetry in America. We delight to linger over this little piece, consisting of only four stanzas of the sort known as "sesta rima," and in spite of its imperfections, read it over and over again until we find that we have learned it by heart. And it is worthy of our praise; the delight it shows in the simple beauty of the flower, embosomed in nature; the thought of the frosts of autumn, and regret for death,—are a foretaste of Bryant and a host of followers. We may read Freneau's volumes through, and find nothing to compare with this; some few pieces faintly recall it, but the vast majority of them are satirical and partisan in spirit.—WHITE, GREENOUGH, 1890, *Sketch of the Philosophy of American Literature*, *p.* 42.

Lived to more than twice the age of Brown, but, with the exception of one imaginative poem, "The House of Night," wrote nothing of more than temporary value. But his political, humorous, and society verses were voluminous, and, in their way and for their time, telling and entertaining. His perceptions were quick, his feelings lively, he wrote rapidly and heedlessly; but now and then he struck a true note or expressed a memorable thought.—HAWTHORNE, JULIAN, AND LEMMON, LEONARD, 1891, *American Literature*, *p.* 25.

Freneau's patriotic verses and political lampoons are now unreadable; but he deserves to rank as the first real American poet, by virtue of his "Wild Honeysuckle," "Indian Burying-Ground," "Indian Student," and a few other little pieces, which exhibit a grace and delicacy inherited, perhaps, with his French blood. Indeed, to speak strictly, all of the "poets" hitherto mentioned were nothing but rhymers; but in Freneau we meet with something of beauty and artistic feeling; something which still keeps his verses fresh.—BEERS, HENRY A., 1895, *Initial Studies in American Letters*, *p.* 62.

Many of his forgotten poems show high imaginative range—touching the landscape (where it appears) with rare tact and grace.—MITCHELL, DONALD G., 1897, *American Lands and Letters, The Mayflower to Rip-Van-Winkle*, *p.* 216.

The review of our early poetry would be disheartening indeed, were it not for the name of Philip Freneau. . . . Captain Freneau's political verse, whether satiric or eulogistic, has vigor and a certain rough originality, but no charm. It is the rare lyric, the sudden grace of phrase or image that the long-baffled seeker for American poetry hails as birdnotes in March. Here and there, the French blood tells. When this noisy sailor softens his tones to sing how

"At Eutaw Springs the valiant died,"

Keltic pathos makes itself felt even through the formalism of the diction. There are touches of "natural magic" in his stanzas to "The Wild Honeysuckle" and "Honey Bee," and the Keltic turn for style, no less than the new poetic vision of "the ancients of these lands," imparts a lasting attraction to his revery upon "The Indian Burying Ground."—BATES, KATHARINE LEE, 1897, *American Literature*, *pp.* 83, 84.

The poet who was capable of producing lines fit to be thus blended with their own by Thomas Campbell and Walter Scott, and of such true lustre as to catch the eye of any critical reader, as they sparkled among those gems of poetic strass with which they were intermingled by the honorable lady who had condescended to claim them as her own, was not forced into the field of satire for lack of genius to succeed in some higher sphere of poetry.—TYLER, MOSES COIT, 1897, *The Literary History of the American Revolution*, 1763–1783, *vol.* I, *p.* 179.

Philip Freneau, who turned out much doggerel and indifferent verse for the newspapers, reaches at times, in some lyric like his "Indian Burying Ground," a level higher than that to which any of his more ambitious brethren attained. His best work is indeed small in quantity, and shines out from a mass of rubbish, but gems like the poem just mentioned, "The Wild Honeysuckle," and "Eutaw Springs" may be said to hold a permanent place in our literature. Such poems bear the stamp of that originality which is one of the marks of a true poet, and they have an unmistakable grace and delicacy of touch.—PANCOAST, HENRY S., 1898, *An Introduction to American Literature, p.* 107.

In one or two of his poems, it now seems probable, we can find more literary merit than in any other work produced in America before the nineteenth century.—WENDELL, BARRETT, 1900, *A Literary History of America, p.* 130.

"The Wild Honeysuckle" is the high-water mark of American poetry of the eighteenth century, in delicacy of feeling and felicity of expression being at least the equal of Bryant's "To the Fringed Gentian." When such lines were possible in the very infancy of the national life, there was no reason to despair for the future of American literature.—BRONSON, WALTER C., 1900, *A Short History of American Literature, p.* 65.

Sir John Leslie

1766–1832.

Sir John Leslie, natural philosopher, born at Largo, 16th April 1766, studied at St. Andrews and Edinburgh, and travelled as tutor in America and on the Continent, meanwhile engaging in experimental research. The fruits of his labors were a translation of Buffon's "Birds" (1793), the invention of a differential thermometer, a hygrometer, and a photometer, and "Inquiry into Heat" (1804). In 1805 he obtained the chair of Mathematics at Edinburgh, though keenly opposed by the ministers as a follower of Hume. In 1810 he invented artificial refrigeration. Transferred to the chair of Natural Philosophy (1819), he invented the pyroscope, atmometer, and æthrioscope. Knighted in 1832, on 3rd November he died. See Memoir by Macvey Napier (1838).—PATRICK AND GROOME, *eds.*, 1897, *Chambers's Biographical Dictionary, p.* 587.

PERSONAL

In 1819 the death of Playfair was followed by Leslie's election to the chair of natural philosophy at Edinburgh without oppositon. He devoted himself to improving the experimental equipment of the physical laboratory, and to the work of teaching his favourite science, but he is said to have been wanting, like so many original workers, in the power of lucid exposition. Of all his "great and varied gifts, none was more remarkable than the delicacy and success with which he performed the most delicate experiments, excepting perhaps his intuitive sagacity in instantly detecting the cause of an accidental failure."—PLATTS, CHARLES, 1893, *Dictionary of National Biography, vol.* XXXIII, *p.* 106.

GENERAL

Mr. Leslie is well known to the scientific world, by the ingenuity he has displayed in the contrivance of his methods and instruments, in those experimental investigations to which he has directed his attention. . . . Mr. Leslie's experimental results are sometimes too briefly stated, and the grounds on which his conclusions rest, are not always brought sufficiently forward: the evidence for them, therefore, frequently appears not equal to the confidence with which they are delivered; and objections occur, which a more ample statement or illustration might perhaps have obviated. We need scarcely add, that the whole work is marked by that ingenuity of invention, and that minute discrimination, which have always distinguished Mr. Leslie's investigations.—MURRAY, JOHN, 1815, *Leslie on Heat and Moisture, Edinburgh Review, vol.* 24, *pp.* 339, 353.

It would be impossible, we think, for any intelligent and well-constituted mind, thoroughly acquainted with the powers and attainments of Sir John Leslie, to view them without a strong feeling of admiration for his vigorous and inventive genius, and of respect for that extensive and varied knowledge which his active curiosity, his excursive reading, and his happy memory had enabled him to amass and digest. His theoretical notions may be thrown aside or condemned; but his exquisite instruments and his experimental combinations will ever attest the utility no less than the originality of his labours, and continue to act as helps to farther discovery.—NAPIER, MACVEY, 1838, *Encyclopædia Britannica.*

His real merit was, that, notwithstanding the difficulties which beset his path, he firmly seized the great truth, that there is no fundamental difference between light and heat. As he puts it, each is merely a metamorphosis of the other. Heat is light in complete repose. Light is heat in rapid motion. Directly light is combined with a body, it becomes heat; but when it is thrown off from that body, it again becomes light. Whether this is true or false, we cannot tell; and many years, perhaps many generations, will have to elapse before we shall be able to tell. But the service rendered by Leslie is quite independent of the accuracy of his opinion, as to the manner in which light and heat are interchanged. That they are interchanged, is the essential and paramount idea. And we must remember, that he made this idea the basis of his researches, at a period when some very important facts, or, I should rather say, some very conspicuous facts, were opposed to it; while the main facts which favoured it were still unknown. When he composed his work, the analogies between light and heat, with which we are now acquainted, had not been discovered; no one being aware, that double refraction, polarization, and other curious properties, are common to both. To grasp so wide a truth in the face of such obstacles, was a rare stroke of sagacity. But, on account of the obstacles, the inductive mind of England refused to receive the truth, as it was not generalized from a survey of all the facts. And Leslie, unfortunately for himself, died too soon to enjoy the exquisite pleasure of witnessing the empirical corroboration of his doctrine by direct experiment, although he clearly perceived that the march of discovery, in reference to polarization, was leading the scientific world to a point, of which his keen eye had discerned the nature, when, to others, it was an almost invisible speck, dim in the distant offing.—BUCKLE, HENRY THOMAS, 1862–66, *History of Civilization in England, vol.* III, *p.* 384.

Hannah More

1745–1833

Born, at Stapleton, Gloucestershire, 2 Feb. 1745. Precocious abilities in childhood. Adopted literary career. Visit to London, 1774; friendship with Garrick begun. Play, "The Inflexible Captive," translated from Metastasio, performed at Exeter and Bath, 1775. Tragedy, "Percy," produced at Covent Garden, 10 Dec. 1777. "The Fatal Falsehood," Covent Garden, 6 May 1779. Gave up connection with stage after Garrick's death. Settled at Cowslip Green, near Bristol, 1785. Started Sunday-schools, with her sisters' help, in her parish of Blagdon, 1789. Took part in "Blagdon Controversy," 1800–02. Removed to Barley Wood, 1802; to Clifton, 1828. Died, at Clifton, 7 Sept. 1833. Buried at Wrington, Gloucestershire. *Works:* "The Search after Happiness," 1773 (2nd edn. same year); "The Inflexible Captive," 1774 (3rd edn. same year); "Sir Eldred of the Bower and the Bleeding Rock," 1776; "Ode to Dragon" (anon.), 1777; "Essays on Various Subjects," 1777; "Percy" (anon.), 1778; "Works . . . in prose and verse," 1778; "The Fatal Falsehood," 1779; "Sacred Dramas," 1782; "Florio . . . and The Bas Bleu," 1786; "Slavery," 1788; "Thoughts on the Importance of the Manners of the Great" (anon.), 1788; "Bishop Bonner's Ghost" (anon.), 1789; "An Estimate of the Religion of the Fashionable World" (anon), 1791; "Remarks on the Speech of M. Dupont," 1793 (3rd edn. same year); "Village Politics" (under pseud. "Will Chip"), 1793; "Hints to all Ranks of People" (anon.), [1795]; Tracts signed "Z," in "Cheap Repository Tracts" 1795–98; "A Hymn of Praise" (anon.), [1796]; "Strictures on the Modern System of Female Education" (2 vols.), 1799 (3rd edn. same year); "Works (8 vols.), 1801; "Hints towards forming the character of a Young Princess" (anon.; 2 vols.), 1805; "Cœlebs in search of a Wife" (anon.), 1808; "Practical Piety" (2 vols.), 1811 (4th edn. same year); "Christian Morals" (2 vols.), 1813 (5th edn. same year); "Essay on the Character and Practical Writings of St. Paul," 1815 (3rd edn. same year); "Poems" (collected), 1816; "Works" (19 vols.), 1818–19; "Stories for the Middle Ranks of Society," 1819; "Moral Sketches of prevailing Opinions and Manners," 1819 (5th edn. same year); "Bible Rhymes on the Names of all the Books of the Old and New Testaments," 1821; "The Spirit of Prayer," 1825 (3rd edn. same year); "The Feast of Freedom," 1827; "Poems" (collected), 1829; "Works" (11 vols.), 1830.

MARIA EDGEWORTH

From the Original Painting by Chappel.

HANNAH MORE

Engraving by J. C. Buttre, Painting by John Opie, R. A.

She *edited:* "Poems" by Ann Yearsley, 1785. *Collected Works:* "Miscellaneous Works" (2 vols.), 1840. *Life:* by H. Thompson, 1838. *Posthumous:* "Letters . . . to Zackary Macaulay," ed. by A. Roberts, 1860.—SHARP, R. FARQUHARSON, 1897, *A Dictionary of English Authors, p.* 202.

PERSONAL

I visited Hannah More, at Cowslip Green, on Monday last, and seldom have I lived a pleasanter day. She knew my opinions, and treated them with a flattering deference. Her manners are mild, her information considerable, and her taste correct. There are five sisters, and each of them would be remarked in a mixed company. . . . They pay for and direct the education of 1,000 poor children.—SOUTHEY, ROBERT, 1795, *Letter To Grosvenor C. Redford, Oct.* 10; *Life and Correspondence, ed. C. C. Southey.*

When she chose, or when she was adequately excited, could really perform with effect and execution; and, at times, she executed *bravuras,* or passages of colloquial effect, which electrified all who heard. Mrs. H. More was the most opposite creature in the world. She was modest, feminine, and, by nature, retiring. Her manners, which were those of a well-bred woman, accustomed to good society, and therefore free from all bustle, hurry, and excitement, supported the natural expression of her mind. It was only by a most unnatural and transient effort that she ever attempted to shine. On the other hand, to the eye, she was a far more pleasing woman than the masculine De Staël. . . . Mrs. H. More was soft, delicate, and agreeable; and, in youth, must have been pretty. Her eyes only too bright for absolute repose of countenance; else hers would have been nearly quiescent. Her sisters were, if not more interesting, at least more entertaining; especially Mrs. Sally, who had exuberant spirits, mirth, and good nature: and Mrs. Patty, who was distinguished for humour, or at least drollery.—DE QUINCEY, THOMAS, 1833, *Recollections of Hannah More, Works, ed. Masson, vol.* XIV, *pp.* 111, 112.

It may be questioned whether any one in modern times has lived so long with less waste of existence, or written so much with less abuse of ability; whether wisdom has been better consecrated or religion better seconded, in this our day at least, by the pure and prudent application of popular talents.—ROBERTS, WILLIAM, 1834, *Memoirs of the Life and Correspondence of Mrs. Hannah More, pt.* v, *ch.* iii.

Though I think that Mrs. More's very great notoriety was more the work of circumstances, and the popular turn of her mind, than owing to a strong original genius, I am far from thinking her an *ordinary* woman. She must have had great energy of character, and a spritely, versatile mind, which did not originate much, but which readily caught the spirit of the day, and reflected all phases of opinion in the pious and well-disposed portion of society in a clear and lively manner.—COLERIDGE, SARA, 1834, *Letter to Miss E. Trevenen, Aug.; Memoirs and Letters, ed. Daughter.*

I never, to the best of my recollection, proposed to review Hannah More's Life or Works. If I did, it must have been in jest. She was exactly the very last person in the world about whom I should choose to write a critique. She was a very kind friend to me from childhood. Her notice first called out my literary tastes. Her presents laid the foundation of my library. She was to me what Ninon was to Voltaire,—begging her pardon for comparing her to a bad woman, and yours for comparing myself to a great man. She really was a second mother to me. I have a real affection for her memory. I therefore could not possibly write about her unless I wrote in her praise; and all the praise which I could give to her writings, even after straining my conscience in her favor, would be far indeed from satisfying any of her admirers.—MACAULAY, THOMAS BABINGTON, 1837, *To Napier, June* 15; *Life and Letters, ed. Trevelyan.*

The cottage, except by the growth of the trees then planted, is little altered from its appearance in 1785, when Miss More first took possession of it. It is only one story high; the roof is thatch; a smooth lawn, with a few shrubs and trees, fronts the window of the drawing-room, which looks towards the south. A border of flowers runs nearly round the walls. Situate in the midst of the bright and fertile vale of Wrington, Cowslip Green commands a variety of exquisite views.

On one side of the lawn rises the abrupt hill on which the noble mansion of Aldwick Court has since been erected. To the south spreads the rich and sylvan valley, bounded by the dark outline of the Mendips, with their warm-tinted herbage and dusky woods, casting out in bold relief the picturesque village of Blagdon, and the "Magick Garden" of Mendip Lodge with its noble terraces of "Shade above shade, a woody theatre of stateliest view;" while between them the cottage roofs and venerable tower of Burrington shelter in the leafy skirts of their bold and rocky coomb. —THOMPSON, HENRY, 1838, *Life of Hannah More.*

I like neither her letters, nor her books, nor her character. She was that most disagreeable of all monsters, a blue-stocking—a monster that can only exist in a miserably false state of society, in which a woman with but a smattering of learning or philosophy is classed along with singing mice or card-playing pigs. —ELIOT, GEORGE, 1848, *Letter to J. Sibree, Life, ed. Cross, vol.* I, *p.* 123.

Her form was small and slight, her features wrinkled with age; but the burden of eighty years had not impaired her gracious smile, nor lessened the fire of her eyes, the clearest, the brightest, and the most searching I have ever seen. They were singularlarly dark—positively black they seemed as they looked forth among carefully-trained tresses of her own white hair; and absolutely sparkled while she spoke of those of whom she was the venerated link between the present and the long past. Her manner on entering the room, while conversing, and at our departure, was positively spritely; she tripped about from console to console, from window to window, to show us some gift that bore a name immortal, some cherished reminder of other days—almost of another world, certainly of another age; for they were memories of those whose deaths were registered before the present century had birth. She was clad, I well remember, in a rich dress of pea-green silk. It was an odd whim, and contrasted somewhat oddly with her patriarchal age and venerable countenance, yet was in harmony with the youth of her step and her increasing vivacity, as she laughed and chatted, chatted and laughed; her voice strong and clear as that of a girl.—HALL, S. C., 1871, *A Book of Memoirs of Great Men and Women of the Age.*

Free from vanity she scarcely was, even in her latter days, though she had forsaken, as she supposed, the vain and frivolous world; but she was singularly amiable, thoroughly guileless, and sincere; hence the number of her devoted friends. Her intellectual abilities were confessedly of a high order, her piety unaffected, and her benevolence conspicuous.—COPNER, JAMES, 1885, *Sketches of Celibate Worthies, p.* 327.

Hannah More did get unendurably poky, narrow, and solemn in her last days, and not a little sanctimonious; and we naturally think of her as an aged spinster with black mitts, corkscrew curls, and a mob cap, always writing or presenting a tedious tract, forgetting her brilliant youth, when she was quite good enough, and lively, too.—SANBORN, KATE, 1885, *The Wit of Women, p.* 33.

Strict and consistent as a moralist, she was never led into any extravagances or fanaticisms. Stern even as a disciplinarian, she did not proscribe healthy and natural amusements. Strong-minded,—if I may use a modern contemptuous phrase,—she never rebelled against the ordinances of nature or the laws dictated by inspiration. She was a model woman: beautiful, yet not vain; witty, yet never irreverent; independent, yet respectful to authority; exercising private judgment, yet admired by bishops; learned, without pedantry; hospitable, without extravagance; fond of the society of the great, yet spending her life among the poor; alive to the fascinations of society, yet consecrating all her energies of mind and body to the good of those with whom she was brought in contact; as capable of friendship as Paula, as religious as Madame Guyon, as charming in conversation as Récamier, as practical as Elizabeth, as broad and tolerant as Fénelon.—LORD, JOHN, 1886, *Beacon Lights of History, vol.* V, *p.* 425.

On the 13th, the worn-out body was laid to rest beside those of her four sisters in the church-yard at Wrington. Her directions had been to avoid all pomp and display—only that suits of mourning were to be given to fifteen old men whom she had selected—but there were endless spontaneous tokens of respect. Every church in

Bristol tolled its bell as the funeral passed through the streets. All the neighboring gentlemen met the procession a mile from the church, and fell into the rear; and for half a mile the road was crowded with country people mostly in mourning, and two hundred school-children, with a large number of clergy, preceded the coffin into church. Hannah More's property was worth about thirty thousand pounds. Having no near relations, she left ten thousand pounds between various charities in London and at Bristol, with bequests to her clubs at Cheddar and Shipham. But her truly valuable legacy was not only the example of what one woman could be and could do, but a real influence on the tone of education in all classes of English women.—YONGE, CHARLOTTE M., 1888, *Hannah More (Famous Women), p.* 226.

He [Freeman] always looked back with interest to this early friendship with Hannah More, and was accustomed to say that she was a direct link between himself and Samuel Johnson, for he had been a pet of Hannah More, as she had been a favourite of the learned Doctor. He was also fond of referring to Lord Macaulay's acquaintance with her when he was a boy, only observing that he himself had not, like Macaulay, offered her a glass of old spirits.—STEPHENS, W. R. W., 1895, *The Life and Letters of Edward A. Freeman, vol.* I, *p.* 6.

CŒLEBS IN SEARCH OF A WIFE
1808

This book is written, or supposed to be written, (for we would speak timidly of the mysteries of superior beings), by the celebrated Mrs. Hannah Moore! We shall probably give great offence by such indiscretion; but still we must be excused for treating it as a book merely human,—an uninspired production,—the result of mortality left to itself, and depending on its own limited resources. In taking up the subject in this point of view, we solemnly disclaim the slightest intention of indulging in any indecorous levity, or of wounding the religious feelings of a large class of very respectable persons. It is the only method in which we can possibly make this work a proper object of criticism. We have the strongest possible doubts of the attributes usually ascribed to this authoress; and we think it more simple and manly to say so at once, than to admit nominally superlunary claims, which, in the progress of our remarks, we should virtually deny.—SMITH, SYDNEY, 1809, *Cœlebs in Search of a Wife, Edinburgh Review, vol.* 14, *p.* 145.

Have you read "Celebs"? It has reached eight editions in so many weeks, yet literally it is one of the very poorest sort of common novels, with the drawback of dull religion in it. Had the religion been high and flavored, it would have been something. I borrowed this "Celebs in Search of a Wife," of a very careful, neat lady, and returned it with this stuff written in the beginning:—

If ever I marry a wife
I'd marry a landlord's daughter,
For then I may sit in the bar,
And drink cold brandy-and-water.

—LAMB, CHARLES, 1809, *Letter to Coleridge, Final Memorials, ed. Talfourd.*

Mrs. Clifford tells me that Mrs. Hannah More was lately at Dawlish, and excited more curiosity there, and engrossed more attention, than any of the distinguished personages who were there, not excepting the Prince of Orange. The gentleman from whom she drew "Cœlebs" was there, but most of those who saw him did him the justice to declare that he was a much more agreeable man than Cœlebs. If you have any curiosity to know his name, I can tell you that—young Mr. Harford, of Blaise Castle. — EDGEWORTH, MARIA, 1810, *To Mrs. Ruxton, Jan.; Life and Letters, ed. Hare, vol.* I, *p.* 170.

Her novel, "Cœlebs in Search of a Wife," has a great deal of shrewdness and caustic wit about it. It was *the* book of its year, and was quoted everywhere. Notwithstanding many expenses and disadvantages, she cleared £2,000 by it in a single year. This sum was paid in the instalments of £500 a quarter, and the copyright remained in her own hands.—HAMILTON, CATHERINE J., 1892, *Women Writers, First Series, p.* 94.

She wrote a novel called "Cœlebs in Search of a Wife." Do you happen to have read it? I hardly know whether to advise it, or not; there is so much to read! But if you do, you will find most excellent English in it, and a great deal of very good preaching; and many hints about the social habits of that time—trustworthy even to the dinner hour and the lunch hour; and maxims good enough for a copy book, or a calendar; and you will find—what you will not find in all stories nowadays—a definite beginning and a definite end. I know what you may say, if you do read it. You would say that the sermons are too long, and that the hero is a prig; and that you would never marry him if he were worth twice his fortune, and were to offer himself ten times over. Well—perhaps not; but he had a deal of money. And that book of "Cœlebs"—whatever you may choose to say of it, had a tremendous success; it ran over Europe like wildfire; was translated into French, into German, into Dutch, into Polish, and I know not what language besides; and across the Atlantic—in those colonial days, when bookshops were not, as now, at every corner—over thirty thousand copies were sold.—MITCHELL, DONALD G., 1895, *English Lands Letters and Kings, Queen Anne and the Georges, p.* 175.

GENERAL

I am very much pleased to find that "Percy" meets with your approbation. It has been extremely successful, far beyond my expectation, and more so than any *tragedy* has been for many years. The profits were not so great as they would have been, had it been brought out when the town was full; yet they were such as I have no reason to complain of. The author's nights, sale of the copy, etc., amounted to near six hundred pounds (this is *entre nous*); and as my friend Mr. Garrick has been so good as to lay it out for me on the best security, and at five per cent., it makes a decent little addition to my small income. Cadell gave £150—a very handsome price, with conditional promises. He confesses (a thing not usual) that it has had a very great sale, and that he shall get a good deal of money by it. The first impression was near four thousand, and the second is almost sold.—MORE, HANNAH, 1778, *Letter to Mrs. Gwatkin, March* 5; *Memoirs, ed. Roberts, pt.* i, *ch.* iv.

Miss Moore has written a poem called "Le Bas Bleu;" which is in my opinion a very great performance. It wanders about in manuscript, and surely will soon find its way to Bath.—JOHNSON, SAMUEL, 1784, *To Mrs. Thrale, Apr.* 19; *Letters, ed. Hill, vol.* II, *p.* 390.

She is a favourite writer with me, and has more nerve and energy, both in her thoughts and language, than half the he-rhymers in the kingdom.—COWPER, WILLIAM, 1788, *To Lady Hesketh, Feb.* 16; *Life of Cowper by Hayley, vol.* I, *p.* 160.

How unlike are these lines to the chymical preparations of our modern poetasters, cock and hen! who leave one with no images but of garlands of flowers and necklaces of coloured stones. Every stanza of "Bonner's Ghost" furnishes you with a theme of ideas. I have read them twenty times, and every time they improve on me. How easy, how well kept up the irony! how sensible the satire! how delicate and genteel the compliments! I hold "Jekyll" and "Bonner's Ghost" perfect compositions, in their different kinds—a great deal to say, when poetry has been so much exhausted.—WALPOLE, HORACE, 1789, *Letter to Miss Berry, July* 10; *Journals and Correspondence of Miss Berry, ed. Lewis, vol.* I, *p.* 172.

As a writer, how eminently artificial she was, notwithstanding some imaginary admiration which she always professed for simplicity, is evident from the very structure of her sentences; which are all turned as in a lathe, and are so entirely dependent for their effect upon antithesis, or direct contraposition in the words, even where there is little or none in the thoughts, that once a great poet, opening one of her works and reading a paragraph, made this remark to me,—"These feeble thinkers dare not trust a single thought to its native powers: so afraid are they of seeming dull, and so conscious of no innate right to challenge or support attention, that each particular sentence is polished into a sparkling and independent whole; so that, open the book where you will, all has an exterior brilliancy, and will bear being detached without any injury to its effect, having no sort of natural cohesion with the context, or dependency upon what goes before." . . . With all these ineradicable disadvantages, Mrs. More's works have their value. The very dilution of their thoughts recommends them, and adapts them to those who would shrink from severer or profounder speculations, and who seek, in all they read, to see their own ordinary sentiments reflected. Still, even thus, Mrs. H. More is not destined to any long existence.—DE QUINCEY, THOMAS, 1833, *Recollections of Hannah More, Works, ed. Masson, vol.* XIV, *pp.* 130, 131.

Miss Hannah More, a lady not out of harmony with these discords which mankind have been so long taking for their melancholy music. . . . It is the first time we ever read any of her verses; and she has fairly surprised us not only with some capital good sense, but with liberal and feeling sentiments! How could a heart, capable of uttering such things, get incrusted with Calvinism! and that, too, not out of fear and bad health, but in full possession, as it should seem, both of cheerfulness and sensibility!—HUNT, LEIGH, 1847, *British Poetesses; Men, Women and Books.*

So low was the standard of poetical taste about the last quarter of the last century that Hannah More was regarded by a nation of admirers as a tenth muse. . . . We do not mean to deny her the possession of very considerable talent. She was the means of circulating through society much good sense in prose and verse very fairly written; her ideas also, on more than one great political question were sound and clear, but her knowledge was limited, and her reading very confined and much too sectarian.—WARBURTON, ELIOT, 1852, *ed., Memoirs of Horace Walpole and His Contemporaries, vol.* II, *p.* 542.

We venture to affirm that her books were more numerous, that they passed through more editions, that they were printed in more languages, and that they were read by more people, than those of any other authoress upon record.—ANDERSON, WILLIAM, 1871, *Model Women, p.* 133.

Not many months ago, at a book depot not many miles from Paternoster Row, an application was made for a tract of Mrs. Hannah More's entitled "Will Chip; or Village Politics." The answer returned was that "*Will Chip and Hannah Moor* were both out of print." . . . To be "out of print" is little; but to be turned into the title of a tract, to be misspelt into "Hannah Moor," and set down amongst the shavings with one's own "Will Chip," is a fate to reconcile the majority of us to oblivion. Yet since oblivion has not yet flowed over this good woman's name, or has merely flowed over it to tarnish it with a little rust, it may be worth while, to spend a few moments in rubbing up the old lamp. If it cannot work wonders any more for us, or be lit up with its old light, it may be well to see how it looked and shone in the season when men were so willing to rejoice in its light—not religious or "evangelical" men only, but poets, wits, actors, men and women of the world.—CHARLES, ELIZABETH RUNDLE, 1874, *Mrs. Hannah More, Good Words, vol.* 15, *p.* 699.

By writings and by her own personal example Hannah More drew the sympathy of England to the poverty and crime of the agricultural laborer.—GREEN, JOHN RICHARD, 1874, *A Short History of the English People, ch.* x, *sec.* i.

She forestalled nearly everything which has been written in our times pertaining to the life of woman, both at school and in society. And she evinced in her writings on this great subject an acuteness of observation, a good sense, a breadth and catholicity of judgment, a richness of experience, and a high moral tone which have never been surpassed.—LORD, JOHN, 1886, *Beacon Lights of History, vol.* V, *p.* 422.

No one could wire-draw sentences and spin high-sounding platitudes full of long words and far-fetched similes, better than Hannah More.—HAMILTON, CATHERINE J., 1892, *Women Writers, First Series, p.* 84.

I freely admit that the celebrated Mrs. Hannah More is one of the most detestable writers that ever held a pen. She flounders like a huge conger-eel in an ocean of dingy morality. She may have been a wit in her youth, though I am not aware of any evidence of it—certainly her poem, "Bas Bleu," is none—but for all the rest of her days, and they were many, she was an encyclopædia of all literary vices. You may search her nineteen volumes through without lighting upon one original thought, one happy phrase. Her religion lacks reality. Not a single expression of genuine piety, of heart-felt emotion, ever escapes her lips. She is never pathetic, never terrible. Her creed is powerless either to attract the well-disposed or make the guilty tremble. No naughty child ever read "The Fairchild Family" or "Stories from the Church Catechism" without quaking and quivering like a short-haired puppy after a ducking; but, then, Mrs. Sherwood was a woman of genius, whilst Mrs. Hannah More was a pompous failure. Still, she has a merit of her own, just enough to enable a middle-aged man to chew the cud of reflection as he hastily turns her endless pages. She is an explanatory author, helping you to understand how sundry people who were old when you were young came to be the folk they were, and to have the books upon their shelves they had.—BIRRELL, AUGUSTINE, 1894, *Essays about Men, Women and Books, p.* 70.

Her writings have the old-fashioned flavour of the eighteenth century; while they now represent the teaching of the evangelical school, which looked up to Newton and Cecil, and of which William Wilberforce and his friends were the recognised political and social leaders. Though now out of fashion, they show not only high moral and religious purpose, but strong sense, as well as considerable intellectual vivacity. If their author showed a little self-complacency, the wonder is that her strong sense kept her from being spoilt by the uniform flattery poured upon her by her contemporaries. Her services to education at a time of general indiffence deserve the highest praise, though her decided desire to keep the poor in their place is now out of fashion.—STEPHEN, LESLIE, 1894, *Dictionary of National Biography, vol.* XXXVIII, *p.* 419.

Hannah More's style is almost always conventional, and generally careless, but "The Cheap Repository Tracts" are simple, forcible, and dramatic; and her faults of manner never entirely obscure her natural vigour and good sense. She is animated and fluent, possessing an extensive, though not a pure vocabulary, and some turn for epigram. Her heaviest works are sprinkled with admirable phrases, reflections, and descriptions, as happy as those which make many of her letters so delightful. She was a thoroughly cultivated and charming woman, who could hold her own in the best society of her day, at once observant, sympathetic, and tactful, with a capacity for unfailing enthusiasm. — JOHNSON, REGINALD BRIMLEY, 1895, *English Prose, ed. Craik, vol.* IV, *p.* 514.

She was very unfortunately parted in respect of time, coming just before the days when it became possible for a lady to be decent in literature without being dull.—SAINTSBURY, GEORGE, 1896, *A History of Nineteenth Century Literature, p.* 45.

John O'Keeffe

1747-1833

A native of Dublin, commenced writing plays at the age of sixteen, and practised dramatic composition with such rapidity that the Biographia Dramatica enumerates nearly fifty of his plays produced before the end of the century. A collection of his "Dramatic Works," in 4 vols. 8vo, was pub. in 1798; his "Recollections of his Life" appeared in 1826, 2 vols. 8vo; and a small volume of his poems, with autobiographical reminiscences, entitled "O'Keefe's Legacy to his Daughters," was pub. in 1834, 12mo. Of his plays, "Tony Lumpkin in Town," "The Agreeable Surprise," "Wild Oats," "Modern Antiques," "Fontainebleau," "The Highland Reed," "Love in a Camp," "The Poor Soldier," and "Sprigs of Laurel," still keep their place on the stage. O'Keefe became blind in his fiftieth year.—ALLIBONE, S. AUSTIN, 1870, *Critical Dictionary of English Literature, vol.* II, *p.* 1451.

GENERAL

If Foote has been called our English Aristophanes, O'Keefe might well be called our English Moliere. The scale of the modern writer was smaller, but the spirit is the same. In light, careless laughter, and pleasant exaggerations of the humourous, we have had no one equal to him. There is no labour or contrivance in his scenes, but the drollery of his subject seems to strike irresistibly upon his fancy, and run away with his discretion as it does with ours. His "Cowslip" and "Lingo" are "Touchstone" and "Audry" revived. He is himself a modern antique. His fancy has all the quaintness and extravagance of the old writers, with the ease and lightness which the moderns arrogate to themselves. All his pieces are delightful, but the "Agreeable Surprise" is the most so. There are in this some of the most irresistible *double entendres,* the most felicitous blunders in situation and character, that can be conceived; and in Lingo's superb replication, "A scholar! I was a master of scholars," he has hit the height of the ridiculous.—HAZLITT, WILLIAM, 1818, *Lectures on the English Comic Writers, Lecture* viii.

His [Goldsmith's] comic writing is of the class which is perhaps as much preferred to that of a staider sort by people in general, as it is by the writer of these pages,—comedy running into farce; that is to say, truth richly coloured and overflowing with animal spirits. It is that of the prince of comic writers, Molierè (always bearing in mind that Molierè beats every one of them in expression, and is a great verse writer to boot). The English have no dramatists to compare in this respect with the Irish. Farquhar, Goldsmith, and Sheridan surpass them all; and O'Keefe, as a farce-writer, stands alone. —HUNT, LEIGH, 1846, *Wit and Humour*, *p.* 339.

The choicest and most popular farce-writer since the career of Foote; and as a pure farcist, as a dispenser of reckless fun, his rival, even his surpasser.—CLARKE, CHARLES COWDEN, 1872, *On the Comic Writers of England, Gentleman's Magazine, n. s., vol.* 8, *p.* 317.

O'Keeffe's "Wild Oats" is played to this day, and one of the most successful of Buckstone's revivals was "The Castle of Andalusia," in which that actor took a leading part. But O'Keeffe's popularity has not proved permanent, and his unpublished and unacted pieces, which his daughter offered for sale at his death, did not find a purchaser.—FITZPATRICK, W. J., 1895, *Dictionary of National Biography, vol.* XLII, *p.* 74.

O'Keefe was to a certain extent a follower of Foote; but his pieces—though he was a practised actor—depended less upon his own powers of exposition than Foote's. They range from rather farcical comedies to pure farces and comediettas much interspersed with songs for music; and their strictly literary merit is not often great, while for sheer extravagance they require the utmost license of the boards to excuse them. There is, however, something much more taking in them than in most of the dramatic work of the time. For instance, the "wild farce" (referred to but not named by Lamb in his paper on Munden) of "The Merry Mourners," though as "improbable" as Mrs. Barbauld thought "The Ancient Mariner" to be, has a singular hustle and bustle of sustained interest, and not a few shrewd strokes. . . . O'Keefe has few gifts beyond knowledge of the stage, Irish shrewdness, Irish rattle, and an honest, straightforward simplicity; and that one turns to him from other dramatists of the period with some relief, is even more to their discredit than to his credit. —SAINTSBURY, GEORGE, 1896, *A History of Nineteenth Century Literature, pp.*418, 419.

Arthur Henry Hallam

1811–1833

[Son of Henry Hallam.] Born, in London, 1 Feb. 1811. Visit to Germany and Switzerland, 1818. At first privately educated; afterwards at Eton, till 1827. Contrib. to "Eton Miscellany," 1827. In Italy, winter 1827–28. Returned to England, June 1828. To Trin. Coll., Camb., Oct. 1828 Friendship with Tennyson formed there. B. A., 1832. Contrib. to "Englishman's Mag.," 1831. Student of Inner Temple, 1832. With father in Germany, 1833. Died suddenly, at Vienna, 15 Sept. 1833. *Works:* "Remarks on Prof. Rossetti's 'Disquisizioni sullo Spirito Antipapale'" (under initials: T. H. E. A.), 1832. *Posthumous:* "Remains in Prose and Verse," ed. by his father (priv. ptd.), 1834.—SHARP, R. FARQUHARSON, 1897, *A Dictionary of English Authors, p.* 122.

PERSONAL

More ought, perhaps, to be said; but it is very difficult to proceed. From the earliest years of this extraordinary young man, his premature abilities were not more conspicuous than an almost faultless disposition, sustained by a more calm self-command than has often been witnessed in that season of life. The sweetness of temper that distinguished his childhood, became, with the advance of manhood, an habitual benevolence, and ultimately ripened into that exalted principle of love towards God and man, which animated and almost absorbed his soul during the latter period of his life, and to which most of the following compositions bear such emphatic testimony. He seemed to tread the earth as a spirit from some better world; and in bowing to the mysterious will which has in mercy removed him, perfected by so short a trial, and passing over the bridge which separates the seen from the unseen life in a moment, and, as we believe, without a moment's pang, we must feel not only the bereavement of those to whom he was dear, but the loss which mankind have sustained by the withdrawing of such light.—HALLAM, HENRY, 1834, *Remains in Verse and Prose of Arthur Henry Hallam, Memoir.*

My Arthur, whom I shall not see
Till all my widow'd race be run;
Dear as the mother to the son,
More than my brothers are to me.

. . . .

Thy converse drew us with delight,
The men of rathe and riper years:
The feeble soul, a haunt of fears,
Forgot his weakness in thy sight.
On thee the loyal-hearted hung,
The proud was half disarm'd of pride,
Nor cared the serpent at thy side
To flicker with his double tongue.
The stern were mild when thou wert by,
The flippant put himself to school
And heard thee, and the brazen fool
Was soften'd, and he knew not why.

—TENNYSON, ALFRED LORD, 1850, *In Memoriam.*

And now what shall I say of Arthur Hallam? I have been somewhat taken by surprise, though probably without sufficient cause, to find how much of his memory has ceased to exist for the younger men who sway the present time. He has remained so vividly before all of us, first as the most charming and perhaps the most promising of our contemporaries, and secondly, as the hero of the great poem "In Memoriam," that we thought his name an imperishable one; but a poem is one thing, the man in whose honour it is written, quite another. We now read "Lycidas" without taking any great interest in Mr. King, and those who come after us may go on admiring Tennyson's verses, without dwelling much on the image of Tennyson's friend. . . . A son of Mr. Tennyson's, though born many years after he left us, has been called Hallam, and a son of mine has been called Arthur. It seemed as if neither he nor I could bear to let the name pass quite away from us, and I have no doubt that the same thing has happened in many other families, as he was regarded by all who knew him with unusual affection. . . . We all of us, even Mr. Gladstone, I think, felt whilst conversing with him, that we were in the presence of a larger, profounder, and more thoughtful mind than any one of us could claim for himself.—DOYLE, SIR FRANCIS HASTINGS, 1886, *Reminiscences and Opinions, pp.* 40, 41.

It is the simple truth that Arthur Henry Hallam was a spirit so exceptional, that everything with which he was brought into relation during his shortened passage through this world came to be, through this contact, glorified by a touch of the ideal. Among his contemporaries at Eton, that queen of visible homes for the ideal schoolboy, he stood supreme among all his fellows; and the long life which I have since wound my way, and which has brought me into contact with so many men of rich endowments, leaves him where he then stood, as to natural gifts, so far as my estimation is concerned.—GLADSTONE, WILLIAM EWART, 1898, *Arthur Henry Hallam, Companion Classics, p.* 7.

GENERAL

We do not remember when we have been more impressed than by these "Remains" of this young man, especially when taken along with his friend's Memorial; and instead of trying to tell our readers what this impression is, we have preferred giving them as copious extracts as our space allows, that they may judge and enjoy for themselves. . . . We can promise them few finer, deeper, and better pleasures than reading, and detaining their minds over these two books together, filling their hearts with the fullness of their truth and tenderness.—BROWN, JOHN, 1862, *Arthur H. Hallam, Horæ Subsecivæ, Second Series, p.* 427.

His very depth and originality rendered it more difficult for him to bring his ideas to the surface, and give them their adequate expression. He required more time for his full development than we did. For instance, his poems, as poems of promise, gave greater hopes for the future than my diluted Scott and water or Byron and water. But just because they were his own, and not borrowed, they seemed (naturally enough, because he was yet but a boy) stiff as to the language, and imperfect in point of form. Before he died, these defects had almost disappeared, or at any rate were rapidly disappearing; I would particularly mention a dramatic scene preserved in his Remains, between the painter Raphael and his mistress (the Fornarina she was called), which strikes me as not only beautifully conceived, but excellent in point of execution. His prose writings were vigorous and effective, but still somewhat wanting in ease, grace, and lightness. Here again, he was moving onward with rapid strides. In proof of this I may refer to the fine analysis of Cicero's character and writings, also preserved in his Remains. . . . It is a critical and philosophical dissertation in the very first rank of such dissertations. —DOYLE, SIR FRANCIS HASTINGS, 1886, *Reminiscences and Opinions, p.* 42.

Arthur Hallam was himself little more than a hope unfulfilled. His pathetic little "Remains" do not even seem to convey to the reader the promises which all his youthful circle saw in him:—a conclusion not by any means unusual—yet in inspiring and making possible this great poem ["In Memoriam"] he has had an unusual fate.—OLIPHANT, MARGARET O. W., 1892, *The Victorian Age of English Literature, p.* 209.

Arthur Hallam's poems, we are told by his father, were intended to be published along with those of his friend, Alfred Tennyson. They would have been worthy of the association. If, on account of his youth, Arthur Hallam had not fashioned any one great work, there is abundant promise of greatness had life been allowed him. He has learned the power of simplicity; he has reached to Dante's secret, and already knows how to suggest by reserve of language. Some of his sonnets are very perfect—full of melody; and hardly could you either add to, or take away from them. He sees clearly, and his expression is adequate; he will allow no redundancy. . . . Arthur Hallam was not only gifted, a genius and a poet, but he almost seems to have known nothing of that intermediate period of vague and misty aspiration, of which the poet Keats so pathetically speaks in the preface to "Endymion."—JAPP, ALEXANDER H., 1892, *The Poets and Poetry of the Century, Frederick Tennyson to Arthur Hugh Clough, ed. Miles, pp.* 107, 108.

Arthur Hallam, whom "In Memoriam" has made immortal, was credited by the partial judgment of his friends with talents which, they would fain think, were actually shown both in verse and prose. A wiser criticism will content itself with saying that in one sense he produced "In Memoriam" itself, and that this is enough connection with literature for any man. His own work has a suspicious absence of faults, without the presence of any great positive merit,—a combination almost certainly indicating precocity, to be followed by sterility.—SAINTSBURY, GEORGE, 1896, *A History of Nineteenth Century Literature, p.* 299.

William Wilberforce

1759-1833

Born at Hull, 24th August 1759, the son of a wealthy merchant. Educated at Wimbledon, Pocklington, and St. John's College, Cambridge, in 1780 he was returned for Hull, in 1784 for Yorkshire, and was a close friend of Pitt, though he remained independent of party. In 1784-85, during a tour on the Continent with Dean Milner, he became seriously impressed; and in 1787 he founded an association for the reformation of manners. In 1788, supported by Clarkson and the Quakers, he entered on his nineteen years' struggle for the abolition of the slave-trade, crowned with victory in 1807. He next sought to secure the abolition of the slave-trade abroad and the total abolition of slavery itself; but declining health compelled him in 1825 to retire from parliament. Long a central figure in the "Clapham sect" of Evangelicals, he died 29th of July 1833, and was buried in Westminster Abbey. He wrote a "Practical View of Christianity" (1797), helped to found the *Christian Observer* (1801), and promoted many schemes for the welfare of the community. See the *Life* by his sons (1838), and his "Private Papers," edited by Mrs. A. M. Wilberforce (1898).—PATRICK AND GROOME, *eds.*, 1897, *Chambers's Biographical Dictionary, p.* 970.

PERSONAL

My Dear Sir—Unless Divine Power has raised you up to be as *Athanasius contra mundum*, I see not how you can go through your glorious enterprise, in opposing that execrable villainy which is the scandal of religion, of England, and of human nature. Unless God has raised you up for this very thing, you will be worn out by the opposition of men and devils; and if God be for you, who can be against you? Are all of them together stronger than God? Oh!

be not weary of well-doing. Go on in the name of God, and in the power of his might, till even American slavery, "The Vilest Thing That Ever Saw The Sun," shall vanish away before it. That He who has guided you from your youth up may continue to strengthen you in this and all things, is the prayer of, dear sir, your affectionate servant.—WESLEY, JOHN, 1791, *Letter to Wilberforce, Feb.* 24.

Thy country, Wilberforce, with just disdain,
Hears thee by cruel men and impious, called
Fanatic, for thy zeal to loose the enthralled
From exile, public sale, and slavery's chain.
Friend of the poor, the wronged, the fetter-galled,
Fear not lest labour such as thine be vain!
Thou hast achieved a part; hast gained the ear
Of Britain's Senate to thy glorious cause:
Hope smiles, joy springs, and though cold caution pause
And weave delay, the better hour is near
That shall renumerate thy toils severe
By peace for Afric, fenced with British laws.
Enjoy what thou hast won, esteem and love
From all the just on earth and all the blest above!

—COWPER, WILLIAM, 1792, *To William Wilberforce.*

He is the very model of a reformer. Ardent without turbulence, mild without timidity or coldness, neither yielding to difficulties, nor disturbed or exasperated by them; patient and meek, yet intrepid: persisting for twenty years through good report and evil report; just and charitable even to his most malignant enemies; unwearied in every experiment to disarm the prejudices of his more rational and disinterested opponents, and supporting the zeal without dangerously exciting the passion of his adherents.—MACKINTOSH, SIR JAMES, 1808, *Journal, May* 23; *Life by his Son, vol.* I, *ch.* viii, *p.* 403.

The fashionable part of my life in London was so laboriously dull in itself that I will not describe it. . . . But there was one place where I went several times, which was so unlike the others that it should not be mentioned with them,—I mean Mr. Wilberforce's. He lives at Kensington. . . . Everything in his house seemed to speak of quiet and peace. . . . He is about sixty years old, small, and altogether an ordinary man in his personal appearance. His voice has a whine in it, and his conversation is broken and desultory. In general, he talks most and is most attentive to those who talk most to him, . . . for his benevolence has so long been his governing principle, that he lends his ear mechanically to all who address him. Yet now and then he starts a subject of conversation, and pursues it with earnestness, quotes Horace and Virgil, and almost rattles with a gay good-humor and vivacity, which strongly and uniformly mark his character. But, in general, he leaves himself much in the hands of those about him, or, if he attempts to direct the conversation, it is only by making inquiries to gratify his curiosity. —TICKNOR, GEORGE, 1819, *Journal; Life, Letters and Journals, vol.* I, *p.* 297.

He acts from mixed motives. He would willingly serve two masters, God and Mammon. He is a person of many excellent and admirable qualifications, but he has made a mistake in wishing to reconcile those that are incompatible. He has a most winning eloquence, specious, persuasive, familiar, silver-tongued, is amiable, charitable, conscientious, pious, loyal, humane, tractable to power, accessible to popularity, honouring the king, and no less charmed with the homage of his fellow-citizens. "What lacks he then?" Nothing but an economy of good parts. By aiming at too much, he has spoiled all, and neutralised what might have been an estimable character, distinguished by signal services to mankind. . . . We can readily believe that Mr. Wilberforce's first object and principle of action is to do what he thinks right: his next (and that we fear is of almost equal weight with the first) is to do what will be thought so by other people. He is always at a game of *hawk and buzzard* between these two: his "conscience will not budge," unless the world goes with it. . . . Mr. Wilberforce has the pride of being familiar with the great; the vanity of being popular, the conceit of an approving conscience. He is coy in his approaches to power: his public spirit is, in a manner, *under the rose.* He thus reaps the credit of independence, without the obloquy; and secures the advantages of servility, without incurring any obligations. He has two strings to his bow:—he by no means nelgects his worldly interests, while he expects a bright reversion in the skies. Mr. Wilberforce is far from being a hypocrite; but he is, we think, as fine a specimen of *moral equivocation* as can well be conceived.—HAZLITT, WILLIAM, 1825, *The Spirit of the Age, pp.* 211, 212, 213.

Wilberforce kept his faculties, and (except when he was actually in fits), his spirits, to the very last. He was cheerful and full of anecdote only last Saturday. He owned that he enjoyed life much, and that he had a great desire to live longer. Strange in a man who had, I should have said, so little to attach him to this world, and so firm a belief in another: in a man with an impaired fortune, a weak spine, and a worn-out stomach!—MACAULAY, THOMAS BABINGTON, 1833, *To Hannah M. Macaulay, July* 31; *Life and Letters, ed. Trevelyan.*

His Christianity was of the most amiable and attractive character—his temper was cheerful even to playfulness—his pleasantry, though measured, was copious—and his wit, though chastened, ready and enlivening.—CROKER, JOHN WILSON, 1838, *Life of Wilberforce, Quarterly Review, vol.* 62, *p.* 285.

Few persons have ever either reached a higher and more enviable place in the esteem of their fellow-creatures, or have better deserved the place they had gained, than William Wilberforce. . . . His nature was mild and amiable beyond that of most men; fearful of giving the least pain, in any quarter, even while heated with the zeal of controversy on questions that roused all his passions; and more anxious, if it were possible, to gain over rather than to overpower an adversary—to disarm him by kindness, or the force of reason, or awakening appeals to his feelings, rather than defeat him by hostile attack. . . . His eloquence was of a very high order. It was persuasive and pathetic in an eminent degree; but it was occasionally bold and impassioned, animated with the inspiration which deep feeling alone can breathe into spoken thought, chastened by pure taste, varied by extensive information, enriched by classical illusion, sometimes elevated by the more sublime topics of Holy Writ—the thoughts and the spirit

"That touch'd Isaiah's hallow'd lips with fire."

—BROUGHAM, HENRY LORD, 1839-43, *Historical Sketches of Statesmen who Flourished in the Time of George III.*

Who that knew him, can fail to recall the rapid movements of his somewhat diminutive form, the illumination of his expressive countenance, and the nimble finger with which he used to seize on every little object which happened to adorn or diversify his path? Much less can we forget his vivacious wit—so playful, yet so harmless; the glow of his affections; the urbanity of his manners; and the wondrous celerity with which he was ever wont to turn from one bright thought to another. Above all, however, his friends will never cease to remember that peculiar sunshine which he threw over a company by the influence of a mind perpetually tuned to love and praise. I am ready to think there could be no greater luxury than that of roaming with him in solitude over green fields and gardens, and drawing out of his treasury things new and old.—GURNEY, JOSEPH JOHN, 1838, *Familiar Sketch, Life of William Wilberforce by his Sons, vol.* V, *p.* 286.

When his funeral reached Westminster Abbey on Saturday, Aug. 5th, the procession was joined by the members then attending the two Houses of parliament. Public business was suspended; the Speaker of the House of Commons, the Lord Chancellor, one Prince of the Blood, with others of the highest rank, took their place as pall-bearers beside the bier. It was followed by his sons, his relations, and immediate friends. The Prebendary then in residence, one of his few surviving college friends, met it at the Minster gate with the Church's funeral office; and whilst the vaulted roof gave back the anthem his body was laid in the north transept, close to the tombs of Pitt, Fox, and Canning. It was remarked by one of the prelates who took part in this striking scene, that considering how long he had retired from active life, and that his intellectual superiority could be known only by tradition to the generation which thus celebrated his obsequies, there was a sort of testimony to the moral sublimity of his Christian character in this unequalled mark of public approbation. For while a public funeral had been matter of customary compliment to those who died in official situations, this voluntary tribute of individual respect from the mass of the great legislative bodies of the land, was an unprecedented honour. It was one moreover to which the general voice responded. —WILBERFORCE, ROBERT ISAAC AND SAMUEL, 1838, *The Life of William Wilberforce, vol.* V, *p.* 375.

I recall the great man as delicate in features, nothwithstanding a somewhat strongly marked outline, and in form the opposite of powerful; the head seemed a little "awry," and is so shown in portraits and the statue at Westminster Abbey. But those features spoke, and that form dilated, when at his work in the house of Commons. It was, however, undoubtedly a disadvantage to the orator, whose business it is to persuade rather than convince —a disadvantage his distinguished son had not, and his grandsons have not—owing more to external advantages than did the illustrious and victorious combatant for the veritable rights of man. He was far past his prime when I knew him, but his voice continued clear, ringing, strong yet melodious, and his eye retained the brilliancy that indicates creative genius.—HALL, SAMUEL CARTER, 1883, *Retrospect of a Long Life, p.* 112.

His transparent kindliness and simplicity made him, like Fox, lovable even to his antagonists. His freedom from the coarser indulgences which stained Fox's private life implied also a certain unfitness for the rough game of politics. He escaped contamination at the cost of standing aside from the world of corruption and devoting himself to purely philanthropical measures. The charm of his character enabled him to take the part of moral censor without being morose; and the religious views which in other members of his sect were generally regarded as gloomy, if not pharisaical, were shown by his example to be compatible with indomitable gaiety and sociability. . . . His extraordinary breadth and quickness of sympathy led to his taking part in a vast variety of undertakings, which taxed the strength of a delicate constitution and prompted an almost reckless generosity. The slavery agitation happily concentrated his powers upon one main question of the day. His more one-sided supporters, who sometimes lamented the versatility which prevented him from confining his powers to one object, perhaps failed to observe how much his influence even in that direction was strengthened by his sensibility to other claims. He could not be regarded as a fanatic of one idea. He held a unique position in his time as one who was equally respected by his tory allies, by such orthodox whigs as Brougham and Sydney Smith, and by such radicals as Romilly and Bentham. His relations to his own family seem to have been perfect, and no one had warmer or more lasting friendships.—STEPHEN, LESLIE, 1900, *Dictionary of National Biography, vol.* LXI, *p.* 216.

PRACTICAL VIEW OF CHRISTIANITY
1797

Some very serious persons have their doubts as to the theological principles of this work in their *full* extent, and I fear it is *too rigid and exclusive* in it's doctrines. There is also too much of a *sectarian* language, which cannot be approved. But of the intention, virtue, learning, and patriotism of the eloquent and well informed Senator, I have the most honourable and decided opinion. His work is vehement, impassioned, urgent, fervid, instant; though sometimes copious to prolixity, and in a few parts even to tediousness. Perhaps it is the production of an orator rather than of a writer. I should think it had been *dictated.* Throughout the whole, there is a manly fortitude of thought, firm and unshrinking.—MATTHIAS, THOMAS JAMES, 1798, *The Pursuits of Literature, Eighth ed., p.* 414.

A work which, for excellency of plan, a strain of masculine eloquence, acuteness of discernment, and force of reasoning, and, above all, for sublime devotion, is not equalled in our language.—WILLIAMS, EDWARD, 1800, *The Christian Preacher.*

It is the expostulation of a brother. Unwelcome truth is delivered with scrupulous fidelity, and yet with a tenderness which demonstrates that the monitor feels the pain which he reluctantly inflicts. It is this tone of human sympathy breathing in every page which constitutes the essential charm of this book.—STEPHEN, SIR JAMES, 1838, *Life of William Wilberforce, Edinburgh Review, vol.* 67, *p.* 163.

We are happy that, having been obliged to dissent on so many occasions from Mr. Wilberforce's peculiar views, we can give to this his most important work—and we really believe the most unquestionable and lasting benefit he conferred on mankind—our almost unlimited approbation. We do not pretend to enter into anything like a critical, or still less a theological examination of this work—twenty editions before the copyright had expired, and a great many since, attest its popularity, and in the case of such a book popularity is a high criterion of merit . . . Produced not only a sudden, but a permanent effect—his station, his reputation, the lucidity, if not the force of his reasoning, the practical character of his means and object, and the persuasive earnestness, yet simplicity of his style, combined to command the attention, to conciliate the feelings, and finally to convince and convert to the vital truths he inculcated, the hearts of many, on whom a drier, more doctrinal, and more argumentive appeal might have been made in vain. And if he fixes the standard of conduct too high for general attainment, he places it, at least, so clearly in sight, that it seems nearer than it is—and many will be tempted to climb and some will be encouraged to approach the summit, though few or none may be destined to reach it; but, in proportion to whatever height any one may attain, his views will be extended and brightened, and he will be, at last, by so much the nearer to heaven.—CROKER, JOHN WILSON, 1838, *Life of Wilberforce, Quarterly Review, vol.* 62, *pp.* 266, 267.

The persons he addressed were men such as those whom St. Paul addressed on Mars' Hill, but whom few preachers were bold enough to summon to the bar, with the same unhesitating plainness with which they arraigned their humbler neighbours. Wilberforce did not appeal to infidels or unbelievers. He made no assault upon scepticism. His object was to show the respectable and intelligent how far their calm and easy ignoring of religion, even while professing it, was unlike the spirit of Christianity. There is no special charm of style to redeem his treatise from the respectful oblivion into which—after a popularity greater in degree than that which almost any other kind of literary production enjoys in its day—religious books are apt to fall. And nothing can be more unlike the works which have gained something of a similar influence in our own time. It is to be feared that to Wilberforce that broad and conciliatory treatment which translated the time-worn language of Christianity into the phraseology of its philosophical opponents, by way of betraying these latter tenderly into something like faith, or approval at least—would have appeared flat blasphemy. He would have had no understanding of the process which turns the love of Christ into the Enthusiasm of Humanity. The society which he addressed was not one which required such methods.—OLIPHANT, MARGARET O. W., 1882, *Literary History of England, XVIII-XIX Century, vol.* III, *p.* 313.

GENERAL

As these are letters addressed to friends, we cannot expect to find in them any depth of thought; yet they indicate critical discrimination in reading, a sagacious perception of merits or demerits in political organizations, a penetrating judgment of real oratory, liveliness of fancy, and felicity of diction. Such elements of literary merit may be found scattered through a correspondence comprising many hundred letters, some of which run into too great diffuseness of expression; but all are written in a pleasant, easy style, leading the reader on from page to page without weariness. . . . The earlier stage of Wilberforce's life was in the very *age of correspondence*, contemporary with two eminent masters of the art, Cowper and Newton. . . . With neither of these writers, in some respects, is Wilberforce to be placed on a level: certainly one misses in his letters the indescribable sort of charm which invests those of his contemporaries, but in other respects—such as knowledge of the world, large experience gathered from varied intercourse, a comprehensive and many-sided sympathy, and a peculiar habit of rapidly passing from one subject to another, as graceful as it is characteristic of his extraordinary versatility—Wilberforce is superior to either of his contemporaries.—STOUGHTON, JOHN, 1880, *William Wilberforce (Men Worth Remembering), pp.* 152, 153.

The few and trifling faults of Wilberforce as an orator and a man are scarcely worth mentioning. The extraordinary discursiveness and versatility of his mind made him sometimes attempt to keep too many irons in the fire—to shift too rapidly from one subject to another—and occasionally gave an appearance of inconsistency to his conduct.—NICOLL, HENRY J., 1881, *Great Movements and Those who Achieved Them, p.* 68.

William Sotheby

1757-1833

William Sotheby, an accomplished scholar and translator, was born in London on the 9th of November 1757. He was of good family, and educated at Harrow School. At the age of seventeen he entered the army as an officer in the 10th Dragoons. He quitted the army in the year 1780, and purchased Bevis Mount, near Southampton, where he continued to reside for the next ten years. Here Mr. Sotheby cultivated his taste for literature, and translated some of the minor Greek and Latin poets. In 1788, he made a pedestrian tour through Wales, of which he wrote a poetical description, published, together with some odes and sonnets, in 1789. In 1798, he published a translation from the "Oberon" of Wieland, which greatly extended his reputation, and procured him the thanks and friendship of the German poet. He now became a frequent competitor for poetical fame. In 1799, he wrote a poem commemorative of the battle of the Nile; in 1800, appeared his translation of the "Georgics" of Virgil; in 1801, he produced a "Poetical Epistle on the Encouragement of the British School of Painting;" and in 1802, a tragedy on the model of the ancient Greek drama, entitled "Orestes." He next devoted himself to the composition of an original sacred poem, in blank verse, under the title of "Saul," which appeared in 1807. The fame of Scott induced him to attempt the romantic metrical style of narrative and description, and in 1810, he published "Constance de Castille," a poem in ten cantos. In 1814, he republished his "Orestes," together with four other tragedies; and in 1815, a second corrected edition of the "Georgics." This translation is one of the best of a classic poet in our language. A tour on the continent gave occasion to another poetical work, "Italy." He next began a labour which he had long contemplated, the translation of the "Iliad" and "Odyssey," though he was upwards of seventy years of age before he entered upon the Herculean task. . . . Mr. Sotheby's translation of the "Iliad" was published in 1831, and was generally esteemed spirited and faithful. The "Odyssey" he completed in the following year. He died on the 30th of December, 1833.—CHAMBERS, ROBERT, 1876, *Cyclopædia of English Literature, ed. Carruthers.*

GENERAL

My acquaintance with this admirable poem, ["Oberon"] being hitherto through the medium of a very different French version, it was with much pleasure and expectation I took up the volumes of Mr. Sotheby; nor have I been disappointed. The versification is usually free and harmonious, and the diction in many places glows with a curious felicity of expression. The various descriptions of female beauty, and the numerous sketchings in landscape with which the "Oberon" abounds, are given *con amore.* The elegant and happy machinery, too, of this poem, unfolding to so much advantage the luxuriant and sportive imagination of Wieland, has been transfused with energy and ease.—DRAKE, NATHAN, 1798-1820, *Literary Hours, vol.* II, *p.* 103.

A scriptural subject treated in blank verse unfortunately brings Milton to the thoughts of most readers; and the name of the translator of Oberon raises expectations which it is not easy to answer. This poem has certainly disappointed us. It is not very like Milton; except in the multitude of Hebrew names: and it is strikingly inferior to Mr. Sotheby's other composition, even in those points where we reckoned with certainty on improvement. There was great beauty of diction in the Oberon; and, considering the difficulty of the measure, an unusual flow and facility of versification. When we found the author writing in blank verse, therefore, we naturally looked for still greater freedom and variety of composition; and expected to be charmed with all those natural graces of expression, which are necessarily excluded, to a certain degree, by the bondage of an intricate stanza. The very reverse is the case, however, with the work now before us. Mr. Sotheby's blank verse is as remarkable for harshness, constraint, and abruptness, as his stanzas were for ease and melody; and his muse, we are afraid, is like one of those old beauties, who, having been long accustomed to move gracefully in tight stays, high shoes, and hooped petticoats, feels her supports withdrawn when disencumbered of her shackles, and totters and stumbles when there are no longer any restraints on

SAMUEL TAYLOR COLERIDGE

From the Original Painting by Peter Vandyke,
now in the National Portrait Gallery, London

CHARLES LAMB

her movements.—JEFFREY, FRANCIS LORD, 1807, *Sotheby's Saul, Edinburgh Review, vol.* 10, *p.* 206.

Sotheby was full of his translation of Homer's Iliad, some specimens of which he has already published. It is a complete failure, more literal than that of Pope, but still tainted with the deep radical vice of Pope's version, a thoroughly modern and artificial manner. It bears the same kind of relation to the Iliad that Robertson's narrative bears to the story of Joseph in the book of Genesis. — MACAULAY, THOMAS BABINGTON, 1831, *To Hannah M. Macaulay, June 10th; Life and Letters, ed. Trevelyan.*

Mr. Sotheby was a man of rare scholarship, deeply imbued with the spirit of classical literature, and his numerous writings, consisting of translations from the Greek, Latin, and German, and original English poems, ill deserve the neglect to which they have recently been consigned. —GRISWOLD, RUFUS W., 1844, *The Poets and Poetry of England in the Nineteenth Century, p.* 22.

Sotheby was never great, except when treading in some beaten path. His "Saul," an epic poem, and his "Constance de Castille," a romance in the manner of Scott, as well as his "Italy," a descriptive poem, contain each fine and spirited passages; but even these are almost always reflections of what has attracted his own particular admiration in others. As a translator, it would be difficult to name his superior. He had the good sense to discover that his great forte lay in the transfusion of ideas from one language into another; and he not only enthusiastically, but industriously, employed himself in the enriching English Literature.—MOIR, D. M., 1850–51, *Sketches of the Poetical Literature of the Past Half-Century, p.* 38.

Sotheby, wrote Byron, "has imitated everybody, and occasionally surpassed his models." Although his poems and plays were held in high esteem by his friends, his translations of Virgil and Wieland alone deserve posthumous consideration. They are faitful to their originals and betray much literary taste, if they are not of the stuff of which classics are made. As a translator of Homer, Sotheby, who owed much to Pope, failed to reproduce Homer's directness of style and diction. The translation, although eminently readable, was a work of supererogation. Sotheby's intimate relations with men of high distinction in literature give his career its chief interest.—LEE, SIDNEY, 1898, *Dictionary of National Biography, vol.* LIII, *p.* 268.

Samuel Taylor Coleridge

1772–1834

1772—Born at Ottery St. Mary, Oct. 21. 1782—Admitted to Christ's Hospital. 1791—Enters Cambridge University. 1793—Enlists in the Light Dragoons. 1794—Returns to Cambridge; meets Southey at Oxford; Pantisocracy hatched; leaves Cambridge and goes to London. 1795—Goes to Bristol; marries Miss Fricker, and settles at Clevedon. 1796—First volume of poems; *The Watchman.* 1797—Removes to Nether Stowey; first meeting with Wordsworth; the "Lyrical Ballads" begun. 1798—"Lyrical Ballads" published; visits Germany with the Wordsworths. 1799—Returns to England; *Morning Post* and "Wallenstein." 1800—Removes to Greta Hall, Keswick. 1801—Broken health; the "Kendal Black Drop." 1802—Dejection and family discord. 1803—Visits Scotland with the Wordsworths. 1804—Sails for Malta; made secretary to Sir Alexander Ball. 1805—Visits Sicily and Rome. 1806–10—At Coleorton with Wordsworth; lectures on the poets at the Royal Institution, London; at Grasmere; projects the *Friend.* 1811–12—In London; lectures on Shakespeare and Milton. 1813–16—"Remorse" at Drury Lane; lectures at Bristol; goes to Calne; settles at Highgate with the Gillmans; publishes "Christabel." 1817—"Biographia Literaria" and "Sibylline Leaves." 1818—Lectures in London; meets Thomas Allsop and Keats. 1818—Failure of publishers. 1820–22—Hackwork. 1825—"Aids to Reflection"; Pension. 1825–34—Last years at Highate.—GEORGE, ANDREW J., 1897, *ed. Coleridge's The Ancient Mariner, p.* 27.

Works: "Fall of Robespierre" (act I. by Coleridge; acts ii., iii. by Southey), 1794; "Moral and Political Lecture delivered at Bristol," 1795; "Conciones ad Populum,"

1795; "The Plot Discovered," 1795; "The Watchman," 1796; "Ode on the Departing Year," 1796; "Poems on various subjects," 1796; "Fears in Solitude," 1798; "France," 1798; "Frost at Midnight," 1798; "Ancient Mariner" contributed to "Lyrical Ballads," 1798; Poems contributed to "Annual Anthology," 1800; "The Friend," 1809-10; contributions to Southey's "Omniana," 1812; "Remorse," 1813; "Christabel, Kubla Khan and Pains of Sleep," 1816; "The Statesman's Manual," 1816; "Blessed are ye that sow beside all waters: a lay Sermon," 1817; "Biographia Literaria," 1817; "Sibylline Leaves," 1817; "Zapolya," 1817; "Aids to Reflection in the formation of a Manly Character," 1825; "Poetical Works, including Dramas," 1829; "On the Constitution of Church and State," 1830. *Posthumous:* "Table-Talk," 1835; "Literary Remains," 1836-38; "Letters, ed. by T. Allsop," 1836; "Confessions of an Enquiring Spirit," 1840; "Treatises on Method" (from "Encyclopædia Metropolitana"), 1845; "Hints towards a formation of a more comprehensive Theory of Life," 1848; "Notes and Lectures upon Shakespeare," 1849; "Essays on his Own Times, forming a second series of 'The Friend,'" 1850; "The Relation of Philosophy to Theology," 1851; "Lay Sermons," 1852; "Notes upon English Divines," 1853; "Notes theological, political and miscellaneous," 1853; "Anima Poetæ; from the unpublished notebooks of S. T. Coleridge, ed. by E. H. Coleridge," 1895; "Letters; edited by E. H. Coleridge," 1895. He *translated:* Schiller's "Wallenstein," 1800. *Collected Works:* in 7 vols., ed. by W. G. T. Stedd, 1884; "Poems," ed. by W. Bell Scott, 1894. *Life:* by H. D. Traill, 1884.—SHARP, R. FARQUHARSON, 1897, *A Dictionary of English Authors, p.* 60.

PERSONAL

My Father was very fond of me, and I was my Mother's darling: in consequence whereof I was very miserable. For Molly, who had nursed my brother Francis, and was immoderately fond of him, hated me because my Mother took more notice of me than of Frank; and Frank hated me because my Mother gave me now and then a bit of cake when he had none. . . . So I became fretful and timorous, and a tell-tale; and the school-boys drove me from play, and were always tormenting me. And hence I took no pleasure in boyish sports, but read incessantly. . . . And I used to lie by the wall, and mope; and my spirits used to come upon me suddenly, and in a flood;—and then I was accustomed to run up and down the church-yard, and act over again all I had been reading on the docks, the nettles and the rank grass. At six years of age I remember to have read Belisarius, Robinson Crusoe, and Philip Quarles; and then I found the Arabian Nights' Entertainments, one tale of which . . . made so deep an impression on me . . . that I was haunted by spectres, whenever I was in the dark: . . . So I became a dreamer, and acquired an indispositon to all bodily activity; and I was fretful and inordinately passionate; and as I could not play at anything, and was slothful, I was despised and hated by the boys; and because I could read and spell, and had, I may truly say, a memory and understanding forced into almost unnatural ripeness, I was flattered and wondered at by all the old women.—COLERIDGE, SAMUEL TAYLOR, 1797, *Letter to Mr. Poole, Oct.* 9; *Biographia Literaria, Biographical Supplement, ed. H. N. Coleridge.*

Every sight and every sound reminded me of him—dear, dear fellow, of his many talks to us, by day and by night, of all dear things. I was melancholy, and could not talk, but at last I eased my heart by weeping—nervous blubbering says William. It is not so. O! how many, many reasons have I to be anxious for him.—WORDSWORTH, DOROTHY, 1801, *Journals, Nov.* 10, *ed. Knight, vol.* I, *p.* 64.

O capacious Soul!
Placed on this earth to love and understand,
And from thy presence shed the light of love,
Shall I be mute, ere thou be spoken of ?
Thy kindred influence to my heart of hearts
Did also find its way.
—WORDSWORTH, WILLIAM, 1805, *The Prelude, bk.* xiv.

His countenance is the most variable that I have ever seen; sometimes it is kindled with the brightest expression, and sometimes all its light goes out, and is utterly extinguished. Nothing can convey stronger indications of power than his eye, eyebrow, and forehead. Nothing can be more imbecile than all the rest of the face; look at them separately, you would hardly think it possible that they could belong to one head; look at them together, you wonder how they came so, and are puzzled what to expect from a character whose outward and visible signs are so contradictory.—SOUTHEY, ROBERT, 1808, *Letter to Matilda Betham, June* 3; *Fraser's Magazine, vol.* 98, *p.* 80.

Coleridge has been lecturing against Campbell. Rogers was present, and from him I derive the information. We are going to make a party to hear this Manichean of poesy.—BYRON, LORD, 1811, *Letters To Mr. Harness, Dec.* 8.

He confined himself to "Romeo and Juliet" for a time, treated of the inferior characters, and delivered a most eloquent discourse on love, with a promise to point out how Shakespeare has shown the same truths in the persons of the lovers. Yesterday we were to have a continuation of the theme. Alas! Coleridge began with a parallel between religion and love, which, though one of his favorite themes, he did not manage successfully. Romeo and Juliet were forgotten. And in the next lecture we are really to hear something of these lovers. Now this will be the fourth time that his hearers have been invited expressly to hear of this play. There are to be only fifteen lectures altogether (half have been delivered), and the course is to include Shakespeare and Milton, the modern poets, etc.!!! Instead of a lecture on a definite subject we have an immethodical rhapsody, very delightful to you and me, and only offensive from the certainty that it may and ought to offend those who come with other expectations. Yet, with all this, I cannot but be charmed with these *splendida vitia*, and my chief displeasure is occasioned by my being forced to hear the strictures of persons infinitely below Coleridge, without any power of refuting or contradicting them.—ROBINSON, HENRY CRABB, 1811, *To Mrs. Clarkson, Dec.* 13; *Diary, Reminiscences and Correspondence, ed. Sadler, vol.* I, *p.* 227.

Coleridge has a grand head, but very ill balanced, and the features of the face are coarse—although, to be sure, nothing can surpass the depth of meaning in his eyes, and the unutterable dreamy luxury in his lips.—LOCKHART, JOHN GIBSON, 1819, *Peter's Letters to His Kinsfolk, Letter* liv.

Come back into memory, like as thou wert in the day-spring of thy fancies, with hope like a fiery column before thee—the dark pillar not yet turned—Samuel Taylor Coleridge—Logician, Metaphysician, Bard!—How have I seen the casual passer through the Cloisters stand still, entranced with admiration (while he weighed the disproportion between the *speech* and the *garb* of the young Mirandula), to hear thee unfold, in thy deep and sweet intonations, the mysteries of Jamblichus, or Plotinus (for even in those years thou waxedst not pale at such philosophic draughts), or reciting Homer in his Greek, or Pindar—while the walls of the old Grey Friars reechoed to the accents of the *inspired charity-boy!* — LAMB, CHARLES, 1820, *Christ's Hospital Five and Thirty Years Ago.*

His complexion was at that time [1798] clear, and even bright—

"As are the children of yon azure sheen."

His forehead was broad and high, light as if built of ivory, with large projecting eyebrows, and his eyes rolling beneath them, like a sea with darkened lustre. "A certain tender bloom his face o'erspread," a purple tinge as we see it in the pale thoughtful complexions of the Spanish portrait-painters, Murillo and Velasquez. His mouth was gross, voluptuous, open, eloquent; his chin good-humoured and round; but his nose, the rudder of the face, the index of the will, was small, feeble, nothing—like what he has done. . . . His hair (now, alas! gray) was then black and glossy as the raven's, and fell in smooth masses over his forehead. —HAZLITT, WILLIAM, 1821-22, *My First Acquaintance with Poets, Table Talk.*

Father, and Bard revered! to whom I owe,
Whate'er it be, my little art of numbers,
Thou in thy night-watch o'er my cradled slumbers,
Didst meditate the verse that lives to shew,
(And long shall live, when we alike are low)
Thy prayer how ardent, and thy hope how strong,
That I should learn of Nature's self the song,
The lore which none but Nature's pupils know.

— COLERIDGE, HARTLEY, 1833, *Poems, Dedicatory Sonnet.*

Stop, Christian passer-by: Stop, child of God,
And read, with gentle breast. Beneath this sod
A poet lies, or that which once seemed he—
O, lift one thought in prayer for S. T. C.—
That he who many a year with toil of breath

Found death in life, may here find life in death:
Mercy for praise,—to be forgiven for fame,—
He asked, and hoped, through Christ. Do thou the same.
—COLERIDGE, SAMUEL TAYLOR, 1833, *Epitaph.*

You know how long and severely he suffered in his health; yet, to the last, he appeared to have such high intellectual gratifications that we felt little impulse to pray for his immediate release; and though his infirmities had been grievously increasing of late years, the life and vigor of his mind were so great that they hardly led those around him to think of his dissolution. His frail house of clay was so illumined that its decaying condition was the less perceptible. His departure, after all, seemed to come suddenly upon us. We were first informed of his danger on Sunday, the 20th of July, and on Friday, the 25th, he was taken from us. . . . When he knew that his time was come, he said that he hoped by the manner of his death to testify the sincerity of his faith; and hoped that all who had heard of his name would know that he died in that of the English Church.—COLERIDGE, SARA, 1834, *To Mrs. Plummer, Oct., Memoir and Letters, ed. her Daughter, p.* 98.

After trial and temptation; after sorrow and pain; after daily dyings to the world; after daily risings into holiness; at length comes that "rest that remaineth unto the people of God." After the fever of life; after wearinesses and sicknesses; fightings and despondings; struggling and failing, struggling and succeeding; after all the changes and chances of this troubled and unhealthy state, at length comes death, at length the White Throne of God, at length the Beatific Vision. —NEWMAN, JOHN HENRY, 1834–42, *Parochial Sermons.*

In height he might seem to be about five feet eight (he was, in reality, about an inch and a-half taller, but his figure was of an order which drowns the height); his person was broad and full, and tended even to corpulence; his complexion was fair, though not what painters technically style fair, because it was associated with black hair; his eyes were large, and soft in their expression; and it was from the peculiar appearance of haze or dreaminess which mixed with their light that I recognised my object. . . . I examined him steadfastly for a minute or more; and it struck me that he saw neither myself nor any other object in the street. He was in a deep reverie; for I had dismounted, made two or three trifling arrangements at an inn-door, and advanced close to him, before he had apparently become conscious of my presence. The sound of my voice, announcing my own name, first awoke him: he started, and for a moment seemed at a loss to understand my purpose or his own situation; for he repeated rapidly a number of words which had no relation to either of us. There was no *mauvaise honte* in his manner, but simple perplexity, and an apparent difficulty in recovering his position amongst daylight realities. This little scene over, he received me with a kindness of manner so marked that it might be called gracious. . . . In the evening, when the heat of the day had declined, I walked out with him; and rarely, perhaps never, have I seen a person so much interrupted in one hour's space as Coleridge, on this occasion, by the courteous attentions of young and old.—DE QUINCEY, THOMAS, 1834–54, *Autobiography from* 1803 *to* 1808, *Collected Writings, ed. Masson, vol.* II, *pp.* 150, 151.

[To] pass an entire day with Coleridge, was a marvellous change indeed. It was a Sabbath past expression deep, and tranquil, and serene. You came to a man who had travelled in many countries, and in critical times; who had seen and felt the world in most of its ranks and in many of its vicissitudes and weaknesses; one to whom all literature and genial art were absolutely subject, and to whom, with a reasonable allowance as to technical details, all science was in a most extraordinary degree familiar. Throughout a long-drawn summer's day would this man talk to you in low, equable, but clear and musical tones, concerning things human and divine; marshalling all history, harmonizing all experiment, probing the depths of your consciousness, and revealing visions of glory and of terror to the imagination; but pouring withal such floods of light upon the mind, that you might, for a season, like Paul, become blind in the very act of conversion. And this he would do, without so much as one allusion to himself, without a word of reflection on others, save when any given act fell naturally in the way of his discourse,—without one anecdote that was not proof and illustration of a previous position;—gratifying no passion, indulging no caprice, but, with a calm mastery over your soul, leading you onward and onward for ever through a thousand windings, yet with no pause, to some magnificent point in which, as in a focus, all the parti-coloured rays of his discourse should converge in light. In all this he was, in truth, your teacher and guide; but in a little while you might forget that he was other than a fellow-student and the companion of your way,—so playful was his manner, so simple his language, so affectionate the glance of his pleasant eye!—COLERIDGE, HENRY NELSON, 1835, *ed., Specimens of the Table Talk of Samuel Taylor Coleridge, Preface.*

The manner of Coleridge was rather *emphatic* than *dogmatic*, and thus he was generally and satisfactorily listened to. There was neither the *bow-wow* nor the growl which seemed usually to characterize Johnson's method of speaking; and his periods were more lengthened and continuous. . . . Coleridge was a *mannerist.* It was always the same tone—in the same style of expression—not quick and bounding enough to diffuse instant and general vivacity. . . . There was always *this* characteristic feature in his multifarious conversation—it was delicate, reverend, and courteous.—DIBDIN, THOMAS FROGNALL, 1836, *Reminiscences of a Literary Life, pp.* 255, 256.

William Coope tells us that he used often to see S. T. Coleridge till within a month of his death, and was an ardent admirer of his prominent blue eyes, reverend hair and rapt expression. He has met Charles Lamb at his house. On one occasion Coleridge was holding forth on the effects produced by his preaching, and appealed to Lamb, "You have heard me preach, I think?" "I have never heard you do anything else," was the urbane reply.—FOX, CAROLINE, 1836, *Memories of Old Friends, ed. Pym, Journals, Dec.* 18, *p.* 14.

His benignity of manner placed his auditors entirely at their ease; and inclined them to listen delighted to the sweet, low tone in which he began to discourse on some high theme. Whether he had won for his greedy listener only some raw lad, or charmed a circle of beauty, rank, and wit, who hung breathless on his words, he talked with equal eloquence; for his subject, not his audience, inspired him. At first his tones were conversational; he seemed to dally with the shadows of the subject and with fantastic images which bordered it; but gradually the thought grew deeper, and the voice deepened with the thought; the stream gathering strength, seemed to bear along with it all things which opposed its progress, and blended them with its current; and stretching away among regions tinted with ethereal colors, was lost at airy distance in the horizon of fancy. His hearers were unable to grasp his theories, which were indeed too vast to be exhibited in the longest conversation; but they perceived noble images, generous suggestions, affecting pictures of virtue, which enriched their minds and nurtured their best affections. . . . He usually met opposition by conceding the point to the objector, and then went on with his high argument as if it had never been raised; thus satisfying his antagonist, himself, and all who heard him; none of whom desired to hear his discourse frittered into points, or displaced by the near encounter even of the most brilliant wits.—TALFOURD, THOMAS NOON, 1837, *The Life and Letters of Charles Lamb, p.* 223.

Whatever might have been his habits in boyhood, in manhood he was scrupulously clean in his person, and especially took great care of his hands. . . . In his dress also he was as cleanly as the liberal use of snuff would permit, though the clothes-brush was often in requisition to remove the wasted snuff. "Snuff," he would facetiously say, "was the final cause of the nose, though troublesome and expensive in its use."—GILLMAN, JAMES, 1838, *The Life of Samuel Taylor Coleridge, p.* 19, *note.*

After dinner he got up, and began pacing to and fro, with his hands behind his back, talking and walking, as Lamb laughingly hinted, as if qualifying for an itinerant preacher; now fetching a simile from Loddige's garden, at Hackney; and then driving off for an illustration to the sugar-making in Jamaica. With his fine, flowing voice, it was glorious music, of the "never-ending, still-beginning" kind and you did not wish it to end. It was rare flying, as in the Nassau Balloon; you knew not whither, nor did you care. Like his own bright-eyed Marinere, he had a spell in his voice that would not let you go. To describe my own feeling afterward, I had been carried, spiralling, up to heaven by a whirlwind intertwisted with sunbeams, giddy and dazzled, but not displeased, and had then been rained down again with a shower of mundane sticks and stones that battered out of me all recollection of what I had heard, and what I had seen!—HOOD, THOMAS, 1845? *Literary Reminiscenses.*

The Mercury at these times was generally Mr. Coleridge, who, as has been stated, ingeniously parried every adverse argument, and after silencing his hardy disputants, announced to them that he was about to write and publish a quarto volume in favor of Pantisocracy, in which a variety of arguments would be advanced in defence of his system, too subtile and recondite to comport with conversation. It would then, he said, become manifest that he was not a projector raw from his cloister, but a cool calculating reasoner, whose efforts and example would secure to him and his friends the permanent gratitude of mankind. From the sentiments thus entertained I shall represent Mr. Coleridge, in the section of his days which devolves on me to exhibit, just as he was, and that with a firm belief that by so doing, without injuring his legitimate reputation, I shall confer an essential benefit on those to come, who will behold in Mr. C. much to admire and imitate; and certainly some things to regret. For it should be remembered, Mr. Coleridge, from universal admission, possessed some of the highest mental endowments, and many pertaining to the heart; but if a man's life be valuable, not for the incense it consumes, but for the instruction it affords, to state even defects, (in one like Mr. C. who can so well afford deductions without serious loss), becomes in his biographer, not optional, but a serious obligation.—COTTLE, JOSEPH, 1847, *Reminiscences of Samuel Taylor Coleridge and Robert Southey, p.* 6.

The house which Mr. Gillman occupied is now occupied by a Mr. Brendon. There is nothing remarkable about the house except its view. Coleridge's room looked upon a delicious prospect of wood and meadow, with a gay garden full of color under the window. When a friend of his first saw him there, he said he thought he had taken his dwelling-place like an abbot. There he cultivated his flowers, and had a set of birds for his pensioners, who came to breakfast with him. He might be seen taking his daily stroll up and down near Highgate, with his black coat and white locks, and a book in his hand; and was a great acquaintance of the little children.—HOWITT, WILLIAM, 1847, *Homes and Haunts of the Most Eminent British Poets, vol.* II, *p.* 121.

Coleridge was as little fitted for action as Lamb, but on a different account. His person was of a good height, but as sluggish and solid as the other's was light and fragile. He had, perhaps, suffered it to look old before its time, for want of exercise. His hair was white at fifty; and as he generally dressed in black, and had a very tranquil demeanor, his appearance was gentlemanly, and for several years before his death was reverend. Nevertheless, there was something invincibly young in the look of his face. It was round and fresh-colored, with agreeable features, and an open, indolent, good-natured mouth. This boy-like expression was very becoming in one who dreamed and speculated as he did when he was really a boy, and who passed his life apart from the rest of the world, with a book, and his flowers. His forehead was prodigious—a great piece of placid marble; and his fine eyes, in which all the activity of his mind seemed to concentrate, moved under it with a sprightly ease, as if it was pastime to them to carry all that thought.—HUNT, LEIGH, 1850-60, *Autobiography.*

Every body has heard the often told story of Coleridge's enlisting in a cavalry regiment under a feigned name, and being detected as a Cambridge scholar in consequence of his writing some Greek lines, or rather, I believe, some Greek words, over the bed of a sick comrade, whom, not knowing how else to dispose of him, he had been apppointed to nurse. It has not been stated that the arrangement for his discharge took place at my father's house at Reading. Such, however, was the case.—MITFORD, MARY RUSSELL, 1851, *Recollections of a Literary Life, p.* 394.

Coleridge sat on the brow of Highgate Hill, in those years, looking down on London and its smoke-tumult, like a sage escaped from the inanity of life's battle;

attracting towards him the thoughts of innumerable brave souls still engaged there. . . . The good man, he was now getting old, sixty perhaps; and gave you an idea of a life that had been full of sufferings; a life heavy-laden, half-vanquished, still swimming painfully in seas of manifold physical and other bewilderment. Brow and head were round and of massive weight, but the face was flabby and irresolute. The deep eyes, of a light hazel, were as full of sorrow as of inspiration; confused pain looked mildly from them, as in a kind of mild astonishment. The whole figure and air, good and amiable otherwise, might be called flabby and irresolute; expressive of weakness under possibility of strength. He hung loosely on his limbs, with knees bent, and stooping attitude; in walking, he rather shuffled than decisively stept; and a lady once remarked, he never could fix which side of the garden walk would suit him best, but continually shifted, in corkscrew fashion, and kept trying both. A heavy-laden, high-aspiring, and surely much-suffering man. His voice, naturally soft and good, had contracted itself into a plaintive snuffle and singsong; he spoke as if preaching,—you would have said, preaching earnestly and almost hopelessly the weightest things. I still recollect his "object" and "subject," terms of continual recurrence in the Kantean province; and how he sang and snuffled them into "om-m-mject" and "sum-m-mject," with a kind of solemn shake or quaver, as he rolled along. No talk, in his century or in any other, could be more surprising.—CARLYLE, THOMAS, 1851, *The Life of John Sterling.*

Coleridge was a marvellous talker. One morning he talked three hours without intermission about poetry, and so admirably that I wished every word he uttered had been written down. But sometimes his harangues were quite unintelligible, not only to myself but to others. Wordsworth and I called upon him one forenoon when he was lodging in Pall Mall. He talked uninterruptedly for about two hours, during which Wordsworth listened to him with profound attention, every now and then nodding his head as if in assent. On quitting the lodging I said to Wordsworth, "Well, for my own part I could not make head or tail of Coleridge's oration; pray, did you understand it?" "Not one syllable of it," was Wordsworth's reply. —ROGERS, SAMUEL, 1855, *Recollections of Table Talk, ed. Dyce.*

"What do you think of Dr. Channing, Mr. Coleridge?" said a brisk young gentleman to the mighty discourser, as he sat next him at a small tea-party. "Before entering upon that question, sir," said Coleridge, opening upon his inquirer those "noticeable gray eyes," with a vague and placid stare, and settling himself in his seat for the night, "I must put you in possession of my views, *in extenso* on the origin, progress, present condition, future likelihoods, and absolute essence of the Unitarian controversy, and especially the conclusions I have, upon the whole, come to on the great question of what may be termed the philosophy of religious difference."—BROWN, JOHN, 1858–61, *Horæ Subsecivæ.*

His voice was deep and musical, and his words followed each other in an unbroken flow, yet free from monotony. There was indeed a peculiar charm in his utterance. His pronunciation was remarkably correct; in some respects pedantically so. He gave the full sound of the *l* in *talk*, and *should*, and *would*.—LESLIE, CHARLES R., 1860, *Autobiographical Recollections, ed. Taylor.*

In all, he was physically of an enervated nature—I mean the reverse of muscular. His action was most quiet and subdued, even when most energetically declaiming: and his hand . . . was as velvety as the sheathed paw of cat or mole, and might have manifested the veriest Sybarite that ever lived for luxury alone.—JERDAN, WILLIAM, 1866, *Men I have Known.*

Meadows, in these our pleasant perambulations, was wont to speak of an old lady who kept the Lion and Sun Hotel in that neighborhood [Highgate]. This was a favorite resort of Coleridge; and the communicative landlady used to remark that he was a great talker, and "when he began there was no stopping him." Whenever she returned to the room, she said, after leaving it for a short time, he would still "be going on," and sometimes he made such a noise that she wished him further.—HODDER, GEORGE, 1870, *Memoirs of My Time, ch.* v.

I recollect him only as an eloquent but intolerable talker; impatient of the speech and opinions of others; very inconsecutive, and putting forth with a plethora of words misty dogmas in theology and metaphysics, partly of German origin, which he never seemed to me to clear up to his own understanding or to that of others. What has come out posthumously of his philosophy has not removed this imputation upon it.—HOLLAND, SIR HENRY, 1871, *Recollections of Past Life, p.* 205.

Samuel Taylor Coleridge was like the Rhine,

That exulting and abounding river.

He was full of words, full of thought; yielding both in an unfailing flow, that delighted many, and perplexed a few of his hearers. He was a man of prodigious miscellaneous reading, always ready to communicate all he knew. From Alpha to Omega, all was familiar to him. He was deep in Jacob Behmen. He was intimate with Thomas Aquinas and Quevedo; with Bacon and Kant, with "Peter Simple" and "Tom Cringle's Log;" and with all the old divines of both England and France. The pages of all the infidels had passed under his eye and made their legitimate (and not more than their legitimate) impression. He went from flower to flower, throughout the whole garden of learning, like the butterfly or the bee,—most like the bee. He talked with everybody, about anything. He was so full of information that it was a relief to him to part with some portion of it to others. It was like laying down part of his burden.—PROCTER, BRYAN WALLER, 1874? *Recollections of Men of Letters, p.* 144.

The upper part of Coleridge's face was excessively fine. His eyes were large, light gray, prominent, and of liquid brilliancy, which some eyes of fine character may be observed to possess, as though the orb itself retreated to the innermost recesses of the brain. The lower part of his face was somewhat dragged, indicating the presence of habitual pain; but his forehead was prodigious, and like a smooth slab of alabaster.—CLARKE, CHARLES AND MARY COWDEN, 1878, *Recollections of Writers, p.* 35.

Like desert pools that show the stars
Once in long leagues,—even such the scarce-snatched hours
Which deepening pain left to his lordliest powers:—
Heaven lost through spider-trammelled prison-bars.
Six years, from sixty saved! Yet kindling skies
Own them, a beacon to our centuries.

—ROSSETTI, DANTE GABRIEL, 1881, *Samuel Taylor Coleridge, Five English Poets, Ballads and Sonnets.*

Recently an old laborer here, very old and fearing death, sent for the curate of the parish, who discovered that he was using laudanum for his rheumatism, and warned him of the risks he ran. The old man replied: "Why, I know better, Parson; my brother was doctor's boy to Mr. Gillman fifty years or more ago, and there was an old chap there called Colingrigs, or some such name, as Mr. Gillman thought he was a-curing of drinking laudanum, and my brother he used to fill a bottle with that stuff from Mr. Gillman's own bottles, and hand it to me, and I used to put it under my jacket and give it to h'old Colingrigs, and we did that for years and it never hurted him." . . . Mrs. Dutton, a charming old lady greatly respected in Highgate, lives in an ivy-covered cottage on the Grove, and remembers Coleridge well. She used to sit on his knee and prattle to him, and she tells how he was followed about the Grove by troops of children for the sake of the sweeties of which his pockets were always full.—MARTIN, DR. E. B., 1884, *Literary Landmarks of London, by Hutton, Letter, p.* 58.

If Coleridge was at any period guilty of offence against the moral law it must have been in those early days when, as he says, he knew "just so much of folly" as "made maturer years more wise." In later years his walk became, more than ever, that of a man who had never so much as a temptation to such offence. It is a curious fact, which any careful reader of his letters may verify, that when he became a slave to opium, his spiritual consciousness became more active, and his watchfulness of the encroachments of the baser impulses of his nature more keen. If his excesses in this regard were what Southey described them, guilty animal indulgences, it is a strange problem in psychology why the whole spiritual nature of the man should undergo a manifest exaltation. Every one who was brought into contact with Coleridge in the darkest days of his subjection to opium, observed this extraordinary moral transfiguration.—CAINE, HALL, 1887, *Life of Samuel Taylor Coleridge (Great Writers), p.* 136.

A gentle peace soothed these last years. He had fought a terrible battle against the most insidious foe that can attack man. He had suffered many a defeat, and had gained many a victory, but at last the soul rose triumphant over the weakened body. In the days of his humiliation he had written books that are sought and studied by scholars, for their clear philosophy and their Christian teaching. The mists of doubt and questioning had long since cleared away, and his faith grasped the Bible and all its teachings as the only sure guide. . . . At this time, during the long days and nights, when the Past with all its phases and mistakes rose before him, he could feel that at least he had always believed and written honestly, and that the principles of his youth were the principles of his age, only modified by the clearer vision gained by life's varied experiences. His early friends were still the friends of his last years, and he had never stooped to truckle for favor or influence.—LORD, ALICE E., 1893, *The Days of Lamb and Coleridge, A Historical Romance*, p. 368.

In writing of the man of the "graspless hand," the biographer's own hand in time grows graspless on the pen; and in reading of him our hands too grow graspless on the page. We pursue the man and come upon group after group of his friends; and each, as we demand, "What have you done with Coleridge?" answers, "He was here just now and we helped him forward a little way." Our best biographies are all of men and women of character—and, it may be added, of beautiful character—of Johnson, Scott, and Charlotte Brontë.—QUILLER-COUCH, A. T., 1893, *Adventures in Criticism.*

A brief dawn of unsurpassed promise and achievement; "a trouble" as of "clouds and weeping rain;" then, a long summer evening's work done by "the setting sun's pathetic light"—such was Coleridge's day, the after-glow of which is still in the sky. I am sure that the temple, with all the rubble which blended with its marble, must have been a grander whole than any we are able to reconstruct for ourselves from the stones that lie about the field. The living Coleridge was ever his own apology—men and women who neither shared nor ignored his shortcomings, not only loved him, but honored and followed him.—CAMPBELL, JAMES DYKES, 1894, *Samuel Taylor Coleridge*, p. 281.

Coleridge's domestic life was not fortunate or wisely managed, but at Clevedon, for some time after his early marriage, he was as happy as a lover. Every one who knows his early verse remembers the frequent references to his beloved Sara, which are provoking in their lack of real characterisation. With the most exquisite feeling for womanhood in its general features, he seems to have been incapable of drawing strongly the features of any individual woman. His nearest approach to the creation of a heroine is perhaps in his Illyrian queen, Zapolya. Even Christabel is a figure somewhat too faintly drawn, a figure expressing indeed the beauty, innocence, and gentleness of maidenhood, but without any of the traits of a distinctive personality. All his other imaginings of women are exquisite abstractions, framed of purely feminine elements, but representing Woman rather than being themselves veritable women.—DOWDEN, EDWARD, 1895, *New Studies in Literature*, p. 321.

Domesticity was never a shining virtue in him; and wife, and cottage, and Arcadia somehow fade out from the story of his life—as pointless, unsaving, and ineffective for him, all these, as the blurred lines with which we begin a story, and cross them out.—MITCHELL, DONALD G., 1895, *English Lands Letters and Kings, Queen Anne and the Georges*, p. 312.

Coleridge's life gilded slowly away, calm outwardly, but animated by inner and never resting intellectual and emotional forces. The close of his life was attended with many physical sufferings. He was troubled greatly by nightmare. . . . What Coleridge appeared to me to lack was force of character and individuality. His life was centred in his imagination. His world was not our every-day working world, but one created out of his own inner consciousness. Coleridge was a Richter without his vivid humanity and humour. He was about 5 feet 9½ inches in height, but looked shorter. When a youth, his hair was black and glossy; but it was white at fifty. His complexion was fair; his countenance thoughtful and benevolent. In advanced years he was a great snuff-taker; but always scrupulously clean. —FORSTER, JOSEPH, 1897, *Great Teachers.*

POETRY

Shall gentle Coleridge pass unnoticed here.
To turgid ode and tumid stanza dear?
Though themes of innocence amuse him best,
Yet still obscurity's a welcome guest.
If Inspiration should her aid refuse
To him who takes a pixy for a muse,
Yet none in lofty numbers can surpass
The bard who soars to elegize an ass.
How well the subject suits his noble mind,
He brays, the laureat of the long-ear'd kind.
—BYRON, LORD, 1809, *English Bards and Scotch Reviewers.*

He was a mighty poet—and
A subtle-soul'd psychologist;
All things he seem'd to understand,
Of old or new—of sea or land—
But his own mind—which was a mist.
This was a man who might have turn'd
Hell into Heaven—and so in gladness
A Heaven unto himself have earn'd;
But he in shadows undiscern'd
Trusted,—and damn'd himself to madness.
—SHELLEY, PERCY BYSSHE, 1819, *Peter Bell the Third.*

He is superior, I think, to almost all our poets, except Spenser, in the deliciousness of his numbers. This charm results more from melody than measure, from a continuity of sweet sounds than from an apt division or skilful variation of them. There is no appearance of preparation, effort or artifice; they rise or fall with his feelings, like the unbidden breathings of an Æolian harp, from the deep intonations of passion to the light skirmishes of fancy. On the generality of readers it is to be feared this is all so much thrown away. Rapidity of reading hinders attraction to it. To enjoy the instrument one had need be in some such happy Castle of Indolence as Thomson has placed it in.—CARY, HENRY FRANCIS, 1823, *Notices of Miscellaneous English Poets, Memoir, ed. Cary, vol.* II, *p.* 299.

. . . dreamy Coleridge, of the wizard lay!
—ELLIOTT, EBENEZER, 1829, *The Village Patriarch, bk.* iv.

It is to Mr. Coleridge that I am bound to make the acknowledgement due from the pupil to his master.—SCOTT, SIR WALTER, 1830, *Lay of the Last Minstrel, Introduction.*

O! Heart that like a fount with freshness ran,
O! Thought beyond the stature given to man,
Although thy page had blots on many a line,
Yet Faith remedial made the tale divine.
With all the poet's fusing, kindling blaze,
And sage's skill to thread each tangled maze,
Thy fair expressive image meets the view,
Bearing the sunlike torch, and subtle clew.
—STERLING, JOHN, 1839, *Coleridge, Poems, p.* 154.

And visionary Coleridge, who
Did sweep his thoughts as angels do
Their wings with cadence up the Blue.
—BROWNING, ELIZABETH BARRETT, 1844, *A Vision of Poets.*

His poetry is another matter. It is so beautiful, and was so quietly content with its beauty, making no call on the critics, and receiving hardly any notice, that people are but now beginning to awake to a full sense of its merits. Of pure poetry, strictly so called, that is to say, consisting of nothing but its essential self, without conventional and perishing helps, he was the greatest master of his time. If you could see it in a phial, like a distillation of roses (taking it, I mean, at its best), it would be found without a speck. . . . Oh! it is too late now; and habit and self-love blinded me at the time, and I did not know (much as I admired him) how great a poet lived in that grove at Highgate; or I would have cultivated its walks more, as I might have done, and endeavoured to return him, with my gratitude, a small portion of the delight his verses have given me.—HUNT, LEIGH, 1844, *Imagination and Fancy, pp.* 250, 255.

Lazy Coleridge, by the morning's light,
Gazed for a moment on the fields of white,
And lo! the glaciers found at length a tongue,
Mont Blanc was vocal, and Chamouni sung!
—HOLMES, OLIVER WENDELL, 1846, *A Rhymed Lesson.*

Few minds are capable of fathoming his by their own sympathies, and he has left us no adequate manifestation of himself as a poet by which to judge him. For his dramas, I consider them complete failures, and more like visions than dramas. For a metaphysical mind like his to attempt that walk, was scarcely more judicious than it would be for a blind man to essay painting the bay of Naples. Many of his smaller pieces are perfect in their way, indeed no writer could excel him in depicting a single mood of mind, as Dejection, for instance. . . . Give Coleridge a canvass, and he will paint a single mood as if his colors were made of the mind's own atoms. Here he is very unlike Southey. There is nothing of the spectator about Coleridge; he is all life; not impassioned, not vehement, but searching, intellectual life, which seems "listening through the frame" to its own pulses.—OSSOLI, MARGARET FULLER, 1850? *Art, Literature and the Drama, pp.* 97, 98.

Let me say here that I know of no English translation of a poem of any length which, a few passages excepted, so perfectly reproduces the original as this, ["Wallenstein"] and that if the same hand had given us in our language the other dramas of this author, we should have had an English Schiller worthy to be placed by the side of the German.—BRYANT, WILLIAM CULLEN, 1859, *Schiller, Orations and Addresses, p.* 299.

A warm poetic joy in everything beautiful, whether it be a moral sentiment, like the friendship of Roland and Leoline, or only the flakes of failing light from the water-snakes—this joy, visiting him, now and again, after sickly dreams, in sleep or waking, as a relief not to be forgotten, and with such a power of felicitous expression that the infection of it passes irresistibly to the reader—such is the predominant element in the matter of his poetry, as cadence is the predominant quality of its form.—PATER, WALTER, 1865-80, *Appreciations, p.* 103.

His utterances were but part of his system; like the leaves of the Sibyl, they but scattered forth part of the fulness, inwardness, warmth, and completeness of his convictions; and his philosophy has been lost to us—save that he himself was the father of a school of earnest and humble thinkers, and will yet beget more. Of true poets he is one:—he has dared, and known, and doubted—has penetrated into the sanctuary of poetry, and trod the utmost limits of the knowable—and yet dares humbly to write himself a Christian. The example of Coleridge was great, valuable, beyond price, to the young men at the beginning of this century of doubt.—FRISWELL, JAMES HAIN, 1869, *Essays on English Writers, p.* 313.

From natural fineness of ear, was the best metrist among modern English poets.—LOWELL, JAMES RUSSELL, 1870, *Chaucer, My Study Windows, p.* 267.

It is like distant music when the tone comes to us pure and without any coarser sound of wood or wire; or like the odour on the air when we smell the flower without detecting in it that of the stalk or of the earth.—DEVERE, AUBREY, 1873-97, *Letters, Recollections, p.* 197.

As a poet his place is indisputable. It is high among the highest of all time. An age that should forget or neglect him might neglect or forget any poet that ever lived. At least, any poet whom it did remember such an age would remember as something other than a poet; it would prize and praise in him, not the absolute and distinctive quality, but something empirical or accidental. That may be said of this one which can hardly be said of any but the greatest among men; that come what may to the world in course of time, it will never see his place filled. Other and stronger men, with fuller control and concentration of genius, may do more service, may bear more fruit; but such as his was they will not have in them to give. The highest lyric work is either passionate or imaginative; of passion Coleridge's has nothing; but for height and perfection of imaginative quality he is the greatest of lyric poets. This was his special power, and this is his special praise.—SWINBURNE, ALGERNON CHARLES, 1875, *Essays and Studies, p.* 274.

His best work is but little, but of its kind it is perfect and unique. For exquisite music of metrical movement and for an imaginative phantasy, such as might belong to a world where men always dreamt, there is nothing in our language to be compared with "Christabel," 1805, and "Kubla Khan," and to the "Ancient Mariner" published as one of the "Lyrical Ballads," in 1798. The little poem called "Love" is not so good, but it touches with great grace that with which all sympathise. All that he did excellently might be bound up in twenty pages, but it should be bound in pure gold.—BROOKE, STOPFORD A., 1876, *English Literature (Primer), p.* 152.

As a poet, Coleridge's own place is safe. His niche in the great gallery of English poets is secure. Of no one can it be more emphatically said that he was "of imagination all compact." His peculiar touch of melancholy tenderness may prevent his attaining a high place in popular estimation. He does not possess the fiery pulse and humaneness of Burns, but the exquisite perfection of his metre and the subtle alliance of his thought and expression must always secure for him the warmest admiration of true lovers of poetic art.—BOYLE, G. D., 1877, *Encyclopædia Britannica, Ninth ed., vol.* VI, *p.* 124.

But it is less easy to follow Coleridge than to follow Southey, because it is more difficult to appreciate the full meaning of his conclusions. He loved to be mysterious and obscure; and this mystery and obscurity is constantly visible in his most beautiful poetry. Why was the Ancient Mariner to be doomed to perpetual mystery because he had shot an albatross? Why was the exquisitely pure Lady Christabel to be cursed for the performance of an act of Christian charity? The argument offends the reason as much as the language charms the sense.—WALPOLE, SPENCER, 1878, *A History of England from the Conclusion of the Great War in* 1815, *vol.* I, *p.* 357.

He is perhaps the finest instance we have in England of the critical and poetical power combined.—SHAIRP, JOHN CAMPBELL, 1881, *Poetic Style in Modern English Poetry, Aspects of Poetry.*

Endowed with so glorious a gift of song, and only not fully master of his poetic means because of the very versatility of his artistic power and the very variety and catholicity of his youthful sympathies, it is unhappily but too certain that the world has lost much by that perversity of conspiring accidents which so untimely silenced Coleridge's muse. And the loss is the more trying to posterity because he seems, to a not, I think, too curiously considering criticism, to have once actually struck that very chord which would have sounded most movingly beneath his touch. —TRAILL, HENRY DUFF, 1884, *Coleridge (English Men of Letters), p.* 65.

There is no one of Coleridge's sonnets which can be pronounced distinctly satisfactory. The one I have given seems to me on the whole the best. The famous one on Schiller's "Robbers" has been much overrated—though Coleridge himself had a high opinion of it. Wordsworth showed his critical faculty when, on receipt of Dyce's "Sonnet-Anthology," he referred to the insertion of "The Robbers" as a mistake, on the ground of "rant." . . . There are probably few readers of mature taste who would not consider Wordsworth's epithet "rant" as literally applicable. One learns with a sense of uncomfortable wonder that Coleridge himself—this supreme master of metrical music—considered the last six lines "strong and fiery!" What a difference between this Schiller sonnet and the beautiful poem in fourteen lines entitled "Work without Hope." If these lines had only been adequately set in sonnet-mould, the result would have been a place for this poetic gem among the finest sonnets in the language.—SHARP, WILLIAM, 1886, *Sonnets of this Century, p.* 238, *note.*

Coleridge, who had little technical knowledge of any art but that in which, when he was himself, he supremely excelled—poetry—had nevertheless a deeper insight into the fundamental principles of art than any modern writer, with the sole exception of Goethe.—PATMORE, COVENTRY, 1889–98, *Principle in Art, p.* 12.

Coleridge, the poet, sees clearer than Coleridge, the metaphysician.—CHENEY, JOHN VANCE, 1891, *The Golden Guess, p.* 29.

Those songs half-sung that yet were all-divine—
 That woke Romance, the queen, to reign afresh—
Had been but preludes from that lyre of thine,
 Could thy rare spirit's wings have pierced the mesh
Spun by the wizard who compels the flesh,
But lets the poet see how heav'n can shine.
—WATTS, THEODORE, 1892? *Coleridge.*

The greatest master of the poetry of pure wonder which English literature has ever had is undoubtedly Coleridge. There is a subtle charm and magic, a witchery of sound and vision, in such poems as "Kubla Khan" and "Christabel" which has never been approached by any other English poet; and "The Ancient Mariner" still remains the most splendid effort of pure imaginative poetry in modern literature. —DAWSON, W. J.. 1892, *Quest and Vision, p.* 269.

Coleridge never met with a patron; he who surpassed every poet but one in genius; so he famished, exclaiming, "Work without hope, draws nectar in a sieve!"—HAKE, GORDON, 1892, *Memoirs of Eighty Years, p.* 77.

The debt was not all on one side. It was during the memorable year of his companionship with Wordsworth that Coleridge wrote nearly every thing that now remains as a measure of his wonderful poetic gifts. "The Rime of the Ancient Mariner" and "Christabel" were both written in that year, besides most of the short poems that make up the small volume of his poetical works. The presence by his side of the steady, resolute will of the Westmoreland dalesman seems to have for the time constrained his imagination from aimless wandering; and the lofty, unwavering self-confidence of his friend inspired him with a similar energy. Away from Wordsworth after that year he lost himself in visions of work to be done that always remained to be done. Coleridge had every poetic gift but one—the will for sustained and concentrated effort.—MINTO, WILLIAM, 1894, *The Literature of the Georgian Era, ed. Knight, p.* 212.

Even Shakespeare's grasp of Nature, though wider, is not, I think, more intimate than Coleridge's. To take a figure from physical science, the union of Nature with the soul in him is chemical, not mechanical combination.—PALGRAVE, FRANCIS TURNER, 1896, *Landscape in Poetry, p.* 203.

The poetic genius of Coleridge, the highest of his many gifts, found brilliant and fascinating expression. His poems—those in which his fame lives—are as unique as they are memorable; and though their small number, their confined range, and the brief period during which his faculty was exercised with full freedom and power, seem to indicate a narrow vein, yet the remainder of his work in prose and verse leaves an impression of extraordinary and abundant intellectual force. In proportion as his imaginative creations stand apart, the spirit out of which they came must have possessed some singularity: and if the reader is not content with simple æsthetic appreciation of what the gods provide, but has some touch of curiosity leading him to look into the source of such remarkable achievement and its human history, he is at once interested in the personality of the "subtle-souled psychologist," as Shelley with his accurate critical insight first named him.—WOODBERRY, GEORGE E., 1897, *Library of the World's Best Literature, ed. Warner, vol.* VII, *p.* 3844.

No other poet, perhaps, except Spenser, has been an initial influence, a generative influence, on so many poets. Having with that mild Elizabethan much affinity, it is natural that he also should be "a poets' poet" in the rarer sense—the sense of fecundating other poets. As with Spenser, it is not that other poets have made him their model, have reproduced essentials of his style (accidents no great poet will consciously perpetuate). The progeny are sufficiently unlike the parent. It is that he has incited the very sprouting in them of the laurel-bough, has been to them a fostering sun of song. Such a primary influence he was to Rossetti—Rossetti, whose model was far more Keats than Coleridge. Such he was to Coventry Patmore, in whose work one might trace many masters rather than Coleridge. . . . For the last thirty years criticism has unburdened its suppressed feelings about Coleridge, which it considerately spared him while he was alive; and his position is clear, unquestioned; his reputation beyond the power of wax or wane. Alone of modern poets, his fame sits above the power of fluctuation. Wordsworth has fluctuated; Tennyson stands not exactly as he did; there is reaction in some quarters against the worship of Shelley; though all are agreed Keats is a great poet, not all are agreed as to his place. But around Coleridge the clamour of partisans is silent: none attacks, none has need to defend. . . . Over that wreck, most piteous and terrible in all our literary history, shines, and will shine for ever, the five-pointed star, of his glorious youth; those poor five resplendent poems, for which he paid the devil's price of a desolated life and unthinkably blasted powers. Other poets may have done greater things; none a thing more perfect and uncompanioned. Other poets belong to this class or that; he to the class of Samuel Taylor Coleridge.—THOMPSON, FRANCIS, 1897, *Academy Portraits, The Academy, vol.* 51, *pp.* 179, 180.

THE ANCIENT MARINER
1798

His "Ancient Mariner" is the most remarkable performance, and the only one that I could point out to any one as giving an adequate idea of his great natural powers. It is high German, however, and in it he seems to "conceive of poetry but as a drunken dream, reckless, careless, and heedless, of past, present, and to come."—HAZLITT, WILLIAM, 1818, *Lectures on the English Poets, Lecture* viii.

A wild, mystical, phantasmagoric narrative, most picturesquely related in the old English ballad measure, and in language to which is skillfully given an air of antiquity in admirable harmony with the spectral character of the events. The whole poem is a splendid dream, filling the ear with the strange and floating melodies of sleep, and the eye with a shifting, vaporous succession of fantastic images, gloomy or radiant.—SHAW, THOMAS B., 1847, *English Literature, p.* 426.

It is Coleridge's one great complete work, the one really finished thing, in a life of many beginnings.—PATER, WALTER, 1865–80, *Appreciations, p.* 101.

The "Ancient Mariner" has doubtless more of breadth and space, more of material force and motion, than anything else of the poet's. And the tenderness of sentiment which touches with significant colour the pure white imagination is here no longer morbid or languid, as in the earlier poems of feeling and emotion. It is soft and piteous enough, but womanly rather than effeminate; and thus serves indeed to set off the strange splendours and boundless beauties of the story. For the execution, I presume no human eye is too dull to see how perfect it is, and how high in kind of perfection. Here is not the speckless and elaborate finish which shows everywhere the fresh rasp of file or chisel on its smooth and spruce excellence; this is faultless after the fashion of a flower or a tree. Thus it has grown: not thus has it been carved.—SWINBURNE, ALGERNON CHARLES, 1875, *Essays and Studies, p.* 264.

The "Ancient Mariner" is a poem of which (in the experience of most of us) the first impression dates back to those earliest years when the Bible and the "Pilgrim's Progress" made up the whole body of serious reading; but if we could encounter it first of all late in life, after the stream of more modern literature had filtered into our minds, it would probably seem to us like meeting for the first time in person some great writer of whom we have known much through his books. For just as in the one case, many qualities of mind and heart which have endeared the writer to us, find to our heightened sense a kind of visible embodiment in the face, voice, gait and gesture of the man in whose work we recognised them; so in the other, many exquisite and original imaginative fantasies which we must have seen wandering through uncertain channels, would find their true place and fitting mission in the beautiful and complete conception from which they were borrowed.—CAINE, HALL, 1883, *Cobwebs of Criticism, p.* 59.

It is enough for us here that he has written some of the most poetical poetry in the language, and one poem, the "Ancient Mariner," not only unparalleled, but unapproached in its kind, and that kind of the rarest. It is marvellous in its mastery over that delightfully fortuitous inconsequence that is the adamantine logic of dreamland. Coleridge has taken the old ballad measure and given to it by an indefinable charm wholly his own all the sweetness, all the melody and compass of a symphony. And how picturesque it is in the proper sense of the word. I know nothing like it. There is not a description in it. It is all picture.—LOWELL, JAMES RUSSELL, 1885–90, *Address on Unveiling the Bust of Coleridge in Westminster Abbey, 7 May; Prose Works, Riverside ed., vol.* VI, *p.* 73.

The component parts were supplied to him, but their novel and organic combination was his own; and in art all depends on this power of construction. The real artist comprehends these things intuitively; but to the conscious psychologist they are as hidden as is the origin of life to the biologist. At the same time, it is well worth our while to track the artist's footsteps; for the nearer we can come to him, the more we instinctively feel the action of genius, both in detail and in general laws. —BRANDL, ALOIS, 1887, *Samuel Taylor Coleridge and the English Romantic School, tr. Lady Eastlake, p.* 204.

In "The Ancient Mariner," his powers are revealed at their highest. As a mere story the subject matter is fanciful, but under the subtle alchemy of so exquisite a genius the unreality is lost, and the effect is irresistible. We feel it not the least in passages that surprise us by their quaint simplicity and unsophisticated truthfulness. Brevity and conciseness never fail, restraint is never relaxed. There is no rambling away into commonplace; even in the imagery the reader has scarcely realised the beauty of one figure before the narrative resumes its interest, or yet another simile claims his admiration. All is quick, tense, and nervous; sprightly in rhythm, concentrated in effect, apt and succinct in expression. The charm of its Saxon English never seems assumed or strained. Its scenes of weird horror fascinate but never repel. The cry of despair from that scorched deck in mid-ocean is utterly free from theatrical impressiveness; even in those parts that most abound with ornament we are hurried away from their contemplation with an impetuosity which forbids us to look back; half a dozen short verses bring us from the fogs and ice-floes of arctic seas to the hot silence of a tropic calm.—GROSER, HORACE G., 1891, *The Poets and the Poetry of the Century, Crabbe to Coleridge, ed. Miles, p.* 442.

If in outward form the poem cannot be called religious, in its spirit it is steeped in religious thought and conviction. Into it has passed, perhaps unconsciously to the poet himself, the profoundest human experiences which are indicative of the energy of the religious consciousness.—CARPENTER, W. BOYD, 1901, *The Religious Spirit in the Poets, p.* 150.

CHRISTABEL
1805–16

"Christabel"—I won't have any one sneer at "Christabel:" it is a fine wild poem.—BYRON, LORD, 1816, *Letter to Mr. Murray, Sept.* 30.

It is common to hear everything which Mr. Coleridge has written condemned with bitterness and boldness. His poems are called extravagant; and his prose works, poems too, and of the noblest breed, are pronounced to be mystical, obscure, metaphysical, theoretical, unintelligible, and so forth; just as the same phrases have over and over been applied, with as much sagacity, to Plato, St. Paul, Cudworth, and Kant. But "Christabel" is the only one of his writings which is ever treated with unmingled contempt. . . . Throughout the poem there runs and lives one especial excellence, the beauty of single lines and expressions, perfect flowers in themselves, yet interfering as little with the breadth and unity of the general effect, as the primroses and hawthorns of the valley with its sweeping perspective of light and shadow. No one, I imagine, can fail to recognise in it the original germ of the "Lay of the Last Minstrel;" but how superior is it to that spirited and brilliant tale, in the utter absence both of defect and superfluity in the diction,—in the thrilling interest and beauty of every, the slightest circumstance,—in the relation of each atom to the whole,—and in the deep reflection, which is the very atmosphere and vital air of the whole composition!—STERLING, JOHN, 1828–58, *On Coleridge's Christabel, Essays and Tales, ed. Hare, vol.* I, *pp.* 101, 110.

The thing attempted in "Christabel" is the most difficult of execution in the whole field of romance—witchery by daylight; and the success is complete. Geraldine, so far as she goes, is perfect. She is *sui generis*. The reader feels the same terror and perplexity that Christabel in vain struggles to express, and the same spell that fascinates her eyes. Who and what is Geraldine—whence come, whither going, and what designing? What did the poet mean to make of her? What could he have made of her? Could he have gone on much farther without having had recourse to some of the ordinary shifts of witch tales? Was she really the daughter of Roland de Vaux, and would the friends have met again and embraced? . . . We are not amongst those who wish to have "Christabel" finished. It cannot be finished. The poet has spun all he could without snapping. The theme is too fine and subtle to bear much extension. It is better as it is, imperfect as a story, but complete as an exquisite production of the imagination, differing in form and colour from the "Ancient Mariner," yet differing in effect from it only so as the same powerful faculty is directed to the feudal or the mundane phases of the preternatural.—LOCKHART, JOHN GIBSON, 1834, *The Poetical Works of S. T. Coleridge, Quarterly Review, vol.* 52, *pp.* 29, 30.

Out of a hundred readers of "Christabel," fifty will be able to make nothing of its rhythm, while forty-nine of the remaining fifty will, with some ado, fancy they comprehend it after the fourth or fifth perusal. The one out of the whole hundred who shall both comprehend and admire it at first sight must be an unaccountably clever person; and I am by far too modest to assume, for a moment, that that very clever person is myself.—POE, EDGAR ALLAN, 1848, *The Rationale of Verse, Works of Poe, ed. Stedman and Woodberry, vol.* VI, *p.* 76.

For my part, I cannot compare "Kubla Khan" with "Christabel." The magical beauty of the latter has been so long canonized in the world's estimate, that to praise it now would be unseemly. It brought into English poetry an atmosphere of wonder and mystery, of weird beauty and pity combined, which was quite new at the time it appeared, and has never since been approached. The movement of its subtle cadences has a union of grace with power, which only the finest lines of Shakespeare can parallel. As we read "Christabel" and a few other of Coleridge's pieces, we recall his own words:

"In a half-sleep we dream,
And dreaming hear thee still, O singing lark!
That singest like an angel in the clouds."

—SHAIRP, JOHN CAMPBELL, 1881, *Poetic Style in Modern English Poetry, Aspects of Poetry.*

I confess that I prefer the "Ancient Mariner" to "Christabel," fine as that poem is in parts and tantalizing as it is in the suggestion of deeper meanings than were ever there. The "Ancient Mariner" seems to have come of itself. In "Christabel" I fancy him saying, "Go to, let us write an imaginative poem." It never could be finished on those terms.—LOWELL, JAMES RUSSELL, 1885–90, *Address on Unveiling the Bust of Coleridge in Westminster Abbey*, 7 *May; Prose Works, Riverside ed., vol.* VI, *p.* 76.

Inhospitably hast thou entertained,
O Poet, us the bidden to thy board,
Whom in mid-feast, and while our thousand mouths
Are one laudation of the festal cheer,
Thou from thy table dost dismiss, unfilled.
Yet lordlier thee than many a lavish host
We praise, and oftener thy repast half-served
Than many a stintless banquet, prodigally
Through satiate hours prolonged; nor praise less well
Because with tongues thou hast not cloyed, and lips
That mourn the parsimony of affluent souls,
And mix the lamentation with the laud.

—WATSON, WILLIAM, 1893, *Lines in a Flyleaf of "Christabel," Poems, p.* 145.

"Christabel" is a fragment of most wonderful quality, and exhibits another singular feature of Coleridge's poetry—his marvellous power of touching the sense of the supernatural.—MINTO, WILLIAM, 1894, *The Literature of the Georgian Era, ed. Knight, p.* 213.

KUBLA KHAN
1816

Were we compelled to the choice, I for one would rather preserve "Kubla Khan" and "Christabel" than any other of Coleridge's poems. It is more conceivable that another man should be born capable of writing the "Ancient Mariner" than one capable of writing these. The former is perhaps the most wonderful of all poems. In reading it we seem rapt into that paradise revealed to Swedenborg, where music and colour and perfume were one, where you could hear the hues and see the harmonies of heaven. For absolute melody and splendour it were hardly rash to call it the first poem in the language. —SWINBURNE, ALGERNON CHARLES, 1875, *Essays and Studies, p.* 264.

Were there left of Coleridge nothing but "Kubla Khan," from this gem one might almost reconstruct, in full brightness, its great author's poetic work, just as the expert zoölogist reconstructs the extinct megatherium from a single fossil bone. Of this masterpiece, the chief beauty is not the noted music of the versification, but the range and quality of the imaginings embodied in this music. Were there in these no unearthly breathings, no mysterious grandeur, the verse could not have been made to pulsate so rhythmically. The essence of the melody is in the fineness of the conception, in the poetic imaginations. —CALVERT, GEORGE H., 1880, *Coleridge, Shelley, Goethe, p.* 12.

To us "Kubla Khan" is a splendid curiosity, a lyrical landscape fairy tale, which we know not what to make of. Ninety years ago this specimen of emotional inspiration evinced a bold and powerful reaction. Shelley borrowed many a curiosity from it; for example, in "Marianne's Dream" we have the Fata Morgana towers —the half-joyful, half-demoniacal sound in the lady's ears—the bursting streams of light, and the feverishly-tossing floods —all without any practical object. And again, in the "Skylark," the "high-born maiden" in a palace, and the harmonious madness of the singer. This is why Byron, Shelley, and Keats indulge so commonly in visions, distinctly so entitled—for example, "Darkness," "Vision of the Sea," "On a Dream"—seeking in all seriousness to forecast the future, and even placing the truth of the dream before that of the waking eye. The poetic atmosphere became purified, but, in the zeal for reform, too much rarefied.—BRANDL, ALOIS, 1887, *Samuel Taylor Coleridge and the English Romantic School, tr. Lady Eastlake, p.* 186.

AIDS TO REFLECTION
1825

Omitting, of course, one's Bible and Shakespeare, which, if one really loves them, are mightier and more penetrating than any other books, the first that really went far—farther, perhaps, than any other—to the making of me was Coleridge's "Aids to Reflection," which I came across early in college days. I was still only a boy, and should have been at school for some years yet. I had no one to guide my reading, and came on the book by chance, for I read just whatever happened to fall in my way. Brought up in the strictest sect of Calvinists, I had all along entered a silent protest against the thing I was taught for truth; but till now had never got any help in formulating that protest and obtaining a larger faith. On the religious side of my nature, this was the work that did most for me, and I soon found that my friend the impecunious grocer was quite as devoted to it as myself. We read it, quoted it, annotated it, and scraped enough money to get also "The Confessions of an Inquiring Spirit" and Leighton's "St. Peter." But Leighton was not so much to me as Coleridge; the commentary touched me more nearly than the text, and there were times when I even thought they had little or no connection. But be that as it may. It is not my present business to criticise the book, but only to tell what it was to me in those years. Of course it led me soon to read his poems; but here again, as with Shelley, I had little affinity with the weird and eerie genius that sang "The Ancient Mariner" and "Christabel," and was chiefly affected by the wonderful melody of his verse. I speak now only of those early years. Later, I came to see that the same mind was at work in the poems as in the thoughtful prose. On the whole, I am more indebted to Coleridge than to any one else for what is deepest and best in me.—SMITH, WALTER C., 1887, *Books which Have Influenced Me, p.* 92.

It was just after I left school, and before I went up to the university, that the first great crisis in my intellectual life occurred. I was introduced to the writings of Samuel Taylor Coleridge. I do not, of course, refer to the poetical works, but to that entirely unique collection of theologico philosophical dogmatism, of profoundly suggestive hints and speculations, of hybrid mysticism, of subtile and pregnant criticism, of dreams and lightning flashes of genius to be found in the prose writings of the Highgate sage. To me, as to many another young man at that time (1844), the "Aids to Reflection" came as a new revelation. I cannot stop to explain how it was so, but the book took such hold of me that for years I rarely passed a week without reading out of it. —JESSOPP, AUGUSTUS, 1888, *Books that Have Helped Me, p.* 62.

No less devout adherent of that theology could have penetrated it so powerfully with his influence. But what was a condition of his immediate success has told fatally upon his lasting fame. Gold and clay are mingled, even more than in his political tracts, in the fragmentary records of his religious thought. In the "Aids to Reflection," a profound spiritual emotion struggles for utterance among concatenated pedantries of phrase, and the terminology of Kant is constrained to the service of Anglican orthodoxy.—HERFORD, C. H. 1897, *The Age of Wordsworth, p.* 32.

GENERAL

Beyond all other political speculators, our author mingles important moral philosophical principles with his reasonings. . . . We cannot conclude without expressing an earnest wish, that this original thinker and eloquent writer may be persuaded to put the literary public speedily in possession, by successive volumes of essays, of an ample portion of those refined speculations, the argument and the strongest illustrations of which he is well known to have in an almost complete state in his mind—and many of which will never be in any other mind, otherwise than as communicated from him. The chief alteration desirable, for his reader's sake, to be made in his mode of writing, is a resolute restriction on that mighty profusion and excursiveness of thought, in which he is tempted to suspend the pursuit and retard the attainment of the one distinct object which should be clearly kept in view; and, added to this, a more patient and prolonged effort to reduce the abstruser part of his ideas, as much as their subtle quality will possibly admit, to a substantial and definable form.—FOSTER, JOHN, 1811, *Coleridge, Critical Essays, ed. Ryland, vol.* II, *pp.* 20, 23.

A metaphysical dilettante.—TENNEMANN, WILLIAM GOTTLIEB, 1812-52, *A Manual of the History of Philosophy, tr. Johnson, ed. Morell, p.* 490.

Coleridge, too, has lately taken wing,
But like a hawk encumber'd with his hood,—
Explaining metaphysics to the nation—
I wish he would explain his Explanation.
—BYRON, LORD, 1819, *Don Juan, Dedication.*

You will see Coleridge—he who sits obscure
In the exceeding lustre and the pure
Intense irradiation of a mind,
Which, with its own internal lightning blind,
Flags wearily through darkness and despair—
A cloud-encircled meteor of the air,
A hooded eagle among blinking owls.
—SHELLEY, PERCY BYSSHE, 1820, *Letter to Maria Gisborne.*

Very great but rather mystical, sometimes absurd.—CARLYLE, THOMAS, 1823, *Letter to John A. Carlyle, Nov.* 11; *Early Letters, ed. Norton, p.* 294.

If Mr. Coleridge had not been the most impressive talker of his age, he would probably have been the finest writer; but he lays down his pen to make sure of an auditor, and mortgages the admiration of posterity for the stare of an idler. If he had not been a poet, he would have been a powerful logician; if he had not dipped his wing in the Unitarian controversy, he might have soared to the very summit of fancy. But in writing verse, he is trying to subject the Muse to *transcendental* theories: in his abstract reasoning, he misses his way by strewing it with flowers. All that he has done of moment, he had done twenty years ago: since then, he may be said to have lived on the sound of his own voice. . . . He walks abroad in the majesty of an universal understanding, eyeing the "rich strond," or golden sky above him, and "goes sounding on his way," in eloquent accents, uncompelled and free!—HAZLITT, WILLIAM, 1825, *The Spirit of the Age, pp.* 38, 39.

Taken absolutely and in itself, the "Remorse" is more fitted for the study than the stage; its character is romantic and pastoral in a high degree, and there is a profusion of poetry in the minor parts, the effect of which could never be preserved in the common routine of representation. What this play wants is dramatic movement; there is energetic dialogue and a crisis of great interest, but the action does not sufficiently grow on the stage itself.—LOCKHART, JOHN GIBSON, 1834, *The Poetical Works of S. T. Coleridge, Quarterly Review, vol.* 52, *p.* 23.

Spirit! so oft in radiant freedom soaring
High through seraphic mysteries unconfined,
And oft, a diver through the deeps of mind,
Its caverns, far below its waves, exploring;
And oft such strains of breezy music pouring,
As, with the floating sweetness of their sighs,
Could still all fevers of the heart, restoring
Awhile that freshness left in Paradise;
Say, of those glorious wanderings what the goal?
What the rich fruitage to man's kindred soul
From wealth of thine bequeathed? Oh, strong and high,
And sceptred intellect! thy goal confessed
Was the Redeemer's Cross—thy last bequest
One lesson breathing thence profound humility!
—HEMANS, FELICIA DOROTHEA, 1834, *On Reading Coleridge's Epitaph Written by Himself.*

Coleridge was, like Moses, forbid to enter into the promised land; but, from a Pisgah of his own, he saw it in clear vision.—GRANT, ANNE, 1835, *Letter, March* 18; *Memoir and Correspondence, ed. Grant, vol.* III, *p.* 252.

The Opium-eater calls Coleridge "the largest and most spacious intellect, the subtlest and most comprehensive that has yet existed among men." Impiety to Shakspeare! treason to Milton! I give up the rest, even Bacon. Certainly, since their day, we have seen nothing at all comparable to him. Byron and Scott were but as gunflints to a granite mountain! Wordsworth has one angle of resemblance.—LANDOR, WALTER SAVAGE, 1835, *Letter to Lady Blessington, March* 16; *Literary Life and Correspondence, ed. Madden, vol.* II. *p.* 123.

I think with all his faults Old Sam was more of a great man than any one that has lived within the four seas in my memory. It is refreshing to see such a union of the highest philosophy and poetry, with so full a knowledge, in so many points at least, of particular facts.—ARNOLD, THOMAS, 1836, *Letter to W. W. Hull, Nov.* 16; *Life and Correspondence, ed. Stanley, vol.* II, *p.* 61.

No loftier, purer soul than his hath ever
With awe revolved the planetary page,
From infancy to age,
Of Knowledge; sedulous and proud to give her
The whole of his great heart for her own sake;
For what she is; not what she does, or what can make.
—DEVERE, AUBREY, 1839, *Coleridge, The Search after Proserpine and other Poems, p.* 206.

The name of Coleridge is one of the few English names of our own time which are likely to be oftener pronounced, and to become symbolical of more important things, in proportion as the inward workings of the age manifest themselves more and more in outward facts. Bentham excepted, no Englishman of recent date has left his impress so deeply in the opinions and mental tendencies of those among us who attempt to enlighten their practice by philosophical meditation. . . . The influence of Coleridge, like that of Bentham, extends far beyond those who share in the peculiarities of his religious or philosophical creed. He has been the great awakener in this country of the spirit of philosophy, within the bounds of traditional opinions. . . . It is hardly possible to speak of Coleridge, and his position among his contemporaries, without reverting to Bentham: they are connected by two of the closest bonds of association—resemblance and contrast. It would be difficult to find two persons of philosophic eminence more exactly the contrary of one another. Compare their modes of treatment of any subject, and you might fancy them inhabitants of different worlds. They seem to have scarcely a principle or a premiss in common. Each of them sees scarcely anything but what the other does not see. Bentham would have regarded Coleridge with a peculiar measure of the good-humoured contempt with which he was accustomed to regard all modes of philosophizing different from his own. Coleridge would probably have made Bentham one of the exceptions to the enlarged and liberal appreciation which (to the credit of *his* mode of philosophizing) he extended to most thinkers of any eminence, from whom he differed.—MILL, JOHN STUART, 1840, *Coleridge, London and Westminster Review, vol.* 33, *pp.* 257, 258, 259.

A new era of critical opinion upon Shakspere, as propounded by Englishmen, may be dated from the delivery of the lectures of Samuel Taylor Coleridge, at the Surrey Insitution, in 1814. What that great man did for Shakspere during the remainder of his valuable life can scarcely be appreciated by the public. For his opinions were not given to the world in formal treatises and ponderous volumes. They were fragmentary; they were scattered, as it were, at random; many of them were the oral lessons of that wisdom and knowledge which he poured out to a few admiring disciples. But they have had their effect. For ourselves, personally, we owe a debt of gratitude to that illustrious man that can never be repaid. If in any degree we have been enabled to present Shakspere to the popular mind under new aspects, looking at him from a central point, which should permit us, however imperfectly, to comprehend something of his wondrous *system*, we owe the desire so to understand him ourselves to the germs of thought which are scattered through the works of that philosopher; to whom the homage of future times will abundantly compensate for the partial neglect of his contemporaries. We desire to conclude this outline of the opinions of others upon the works of Shakspere, in connection with the imperfect expression of our own sense of those opinions, with the name of COLERIDGE.—KNIGHT, CHARLES, 1845, *Studies of Shakspere, p.* 560.

To
the honored memory
OF SAMUEL TAYLOR COLERIDGE,
the Christian Philosopher,
who through dark and winding paths of speculation
was led to the light
in order that others by his guidance might reach that light,
without passing through the darkness,
these Sermons on the Work of the Spirit
are dedicated
with deep thankfulness and reverence
by one of the many pupils
whom his writings have helped to discern
the sacred concord and unity of
human and divine truth.
—HARE, JULIUS CHARLES, 1846, *The Mission of the Comforter, Dedication.*

Coleridge was the first who made criticism interpretative both of the spirit and the form of works of genius, the first who founded his principles in the nature of things. . . . He had a clear notion of the difference lying at the base of all poetic criticism, between *mechanical regularity* and *organic form*.—WHIPPLE, EDWIN P., 1846, *Essays and Reviews, vol.* II, *pp.* 183, 184.

A brook glancing under green leaves, self-delighting, exulting,
And full of a gurgling melody ever renewed—
Renewed thro' all changes of Heaven, unceasing in sunlight,
Unceasing in moonlight, but hushed in the beams of the holier orb.
—MEREDITH, GEORGE, 1851, *Works, vol.* 31, *p.* 140.

A man resembling Shakspeare in width and subtlety, although not in clearness and masculine strength and directness.—GILFILLAN, GEORGE, 1855, *A Third Gallery of Portraits, p.* 181.

Atherton—You quoted Coleridge a minute since. He first, and after him Carlyle, familiarized England with the German distinction between reason and understanding. In fact, what the Epicureans and the Stoics were to Plotinus in his day, that were Priestley and Paley to Coleridge. The spiritualist is the sworn foe of your rationalist and pleasures-of-virtue man. Romance must loathe utilitarianism, enthusiasm scorn expediency. Hence the reaction which gives us Schelling as the Plotinus of Berlin, and Coleridge as the Schelling of Higate.—VAUGHAN, ROBERT ALFRED, 1856–60, *Hours with the Mystics, vol.* I, *p.* 70.

Coleridge, a catholic mind, with a hunger for ideas; with eyes looking before and after to the highest bards and sages, and who wrote and spoke the only high criticism in his time, is one of those who save England from the reproach of no longer possessing the capacity to appreciate what rarest wit the island has yielded. Yet the misfortune of his life, his vast attempts but most inadequate performings, failing to accomplish any one masterpiece,—seems to mark the closing of an era. Even in him, the traditional Englishman was too strong for the philosopher, and he fell into *accommodations;* and as Burke had striven to idealize the English State, so Coleridge "narrowed his mind" in the attempt to reconcile the Gothic rule and dogma of the Anglican Church, with eternal ideas. But for Coleridge, and a lurking taciturn minority uttering itself in occasional criticism, oftener in private discourse, one would say that in Germany and in America is the best mind in England rightly respected.—EMERSON, RALPH WALDO, 1856–84, *Literature, English Traits; Works, Riverside ed., vol.* V, *p.* 236.

Some of the peculiarities of Coleridge most familiar to theologians,—his tetrads and pentads, his doctrine of Church and State, his denial of the documentary inspiration of the whole Bible,—we pass by; not from any slighting estimate of their importance as parts of an organic whole, but in order to insulate the one character, —of *religious Realism,*—which is the inner essence of the system itself, and the living seed of its development in the school of Mr. Maurice.—MARTINEAU, JAMES, 1856–90, *Personal Influence on Present Theology; Essays, Reviews and Addresses, vol.* I, *p.* 258.

Among the men who have led the van of British thought during the present century, who have stamped the impress of their genius upon the forehead of the age, and moulded the intellectual destinies of our time, there is one name preëminently fraught with interest to the student of our internal history. That name is Samuel Taylor Coleridge. In our schools of poetry, of philosophy, of theology—among our critics and our ecclesiastics, our moralists and our politicians—the influence of Coleridge has worked, silently and viewlessly, but with wide-spread and mighty power. As by a verbal talisman, his name opens to our mental gaze vast and varied fields of reflection, invokes grave, important, and thickly-crowding thoughts, and forms the centre round which countless subjects of discussion and investigation group themselves.—BAYNE, PETER, 1858, *Essays in Biography and Criticism, Second Series, p.* 108.

In point of thorough knowledge of the meaning, and constant and scrupulous precision in the use, of individual words, I suppose Coleridge surpasses all other English writers, of whatever period.—MARSH, GEORGE P., 1859, *Lectures on the English Language, First Series, p.* 115.

Those, indeed, who learnt, and still learn, from the "Friend," perceive that it had one main purpose; that whether Coleridge discussed questions of art or questions of ethics, or—what have the largest place in the book—questions of politics, he was seeking to distinguish between those principles which are universal, which belong to one man as much as another, and those rules and maxims which are generalized from experience. Having this end in view he accepted Kant's distinction between the understanding and the reason as of inestimable worth. . . . What we have said may help to remove the impression that any part of Coleridge's influence arose from the unpractical qualities of his mind. Just in proportion as he yielded to these, or they prevailed over him, his influence was weakened. Whatever has been said, or may be said, to the contrary, he exercised *no* power through them. It is only by being in contact with the actual things which other men were thinking of, and with the thoughts which those things were awakening, that he gained a hearing in any quarter.—MAURICE, FREDERICK DENISON, 1862, *Moral and Metaphysical Philosophy, vol.* II, *pp.* 665, 666.

Coleridge had less delicacy and penetration than Joubert, but more richness and power; his production, though far inferior to what his nature at first seemed to promise, was abundant and varied. Yet in all his production how much is there to dissatisfy us! How many reserves must be made in praising either his poetry, or his criticism, or his philosophy! How little either of his poetry, or of his criticism, or of his philosophy, can we expect permanently to stand! But that which will stand of Coleridge is this; the stimulus of his continual effort,—not a moral effort, for he had no morals,—but of his continual instinctive effort, crowned often with rich success, to get at and to lay bare the real truth of his matter in hand, whether that matter were literary, or philosophical, or political, or religious; and this in a country where at that moment such an effort was almost unknown. . . . Coleridge's great action lay in his supplying in England, for many years and under critical circumstances, by the spectacle of this effort of his, a stimulus to all minds, in the generation which grew up round him, capable of profiting by it. His action will still be felt as long as the need for it continues. When, with the cessation of the need, the action too has ceased, Coleridge's memory, in spite of the disesteem,—nay, repugance,—which his character may and must inspire, will yet forever remain invested with that interest and gratitude which invests the memory of founders.—ARNOLD, MATTHEW, 1865, *Joubert, Essays in Criticism.*

The literary life of Coleridge was a disinterested struggle against the relative spirit. With a strong native bent towards the tracking of all questions, critical or practical, to first principles, he is ever restlessly scheming to "apprehend the absolute," to affirm it effectively, to get it acknowledged. It was an effort, surely, an effort of sickly thought, that saddened his mind, and limited the operation of his unique poetic gift. . . . Perhaps the chief offence in Coleridge is an excess of seriousness, a seriousness arising not from any moral principle, but from a misconception of the perfect manner.—PATER, WALTER, 1865–80, *Appreciations, pp.* 67, 68.

He explored the wide field of literature and philosophy, and brought to light richer spoils than any scholar of his time, or since. . . . To follow him were an education in itself.—ALCOTT, A. BRONSON, 1869–72, *Concord Days, pp.* 136, 137.

The greatest imaginative intellect of the age.—TAYLOR, SIR HENRY, 1885, *Autobiography, vol.* I, *p.* 156.

His positions as a poet and a prose writer are entirely independent. He is the only man that is very great as an imaginative writer and as a logician, for though Plato is a great literary artist, we do not know that he was a poet of the first rank. Coleridge does not mix his reasoning and his poetry as Milton did, and as Wordsworth did. While his prose abounds in graphic and suggestive images, it is strictly argumentative prose; it holds no artistic element in solution. It is addressed primarily to the intellect. His poetry on the other hand is strictly representative, purely an art product. It makes no appeal to the understanding, but is the language of something higher.—JOHNSON, CHARLES F., 1885, *Three Americans and Three Englishmen, p.* 43.

Our business is not so much to attempt any criticism of the value of Coleridge's thought as to describe it as a new power. That it was such a power is beyond all question. It is not merely the testimony of such men as Archdeacon Hare and John

Sterling, of Newman and of John Stuart Mill, but it is the fact that the later streams of religious thought in England are all more or less colored by his influence. They flow in deeper and different channels since he lived. Not only are some of those streams directly traceable to him, and said to derive all their vitality from his principles, but those which are most opposed to him have been moulded more or less by the impress of his religious genius. There was much in the man Coleridge himself to provoke animadversion; there may have been aspects of his teaching that lend themselves to ridicule; but if a genius, seminal as his has been in the world of thought and of criticism as well as poetry, it is not to excite our reverence, there is little that remains for us to reverence in the intellectual world. And when literature regains the higher tone of our earlier national life, the tone of Hooker and of Milton, Samuel Taylor Coleridge will be again acknowledged, in Julius Hare's words, as "a true sovereign of English thought." He will take rank in the same line of spiritual genius. He has the same elevation of feeling, the same profound grasp of moral and spiritual ideas, the same wide range of vision. He has, in short, the same love of wisdom, the same insight, the same largeness—never despising nature or art or literature for the sake of religion, still less ever despising religion for the sake of culture.—TULLOCH, JOHN, 1885, *Movements of Religious Thought in Britain During the Nineteenth Century*, *p.* 11.

Coleridge's prose, less unique than his verse, is more uniformly excellent, and has an almost unparalleled range of application to subjects grave and gay, easy and abstruse. — SAINTSBURY, GEORGE, 1886, *Specimens of English Prose Style*, *p.* 288.

Characteristically a poet, and never more so than when pouring forth his "divine philosophy," he had the poet's power to make the ideal life the real. Everything that passed through his mind suffered "a change into something rich and strange," so that it could neither be identified nor reclaimed; but he would have acknowledged Kant as his master, and, whether or not he was an accurate teacher, he made the great outlines of his master's philosophy known to English thought.—PITMAN, ROBERT C., 1888, *Books that have Helped Me, The Forum, vol.* 4, *p.* 604.

A man to-morrow weak as are the worst,
  A man to whom all depths, all heights belong,
Now with too bitter hours of weakness cursed,
  Now winged with vigor, as a giant strong
To take our groping hearts with tender hand,
And set them surely where God's angels stand.

—MITCHELL, S. WEIR, 1888, *Coleridge at Chamouny, Collected Poems, p.* 252.

Milton and Coleridge have certainly exercised deeper influence over my life and opinions than any other authors. I received the entire works of Coleridge, both prose and poety, as a college prize, and became thoroughly familiar with them all. I have no space to mention the permanent lessons of philosophy and theology which I learnt from him, though I have never seen reason to alter the views which he taught me on two subjects of the utmost theological importance—the doctrines of the atonement and the inspiration of the Scriptures.—FARRAR, F. W., 1890, *Formative Influences, The Forum, vol.* 10, *p.* 382.

Samuel Taylor Coleridge was a true representative of Romanticism with all its bright and dark sides. He was a man of wide culture, of fine sensibility, of vivid imagination, of ready intellect; but as a thinker his efforts were spasmodic and fragmentary, lacking steadiness, consistency, and thoroughness; and he displayed a surprising want of moral strength.—PFLEIDERER, OTTO, 1890, *The Development of Theology in Germany since Kant, and its Progress in Great Britain since* 1825, *tr. Smith, p.* 308.

The influence of Coleridge has been scattered and fragmentary. In church, in state, in literature, his spirit has descended to many whose theories and purposes are otherwise widely different. John Henry Newman and Frederick D. Maurice alike owe their inspiration to him; John Stuart Mill can call him one of the two great moving forces of the century; Thomas Carlyle and Matthew Arnold carried on in their different fashions his European and cosmopolitan culture of England. His literary criticism is of the same scattered and frutiful sort. In his suggestions lies the germ of a higer development, the spirit that must inform the great and enduring work of the future. Fragmentary as his writings are, there is yet opened through them an ideal criticism that has never been reached, and for which we can only hope if the clear intellectuality of the eighteenth century shall come to blend with the spirituality that complemented and destroyed it.—WYLIE, LAURA JOHNSON, 1894, *Evolution of English Criticism, p.* 204.

One is a little apt to forget that his metaphysical bent was no less innate than his poetical,—even at Christ's Hospital, his spiritual potation was a half-and-half in which the waters of a more or less authentic Castaly, and the "philosophic draughts" from such fountains as Jamblichus and Plotinus, were equally mingled. Whether or not a born "maker," he was certainly a born theorist; and we believe not only that under all his most important artistic achievements there was a basis of intellectual theory, but that the theory, so far from being an alien and disturbing presence, did duty as the unifying principle which co-ordinated the whole.—WATSON, WILLIAM, 1893, *Excursions in Criticism, p.* 98.

One of the greatest among poets, who was also—now and then, by fits and starts —a very great critic. . . . Coleridge was never systematic or coherent in criticism; on poetry, on philosophy, on theology, on politics, he delivered his soul at random, and after such a fashion as to call up the fancy of a first-rate player at billards or at chess who took pleasure in playing blindfold. His good hits, or his good moves, are naturally nothing less than admirable; indeed, no subsequent player can hope to follow them; but when he goes wrong he is more hopelessly wrong than the most incompetent novice.—SWINBURNE, ALGERNON CHARLES, 1894, *Studies in Prose and Poetry, p.* 81.

Coleridge is "'sequacious," even when he rambles; seer though he is, he omits no step; his style is not only redintegrating, but, at times, almost impartially so—as if narcotism had touched his selective faculty. He uses more "hooks-and-eyes" than any writer of his time, more, I presume, than any great English *littérateur* of the century. Of 300 sentences in the "Friend," 100 are formally connected—up to that day a higer proportion than that of any man after Walton.—LEWIS, EDWIN HERBERT, 1894, *The History of the English Paragraph, p.* 128.

The contributions which Coleridge made to modern thought, rich, ample, and suggestive as they are, have all the characteristics of his varied and eventful life. In Poetry, Criticism, and Philosophy he drove the shaft deep and gave us samples of the wealth of ore lying in their confines. Although he worked these mines only at irregular intervals and passed rapidly from one to the other, yet, by stimulating and quickening activity in his associates and followers, he caused the entire territory to be explored as it never was before in English history. If it cannot be said of him that he left us a rounded and complete system, yet it can be said—and it is a far nobler tribute—that he made it possible for us to grasp those principles which underlie all systems. His contribution to the literature of power is certainly unsurpassed by that of any writer of modern times.—GEORGE, ANDREW J., 1895, *ed. Coleridge's Principles of Criticism, p.* vii.

Like Nelson's letter to Lady Hamilton, Coleridge's "Letters," to everybody almost, are not always agreeable reading. One lesson of Mr. Carlyle's, a lesson which he preached by precept rather than example, we have partly learned. "Consume your own smoke," said the sage. Coleridge, in his private correspondence, blew abroad the vapor of smoke which rose from, and often dimmed the fire of his unexampled genius. On that sacred flame it is no metaphor to say that he poured too many drugs, heaped "poppy buds and labdanum." Hence ascended the smoke which he did not restrain or consume, but allowed to take its free way through heaven and earth. It may be said that there is an affectation, now, of reticence, and an affectation of manliness. Affectations if they be, these at least are imitations of virtues which Coleridge did not possess. He had a kind of mania for confessing himself, and crying *mea culpa*. Like the bad man in Aristotle, he is "full of repentance," or of remorse. He is an erring creature, and knows it, and his confessions occasionally suggest, in a sense, the Scotch proverbial policy of "taking the first word of flyting." One would rather see him more hardened, less "sensible." To moralise about Coleridge is temptingly easy and absolutely useless.

—LANG, ANDREW, 1895, *The Letters of Coleridge, Contemporary Review, vol.* 67, *p.* 876.

In disburthening himself of the ideas and imaginations which pressed upon his consciousness, in committing them to writing and carefully preserving them through all his wanderings, Coleridge had no mind that they should perish utterly. The invisible pageantry of thought and passion which forever floated into his spiritual ken, the perpetual hope, the half belief that the veil of the senses would be rent in twain, and that he and not another would be the first to lay bare the mysteries of being, and to solve the problem of the ages—of these was the breath of his soul. It was his fate to wrestle from night to morn with the Angel of the Vision, and of that unequal combat he has left, by way of warning or encouragement, a broken but an inspired and inspiring record.—COLERIDGE, ERNEST HARTLEY, 1895, *Anima Poetæ from the Unpublished Note-Books of Samuel Taylor Coleridge, Preface, p.* ix.

No English prose is nearer to that of Goethe in its power of carrying the reader along, with or without his consent, till he is left wondering what it is that has got hold of him. The spell that drew so many people, of all orders of intellectual constitution, to listen to Coleridge talking, may still be found in his philosophical and critical writings; and, in spite of the scorner, it is still possible to "sit under" the eloquence of his sermons, merely because it is true eloquence, and not a battery of separate notes and epigrams. . . . It is seldom that the prose of Coleridge is decorated in any adventitious way. There are many illustrations, but rarely any that look as if they had been stuck on for effect.—KER, W. P., *English Prose,* 1896, *ed. Craik, vol.* v, *pp.* 76, 79.

Coleridge's Shakespeare criticism is from first to last a continual quest of the evidences of organic structure, thus conceived. It illustrates both the value of the method and its perils. He made the first serious effort to grasp the totality of Shakespeare's work, and to trace out the inner history of his mind through the chronological chaos in which the dramas were still involved. The method gives subtlety, sometimes over-subtlety, to his appreciation of character. Every obvious trait becomes the mask of an alien quality which it conceals. He insists upon the inadequacy of the traditional classifications. He refuses to see sheer folly or villainy; dwells on the intellectual greatness of Iago, of Richard; repudiates the "cowardice" of Falstaff, and finds in Polonius a wise man past his prime. He elicits the hidden pathos of humour, and is somewhat too prone to find profound judgment in a pun.—HERFORD, C. H., 1897, *The Age of Wordsworth, p.* 87.

Charles Lamb

1775-1834

1775—Born February 10, Crown Office Row, Temple. 1782—Enters Christ's Hospital School. 1789—Leaves school and enters service of South Sea House. 1792—Enters service East India Company. 1795—Resides at No. 7 Little Queen St., Holborn. 1796—Publishes four Sonnets in volume of "Poems by S. T. Coleridge." 1797—Removes to No. 45 Chappel St., Pentonville.—Contributes to "Poems by S. T. Coleridge, Charles Lamb, and Charles Lloyd." 1800—Writes Epilogue to Godwin's "Antonio." 1801—Removes to No. 16 Mitre-Court Buildings, Temple. 1802—Publishes "John Woodvil." 1806—Produces "Mr. H."—a Farce, at Drury Lane. 1807—Publishes "Tales from Shakespear"—"Mrs. Leicester's School."—Writes Prologue for "Faulkener," by Godwin. 1808—Publishes "Specimens of Dramatic Poets"—"The Adventures of Ulysses." 1809—Publishes "Poetry for Children."—Removes to No. 4 Inner Temple Lane.—Lives at No. 34 Southampton Buildings. 1811—Publishes "Prince Dorus." 1813—Writes Prologue for Coleridge's "Remorse." 1817—Removes to No. 20 Russell St., Covent Garden. 1818—Publishes "Collected Works," 2 vols. 1820—Contributes to the *London Magazine.* 1823—Removes to Colebrooke (Colnbrooke) Row, Islington.—Publishes "Essays of Elia," First Series. 1825—Retires from East India House.—Contributes numerous articles to Hone's "Every Day Book." 1826—Removes to Enfield. 1827—Contributes Introduction to "The Garrick Plays," in Hone's "Table Book." 1829—Lodges in Enfield. 1830—Publishes "Album

Verses."—Contributes "De Foe's Works of Genius" to Wilson's "Memoirs of Daniel De Foe." 1831—Publishes "Satan in Search of a Wife." 1832—Removes to Bay Cottage, Edmonton. 1833—Publishes "Last Essays of Elia."—Contributes Epilogue to "The Wife," by J. Sheridan Knowles. 1834—Charles Lamb dies, December 27, at Edmonton.—NORTH, ERNEST D., 1890–94, *In the Footprints of Charles Lamb, by Benjamin Ellis Martin, Bibliography, p.* 149.

PERSONAL

Dear Charles! whilst yet thou wert a babe, I ween
That Genius plunged thee in that wizard fount
Hight Castalie: and (sureties of thy faith)
That Pity and Simplicity stood by,
And promised for thee, that thou shouldst renounce
The world's low cares and lying vanities,
Steadfast and rooted in the heavenly Muse,
And washed and sanctified to Poesy.
—COLERIDGE, SAMUEL TAYLOR, 1800, *To a Friend who had declared his intention of writing no more Poetry.*

I am glad that you think of him as I think; he has an affectionate heart, a mind *sui generis;* his taste acts so as to appear like the unmechanic simplicity of an instinct—in brief, he is worth an hundred men of *mere* talents. Conversation with the later tribe is like the use of leaden bells—one warms by exercise, Lamb every now and then *irradiates*, and the beam, though single and fine as a hair, is yet rich with colours, and I both see and feel.—COLERIDGE, SAMUEL TAYLOR, 1800, *Letter to William Godwin, May* 21; *William Godwin his Friends and Contemporaries, ed. Paul, vol.* II, *p.* 3.

A day of great pleasure. Charles Lamb and I walked to Enfield by Southgate, after an early breakfast in his chambers. . . . After tea, Lamb and I returned. The whole day most delightfully fine, and the scenery very agreeable. Lamb cared for the walk more than the scenery, for the enjoyment of which he seems to have no great susceptibility. His great delight, even in preference to a country walk, is a stroll in London. The shops and the busy streets, such as Thames Street, Bankside, etc., are his great favorites. He, for the same reason, has no great relish for landscape painting. But his relish for historic painting is exquisite.—ROBINSON, HENRY CRABBE, 1814, *Diary, July* 3; *Reminiscences, ed. Sadler, vol.* I, *p.* 278.

I forget whether I had written my last before my Sunday evening at Haydon's—no, I did not, or I should have told you, Tom, of a young man you met at Paris, at Scott's, of the [name of] Ritchie. I think he is going to Fezan, in Africa; then to proceed if possible like Mungo Park. He was very polite to me, and inquired very particularly after you. Then there was Wordsworth, Lamb, Monkhouse, Landseer, Kingston, and your humble servant. Lamb got tipsy and blew up Kingston—proceeding so far as to take the candle across the room, hold it to his face, and show us what a soft fellow he was.—KEATS, JOHN, 1818, *Letter to his Brothers, Jan.* 5; *Poetry and Prose, ed. Forman, vol.* V, *p.* 78.

There was L— himself, the most delightful, the most provoking, the most witty and sensible of men. He always made the best pun, and the best remark in the course of the evening. His serious conversation, like his serious writing, is his best. No one ever stammered out such fine, piquant, deep, eloquent things in half a dozen half-sentences as he does. His jests scald like tears: and he probes a question with a play upon words. . . . There was no fuss of cant about him: nor were his sweets or his sours ever diluted with one particle of affectation.—HAZLITT, WILLIAM, 1821–22, *On the Conversation of Authors, Table Talk.*

Charles Lamb, born in the Inner Temple, 10th February, 1775; educated in Christ's Hospital; afterwards a clerk in the Accountants' Office, East India House; pensioned off from that service, 1825, after thirty-three years' service; is now a gentleman at large; can remember few specialities in his life worth noting, except that he once caught a swallow flying (*teste suā manu*). Below the middle stature; cast of face slightly Jewish, with no Judaic tinge in his complexional religion; stammers abominably, and is therefore more apt to discharge his occasional conversation in a quaint aphorism, or a poor quibble, than in set and edifying speeches; has consequently been libelled as a person always aiming at wit; which, as he told a dull fellow who charged him with it, is at least as good as aiming at dullness. A small eater, but not drinker; confesses a partiality for the production of the juniper berry; was a fierce smoker of tobacco, but may be resembled to a volcano burnt out, emitting only now and then an occasional puff. Has been guilty of obtruding upon the public a tale in prose, called "Rosamond Gray," a dramatic sketch named "John Woodvil," a "Farewell Ode to Tobacco," with sundry other poems and light prose matter, collected in two slight crown octavos, and pompously christened his works, though, in fact, they were his recreations; and his true works may be found on the shelves of Leadenhall Street, filling some hundred folios. He is also the true Elia, whose essays are extant in a little volume. He died 18— much lamented. *Witness his hand.*—LAMB, CHARLES, 1827, *Autobiography, April* 18.

Heigh ho! Charles Lamb I sincerely believe to be in some considerable degree insane. A more pitiful, ricketty, gasping, staggering, stammering Tomfool I do not know. He is witty by denying truisms and abjuring good manners. His speech wriggles hither and thither with an incessant painful fluctuation, not an opinion in it, or a fact, or a phrase that you can thank him for—more like a convulsion fit than a natural systole and diastole. Besides, he is now a confirmed, shameless drunkard; *asks* vehemently for gin and water in strangers' houses, tipples till he is utterly mad, and is only not thrown out of doors because he is too much despised for taking such trouble with him. Poor Lamb! Poor England, when such a despicable abortion is named genius!—CARLYLE, THOMAS, 1831, *Journal, Life by Froude, vol.* II, *p.* 170.

Once, and once only have I seen thy face,
Elia! once only has thy tripping tongue
Run o'er my heart, yet never has been left
Impression on it stronger and more sweet,
Cordial old man! what youth was in thy years,
What wisdom in thy levity, what soul
In every utterance of thy purest breast!
Of all that ever wore man's form, 'tis thee
I first would spring to at the gate of Heaven.

I say *tripping* tongue for Charles Lamb stammered and spoke hurriedly. He did not think it worth while to put on a fine new coat to come down to see me in, as poor Coleridge did, but met me as if I had been a friend of twenty years' standing; indeed, he told me I had been so, and showed me some things I had written much longer ago and had utterly forgotten. The world will never see again two such delightful volumes as "The Essays of Elia;" no man living is capable of writing the worst twenty pages of them. The Continent has Zadig and Gil Blas, we have Elia and Sir Roger de Coverley.—LANDOR, WALTER SAVAGE, 1834, *Letter to the Countess of Blessington, Literary Life and Correspondence, ed. Madden, vol.* II, *p.* 381.

Genius triumphed over seeming wrong,
And poured out truth in works by thoughtful love
Inspired—works potent over smiles and tears.
And as round mountain-tops thy lightning plays,
Thus innocently sported, breaking forth
As from a cloud of some grave sympathy,
Humour and wild instinctive wit, and all
The vivid flashes of his spoken words. . . .
At the centre of his being, lodged
A soul by resignation sanctified:
And if too often, self-reproached, he felt
That innocence belongs not to our kind,
A power that never ceased to abide in him,
Charity, 'mid the multitude of sins
That she can cover, left not his exposed
To an unforgiving judgment from just Heaven,
Oh, he was good, if e'er a good Man lived.
—WORDSWORTH, WILLIAM, 1835, *Written After the Death of Charles Lamb.*

Mr. Lamb's personal appearance was remarkable. It quite realized the expectations of those who think that an author and a wit should have a distinct air, a separate costume, a particular cloth, something positive and singular about him. Such unqestionably had Mr. Lamb. Once he rejoiced in snuff-color, but lattery his costume was inveterately black—with gaiters which seemed longing for something more substantial to close in. His legs were remarkably slight,—so indeed was his whole body, which was of short stature, but surmounted by a head of amazing fineness. . . . His face was deeply marked and full of noble lines—traces of sensibility, imagination, suffering, and much thought. His wit was in his eye, luminous, quick, and restless. The smile that played about his mouth was ever cordial and good-humored; and the most cordial and delightful of his smiles were those which he accompanied his affectionate talk with his sister, or his jokes against her.—FORSTER, JOHN, 1835, *Charles Lamb, New Monthly Magazine, vol.* 43, *p.* 205.

Here sleeps beneath this bank, where daisies grow,
The kindliest sprite earth holds within her breast;
In such a spot I would this frame should rest,
When I to join my friend far hence shall go.
His only mate is now the minstrel lark,
Who chaunts her morning music o'er his bed,
Save she who comes each evening, ere the bark
Of watch-dog gathers drowsy folds, to shed
A sister's tears. Kind Heaven, upon her head
Do thou in dove-like guise thy spirit pour,
And in her aged path some flow'rets spread
Of earthly joy, should Time for her in store
Have weary days and nights, ere she shall greet
Him whom she longs in Paradise to meet.

—MOXON, EDWARD, 1835, *Sonnets, Part Second, p.* 18.

His angry letter to me in the Magazine arose out of a notion that an expression of mine in the *Quarterly Review* would hurt the sale of Elia: some one, no doubt, had said that it would. I meant to serve the book, and very well remember how the offense happened. I had written that it wanted nothing to render it altogether delightful but a *saner* religious feeling. *This* would have been the proper word if any other person had written the book. Feeling its extreme unfitness as soon as it was written, I altered it immediately for the first word which came into my head, intending to remodel the sentence when it should come to me in proof; and that proof never came.—SOUTHEY, ROBERT, 1836, *To Edward Moxon, Feb.* 2; *Life and Correspondence, ed. C. C. Southey, ch.* xxxvi.

It cannot be denied or concealed that Lamb's excellences, moral and intellectual, were blended with a single frailty; so intimately associating itself with all that was most charming in the one, and sweetest in the other, that, even if it were right to withdraw it wholly from notice, it would be impossible without it to do justice to his virtues. The eagerness with which he would quaff exciting liquors, from an early period of life, proved that to a physical peculiarity of constitution was to be ascribed, in the first instance, the strength of the temptation with which he was assailed. This kind of corporeal need; the struggles of deep thought to overcome the bashfulness and the impediment of speech which obstructed its utterance; the dull, heavy, irksome labors which hung heavy on his mornings, and dried up his spirits; and still more, the sorrows which had environed him, and which prompted him to snatch a fearful joy; and the unbounded craving after sympathy with human feelings, conspired to disarm his power of resisting when the means of indulgence were actually before him. Great exaggerations have been prevalent on this subject, countenanced, no doubt, by the "Confessions" which, in the prodigality of his kindness, he contributed to his friend's collection of essays and authorities against the use of spirituous liquors; for, although he had rarely the power to overcome the temptation when presented, he made heroic sacrifices in flight. His final abandonment of tobacco, after many ineffectual attempts, was one of these—a princely sacrifice.—TALFOURD, THOMAS, NOON, 1837–59, *The Life and Letters of Charles Lamb, p.* 399.

He was *petite* and ordinary in his person and appearance. I have seen him sometimes in what is called good company, but where he has been a stranger, sit silent, and be suspected for an odd fellow.—CHORLEY, HENRY F., 1838–61, *Authors of England, p.* 60.

In the words of our dear departed friend, Charles Lamb, "You good-for-nothing old Lake Poet," what has become of you? Do you remember his saying that at my table in 1819, with "Jerusalem" towering behind us in the painting room, and Keats and your friend Monkhouse of the party? Do you remember Lamb voting me absent, and then making a speech descanting on my excellent port, and proposing a vote of thanks? Do you remember his then voting me present? I had never left my chair—and informing me of what had been done during my retirement, and hoping I was duly sensible of the honor? Do you remember the Commissioner (of Stamps and Taxes) who asked you if you did not think Milton a great genius, and Lamb getting up and asking leave with a candle to examine his phrenological development? Do you remember poor dear Lamb, whenever the Commissioner was equally profound, saying: "My son John went to bed with his breeches on," to the dismay of the learned man? Do you remember you and I and Monkhouse getting Lamb out of the room by force, and putting on his greatcoat, he reiterating his earnest desire to examine the Commissioner's skull? . . . Ah! my dear old friend, you and I shall never see such days again! The peaches are not so big now as they were in our days.—HAYDON, BENJAMIN ROBERT, 1842, *Letter to Wordsworth, Oct.* 16; *Life, Letters and Table Talk, ed. Stoddard, p.* 201.

I was sitting one morning beside our editor, busily correcting proofs, when a visitor was announced, whose name, grumbled by a low ventriloquial voice, like Tom Pipes calling down the hold through the hatchway, did not resound distinctly on my tympanum. However, the door opened, and in came a stranger,—a figure remarkable at a glance, with a fine head, on a small spare body, supported by two almost immaterial legs. He was clothed in sables, of a by-gone fashion, but there was something wanting, or somethig present about him, that certified he was neither a divine, nor a physician, nor a school-master: from a certain neatness and sobriety in his dress, coupled with his sedate bearing, he might have been taken, but that such a costume would be anomalous, for a *Quaker* in black. He looked still more (what he really was) a literary Modern Antique, a New Old Author, a living Anachronism, contemporary at once with Burton the Elder and Colman the Younger. Meanwhile he advanced with rather a peculiar gait, his walk was plantigrade, and with a cheerful "How d'ye," and one of the blandest, sweetest smiles, that ever brightened a manly countenance, held out two fingers to the editor. The two gentlemen in black soon fell into discourse; and whilst they conferred, the Lavater principle within me set to work upon the interesting specimen thus presented to its speculations. It was a striking intellectual face, full of wiry lines, physiognomical quips and cranks, that gave it great character. There was much earnestness about the brows, and a great deal of speculation in the eyes, which were brown and bright, and "quick in turning;" the nose, a decided one, though of no established order; and there was a handsome smartness about the mouth. Altogether, it was no common face—none of those *willow-pattern* ones, which Nature turns out by thousands at her potteries;—but more like a chance specimen of the Chinese ware, one to the set—unique, quaint. No one who had once seen it could pretend not to know it again. It was no face to lend its countenance to any confusion of persons in a Comedy of Errors. You might have sworn to it piecemeal—a separate affidavit for every feature. — HOOD, THOMAS, 1845? *Literary Reminiscences.*

In these miscellaneous gatherings, Lamb said little, except when an opening arose for a pun. And how effectual that sort of small shot was from *him*, I need not say to anybody who remembers his infirmity of stammering, and his dexterous management of it for purposes of light and shade. He was often able to train the roll of stammers into settling upon the words immediately preceding the effective one; by which means the key-note of the jest or sarcasm, benefiting by the sudden liberation of his embargoed voice, was delivered with the force of a pistol shot. That stammer was worth an annuity to him as an ally of his wit. Firing under cover of that advantage, he did triple execution; for, in the first place, the distressing sympathy of the hearers with *his* distress of utterance won for him unavoidably the silence of deep attention; and then, whilst he had us all hoaxed into this attitude of mute suspense by an appearance of distress that he perhaps did not really feel, down came a plunging shot into the very thick of us, with ten times the effect it would else have had.—DE QUINCEY, THOMAS, 1850, *Charles Lamb, Biographical Essays.*

I have spoken of the distinguished individuals bred at Christ-Hospital, including Coleridge and Lamb, who left the school not long before I entered it. Coleridge I never saw till he was old. Lamb I recollect coming to see the boys, with a pensive, brown, handsome, and kingly face, and a gait advancing with a motion from side to side, between involuntary consciousness and attempted ease. His brown complexion may have been owing to a visit in the country, his air of uneasiness to a great burden of sorrow. He dressed with a Quaker-like plainness.—HUNT, LEIGH, 1850, *Autobiography, vol.* I, *p.* 117.

In point of intellectual character and expression, a finer face was never seen, nor one more fully, however vaguely, corresponding with the mind whose features it interpreted. There was the gravity usually engendered by a life passed in book-learning, without the slightest tinge of that assumption and affectation which almost always attend the gravity *so* engendered; the intensity and elevation of general expression that mark high genius, without any of its pretension and its oddity; the sadness waiting on fruitless thoughts and baffled aspirations, but no evidences of that spirit of scorning and contempt which these are apt to engender. Above all, there was a pervading sweetness and gentleness which went straight to the heart of every one who looked on it; and not the less so, perhaps, that it bore about it an air, a something, seeming to tell that it was not *put on*—for nothing would be more unjust than to tax Lamb with assuming anything, even a virtue, which he did not possess—but preserved and persevered in, spite of opposing and contradictory feelings within, that struggled in vain for mastery. It was a thing to remind you of that painful smile which bodily disease and agony will sometimes put on, to conceal their sufferings from the observation of those they love. . . . His head might have belonged to a full-sized person, but it was set upon a figure so *petite* that it took an appearance of inappropriate largeness by comparison. This was the only striking peculiarity in the *ensemble* of his figure; in other respects it was pleasing and well-formed, but so slight and delicate as to bear the appearance of extreme spareness, as if of a man air-fed, instead of one rejoicing in a proverbial predilection for "roast-pig." The only defect of his figure was that the legs were too slight even for the slight body. —PATMORE, PETER GEORGE, 1854, *My Friends and Acquaintances, vol.* I, *pp.* 15, 17.

Of middle height, with brown, and rather ruddy complexion, gray eyes expressive of sense and shrewdness, but neither large nor brilliant; his head and features well-shaped, and the general expression of his countenance quiet, kind, and observant, undergoing rapid changes in conversation, as did his manner, variable as an April day, particularly to his sister, whose saint-like good humor and patience were as remarkable as his strange and whimsical modes of trying them. But the brother and sister perfectly understood each other, and "Charles," as she always called him, would not have been the "Charles" of her loving heart without the pranks and oddities which he was continually playing off upon her—and which were only outnumbered by the instances of affection, and evidences of ever watchful solicitude with which he surrounded her. —BALMANNO, MARY, 1858, *Pen and Pencil.*

Lamb, from the dread of appearing affected, sometimes injured himself by his behaviour before persons who were slightly acquainted with him. With the finest and tenderest feelings ever possessed by man, he seemed carefully to avoid any display of sentimentality in his talk.—LESLIE, CHARLES ROBERT, 1860, *Autobiographical Recollections, ed. Taylor, p.* 35.

The fact that distinguished Charles Lamb from other men was his entire devotion to one grand and tender purpose. There is, probably, a romance involved in every life. In his life it exceded that of others. In gravity, in acuteness, in his noble battle with a great calamity, it was beyond the rest. Neither pleasure, nor toil ever distracted him from his holy purpose. Everything was made subservient to it. He had an insane sister, who, in a moment of uncontrollable madness, had unconsciously destroyed her own mother; and to protect and save his sister—a gentlewoman, who had watched like a mother over his own infancy—the whole length of his life was devoted. What he endured, through the space of nearly forty years, from the incessant fear and frequent recurrence of his sister's insanity, can now only be conjectured. In this constant and uncomplaining endurance, and in his steady adherence to a great principle of conduct, his life was heroic.—PROCTER, BRYAN WALLER (BARRY CORNWALL), 1866, *Charles Lamb, A Memoir, p.* 2.

He never kept a letter; except a couple or so: and heartily despised "relics," especially of the sentimental sort. Thus, when a traveller brought him acorns, from Virgil's tomb, he amused himself with throwing them at the hackney coachmen that passed by.—FITZGERALD, PERCY, 1866, *Charles Lamb: his Friends, his Haunts and his Books.*

There were few modern volumes in his collection; and subsequently, such presentation copies as he received were wont to find their way into my own book-case, and often through eccentric channels. A

Leigh Hunt, for instance, would come skimming to my feet through the branches of the apple-trees (our gardens were contiguous); or a Bernard Barton would be rolled down stairs after me, from the library door. "Marcian Colonna" I remember finding on my window-sill, damp with the night's fog; and the "Plea of the Midsummer Fairies" I picked out of the strawberry bed.—WESTWOOD, THOMAS, 1866, *Recollections of Charles Lamb, Notes and Queries, Third Series, vol.* 9, *p.* 221.

Lamb was not a saint. He drank sometimes to excess. He also smoked tobacco. But if ever a good, great man walked the earth—good and great in the profoundest and noblest sense—full of that simple human charity, and utter renunciation of self, which is the fulfilling of the highest law and the holiest instinct—it was that man with a face of "quivering sweetness," nervous, tremulous; . . . so slight of frame that he looked only fit for the most placid fortune,—but who conquered poverty and hereditary madness, and won an imperishable name in English literature, and a sacred place in every generous heart, all in silence, and with a smile.—CURTIS, GEORGE WILLIAM, 1859, *Notes of Charles Lamb to Thomas Allsop, Harper's Magazine, vol.* 20, *p.* 97.

With all the light that has been thrown upon every circumstance of Lamb's life, and with the best disposition of the part of the biographers to find evidence that he sacrificed a conjugal happiness which was within his reach for the sake of his sister, no other facts bearing upon the question, however remotely, have been brought to light. It is surprising that a man of Lamb's sensibility—it would be surprising in the case of any man—should not once, during the forty years that elapsed between his rejection by Alice and his death, have "fallen in love," in any sense authorized by the most liberal construction of those words. Had he been in love with a dozen women in the course of that long period, he would only have resembled his fellow-bachelors, and it would by no means have followed that, in continuing single, he practised heroic self-denial. The biographers and reviewers who are so fond of ringing changes upon Lamb's imputed self-sacrifice, and upon the happiness which wife and children might have added to his life, strangely neglect to advert to a circumstance which would have raised grave doubts as to the propriety of his marrying had there been no other obstacle. We refer, of course, to his liability to madness.—HILL, A. S., 1867, *Charles Lamb and his Biographers, North American Review, vol.* 104, *p.* 396.

His style of playful bluntness when speaking to his intimates was strangely pleasant—nay, welcome: it gave you the impression of his liking you well enough to be rough and unceremonious with you: it showed you that he felt at home with you. It accorded with what you knew to be at the root of an ironical assertion he made—that he always gave away gifts, parted with presents, and *sold* keepsakes. It underlay in sentiment the drollery and reversed truth of his saying to us, "I always call my sister Maria when we are alone together, Mary when we are with our friends, and Moll before the servants." —CLARKE, MARY COWDEN, 1874–78, *Recollections of Writers.*

As to his kindness and practical benevolence, Mr. Ogilvie declared that it could not be overstated. His sympathies were so easily won that he was often imposed upon, yet he never learned to be suspicious. He had been known to wear a coat six months longer, that he might spare a little money to some needy acquaintance. There was hardly ever a time when he did not have somebody living upon him. If he was freed from one client, another would soon arise to take his place. A poor literary aspirant, or vagabond, especially, he could not resist, and he regularly had one or more on his hands. He would even take them to his house, and let them stay there weeks and months together.—TWICHELL, JOSEPH H., 1876, *Concerning Charles Lamb, Scribner's Monthly, vol.* 11, *p.* 276.

I must say I think his Letters infinitely better than his Essays; and Patmore says his Conversation, when just enough animated by Gin and Water, was better than either: which I believe too. Procter said he was far beyond the Coleridges, Wordsworths, Southeys, &c. And I am afraid I believe that also.—FITZGERALD, EDWARD, 1876, *To C. E. Norton, June* 10; *Letters and Literary Remains, ed. Wright, vol.* I, *p.* 385.

No one who has passed an hour in the company of Charles Lamb's "dear boy" can ever lose the impression made upon him by that simple, sincere, shy, and delicate soul. His small figure, his head, not remarkable for much besides its expression of intelligent and warm good-will, and its singular likeness to that of Sir Walter Scott; his conversation, which had little decision or "point" in the ordinary sense, and often dwelt on truths which a novelty-loving society banishes from its repertory as truisms, never disturbed the effect, in any assemblage, of his real distinction. His silence seemed wiser, his simplicity subtler, his shyness more courageous than the wit, philosophy, and assurance of others.—PATMORE, COVENTRY, 1877, *ed., Bryan Waller Procter, Autobiographical Fragment, p.* 5.

I availed myself of Charles Lamb's friendly invitation on Tuesday, August 5, 1834. On reaching his cottage—which stood back from the road (nearly opposite the church), between two houses which projected beyond it, and was screened by shrubs and trees—I found that he was out, taking his morning's stroll. I was admitted into a small, panelled, and agreeably shaded parlour. The modest room was hung round with engravings by Hogarth in dark frames. Books and magazines were scattered on the table and on the old-fashioned window seat. I chatted awhile with Miss Lamb—a meek, intelligent, very pleasant, but rather deaf elderly lady, who told me that her brother had been gratified by parts of my poem ("Emily de Wilton") and had read them to her. "Elia" came in soon after—a short, thin man. His dress was black, and he wore a capacious coat, breeches and gaiters, and a white neck-handkerchief. His dark and shaggy hair and eyebrows, heated face and very piercing jet-black eyes gave to his appearance a singularly wild and striking expression. The sketch of him in *Fraser's Magazine* gives a true idea of his dress and figure, but his portraits fail to represent adequately his remarkably "fine Titian head, full of dumb eloquence," as Hazlitt described it. He grasped me cordially by the hand, sat down, and taking a bottle from a cupboard behind him, mixed some rum and water. On another occasion his sister objected to this operation, and he refrained. Presently after he said, "May I have a little drop now? only a *leetle* drop?" "No," said she; "be a good boy." At last, however, he prevailed, and took his usual draught.—RUSSEL, J. FULLER, 1882, *Charles Lamb at Home, Notes and Queries, Sixth Series, vol.* 5, *p.* 241.

Very often, Charles Lamb was one of the party at the residence of Coleridge, with his gentle, sweet, yet melancholy countenance; for I can recall it only as bearing the stamp of mournfulness, rather than of mirth. Even when he said a witty thing, or made a pun, which he was too apt to do, it came from his lips (jerked out in the well-known semi-stutter) as if it had been a foreboding of evil; certainly, his merriment seemed forced.—HALL, SAMUEL CARTER, 1883, *Retrospect of a Long Life, p.* 316.

Lamb was buried in the quiet little churchyard at Edmonton. A tall, flat stone, with an inscription by Cary, the translator of Dante, which is neither happy nor quite coherent, marks the spot, which is just beyond the path on the southwest of the church.—HUTTON, LAURENCE, 1885, *Literary Landmarks of London, p.* 192.

Lamb's letters from first to last are full of the philosophy of life; he was as sensible a man as Dr. Johnson. One grows sick of the expressions, "poor Charles Lamb," "gentle Charles Lamb," as if he were one of those grown-up children of the Leigh Hunt type, who were perpetually begging and borrowing through the round of every man's acquaintance. Charles Lamb earned his own living, paid his own way, was the helper, not the helped; a man who was beholden to no one, who always came with gifts in his hand, a shrewd man capable of advice, strong in council. Poor Lamb indeed! Poor Coleridge, robbed of his will; poor Wordsworth, devoured by his own *ego*; poor Southey, writing his tomes and deeming himself a classic; poor Carlyle, with his nine volumes of memoirs, where he

"Lies like a hedgehog rolled up the wrong way,
Tormenting himself with his prickles"—

call these men poor, if you feel it decent to do so, but not Lamb, who was rich in all that makes life valuable or memory sweet. But he used to get drunk. This explains all.—BIRRELL, AUGUSTINE, 1887, *Obiter Dicta, Second Series, p.* 230.

A man of noticeable and impressive presence:—small of stature, fragile of frame, clad in clothing of tightly fitting black, which was clerical as to cut and well-worn as to texture; his "almost immaterial legs," in Tom Hood's phrase, ending in gaiters and straps; his dark hair, not quite black, curling crisply about a noble head and brow—"a head worthy of Aristotle," Leigh Hunt tells us; "full of dumb eloquence," are Hazlitt's words; "such only may be seen in the finer portraits of Titian" John Forster put it; "a long, melancholy face, with keen, penetrating eyes," we learn from Barry Cornwall; brown eyes, kindly, quick, observant; his dark complexion and grave expression brightened by the frequent "sweet smile, with a touch of sadness in it." This visitor, of such peculiar and piquant personality—externally, "a rare composition of the Jew, the gentleman, and the angel," to use his own words of the singer Braham—is Charles Lamb.—MARTIN, BENJAMIN ELLIS, 1890-94, *In the Footprints of Charles Lamb*, p. 4.

Not here, O teeming City, was it meet
Thy lover, thy most faithful, should repose,
But where the multitudinous life-tide flows
Whose ocean-murmur was to him more sweet
Than melody of birds at morn, or bleat
Of flocks in Spring-time, *there* should Earth enclose
His earth, amid thy thronging joys and woes,
There, 'neath the music of thy million feet.
In love of thee this lover knew no peer.
Thine eastern or thy western fane had made
Fit habitation for his noble shade.
Mother of mightier, nurse of none more dear,
Not here, in rustic exile, O not here,
Thy Elia like an alien should be laid!
—WATSON, WILLIAM, 1893, *At the Grave of Charles Lamb in Edmonton, Poems*, p. 144.

The Blue-coat boy had already become known and famous far beyond his modest ambition. Little by little his quaint fancies had taken hold in the popular heart, and being so unpretending the critics gave him help rather than hindrance. When he died, his heroic life of self-sacrifice and self-surrender was known to few besides his intimate friends. He never claimed the least merit for surrendering life's ambitions at the very start, taking up its burdens in the path of duty. His quiet generosity to friends in need was known only to himself and the recipients of his charities; but the fragrance of his sweet, blameless life clung around his memory, and expanded as the years passed, until his life, as well as his works, gave him his place among the best beloved of the English essayists.—LORD, ALICE E., 1893, *The Days of Lamb and Coleridge, A Historical Romance*, p. 376.

Past cheat of years the comrades of his mood—
The quiet old men sitting in the sun;
Strict maids; gray clerks; and children fair and blest;
And that sad woman of his house and blood—
And still he hides his hurts from dearest one;
But with the whole world shares the stingless jest!
—REESE, LIZETTE WOODWORTH, 1896, *A Quiet Road.*

TO THE MEMORY
of
CHARLES LAMB,
Died 27th Decr. 1834, aged 59.

Farewell, dear friend: That smile, that harmless mirth
No more shall gladden our domestic hearth;
That rising tear with pain forbid to flow
Better than words, no more assuage our woe;
That hand outstretched, from small but well-earned store
Yield succour to the destitute no more.
Yet art thou not all lost; thro' many an age
With sterling sense and humour shall thy page
With many an English bosom, pleased to see
That old and happier vein revived in thee
This for our earth, and if with friends we share
Our joys in heaven, we hope to meet thee there.

Also, MARY ANNE LAMB,
Sister of the above,
Born 3rd Decr. 1767, Died 20th May 1847.
—LINES ON TOMB.

POETRY

Mr. C. Lamb has produced no poems equal to his prose writings: but I could not resist the temptation of transferring into this collection his "Farewell to Tobacco," and some of the sketches in his "John Woodvil;" the first of which is rarely surpassed in quaint wit, and the last in pure feeling.—HAZLITT, WILLIAM, 1824, *Select British Poets.*

There is much quaint feeling in his verses: he has used the style of the good old days of Elizabeth in giving form and utterance to his own emotions; and, though often unelevated and prosaic, every line is informed with thought or with some vagrant impulse of fancy. . . . He gives portraits of men whose manners have undergone a city change; records sentiments which are the true offspring of the mart and the custom-house, and attunes his measure to the harmony of other matter than musical breezes and melodious brooks, —CUNNINGHAM, ALLAN, 1833, *Biographical and Critical History of the Literature of the Last Fifty Years.*

"John Woodvil" contains passages which would not have done dishonour to the great dramatists of Shakspeare's golden age; and "The Farewell to Tobacco," in these pages, is such a piece of verse as one might imagine "Elia" would write.—GRISWOLD, RUFUS W., 1844, *The Poets and Poetry of England in the Nineteenth Century, p.* 111.

Charles Lamb was a true poet, but not a great one. His genius was peculiar and wayward, and his mind seemed so impregnated with the dramatists preceding or contemporary with Shakspeare—Marlowe, Webster, Ford, Shirley, Marston, Massinger, and their compeers—that he could not help imitating their trains of thought. Yet he struck out a few exquisite things, —sparks from true genius, which can never be extinguished; as "The Old Familiar Faces;" "To Hester;" "The Virgin of the Rocks;" and the descriptive forest-scene in "John Woodvil," which, it is said, Godwin, having found somewhere extracted, was so enchanted with, that he hunted—of course vainly—through almost all the earlier poets in search of it:

"To see the sun to bed, and to arise," &c.

—MOIR, D. M., 1850–51, *Poetical Literature of the Past Half-Century, p.* 89.

Lamb's poems, as a rule, are insipid, and *artificially natural;* he belongs to that school of which Ambrose Phillips is generally—though without sufficient ground, perhaps—regarded as the founder. Namby-pambyism is surely not so modern.—HAZLITT, WILLIAM CAREW, 1874, *Mary and Charles Lamb, p.* 172.

As a Poet, Charles Lamb is once again original. He has produced but little, it is true; but that little is perfect in its own way, and ensures for its author a niche all to himself in the temple of Parnassus. What more pathetic than his lines on his mother, first printed in the "Final Memorials;" his "Old Familiar Faces;" "The Three Friends;" and "The Sabbath Bells"? Then there is the fierce energy of the "Farewell to Tobacco," and "The Gipsy's Malison," with its almost demoniacal force of expression. These are all pieces of perfect finish, and are marked by a wondrously refined artifice of rhyme, rhythm, phrase, and condensation of thought. —BATES, WILLIAM, 1874–98, *The Maclise Portrait Gallery of Illustrious Literary Characters, with Memoirs, p.* 295.

Charles Lamb's nosegay of verse may be held by the small hand of a maiden, and there is not in it one flaunting, gallant flower; it is, however, fragrant with the charities of home, like blossoms gathered in some old cottage croft.—DOWDEN, EDWARD, 1880, *The English Poets, ed. Ward, vol.* IV, *p.* 326.

In the literary tribunal, Lamb the essayist and Lamb the poet are two individualities, and it is well that for the present at least the distinction should be kept clear. Rightly perceived—and Lamb himself would have so perceived it—he was more of a lay-assistant than a priest at the high altar of poetry. While Coleridge and Wordsworth performed the rites, he witnessed, worshipped, and aided, but did not officiate—unless it were in the humble capacity of censer-bearer. It is true he has written in metre and in rhyme, but the result, generally, is verse rather than poetry, and some may add, and not very good verse either.—TIREBUCK, WILLIAM, 1887, *ed., The Political Works of Bowles, Lamb, and Hartley Coleridge, Introduction, p.* xiv.

Lamb's poems are not of the best; they have a haltingness—like that in his speech, —with none of Rogers's glibness and currency, and none of his shallowness either. Constraint of rhyme sat on Elia no easier than a dress-coat.—MITCHELL, DONALD G., 1895, *English Lands Letters and Kings, Queen Anne and the Georges, p.* 320.

It is of course true that his popularity rests more with his essays than with his poems, which form only the smaller portion of his writings, but the same qualities which make his prose such delightful reading are found crystallised and perfected in his verse. His distinctive characteristic is quaint originality, coloured, but not formed by his keen appreciation of, and familiar acquaintance with, the works of our old poets and dramatists. He never has any tendency to fall into the manner of "the lake poets," though he was the intimate friend of Wordsworth, Coleridge, and Southey. He was not insensible to the beauties of nature, or to the charm of fine scenery; but he was more at home amidst the world of books and the haunts of men. . . . As an original humourist he has never been surpassed, and this quality, no less than the depth of sensibility and pathetic power, in his poems attests that the mild jocularity of Wordsworth, who called him "Lamb, the frolic and the gentle," was not misplaced.—ARCHER, THOMAS, 1895, *The Poets and Poetry of the Century, Robert Southey to Percy Bysshe Shelley, ed. Miles, pp.* 131, 136.

ROSAMUND GRAY
1798

A TALE | of | ROSAMUND GRAY | and | OLD BLIND MARGARET. | by CHARLES LAMB. | London, | Printed for Lee and Hurst, | No. 32, Pater-noster Row, | 1798.—TITLE PAGE OF FIRST EDITION, 1798.

With it came, too, Lamb's works. . . . What a lovely thing is his "Rosamund Gray!" How much knowledge of the sweetest and deepest parts of our nature in it! When I think of such a mind as Lamb's—when I see how unnoticed remain things of such exquisite and complete perfection—what should I hope for myself, if I had not higher objects in view than fame!—SHELLEY, PERCY BYSSHE, 1819, *Letter to Hunt, Sep.* 8; *Correspondence of Leigh Hunt, ed. by his Son.*

Rosamund, with the pale blue eyes and the "yellow Hertfordshire hair," is but a fresh copy of his Anna and his Alice. That Rosamund Gray had an actual counterpart in real life seems certain, and the little group of cottages, in one of which she dwelt with her old grandmother, is still shown in the village of Widford, about half a mile from the site of the old mansion of Blakesware. And it is the tradition of the village, and believed by those who have the best means of judging, that "Rosamund Gray" (her real name was equally remote from this, and from Alice W—n) was Charles Lamb's first and only love. Her fair hair and eyes, her goodness, and (we may assume) her poverty, were drawn from life. The rest of the story in which she bears a part is of course pure fiction. The real Anna of the sonnets made a prosperous marriage, and lived to a good old age.—AINGER, ALFRED, 1882, *Charles Lamb (English Men of Letters), p.* 39.

It is crude and formless, the raw elements of a story clumsily thrust into a common frame. The idyllic picture of Rosamund and her grandmother (embalming probably a memory of his Anna Simmons) has a charm; but the horrible fate of the young girl is a jarring dissonance, sudden and arbitrary as the invading shock of madness in which that early love had issued.—HERFORD, C. H., 1897, *The Age of Wordsworth, p.* 61.

LETTERS

Lamb's letters are not indeed model letters like Cowper's. Though natural to Lamb, they cannot be called easy. "Divine chit-chat" is not the epithet to describe them. His notes are all high. He is sublime, heartrending, excruciatingly funny, outrageously ridiculous, sometimes possibly an inch or two overdrawn. He carries the charm of incongruity and total unexpectedness to the highest pitch imaginable.—BIRRELL, AUGUSTINE, 1892, *Res Judicatæ, p.* 240.

As for Lamb, those who love him at all love him so well that it matters little which of his letters they read, or how often they have read them before. Only it is best to select those written in the meridian of his life. The earlier ones are too painful, the later ones too sad. Let us take him at his happiest, and be happy with him for an hour; for, unless we go cheerfully to bed, the portals of morn open for us with sullen murmur, and fretful dreams, more disquieting than even the troubled thoughts of day, flit batlike round our melancholy pillows.—REPPLIER, AGNES, 1894, *In the Dozy Hours, p.* 8.

His correspondence must remain an integral part of the age, which it immediately concerns, as much as that of Walpole; and in this capacity and aspect, if in no other, he has laid himself, so to speak, across an epoch. Any one who bestows even a cursory study on these inimitable productions must perceive and allow that the serious style largely preponderates, and that of broad fun there is little more than an occasional vein. His wit is more usually delicate and playful—sometimes bordering on pathos. Here and there, among the letters, there are spasms of boisterous and rollicking gaiety parallel with the horse-play in the Inner Temple Lane times; but it makes little indeed in so voluminous a body of matter.—HAZLITT, WILLIAM CAREW, 1897, *The Lambs, their Lives, their Friends and their Correspondence, p.* 13.

GENERAL

The person you have thus leagued in a partnership of infamy with me is Mr. Charles Lamb, a man who, so far from being a democrat, would be the first person to assent to the opinions contained in the foregoing pages: he is a man too much occupied with real and painful duties—duties of high personal self denial—to trouble himself about speculative matters. Whenever he has thrown his ideas together, it has been from the irresistible impulse of the moment, never from any intention to propagate a system, much less any "of folly and wickedness."—LLOYD, CHARLES, 1799, *A Letter to the Anti-Jacobin Reviewers, Appendix.*

Elia in his happiest moods delights me: he is a fine soul; but when he is dull, his dulness sets human stupidity at defiance. He is like a well-bred, ill-trained pointer. He has a fine nose, but he won't or he can't range. He keeps always close to your foot, and then he points larks and titmice. You see him snuffing and smoking and brandishing his tail with the most impassioned enthusiasm, and then drawn round into a semicircle, he stands beautifully—dead-set. You expect a burst of partridges or a towering cock-pheasant, when lo, and behold! away flits a lark, or you discover a mouse's nest, or there is absolutely nothing at all. Perhaps a shrew has been there the day before. Yet if Elia were mine, I would not part with him, for all his faults.—WILSON, JOHN, 1822, *Noctes Ambrosianæ, April.*

Read "Elia," if the book has not fallen in your way. It is by my old friend Charles Lamb. There are some things in it which will offend, and some which will pain you, as they do me; but you will find in it a rich vein of pure gold.—SOUTHEY, ROBERT, 1823, *Letters.*

His style runs pure and clear, though it may often take an underground course, or be conveyed through old-fashioned conduit-pipes. . . . There is a fine tone of *chiaro-scuro*, a moral perspective in his writings. He delights to dwell on that which is fresh to the eye of memory; he yearns after and covets what soothes the frailty of human nature. That touches him most nearly which is withdrawn to a certain distance, which verges on the borders of oblivion:—that piques and provokes his fancy most, which is hid from a superficial glance. That which, though gone by, is still remembered, is in his view more genuine, and has given more "vital signs that it will live," than a thing of yesterday, that may be forgotten to-morrow. Death has in this sense the spirit of life in it; and the shadowy has to our author something substantial in it.—HAZLITT, WILLIAM, 1825, *The Spirit of the Age, pp.* 262, 263.

Poor Charles Lamb, what a tender, good, joyous heart had he! What playfulness! what purity of style and thought!—LANDOR, WALTER SAVAGE, 1835, *Letter to Lady Blessington, March* 16; *Literary Life and Correspondence of the Countess of Blessington, ed. Madden, vol.* II, *p.* 123.

Of his own writings it is now superfluous to speak; for, after having encountered long derision and neglect, they have taken their place among the classics of his language. They stand alone, at once singular and delightful. They are all carefully elaborated; yet never were works written in a higher defiance to the conventional pomp of style. A sly hit, a happy pun, a humorous combination, lets the light into the intricacies of the subject, and supplies the place of ponderous sentences. . . . In all things he is most human. Of all modern writers, his works are most immediately directed to give us heart-ease and to make us happy.—TALFOURD, THOMAS NOON, 1837, *The Life and Letters of Charles Lamb.*

Charles Lamb's "Specimens of English Dramatic Poets" is of deeper interest. He was a nobler workman, and he carries us on through whole scenes by a true unerring emotion. He was a poetical mind laboring in poetry.—DISRAELI, ISAAC, 1841, *Predecessors and Contemporaries of Shakspeare, Amenities of Literature.*

We never rise from one of his essays without a feeling of contentment. He leads our thoughts to the actual, available springs of enjoyment. He reconciles us to ourselves; causing home-pleasures, and the charms of the wayside, and the mere comforts of existence, to emerge from the shadow into which our indifference has cast them, into the light of fond recognition. The flat dull surface of common life, he causes to rise into beautiful *basso-relievo.* In truth, there are few better teachers of gratitude than Lamb.—TUCKERMAN, HENRY T., 1849, *Characteristics of Literature, p.* 167.

Such wit, such humor, such imagination, such intelligence, such sentiment, such kindliness, such heroism, all so quaintly mixed and mingled, and stuttering out in so freakish a fashion, and all blending so finely in that exquisite eccentric something which we call the character of Charles Lamb, make him the most lovable of writers and men.—WHIPPLE, EDWIN P., 1857–66, *Eccentric Character, Character and Characteristic Men, p.* 60.

Their ["Essays"] egotism is chastened and subdued, but their personality is never relinquished: it is not philosophy that selects its problem, and proceeds to solve it—it is Charles Lamb who, philosophising through whim and fancy, allures you to listen to Charles Lamb.—LYTTON, EDWARD BULWER LORD, 1863–68, *Caxtoniana, Miscellaneous Prose Works, vol.* III, *p.* 162.

There is a healthy Gascon flavour in Montaigne's Essays; and Charles Lamb's are scented with the primroses of Covent Garden. — SMITH, ALEXANDER, 1863, *Dreamthorp, p.* 30.

Charles Lamb was no teacher of his time, and had no commanding or immediate influence on his contemporaries. He lifted up no banner, summoned no contending hosts to the conflict, did no battle on the side of faction or party, and was possessed of no vast intellectual powers. But this he *was*—one of the most affectionate, most lovable, most piquantly imperfect of dear, good fellows that ever won their way into the human heart, and one of the most hearty, most English, most curiously felicitous humourists—emphatically one of the *best* that ever lived. He has left us in his works a perennial source of refining pleasure, full of freshness and moral health, and kindly communicative warmth, over which countless readers will bend with smiling face or moistened eye; and the sad will feel a solace, the weary gather heart's-ease, the cold and narrow of nature may warm them and expand in the generous glow to be found in the writings of Charles Lamb.—MASSEY, GERALD, 1867, *Charles Lamb, Fraser's Magazine, vol.* 75, *p.* 672.

The most supremely competent judge and exquisite critic of lyrical and dramatic art that we have ever had.—SWINBURNE, ALGERNON CHARLES, 1868, *William Blake: a Critical Essay, p.* 8.

The restorer of the old drama.—TAINE, H. A., 1871, *History of English Literature, tr. Van Laun, vol.* II, *bk.* iv, *ch.* i, *p.* 250.

His humor was thoroughly original; his command of language, though peculiar, was perfect; an air of genuine good feeling pervaded every essay as unmistakably as his wit.—YONGE, CHARLES DUKE, 1872, *Three Centuries of English Literature, p.* 408.

With all Lamb's whims and oddities, the foundations of his being were serious and substantial.—MINTO, WILLIAM, 1872–80, *Manual of English Prose Literature, p.* 535.

He was not one of those voluminous writers of whom we possess such a goodly array of tomes, that we are content to let the waifs and strays take their chance and float whither they will. He was never, indeed, a professional writer. Tied down during the best years of his life to office-duties, and not reaching the age of three-score, the total sum of his writings, after every nook and cranny has been searched that could yield anything buried and forgotten, is still comprisable in less than eight hundred pages, though one or two little items are still unavoidably wanting.—SHEPHERD, RICHARD HERNE, 1874, *ed., The Complete Works in Prose and Verse of Charles Lamb, Introduction, p.* vii.

The exquisite literary faculty of Charles Lamb revelled in detecting beauties which had been covered with the dust of oblivion during the reign of Pope. His appreciation was intensified by that charm of discovery which finds its typical utterance in Keats's famous sonnet. He was scarcely a more impartial judge of Fletcher or Ford than "Stout Cortes" of the new world revealed by his enterprise. We may willingly defer to his judgment of the relative value of the writers whom he discusses, but we must qualify his judgment of their intrinsic excellence by the recollection that he speaks as a lover.—STEPHEN, LESLIE, 1874–78, *Hours in a Library, vol.* II, *p.* 142.

In the making of prose he realises the principle of art for its own sake, as completely as Keats in the making of verse. And, working ever close to the concrete, to the details, great or small, of actual things, books, persons, and with no part of them blurred to his vision by the intervention of mere abstract theories, he has reached an enduring moral effect also, in a sort of boundless sympathy. Unoccupied, as he might seem, with great matters, he is in immediate contact with what is real, especially in its caressing littleness, that littleness in which there is much of the whole woeful heart of things, and meets it more than half-way with a perfect understanding of it. What sudden, unexpected touches of pathos in him!—bearing witness how the sorrow of humanity, the *Welt-schmerz*, the constant aching of its wounds, is ever present with him; but what a gift also for the enjoyment of life in its subtleties, of enjoyment actually refined by the need of some thoughtful economies and making the most of things!—PATER, WALTER, 1878, *Appreciations.*

Poor Lamb has not a little to answer for, in the revived relish for garbage unearthed from old theatrical dung-heaps. Be it jest or earnest, I have little patience with the Elia-tic philosophy of the frivolous.—HARRISON, FREDERIC, 1879, *The Choice of Books and Other Literary Pieces, p.* 6.

How . . . the shyness of Lamb's nature,—his love of quip, and whimsey, and old black-letter authors,—peeps out in his style, with its antique words, and quaint convolutions, and doublings back on itself! Dean Swift would have torn to pieces a lamb like a wolf; but the loving "Elia" would have tried to coax a wolf into a lamb.—MATHEWS, WILLIAM, 1881, *Literary Style, p.* 21.

Let anyone who wants a true alterative or relief from Carlyle's grim and black-browed chuckle of almost brutal self-satisfaction in such self-revelation, take down Elia's essays, and read that on "Poor Relations" carefully to the end; and then thank Heaven for the beautiful, bountiful gift of true humorous geniality, and, what is yet higher and better, faith in human nature, which is, *pace* Carlyle, happily preserved to us in literature that he would dub cockney and treat with a malignant scowl; as if it were possible for a cockney to have a heart, or that it were always possible even for a great Scotchman to have a big one.—JAPP, ALEXANDER H., 1881, *Charles Lamb, The Gentleman's Magazine, vol.* 250, *p.* 711.

He is one of those writers whom we would not have changed in the least degree—whom, indeed, we cannot conceive of being changed. Had he been greater in certain directions than he was, he would have been, as a whole, less perfect. For instance, he was not possessed of very profound perceptions, but had he been a man of greater penetration than he was, his mind might have been marked by a difficulty and painful gravity from which he was altogether free; facility and lightness were essential parts of his character, as we now know him. Then Lamb had a mind that was very fully flowered out. There is nothing in his character to demand or to reward a painstaking inquiry. For this reason, perhaps, he is less attractive to the critic than many other less perfect and less distinguished characters. But most readers are not critics. They read for amusement, and not for the pleasure of investigation. To them, therefore, the fact that they can understand Lamb at a glance, and that he is almost as familiar to them as one of their own family, is the cause of their liking to read him.—ARBUCKLE, JOHN, 1881, *Charles and Mary Lamb, Scribner's Monthly, vol.* 21, *p.* 696.

He was the acutest as well as most tolerant of critics. Not even Coleridge, though covering larger ground in literature, has surpassed Lamb in his special department of poetical criticism. His comments on the English dramatic poets of the Elizabethan age are, indeed, unequalled in suggestiveness and masterly appreciation of character.—DENNIS, JOHN, 1882, *Charles Lamb and his Friends, Fraser's Magazine, vol.* 105, *p.* 612.

No true reader, wherever found, can fail to acknowledge the power of Elia. He is, in the best sense of the word, one who writes for writing's sake—not because he has much to tell us, but because it is a pleasure to him to make friends with us, to jest and sigh and trifle, to play some whimsical trick upon us, to transport us in a moment, all unwittingly, from laughter into weeping, to play upon all the strings of our hearts.—OLIPHANT, MARGARET O. W., 1882, *The Literary History of England, XVIII-XIX Century, vol.* II, *p.* 10.

Beloved beyond all names of English birth,
More dear than mightier memories! gentlest name
That ever clothed itself with flower sweet fame,
Or linked itself with loftiest names of old
By right and might of loving; I, that am
Less than the least of those within thy fold,
Give only thanks for them to thee, Charles Lamb.

—SWINBURNE, ALGERNON CHARLES, 1882, *On Lamb's Specimens of Dramatic Poets.*

It is in vain to attempt to convey an idea of the impression left by Lamb's style. It evades analysis. One might as well seek to account for the perfume of lavender, or the flavour of quince. It is in truth an essence, prepared from flowers and herbs gathered in fields where the ordinary reader does not often range. And the nature of the writer—the alembic in which these various simples were distilled—was as rare for sweetness and purity as the best of those enshrined in the old folios—his "midnight darlings." If he had by nature the delicate grace of Marvell, and the quaint fancy of Quarles, he also shared the chivalry of Sidney, and could lay on himself "the lowliest duties," in the spirit of his best-beloved of all, John Milton. It is the man, Charles Lamb, that constitutes the enduring charm of his written words. He is, as I have said, an egotist—but an egotist without a touch of vanity or self-assertion—an egotist without a grain of envy or ill-nature.—AINGER, ALFRED, 1882, *Charles Lamb (English Men of Letters), p.* 120.

In some respects, though in some only, Charles Lamb's humour anticipates the type of humour which we now call, in the main, American. When, for instance, he gravely narrated the origin of the Chinese invention of roast pig, in the burning down of a house,—when he told a friend that he had moved just forty-two inches nearer his beloved London,—and again, when he wrote to Manning in China that the new Persian Ambassador was called "Shaw Ali Mirza," but that the common people called him "Shaw Nonsense," we might think we were listening to Artemus Ward's or Mark Twain's minute and serious nonsense. But for the most part, Charles Lamb's humour is more frolicsome, more whimsical, and less subdued in its extravagance; more like the gambolling of a mind which did not care to conceal its enjoyment of paradox, and less like the inward invisible laughter in which the Yankees most delight.—HUTTON, RICHARD HOLT, 1882–94, *Criticisms on Contemporary Thought and Thinkers, vol.* I, *p.* 105.

Americans take a peculiar delight in the humor of Charles Lamb, for he is one of the foremost of American humorists. On the roll which is headed by Benjamin Franklin, and on which the latest signatures were made by "Mark Twain" and Mr. Bret Harte, no name shines more brightly than Lamb's. It may be objected by the captious that he was not an American at all; but surely this should not be remembered to his discredit: it was a mere accident of birth. Elia could have taken out his naturalization-papers at any time. . . . He was an Englishman,—nay, more, a Cockney,—indeed, a Cockney of the strictest sect; but he had parts not unworthy of American adoption. He had humour, high and dry, like that which England is won't to import from America in the original package.—MATTHEWS, BRANDER, 1883, *Charles Lamb's Dramatic Attempts, Lippincott's Magazine, vol.* 31, *p.* 493.

With a wit that was almost unrivalled, he had the indigenous faculties of courtesy, generosity, humanity, and benignity. Scarcely any modern essayist so feeds and fertilizes the mind as Charles Lamb; for he was endowed with that inexplicable power called charm, which holds the reader like a spell. He makes us love him, as we turn his pages, as few authors are ever enabled to do.—FIELDS, JAMES T., 1885, *Charles Lamb, Some Noted Princes, Authors and Statesmen of Our Time, ed. Parton, p.* 146.

It detracts nothing from the unique charm of "Elia," and it will be most clearly recognised by those who know "Elia" best, that Lamb constantly borrows from Browne, that the mould and shape of his most characteristic phrases is frequently suggested directly by Sir Thomas, and that though there seldom can have been a follower who put more of his own in his following, it may be pronounced with confidence, "no Browne, no Lamb," at least in the forms in which we know the author of "Elia" best, and in which all those who know him best, though they may love him always, love him most.—SAINTSBURY, GEORGE, 1887, *History of Elizabethan Literature*, p. 339.

He is and will forever be more than a mere author to those that know him. He is a presence, a presiding genius; he goes in and out with you, haunts you in the kindest, gentlest way.—JESSOPP, AUGUSTUS, 1887, *Books that have Helped Me, The Forum, vol.* 4, *p.* 33.

What I felt most keenly was the intellectual starvation I suffered in the strenuous pioneer life of Minnesota in 1856. About this time there came along a man who conducted the book business on a plan I have never heard of since. He carried the priced catalogue of Derby & Jackson, and took orders for any book on the list. I bought in this way a copy of Charles Lamb's Works. It was my only book in a land where books were not, and it was no end of advantage to me. I was, just at this period of my life, deeply interested in settling the six days of creation; for in that time, when Darwin and evolution were yet below the horizon, our chief bother was to get the stratified rocks correctly created according to Moses. I had read Hugh Miller with eagerness, and had even followed the wire-drawn speculations in Hitchcock's "Religion of Geology." To a youth who has assumed such cosmical tasks Lamb could not but be wholesome. His delicious and whimsical humor is a great prophylactic against priggery. I cleave still to my stout one-volume copy of Lamb. There are many better editions, but none so good for me as this, with its margins covered by pencil notes, humiliating enough now, for they reveal the crudities, prejudices, immaturities of the young man who wrote them.—EGGLESTON, EDWARD, 1888, *Books that have Helped Me*, p. 54.

The most striking note of Lamb's literary criticism is its veracity. He is perhaps never mistaken. His judgments are apt to be somewhat too much coloured with his own idiosyncrasy to be what the judicious persons of the period call final and classical, but when did he ever go utterly wrong either in praise or in dispraise?—BIRRELL, AUGUSTINE, 1892, *Res Judicatæ, p.* 249.

It is not easy to discuss that love for books, which in some men is indeed wonderful, passing the love of women, without quoting Charles Lamb. For he is of all later classics the ideal book-lover; one who adores not only their mental but their physical beauty: no mere æsthetic admirer, content to "worship from afar with distant reverence;" but one who must fondle his treasures.—WHITE, GLEESON, 1893, *ed., Book-Song, p.* vii.

In accents sublime,
In sweetness of diction that touches our hearts,
In mirth, which a flavor of sadness imparts,
In a jest, or a pun, or a sharp epigram,
There is none like our dear, witty, charming Charles Lamb.

—EVANS, M. A. B., 1893, *In Various Moods, p.* 40.

Lamb's use of the short sentence was incomparably freer, and as Mr. Pater might have said, "blither" than that of any of his predecessors. In sentence-length, indeed, he exhibits all the variability of insanity. . . . In spite of now and then a long but harmless parenthesis, Lamb knew the value of the paragraph structure—knew it better than Coleridge did, or DeQuincey. Hardly one of his shorter sections but is an artistic whole. The order is loose. The mass is often perfect—the topic striking the eye instantly, and the paragraph ending with words that deserves emphasis. . . . The fact is that Lamb's style, on any subject Lamb would have been willing to touch, would be easier to follow than Coleridge's, no matter how far afield the whimsical Elia might wander. For there are no long intervals between Lamb's propositions, no involved restrictions of those propositions, no necessity of supplying anything except a few obvious verbs and the sense of a few freakish vocables. —LEWIS, EDWIN HERBERT, 1894, *The History of the English Paragraph, pp.* 132, 133.

I love Charles Lamb and his writings so much, that I think everybody else ought to love them. There is not great weight in those essays of his; you cannot learn from them what the capital of Hindostan is, or what Buddhism is, nor the date of the capture of Constantinople. Measured by the Dry-as-Dust standard, and there is scarce more in them than in a field of daisies, over which the sunshine and the summer breezes are at play. But what delicacy there is! What a tender humor; what gentle and regaling lapses of quaint thought that beguiles and invites and is soothing and never wearies.—MITCHELL, DONALD G., 1895, *English Lands Letters and Kings, Queen Anne and the Georges, p.* 319.

His most original work was the "Essays of Elia," in which he renewed the lost grace of the Essay, and with a humour not less gentle, more surprising, more self-pleased than Addison's.—BROOKE, STOPFORD A., 1896, *English Literature, p.* 208.

With Charles Lamb we have a quaintness of archaism which loses all trace of artificiality only by the magic touch of genius.—CRAIK, HENRY, 1896, *English Prose, Introduction, vol.* V, *p.* 5.

Lamb can scarcely be classed along with any other essayist; the archness and piquancy of his humour, if they sometimes remind one of Sterne, had for the most part an ancestry older than Addison and Steele, and it is only by going back to the writers of the seventeenth century that one fully detects the atavism of his style. . . . The obliquity of Lamb's genius precluded in his own day, as it still precludes, the possibility of successful imitation; he created no new school of essayists, and he left no abiding mark on the development of English prose; but he is within certain well-defined limits one of the most artistic exponents of the essay, and the power of fully appreciating the delicacy of his work is one of the surest indications of a literary epicure.—LOBBAN, J. H., 1896, *English Essays, Introduction, p.* lix.

A still better critic than either Cowper or Landor, the sure-footed Charles Lamb, who in his innumerable appreciations of writers both in verse and prose, hardly ever makes a false step, save from some affectionate bias of the heart, hardly ever pronounces a judgment that has not been cordially endorsed by posterity.—BENSON, ARTHUR CHRISTOPHER, 1896, *Essays, p.* 97.

He had a poetry of his own, wholly distinct from that of either of his friends, though allied to both; the poetry of great cities, which Wordsworth did not know, the poetry of the local, from which Coleridge's "thirst for the absolute" perpetually estranged him. In spiritual beauty of character neither they nor any other, save Shelley, of his greater contemporaries approached him. The tragic horror of fear and memory which underlay his life, and the exquisite wit and humour which irradiated its surface, were his alone. . . . Imagination of a more ethereal kind, as in Shelley, or of a grosser and more concrete kind, as in Scott, or of the remote and mythological kind as in Southey, attracted him little. His own imagination glances off, as it were, upon the edge of humour, and becomes a glittering spray of freaks and sallies. He has, from first to last, a boyish delight in play. His overflowing charity was materially helped by his gift for constructing comedy out of the meanest stuff of human nature. In the beggar who cheated him he saw a comedian playing a part, and joyously paid his money for the performance; he was peculiarly ready to believe in the art which plays with the elements of life—which creates a fantastic world of its own—like humanity, but detached from the conditions of human beings.—HERFORD, C. H., 1897, *The Age of Wordsworth, pp.* 59, 68.

Whose humour delighted in floating a galleon paradox and wafting it as far as it would go.—MEREDITH, GEORGE, 1897, *An Essay on Comedy and the Uses of the Comic Spirit, p.* 11.

Elia is a name of the imagination; but it was borne by an old acquaintance, an Italian who was a fellow-clerk at the South-Sea House when Lamb was a boy there, thirty years before he sat down to write these Essays; and, as a piece of pleasantry, he borrowed his friend's true face to mask his own. He went, he tells us, to see the Elia of flesh and blood, and laugh over the liberty he had taken, but found the Italian dead; and the incident—the playfulness of the odd plagiarism ending unexpectedly in a solemn moment, a pathetic close—is so in character with the moods of these pages, that even their maker could not have invented better what life gave into his hands. The name had devolved upon him now, he said; he had, as it were, unknowingly adopted a shade, and it was to go about with him thenceforth, and watch at his grave after he too should depart. For two years he used the ruse of this ghost of a name, but the uncanniness of it was his own secret; to the reader of the *London Magazine*, in which he published, Elia was—what it is to us—a name of the eternal humorist in life's various crowd.—WOODBERRY, GEORGE EDWARD, 1900, *Makers of Literature, p.* 109.

Edward Irving

1792-1834.

Born at Annan, August 4, 1792, at thirteen entered Edinburgh University, and in 1810 became a schoolmaster at Haddington, in 1812 at Kirkcaldy. Here three years later he was licensed to preach, and in 1819 he was appointed assistant to Dr. Chalmers in Glasgow. In 1822 he was called to the Caledonian Church, Hatton Garden, London; his success as a preacher there was such as had never been known. In 1825 he began to announce his convictions in regard to the imminent second advent of Christ; this was followed up by the translation of "The Coming of the Messiah" (1827), professedly written by a Christian Jew, but really by a Spanish Jesuit. By 1828, when his "Homilies on the Sacraments" appeared, he had begun to elaborate his views of the Incarnation, asserting Christ's oneness with us all in the attributes of humanity; and he was charged with heresy as maintaining the sinfulness of Christ's nature. He was now deep in the prophecies, and when in the beginning of 1830 he heard of extraordinary manifestations of prophetic power in Dumbartonshire, he believed them. He was arraigned before the presbytery of London in 1830 and convicted of heresy, ejected from his new church in Regent's Square in 1832, and finally deposed in 1833 by the presbytery of Annan, which had licensed him. The majority of his congregation adhered to him, and a new communion, the Catholic Apostolic, was developed, commonly known as Irvingite, though Irving had little to do with its development. Shortly after his health failed, and he went down to Glasgow, where he died of consumption, December 8, 1834. He is buried in the crypt of the cathedral. See Life by Mrs. Oliphant (1862) and Carlyle's "Essays" and "Reminiscences."—PATRICK AND GROOME, *eds.*, 1897, *Chambers's Biographical Dictionary, p.* 521.

PERSONAL

I spent Sunday at Glasgow, and I believe saw everything very remarkable. . . . Unluckily Dr. Chalmers was out of town, a circumstance which I did not learn till the afternoon, and attended his church both services in hopes of hearing him. In the morning I heard a very heavy piece of Presbyterian divinity, which I had hardly time to digest in the interval. I was, however, highly gratified in the afternoon by Dr. Chalmers's coadjutor (a Mr. Irving, I think), who is one of the very small number of powerful and original thinkers I have heard from the pulpit, and whom I should be willing constantly to attend.—THIRLWALL, CONNOP, 1821, *To John Thirlwall, Aug.* 15; *Letters Literary and Theological, ed. Perowne and Stokes, p.* 58.

You have doubtless heard of the prevailing *fashion* of resorting to the conventicle to hear Dr. Chalmers's late assistant, Mr. Irving. It is not merely the opposition members of both Houses, Lord Lansdown, Mackintosh, &c., that attend him; their political nonconformity might be supposed to endear to them his ecclesiastical dissent: but the orthodox Lord Liverpool, the vindicator of existing institutions Mr. Canning, press into his meeting-house; and even with tickets you must be at the door an hour before the service commences, if you wish to get in without losing one of your coat pockets by mere mobbing.—WILBERFORCE, WILLIAM, 1823, *Letters to Hannah More, July* 14; *Life by Sons, vol.* v, *p.* 188.

I have got acquainted with Mr. Irving the Scotch preacher, whose fame must have reached you. He is an humble disciple at the foot of Gamaliel S. T. C. Judge how his own sectaries must stare, when I tell you he has dedicated a book to S. T. C., acknowledging to have learnt more of the nature of faith, Christianity, and Christian Church, from him than from all the men he ever conversed with! He is a most amiable, sincere, modest man in a room, this Boanerges in the temple. Mrs. Montague told him the dedication would do him no good. "That shall be a reason for doing it," was his answer. Judge, now, whether this man be a quack.—LAMB, CHARLES, 1824, *To Leigh Hunt, Letters, ed. Ainger, vol.* II, *p.* 121.

I must not forget to tell you of an exploit of mine, which I think I should not have undertaken unless I had been prompted by my son. I was going last Saturday, *at six in the morning*, to hear the celebrated Mr Edward Irving. He preached at seven in Sir Harry Moncrieff's church, which suited him from its great size, and me from its proximity. It was necessary to take possession of a seat an hour before the service began; my son went with me, and we were accommodated with a seat within good seeing and hearing distance, for seeing is indispensable. I should tell you that the sensation created by this setter forth of new doctrines in the new Athens reminds one of a more authentic preacher's influence in the old. I heard nothing that raised him above the place he formerly held in my opinion; but, in justice, I must add that the prophet is less affected and theatrical than I expected; that he has a very pleasing and well-modulated voice; and that his action is not unsuited to his doctrine, which he evidently supposes to be authorised by inspiration. Of his discourse, I will only say at present that it has little coherence, a great deal of verbiage, and no indication, that I can discover, of high imagination or sound reasoning.—GRANT, ANNE, 1828, *Letter, June* 4; *Memoir and Correspondence, ed. Grant, vol.* III, *p.* 119.

I met to-day the celebrated divine and *soi-disant* prophet, Irving. He is a fine-looking man (bating a diabolical squint) with talent on his brow and madness in his eye. His dress, and the arrangement of his hair, indicated that. I could hardly keep my eyes off of him while we were at table. He put me in mind of the devil disguised as an angel of light, so ill did that horrible obliquity of vision harmonize with the dark tranquil features of his face, resembling that of our Saviour in Italian pictures, with the hair carefully arranged in the same manner. There was much real or affected simplicity in the manner in which he spoke. He rather *made play*, spoke much, and seemed to be good-humoured. But he spoke with that kind of unction which is nearly allied to *cajolerie.*—SCOTT, SIR WALTER, 1829, *Journal, Aug; Life by Lockhart, ch.* lxxvii.

Irving caught many things from me; but he would never attend to anything which he thought he could not use in the pulpit. I told him the certain consequence would be, that he would fall into grievous errors. Sometimes he has five or six pages together of the purest eloquence, and then an outbreak of almost madman's babble.—COLERIDGE, SAMUEL TAYLOR, 1830, *Table Talk, ed. Ashe, May* 15, *p.* 76.

You will have heard of the death of Irving. You cannot enter into my feelings on this event, as you did not know him or regard him as I did. He has been a remarkable man in a remarkable age. He was a man of much child-like feeling to God, and personal dependence on Him, amidst things which may well appear unintelligible and strange in his history.—ERSKINE, THOMAS, 1834, *To Miss Stuart, Dec.* 13; *Letters, ed. Hanna, p.* 165.

He was one of those whom Burns calls the nobles of nature. His talents were so commanding, that you could not but admire him; and he was so open and generous, that it was impossible not to love him. He was an evangelical Christian grafted on the old Roman—with the lofty stern virtues of the one, he possessed the humble graces of the other. The constitutional basis and ground-work of his character was virtue alone; and, notwithstanding all his errors and extravagances, which both injured his character in the estimation of the world, and threw discredit upon much that was good and useful in his writings, I believe him to be a man of deep and devoted piety.—CHALMERS, THOMAS, 1834, *Remarks before the Senior Class at Glasgow.*

Dr. Rainy, who attended him, informed me of various particulars in these days; but, indeed, so touched with tears, after nearly thirty years' interval, was even the physician's voice, and so vivid the presentment of that noble, wasted figure, stretched in utter weakness, but utter faith, waiting for the moment when God, out of visible dying, should bring life and strength, that I can not venture to record with any distinctness those heart-breaking details. . . . As the gloomy December Sunday sank into the night shadows, his last audible words on earth fell from his pale lips. "The last thing like a sentence we could make out was, 'If I die, I die unto the Lord. Amen.'" And so, at the wintry midnight hour which ended that last Sabbath on earth, the last bonds of mortal trouble dropped asunder, and the saint and martyr entered into the rest of his Lord. . . . He was laid in his grave in the December of 1834—a life time since; but scarce any man who knew him can yet name, without a softened voice and a dimmed eye, the name of Edward Irving — true friend and tender heart—martyr and saint.—OLIPHANT, MARGARET O. W., 1862, *The Life of Edward Irving, pp.* 557, 559, 560.

We ourselves saw less and less of Irving; but one night, in one of our walks, we did make a call; and actually heard what they called the Tongues. It was in a neighbouring room, larger part of the drawing room belike. Mrs. Irving had retired thither with the devotees; Irving for our sake had staid, and was pacing about the floor, dandling his youngest child, and talking to us of this and that, probably about the Tongues withal,—when there burst forth a shrieky hysterical "Lall-lall-lall!" (little or nothing else but *l*'s and *a*'s continued for several minutes); to which Irving, with singular calmness, said only, "There, hear you; there are the Tongues!" and we two, except by our looks which probably were eloquent, answered him nothing; but soon came away, full of distress, provocation and a kind of shame. "Why wasn't there a bucket of cold water to fling on that *lall-lalling* hysterical mad-woman?" thought we, or said, to one another: "Oh Heavens, that it should come to this!"—I do not remember any call we made there afterwards; of course there was a Farewell call; but that too I recollect only obliquely. . . . Seldom was seen a more tragical scene to us, than this of Irving's London life was now becoming! — CARLYLE, THOMAS, 1866, *Edward Irving, Reminiscences, ed. Norton, vol.* II, *p.* 205.

Few of the present generation think of the Rev. Edward Irving except, perhaps, as a superstitious enthusiast; yet, with all his eccentricities, he was a man eminently worth knowing and listening to. . . . The personal appearance of the speaker at once arrested my attention. Over six feet high, limbs and body finely proportioned, the ample forehead surmounted by a mass of jet-black hair, parted in the centre and dropping in curls on his shoulders: the features regular and expressive, especially the piercing dark eyes (their effect somewhat marred, however, by a squint); a stately bearing, and a majestic style of eloquence, such as might befit an apostle, conscious of a mission from on high; gestures sometimes, indeed, *outré*, even fantastic, yet often startlingly emphatic,—everything about him was strange, strong, telling. The man himself and his weird aspect at first engrossed one's thoughts; yet when he fairly warmed to his subject, and the stirring tones of a voice at once persuasive and commanding gradually asserted their magnetic power, one forgot the speaker and all his peculiarities, listening, not to the words, but to the thoughts, fiery and earnest,—thoughts, one instinctively felt, that had their origin down in the depths of conscientious conviction.—OWEN, ROBERT DALE, 1874, *Threading My Way, p.* 337.

I never heard him utter a harsh or uncharitable word. I never heard from him a word or sentiment which a good man could have wished unsaid. His words were at once gentle and heroic. . . . He loved to dwell on great and good men, and on noble actions His memory could not apparently retain anything that was mean.—PROCTER, BRYAN WALLER, 1874? *Recollections of Men of Letters, pp.* 158, 159.

The rumor of his burning eloquence and marked peculiarities had preceded him to London; crowds, on his appearance in the Metropolis in 1822, flocked to hear him preach; and finding that the Scottish clergyman was indeed something strange and startling, came again, and in ever-increasing numbers. Irving drew for a while the attention of men of all faiths—or of none; but it was as a meteor that shoots across the heavens, and then is quenched in darkest night. Soon there came a time when the enthusiasm, bordering on extravagance, of the preacher provoked yet more extravagant responses from a devoted few of his hearers; when to the Scottish Kirk Irving became a stumbling-block, and to the polite world of London foolishness. The former cast him out; the latter sneered at him, ceasing to throng and hear a preacher whom some called a hypocrite and others a madman, and whose peculiar eloquence had no longer the attraction of novelty. A brief season of mockery and persecution, and the sensitive nature of the man gave way. The disease that Edward Irving died of was, practically, a broken heart. . . . At the time to which I refer, Irving was in the prime of manhood and of striking presence: tall, slender, but by no means attenuated, with strongly marked features of the Roman type, and a profusion of long, black, wavy hair that hung partly over his shoulders. On looking closely into his face, you saw how grievously its expression was marred by an obliquity of vision, amounting in fact to a decided "squint." It is said to have been in only one of his eyes; but its effect was fatal to the claim that might otherwise have been advanced in his behalf of possessing an awe-inspiring mien, a countenance such as one might indeed associate in fancy with a Boanerges.—HALL, SAMUEL CARTER, 1883, *Retrospect of a Long Life, pp.* 311, 312.

Her letters [Mrs. Carlyle] show that her feelings for Irving, first controlled by principle and honour, soon underwent a very natural change. Her love for him was the passion of an ardent and inexperienced girl, twenty or twenty-one years old, whose character was undeveloped, and who had but an imperfect understanding of the capacities and demands of her own nature. In the years that followed upon this incident she made rapid progress in self-knowledge and in the knowledge of others, chiefly through Carlyle's influence, and she came to a more just estimate of Irving's character than she originally had formed. Irving's letters to her, his career in London, his published writings, revealed to her clear discernment his essential weakness,—his vanity, his mawkish sentimentality, his self-deception, his extravagance verging to cant in matters of religion. The contrast between his nature and Carlyle's did "affect her profoundly," and her temporary passion for Irving was succeeded by a far deeper and healthier love.—NORTON, CHARLES ELIOT, 1886, *Early Letters of Thomas Carlyle, Appendix, p.* 356.

Edward Irving had, as we have seen, left Kirkcaldy an engaged man, pledged to Miss Isabella Martin, who afterwards became his wife. Yet was there an unsatisfied longing in his heart also, for the image of the bright, eager face of Jeannie Welsh, his former pupil, haunted his mind and thoughts, and refused to be banished. Parting from her while she was still almost a child, he had yet had opportunities of seeing her while she ripened into her lovely womanhood, and he had learned to know his own heart, whose deep strong love was, alas! given to her, and not by any means to be taken away and bestowed on Miss Martin, or any other woman. Irving knew it, blinded himself to it, perhaps, in a measure, and at one time desperately hoped against hope. But the days of hope were over before 1821, and he knew he was only looking at the roses in another man's garden.—IRELAND, ANNIE E., 1891, *The Life of Jane Welsh Carlyle, p.* 27.

GENERAL

Irving's book is come three days ago. Mrs. Buller bought it. I fear it will hardly do. There is a fierce and very spiteful review of it and him in the last "Blackwood." There is strong talent in it, true eloquence and vigorous thought, but the foundation is rotten, and the building itself a kind of monster in architecture, beautiful in parts, vast in dimensions, but on the whole decidedly a monster. Buller has stuck in the middle of it, "Can't fall in with your friend at all, Mr. C." Mrs. Buller is very near sticking; sometimes I burst right out laughing when reading it. At other times I admired it sincerely.—CARLYLE, THOMAS, 1823, *Letter to John Carlyle, Early Life by Froude, vol.* I, *p.* 151.

Take the volume of "Sermons on Astronomy," by Dr. Chalmers, and the "Four Orations for the Oracles of God" which Mr. Irving lately published, and we apprehend there can be no comparison as to their success. The first ran like wild-fire through the country, were the darlings of watering-places, were laid in the windows of inns, and were to be met with in all places of public resort; while the "Orations" get on but slowly, on Milton's stilts, and are pompously announced as in a Third Edition. We believe the fairest and fondest of his admirers would rather see and hear Mr. Irving than read him. The reason is, that the ground-work of his compositions is trashy and hackneyed, though set off by extravagant metaphors and an affected phraseology; that without the turn of his head and wave of his hand, his periods have nothing in them; and that he himself is the only *idea* with which he has yet enriched the public mind! He must play off his person, as Orator Henley used to dazzle his hearers with his diamond-ring.—HAZLITT, WILLIAM, 1825. *The Spirit of the Age*, p. 58.

We mean not to deny that some of Irving's productions are worthy, not only of his floating reputation, but of that gift in him which was never fully developed, or at least never completely displayed. In all his writings you see a man of the present wearing the armor of the past; but it is a proof of his power, that, although he wears it awkardly, he never sinks under the load. It is not a David clad in a Goliath's arms, and overwhelmed by them; it is the shepherd-giant, Eliab, David's brother, not yet at home in a panoply which is not too large for his limbs, but for wearing which a peaceful profession and period had not prepared him. Irving, in native power, was only, we think, a little lower than the men of the Elizabethan period, and of the next two reigns. He was originally of a similar order of genius, but he had given that genius a less severe and laborious culture, and he had fallen upon an age adverse for its display. Hence, even his best writings, when compared to theirs, have a certain stiff, imitative, and convulsive air. There is nothing false in any of them, but there is something *forced* in most. You feel always how much better Irving's noble, generous thoughts would have looked, had he expressed them in the language of his own day. Burke had as big a heart, a far subtler intellect, and richer imagination than Irving, and yet how few innovations, and fewer archaisms, has he ventured to introduce into his style.—GILFILLAN, GEORGE, 1855, *A Third Gallery of Portraits*, p. 62.

Irving's sermons were for a time one of the wonders of London; when read they perhaps hardly sustain their reputation, yet they are noteworthy among the comparatively few really remarkable examples of recent English homiletics.—SAINTSBURY, GEORGE, 1886, *Specimens of English Prose Style*, p. 347.

Had Irving set himself with anything like the devotion of Chalmers to the "excavation" of the heathen in some district of London, instead of curiously prying into the unfulfilled prophecies of the future, there might have been no tongues, but there would have been more good effected, and the Church might not have had to mourn over the aberration of one of her noblest sons. It is the aggressiveness of the Church that is to keep it orthodox, and whenever schemes of prophetic fulfillment, or indeed speculations of any sort, take the place of efforts for the evangelization of the unconverted, we may look out for the uprising of some form of Irvingism.—TAYLOR, WILLIAM M., 1887, *The Scottish Pulpit*, p. 213.

His works in theology, if they can be so called, Sermons and Addresses, are in most cases poems of passionate fervour with an antique touch as if of the Prophets and Seers.—OLIPHANT, MARGARET O. W., 1892, *The Victorian Age of English Literature*, p. 332.

His "Orations" (1823) at times come as near to the rolling majesty of Milton's impassioned prose as rhetoric that rarely rings quite true well can. But the intellectual substance is of a meagerness which ill corresponds to its sumptuous clothing. He was rather a visionary than a prophet. His imagination did not so much interpret life as envelope it in a cloudy effulgence; and unable to read, like the author of "Sartor" the "eternal miracle of creation," flung the glory of miracle over imposture and delusion.—HERFORD, C. H., 1897, *The Age of Wordsworth*, p. 33.

Thomas Robert Malthus

1765-1834

Born, near Guildford, 17 Feb. 1766. Educated privately. To Jesus Coll., Camb., as Pensioner, 8 June 1784; B. A., 1788; M. A., 1791; Fellow, 10 June 1793 to March 1804. Ordained Curate of Albury, Surrey, 1795 [?]. Travelled in Northern Europe, 1799; in France and Switzerland, 1802. Married Harriet Eckersall, 13 March 1804. Prof. of Hist. and Polit. Econ. at Haileybury Coll., 1805; lived there till his death. Visit to Ireland, 1817. F. R. S., 1819. Associate of Royal Soc. of Literature, 1824. Travelled on Continent, 1825. Foreign Associate of Académie des

Sciences morales et politiques, 1833. Mem. of Royal Acad. of Berlin, 1833. Mem. of Statistical Soc., 1834. Mem. of French Institute. Died, suddenly, at St. Catherine's, near Bath, 23 Dec. 1834. Buried in Bath Abbey Church. *Works:* "Essay on the Principle of Population" (anon.), 1798; "An Investigation of the cause of the present High Price of Provisions" (anon.), 1800 (2nd edn. same year); "Letter to Samuel Whitbread, Esq., M. P.," 1807; "Letter to . . . Lord Granville," 1813; "Observations on the Effects of the Corn Laws," 1814 (2nd edn. same year); "Grounds of an Opinion on the Policy of Restricting the Importation of Foreign Corn," 1815; "An Inquiry into the Nature and Progress of Rent," 1815; "Statements respecting the East India College," 1817; "Principles of Political Economy," 1820; "The Measure of Value," 1823; "On the Measure of the Conditions necessary to the supply of Commodities," 1825; "On the meaning . . . attached to the term Value of Commodities," 1827; "Definitions in Political Economy," 1827; "Summary View of the Principle of Population," 1830. *Life:* "Malthus and his Work," by J. Bonar, 1885.—SHARP, R. FARQUHARSON, 1897, *A Dictionary of English Authors, p.* 184.

PERSONAL

By-the-by that fellow has the impudence to marry, after writing upon the miseries of population.—SOUTHEY, ROBERT, 1804, *Letter to Coleridge, June* 11; *Life and Correspondence, ed. C. C. Southey, ch.* v.

Since you left us, Malthus has been a day or two in town; and gave me a little of his society, enough to enable me to judge of him; and I am happy to say, that a more philosophic candour, calm love of truth, and ingenious turn for speculation in his important branch, I have seldom met with. It is quite delightful to find, how closely he has taught himself to examine the circumstances of the lower classes of society, and what a scientific turn he gives the subject. There is a new speculation of his, about the importance of the people being fed dear, which I wish you were here to discuss; it has the look of a paradox, and, like most of his views, is revolting to the common belief; but I have not yet detected the fallacy, if there is one.—HORNER, FRANCIS, 1807, *To Lord Webb Seymour, July* 6; *Memoirs and Correspondence, vol.* I, *p.* 433.

Malthus is, what anybody might anticipate, a plain man, with plain manners, apparently troubled by few prejudices, and not much by the irritability of authorship, but still talking occasionally with earnestness. In general, however, I thought he needed opposition, but he rose to the occasion, whatever it might be.—TICKNOR, GEORGE, 1819, *Journal, April; Life, Letters and Journals, vol.* I, *p.* 290.

Philosopher Malthus came here last week. I got an agreeable party for him of unmarried people. There was only one lady who had had a child; but he is a good-natured man, and, if there are no appearance of approaching fertility, is civil to every lady. Malthus is a real moral philosopher, and I would almost consent to speak as inarticulately, if I could think and act as wisely.—SMITH, SYDNEY, 1831, *To Lady Holland, July; Letters, ed. Mrs. Austin, p.* 73.

Of all the people in the world, Malthus was the one whom I heard quite easily without it [trumpet];—Malthus, whose speech was hopelessly imperfect, from defect in the palate. . . . I could not decline such an invitation as this: but when I considered my own deafness, and his inability to pronounce half the consonants in the alphabet, and his hare-lip which must prevent my offering him my tube, I feared we should make a terrible business of it. I was delightfully wrong. His first sentence,—slow and gentle, with the vowels sonorous, whatever might become of the consonants,—set me at ease completely. I soon found that the vowels are in fact all that I ever hear. His worst letter was *l:* and when I had no difficulty with his question,—"Would not you like to have a look at the Lakes of Killarney?" I had nothing more to fear. It really gratified him that I heard him better than any body else; and whenever we met at dinner, I somehow found myself beside him, with my best ear next him; and then I heard all he said to every body at table.—MARTINEAU, HARRIET, 1855–77, *Autobiography.*

The personal aspect of Malthus, to those who had known him only through the "Essay on Population" (a book however more railed at than read), generally excited some surprise. With genial, even gentle expression of features, he had a tremulous stammering voice, seemingly little fitted for the utterance of any doctrine which could be deemed dangerous to social welfare.—HOLLAND, SIR HENRY, 1871, *Recollections of Past Life, p.* 241.

There is nothing in Mr. Malthus's life which is worth mentioning, or which illustrated his doctrines. He was an estimable gentleman and clerical professor; "a mild pottering person," I think, Carlyle would have called him. Neither his occupation nor his turn of mind particularly fitted him to write on money matters: he was not a man of business, nor had he, like Paley and similar clergymen, a hard-headed liking for and an innate insight into the theory of business. He was a sensible man educated in the midst of illusions; he felt a reaction against them, and devoted the vigor of his youth to disprove and dispel them: and he made many sensible and acute remarks on kindred topics. But he has been among the luckiest of authors, for he has connected his name with the foundation of a lasting science which he did not plan and would by no means have agreed in.—BAGEHOT, WALTER, 1876? *Malthus, Works, ed. Morgan, vol.* V, *p.* 400.

Malthus was the student, of quiet settled life, sharing his domestic happiness with his friends in unobtrusive hospitality, and constantly using his pen for the good, as he believed, of the English poor, that in these wretched times they might have a family life as happy as his own. There never was a more curious delusion than the traditional belief in the hard-heartedness of Malthus. Besides the unamimous voice of private friends, he has left testimony enough in his own books to absolve him. While Adam Smith and others owe their errors to mere intellectual fallibility, Malthus actually owes most of his to his tender heart. His motive for studying political economy was no doubt a mixed motive; it was partly the interest of an intelligent man in abstract questions. But it was chiefly the desire to advance the greatest happiness of the greatest number. In his eyes the elevation of human life was much more important than the solution of a scientific problem.—BONAR, JAMES, 1881, *Parson Malthus, p.* 55.

At all events, though Malthus still remains "the best abused man of the age," it is pleasant to remember that he told Miss Martineau that except for the first fortnight after the publication of the essay, during which time he was somewhat grieved at the general misunderstanding, he remained wholly undisturbed by all the railings of his adversaries. It is pleasant to remember this, because Malthus was among the best of men.—MEANS, D. McG., 1885, *The Nation, vol.* 41, *p.* 345.

ESSAY ON THE PRINCIPLE OF POPULATION
1798–1803–1817

"Go, my son,"—said a Swedish chancellor to his son,—"go and see with how little cost of wisdom this world is governed." "Go," might a scholar in like manner say after a thoughtful review of literature, "go and see how little logic is required to the composition of most books." Of the many attestations to this fact, furnished by the history of opinions in our hasty and unmeditative age, I know of none more striking than the case of Mr. Malthus, both as regards himself and his critics. About a quarter of a century ago Mr. Malthus wrote his "Essay on Population," which soon rose into great reputation. And why? Not for the truth it contained; *that* is but imperfectly understood even at present; but for the false semblance of systematic form with which he had invested the truth. Without any necessity he placed his whole doctrine on the following basis: man increases in a geometrical ratio—the food of man in an arithmetical ratio.—DE QUINCEY, THOMAS, 1823, *Malthus on Population, Works, ed. Masson, vol.* IX, *p.* 11.

There is this to be said for Mr. Malthus, that in speaking of him, one knows what one is talking about. He is something beyond a mere name—one has not to *beat the bush* about his talents, his attainments, his vast reputation, and leave off without knowing what it all amounts to—he is not one of those great men, who set themselves off and strut and fret an hour upon the stage, during a day-dream of popularity, with the ornaments and jewels borrowed from the common stock, to which nothing but their vanity and presumption gives them the least individual claim, he has dug into the mine of truth, and brought up ore mixed with dross! In weighing his merits we come at once to the question of what he has done or failed to do. It is a specific claim that he sets up. When we speak of Mr. Malthus, we mean the "Essay on Population;" and when we mention the Essay on Population, we mean a distinct leading proposition, that stands out intelligibly from all trashy pretence, and is a ground on which to fix the levers that may move the world, backwards or forwards. He has not left opinion where he found it; he has advanced or given it a wrong bias, or thrown a stumbling-block in its way.—HAZLITT, WILLIAM, 1825, *The Spirit of the Age, p.* 149.

Into the Hofrath's *Institute*, with its extraordinary schemes, and machinery of Corresponding Boards and the like, we shall not so much as glance. Enough for us to understand that Heuschrecke is a disciple of Malthus; and so zealous for the doctrine, that his zeal almost literally eats him up. A deadly fear of Population possesses the Hofrath; something like a fixed-idea; undoubtedly akin to the more diluted forms of Madness. Nowhere, in that quarter of his intellectual world, is there light; nothing but a grim shadow of Hunger; open mouths opening wider and wider; a world to terminate by the frightfullest consummation: by its too dense inhabitants, famished into delirium, universally eating one another. To make air for himself in which strangulation, choking enough to a benevolent heart, the Hofrath founds, or proposes to found, this *Institute* of his, as the best he can do.—CARLYLE, THOMAS, 1831–38, *Sartor Resartus, bk.* iii, *ch.* iv.

Mr. Malthus published his essay in June, 1798; and, in the revolutionary state of the world at the time, the importance of the principle on which he depended was instantly perceived, and it has formed the groundwork of the reasonings of all intelligent men on the affairs of mankind ever since.—SMYTH, WILLIAM, 1840–55, *Lectures on the History of the French Revolution, vol.* II, *p.* 228.

This work made, when published, a powerful impression, and was supposed, for a while, to have exhausted the important department of the science of which it treats. It had, however, but few claims to attention on the score of originality, the fundamental principle maintained by Mr. Malthus—that population never fails, without any artificial stimulus, to rise to the level of subsistence—having been already set in the clearest point of view by a great number of the most eminent writers. But Mr. Malthus did not stop here.—MCCULLOCH, JOHN RAMSAY, 1845, *Literature of Political Economy, p.* 259.

His works will probably be little read henceforth; for the first and chief, his "Essay on Population," has answered its purpose.—MARTINEAU, HARRIET, 1849, *A History of the Thirty Years' Peace, A. D.* 1815-1846, *p.* 78.

Notwithstanding this fundamental error [respecting population], Malthus was a great political philosopher, and the very promulgation of his error was an important step in the advance to truth.—ALISON, SIR ARCHIBALD, 1853–59, *History of Europe,* 1815–52, *ch.* v.

It seemed to me probable that allied species were descended from a common ancestor. But during several years I could not conceive how each form could have been modified so as to become admirably adapted to its place in nature. I began therefore to study domesticated animals and cultivated plants, and after a time perceived that man's power of selecting and breeding from certain individuals was the most powerful of all means in the production of new races. Having attended to the habits of animals and their relations to the surrounding conditions, I was able to realise the severe struggle for existence to which all organisms are subjected; and my geological observations had allowed me to appreciate to a certain extent the duration of past geological periods. With my mind thus prepared I fortunately happened to read Malthus's "Essay on Population;" and the idea of a natural selection through the struggle for existence at once occurred to me. Of all the subordinate points in the theory, the last which I understood was the cause of the tendency in the descendants from a common progenitor to diverge in character.—DARWIN, CHARLES, 1868–89, *History of Creation by Ernst Heinrich Haeckel, Preface.*

Mr. Malthus unquestionably committed some errors of statement and faults of reasoning in his original enunciation of the principles of population, as is likely to be the case on the first promulgation of great economical or social laws; and during his whole life he was closely followed up by criticism and abuse. Since

Mr. Malthus' death has taken all personal interest out of the controversy over the principles of population, and Malthusianism has come to be merely a name for a body of doctrine, the views here presented have been a butt for the headless arrows of beginners in economics and of sundry sentimental sociologists. The amount of cheap wit and cheaper logic which has been expended on this theme gives the student of the principles of population a new idea of the capabilities of the human intellect.—WALKER, FRANCIS A., 1883, *Political Economy*, p. 313.

Fawcett, in particular, was profoundly impressed by the teaching of Malthus. He always speaks of Malthus with especial respect, and retorts the scorn of the popular assailants of his vital principle. Malthus was not the first to call attention to the evils which he specially denounced. Nobody is ever first in such discoveries. Nor was he aware—no one is ever aware—of the full import of his own theories. But his theory was of the highest importance because it involved the implicit recognition of a cardinal truth.—STEPHEN, LESLIE, 1885, *Life of Henry Fawcett*, p. 150.

He investigated the economic aspects of population with a masterly idea of the right method for scrutinising the fundamental principle involved under all existing and widely-divergent cases by which it is exemplified. Thus he founded on solid ground a doctrine which, when stripped entirely of its pseudo-mathematical integument, and stated with greater precision statistically and psychologically, has held its own up to the present hour against a horde of cavils which turn for the most part upon a loose employment of terms; it has even weathered the shock given to it by certain incompetent friends who have fastened upon it the heavy burden of their own false conclusions, and have not shrunk from promoting the passage of laws aimed at the restriction of marriages. This was bad enough in all conscience; but what shall we say to men who have dared to call themselves "Neo-Malthusians," and then have indulged in immoral disquisitions on "preventive intercourse?" . . . The essay of Malthus still remains the leading work on the economic problem of population, which is still far from any final solution. Not that flaws have not been found in the essay; on the contrary, its faults have been frequently adverted to in subtle arguments advanced by various writers, not a few of whom have been Italians.—COSSA, LUIGI, 1891–93, *An Introduction to the Study of Political Economy, tr. Dyer*, pp. 303, 305.

It is impossible, indeed, to overrate the importance of Malthus, viewed as a schoolmaster to bring men to Darwin, and to bring Darwin himself to the truth. Without the "Essay on the Principle of Population" it is quite conceivable that we should never have had the "Origin of Species" or the "Descent of Man."—ALLEN, GRANT, 1893, *Charles Darwin (English Worthies)*, p. 67.

GENERAL

The want of perspicuity and precision, and of thoroughness in following out the consequences of his doctrines, which has hindered the reception of the writings of Malthus, and caused him to be singularly misrepresented even to this day, was then perceived and lamented by those who knew how to value him: but he was in full career of social discovery; and it is a consolation, in the retrospect of that melancholy season, to see him meditating and speaking in the spirit of benevolence and candour, and the best men of the time listening to him with searching attention and earnest respect.—MARTINEAU, HARRIET, 1851, *History of England, A. D.* 1800-1815, p. 258.

Malthus, the economist, deserves a higher place than he generally receives, but it is as a practical reformer that he is most worthy of remembrance. The consequences of his teaching were fully appreciated in his own day, when the administration of the poor law was bidding fair to sap the strength of the people and to ruin the country. Pauperism was steadily increasing. The morals of the people were steadily deteriorating. Almost every incentive to prudence was removed, for the industrious and independent labourer could look forward to no better future than the idle and careless. It was in struggling against this iniquity that Malthus spent his life, and it was due to him more than to any other man that its causes were at length understood. Though other hands carried it out, the Poor Law Amendment Act of 1834 was his work.—MACDONELL, G. P., 1885, *Malthus, The Academy*, vol. 28, p. 81.

Felicia Dorothea Hemans

1793-1835

Born [Felicia Dorothea Browne], in Liverpool, 25 Sept. 1793. Family removed to Gwrych, North Wales, 1800. Educated there. Early precocity; a volume of poems pub., 1808. Married to Capt. Hemans, 1812; separated from him, 1818. Contrib. to "Edinburgh Monthly Mag.," 1820. Prize Poem, Royal Soc. of Literature, 1821. Tragedy, "The Vespers of Palermo," produced at Covent Garden, 12 Dec. 1823. Contrib. to "Blackwood's Mag.," and "Colburn's Mag." Life mainly spent in Wales till 1828; removed to Liverpool, 1828; to Dublin, 1831. Died, in Dublin, 16 May 1835; buried in St. Anne's Church. *Works:* "Poems," 1808; "England and Spain," 1808; "The Domestic Affections," 1812; "The Restoration of the Works of Art to Italy," 1816; "Modern Greece" (anon.), 1817; "Translations from Camoens and other poets" (anon.), 1818; "Tales and Historic Scenes," 1819; "The Meeting of Bruce and Wallace," 1819; "The Sceptic," 1820; "Superstition and Error," 1820; "Stanzas on the Death of the late King," 1820; "Dartmoor," 1821; "Welsh Melodies," 1822; "The Vespers of Palermo" (anon.), 1823; "The Siege of Valencia," 1823; "Lays of Many Lands," 1825; "The Forest Sanctuary," 1825; "Poems" (American edn.), 1825; "Records of Women," 1828 (2nd edn. same year); "Songs of the Affections," 1830; "Hymns on the Works of Nature," 1833; "Hymns for Childhood," 1834; "National Lyrics and Songs for Music," 1834; "Scenes and Hymns of Life," 1834; *Collected Works:* ed. by Mrs. Hughes (7 vols.), 1839. *Life:* by Mrs. Hughes, 1839; by W. M. Rossetti, in 1873 edn. of "Works."—SHARP, R. FARQUHARSON, 1897, *A Dictionary of English Authors, p.* 130.

PERSONAL

She is entirely feminine, and her language has a charm like that of her verse,—the same ease and peculiar grace, with more vivacity. If affliction had not laid a heavy hand upon her, she would be playful: she has not the slightest tinge of affectation, and is so refined, so gentle, that you must both love and respect her.—GRANT, ANNE, 1829, *Letters, Aug.* 26; *Memoir and Correspondence, ed. Grant, vol.* III, *p.* 137.

Egeria was totally different from any other woman I had ever seen, either in Italy or England. She did not dazzle, she subdued me. Other women might be more commanding, more versatile, more acute: but I never saw one so exquisitely feminine. Her birth, her education, but above all the genius with which she was gifted, combined to inspire a passion for the ethereal, the tender, the imaginative, the heroic—in one word, the beautiful. It was in her a faculty divine, and yet of daily life; it touched all things, but, like a sunbeam, touched them with a "golden finger." Anything abstract or scientific was unintelligible and distasteful to her. Her knowledge was extensive and various; but true to the first principle of her nature, it was poetry that she sought in history, scenery, character, and religious belief—poetry that guided all her studies, governed all her thoughts, coloured all her conversation. Her nature was at once simple and profound: there was no room in her mind for philosophy, nor in her heart for ambition; the one was filled by imagination, the other engrossed by tenderness. She had a passive temper, but decided tastes; any one might influence, but very few impressed her. Her strength and her weakness alike lay in her affections. These would sometimes make her weep at a word,—at others, imbue her with courage; so that she was alternately a "falcon-hearted dove," and "a reed shaken with the wind." Her voice was a sad sweet melody, and her spirits reminded me of an old poet's description of the orange-tree, with its

"Golden lamps hid in a night of green,"

or of those Spanish gardens where the pomegranate grows beside the cypress. Her gladness was like a burst of sunlight; and, if in her depression she resembled night, it was night bearing her stars. I might describe and describe forever, but I should never succeed in portraying Egeria. She was a Muse, a Grace, a variable child, a dependent woman, the Italy of human beings. — JEWSBURY, MARIA JANE (MRS. FLETCHER), 1830, *The Three Histories.*

One loves her as a Christian woman even more than one admires her as a

LETITIA ELIZABETH LANDON

Engraving by J. Thomson. Painting

FELICIA DOROTHEA HEMANS

Engraving by Edward Smith. From a Miniature by Edward Robertson.

writer.—KEMBLE, FRANCES ANN, 1831, *Letter, March* 13; *Records of a Girlhood*, *p.* 358.

> Mourn rather for that holy Spirit,
> Sweet as the spring, as ocean deep;
> For Her who, ere her summer faded,
> Has sunk into a breathless sleep.

—WORDSWORTH, WILLIAM, 1835, *Extempore Effusion upon the Death of James Hogg.*

> Nor mourn, O living One, because her part in life was mourning:
> Would she have lost the poet's fire for anguish of the burning?—
> The minstrel harp, for the strained string? the tripod, for the afflated
> Woe? or the vision, for those tears in which it shone dilated?
> Perhaps she shuddered while the world's cold hand her brow was wreathing,
> But never wronged that mystic breath which breathed in all her breathing,
> Which drew from rocky earth and man, abstractions high and moving—
> Beauty, if not the beautiful, and love, if not the loving. . . .
> Be happy, crowned and living One! and, as thy dust decayeth
> May thine own England say for thee, what now for Her it sayeth—
> "Albeit softly in our ears her silver song was ringing,
> The foot-fall of her parting soul is softer than her singing."

—BROWNING, ELIZABETH BARRETT, 1835, *Felicia Hemans* (*To L. E. L.*)

She was little understood, even by her friends, and as too blindly admired by some, as she was foolishly and unjustly commented upon by those who would not know her, or could not understand her. Her life was one of misfortune, and false influence on the part of those who had her character in their hands at a time when it might have taken any form; and had they taught her that the imagination gains strength and scope from the reason being cultivated in proportion with it; that nothing is *first rate* and marked for an enduring fame but something which shall profit the world and expand its sympathies, as well as please its ear and its fancy, she might, I know, have taken a stand in our literature far higher than she did. As it was, she was coming to this calmer and loftier state of mind when she died.—CHORLEY, HENRY FOTHERGILL, 1835, *Letter; Autobiography, Memoir and Letters, ed, Hewlett, p.* 129.

I have been reading Mrs. Hemans's "Life," and am disappointed in her. She seems to me to have belonged to another age of the world—to have been a Sappho or a Corinne—a creature of those times when the elect few had no sympathy with their race, when they were born for music and song, for *pas seuls* and *pas de deux*, and *not* to be linked in with their kind, to lean on the strong and sustain the feeble. She shows how inadequate sentiment is, how feeble the theory of beauty compared with that sense of duty, that perception and love of the image of God, which gives an interest to the meanest of our fellow-creatures, and a dignity to the commonest office of social life. In our practical, working-day world we can scarcely conceive such an existence as Mrs. H's.—SEDGWICK, CATHARINE M., 1837, *To Miss K. M. Sedgwick, May* 19; *Life and Letters, ed. Dewey, p.* 266.

The mantling bloom of her cheeks was shaded by a profusion of natural ringlets, of a rich golden brown; and the ever-varying expression of her brilliant eyes gave a changeful play to her countenance, which would have made it impossible for any painter to do justice to it. . . . Some of the happiest days the young poetess ever passed were during the occasional visits to some friends at Conway, where the charms of the scenery, combining all that is most beautiful in wood, water, and ruin, are sufficient to inspire the most prosaic temperament with a certain degree of enthusiasm; and it may therefore well be supposed, how fervently a soul, constituted like hers, would worship Nature at so fitting a shrine. With that happy versatility, which was at all times a leading characteristic of her mind, she would now enter with child-like playfulness into the enjoyments of a mountain scramble, or a picnic water party, the gayest of the merry band, of whom some are now, like herself, laid low, some far away in foreign lands, some changed by sorrow, and all by time; and then, in a graver mood, dream away hours of pensive contemplation amidst the grey ruins of that noblest of Welsh castles, standing, as it then did, in solitary grandeur, unapproached by bridge or causeway, flinging its broad shadow across the tributary waves which washed its regal walls.—HUGHES, MRS., 1839, *Memoir of the Life and Writings of Mrs. Hemans.*

Her remains were interred in a vault beneath St. Ann's Church [Dublin] but a short distance from her house, on the same side of the street; where, on the wall, under the gallery, on the right hand, as you enter, you observe a tablet, bearing this inscription—"In the vault beneath are deposited the Mortal Remains of Felicia Hemans, who died, May 16, 1835."—HOWITT, WILLIAM, 1847, *Homes and Haunts of the Most Eminent British Poets, vol.* II, *p.* 143.

As a woman she was to a considerable degree a spoilt child of the world. She had been early in life distinguished for talents, and poems of hers were published whilst she was a girl. She had also been handsome in her youth, but her education had been most unfortunate. She was totally ignorant of housewifery, and could as easily have managed the spear of Minerva as her needle. . . . These notices of Mrs. Hemans would be very unsatisfactory to her intimate friends, as indeed they are to myself, not so much for what is said, but what for brevity's sake is left unsaid. Let it suffice to add there was much sympathy between us, and if opportunity had been allowed me to see more of her, I should have loved and valued her accordingly. As it is, I remember her with true affection for her amiable qualities, and above all for her delicate and irreproachable conduct during her long separation from an unfeeling husband, whom she had been led to marry from the romantic notions of inexperienced youth. Upon this husband I never heard her cast the least reproach, nor did I ever hear her even name him, though she did not forbear wholly to touch upon her domestic position; but never so as that any fault could be found with her manner of adverting to it.—WORDSWORTH, WILLIAM, 1850? *Notes and Illustrations of the Poems, ed. Grosart, p.* 193.

Mrs. Hemans in private society was just what you might expect from the impassioned and yet melancholy style of her writings. She was ardent rather than amusing; enthusiastic rather than animated. Her imagination was vivid, her language energetic, her sentiments elevated; but the private sorrow she had experienced had given a sombre cast to her thoughts, which formed as it were a dark setting to the flashes of genius that shone through her conversation.—ALISON, SIR ARCHIBALD, 1867–83, *Some Account of My Life and Writings, ed. Lady Alison, vol.* I, *p.* 282.

An engraved portrait of her by the American artist William E. West, one of the three which he painted in 1827, shows us that Mrs. Hemans, at the age of thirty-four, was eminently pleasing and good-looking, with an air of amiability and sprightly gentleness, and of confiding candour which, while none the less perfectly womanly, might almost be termed childlike in its limpid depth. The features are correct and harmonious; the eyes full; the contour amply and elegantly rounded. In height she was neither tall nor short. A sufficient wealth of naturally clustering hair, golden in early youth, but by this time of a rich auburn, shades the capacious but not over-developed forehead, and the lightly penciled eyebrows. The bust and form have the fullness of a mature period of life; and it would appear that Mrs. Hemans was somewhat short-necked and high-shouldered, partly detracting from delicacy of proportion, and of general aspect or impression on the eye. We would rather judge of her by this portrait (which her sister pronounces a good likeness) than by another engraved in Mr. Chorley's "Memorials." This latter was executed in Dublin in 1831 by a young artist named Edward Robinson. It makes Mrs. Hemans look younger than in the earlier portrait by West, and may on that ground alone be surmised unfaithful; and, though younger, it also makes her heavier and less refined.—ROSSETTI, WILLIAM MICHAEL, 1878, *Lives of Famous Poets, p.* 332.

Hers has not been a happy life here. In her eighteenth year she married Captain Hemans, an Irish gentleman of good family. A few years after they were wedded he became a permanent resident in Italy, his wife continuing to reside in Wales, rearing and educating five sons who were born to them, working for her own and their honorable independence. The eldest son was George Willoughby Hemans, afterward the distinguished civil engineer. The reasons of their separation remain inexplicable; and surely had now better not be inquired into. But it does not seem that any shadow of blame was attributable to the admirable woman who taught so much, and taught so well, in imperishable verse: no cloud rests upon her memory. That parting is a mystery, and must remain so. Yet there have been few women more calculated to win and retain the love of man; being—as she was—handsome, gracefully formed, her personal charms considerable; while her mind, at once of the highest and finest order, could not have failed to render her a delightful companion and a sympathetic helpmeet. Hers was that beauty that depends mainly on expression. Like her writings, it was thoroughly womanly. Her auburn hair, parted over her brow, fell on either side in luxuriant curls. Her eyes are described as "dove-like," with a chastened character that appertained to sadness. "A calm repose," so writes one of her friends, "not unmingled with melancholy, was the characteristic expression of her face."—HALL, SAMUEL CARTER, 1883, *Retrospect of a Long Life, p.* 337.

Many years ago some one gave the writer a little miniature of Mrs. Hemans, by the help of which it is still quite possible to conjure up an outward semblance, and to put a shape to one's impression of the impulsive being who paid so dearly for her happiness, her sensibility, her undoubted powers and beauty, and her charming poetical gifts. . . . The picture represents a woman of about twenty-eight; she has dark glossy curls, delicately marked features, a high color; her bright, full, sad eyes, her laughing lips, give one an impression of womanly predominance, and melancholy and gayety all at once. She wears a black dress with gigot sleeves and the jewelry of her time—the buckle, the hair chain and locket, and also a golden ornament in her dark hair. There is perhaps (but this is merest guess-work), a certain sense of limitation—shall I call it persistency?—in the general expression of the countenance. It is hard to generalize from so slight a sketch, but perhaps something of this impulsiveness and inadaptability may have been the secret of much of the trouble of her life.—RITCHIE, ANNE ISABELLA THACKERAY, 1901, *Blackstick Papers, The Critic, vol.* 38, *p.* 119.

GENERAL

I do not despise Mrs. Hemans; but if she knit blue stockings instead of wearing them, it would be better. *You* are taken in by that false stilted trashy style, which is a mixture of all the styles of the day, which are *all bombastic* (I don't except my *own*—no one has done more through negligence to corrupt the language); but it is neither English nor poetry.—BYRON, LORD, 1820, *Letter to Mr. Murray, Sept.* 28.

I really do not know how I can advise you respecting Mrs. H. It seems a case on which you alone can decide—to wit, whether her contributions are or are not worth the money. My opinion, *on the whole*, is as follows: She is the best of our female writers of what is called Poetry. Her verses are often beautiful, always melodious, but—I think they should either be *all* accepted or *all* declined. For *none* of them that I have read are unworthy of a place in that department of a Magazine, as verses go—and she is a popular enough writer, entitled, I think, to that right. It would be offensive to her to have them returned; and I scarcely think *any of them* should be rejected. Are they then worth the money? Confound me if I know! To me they are not. But, I believe, to many readers they give much pleasure. They make an agreeable break, and they are generally pleasant reading. Besides, she was, I presume, flattered by their reception, and perhaps might feel hurt by being cut off, as well as injured by the loss of the coin. I am rather disposed to think you should go on with her; but I will converse with you about it, as it certainly is a point rather perplexing. It is surprising that she is not run out entirely, and dry as a whistle. Poetry is certainly a drug—but hers don't seem to disgust. I conclude my unsatisfactory epistle.—WILSON, JOHN, 1822, *Letter to W. Blackwood; William Blackwood and his Sons, ed. Oliphant, vol.* I, *p.* 309.

Mrs. Hemans is somewhat too poetical for my taste—too many flowers I mean, and too little fruit.—SCOTT, SIR WALTER, 1823, *Letter to Miss Joanna Baillie, July* 11; *Life by Lockhart, ch.* lix.

Mrs. Hemans's favourable opinion of my little books is worth that of twenty mobs as far as one's intellectual gratification is concerned, and I am obliged to you for communicating it to me. Next to your own unrivalled Joanna Baillie, Mrs. H. is surely entitled to rank first among all our female writers. Many write with as much feeling, some with taste as refined and as melodious diction, but no other woman that I know of with such loftiness and holiness of thought as Mrs. Hemans, always saving and excepting the gifted Joanna. —BOWLES, CAROLINE, 1827, *Letter to Blackwood, July* 9; *William Blackwood and his Sons, ed. Oliphant, vol.* I, *p.* 494.

Had her writings been merely harmless, we should not have entered into an analysis of them; but the moral charm which is spread over them is so peculiar, so full of nature and truth and deep feeling, that her productions claim at once the praise of exquisite purity and poetic excellence. She adds the dignity of her sex to a high sense of the duties of a poet; she writes with buoyancy, yet with earnestness; her poems bear the impress of a character worthy of admiration. In the pursuit of literary renown she never forgets what is due to feminine reserve. We perceive a mind, endowed with powers to aspire; and are still further pleased to find no unsatisfied cravings, no passionate pursuit of remote objects, but high endowments, graced by contentment.—BANCROFT, GEORGE, 1827, *Mrs. Hemans's Poems, North American Review, vol.* 24, *p.* 449.

If taste and elegance be titles to enduring fame, we might venture securely to promise that rich boon to the author before us; who adds to those great merits a tenderness and loftiness of feeling, and an ethereal purity of sentiment, which could only emanate from the soul of woman. She must beware, however, of becoming too voluminous; and must not venture again on anything so long as the "Forest Sanctuary." But, if the next generation inherits our taste for short poems, we are persuaded it will not readily allow her to be forgotten. For we do not hesitate to say, that she is, beyond all comparison, the most touching and accomplished writer of occasional verses that our literature has yet to boast of.—JEFFREY, FRANCIS, 1829-44, *Felicia Hemans, Contributions to the Edinburgh Review, vol.* III, *p.* 297.

Thou art quite right about Mrs. Hemans's poetry, and thou art not by any means peculiar. But it is no stately undertone of *German* in it that offends thee. She wants true simplicity. Her heart is right, but her taste is rather vitiated. It is just like her dress; it has too much glare and contrast of colour to be in pure taste. I *felt* this when I saw her.—HOWITT, MARY, 1829, *Letter to her Sister, Dec.* 13; *Autobiography, ed., her Daughter, vol.* I, *p.* 212.

Felicia Hemans is the authoress of many a plaintive and mournful strain. She has shown high sentiment and heroic feelings occasionally, but her affections are with the gentle, the meek, and the wounded in spirit.—CUNNINGHAM, ALLAN, 1833, *Biographical and Critical History of the Literature of the Last Fifty Years.*

Thy song around our daily path
Flung beauty born of dreams,
And scattered o'er the actual world
The spirit's sunny gleams.
Mysterious influence, that to earth
Brings down the heaven above,
And fills the universal heart
With universal love.
Such gifts were thine,—as from the block,
The unformed and the cold,
The sculptor calls to breathing life
Some shape of perfect mould,
So thou from common thoughts and things
Didst call a charmed song,
Which on a sweet and swelling tide
Bore the full soul along.

—LANDON, LETITIA ELIZABETH, 1835, *Stanzas on the Death of Mrs. Hemans, The New Monthly Magazine, vol.* 44, *p.* 286.

It ["Records of Women"] was, indeed, written from the fulness of her heart; and the execution of most of the sketches which it contains admirably seconds the emotions under the strong influence of which it was undertaken and completed. This has been the most popular of Mrs. Hemans' works. The last written of its poems are composed with the depressing prospect before her of a dispersion of the home-circle wherein she had always found shelter, and leisure to pursue her engrossing calling undisturbed—which was to send her forth into the world, for the first time—alone, and as innocent of its ways and wisdom as a child.—CHORLEY, HENRY F., 1838, *Authors of England, p.* 4.

Why should we say
Farewell to thee, since every unborn age
Shall mix thee with its household charities?
The hoary sire shall bow his deafened ear,
And greet thy sweet words with his benison;
The mother shrine thee as a vestal-flame
In the lone temple of her sanctity,
And the young child who takes thee by the hand
Shall travel with a surer step to heaven.

—SIGOURNEY, LYDIA H., 1840, *Monody on Mrs. Hemans.*

Her inspiration always pauses at the feminine point. It never "oversteps the modesty of nature," nor the dignity and decorum of womanhood. She is no Sibyl, tossed to and fro in the tempest of furious excitement, but ever a "deep, majestical, and high-souled woman"—the calm mistress of the highest and stormiest of her emotions. The finest compliment we can pay her—perhaps the finest compliment that it is possible to pay to a woman as a moral being,—is to compare hér to "one of Shakspere's women," and to say, had Imogen, or Isabella or Cornelia become an authoress, she had so written.—GILFILLAN, GEORGE, 1847, *Mrs. Hemans, Second Gallery of Literary Portraits, Tait's Edinburgh Magazine, vol.* 14, *p.* 360.

Showed Shelley some poems to which I had subscribed, by Felicia Browne, whom I had met in North Wales, where she had been on a visit at the house of a connexion of mine. She was then sixteen, and it was impossible not to be struck with the beauty (for beautiful she was), the grace, and charming simplicity and *naïveté* of this interesting girl; and on my return from Denbighshire I made her and her works frequent subjects of conversation with Shelley. Her juvenile productions, remarkable certainly for her age—and some of those which the volume contained were written when she was a mere child—made a powerful impression on Shelley, ever enthusiastic in his admiration of talent; and with a prophetic spirit he foresaw the coming greatness of that genius which, under the name of Hemans, afterward electrified the world.—MEDWIN, THOMAS, 1847, *The Life of Percy Bysshe Shelley.*

Is the most generally admired of all English female poets, and deservedly so. . . . She seldom reached the sublime, but her thought was often profound, and her nice analysis of the best affections, her delicate perception of the minute circumstances that awaken and guide the sensibilities, the readiness with which she seized upon the noble, the picturesque, the graceful and the tender, designate her above every English writer but *one* as the "poet of the heart."—BETHUNE, GEORGE WASHINGTON, 1848, *The British Female Poets.*

Mrs. Hemans's poetry was of a far higher order. It was deformed by a mannerism of that degree which is fatal to permanence of popularity; and there is not much substance of thought. But the sentiment is commonly as true and natural as the expression of it is otherwise; and of a depth which always insures its freshness. The substantial power of Mrs. Hemans is, perhaps, best shown in the choice of the subjects of her smaller pieces, which is so rich in suggestion, and so full of the keen and sagacious apprehension that belongs to genius, that it is almost a greater treat to look over the table of contents of her minor poems, than to read the poems themselves. Her fame—a genuine and reasonable fame, depending upon her qualities, and not upon any accident of the time—had spread widely over the European and American continents, many years before her death; and there are thousands living to whom the slightest casual recollection of some of her poems will be, to the day of their death, like the singing of a dirge in the recesses of their hearts.—MARTINEAU, HARRIET, 1849, *A History of the Thirty Years' Peace, p.* 76.

By far the most popular of our poetesses, alike at home and beyond the Atlantic; nor do I say undeservedly. . . . In her poetry, religious truth, moral purity, and intellectual beauty ever meet together; and assuredly it is not less calculated to refine the taste and exalt the imagination because it addresses itself almost exclusively to the better feelings of our nature. Over all her pictures of humanity are spread the glory and the grace reflected from virtuous purity, delicacy of perception and conception, sublimity of religious faith, home-bred delights, and the generous, expansive ardour of patriotism; while, turning from the dark and degraded, whether in subject or sentiment, she seeks out those verdant oases in the desert of human life, on which the affections may most pleasantly rest. Her poetry is intensely and entirely feminine; and, in my estimation, this is the highest praise which, in one point of view, could be awarded it. It could have been written by a woman only. . . . Mrs. Hemans, above all female writers, was distinguished for her rich tones—the voice at once sweet and full—that carried them to the heart, awakening the feelings as well as the imagination.—MOIR, D. M, 1851–52, *Sketches of the Poetical Literature of the Past Half-Century, pp.* 261, 263, 282.

Gone is she
Who shrouded *Casa-Bianca*, she who cast
The iron mould of *Ivan*, yet whose song
Was soft and varied as the nightingale's,
And heard above all others.

—LANDOR, WALTER SAVAGE, 1853, *The Heroines of England, The Last Fruit off an Old Tree.*

I got a little chance to retort, by telling him [Dr. Whewell] that we had outgrown Mrs. Hemans in America, and that we now read Mrs. Browning more. He laughed at it, and said that Mrs. Browning's poetry was so coarse that he could not tolerate it, and he was amused to hear that any people had got above Mrs. Hemans; and he asked me if we had outgrown Homer. —MITCHELL, MARIA, 1857, *Life, Letters and Journals, p.* 116.

Her character as an author is now fixed in public estimation: she is decidedly one of the first lyric poets which England has produced. Without the classic charm of Gray, or the burning thoughts of Campbell, she has produced some pieces which have struck nearly as deep into the national heart as the verses of either of these writers. She is eminently national in her ideas; the most beautiful of her odes are those which—founded on domestic feelings, rekindling the family affections, appealing to the images of the country, the national associations, the patriotic emotions—have touched a chord which is responded to in every generous heart. The great objection to her poems, which has chiefly prevented them hitherto from taking their place beside the most popular British classics, is their number.—ALISON, SIR ARCHIBALD, 1867–83, *Some Account of My Life and Writings, ed. Lady Alison, vol.* I, *p.* 281.

As to the effective utterance of original truth, Mrs. Hemans is silent; but for pathos, sentiment, and gorgeous richness of language, we know no lyrics superior to her little pieces.—ANDERSON, WILLIAM, 1871, *Model Women, p.* 184.

According to the spiritual or emotional condition of those who peruse, it would be found that a poem by this authoress which to one reader would be graceful and tender would to another be touching, and to a third poignantly pathetic. The first we can suppose to be a man, and the third a woman; or the first a critic, the second a "poetical reader," and the third a sensitive nature attuned to sympathy by suffering.—ROSSETTI, WILLIAM MICHAEL, 1878, *Lives of Famous Poets, p.* 348.

I know that it has long been out of fashion to admire Mrs. Hemans, or even to read her poems; and one must admit that it is before a higher literary canon that her writings have declined in value. But there are regions of experience where literary taste blends with memories of past emotion. No criticism can demonstrate out of existence the facts of human nature. I have heard a learned symphony that left me critical, approving, cold; then heard a child singing with reedy voice some little song familiar in early days, which quickened the pulse and started tears to the eyes. green fields were in it, and the sweet playmates, and the long-lost realm of childhood's sunshine. What can art do better than to raise the happiest emotions? What can I read on the page of Goethe, of Wordsworth, or Tennyson, which can set all these birds and flowers and laden bees around Dovenest singing the songs that evoke from the shadowy past sweet loving faces of those who sang them to me in life's rosy morning-time?—CONWAY, MONCURE D., 1880, *The English Lakes and their Genii, Harper's Magazine, vol.* 62, *p.* 26.

Fifty years ago few poets were more popular than Mrs. Hemans; her verses were familiar to all hearts, and won praise from such fastidious critics as Gifford and Jeffrey, no less than from Wordsworth, Scott and Byron. Yet now they are chiefly forgotten, and without injustice. Her tedious romantic tales, her dramas characterless and without invention, are more frequently below than above the mean of merit. Her lyric poetry is more memorable; yet this, even, is less to be valued for its own sake than as the revelation of a delicate and attractive personality. . . . Her simplicity was never the result of an inspired clearness of vision, as with Wordsworth or with Blake, but was rather the expression of a nature whose vistas were not wide enough to be indistinct, and whose plan of the globe ignored the unseen side.—ROBINSON, A. MARY F., 1880, *English Poets, ed. Ward, vol.* IV, *pp.* 334, 335.

Her poems are like this description of herself. They are always sweet, liquid, and melodious: they mean as much as so soft and beautiful a nature ever requires to mean: "Sweet records, promises as sweet"—the gentle sentiments that lie on the surface, subdued sorrows, chastened happiness.—OLIPHANT, MARGARET O. W., 1882, *Literary History of England, XVIII-XIX Century, vol.* II, *p.* 317.

It was much that Mrs. Hemans was the first poetess to devote her verse to nature, as Wordsworth was the first poet to do so. But Wordsworth had a healthier way of studying it; he may be said to have gone to nature for teaching, while Mrs. Hemans went to it for sympathy. There is as much difference between the outlook of the poetess and that of the poet upon the external universe, as there is between the way in which Longfellow and the way in which Emerson regarded it.—ROBERTSON, ERIC S., 1883, *English Poetesses, p.* 185.

Surely the reader is impressed with the way in which a woman's genius, even if not of the very highest order, may retain its hold after her death, on seeing the late statements of Mr. Routledge, the great publisher of cheap books in England, as to the continued demand for Mrs. Hemans's poetry. In the last generation the pure and melodious muse of this lady had great reputation; her American editor was Professor Andrews Norton, father of the present Professor Charles Eliot Norton, and one of the most cultivated critics of his day; and it appears from the late memoirs of Garrison that her verses were long the favorite food of that strong and heroic mind. Yet it has been the custom to speak of her popularity as a thing of the past. Now arrives Mr. Routledge, and gives the figures as to his sales of the different poets in a single calendar year. First comes Longfellow, with the extraordinary sale of 6,000 copies; then we drop to Scott, with 3,170; Shakespeare, 2,700; Byron, 2,380; Moore, 2,276; Burns, 2,250. To these succeeds Mrs. Hemans, with a sale of 1,900 copies, Milton falling short of her by 50, and no one else showing much more than half that demand. Hood had 980 purchasers, Cowper, 800, and all others less; Shelley had 500 and Keats but 40. Of course this is hardly even an approximate estimate of the comparative popularity of these poets, since much would depend, for instance, on the multiplicity or value of rival editions; but it proves in a general way that Mrs. Hemans holds her own, in point of readers, fifty years after her death. What other form of influence for man or woman equals this?—HIGGINSON, THOMAS WENTWORTH, 1887, *Women and Men, p.* 18.

It is usual to couple her [Miss Landon] with Mrs. Hemans; but this, I think, without justice. Mrs. Hemans was unquestionably her superior in poetic energy, variety, and rhythmic power. Although this writer's poems are weakened by the sentimentality of her epoch, much of her work has true poetic qualities and lyrical impulse. Her wide popularity has not extended to the present generation, and she now runs the risk of being unduly overlooked.—SHARP, ELIZABETH A., 1890, *Women Poets of the Victorian Era, Preface, p.* xxii.

Her poetry lacks deep thought or subtle emotion, and although it had immense popularity in its day, its sweetness and fluency have long palled upon the taste of thoughtful readers.—SUTTON, C. W., 1891, *Dictionary of National Biography, vol.* XXV, *p.* 383.

Her verse at its best was spontaneous, simple, and direct. Her descriptions of nature, though, of course, lacking the profound insight and sense of communion which are the chief attributes of Wordsworth's descriptions, were true to fact and free from any touch of pedantry. . . . Felicia Hemans has now ceased to be a poet for poets. Her diffuseness alone would prevent her from being this. She not only rarely achieved concentration: she seems rarely to have tried to achieve it. Diffuseness such as hers is fatal to the life of poetry. . . . No body of verse ever survived that was as diffuse as is much of Felicia Hemans's poetry. Her name will still be held in honour however because of a few of her poems. For so universal is the human interest of some of her themes that it is difficult to believe a time will come when she will cease to be read by the people.—BELL, MACKENZIE, 1892, *The Poets and the Poetry of the Century, Joanna Baillle to Mathilde Blind, ed. Miles, pp.* 53, 55.

Mrs. Hemans is now unduly depreciated, but the difference between the most favourable and the least favourable critic can only be with regard to the degree of weakness charged against her.—WALKER, HUGH, 1897, *The Age of Tennyson, p.* 53.

Accomplishment without genius, and amiability without passion, reappear, translated into an atmosphere of lyric exaltation, in the once famous poetry of Mrs. Hemans. . . . Of all the English Romantic poets, Mrs. Hemans expresses with the richest intensity the more superficial and transient elements of Romanticism. She is at the beck and call of whatever is touched with the pathos of the far away, of the bygone—scenes of reminiscence or farewell, laments of exiles and dirges for the dead. Her imagination floats romantically aloof from actuality, but it quite lacks the creative energy of the great Romantics, and her fabrics are neither real substance nor right dreams. Her expression is spontaneously picturesque and spontaneously melodious; and both qualities captivated her public; but she never learned either to modulate or to subdue her effects. She paints with few colours, all bright. Her pages are a tissue of blue sky, golden corn, flashing swords and waving banners, the murmur of pines, and the voices of children.—HERFORD, C. H., 1897, *The Age of Wordsworth*, *pp.* 211, 212.

James Hogg

1770-1835

Born, at Ettrick, Selkirkshire, 1770; baptised, 9 Dec. 1770. Employed as shepherd in various quarters till 1800. Managed his father's farm at Ettrick, 1801-03. Made unsuccessful attempts at sheep-farming on his own account. Having by this time published some poems, settled in Edinburgh, 1810, to take up literary career. Ed. "The Spy," Sept. 1810 to 1811. Presented by Duke of Buccleuch with the farm of Altrive Lake, Yarrow, 1816. Settled there. Helped to start "Blackwood's Mag.," 1817; became frequent contributor. Married Margaret Phillips, 1820. Visit to London, 1832. Entertained at a public dinner there; also at Peebles in 1833. Died, 21 Nov. 1835. Buried in Ettrick churchyard. *Works:* "Scottish Pastorals," 1801; "The Shepherd's Guide," 1807; "The Mountain Bard," 1807; "The Forest Minstrel" (mainly by Hogg), 1810; "The Queen's Wake," 1813; "The Hunting of Badlewe" (under pseud. of "J. H. Craig"), 1814; "The Pilgrims of the Sun," 1815; "Madoc of the Moor," 1816; "The Poetic Mirror" (anon.), 1816; "Dramatic Tales" (anon.), 1817; "Long Pack" (anon.), 1817; "The Brownie of Bodsbeck" (2 vols.), 1818; "Jacobite Relics of Scotland" (2 vols.), 1819-20; "Winter Evening Tales," 1820; "The Royal Jubilee" (anon.), 1822; "The Three Perils of Man" (3 vols.), 1822; "The Three Perils of Woman" (3 vols.), 1823; "The Private Memoirs and Confessions of a Justified Sinner," (anon.), 1824; "Queen Hynde," 1825; "The Shepherd's Calendar," 1829; "Songs" (anon.), 1831; "Altrive Tales," 1832; "A Queer Book" (anon.), 1832; "A Series of Lay Sermons," 1834; "The Domestic Manners and Private Life of Sir Walter Scott," 1834; "Tales of the Wars of Montrose," 1835. *Collected Works:* in 2 vols., ed. by Blackie, with *life* by Rev. T. Thomson, 1865-66.—SHARP, R. FARQUHARSON, 1897, *A Dictionary of English Authors*, *p.* 134.

PERSONAL

I have had the most amusing letter from Hogg, the Ettrick minstrel and shepherd. He wants me to recommend him to Murray; and, speaking of his present bookseller, whose "bills" are never "lifted," he adds, *totidem verbist*, "God d—n him and them both." I laughed, and so would you too, at the way in which this execration is introduced. The said Hogg is a strange being, but of great, though uncouth, powers. I think very highly of him, as a poet; but he, and half of these Scotch and Lake troubadours, are spoilt by living in little circles and petty societies.—BYRON, LORD, 1814, *Letter to Moore, Aug.* 3.

I had no method of learning to write save by following the Italian alphabet; and though I always stripped myself of coat and vest when I began to pen a song, yet my wrist took a cramp, so that I could rarely make above four or five lines at a sitting. Whether my manner of writing it out was new, I knew not, but it was not without singularity. Having very little spare time from my flock, which was unruly enough, I folded and stitched a few sheets of paper, which I carried in my pocket. I had no ink-horn, but in place of it I borrowed a small phial, which I fixed in a hole in the breast of my waistcoat; and having a cork fastened by a piece of twine, it answered my purpose fully as well. Thus equipped, whenever a leisure minute or two offered, and I had nothing else to do, I sat down and wrote out my thoughts as I found them. This is still my invariable practice in writing prose. I cannot make out one sentence by study without the pen in my hand to catch the ideas as they rise, and I never write two copies of the same thing. My manner of composing poetry is very different, and, I believe, much more singular. Let the piece be of what length it will, I compose and correct it wholly in my mind, or on a slate, ere ever I put pen to paper; and then I write it down as fast as the A, B, C. When once it is written, it remains in that state; it being with the utmost difficulty that I can be brought to alter one syllable.—HOGG, JAMES, 1832? *Autobiography.*

Hogg is a little red-skinned stiff sack of a body, with quite the common air of an Ettrick shepherd, except that he has highish though sloping brow (among his yellow grizzled hair), and two clear little beads of blue or grey eyes that sparkle, if not with thought, yet with animation. Behaves himself quite easily and well; speaks Scotch, and mostly narrative absurdity (or even obscenity) therewith. Appears in the mingled character of zany and raree show. All bent on bantering him, especially Lockhart; Hogg walking through it as if unconscious, or almost flattered. His vanity seems to be immense, but also his good-nature. I felt interest for the poor "herd body," wondered to see him blown hither from his sheepfolds, and how, quite friendless as he was, he went along cheerful, mirthful, and musical. I do not well understand the man; his significance is perhaps considerable. His poetic talent is authentic, yet his intellect seems of the weakest; his morality also limits itself to the precept "be not angry." Is the charm of this poor man chiefly to be found herein, that he *is* a real product of nature, and able to speak naturally, which not one in a thousand is? An "unconscious talent," though of the smallest, emphatically *naïve.* Once or twice in singing (for he sung of his own) there was an emphasis in poor Hogg's look —expression of feeling, almost of enthusiasm.—CARLYLE, THOMAS, 1832, *Journal, Jan.* 21; *Life by Froude, vol.* II, *p.* 189.

When first, descending from the moorlands,
I saw the Stream of Yarrow glide
Along a bare and open valley,
The Ettrick Shepherd was my guide.
When last along its banks I wandered,
Through groves that had begun to shed
Their golden leaves upon the pathways,
My steps the Border-minstrel led. . . .
No more of old romantic sorrows,
For slaughtered Youth or love-lorn Maid!
With sharper grief is Yarrow smitten,
And Ettrick mourns with her their Poet dead.

—WORDSWORTH, WILLIAM, 1835, *Extempore Effusion upon the Death of James Hogg.*

Scott . . . invited him to dinner in Castle Street. . . . When Hogg entered the drawingroom, Mrs. Scott, being at the time in a delicate state of health, was reclining on a sofa. The Shepherd, after being presented, and making his best bow, forthwith took possession of another sofa, placed opposite to hers, and stretched himself thereupon at all his length; for, as he said afterwards, "I thought I could never do wrong to copy the lady of the house." As his dress at this period was precisely that in which any ordinary herdsman attends cattle to the market, and as his hands, moreover, bore most legible marks of a recent sheep-smearing, the lady of the house did not observe with perfect equanimity the novel usage to which her chintz was exposed. The Shepherd, however, remarked nothing of all this—dined heartily, and drank freely, and, by jest, anecdote, and song, afforded plentiful merriment to the more civilized part of the company. As the liquor operated, his familiarity increased and strengthened; from "Mr. Scott," he advanced to "Sherra," and thence to "Scott," "Walter," and "Wattie," until, at supper, he fairly convulsed the whole party by addressing Mrs. Scott as "Charlotte."—LOCKHART, JOHN GIBSON, 1836, *The Life of Scott, ch.* xii.

I have seen him many times by the banks of his own romantic Yarrow; I have sat with him in the calm and sunny weather by the margin of St. Mary's Lake; I have seen his eye sparkle and his cheek flush as he spoke out some old heroic ballad of the days of the Douglas and the Græme; and I have felt, as I listened to the accents of his manly voice, that whilst Scotland could produce amongst her children such men as him beside me, her ancient spirit had not departed from her, nor the star of her glory grown pale! For he was a man, indeed, cast in nature's happiest mould. True-hearted, and brave, and generous, and sincere, alive to every kindly impulse, and fresh at the core to the last, he lived among his native hills the blameless life of the shepherd and the poet; and on the day when he was laid beneath the sod in the lonely kirkyard of Ettrick, there was not one dry eye amongst the hundreds that lingered round his grave.—AYTOUN, WILLIAM EDMONDSTOUNE, 1844, *The Burns Festival, Memoir, ed. Martin, p.* 102.

Hogg's birthplace and his grave are but a few hundred yards asunder. The kirkyard of Ettrick is old, but the kirk is recent; 1824 is inscribed over the door. Like most of the country churches of Scotland, it is a plain fabric, plainly fitted up within with seats, and a plain pulpit. . . . Ettrick kirk lifts its head in this quiet vale with a friendly air. It is built of the native adamantine rock, the whinstone; has a square battlemented tower; and, what looks singular, has, instead of Gothic ones, square doorways, and square, very tall sash windows. Hogg's grave lies in the middle of the kirk-yard. At its head stands a rather handsome headstone, with a harp sculptured on a border at the top, and this inscription beneath it:—"James Hogg, the Ettrick Shepherd, who was born at Ettrick Hall, 1770, and died at Altrive Lake, the 21st day of November, 1835."—HOWITT, WILLIAM, 1847, *Homes and Haunts of the Most Eminent British Poets, vol.* II, *p.* 66.

Hogg had his joyous moods seemingly without any reaction of gloom; with the help of "the sclate," he composed with great facility, and had a dislike to corrections afterwards; his temper was sustained and equable; his ambition, though steadfast, was of a quiet character, and though baffled, as it often happened, in his purpose, he was never for a moment cast down. Surely there never has been any instance of the pursuit of literature under circumstances more untoward than those which the Shepherd so cheerfully encountered. Take, for example, the difficulties attending his first attempt at publication. Being appointed to the vastly pleasant and poetical task of driving a herd of cattle from Ettrick to Edinburgh . . . in the dreary month of November, he suddenly conceived the notion of getting a volume into print, but having no manuscript in hand, he tried during his walks to remember the verses, and as often as they recurred ran into a shop to borrow a stump of pen and morsel of paper to note them down. In this way copy was provided; luckily for his purpose, he found a good-natured printer, and an octavo volume, or pamphlet was produced in a week, with which he returned in triumph to the forest.—GILLIES, ROBERT PEARCE, 1851, *Memoirs of a Literary Veteran.*

There was a homely heartiness of manner about Hogg and a Doric simplicity in his address, which was exceedingly prepossessing. He sometimes carried a little too far the privileges of an innocent rusticity, as Mr. Lockhart has not failed to note in his life of Scott; but, in general his slight deviations from etiquette were rather amusing than otherwise. When we consider the disadvantages with which he had to contend, it must be admitted that Hogg was in all respects a very remarkable man. In his social hours, a naïvete, and a vanity which disarmed displeasure by the openness and good-humour with which it was avowed, played over the surface of a nature which at bottom was sufficiently shrewd and sagacious; but his conversational powers were by no means pre-eminent. He never indeed attempted any colloquial display, although there was sometimes a quaintness in his remarks, a glimmering of drollery, a rural freshness, and a tinge of poetical colouring, which redeemed his discourse from commonplace, and supplied to the consummate artist who took him in hand the hints out of which to construct a character at once original, extraordinary, and delightful—a character of which James Hogg undoubtedly furnished the germ, but which, as it expanded under the hands of its artificer, acquired a breadth, a firmness and a power to which the bard of Mount Benger had certainly no pretension.—FERRIER, JAMES F., 1855, *Works of John Wilson, Preface.*

In the latter period of his life, when brought to mix with the most refined circles of London for a brief season, his ready adaptation of his manners to the company was absolutely marvellous. Never forgetting, and never obtruding himself when urged to a display of his talents, he so acquitted himself as to become an object of genuine admiration and interest to all who had the pleasure to witness these coruscations of genius.—JERDAN, WILLIAM, 1866, *Men I Have Known.*

You will perhaps wonder to hear me assert that it was the simplicity and the single-heartedness—if I may so word it—of his character which rendered it to many so difficult to understand. At least so have I always thought. Men of the world, I mean simply of the every-day world, expecting to meet with one who, a poet, was yet in other respects quite of their own cast, could not understand why it should turn out so far otherwise, and much less could they readily comprehend the unassuming simplicity both of manners and language which constituted the cause of anomaly. . . . Nothing ever hurt his feelings so much as to hear one man speaking disrespectfully of another. . . . I do not think that he was apt to entertain bitter or unrelenting feelings towards any of his fellow kind, and this is how, I suppose, not a few took unwarrantable advantage of his good nature. Yet if dissatisfied with any one he would not scruple to express his sentiments as opportunity might serve. . . . He would not seek to alter your opinion, and most likely you have failed to alter his. There was a deep and earnest stamina of mental firmness in him after all.—RIDDELL, HENRY SCOTT, 1866, *Lectures, Memorials of James Hogg, ed. Mrs. Garden, p.* 332.

Thirty years ago many of those whom I now address knew the Shepherd well. We remember among the things of this life that are worth remembering, his sturdy form, and shrewd, familiar face; his kindly greetings, and his social cheer; his summer angling, and his winter curling; his welcome presence at kirk and market and border game; and above all, we remember how his grey eye sparkled as he sang, in his own simple and unadorned fashion, those rustic ditties in which a manly vigour of sentiment was combined with unexpected grace, sweetness and tenderness. It is now a quarter of a century since he ceased to be seen among us, and since a large assemblage of sorrowing friends bore him past these waters to his grave in Ettrick.—BELL, HENRY GLASSFORD, 1869, *Address at the Unveiling of the Statue to Hogg at St. Mary's Loch, Memorials of James Hogg, ed. Mrs. Garden.*

In 1824 Christopher North predicted, in the ever memorable "Noctes," that a monument would be erected to his honour. "My beloved Shepherd, some half-century hence your effigy will be seen on some bonnie green knowe in the Forest, with its honest freestone face looking across St. Mary's Loch, and up towards the Gray Mare's Tail, while by moonlight all your own fairies will weave a dance around its pedestal." His prediction was verified June 28, 1860, when a handsome freestone statue, executed by Andrew Currie, was erected in the Vale of Yarrow, on the hillside between St. Mary's Loch and the Loch of the Lowes, and immediately opposite to Tibby Shiel's cottage.—WILSON, JAMES GRANT, 1876, *The Poets and Poetry of Scotland, vol.* I, *p.* 450.

I likewise formed an acquaintance with James Hogg, the Ettrick Shepherd, and was amused with his blunt simplicity of character and good-nature. It did not seem as if he had the slightest veneration for any one more than another whom he addressed, no matter what was their rank or position; and I could quite believe that he sometimes took the liberty, as is alleged of him, of familiarly addressing Sir Walter Scott as "Watty," and Lady Scott as "Charlotte." The Shepherd, however, was a genuinely good creature, and an agreeable acquaintance.—CHAMBERS, WILLIAM, 1882, *Story of a Long and Busy Life, p.* 46.

Mrs. Hogg survived her husband for the long period of five-and-thirty years, but to the last day of her gentle life the recollection of the "Noctes" of that period brought back to her mind the *bête noir* that had made her pulse beat faster and her eye sparkle with a wife's indignation. Was she wrong; or did it happen that the world, being wiser than she, detected the conceit and saw through the mask? Doing so they would know that the "Shepherd" of the "Noctes" was, after all, but a creation of the wild and somewhat jovial fancy of Christopher North, having little or no real existence.—GARDEN, MRS., 1885, *Memorials of James Hogg, p.* 139.

Hogg was essentially a kindly, generous, and warm-affectioned man, capable of attaching to himself friends of very opposite characters; genial in society, though not a copious or brilliant talker, and, in his own home at Eltrive and Mount

Benger, hospitable almost to a fault. Obviously, too, he was a loving and well-loved man in his home circle, where he found his best happiness. His shrewd views of people and things, and his quaint modes of expression, redolent of the vernacular of the Forest and tinged with poetry,—in a word, the singular individuality of his character made him an object of interest to numerous friends and acquaintances all over Britain.—VEITCH, JOHN, 1885, *Memorials of James Hogg, ed. Mrs. Garden, Preface, p.* x.

According to an old Border character who knew him in the flesh, James Hogg had no right to the title of Shepherd at all. "Though kind o'clever," says this worthy, "he was nae shepherd, for the useless body let a' his sheep get scabbed, and though he had his farm free from the Duke o' Buccleuch, he made naething o't, but was aye lettin' his bills be overdue." The old worthy is probably right, but we shall e'en let the title pass without question. It is something to have the admission that, though he was no shepherd, Hogg was "kind o' clever," and that he wrote "several fine songs," which his countrymen have placed on a level with the best lyrics of Burns himself. His cleverness was, indeed, of a kind that is very rarely met with, even in the case of men of the highest genius. He was entirely an untutored singer, an uncultivated child of Nature, who certainly owed as much to his own industry and indomitable perseverance as to the inborn talent which he undoubtedly possessed.—HADDEN, J. CUTHBERT, 1892, *The Ettrick Shepherd, The Gentleman's Magazine, vol.* 273, *p.* 283.

THE QUEEN'S WAKE
1813

The specimens we have already given (of "Kilmeny") will enable the reader to judge of the style and manner of the singular composition; upon the strength of which alone we should feel ourselves completely justified, in assuring the author, that no doubt can be entertained that he is a poet—in the highest acceptation of the name.—JEFFREY, FRANCIS LORD, 1814, *Hogg's Queen's Wake, Edinburgh Review, vol.* 24, *p.* 167.

"The Queen's Wake" is a garland of fair forest-flowers, bound with a band of rushes from the moor. It is not a poem, —not it; nor was it intended to be so; you might as well call a bright boquet of flowers a flower, which, by-the-by, we do in Scotland. Some of the ballads are very beautiful; one or two even splendid; most of them spirited; and the worst far better than the best that ever was written by any bard in danger of being a blockhead. "Kilmeny" alone places our (*ay, our*) Shepherd among the Undying Ones.—WILSON, JOHN, 1831, *Christopher North's Recreations: An Hour's Talk about Poetry.*

The poem is unequal, and it could not well be otherwise; it consists of the songs of many minstrels in honour of Queen Mary, united together by a sort of recitative, very rambling, amusing, and characteristic. Some of the strains of the contending Bards are of the highest order, both of conception and execution; the Abbot of Eye has great ease, vigour, and harmony, and the story of the Fair Kilmeny, for true simplicity, exquisite loveliness, and graceful and original fancy, cannot be matched in the whole compass of British song.—CUNNINGHAM, ALLAN, 1833, *Biographical and Critical History of the Literature of the Last Fifty Years.*

"Kilmeny" has been the theme of universal admiration, and deservedly so, for it is what Wharton would have denominated "pure poetry." It is, for the most part, the glorious emanation of a sublime fancy —the spontaneous sprouting forth of amaranthine flowers of sentiment—the bubbling out and welling over of inspiration's fountain.—MOIR, D. M., 1851-52, *Poetical Literature of the Past Half-Century.*

After a few hits and misses in various departments of literature, he succeeded in striking the right chord in "The Queen's Wake," which was published in 1813. This stamped Hogg as, after Burns (*proximus sed longo intervallo*) the greatest poet that had ever sprung from the bosom of the people. It became at once, and deservedly, popular.—FERRIER, JAMES F., 1855, *Works of John Wilson, Preface.*

Full of beautiful things.—VICTORIA, QUEEN, 1871, *Diary, Aug.* 15.

That one so ignorant as he should have written it excited the wonder of all who knew him, and gave it a distinction which readers of to-day fail to find in it. It was remarkable as the work of an unlettered man, but not so remarkable, all things considered, as a work of the period when it appeared.—STODDARD, RICHARD HENRY, 1892, *Under the Eveniug Lamp, p.* 68.

His songs will not bear comparison with the best of his master's, and as a poet generally he takes much lower rank; some, indeed, in our day denying him all poetic rank whatever; but, without instituting comparisons where none are necessary, the reader may enjoy "the Witch of Fife" as an example of Northern wit and humour, well worthy of a place in any collection of humorous poetry. "The Queen's Wake," in which it appears, was first published in 1813, and became an immediate success. Its author was a born balladist, and the form of this effort exactly suited his powers. In the result he produced a work which can hardly fail to give him a permanent place in literature.—MILES, ALFRED H., 1894, *The Poets and the Poetry of the Century, Humour, Society, Parody and Occasional Verse, p* 78.

There is a balance-sheet of the transaction between Goldie and Hogg enclosed with these old letters—by which it appears that Hogg received for the slim volume of poetry no less a sum than £245, a reward which a minor poet in our own day would certainly think no unsubstantial one.—OLLIPHANT, MARGARET O. W., 1897, *William Blackwood and His Sons, vol.* I, *p.* 36.

GENERAL

Unlike those puny productions of pastoral bards, which the injudicious flattery of admirers, incompetent to form a judgment, has so often obtruded on the public, his compositions many bear comparison with many of the happiest flights of the more cultivated geniuses of this truly poetic age. In almost every style of verse which he has attempted, and there are few which he has left untried, he has succeeded.—RYAN, RICHARD, 1826, *Poetry and Poets, vol.* I, *p.* 240.

Who is there that has not heard of the Ettrick Shepherd—of him whose inspiration descended as lightly as the breeze that blows along the mountain-side—who saw, amongst the lonely and sequestered glens of the south, from eyelids touched with fairy ointment, such visions as are vouchsafed to the minstrel alone—the dream of sweet Kilmeny, too spiritual for the taint of earth? I shall not attempt any comparison—for I am not here to criticise—between his genius and that of other men, on whom God in His bounty has bestowed the great and the marvellous gift. The songs and the poetry of the Shepherd are now the nation's own, as indeed they long have been; and amidst the ministrelsy of the choir who have made the name of Scotland and her peasantry familiar throughout the wide reach of the habitable world, the clear wild notes of the forest will forever be heard to ring.—AYTOUN, WILLIAM EDMONDSTOUNE, 1844, *The Burns Festival, Memoir, ed. Martin, p.* 102.

A man of stubborn and graceful imagination—of unscrupulous manners and delicate sentiment; a man who taught himself to write with such labour, that he began his task by taking off his coat and waistcoat, but who produced his songs with such facility, that they seem to have presented themselves to him like a group of sun-touches on the prominences of his native valleys and hillsides. His life was one of painful vicissitudes, from his want of prudence, and of knowledge of the world.—MARTINEAU, HARRIET, 1849, *A History of the Thirty Years' Peace, A. D.* 1815-1846, *p.* 76.

All the verses of Hogg exhibit that kind of imaginative awe which lives on the fruit and food yielded by Superstition. His images from Nature are all surrounded with the beings of another day: what an array of fairies, witches, bogies, ghosts, we have! He seems to transport his mind back to the time when every object in Nature was the home, and beneath the guardianship of some spiritual being; when there was a spirit in every dingle, and the muttering of some potent power in every gale; when Superstition was privileged to erect her gibbets, and kindle her fires in every village and town. . . . His eye had beheld, his soul had sported, in all the strange amplitude of nature's vast boundless theatre. Whatever else he felt, the soul of the forest was strong within him; he wrote beneath the glare of its lightnings, and the gleam of its sunsets and sunrisings. The roar of its woods and waters was forever sounding on his ear; the snatches of old songs, the carol and the lilt of old wild lyrics, these were the pages of the book whence he gathered his ideas.—HOOD, EDWIN PAXTON, 1859-70, *The Peerage of Poverty, pp.* 338, 339.

Halleck ever held James Hogg in high

estimation as a poet, and he once told me that few poems had afforded him so much delight as "The Queen's Wake." He deemed the Shepherd's lines, written for the famous Buccleugh Border celebration, much superior to Sir Walter Scott's.—WILSON, JAMES GRANT, 1869, *Life and Letters of Fitz-Greene Halleck*, p. 255.

No Scottish poet has dealt with the power and the realm of Fairy more vividly and impressively than the Bard of Ettrick. He caught up several of the floating traditions which actually localised the fairy doings, and this, as he haunted the hills and moors where they were said to have taken place, brought the old legend home to his every day life and feeling. He was thus led to an accurate observation and description of the reputed scenes of the story, and of the haunts of the Fairies. These had received only bare mention in the tradition itself, and little more than this even when they had been put into verse in the older time. But all these spots he knew well; many of them were the daily round of the shepherd and his collie. The legends he had learned thus acquired something of the reality which he felt. Hence Hogg's poems of Fairy are remarkable for the fulness, the richness, and the accuracy of the description of the country—of hill, glen, and moor.—VEITCH, JOHN, 1878, *The History and Poetry of the Scottish Border*, p. 358.

Hogg wrote certain short poems, the beauty of which in their kind Sir Walter himself never approached. — HUTTON, RICHARD HOLT, 1879, *Sir Walter Scott (English Men of Letters)*, p. 67.

The combination of rough humour with sweetness of purity and sentiment is by no means rare; but Hogg is one of the most eminent examples of it; all the more striking that both qualities were in him strongly acccentuated by his demonstrative temperament. His humour often degenerates into deliberate loutishness, affected oddity; and his tenderness of fancy sometimes approaches "childishness," or, as the Scotch call it, "bairnliness." But with all his extravagances, there is a marked individuality in the Shepherd's songs and poems; he was a singer by genuine impulse, and there was an open-air freshness in his note.—MINTO, WILLIAM, 1880, *The English Poets, ed. Ward, vol.* IV, *p.* 227.

The moving tales and strange legends from the fertile pen of the Shepherd, for generations to come, will help innocently to entertain the fancy of many an honest cottar's fireside in the long winter nights; while the strange unearthly weirdness of his "Fife Witch's" nocturnal ride, and the spiritual sweetness of his "Bonnie Kilmeny," will secure their author a high place among the classical masters of imaginative narrative in British literature; but his appearance on the field of narrative poetry in the same age with the more rich and powerful genius of Scott, was unfavourable to his asserting a permanent position as a poetical story-teller. It is as a song-writer, therefore, that he is likely to remain best known to the general public; for, though in this department he has no pretensions to the wealth or the power or the fire of Burns, he has prevailed to strike out a few strains of no common excellence, that have touched a chord in the popular heart and found an echo in the public ear: and this, indeed, is the special boast of good popular songs, that they are carried about as jewels and as charms in the breast of every man that has a heart, while intellectual works of a more imposing magnitude, like palatial castles, are seen only by the few who purposely go to see them or accidentally pass by them. Small songs are the circulating medium of the people. The big bullion lies in the bank.—BLACKIE, JOHN STUART, 1889, *Scottish Song*, p. 45.

Hogg deserved the approbation he received from his distinguished compeers. Scott probably understood him best, and invariably advised him well, receiving him heartily after a period of alienation owing to the "Poetic Mirror," and acting as peacemaker when Hogg became exasperated with Blackwood and the magazine. Wilson had a real and deep affection for the Ettrick Shepherd, as the idealism of the "Noctes" shows, and it is to be regretted that he did not write Hogg's biography, as at one time he intended. Southey's honest outspoken criticism and commendation were as heartily received by Hogg as they were given, and Wordsworth's memorial tribute strikes a true note of appreciation in crediting him with a "mighty minstrelsy."—BAYNE, THOMAS, 1891, *Dictionary of National Biography, vol.* XXVII, *p.* 101.

What Hogg was up to this time he remained to the end of his days. A man with a poetic gift—one may almost say with a certain literary gift—but with no skill in literature. He was ignorant and confident—ignorant of the world and its ways, and confident of himself and what he could do. If Scott could write metrical romances, he could; if the author of "Waverley" could write stories, he could; whatever anybody could do, he could do.—STODDARD, RICHARD HENRY, 1892, *Under the Evening Lamp, p.* 75.

Though the Shepherd's popularity among his countrymen has been wide and promises to be enduring, his work has received less attention than it merits at the hands of the literary critic. Much that he wrote is of little or no worth; his long ambitious tales in verse, "Queen Hynde," "Madoc of the Moor," and "The Pilgrims of the Sun," have fallen into the limbo of the unread, and for them there is no resurrection. His defects are glaring; he is often affected and over-ambitious; he uses words with a pedantic ineptitude, a comic infelicity which it would be hard to parallel in the works of any writer of corresponding genius. Compare him, not to Burns or Scott—which would be grotesquely unjust—but to such a minor singer as Tannahill, and you find that the verses of the west-country weaver have a depth of feeling, a glow and tremor of lyric passion, which moves you as you are never moved by aught that Hogg has written. But he was a most musical song-writer and a master of the ballad; he had a gift of humour both playful and grimly fantastic; and in one sphere of work he has hardly been excelled.—WHYTE, WALTER, 1891, *The Poets and the Poetry of the Century, Crabbe to Coleridge, ed. Miles, p.* 177.

Hogg's notes [Edition of Burns] are more amusing than instructive. Some notes were counted so personal or so improper that alternative leaves were supplied for substitution in binding.—HENLEY, WILLIAM ERNEST, AND HENDERSON, THOMAS F., 1896, *ed., The Poetry of Robert Burns, vol.* II, *p.* 288, *note.*

If Leyden surpassed Scott in versatility of intellect, James Hogg, with all his grotesque eccentricities, surpassed him in ultimate poetical quality.—HERFORD, C. H., 1897, *The Age of Wordsworth, p.* 195.

Willam Cobbett

1762-1835

Born at Farnham, Surrey, England, March 9, 1762: died near Farnham, June 18, 1835. A noted English political writer. He was the son of a peasant, obtained a meager education, enlisted in the army about 1783, obtained his discharge about 1791, and in 1792 emigrated to America. From 1797 to 1799 he published at Philadelphia "Porcupine's Gazette," a Federalist daily newspaper. He returned to England in 1800. In January, 1802, he began at London the publication of "Cobbett's Weekly Political Register," which, with trifling interruptions, was continued until his death; and in 1803 began to publish the "Parliamentary Debates," which in 1812 passed into the hands of T. C. Hansard. He at first supported the government, but about 1804 joined the opposition, with the result that he was several times fined for libel, and in 1810 sentenced to imprisonment for two years. He was elected to Parliament as member for Oldham in 1832, and again in 1834. Author of "Porcupine's Works" (1801-02), "A Grammar of the English Language" (1818), a grammar and a dictionary of the French language, "Cottage Economy" (1821), "The Emigrant's Guide" (1828), "Advice to Young Men and, incidentally, to Young Women" (1830), etc.—SMITH, BENJAMIN E., *ed.* 1894-97, *The Century Cyclopedia of Names, p.* 262.

PERSONAL

I had this day as a visitor one of the most distinguished literary and political characters which ever adorned this or any other country, namely Mr. William Cobbett. . . . Mr. Cobbett is now in his sixty-seventh year. He is above six feet high, stout made, of a plump, ruddy countenance, and has a most winning and engaging smile. His hair is as white as the driven snow. His whole appearance is of the most engaging and gentlemanly kind. He is a singularly abstemious and temperate man; never eating anything after dinner, with the exception of a little bread to his tea. He avoids spirits, wine, ale, porter.

His dislike to all these things is so great that he will not sit down in a room where they are used. His common drink is a little skim milk. He goes to bed at eight or nine o'clock, and rises by four or five in the morning.—BLAKEY, ROBERT, 1832, *Memoirs, pp.* 68, 70.

He presented himself before an impatient house, filled from floor to ceiling, which rose to greet him in a tumultuous rapture. His appearance is highly favourable; his ease, tact, and self-possession, are unrivalled. He was neither overpowered nor taken by surprise with these demonstrations of the Modern Athenians, but received them all as matter of course, which came a little in the way of proceeding to business. Mr. Cobbett is still of stately stature, and must, in youth, have been tall. He must then in physiognomy, person, and bearing, have been a fine specimen of the true Saxon breed,—

The eyes of azure, and the locks of brown,
And the blunt speech, that bursts without a pause,
And free-born thoughts, which league the soldier with the laws.

As, with the "Ciceronian suavity" he had promised to assume, he presented himself before the "critical audience of Edinburgh," he looked like an old English gentleman

Of the good olden time—

a hearty Essex or Hampshire squire, of the fourth magnitude, whose woods are flourishing, and his paternal acres unmortgaged, dressed for a dinner of some ceremony, in a coat of the best Saxon blue broadcloth, with its full complement of gilt buttons, and an ample white waistcoat, with flowing skirts. His thin, white hairs, and high forehead—the humour lurking in the eye, and playing about the lips, betokened something more than the squire in his gala-suit; still he altogether was of this respectable and responsible kind. His voice is low-toned, clear, and flexible; and so skillfully modulated, that not an aspiration was lost of his nervous, fluent, unhesitating, and perfectly correct discourse.—ANON, 1832, *Cobbett in Edinburgh, Tait's Edinburgh Magazine, vol.* 2, *p.* 236.

Mr. Cobbett, in personal stature, was tall and athletic. I should think he could not have been less than six feet, while his breadth was proportionally great. He was, indeed, one of the stoutest men in the house. I have said there was a tendency to corpulency about him. His hair was of a milk-white colour, and his complexion ruddy. His features were not strongly marked. What struck you most about his face was his small, sparkling, laughing eyes. When disposed to be humorous himself, you had only to look at his eyes and you were sure to sympathise in his merriment. When not speaking, the expression of his eyes and his countenance was very different. He was one of the most striking refutations of the principles of Lavater I ever witnessed. Never were the books of any man more completely at variance with his character. There was something so dull and heavy about his whole appearance, that any one who did not know him, would at once have set him down for some country clodpole—to use a favourite expression of his own—who not only never read a book, or had a single idea in his head, but who was a mere mass of mortality, without a particle of sensibility of any kind in his composition. He usually sat with one leg over the other, his head slightly drooping, as if sleeping, on his breast, and his hat down almost to his eyes.—GRANT, JAMES, 1835, *Random Recollections of the House of Commons from the Year* 1830 *to the Close of* 1835, *p.* 198.

O bear him where the rain can fall,
And where the winds can blow;
And let the sun weep o'er his pall
As to the grave ye go!
And in some little lone churchyard,
Beside the growing corn,
Lay gentle Nature's stern prose bard,
Her mightiest peasant-born.
Yes! let the wild-flower wed his grave,
That bees may murmur near,
When o'er his last home bend the brave,
And say—"A man lies here!"
For Britons honor Cobbett's name,
Though rashly oft he spoke;
And none can scorn, and few will blame
The low-laid heart of oak.
See, o'er his prostrate branches, see!
E'en factious hate consents
To reverence, in the fallen tree,
His British lineaments.

—ELLIOTT, EBENEZER, 1835, *Elegy on William Cobbett.*

Cobbett was not only an example of self-instruction, but of public teaching. He said, on some occasion, many years ago, "It is certain that I have been the great enlightener of the people of England;"

and so he was. The newspapers have not, that we are aware, adverted to our deepest obligation to him. He was the inventor of Twopenny Tracts. Let the title be inscribed on his monument. The infamous Six Acts, although they suspend the machinery for awhile of cheap political publications, could not undo what had been done, nor avert its great immediate, and far greater eventual utility. If only for that good work, honoured be the memory of old Cobbett.—FOX, W. J., 1835, *Monthly Repository, p.* 487.

A labourer's son, 'mid squires and lords
Strong on his own stout legs he stood,
Well-armed in bold and trenchant wit;
And well they learned that tempted it,
That his was English blood.
And every wound his victim felt
Had in his eyes a separate charm;
Yet, better than successful strife
He loved the memory of his life,
In boyhood, on the farm.

—LUSHINGTON, HENRY, 1838–48, *Cobbett; or A Rural Ride.*

With two or three qualities more, Cobbett would have been a very great man in the world; as it was, he made a great noise in it. . . . The immediate cause of his death was water on the chest. He was buried, according to his own desire, in a simple manner in the churchyard of Farnham, in the same mould as that in which his father and grandfather had been laid before him. His death struck people with surprise, for few could remember the commencement of his course, and there had seemed in it no middle and no decline; for though he went down to the grave an old man, he was young in the path he had lately started upon. He left a gap in the public mind which no one else could fill or attempt to fill up, for his loss was not merely that of a man, but of a habit—of a dose of strong drink which all of us had been taking for years, most of us during our lives, and which it was impossible for any one again to concoct so strongly, so strangely, with so much spice and flavour, or with such a variety of ingredients. And there was this peculiarity in the general regret—it extended to all persons.—BULWER, SIR HENRY LYTTON, 1867, *Historical Characters, vol.* II, *pp.* 101, 178.

Cobbett rose, under singular difficulties, many of which were of his own creation, from the condition of a farmer's boy to that of a member of the British Parliament. . . . Cobbett's marriage was eminently characteristic. When he was in New Brunswick, he saw, on an early December morning, a girl, not more than thirteen years of age, scrubbing a washtub in the snow. She was the daughter of a soldier, a serjeant-major like Cobbett himself. He resolved to marry her in due time. It seems that his project was favoured by the girl's father. Three or four years after he made this resolve, the parents of the girl were ordered back to Woolwich. Cobbett, thinking the risks of a residence in this town were neither few nor slight, recommended her to take up her residence with some decent people who would board her; and to meet this expense he handed her over all his savings, amounting to 150 guineas. They then parted for three or four years. When he returned to England, he found her engaged as a maid-of-all-work in a family. She returned him his 150 guineas unbroken, and in a few weeks they were married. — ROGERS, JAMES E. THOROLD, 1869, *Historical Gleanings, First Series, vol.* I, *pp.* 160, 161.

Much of Cobbett's wonderful staying-power lay in his splendid mental and physical health. An active and temperate existence, in which nothing was allowed to run to waste, warded off the approaches of senility. Excepting only a tumour which gave some trouble for a few months during 1824, he had known nothing of illness; beyond those trifling matters to which even the best constitutions are liable under given circumstances. After reaching his three score-and-ten, he could still boast of riding over the country with the youngest; or doing a day's work against any one of his labourers. This was an astonishingly active, fully-worked life; in which nothing of the morbid could possibly find entrance. An early riser, and no lingerer at meals, Cobbett never confessed to having any leisure time. Social pleasures, as such, would seem to have been almost unheeded, if not despised. Yet his hospitality was unbounded, and overflowing with good nature; and he was always at the service of persons who applied to him for advice, or, even, of those nondescript individuals who would claim the privileges of half-acquaintanceship, and call upon him to indulge a sort of curiosity.—SMITH, EDWARD, 1878, *William Cobbett: A Biography, vol.* II, *p.* 299.

The round, rosy, rather heavy face, the flaxen hair, the powerful and thick-set frame, the general air of hearty animal vigor,—all bespeak his nationality; and mind and character corresponded to the body which inclosed them. In every incident of Cobbett's life, the sturdy, stubborn persistence, the love of home and independence, the delight in fighting for fighting's sake, and the utter incapacity to recognize defeat,—all of which mark the Anglo-Saxon,—come out with wonderful clearness, and form a combination of qualities for which one may look in vain among other nations.—LODGE, HENRY CABOT, 1880-84, *Studies in History, p.* 113.

He made but a poor figure in the House; had not a scintillation of eloquence, and his manner was brusque almost to coarseness. The rudeness that is so often mistaken for independence never at any time "told" there, where the greatest and the humblest are certain to find their true level; and if there be any who recall him to memory, with a faint idea that they may accord to it respect, it will not be as seated on the Opposition bench of the House of Commons. Though he spoke often, he never made what might have been called "a speech." He seemed always on guard lest he might commit himself; indeed, in the House he never seemed at home, and was by no means the virtuous contemner of his superiors he was expected to have been; few who listened to him would have thought they heard the author of much envenomed bitterness—the quality that so continually characterized his written words.—HALL, SAMUEL CARTER, 1883, *Retrospect of a Long Life, p.* 137.

GENERAL

Have you seen Cobbett's last number? It is the most plausible and the best written of anything I have seen from his pen, and apparently written in a less fiendish spirit than the average of his weekly effusions. The self-complacency with which he assumes to himself exclusively, truths which he can call his own only as a horse-stealer can appropriate a stolen horse, by adding mutilation and deformities to robbery, is as artful as it is amusing.—COLERIDGE, SAMUEL TAYLOR, 1819, *Table Talk, ed. Ashe, Dec.* 13, *p.* 308.

This ["Cottage Economy"] is an excellent little book—written not only with admirable clearness and good sense, but in a very earnest and entertaining manner—and abounding with kind and good feelings, as well as with most valuable information: And as we have never scrupled openly to express our disapprobation of Mr. Cobbett's conduct and writings, when we thought him in the wrong, we shall scarcely be suspected of partiality in the gratitude we now profess to him, and the endeavour we make to asssist his exertions for the benefit of by far the most numerous and important part of society—the labouring classes.—JEFFREY, FRANCIS LORD, 1823, *Cobbett's Cottage Economy, Edinburgh Review, vol.* 38, *p.* 105.

People have about as substantial an idea of Cobbett as they have of Cribb. His blows are as hard, and he himself is as impenetrable. One has no notion of him as making use of a fine pen, but a great mutton-fist; his style stuns his readers, and he "fillips the ear of the public with a three-man beetle." . . . He is one of those writers who can never tire us—not even of himself; and the reason is, he is always "full of matter." He never runs to lees, never gives us the vapid leavings of himself, is never "weary, stale and unprofitable," but always setting out afresh on his journey, clearing away some old nuisance, and turning up new mould. His egotism is delightful, for there is no affectation in it. He does not talk of himself for lack of something to write about, but because some circumstance that has happened to himself is the best possible illustration of the subject, and he is not the man to shrink from giving the best possible illustration of the subject from a squeamish delicacy. He likes both himself and his subject too well. . . . He throws his head into his adversary's stomach, and takes away from him all inclination for the fight, hits fair or foul, strikes at every thing, and as you come up to his aid or stand ready to pursue his advantage, trips up your heels or lays you sprawling, and pummels you when down as much to his heart's content as ever the Yanguesian carriers belaboured Rosinante with their pack-staves. *"He has the back-trick simply the best of any man in Illyria."* He pays off both scores of old friendship and new-acquired enmity in a breath, in one perpetual volley, one raking fire of "arrowy sleet" shot from his pen.

However his own reputation or the cause may suffer in consequence, he cares not one pin about that, so that he disables all who oppose or who pretend to help him. —HAZLITT, WILLIAM, 1825, *The Spirit of the Age, pp.* 219, 221, 223.

I am reading Cobbett's work on gardening, and it makes me long for a plot to sow endive and cauliflower in. I am not yet come to his remarks on flower-gardening, but I expect that it will be more disquieting than the cabbage and salad dispensation. What a clever writer he is! Whatever his faults may be as a politician, he has true genius, and that he shows by the extraordinary interest he gives to common subjects.—HOWITT, MARY, 1832, *Letter to Sister Anna, Feb.* 4; *Autobiography, ed. her Daughter, vol.* I, *p.* 229.

This author did not in any way advance the practice of agriculture, either by precept or example; but he adorned the parts that have been mentioned, by his homely knowledge of the art, and most agreeable delineation. He did not grasp the art as a comprehensive whole, nor did he aspire to the higher branches, among which to indulge a lofty seat of view and ideal elevation.—DONALDSON, JOHN, 1854, *Agricultural Biography.*

It would be well worth the while of some competent editor to form a selection from Cobbett's multifarious writings. Since Swift, from whom he derived his style, there has been no more remarkable writer of terse, idiomatic English, and especially of the language of vituperation. When he was seeking work in Kew Gardens, at ten years old, he slept under a haystack, reading the "Tale of a Tub" as long as daylight lasted. His mind was not reserved or thoughtful enough to appropriate the irony of his great master; but in the "Political Register" there are lampoons as bitter, and almost as forcible and witty, as those of Swift himself. In his miscellaneous writings, such as his "English Grammar," Cobbett always digresses, from time to time, into gratuitous attacks on the multitudinous objects of his indignation. . . . In the "Rural Rides," which are perhaps the most peaceable and pleasant of his works, he interrupts a receipt for curing bacon, by an exhortation to the farmer's wife, not to let the Methodist preacher wheedle her out of a rasher when her husband is from home. In his writings, with all their faults, there is unfailing vigour, and a total absence of the maudlin sentimentality which disgraces, in the present day, the degenerate literature of agitation and discontent.—VENABLES, GEORGE STOVIN, 1859, *Macmillan's Magazine, vol.* 1, *p.* 41.

As a political writer Cobbett, who occupied a first place in the criticism of current politics for more than forty years, had few rivals. He was a great master of that homely, idiomatic English, which is persuasive by its very plainness and lack of ornament, and which is exhibited in its perfection by another farmer's son—another politician, but also a statesman of the highest and noblest type.—ROGERS, JAMES E. THOROLD, 1869, *Historical Gleanings, First Series, vol.* I, *p.* 176.

Had he full scholastic instruction, and the benefit of extensive reading, his abilities, cultivated and improved, might have placed his name with many of the highest in literature. As it was, his boldness wanted knowledge and judgment to control it; he was ignorant of much that the most ordinary writers ought to understand; he had no proper conception of the estimate in which the giants of literature are to be held. He pronounced it easy to imitate Shakspeare because the public had been partially deluded for a while by Ireland's "Vortigern;" and easy to copy Milton, because any one could make angels and devils fight like men. Having sense to see the vanity of pretending to be what he was not, he affected to decry what he did not possess; and yet, though he proclaimed his contempt for the learned languages as useless, he would fain have had his public think that he was not altogether ignorant of them, as was shown by his writing always *per centum,* and introducing now and then a Latin expression. . . . In the style in which he set forth his declarations, however extravagant, there was sure to be something attractive; whatever he supported or assailed, his readers would never fail to find something to interest or amuse them.—WATSON, JOHN SELBY, 1870, *Biographies of John Wilkes and William Cobbett, pp.* 397, 399.

He was a great master of clear and forcible idiomatic English. His "Rural Rides" expounds the homely aspects of English scenery with much picturesqueness and graphic neatness of touch. In his political diatribes he indulged in a licence of invective and abuse almost incredible to newspaper readers of this generation, although it was not so much above the ordinary heat of his time.—MINTO, WILLIAM, 1872-80, *Manual of English Prose Literature*, p. 517.

He was the comet of the literary hemisphere, dazzling the world with his brilliancy, perplexing it with his eccentricity, and alarming it with his apparent inflammability.—WALPOLE, SPENCER, 1878, *A History of England from the Conclusion of the Great War in* 1815, *vol.* I, *p.* 391.

As a writer Cobbett belongs to the school of Swift, for whose "Tale of a Tub" he sacrificed his supper; but he is far from being Swift's equal, for the Dean was a great genius and Cobbett was not. The pupil has neither the refinements of style nor the keenness of satire for which the master is still preëminent. But Cobbett possessed in ample measure Swift's simplicity of diction and strength of phrase, and he used pure Saxton to an extent and with a power which is well worth study at the present day.—LODGE, HENRY CABOT, 1880-84, *Studies in History*, *p.* 131.

Even his long expositions of past quarrels, and spiteful, personal attacks upon men dead and forgotten, have a certain interest, so living is the narrative, full of hot impulse and feeling, and boundless graphic detail. And in the foreground of everything he writes, the centre of all, is always that lively, amusing, hot-headed, wrong-headed self, a being inaccessible to reason, swayed by sudden impulses, by rapid mistaken impressions, by side gleams of confused reflection and distorted perspective so far as concerned the great public affairs into which he rashly threw himself without training for the work or understanding of its real bearings. But when we turn to the other side of his character, and find him in scenes which he thoroughly understands, in the fresh rural landscapes, and humble thrifty houses, and village economics among which he was bred, he is a very different person. Occasionally we come to a bit of fine observation of nature which would not have misbecome White of Selborne: and his pictures of home-scenery are often as touching and real in English sweetness and homely subdued beauty as if they had come from the hands of Gainsborough or Constable.—OLIPHANT, MARGARET O. W., 1882, *Literary History of England, XVIII-XIX Century*, *vol.* II, *p.* 302.

We believe him to be the most voluminous writer in our language, with the exception—if, indeed, he be an exception—of William Prynne; and we would take this opportunity of saying that if any one would know of what our language is capable, then let him study the writings of William Cobbett.—HOOD, E. PAXTON, 1884, *William Cobbett, The Leisure Hour*, *vol.* 33, *p.* 696.

Were the well-meaning persons to have their way who long for the establishment of an English Academy, one wonders what would be the attitude of such an august body towards a writer like Cobbett. And yet his claim to rank as a classic admits, I suppose, of little question. The position he holds among the immortals he has taken, as it were, by storm; and what no favour of literary clique helped to gain, no passing whim of favour can take away. . . . Of the merits of Cobbett's style there can be no question. In his moods of most frantic violence, dancing a war-dance around Lord Castlereagh's dead body, or covering with the foulest abuse the honoured name of Burke, the manner of his writing never lacks in skill. We may not approve the music it gives forth, but we cannot but allow that the pipe is never out of tune. Nor is the secret of the merits of his style far to seek. Of none other does the saying of Buffon hold more profoundly true that "*le style c'est l'homme.*" His very weaknesses as a man lent strength to his writing. Because he was obstinate, narrow-minded, and could see only the one side of a question, therefore his sight had nothing to distract it from seeing what he did see with perfect distinctness, and from describing that with perfect accuracy. It is surely no mere coincidence that in our times a similar intellectual harvest, and that the greatest of living English orators recalls in his obstinacy and in his self-sufficiency, no less than by the spell of his eloquence, the memory of Cobbett.—EGERTON, HUGH E., 1885, *A Scarce Book, The National Review*, *vol.* 5, *p.* 413.

As a writer of pure English, Cobbett stands out almost unrivalled, and hundreds of passages might be quoted from his writings which are masterpieces of diction.

He did not draw his illustrations from the fantasies of a perplexed brain, but from that nature which is always ready to reveal her secrets to those who love her. You will find his descriptions of scenery as true as those of Sir Walter Scott, and flowers and trees and coppices and wolds and woodlands and the birds and beasts that belong to them, are all put in their proper places. His word-paintings savour sometimes of almost an excessive realism. —GASKELL, CHARLES MILNES, 1886, *William Cobbett, The Nineteenth Century, vol.* 19, *p.* 255.

Nobody now would say of him as William Hazlitt said, under the more direct influence of his personal energy and power, that "he might be said to have the cleverness of Swift, the naturalness of Defoe, and the picturesque satirical description of Mandeville." He was perhaps as strong a man as Bernard Mandeville; but he had the cleverness of Swift without the genius, and Defoe's naturalness without the imagination that enabled Defoe to shape the real into an ideal, and in "Robinson Crusoe" to produce a work having some part of the nature of a poem, though Defoe, like Cobbett, was essentially a man of prose. Cobbett belaboured to good purpose the big drum of politics, and blew a trumpet all his own. But the plain speech of Cobbett was as honest and as resolute as the plain speech of Luther; and Luther in the conflict did not measure his words.—MORLEY, HENRY, 1887, *ed., Advice to Young Men by William Cobbett, Introduction, p.* 6.

The total is huge; for Cobbett's industry and facility of work were both appalling, and while his good work is constantly disfigured by rubbish, there is hardly a single parcel of his rubbish in which there is not good work. . . . As happens with all writers of his kindney he is not easily to be characterised. Like certain wines he has the *goût du terroir;* and that gust is rarely or never definable in words. It is however I think critically safe to say that the intensity and peculiarity of Cobbett's literary savour are in the ratio of his limitation. He was content to ignore so vast a number of things, he so bravely pushed his ignorance into contempt of them and almost into denial of their real existence, that the other things are real for him and in his writings to a degree almost unexampled. I am not the first by many to suggest that we are too diffuse in our modern imagination, that we are cumbered about too many things. No one could bring this accusation against Cobbett; for immense as his variety is in particulars, these particulars group themselves under comparatively few general heads. I do not think I have been unjust in suggesting that this ideal was little more than the bellyful, that Messer Gaster was not only his first but his one and sufficient master of arts.—SAINTSBURY, GEORGE, 1891, *William Cobbett, Macmillan's Magazine, vol.* 65, *pp.* 95, 108.

In Cobbett we have little of refinement, little of resource, little liberal equipment; but the tradition of common sense is still a vigorous force, and in his almost enthusiastic inculcation of lucidity and correctness of style, he keeps alive one of the best inheritances from the eighteenth century.—CRAIK, HENRY, 1895, *ed., English Prose, Introduction, vol.* IV, *p.* 5.

His words flowed as easily as his thoughts. His anecdotes, and especially his epithets, clung to the memory. He made no pretence of profound learning. He dealt out facts and arguments closely within the range of the ideas and experience of ordinary Englishmen; and he was a "popular writer" in the sense of one who wrote what all could understand. The *naïveté* of his egotism disarmed his critics. He rivalled Junius in the rich discursiveness of his vituperation. He had all the infallibility of a newspaper editor, without wearing the usual mask of one.—BONAR, JAMES, 1895, *English Prose, ed. Craik, vol.* IV, *p.* 577.

A brutal personality, excellently muscular, snatching at words as the handiest weapons wherewith to inflict itself, and the whole body of its thoughts and preferences, on suffering humanity, is likely enough to deride the daintiness of conscious art. Such a writer is William Cobbett, who has often been praised for the manly simplicity of his style, which he raised into a kind of creed. His power is undeniable; his diction, though he knew it not, both choice and chaste; yet page after page of his writing suggests only the reflection that here is a prodigal waste of good English. He bludgeons all he touches, and spends the same monotonous emphasis on his dislike of tea and on his hatred of the Government. His is the simplicity of a crude and violent mind, concerned only with giving forcible expression to its unquestioned prejudices. Irrelevance, the besetting sin of the ill-educated, he glories in, so that his very weakness puts on the semblance of strength, and helps to wield the hammer. —RALEIGH, WALTER, 1897, *Style*, *p.* 106.

Cobbett's inconsistencies are a proverb. Few publicists have contradicted themselves so flatly and so often, and yet produced so powerful an impression of tenacity and honesty. His opinions shifted like a kaleidoscope, but the man was hewn out of rock. His copiousness was enormous, and though he did not adorn all that he touched, he touched nothing without setting his unmistakable stamp upon it. Grammar, finance, church history, farming, practical morality, and a score of other subjects Cobbett stripped of pedantry and technique for the behoof of the vast uneducated mob of Georgian England. . . . All that is strong, sinewy, and simple in Cobbett seems to have filtered through, unalloyed, into his English style, which his harshest critics have accordingly praised without reserve. He may swell with arrogance, but his prose never becomes timid; his facts and his reasons may be grotesque, but he never chooses the wrong word. His fundamentally concrete mind was too ready to brandish scientific formulas of which he half grasped the scope; but the same fundamentally concrete quality of mind which prevented him from being a master of theory, or a shaper of ideas, preserved him, as a writer, from the abstract formalism of style which the later eighteenth century bequeathed to the early nineteenth. His style is himself, full of personal flavour, anecdote, colloquial turns, questions, gibes, nick names, apparently distaining all literary distinction. In function, if not in genius, he is the Burns of modern prose, and his example, though less efficacious, was not less salutary, in the generation which gathered its political teaching among the technicalities of Bentham, the verbosities of Mackintosh, and the involutions of Coleridge. —HERFORD, C. H., 1897, *The Age of Wordsworth*, *pp.* 9, 10.

For years displayed, amid many extravagances of prejudice and crudities of utterance, a command of racy, homely, and vigorous English which made him the most popular, if not the most powerful, political writer of his time.—TRAILL, HENRY DUFF, 1897, *Social England*, *vol.* VI, *p.* 32.

William Motherwell

1797–1835

Born, in Glasgow, 13 Oct. 1797. At school in Edinburgh, 1805–08; in Paisley, 1809–14. At Glasgow Univ., 1818–19. Contrib. verses to the Greenock "Visitor," 1818. In Sheriff-Clerk's office, Paisley, 1819. Sheriff-Clerk Depute of Renfrewshire, May 1819 to Nov. 1829. Edited "Paisley Mag." 1828; "Paisley Advertiser," 1828–30; "Glasgow Courier," 1830–35. Contrib. to "The Day," 1832–35. To London, to give evidence before a Committee of House of Commons, Aug. 1835. Died, in Glasgow, 1 Nov. 1835. Buried in Necropolis, Glasgow. *Works:* "Renfrewshire Characters and Scenery" (under pseud. "Isaac Brown"), 1824; "Minstrelsy, Ancient and Modern," 1827; "Jeanie Morrison" (1832); "Poems, Narrative and Lyrical," 1832. He *edited* "The Harp of Renfrewshire," 1819; A. Henderson's "Scottish Proverbs," 1832; Burns' "Poems" (with Hogg), 1835. *Collected Works:* ed. by J. M'Conechy, with *life*, 1846.—SHARP, R. FARQUHARSON, 1897, *A Dictionary of English Authors*, *p.* 206.

PERSONAL

Lay me then gently in my narrow dwelling,
Thou gentle heart;
And though thy bosom should with grief be swelling,
Let no tear start;
It were in vain,—for Time hath long been knelling,—
"Sad one, depart!"

—MOTHERWELL, WILLIAM, 1835, *Last Verses, Given to a Friend.*

He was small, well formed, and muscular, with a large head, was an accomplished boxer and fencer, and had a local reputation as an antiquary.—JOHNSON, ROSSITER, 1875, *Little Classics*, *Authors*, *p.* 189.

Motherwell was the most genial creature, with a Conservative craze. In his mind Toryism was bound up with poetry, that is with antiquarian romance and

"Bonnie Prince Charlie" rubbish. — SCOTT, . WILLIAM BELL, 1882, *Autobiographical Notes, ed. Minto, vol.* I, *p.* 79.

A restrained conversationalist, Motherwell could be eager and even vehement when deeply moved, and with kindred spirits—such as R. A. Smith, the musician, and others of the "Whistle Binkie" circle —he was both easy and affable. His social instinct and public spirit are illustrated in his spirited cavalier lyrics. His essentially superstitious temperament, clinging to the Scottish mythology that amused Burns, specially qualified him for writing weird lyrics like his "Demon Lady" and such a successful fairy ballad as "Elfinland Wud."—BAYNE, THOMAS, 1894, *Dictionary of National Biography, vol.* XXXIX, *p.* 193.

GENERAL

When Aaron's rod sprang out and budded, those who saw it could not marvel more at the dry timber producing leaf and bloom than we did when Motherwell, an acute and fastidious antiquarian, appeared as a poet, original and vigorous. His lyrics are forceful and flowing,—with more of the strength of Burns than of his simplicity and passion. — CUNNINGHAM, ALLAN, 1833, *Biographical and Critical History of the Literature of the Last Fifty Years.*

All his perceptions are clear, for all his senses are sound; he has fine and strong sensibilities and a powerful intellect. . . . His style is simple, but, in his tenderest movements, masculine; he strikes a few bold knocks at the door of the heart, which is instantly opened by the master or mistress of the house, or by son or daughter, and the welcome visitor at once becomes one of the family. — WILSON, JOHN (CHRISTOPHER NORTH), 1833, *Motherwell's Poems, Blackwood's Magazine, vol.* 33, *p.* 670.

"Jeannie Morison" and "My heid is like to rend, Willie," are scarcely surpassed for simplicity and tenderness in the whole range of Scottish poetry.—GRISWOLD, RUFUS W., 1844, *The Poets and Poetry of England in the Nineteenth Century, p.* 329.

He was about equally successful in two departments,—the martial and the plaintive; yet stirring as are his "Sword Chant of Thorstein Raudi" and his "Battle-Flag of Sigurd," I doubt much whether they are entitled to the same praise, or have gained the same deserved acceptance, as his "Jeanie Morrison" or his striking stanzas commencing "My heid is like to rend." . . . Several of his lyrics also verge on excellence; but it must be acknowledged of his poetry generally, that ingenious although it be, it rather excites expectation than fairly satisfies it.—MOIR, D. M., 1851–52, *Sketches of the Poetical Literature of the Past Half-Century, pp.* 247, 248.

Two of the ballads of William Motherwell are among the most beautiful in the Scottish dialect, so full of lyrical beauty; and yet the one which is the most touching is scarcely known, except to a few lovers of poetry. "Jeanie Morrison," indeed, has an extensive popularity in Scotland, and yet even that charming song is comparatively little known in this country. Burns is the only poet with whom, for tenderness and pathos, Motherwell can be compared. . . . By touching and retouching, during many years, did "Jeanie Morrison" attain her perfection, and yet how completely has art concealed art! How entirely does that charming song appear like an irrepressible gush of feeling that *would* find vent. In "My heid is like to rend, Willie," the appearance of spontaneity is still more striking, as the passion is more intense,—intense, indeed, almost to painfulness.—MITFORD, MARY RUSSELL, 1851, *Recollectious of a Literary Life, p.* 540.

His martial lyrics are among the finest ever written.—JOHNSON, ROSSITER, 1875, *Little Classics, Authors, p.* 189.

As an antiquary, he was shrewd, indefatigable, and truthful. As a poet, he was happiest in pathetic or sentimental lyrics, though his own inclinations led him to prefer the chivalrous and martial style of the old minstrels.—CHAMBERS, ROBERT, 1876, *Cyclopædia of English Literature, ed. Carruthers.*

Motherwell's reputation in his own country as a poet was made by the plaintive song of "Jeanie Morrison," a sweet and touching reminiscence of pleasant days spent with a school playfellow and child sweetheart. This and another song in the Scotch dialect, "My heid is like to break," in which a betrayed damsel harrows up the feelings of her seducers with pitiless pathos, may be said to be the only two lyrics of his that have taken any hold of fame. They prove him to have been a man of keen sensibility; he was also a man of vigorous intellect and large culture, more of a student and a scholar than any contemporary Scotch lyrist.—MINTO, WILLIAM, 1880, *English Poets, ed. Ward, vol.* IV, *p.* 524.

There are very few Scottish songs of modern date that can equal "Jeanie Morrison" in tenderness and feeling. The heroine was a real schoolmate of Motherwell's, whose beauty and childish companionship left so indelible an impression on his young heart that he retained his love for her during all the future years of his existence. They never met, however, after separating in childhood.—ROSS, JOHN D., 1886, *Celebrated Songs of Scotland, p.* 329.

Such was William Motherwell, whose poetry I read over and over in my nonage, in summer when the days were long, and my work ended before the setting of the sun, and under my evening lamp, when it was too dark and cold to be out-of-doors. It attracted me, and it repelled me. I knew then why it attracted me, and I know now, what I did not then, why it repelled me. It was because a great deal of it was a forced, not a natural, growth—a simulation of moods and feelings which did not exist in the mind or heart of the poet, a make-believe of love and loss, of sin and sorrow. It was not a creation, but a production, a manufactured melancholy, an elaborated gloom. It is studiedly morbid and predeterminedly unhealthy, darkened with imaginary infamy, convulsive with pretended pangs. It was, in short, merely literary verse, and was, therefore, a sham and a fraud. But this is only one side of it; for there is another side, and that, within the limitations of Motherwell's genius, is glorious and noble. Many poets have sung of childish love, but none so well as Motherwell in "Jeanie Morrison," which is full of feeling and pathetic tenderness. Many poets have sung of betrayed womanliness (for lovely woman *will* stoop to folly), but none so well as Motherwell in "My heid is like to rend, Willie," the sorrow of which is heartfelt and profound.—STODDARD, RICHARD HENRY, 1892, *Under the Evening Lamp, p.* 87.

Among the minor poets of Great Britain, Motherwell should maintain a leading position. Without that supreme adaptability to the genius of his countrymen which made Burns *facile princeps* in their hearts, Motherwell possesses an individuality such as all poets, as distinguished from mere versifiers have. A fondness for archaic words and forms of speech gives an air of affectation to many of his productions; but even this may be forgiven when it has such splendid results as "The Cavalier's Song," which, had it been really written by Lovelace or Suckling, would have figured in every anthology. Unfortunately, Motherwell wrote too much—that is, too much in one vein.—INGRAM, JOHN H., 1894, *The Poets and the Poetry of the Century, John Keats to Edward Lord Lytton, ed. Miles, p.* 185.

Of his original work, "Jeanie Morrison" is the best known; and those who have read, especially if they have read it in youth, "The Sword Chant of Thorstein Raudi," will not dismiss it as Wardour Street; while he did some other delightful things.—SAINTSBURY, GEORGE, 1896, *A History of Nineteenth Century Literature, p.* 109.

He had a taste for research in old popular poetry, but he took such liberties that his versions are not to be trusted. He also allowed the pseudo-antique to mar some of his own work, especially the fine "Cavalier Song." He is happiest in the vein of pathetic Scotch verse, of which the best specimen he left is his "Jeanie Morrison." He had the feeling and sensibility of a minor Burns, but not the force. —WALKER, HUGH, 1897, *The Age of Tennyson, p.* 61.

Michael Scott

1789–1835

Michael Scott (born 1789, died 1835), humorist, was educated at the High School and University of Glasgow, his native town, and in 1806 went to Jamaica, where he remained until 1822. He returned to Scotland, and became engaged in mercantile transactions. His admirably conceived sketches, "Tom Cringle's Log," were at first published incognito in *Blackwood's Magazine*, and appeared in volume form in 1834; "The Cruise of the Midge," which was hardly so successful, appeared in 1836.—SANDERS, LLOYD C., *ed.*, 1887, *Celebrities of the Century, p.* 908.

PERSONAL

Of what manner of man he was, how he bore himself among his fellows, his comrades in pleasure and business, in sport, travel, and adventure by sea and land, no memory remains. His name alone survives as the author of two works which have taken their place among the classics of English fiction, and in their pages, if anywhere, must this shadowy figure find shape and substance. It is but sixty years since he died, a mere moment of time in the world's history; and yet we know no more of him than, after six hundred years, we know of his namesake, the great wizard who spoke.

"The words that cleft Eildon hills in three,
And bridled the Tweed with a curb of stone."

—MORRIS, MOWBRAY, 1895, *ed. Tom Cringle's Log, Introduction, p.* xii.

There used to be a tradition at Cambridge to the effect that an undergraduate, being called on in examination to give some account of John the Baptist, returned the answer, "Little or nothing is known of this extraordinary man,"—a reply which probably did not go far enough to satisfy the examiner. Scarcely more satisfying, however, must be the response of the biographer who is called on to gratify natural curiosity regarding the author of "Tom Cringle's Log"—scarcely more satisfying, though with apparently so much less of excuse. For it is only a little over sixty years since the death of Michael Scott. Neither was his a case of posthumous reputation, or a rehabilitation after long neglect, which might have accounted for the obscuring of biographical detail—his work, though it has lost nothing of popularity, or certainly of readableness in the interim, having been received with acclamation on its first appearance. And yet, after diligent and eager inquiry, the present writer finds himself forced to acknowledge that all but a meagre outline of the facts of Scott's life is lost. This is the more remarkable in that he was obviously no bookworm or literary recluse, and that all who know his writings will feel instinctively that one so characterised by humor and the love of good company—to say nothing of practical joking—should have strewn anecdote thick behind him wherever he went. . . . He is buried in the Necropolis, where an unpretending monument marks his resting-place and that of his wife and several of their children. In the inscription which it bears, no allusion whatever is made to his literary achievements. I have been told that in private life Scott was a quiet, easy-going man, of modest and retiring disposition, and also, on the authority of an old lady who remembers his death, that great was the surprise in Glasgow when it became known that he had been the author of thrilling tales of adventure by sea and land.—DOUGLAS, SIR GEORGE, 1897, *The Blackwood Group (Famous Scots), pp.* 134, 140.

GENERAL

Mullion. "Marryat himself is enough almost to bear the concern through. A capital writer, sir—beats the American, Cooper, to shivers—he's only second, in fact, to Tom Cringle." *North.* "That's high praise, I promise you, sir. Cringle, indeed, is a giant."—WILSON, JOHN, 1832, *Noctes Ambrosianæ, Oct.*

"Tom Cringle's Log," by Michael Scott, and "The Cruise of the Midge"—both originally published in "Blackwood's Magazine"—are veritable productions of the sea—a little coarse, but spirited and showing us "things as they are."—CHAMBERS, ROBERT, 1876, *Cyclopædia of English Literature, ed. Carruthers.*

Two sea tales of Mr. Michael Scott still worthily survive in "Tom Cringle's Log" and the "Cruise of the Midge."—RUSSELL, PERCY, 1894, *A Guide to British and American Novels, p.* 68.

It is not only, nor even mainly, perhaps, for the qualities assigned to him by the critics of the "Noctes Ambrosianæ" that Michael Scott has won and kept his place in fiction. His pictures of the sea and seafaring life are, beyond question, extremely vivid and striking; startling, indeed, they might sometimes be called, with a wild, lurid picturesqueness which, no doubt, gave Fonblanque his idea of Salvator Rosa. No landsman has ever matched him in this respect, nor come near to him; but Marryat and Cooper were not landsmen, and it would be hard to grant Scott all the superiority that Wilson assumed for him. Good as his sea-pieces certainly are, he was as much a master on land,—in that wonderful panorama, for instance, unfolding scene after scene through all the phases of the great storm in Cuba. Scott surely holds his place by right of many qualities rather than of pre-eminence in one. He had a keen eye for the picturesque, wherever it was to be found; but, liberally as he loved her, he was no mere court-painter of nature. Always, wherever his scene is laid,—among the fogs and shoals of the North Sea or the sunny waters of the Caribbean Archipelago, in the breezy highlands of Jamaica, on the wooded slopes of Hayti, or the sweltering lowlands of the Spanish Main,—there are human figures in the foreground, always through his pages beats the pulse of human life.—MORRIS, MOWBRAY, 1895, *ed. Tom Cringle's Log, Introduction, p.* xv.

He employed his experiences in composing for *Blackwood's Magazine*, and afterwards reducing to book shape, the admirable miscellanies in fiction entitled "Tom Cringle's Log" and "The Cruise of the Midge," which contain some of the best fighting, fun, tropical scenery, and description generally, to be found outside the greatest masters. Very little is known of Scott, and he wrote nothing else.—SAINTSBURY, GEORGE, 1896, *A History of Nineteenth Century Literature, p.* 160.

Would be not unworthy to be bracketed with Marryat if a man could be judged by parts of his books without regard to the whole; but unfortunately "Tom Cringle's Log" (1829–30) and "The Cruise of the Midge" (1836) are little more than scenes and incidents loosely strung together. Perhaps Scott was influenced by the *genius loci;* at any rate his books resemble the "Noctes Ambrosianæ" in so far as they are the outlet to every riotous fancy and every lawless freak of the writer's humour. —WALKER, HUGH, 1897, *The Age of Tennyson, p.* 80.

"Tom Cringle's Log" appeared in "Blackwood's Magazine," beginning with the September number of 1829; the final chapters appeared in August 1833. The instalments were intermittent at first, and each had its own title. Blackwood advised that the papers should be connected so as to make a continuous narrative, and in the June issue of 1831 "Tom Cringle's Log" was first used as a title, but then only as the title of a single paper. As the story appeared it received a warm welcome. Coleridge pronounced it to be "most excellent," but Captain Marryat thought it melodramatic. There is some doubt as to where the chapters were written, and Anthony Trollope in "The West Indies and the Spanish Main" refers to a tradition that the work was written at Raymond Lodge, the house which Scott occupied in Jamaica. It was probably written in Glasgow in the intervals of business. It first appeared in book form at Paris in 1836, after Scott's death. Scott so successfully concealed his identity that he was dead before his authorship of "Tom Cringle" was known.—MACDONALD, J. R., 1897, *Dictionary of National Biography, vol.* LI, *p.* 62.

Granting, then, that rarely if ever have more brilliant pictures of more interesting incidents been more lavishly set before a reader than in the pages of "Tom Cringle's Log," we are impelled to enquire what are the corresponding weaknesses which have debarred the author from taking the highest rank as a writer. The answer is not far to seek; it is a defect of constructive power. If he possessed much genius, Michael Scott had but little art. The effect of his fine pictures is not cumulative; each is alike revealed, as it were, by a powerful flash, and the result is that they obliterate one another. . . . Scott's stories have here been considered together, for though the "Log" is on the whole justly the favourite of the two, in general characteristics they are almost identical. Quite towards the close, both books display some slight tendency to "drag," but in this respect the "Cruise" is the worse transgressor. It is also the more loosely put together, and this despite the fact that in the relations subsisting between Lennox and Adderfang, and the mystery which surrounds young De Walden, the author has obviously been at pains to sustain interest by something in the nature of a plot. . . . On the whole, such fine books are they both that to criticise either is deservedly to incur the imputation of being spoiled with good things.— DOUGLAS, SIR GEORGE, 1897, *The Blackwood Group (Famous Scots), pp.* 146, 150.

John Marshall

1755-1835

Born in Fauquier County, Va., Sep 24, 1755: died at Philadelphia, July 6, 1835. A celebrated American jurist. He served in the Revolutionary War; was a member of the Virginia convention to ratify the constitution in 1788; was a United States envoy to France 1797-98; was a member of Congress from Virginia 1799-1800; was secretary of state 1800-1801; and was chief justice of the United States Supreme Court 1801-35. He published a "Life of Washington" (5 vols. 1804-07), the first volume of which was published separately under the title of "A History of the American Colonies" (1824).—SMITH, BENJAMIN E., *ed.*, 1894-97, *The Century Cyclopedia of Names, p.* 659.

PERSONAL

The . . . of the United States is, in his person, tall, meager, emaciated; his muscles relaxed, and his joints so loosely connected, as not only to disqualify him, apparently, for any vigorous exertion of body, but to destroy every thing like elegance and harmony in his air and movements. Indeed, in his whole appearance and demeanor; dress, attitudes, gesture; sitting, standing or walking; he is as far removed from the idolized graces of Lord Chesterfield, as any other gentleman on earth. To continue the portrait; his head and face are small in proportion to his height; his complexion swarthy; the muscles of his face, being relaxed, give him the appearance of a man of fifty years of age, nor can he be much younger, his countenance has a faithful expression of great good humor and hilarity; while his black eyes—that unerring index—possess an irradiating spirit, which proclaims the imperial powers of the mind that sits enthroned within.—WIRT, WILLIAM, 1803, *The Letters of the British Spy.*

Marshall is of a tall, slender figure, not graceful nor imposing, but erect and steady. His hair is black, his eyes small and twinkling, his forehead rather low; but his features are in general harmonious. His manners are plain, yet dignified; and an unaffected modesty diffuses itself through all his actions. His dress is very simple, yet neat; his language chaste, but hardly elegant; it does not flow rapidly, but it seldom wants precision. . . . He has not the majesty and compactness of thought of Dr. Johnson; but in subtle logic he is no unworthy disciple of David Hume.—STORY, JOSEPH, 1808, *To S. P. P. Fay, Feb.* 25; *Life and Letters, vol.* I, *pp.* 166, 167.

We then went into the Supreme Court. Your father will tell you that it is the most dignified body in the United States. It is a small room, and looks like a handsome cell in a monastery. The ceiling is like a scallop-shell: all is marble. Chief Justice Marshall was presiding, and reading an opinion. His voice is feeble. His face has a fine union of intellect and tranquility, the seal of a well-spent life upon it.—SEDGWICK, CATHERINE M., 1831, *To K. M. Sedgwick, Feb.* 2; *Life and Letters, ed. Dewey, p.* 214.

He had no frays in boyhood. He had no quarrels or outbreakings in manhood. He was the composer of strifes. He spoke ill of no man. He meddled not with their affairs. He viewed their worst deeds through the medium of charity. He had eight sisters and six brothers, with all of whom, from youth to age, his intercourse was marked by the utmost kindness and affection; and, although his eminent talents, high public character, and acknowledged usefulness, could not fail to be a subject of pride and admiration to all of them, there is no one of his numerous relatives, who has had the happiness of a personal association with him, in whom his purity, simplicity, and affectionate benevolence did not produce a deeper and more cherished impression than all the achievements of his powerful intellect.—BINNEY, HORACE, 1835, *Address before the Councils of Philadelphia.*

With Judge Story sometimes came the man to whom he looked up with feelings little short of adoration; the aged Chief-Justice Marshall. There was almost too much mutual respect in our first meeting; we knew something of his individual merits and services; and he maintained through life, and carried to his grave, a reverence for woman as rare in its kind as in its degree. It had all the theoretical fervour and magnificence of Uncle Toby's, with the advantage of being grounded upon an extensive knowledge of the sex. He was the father and the grandfather of women; and out of this experience he brought, not only the love and pity which their offices and position command, and the awe of purity which they excite in the minds of the pure, but a steady conviction of their intellectual equality with men; and, with this, a deep sense of their social injuries. Throughout life he so invariably sustained their cause, that no indulgent libertine dared to flatter and humor, no sceptic, secure in the possession of power, dared to scoff at the claims of woman in the presence of Marshall, who, made clear-sighted by his purity, knew the sex far better than either. How delighted we were to see Judge Story bring in the tall, majestic, bright-eyed old man!—old by chronology, by the lines on his composed face, and by his services to the republic; but so dignified, so fresh, so present to the time, that no feeling of compassionate consideration for age dared to mix with the contemplation of him.—MARTINEAU, HARRIET, 1838, *Western Travel, vol.* I, *p.* 247.

A tall, venerable man; his hair tied in a cue, according to olden custom, and with a countenance indicating that simplicity of mind and benignity which so eminently distinguish his character. I had the pleasure of several long conversations with him, and was struck with admiration at the extraordinary union of modesty and power, gentleness and force which his mind displays. His house is small, and more humble in appearance than those of the average of successful lawyers or merchants. I called three times upon him; there is no bell to the door; once I turned the handle of it, and walked in unannounced; on the other two occasions he had seen me coming, and lifted the latch and received me at the door, although he was at the time suffering from some very severe contusions received in the stage while travelling on the road from Fredericksburg to Richmond. I verily believe there is not a particle of vanity in his composition, unless it be of that venial and hospitable nature which induces him to pride himself on giving to his friends the best glass of Madeira in Virginia.—MURRAY, CHARLES AUGUSTUS, 1839, *Travels in North America During the Years* 1834–5–6, *ch.* ix.

I can never forget how he would prostrate his tall form before the rude low benches without backs at Cool Spring Meeting-House, in the midst of his children and grandchildren, and his old neighbours. In Richmond he always set an example to the gentlemen of the same conformity, though many of them did not follow it.—MEADE, WILLIAM, 1857, *Recollections of Old Churches, Ministers and Families of Virginia.*

The residence of the Chief Justice in Richmond was built by himself, and situated on Shockhoe Hill. Though without the slightest architectural pretensions, it was commodious, and the grounds were ample. No man was more attached to his home, and his judicial labors were so distributed, that he was enabled to spend the most of each year in the midst of his family. The session of the Supreme Court at Washington, and the Circuit Courts for Virginia and North Carolina completed the annual round of his judicial duties. Having considerable leisure, and being fond of agriculture, he purchased a farm three or four miles from Richmond, which he visited frequently, often on foot. He also owned a farm in Fauquier, his native county, to which he made an annual visit. His family and social attachments were warm and constant, and his periodical visits to Fauquier were always highly enjoyed both by himself and his numerous relatives and friends. He took great delight in social, and even convivial, pleasures. He was a member of the Barbecue, or Quoit Club, at Richmond, for more than forty years; and no one participated in the exercise and recreation that took place at their meetings with more zest and enthusiasm than himself.—FLANDERS, HENRY, 1857, *The Lives and Times of the Chief Justices of the Supreme Court of the United States, vol.* II, *p.* 516.

The day after my arrival at the capital [1826] I called upon Judge Story, at the Supreme Court, as he had requested me to do. Immediately upon adjournment he presented me to the Chief Justice and Judge Bushrod Washington, both gentlemen whom I had much desired to meet. The first view of Judge Marshall was not impressive. He struck me as a tall man who regretted his height, because he had not the knack of carrying it off with ease and dignity. His manner was so simple as to be almost rustic; and, were it not for the brilliancy of his eyes, he might have been taken for a mere political judge instead of the recognized expositor of the Constitution. — QUINCY, JOSIAH, 1883, *Figures of the Past from the Leaves of Old Journals*, *p.* 242.

He presided for the last time in the Supreme Court in the winter season of 1835. . . . His tomb in Shocko Hill Cemetery consists of a marble slab, held by four upright columns. Upon the slab is the simple inscription he wrote two days before his death: "John Marshall, son of Thomas and Mary Marshall, was born on the 24th of September, 1755; intermarried with Mary Willis Ambler, the 3d of January, 1783; departed this life the 6th of July, 1835.—MARSHALL, S. E., 1884, *Chief-Justice John Marshall, Magazine of American History, vol.* 12, *p.* 71.

As the years pass, the fame of this great man continues to shine with undiminished lustre, and so will continue until the firmament from whence beam the glories of Tribonian and D'Aguesseau, of Hale and Mansfield, is rolled together like a scroll.—FULLER, MELVILLE W., 1885, *Chief-Justice Marshall, The Dial, vol.* 6, *p.* 12.

The hundreth anniversary of the day, February 4, 1801, when John Marshall took oath as Chief Justice of the United States was honored in the centres of population in this country by many meetings, especially of lawyers, by many addresses of weight and significance, by dinners, by many articles in the magazines, and due attention from the newspapers. Marshall's reputation is vastly greater than it was a hundred years ago. . . . It is reassuring that such a public servant as he, whose service was intellectual, and was concerned with fundamental principles, should be remembered and honored as he has been so long after his death. It is a wholesome thing that a great judge should be so honored. Most of the judges of our Supreme Court devote themselves to the public service at great sacrifice of their private interests. They are hard-worked and meagrely paid. It is well that they should have such assurance as may come from these late tributes paid to Marshall that the work of a great judge is not forgotten.—MARTIN, E. S., 1901, *This Busy World, Harper's Weekly, vol.* 45, *p.* 186.

CHIEF JUSTICE

The character of his mind, its patience, its calmness, its power of analysis and generalization, and the steadiness of its movements, made him peculiarly fitted for the exposition of constitutional law. Whatever rank may be assigned to him as a common lawyer, in this department he stands confessedly alone and without a rival.—HILLARD, GEORGE S., 1836, *Chief-Justice Marshall, North American Review, vol.* 42, *p.* 227.

He was supremely fitted for high judicial station—a solid judgment, great reasoning powers, acute and penetrating mind; with manners and habits to suit the purity and the sanctity of the ermine; attentive, patient, laborious; grave on the bench, social in the intercourse of life; simple in his tastes, and inexorably just. Seen by a stranger come into a room, and he would be taken for a modest country gentleman, without claims to attention, and ready to take the lowest place in company or at table, and to act his part without trouble to anybody. Spoken to and closely observed, he could be seen to be a gentleman of finished breeding, of winning and prepossessing talk, and just as much mind as the occasion required him to show. —BENTON, THOMAS HART, 1854–56, *Thirty Years' View, vol.* I, *p.* 681.

His opinions do not abound in displays of learning. His simplicity—a character so conspicuous in all his writings and actions—that first and highest characteristic of true greatness—led him to say and do just what was necessary and proper to the purpose in hand. Its reflected consequences on his own fame as a scholar, a statesman, or a jurist seem never once to have occurred to him. As a judge, the Old World may be fairly challenged to produce his superior. His style is a model,—simple and masculine; his reasoning direct, cogent, demonstrative, advancing with a giant's pace and power, and yet withal so easy evidently to him as to show clearly a mind in the constant habit of such efforts.—SHARSWOOD, GEORGE, 1854, *Professional Ethics*, *p.* 103.

His judicial career alone extends through a continuous period of thirty-five years. I believe, if not the longest, it is the most successful, the most brilliant, the most honorable of any on record. Its history is the history of the Supreme

Court through this entire period. Its published decisions alone fill more than thirty volumes of Reports.—VAN SANTVOORD, GEORGE, 1854, *Sketches of the Lives and Judicial Services of the Chief-Justices of the Supreme Court of the United States*, *p.* 296.

Who among them [the ancient Greeks and Romans] dispensed public justice and laid broad and deep the foundations of constitutional law like John Marshall?—BARNES, ALBERT, 1855, *Essays and Reviews, vol.* II, *p.* 264.

He kept himself at the front on all questions of constitutional law, and, consequently, his master hand is seen in every case which involved that subject. At the same time he and his co-workers, whose names are, some of them, almost as familiar as his own, were engaged in laying, deep and strong, the foundations on which the jurisprudence of the country has since been built. Hardly a day now passes in the court he so dignified and adorned without reference to some decision of his time as establishing a principle which, from that day to this, has been accepted as undoubted law.—WAITE, MORRISON R., 1884, *Address at the Unveiling of the Statue of Chief Justice Marshall, p.* 18.

"The Expounder of the Constitution." A title given to John Marshall, chief justice of the United States from 1801 till his death. His decisions in the supreme court raised that court to a point of public respect and professional reputation which has not since been surpassed, and particularly in the departments of constitutional and commercial law he is considered of the highest authority.—FREY, ALBERT R., 1888, *Sobriquets and Nicknames, p.* 104.

That which Hamilton, in the bitterness of defeat, had called "a frail and worthless fabric," Marshall converted into a mighty instrument of government. The Constitution which began as an agreement between conflicting States, Marshall, continuing the work of Washington and Hamilton, transformed into a charter of national life. When his life closed, his work was done—a nation had been made. Before he died, he heard this great fact declared with unrivalled eloquence by Webster. It was reserved to another generation to put Marshall's work to the last and awful test of war, and to behold it come forth from that dark ordeal triumphant and supreme. John Marshall stands in history as one of that small group of men who have founded states. He was a nation-maker, a state-builder. His monument is in the history of the United States, and his name is written upon the Constitution of his country.—LODGE, HENRY CABOT, 1901, *John Marshall, Statesman, North American Review, vol.* 172, *p.* 204.

If it be true—as it is beyond cavil—that to Washington more than to any other man is due the birth of the American nation, it is equally true beyond cavil that to Marshall more than to any other man is it due that the Nation has come safely through the trying ordeals of infantile weakness and youthful effervescence, and has triumphantly emerged into well-developed and lusty manhood.—OLNEY, RICHARD, 1901, *Chief Justice Marshall, The Outlook, vol.* 67, *p.* 575.

THE LIFE OF GEORGE WASHINGTON
1804–07

Mr. Madison and myself have cut out a piece of work for you, which is, to write the history of the United States, from the close of the war downwards. We are rich ourselves in materials, and can open all the public archives to you; but your residence here is essential, because a great deal of the knowledge of things is not on paper, but only within ourselves, for verbal communication. John Marshall is writing the Life of General Washington from his papers. It is intended to come out just in time to influence the next Presidential election. It is written, therefore, principally with a view to electioneering purposes. But it will, consequently, be out in time to aid you with information, as well as to point out the perversions of truth necessary to be rectified. Think of this, and agree to it.—JEFFERSON, THOMAS, 1802, *Letter to Joel Barlow, May* 3.

The life of Washington by Judge Marshall, like the life of Chaucer by Godwin, is rather a history of the period when he flourished than the real biography of the individual.—LAMBERT, JOHN, 1811, *Salmagundi, vol.* I, *p.* 126, *note.*

Mr. Marshall is not one of those ready writers, who run over a large mass of materials with a careless or indifferent eye, and sit down to write their first impressions, and fill up the spaces left vacant of facts with plausible conjectures, or imaginary events. He does not listen with implicit faith to every idle tale told by artless credulity or vulgar prejudice. He does not seek the title of superior wisdom by unsettling the truths of history, and proving, that all writers, but himself, have mistaken the facts and the characters of former times. He does not construct any new narrative of events, and in his own closet show how fields were lost or won, by drawing upon the resources of his own fancy. He does not dispute the veracity of persons nearest the scenes, simply because his own theory would be broken down by any admission in their favor. Far different is his course, and far different his ambition. The habits of his mind are close investigation, caution, patience, and a steady devotion to the weight of evidence. He examines all the materials before him with the sobriety and impartiality of judicial life. His conclusions, therefore, if they are not always absolutely correct, are such as it is difficult to resist, and never without very strong historical support. We have no hesitation in declaring, that the present work contains the most authentic history of the colonies, which is extant; and that it may be relied on with entire safety, as combining accuracy with variety of information.—STORY, JOSEPH, 1828, *Chief Justice Marshall's History of the American Colonies, North American Review, vol.* 26, *p.* 38.

After the able, accurate, and comprehensive work of Chief-Justice Marshall, it would be presumptuous to attempt a historical biography of Washington.—SPARKS, JARED, 1834, *Life of George Washington, Preface.*

Ramsay was a fluent, graceful, and eloquent writer of history, perhaps excelling, in ease and perspicuity, Marshall, the celebrated writer of the "Life of Washington;" a work which is highly valuable, as interweaving in the life of that great man the most material points of American history during his long and eventful career It evinces more strength of mind and detail of research than eloquence and interest, but will always remain the first authority for that period of our annals.—FLINT, TIMOTHY, 1835, *Sketches of the Literature of the United States, London Athenæum, p.* 803.

To judge of the service which Mr. Sparks has rendered the country, we must compare the previous accounts of Washington's career with that which we now possess. All that is contained in Marshall is meagre and incomplete in comparison with the copious details and ample illustrations with which we are at present furnished.—BANCROFT, GEORGE, 1838, *Documentary History of the Revolution, North American Review, vol.* 46, *p.* 483.

In 1804, he published the "Biography of Washington," which for candour, accuracy, and comprehension, will forever be the most authentic history of the Revolution.—GRISWOLD, RUFUS W., 1846–52, *Prose Writers of America, p.* 86.

There is no attempt to dazzle by studied elegance, harmonious diction, or brilliant ornament, but they are written in a plain and unpretending style, substantiated by historical facts, and possess great weight on account of conclusions so well drawn as to be extremely difficult of resistance, even when not borne out by their antecedent propositions. His own reflections are presented in such an unostentatious mode as not to offend, but to add a charm to the facts he narrates; yet while we must admit their ability, and the candor with which they are expressed, we cannot deny, that like some of his legal opinions, they are colored by the political sentiments which were so firmly rooted in his breast. —WYNNE, JAMES, 1850, *Lives of Eminent Literary and Scientific Men of America, p.* 298.

This work is very authentic and accurate, except the first volume on Colonial History. It is written with great simplicity and perspicuity; but it has lost much of its interest and attraction since the appearance of Sparks's immortal work.—KENT, JAMES, 1853, *Course of English Reading, p.* 44.

This author had not so large advantages in the way of materials as some of the later writers, but his political acumen and his judicial equipoise were such as to give his work a great and a permanent importance. The first volume is devoted to a description of the colonial period, and it still remains one of the most satisfactory works we have on the subject. The last volume is also of great importance as a view of Washington's administration.—ADAMS, CHARLES KENDALL, 1882, *A Manual of Historical Literature*, p. 582.

The first great contribution to American historical literature.—COOKE, JOHN ESTEN, 1883, *Virginia (American Commonwealths)*, p. 490.

Neither was Marshall altogether fitted to write a great book; he was not a literary man nor a scholar; he did not understand the art of composition, and of making a vivid, condensed, attractive narrative. He wrote a useful book, as a man of his ability could not fail to do in dealing with subjects with which he was thoroughly familiar, and in which he was deeply interested; he had further the advantage which arises always from personal acquaintance with the subject of the memoir and from entire sympathy with him. For the student of American history the book must thus have a value; but general readers have long since forgottten it, and leave it neglected on the shelves of the old libraries. It has long been out of print, and copies of it are not in demand even by reason of rarity. Jefferson was so far right in his prognostications concerning it that it is now universally regarded as a decidedly Federalist biography.—MAGRUDER, ALLAN B., 1885, *John Marshall (American Statesmen)*, p. 240.

Our first American biography of scope and dignity.—BATES, KATHARINE LEE, 1897, *American Literature*, p. 239.

Michael Thomas Sadler

1780–1835

Michael Thomas Sadler, M. P., 1780–1835, a native of Snelston, Derbyshire, for some time a merchant of Leeds, was M. P. for Newark-upon-Trent, 1829, and again in 1830 and in 1831 for Aldborough, Yorkshire. He was noted for his philanthropic interest on behalf of the agricultural poor and the children in factories, and his opposition to Roman Catholic Emancipation and Parliamentary Reform. 1. "Ireland: its Evils and their Remedies," London, 1828, 8vo. . . . 2. "Speech on the State and Prospects of the Country, delivered at Whitby," 1829, 8vo. Ridiculed by *Edinburgh Review*, 50, 344. "The Law of Population: a Treatise, in Six Books, in Disproof of the Superfecundity of Human Beings, and Developing the Real Principle of their Increase," 1830, 2 vols. 8vo. Vol. iii. never appeared.—ALLIBONE, S. AUSTIN, 1870, *A Critical Dictionary of English Literature*, vol. II, p. 1911.

PERSONAL

Sadler is a loss; he might not be popular in the house, or in London society, but his speeches did much good in the country, and he is a singularly able, right-minded, and religious man. Who is there that will take up the question of our white slave-trade with equal feeling?—SOUTHEY, ROBERT, 1833, *Letter to Lord Ashley, Jan.* 13.

His fame, however, is of a higher class than that of a parliamentarian. His was the hand which, after a hundred fruitless attempts, and those by men of no mean rank—his was the hand that threw down, and broke to pieces, and stamped into powder, that Moloch principle, long worshipped as an idol by many, of *the superfecundity of the human species*. The Malthusian theory was by him, at once and for ever, put an end to. It is true that the numerous disciples of that heresy will still adhere to it "for the term of their natural lives." But it is now a detected imposture, and its fate is sealed. . . . He was a man of rare natural endowments, and of extraordinary accomplishments; but these qualities could only be known in their variety, to his private circle and friends. His enthusiastic devotion to the welfare of the poor was the leading feature of his character; and in this point his value was felt and appreciated by the people generally. We perceive that the men of Leeds are claiming the honour of rearing and possessing his monument. But there must be a record of his labours and his doings, of a more extensive and durable character than a local column, or tablet, or statue. Seldom has a nobler subject for the pen of the biographer been afforded, and we are glad to hear that it will not be allowed to pass unnoticed.—MAGINN, WILLIAM, 1835, *Michael Thomas Sadler, Fraser's Magazine*, vol. 12, p. 280.

Michael Thomas Sadler was a good speaker—too fond, sometimes, of the abomination of delivering cut-and-dry orations which he had carefully elaborated beforehand. His delivery was good, and his language not only clear, but elegant. —MACKENZIE, R. SHELTON, 1854, *ed., Noctes Ambrosianæ, vol.* III, *p.* 393, *note.*

Sadler's brief public life deeply impressed his contemporaries. He was one of those philanthropic statesmen whose inspiration may be traced to the evangelical movement and the necessities of the industrial revolution. He did not believe in any purely political remedy for the discontent caused by the unregulated growth of the factory system, but underrated the need for political reform, and was too sanguine in his belief that the territorial aristocracy would realise the necessity of social readjustments, and force the needed changes on the manufacturing element of the middle class. He met with as much opposition from his own side as from his opponents. Lloyd Jones, who knew him well, bore testimony to his eloquence, marked ability, and "modest honesty of purpose plain to the eye of the most careless observer in every look and action of the man."—SADLER, MICHAEL E., 1897, *Dictionary of National Biography, vol.* L, *p.* 109.

THE LAW OF POPULATION
1830

We did not expect a good book from Mr. Sadler: and it is well that we did not; for he has given us a very bad one. The matter of his treatise is extraordinary; the manner more extraordinary still. His arrangement is confused, his repetitions endless, his style everything which it ought not to be. Instead of saying what he has to say with the perspicuity, the precision, and the simplicity in which consists the eloquence proper to scientific writing, he indulges without measure in vague, bombastic declamation, made up of those fine things which boys of fifteen admire, and which everybody who is not destined to be a boy all his life, weeds vigorously out of his compositions after five-and-twenty. That portion of his two thick volumes which is not made up of statistical tables, consists principally of ejaculations, apostrophes, metaphors, similes,—all the worst of their respective kinds. His thoughts are dressed up in this shabby finery with so much profusion and so little discrimination, that they remind us of a company of wretched strolling players, who have huddled on suits of ragged and faded tinsel, taken from a common wardrobe, and fitting neither their persons nor their parts; and who then exhibit themselves to the laughing and pitying spectators, in a state of strutting, ranting, painted, gilded beggary. The spirit of this work is as bad as its style. —MACAULAY, THOMAS BABINGTON, 1830, *Sadler's Law of Population, Critical and Miscellaneous Essays.*

His book is a most important one. He has trampled upon Malthus's theory, proving its absurdity and falsehood.—SOUTHEY, ROBERT, 1830, *To Henry Taylor, May* 3; *Life and Correspondence, ed. C. C. Southey, ch.* xxxiii.

Mr. Sadler, on whom his Godfathers bestowed the most just of all epithets by the most prophetic of all initials—Mr. M. T. (commonly pronounced *Empty*) Sadler, has lately published a book in opposition to the followers of Malthus; the size of it is very remarkable.—LYTTON, EDWARD GEORGE BULWER LORD, 1831, *The Siamese Twins, p.* 11, *note.*

Quite unworthy of the subject.—MCCULLOCH, JOHN RAMSAY, 1845, *Literature of Political Economy, p.* 261.

His very able work.—MACKENZIE, R. SHELTON, 1854, *ed., Noctes Ambrosianæ, vol.* V, *p.* 158, *note.*

Mr. Sadler was an ardent benevolent man, an impracticable politician, and a florid speaker. His literary pursuits and oratorical talents were honourable and graceful additions to his character as a man of business, but in knowledge and argument he was greatly inferior to Malthus and Ricardo.—CHAMBERS, ROBERT, 1876, *Cyclopædia of English Literature, ed. Carruthers.*

Thomas James Mathias
1754?-1835

Born about 1754: died at Naples, Aug., 1835. An English satirist and Italian scholar. He graduated at Trinity College, Cambridge. He went to Italy in 1817, and remained there the rest of his life. His "Pursuits of Literature" was begun in 1794.

Other satires are "The Political Dramatist" (1795), "An Equestrian Epistle in Verse to the Earl of Jersey" (1796), "An Imperial Epistle from Kien Long, Emperor of China, to George III. in 1794." His "Works of Gray" were published in 1814. In Italian he wrote "Poesie Liriche" and "Canzone Toscane."—SMITH, BENJAMIN E., *ed.*, 1894–97, *The Century Cyclopedia of Names, p.* 665.

PERSONAL

Matthias, aged eighty-one, is rather younger than ever, but complains that he sees nobody. Craven had him to dinner, and remarked how clever he was at contriving to ask questions without ceasing, yet never to profit in the least by the answer.—GELL, SIR WILLIAM, 1833, *Letter to Lady Blessington, Nov.* 19; *Literary Life and Correspondence, ed. Madden, vol.* I, *p.* 369.

The *Examiner*, which I read, records his death. I knew him; he was of a kind and courteous disposition, of more acquirement than genius, and living latterly upon the reputation of having had a reputation from the "Pursuits of Literature," which his Italian translations and complimentary sonnets did not enhance nor support.—MACREADY, W. C., 1835, *Diary, Aug.* 23; *Reminiscences, ed. Pollock, p.* 355.

PURSUITS OF LITERATURE
1794–98

Mr. Mathias's "Pursuits of Literature" were purchased with avidity, not as I conceive from the work being so generally read and understood, but in consequence of the unvarying ill-nature which characterised its pages, and the fame which it acquired with a set of scholastic critics who haunt the shops of the Piccadilly publishers, and gave it celebrity as a most classical production. For my own part, I must confess this work did not appear to me as deserving of the encomiums lavished upon its style, particularly on reference to the poetry, which never struck me as being above a certain degree of mediocrity; but when the candour of its decisions are examined, no man can regard the "Pursuits of Literature" but as a vehicle of the most unprovoked abuse, and rancorous ill-nature.—IRELAND, S. W. H., 1815, *Scribbleomania, p.* 97, *note.*

In 1794 appeared the first part of an anonymous poem entitled the "Pursuits of Literature," which, when completed in four parts, attracted universal notice, chiefly on account of the notes, which abound in deep and extensive learning, with keen and discriminating criticism on public men and opinions. It has been truly observed that "the cause of literature has never been supported in a day of danger and perversion, upon principles more excellent, or with powers better adapted to their object." After ascribing this work to various writers of high rank, the general voice united in fixing it upon Mr. Mathias, who has been supposed to have received some material assistance in it from some leading members of his own college. — UPCOTT AND SHOBERL, 1816, *A Biographical Dictionary of the Living Authors of Great Britain and Ireland, p.* 227.

The poem, which consists in all of only between 1500 and 1600 lines, spread over a volume of 450 pages, takes a general survey both of the literature and politics of its day; but the interest of the work lies chiefly in the prose prefaces and notes, the quantity of which amounts to about ten times that of the verse. Mathias's gift of song was not of a high order; his poetry is of the same school with Gifford's, but the verse of the "Pursuits of Literature" has neither the terseness and pungency nor the occasional dignity and elegance which make that of the "Baviad" and "Mæviad" so successful an echo of Pope—the common master of both writers. The notes, however, though splenetic, and avowing throughout a spirit of the most uncompromising partisanship, are written with a sharp pen, as well as in a scholarly style, and, in addition to much Greek and Latin learning, contain a good deal of curious disquisition and anecdote. —CRAIK, GEORGE L., 1861, *A Compendious History of English Literature and of the English Language, vol.* II, *p.* 409.

The poem contained some slashing lines scattered among a mass of affected criticism, and as its sole idea was to ridicule those trading on literature, it soon proved wanting in life. George Steevens called it "a peg to hang the notes on," and these were often of portentous length, though Rogers thought them "rather piquant." De Quincey, in his "Essay on Parr," speaks of it as marred by "much licence of tongue, much mean and impotent spite, and by a systematic pedantry without parallel in literature," and he might have added, by the shameless puffing of his own works by Mathias. Cobbett, who shared many of his prejudices, called it a "matchless poem," but Dr. Wolcot dubbed him "that miserable imp Mathias."—COURTNEY, W. P., 1894, *Dictionary of National Biography, vol.* XXXVII, *p.* 48.

Thomas James Mathias, the author of "The Pursuits of Literature," was a much nearer approach to the pedant pure and simple. For he did not, like Gifford, redeem his rather indiscriminate attacks on contemporaries by a sincere and intelligent devotion to older work; and he was, much more than Gifford, ostentatious of such learning as he possessed. Accordingly the immense popularity of his only book of moment is a most remarkable sign of the times. De Quincey, who had seen its rise and its fall, declares that for a certain time, and not a very short one, at the end of the last century and the beginning of this, "The Pursuits of Literature" was the most popular book of its own day, and as popular as any which had appeared since; and that there is not very much hyperbole in this is proved by its numerous editions, and by the constant references to it in the books of the time. Colman, who was one of Mathias' victims, declared that the verse was a "peg to hang the notes on;" and the habit above referred to certainly justified the gibe to no small extent. If the book is rather hard reading nowadays (and it is certainly rather difficult to recognise in it even the "demon of originality" which De Quincey himself grants rather grudgingly as an offset to its defects of taste and scholarship), it is perhaps chiefly obscured by the extreme desultoriness of the author's attacks and the absence of any consistent and persistent target. Much that Mathias reprehends in Godwin and Priestley, in Colman and Wolcot, and a whole crowd of lesser men, is justifiably censured; much that he lays down is sound and good enough. But the whole—which, after the wont of the time, consists of several pieces jointed on to each other and all flooded with notes—suffers from the twin vices of negation and divagation. Indeed, its chief value is that, both by its composition and its reception, it shows the general sense that literature was not in a healthy state, and that some renaissance, some reaction, was necessary.—SAINTSBURY, GEORGE, 1896, *A History of Nineteenth Century Literature, p.* 25.

GENERAL

Talked of the "Pursuits of Literature," and the sensation it produced when published. Matthias's Italian poetry: Mr. Oakden said he had heard Florentines own he came nearer their poetry than any other foreigner had done, but that still he was *but* a foreigner at it.—MOORE, THOMAS, 1818, *Journal, Oct.* 27; *Memoirs, ed. Russell, vol.* II, *p.* 205.

The name of Mathias is well known to every lover of the Italian tongue; his poetical productions rank with those of Milton in merit, and far exceed them in quantity.—PRESCOTT, WILLIAM HICKLING, 1824, *Italian Narrative Poetry, Biographical and Critical Miscellanies, p.* 413.

Mr. Mathias also wrote some Latin odes, and translated into Italian several English poems. He wrote Italian with elegance and purity, and it has been said that no Englishman, since the days of Milton, has cultivated that language with so much success.—CHAMBERS, ROBERT, 1876, *Cyclopædia of English Literature, ed. Carruthers.*

William Henry Ireland

1777–1835

Samuel William Henry Ireland, was born in London in 1777, the son of a dealer in old books and prints. Articled at seventeen to a London conveyancer, he was tempted by his father's unintelligent enthusiasm for Shakespeare to forge an autograph of the poet on a carefully-copied old lease. His audacity grew with the credulity of his dupes, and ere long locks of hair, private letters, annotated books, &c., were plentifully produced. Boswell, Warton, Dr. Parr, and hundreds more came, saw, and believed; but those like Malone, really qualified to judge, denounced the imposture. Ireland now produced a deed of Shakespeare's bequeathing his books and papers to a William-Henrye Irelaunde, an assumed ancestor. Next a new historical play entitled

"Vortigern" was announced, and produced by Sheridan at Drury Lane, 2d April 1796. Vapid and un-Shakespearian, it was damned at once; and this nipped in the bud a projected series of historical plays. The uneasiness of Ireland's father at length getting the better of his credulity, the young man was forced to confess; he published a statement in 1796, and expanded it in his "Confessions" (1805). He soon sank into poverty, eking out a living as a bookseller's hack till his death, 17th April 1835. He produced a dozen poems, four or five novels, and ten or more biographical and miscellaneous compilations.—PATRICK AND GROOME, *eds.*, 1897, *Chambers's Biographical Dictionary, p.* 521.

FORGERIES

In the year 1796 I gave to the world a concise pamphlet, in which I avowed myself the fabricator of the manuscripts attributed by me to Shakspeare. The papers themselves, and the circumstances attending their production, had so highly excited the public curiosity that the whole edition was disposed of in a few hours: and so great has since been the eagerness to procure a copy that, though originally published at one shilling, a single impression has been sold, in a public auction-room, at the extravagant price of a guinea. This fact was known to many of my friends, who in consequence have often expressed surprise that I did not republish the pamphlet, and have frequently importuned me to do so: but the revival of the subject, I conceived, might rather tend to injure than benefit me as a literary character: besides, I had already suffered much from the agitation of the question, and had reason to wish it might for ever rest in peace.—IRELAND, WILLIAM-HENRY, 1805, *Confessions, Preface.*

When there was considerable fermentation in the literary world on the subject of the supposed Shakspeare Manuscripts, and many of the most distinguished individuals had visited Mr. Ireland's house to inspect them, Porson, accompanied by a friend, went also. Many persons had been so imposed upon as to be induced to subscribe their names to a form, previously drawn up, avowing their belief in the authenticity of the papers exhibited. Porson was called upon to do so likewise. "No," replied the Professor, "I am always very reluctant in subscribing my name, and more particularly to articles of faith." —BELOE, WILLIAM, 1817, *The Sexagenarian, vol.* I, *p.* 231.

Several other novels, some poems, and attempts at satire, proceeded from the pen of Ireland; but they are unworthy of notice; and the last thirty years of the life of this industrious but unprincipled littérateur were passed in obscurity and poverty.—CHAMBERS, ROBERT, 1876, *Cyclopædia of English Literature, ed. Carruthers.*

Was a liar and a solicitor's clerk, so versatile and accomplished that we cannot always believe him, even when he is narrating the tale of his own iniquities. The temporary but wide and turbulent success of the Ireland forgeries suggests the disagreeable reflection that criticism and learning are (or a hundred years ago were) worth very little as literary touchstones. A polished and learned society, a society devoted to Shakespeare and to the stage, was taken in by a boy of eighteen. Young Ireland not only palmed off his sham documents, most makeshift imitations of the antique, but even his ridiculous verse on the experts. James Boswell went down on his knees and thanked Heaven for the sight of them, and feeling thirsty after these devotions, drank hot brandy and water. Dr. Parr was as readily gulled, and probably the experts, like Malone, who held aloof, were as much influenced by jealousy as by science. The whole story of young Ireland's forgeries is not only too long to be told here, but forms the topic of a novel ("The Talk of the Town") by Mr. James Payn. The frauds in his hands lose neither their humor nor their complicated interest of plot.—LANG, ANDREW, 1886, *Books and Bookmen, p.* 28.

Thomas Taylor

1758-1835

"The Platonist," a Londoner bred at St. Paul's School, entered Lubbock's bank as a clerk. He left his desk to teach private pupils and to become assistant-secretary to the Society for the Encouragement of Arts, &c. During his last forty years he lived at Walworth, immersed in Plato and the Platonists, on £100 a year from Mr. Meredith, a retired tradesman. His fifty works include translations of the Orphic Hymns, parts of Plotinus, Proclus, Pausanias, Apuleius, Iamblichus, Porphyry, &c., Plato (nine of the Dialogues by Floyer Sydenham, 1804), and Aristotle (1806-12). "The Spirit of All Religions" (1790) expresses his strange polytheistic creed.—PATRICK AND GROOME, *eds.*, 1897, *Chambers's Biographical Dictionary, p.* 904.

GENERAL

Taylor's book was shown to me this summer. . . . I find that the world's future religion is to be founded on a blundered translation of an almost unintelligible commentator on Plato. . . . Taylor will have no success.—WALPOLE, HORACE, 1789, *To the Countess of Ossory, Nov.* 26; *Letters, ed. Cunningham, vol.* IX, *p.* 227.

Without staying even to learn the inflexions of Greek words, has plunged to the very bottom of pagan philosophy, *taught by the heavenly muse to venture down the dark descent, and up to reascend, though hard and rare.*—PORSON, RICHARD, 1794, *To the Editor of the "Morning Chronicle."*

Thomas Taylor, . . . the would-be restorer of unintelligible mysticism and superstitious pagan nonsense. All that Iamblichus revealed to Ædesius.—MATHIAS, THOMAS JAMES, 1794-98, *The Pursuits of Literature, Eighth ed., p.* 181.

Thomas Taylor, sometimes called "Plato Taylor," is a name justly entitled to honourable mention in any history of mental speculation. He spent above forty years in an exclusive devotion to what he considered the first and most august philosophy; and is the only modern, since the days of the Emperor Julian or the age immediately succeeding, who has penetrated to its remotest sources, and effected its perfect mastership. . . . The Platonic Philosophy being strictly and essentially theological—in which, accordingly, all other principles and knowledge become themselves religionised, so to speak—Mr. Taylor adopts it in its fullest extent, with all the old profoundly significant and representative mythology attached to it; and perhaps (I speak with diffidence) in a more absolute and dogmatic sense than even the Platonists themselves intended. As a consequence of this, Taylor looks with coldness and distrust on the principles of Christian theology. He understands Plato thoroughly, but it is quite clear that he has studied the principles of natural and revealed religion through a miserably corrupted and distorted medium. This has led him to throw a gorgeous halo around the Grecian system; and to look at pure and undefiled truth through a dim and hazy atmosphere.—BLAKEY, ROBERT, 1850, *History of the Philosophy of Mind, vol.* IV, *pp.* 66, 68.

His translations are very numerous; some rather good, the majority poor, and all anathematized by each successive generation of scholars and reviewers. The principal are "The Works of Plato" (in which Taylor was assisted by Sydenham), and "The Works of Aristotle." These voluminous contributions to the history of philosophy had some value, not because of their intrinsic merits, but because until lately nothing better had taken their place. They are very carelessly executed, and full of errors. Taylor seems to have regarded it as his life-mission to reproduce in English all that related to the Platonic and Neo-Platonic school. The complete list of his works covers nearly forty translations, on all subjects, from the "Hymns of Orpheus" to the "Golden Ass of Apuleius." The translation of Plato by Prof. Jowett, completed in 1871, supersedes entirely that by Taylor.—HART, JOHN S., 1872, *A Manual of English Literature, p.* 498.

Thomas Taylor, the Platonist, for instance, is really a better man of imagination, a better poet, or perhaps I should say a better feeder to a poet, than any man between Milton and Wordsworth.—EMERSON, RALPH WALDO, 1876, *Poetry and Imagination, Letters and Social Aims.*

Talyor resigned his clerkship, and obtained in 1798 the post of assistant secretary to the Society of Arts, which he resigned in 1806 in order to devote himself more assiduously to the work of translating and expounding the ancient thinkers. His equipment for this enterprise left much to be desired. Critical faculty he had none. No doubt of the historic personality of Orpheus or the authenticity of the hymns ascribed to him ever crossed his mind; the mystical neo-Pythagorean mathematics he esteemed the true science, which the Arabians and their European successors had corrupted; and he rejected the common opinion of an essential antagonism between the Platonic and Peripatetic philosophies, only to resuscitate the forced and fanciful syncretism of the ancient commentators. His style, formed on the Johnsonian model, retained its stiffness to the last. But with an ardour which neither neglect nor contempt could damp, he plodded laboriously on until he had achieved a work never so much as contemplated in its entirety by any of his predecessors. Widely read in America, his works had never much vogue in England, where his frank avowal of philosophic polytheism created a strong feeling against him.—RIGG, J. M., 1898, *Dictionary of National Biography, vol.* LV, *p.* 468.

William Godwin

1756–1836

Born, at Wisbeach, Cambs., 3 March, 1756. Family removed to Debenham, Suffolk, 1758; to Guestwick, Norfolk, 1760. At school at Guestwick, 1760–64; at Hindolveston, 1764–67; with tutor, 1767–71. Master at Hindolveston School, 1771–73. To Hoxton Academy, London, 1773. Minister at Ware, Herts, 1778. In London, 1779. Minister at Stowmarket, Suffolk, 1780–82; returned to London, 1782. Minister at Beaconsfield in 1783; gave up ministry that year and took to literature. Intimacy with Mary Wollstonecraft begun, 1796; married her, 29 March 1797. Daughter Mary (afterwards Mrs. Shelley) born 30 Aug. 1797; wife died, 10 Sept. 1797. Married Mrs. Mary Jane Clairmont, Dec. 1801. Friendship with Coleridge, Lamb, Wordsworth. "Tragedy of Antonio" produced at Drury Lane, 13 Dec. 1800; "Faulkener" produced, Dec. 1807. Financial troubles. Wife started publishing business. Friendship with Shelley begun, 1811. Bankrupt, 1822. Yeoman Usher of Exchequer, 1833–36. Died, in London, 7 April 1836. Buried in Old St. Pancras Churchyard. *Works:* "Life of Chatham" (anon.), 1783; "Sketches of History" 1784; "Enquiry concerning Political Justice," 1793; "Things as they are; or, the Adventures of Caleb Williams," 1794; "Cursory Strictures on the Charge of Chief-Justice Eyre," 1794; "The Enquirer," 1797; "Memoirs of the Author of a Vindication of the Rights of Women," 1798 (2nd edn. same year); "St. Leon," 1799; "Antonio," 1800; "Thoughts occasioned by . . . Dr. Parr's Spital Sermon," 1801; "Life of Geoffrey Chaucer," 1803; "Fleetwood," 1805 (French trans. same year); "Fables" (under pseud. "Edward Baldwin"), 1805; "The Looking-Glass" (under pseud. "Theophilus Marcliffe," attrib. to Godwin), 1805; "Faulkener," 1807; "Essay on Sepulchres," 1809; "Dramas for Children" (anon.), 1809; "History of Rome" (by "E. Baldwin"), 1809; "New and improved Grammar of the English Language" (anon.), 1812; "Lives of Edward and John Philips," 1815; "Mandeville," 1817; "Of Population," 1820; "Life of Lady Jane Grey" (by "E. Baldwin"), 1824; "History of the Commonwealth of England" (4 vols.), 1824–28; "The History of England for the use of Schools" (by "E. Baldwin"), 1827; "History of Greece" (by "E. Baldwin"), 1828; "Cloudesley" (anon.), 1830; "Thoughts on Man," 1831; "Deloraine," 1833; "Lives of the Necromancers," 1834. *Posthumous:* "Essays," 1873. He *translated:* Lord Lovat's "Memoirs," 1797; and *edited:* Mary Godwin's "Posthumous Works," 1798; his son (W. Godwin's) "Transfusion," 1835. *Life: by C. Kegan Paul,* 1876.—SHARP, R. FARQUHARSON, 1897, *A Dictionary of English Authors, p.* 113.

PERSONAL

You distress me, sir, extremely, by again agitating a question which ought to be considered as decided. I had full opportunity, when in Town, to hear, and attentively to weigh your opinions concerning the point on which we most differ: for perhaps I do not fully agree with you in supposing our minds at unison on many others; but that is immaterial—the matter before us is decisive. . . . You tell me that you are individually beloved by those who know you, and I can easily believe it, but I will tell you that even among the number of your friends, or at least well-wishers, there are to my knowledge those who much lament, and even blame the lengths to which your systems of thinking have carried you, and who recede insensibly from your oppinions, while they

WILLIAM GODWIN

From the Original Painting by Northcote.

WILLIAM BLAKE

Engraving by A. L. Dick. From a Portrait by William Blake.

preserve a respect for your intentions.—LEE, HARRIET, 1798, *Letter to Godwin, July* 31; *William Godwin by Paul, vol.* I, *pp.* 307, 308.

I was disgusted at heart with the grossness and vulgar insanocecity of this dim-headed prig of a philosophocide, when, after supper, his ill stars impelled him to renew the contest. I begged him not to goad me, for that I feared my feelings would not long remain in my power. He (to my wonder and indignation) persisted (I had not deciphered the cause), and then, as he well said, I did "thunder and lighten at him" with a vengeance for more than an hour and a half. Every effort of self-defence only made him more ridiculous. If I had been Truth in person, I could not have spoken more accurately; but it was Truth in a war chariot, drawn by the three Furies, and the reins had slipped out of the goddess's hands!—COLERIDGE, SAMUEL TAYLOR, 1804, *To Robert Southey, Feb.* 20; *Letters, ed. E. H. Coleridge, vol.* II, *p.* 465.

The name of Godwin has been accustomed to excite in me feelings of reverence and admiration. I have been accustomed to consider him as a luminary too dazzling for the darkness which surrounds him, and from the earliest period of my knowledge of his principles, I have ardently desired to share in the footing of intimacy that intellect which I have delighted to contemplate in its emanations. Considering, then, these feelings, you will not be surprised at the inconceivable emotion with which I learned your existence and your dwelling. I had enrolled your name on the list of the honourable dead. I had felt regret that the glory of your being had passed from this earth of ours. It is not so. You still live, and I firmly believe are still planning the welfare of human kind. . . . When I come to London I shall seek for you. I am convinced I could represent myself to you in such terms as not to be thought wholly unworthy of your friendship. At least, if any desire for universal happiness has any claim upon your preference, that desire I can exhibit.—SHELLEY, PERCY BYSSHE, 1811, *Letter to Godwin, Jan.* 3; *William Godwin by Paul, vol.* II, *p.* 202.

Godwin is as far removed from everything feverish and exciting as if his head had never been filled with anything but geometry. He is now about sixty-five, stout, well-built, and unbroken by age, with a cool, dogged manner, exactly opposite to everything I had imagined of the author of "St. Leon" and "Caleb Williams." He lives on Snowhill, just about where Evelina's vulgar relations lived. His family is supported partly by the labors of his own pen and partly by those of his wife's, but chiefly by the profits of a shop for children's books, which she keeps and manages to considerable advantage. She is a spirited, active woman, who controls the house, I suspect, pretty well; and when I looked at Godwin, and saw with what cool obstinacy he adhered to everything he had once assumed, and what a cold selfishness lay at the bottom of his character, I felt a satisfaction in the thought that he had a wife who must sometimes give a start to his blood and a stir to his nervous system.—TICKNOR, GEORGE, 1819, *Journal; Life, Letters and Journals, vol.* I, *p.* 294.

The Spirit of the Age was never more fully shown than in its treatment of this writer—its love of paradox and change, its dastard submission to prejudice and to the fashion of the day. Five-and-twenty years ago he was in the very zenith of a sultry and unwholesome popularity; he blazed as a sun in the firmament of reputation; no one was more talked of, more looked up to, more sought after, and wherever liberty, truth, justice was the theme, his name was not far off:—now he has sunk below the horizon, and enjoys the supreme delight of a doubtful immortality. Mr. Godwin, during his lifetime, has secured to himself the triumphs and the mortifications of an extreme notoriety and of a sort of posthumous fame. . . . In size Mr. Godwin is below the common stature, nor is his deportment graceful or animated. His face is, however, fine, with an expression of placid temper and recondite thought. He is not unlike the common portraits of Locke.—HAZLITT, WILLIAM, 1825, *The Spirit of the Age, pp.* 19, 33.

Next came Godwin. Did you not grudge me that pleasure, now? At least, mourn that you were not there with me? Grudge not, mourn not, dearest Jeannie; it was the most unutterable stupidity ever enacted on this earth. . . Mrs. Godwin already sate gossiping in the dusk—an old woman of no significance. . . .

Shortly before candles, Godwin himself (who had been drinking *good* green tea by his own hearth before stirring out). He is a bald, bushy-browed, thick, hoary, hale little figure, taciturn enough, and speaking when he does speak with a certain *epigrammatic* spirit, wherein, except a little shrewdness, there is nothing but the most commonplace character. (I should have added that he wears spectacles, has full grey eyes, a very large blunt characterless nose, and ditto chin).—CARLYLE, THOMAS, 1831, *To Mrs. Carlyle, Aug.* 17; *Early Life of Thomas Carlyle, ed. Froude, vol.* II, *p.* 139,

Godwin's name seems sinking out of remembrance; and he is remembered less by the novels that succeeded, or by the philosophy that he abjured, than as the man that had Mary Wollstonecraft for his wife, Mrs. Shelley for his daughter, and the immortal Shelley as his son-in-law.—DE QUINCEY, THOMAS, 1845–59, *Gilfillan's Literary Portraits, Works, ed. Masson, vol.* XI, *p.* 335.

He rose between seven and eight, and read some classic author before breakfast. From nine till twelve or one he occupied himself with his pen. He found that he could not exceed this measure of labour with any advantage to his own health, or the work in hand. While writing "Political Justice," there was one paragraph which he wrote eight times over before he could satisfy himself with the strength and perspicuity of his expressions. On this occasion a sense of confusion of the brain came over him, and he applied to his friend Mr. Carlisle, afterwards Sir Anthony Carlisle, the celebrated surgeon, who warned him that he had exerted his intellectual faculties to their limit. In compliance with his direction, Mr. Godwin reduced his hours of composition within what many will consider narrow bounds. The rest of the morning was spent in reading and seeing his friends. When at home he dined at four, but during his bachelor life he frequently dined out. His dinner at home at this time was simple enough. He had no regular servant; an old woman came in the morning to clean and arrange his rooms, and if necessary she prepared a mutton chop, which was put in a Dutch oven.—SHELLEY, MARY WOLLSTONECRAFT, 1851? *Fragmentary Notes, William Godwin, by Paul, vol.* I, *p.* 79.

It was in the year 1813 that I first became acquainted with William Godwin. . . . I had expressed a wish to know him, and I was soon invited by a charming family, with whom he was intimate, to dine at their house, where I should find him and Bysshe. I repaired thither, to a somewhat early dinner, in accordance with the habits of the philosopher. I was not on any account to be late, for it was unpleasant to him to dine later than four o'clock. It was a fine Sunday. I set out betimes, and arrived at the appointed place at half-past three. I found a short, stout, thickset old man, of very fair complexion, and with a bald and very large head, in the drawing-room, alone, where he had been for some time by himself, and he appeared to be rather uneasy at being alone. He made himself known to me as William Godwin; it was thus he styled himself. His dress was dark, and very plain, of an old-fashioned cut, even for an old man. His appearance, indeed, was altogether that of a dissenting minister. . . . William Godwin, according to my observation, always eat meat, and rather sparingly, and little else besides. He drank a glass or two of sherry, wherein I did not join him. Soon after dinner, a large cup of very strong green tea,—of gunpowder tea, intensely strong,—was brought to him; this he took with evident satisfaction, and it was the only thing that he appeared to enjoy, although our fare was excellent. Having drunken the tea, he set the cup and saucer forcibly upon the table, at a great distance from him, according to the usages of that old school of manners, to which he so plainly belonged. He presently fell into a sound sleep, sitting very forward in his chair, and leaning forward, so that at times he threatened to fall forward; but no harm came to him. Not only did the old philosopher sleep soundly, deeply, but he snored loudly.—HOGG, THOMAS JEFFERSON, 1858, *The Life of Percy Bysshe Shelley, vol.* II, *pp.* 444, 447.

I remember vividly accompanying my father to the dark rooms in the New Palace Yard, where I saw an old vivacious lady and an old gentleman. My father was most anxious that I should remember them; and I do remember well that he appeared to bear a strong regard for them. . . . One morning he called on the Godwins, and was kept for some minutes waiting in their drawing-room. It was irresistible, he could never think of these things. Whistle in a lady's drawing-room! . . . Still he did whistle,—not only *pianissimo*, but *fortissimo*, with variations enough to satisfy the most ambitious of thrushes. Suddenly good little Mrs. Godwin gently opened the door, paused still—not seen by the performer—to catch the dying notes of the air, and then, coming up to her visitor, startled him with the request, made in all seriousness, "You *couldn't whistle* that again, could you?"—JERROLD, BLANCHARD, 1859, *Life and Remains of Douglas Jerrold, ch.* vi.

William Godwin was then seventy years old; but he seemed to me older than Bentham. Feeble and bent, he had neither the bright eye nor the elastic step of the utilitarian philosopher. In person he was small and insignificant. His capacious forehead, seeming to weigh down the aged head, alone remained to indicate the talent which even his opponents confessed that he had shown, alike in his novels and in his graver works. His conversation gave me the impression of intellect without warmth of heart; it touched on great principles, but was measured and unimpulsive; as great a contrast to Bentham's as could well be imagined.—OWEN, ROBERT DALE, 1874, *Threading My Way, p.* 207.

Was always the same; very cold, very selfish, very calculating. His philosophy, such as it was, never generated pity or gratitude. His sympathies and generosities and liberal qualities showed themselves only in print. His conduct towards Shelley was merely an endeavor to extract from him as much money as was possible. His conduct toward Mr. —, whom I have heard speak of it, in denying a pecuniary liability, because as he said, "there was no witness to the loan;" his pedantic cavilling at his wife's unscientific expression when dying, "Oh, Godwin, I am in heaven!" (expressive of her relief from extreme pain), all indicate an unamiable character. I have known several persons who were intimate with him, none of whom ever pretended to endue him with a single good quality. He was very pragmatic, very sceptical of God and men and virtue. And yet this man has in his study compiled fine rhetorical sentences, which strangers have been ready to believe flowed warm from his heart. I have always thought him like one of those cold intellectual demons of whom we read in French and German stories, who come upon earth to do good to no one and harm to many.—PROCTER, BRYAN WALLER, 1874? *Recollections of Men of Letters, p.* 203.

The same calm temperament which enabled him to dispense with much which is often thought of the essence of religion, seems to have kept him free also from any feeling which can be called love. Except the one great passion of his life, and even this was conducted with extreme outward and apparent phlegm, friendship stood to him in the place of passion, as morality was to him in the room of devotion. All the jealousies, misunderstandings, wounded feelings and the like, which some men experience in their love affairs, Godwin suffered in his relations with his friends. Fancied slights were exaggerated; quarrels, expostulations, reconciliations followed quickly on each other, as though they were true *amantiam irae*. And his relations with women were for the most part the same as those with men. His frendships were as real with the one sex as with the other, but they were no more than friendships. Marriage seemed to him a thing to be arranged, "adjusted," as Mr. Tennyson says of the loves of vegetables.—PAUL, C. KEGAN, 1876, *William Godwin: his Friends and Contemporaries, vol.* I, *p.* 29.

Godwin, though overrated in his generation, and almost ludicrously idealized by Shelley, was a man whose talents verged on genius. But he was by no means consistent. His conduct in money-matters shows that he could not live the life of a self-sufficing philosopher; while the irritation he expressed when Shelley omitted to address him as Esquire, stood in comic contradiction with his published doctrines. —SYMONDS, JOHN ADDINGTON, 1879, *Shelley (English Men of Letters), p.* 93.

It would be difficult to find a greater contrast than that between Irving and Godwin. In persons, in manners, in features, in mind, in spirit, they were uttermost opposites. The free-thinking husband of Mary Wollstonecraft—whose union was the slender one of a love-bond, until in later life, they took upon them the bonds of wedlock—was of awkard, ungainly form; a broad, intellectual forehead redeemed a flat, coarse, inexpressive face; his dress was clumsy; his habits careless—of cleanliness at least.—HALL, SAMUEL CARTER, 1883, *Retrospect of a Long Life*, p. 313.

Of a cool, unemotional temperament, safe from any snares of passion or imagination, he became the very type of a town philosopher. Abstractions of the intellect and the philosophy of politics were his world. He had a true townsman's love of the theatre, but external nature for the most part left him unaffected, as it found him. With the most exalted opinion of his own genius and merit, he was nervously susceptible to the criticism of others, yet always ready to combat any judgment unfavourable to himself. Never weary of argument, he thought that by its means, conducted on lines of reason, all questions might be finally settled, all problems satisfactorily and speedily solved. Hence the fascination he possessed for those in doubt and distress of mind. Cool rather than cold-hearted, he had a certain benignity of nature which, joined to intellectual exaltation, passed as warmth and fervour.—MARSHALL, MRS. JULIAN, 1889, *The Life and Letters of Mary Wollstonecraft Shelley, vol.* I, *p.* 4.

Affecting the virtues of calmness and impartiality, he was yet irritable under criticism, and his friendships were interrupted by a series of quarrels. His self-respect was destroyed in later life under the pressure of debt and an unfortunate marriage; but, though his character wanted in strength and elevation, and incapable of the loftier passions, he seems to have been mildly affectionate, and, in many cases, a judicious friend to more impulsive people.—STEPHEN, LESLIE, 1894, *Dictionary of National Biography, vol.* XXII, *p.* 67.

First and last, Shelley emptied into that rapacious mendicant's lap a sum which cost him—for he borrowed it at ruinous rates—from eighty to one hundred thousand dollars. —CLEMENS, S. M. (MARK TWAIN), 1897, *In Defence of Harriet Shelley, How to tell a Story and Other Essays, p.*49.

ENQUIRY CONCERNING POLITICAL JUSTICE

1793

Dr. Priestley says my book contains a vast extent of ability—Monarchy and Aristocaracy, to be sure, were never so painted before—he agrees with me respecting gratitude and contracts absolutely considered, but thinks the principles too refined for practice—he felt uncommon approbation of my investigation of the first principles of government, which were never so well explained before—he admits fully my first principle of the omnipotence of instruction and that all vice is error—he admits all my principles, but cannot follow them into all my conclusions with me respecting self-love—he thinks mind will never so far get the better of matter as I suppose; he is of opinion that the book contains a great quantity of original thinking, and will be uncommonly useful. Horne Tooke tells me that my book is a bad book, and will do a great deal of harm—Holcroft and Jardine had previously informed me, the first, that he said the book was written with very good intentions, but to be sure nothing could be so foolish; the second, that Holcroft and I had our heads full of plays and novels, and then thought ourselves philosophers.—GODWIN, WILLIAM, 1793, *Supplement to Journal, March* 23; *William Godwin by Paul, vol.* I, *p.*116.

You supped upon Godwin and oysters with Carlisle. Have you, then, read Godwin, and that with attention? Give me your thoughts upon his book; for, faulty as it is in many parts, there is a mass of truth in it that must make every man think. Godwin, as a man, is very contemptible. I am afraid that most public characters will ill endure examination in their private lives.—SOUTHEY, ROBERT, 1795, *To Grosvenor C. Bedford, Nov.* 22; *Life and Correspondence, ed. C. C. Southey, ch.* iii.

While everybody was abusing and despising Mr. Godwin, and while Mr. Godwin was, among a certain description of understandings, increasing every day in popularity, Mr. Malthus took the trouble of refuting him; and we hear no more of Mr. Godwin.—SMITH, SYDNEY, 1802, *Dr. Rennel, Edinburgh Review, Essays, p.* 9.

I cannot but consider the author of "Political Justice" as a philosophical reasoner of no ordinary stamp or pretensions. That work, whatever its defects may be, is distinguished by the most acute and severe logic, and by the utmost boldness of thinking, founded on a love and conviction of truth.—HAZLITT, WILLIAM, 1818, *Lecture on the English Novelists.*

He carried one single shock into the bosom of English society, fearful but momentary, like that from the electric blow of the gymnotus; or, perhaps, the intensity of the brief panic which, fifty years ago, he impressed on the pubic mind may be more adequately expressed by the case of a ship in the middle ocean suddenly scraping with her keel a ragged rock, hanging for one moment as if impaled upon the teeth of the dreadful *sierra*,—then, by the mere *impetus* of her mighty sails, grinding audibly to powder the fangs of this accursed submarine harrow, leaping into deep water again, and causing the panic of ruin to be simultaneous with the deep sense of deliverance.—De Quincey, Thomas, 1845–59, *Gilfillan's Literary Portraits, Works, ed. Masson, vol.* xi, *p.* 327.

It was in the spring of this year and before I left Colchester that I read a book which gave a turn to my mind, and in effect directed the whole course of my life,—a book which, after producing a powerful effect on the youth of that generation, has now sunk into unmerited oblivion. This was Godwin's "Political Justice." I was in some measure prepared for it by an acquaintance with Holcroft's novels, and it came recommended to me by the praise of Catherine Buck. I entered fully into its spirit, it left all others behind in my admiration, and I was willing even to become a martyr for it; for it soon became a reproach to be a follower of Godwin, on account of his supposed atheism. I never became an atheist, but I could not feel aversion or contempt towards G. on account of any of his views. In one respect the book had an excellent effect on my mind,—it made me feel more *generously*. I had never before, nor, I am afraid, have I ever since felt so strongly the duty of not living to one's self, but of having for one's sole object the good of the community. His idea of justice I then adopted and still retain; nor was I alarmed by the declamations so generally uttered against his opinions on the obligations of gratitude, the fulfillment of promises, and the duties arising out of the personal relations of life.—Robinson, Henry Crabb, 1867? *Reminiscences for* 1795, *Diary, Reminiscences and Correspondence, ed. Sadler, vol.* i, *p.* 20.

No more abstract work on political science ever took hold of the English public mind with more tenacity than this publication. It was in everybody's hands.—Blakey, Robert, 1873, *Memoirs, p.* 58.

His mind, clear, systematic, and passionless, speedily threw off the prejudices from which Price and Priestley never emancipated themselves. More than any English thinker, he resembles in intellectual temperament those French theorists who represented the early revolutionary impulse. His doctrines are developed with a logical precision which shrinks from no consequences, and which placidly ignores all inconvenient facts. The Utopia in which his imagination delights is laid out with geometrical symmetry and simplicity. Godwin believes as firmly as any early Christian in the speedy revelation of a new Jerusalem, four-square and perfect in its plan. Three editions of his "Political Justice" were published, in 1793, 1796, and 1798. Between those dates events had occurred calculated to upset the faith of may enthusiasts. Godwin's opinions, however, were rooted too deeply in abstract speculation to be effected by any storms raging in the region of concrete phenomena. . . . Godwin's intellectual genealogy may be traced to three sources. From Swift, Mandeville, and the Latin historians, he had learnt to regard the whole body of ancient institutions as corrupt; from Hume and Hartley, of whom he speaks with enthusiam, he derived the means of assault upon the old theories; from the French writers, such as Rousseau, Helvetius, and Holbach, he caught, as he tells us, the contagion of revolutionary zeal. The "Political Justice" is an attempt to frame into a systematic whole the principles gathered from these various sources, and may be regarded as an exposition of the extremest form of revolutionary dogma. Though Godwin's idiosyncrasy is perceptible in some of the conclusions, the book is instructive, as showing, with a clearness paralleled in no other English writing, the true nature of those principles which excited the horror of Burke and the Conservatives.—Stephen, Leslie, 1876, *History of English Thought in the Eighteenth Century, vol.* ii, *pp.* 264, 265.

He never could have been a worker on the active stage of life. But he was none the less a motive power behind the workers, and "Political Justice" may take its place with the "Speech for Unlicensed Printing," the "Essay on Education," and "Emile," among the unseen levers which have moved the changes of the times.—PAUL, C. KEGAN, 1876, *William Godwin: his Friends and Contemporaries, vol.* I, *p.* 105.

I thought of Shelley—so we all think of him—as a man of extraordinary sensitiveness and susceptibility, susceptibility above all to ideal impressions; and I further thought of him as instinctively craving something to balance his own excessive sensitiveness, something to control his mobility of feeling, something to steady his advance and give him poise. A law he needed, but a law which should steady his advance, not one which should trammel his advance or hold him in motionless equilibrium. Coming at a time when the ideas of the Revolution were in the air, he found what served him as a law in those ideas, as declared by their most eminent English spokesman, William Godwin. A lyrical nature attempting to steady its advance by the revolutionary abstractions—such was Shelley. And his work in literature represents on the one hand his own mobile temperament, his extraordinary sensitiveness and marvellous imagination, and on the other hand the *zeit-geist*, the spirit of 1789, as formulated by Godwin in a code of morals, rigid, passionless, and doctrinaire, yet containing a hidden fire, and glowing inwardly with ardent anticipations. The volumes of "Political Justice" were thus for Shelley at once a law and a gospel.—DOWDEN, EDWARD, 1887, *Last Words on Shelley, Fortnightly Review, vol.* 48, *p.* 461.

Shows a great advance in lucidity and command of logical language. He has been compared, surely to his own moral advantage, with Condorcet; but there is no question that he was curiously related to the French precursors of the Revolution, and particularly to Rousseau and Helvetius, from whom he caught, with their republican ardour, not a little of the clear merit of their style.—GOSSE, EDMUND, 1897, *A Short History of Modern English Literature, p.* 293.

CALEB WILLIAMS

1794

One word respecting the MS. itself, and I have done. The incidents are ill chosen; the characters unnatural, distorted; the phraseology intended to mark the humorous ones inappropriate; the style uncouth; everything upon stilts; the whole uninteresting; written as a man would make a chair or a table that had never handled a tool. I got through it, but it was as I get over a piece of ploughed-up ground, with labour and toil. By the way, judging from the work in question, one might suppose some minds not to be unlike a piece of ground. Having produced a rich crop, it must lie fallow for a season, that it may gain sufficient vigour for a new crop. You were speaking for a motto for this work—the best motto in my opinion would be a *Hic jacet;* for depend upon it, the world will suppose you to be exhausted; or rather what a few only think at present, will become a general opinion, that the Hercules you have fathered is not of your begetting.—MARSHAL, JAMES, 1793, *Letter to Godwin, May* 31; *William Godwin by Paul, vol.* I, *p.* 90.

In the writings of Godwin, some of the strongest of our feelings are most forcibly awakened, and there are few novels which display more powerful painting, or excite higher interest, than his "Caleb Williams." The character of Falkland, the chief actor, which is formed on visionary principles of honour, is perhaps not strictly an invention, as it closely resembles that of Shamont, in Beaumont and Fletcher's "Nice Valour." But the accumulated wretchedness with which he is overwhelmed, the inscrutable mystery by which he is surrounded, and the frightful persecutions to which he subjects the suspected possessor of his dreadful secret, are peculiar to the author, and are represented with a force which has not been surpassed in the finest passages and scenes of poetic or dramatic fiction.—DUNLOP, JOHN, 1814–42, *The History of Fiction, vol.* II, *p.* 405.

"Caleb Williams" is probably the finest novel produced by a man—at least since the "Vicar of Wakefield." The sentiments, if not the opinions, from which it arose, were transient. Local usages and institutions were the subjects of its satire, exaggerated beyond the usual privilege of that species of writing. Yet it has been translated into most languages, and it has appeared in various forms, on the theatres, not only of England, but of France and Germany. There is scarcely a continental circulating library in which it is not one of the books which most quickly require to be replaced. . . . There is scarcely a fiction in any language which it is so difficult to lay by. . . . The passages which betray the metaphysician more than the novelist, ought to be weeded out with more than ordinary care.—MACKINTOSH, SIR JAMES, 1815, *Godwin's Lives of Milton's Nephews, Edinburgh Review, vol.* 25, *pp.* 486, 487.

Few there are who do not enter into and understand the workings of the mind of Caleb Williams, where the demon of curiosity, finding a youth of an active and speculative disposition, without guide to advise, or business to occupy him, engages his thoughts and his time upon the task of prying into a mystery which no way concerned him, and which from the beginning he had a well-founded conviction might prove fatal to him, should he ever penetrate it. The chivalrous frenzy of Falkland, in the same piece, though perhaps awkwardly united with the character of an assassin, that love of fame to which he sacrifices honour and virtue, is another instance of a *humour*, or turn of mind, which, like stained glass, colours with its own peculiar tinge every object beheld by the party.—SCOTT, SIR WALTER, 1826, *The Omen, Blackwood's Magazine, vol.* 20, *p.* 53.

"Caleb Williams" is the cream of his mind, the rest are the skimmed milk; yet in that wondrous novel all must be offended with the unnatural and improbable character of Falkland; the most accomplished, the most heroical and lofty-minded of men murders one who has affronted him, allows others to hang for the deed, and persecutes to the brink of ruin a man whose sole sin was a desire to penetrate through the mystery in which this prodigy of vice and virtue had wrapped himself. Williams suffers merely because it was necessary for the story that he should; a single word would have set all right and saved him from much unnatural terror. In short, the fault is, that the actions which the *dramatis personæ* perform are not in keeping with their characters.—CUNNINGHAM, ALLAN, 1833, *Biographical and Critical History of the Literature of the Last Fifty Years.*

"Caleb Williams," the earliest, is also the most popular, of our author's romances, not because his latter works have been less rich in sentiment and passion, but because they are, for the most part, confined to the development of single characters; while in this there is the opposition and death-grapple of two beings, each endowed with poignant sensibilities and quenchless energy. There is no work of fiction which more rivets the attention—no tragedy which exhibits a struggle more sublime or sufferings more intense than this; yet to produce the effect, no complicated machinery is employed, but the springs of action are few and simple. The motives are at once common and elevated, and are purely intellectual, without appearing for an instant inadequate to their mighty issues.—TALFOURD, THOMAS NOON, 1842, *Critical and Miscellaneous Writings, p,* 38.

The interest of this wonderful tale is indescribable. . . . This author possesses no humour, no powers of description, at least of nature—none of that magic which communicates to inanimate objects the light and glow of sentiment—very little pathos; but, on the other hand, few have possessed a more penetrating eye for that recondite causation which links together motive and action, a more watchful and determined consistency in tracing the manifestations of such characters as he has once conceived, or a more prevailing spirit of self-persuasion as to the reality of what he relates. The romance of "Caleb Williams" is indeed ideal; but it is an ideal totally destitute of all the trappings and ornaments of the ideal: it is like some grand picture painted in dead colour.—SHAW, THOMAS B., 1847, *Outlines of English Literature, pp.* 382, 383.

One of the most powerful and fascinating novels in the language, the plot, and its evolution, being invested with such intense interest that the didactic purpose of the work is not noticed by an ordinary reader, and may, indeed, be entirely ignored, without any detriment.—DAVIES, JAMES, 1873, *English Literature from the Accession of George III. to the Battle of Waterloo, p.* 139.

The novel had very great success, and was dramatized by Colman under the name of "The Iron Chest." In spite of the amazing impossibilities of the story and its unrelieved gloom; in spite of the want of almost any character to admire—since Mr. Clare, by whom Godwin probably intended to represent his friend Fawcet, dies early in the tale; though there is no real heroine and scarcely mention of love, the story has survived and has probably been read by very many persons who, but for it, have never heard of Godwin. It is a very powerful book, and the character of Falkland the murderer is unique in literature.—PAUL, C. KEGAN, 1876, *William Godwin: his Friends and Contemporaries, vol.* I, *p.* 117.

The most obvious moral is that you ought not to have half a conscience. If Falkland had been thoroughly virtuous, he would not have committed murder; if thoroughly vicious, he would not have been tortured to death by remorse. But fortunately this childish design of enforcing a political theory did not spoil Godwin's story. The situation is impressive, and, in spite of many clumsy details, is impressively represented. The spectacle of a man of delicate sense of honour writhing under the dread of detection, and opposed by an incarnation of vulgar curiosity, moves us to forget the superfluous moral. —STEPHEN, LESLIE, 1876, *William Godwin, The Fortnightly Review, vol.* 26, *p.* 459.

The interest of "Caleb Williams" is very real and very well maintained. The character of Falkland, in which all the milder virtues have been overshadowed by the memory of his crime, the sleepless curiosity of Williams in the effort to ascertain his master's secret, the price he pays for success in the persecution that dogs him unremittingly, together make up a story of an interest too powerful to permit it to be enslaved to a frigid scheme of Utopian politics.—RALEIGH, WALTER, 1894, *The English Novel, p.* 245.

In "Caleb Williams" we have before us a revolutionary work of art, the imaginative work of a theorist, a tale which enforces a doctrine. It gains and loses by the concentration of spirit with which Godwin in it studies and works out a moral problem. To read it is to enter and explore a cavern; it is narrow; it is dark; we lose the light and air, and the clear spaces of the firmament; but the explorer's passion seizes upon us, and we grope along the narrowing walls with an intensity of curious desire. As the work of a political thinker, the book is an indictment of society. . . . "Caleb Williams" is the one novel of the days of Revolution, embodying the new doctrine of the time, which can be said to survive.—DOWDEN, EDWARD, 1897, *The French Revolution and English Literature, pp.* 66, 76.

ST. LEON
1799

Men must have arrived at an uncommon degree of general wisdom, when "St. Leon" shall no longer be read. Your Marguerite is inimitable. Knowing the model after which you drew, as often as I recollected it, my heart ached while I read. Your Bethlem Gabor is wonderfully drawn. It is like the figures of Michel Angelo, any section of an outline of which taken apart would be improbable and false, but which are so combined as to form a sublime whole. Having read I could coldly come back, and point to the caricature traits of the portrait, but while reading I could feel nothing but astonishment and admiration. Through the whole work there is so much to censure, and so much to astonish, that in my opinion it is in every sense highly interesting. Its faults and its beauties are worthy the attention of the most acute critic.—HOLCROFT, THOMAS, 1800, *Letter to Godwin, Sept.* 9; *William Godwin by Paul, vol.* II, *p.* 25.

I have been reading (for the little I could read) a new novel of Godwin's, in four vols., called "The Travels of St. Leon." It is an odd work, like all his, and, like all his, interesting, tho' hardly ever pleasantly so; and while one's head often agrees with his observations, and sometimes with his reasoning, never does one's heart thoroughly agree with his sentiments on any subject or in any character. He now *allows* that the social affections may be cultivated to advantage in human life, and upon this plan his present novel is formed. I should tell you, which I know from Edwards, that it was written for bread, agreed for by the book-sellers beforehand, and actually composed and written as the printers wanted it. I think you will see many marks of this throughout the work if you read it, which I should recommend to you, if, like me, you have not seen a *readable* novel for this age.—BERRY, MARY, 1800, *To Miss Cholmeley, Jan.* 2; *Extracts from Journals and Correspondence, ed. Lady Lewis, vol.* II, *p.* 111.

The character, too, of St. Leon is ably sustained—we are charmed with his early loyalty and patriotism—his elevation of soul and tender attachment to his family; while, at the same time, his fondness for magnificence and admiration naturally prepares his acceptance of the pernicious gifts of the alchymist. Through the whole romance the dialogues are full of eloquence, and almost every scene is sketched with the strong and vivid pencil of a master. Never was escape more interesting than that of St. Leon from the *Auto da Fe* at Valladolid, or landscape more heart-reviving than that of his subsequent journey to the mansion of his fathers! Never did human genius portray a more frightful picture of solitude and mental desolation, than that of the mysterious stranger who arrives at the cottage of St. Leon, and leaves him the fatal bequest! At the conculsion we are left with the strongest impressions of those feelings of desertion and deadness of heart experienced by St. Leon, and which were aggravated by his constant remembrance of scenes of former happiness.—DUNLOP, JOHN, 1814–42, *The History of Fiction, vol.* II, *p.* 406.

In "St. Leon," Mr. Godwin has sought the stores of the supernatural;—but the "metaphysical aid" which he has condescended to accept, is not adapted to carry him farther from nature, but to ensure a more intimate and wide communion with its mysteries. His hero does not acquire the philosopher's stone and the elixir of immortality to furnish out for himself a dainty solitude, where he may dwell, soothed with the music of his own undying thoughts, and rejoicing in his severance from his frail and transitory fellows.—TALFOURD, THOMAS NOON, 1842, *Critical and Miscellaneous Writings, p.* 39.

Though it had a considerable reputation, and went through many editions, it never had the popularity of "Caleb Williams;" its even greater improbability removed it still more from the region of human sympathies. But the description of Marguerite, drawn from the character of Mary Wollstonecraft, and of St. Leon's married life with her, idealized from that which Godwin had himself enjoyed, are among the most beautiful passages in English fiction, while the portrait of Charles, St. Leon's son, stands alone. No such picture has elsewhere been drawn of a perfectly noble, self-sacrificing boy.—PAUL, C. KEGAN, 1876, *William Godwin: his Friends and Contemporaries, vol.* I, *p.* 331.

LIFE OF GEOFFREY CHAUCER
1803

I may be wrong, but I think there is one considerable error runs through it, which is a conjecturing spirit, a fondness for filling out the picture by supposing what Chaucer did and how he felt where the materials are scanty.—LAMB, CHARLES, 1803, *Letter to William Godwin, Nov.* 10; *William Godwin by Paul, vol.* II, *p.* 103.

The perusal of this title excited no small surprise in our critical fraternity. The authenticated passages of Chaucer's life may be comprised in half a dozen pages; and behold two voluminous quartos! . . . We have said that Mr. Godwin had two modes of wire-drawing and prolonging his narrative. The first is, as we have seen, by hooking in the description and history of everything that existed upon the earth at the same time with Chaucer. In this kind of composition, we usually lose sight entirely of the proposed subject of Mr. Godwin's lucubrations, travelling to Rome or Palestine with as little remorse as if poor Chaucer had never been mentioned in the title-page. The second mode is considerably more ingenious, and consists in making old Geoffrey accompany the author upon these frisking excursions. For example, Mr. Godwin has a fancy to describe a judicial trial. Nothing can be more easily introduced; for Chaucer certainly studied at the Temple, and is supposed to have been bred to the bar.—SCOTT, SIR WALTER, 1804, *Godwin's Life of Chaucer, Edinburgh Review, vol.* 3, *pp.* 437, 440.

In his Life of Mary Wollstonecraft he has written little and said much; and in his account of Chaucer, he has written much and said little. . . . It has been said that a spoonful of truth will colour an ocean of fiction; and so it is seen in Godwin's "Life of Chaucer;" he heaps conjecture upon conjecture—dream upon dream—theory upon theory; scatters learning all around, and shows everywhere a deep sense of the merits of the poet; yet all that he has related might have been told in a twentieth part of the space which he has taken.—CUNNINGHAM, ALLAN, 1833, *Biographical and Critical History of the Literature of the Last Fifty Years.*

Godwin's "Life of Chaucer," which

appeared in 1803, in two large quarto volumes, is in many ways an extraordinary specimen of biography. The perusal of the work, when for any reason that becomes an absolute necessity, is as much of the nature of a solemn literary undertaking as was its composition. It is perhaps the earliest, though unhappily not the latest or even the largest, illustration of that species of biography in which the lack of information about the man who is its alleged subject is counterbalanced by long disquisitions about anything or everything he shared in or saw, or may have shared in or seen. . . . Godwin was always ready to tell what he did not know, to describe what he had not seen, and to explain what he did not understand. . . . May indeed be declared to deserve the distinction of being the most worthless piece of biography in the English language—certainly the most worthless produced by a man of real ability.—LOUNSBURY, THOMAS R., 1892, *Studies in Chaucer, vol.* I, *pp.* 191, 194.

FLEETWOOD
1805

There is, perhaps, little general sympathy with the overstrained delicacies of Fleetwood, who, like Falkland in the "School for Scandal," is too extravagant in his peculiarities to deserve the reader's pity.—SCOTT, SIR WALTER, 1826, *The Omen, Blackwood's Magazine, vol.* 20, *p.* 53.

"Fleetwood" has less of our author's characteristic energy than any other of his works.—TALFOURD, THOMAS NOON, 1842, *Critical and Miscellaneous Writings, p.* 40.

The best of his imaginative work is to be found in "Fleetwood;" not so much in the main story, with its stock villain and maligned wife, as in the early reminiscences of Feetwood and the episodical autobiography of Ruffigny, where the author displays a sensibility to scenery and a vivid remembrance of the feelings of childhood that would be remarkable even in a less arid mind.—RALEIGH, WALTER, 1894, *The English Novel, p.* 247.

MANDEVILLE
1817

Powerful but unnatural and bombastic novel.—CARLYLE, THOMAS, 1818, *To Mr. R. Mitchell, Feb.* 16; *Early Letters, ed. Norton, p.* 70.

Of "Mandeville," I shall say only one word. It appears to me to be a falling off in the subject, not in the ability. The style and declamation are even more powerful than ever. But unless an author surpasses himself, and surprises the public as much the fourth or fifth time as he did the first, he is said to fall off, because there is not the same stimulus of novelty. A great deal is here made out of nothing, or out of a very disagreeable subject. I cannot agree that the story is out of nature. The feeling is very common indeed; though carried to an unusual and improbable excess, or to one with which from the individuality and minuteness of the cicumstances, we cannot readily sympathise.—HAZLITT, WILLIAM, 1818, *Lecture on the English Novelists.*

Like his other novels, it contains an important lesson, forcibly inculcated—it shows the forlornness and misery of a jealous, sullen, aspiring mind, that makes great claims on the world, without proper efforts to justify or enforce them. The author in this, as in his previous works, displays, with appalling truth, the despotic sovereignty and all searching observation of publick opinion, in so much, that one trembles with the consciousness of being subject to this tremendous power, which he cannot fly from or resist. No writer has perhaps more adequately expressed, what every body feels,—how much of the good and ill of life is involved in reputation.—PHILLIPS, W., 1818, *Godwin's Mandeville, North American Review, vol.* 7, *p.* 105.

His St. Leon and his Mandeville are ten degrees darker than his Falkland: in the latter, there are many ties to connect us with truth and nature, and we go on—as the sailors keep by a sinking vessel—in the hope that all must be righted soon. Mandeville is one of those unhappy persons whose minds are never so free from the storms of passion as to be fully rational, and yet cannot, save in fits of fury, be considered wholly mad.—CUNNINGHAM, ALLAN, 1833, *Biographical and Critical History of the Literature of the Last Fifty Years.*

"Mandeville" has all the power of its author's earliest writings, but its main subject—the development of an engrossing and maddening hatred—is not one which can excite human sympathy. There is, however, a bright relief to the gloom of the picture, in the angelic disposition of Clifford, and the sparkling loveliness of Henrietta, who appears "full of life, and splendour and joy."—TALFOURD, THOMAS NOON, 1842, *Critical and Miscellaneous Writings, p.* 41.

GENERAL

O form'd t' illume a sunless world forlorn,
As o'er the chill and dusky brow of Night,
In Finland's wintry skies the mimic morn
Electric pours a stream of rosy light,
Pleased I have mark'd Oppression, terror-pale,
Since, thro' the windings of her dark machine,
Thy steady eye has shot its glances keen—
And bade th' all-lovely "scenes at distance hail."
Nor will I not thy holy guidance bless,
And hymn thee, Godwin! with an ardent lay;
For that thy voice, in Passion's stormy day,
When wild I roam'd the bleak Heath of Distress,
Bade the bright form of Justice meet my way—
And told me that her name was Happiness.
—COLERIDGE, SAMUEL TAYLOR, 1795, *Sonnet to William Godwin, Jan.* 10.

You will find much to blame in his style, and you will be surprised that he should have written a dissertation upon English style.—EDGEWORTH, MARIA, 1797, *To Miss Sophy Ruxton, Oct.; Letters, vol.* I, *p.* 47.

Dear Sir,—I thank you for the play of "Antonio," as I feel myself flattered by your remembrance of me; and I most sincerely wish you joy of having produced a work which will protect you from being classed with the successful dramatists of the present day, but which will hand you down to posterity among the honoured few who, during the past century, have totally failed in writing for the stage.—INCHBALD, ELIZABETH, 1801, *Letter to Godwin, Jan.* 5; *William Godwin by Paul, vol.* II, *p.* 77.

You will have heard, I presume, that your friend Godwin's tragedy of "Antonio," which he expected to produce him 500*l*. was universally and completely damned.—RITSON, JOSEPH, 1801, *Letters, Feb.* 26, *vol.* II, *p.* 201.

Indeed at this period (1798) of Mr. Brown's life, he was an avowed admirer of Godwin's style, and the effects of that admiration, may be discerned in many of his early compositions.—DUNLAP, WILLIAM, 1815, *Life of Charles Brockden Brown, vol.* II, *p.* 15.

Greater none than he
Though fallen—and fallen on evil times—to stand
Among the spirits of our age and land,
Before the dread tribunal of *To come*
The foremost, while Rebuke cowers pale and dumb.
—SHELLEY, PERCY BYSSHE, 1820, *Letter to Maria Gisborne.*

I dissent from Mr. Godwin's theory of politics and morality as sincerely as I admire his genius.—SCOTT, SIR WALTER, 1826? *Letter to B. R. Haydon; Life, Letters and Table Talk, ed. Stoddard, p.* 160.

Mr. Godwin was by no means turned to tragedy. He was either weak in his fable, or impure in his interest, careless about received opinions, and not so much a master of the passions as to move them in spite of all the indecorum in the world. He was not a Kotzebue.—BOADEN, JAMES, 1831, *The Life of Mrs. Jordan, vol.* II, *p.* 65.

Godwin was a man of great powers, insufficiently balanced; and, as the European world was, in his youth, a mighty conflict of great powers insufficiently balanced, he was just the man to make an impression of vast force on the society of his day. Soon after his "Political Justice" was published, working-men were seen to club their earnings to buy it, and to meet under a tree or in an ale-house to read it. It wrought so violently that Godwin saw there must be unsoundness in it; and he modified it considerably before he reissued it. His mind was acute, and, through the generosity of his heart, profound; but it was one-sided.—MARTINEAU, HARRIET, 1849, *A History of the Thirty Years' Peace, A. D.* 1815–1846, *vol.* IV, *p.* 79.

As Godwin's was no vulgar intellect, and as his politics were of an ardent and speculative cast, so, even now, when his novels are read for their purely imaginative interest, they impress powerfully.—MASSON, DAVID, 1859, *British Novelists and Their Styles, p.* 185.

The "Enquirer" was less popular than the "Political Justice." Part of the charm of the latter undoubtedly lay in the elaborate completeness and systematic order of the whole discussion. The foundations were laid in the psychology of Locke; and then the building was raised, stone by stone, until the whole was finished. But in the "Enquirer" Godwin's dislike of law had extended even to the form of composition. He had been wrong, he said, in trying to write a systematic treatise on Society; and he would now confine himself to detached essays, wholly experimental and not necessarily in harmony with one another. The contrast between these two styles is the contrast between a whole oratorio and a miscellaneous concert, or between a complete poem and a volume of extracts.—BONAR, JAMES, 1881, *Parson Malthus, p.* 15.

I believe my father's ride of between two and three hundred miles to London was chiefly with a view to make Godwin's acquaintance. He was then supposed, by a large party in the country, to be a political philosopher who had achieved imperishable renown. His two large volumes sleep on my shelves, and, written in the fly-leaf, in the hand of one of my uncles, is "Hoc nescire nefas."—TAYLOR, SIR HENRY, 1885, *Autobiography, vol.* I, *p.* 16.

Godwin at his best far surpasses the other English revolutionary novelists in the art of fusing ethical doctrine with imaginative form; but as he grew older, and the fire burnt low, the two elements gradually disintegrated.—HERFORD, C. H., 1897, *The Age of Wordsworth, p.* 100.

Godwin was an advanced thinker and an able writer. One of his romances is still read, but his philosophical works, once so esteemed, are out of vogue now; their authority was already declining when Shelley made his acquaintance—that is, it was declining with the public, but not with Shelley. They had been his moral and political Bible, and they were that yet. Shelley the infidel would himself have claimed to be less a work of God than a work of Godwin. Godwin's philosophies had formed his mind and interwoven themselves into it and become a part of its texture; he regarded himself as Godwin's spiritual son. Godwin was not without self-appreciation; indeed, it may be conjectured that from his point of view the last syllable of his name was surplusage. He lived serene in his lofty world of philosophy, far above the mean interests that absorbed smaller men, and only came down to the ground at intervals to pass the hat for alms to pay his debts with, and insult the man that relieved him. —CLEMENS, S. M. (MARK TWAIN), 1897, *How to Tell a Story and Other Essays, p.* 75.

Godwin is essentially a prose-writer, and his style, though it has been over-praised, is of considerable merit. Although his exaggerated anarchism and determination to regard everything as an open question are absurd enough in principle and lead to the most unimaginable absurdities in detail, yet they give his thought always the appearance, and sometimes the reality of freer play than had been enjoyed by any English writer since Hobbes. . . . It was Godwin, more than any one else, who introduced the mischievous but popular practice of bolstering out history by describing at great length the places and scenes which his heroes might have seen, the transactions in which, being contemporary, they might have taken an interest, and the persons with whom they either were, or conceivably might have been, acquainted. In this, as in other things, he belonged to the class of "germinal" writers. And his influence on the early, although impermanent, creeds and tempers of the most brilliant young men of his day was quite extraordinary. — SAINTSBURY, GEORGE, 1898, *A Short History of English Literature, pp.* 634, 635.

Godwin is partly remembered because of his great influence on Shelley, which resulted in the poet's application to the philosopher's own family of those principles concerning love and marriage which Godwin so coolly set forth. Really, however, the man had power enough to be remembered for himself; deeply influenced by the rationalistic philosophy of the eighteenth century, he devoted himself both in such direct writings as his "Political Justice," and in such medicated fiction as "Caleb Williams," to expounding deeply revolutionary ideas. — WENDELL, BARRETT, 1900, *A Literary History of America, p.* 160.

James Mill

1773–1836

Born, at Northwater Bridge, Forfarshire, 6 April 1773. Educated at Parish School; and at Montrose Academy. Friendship with Hume begun at latter. Tutor for some time to the daughter of Sir James Stuart. To Edinburgh Univ., 1790.

Licensed to preach, 4 Oct. 1798. To London, 1802. Contrib. to "Anti-Jacobin Review," 1802; and other periodicals. Edited "The Literary Journal," 1802-06; edited "St. James's Chronicle," 1805-08[?]. Married Harriet Burrow, 5 June 1805. Contrib. to "British Rev." "Monthly Rev.," "Eclectic Rev." to "Edinburgh Rev.," 1808-13; to "The Philanthropist," 1811-17. Friendship with Bentham begun, 1808; with Ricardo, 1811. Assistant to Examiner of India Correspondence, India House, May 1819; Second Assistant, April 1821; Assistant Examiner, April 1823; Examiner, Dec. 1830. Contrib. to "Encycl. Brit.," 1816-23. Political Economy Club founded, 1820. Helped to found "Westminster Rev." 1824; frequent contributor, 1824-29. One of founders of London University; member of original Council, 1825. Contrib. to "London Rev.," 1835-36. Died, in London, 23 June 1836. Buried at Kensington Church. *Works:* "Essay on the Impolicy of a Bounty on the Exportation of Grain" (anon.), 1804; "Commerce Defended," 1808; "History of British India" (3 vols.), 1817; "Elements of Political Economy," 1821; "Essays" (priv. ptd.), [1825?]; "Analyses of the Phenomena of the Human Mind," 1829; "On the Ballot" (anon.), [1830]; "Fragment on Mackintosh" (anon.), 1835. *Posthumous:* "The Principles of Toleration," 1837. He *translated:* C. F. D. de Villers' "Essay on the Spirit and influence of the Reformation," 1805. *Life:* by Prof. Bain, 1882.—SHARP, R. FARQUHARSON, 1897, *A Dictionary of English Authors*, p. 196.

PERSONAL

With profound grief we have to record the death of one of the first men of our time; the loss of one of our master-minds, of one that has given the most powerful impulse, and the most correct direction to thought. Wherever talent and good purpose were found conjoined—the power and the will to serve the cause of truth—the ability and the disposition to be useful to society, to weed out error, and advance improvement—wherever these qualities were united, the possessor found a friend, a supporter to fortify, cheer, and encourage him in his course, in James Mill. He fanned every flame of public virtue, he strengthened every good purpose that came within the range of his influence. His conversation was full of instruction, and his mind was rich in suggestion, to a degree that we have never found equalled. His writings, with all their solid value, would convey but an imperfect notion of the character and powers of his mind. His conversation was so energetic and complete in thought, so succinct, and exact *ad unguem* in expression, that, if reported as uttered, his colloquial observations or arguments would have been perfect compositions. His thoughts, conveyed to paper, lost some of the excellences we have mentioned. Yet his works will be stores of valuable doctrine. . . . It was hardly possible for an intelligent man to know James Mill without feeling an obligation for the profit derived from his mind.—FONBLANQUE, ALBANY WILLIAM, 1836, *The Examiner*.

In all the relations of private life he was irreproachable; and he afforded a rare example of one born in humble circumstances, and struggling, during the greater part of his laborious life, with the inconveniences of restricted means, nobly maintaining an independence as absolute in all respects as that of the first subject in the land—an independence, indeed, which but few of the pampered children of rank and wealth are ever seen to enjoy. For he could at all times restrain his wishes within the limits of his resources; was firmly resolved that his own hands alone should ever minister to his wants; and would, at every period of his useful and virtuous life, have treated with indignation any project that should trammel his opinions or his conduct with the restraints which external influence, of whatever kind, could impose.—BROUGHAM, HENRY LORD, 1838, *Speech on Law Reform*.

His unpremeditated oral exposition was hardly less effective than his prepared work with the pen; his colloquial fertility on philosophical subjects, his power of discussing himself, and of stimulating others to discuss, his ready responsive inspirations through all the shifts and windings of a sort of Platonic dialogue—all these accomplishments were, to those who knew him, even more impressive than what he composed for the press. Conversation with him was not merely instructive, but provocative to the dormant intelligence. Of all persons whom we have known Mr. James Mill was the one who stood least remote from the lofty Platonic ideal of

Dialectic—Τοῦ διδόναι καὶ δέχεσθαὶ λόγου—(the giving and receiving of reasons)—competent alike to examine others, or to be examined by them on philosophy. When to this we add a strenuous character, earnest convictions, and single-minded devotion to truth, with an utter disdain of mere paradox, it may be conceived that such a man exercised powerful intellectual ascendancy over younger minds.—GROTE, GEORGE, 1865, *Examination of Sir William Hamilton's Philosophy by John Stuart Mill*

He *was* sought for the vigour and instructiveness of his conversation, and did use it largely as an instrument for the diffusion of his opinions. I have never known any man who could do such ample justice to his best thoughts in colloquial discussion. His perfect command over his great mental resources, the terseness and expressiveness of his language and the moral earnestness as well as intellectual force of his delivery, made him one of the most striking of all argumentative conversers: and he was full of anecdote, a hearty laugher, and, when with people whom he liked, a most lively and amusing companion. It was not solely, or even chiefly, in diffusing his merely intellectual convictions that his power showed itself: it was still more through the influence of a quality, of which I have only since learnt to appreciate the extreme rarity: that exalted public spirit, and regard above all things to the good of the whole, which warmed into life and activity every germ of similar virtue that existed in the minds he came in contact with: the desire he made them feel for his approbation, the shame at his disapproval; the moral support which his conversation and his very existence gave to those who were aiming at the same objects, and the encouragement he afforded to the faint-hearted or desponding among them, by the firm confidence which (though the reverse of sanguine as to the results to be expected in any one particular case) he always felt in the power of reason, the general progress of improvement, and the good which individuals could do by judicious effort.—MILL, JOHN STUART, 1873, *Autobiography, p.* 101.

She [Mrs. Mill] was an exceedingly pretty woman; had a small fine figure, an aquiline type of face (seen in her eldest son), and a pink and dun complexion. One letter of Mill's to her she preserved, as perhaps the fullest and strongest of all his affectionate outpourings. The depth and tenderness of the feeling could not well be exceeded; but, in the light of after years, we can see that he too readily took for granted that she would be an intellectual companion to himself. . . . Mrs. Mill was not wanting in any of the domestic virtues of an English mother. She toiled hard for her house and her children, and became thoroughly obedient to her lord. As an admired beauty, she seems to have been chagrined at the discovery at her position after marriage. There was disappointment on both sides: the union was never happy.—BAIN, ALEXANDER, 1882, *James Mill, a Biography, pp.* 59, 60.

James Mill's greatest achievement was, it has been said, to have produced John Mill. This dictum has a certain amount of epigrammatic force, but it contains at least as much falsehood as truth. For no error would be greater than to suppose that James Mill was nothing but the father of his better-known son. If the word "noteworthy" could be used in a strictly neutral sense, as meaning, without any implication either of praise or of blame, "worthy to be noticed," a fair critic would, without much hesitation, pronounce James Mill a more noteworthy person than the writer who, to the generation who have grown up within the last thirty or forty years, will always be emphatically known as "Mill." The truth is, that James Mill was a man who, for bad or good, possessed a strength, energy, and individuality of character far exceeding that of the author whose somewhat morbid passion for liberty, or even eccentricity, is, we take it, an unconscious reaction against the overpowering sway exercised over his mind and will by the unconquerable volition of his father. The one word which James Mill's whole character and career suggests is "force." He was not a lovable man; he was not a man of genius; he was not, with all his talent and capacity, a man of original conceptions, but he was a man of strength.—DICEY, A. V., 1882, *James Mill, The Nation, vol.* 35, *p.* 204.

James Mill was of the same country as Mackintosh—a Northern Scot, though not of Celtic race. This latter circumstance may partly account for the difference between them, which was as great as if half a world had lain between their places of birth. To come suddenly out of the genial presence of the one into the gloomy companionship of the other involves a greater shock of difference than could we pass in a moment from Italy to Iceland. Mill was one of the sternest and most rigid representatives of that northern race which, notwithstanding the very different qualities of the names which make it illustrious, has so continued to retain its conventional character for harshness and coldness that we are almost forced to believe there must be some truth in the imputation. There would be so, if the Devil's advocate could produce many such men as James Mill to counterbalance Scott and Mackintosh as specimens of the character of their countrymen.—OLIPHANT, MARGARET O. W., 1882, *Literary History of England, XVIII-XIX Century, vol.* III, *p.* 282.

HISTORY OF BRITISH INDIA
1817

In the evening looked through the first volume of Mill's "India:". a rich display of learning; combats all the flattering theories and notices that have been held with respect to the Hindoos; exposes many instances of weakness in Sir W. Jones on this subject.—MOORE, THOMAS, 1819, *Diary, March* 17, *ed. Russell, vol.* II, *p.*277.

A great many of the details about the squabbles and wars with the petty Indian princes are invincibly dull, but the work is, on the whole, both interesting and instructive.—LEWIS, SIR GEORGE CORNEWALL, 1837, *To E. W. Head, Jan.* 10; *Letters, ed. Lewis, p.* 72.

We may and must have others, written by men who have seen India, and who can contribute much that did not lie in Mr. Mill's way; but nothing can now prevent his being the history which first presented the great subject of India to the best part of the mind of England, and largely influenced the administration of that great dependency. — MARTINEAU, HARRIET, 1849, *A History of the Thirty Years' Peace, A. D.* 1815–1846, *vol.* IV, *p.* 77.

At this time of day, I am not called upon to criticize the "History of India." It has exercised its influence, and found its place. Any observations that are needful are such as will aid us in appreciating the character of the author. Coming to the subject with his peculiar powers and his acquired knowledge, and expending upon it such an amout of labour, he could not but produce a work of originality and grasp. If the whole of his time for twelve years was not literally devoted to the task, it was, we may say, substantially devoted; for his diversions consisted mostly in discussing topics allied to the problems that the History had to deal with.—BAIN, ALEXANDER, 1882, *James Mill, A Biography, p.* 176.

Surely it is not merely that various mistakes and shortcomings have been discovered, but that the whole point of view is wrong. Mill was violently knocking his head against a stone wall, instead of patiently seeking for a door and a key. Along with the "best ideas of the sociological writers of the eighteenth century," he had their worst. He views Hindoo religion, manners, and institutions from an absolute instead of a relative and historic standpoint. This is exactly the same fatal error as was made by the school of the eighteenth century about Christianity itself, and in the light of modern philosophy Mill's Second Book is as profoundly unsatisfactory as Gibbon's Fifteenth and Sixteenth Chapters. He speaks of the Hindoos, their superstition and their degradation, with the bitterness of the most ferocious evangelical missionary. There was some provocation, no doubt, in the exaggerated pictures which had been painted of the sublimity of the Hindoo religion; for this again was a mark of the eighteenth century, to extol the virtues and the philosophy of Chinamen, Persians, and all other sorts and conditions of unknown peoples. . . . It is odd that he should not have felt the necessity, as a positive thinker, of seeking some explanation of these superstitious beliefs, grovelling customs, and backward institutions, in the facts of human nature, history, and surrounding circumstances. The time was not then ripe for adequate theories on these matters, but Mill rushed further away from the track than he ought in reason and consistency to have done.—MORLEY, JOHN, 1882, *The Life of James Mill, Fortnightly Review, vol.* 37, *p.* 501.

A book of great ability, of strong prejudices, and of very extensive learning.

The author plunged deep into the most obscure sources of knowledge, and, for such information as he desired, followed out every clew to its end. He culled from old despatches everything that could throw light on the subject in hand. The point of view from which he wrote was that of an opponent of the purposes and methods of the East India Company. The volumes might be called an elaborate and sustained arraignment of the entire policy of the Company. . . . Though the work, as a whole, is a monument of learning, if not of historical skill, it ought to be said, perhaps, that in point of style it lacks animation and picturesqueness. This characteristic will always prevent it from attracting and holding a very large number of general readers. On this account its popularity can never equal its intrinsic merits. For the special student of the English policy in the East it is invaluable.—ADAMS, CHARLES KENDALL, 1882, *A Manual of Historical Literature, p.* 441.

The "History" succeeded at once, and has become a standard work. Mill unfortunately left his share of the profits in the hands of the publisher, Baldwin, and though he received the interest during his life, the capital was afterwards lost to his family by Baldwin's bankruptcy. The book, though dry and severe in tone, supplied a want, and contained many interesting reflections upon social questions. He has been accused of unfairness, and his prejudices were undoubtedly strong. His merits, however, met with an unexpected recognition. — STEPHEN, LESLIE, 1894, *Dictionary of National Biography, vol.* XXXVII, *p.* 385.

Has interest and even piquancy, for the literary historian. . . . His disabilities were considerable. He had never been in India; he knew no Indian language. He shows his entire divergence from the Romantic school of history by making light of both facts. To enter into the genius of a strange civilization and judge it in the light of its own aims and aspirations was no business of his; he desired to bring it to the bar of his own trained and peremptory judgment, and try it by "the grand test of civilization"—utility. The historian has with him not only to judge, but to give his reasons at length, which he does with an amplitude reproduced by Grote, rudely ignoring in this and other respects the artistic presentment of history made current by Voltaire and Montesquieu. Yet his account of Hindoo civilization, though bitterly contemptuous, is in many points a wholesome corrective to the uncritical rhapsodies of the early Sanscritists—of Sir W. Jones and F. Schlegel; and the entire exemption from vulgar patriotism which prompts his incisive criticisms of the Company, was a most salutary application of Bentham's mechanical formula: everyone to count as one, and no one for more than one.—HERFORD, C. H., 1897, *The Age of Wordsworth, p.* 45.

PHILOSOPHY

It would be difficult to overrate the importance of the service which James Mill did to philosophy by his analysis of the elementary laws of the association of ideas; for an ignorance of those laws has led to more false philosophy than probably anything else.—BISSET, ANDREW, 1871, *Essays on Historical Truth, p.* 105.

The work with which we have to do, is his "Analysis of the Human Mind." The title indicates the aim of the treatise. It is not an inductive observation of facts; it is not a classification of facts in a cautious and careful manner; it is a determined attempt to resolve the complex phenomena of the mind into as few elements as possible. . . . He closes the work with a discussion as to will and intention. Will is the peculiar state of mind or consciousness by which action is preceded. He treats of its influence over the actions of the body, and over the actions of the mind. He shows that sensations and ideas are the true antecedents of the bodily actions, and so he does not need to call in a separate capacity called the will. He then turns to the power which the mind seems to possess over its associations. He proves, as Brown and others had done, that we cannot will an absent idea before us,—for to will it is already to have it; and the recalling is always a process of association. He does not see that, by a stern act of will, we can detain a present thought, and thus gather around it a whole host of associations. He speaks of ends, but has no idea of the way in which ends spring up and influence the mind. He takes no notice of the essential freedom belonging to the will, and thus leaves no ground on which to rear the doctrine of human responsibility.—McCosh, James, 1874, *Scottish Philosophy*, pp. 378, 388.

The date of this book ["Analysis"] makes it curious. It is too new, and yet not new enough to obtain a great success. It is a transitional work which is not well understood until *after*. Clear, lucid, methodical, well put together, the book errs from want of width and insufficiency of development. Now, opinion does not understand, and above all does not accept a doctrine except by dint of hearing it repeated. Contemporary labours, directed in the same sense, but less concise, and more familiar with the sciences, seem to have lent to his a retrospective value. . . . What is his method? He does not tell us that; but he almost always proceeds subjectively. In this respect he belongs to the eighteenth century. We do not find in his works any trace of a comparative psychology. He also belongs to this century by his tendency to consider phenomena only in adult minds, and among a cvilized people. Carrying the practical spirit of his nation into psychological studies, he thinks, with reason, that education would be more enlightened and more systematic if psychology were more advanced; and that a good analysis of the phenomena of mind ought to serve as the basis of three practical treatises,—one Logical, to lead us to the true, one Moral, to regulate our actions, one Emotional, to develop the individual and the species.—Ribot, Th., 1874, *English Psychology*, p. 45.

The differences in point of matter between the two philosophers were not great. Such as they were, they arose partly from the peculiarities of the men, partly from the characteristics of the times in which they severally lived. Mill was more bent on the practical application of his views than Hartley, and wrote more with the fervour of a man who expected his creeds to be turned into deeds, and who attached an educational or social value to every opinion which he expressed. Mill composed with the rigour and simplicity of a schoolmaster of the world; Hartley with the ingenuous babbling of a pupil of the world. Consequently the former at once discarded vibrations; for, provided that people can be brought to perceive the uses of association in education, it does not matter what physical theory is put behind it as the cause of the cause. Nor on the other hand will he follow his theory out into the nebulous region of theopathy and theology; for if men can be induced to construct a morality on better associations, they will not be long in constructing a better religion.—Bower, George Spencer, 1881, *Hartley and James Mill (English Philosophers)*, p. 221.

By his "Analysis of the Mind" and his "Fragment on Mackintosh" Mill acquired a position in the history of psychology and ethics. Attached to the *a posteriori* school, he vindicated its claims with conspicuous ability. He took up the problems of mind very much after the fashion of the Scotch school, as then represented by Reid, Stewart, and Brown, but made a new start, due in part to Hartley, and still more to his own independent thinking. He carried out the principle of association into the analysis of the complex emotional states, as the affections, the æsthetic emotions, and the moral sentiment, all which he endeavored to resolve into pleasurable and painful sensations. But the salient merit of the "Analysis" is the constant endeavor after precise definition of terms and clear statement of doctrines. The "Fragment on Mackintosh" is a severe exposure of the flimsiness and misrepresentations of Mackintosh's famous dissertation on ethical philosophy. It discusses, in a very thorough way, the foundations of ethics from the author's point of view of utility.—Bain, Alexander, 1884, *Encyclopædia Britannica, Ninth ed., vol.* xvi, *p.* 320.

James Mill's dogmatism was at all times narrow and one-sided. . . . A man so non-religious as James Mill could hardly be expected to understand Christianity any more than a man without any soul or faculty for music could understand harmony. There are men, and James Mill was one of them, so utterly lacking in spiritual instinct that their judgments as to religion really merit no more attention than other men's judgments about music.—Tulloch, John, 1885, *Movements of Religious Thought in Britain During the Nineteenth Century*, pp. 134, 136.

Mill's "Analysis," though not widely read, made a deep impression upon Mill's own disciples. It is terse, trenchant, and uncompromising. It reminds us in point of style of the French writers, with whom he sympathised, rather than of the

English predecessors, to whom much of the substance was owing. The discursive rhetoric of Brown or Stewart is replaced by good, hard, sinewy logic. The writer is plainly in earnest. If over confident, he has no petty vanity, and at least believes every word that he says. Certain limitations are at once obvious. Mill, as a publicist, a historian, and a busy official, had not had much time to spare for purely philosophic reading. He was not a professor in want of a system, but an energetic man of business, wishing to strike at the root of the superstitions to which his political opponents appealed for support. He had heard of Kant, and seen what "the poor man would be at." Later German systems, had he heard of them, would have been summarily rejected by him as so much transcendental moonshine. The problem of philosophy was, he held, a very simple one, if attacked in a straightforward, scientific method. — STEPHEN, LESLIE, 1900, *The English Utilitarians, vol.* II, *p.* 288.

GENERAL

We know of no writer who takes so much pleasure in the truly useful, noble, and philosophical employment of tracing the progress of sound opinions from their embryo state to their full maturity. He eagerly culls from old despatches and minutes every expression in which he can discern the imperfect germ of any great truth which has since been fully developed. He never fails to bestow praise on those who, though far from coming up to his standard of perfection, yet rose in a small degree above the common level of their contemporaries. It is thus that the annals of past times ought to be written. It is thus, especially, that the annals of our own country ought to be written.—MACAULAY, THOMAS BABINGTON, 1835, *Mackintosh's History, Critical and Miscellaneous Essays.*

When the system of legal polity was to be taught, and the cause of Law Reform to be supported in this country, no one could be found more fitted for the service than Mr. Mill; and to him more than to any other person has been owing the diffusion of those important principles and their rapid progress in England. He was a man of extensive and profound learning, thoroughly imbued with the doctrines of metaphysical and ethical science; conversant above most men with the writings of the ancient philosophers, whose language he familiarly knew; and gifted with an extraordinary power of application, which had made entirely natural to him a life of severe and unremitting study. . . . His admirable works on the Principles of Political Economy, and of Moral Philosophy, entitle him, perhaps, to a higher place among the writers of his age; but neither these nor his "History of British India," the greatest monument of his learning and industry, can vie with his discourses on Jurisprudence in usefulness to the cause of general improvement, which first awakened the ardour of his vigorous mind, and on which its latest efforts reposed. His style was better adapted to didactic works, and works of abstract science, than to history; for he had no powers of narrative, and was not successful in any kind of ornamental composition. He was slenderly furnished with fancy, and far more capable of following a train of reasoning, expounding the theories of others, and pursuing them to their legitimate consequences, than of striking out new paths, and creating new objects, or even adorning the creations of other men's genius.—BROUGHAM, HENRY LORD, 1838, *Speech on Law Reform.*

This work ["Elements of Political Economy"], is a resume of the doctrines of Smith and of Ricardo with respect to the production and distribution of wealth, and of those of Malthus with respect to population. But it is of too abstract a character to be either popular or of much utility. . . . The science is very far from having arrived at the perfection Mr. Mill supposed.—MCCULLOCH, JOHN RAMSAY, 1845, *Literature of Political Economy, pp.* 17, 18.

John Mill tells us also that James Mill considered the friendship of Ricardo to have been the most valuable of his whole life. To a genius like Ricardo, with Ricardo's time and circumstances, the doctrines of James Mill must have come like fire to fuel; they must have stimulated the innate desire to deduce in systematic connection, from the fewest possible principles, the truths which he had long been considering disconnectedly. If Ricardo had never seen James Mill, he would probably have written many special pamphlets of great value on passing economical problems, but he would probably not have written "On the Principles of Political Economy and Taxation," and thus founded an abstract science; it takes a great effort to breathe for long together the "thin air" of abstract reasoning.—BAGEHOT, WALTER, 1876? *Ricardo, Works, ed. Morgan, vol.* V, *p.* 408.

As a writer, his style has been found fault with, especially by Bentham; who spoke of the History in particular, as abounding in bad English. The fact I believe to be that, although he took great pains to get rid of Scotticisms, he did not attain a mastery of good English idiom. . . . It is needless to remark that his composition was essentially cast for scientific subjects. He had practised narrative style in his long historical work, and attained a certain success; but it was not carried to the pitch of art. The truth is, although a man of great general accomplishment, language was not his *forte.*—BAIN, ALEXANDER, 1882, *James Mill, a Biography, pp.* 425, 426.

James Madison

1751-1836

Fourth President of the United States, was born in King George county, Virginia, educated at Princeton College, and was afterwards admitted a lawyer. After some experience in the local legislature, he became a member of the first Congress under the Constitution in 1789, when he gained the friendship of Washington, and took a leading part in the organisation of the United States Constitution. He next became Secretary of State (1801-8), under President Jefferson, and distinguished himself by upholding the rights of the United States as a neutral Power in the great European war. His "Examination of the Doctrines of National Law" has the reputation of being one of the ablest of existing treatises on the relative rights of neutral and belligerent Powers. In 1809 he was elected to the Presidency, which he held for two terms. . . . Madison was not a great war administrator, and the period of his Presidency is less to his credit than the period of his Secretaryship of State. In 1817 Madison retired from the Presidency with a name for eminent ability and spotless integrity. He spent the remainder of his days in discharging the academic duties in connection with Virginia University. His speeches, letters, papers, and essays were purchased by Congress for 30,000 dollars, and published in 1840 under the editorial superintendence of H. D. Gilpin.—SANDERS, LLOYD C., *ed.*, 1887, *Celebrities of the Century, p.* 709.

PERSONAL

I made two speeches, the latter in reply to Madison, who is a man of sense, reading, address, and integrity, as 'tis allowed. Very much Frenchified in his politics. He speaks low, his person is little, and ordinary. He speaks decently, as to manner, and no more. His language is very pure, perspicuous, and to the point. Pardon me, if I add, that I think him a little too much of a book politician, and too timid in his politics, for prudence and caution are opposites of timidity. He is not a little of a Virginian, and thinks that state the land of promise, but is afraid of their State politics, and of his popularity there, more than I think he should be. His manner is *something* like John Choate's. He is our first man.—AMES, FISHER, 1789, *Letter to George Richards Minot, May* 3; *Works, ed. Ames, vol.* I, *p.* 35.

Mrs. Madison is a large, dignified lady, with excellent manners, obviously well practised in the ways of the world. Her conversation was somewhat formal, but on the whole appropriate to her position, and now and then amusing. I found the President more free and open than I expected, starting subjects of conversation and making remarks that sometimes savored of humor and levity. He sometimes laughed, and I was glad to hear it; but his face was always grave. He talked of religious sects and parties, and was curious to know how the cause of liberal Christianity stood with us, and if the Athanasian creed was well received by our Episcopalians. He pretty distinctly intimated to me his own regard for the Unitarian doctrines.—TICKNOR, GEORGE, 1815, *Letter to his Father, Jan.* 21; *Life, Letters and Journals, vol.* I, *p.* 30.

James Madison succeeded Jefferson in the Presidency, serving for eight years, from March 4, 1809. He almost broke down his health by severe studies, and, although undoubtedly a horseman, as proved by his military services when the British attacked Washington during his Administration, in 1814, he was so devoted to books that during his novitiate at Princeton College, in New Jersey, he allowed himself but three hours' sleep and devoted the day to study.—FORNEY, JOHN W., 1881, *Anecdotes of Public Men, vol.* II, *p.* 416.

The sentiment of veneration for Madison, entertained by all in the vicinity of my birth place, was deeply imbedded in their minds. His praises were so frequently sounded in my hearing that among my earliest recollections of public men and events are those with which his name is associated. The purity of his life was such and the prominence of his virtues so conspicuous, that this sentiment was imparted to my own mind, and became so indelibly fixed that, in my early estimate of founders of the republic, I was accustomed to place him next to Washington, esteeming him as the Father of the Constitution and Washington as the Father of the Nation. His country residence was known as Montpelier. It was situated in Orange county, Virginia, within less than thirty miles from the place of my nativity. As all travel at that time was on horse back and I was too young to visit him alone, my opportunities for seeing him were "like angels' visits, few and far between." There having been, however, several occasions when I could do so, I was enabled, much to my gratification, to realize for myself that his personal appearance indicated the possession of the high qualities universally assigned to him. After I had seen Jefferson, I could not avoid observing the contrast between them—Madison being below the average height, while Jefferson was tall. I was more attracted by the expression of his countenance than by that of Jefferson. It seemed to me, each time I observed him, that I had rarely seen a face in which more benignity and quiet composure was expressed. It was a complete personification of gentleness and benevolence. This, however, was altogether consistent with the prominent characteristics assigned to him by the whole community—characteristics which made him as influential in the limited circle around his home as he had been in the broader field of national affairs. —THOMPSON, RICHARD W., 1894, *Recollections of Sixteen Presidents, vol.* I, *p.* 65.

STATESMAN

Mr. Madison is a character who has long been in public life; and what is very remarkable every person seems to acknowledge his greatness. He blends together the profound politician with the Scholar. In the management of every great question he evidently took the lead in the Convention, and tho' he cannot be called an Orator, he is a most agreeable, eloquent, and convincing Speaker. From a spirit of industry and application which he possesses in a most eminent degree, he always comes forward the best informed Man on any point in debate. The affairs of the United States he, perhaps, has the most correct knowledge of, of any Man in the Union. He has been twice a Member of Congress, and was always thought one of the ablest Members that ever sat in that Council. Mr. Madison is about 37 years of age, a Gentleman of great modesty,—with a remarkable sweet temper. He is easy and unreserved among his acquaintance, and has a most agreable style of conversation. —PIERCE, WILLIAM, 1787, *Characters of the Federal Convention.*

Trained in these successive schools, he acquired a habit of self-possession which placed at ready command the rich resources of his luminous and discriminating mind, and of his extensive information. and rendered him first of every assembly afterwards of which he became a member. . . . With these consummate powers, were united a pure and spotless virtue, which no calumny has ever attempted to sully. Of the powers and polish of his pen, and of the wisdom of his administration in the highest office of the nation, I need say nothing; they have spoken, and will forever speak for themselves.—JEFFERSON, THOMAS, 1826? *Autobiography, Writings, vol.* I, *p.* 41.

Of the public life of James Madison what could I say that is not deeply impressed upon the memory and upon the heart of every one within the sound of my voice? Of his private life, what but must meet an echoing shout of applause from every voice within this hall? Is it not, in a pre-eminent degree, by emanations from his mind that we are assembled here as the representatives of the people and States of this Union? Is it not transcendently by his exertions that we address each other here by the endearing appellation of countrymen and fellow-citizens?—ADAMS, JOHN QUINCY, 1836, *Speech in the National House of Representatives, on the announcement of the death of Mr. Madison.*

I entirely concur with you in your estimate of Mr. Madison,—his private virtues, his extraordinary talents, his comprehensive and statesmanlike views. To him and Hamilton, I think, we are mainly indebted for the Constitution of the United States, and in wisdom I have long been accustomed to place him before Jefferson. You and I know something more of each of them in trying times, than the common politicians of our day can possibly arrive at. I wish some one who was perfectly fitted for the task, would write a full and accurate biography of Madison. I fear that it can hardly be done now; for the men who best appreciated his excellences have nearly all passed away. What shadows we are!—STORY, JOSEPH, 1842, *To Hon. Ezekiel Bacon, April* 30; *Life and Letters, vol.* II, *p.* 420.

From the leading agency of Mr. Madison in the initiation, conduct, and consummation of this great organic change, the history of his public life becomes necessarily a history of the Constitution of the United States, and under a form, which, combining a concrete narrative of individual exertions and individual opinions with the more abstract process of national deliberations, may impart to the latter a livelier and more attractive interest.—RIVES, WILLIAM CABELL, 1865, *History of the Life and Times of James Madison, Preface, vol.* II, *p.* vi.

His was not a character so thoroughly and harmoniously constituted and developed as Washington's. He, too, concealed the depth of his ambition under a plain and modest exterior. When it or his oversensitiveness was wounded, he, too, could be unjust to his opponents. The violence with which the party struggle was conducted by degrees carried him, also, so far away that he played a more covert game than can be entirely justified by the excuse of political necessity. And when it was a question of opposing a measure in too great conflict with his own party programme, he could descend to the letter, and to petty quibbling, if he could not give his attack the necessary energy from the higher standpoint of the statesman. Spite of this, however, there was nothing of the demagogue about him. He is a purely constituted character, spite of the fact that his moral principles did not so unconditionally govern him as to leave his judgment entirely uninfluenced by his desires. It cannot be charged that he ever consciously approached the constitution with the intention of discovering in it a word which he might make to serve his purposes by dialectical legerdemain.—VON HOLST, DR. H., 1875–76, *The Constitutional and Political History of the United States, vol.* I, *p.* 160.

He is usually and most justly regarded as a man of great amiability of character; of unquestionable integrity in all the purely personal relations of life; of more than ordinary intellectual ability of a solid, though not brilliant, quality; and a diligent student of the science of government, the practice of which he made a profession. But he was better fitted by nature for a legislator than for excutive office, and his fame would have been more spotless, though his position would have been less exalted, had his life been exclusively devoted to that branch of government for which he was best fitted. It was not merely that for the sake of the Presidency he plunged the country into an unnecessary war; but when it was on his hands he neither knew what to do with it himself or how to choose the right men who did know.—GAY, SYDNEY HOWARD, 1884, *James Madison (American Statesmen), p.* 325.

Madison's political career is, in some ways, a very curious one, and can be summed up in very few words. By nature and reason he was a Federalist and a nationalist. By circumstances he became a Democrat, and at one time a separatist. He was entirely faithful to the party which he espoused, but he was not in full and entire sympathy with it. The result was, that he founded no school and had no personal following. The party which he led honored and trusted him, and it is to their honor and credit that they did so. But they neither loved him nor were in sympathy with him. The party with which he really sympathized opposed him throughout his life. Politically speaking, he was a lonely man, and that loneliness has continued until to-day. No party has placed him among its heroes for stated or occasional worship. He seems to stand aloof in history as he did in life, respected and honored by all, loved and followed by none. With such a nature as Madison's it could not well be otherwise, and his career was possible only to a man as cold, as conscientious, and as liberal as he was. He was a poor partisan, but a great and useful statesman. He did some unworthy things, he made mistakes, like the rest of humanity, but his abilities and his character are an honor to his country and to his State. Statues may not rise to him in the market-place, political parties may not enshrine him as a patron saint, but by his labors in the establishment of the government and the Constitution of the United States, and by a pure and dignified character and career, he has built himself a monument more enduring than any of brass or marble.—LODGE, HENRY CABOT, 1885, *James Madison, The Andover Review, vol.* 4, *p.* 245.

By American writers he is invested with the highest mental gifts. Yet the impression which he makes on the ordinary reader is rather that of a cultivated and somewhat prim mediocrity, though combined with a clear understanding, a scientific knowledge of politics, statesmanlike training, and a surefooted ambition.—SMITH, GOLDWIN, 1893, *The United States, An Outline of Political History, p.* 165.

GENERAL

Although we attach very great value to the Madison papers, we are by no means disposed to go the length of Mr. Robbins, the Senator from Rhode Island, who in his place described them as "the most valuable work that has appeared since the days when Bacon gave to the world his Novum Organum." This is a fair specimen of the magniloquence for which this country is so remarkable, and which has its focus in the Congress of the United States. It is altogether too long a period of time to look back upon, and too many profound men and brilliant geniuses have lived and written in the interval, for us to like to venture upon such a comparison. Besides, it appears to us to be doing great injustice to the work and its author, to take it up in this tone. It is neither a work of genius, nor does it treat very profoundly of any department of human knowledge. Its value, so far as we can understand, is of a peculiar and somewhat unique character. It is the record of an extraordinary coincidence, in the same assembly, of men of practical skill, legislative talent, and disinterested purposes, such as the world had not often seen before, and such as it may never see again. . . . The Madison Papers will scarcely teach the inquirer after truth any new and marvellous axioms in the science of government, so much as the application of old and established ones to the peculiar condition of a people already organized into separate communities, and seeking no more than for certain definite objects, expected to be gained thereby, to engraft upon their established system a few features of consolidation.—ADAMS, CHARLES FRANCIS, 1841, *The Madison Papers, North American Review, vol.* 53, *pp.* 42, 43.

Madison lacked neither ability nor inclination for speculative inquiries, and had a mind capable of enforcing the application of whatever principles he espoused. Yet his calm good sense, and the tact with which he could adapt theory to practice, were no less among his prominent characteristics.—CURTIS, GEORGE TICKNOR, 1855, *History of the Origin, Formation and Adoption of the Constitution of the United States, vol.* I, *p.* 388.

The name of Madison is identified with the political literature of the country, beyond the share which his official state papers must claim, by his defence of the Constitution in the *Federalist,* and his faithful history of the Debates in the great Assembly which gave bounds and authority to our national government. In these he will be remembered by the political student in the library, when the eye is withdrawn from the public acts of his administration.—DUYCKINCK, EVERT A. AND GEORGE L., 1855–65–75, *Cyclopædia of American Literature, ed. Simons, vol.* I, *p.* 336.

Madison's claims to literary distinction are neither transcendent nor contemptible. He is entitled to be remembered as having had a share in the form, as well as the matter, of the Declaration of Independence, of the Constitution, and of Washington's retiring address.—NICHOL, JOHN, 1880–85, *American Literature, p.* 80.

"The Federalist," their joint production, is probably the greatest treatise of political science that has ever appeared in the world, at once the most practical and the most profound. The evenness with which the merits of this work are shared between Madison and Hamilton, is well illustrated by the fact that it is not always easy to distinguish between the two, so that there has been considerable controversy as to the number of papers contributed by each. According to Madison's own memorandum, he was the author of twenty-nine of the papers, while fifty-one were written by Hamilton, and five by Jay. The question is not of great importance. Very probably Mr. Madison would have had a larger share in the work had he not been obliged, in March, 1788, to return to Virginia, in order to take part in the state convention for deciding upon the ratification of the constitution.—FISKE, JOHN, 1886-1900, *The Presidents of the United States* 1789-1900, *ed. Wilson, p.* 98.

Judge Story once said that to James Madison and Alexander Hamilton we were mainly indebted for the Constitution of the United States. It is curious that to Madison we are also mainly indebted for those Virginia "Resolutions of '98," which have been used to justify nullification and secession. With all his mental ability, Madison had not much original force of nature. He leaned now to Hamilton, now to Jefferson, and at last fell permanently under the influence of the genius of the latter. He was lacking in that grand moral and intellectual impulse, underlying mere knowledge and logic, which distinguishes the man who reasons from the mere reasoner. His character was not on a level with his talents and acquirements; his much-vaunted moderation came from the absence rather than from the control of passion: and his understanding, though broad, was somewhat mechanical in its operations, and had no foundation in a corresponding breath of nature. The "Resolutions of '98," which Southern Democrats came gradually to consider as of equal authority with the Constitution, were originally devised for transient party purpose. . . . The "Resolutions of '98" must be considered an important portion of our national literature, for they were exultingly adduced as the logical justification of the gigantic rebellion of 1861. It is rare, even in the history of political factions, that a string of cunningly written resolves, designed to meet a mere party emergency, should thus cost a nation thousands of millions of treasure and hundred of thousands of lives.—WHIPPLE, EDWIN PERCY, 1886, *American Literature and Other Papers, ed. Whittier, pp.* 17, 19.

The time and purpose hardly favored the production of a calm and dispassionate treatise on government, which "The Federalist" certainly is not; but it contains, despite its lack of system, able discussions of many questions of national life and political science. The closing words of Number XIV., printed in the *New York Packet*, November 30, 1787, and known to be one of Madison's contributions, illustrate the rhetorical and literary characteristics of the work at their best. This is Johnsonian English, already feeling the breath of a fresher day, and stirring with the intense purpose which pushed the Americans forward.—RICHARDSON, CHARLES F., 1887, *American Literature*, 1607-1885, *vol.* I, *p.* 198.

His style lacks imaginative charm; it is high-sounding and mechanical and sometimes lacking in clearness. But there is a grave and well-considered purpose apparent in many of his papers; and upon the audience he addressed they produced a weighty effect.—HAWTHORNE, JULIAN, AND LEMMON, LEONARD, 1891, *American Literature, p.* 33.

Madison's notes on the debates of the Congress of the Confederation and of the Federal Convention are invaluable and almost unique records of these critical episodes. — HART, ALBERT BUSHNELL, 1901, *American History told by Contemporaries, vol.* III, *p.* 126.

George Colman

The Younger

1762-1836

Born, in London, 21 Oct. 1762. Educated at Marylebone School, Christmas 1770 to March 1771; at Westminster School, 30 June 1772 to 1778. To Christ Church, Oxford, 28 Jan. 1779; removed from Oxford, autumn of 1781. At King's Coll., Aberdeen, 1781-83. Farce "The Female Dramatist" anonymously produced at Haymarket, 16 Aug. 1782. Admitted Mem. of Lincoln's Inn, 1784. "Two to One," produced at Haymarket, 19 June 1784; "Turk and no Turk," 9 July 1785; "Inkle and Yarico," 4 Aug. 1787; "Ways and Means," 10 July 1788; "Battle of Hexham," 11 Aug. 1789; "Surrender of Calais," 30 July 1791; "Poor old Haymarket," 15 June 1792; "Mountaineers," 3 Aug. 1793; "New Hay at the Old Market" (afterwards known as "Sylvester Daggerwood"), 9 June 1795; "The Heir at Law," 15 July 1797. Married Clara Morris, 3 Oct. 1784, at Gretna Green; remarried publicly, at Chelsea Church, 10 Nov. 1788. Manager of Haymarket, 1789. Purchased patent of Haymarket, 1794. "The Iron Chest" produced at Drury Lane, 12 March 1796; "Blue Beard," 23 Jan. 1798; "Feudal Times," 19 Jan. 1799. "Blue Devils" produced at Covent Garden, 24 April 1798; "Poor Gentleman," 11 Feb. 1801; "John Bull," 5 March 1803; "Who wants a Guinea?" 18 April 1805; "We Fly by Night," 28 Jan. 1806; "X. Y. Z.," 11 Dec. 1810; "The Law of Java," 11 May 1822. "Review" produced at Haymarket, 2 Sept. 1800; "Gay Deceivers," 22 Aug. 1804; "Love Laughs at Locksmiths," 25 July 1803; "The Africans," 29 July 1808. Reckless management of Haymarket, and constant financial difficulties. Lieutenant of Yeoman of the Guard, 13 May 1820 to 1831. Examiner of Plays, 19 Jan. 1824 till death. Possibly a second time married to Mrs. Gibbs, with whom he had lived [since 1795?]. Died, in Brompton Square, 17 Oct. 1836. Buried in vaults of Kensington Church. *Works:* "The Man of the People" (anon.), 1782, "Two to One," 1785; "Inkle and Yarico," [1787]; "Ways and Means," 1788 (2nd edn. same year); "The Battle of Hexham" (anon.), 1790; "The Surrender of Calais," 1792; "The Mountaineers" (anon.), 1794; "New Hay at the Old Market," 1795 (2nd. end. under title "Sylvester Daggerwood," 1808); "The Iron Chest," 1796 (2nd edn. same year); "My Night-Gown and Slippers," 1797 (other edns. under title "Broad Grins," 1802, etc.); "Blue-Beard," 1798 (2nd, 3rd, 4th edns. same year); "Feudal Times," 1799 (2nd edn. same year); "The Heir at Law," 1800; "The Poor Gentleman," (1801); "Epilogue to the . . . Maid of Bristol," [1803]; "John Bull," 1805; "Who Wants a Guinea?" 1805; "The Africans," 1808; "Blue Devils," 1808; "The Gay Deceivers," 1808; "Love Laughs at Locksmiths," 1808; "The Review," 1808; "Poetical Vagaries," 1812; "The Maskers of Moorfields," 1815; Eccentricities for Edinburgh," 1816; "The Gnome King" (anon.), 1819; "X. Y. Z." (anon.), 1820; "The Law of Java," 1822; "The Circle of Anecdote and Wit," 1823; "Dramatic Works," ed. with life, by J. W. Lake, 1827; "Random Records," 1830; "Sermons for a General Fast . . . by a Layman" [no date]. *He edited:* Gay's "Achilles in Petticoats," with alterations, 1774; Palmer's "Like Master, like Man," 1811; "Posthumous Letters . . . addressed to F. Colman and G. Colman the elder," 1820. *Life:* in Peake's "Memoirs of the Colman Family," 1841.—SHARP, R. FARQUHARSON, 1897, *A Dictionary of English Authors, p.* 64.

PERSONAL

I have met George Colman occasionally, and thought him extremely pleasant and convivial. . . . Sheridan was a grenadier company of life-guards, but Colman a whole regiment—of *light infantry,* to be sure, but still a regiment.—BYRON, LORD, 1813, *Detached Thoughts.*

It has never fallen to my lot to witness "in the hour of death," so much serenity of mind, such perfect philosophy, or resignation more complete. Up to within one hour of his decease, he was perfectly sensible of his danger, and bore excruciating pain with the utmost fortitude. . . . It is remarkable, that although the disease of Colman was of a most painful and irritating nature, yet his mind and temper were seldom disturbed: it appeared often to me, that in the same ratio he lost physical power and suffered bodily pain, there was increased cerebral energy, intellectual activity, and wit of the most genuine character. . . . His funeral was private: he was buried in the vaults under Kensington church, by the side of his father; his old friends General Lewis, Mr. Harris, myself, and one or two others only attending. —CHINNOCK, DR. H. S., 1841, *Letter to R. B. Peake, Jan.* 18; *Peake's Memoirs of the Colman Family, vol.* II, *pp.* 451, 453.

As a manager, Colman the younger was liberal, affable, and assiduous; he assumed no affected reserve or superiority, but was with all his performers familiar and friendly, though he never lost sight of the respect due to the audience, and of the proper interests of the theatre; and though, as Sir Fretful Plagiary says, "he writes himself," yet he was exempt from the narrow jealousy too often prevalent in the literary character, and they who aspired at dramatic distinction were sure to meet at his theatre with counsel, assistance, and protection. . . . Although Colman was more nearly allied to the character of a punster than that of a wit, he was more than either, that of a humorist; he said thousands of good things which would entirely lose their poignancy by repetition, since the inimitable chuckle of his voice, and the remarkable expression of his countenance, would be wanting. The intelligent roll of his large and almost glaring eyes, with the concurrent expression of his handsome face, were ever the unerring *avant couriers* of his forthcoming joke; and if anything curtailed the mirth he had provoked, it was the almost interminable laughter with which he honoured his own effusion. — PEAKE, RICHARD BRINSLEY, 1841, *Memoirs of the Colman Family, vol.* II, *pp.* 415, 419.

His vanity and his desire to be talked about were inordinate. When in his later years he was in danger of being forgotten, he wrote anonymous abuse of himself to bring his name before the public again. As a manager he was jovial and pleasant; but in his business transactions he was selfish and ungenerous. When poor O'Keefe, who had lost his sight, was preparing an edition of his dramatic works to be published by subscription, he applied to Colman for permission to reprint some farces which he had sold to his father for a mere trifle, and was refused. His later managerial career was not prosperous.—BAKER, H. BARTON, 1882, *George Colman, Elder and Younger, Belgravia, vol.* 46, *p.* 200.

Colman was an entertaining companion and a genuine humourist. He was, however, disorderly if not profligate in his writings and in his life. The trustworthiness and stability of his father did not descend to him. As a manager he was capable, but his extravagance led to constant difficulties and feuds.—KNIGHT, JOSEPH, 1887, *Dictionary of National Biography, vol.* XI, *p.* 396.

GENERAL

The pertinacious ribaldry of Mr. Colman, and his affectation of regarding its reprovers as hypocrites,—things which look more like the robust ignorance of a vulgar young rake, than the proceeding of even an old man of the world who is approaching his grave,—have met with their just reprobation from every reader of common sense. The truth is, that Mr. Colman the *Younger*, as he calls himself, has been prodigiously overrated in his time, partly perhaps from his real superiority to the Dibdins and Reynoldses as a writer of huge farces, and partly from the applauses of a set of interested actors and gratuitous playwrights, whom he has helped to spoil in return; so that it really seems to be half vanity as well as sottishness, that persuades him he has a right to talk as he pleases, and to make us acquainted with this obscene dotage of his over his cups. —HUNT, LEIGH, 1814–15, *Feast of the Poets, p.* 45, *note.*

Within this monumental bed
Apollo's favourite rests his head;
Ye Muses, cease your grieving.
A son the father's loss supplies;—
Be comforted; though Colman dies,
His "Heir-at-Law" is living.

—SMITH, JAMES, 1836, *On George Colman the Younger.*

"The Heir at Law" was his first regular comedy; and we doubt very much whether he ever excelled it, or, indeed, if it has been excelled by more than a very few plays in the English language. We know that the theatrical world, and we believe the author himself, gave a decided preference to "John Bull;" but we admit that as we are unfashionable enough to prefer Sheridan's "Rivals" to his "School for Scandal," so are we prepared unhesitatingly to declare our opinion that "The Heir at Law" is Colman's *chef-d'œuvre.*—HOOK, THEODORE, 1837, *George Colman, Bentley's Miscellany, vol.* I, *p.* 10.

No modern dramatist has added so many stock pieces to the theatre as Colman, or imparted so much genuine mirth and humour to all play-goers. . . . The comedies of Colman abound in witty and ludicrous delineations of character, interspersed with bursts of tenderness and feeling, somewhat in the style of Sterne, whom, indeed, he has closely copied in his "Poor Gentleman."—CHAMBERS, ROBERT, 1876, *Cyclopædia of English Literature, ed. Carruthers.*

His humour was of the broad kind, popular in his day, and as such was marred by indelicacies of subject and allusion, which make the reproduction of it impossible. Of his longer efforts, "The Lady of the Wreck," a clever parody, dedicated to the author of "The Lady of the Lake" is perhaps the best; of his shorter pieces, "The Newcastle Apothecary" and "Lodgings for a Single Gentleman" have been immensely popular as recitations.—MILES, ALFRED H., 1895, *The Poets and the Poetry of the Century, Humour, Society, Parody and Occasional Verse, p.* 11.

Coleman was a very clever manufacturer of comedy. His best characters are ingenious mechanisms constructed upon methods which he is not artist enough to be at any pains to disguise; an oddity, incessantly repeated, a professional trait harped upon in every sentence, are the formulas which, expanded, become a Pangloss ("Heir at Law") or an Ollapod ("Poor Gentleman"). Colman's sentiment is still more theatrical than his humour. . . . Besides his plays he adventured in the field of burlesque verses, in the manner of Peter Pindar; his "Broad Grins" (1802), "Poetical Vagaries," and similar collections, have a certain coarse effectiveness, but scarcely belong to literature. Compared with the classical work of Goldsmith in humorous verse they fairly measure the literary decline of the drama in the generation between "She Stoops to Conquer" and "John Bull."—HERFORD, C. H., 1897, *The Age of Wordsworth, p.* 137.

William Taylor

1765–1836

William Taylor, "of Norwich," son of a Unitarian Merchant, entered his father's counting house in 1779, and, sent next year to the Continent, mastered French, Italian and German. The French Revolution indoctrined him with democratic ideas and began the ruin of his father's business, and Taylor turned to literature. He introduced to English readers the poetry drama of Germany, mainly through criticisms and translations in periodicals, collected in his "Historic Survey of German Poetry" (1828–30). Another work was "English Synonyms" (1813). Borrow's "Lavengro" describes his philosophy, scepticism, and inveterate smoking; his correspondence with Southey, Scott, Mackintosh, Godwin, &c., is given in the "Life" of him by Robberds, (1843).—PATRICK AND GROOME, *eds.*, 1897, *Chambers's Biographical Dictionary, p.* 904.

PERSONAL

William Taylor was then at his best; when there was something like fulfillment of his early promise, when his exemplary filial duty was a fine spectacle to the whole city, and before the vice which destroyed him had coarsened his *morale*, and drowned his intellect. During the war, it was a great distinction to know anything of German literature; and in Mr. Taylor's case it proved a ruinous distinction. He was completely spoiled by the flatteries of the shallow men, pedantic women, and conceited lads. . . . When William Taylor began with "I firmly believe" we knew that something particularly incredible was coming. We escaped without injury from hearing such things half a dozen times in a year; and from a man who was often seen to have taken too much wine; and we knew, too, that he came to our house because he had been my father's schoolfellow, and because there had always been a friendship between his excellent mother and our clan. His virtues as a son were before our eyes when we witnessed his endurance of his father's brutality of temper and manners, and his watchfulness in ministering to the old man's comfort in his infirmities. When we saw, on a Sunday morning, William Taylor guiding his blind mother to chapel, and getting her there with her shoes as clean as if she had crossed no gutters in those flint paved streets, we could forgive anything that had shocked or disgusted us at the dinner table. But matters grew worse in his old age, when his habits of intemperance kept him out of sight of ladies, and he got round him a set of ignorant and conceited young men, who thought they could set the world right by their destructive propensities. One of his chief favorites was George Borrow, as George Borrow has himself given the world to understand. When this polyglot gentleman appeared in public as a devout agent of the Bible-society in foreign parts, there was one burst of laughter from all who remembered the old Norwich days. At intervals, Southey came to see his old friend.—MARTINEAU, HARRIET, 1855–77, *Autobiography, ed. Chapman, vol.* I, *pp.* 225, 227.

William Taylor was one of the liberals of liberal Norwich, and dangled abroad whatever happened to be the newest paradox in religion. But neither his radicalism, nor his Pyrrhonism, nor his paradoxes, could estrange Southey. The last time the oddly-assorted pair met was in Taylor's house: the student of German criticism had found some theological novelty, and wished to draw his guest into argument; Southey parried the thrusts good-humouredly, and at last put an end to them with the words, "Taylor, come and see me at Keswick. We will ascend Skiddaw, where I shall have you nearer heaven, and we will then discuss such questions as these."—DOWDEN, EDWARD, 1880, *Southey (English Men of Letters), p.* 134.

Taylor was a devoted son and a generous friend. It delighted him to encourage the studies of young men; George Borrow learned German from him "with extraordinary rapidity" before he was eighteen, and has described him in "Lavengro." After his losses he cultivated chiefly the society of his juniors; hence Harriet Martineau's rather harsh judgment that he was spoiled by flattery. He was accused of initiating young men into habits of conviviality; what his censors really feared was the influence of his erratic opinions, but these were not always taken seriously. He was known to argue for an hour in proof that Adam was a negro; no one venturing to reply, he spent the next hour in answering himself and proving that Adam was white.—GORDON, ALEXANDER, 1898, *Dictionary of National Biography, vol.* LV. *p.* 477.

GENERAL

Mr. Taylor is so considerable a person, that no Book deliberately published by him, on any subject, can be without weight. On German poetry, such is the actual state of public information and curiosity, his guidance will be sure to lead or mislead a numerous class of inquirers. We are therefore called on to examine him with more than usual strictness and minuteness. . . . Mr. Taylor, in respect of general talent and acquirement, takes his place above all our expositors of German things; that his Book is greatly the most important we have yet on this subject. Here are upwards of fourteen hundred solid pages of commentary, narrative and translation, submitted to the English reader; numerous statements and personages, hitherto unheard of, stand here in fixed shape; there is, if no map of intellectual Germany, some first attempt at such. Farther, we are to state that our Author is a zealous, earnest man; no hollow dilettante hunting after shadows, and prating he knows not what; but a substantial, distinct, remarkably decisive man; has his own opinion on many subjects, and can express it adequately. . . . The truth is, this "Historic Survey" has not anything historical in it; but is a mere aggregate of Dissertations, Translations, Notices and Notes, bound together indeed by the circumstance that they are all about German Poetry, "about it and about it;" also by the sequence of time, and still more strongly by the Bookbinder's packthread; but by no other sufficient tie whatever. The authentic title, were not some mercantile varnish allowable in such cases, might be; "General Jail-delivery of all Publications and Manuscripts, original or translated, composed or borrowed, on the subject of German Poetry; by" &c. . . . But on the whole, what struck us most in these errors is their surprising number. In the way of our calling, we at first took pencil, with intent to mark such transgressions; but soon found it too appalling a task, and so laid aside our black-lead and our art (*cæstus artemque*). Happily, however, a little natural invention, assisted by some tincture of arithmetic, came to our aid. Six pages, studied for that end, we did mark; finding therein thirteen errors: the pages are 167–173 of Volume Third, and still in our copy have their marginal stigmas, which can be vindicated before a jury of Authors. Now if 6 give 13, who sees not that 1455, the entire number of pages, will give 3512 and a fraction? or, allowing for Translations, which are freer from errors, and for philosophical Discussions, wherein the errors are of another sort; nay, granting with a perhaps unwarranted liberality, that these six pages may yield too high an average, which we know not that they do,—may not, in round numbers, Fifteen Hundred be given as the approximate amount, not of errors indeed, yet of mistakes and misstatements, in these three octavos?—CARLYLE, THOMAS, 1831, *Critical and Miscellaneous Essays.*

His *magnum opus*, the "Historic Survey of German Poetry," 1828–30, 3 vols. 8vo., was somewhat belated. It is a patchwork (Carlyle calls it a "jail-delivery") of his previous articles and translations, with digressions on Homer, the Zendavesta, and other literary gleanings, while the "survey" itself was not brought up to date. But it shows what Taylor had been doing for German studies during a literary life of forty years, and its value is that of a permanent conspectus of his work.—GORDON, ALEXANDER, 1898, *Dictionary of National Biography, vol.* LV, *p.* 477.

Taylor of Norwich did more than any man of his generation, by his translations and critical papers in the *Monthly Magazine* and *Monthly Review*, to spread a knowledge of the new German literature in England. . . . Taylor's tastes were one-sided, not to say eccentric; he had not kept up with the later movement of German thought; his critical opinions were out of date, and his book was sadly wanting in unity and a proper perspective. Carlyle was especially scandalized by the slight space accorded to Goethe. But Taylor's really brilliant talent in translation, and his important service as an introducer and interpreter of German poetry to his own countrymen, deserve always to be gratefully remembered. "You have made me hunger and thirst after German poetry," wrote Southey to him, February 24, 1799. —BEERS, HENRY A., 1898, *A History of English Romanticism in the Eighteenth Century, p.* 397.

To the periodicals of the day, he was a toilsome contributor on subjects of foreign literature. He was among the first to introduce German poetry to English readers. He translated the "Nathan der Weise," and gave a rendering of the ballad of "Ellenore" which found favor in the eyes of Longfellow, and from which Sir Walter Scott derived some inspiration. He also wrote an "Historic Survey of German Poetry," and a work on English synonyms. His style was quaint, involved, harsh,—no mortal could read him now; but the fact stands that he was read, and not without profit, then.—JACKSON, A. W., 1900, *James Martineau, A Biography and Study, p.* 8.

Sir Samuel Egerton Brydges

1762–1837

A miscellaneous writer, was born 30th November, 1762. He studied at Queen's College, Cambridge, and adopted the profession of law. In 1790 he persuaded his elder brother that their family were the heirs to the barony of Chandos, being descended from a younger branch of the Brydges who first held the title. The case was tried and lost, but Brydges never gave up his claim, and used to sign himself *Perlegem terræ* B. C. of S. (*i. e.*, Baron Chandos of Sudeley). It has been said that he underwent the labor of re-editing Collins's Peerage, for the sole purpose of inserting a statement about his supposed right. In 1814 he was made a baronet and in 1818 he left England. He died at Geneva in 1837. Sir Egerton was a most prolific author; he is said to have written 2,000 sonnets in one year. His first volume of poems was published in 1785; of his other numerous works including novels, political pamphlets, and bibliographies, perhaps the most important are "Censura Literaria," 10 vols. 1805–9, and "Autobiography, Times, Opinions, and Contemporaries of Sir S. E. Brydges," 1834.—BAYNES, THOMAS SPENCER, *ed.*, 1876, *Encyclopædia Britannica, Ninth ed., vol.* IV, *p.* 366.

PERSONAL

I aim to strengthen the hopes of younger minds against the fear of the approaches of old age, by assuring them, with the utmost sincerity, that in the midst of privations, neglects, calumnies, and tremendous injuries, I have the conviction that life is altogether joyous to me,—perhaps more satisfactory and even delightful than in the effervescence of youth and strength of mature manhood. My eye is as delighted with the grandeur and variety of inanimate nature, and my heart is as open to all the virtues and friendships of human society. I boast that I am not deficient in the magnanimity of moral courage. I have calmly stood tremendous shocks, from which they who have faced without trembling the onset of the most furious battle would have shrunk; and I have passed, by the aid of an unswerving spirit, over pits and mines which would have subdued the hearts of the stoutest warriors. Of the little passions which tormented me in my junior days, in common with the multitude, I have overcome the greater part. I believe that I am mild, well-wishing, still warm and energetic, with a glowing imagination and a trembling heart; not unenlarged in my views of society and human nature; ready to be pleased; melting to kindness; visionary as a child, yet not unskilled in life; more ductile than becomes my years; more solitary than is consistent with worldly wisdom.—BRYDGES, SIR SAMUEL EGERTON, 1834, *Autobiography, vol.* II, *p.* 430.

GENERAL

We have read this work ["Autobiography"] with feelings of considerable pain. It presents to us an elaborate picture of a species of literary character, that may be expected to appear, at times, in that heated and high-wrought civilisation, to which the world has attained;—a character that has all the acute sensibilities of poetical genius, without its energy and its power—its irritable temper—its wayward self-engrossment—its early relinquishment of the common pleasures of life, for one feverish and jealous object. This is often a painful picture, even when, as in the case of Byron or Rousseau, it is gilded with all the glory of success, placed in the long gallery of fame, and destined to become immortal. But how much deeper is the pain with which we gaze on these melancholy colours, when we feel them fading as we gaze; or when we know that in a little while the picture will be thrown aside, amidst the lumber of the age, to perish and be forgotten.—LYTTON, S. E. B., 1834, *Sir Egerton Brydges's Autobiography, Edinburgh Review, vol.* 59, *p.* 439.

Do you know anything of poor Sir Egerton Brydges?—this, in talking of sonnets—poor fellow, he wrote them for seventy years, fully convinced of their goodness, and only lamenting that the public were unjust and stupid enough not to admire them also. He lived in haughty seclusion, and at the end of life wrote a doting Autobiography. He writes good prose however, and shews himself as he is very candidly: indeed he is proud of the display.—FITZGERALD, EDWARD, 1841, *To F. Tennyson, July* 26; *Letters, vol.* I, *p.* 72.

To no author of the present century is English Literature more deeply indebted than to Sir Egerton Brydges, and in no one can be found finer passages of just thought, genial and tasteful criticism, pure and ennobling sentiment, and beautiful and eloquent writing. . . . Indeed, I know of no one who has written so much himself, and who, at the same time, has done so much to bring forward the writings of others—to bring out the hidden, to revive the forgotten—and to honor the neglected, but true genius. We are most deeply indebted to him, too, for his labors of love upon our great Epic; for no critic, not excepting Addison himself, has had a more just appreciation of the genius of Milton, or has criticised him with truer taste or sounder judgment.—CLEVELAND, CHARLES D., 1853, *English Literature of the Nineteenth Century, pp.* 346, 348.

The name of this literary veteran is especially sweet to the ear of the bibliophile, not from the number of books he has written, but the small number he has printed,—not from the productions of his own intellect, but rather the "restitution" he has afforded to those of others, by his critical notices or his elegant reprints. Many of these were fifty years ago, black swans of the book-hunter. . . . He was always ready to swim with the stream of popular taste. During the rage for poetry, from the time of Cowper to Byron, he courted the Muses with toil and ardour; when Minerva-press novels were the rage, Sir Egerton was ready with a whole shelf-full of sentimental fictions; when Charlotte Smith and W. L. Bowles had made the "sonnet" fashionable, our poet cultivated this form of poetic composition; and when Lord Byron died, our aspirant was soon ready with a bulky volume of "Letters on the Character and Poetical Genius" of the lamented bard, of which Moore says that "they contain many just and striking views." Among other causes of failure were haste and want of concentration. . . . Like Rousseau, he seems to have believed that all the world was in a conspiracy against him, and that just as the Lords had debarred his access to the House of Peers, the critics were striving to exclude him from the Temple of the Muses.—BATES, WILLIAM, 1874–98, *The Maclise Portrait Gallery of Illustrious Literary Characters, pp.* 217, 218.

This sonnet ["On Echo and Silence"]

like those of Bowles, owes much of its reputation to the warm praise it received from certain eminent contemporaries of its author, including Wordsworth and Coleridge. It has, of course, genuine merit, though this is not one of those instances where we are likely to be induced to consider the Alexandrine at the close an unexpected charm (an Alexandrine also ends the octavo). The somewhat pompous author never, however, wrote anything better, though that he had some faculty for his art will be evident to anyone who glances through his "Poems" (1807).—SHARP, WILLIAM, 1883, *Sonnets of this Century, p.* 281, *note.*

Letitia Elizabeth Landon

Mrs. George Maclean

1802–1838

Letitia Elizabeth Landon (born 1802, died 1838), perhaps better known as "L. E. L.," was the daughter of John Landon, of an old Herefordshire family. Her earliest poems were published in the "Literary Gazette," the editor of which, Mr. Jerdan, afforded her valuable critical and literary assistance. Her first long poem, "The Fate of Adelaide" (1820), a very immature production, was followed by the "Poetical Sketches" contributed to the "Literary Gazette," and during the whole of her career she continued to write for this and other periodicals. Of her longer poems, "The Improvisatrice" appeared in 1824, "The Troubadour" in 1825, "The Golden Violet" in 1826, "The Venetian Bracelet," "Lost Pleiad," and other poems in 1829. "The Zenana" was one of the longest contributions to Fisher's "Drawing-room Scrap-book," which Miss Landon edited from 1830 until her departure for Africa. In 1831 appeared her first prose work, "Romance and Reality;" it was followed by "Francesca Carrara." "Ethel Churchill" (1836), her most powerful work, as well as the tragedy "The Fortunes of Castruccio Castracani," gave evidence of maturing forces which might have produced greater results than those by which she is now known. Having spent the greater part of her life in London, Miss Landon married, on June 7th, 1838, George Maclean, Governor of Cape Coast, and sailed with him shortly after for Africa. The separation from her friends and admirers in England was destined to be a lasting one, for she died in the following year [?] from an overdose of prussic acid administered medicinally by herself. Unlike her writings, which are tinged with a uniform gloom and melancholy, she was of a most sociable and animated nature.—SANDERS, LLOYD C., *ed.*, 1887, *Celebrities of the Century, p.* 651.

PERSONAL

Pickersgill's portrait of her, which was exhibited at the Royal Academy, is allowed, by every body who has seen her, to be any thing but a flattering likeness, except in the talent and animation which it indicates. . . . Her life can as yet afford but few events to chronicle; and we hope it will never be chequered by any of an unpleasant character.—RYAN, RICHARD, 1826, *Poetry and Poets, vol.* II, *pp.* 99, 100.

So Daniel has bought the "Improvisatrice." Did thou know that L. E. L. was a ward of Jerdan's, the editor of the *Literary Gazette?* whence his abundant and extravagant puffs of her. She is, I understand, rather short, but interesting-looking, a most thoughtless girl in company, doing strangely extravagant things; for instance, making a wreath of flowers, then rushing with it into a grave and numerous party, and placing it on her patron's head. Bernard Barton sent her one of his last volumes, and in reply, after some remarks on the poetry it contained, she sent him, in high glee, a full account of a ball she had just attended, particularising all the dresses, forgetting she was writing to a sober Quaker. However, she is but a girl of twenty, a genius and therefore she must be excused.—HOWITT, MARY, 1824, *Letter to her Sister, Oct.* 28; *Autobiography, ed. her Daughter, vol.* I, *p.* 187.

I avoided L. E. L., who looked the very personification of Brompton—pink satin dress and white satin shoes, red cheeks, snub nose, and her hair *à la* Sappho.—BEACONSFIELD, BENJAMIN DISRAELI LORD, 1832, *Correspondence with his Sister, Feb.* 18, *p.* 2.

Oh! I saw L. E. L. to-day. She avows her love to her betrothed frankly, and is going to Africa, where *he* is governor of a fortress. Is not that grand? It is on the Gold Coast, and his duty is to protect black people from being made slaves. The whole thing is a romance for Lamartine—half Paul and Virgina, half Inkle and Yarico. Poor Miss Landon! I do like and shall miss her. But she will be happier than in writing, which seems to me like shooting arrows and never hitting the right mark, but now and then putting out one's own little boy's eye.—LYTTON, EDWARD GEORGE LORD, 1838, *Letter to Lady Blessington; Literary Life and Correspondence of the Countess of Blessington, ed. Madden, vol.* II, *p.* 183.

Hic jacet sepultum
omne quod mortale fuit
LETITIAE ELIZABETHAE McLEAN,
quam, egregià ornatam indole,
musis unicè amatam,
omniumque amores secum trahentem,
in ipso aetatis flore,
mors immatura rapuit,
Die Octobris xv., A. D., MDCCCXXXVIII.,
Ætat. 36.

Quod spectas viator marmor,
Vanum heu doloris monumentum,
Conjux moerens erexit.

—INSCRIPTION ON TABLET, 1838, *Cape Coast Castle.*

Our far-off England! ofttimes would she sit
With moist eyes gazing o'er the lustrous deep,
Through distance, change, and time beholding it
In its green beauty, while the sea did keep
A whispering noise, to lull her spirit's visioned sleep.
And fondly would she watch the evening breeze
Steal, crushing the smooth ocean's sultry blue,
As 'twere a message from her own tall trees,
Waving her back to them, and flowers, and bees,
And loving looks, from which her young heart drew
Its riches, and all the joys her winged childhood knew. . . .
Spring shall return to that beloved shore,
With health of leaves, and buds, and wild wood songs,
But hers the sweetest, with its tearful lore,
Its womanly fond gushes come no more,
Breathing the cadenced poesy that throngs
To pure and fervid lips unstained by cares and wrongs.

—LANDOR, WALTER SAVAGE? 1838, *A Lament for L. E. L., The Literary Life and Correspondence of the Countess of Blessington, ed. Madden, vol.* II, *p.* 68.

There was no slander too vile, and no assertion too wicked, to heap on the fame of this injured creature. Mr. [ ], a married man, and the father of a large family, many of whom were older than L. E. L., was said to have been her lover, and it was publicly stated that she had become too intimately connected with him. Those who disbelieved the calumny refrained not from repeating it, until it became a general topic of conversation. Her own sex, fearful of censure, had not courage to defend her; and this highly-gifted and sensitive creature, without having committed a single error, found herself a victim to slander. . . . Pride led her to conceal what she suffered, but those who best knew her were aware that for many months sleep could only be obtained by the aid of narcotics, and that violent spasms and frequent attacks of the nerves left her seldom free from acute suffering. The effort to force a gayety she was far from feeling increased her sufferings even to the last. The first use she made of the money produced by her writings was to buy an annuity for her grandmother—that grandmother whose acerbity of temper and wearying *exigeance* had embittered her home. She then went to reside in Hans Place with some elderly ladies who kept a school, and here again calumny assailed her. Dr. M—, a married man, and father of grown daughters, was now named as her paramour; and though his habits, age, appearance, and attachment to his wife ought to have precluded the possibility of attaching credence to so absurd a piece of scandal, poor L. E. L. was again attacked in a manner that nearly sent her to the grave. This last falsehood was invented a little more than four years agc, when some of those who disbelieved the other scandal affected to give credit to this, and stung the sensitive mind of poor L. E. L. almost to madness by their hypocritical conduct. About this time Mr. Maclean became acquainted with her, and after some months proposed for her hand.—BLESSINGTON, COUNTESS, 1839, *Letter to Lady W——, Jan.* 29; *Literary Life and Correspondence, ed. Madden, vol.* II, *p.* 70.

Her easy carriage and careless movements would seem to imply an insensibility to the feminine passion of dress; yet she had a proper sense of it, and never disdained the foreign aid of ornament, always provided it was simple, quiet, and becoming. Her hair was darkly brown, very soft and beautiful, and always tastefully arranged; her figure slight, but well-formed and graceful; her feet small, but her hands especially so, and faultlessly white and finely shaped; her fingers were fairy fingers; her ears also were observably little. Her face, though not regular in any feature, became beautiful by expression; every flash of thought, every change and colour of feeling, lightened over it as she spoke, when she spoke earnestly. The forehead was not high, but broad and full; the eyes had no overpowering brilliancy, but their clear intellectual light penetrated by its exquisite softness; her mouth was not less marked by character; and besides the glorious faculty of uttering the pearls and diamonds of fancy and wit, knew how to express scorn, or anger, or pride, as well as it knew how to smile winningly, or to pour forth those quick, ringing laughs which, not even excepting her *bon-mots* and aphorisms, were the most delightful things that issued from it.—BLANCHARD, LAMAN, 1841, *The Life and Literary Remains of L. E. L.*

A more mournful story than hers is seldom heard—illustrative as it is of the perils, snares, and sufferings of a literary life, where the responsibility of the vocation is not felt with the seriousness which shames cupidity, and silences flattery. People inferior to herself made money and amusement out of her talent and herself; and she permitted them to do it—partly out of careless generosity, and partly because she was too little aware of the responsibility of genius. Carefully cultivated, her genius might have accomplished great things. As it was, her early and wonderful facility is nearly all that remains for admiration. By her personal friends she is remembered with an affection which has nothing to do with her writings; and by those who did not know her, her writings are regarded with an indifference almost as great as her own.—MARTINEAU, HARRIET, 1849, *A History of the Thirty Years' Peace, A. D.* 1815-1846, *vol.* IV, *p.* 75.

The verdict, therefore, was, that she died from an overdose of Scheele's preparation of prussic acid, taken inadvertently. In those warm latitudes interment follows death with a haste which often cruelly shocks the feelings. Mrs. Maclean was buried the same evening, within the precincts of the castle. Mr. Topp read the funeral service, and the whole of the residents assisted at the solemn ceremony. The grave was lined with walls of brick and mortar, with an arch over the coffin. Soon after the conclusion of the service, one of those heavy showers only known in tropical climates suddenly came on. All departed for their houses. I remained to see the arch completed. The bricklayers were obliged to get a covering to protect them and their work from the rain. Night had come on before the paving-stones were all put down over the grave, and the workmen finished their business by torchlight. How sadly yet does that night of gloom return to my remembrance! How sad were then my thoughts, as, wrapped up in my cloak, I stood beside the grave of L. E. L. under that pitiless torrent of rain! I fancied what would be the thoughts of thousands in England if they could see and know the meaning of that flickering light, of those busy workmen, and of that silent watcher! I thought of yesterday, when at the same time I was taking my seat beside her at dinner, and now—oh, how very, very sad the change!—CRUICKSHANK, BRODIE, 1853, *Eighteen Years in the Gold Coast of Africa, including an Account of the Native Tribes and their Intercourse with Europeans.*

I can recollect her when she lived in Sloane Street with her grandmother; indeed, I remember her before that time. I recall her exactly; short, not slight, with a most blooming, glowing complexion, beautiful teeth, expression; everything but features—that is, the features were insignificant—they were not unpleasing. She could not have been above eighteen, but she had a fashion of wearing a fanciful little cap on the top of her head, and that suited her exactly. It was an eccentric appearance that she made. She dressed then upon an idea—a sweeter voice I never heard; I mean in speaking. I do not believe that she sang, or that she had any knowledge of music. She had an inborn courtesy of manner, that flattered you whether she wished it or not: a warm, excitable nature. We met, one evening—but stay—I must sit and think of her awhile. She is too precious a remembrance to be merely made notes of. I should like here to record all that I knew of her, felt for her, heard of her. What is the street, in all that there really *is*, of London, (that is, west of Portland Place and south of Oxford Street), in which her pleasant voice, her quick step, are *not* at some moment or other present with me? —THOMSON, KATHERINE, 1854, *Recollections of Literary Characters and Celebrated Places, vol.* II, *p.* 71.

The spot that was chosen for the grave of this accomplished but unhappy lady could not be more inappropriate; a few common tiles distinguish it from the graves of the various military men who have perished in this stronghold of pestilence. Her grave is daily trampled over by the soldiers of the fort. The morning blast of the bugle and roll of the drum are the sounds that have been thought most in unison with the spirit of the gentle being who sleeps below the few red tiles where the soldiers on parade do congregate. There is not a plant, nor a blade of grass, nor of any thing green, in that court-yard, on which the burning sun blazes down all day long. And this is the place where they have buried L. E. L.—MADDEN, R. R., 1855, *The Literary Life and Correspondence of the Countess of Blessington, vol.* II, *p.* 57.

In spite of the miserably low standard of her literary morality, Miss Landon (for awhile put forward as Mrs. Hemans's rival) was meant for better things. She was incomplete, but she was worthy of being completed; she was ignorant, but she was quick, and capable of receiving culture, had she been allowed a chance. If she was unrefined, it was because she had fallen into the hands of a coarse set of men—the Tories of a provincial capital —such as then made a noise and a flare in the "Noctes Ambrosianæ" of "Blackwood's Magazine," second-hand followers of Lockhart and Professor Wilson, and Theodore Hook; the most noisy and most reprehensible of whom—and yet one of the cleverest—was Dr. Maginn. Not merely did they, at a very early period of the girl's career, succeed in bringing her name into a coarse repute, from which it never wholly extricated itself, but, by the ridiculous exaggeration of such natural gifts as she possessed (no doubt accompanied by immediate gain), flattered her into the idea that small further cultivation was required by one who could rank with a Baillie, a Tighe, a Hemans—if not their superior, at least their equal. Further, she was not fortunate in her home position, called on to labour incessantly for the support of those around her. All this resulted in what may be called a *bravado* in her intercourse with the public, which excited immense distaste among those who were not of the coterie to which she belonged.—CHORLEY, HENRY FOTHERGILL, 1873, *Autobiography, Memoirs and Letters, vol.* I, *p.* 249.

I knew her well and attended her from her infancy; she was the last woman whom I should have supposed likely to destroy herself. She was said to have died from prussic acid. Now I fitted out the medicine chest she took with her to Cape Coast Castle, and know that there was no prussic acid in her possession. I am convinced that she did not die from its effects, and we must seek for her death from some other cause.—THOMSON, DR. ANTHONY TODD, 1874, *Autobiographical Reminiscences of the Medical Profession, p.* 308.

Mr. Landon was a character of no ordinary cast, and like his sister (though not in the same way) possessed very superior talents, cultivated by study, and no less by the opportunities of mingling much in the literary circles of London. His love for his sister was most warm and marked. When he came first to see us, his sister was living, in the bloom of womanhood, the height of fame, and indulging in the creations of her genius. She could not be unconscious of her uncommon powers, for success from the very first had attended her steps. She never experienced opposition and adversities, which humble often even the most gifted. She knew no jealousy of others; on the contrary she was ever ready to do a kind act for any one. —BRAY, ANNA ELIZA, 1883, *Autobiography, ed. Kempe, p.* 236.

Her fame, like herself, is but a memory now. But how bright it was half a century ago!—how intoxicating! So quickly won, too, that she might, like Byron, have written, "I awoke one morning and found myself famous." Alas! Dead-Sea fruit, indeed, was to her the fruit of genius—of all the women of letters whose pens have assisted feminine charms to make them famous and flattered, few have been more completely miserable; none can I bring to mind who ever closed a career of brilliant unhappiness by a death so tragical. Her marriage wrecked her life; but before that fatal mistake was made, slander had been busy with her fair fame—the slander that most cruelly wounds a woman. She took refuge from it in union with a man utterly incapable of appreciating her or making her happy, and went out with him to his government at the Gold Coast—to die. And not even—tragical as such an ending would have been to the career of the applauded writer, the flattered woman—to wither before the pestilential influences that steam up from that wilderness of swamp and jungle; but to die a violent death—a fearful one—and to leave to the coroner's inquest, that the manner of her end made necessary, the task of delicately veiling under a verdict of accident the horrid doubts that her fate suggested. Suicide or murder—which was it, the voice of the public of that day asked, that had so tragically closed the career of the gifted "L. E. L.?" For my part, that unhappy "L. E. L." was murdered I never had a doubt. . . . When the ship that bore them to Africa arrived in port, Maclean left her on board while he went to arrange matters on shore. A negro woman was there, with four or five children—*his* children; she had to be sent into the interior to make room for her legitimate successor. It is understood the negress was the daughter of a king; at all events she was of a race "with whom revenge is a virtue," and from the moment "L. E. L." landed, her life was at the mercy of her rival; that by her hand she was done to death I am all but certain, although in the only letter she wrote to Mrs. Hall from Africa she assumed an air of cheerfulness and content. . . . Poor child, poor girl, poor woman, poor wife, poor victim—from the cradle to the grave, it was an unhappy life! I have seldom seen her merry, that the laugh was not followed by a sigh.—HALL, SAMUEL CARTER, 1883, *Retrospect of a Long Life, pp.* 395, 396.

No circumstance respecting "L. E. L." has occasioned so much discussion as her sudden and mysterious death at Cape Coast Castle on 15 Oct. 1838. That she died of taking prussic acid can hardly be disputed, though the surgeon's neglect to institute a post-mortem examination left an opening for doubt. That she was found lying in her room with an empty bottle, which had contained a preparation of prussic acid, in her hand seems equally certain, and the circumstance, if proved, negatives the not unnatural suspicion that her death was the effect of the vengeance of her husband's discarded mistress, while there is no ground in any case for suspecting him. There remain, therefore, only the hypotheses of suicide and of accident; and the general tone of her letters to England, even though betraying some disappointment with her husband, is so cheerful, and the fact of her having been accustomed to administer a most dangerous medicine to herself is so well established, that accident must be regarded as the more probable supposition.—GARNETT, RICHARD, 1892, *Dictionary of National Biography, vol.* XXXII, *p.* 53.

GENERAL

L. E. L. has too little variety for me; everything is so impassioned: I wish she would mix a little sage with her myrtle garland.—GRANT, ANNE, 1827, *Letter to Mrs. Hook, May* 26; *Memoir and Correspondence, ed. Grant, vol.* III, *p.* 90.

Tickler. I love L. E. L.

North. So do I; and, being old gentlemen, we may blamelessly make the public our confidante. There is a *passionate purity* in all her feelings that endears to me both her human and poetical character. She is a true enthusiast. Her affections overflow the imagery her fancy lavishes on all the subjects of her song, and colour it with a rich and tender light which makes even confusion beautiful, gives a glowing charm even to indistinct conception, and when the thoughts themselves are full-formed and substantial, which they often are, brings them prominently out upon the eye of the soul in flashes that startle us into sudden admiration. The originality of her genius, methinks, is conspicuous in the choice of its subjects:—they are unborrowed—and in her least successful poems—as wholes—there is no dearth of poetry. Her execution has not the consummate elegance and grace of Felicia Hemans; but she is very young, and becoming, every year she lives, more mistress of her art,—and has chiefly to learn now how to use her treasures, which, profuse as she has been, are in abundant store. And, in good truth, the fair and happy being has a fertile imagination: the soil of her soul, if allowed to lie fallow for one sunny summer, would, I predict, yield a still richer and more glorious harvest. I love Miss Landon; for in her genius does the work of duty—the union of the two is "beautiful exceedingly,"—and virtue is its own reward; far beyond the highest meed of praise ever bestowed by critic, though round her fair forehead is already wreathed the immortal laurel. —WILSON, JOHN, 1832, *Noctes Ambrosianæ, Feb.*

The brilliant parterres of Miss Landon's enclosure, on the south of Parnassus, where ideas, like humming-birds, are seen flying about in tropical sunshine, or fluttering over blossoms of all hues and all climes.—MONTGOMERY, JAMES, 1833, *Lectures on General Literature, Poetry, etc., p.* 161.

Next to Sister Joanna, the most successful poetess of our day. She is the L.E.L. of many a pretty poem: nor has she sung only a tender ditty or two and then shut her lips to listen to the applause they brought; she has written much,—sometimes loftily, sometimes touchingly, and always fluently and gracefully. She excels in short and neat things; yet she has poured out her fancy and her feelings through the evolutions of a continuous narrative and intricate story. The flow of her language is remarkable: her fancy is ever ready, and never extravagant.—CUNNINGHAM, ALLAN, 1833, *Biographical and Critical History of the Literature of the Last Fifty Years.*

The career of Mrs. Maclean commenced brilliantly, but the promise of her earlier efforts was scarcely fulfilled in her subsequent productions, which were generally written under circumstances that prevented study and elaboration. She had a deep feeling of affection, a lively fancy, a fine eye for the picturesque, and an unusual command of poetical language; and notwithstanding the haste and carelessness with which she wrote, she was improving in taste and execution, and would probably have gained a far higher reputation had she lived a few years more. With all her faults she will be remembered as one of the sweetest poets of the age.—GRISWOLD, RUFUS W., 1844, *The Poets and Poetry of England in the Nineteenth Century, p.* 388.

But you shall not think me exclusive. Of poor L. E. L. for instance, I could write with *more* praiseful appreciation than you can. It appears to me that she had the gift—though in certain respects she dishonored the art—and her latter lyrics are, many of them, of great beauty and melody, such as, having once touched the ear of a reader, live on in it.—BROWNING, ELIZABETH BARRETT, 1845, *To Mr. Chorley, Jan.* 7; *Letters, ed. Kenyon, vol.* I, *p.* 232.

I should say that it is the young and ardent who must always be the warmest admirers of the larger poems of L.E.L. They are filled with the faith and the fancies of the young. The very scenery and ornaments are of that rich and showy kind which belongs to the youthful taste;—the white rose, the jasmine, the summer garniture of deep grass and glades of greenest foliage; festal gardens with lamps and bowers; gay cavaliers, and jewelled dames, and all that glitters in young eyes and love-haunted fancies. But, among these, numbers of her smaller poems from the first dealt with subjects and sympathies of a more general kind, and gave glimpses of a nobility of sentiment, and a bold expression of her feeling of the unequal lot of humanity, of a far higher character. . . . Her prose stories have all the leading characteristics of her poetry. Their theme is love, and their demonstration that all love is fraught with destruction and desolation. But there are other qualities manifested in the tales. The prose page was for her a wider tablet, on which she could, with more freedom and ampler display, record her views of society.—HOWITT, WILLIAM, 1847, *Homes and Haunts of the Most Eminent British Poets, vol.* II, *pp.* 156, 157.

This remarkable writer, better known perhaps as Miss Landon, or L. E. L., may, I think, be considered the Byron of our poetesses. . . . Of Mrs. Maclean's genius there can be but one opinion. It is distinguished by very great intellectual power, a highly sensitive and ardent imagination, an intense fervour of passionate emotion, and almost unequalled eloquence and fluency. Of mere art she displays but little. Her style is irregular and careless, and her painting sketchy and rough: but there is genius in every line she has written.—ROWTON, FREDERIC,

1848, *The Female Poets of Great Britain*, *p.* 424.

Some of her smaller pieces, as "Crescentius," show her to have been capable of higher classic power, if she had had the patience to cultivate a greater severity of criticism on her own productions. The editor has far greater pleasure in speaking of her writings, as they struck his youthful fancy, than with the cool judgment of more mature years; but he believes that there are few who will not join him in a willing tribute to the minstrel power of one, who, whatever her defects may have been, had the true fire and gush of poetic inspiration.—BETHUNE, GEORGE WASHINGTON, 1848, *The British Female Poets*, *p.* 275.

Her deficiency alike in judgment and taste made her wayward and capricious, and her efforts seemed frequently impulsive. Hence she gave to the public a great deal too much,—a large part of her writings being destitute of that elaboration, care, and finish essentially necessary in the fine arts, even when in combination with the highest genius, to secure permanent success . . . L. E. L. had opened her eyes to these her defects, and was rapidly overcoming them; for her very last things—those published in her "Remains" by Laman Blanchard—are incomparably her best, whether we regard vigorous conception, concentration of idea, or judicious selection of subject. Her faults originated in an enthusiastic temperament and an efflorescent fancy; and showed themselves, as might have been expected, in an uncurbed prodigality of glittering imagery,—her muse, untamed and untutored, ever darting in dalliance from one object to another, like the talismanic bird in the Arabian story.—MOIR, D. M., 1851–52, *Sketches of the Poetical Literature of the Past Half-Century*, *pp.* 274, 275.

The poems of L. E. L. of surpassing sweetness and pathos, rivaling those of Mrs. Norton herself in heartrending sentiment, will long survive their unhappy author, and speak to the heart of generations to which her premature fate will be a lasting subject of commiseration.—ALISON, SIR ARCHIBALD, 1853–59, *History of Europe*, 1815–1852, *ch.* v.

The chief characteristics of the poetry of L. E. L. consist in imaginative power, tenderness, and geniality of feeling, and harmony of versification.—MADDEN, R. R., 1855, *The Literary Life and Correspondence of the Countess of Blessington*, *vol.* II, *p.* 42.

As a poetess Letitia Elizabeth Landon can only rank as a gifted improvisatrice. She had too little culture, too little discipline, too low an ideal of her art, to produce anything of very great value. All this she might and probably would have acquired under happier circumstances.—GARNETT, RICHARD, 1892, *Dictionary of National Biography*, *vol.* XXXII, *p.* 54.

It is tolerably exact, and it is not harsh, to say that "L. E. L." is a Mrs. Hemans with the influence of Byron added, not to the extent of any "impropriety," but to the heightening of the Romantic tone and of a native sentimentality. Her verse is generally musical and sweet: it is only sometimes silly. But it is too often characterised by what can but be called the "gush" which seems to have affected all the poetesses of this period except Sara Coleridge.—SAINTSBURY, GEORGE, 1896, *A History of Nineteenth Century Literature*, *p.* 119.

Though her verse is of little value, she is one of the best examples of the tendencies of the time. She followed Byron as far as her talents and the restraints of her sex would allow. Her longer poems are on the whole poor; some of her shorter pieces are very readable, but they are chargeable with the fault of an excess of rhetoric.—WALKER, HUGH, 1897, *The Age of Tennyson*, *p.* 53.

Anne Grant

1755–1838

Born in Glasgow, the daughter of Duncan M'Vicar, an army officer, was in America, 1758–68, and in 1779 married the Rev. James Grant, minister of Laggan. Left a widow in 1801, she published "Poems" (1803), "Letters from the Mountains" (1806), "Superstitions of the Highlanders" (1811), &c. In 1825 she received a pension of £100. See memoir by her son (1844).—PATRICK AND GROOME, *eds.*, 1897, *Chambers's Biographical Dictionary*, *p.* 429.

PERSONAL

I went quite as often to Mrs. Grant's, where an American, I imagine, finds himself at home more easily than anywhere else in Edinburgh. She is an old lady of such great good-nature and such strong good-sense, mingled with a natural talent, plain knowledge, and good taste, derived from English reading alone, that when she chooses to be pleasant she can be so to a high degree. Age and sorrow have fallen pretty heavily upon her. She is about seventy, and has lost several of her children, but still she is interested in what is going forward in the world, tells a great number of amusing stories about the past generation, and gives striking sketches of Highland manners and feelings, of which she is herself an interesting representative.—TICKNOR, GEORGE, 1819, *Journal, March; Life, Letters and Journals, vol.* I, *p.* 278.

Some months since, I joined with other literary folks in subscribing a petition for a pension to Mrs. Grant of Laggan, which we thought was a tribute merited by her as an authoress; and, in my opinion, much more by the firmness and elasticity of mind with which she had borne a succession of great domestic calamities. Unhappily there was only about £100 open on the pension list, and this the ministers assigned in equal portions to Mrs. G— and a distressed lady, granddaughter of a forfeited Scottish nobleman. Mrs. G—, proud as a Highland-woman, vain as a poetess, and absurd as a bluestocking, has taken this partition in *malam partem*, and written to Lord Melville about her merits, and that her friends do not consider her claims as being fairly canvassed, with something like a demand that her petition be submitted to the King. This is not the way to make her *plack a bawbee*, and Lord M., a little *miffed* in turn, sends the whole correspondence to me, to know whether Mrs. G— will accept the £50 or not. Now, hating to deal with ladies when they are in an unreasonable humour, I have got the good-humoured Man of Feeling to find out the lady's mind, and I take on myself the task of making her peace with Lord M. There is no great doubt how it will end, for your scornful dog will always eat your dirty pudding. After all the poor lady is greatly to be pitied;—her sole remaining daughter deep and far gone in a decline.—SCOTT, SIR WALTER, 1825, *Journal, Nov.* 30; *Life by Lockhart, ch.* lxv.

Mrs. Grant was a tall, dark woman, of very considerable intellect, great spirit, and the warmest benevolence. Her love of individual Whigs, particularly of Jeffrey, in spite of her amusing horror of their principles, was honorable to her heart. She was always under the influence of an affectionate and delightful enthusiasm, which, unquenched by time or sorrow, survived the wreck of many domestic attachments, and shed a glow over the close of a very protracted life.—COCKBURN, HENRY, 1830–54, *Memorials of His Time, p.* 255.

Mrs. Grant was tall, and, in her youth, slender, but after her accident she became rather corpulent. In her later years she was described as a venerable ruin; so lame as to be obliged to walk with crutches, and even with that assistance her motions were slow and languid. Her broad and noble forehead, relieved by the parted gray hair, excelled even youthful beauty. There was a dignity and a sedateness in her carriage which rendered her highly interesting, and her excellent constitution bore her through a great deal. Her conversation was original and characteristic; frank, yet far from rude; replete at once with amusement and instruction. For nearly thirty years she was a principal figure in the best and most intellectual society of the Scottish metropolis; and to the last her literary celebrity made her an object of curiosity and attraction to strangers from all parts of the world. The native simplicity of her mind, and an entire freedom from all attempt at display, made the youngest person feel in the presence of a friend.—ANDERSON, WILLIAM, 1871, *Model Women, p.* 147.

GENERAL

Her "Letters from the Mountains," notwithstanding the repulsive affectation of the title, are among the most interesting collections of real letters that have lately been given to the public; and, being indebted for no part of their interest to the celebrity of the names they contain or the importance of the events they narrate, afford, in their success, a more honourable testimony to the talents of the author. The great charm of the correspondence, indeed, is its perfect independence of artificial helps; and the air of fearlessness and originality which it has consequently assumed. . . . Her Poetry . . . is really not very good; and the most tedious, and certainly the least poetical, volume which she has produced, is that which contains her verses. The longest piece,—which she has entitled "The Highlanders,"—is heavy and uninteresting; and there is a want of compression and finish—a sort of loose, rambling, and indigested air—in most of the others. Yet the whole collection is enlivened with the sparklings of a prolific fancy, and displays great command of language and facility of versification. When we write our article upon unsuccessful poetry, we shall endeavour to explain how these qualities may fail of success:—but in the meantime, we think there is an elegy upon an humble friend, and an address from a fountain, and two or three other little pieces, which very fully deserve it;—and are written with great beauty, tenderness, and delicacy.—JEFFREY, FRANCIS LORD, 1811, *Mrs. Grant on Highlanders, Edinburgh Review, vol.* 18, *pp.* 480, 481.

Mrs. Grant in her "Highlanders and other Poems" respectably assisted in sustaining the honours of the Scottish muse.—MOIR, D. M., 1851–52, *Sketches of the Poetical Literature of the Past Half-Century.*

Honestly, we cannot believe that it was expected or desired, and certainly it was not necessary in the case of Mrs. Grant, for the illustration of character, to illuminate, during a period of years, for the common gaze, the privacies of a heart too constantly and deeply acquainted with affliction in its sharpest earthly form, or for the confirmation of fame, to make the million confidants in the casual unimportant intercommunication of female friendship, or in other mysteries of equal moment. On the first of these subjects, we have a very decided opinion. Grief in itself is a sacred thing, while the language of grief is that probably most universally spoken by mankind. Where, therefore, there is an objection—and, to our mind, there is *always* an objection—to perpetually, or at least over-frequently obtruding the *thing*, little or nothing is to be gained by parading its *language*, which blunts its edge by monotonous repetition. On the other matter, we are inclined to be not a whit more tolerant or less severe, regarding it conscientiously as a besetting sin of the day, against the prevalence of which we unreservedly and energetically protest.—GORDON, J. T., 1844, *Memoir and Correspondence of Mrs. Grant of Laggan, North British Review, vol.* 1, *p.* 102.

A woman of extraordinary good sense, and of uncommon powers of mind; whose letters, embracing a wide variety of subjects, are as truly valuable as those of any other writer, and likely to be of as permanent interest, and to afford as lasting gratification; but especially of a woman of great strength of character, formed by religious principle and penetrated by religious sentiment, the vital principle of whose moral being was faith in God and immortality, whose sympathies were warm and diffusive, and who was full of disinterested kindness.—NORTON, ANDREWS, 1845, *Memoir of Mrs. Grant of Laggan, North American Review, vol.* 60, *p.* 156.

An education of rough experience, combined with a naturally shrewd, powerful, and sensitive mind, made Mrs. Grant a highly effective and successful writer; and the fame of her literary abilities (even before she published any fruits of them) was so great, that three thousand persons gave her their names as subscribers to her poem of the "Highlanders."—ROWTON, FREDERIC, 1848, *The Female Poets of Great Britain, p.* 254.

The writings of this lady display a lively and observant fancy, and considerable powers of landscape painting. They first drew attention to the more striking and romantic features of the Scottish Highlands, afterwards so fertile a theme for the genius of Scott.—CHAMBERS, ROBERT, 1876, *Cyclopædia of English Literature, ed. Carruthers.*

Winthrop Mackworth Praed

1802–1839

Born, in London, 26 July 1802. At school at Langley Broom, 1810–14; at Eton, March 1814 to 1821. Edited "The Etonian," with W. Blunt, 1821. To Trin. Coll., Camb., Oct. 1821; Browne Medallist for Greek Ode, 1822 and 1823; for Greek

Epigrams, 1822 and 1824; Chancellor's Medal for English Poem, 1823 and 1824; B.A., 1825. Contrib. to Knight's "Quarterly Mag.," 1822. Part editor of "The Brazen Head," 1826. At Eton, as private tutor to Lord Ernest Bruce, 1825-27. Fellow, Trin. Coll., Camb., 1827; Seatonian prize poem, 1830. Called to Bar at Middle Temple, 29 May, 1829. Contrib. to "Times," "Morning Post," "Albion," etc. M. P. for St. Germans, by purchasing seat, Dec. 1832; constituency disfranchised same year by Reform Bill. M. P. for Great Yarmouth, 1834-37. Sec. to Board of Control, Dec. 1834 to April 1835. Married Helen Bogle, 1835. M. P. for Aylesbury, 1837. Deputy High Steward to Univ. of Cambridge. Died, in London, 15 July 1839. Buried at Kensal Green. *Works:* "Carmen Græcum: Pyramides Ægyptiacæ" [1822]; "Epigrammata" [1822]; "Australasia" [1823]; "Carmen Græcum: In Obitum T. F. Middleton" [1823]; "Lillian," 1823; "Athens" [1824]; "Epigrammata [1824]; "Speech in Committee on the Reform Bill," 1832; "Trash" (anon.), 1833. *Collected Works:* "Poetical Works," ed. by R. W. Griswold (New York), 1844; ed. by Derwent Coleridge, revised edn. (2 vols.), 1885; "Essays," ed. by Sir G. Young, 1887; "Political and Occasional Poems," ed. by Sir G. Young, 1888.—SHARP, R. FARQUHARSON, 1897, *A Dictionary of English Authors, p.* 231.

PERSONAL

What he might have become had life been spared it were now vain to conjecture. He married happily; he died young. Light, lively, brilliant, the darling of every society that he entered, he was yet most beloved by those who knew him best. To me it seems that had he outlived the impetuosity of youth, he would have become something higher and better than a political partisan, however clever, or a fashionable poet, however elegant.—MITFORD, MARY RUSSELL, 1851, *Recollections of a Literary Life, p.* 101.

It is not easy to separate my recollections of the Praed of Eton from those of the Praed of Cambridge. The Etonian of 1820 was natural and unaffected in his ordinary talk; neither shy nor presuming; proud, without a tinge of vanity; somewhat reserved, but ever courteous; giving few indications of the susceptibility of the poet, but ample evidence of the laughing satirist; a pale and slight youth, who had looked upon the aspects of society with the keen perception of a clever manhood; one who had, moreover, seen in human life something more than follies to be ridiculed by the gay jest or scouted by the sarcastic sneer.—KNIGHT, CHARLES, 1863, *Passages of a Working Life During Half a Century.*

To his contemporaries, to all by whom he was intimately known, to very many who knew him mainly by report, and who perhaps cherish the remembrance of a casual meeting, the name of Winthrop Praed is still as the sound of music. The depths of his nature were indeed opened but to few; not often or willingly to them: but he had a special faculty and privilege, better than any craft of will, by which he attracted even when he seemed to repel,—and was more than popular even when, in his younger and gayer days, he appeared to court animadversion and defy dislike. —COLERIDGE, DERWENT, 1864, *ed., The Poems of Winthrop Mackworth Praed, Memoir.*

His nature might be compared to an Æolian lyre that is stirred by inspiration from without, rather than a harp that vibrates to the touch of human fingers. Or one may see in him a likeness to that type of character which the greatest of modern masters has portrayed in "Tristram," whose mind, even when haunted by an object of real passion, was prone to yield to any transient distraction. — HEWLETT, HENRY G., 1872, *Poets of Society, The Contemporary Review, vol.* 20, *p.* 259.

A common interest in that debating society brought together in joyous social life the most ardent and ambitious youths of the University. What robust and sanguine society exhilarated the suppers to which we adjourned from our mimic senate! There, foremost in ready wit, as the hour before he had been in brilliant extempore eloquence, was Winthrop Mackworth Praed. There was a fascination in the very name of this young man which eclipsed the repute of all his contemporaries. Sweeping away prizes and scholarships from the competition of perhaps sounder and more copious learning; the quickest and easiest debater in the Union, without study or preparation;

carrying everywhere into our private circles a petulant yet graceful vivacity; matchless in repartee; passionately fond of dancing; never missing a ball, though it were the night before an examination; there was in his mind a restless exuberance of energy and life, all the more striking from its contrast with a frame and countenance painfully delicate and marked by the symptoms of consumption. He excited at the University the same kind of haunting personal interest that Byron was then exciting in the world. All were fond of speculating about his future. For the outlines of his genius were not definitely marked. They vanished away when you ought to seize them —LYTTON, EDWARD BULWER LORD, 1873–83, *Life, Letters and Literary Remains, ed. his Son, vol.* I, *p.* 233.

GENERAL

There was through all his poetry—and it is its deepest although not its most obvious charm—a love of the genuine and the true, a scorn for the false and the pretending, which is the foundation of all that is really good in eloquence as well as in poetry, in conduct and in character, as well as in art. The germ of the patriot and the statesman is to be found in the love of truth and the hatred of pretense; and never were they more developed than in the poems of Winthrop Mackworth Praed.—MITFORD, MARY RUSSELL, 1851, *Recollections of a Literary Life, p.* 101.

In his early poems there is a buoyancy which afterward is wanting in his lines. . . . While few poets have written purer verse than he, few satirists have done their task with more gentleness. While we laugh at the follies of the day as he portrays them, we feel that the very subject of the picture would read the lines with complacent thoughts, and with admiration at the skill which had individualized him as his own ideal.—WHITMORE, W. H., 1859, *Praed and his Poems, North American Review, vol.* 89, *pp.* 545, 546.

Much that Praed wrote was written hastily; much of it was written while he was yet very young. Of much, then, the intrinsic value is small. . . . Praed was not without a certain measure of the poetic faculty. But, aside from that, but two things seem to have made him a writer of verse: his imitative ability, of which the reader is made aware by being often reminded of other writers, as Byron, Scott, Hood, while never arrested by any strong marks of originality; and, secondly, the persistent cultivation given to such poetic ability as he had by his father at home, by his tutors at school and college, and at the university by the competition for prizes, of which honors he bore off many. He thus acquired all the arts of versification. The precocity of his parts was, perhaps, their most distinguishing feature, and his early productions are characterized by that neat finish which appears rarely in the first essays of genius but is often found in the works of youthful talent. . . . It would be wrong to say that Praed is a mere versifier. If he is tried by his thoughts, if we enquire what, amidst much that is temporary and trivial, we may find that is noble, beautiful, and enduring, we shall discover here and there amid the prose some gleams of golden poetry. He is the possessor of a fancy not powerful and capable of sustained flights, but very quick and fertile in details. It can create for us the nymph of a single tree, but if we would wander in enchanted forests we must commit ourselves to some mightier master of the spell than he.—DENNETT, J. R., 1865, *Winthrop Mackworth Praed, The Nation, vol.* 1, *pp.* 52, 53.

His spirit was keen and eager, and the great incentive to all he did was the desire to excel. This passion mastered his whole being; and the momentary earnestness he threw into every successive undertaking was probably instrumental in undermining his constitution. Praed takes us into another atmosphere altogether from that in which Swift and Prior moved. Even satire had become good-natured and love decorous. We discover no single line which could not be read aloud in the most fastidious circle. Praed has the sweetness of a summer's night, and his wit represents the twinkling of the stars. Yet, in the midst of all his gaiety, in some of his poems a tinge of melancholy seems to indicate a premature weariness of life. —SMITH, GEORGE BARNETT, 1875, *English Fugitive Poets, Poets and Novelists, p.* 395.

. . . In these days of maudlin rhyme,
When half our poets are Empirics,
I've read for the five hundredth time
His "Characters," your "London Lyrics."

Trifles in truth, no passion there,
  No frightful advent of sensation,
But a most calm and classic air,
  A grace and beauty quite Horatian.
As Homer's lay of Ilion's towers
  Shines through the Past with god-like lustre,
So our Anacreon, crown'd with flowers,
  Will live as long as vine-leaves cluster.
—COLLINS, MORTIMER, 1876? *To Frederick Locker.*

The "Vicar" is a beautiful bit of verse, but its touch of tenderness sets it apart from all Praed's other work, which is brilliant with a hard and metallic brilliancy. Praed dazzles almost to weariness; his lines stand out sharply like fireworks at midnight. More brilliant than Praed no poet well could be.—MATTHEWS, BRANDER, 1883, *Frederick Locker, The Century, vol.* 25, *p.* 594.

As we pass from book to book, it is a long leap from Euripides to the brilliant young Etonian who brought all the grace of happy youth into such work as we have here. Happy the old who can grow young again with this book in their hands. If we all came into the world mature, and there were no childhood and youth about us, what a dull world it would be! Any book is a prize that brings the fresh and cheerful voice of youth into the region of true Literature.—MORLEY, HENRY, 1887, *Essays by Winthrop Mackworth Praed, ed. Young, Introduction, p.* 5.

Among the characteristics of these pieces will be found an almost unfailing good taste; a polished style, exhibiting a sparkle, as of finely constructed verse; a strong love of sheer fun, not ungracefully indulged; a dash of affectation, inoffensive, and such as is natural in a new-comer, upon whom the eyes of his circle have, by no fault of his, been drawn; a healthy, breezy spirit, redolent of the playing-fields; and a hearty appreciation of the pleasures arising from a first fresh plunge into the waters of literature. Powers of observation are shown of no mean order, and powers, also of putting in a strong light, whether attractive or ridiculous, the more obvious features of every-day characters. These powers afterwards ripened into a truly admirable skill of political and social verse-writing; and they showed signs of deepening into a more forcible satiric power, tempered with humour, as his too short career drew towards its end. Praed is moreover especially to be commended in that he is never dull. Although free from "sensationalism," he is not forgetful that the first business of a writer is—to be read.—YOUNG, SIR GEORGE, 1887, *ed., Essays by Winthrop Mackworth Praed, Preface, p.* x.

Unhappy is the person of whom it can be said that he neither has been, is, nor ever will be in the temper and circumstances of which Praed's verse is the exact and consummate expression; not much less unhappy he for whom that verse does not perform the best perhaps of all the offices of literature, and call up, it may be in happier guise than that in which they once really existed, the "many beloved shadows" of the past.—SAINTSBURY, GEORGE, 1888, *Winthrop Mackworth Praed, Macmillan's Magazine, vol.* 58, *p.* 355.

It has generally been the custom to regard Praed as the foremost exponent of what, for want of an exacter term, is known as "society verse,"—by society verse being intended, not so much the verse that treats of man as a social animal as the verse that treats of man (and woman) as they appear in that fashionable world. Many of Praed's pieces do undoubtedly come in this category, and they are numerous enough to justify his claim to be the Corphæus of his kind. But it is unjust to class him solely as the laureate of county balls and archery meetings. . . . His command of his instrument was so great, and his epigrammatic faculty so perfected by use, that the slightest provocation was sufficient to enable him to throw off a creditable "copy of verses." Thus it now and then fell out that the lines were finished before he had time to think whether the motive was adequate, or whether they included that beginning, middle, and end which even the trifles of metre require for their preservation. Also it occurred to him at times to write variations on himself, which, in his own interest, it had been wiser to withhold. But these are the objections of those who admire him so much that they would never have him below his best. When he is at his best—and we take that best to be exemplified by "The Red Fisherman," "The Vicar," "Quince," "My Own Araminta," "Our Ball," "Good Night to the Season," and some twenty more pieces, political and otherwise—he is unsurpassed and unsurpassable. In ease of wit and humour, in spontaneity and unflagging vivacity of rhythm, in sparkle of banter and felicity of rhyme, no imitator, whom we can recall, has ever come within measurable distance of Winthrop Mackworth Praed. —DOBSON, AUSTIN, 1894, *The Poets and the Poetry of the Century, John Keats to Edward Lord Lytton, ed. Miles.*

If Praed had been more of a colourist, he would have been our Watteau of the pen.—LOCKER-LAMPSON, FREDERICK, 1895, *My Confidences, p.* 180.

Praed's best poetry shows very remarkable grace and lightness of touch. His political squibs would perhaps have been more effective had they been more brutal; but Praed could not cease to be a gentleman even as a politician. The delicacy of feeling, with a dash of acid though never coarse satire, gives a pleasant flavour to his work; and in such work as the "Red Fisherman" he shows an imaginative power which tempts a regret for the diffidence which limited his aspirations. Probably, however, he judged rightly that his powers were best fitted for the lighter kinds of verse.—STEPHEN, LESLIE, 1896, *Dictionary of National Biography, vol.* XLVI, *p.* 283.

Praed belongs to the class of writers of *vers de société* of which Prior is the earlier and Locker-Lampson the later master; and it is not too much to say that he surpasses both.—WALKER, HUGH, 1897, *The Age of Tennyson, p.* 57.

John Galt

1779-1839

John Galt, Scotch novelist, was born at Irvine, May 2, 1779, and educated at Greenock. He was then placed in the Custom-house, but in 1804 proceeded to London with an epic poem on the battle of Largs in his portmanteau, a poem he printed but soon withdrew from circulation. After a few years his health failed, and he travelled for some time in the Levant, where he met Byron. On his return he published his "Letters from the Levant," a Life of Wolsey, several plays, and much miscellaneous work; but he first displayed individual power in "The Ayshire Legatees," which appeared in "Blackwood's Magazine" in 1820. Its successor, "The Annals of the Parish" (1821), remains his masterpiece. He produced in quick succession "Sir Andrew Wylie," "The Entail," "The Steamboat," and "The Provost." The historical romances, "Ringan Gilhaize" (a tale of the Covenanters), "The Spaewife," "Rothelan," and "The Omen," although full of striking scenes, were not so successful. Galt was now busily engaged in the formation of the Canada Company; but before he left England he published "The Last of the Lairds." He departed for Canada in 1826, but three years later returned to England a ruined man, and produced a new novel, "Lawrie Todd," followed by "Southennan," a romance of the days of Queen Mary, and a "Life of Lord Byron," which ran through several editions, but was roughly handled by the critics. In 1834 he issued his "Literary Life and Miscellanies." He now returned to Scotland, utterly broken in health and spirits, and died at Greenock, 11th April 1839.—PATRICK AND GROOME, *eds.*, 1897, *Chambers's Biographical Dictionary, p.* 394.

PERSONAL

We are old fellow-travellers, and, with all his eccentricities, he has much strong sense, experience of the world, and is, as far as I have seen, a good-natured, philosophical fellow.—BYRON, LORD, 1813, *Journals, Dec.* 6.

I first met with this most original and most careless writer at Greenock, in the summer of 1804. . . . He was dressed in a frock coat and new top-boots; and it being then the fashion to wear the shirt collars as high as the eyes, Galt wore his the whole of that night with the one side considerably above his ear, and the other flapped over the collar of his frock-coat down to his shoulder. He had another peculiarity, which appeared to me a singular instance of perversity. He walked with his spectacles on, and conversed with them on; but when he read he took them off. In short, from his first appearance, one would scarcely have guessed him to be a man of genius.—HOGG, JAMES, 1832? *Autobiography.*

Galt seemed to me to be by nature a

male Scherazaide. He had the gift of narrative, so rare, so fine, so seemingly simple, but so inexplicably difficult; repartee is nothing to it: the power of relating a story, without affectation, or weariness to your listener, is one above all price. . . . The last time I saw him he called upon me alone. He came, even in his low and feeble state, and got out of the cab which brought him, and entered the house leaning upon the arm of my servant. He could scarcely walk. When seated, Galt retained little appearance of disease. His complexion was clear, his articulation was then restored, his eyes sparkled; it was when he arose and walked that one saw that the axe had been laid to the root of the tree.—THOMSON, KATHERINE, 1854, *Recollections of Literary Characters and Celebrated Places, vol.* II, *pp.* 103, 112.

Galt, with his curious, limited, but very remarkable talent, had always a serious purpose before him, and worked soberly for such modest fame as might be procurable, and the more substantial reward which helped him forward through the mingled course of his career—a little reputation which often helped him, and money which was of still greater use.—OLIPHANT, MARGARET O. W., 1897, *William Blackwood and His Sons, vol.* I, *p.*446.

Galt remains in obscurity. And yet it is easy to understand how his qualities have failed of recognition. For though his character was in the ordinary sense of the word exemplary, his genius extraordinary, yet in either there was something lacking. Indeed the study of his life and works reveals almost as much to be blamed as to be praised.—DOUGLAS, SIR GEORGE, 1897, *The Blackwood Group* (*Famous Scots Series*), *p.* 47.

GENERAL

My dear Hodgson,—There is a book entituled "Galt," his Travels in ye Archipelago," daintily printed by Cadell and Davies, ye which I could desiderate might be criticised by you, inasmuch as ye author is a well-respected esquire of mine acquaintance, but I fear will meet with little mercy as a writer, unless a friend passeth judgment. Truth to say, ye boke is ye boke of a cock-brained man, and is full of devices crude and conceitede, but peradventure for my sake this grace may be vouchsafed unto him. Review him myself I can not, will not, and if you are likewize hard of heart, woe unto ye boke, ye which is a comely quarto.—BYRON, LORD, 1812, *Letters, ed. Henley, February* 21.

There are pages in the "Annals" and spots in the "Legatees" which would be shining places in the "Pirate." If he be a young author he may scatter his wild oats about; but if he be anything like a veteran, he should husband his resources and make not more than one great effort per annum.—CROKER, J. W., 1821, *Letter to Blackwood; William Blackwood and His Sons, ed. Oliphant, vol.* I, *p.* 475.

Pray read or have read to you by Mrs. Agnes, the "Annals of the Parish." Mr. Galt wrote the worst tragedies ever seen, and has now written a most excellent novel, if it can be called so.—SCOTT, SIR WALTER, 1821, *Letter to Joanna Baillie, June* 11: *Life by Lockhart, ch.* lii.

The great charm of the work ["Annals of the Parish"] is in the traits of character which it discloses, and the commendable brevity with which the whole chronicle is digested. We know scarcely any instance in which a modern writer has shown such forbearance and consideration for his readers. With very considerable powers of humour, the ludicrous incidents are never dwelt upon with any tediousness, nor pushed to the length of burlesque or caricature—and the more seducing touches of pathos with which the work abounds, are intermingled and cut short, with the same sparing and judicious hand. . . . Though the conception of the "Ayrshire Legatees," however, is not new, the execution and details must be allowed to be original; and, along with a good deal of *twaddle*, and too much vulgarity, certainly display very considerable powers both of humour, invention, and acute observation. . . . "The Steam-Boat," which has really no merit at all; and should never have been transplanted from the Magazine in which we are informed it first made its appearance. With the exception of some trash about the Coronation, which nobody of course could ever look at three months after the thing itself was over, it consists of a series of vulgar stories, with little either of probability or originality to recommend them. The attempt at a parallel or paraphrase on the story of Jeanie Deans, is, without any exception, the boldest and the most unsuccessful speculation we have ever seen in literary adventure. —JEFFREY, FRANCIS LORD, 1823–44, *Secondary Scotch Novels, Contributions to the Edinburgh Review, vol.* III, *pp.* 502, 510, 517.

Read "Lawrie Todd" by Galt. It is excellent; no surprising events, or very striking characters, but the humorous and entertaining parts of common life brought forward in a tenor of probable circumstances.—SMITH, SYDNEY, 1829, *To Sir George Philips; Memoir by Lady Holland.*

North.—Mr. Galt is a man of genius, and some of his happiest productions will live in the literature of his country. His humour is rich, rare, and racy, and peculiar withal, entitling him to the character of originality—a charm that never fadeth away—he has great power in the humble, the homely pathetic—and he is conversant, not only with many modes and manners of life, but with much of its hidden and more mysterious spirit.—WILSON, JOHN, 1830, *Noctes Ambrosianæ, Nov.*

Is rather a murder ["Life of Byron"] and the crime is perpetrated with a coarse weapon.—LOCKHART, JOHN GIBSON, 1831, *To Milman, Sept.* 12; *Life and Letters, ed. Lang, vol.* II, *p.* 96.

He has no classic predilections, and sets up no favourite author as a model; he aims at no studied elegance of phrase, cares nothing for formal accuracy of costume, seems not at all solicitous about the dignity of human nature, and thinks chivalry a joke. He leaves all these matters to take care of themselves, and sets to work to read us a chapter of living life, like one sure of securing listeners. —CUNNINGHAM, ALLAN, 1833, *Biographical and Critical History of the Literature of the Last Fifty Years.*

The "Annals of the Parish," the supposed journal of a quaint, simple-minded Presbyterian pastor, give us a singularly amusing insight into the microscopic details of Scottish life in the lower classes. Galt's primary characteristic is a dry, subdued, quaint humour—a quality very perceptible in the lower orders of Scotland, and which in his works, as in the national character of his countrymen, is often accompanied by a very profound and true sense of the pathetic.—SHAW, THOMAS B., 1847, *Outlines of English Literature, p.* 385.

The sphere within which Galt's genius works most smoothly and profitably is a comparatively limited one. There never was a book written by mortal man which spoke so plainly of unwearied labour, of unremitting care, of painstaking conscientiousness, as "The Omen." Yet, despite the scrupulously chosen diction and the deliberately-calculated effects, "The Omen" is, upon the whole, a failure; a highly respectable bit of work, no doubt, but one in which there is much effort and little achievement; much cry and scarce sixpenn'orth of wool. The same may be said of almost all the passages in his best works where, so to speak, he goes beyond the instructions of Nature. Neither the burning of the ship in "The Last of the Lairds" nor the shipwreck in "The Entail," produces any impression proportionate to the pains lavished on it, or worthy to be named in the same breath with that produced by the memorable Windy Yule in "The Provost." . . . The creator of Mrs. Mailsetter and of Mrs. Heukbane, of the Mucklebackits, and of John Girder, can assuredly never be surpassed by anyone in the representation of Scottish life and character.—MILLAR, J. H., 1895, *The Novels of John Galt, The New Review, vol.* 13, *pp.* 209, 214.

His literary production was vast and totally uncritical; his poems, dramas, etc., being admittedly worthless, his miscellaneous writing mostly book-making, while his historical novels are given up by all but devotees. He had, however, a special walk—the delineation of the small humours and ways of his native town and country—in which, if not exactly supreme, he has seldom been equalled. The "Ayrshire Legatees" is in main scheme a pretty direct and not very brilliant following of "Humphrey Clinker;" but the letters of the worthy family who visit London are read in a home circle which shows Galt's peculiar talent. It is shown better still in his next published work, the "Annals of the Parish" which is said to have been written long before, and in the pre-Waverly days to have been rejected by the publishers, because "Scotch novels could not pay." —SAINTSBURY, GEORGE, 1896, *A History of Nineteenth Century Literature, p.* 140.

In describing the unromantic detail of provincial or parish life, Galt is hardly inferior to Scott, but the province or the parish is his exclusive dominion; while in the back ground of Scott's most vivid pictures of the country-side we are aware of the moving pageant of national life.—HERFORD, C. H., 1897, *The Age of Wordsworth, p.* 124.

His works were the first of their kind, and have been the model of all those successive works—always curiously popular in England as well as in Scotland, for it is difficult to tell what reason—which have expounded so often, and notably in our own day, the life from within of the Scottish peasant, with its humours and sagacities and roughnesses. We do not compare any of the recent exponents of the native farmer, clodhopper, or shepherd, from his own point of view, with Scott: but we do compare them with Galt, although with reservations, seeing that he is their originator and the chief of their tribe. It was not, however, the Scottish peasant with whom he was chiefly concerned. It was with the middle class, the smaller order of lairds, the rural clergy, the country writers and civic dignitaries, most of them with certain pretentions to gentility, but all with those views—original by force of their extreme limitation, and the quaint incomprehension which mingled with their native judgment—with which an intelligence trained in a village looks out upon the bigger world.—OLIPHANT, MARGARET O. W., 1897, *William Blackwood and his Sons, vol.* I, *p.* 446.

In 1820, Mr. Blackwood accepted "The Ayrshire Legatees" for his magazine, and this book proved to be Galt's first real literary success. Perhaps it is also the first deliberate attempt in our literature to delineate, for their own sake, contemporary Scottish manners and character. It will be seen that the mechanism of the story, though of the simplest, is well contrived for supplying to these the necessary relief. . . . Few writers have possessed a greater native gift of story-telling than Galt, and few, it must, alas! be added, have used their gift more carelessly. In the very slightest of his numberless tales, traces of this gift are apt to appear, and perhaps in none of his writings is it seen to greater advantage than in the incidental reminiscences of "The Provost." But, in fact, this little book possesses the merit, so rare among our author's writings, of perfection as an artistic whole. . . . It is not enough to say, as has been said, that in him there were two men, the man of letters and the man of affairs: there were two literary men in him, the creative artist and the book-maker. And the fact that, of these two, the latter had things too much his own way was due to Galt's defective appreciation of his high calling. . . . "The Provost" and "The Annals" might almost belong to the age of Tourguenieff and Mr. Henry James, and in this respect his works have been more studied than they have been praised, their influence has been greater than their reputation. —DOUGLAS, SIR GEORGE, 1897, *The Blackwood Group* (*Famous Scots Series*).

James Smith

1775–1839

James Smith (born 1775, died 1839), and Horace (born 1779, died 1849), sons of Robert Smith, solicitor to the Board of Ordnance, are chiefly to be remembered for their joint-work, "Rejected Addresses," which appeared in 1812. They were suggested by the management of Drury Lane offering a prize of £20 for an address to be spoken on the re-opening of the theatre, and consisted of some wonderful parodies of the chief poets of the day. Scott said of his, "I must have done this myself, but I can't remember when." Their earliest literary efforts appeared in the *Pic-Nic* newspaper (1802), and *Mirror* (1807–10). James had followed in the footsteps of his father as a solicitor, receiving the latter's business and official appointment. Horace, who joined the Stock Exchange, wrote some twenty novels, among them being "Gaieties and Gravities," "Brambletye House," "Reuben Apsley," "Zillah," and "Heads and Tails," perhaps his best (1836).—SANDERS, LLOYD C., *ed.*, 1887, *Celebrities of the Century, p.* 934.

PERSONAL

A pleasant, twaddling, pun-making, epigram-manufacturing, extempore-grinding, and painstaking elderly joker. He made one hit, and that was a good one; on the strength of which he has lived ever since, as indeed he deserved to live. We cannot recollect that he wrote anything in the book line except his contributions to the "Rejected Addresses," unless he had a hand in such stuff as "Jokeby," or "Horace in London." His magazine papers in the *New Monthly* were rather monotonous; and his continually quoting of them for years afterwards has contributed in a great measure towards getting him, so generally as he is, considered to be a bore. But let him have his praise. His single talent was a *good* talent, and there is no reason why he should wrap it up in a napkin. We have already alluded to the universal diffusion of his name among us English folk, and its trite and ordinary sound in our ears. It is perhaps more congruous on that account with the station which he has chosen to hold in our literature. His place there is of the Smiths, Smithish.—MAGINN, WILLIAM, 1834, *James Smith, Fraser's Magazine, vol.* 10, *p.* 538.

A fair, stout, fresh-coloured man, with round features, . . . he used to read us trim verses, with rhymes as pat as butter.—HUNT, LEIGH, 1850, *Autobiography, ch.* x.

James Smith, was very different from his brother Horace in all the qualities and attributes of his mind and intellectual character, with the exception of his lively wit, amiable and popular manners, and singularly gentlemanly bearing and personal appearance. In this latter respect James Smith was all his life a model; and this, although he had been bred and brought up in the city, and passed nearly the whole of his life there. I have never seen a man on whom was more legibly and eloquently written that comprehensive title, "Gentleman." . . . James Smith, though certainly not possessing a larger amount of wit and humour than his brother Horace, was essentially and emphatically "a wit"—in the old-fashioned sense of the age of Anne and her immediate successor. Had he lived in those days, he would have been among the favourite *habitués* of Button's and Wills's, and would have manfully asserted and maintained his station among the best of that brilliant day. As it was—though, like his brother, associating with the highest and most cultivated spirits of the day in which he lived, and fully qualified to take a distinguished place among them—unlike that gentle and genial spirit, he preferred those lower and more limited circles in which his intellectual pretensions were paramount and his supremacy undisputed: he preferred the green-rooms of Covent Garden and Drury Lane to Holland House; and so anxious and determined was he to succeed in establishing the social reputation at which he aimed in both these circles, that I'm afraid there is little doubt of his having made it no unimportant part of the business of his life to manufacture beforehand the appliances and means proper to his success; so that you could never be sure of any one of his droll anecdotes, lively sallies, bitter jests, or biting repartees, that it was not *fait à loisir.*—PATMORE, P. G., 1854, *My Friends and Acquaintance, vol.* II, *pp.* 239, 241.

The nervous terror which I experienced when singing or playing before my mother was carried to a climax when I was occasionally called upon to accompany the vocal performances of our friendly acquaintance, James Smith (one of the authors of the "Rejected Addresses"). He was famous for his humorous songs and his own capital rendering of them, but the anguish I endured in accompanying him made those comical performances of his absolutely tragical to me; the more so that he had a lion-like cast of countenance, with square jaws and rather staring eyes. But perhaps he appeared so stern-visaged only to me; while he sang everybody laughed, but I perspired coldly and felt ready to cry, and so have but a lugubrious impression of some of the most amusing productions of that description, heard to the very best advantage (if I could have listened to them at all) as executed by their author.—KEMBLE, FRANCES ANN, 1879, *Records of a Girlhood, p.* 86.

GENERAL

A conversational wit of high rank, and beyond comparison the best epigrammatist of the day. . . . His reputation may well rest upon the "Rejected Addresses," of which he contributed the larger portion; a series of poems, &c., which, as a fellow-traveller once gravely informed him, did not appear so *very bad*—he did not think that they ought *all* to have been rejected!—BARHAM, R. H. DALTON, 1848, *The Life and Remains of Theodore Edward Hook, pp.* 162, 163.

Spencer and Praed were not more felicitous in their poetry of fashion than James Smith. The topics show the man and his associations, and his poems are so many finished daguerreotypes of London society in the first half of the nineteenth century. In this light they will always be interesting and amusing—and may be admitted into collections of British poetry, from which similar sketches by Swift and Prior, of a grosser period, aught to be excluded. —SARGENT, EPES, 1871, *Rejected Addresses and Other Poems by James Smith and Horace Smith, Preface, p.* iii.

The best of the thing was that there was no gall in the ink of which the happy parodists made use; their satire was of such genial character that it "procured for the authors,"—as they boasted,—"the acquaintance, and conciliated the good-will of those whom they had the most audaciously burlesqued." Sir Walter Scott said to one of them that he certainly must have written himself the piece that bears his initials, "though he forgot on what occasion;" William Spencer, when warned by Lydia White, a notorious feeder of London lions, that he would meet at her table "one of those men who made that shameful attack," replied that this "was the very man upon earth he should like to know;" and Lord Byron wrote to Murray from Italy, "Tell him we forgive him, were he twenty times our satirist,"—adding that the Imitations were "the best things after the 'Rolliad.'" Indeed, the only people offended or discontented were, as Mr. Hayward says, those who were left out! Few books are better known, even at the present day, than this of which I have been speaking; and I should not have felt it necessary to say so much about it, if I had not learnt by experience that, *in re literariâ* at least, it is more satisfactory to assume the ignorance than the knowledge of one's readers. The book, indeed, has more than one point of attraction. Collectors prize it for the exquisite woodcut illustrations by George Cruikshank which are to be found in the later editions; lovers of wit and humour for the truly attic salt wherewith it is savoured; while all that know it will readily endorse the opinion of Jeffrey, who says, "I take the 'Rejected Addresses' to be the very best imitations, and often of difficult originals, that ever were made."—BATES, WILLIAM, 1874–98, *The Maclise Portrait Gallery of Illustrious Literary Characters, p.* 279.

The honours of the authorship were pretty fairly divided between James and Horace. The parodies on Wordsworth, Crabbe, Southey, and Coleridge, and the first stanza of the parody on Byron, were contributed by James. He was especially happy in burlesquing Wordsworth and Crabbe. . . . James Smith wrote a number of verses, which were collected after his death by his brother, but he is only remembered for his parodies.—WHYTE, WALTER, 1894, *The Poets and the Poetry of the Century, Humour, Society, Parody and Occasional Verse, ed. Miles, pp.* 102, 103.

James Smith's contributions to these famous parodies were perhaps the best, though not the most numerous, but he appeared contented with the celebrity they had brought him, and never again produced anything considerable. Universally known, and everywhere socially acceptable, "he wanted," says his brother, "all motive for further and more serious exertion." . . . He also produced much comic verse and prose for periodicals, not generally of a very high order, but occasionally including an epigram turned with point and neatness. His reputation rather rested upon his character as a wit and diner-out; most of the excellent things attributed to him, however, were, in the opinion of his biographer in the "Law Magazine," *impromptus faits à loisir.*—GARNETT, RICHARD, 1898, *Dictionary of National Biography, vol.* LIII, *p.* 58.

Thomas Haynes Bayly

1797–1839

Thomas Haynes Bayly, song-writer, was born at Bath, October 13, 1797, and was trained for the church at Winchester and St. Mary Hall, Oxford. In 1824, however, he settled in London; and his "I'd be a Butterfly" was quickly followed by "The Soldier's Tear," "We met—'twas in a Crowd," "She wore a Wreath of Roses,"Oh, *no,* we never mention her," &c. He also wrote a novel, several volumes of verse, some tales, and thirty-six dramatic pieces. In his last years afflicted by sickness and loss of fortune, he died April 22, 1839.—PATRICK AND GROOME, *eds.*, 1897, *Chambers's Biographical Dictionary*, p. 76.

PERSONAL

He was a thorough gentleman, of handsome person and refined manners. His talent did not approach genius, but he hit the popular taste, and his verses, wedded to simple music, long delighted ears not over-fastidious. . . . He is one of the numerous worthies whose names are intimately associated with Bath; for, in addition to his having been born there, all, or nearly all, his most popular songs were written in that pleasant city.—HALL, SAMUEL CARTER, 1883, *Retrospect of a Long Life*, p. 408.

Mr. T. H. Bayly was a dandy, who wore white kid gloves in the day time. He was a gentleman; had been a man of fortune; but I suspect that like Dogberry, he had had losses.—SALA, GEORGE AUGUSTUS, 1894, *Things I have Seen and People I have Known*, vol. II, p. 150.

GENERAL

An English critic supposes that he is indebted for much of his popularity to his former position in society; but the estimation in which his compositions are held in this country, where his personal history was unknown, shows the opinion to be erroneous. It is not always easy to discover the true causes of an author's success. Bayly was certainly not one of the first poets of his time—the century in which more true and enduring poetry was written than in any other since the invention of letters; and if he had essayed any thing of a more ambitious character than the simple ballad, doubtless he would have failed; but by her who dallies with a coronet and the maiden at her spinning-wheel, by the soldier, the student, and the cottage Damon, his melodies are sung with equal feeling and admiration. Many have written "songs," exquisitely beautiful as poems, which are never sung; and others, like Dibdin, have produced songs for particular classes; but Bayly touches the universal heart. He is never mawkish, never obscure, and rarely meretricious; his verse is singularly harmonious; every word seems chosen for its musical sound; and his modulation is unsurpassed. Our rough English flows from his pen as smoothly as the soft Italian from that of Bojardo or Metastasio.—GRISWOLD, RUFUS W., 1844, *The Poets and Poetry of England in the Nineteenth Century*, p. 312.

He possessed a playful fancy, a practised ear, a refined taste, and a sentiment which ranged pleasantly from the fanciful to the pathetic, without, however, strictly attaining either the highly imaginative or the deeply passionate.—MOIR, D. M., 1851-52, *Sketches of the Poetical Literature of the Past Half-Century*, p. 289.

He is now mostly known for his exquisite songs, which for sweetness and elegance are second only—if they are second—to those of Burns and Moore; showing the playful fancy, the practised ear, and the refined taste of the author. They are simple, natural and graceful, and tender—descriptive of the feelings of all, in a language which all can appreciate and understand. It is doubtful if any songs in the English language ever attained the popularity of "Oh no, we never mention her!" "I'd be a Butterfly," and the "Soldier's Tear." Other of his songs, as "Why don't the Men propose?" and "My married Daughter could you see," show a different kind of power—that the author possessed that knowledge of human nature, and those powers of keen and delicate satire, which can lay bare the secret workings of the heart of a vain daughter or of a silly mother for the amusement of the world. —CLEVELAND, CHARLES D., 1853, *English Literature of the Nineteenth Century*, p. 369.

There is no lofty strain in any of Bayly's productions, but in nearly all there is lightness and ease in expression, which fully account for their continued popularity.—SMITH, G. BARNETT, 1885, *Dictionary of National Biography*, vol. III, p. 452.

If to be sung everywhere, to hear your verses uttered in harmony with all pianos and quoted by the world at large, be fame, Bayly had it. He was an unaffected poet. He wrote words to airs, and he is almost absolutely forgotten. To read him is to be carried back on the wings of music to the bowers of youth; and to the bowers of youth I have been wafted, and to the old booksellers. You do not find on every stall the poems of Bayly; but a copy in two volumes has been discovered, edited by Mr. Bayly's widow (Bentley, 1844). They saw the light in the same year as the present critic, and perhaps they ceased to be very popular before he was breeched. . . . Of his poems the inevitable criticism must be that he was a Tom Moore of much lower accomplishments. His business was to carol of the most vapid and obvious sentiment, and to string flowers, fruits, trees, breeze, sorrow, to-morrow, knights, coal-black steeds, regret, deception, and so forth, into fervid anapæstics. Perhaps his success lay in knowing exactly how little sense in poetry composers will endure and singers will accept. . . . How does Bayly manage it? What is the trick of it, the obvious, simple, meretricious trick, which somehow, after all, let us mock as we will, Bayly could do, and we cannot? He really had a slim, serviceable, smirking, and sighing little talent of his own; and—well, we have not even that. Nobody forgets

"The lady I love will soon be a bride."

Nobody remembers our cultivated epics and esoteric sonnets, oh brother minor poet, *mon semblable, mon frère!* . . . The moral of all this is that minor poetry has its fashions, and that the butterfly Bayly could versify very successfully in the fashion of a time simpler and less pedantic than our own. On the whole, minor poetry for minor poetry, this artless singer, piping his native drawing-room notes, gave a great deal of perfectly harmless, if highly uncultivated, enjoyment.—LANG, ANDREW, 1891, *Essays in Little, pp.* 36, 42, 46, 47.

It was as a song writer that Bayly attained his greatest success, and some of his songs, partly on their own account, and partly from the felicity of their setting at the hands of musical composers, and of their popularity with vocalists, have been among the most sung songs of the century. . . . His songs and *vers de société* are, however, the more characteristic productions of the Butterfly bard.—MILES, ALFRED H., 1894, *The Poets and the Poetry of the Century, Humour, Society, Parody and Occasional Verse, pp.* 242, 243.

Archibald Alison

1757–1839

Archibald Alison, born at Edinburgh in 1757, studied at Glasgow University and Balliol College, Oxford; was ordained in 1784; from 1800 to 1831 was an Episcopal minister in Edinburgh; and died 17th May 1839. His "Essays on the Nature and Principles of Taste" (1790) advocate the "association" theory of the sublime and beautiful, and are written much in the style of Blair, as are also his "Sermons" (1814–15). —PATRICK AND GROOME, *eds.*, 1897, *Chambers's Biographical Dictionary, p.* 24.

PERSONAL

I am quite taken with his conversation: he appears to me to possess a fund of diversified and miscellaneous information, and to have gradually formed the acquisition not only with the vigour of an original and reflecting mind, but with the temper of a mind happily harmonised and free from all the shackles of theory as well as of prejudice. This information is likewise communicated not only with the most unaffected ease, and with an air of perfect liberality and candour, but with a mixed sensibility and pleasantry which I have seldom seen so well blended together.—HORNER, FRANCIS, 1801, *Memoirs and Correspondence, vol.* I, *p.* 154.

It is long since I was at Edinburgh, and when I was there nothing of importance was a-doing. I heard Alison preach. His elocution is clear—his style elegant—his ideas distinct rather than profound. Some person contrasting him and Chalmers, observed that the Prebendary of Sarum is like a glass of spruce beer,—pure, refreshing, and unsubstantial—the minister of the Tron Kirk, like a draught of Johnnie Dowie's ale,—muddy, thick, and spirit-stirring.—CARLYLE, THOMAS, 1817, *Early Letters, ed. by Charles Eliot Norton, p.* 62.

To me he appears the best preacher I have ever heard.—EDGEWORTH, MARIA, 1823, *Letters, vol.* II, *p.* 101.

My earliest recollections of domestic life are those of the solitude and seclusion of an English parsonage-house. Though visited occasionally by the great, often by the learned, the greater part of our life, even in summer, and the whole winter, was spent alone. A devoted worshipper of Nature, my father was firmly impressed with the conviction, so conspicuous in his writings, that the best feelings of the heart are to be drawn from her influences, and the purest enjoyments of life from her contemplation. He studied her works incessantly. The migration of birds, the changes of the seasons, the progress of vegetation, were the subjects of constant observation, and by keeping an accurate daily register, not only of the weather, but of the blooming of flowers and the changes of vegetation, he maintained a constant interest by comparing the progress of one season with another. Botany, zoology, and ornithology were in his hands not mere unmeaning sciences containing an artificial classification of objects and a dry catalogue of names, but a key to the secret interests of Nature, and commentaries on the wisdom and beneficence of its Author. White's "Natural History of Selborne" was the subject of his study and the object of his imitation. We all grew up with the same habits, and indelibly received the same impressions.—ALISON, SIR ARCHIBALD, 1867? *Some Account of My Life and Writings, vol.* I, *p.* 10.

GENERAL

He has never received fame enough for a book ["Principles of Taste"] which, with many faults, contains many beautiful thoughts and many charms in the writing. —HORNER, FRANCIS, 1805, *Memoirs and Correspondence, vol.* I, *p.* 345.

The style of these "Sermons" is something new, we think, in the literature of this country. It is more uniformly elevated, more profusely figured—and, above all, more curiously modulated, and balanced upon a more exact and delicate rhythm, than any English composition in mere prose with which we are acquainted. In these, as well as in some more substantial characteristics, it reminds us more of the beautiful moral harangues that occur in the Telemaque of Fenelon, or of the celebrated Oraisons funebres of Bossuet, than of any thing of British growth and manufacture:—Nor do we hesitate at all to set Mr. Alison fairly down by the side of the last named of those illustrious Prelates. He is less lofty perhaps; but more tender and more varied—less splendid, but less theatrical—and, with fewer striking reflections on particular occurrences, has unquestionably more of the broad light of philosophy, and the milder glow of religion. In polish and dignity we do not think him at all inferior—though he has not the advantage of enhancing the simple majesty of Christianity by appeals to listening monarchs, and apostrophes to departed princes.—JEFFREY, FRANCIS LORD, 1814, *Alison's Sermons, Edinburgh Review, vol.* 23, *p.* 424.

Alison denied that there is any intrinsic pleasure either in sound, in colour, or in form. He resolved the emotions of sublimity and beauty into associations with primitive sensibilities. The "Essay" is written in a very readable style for a work of abstruse analysis.—MINTO, WILLIAM, 1872–80, *Manual of English Prose Literature, p.* 515.

The arrangement and manner of the work ["Principles of Taste"] are admirable. The style is distinguished by infinite grace, and is worthy of being compared to that of Addison:—indeed I am not sure if we have a more beautiful specimen of the last-century manner of composition, moulded on the "Spectator," on the French classics, and the wits of Queen Anne. Every word is appropriate, and is in its appropriate place; and the sentences glide along like a silvery stream. The descriptions of natural scenery, which are very numerous, are singularly felicitous and graceful: that word *graceful* ever comes up when we would describe his manner. He does not seem to have had an equal opportunity of studying beauty in the fine arts, in architecture, statuary, and painting, though the allusions to the universally known models of these are always appreciative and discriminating. —MCCOSH, JAMES, 1874, *The Scottish Philosophy, p.* 308.

Justly admired ["Sermons"] for the elegance and beauty of their language, and their gentle, persuasive inculcation of Christian duty. On points of doctrine and controversy the author is wholly silent: his writings, as one of his critics remarked, were designed for those who "want to be roused to a sense of the beauty and the good that exist in the universe around them, and who are only indifferent to the feelings of their fellow-creatures and negligent of the duties they impose, for want of some persuasive monitor to awake the dormant capacities of their nature, and to make them see and feel the delights which providence has attached to their exercise."—CHAMBERS, ROBERT, 1876, *Cyclopædia of English Literature, ed. Carruthers.*

The Association school produced as its characteristic æsthetics Alison's "Essays on the Principles of Taste," which had the fatal defect of satisfying Francis Jeffrey.—HERFORD, C. H., 1897, *The Age of Wordsworth, p.* 4.

Frances Burney

Madame D'Arblay

1752-1840

Frances Burney [Madame D'Arblay], 1752-1840. Born, at King's Lynn, 13 June 1752. Family removed to London, 1760. Mother died, 1761. Father married again, 1766. No regular education. Began early to write stories, plays, poems, etc. First novel published anonymously, Jan. 1778. Intimacy with Mrs. Thrale, Dr. Johnson, Sheridan, Burke, etc. Appointed Second Keeper of Robes to Queen, 17 July 1786. Bad health; retired, 7 July 1791, with pension of £100 a year. Travelled in England. Made acquaintance of Gen. D'Arblay at Mickleham, where her sister lived. Married to him, 31 July 1793. Settled at Bookham, near Norbury. Tragedy, "Edwy and Elvina," performed at Drury Lane, 21 March 1795; withdrawn after first night. Built a cottage at West Humble, near Mickleham; removed there, 1797. Comedy, "Love and Fashion," accepted for Covent Garden, but withdrawn before performance, 1800. Husband went to seek employment in France, 1801. In Paris with him, 1802-05; at Passy, 1805-14. Visit to England with son, Aug. 1812. In Paris, 1814-15. In Belgium, March to July, 1815. Returned to England, Oct. 1815. At Bath, Feb. 1816 to June 1817; at Ilfracombe, June to Oct., 1817; at Bath, Oct. 1817 to Sept. 1818. Husband died, 3 May 1818. To London, Oct. 1818. Son died, 19 Jan. 1837. Severe illness, 1839. Died, in London, 6 Jan. 1840. *Works:* "Evelina" (anon.), 1778; "Cecilia" (anon.), 1782; "Brief Reflections relative to the French Emigrant Clergy" (anon.), 1793; "Camilla," 1796; "The Wanderer," 1814; "Memoirs of Dr. Burney," 1832. *Posthumous:* "Diary and Letters" (7 vols.), 1842-46. —SHARP, R. FARQUHARSON, 1897, *A Dictionary of English Authors, p.* 41.

PERSONAL

Mrs. Byron, who really loves me, was disgusted at Miss Burney's carriage to me, who have been such a friend and benefactress to her: not an article of dress, not a ticket for publio places, not a thing in the world that she could not command from me: yet always insolent, always pining for home, always preferring the mode of life in St. Martin's Street to all I could do for her. She is a saucy-spirited little puss, to be sure, but I love her dearly for all that; and I fancy she has a real regard for me, if she did not think it beneath the dignity of a wit, or of what she values more,—the dignity of Dr. Burney's daughter,—to indulge it. Such dignity! the Lady Louisa of Leicester Square! In good time!—THRALE, HESTER LYNCH (MRS. PIOZZI), 1780, *Thraliana, July* 1; *Autobiography, Letters and Literary Remains, ed. Hayward, p.* 485.

There are few—I believe I may say fairly there are none at all—that will not find themselves better informed concerning human nature, and their stock of observation enriched, by reading your "Cecilia." . . . I might trespass upon your delicacy if I should fill my letter to you with what I fill my conversation to others; I should be troublesome to you alone if I should tell you all I feel and think on the natural vein of humour, the tender pathetic, the comprehensive and noble moral and the sagacious observation, that appear quite throughout this extraordinary performance. . . . In an age distinguished by producing extraordinary women, I hardly dare to tell where my opinion would place you amongst them. —BURKE, EDMUND, 1782, *Letter to Miss Burney, July* 29.

Next to the balloon [on exhibition in the Pantheon] Miss Burney is the object of public curiosity; I had the pleasure of meeting her yesterday. She is a very unaffected, modest, sweet, and pleasing young lady: but you, now I think of it, are a Gothe, and have not read "Cecilia." Read, read it, for shame!—BARBAULD, ANNA LÆTITIA, 1784, *Letter to her Brother, Jan.* 2; *Memoir by Ellis, vol.* I, *p,* 115.

At last Madame D'Arblay arrived. I was very glad to see her again. She is wonderfully improved in good looks in ten years, which have usually a very different effect at an age when people begin to fall off. Her face has acquired expression and a charm which it never had before. She has gained an *embompoint* very advantageous to her face. We did not talk much about France; but with her intelligence there was a great deal she could tell, and much she could not, having a husband and a French establishment, to which she was to return after the winter.—BERRY, MARY, 1812, *Journals, Nov.* 10; *Extracts of the Journals and Correspondence, vol.* II, *p.* 508.

Was introduced by Rogers to Mad. D'Arblay, the celebrated authoress of "Evelina" and "Cecilia"—an elderly lady, with no remains of personal beauty, but with a simple and gentle manner, a pleasing expression of countenance, and apparently quick feelings. She told me she had wished to see two persons—myself, of course, being one, the other George Canning. This was really a compliment to be pleased with—a nice little handsome pat of butter, made up by a "neat-handed Phillis" of a dairy-maid, instead of the grease, fit only for cart-wheels, which one is dosed with by the pound. Mad. D'Arblay told us that the common story of Dr. Burney, her father, having brought home her own first work, and recommended it to her perusal, was erroneous. Her father was in the secret of "Evelina" being printed. But the following circumstance may have given rise to the story:—Dr. Burney was at Streatham soon after the publication, where he found Mrs. Thrale recovering from her confinement, low at the moment, and out of spirits. While they were talking together, Johnson, who sat beside in a kind of reverie, suddenly broke out, "You should read this new work, madam—you should read 'Evelina;' every one says it is excellent, and they are right." The delighted father obtained a commission from Mrs. Thrale to purchase his daughter's work and retired the happiest of men. Madame D'Arblay said she was wild with joy at this decisive evidence of her literary success, and that she could only give vent to her rapture by dancing and skipping round a mulberry-tree in the garden. She was very young at this time.—SCOTT, SIR WALTER, 1826, *Journal, Nov.* 18; *Life by Lockhart, ch.* lxxii.

The Queen was persuaded to appoint Miss Burney, Mrs. Delany and Mr. Smelt having deceived themselves into believing her capable of adapting herself to her place, and of performing her new duties satisfactorily; their earnest desire to insure Miss Burney a certain salary instead of the precarious income arising from her works, having blinded their better judgment. Miss Burney was elated to such a degree by the appointment that she gradually lost all consciousness of her actual or relative position. She lived in an ideal world of which she was, in her own imagination, the centre. She believed herself possessed of a spell which fascinated all those she approached. She became convinced that all the equerries were in love with her, although she was continually the object of their ridicule, as they discovered her weaknesses and played upon her credulity for their own amusement. Many entertaining anecdotes might be collected of the ludicrous effect produced by Miss Burney's far-fetched expressions when she desired to be especially eloquent, and *particularly courtly.*—LLANOVER, LADY, 1862, *ed., The Autobiography and Correspondence of Mary Granville, Mrs. Delany, Second Series, vol.* III, *p.* 361.

I attended her during the last twenty years of her long life. . . . She lived in almost total seclusion from all but a few members of her own family; changed her lodgings more frequently than her dresses and occupied herself laboriously in composing those later works which retain so little of the charm of her earlier writings. Mr. Rogers was the only literary man who seemed to know of her existence.—HOLLAND, SIR HENRY, 1871, *Recollections of Past Life, pp.* 204, 205.

For a considerable time the income on which she, her husband, and her child subsisted, did not exceed £125 a year. They were too independent in spirit to accept assistance from friends; too upright to rely on contingencies; and Madame D'Arblay pursued, in all the minutiæ of domestic life, a course of self-denial such as she wrote to her Susanna, "would make you laugh to see, though perhaps cry to hear." With all this, her mind and thoughts were never shut up in her economy. It was at this period that she originated the invitation sent by her and M. D'Arblay to his friend the Comte de Narbonne, to make their cottage his home; and it was also during these straitened circumstances that she withdrew her comedy of "Love and Fashion" from rehersal, in dutiful compliance with the wishes of her father; although the management of Covent Garden had promised her £400 for the manuscript. Queen Charlotte's expression, that she was "true as gold," was abundantly verified in her friendship.—WOOLSEY, SARAH CHAUNCEY, 1880, *ed., Diary and Letters of Frances Burney, Mme. D'Arblay.*

Consider the brilliant and instantaneous success of Frances Burney. Think of the excitement she aroused, and honors heaped thick and fast upon her. A woman of twenty-six when she wrote "Evelina" she was able, by dint of short stature and childish ways, to pass for a girl of seventeen, which increased amazingly the popular interest in her novel. Sheridan swore he could not believe so young a thing could manifest such genius, and begged her to write him a comedy on the spot. Sir Joshua Reynolds professed actual fear of such keen wit and relentless observation. Dr. Johnson vowed that Richardson had written nothing finer, and Fielding nothing so fine as "Evelina," and playfully protested he was too proud to eat cold mutton for dinner when he sat by Miss Burney's side. Posterity, it is true, while preserving "Evelina" with great pride, has declined to place it by the side of "Tom Jones" or "Clarissa Harlowe," but if we had our choice between the praise of posterity which was Miss Austen's portion, and the praise of contemporaries which was Miss Burney's lot, I doubt not we should be wise enough to take our applause off-hand,—"dashed in our faces, sounded in our ears," as Johnson said of Garrick, and leave the future to look after itself.—REPPLIER, AGNES, 1897, *Varia, p.* 208.

The fame of Miss Burney declined pretty rapidly after the publication of her third novel. This did not appear till fourteen years after "Cecilia"—namely, in 1796. But her publishers, from whom she is said to have received a large sum of money for "Camilla," on the strength, it is to be supposed, of her previous reputation, must have burnt their fingers by the venture. It failed to hit the public taste—failed as completely as Miss Burney's subsequent memoirs of her father, and, indeed, as everything else that she subsequently wrote. She seems, in fact, to have been the "*Miss* Betty" of the literary world; and it is as difficult to understand in these days that she could ever have been the admiration of a lettered coterie, as it must have been for the friends of the "Young Roscius'" later years to realise in the person of that stout, middle-aged, respectable gentleman the juvenile prodigy for whom the play-going public had for the time deserted all the great actors of their day.—TRAILL, HENRY DUFF, 1898, *The New Fiction, p.* 154.

EVELINA
1778

This year was ushered in by a grand and most important event! At the latter end of January, the literary world was favored with the first publication of the ingenious, learned, and most profound Fanny Burney! . . . This admirable authoress has named her most elaborate performance, "Evelina; or, a Young Lady's Entrance into the world." Perhaps this may seem a rather bold attempt and title for a female whose knowledge of the world is very confined, and whose inclinations, as well as situation, incline her to a private and domestic life. All I can urge is, that I have only presumed to trace the accidents and adventures to which a "young woman" is liable; I have not pretended to shew the world what it actually *is*, but what it *appears* to a girl of seventeen: and so far as that, surely, any girl who is past seventeen may safely do?—BURNEY, FANNY, 1778, *Early Diary, ed. Ellis, vol.* II, *p.*213.

"Evelina" seems a work that should result from long experience, a deep and intimate knowledge with the world: yet it has been written without either. Miss Burney is a real wonder. What she is, she is intuitively. Dr. Burney told me she had the fewest advantages of any of his daughters, from some peculiar circumstances. And such has been her timidity, that he himself had not any suspicion of her powers. . . . Modesty with her is neither pretense nor decorum; it is an ingredient of her nature; for she who could part with such a work for twenty pounds, could know so little of its worth or of her own, as to leave no possible doubt of her humility.—JOHNSON, SAMUEL, 1778, *On Miss Burney's Evelina.*

The early works of Madame D'Arblay, in spite of the lapse of years, in spite of the change of manners, in spite of the popularity deservedly obtained by some of her rivals, continued to hold a high place in the public esteem. She lived to be a classic. Time set on her fame, before she went hence, that seal which is seldom set except on the fame of the departed. Like Sir Condy Rackrent in the tale, she survived her own wake, and overheard the judgment of posterity.—MACAULAY, THOMAS BABINGTON, 1843, *Madame D'Arblay, Edinburgh Review, Critical and Miscellaneous Essays.*

Now here was a novel which riveted Burke and Sir Joshua; threw Johnson, old, sad, and hypochondriac as he was, into fits of admiration and laughter; made Sheridan dread a rival in the field; and extorted honest compliments from Gibbon, in the full flush of his own reputation. Its phrases became catchwords among the wits and blues; its characters were accepted as real types, and their names affixed to originals in all sorts of societies. The Miss Palmers told Miss Burney, and Miss Reynolds confirmed the story, how Sir Joshua, who began the book one day when he was too much engaged to go on with it, was so much caught that he could think of nothing else, and was quite absent all the day, not knowing a word that was said to him; and when he took it up again, found himself so much interested in it, that he sat up all night to finish it.—LESLIE, CHARLES ROBERT, AND TAYLOR, TOM, 1865, *Life and Times of Sir Joshua Reynolds, vol.* II, *p.* 204.

The publication of "Evelina," in 1778, made a sensation which the merits of the work fully justified. . . . "Evelina" fully deserved the praise and interest which it then obtained and still excites. . . . This novel presents to the reader a variety of social scenes which gives it a value possessed by no other work of fiction of the eighteenth century. No novelist has described so well or so fully the aspect of the theatres, of Vauxhall and Ranelagh, of Bath in the season, of the ridottos and assemblies of the London fashionable world. The shops, the amusements and the manners of the middle classes are made familiar to Evelina by her association with the Brangtons, and add greatly to the breadth of this valuable picture of metropolitan life. With a feminine attention to detail, and a quick perception of salient characteristics, Miss Burney described the world about her so faithfully and picturesquely as to deserve the thanks of every student of social history. . . . In the painting of manners Miss Burney was eminently successful. But she was hardly less so in a point in which excellence could not have been expected in so youthful a writer. The plot of "Evelina" is constructed with a skill worthy of a veteran. Fielding alone, of the eighteenth century novelists, can be said to surpass Miss Burney in this respect. . . . In regard to her sketches of character, it may be objected that Miss Burney lacked breadth of treatment, that she dwelt on one distinctive characteristic at the expense of the others. But still, Lord Orville, though somewhat too much of a model, and Mrs. Selwyn, though somewhat too habitually a wit, are vivid and life-like characters. The Brangtons and Sir Clement Willougby are nature itself, and the girlish nature of Evelina is betrayed in her letters with great felicity.—TUCKERMAN, BAYARD, 1882, *A History of English Prose Fiction, pp.* 251, 252, 253.

She had observed the droll and farcical side of life with great acumen, and the frank laughter which her pages provoked was indescribably welcome after the tear-inspiring episodes of the Sensibility school. It is to be desired that Miss Burney had remained the author of one book. Her "Cecilia" is only read because it is by the creator of "Evelina," and her "Camilla" is never read at all.—GOSSE, EDMUND, 1888, *A History of Eighteenth Century Literature, p.* 361.

Evelina is perhaps rather the principal character of a celebrated story than a great character herself; yet she has in her more of the elements of a great character than her timidity would at first lead us to suppose. She is, when introduced to us, a lovely, but simple and timid girl, well brought up in a retired home; and her good sense and high principle only emerge gradually from a fog of overpowering shyness. . . . The tale is long, and every incident is most minutely described, but it is well worth reading, and if our readers like to ask for it at old bookstalls, they may perhaps obtain it for a modest sum. The characters are broadly drawn; the extremes of fantastic luxury, and of coarse vulgarity, meet in one picture in a way which seems strange to our more educated age, when good manners are the rule in all but the lowest class. But our Evelina moves among them all, simple, right minded, though unwise sometimes from extreme timidity, but coming out safely from many awkward situations by the protecting force of her own inner purity. That which strikes us most in the book is its vivacious style, and the marked contrast between a few refined and delicate-minded women, and the rough practical jokes which were apparently not out of favour in that day even in the highest circles.—MERCIER, MRS. JEROME, 1893, *Great Characters of Fiction, ed. Townsend, pp.* 3, 11.

Miss Burney is no less caustic than Miss Austen; the Holborn beau, Mr. Smith, with his "fine varnish of low politeness," and the two giggling Misses Braughton with their innocently gross confidences and grosser reticences, are as vulgar as anything to be found in the pages of her greater successor. But she is less detached and impersonal,—she cannot smile as Miss Austen smiles over the rabbit-warren of human littlenesses; at times she seems on the point of forgetting that there is nothing tragic in offence given to a peer's sense of propriety—so warmly does she espouse Evelina's grievances. Social miseries, in all their intensity and variety—some of them, by an odd repetition, undergone by herself years later at Windsor—surely never had a more enthusiastic recorder. The tortures Evelina suffers have the vividness of a nightmare; they are not exaggerated in representation, but they are so completely isolated, kept so far from the wash of the larger passions and interests of life, that what might have been a dull discomfort becomes a frightful incubus.—RALEIGH, WALTER, 1894, *The English Novel, p.* 258.

It was the masterly natural freshness of the character-drawing, the clear, unencumbered vivacity of the incidents, the frankness of the humour,—in a word, the originality, the absence of literary artificiality,—that signalized "Evelina" as a work of genius, and set everybody talking about the new writer. Miss Burney was not the first woman novelist, but she was the first with a distinct vein of her own who wrote with her eyes on the subject, and not on any established model of approved style.—MINTO, WILLIAM, 1894, *The Literature of the Georgian Era, ed. Knight, p.* 120.

You should read that story—whatever you may do with "Cecilia" and other later ones—if only to see how good and cleanly a piece of work in the way of society novel can come out of those broiling times, when "Humphrey Clinker" and "Tom Jones" and the prurient and sentimental langours of Richardson were on the toilette tables of the clever and the honest. The book of "Evelina" is, all over, Miss Burney; that gives it the rarest and best sort of realism. Through all her work indeed, we have this over-jubilant and gushing, yet timid and diffident young lady, writing her stories—with all her timidities and large, unspoken hopes, tumbling and twittering in the bosoms of her heroines: if my lady has the fidgets, the fidgets come into her books; and you can always chase back the tremors that smite from time to time the fair Evelina, to the kindred tremors that afflict the clever and sensitive daughter of old Dr. Burney.—MITCHELL, DONALD G., 1895, *English Lands Letters and Kings, Queen Anne and the Georges, p.* 165.

The novel, as we know, was reported, before its author's name was known, to be the work of a girl of seventeen, and perhaps some part of its extraordinary vogue may have been due to this flattering mistake. But the main element in its success must surely, I should think, be sought in the fact that it was the first "novel of manners," in the later sense of the word, that had ever been offered to the public. It was a picture of life in London, life at Bath, life at the Bristol Hot Wells, in the later eighteenth century—principally, indeed, of modish life, but with just so much of a side glance at the gaieties and affectations of the middle class as would give it additional piquancy to the taste of the superiors whom they strove to imitate. . . . No tenderness towards this subject of a hundred-years-old nine-days' wonder ought to induce a candid critic of to-day to conceal his conviction that "Evelina" is a very crude performance.—TRAILL, HENRY DUFF, 1898, *The New Fiction, pp.* 147, 149.

CECILIA
1782

Oh! it beats every other book, even your own other volumes, for "Evelina" was a baby to it. . . . Such a novel! Indeed, I am seriously and sensibly touched by it, and am proud of her friendship who so knows the human heart.—THRALE, HESTER LYNCH, 1782, *Letter to Fanny Burney, Diary and Letters of Fanny Burney.*

I am sure you are acquainted with the novel entitled "Cecilia," much admired for its good sense, variety of character, delicacy of sentiment, etc., etc. There is nothing good, amiable, and agreeable mentioned in the book, that is not possessed by the author of it, Miss Burney. I have now been acquainted with her three years: her *extreme diffidence of herself,* notwithstanding her great genius and the applause she has met with, adds lustre to all her excellences, and all improve on acquaintance.—DELANY, MRS., 1786, *Letter to Mrs. F. Hamilton, July* 3; *Autobiography and Correspondence, ed. Lady Llanover.*

Though the world saw and heard little of Madame D'Arblay during the last forty years of her life, and though that little did not add to her fame, there were thousands, we believe, who felt a singular emotion when they learned that she was no longer among us. The news of her death carried the minds of men back at one leap, clear over two generations, to the time when her first literary triumphs were won. All those whom we had been accustomed to revere as intellectual patriarchs, seemed children when compared with her; for Burke had sat up all night to read her writings, and Johnson had pronounced her superior to Fielding when Rogers was still a school-boy, and Southey still in petticoats. Yet more strange did it seem that we should just have lost one whose name had been widely celebrated before anybody had heard of some illustrious men who, twenty, thirty, or forty years ago, were, after a long and splendid career, borne with honour to the grave. Yet so it was. Frances Burney was at the height of fame and popularity before Cowper had published his first volume, before Porson had gone up to college, before Pitt had taken his seat in the House of Commons, before the voice of Erskine had been once heard in Westminster Hall. Since the appearance of her first work, sixty-two years had passed; and this interval had been crowded, not only with political, but also with intellectual revolutions.—MACAULAY, THOMAS BABINGTON, 1843, *Madame D'Arblay, Edinburgh Review, Critical and Miscellaneous Essays.*

She wrote "Cecilia" because the world told her it was amused by her, and that she could make her fortune by going on amusing it. But even in this second book there were indications that the natural spring was pretty nearly exhausted, while a deterioration of style betrayed the fact that her mastery of the means of literary expression was not sufficient to keep her works up to the mark when the vivacity of the first spontaneous impulse should be spent.—CHRISTIE, MARY ELIZABETH, 1882, *Miss Burney's Novels, Contemporary Review, vol.* 42, *p.* 897.

CAMILLA
1796

How I like "Camilla?" I do not care to say how little. Alas! she has reversed experience, which I have long thought reverses its own utility by coming at the wrong end of our life when we do not want it. This author (Miss Burney) knew the world and penetrated characters before she had stepped over the threshold; and, now she has seen so much of it, she has little or no insight at all: perhaps she apprehended having seen too much, and kept the bags of foul air that she brought from the Caves of Tempests too closely tied.—WALPOLE, HORACE, 1796, *To Miss Hannah More, Aug.* 29; *Letters, ed. Cunningham, vol.* IX, *p.* 470.

Critics have differed about the merits of "Camilla." A small but by no means ill-judging minority prefer it to the author's earlier works. In plot, development of character, and natural pathos it seems to us not inferior to "Evelina" and "Cecilia;" but the style is less easy and flowing, betraying the first symptoms of that falling off which afterwards became so apparent. —CROSLAND, MRS. NEWTON, 1854, *Memorable Women, p.* 153.

The real talent of the authoress shows forth in "Camilla," the least extolled, but certainly the best of her novels. Camilla's character is charming: impulsive, erring, endearing, the old uncle, the spoiled Indiana, the deformed sister, the indulgent pitying father, are perfect. The story is touching and interesting—there are points in it which one can hardly remember without tears; and if we condemn the hard and lofty virtue of the hero, we must admit that it stands in relief to the infirm purpose, and gentle failings of the other characters.—THOMSON, KATHERINE (GRACE WHARTON), 1862, *The Literature of Society, vol.* II, *p.* 260.

THE WANDERER
1814

Betrayed a terrible contrast to her earlier and happier style, and was in every way unworthy of her name.—MOLLOY, FITZGERALD, 1889, *A Fashionable Authoress of the Last Century, Temple Bar, vol.* 85, *p.* 207.

DIARY AND LETTERS

Our conjectures are now too fully verified: the interest is indeed much less than we anticipated, but in all the rest—the diffuseness—the pomposity—the prolixity—the false colouring—the factitious details—and, above all, the personal affectation and vanity of the author, this book exceeds our worst apprehensions. . . . We really have never met anything more curious, nor, if it were not repeated *ad nauseam*, more comical, than the elaborate ingenuity with which—as the ancients used to say that *all roads led to Rome*—every topic, from whatsoever quarter it may start, is ultimately brought home to Miss Burney. . . . The result of all is that we are conscientiously obliged to pronounce these three volumes to be—considering their bulk and pretensions—nearly the most worthless we have ever waded through, and that we do not remember in all our experience to have laid down an unfinished work with less desire for its continuation. That it may not mend as it proceeds, we cannot—where there is such room for improvement—venture to pronounce; and there is thus much to be said for it, that it can hardly grow worse.—CROKER, JOHN WILSON, 1842, *Madame D'Arblay's Diary and Letters, Quarterly Review, vol.* 70, *pp.* 244, 245, 287.

This is believed to be the only published, perhaps the only existing, record of the life of an English girl, written by herself, in a century before that which is now in its wane. Such a portrayal of a young Englishwoman, and her times, would be interesting even if the girl had not been (as was this one) a born author, who lived among men and women more or less distinguished, herself became famous, and was admired by the admired, as well as praised by the common voice; whose brilliant reputation as a novelist was revived, some fifty years ago, by her fresh and still greater renown as a chronicler of English social and court-life, during many and marked years of the long reign of George the Third. The novelist and the chronicler are shown in these still earlier diaries which are now for the first time published, as developing from year to year. Sketches revealing the future "character-monger" alternate here with innocent, tender, and generous thoughts, and feelings of affection to kinsfolk and friends, more than commonly lasting, as well as warm; with traits of a disposition very mobile, but singularly steady; very lively, but very sweet; discreet, and considerate almost to moral precocity.—ELLIS, ANNIE RAINE, 1889, *ed., The Early Diary of Frances Burney, Preface, p.* v.

The greater part of this latter work ("Diary and Letters") has the charm of contemporary narrative written without the primary intention of publication, and inspired by affection and the certainty of meeting with sympathy and interest in the intended recipient of their confidences. Such writings may be full of egotism and trivial detail; but they do not deceive and they do not weary. We come to know thoroughly, to like or dislike naturally, the persons described. We find, as we read, that we are getting new insight into the characters of men and women famous in other ways; and that we are learning something new from the sayings and doings of men and women who have never been famous at all.—SHUCKBURGH, E. S., 1890, *Madame D'Arblay, Macmillan's Magazine, vol.* 61, *p.* 291.

GENERAL

She is a quick, lively, and accurate observer of persons and things; but she always looks at them with a consciousness of her sex, and in that point of view in which it is the particular business and interest of women to observe them. There is little in her works of passion or character, or even manners, in the most extended sense of the word, as implying the sum-total of our habits and pursuits; her *forte* is in describing the absurdities and affectations of external behaviour, or the manners of people in company. . . . In one of her novels, for example, a lady appears regularly every ten pages, to get a lesson in music for nothing. She never appears for any other purpose; this is all you know of her; and in this the whole wit and humour of the character consists. Meadows is the same, who has always the cue of being tired, without any other idea. It has been said of Shakspeare, that you may always assign his speeches to the proper characters; and you may infallibly do the same thing with Madame D'Arblay's, for they always say the same thing. The Braughtons are the best. Mr. Smith is an exquisite city portrait. "Evelina" is also her best novel, because it is the shortest; that is, it has all the liveliness in the sketches of character, and smartness of comic dialogue and repartee, without the tediousness of the story, and endless affectation of sentiment which disfigures the others. . . . There is little other power in Madame D'Arblay's novels than that of immediate observation; her characters, whether of refinement or vulgarity, are equally superficial and confined.—HAZLITT, WILLIAM, 1818, *Lecture on the English Novelists.*

Her works are deficient in original vigour of conception, and her characters in depth and nature. She has considered so anxiously the figured silks and tamboured muslins which flutter about society, that she has made the throbbings of the hearts which they cover a secondary consideration. . . . Fashion passes away, and the manners of the great are unstable, but natural emotion belongs to immortality.—CUNNINGHAM, ALLAN, 1833, *Biographical and Critical History of the Literature of the Last Fifty Years.*

Miss Burney did for the English novel what Jeremy Collier did for the English drama; and she did it in a better way. She first showed that a tale might be written in which both the fashionable and the vulgar life of London might be exhibited with great force, and with broad comic humour, and which yet should not contain a single line inconsistent with rigid morality, or even with virgin delicacy. She took away the reproach which lay on a most useful and delightful species of composition. She vindicated the right of her sex to an equal share in a fair and noble province of letters. Several accomplished women have followed in her track. At present, the novels which we owe to English ladies form no small part of the literary glory of our country. No class of works is more honourably distinguished by fine observation, by grace, by delicate wit, by pure moral feeling. Several among the successors of Madame D'Arblay have equalled her; two, we think, have surpassed her. But the fact that she has been surpassed gives her an additional claim to our respect and gratitude; for in truth we owe to her, not only Evelina, Cecilia, and Camilla, but also Mansfield Park and the Absentee.—MACAULAY, THOMAS BABINGTON, 1843, *Madame D'Arblay, Edinburgh Review, Critical and Miscellaneous Essays.*

Notwithstanding their egotism and prolixity, certainly these volumes are among the most delightful in the language! To the mere novel-reader they are charming; to the student of literary history and English manners, invaluable.—ALLIBONE, S. AUSTIN, 1854–58, *A Critical Dictionary of English Literature, vol.* I, *p.* 475.

Fanny Burney's novels were considered immensely humorous and diverting in their day. Burke complimented her on "her natural vein of humor," and another eminent critic speaks of "her sarcasm, drollery, and humor;" but it would be almost impossible to find a passage for quotation that would now satisfy on these points.—SANBORN, KATE, 1885, *The Wit of Women, p.* 32.

Deriving her inspiration in part from Richardson, she heads the roll of those female novelists whose works form a considerable part of English literature. The purity of her writings first made the circulating library respectable. "We owe to her," says Macaulay very justly, "not only 'Evelina,' 'Cecilia,' *and* 'Camilla,' but 'Mansfield Park' and the 'Absentee.' "—SEELEY, L. B., 1890, *ed. Fanny Burney and Her Friends, p.* 328.

Unfortunately Miss Burney neither restrained her own early simplicity, nor did she adhere to that measured formality which she had learnt from Johnson. By whatever aberration of taste, or ur er whatever stress of circumstance—it n v well be, as Macaulay surmises, by associ tion with the French refugees and he subsequent residence in France—she fel into a style the most intricate, the most laboured, and the most affected that could be conceived. Her later novels had no qualities that could enable them to take their place with "Evelina" and "Cecilia;" but even if their other merits had been greater they would have been crushed into oblivion under the weight of such a style as is seen in the "Wanderer" and in the "Memoirs of Dr. Burney."—CRAIK, HENRY, 1895, *English Prose, vol.* IV, *p.* 540.

Fanny Burney is one of the best examples of what has been called the originality of ignorance. She was positively illiterate. . . . Quick observation, quick fancy, were her chief gifts. A little more study of the writings of others, a few more ideas, would have stifled her genius. Had she had a spark of imagination with her limited intellect, she would probably have been unable to write at all; but the absence of any transcendental quality made her fearless and successful in paths where more distinguished abilities dared not tread.—DAVIDSON, JOHN, 1895, *Sentences and Paragraphs, p.* 42.

The most difficult figure to fit in to any progressive scheme of English fiction is Frances Burney, who was actually alive with Samuel Richardson and with Mr. George Meredith. She wrote seldom, and published at long intervals; her best novels, founded on a judicious study of Marivaux and Rosseau, implanted on a strictly British soil, were produced a little earlier than the moment we have now reached. Yet the "Wanderer" was published simultaneously with "Waverley." She is a social satirist of a very sprightly order, whose early "Evelina" and "Cecilia" were written with an ease which she afterwards unluckily abandoned for an aping of the pomposity of her favourite lexicographer. Miss Burney was a delightful novelist in her youth, but she took no part in the progressive development of English literature.—GOSSE, EDMUND, 1897, *A Short History of Modern English Literature, p.* 294.

Gerald Griffin

1803-1840

Gerald Griffin was born in Limerick, Ireland, December 12, 1803. His family emigrated to United States about 1820, but he remained with an elder brother, who lived at Adare. His earliest poems were contributed to the Limerick newspapers. In 1823, with a manuscript tragedy entitled "Aguire," he went to London as a literary adventurer. But he could get no manager to put the play upon the stage, and with another, entitled "Gisippus," he was no more fortunate. He sustained himself by writing for magazines, and soon acquired a brilliant reputation. In 1827 he published "Holland Tide," and "Tales of the Munster Festivals," stories of Irish peasant life; and in 1828 "The Colleen Bawn; or, The Collegians," his best known and most powerful novel, which has been dramatised as "The Colleen Bawn." His subsequent publications were "The Invasion," "The Rivals," "The Duke of Monmouth," a second series of "Tales of the Munster Festivals," "Tracey's Ambition," "Tales of the Five Senses," and "Tales of the Jury-Room." In the last mentioned, an Irish jury, together with an interloper who had been accidently locked up with them, spent a night in telling stories and singing songs by turns around. . . . Griffin joined the society of the Christian Brothers in 1838, and died in Cork, June 12, 1840. After his death his tragedy of "Gisippus" was brought out at Drury Lane Theatre with great success. His works, edited with a memoir by his brother, have been published in New York in ten volumes, including one volume of poems.—JOHNSON, ROSSITER, 1875, *Little Classics, Authors, p.* 110.

PERSONAL

Until within a short time back I have not had, since I left Ireland, a single moment's peace of mind; constantly running backwards and forwards, and trying a thousand expedients, only to meet disappointments everywhere I turned. . . . I never will think or talk upon the subject again. It was such a year that I did not think it possible I could have outlived, and the very recollection of it puts me into the horrors. . . . When I first came to London my own self-conceit, backed by the opinion of one of the most original geniuses of the age, induced me to set about revolutionising the dramatic taste of the time by writing for the stage. Indeed, the design was formed and the first step taken (a couple of pieces written), in Ireland. I cannot with my present experience conceive anything more comical than my own views and measures at that time. A young gentleman totally unknown even to a single family in London coming into town with a few pounds in one pocket, and a brace of tragedies in the other, supposing that the one will set him up before the others are exhausted, is not a very novel, but a very laughable delusion. I would weary you, or I would carry you through a number of curious scenes into which it led me.—GRIFFIN, GERALD, 1825, *Letter to his Mother*.

About two years after he set off gaily for London with "Gisippus" and I know not how many other plays in his pocket, for his only resource, and his countryman John Banim for his only friend. He was not yet twenty, poor boy, had hardly left his father's roof, and he set out for London full of spirits and of hope to make his fortune by the stage. *Now* we all know what "Gisippus" is—the story of a great benefit, a foul ingratitude, suffering heaped upon suffering, wrong upon wrong, avenged in the last scene by such a pardon, such a reconciliation as would draw tears from the stoniest heart that ever sat in a theatre. We all know the beauty of "Gisippus" now; for after the author's death that very play, in Mr. Macready's hands, achieved perhaps one of the purest successes of the modern drama. But during Gerald Griffin's life it produced nothing but mortifications innumerable and unspeakable. The play and the poet were tossed unread and unheard from actor to actor, from manager to manager, until hope fainted within him, and the theatre was abandoned at once and forever.—MITFORD, MARY RUSSELL, 1851, *Recollections of a Literary Life*, p. 457.

Thus lived and died one whom it would be faint praise to call one of the brightest and purest ornaments which this century has given to English literature. The various creations of his fancy will long hold a high place in the hearts of all who admire the beautiful and revere the good; but the moral of his own life is the noblest heritage he has left us. True to the instincts of his Catholic birth and training, he passed through the temptations of sorrow, poverty, and vanities of a great city for years, preserving his faith unshaken and his morals unsullied; with courage and tenacity of purpose, the attributes of true heroism, he surmounted obstacle after obstacle, which easily have daunted older and stronger men, till he reached a proud position in the literature of his country; and when surrounded by all that is supposed to make life valuable—personal independence, devoted friends, and worldly applause—he gently and after mature self-examination took off his laurels, laid them modestly on the altar of religion, and, clothed in the humble garb of a Christian Brother, prepared to devote his life to unostentatious charity. Even his very name, that he once fondly hoped to write on the enduring tablets of history, he no longer desired to be remembered; for on the plain stone that marks his last resting-place in the little graveyard on the monastery is engraved simply the words, BROTHER JOSEPH. DIED JUNE 12, 1840. —MCGEE, J. G., 1870, *Gerald Griffin, The Catholic World, vol.* 11, *p.* 411.

"Lie lightly on him, earth"—on the dust of one who found the struggle for fame so bitter that he resigned it in very weariness of heart when victory was well-nigh within his grasp. I knew Griffin when I was like him—a young man toiling hard for a future. John Banim—who had, between sickness, disappointment, and poverty, something like the lot of a literary martyr to endure himself—was his useful adviser and steadfast friend; and at Banim's house I met him more than once. He was then a delicate, or, rather, a refined-looking young man, tall and handsome, but with mournful eyes, and that unmistakable something which prognosticates a sad life and an early death. He had come to London at the age of nineteen, with some poems in his pocket and an unfinished tragedy. For a long time he continued to pick up a precarious living by literature, struggling with absolute poverty, without friends, without prospects—almost without hope. Sickened by numberless disappointments, brought face to face with actual starvation—for it had come to that, when a friend once discovered him, and ascertained that he had been three days without food—his pride yet held him back from seeking the aid that relatives he had left in Limerick would certainly have tendered, could he have prevailed on himself to make known to them his extremity of distress. Banim—himself hardly in better circumstances—proffered help, and it was rejected. At last—too late—"The Collegians" and 'The Munster Festivals" found their way into print, and to success; then their author's dreary path was lighted up with the first dawning of fame. Too late—for, though the struggle was at an end, it had crushed him. He determined to burn his manuscripts and write no more, but withdraw himself from the world. Alas! even while he was preparing for long years of penance and prayer, Death came and removed him to heaven.—HALL, SAMUEL CARTER, 1883, *Retrospect of a Long Life*, *p.* 417.

The success of "The Collegians" led to the writing of a number of novels, essays, poems, etc., to the pleasantest of social associations, and to all those pleasures which Griffin as a lad of eighteen facing the world had longed to enjoy. Just how and when the idea of suddenly renouncing them all and entering a religious order came to him his biographer has not stated, but I may venture to quote the opinion given me by Mr. Aubrey De Vere. He assured me that the leading idea in Gerald Griffin's mind was that writing fiction was injurious to his own standard of thought and feeling, and that his higher inspiration was for a life devoted to charitable works. He began to criticise his own novels unsparingly, declaring that he found in some of them tendencies which he disapproved. He was nervous over this, anxious for the work even of a missionary, but by no means either morbid or fantastic in his views, as some of his critics have averred. When he decided to join the Christian Brotherhood to devote himself to a life of simple usefulness, of teaching the poorer classes, and also of writing religious works, he was in the calmest and serenest frame of mind. The call had reached him, and it was not to be resisted or denied. One who lived in the same order years later told me that those among the Christian Brothers who remembered him declared that never was a more joyous or happy spirit among them. He had studied law, theology, and metaphysics; he had mingled with the leading spirits of the day; he had talked philosophy with the followers of Voltaire and Hume; he had listened to every sort of opinion that floated through the London he called his home, and he had of late years been met more than half-way by fame and pecuniary success. There was no depression in his decision, no sudden phase of feeling that there was a tremendous heroism or sacrifice in the step he contemplated. It was as clearly a necessity to him and the scheme of life and salvation he proposed to himself as if it had been a Saul who, listening to the voice in the heavens, answered, "My Lord and my God."—LILLIE, LUCY C., 1890, *The Author of "The Collegians," Lippincott's Magazine, vol.* 45, *p.* 404.

One day his brother found the fireplace black with the cinders of papers recently burned. He had just destroyed the whole of his manuscripts, verse and prose alike, and answered all inquiries by stating that he had devoted the rest of his life to the instruction of little peasant boys, as one of the "Christian Brothers"—the humblest of all religious communities. He laboured assiduously for a few years at Cork; and there, some years later, I saw his grave, and heard his fellow-labourers declare that if Ireland had ever had a saint, Gerald Griffin was one.—DEVERE, AUBREY, 1897, *Recollections*, *p.* 32.

GENERAL

Written as it was ["Gisippus"] in his twentieth year, I do not hesitate to call it one of the marvels of youthful production in literature. The solid grasp of character, the manly depth of thought, the beauties as well as defects of the composition (more than I can here enumerate), wanted only right direction to have given to our English drama another splendid and enduring name. In little London coffee-houses, on little slips of paper, this tragedy was written. But he could get no hearing for it.—FORSTER, JOHN, 1848–71, *The Life and Times of Oliver Goldsmith, vol.* I, *p.* 207, *note.*

Griffin was certainly a man of genius; a man having a certain inborn aptitude, which is not the result of education and industry. . . . It became active in Griffin while he was very young; indeed, when Griffin gave up literature, he was still young, so that Griffin was always a young author; and yet we might say that he was always a ripe one. From the first, he displayed a certain masculine vigor altogether different from the feebleness which sometimes characterizes the compositions of young writers, who afterwards become remarkable for their strength. . . . He had an inventive and bold imagination: to this his power and variety in the creation of character bear witness. He had great fulness of sensibility and fancy, as we observe in the picturesqueness of his style, and in his wealth of imagery. He delighted in outward nature, and is a fine describer of it; but, like Sir Walter Scott, he never describes for the sake of description, but always in connection with human interest and incident. He excels in the pathetic: but it is in passion that he has most power; strong natural passion, and such as it is in those individuals in whom it is strongest and most natural,—individuals in the middle and lower ranks of life, especially in the middle and lower ranks of Irish life. . . . His genius, too, was of the most refined moral purity, without sermonizing or cant; and when we reflect that guilt and sin and passion, low characters, vulgar life, and broad humor, are so constantly the subjects with which it is concerned, this purity is no less remarkable than it is admirable.—GILES, HENRY, 1865, *Gerald Griffin, Christian Examiner, vol.* 78, *pp.* 357, 358.

As a poet, Griffin is remarkable for the beauty of his delineations of natural scenery, his elevation of sentiment and purity of conception. His lyrics remind us of Moore, and are scarcely inferior to some of the best of that immortal bard's in feeling and choiceness of metaphor; but being somewhat deficient in rhythm, they have never found much favor in the drawing or concert-room, "A Place in thy Memory, Dearest," "My Mary of the Curling Hair," and one or two others excepted.—MCGEE, J. G., 1870, *The Works of Gerald Griffin, The Catholic World, vol.* 11, *p.* 678.

A poet, on the one hand, who has both passion and imagination, he can portray some of the most terrible as well as affecting of human struggles; a humorist on the other, he possesses that rarer quality which is both the medium of reality and source of insight into character. But for the strong religious convictions which tore him from the world at the moment his brilliant powers were arriving at maturity, there is very little doubt he would have become the national bard of Ireland, and have enriched our English literature with some of its noblest modern additions. It would be hard indeed to limit the possibilities of one who could write such a play as "Gisippus" before he had reached the age of twenty, and produce, only five years afterwards, such a romance as "The Collegians." . . . The genius of Gerald Griffin was eminently dramatic. This was shown in the spirit of his stories, so many of which were adapted to the stage, and in the fact that all his earliest and most prized attempts were plays. . . . More a poet than a patriot, more affected by what was universal and enduring in his countrymen than what was special and political under the influence of passing systems, whilst feeling deeply the peasant's condition, he was less attracted to his sphere than to that of his own order—the rural middle class of Ireland, with its comparative culture and tranquility, and which had also its romance in its traditions of strange events, that had roused at times its slumbering passions and lashed a peaceful current into momentary surges. Of such traditions were the stories of the "Collegians" and the "Aylmers"—pathetic memories that had long been cherished in remote and quiet neighbourhoods,—tenuous and delicate foundations, but on which the concreting touch of genius could build —at least in one case—an imperishable structure.—BERNARD, BAYLE, 1874, *The Life of Samuel Lover, pp.* 181, 182, 185.

His novels are of a more sustained merit than those of the O'Hara Family, if they do not equal them in detached passages. His poetry, with the exception of his tragedies, was all occasional, and in its fine feeling and frequently admirable felicity is evidence of what he might have accomplished with more leisure and a spirit less perturbed with an incessant and painful struggle for existence. — WILLIAMS, ALFRED M., 1881, *The Poets and Poetry of Ireland, p.* 266.

"The Collegians" established his reputation. This book is perhaps now more widely known by the popular play of the Colleen Bawn, which was founded upon it, than by its own attractions. But the story is the least satisfactory part of it, and the sketches of life and the character to be met with in the book are infinitely more worth the reader's while than the melodramatic fate of Eily O'Connor, and the despair and misery of her lover. Not even Miss Edgeworth's account of the successive squires of "Castle Rackrent" sets forth the wild groups of Irish gentry with so trenchant a touch as that with which Griffin represents his Cregans and Creaghs in their noisy carouses: and his peasants of all discriptions are full of humour and life—more individual and displaying a more intimate knowledge than those of Miss Edgeworth.—OLIPHANT, MARGARET O. W., 1882, *Literary History of England, XVIII-XIX Century, vol.* III, *p.* 226.

"The Collegians" has been frequently reprinted, and presents the best picture existing of Irish peasant life—at once the most vivid and the most accurate. Its comic parts are the most comic, and its tragic the most tragic, to be found in Irish literature.—DEVERE, AUBREY, 1897, *Recollections, p.* 28.

Had he given to the stage the tragic realities of life around him, such as he gave to his novels, he might have formed a successful national drama. His riper mind found fresher paths. It should be counted to him that he was the first to present several of our folk-customs, tales, and ancient legends in English prose. In poetry his longer pieces fail in freshness, vigour, and local colour; they are conventional compositions, carefully worked, with pleasing imagery and pensive reflections. In his lyrics, however, where his native genius is free, he is at his best, impassioned at times (though never passionate), tender, delicate, yet strong with a certain dramatic grasp of his subject. There is a curious prudence, somewhat Edgeworthian, in certain of his verses, which controls passion and may be due to the influence of a Quaker lady whose friend he was.—SIGERSON, GEORGE, 1900, *A Treasury of Irish Poetry, eds. Brooke and Rolleston.*

Theodore Edward Hook

1788-1841

Born, in London 22 Sept. 1788. Early education at private schools. At Harrow, June 1804 to 1810. Wrote opera libretti, farces and melodramas during school days. Matric. St. Mary Hall, Oxford, 2 July 1810. Accountant-General and Treasurer at Mauritius, Oct. 1813. Deprived of office owing to deficit in treasury, and sent back to England, 1818. Imprisoned, 1823–25. Edited "The Arcadian," 1820; edited "John Bull," 1820–41; edited "New Monthly Mag.," 1837–38. F. S. A., 27 Feb. 1840. Died, at Fulham, 24 Aug. 1841. *Works:* "The Soldier's Return" (anon.), 1805; "Catch Him Who Can," 1806; "The Invisible Girl," 1806; "Tekeli," 1806; "The Fortress," 1807; "Siege of St. Quintin," 1807; "Music Mad," 1808; "Killing No Murder," 1809; "Safe and Sound," 1809; "The Man of Sorrow," (3 vols.), 1809; "The Trial by Jury," 1811; "Darkness Visible," 1811 (2nd edn. same year); "Pigeons and Crows," 1819; "Facts illustrative of the treatment of Napoleon Buonaparte in St. Helena" (anon.), 1819; "Exchange No Robbery," (anon.), 1820; "Tentamen" (under pseud. of "Vicesimus Blenkinsop"), 1820; "Peter and Paul," 1821; "Sayings and Doings," 1st series (3 vols.; anon.), 1824; 2nd series (3 vols.; anon.), 1825; 3rd series (3 vols.), 1828; "Reminiscences of Michael Kelly," 1826; "Maxwell" (anon.), 1830; "The Life of Sir David Baird" (2 vols.; anon), 1832; "The Parson's Daughter" (anon.), 1833; "Love and Pride" (anon.), 1833; "Gilbert Gurney"(anon.), 1836; "Jack Brag" (anon.), 1837; "Pascal Bruno," 1837; "Births, Deaths, and Marriages" (anon.), 1839; "Gurney Married," (anon.), 1839; "Cousin Geoffrey," 1840; "Precept and Practice," 1840. *Posthumous:* "Fathers and Sons," 1842; "Peregrine Bunce" (perhaps spurious) 1842; "The Widow and the Marquess," 1842; "The Ramsbottom Letters," 1872; "The Ramsbottom Papers," [1874]. He *edited:* "Peter Priggins," 1841; "The Parish Clerk," 1840. *Collected Works:* "Choice Humourous Works" [1873]. *Life:* "Life and Remains," by R. H. D. Barham, 1877.—SHARP, R. FARQUHARSON, 1897, *A Dictionary of English Authors, p.* 136.

PERSONAL

We have already expressed our opinion, that Theodore Hook's ability in conversation was above what he ever exemplified in his writings. We have seen him in company with very many of the most eminent men of his time; and we never, until he was near his end, carried home with us the impression that he had been surpassed. He was as entirely, as any parent of *bon-mots* that we have known, above the suspicion of having premeditated his point; and he excelled in a greater variety of ways than any of them. No definition either of wit or humour could have been framed that must not have included him; and he often conveyed what was at once felt to be the truest wit in forms, as we believe, entirely new. He could run riot in conundrums—but what seemed at first mere jingle, was often perceived, a moment after, to contain some allusion or insinuation that elevated the vehicle. Memory and knack may suffice to furnish out an amusing narrator; but the teller of good stories seldom amuses long if he cannot also say good things. Hook shone equally in both. In fact he could not tell any story without making it his own by the ever-varying, inexhaustible invention of the details and the aspects, and above all, by the tact that never failed to connect it with the persons, the incidents, the topics of the evening. —LOCKHART, JOHN GIBSON, 1843, *Theodore Hook, Quarterly Review, vol.* 72, *p.* 106.

Thank you for the paper about Theodore Hook. I knew him and disliked him. He was very witty and humorous, certainly; but excessively coarse in his talk and gross in his manners, and was hardly ever strictly sober after dinner.—KEMBLE, FRANCES ANN, 1843, *Letter, Records of Later Life, p.* 398.

Any estimate of the powers of Theodore Hook, drawn from his writings alone, must be fatally inadequate and erroneous. As a novelist he has been not unfrequently equalled, and occasionally surpassed, by more than one of his compeers; and whatever the eminence to which his published works have raised him, it is as nothing compared with the position which, by virtue of his varied talents,—his brilliant and unflagging wit, has been unhesitatingly conceded to him in society. But it is precisely in these its higher qualities, that his genius cannot be appreciated save by those who knew him. . . . His social qualities were only too attractive; he not only delighted by his talents, but charmed by that easy benevolence in trifles, in which true politeness is defined to consist; to men younger and less gifted, his demeanour was gentle and encouraging; to children, those who could sit and listen, all eye and ear to his music and his mirth, he was remarkably indulgent. Unsurpassed as a talker, he was, what perhaps is almost equally appreciated, patient as a listener. . . . In person, Theodore Hook was above the middle height, his frame was powerful and well-proportioned, possessing a breadth and depth of chest, which, joined to a constitution naturally of the strongest order, whould have seemed, under ordinary care, to hold promise of a long and healthy life. His countenance was fine and commanding, his features, when in repose, settling into a somewhat stern and heavy expression, but all alive and alight with genius the instant his lips were opened. His eye was dark, large, and full—to the epithet Βοώπις he, not less justly than the venerable goddess, was entitled. His voice was rich, deep, and melodious.—BARHAM, R. H. DALTON, 1848, *The Life and Remains of Theodore Edward Hook, pp.* 2, 250, 251.

Never, perhaps, was there a man of such precocious and versatile talents. "As a wit, confessed without rival to shine," his company was courted, and he was incessantly flattered by princes, nobles, and the most noted in the world of fashion and of fame. As a writer of novels, farces, songs, and particularly in improvisation, he was, perhaps, unrivalled in the world of genius. Having been several times in his fascinating company, I can bear witness to these qualifications: when in contact and competition with the famed authors of "The Rejected Addresses," he seemed to shine with additional brilliancy. Yet this man, this accomplished wit and novelist, was imprisoned and degraded for disreputable neglect of his duties in a public government office, in which he was misplaced by political friends.—REES, THOMAS, 1853, *Reminiscences of Literary London, p.* 108.

Like many fellows of "most excellent fancy," "wont to set the table in a roar,"

Hook—the humorist all mirth and jocularity abroad—at home was subject to violent revulsions of feeling, to gusts of sadness, and fits of dejection of spirits, which temporary excitement, produced by stimulants, did not much tend to remedy or remove. The results of his disordered and embarrassed circumstances became too manifest to his private friends in impaired energies of mind and body, in his broken health, and depressed spirits, and furnished a melancholy contrast with the public exhibition of apparently irrepressible animal spirits, that rendered him a welcome guest at all tables.—MADDEN, R. R., 1855, *The Literary Life and Correspondence of the Countess of Blessington, vol.* II, *p.* 294.

Hook has been, by common consent, placed at the head of modern wits. . . . Theodore could amuse, Theodore could astonish, Theodore could beat home any where; he had all the impudence, all the readiness, all the indifference of a jester, and a jester he was. Let any one look at his portrait, and he will doubt if this be the king's jester, painted by Holbein, or Mr. Theodore Hook, painted by Eddis. The short, thick nose, the long upper lip, the sensual, whimsical mouth, the twinkling eyes, all belong to the regular maker of fun. Hook was a certificated jester, with a lenient society to hear and applaud him, instead of an irritable tyrant to keep him in order: and he filled his post well. . . . Theodore Hook stands almost alone in this country as an improviser.—THOMSON, KATHERINE AND J. C. (GRACE AND PHILIP WHARTON), 1860, *The Wits and Beaux of Society.*

For the rest, it should not be forgotten that Theodore Hook was a man warm in his friendships; of humane and charitable disposition; and of open-handed, generous nature. He was beloved and regretted by all who knew him; and possessed to the last such charm of grace and manner, that, at the Athenæum, his favourite club, it is said that the dinners fell off to the extent of £300 per annum when he disappeared from his accustomed corner, near the door of the coffee-room.—BATES, WILLIAM, 1874–98, *The Maclise Portrait Gallery of Illustrious Literary Characters, p.* 235.

In the art of punning he was without a rival, as he was also in the exercise of the still less legitimate form of humour contained in hoaxes. . . . It may be noted, in passing, as curious that despite the unanimity with which his improvising powers were spoken of as unique, but few of the improvisations have got committed to paper.—It seemed as if his talent was essentially oral, and refused to give itself wholly to a more permanent means of sustaining his reputation.—The exuberance of his fun was irrepressible.—Unabating spirit and unflagging mirth made him the soul and centre of the convivial circle.—Since the days of Sheridan no more brilliant luminary had flashed across the realm of fashion.—JERROLD, WALTER, 1894, *ed., Bon-Mots of Samuel Foote and Theodore Hook, Introduction, pp.* 10, 11.

GENERAL

Tickler.—"Confound haste and hurry! What else can account for Theodore Hook's position? Who that has read his 'Sayings and Doings,' and, above all, his 'Maxwell,' can doubt that, had he given himself time for consideration and correction, we should have been hailing him ere now, *nem. con.*, as another Smollett, if not another Le Sage?" . . . *North.*—"I agree with you; and I sincerely hope this novel-improvisatore will pause ere it is too late, and attempt something really worthy of his imagination. But, as it is, such is the richness of the *vis comica* showered over these careless extravaganzas, that unless he himself throws them into the shade by subsequent performances, I venture to say they have a better chance of being remembered a hundred years hence than any contemporary productions of their class—except only those of the two great lights of Scotland and Ireland—Jam dudum ad scripta Camœnis."—WILSON, JOHN, 1831, *Noctes Ambrosianæ, Sept.*

It would not be easy to find another artist with ability equal to Hook's for discussing the good and evil, the passions and affectations, the fits of generosity and settled systems of saving, the self-sufficiency and the deplorable weakness, the light and darkness, the virtue and the vice, of this prodigious Babel. The stories which he tells might be invented with little outlay of fancy, for the best of them are far from being consistent; but the characters which live and breathe in them would make the narratives pleasing though they were as crooked as the walls of

Troy.—CUNNINGHAM, ALLAN, 1833, *Biographical and Critical History of the Literature of the Last Fifty Years.*

His name will be preserved. His political songs and *jeux d'esprit*, when the hour comes for collecting them, will form a volume of sterling and lasting attraction; and after many clever romances of this age shall have sufficiently occupied public attention, and sunk, like hundreds of former generations, into utter oblivion, there are tales in his collection which will be read with, we venture to think, even a greater interest than they commanded in their novelty. We are not blind to his defects. The greatest and the most prevailing blemish is traceable to his early habits as a farce-writer: he too often reminds us of that department of the theatre, both in the flagrancy of his contrasts in character, and the extravagant overcharging of particular incidents. He is tempted to pile absurdity on absurdity till all credibility is destroyed—and if it were not for the easy richness of his language, ever pregnant with byeplay, the *incredulus* would toss the volume down with *odi*. . . . His defects are great;—but Theodore Hook is, we apprehend, the only male novelist of this time, except Mr. Dickens, who has drawn portraits of contemporary English society destined for permanent existence. A selection from his too numerous volumes will go down with Miss Edgeworth and Miss Austen. His best works are not to be compared with theirs, either for skilful compactness of fable or general elegance of finish. His pace was too fast for that. But he is never to be confounded for a moment either with their clumsier and weaker followers, or with the still more tedious imitators of their only modern superior.—LOCKHART, JOHN GIBSON, 1843, *Theodore Hook, Quarterly Review, vol.* 72, *pp.* 104, 105.

Mr. Hook had no sympathies with humanity for its own sake, but only as developed and modified by aristocratic circumstances and fashionable tastes. He was devoted to splendid externals. He may be said to have had no inner life—except that the lofty image of a powdered footman, with golden aiguillettes and large white calves, walked with a great air up and down the silent avenues of his soul.—HORNE, RICHARD HENRY, 1844, *ed., A New Spirit of the Age, pp.* 223, 225.

As a dramatic author, his fame was built on a foundation too slight to last; the cleverest of his pieces were written to display the powers, or contrast the peculiarities of particular actors, and with them may be considered to have retired from the stage. But as a novelist, we have ventured to affirm, that his reputation stands high and is broadly based; in the delineation of modern English life, in laying bare the hidden springs of human action, effected the one without mannerism, the other without pretension.—BARHAM, R. H. DALTON, 1848, *The Life and Remains of Theodore Edward Hook, p.* 247.

Doubtless his wit and humour were apt to degenerate into buffoonery, his pathos into sentimentality, and his nature into conventionalism; but his knowledge of city life, in its manners, habits, and language, seemed intuitive, and has been surpassed only by Fielding and Dickens. Many and multifarious, however, as are his volumes, he has left behind him no great creation,—nothing that can be pointed to as a triumphant index of the extraordinary powers which he undoubtedly possessed. —MOIR, D. M., 1851–52, *Sketches of the Poetical Literature of the Past Half-Century.*

I see the merit of the novels of Theodore Hook, whom I held in greater abhorrence than even Croker, stuffed as those novels are with scurrility against my political friends.—MACAULAY, THOMAS BABINGTON, 1858, *Journal; Life and Letters, ed. Trevelyan, vol.* II, *p.* 297.

As a novelist he has fallen into undeserved oblivion. The best of his novels are scarcely inferior in comic power to Dickens's most successful works. Indeed, there is a great similarity between the two humourists, the same tendency to exaggeration and caricature. "In casting our eyes over the volumes," says Barham, "we are at a loss to point out a single character of importance that has not its prototype, or an incident—the most incredible, the most true—that is not in some measure founded upon facts." Some of the best known persons of the day, so little disguised as to be easily recognisable, were introduced in his novels. He himself and Sam Beazley, architect and dramatist, divided Gilbert Gurney and Daly between them; Hull was the noted Tom Hill, before mentioned as the original of

Poole's "Paul Pry;" Godfrey Moss in "Maxwell," the Rev. Edward Canon, the King's Chaplain, &c. Nor was the *vis comica* his only excellence. There is a power in "Maxwell" and "Cousin William" not inferior to the best sensation novelist of the day. Yet all his works were composed hurriedly, under high pressure; the plots are badly constructed, and the whole requires finish. But his powers of observation, his profound knowledge of human nature, his fun, the excellence of his detached scenes must ever place him in a high rank among novelists; and a perusal of his bygone books, were it only for the striking pictures they give of bygone men and manners, would still prove more profitable and amusing than that of three-fourths of those which have no other claim to attention than their being new. —BAKER, H. BARTON, 1877, *Theodore Hook, Belgravia, vol.* 34, *p.* 209.

Hook's novels are not of much higher class than his journalism. They abound in caricature, not even the caricature of invention, but that of actual portraiture, all his broadest sketches being easily identified by those who knew him, and by society in general. They were clever enough to be largely read at the time, but nothing can be more entirely dead than these galvanically vivacious productions are now, nor is there enough even of contemporary life in them to make it worth while to recall them to the reader.—OLIPHANT, MARGARET O. W., 1882, *Literary History of England, XVIII-XIX Century, vol.* III, *p.* 159.

His unflagging literary industry in the midst of so many hindrances and temptations is highly to his credit. Though he sold his pen, he did not prostitute it; the side in support of which his wit and scurrility were inlisted was really his own. His natural powers were extraordinary. "He is," said Coleridge, "as true a genius as Dante." With regular education and mental discipline he might have done great things; his actual reputation is that of a great master in a low style of humour, and the most brilliant improvisatore, whether with the pen or at the piano, that his country has seen.—GARNETT, RICHARD, 1891, *Dictionary of National Biography, vol.* XXVII, *p.* 276.

In "Gilbert Gurney" Hook has painted his own portrait, under the name of Daly. "Fun is to me what ale was to Boniface," says Daly of himself. "I sleep upon fun—I drink for fun—I talk for fun—I live for fun." The practical jokes which that gentleman delights in are in effect the jests which Hook had perpetrated in real life.—WALSH, W. S., 1893, *The Practical Jester, Lippincott's Magazine, vol.* 51, *p.* 760.

Joseph Blanco White

1775-1841

Joseph Blanco White was born in Seville, Spain, July 11, 1775. He was educated for the priesthood, and was ordained in 1799. But he left the communion of the Roman Church a few years later, and in 1810 went to England, where he united with the Anglican Church. In London he edited with great ability a monthly entitled *El Español*, which was discontinued at the close of the Peninsular war in 1814, and thereafter White enjoyed a government pension of £250. He edited *Las Variedades*, a Spanish quarterly, in 1822-25, and the "London Review" in 1829. His publications in book form were: "Letters from Spain," 1822; "Practical and Internal Evidence against Catholicism," 1825; "The Poor Man's Preservative against Popery," 1825; and "Second Travels of an Irish Gentleman in Search of a Religion," as an answer to Moore's, 1833. He removed to Liverpool in 1839, and died there May 20, 1841. His autobiography, with selections from his correspondence, edited by J. H. Thom, appeared in 1845.—JOHNSON, ROSSITER, 1875, *Little Classics, Authors, p.* 243.

PERSONAL

He is remarkably intelligent, and his conversation peculiarly prepossessing. He expresses himself with force and fluency such as one rarely hears from a native Englishman, with the slightest tinge of foreign accent.—MILMAN, HENRY HART, 1826, *A Biographical Sketch by his son, Arthur Milman, p.* 106.

The full value of this Autobiography for those who will *study* it as the religious history of an individual man, endowed with the noblest qualities of Intellect and Heart, but placed in circumstances the most fitted to suppress and limit the natural character. Of the countless thousands similarly situated, how few have burst their original chains, or, if they have seen light, have come forth out of their circumstances to announce the truth of their souls! The history of one who stands out, and by *individual veracity* attracts the notice of mankind, should, and on grounds altogether apart from religious dogmas or doubtful controversies, be as precious to the world as Martyr's blood. . . . So little, indeed, did some of his former friends who had stereotyped their minds, understand his true nature, that they commonly described him as a man intellectually unsteady, fickle, and apt to change. It was a libel. Every page of these "Memoirs" will disprove it, and show that his affections would have made him a Conservative in every thing,—that *Honesty,* not speculativeness, enforced each change,—that he never stepped off any old ground of Faith, until he could no longer stand upon it without moral culpability, and that he never moved away from old friendships at all.—THOM, JOHN HAMILTON, 1845, *ed., The Life of the Rev. Joseph Blanco White, written by Himself, Introduction, vol.* I, *pp.* ix, x.

Such a life as Mr. Blanco White's is, in a minor way, a blow struck at Christianity, and a blow which will not be unfelt, perhaps, in some quarters. Christianity has had many blows struck at it in the course of its earthly career, and more than one in this country within the last century. Hume's argument against miracles was a blow; Gibbon's Roman History was a blow. Christianity simply received them, allowed them to tell and have influence upon this or that portion of society, and went on its way. A feebler blow in the same direction is Mr. Blanco White's autobiography. His mind is a deep, narrow well, out of which infidelity springs up with wonderful genuineness and life. The infidel objection he raises has a clearness and transparency which can result only from the reality of the thought in his mind. It is surprising to see the old objection which Butler's "Analogy" has long ago dealt with, and which one thought had now had its day, springing up again with the freshness of life, and with as seemingly clear a sensation of its unanswerableness as if the fountain-head of truth itself were speaking. In this light the present autobiography is not an unimportant book.—MOZLEY, J. B., 1845, *Essays Historical and Theological, vol.* II, *p.* 71.

Couldst thou in calmness yield thy mortal breath,
Without the Christian's sure and certain hope?
Didst thou to earth confine our being's scope,
Yet, fixed on One Supreme with fervent faith,
Prompt to obey what conscience witnesseth,
As one intent to fly the eternal wrath,
Decline the ways of sin that downward slope!
O thou light-searching spirit, that dist grope
In such bleak shadows here, 'twixt life and death,
To thee dare I bear witness, though in ruth—
Brave witness like thine own—dare hope and pray
That thou, set free from this imprisoning clay,
Now clad in raiment of perpetual youth,
Mayst find that bliss untold 'mid endless day
Awaits each earnest soul that lives for Truth.
—COLERIDGE, SARA, 1845, *Blanco White.*

We cannot then entertain the smallest confidence that, if he had been permitted a few more years of mental activity, he would not have crushed into dust the fragments of belief, which at the period of his death had not yet been decomposed. In that case, the warning which he has left behind him, written by the dispensation of Providence for our learning, would have been even more forcible, but the picture itself would have been in proportion more grievous. And truly, as it is, it has abundant power both to convey instruction and to excite pity. As to the last, what can be more deeply moving than to see one who was endowed from birth upwards with more than an ordinary share of the best worldly goods, and dedicated to the immediate service of God, after he has once fallen into atheism and has been recovered from it, again loosened from his hold, tossed about by every wind of doctrine, pursuing in turn a series of idle phantoms, each more shadowy than that which it succeeds, and terminating his course in a spiritual solitude and darkness absolutely unrelieved but for one single star, and that too of flickering and waning light? And all this under the dismal delusion that he has been a discoverer of truth—that he has been elected from among men to this nakedness and destitution—that with the multitude of his accumulating errors he has acquired a weight of authority, increasing in proportion to the years which he has consumed in weaving the meshes that entangle him.—GLADSTONE, WILLIAM EWART, 1845, *Life of Mr. Blanco White, Quarterly Review, vol.* 76, *p.* 200.

I cannot remember who it was that introduced me to Mr. White, or more correctly to M. Blanco, he having adopted the name of "White," which is merely the transition of his Spanish name Blanco, but I remember that I called upon him for some purpose, the object of which I have forgotten. He resided in lodgings at Chelsea. I found him pale, almost sickly-looking, dressed in black, with much of the character of a Roman Catholic priest. He spoke English well, telling me he had persevered in thinking in that language in place of his own Spanish tongue for the space of several years. There was a character of unhappiness, if not querulousness, depicted in his countenance, and he had much of the peculiar bearing which is characteristic of his countrymen,—that gravity which we attach unconsciously to the hero of Cervantes's immortal satire. I may be mistaken, but, if I recollect aright, he said his mother was an Englishwoman.—REDDING, CYRUS, 1867, *Personal Reminiscences of Eminent Men, vol.* III, *p.* 173.

Every Oriel man of that day may look back with regret at the little use made of what was really the very interesting episode of Blanco White's connection and residence. . . . He was really incapable of rest and composure, for his head and heart alike were in a continual flutter and turmoil, and his memory was heavily charged with painful sores. He had probably never enjoyed a day's thorough rest, or a night's uninterrupted sleep, in his life. A small bottle of cayenne pepper, of exceptional pungency, the gift of some city friend, was his inseparable companion at dinners, and without it his digestion was powerless even for the plainest food. . . . He was the most sensitive of men, and, as is often the case with such men he seemed doomed to small annoyances. . . . Nothing could exceed Blanco White's kindness to those who would receive favors from him, seek information, and show that they valued his opinion. He might have been happy in a world of such cases as long as the illusion lasted or the performances could be kept up.—MOZLEY, T., 1882, *Reminiscences Chiefly of Oriel College and the Oxford Movement, vol.* I, *pp.* 58, 59, 60.

GENERAL

The finest and most grandly conceived Sonnet ["Night and Death"] in our Language,—(at least, it is only in Milton's and in Wordsworth's Sonnets that I recollect any rival).—COLERIDGE, SAMUEL TAYLOR, 1827, *To Joseph Blanco White, Nov.* 28; *Life, ed. Thom, vol.* I, *p.* 439.

Poor Blanco White's book has at length appeared: that is, his first book. I suppose after his death there will be a second. It is as bad as can be. He evidently wishes to be attacked. I hope as far as possible he will be let alone; it will do him most good. He is not contented till he is talked about, and he has a morbid pleasure in being abused.—NEWMAN, JOHN HENRY, 1835, *To his Sister Jemima, Aug.* 9; *Letters and Correspondence, ed. Mozley, vol.* II, *p.* 122.

We do not say that Blanco White's is not a deep mind—far from it; but a literary and a dilettante mind may easily be a deep one. There are different kinds of depth—of *real* depth. Blanco White has one kind, not the most solid. His mind is a penetrating, but not a large one. He perforates, but he does not spread; he grasps particular ideas very tight, but does not take in a field of balance and comparison. He dips under, and comes up again; he disappears, and comes up instantly in the same place; he brings up something solid with him from the metaphysical bottom, but he has not stayed there long enough to see its large and awful extent. He is content with seeing very clearly and pointedly what he does see, and does not feel the enlarging swell and movement of the inner mind, which suspects narrowness, and wants to have as many ideas under its eye at a time as possible—to think as many things at once as possible. We mention it more as a philosophical than a moral fault in him, that he is far too satisfied with the mere clearness of an intellectual view, and luxuriates in metaphysical point and local accuracy.—MOZLEY, J. B., 1845, *Essays Historical and Theological, vol.* II, *p.* 69.

The "Observations on Heresy and Orthodoxy" contain many just, instructive, and profound suggestions, and show that the author's mind, in regard to the subjects here treated of, has been continually advancing. But, we regret to say, it is less likely to be generally read, or generally popular even among those by whom it is read, than either of his preceding works; partly from the nature of the topics, and partly also from an apparent want of a close and logical connexion in the train of ideas, and of a clear and distinct apprehension of the leading and fundamental idea to be enforced.—WALKER, J., 1836, *Blanco White's Life and Writings, Christian Examiner, vol.* 20, *p.* 133.

Blanco White—half English, half Spanish by descent—was one of the most striking cases I have known of "that painful thinking which corrodes the clay." He lived in an atmosphere of doubts and gloomy thoughts, all directed to religious questions and the destinies of man. His writings and the acts of his life show, what his countenance and conversation well depictured, the unceasing and painful restlessness of his mind on these topics. He sent for me frequently; but the inborn temperament of the man was too strong to allow of remedy, and any relief I could give was speedily lost in the chaos of changeful thoughts and speculations, which haunted him to the hour of his death. The persistent kindness of Archbishop Whately to Blanco White, in spite of some obloquy incurred thereby, was one of the many traits which do honour to the memory of that excellent but eccentric prelate.—HOLLAND, SIR HENRY, 1871, *Recollections of Past Life, p.* 255.

Blanco White would make an interesting study by himself, with all his spiritual vicissitudes and pathetic ways. . . . Influenced in some degree he must have been, for he was the most sensitive and radiating of mortals, either giving or receiving light every day of his life. But curious and touching as he is in himself, I have failed to trace any definite impulse communicated by him to the Oriel School, or even to the religious thought of his time. Like many other men who have been trained in close systems of thought, when the spirit of doubt was awakened in him, he merely fell out of one system into another—Romanism, Atheism, Anglicanism, Unitarianism. He had little conception of true inquiry, or of the patience of thought which works through all layers of systems to the core of truth beneath.—TULLOCH, JOHN, 1885, *Movements of Religious Thought in Britain During the Nineteenth Century, p.* 33.

Blanco White owes an enduring fame to a single sonnet—but this sonnet is one of the noblest in any language. There is quite a "Blanco White" literature concerning the famous fourteen lines headed "Night and Death." It is strange that the man who wrote this should do nothing else of any importance, and its composition must either have been a magnificent accident or the outcome of a not very powerful poetic impulse coming unexpectedly and in a moment to white heat, and therein exhausting itself for ever.—SHARP, WILLIAM, 1886, *Sonnets of this Century, p.* 323.

Of Blanco White's positive influence, it is not too much to say that he is the real founder of the modern Latitudinarian school in the English Church. . . . Blanco White's was a much more powerful mind than Whately's. . . . It is within the truth to say that but for Blanco White's visit to Oxford, Hampden's Bampton Lectures could never have been written.—LIDDON, HENRY PARRY, 1893, *Life of Edward Bouverie Pusey, ed. Johnston and Wilson, vol.* I, *pp.* 360, 361.

Eccentricities of inspiration, which sometimes result in productions that may almost be called fortuitous, occur in poetry as in other departments of art; and single poems, like single speeches and single pictures, sometimes baffle all accounting for. Of such the famous sonnet "To Night." . . . is perhaps the most striking example. . . . He wrote little verse, and, with the exception of the sonnet on Night and Death, none that calls for remark. This sonnet Coleridge characterized as "the finest and most greatly conceived sonnet in our language;" and Leigh Hunt declared that for thought it "stands supreme perhaps above all in any language, nor can we ponder it too deeply or with too hopeful a reverence." As Mr. Sharp pointed out . . . quite a Blanco-White literature has grown up around this sonnet.—MILES, ALFRED H., 1897, *The Poets and the Poetry of the Century, Sacred, Moral and Religious Verse.*

James Abraham Hillhouse

1789-1841

James Abraham Hillhouse, a native of Sachem's Head, near New Haven (1789-1841), graduated at Yale College in 1808, and spent many of his early years in New York, engaged in mercantile pursuits. On his return from a visit to Europe he married and retired to Sachem's Head, where he devoted himself to literature rather as an amusement than an occupation. His first poem, entitled "The Judgment," appeared in New York in 1812. "Percy's Masque," the successful attempt of one of the Percys to recover his ancestral home of Alnwick Castle, was issued in London in 1820, and reissued in New York the same year. In 1824 Hillhouse published the sacred drama of "Hadad," and in 1839 a complete edition in two volumes of his poetical writings. He was also the author of numerous addresses and discourses delivered on various occasions.—WILSON, JAMES GRANT, 1885, *Bryant and His Friends*, p. 387.

PERSONAL

Literary celebrity was purchased in those Arcadian days at a much lower price than is at present set upon the article. I do not remember much about Mr. Hillhouse's poem, called "Hadad," yet I shall venture to doubt whether it would make an author conspicuous if published to-day. Nevertheless, Mr. Hillhouse, the distinguished American poet, was pointed out as among the largest lions of the evening. [June 17, 1825] . . . Mr. Hillhouse was a man of great gentleness and refinement, and I afterward enjoyed his society as a visitor in our family circle.—QUINCY, JOSIAH, 1883, *Figures of the Past from the Leaves of Old Journals*, p. 140.

GENERAL

We are glad to meet with so respectable a production in this department of literature from the pen of a native writer; indeed, we are pleased to light upon any modern tragedy in the English language so well worthy of notice. . . . There is no powerful development of character, but the characters are consistent and well sustained. . . . We think that the author of "Percy's Masque" is to be congratulated on having escaped so well the florid and declamatory manner, with so many celebrated and seducing examples before him. We hope, however, that, should he continue to cultivate this department of the drama, he will be led to study a style still more idiomatic and easy, and, particularly (for here he has sinned most) with fewer capricious departures from the natural construction.—BRYANT, WILLIAM CULLEN, 1820, *North American Review*, vol. 11, pp. 384, 392, 393.

In short, such is the approach to excellence, both in the conception and execution of this little poem, that I confess myself more than commonly gratified in the opportunity of doing what lies in my power towards making it further known on this side the Atlantic; especially as the praise to which it is so justly entitled may, in all probability, lead its author to other and more extended efforts. —DRAKE, NATHAN, 1822, *Evenings in Autumn*, vol. II.

He observes all the proprieties of place, time, and character. In persuing "Hadad," we were struck with his constant adherence to historical and geographical truth, and his continual illusions to the customs, manners, events, and superstitions of the people among whom he had laid his scene. His *dramatis personæ* are not merely a list of Jewish names, but they are Jews, clad in Jewish costume, living in Jewish houses, expressing Jewish opinions, and talking, as far as possible, a Jewish language. The people are the descendants of Abraham, and the country is Palestine. . . . Mr. Hillhouse's "Hadad" is an ornament and bright addition to the literature of our country. We can send it abroad without a blush or an apology; not as being of the highest order of excellence, but as a sample of Amercian poetry, full of beauty, dignity and interest.—GREENWOOD, F. W. P., 1826, *Hillhouse's Hadad*, *North American Review*, vol. 22, pp. 25, 27.

Hillhouse, whose music, like his themes,
Lifts earth to heaven; whose poet-dreams
Are pure and holy as the hymn
Echoed from harp of seraphim,
By bards that drank at Zion's fountain,
  When glory, peace, and hope was hers,
And beautiful upon her mountain
  The feet of angel messengers.

—HALLECK, FITZ-GREENE, 1828, *The Recorder*.

Besides the high finish of Mr. Hillhouse's writings, we find another peculiarity in them, as compared with most others which come in our way. While there are no oddities in his style it has, in the best sense, a right to be called original. . . . Our impressions, derived from the reading of "Percy's Masque" and "Hadad" on their first appearance, were in favor of the former, as the superior poem. We now are of a different mind; nor are we induced to change it simply by the important improvements which "Hadad" has undergone, in the course of revision. The two works are, perhaps, equally graceful, but "Hadad" now strikes us as a composition of decidedly more power. Its fable, also, is more faultless, at the same time that it is much more bold. . . . This beautiful poem is certainly not the less effective on account of the perfect simplicity of its plot; nor, on the other hand, has any of the ample time, which has been given to a minute finish of the details, been lost. It is a story of love crossed by jealousy, and is wrought up to that painful degree of interest, which is only within the power of genius and study united.—PALFREY, JOHN G., 1840, *Hillhouse's Poems and Discourses, North American Review, vol.* 50, *pp.* 232, 239, 243.

As a mere work of art, "Percy's Masque" is one of the most faultless in the language. If subjected to scrutiny, it will bear the strictest criticism by which compositions of this kind can be tried. We cannot detect the violation of a single rule which should be observed in the construction of a tragedy. When, therefore, it was republished in this country, it at once gave its author an elevated rank as a dramatic poet. . . . "Hadad" was written in 1824, and printed in the following year. This has generally been esteemed Hillhouse's masterpiece. As a sacred drama, it is probably unsurpassed. The scene is in Judea, in the days of David; and as the agency of evil spirits is introduced, as opportunity is afforded to bring forward passages of strange sublimity and wildness. For a work like this, Hillhouse was peculiarly qualified. A most intimate acquaintance with the Scriptures enabled him to introduce each minute detail in perfect keeping with historical truth, while from the same study he seems also to have imbibed the lofty thoughts, and the majestic style of the ancient Hebrew prophets. . . . As a poet, he possessed qualities seldom found united: a masculine strength of mind, and a most delicate perception of the beautiful. With an imagination of the loftiest order—with "the vision and the faculty divine" in its fullest exercise, the wanderings of his fancy were chastened and controlled by exquisite taste. The grand characteristic of his writings is their classical beauty. Every passage is polished to the utmost, yet there is no exuberance, no sacrifice to false and meretricious taste. He threw aside the gaudy and affected brilliancy with which too many set forth their poems, and left his to stand, like the doric column, charming by its simplicity. Writing not for present popularity, or to catch the senseless applause of the multitude, he was willing to commit his works—as Lord Bacon did his memory—"to the next ages."—GRISWOLD, RUFUS W., 1842–46, *The Poets and Poetry of America, pp.* 81, 82.

"Percy's Masque," while it claims an humbler character than that of "The Judgment," and "Hadad," for boldness of conception, and vigor of thought, is a poem of exceeding merit, and, if we mistake not, is the most beautiful of our author's productions.—EVEREST, CHARLES W., 1843, *The Poets of Connecticut, p.* 170.

"Percy's Masque" reproduces the features of an era more impressed with knightly character than any in the annals of England. Hillhouse moves in that atmosphere quite as gracefully as among the solemn and venerable traditions of the Hebrew faith. His dramatic and other pieces are the first instances in this country of artistic skill in the higher and more elaborate spheres of poetic writing.—TUCKERMAN, HENRY T., 1852, *A Sketch of American Literature.*

The prevalent character of the writings of Hillhouse is a certain spirit of elegance, which characterizes both his prose and poetry, and which is allied to the higher themes of passion and imagination. He felt deeply and expressed his emotions naturally in the dramatic form. His conceptions were submitted to a laborious preparation, and took an artistical shape. Of his three dramatic productions, "Demetria," an Italian tragedy, is a passionate story of perplexed love, jealousy, and intrigue; "Hadad" is a highly wrought dramatic poem, employing the agency of the supernatural; and "Percy's Masque," suggested by an English ballad, Bishop Percy's "Hermit of Warkworth," an historical romance, of much interest in the narrative, the plot being highly effective, at the expense somewhat of character, while the dialogue is filled with choice descriptions of the natural scenery in which the piece is cast, and tender sentiment of the lovers. That, however, which gained the author most repute with his contemporaries, and is the highest proof of his powers, is the two-fold characterization of "Hadad" and "Tamar;" the supernatural fallen angel appearing as the sensual heathen lover, and the Jewish maiden. The dialogue in which these personages are displayed, abounds with rare poetical beauties; with lines and imagery worthy of the old Elizabethan drama. The description, in the conversation between Nathan and Tamar, of the associations of Hadad, who is "of the blood royal of Damascus," is in a rich imaginative vein. —DUYCKINCK, EVERT A. AND GEORGE L., 1855-65-75, *Cyclopædia of American Literature, ed. Simons, vol.* I, *p.* 817.

Excelled in what may be called the written drama, which, though unsuited to representation, is characterized by noble sentiment and imagery. His dramatic and other poems are the first instances in this country of artistic skill in the higher and more elaborate spheres of poetic writing, and have gained for him a permanent place among the American poets.—BOTTA, ANNE C. LYNCH, 1860, *Hand-Book of Universal Literature, p.* 524.

Hillhouse's poetry, although at one time ranked very high by critics, is now but little read by the public.—HART, JOHN S., 1872, *A Manual of American Literature, p.* 106.

The well balanced stanzas of James A. Hillhouse. — NICHOL, JOHN, 1880-85, *American Literature, p.* 251.

William Ellery Channing

1780-1842

William Ellery Channing, preacher and writer, was born 7th April 1780 at Newport, Rhode Island. He graduated at Harvard in 1798, and in 1803 was ordained minister of a Congregational church in Boston, where his sermons were famous for their "fervour, solemnity, and beauty." He was somewhat of a mystic, held Christ to be more than man, but was ultimately the leader of the Unitarians. In 1821 he received the title of D. D. from Harvard University, and next year he visited Europe, and made the acquaintance of Wordsworth and Coleridge. Among his Works (6 vols. 1841-46) were his "Essay on National Literature," "Remarks on Milton," "Character and Writings of Fénélon," "Negro Slavery," and "Self-culture." He died October 2, 1842, at Bennington, Vermont.—PATRICK AND GROOME, *eds.*, 1897, *Chambers's Biographical Dictionary, p.* 199.

PERSONAL

One of the greatest pleasures I have had here, or could have anywhere, has been seeing Mr. Channing. I have twice dined and spent the evening in his company, and sat next to him all the time. There is a superior light in his mind that sheds a pure, bright gleam on every thing that comes from it. He talks freely upon common topics, but they seem no longer to be common topics when he speaks of them. There is the influence of the sanctuary, the holy place about him. . . . It seems to me that it would be impossible to live within the sphere of Mr. Channing's influence without being in some degree spiritualized by it.—SEDGWICK, CATHARINE M., 1826, *Life and Letters, p.* 181.

My Dear H—, I began this letter yesterday, and am this moment returned from a long visit to Dr. Channing. . . . The outward man of the eloquent preacher and teacher is rather insignificant, and produces no impression at first sight of unusual intellectual supremacy; and though his eyes and forehead are fine, they did not seem to me to do justice to the mind expressed in his writings; for though Shakespeare says,

"There is no art to read the mind's construction in the face,"

I think the mental qualities are more often detected there than the moral ones. He is short and slight in figure, and looks, as indeed he is, extremely delicate, an habitual invalid; his eyes, which are gray, are well and deeply set, and the brow and forehead fine, though not, perhaps, as striking as I had expected. The rest of the face has no peculiar character, and is rather plain. He talked to me a great deal about the stage, acting, the dramatic art; and, professing to know nothing about it, maintained some theories which proved he did not, indeed, know much.—KEMBLE, FRANCES ANN, 1833, *Letter, May* 24; *Records of a Girlhood, p.* 576.

I gave Mr. Persico no encouragement to make an experiment on my head. It is too thin, and has too little beauty for this art. Painting, I think, can take greater liberties than sculpture, and even painting has made poor work with my face. I am certainly not vain of my exterior. My countenance would not make me many friends, I fear. What has troubled me in my different portraits is, that they have not given me a more intellectual expression, but that so little benevolence has beamed from the features. I have learned, with the Apostle, to prefer charity to all knowledge; and, if I am to be handed down to posterity, I should be pleased to speak from the stone or canvas, or rather to breathe from it, good-will to mankind.—CHANNING, WILLIAM ELLERY, 1835, *Diary, Nov.* 20.

Thence I went to Boston, where I spent nearly a fortnight very pleasantly, and saw much of Dr. Channing, the good, the wise, the great. Don't you envy me? We will have everlasting talks of him when we meet. I heard him preach—like an apostle!—JAMESON, ANNA, 1837, *Letter, Memoirs, ed. Macpherson, p.* 134.

Here rest the remains of
WILLIAM ELLERY CHANNING,
Born, 7 April, 1780,
at Newport, R. I.;
Ordained, 1 June, 1803,
as a minister of Jesus Christ
to the Society worshipping God
in Federal Street, Boston:
Died, 2 October, 1842,
while on a journey,
at Bennington, Vermont.

In Memory of
WILLIAM ELLERY CHANNING,
honored throughout Christendom,
for his eloquence and courage
in maintaininy and advancing
the Great Cause of
Truth, Religion, and Human Freedom,
This Monument
is gratefully and reverently erected
by the Christian Society,
of which, during nearly forty years,
he was Pastor.

—TICKNOR, GEORGE, 1842, *Inscription on Monument.*

Thou livest in the life of all good things;
What words thou spak'st for Freedom shall not die;
Thou sleepest not, for now thy Love hath wings
To soar where hence thy Hope could hardly fly. . . .
This laurel-leaf I cast upon thy bier;
Let worthier hands than these thy wreath entwine;
Upon thy hearse I shed no useless tear,—
For us weep rather thou in calm divine!

—LOWELL, JAMES RUSSELL, 1842, *Elegy on the Death of Dr. Channing.*

With few of the physical attributes belonging to the orator, he was an orator of surpassing grace. His soul tabernacled in a body that was little more than a filament of clay. He was small in stature; but when he spoke his person seemed to dilate with the majesty of his thoughts,—as the Hercules of Lysippus, a marvel of ancient art, though not more than a foot in height, revived in the mind the superhuman strength which overcame the Nemean lion. . . . His voice was soft and musical, not loud or full in tone; and yet, like conscience, it made itself heard in the inmost chambers of the soul. His eloquence was gentleness and persuasion, reasoning for religion, humanity, and justice. He did not thunder or lighten. The rude elemental forces furnish no proper image of his power. Like sunshine, his words descended upon the souls of his hearers, and under their genial influence the hard in heart were softened, while the closely hugged mantle of prejudice and error dropped to the earth. His eloquence had not the character and fashion of forensic effort or parliamentary debate. It mounted above these, into an atmosphere unattempted by the applauded orators of the world.—SUMNER, CHARLES, 1846, *The Scholar, the Jurist, the Artist, the Philanthropist; Works, vol.* I, *p.* 296.

He sought and longed for a perfectly free communication; and no conversation interested him more than that which, in forgetfulness of him and of one's self and of every thing extraneous, was a kind of monologue, a kind of reverie, the purest and most abstract idealism. Least of all must it be supposed that there was any assumption about him, or any stiff formality or precision,—any thing that said, "Now let us talk great talk." Never. He did talk greatly, because he could not help it. But his manner of doing it, his manner in every thing, was the most simple, the most unpretending, imaginable. At the same time he possessed a nature the most truly social. He regretted any thing in himself or in others that repressed it. More than once has he said to me, "I am *too serious.*" He longed to feel upon his spirit the free and genial breath of society. . . . I wish it were in my power to give any idea of the extraordinary character of this conversation. On my first acquaintance with him, it was my happiness to pass a number of weeks under his own roof. His health was then delicate; he went abroad but little; but his mind was left untouched by the frailty of his body; and I found it constantly occupied and struggling with great questions. On the highest philosophy, on the highest religion, on the highest wisdom of life, all the day long he pursued the questions which these themes present, without ever slackening, or ever turning aside to ordinary and commonplace talk. The range of his subjects was as great as their elevation; from the most recondite point in philosophy—the difference between relative and absolute truth—to the forms of philanthropic enterprise and political development around him. But his favorite themes were *man* and the New Testament; man,—his condition and the philosophy of his condition; the New Testament,—Jesus Christ, his teaching, and the sublimest contemplation of God. —DEWEY, ORVILLE, 1847, *Discourse on the Character and Writings of Channing.*

Thus tranquilly passed Dr. Channing's days at Oakland. Up usually, in the morning, before any of his guests were risen, his quick step was heard upon the gravel walk, and, looking from the window, one saw him, with his shawl or gown wrapped round his shoulders and the dogs gambolling by his side, passing amid the shrubbery, and stopping each moment to gaze, at a newly opened flower, a gleam of sunshine on the dewy lawn, or some passing bird scattering drops from the branches, caught his eye. His own expression—"When I see my friends after the night's separation, let me receive them as new gifts from God, as raised from the dead"—describes precisely the character of his greeting. The beaming eyes, the radiant smile, the grasp of the hand, the joyous tone, all spoke to the spirit, saying, —"What an inestimable privilege it is to live together in this glorious home which our Father gives us each day anew!" Without a word or look that was not as spontaneous as the delight of a child, he seemed so softened with religious sensibility, that his very "good morning" was a welcome to prayer.—CHANNING, WILLIAM HENRY, 1848, *Memoir of William Ellery Channing, vol.* III, *p.* 433.

The most singular thing in his utterance was the extraordinary flexibility of his voice, its vast and "undulating" variety of modulation. It seemed to us like one of those delicate, scientific instruments, invented to detect and measure the subtilest elements in nature, and sensitive to the slightest influence,—as, for instance, those nicely adjusted scales which vibrate under the small dust on the balance or the weight of a hair. It rose and fell so strangely in the course of the simplest and most commonplace sentence, in the utterance of a single word often, that his hearers felt immediately that here was a speaker of a novel kind, and they watched to see how he could possibly become, according to any ordinary sense of the word, eloquent. If our readers who were wont to hear him will recall the word "immortality" as spoken by Dr. Channing, they will understand what we endeavour to describe. His style of speaking, from this peculiarity, was instantly felt to be his own,—not the product of any art, but the gift of nature; if indeed it could be thought a gift, and not a misfortune, when only its singularity was apparent, before its capabilities were witnessed and its wondrous power felt. There was no want of firmness in his tones, and yet they fluctuated continually. And the power of his voice lay in this, that, being thus flexible, it was true to every change of emotion that arose in his mind.—FURNESS, W. H., 1848, *Memoir of Channing, Christian Examiner, vol.* 45, *p.* 274.

Dr. Channing's life is full of interest, but of a calm, thoughtful kind. He had no adventures; nor were his inward struggles, as detailed, at least, very striking. He had taken immense pains with himself, but the nobler element of his nature was so strongly predominant, that his life was steady continuous victory, unmarked by any of those partial victories of evil which give fearful interest to the lives of the greater part of those who have fought their way to uncommon excellence. The purest love for man, the most unconquerable trust in human nature, seem to have been the very basis of his being. He was a Unitarian, but that is a very wide term, including a vast variety of persons thinking very differently on essentials. I can only say that I should be very glad if half of those who recognise the hereditary claims on the Son of God to worship, bowed down before his moral dignity with an adoration half as profound, or a love half as enthusiastic, as Dr. Channing's. I wish I, a Trinitarian, loved and adored Him, and the Divine goodness in Him, anything near the way in which that Unitarian felt. A religious lady found the book on my table a few days ago, and was horror-struck. I told her that if she and I ever got to heaven, we should find Dr. Channing revolving round the central Light in an orbit immeasurably nearer than ours, almost invisible to us, and lost in a blaze of light; which she has no doubt, duly reported to the Brighton inquisition for heretics.—ROBERTSON, FREDERICK W., 1849, *Letter, Nov.* 16; *Life and Letters, ed. Brooke, vol.* I, *p.* 283.

Not vainly did old poets tell,
  Nor vainly did old genius paint
God's great and crowning miracle,—
  The hero and the saint!
For even in a faithless day
  Can we our sainted ones discern;
And feel, while with them on the way
  Our hearts within us burn.
And thus the common tongue and pen
Which, world-wide, echo CHANNING'S fame,
As one of Heaven's anointed men,
  Have sanctified his name.

—WHITTIER, JOHN GREENLEAF, 1850, *Channing, Poetical Works.*

I have often heard him [John Wilson] speak of Americans in terms of admiration. He knew many, and received all who came to see him with much interest and kindness. . . . Of one of them he always spoke with profound respect, as a man whose spiritual life and great accomplishments, pure philosophical inquiries and critical taste, had given him a lofty position among his countrymen—Dr. Channing, the piety of whose character made his life upon earth one of singular beauty.—GORDON, MRS., 1862, *"Christopher North," A Memoir of John Wilson, ed. Mackenzie, p.* 426.

Some men live always on the plane of what is common: they live in averages, and take life at low-water mark. Others rise and fall again, sometimes having a moment of enthusiasm, a sparkle of generosity, and then subsiding into their old routine. But Dr. Channing was always breathing the pure air of the mountain-top. Whenever you went into his room, he would begin some strain of a higher mood, some theme of pure religion, something which would lift you into the realm of eternal truths, something which would make you better and happier during the whole day.—CLARKE, JAMES FREEMAN, 1867-78, *William Ellery Channing, Memorial and Biographical Sketches, p.* 162.

Dr. Channing, between whom and Harriet Martineau a true friendship subsisted to the day of his death, was a good man, but not in any sense a great one. With benevolent intentions, he could not greatly help the nineteenth century, for he knew very little about it or indeed of any other. He had neither insight, courage nor firmness. In his own church had sprung up a vigorous opposition to slavery, which he innocently, in so far as ignorantly, used the little strength he had to stay. He was touched by Brougham's eloquent denial of the right of property in man, and he adopted the idea as a theme: but he dreaded any one who claimed, on behalf of the slaves, that their masters should instantly renounce that right of ownership; he was terror-stricken at the idea of calling on the whole American people to take counsel on so difficult and delicate a matter in anti-slavery associations; and, above all, he deprecated the admission of the colored race to our ranks. He had been selected by a set of money-making men as their representative for piety, as Edward Everett was their representative gentleman and scholar, Judge Story their representative gentleman, jurist, and companion in social life, and Daniel Webster their representative statesman and advocate, looking after their business interests in Congress.—CHAPMAN,

MARIA WESTON, *ed.*, 1877, *Harriet Martineau's Autobiography, vol.* II, *pp.* 272, 273.

During these years (from 1828 to '32), I often heard Doctor Channing preach. His attenuated figure and face, his large luminous eyes, and his sweet but pervading voice, formed a peculiar presence not to be forgotten. His manner was calm and rarely aided by gesture, but earnest and deeply impressive, and he possessed the magnetism that carried the audience side by side with him, from point to point of his discourse. In social life he was not unamiable, but his grand views of humanity seemed to lift his attention above social surroundings. — OAKEY, S. W., 1881, *Recollections of American Society, Scribner's Monthly, vol.* 21, *p.* 783.

Dr. Channing, whilst he lived, was the star of the American Church, and we then thought, if we do not still think, that he left no successor in the pulpit. He could never be reported, for his eye and voice could not be printed, and his discourses lose their best in losing them. He was made for the public; his cold temperament made him the most unprofitable private companion; but all America would have been impoverished in wanting him. We could not then spare a single word he uttered in public, not so much as the reading a lesson in Scripture, or a hymn, and it is curious that his printed writings are almost a history of the times; as there was no great public interest, political, literary, or even economical (for he wrote on the Tariff), on which he did not leave some printed record of his brave and thoughtful opinion. A poor little invalid all his life, he is yet one of those men who vindicate the power of the American race to produce greatness.— EMERSON, RALPH WALDO, 1882? *Historic Notes of Life and Letters in New England, Works, Riverside ed., vol.* X, *p.* 320.

While Parker's and Beecher's pulpits echoed Jonathan Mayhew's morning gun and fired words like cannon-balls, in the highest pulpit of America, foremost among the champions of liberty, stood the slight and radiant figure of the scholarly son of Rhode Island, upon whom more than upon any of her children the mantle of Roger Williams had worthily fallen, William Ellery Channing.—CURTIS, GEORGE WILLIAM, 1882, *Orations and Addresses, ed. Norton, vol.* I, *p.* 329.

No wonder we sometimes heard that from day to day it required the tenderest nursing to keep the soul in the body. See him on Sunday as he moves up the pulpit stairs. His debility fills you with sympathy and anxiety. He sinks exhausted on his seat; and when he rises to give out the hymn, he is too weak, you fear, for the service. The single lock of his soft brown hair, as it falls across his forehead, contrasts strongly with its transparent paleness, and his thin hollow cheeks are covered with pain-caused lines. The first tones of his voice, though feeble and low, are reverential, and stir the hushed congregation to devoutness. After the hymn, read with more strength, is sung, he rises for the sermon. A few sentences are uttered, when you feel that, out of all this weakness, there are coming words of a rare energy. His full eye kindles, his voice gains strength, and, forgetting his delicate figure, you are borne on, with increasing sway, assured that this man is a power to move, thrill, and inspire. Perhaps there was never a more striking demonstration of the power of the human will over the body than in Dr. Channing. . . . Such men as Channing do not grow old with the lapse of years. We who saw him, on and on, from his early manhood to his closing days, remember how little he changed, even in personal appearance, with the approach of age. It seems to me, as I recall him in his meridian, that he showed more the effects of toil and time, and his face was more pallid and careworn, than in the last years of his life. At that time his countenance grew more radiant, and he manifestly felt more at ease, and enjoyed this world as he never had before.—MUZZEY, A. B., 1882, *Reminiscences and Memorials of Men of the Revolution and their Families, pp.* 169, 182.

The fact is, that the man who loomed to such gigantic spiritual stature in the pulpit was not a great pastor. With all his interest in education, he did not personally come near the average youth of his congregation. We revered him and were very proud of him, but the distance between us was impassable. I am speaking of him, of course, as he appeared to the very young. . . . Channing's gift was that of a preacher. His sermons, while coherent and complete as compositions, were given with a warmth and intensity of expression with which scholarship and delicacy of thought are seldom united.—QUINCY, JOSIAH, 1883, *Figures of the Past from the Leaves of Old Journals, p.* 309.

While we were at Boston, at a dinner given him [Gen. Winfield Scott] by that venerable merchant prince, Thomas H. Perkins, he was placed next to Dr. Channing. My seat at the table was too distant to enable me to understand them, but I observed that the general was an attentive listener. They presented a singular contrast—a giant warrior listening with deference to a puny preacher, whose frail body excited compassion. His learning and eloquence, which were ennobled by a spirit of benevolence, secured to Dr. Channing a profound respect even from those men who could not agree with his theology and his restrictive code of morals. Returning from the dinner the general told me the subject of their conversation was the Grecian Philosophy, and he fancied he had been spending the evening with Anaxagoras.—KEYES, GEN. E. D., 1884, *Fifty Years' Observations, p.* 46.

Personally he was amiable, kindly, and courteous, notwithstanding the distance at which he seems to have kept all men.—WOODBERRY, GEORGE EDWARD, 1890, *Studies in Letters and Life, p.* 238.

Newport has honored the memory and name of her illustrious son by the erection of a handsome memorial church and a substantial monument. Perhaps it should be said more precisely that these memorials of the great divine have been erected within her borders; for the church is virtually the gift of the Unitarians of the world, though the movement for its erection was started in Newport, and the monument witnesses to the generosity of a single individual, and he a Newporter only by virtue of his residence in the city during the summer months. But though Newport is only partially and indirectly responsible for these two handsome memorials, she is proud to have them; and with the old house where Channing was born, the old church in which he preached, the farm house and meeting-house on the Island, which he frequented, they are among the most cherished of Newport's points of interest and of the links binding the city of the present day with that of the past and with the great men who have been her sons or who have lived or tarried within her borders.—THURSTON, CHARLES RAWSON, 1896, *The Homes and Haunts of Channing, New England Magazine, vol.* 21, *p.* 429.

GENERAL

He looks through the external forms of things in search of the secret and mysterious principles of thought, action, and being. He takes little notice of the varieties of manners and character that form the favourite topics of the novelist and poet. Mind in the abstract, its nature, proprieties, and destiny, are his constant theme. He looks at material objects chiefly as the visible expressions of the existence, character, and will of the sublime Unseen Intelligence whose power created and whose presence informs and sustains the universe.—EVERETT, ALEXANDER HILL, 1835, *North American Review, vol.* 41, *p.* 366.

Offer my respectful regards to Dr. Channing, whom certainly I could not count on for a reader, or other than a grieved condemnatory one; for I reckoned tolerance had its limits. His own faithful, long-continued striving towards what is best, I knew and honored; that he will let me go my own way thitherward, with a God-speed from him, is surely a new honor to us both.—CARLYLE, THOMAS, 1835, *To Ralph Waldo Emerson, May* 13; *Correspondence, ed. Norton, vol.* I, *p.* 65.

Dr. Channing's little book ["Negro Slavery"] will be received with unhesitating and unmingled consent and applause in Europe, and will add at once to his reputation, which is already much greater than I supposed; not as extensive as that of Washington Irving, but almost as much so, and decidedly higher. My bookseller here told me, to-day, he thought an English edition of his works would sell well on the Continent, they are so frequently asked for in his shop; and Baron Bülow, a young Prussian, brought me the other night a letter from the Duchess of Anhalt Dessau, inquiring earnestly how she could procure them for herself. In England, again and again, where I should least have suspected it, I found him held in the highest estimation; one of the old Besborough family, for instance, looking upon a present of one of his sermons as one of the most agreeable things that could happen to him; and Mrs. Somerville, Miss

Joanna Baillie, and several other persons, of no less note, declaring to me that he was generally regarded by their friends, as well as themselves, as the best writer of English prose alive. If the book on Slavery is written with only the usual talent of his other works, I will venture to predict that it will be more admired than anything he has yet printed.—TICKNOR, GEORGE, 1836, *To William H. Prescott, Feb.* 8; *Life, Letters and Journals of George Ticknor, vol.* I, *p.* 479.

As the name of Dr. Channing stands high in American literature for several works which have shown much vigour of thinking, some talent for declamation, and generally considerable success in composition, we are bound to observe that, had nothing from his pen ever reached us but the tract now before us, we should have been at a loss to comprehend the grounds of the reputation which he enjoys to a certain degree on either side of the Atlantic. The taste which it displays is far from being correct; his diction is exceedingly affected; and the affectation is that of extreme vigour and refinement of thought, often when he is only unmeaning, contradictory, or obscure. His opinions on critical matters likewise indicate a very defective taste, and show that, in his own practice of writing, he goes wrong on a false theory; and in pursuit of the "striking"—the "grand"—the "uncommon." That his style should be perspicuous can, indeed, hardly be expected, when he avows the incredible opinion, that a composition may be too easily understood, and complains of the recent efforts to make science intelligible to the bulk of mankind, that their tendency is to degrade philosophy under the show of seeking after usefulness.—BROUGHAM, HENRY LORD, 1839, *False-Taste—Dr. Channing, Edinburgh Review, vol.* 69, *p.* 214.

Dr. Channing, whose style is irradiated with all the splendours of a glowing imagination, showing, as powerfully as any other example, probably, in English prose, of what melody and compass the language is capable under the touch of genius instinct with genuine enthusiasm.—PRESCOTT, WILLIAM H., 1839, *Chateaubriand's English Literature, Biographical and Critical Miscellanies, p.* 270.

His reputation both at home and abroad is deservedly high, and in regard to the matters of purity, polish, and modulation of style, he may be said to have attained the dignity of a standard and a classic.—POE, EDGAR ALLAN, 1841, *A Chapter on Autography, Works, vol.* V.

There is one word that covers every cause to which Channing devoted his talents and his heart, and that word is FREEDOM. Liberty is the key of his religious, his political, his philanthropic principles. Free the slave, free the serf, free the ignorant, free the sinful. Let there be no chains upon the conscience, the intellect, the pursuits, or the persons of men. Free agency is the prime distinction and privilege of humanity. It is the first necessity of a moral being. Extinguish freedom, and you extinguish humanity. Tyranny is spiritual murder, as sin is moral suicide.—BELLOWS, HENRY W., 1842, *Discourse.*

I think Channing an admirable writer. So much sense and eloquence. Such a command of language. Yet, admirable as his sermon on war is, I have the vanity to think my own equally good, quite as sensible, quite as eloquent, as full of good principle and fine language; and you will be the more inclined to agree with me in this comparison, when I tell you that I preached in St. Paul's the identical sermon which Lord Grey so much admires. I thought I could not write anything half so good, so I preached Channing.—SMITH, SYDNEY, 1844, *To the Countess Grey, March* 27; *Letters, ed. Mrs. Austin.*

From the appearance of his "Discourse on the Evidences of Christianity"—a luminous exposition—till the lamented death of this eminent man, the public expectation which had been raised so high by the character of his earliest performances was continually excited and fulfilled by the appearance of some new and earnest expression of his thoughts on themes which come immediately home to men's business and bosoms,—religion, government, and literature in their widest sense and application.—TAYLER, JOHN JAMES, 1845, *Retrospect of the Religious Life of England.*

We have already observed that a critic of Art places him in an American triumvirate with Allston and Washington. More frequently he is associated with Washington and Franklin. Unlike Washington, he was never general or president; unlike Franklin, he never held high office. But it would be difficult to say that since then any American has exerted greater sway over his fellow-men. And yet, if it be asked what single measure he carried to a successful close, I could not answer. It is on *character* that he has wrought and is still producing incalculable change. So extensive is this influence, that multitudes now feel it although strangers to his spoken or even his written word. The whole country and age feel it. . . . He helped to bring government within the Christian circle, and taught the statesman that there is one comprehensive rule, binding on the conscience in public affairs as in private affairs.—SUMNER, CHARLES, 1846, *The Scholar, the Jurist, the Artist, the Philanthropist, Works, vol.* I, *pp.* 285, 288.

It may be doubted whether another instance can be found of an individual arresting so much attention in the literary world, and yet claiming no place there, finding himself a literary man by accident. The laurels that were showered upon him he took not the slightest pains to gather or preserve. If they appeared to be falling off, he did not even carry himself with the slightest care to keep them on. If a hand was extended to pluck them from him, he showed no sign of resistance, nor did a shade of mortified vanity ever darken those thoughtful and beaming eyes. If his distinguished reviewers thought to wound and humble him, as, from their occasional strength of phrase, would seem to have been their design, never was expectation more completely disappointed. He barely knew of their assaults; they fell far short of his equanimity. He thought even less of the arrows that were discharged at him than the lion of the dewdrops on his mane, for he never stirred to shake them off.—FURNESS, W. H., 1848, *Christian Examiner, vol.* 45, *p.* 272.

He inspired respect more than he won confidence. His thoughts interested his friends more than himself. His name was an exponent of certain principles associated with human progress and moral truth, rather than an endearing household spell. In conversation he appeared mainly intent upon gleaning from his auditors new facts to aid his own speculations. If they had seen a new country, undergone a peculiar experience, or reflected deeply on general truth, he sought, by rigid inquiry, to elicit the result. Thus as a moralist, he pursued the same course as Goethe in his literary vocation—seeking to make his fellow-creatures objective, recoiling from assimilation, and repelling all sympathetic approach, in order to render them subservient to a professional end.—TUCKERMAN, HENRY T., 1849, *Characteristics of Literature, p.* 62.

It was impossible for him to be a learned man. He spread himself sometimes beneath the tree of knowledge; and, for a while, the leaves would drop through the air of motionless attention, and rest upon the silent grass of thought; but the winds that swept over his soul were so frequent and so fresh, that nothing could lie where it fell, and the forms of fancy displaced the order of deposition. There is a peculiarity in his composition, which is traceable to the same cause. His writings exhibit nothing logical, nothing architectoric in their structure. They are not put together in demonstration of a particular truth, or to show the perspective of a complex system; but in exposition of a profound sentiment. He never thinks in a line, but always from a centre, to which he returns again and again, in order to radiate forth in new directions. Thus he does not *survey* a subject, he does not *prosecute* it; he *dwells upon* it.—MARTINEAU, JAMES, 1849, *Life of Channing, The Westminster and Foreign Quarterly Review, vol.* 50, *p.* 346.

I do not place the writings of Dr. Channing as high in the scale of intellectual merit as his Boston friends and admirers are wont to do.—BUSHNELL, HORACE, 1850, *To Dr. Bartol, Jan.* 23; *Life and Letters, p.* 230.

The spiritual beauty of his writings is very great; they are all distinguished for sweetness, elevation, candour, and a severe devotion to truth. On great questions, he took middle ground, and sought a panoramic view; he wished also to stand high, yet never forgot what was above more than what was around and beneath him. He was not well acquainted with man on the impulsive and passionate side of his nature, so that his view of character was sometimes narrow, but it was always noble. He exercised an expansive and purifying power on the atmosphere, and stands a godfather at the baptism of this country. —OSSOLI, MARGARET FULLER, 1850? *Art, Literature and the Drama, p.* 304.

Channing is an antique man, with a Christian heart; in humanity a Greek, in citizenship a Roman, in Christianity an apostle. It would be a misapprehension to conceive of him as a learned and speculative theologian. —BUNSEN, CHRISTIAN KARL JOSIAS, 1858, *God in History.*

Channing never identified himself with any theological party. He called himself a Unitarian, and so in a sense he was, but his views were Arian rather than what are commonly known as Unitarian.—ALEXANDER, WILLIAM L., 1877, *Encyclopædia Britannica, Ninth ed., vol.* V, *p.* 342.

It has been already said that Channing became an author by accident; he himself said so. He never cared to think of himself as a *littérateur;* and yet it is noteworthy that his sermons had a leading part with those of his great contemporaries, Buckminster and the rest, in giving the sermon a place here in literature, as a literary production, and not mere sectarian, theological, political, or historical matter,—a place, in short, in *polite* literature, and among the *humanities.* Channing himself, indeed, repeatedly disclaims paying any special attention to *mere* style. . . . The style of Channing is plain, pure, and perspicuous. It has the transparency of a clear, calm autumn afternoon, when no haze dims the serenity of the atmosphere. Sometimes, though more rarely, it has the sober splendor of those after-summer hours, when a mingled mellowness and brilliancy charm the beholder. But, withal, it is marked by a self-contained quietness and even flow. It has an ease which never degenerates into that inflated and turgid manner which sometimes impairs the style of his classmate, Judge Story. It has a certain chaste elegance, but is remarkably free from ornament; deals very sparingly in figures, and scarcely uses one, excepting where the figure is not mere ornament, but argument; resembling, so far, more the style of Webster than that of Everett.—BROOKS, CHARLES T., 1880, *William Ellery Channing: A Centennial Memory, pp.* 214, 215.

I scarcely need say that I yield to no one in love and reverence for the great and good man whose memory, outliving all prejudices of creed, sect, and party, is the common legacy of Christendom. As the years go on, the value of that legacy will be more and more felt; not so much, perhaps, in doctrine as in spirit, in those utterances of a devout soul which are above and beyond the affirmation or negation of dogma. His ethical severity and Christian tenderness; his hatred of wrong and oppression, with love and pity for the wrongdoer; his noble pleas for self-culture, temperance, peace, and purity; and above all, his precept and example of unquestioning obedience to duty and voice of God in his soul, can never become obsolete. It is very fitting that his memory should be especially cherished with that of Hopkins and Berkeley in the beautiful island to which the common residence of those worthies has lent additional charms and interest.—WHITTIER, JOHN GREENLEAF, 1880, *Read at the Dedication of the Channing Memorial Church at Newport, R. I., March* 13.

In the history of the so-called Transcendental movement of New England I know no name older than Dr. Channing's. I have told how his preaching in 1820 began to emancipate me from the materialistic system of Priestley, and his conversation in 1825 from that of Brown, and his introducing me to Coleridge, from whom I first learned the meaning of the word "transcendental." And when Carlyle's writings and Ralph Waldo Emerson's lectures, in 1832, began to quicken our Boston thinking, it seemed to me that at last Dr. Channing's spiritual philosophy had begun to pervade society, and was about to give it the depth and broad scope of the original Christian faith.—PEABODY, ELIZABETH PALMER, 1880, *Reminiscences of Rev. William Ellery Channing, p.* 364.

A keen practical sense of the duties of life is, in most of his work, more conspicuous than abstract speculative power; but his insight into the position of parties, his charitable view of them, and his forecasts of the probability of future conflicts, are remarkable. Though at variance with the majority of the creeds of christendom, Channing's writings are everywhere marked by a reverential spirit, and not unfrequently by a touch of inherited asceticism. His essays on "Self-Culture" anticipate much said, more recently, by the later school of free-thought, to which he gave the first distinct impulse. . . . Dr. Channing's work is so far from that of a mere intellectual sensualist that he has been called a purist; but he loved

Beauty as well as Virtue for its own sake, and his style is generally free from the defects of taste frequent in the writings of his contemporaries. The "Essay on National Literature" (1824), by which his reputation was first made, is singularly suggestive, and only errs by the intrusion, here and there, of anti-Calvanistic polemic. His review of Fénélon abounds in passages, as the often quoted picture of religious peace, which exhibit the delicacy of his perceptions; but the breadth and force of his sympathy is most manifest in his "Remarks on Milton," à propos of the publication of the posthumous "De Doctrina Christiana."—NICHOL, JOHN, 1880–85, *American Literature, pp.* 133, 184.

Our recognized literature began with Bryant and Irving; but its real sources were in Channing, his associates and disciples, or rather in the intellectual movement that followed the decline of ecclesiastical rule. Channing, so far as he was a conscious agent, was a mild-tempered agitator, remarkable for nobility of character and for a spirituality that was almost angelic. The revolution he led was against the dominant theology, but the influence was felt by millions who never accepted the new doctrines. Clerical limitations became obsolete. People rediscovered Shakespeare, as amateur astronomers discover Jupiter; for the works of the chief of poets had before this been unknown to Puritan libraries. It was found that there were writers and thinkers who were not wearers of Geneva bands. Channing himself was no longer shut up in a remote corner, but was welcomed into the fraternity of lettered men. Until his Essays on Milton, Fénélon, and Napoleon appeared, European scholars had never thought of America except in connection with savages, fish, furs, and rebellion. The breadth and force of this movement can scarcely be overestimated. Excepting Irving, Cooper, and Poe, there has not been an American author of high rank in this century whose intellectual lineage is not traceable, directly or indirectly, to Channing and Emerson.—UNDERWOOD, FRANCIS H., 1882, *James Russell Lowell, a Biographical Sketch, p.* 32.

He was never quite an invalid, but he was always a valetudinarian. In particular, he had a singular sensitiveness to cold; and the recollection of many of his friends will recall his presence, oftenest at the fireside corner of his warmly sheltered and softly furnished room. That soft and warm shelter he seemed always to crave and need as much as a sick child. What to a more vigorous man would be indolent indulgence, with him was a necessity of life and the condition of any working force. Circumstances gave him, through all his working and declining years, this necessary shelter, and screened him from the raw wind of the world by the surroundings and the comforts of sufficient wealth. His virtue lay not in manly struggle with difficulty and hardship, but in the consecration of lifelong leisure and ample opportunity to something very different from a selfish luxury. He had as little of the storm and battle of life as can fall to any serious man to encounter; but was surrounded always by the respectful, affectionate, vigilant, and almost too obsequious homage and love of near friends. Ideally, his thought took in the widest sweep of duty and every sacred sympathy and homely obligation that bind man to his kind: personally, he was perplexed, shrinking, helpless, in the presence of any one of the rougher tasks that would bring him face to face with coarse suffering and want.—ALLEN, JOSEPH HENRY, 1882, *Our Liberal Movement in Theology, p.* 47.

Loftiness of conception raised him and his disciples into the region of art; and, with much that was produced in the charged atmosphere of Unitarian revolt, their discourses, overleaping the boundaries of sect, form additions to American literature.—WELSH, ALFRED H., 1883, *Development of English Literature and Language, vol.* II, *p.* 314.

Channing, however, was still the legitimate spiritual successor of Jonathan Edwards in affirming, with new emphasis, the fundamental doctrine of Christianity, that God is in direct communication with the souls of His creatures. The difference is that Edwards holds the doors of communication so nearly closed that only the elect can pass in; Channing throws them wide open, and invites everybody to be illumined in thought and vitalized in will by the ever-fresh outpourings of celestial light and warmth. But Channing wrote on human nature as though the world was tenanted by actual or possible Channings, who possessed his exceptional delicacy of spiritual perception and his exceptional exemption from the temptations of practical life. He was, as far as a constant contemplation of the Divine perfections was concerned, a meditative saint; and had he belonged to the Roman Catholic Church, he probably would, on the ground of his spiritual gifts, have been eventually canonized. — WHIPPLE, EDWIN PERCY, 1886, *American Literature and Other Papers, ed. Whittier, p.* 56.

Of all those who, on either side, took part in the Unitarian controversy, William Ellery Channing put forth the writings most deserving of notice by the literary student. . . . As a writer, Channing seemed to produce his sentences spontaneously rather than with *labor limæ*, but his natural grace and acquired art stood him in good stead. Behind his straightforward and seemingly artless words were strength of opinion and a well-stored mind; in his own idea he was simply delivering his message and saying his say; but his hearers knew him to be eloquent. —RICHARDSON, CHARLES F., 1887, *American Literature* 1607–1885, *vol.* I.

A man many years my junior, who is himself winning a foremost place among the pioneer minds of our time, asked me a few days ago if Channing had not been greatly overrated. In blended surprise and indignation I was hardly able to reply by a civil negative. Yet when I pondered on the question it no longer surprised me; for it was in the enunciation and defense of principles now regarded as axioms by men of all sects and parties, classes and conditions, that Channing, more than half a century ago, encountered the bitter repugnancy of the many and gained the superlative admiration of the few.—PEABODY, ANDREW P., 1888, *Books That Have Helped Me, p.* 46.

Channing seems to have preached more sermons to himself than to the world. His love of rectitude led him to this excessive conscientiousness, but it brought him great good in other directions. It gave him a respect for the opinions of other men as catholic as it was humble. . . . He was a moral, not an intellectual, reformer; his work was not the destruction of a theology, but the spread of charity. He felt more than he reasoned, and hence his rationalism was bounded, not by the unknown, but by the mystical. He was satisfied with this, and does not seem to have wished to make a definite statement of his beliefs.—WOODBERRY, GEORGE EDWARD, 1890, *Studies in Letters and Life, pp.* 230, 235.

To my mind Channing's emphasis-proportion in the paragraph is more rational, though less brilliant, than Macaulay's. Channing knew the worth of the semicolon; Macaulay did not. On the other hand Channing's paragraphs are too long to be well massed. Nor is the right bulk always assigned to the main ideas. We can find little fault with Channing's unity, and little with his coherence.—LEWIS, EDWIN HERBERT, 1894, *The History of the English Paragraph, p.* 154.

Aside from his work as a religious and social reformer in the van of a movement that was destined to accomplish great things, Channing was a man of letters of high rank, exerting an influence on pure literature in New England equalled by no one before the time of Emerson.—PATTEE, FRED LEWIS, 1896, *A History of American Literature, p.* 206.

Channing is the most eminent representative of the Unitarian movement of this country. . . . A clear mind, not wanting in imaginative warmth, a transparent, natural style, neither slovenly nor overwrought, the sympathies and attainments of a man of letters, even though he was not widely read—are manifest in his writings. Superadded to these qualities, there was a sanctity of spirit which was felt by those who heard him in the pulpit, or met him even casually in conversation. It was not simply that he was sincere, and that he spoke in the accents of conviction. . . . Channing's eminence is chiefly due, first, to the elevated fervor which inspired his teaching, and which was of inestimable advantage in a movement in which the intellectual factor stood in so high a ratio to the religious; and, secondly, to the circumstance that he embodied in himself so fully the ethical and philanthropic impulse which principally constituted the positive living force of the Unitarian cause. Following out the humanitarian tendency, he acquired, at home and abroad, a high and, in the main, a deserved fame as the champion of justice in opposition to slavery and other social evils.—FISHER, GEORGE PARK, 1896, *History of Christian Doctrine, pp.* 421, 422.

Thomas Arnold

1795–1842

Born, at East Cowes, 13 June 1795. At school in Warminster, 1803–07; at Winchester, 1807–11. To Corpus Christi Coll., Oxford, as scholar, 1811; B. A., 27 Oct. 1814; M. A., 19 June 1817; Chancellor's Latin Essay Prize, 1815; Chancellor's English Essay Prize, 1817; Fellow of Oriel Coll., 1815–19. Ordained Deacon, Dec. 1818. Settled at Laleham-on-Thames to take pupils, 1819. Contrib. to "British Critic," 1819–20. Married Mary Penrose, 11 Aug. 1820. Contrib. to "Quarterly Review," 1825; to "Edinburgh Review," 1826 and 1836. Wrote "History of the later Roman Commonwealth," for "Encyclopædia Metropolitana," 1821–27. B. D., 29 March 1828; D. D., 17 Dec. 1828. Ordained Priest, June 1828; Head Master of Rugby, Aug. 1828 to June 1842. Contrib. to "Sheffield Courant," 1831–32; to "Quarterly Journal of Education," 1834–35. Purchased Fox How, Westmoreland, 1832. Contrib. to "Hertford Reformer," 1839–41. Regius Professor of History at Oxford, 1841. Died suddenly, at Rugby, 12 June 1842. *Works:* "The Effects of Distant Colonization on the Parent State" (privately printed), 1815; "The Christian Duty of Granting the Claims of the Roman Catholics," 1829; "Sermons" (3 vols.), 1829–34; "Tract on the Cholera," 1831; "Thirteen Letters on our Social Condition" (anon.), 1832; "Principles of Church Reform," 1833 (2nd and 3rd edns., same year); "Postscript" to preceding, 1833; "History of Rome" (3 vols.), 1838–43; "On the Divisions and Mutual Relations of Knowledge," 1839; "Two Sermons on the Interpretation of Prophecy," 1839; "On the Revival of the Order of Deacons," 1841; "Christian Life" 1841; "Inaugural Lecture on the Study of Modern History," 1841 (2nd edn. same year); "Introductory Lectures on Modern History," 1842. *Posthumous:* "Fragment on the Church," 1844; "Sermons," 1845; "Miscellaneous Works," ed. by A. P. Stanley, 1845; "History of the later Roman Commonwealth" (from "Encyclopædia Metropolitana"), 1845; "Travelling Journals," ed. by A. P. Stanley, 1852. He *edited:* "Poetry of Common Life," 1844; "Thucydides" 1830, etc. *Life:* by A. P. Stanley.—SHARP, R. FARQUHARSON, 1897, *A Dictionary of English Authors, p.* 9.

PERSONAL

The great lion at present is Arnold and his lectures which have created a great stir in the exalted, the literary, and the fashionable word of Oxford. He is here with his whole family, and people look forward to his lectures in the theatre day after day, as they might to a play. He will be quite missed when he goes. Almost every Head goes with his wife and daughters, if he has any, and so powerful is Arnold's eloquence, that the Master of Balliol was, on one occasion, quite overcome, and fairly went—not quite into hysterics, but into tears—upon which the Provost remarked at a large party, that he supposed it was the gout. However, they are very striking lectures. He is working out his inaugural. Everything he does, he does with life and force, and I cannot help liking his manly and open way, and the great reality which he throws about such things as description of country, military laws and operations, and such like low concerns. He has exercised on the whole a generous forbearance towards us and let us off with a few angular points about Priesthood and the Puritans in one lecture, while he has been immensely liberal in other ways, and I should think not to the taste of the Capitular body, *e. g.* puffing with all his might the magnificent age and intensely interesting contests of Innocent III, and in allowing any one to believe, without any suspicion of superstition, a very great many of Bede's miracles and some others beside.—CHURCH, R. W., 1842, *Letter, Feb.; Life and Letters, p.* 35.

My heart has been with you, as I am sure yours has been with me. I returned last night from Rugby. O, what is the death of a great and good man! What distraction (humanly) and yet what consolation! Read the enclosed—I add nothing. All who saw him during the last month were struck by something more than usually heavenly-minded and awfully unearthly.—BUNSEN, CHRISTIAN KARL JOSIAS BARON, 1842, *Letter to Julius Hare, June* 19; *Memoir of Bunsen by his Widow, vol.* II, *p.* 18.

He came to us in Lent Term, 1811, from

THOMAS CHALMERS

Engraving by W. G. Jackman. From a daguerreotype by Claudets.

THOMAS ARNOLD

From Steel Engraving.

Winchester, winning his election against several very respectable candidates. He was a mere boy in appearance as well as in age; but we saw in a very short time that he was quite equal to take his part in the arguments of the common room; and he was, I rather think, admitted by Mr. Cooke at once into his senior class. As he was equal, so was he ready to take part in our discussions: he was fond of conversation on serious matters, and vehement in argument; fearless in advancing his opinions—which, to say the truth, often startled us a good deal; but he was ingenuous and candid, and though the fearlessness with which, so young as he was, he advanced his opinions might have seemed to betoken presumption, yet the good temper with which he bore retort or rebuke relieved him from that imputation; he was bold and warm, because so far as his knowledge went he saw very clearly, and he was an ardent lover of truth, but I never saw in him even then a grain of vanity or conceit. . . . Arnold's bodily recreations were walking and bathing. It was a particular delight to him, with two or three companions, to make what he called a skirmish across the country; on these occasions we deserted the road, crossed fences, and leaped ditches, or fell into them: he enjoyed the country round Oxford, and while out in this way his spirits would rise and his mirth overflowed. Though delicate in appearance, and not giving promise of great muscular strength, yet his form was light, and he was capable of going long distances and bearing much fatigue.—COLERIDGE, JOHN TAYLOR, 1843, *Letter to A. P. Stanley, Sep.; Life and Correspondence of Thomas Arnold, vol.* I, *pp.* 26, 31.

But more than either matter or manner of his preaching, was the impression of himself. Even the mere readers of his sermons will derive from them the history of his whole mind, and of his whole management of the school. But to his hearers it was more than this. It was the man himself, there more than in any other place, concentrating all his various faculties and feelings on one sole object, combating face to face the evil, with which directly or indirectly he was elsewhere perpetually struggling. He was not the preacher or the clergyman who had left behind all his thoughts and occupations as soon as he had ascended the pulpit. He was still the scholar, the historian, and theologian, basing all that he said, not indeed ostensibly, but consciously, and often visibly, on the deepest principles of the past and present. He was still the instructor and the schoolmaster, only teaching and educating with increased solemnity and energy. He was still the simple-hearted and earnest man, laboring to win others to share in his own personal feelings of disgust at sin, and love of goodness, and to trust to the same faith, in which he hoped to live and die himself.—STANLEY, ARTHUR PENRHYN, 1844, *The Life and Correspondence of Thomas Arnold, vol.* I, *p.* 156.

As to Arnold's "Remains," I cannot put myself enough in your place to know the precise point which pains you so much, but for myself there seems much to take comfort in, in things as they are. I do not think that the book will take any great effect in a wrong direction. Of course there is a great deal in it to touch people, but there is so little *consistency* in his intellectual basis that I cannot think that he will affect readers permanently; and then it is very pleasant to think that his work has been so good a one—the reformation of public schools. This seems to have been blessed, and will survive him, and forms the principal, or one of the two principal, subjects of the books. And, further, if it is right to speculate on such serious matters, there is something quite of comfort to be gathered from his removal from the scene of action at the time it took place, as if so good a man should not be suffered to commit himself cominus against truth which he so little understood.—NEWMAN, JOHN HENRY, 1844, *To Rev. J. Keble, June* 12; *Letters and Correspondence During his Life in the English Church, ed. Mozley, vol.* II, *p.* 388.

It does one's heart good to contemplate the life of such a man as Dr. Arnold of Rugby. He possessed that quality of earnestness which gives force to every purpose in life. He was full of strong sympathy for all that was true and good in our modern social movements, and of as strong antipathy for all that he conceived to be false and unjust. He did battle in the cause that he conscientiously felt to be right, with his whole heart and soul; and waged an uncompromising war against what seemed to him to be shams and falsities. He was of the stern stuff of which martyrs are made; for when he saw his way clear, and his conscience approved, he never hesitated at once to act boldly and energetically. We may not agree with him in all the views that he held and advocated; but we never fail to admire the undeviating and high-minded consistency of his life, and the purity of the motives on which he acted.—SMILES, SAMUEL, 1860, *Brief Biographies.*

The great peculiarity and charm of his nature seemed to lie in the regal supremacy of the moral and the spiritual element over his whole being and powers. His intellectual faculties were not such as to surpass those of many who were his contemporaries; in scholarship he occupied a subordinate place to several who filled situations like his; and he had not much of what is called tact in his dealings either with the juvenile or the adult mind. What gave him his power, and secured for him so deeply the respect and veneration of his pupils and acquaintances, was the intensely religious character of his whole life. He seemed ever to act from a severe and lofty estimate of duty. To be just, honest, and truthful, he ever held to be the first aim of his being. With all this, there was intense sympathy with his fellows, the tenderest domestic affections, and the most generous friendship, the most expansive benevolence.—ALEXANDER, WILLIAM L., 1875, *Encyclopædia Britannica, Ninth ed., vol.* II, *p.* 548.

Arnold's life, no less pure and spiritual and fragrant than Keble's, was a life infinitely truer to the actual state of things in the world, infinitely richer in practical aims, infinitely fuller of the heroic and inspiring, a life great in its faithfulness to the present and with the promise of the future. If the opposing tendencies in religious thought were to have their fate settled by the character of the two representatives, there is little doubt, we think, as to which has the more virtue in it, and the greater fitness for the work of the world.—MEAD, EDWIN D., 1884, *Arnold of Rugby and the Oxford Movement, The Andover Review, vol.* I, *p.* 508.

In person he was a little above the middle height; spare, but vigorous, and healthy without being robust. A slightly projecting underlip, and eyes deep set beneath strongly marked eyebrows, gave to his countenance when at rest a somewhat stern expression, which became formidable when he was moved to anger; but the effect was all the greater when, in the playful or tender moods which were frequent with him, or on meeting in a book or in conversation with a noble sentiment or a striking thought, his eye gleamed, and his whole face lighted up. Simple in his tastes and habits, never idle and never hurried, he made his home a "temple of industrious peace;" and he rarely left it except to travel occasionally on the continent, with an eye enlightened by lifelong studies in history and geography. He had an intense delight in beautiful scenery, and took pleasure in the fine arts, and in some of the natural sciences, but chiefly as bearing on the life and history of man. For science as such, for art as such, he cared comparatively little; for music not at all. "Flowers," he used to say, "are my music," and his love for them was like that of a child.—WALROND, THEODORE, 1885, *Dictionary of National Biography, vol.* II, *p.* 117.

Of those whom he left behind him, Jane, the eldest daughter, became the wife of William Edward Foster, afterwards M. P. for Bradford and Vice-President of the Committee of Council on Education; Matthew was the eldest son; Thomas, the second son, became a Fellow of his college at Oxford, and has devoted himself to literary and educational work; William Delafield Arnold was for a time director of public instruction in the Punjaub, and died on his way homewards in 1859; and Edward was a clergyman and inspector of schools. In the next generation, Mrs. Humphry Ward, the gifted daughter of Thomas, and the author of "Robert Elsmere," and Mr. H. O. Arnold Forster, M. P. for Belfast, the son of W. D. Arnold, have in different ways achieved honourable reputation.—FITCH, SIR JOSHUA, 1897, *Thomas and Matthew Arnold (Great Educators), p.* 149.

EDUCATOR

'Twas his to teach,
Day after day, from pulpit and from desk,
That the most childish sin which man can do
Is yet a sin which Jesus never did
When Jesus was a child, and yet a sin
For which, in lowly pain, He lived and died:
That for the bravest sin that e'er was praised
The King Eternal wore the crown of thorns.
In him was Jesus crucified again;
For every fault which he could not prevent

Stuck in him like a nail. His heart bled for it
As it had been a foul sin of his own.
Heavy his cross, and stoutly did he bear it,
Even to the foot of holy Calvary;
And if at last he sank beneath the weight,
There were not wanting souls whom he had taught
The way to Paradise, that, in white robes,
Throng'd to the gate to hail their shepherd home!
—COLERIDGE, HARTLEY, 1842, *On the Late Dr. Arnold, Poems.*

This unsound and unhealthy tone of public morality carries with it a species of contagious virus which stains the honour of the State, and poisons the very fountains of political philosophy. Against this Dr. Arnold exclaimed with characteristic energy; and had he lived to shed credit over Oxford, and infuse a manlier and more honourable spirit among the rising generation of statesmen, he might have done much to arrest and antagonize the mischief. But since he has been called away, we know not where to turn for a Teacher fitted to "take his stand," like the Prophet, "between the Living and the Dead," and stay the progress of the moral plague.—GREG, W. R., 1844, *Life and Correspondence of Thomas Arnold, D. D., Westminster Review, vol.* 42, *p.* 381.

The striking feature of Arnold's mind—and we notice it as being literally a phenomenon, a remarkable specimen of that particular internal power—is his confidence; we mean a rare, esoteric intensity of assurance in his own views. He is *omnia magna;* has every quality that there is in him forcibly, and confidence among the rest. A firm faith is one thing; what we mean is another. A brilliancy of the whole chamber of the mind—a dance of light—a clearness which made his own view of truth to him an object of the keenest internal ocular demonstration rather than of faith, carried him into conflicts and controversies with a boldness that an evident warrant from the invisible world might produce. A phantasmagoric halo of truth accompanied him, and the flame played upon his helmet, as it did on that of Diomede; he was invulnerable; his armour was proof against sword-cut and thrust; a dip in the magical pool had achieved the same security for him that it had done for the hero of old. . . . At Rugby he is great, because at Rugby only the power of self-expansion and self-imparting was wanted. A school of boys is a great receptacle of ideas, and not a counter-stream; they lean upon the master mind, treasure up the thought, suck in the hint, but oppose no standard of their own to exercise and try the master's apprehension, and to be penetrated and surmounted by it. Arnold could watch with genuine tutorial sympathy every stage of the ingress of the idea from his own mind into the pupil's; and all the issues from himself were keenly and minutely seen. That answered perfectly for Rugby; that showed the accomplished schoolmaster. But the schoolmaster came out into the world, and then the scene was changed. In order to implant his ideas in men and equals, he had first to understand theirs, and be the learner and the listener that he might be the teacher; and that he could not be, or would not try to be. He came out into the world, and immediately spoke *ex cathedra*, as if he were in his school-seat. He pictured the world a large Rugby, a grand receptacle of his ideas, and did not think of it in any other light. But the world turned out to be no passive receptacle; it started back and was restive, and then Arnold could not deal with it. Then Arnold was a child. He saw that he had disturbed people indefinitely, but he saw no more. He could not explain, meet objections, soften, accommodate. He could not see why people objected; the mind without was a blank to him; and he could only stare and complain of the unreasoning mass. He was out of his element. Triumphant at Rugby, his exhibition in the world was a failure.—MOZLEY, J. B., 1845, *Essays Historical and Theological, vol.* II, *pp.* 59, 63.

He communicated this earnestness and sincerity to a large number of those who are becoming the men of a later time. As an educator, he put his heart into his work, and laboured there as elsewhere, for truth and good. The views which he considered invaluable may not be in every case held by those whom he trained to hold ideas on conviction only; points which he insisted on as indispensable may appear otherwise to his pupils in their maturity; but they owe to him the power and the conscience to think for themselves, and the earnest habit of mind which makes their conviction a part of their life. By this exalted view and method as an educator, Dr. Arnold did more for education than even by his express and unintermitting assertion of the importance of the function—powerful as his testimony was.—MARTINEAU, HARRIET, 1849, *A History of the Thirty Years' Peace, A. D.* 1815–1846, *p.* 272.

He certainly *did* teach us—thank God for it!—that we could not cut our life into slices and say, "In this slice your actions are indifferent, and you needn't trouble your heads about them one way or another; but in this slice mind what you are about, for they are important"—a pretty muddle we should have been in had he done so. He taught us that in this wonderful world, no boy or man can tell which of his actions is indifferent and which not; that by a thoughtless word or look we may lead astray a brother for whom Christ died. He taught us that life is a whole, made up of actions and thoughts and longings, great and small, noble and ignoble; therefore the only true wisdom for boy or man is to bring the whole life into obedience to Him whose world we live in, and who has purchased us with His blood; and that whether we eat or drink, or whatsoever we do, we are to do all in His name and to His glory; in such teaching, faithfully, as it seems to me, following that of Paul of Tarsus, who was in the habit of meaning what he said, and who laid down this standard for every man and boy in his time.—HUGHES, THOMAS, 1858? *Tom Brown's School Days, Preface to the Sixth Edition, p.* xxiii.

Dr. Arnold will be more widely remembered as a shaper of men than of books.—MORLEY, HENRY, 1881, *Of English Literature in the Reign of Victoria with a Glance at the Past, p.* 292.

We cannot concede to him the character of a great reformer or revolutionist in the sense in which Comenius, Rousseau, Locke, or Pestalozzi was entitled to one of those designations. He was not a realist, but essentially a "humanist" of the type of Milton. He accepted the traditions of the long succession of English teachers, from Ascham and Colet down to Busby and Keate, in favour of making the study of language, and particularly the languages of Greece and Rome, the staple of a liberal education. But, like Milton, he rebelled strongly against the wooden, mechanical, and pedantic fashion in which those languages were often taught, as if the attainment of proficiency in them were an end in itself and not the means to some higher end. . . . The characteristic of Arnold as a schoolmaster was that he was much more concerned to put new life, freshness, and meaning into the received methods than to invent new ones.—FITCH, SIR JOSHUA, 1897, *Thomas and Matthew Arnold* (*Great Educators*), *pp.* 30, 37.

It is in this department of the theory of Education, that Arnold's permanent contribution will be found. Many other Public School masters before and after his time have worked in the same cause, but none have so set their mark upon the work, and no one has expounded the system as clearly as himself, and his biographer. Since his day, new conceptions of education and of teaching have become popular—conceptions which would limit the function of the school to the attainment of knowledge or of manual skill, confusing the office of the teacher with that of an instructor. Against all such doctrine Arnold asserts an eloquent *Non possumus.* The boy is a moral being and the school is a human society; the teacher moving in and out of this society, is required not only to train the intelligence and inform the mind, but to touch the springs of character. First of all, as we have seen, in this conception of the aim of education, he declares the teacher's duty, and now, in his exposition of practice, we observe how he laboured to discharge it.—FINDLAY, J. J., 1897, *Arnold of Rugby: His School Life and Contributions to Education, Preface, p.* xiii.

It is by virtue of great qualities and an intensity and ardor of spirit which would have made him great in any sphere, that he was a great teacher. Consequently his real position is not so much that of a schoolmaster as of a prophet among schoolmasters, a man whose special mission it was to unveil and interpret the higher possibilities, responsibilities, and duties of the schoolmaster's life. Through the intensity of his moral and spiritual feeling and his "radiant vigour" he vitalised ideas of which weaker men had been but dimly conscious, or which they had merely carried about with them as inert or pious opinions. Thus the value of his example to all teachers is to be sought in his unconventional attitude of mind, his striving for reality, his desire to improve upon what has been already attained, his high moral aim, his intense religious purpose, his sense of the responsibility undertaken by every trainer of young lives, and his magnetic and inspiring personality. In one word it is that influence of the prophet which is the salt of society in every age. . . . He rises before us like an inspired prophet, preaching to every schoolmaster sacredness of his calling, and bidding him always remember that formation of character is the primary aim of every good teacher, that it is the duty of the teacher to hasten growth out of the immature and dangerous period of boyhood, and that to do this we should give direct responsibility for the moral conduct and the honour of the whole school to those members of it who are the ablest and most advanced, thus instilling from early years the Christian principle of service as the guiding rule of life; and finally that for these ends the schoolmaster's ideal aim must always be to cultivate in his pupils the habit of moral thoughtfulness, and the conviction that life in Christ is the true goal of all human endeavour.—PERCIVAL, JOHN, 1897, *Arnold of Rugby: His School Life and Contributions to Education, ed. Findlay, Introduction, pp.* xv, xx.

HISTORY OF ROME
1838–43

His "History of Rome" is undoubtedly the best history in the language.—CLEVELAND, CHARLES D., 1853, *English Literature of the Nineteenth Century, p.* 387.

Dr. Arnold lived to complete his history only as far as to the end of the Spanish Campaign in the Second Punic War. The work, therefore, breaks off just after its distinguishing merits began to be conspicuously manifest. The portion of the work that had to deal with the early periods of Roman history was founded on the investigations of Niebuhr, in whose genius as a guide Arnold placed implicit trust. The consequence inevitably was that as Niebuhr's conclusions one after another came to be rejected, those of Arnold fell with them. But from the time of Pyrrhus the author emerges upon ground where independent research becomes possible and fruitful. His account of the First Punic War, and of the Second, as far as to the return of Scipio from Spain, is the most satisfactory yet written in English. It has all the qualities of a great history. But the work is to be regarded only as a fragment, and one of which the last part only is of great value.—ADAMS, CHARLES KENDALL, 1882, *A Manual of Historical Literature, p.* 127.

His style is undoubtedly of its own kind scholarly and excellent; the matter of his history suffers from the common fault of taking Niebuhr at too high a valuation.—SAINTSBURY, GEORGE, 1896, *A History of Nineteenth Century Literature, p.* 224.

Arnold's English is always forcible, and in the best passages it is eloquent. He is strongest in his account of military operations, and his description of the campaigns of the Second Punic War remains still the most vivid and readable in our language, and probably in modern literature. Certainly Mommsen, powerful as his work is, cannot rival Arnold as a military historian.—WALKER, HUGH, 1897, *The Age of Tennyson, p.* 122.

GENERAL

I admire, and, what is more, deeply honor him as a man, and as a writer so far as the man appears in his writings. As a reasoner and speculator I surmise that he was not *great*, though what he does see clearly he expresses with great energy and lifesomeness. It seems to me that he arrived at much truth which subtler men miss through sheer honesty and singleness of heart and mind, through sheer impatience and imprudence, not through philosophy. His views of Church and State I can well understand (I have not seen his fragment on the Church): so far as I *can* understand them, I imagine (it seems presumptuous for such as I to *opine* positively on such a subject) that they are incorrect and inadequate. He was a great historian; yet I would fain see how he reconciled them with history, let alone philosophy.—COLERIDGE, SARA, 1845, *To Hartley Coleridge, Jan.* 20; *Memoirs and Letters, ed. her Daughter, p.* 224.

The merits and influence of Arnold as a theologian have, I think, been underrated. At any rate I can recall but few modern clergymen whose opinions would furnish a more wholesome study. . . . To read Arnold's sermons, after reading too many of those which are now in vogue, is like passing out of the conservatory into the free air and eager breeze of heaven.—FARRAR, FREDERIC WILLIAM, 1878, *Thomas Arnold,*

D. D., Macmillan's Magazine, vol. 37, *pp.* 458, 459.

These eight lectures [on history] though forming Dr. Arnold's Inaugural Course at the University of Oxford, were prepared and delivered in the last year of the author's life, and, consequently, were the ripe fruit of a profound scholarship. The author's object was not to impart historical knowledge, but rather to awaken a greater interest in the study of history. The first lecture is devoted to a definition of history in general, and of modern history in particular; while the body of the work is an expansion of these definitions, and a description of the proper manner of studying the external and the internal life of nations.—ADAMS, CHARLES KENDALL, 1882, *A Manual of Historical Literature, p.* 187.

None of his writings made more noise, or gave more offence, than the "Principles of Church Reform." It offended equally churchmen and dissenters. Its latitudinarianism was obnoxious to the one; its defence of an Established Church, and its assaults upon sectarianism, obnoxious to the other. Its advocacy of large and liberal changes repelled the Conservatives; its severe religious tone displeased the Liberals. . . . If ever, indeed, there was a mind intensely English in the practical, ethical bent underlying all his studies and all his work, it was Arnold's. His powers as an interpreter of Scripture, therefore, sprang from his own native instincts of inquiry and the clear moral sense which made him hate confusion of thought in all directions.—TULLOCH, JOHN, 1885, *Movements of Religious Thought in Britain During the Nineteenth Century, pp.* 42, 43.

Though in my opinion inferior to Whately in intellectual power, was far his superior in the moral influence which he exercised. —OVERTON, JOHN HENRY, 1897, *The Church in England, vol.* II, *p.* 312.

Allan Cunningham

1784–1842

Born, at Keir, Dumfriesshire, 7 Dec. 1784. Educated at village school. Apprenticed to his brother James, stonemason, 1795. Wrote songs and verses. To London, April 1810. Obtained employment from sculptor. Employed on staff of "The Day" to write poetry and political reports. Married Jean Walker, 1 July 1811. Acted as secretary to Francis Chantrey, 1814–41. Worked at literature in spare time. Contributed to "Blackwood," 1819–21; to "London Magazine;" to "The Popular Encyclopædia," 1841. Edited "The Anniversary," 1829–30. Presented with Freedom of Dumfries, 1831. Died, in London, 30 Oct. 1842. Buried at Kensal Green. *Works:* "Songs," 1813; "Sir Marmaduke Maxwell, etc.," 1822; "Traditional Tales of the English and Scottish Peasantry," 1822; "The Songs of Scotland," 1825; "Paul Jones," 1826; "Sir Michael Scott," 1828; "The Lives of the most eminent British Painters, etc." 1829; "The Maid of Elvar," 1833; "Biographical and Critical History of the British Literature of the last Fifty Years" (from "The Athenæum"), 1834; "The Cabinet Gallery of Pictures," 1834; "Lord Roldan," 1836. *Posthumous:* "The Life of Sir David Wilkie" (ed. by P. Cunningham), 1843; "Poems and Songs" (ed. by P. Cunningham), 1847. He *edited:* "Burns' Works," 1834; Pilkington's "General Dictionary of Painters," 1840; Thomson's "The Seasons," 1841. *Life:* by David Hogg, 1875. —SHARP, R. FARQUHARSON, 1897, *A Dictionary of English Authors, p.* 72.

PERSONAL

We breakfasted at honest Allan Cunningham's—honest Allan—a real and true Scotsman of the old cast.—SCOTT, SIR WALTER, 1826, *Journal, Nov.* 14; *Life by Lockhart, ch.* lxxii.

Allan Cunningham was with us last night. Jane calls him a genuine Dumfriesshire mason still; and adds that it is delightful to see a genuine man of any sort. Allan was, as usual, full of Scottish anecdotic talk. Right by instinct; has *no* principles or *creed* that I can see, but excellent old Scottish *habits* of character. An interesting man.—CARLYLE, THOMAS, 1831, *Journal, Oct.; Early Life of Thomas Carlyle, ed. Froude, vol.* II, *p.* 168.

Allan has none of that proverbial Scottish caution about him; he is all heart together, without reserve either of expression or manner; you at once see the unaffected benevolence, warmth of feeling, and firm independence of a man conscious of his own rectitude and mental energies. —HOGG, THOMAS, 1832, *Autobiography*, p. 464.

He is a very tall, stout and rustic-looking person; and while we were conversing together I could not help scanning his bulky frame over, to see if I could discover the outward visible signs of the poet and painter. But with the exception of his eye, which is rather expressive, and of a dark hazel colour, there is little in his looks or demeanour which would indicate a first-rate literary man. His conversation, however, was very sensible, and he talks with ease, and without any of that studied and set manner which we see in some distinguished men, who always seem, when talking even to a single friend in private, as if they were delivering an harangue to a numerous audience. I should think Mr. Cunningham is a plain, honest, unassuming, and clever man, and well worthy of the reputation he at present enjoys in the periodical and lighter literature of the day.—BLAKEY, ROBERT, 1832, *Memoirs, ed. Miller*, p. 74.

This very sudden news of poor Allan Cunningham's death has both shocked and grieved me. I had a letter from him on Friday morning last—I suspect the last he wrote—it was in his old cordial, kindly tone, but evidently written by an invalid. So I sat me down on Saturday night, and wrote him a long epistle, urging him to come down to Lucy and me for a week, as I was quite in hopes a few days' country air and quiet relaxation would do him good. I exerted all my powers of persuasion as eloquently as I could, of course to no purpose, for at the very time I was writing he was dying. And so I have lost my old favourite—him whom Charles Lamb used to call the "large-hearted Scott"—and a large and warm heart he had of his own.—BARTON, BERNARD, 1842, *Memoir, Letters and Poems, ed. his Daughter*, p. 122.

From the light of a November fire, I first saw reflected the dark flashing guerilla eye of Allan Cunningham. Dark it was, and deep with meaning; and the meaning, as in all cases of expressive eyes, was comprehensive, and therefore equivocal. On the whole, however, Allan Cunningham's expression did not belie his character, as afterwards made known to me: he was kind, liberal, hospitable, friendly; and his whole natural disposition, as opposed to his acquired, was genial and fervent. But he had acquired feelings in which I, as an Englishman, was interested painfully. In particular, like so many Scotsmen of *his* original rank, he had a prejudice—or, perhaps, that is not the word: it was no feeling that he derived from experience—it was an old Scottish grudge: not a feeling that he indulged to his own private sensibilities, but to his *national* conscience—a prejudice against Englishmen. He loved, perhaps, this and that Englishman, Tom and Jack; but he hated us English as a body: it was in vain to deny it.—DE QUINCEY, THOMAS, 1853, *Literary Reminiscences, ch.* xxii.

He was a tall man, powerful of frame, and apparently of an iron constitution. Of a genial, kindly, courteous nature, these qualities gained for him not only esteem but affection, yet to the last he gave the idea of a man self-taught, or rather whose teacher was Nature; and his tongue, always when he warmed to a subject, smacked of the heather. There is a pile of granite reared over his grave in Kensal Green—granite from Aberdeen it is true—but it would seem more in keeping with the memory of Allan Cunningham if daisies grew where he was laid: or as his friend Theodore Martin wrote, in a noble poem that commemorated the burial of Campbell:

"Better after-times should find him—
To his rest in homage bound,
Lying in the land that bore him, with its
glories piled around."

His admirable wife, the bonnie Jean of his earlier poems, rests by his side.—HALL, SAMUEL CARTER, 1883, *Retrospect of a Long Life*, p. 400.

GENERAL

A man of genius, besides, who only requires the tact of knowing when and where to stop, to attain the universal praise which ought to follow it. I look upon the alteration of "It's hame and it's hame," and "A wet sheet and a flowing sea," as among the best songs going. His prose has often admirable passages; but he is obscure, and overlays his meaning, which will not do now-a-days, when he who runs must read.—SCOTT, SIR WALTER, 1826, *Journal, Nov.* 14; *Life by Lockhart, ch.* lxxii.

Our author's prose, consisting of a copious preface and critical notices, is both florid and pedantic; it continually aspires to the vicious affectation of poetry, and explains the most common sentiments by a host of illustrations and images, thus perpetually reminding us of the children's play of "What is it like?" As a poet, his fame has long been established, and the few original pieces which he has introduced into the present collection have the ease and natural vivacity conspicuous in his former compositions.—PRESCOTT, WILLIAM H., 1826, *Scottish Song, Biographical and Critical Miscellanies, p.* 589.

North—"Allan Cunningham's 'Lives of the Painters'—I know not which of the two volumes is best—are full of a fine and instructed enthusiasm. He speaks boldly, but reverentially, of genius, and of men of genius; strews his narrative with many flowers of poetry; disposes and arranges his materials skilfully; and is, in few words, an admirable critic on art—an admirable biographer of artists."—WILSON, JOHN, 1830, *Noctes Ambrosianæ, April.*

I was astonished at the luxuriousness of his fancy. It was boundless; but it was the luxury of a rich garden overrun with rampant weeds. He was likewise then a great mannerist in expression, and no man could mistake his verses for those of any other man. I remember seeing some imitations of Ossian by him, which I thought exceedingly good; and it struck me that the style of composition was peculiarly fitted for his vast and fervent imagination. . . . Mr. Cunningham's style of poetry is greatly changed of late for the better. I have never seen any style improved so much. It is free of all that crudeness and mannerism that once marked it so decidedly. He is now uniformly lively, serious, descriptive, or pathetic, as he changes his subject; but formerly he jumbled all these together, as in a boiling caldron, and when once he began, it was impossible to calculate where or when he was going to end.—HOGG, JAMES, 1832, *Autobiography, p.* 465.

Does not his name alone recall to your recollection many a sweet song that has thrilled the bosom of the village maiden with an emotion that a princess need not blush to own?—AYTOUN, WILLIAM EDMONDSTOUNE, 1844, *The Burns Festival, Memoirs, ed. Martin, p.* 103.

Whether from defective opportunities (he had never, I believe, set his foot in Ayrshire), or a failure to apprehend and grapple with the difficulties of the subject, this honest-hearted writer seems to have also failed to produce a work ["Life of Burns"] which could leave nothing to be desired.—CHAMBERS, ROBERT, 1850, *The Life and Works of Robert Burns, Preface, vol.* I, *p.* vi.

He evidently puts his soul in all that he writes, and makes us feel because he feels first himself. Some of his smaller poems are perfect gems, and his dissertation upon the history and peculiarities of Scottish song exhibits a prose style of great clearness, eloquence and power.—CLEVELAND, CHARLES D., 1853, *English Literature of the Nineteenth Century, p.* 398.

Under pretense of collecting a world of previously unknown local song from the well-gleaned land of Burns and Scott, the young man, finding in Cromek (who had more natural taste than reading or acumen) a good subject for the cheat, and a willing one, palmed off, as undoubted originals, a whole deskful of his own verse in slightly antique mould. Verse, it proved bold, energetic, and stirring, or tender, sentimental and graceful; the best of modern Scottish songs and ballads since those of the Ayrshire peasant, though wide the interval!—GILCHRIST, ALEXANDER, 1863, *Life of William Blake, p.* 236.

The genius of Cunningham, unlike that of Hogg was essentially lyrical. It was incapable of continued flight, and was best evinced in the poetry of songs and ballads, where concentration was necessitated, as Allen did not know when to hold his hand. Scott classed "among the best songs going," "The Wet Sheet and a Flowing Sea," and the touching piece "It's Hame, and it's Hame," which Mrs. Lockhart, his daughter, sang so charmingly. The magnificent ballad "Sir Roland Græme" is one of the finest specimens of word-painting out of Homer,—full of dash, vigour, and energy. Then there are "The Mermaid of Galloway,"—which suggested to Hilton, the Royal Academician, a picture which once formed part of the collection of Sir John Fleming Leicester, "She's gane to dwell in Heaven," "Bonnie Lady Anne," "The Lord's Marie" and many others, which are, in their way, of the very highest order of merit. It is, indeed, upon these, and his contributions to Cromek's *Relics*, that his reputation must rest.—BATES, WILLIAM, 1874–98, *The Maclise Portrait Gallery of Illustrious Literary Characters, p.* 136.

No more genuine Scot could be, either in his works or sentiments, than Allan Cunningham, "honest Allan," one of those men, peasant-born and but barely educated, who, by dint of something which we must call genius, though not great enough to reach an exalted rank, have made their way out of the fields and workshops into the world of literature. Nothing but a spark of a divinity uncontrollable and subject to no laws, which, like the winds, goes "where it listeth," could account for the appearance here and there of such a simple and stalwart figure, in regions so different from those which brought him forth. Allan Cunningham was all the more remarkable that he had not only brought out of a gardener's cottage enough of the faculty of Song to find him a place in the poetic records of his country, but also out of the stonemason's yard some perception of art which made him capable of becoming the trusty assistant and head workman of a great sculptor. His connection with Chantrey is still more remarkable than his connection with literature, for art exacts a harder apprenticeship than has ever been required for authorship.—OLIPHANT, MARGARET O. W., 1882, *The Literary History of England, XVIII-XIX Century, vol.* III, *p.* 164.

Cunningham began—following a taste very rife at the time—with imitated, or to speak plainly, forged ballads; but the merit of them deserved on true grounds the recognition it obtained on false, and he became a not inconsiderable man of letters of all work. His best known prose work is the "Lives of the Painters." In verse he is ranked, as a song writer in Scots, by some next to Burns, and by few lower than Hogg. Some of his pieces, such as "Fair shines the sun in France," have the real, the inexplicable, the irresistible song-gift. —SAINTSBURY, GEORGE, 1896, *A History of Nineteenth Century Literature, p.* 108.

William Maginn

1793–1842

Born at Cork, 10th July 1793, and educated at Trinity College, Dublin, at twenty six took his LL. D., taught in Cork for ten years, and in 1823 removed to London. His first of many contributions to *Blackwood's Magazine*—a Latin translation of "Chevy Chase"—appeared in 1819. In 1828 he joined the staff of the *Standard*, and he was one of the originators of *Fraser's Magazine* in 1830. He wrote his "Shakespeare Papers" for Blackwood in 1837, and in 1840 began his "Magazine Miscellanies." His life was irregular, and he was often in jail for debt. He died 21st August 1842. His "Whitehall, or the Days of George IV" (1827), is a parody on the historical novel; "John Manesty" (1844) was completed after his death by Charles Ollier. His "Homeric Ballads" were published in 1849. A collection of his papers was edited by R. S. Mackenzie (New York, 1855–57), and his "Miscellanies" by Montagu (1885).—PATRICK AND GROOME, *eds.*, 1897, *Chambers's Biographical Dictionary, p.* 620.

PERSONAL

I wish I had it in my power to show you in any way how deeply I and my friends feel indebted to you. I have no wish you should give up your incognito unless you find it perfectly agreeable to do so; but I hope you some day will, or at all events that you will point out to me how I can make you any return for all your kindnesses. It is not merely that it would give me satisfaction were you to allow me to offer you the remuneration we make to our ordinary contributors; but the hearty good will with which you enter into the very spirit of "Maga" lays me under a weight of obligation which I cannot repay you.—BLACKWOOD, WILLIAM, 1820, *Letter to Maginn, William Blackwood and His Sons, ed. Oliphant, vol.* I, *p.* 377.

Here early to bed lies kind William Maginn,
Who with genius, wit, learning, life's trophies to win,
Had neither great lord nor rich cit of his kin,
Nor discretion to set himself up as to tin.
So his portion soon spent, like the poor heir of Lynn,
He turned author while yet was no beard on his chin.
And whoever was out or whoever was in,
For your Tories his fine Irish brains he would spin,

Who received rhyme and prose with a promising grin:
"Go ahead, you queer fish, and more power to your fin!"
But to save from starvation stirred never a pin.
Light for long was his heart, though his breeches were thin;
But at last he was beat, and sought help from the bin
(All the same to the Doctor, from claret to gin),
Which led swiftly to gaol, with consumption within:
It was much, when the bones rattled loose in his skin,
He got leave to die here, out of Babylon's din.
Barring drink and the girls, I ne'er heard of a sin:
Many worse, better few, than bright broken Maginn.

—LOCKHART, JOHN GIBSON, 1842, *On the Death of William Maginn.*

His manners, devoid of all affectation, simple and unstudied, were singularly engaging. No robe of reserve did he draw round him, like too many men of celebrity, whose silence is perhaps the best safeguard of their fame. None of these absurd misanthropic monkey airs, which almost established the reputation of Byron, and certainly veiled the poverty of his mind, did he ever display. He maintained a certain boyishness of heart and character to the very last, and though his knowledge of mankind was extensive and accurate, he could be as easily deceived, as if he were only a raw youth. There was a snowy candor in his manner, which lent a perfect charm to all he said and did, and the most unlettered person felt as much at ease in his company as the most learned.—KENEALY, EDWARD VAUGHAN HYDE, 1844, *William Maginn, Dublin University Magazine, vol.* 23, *p.* 77.

In person, Dr. Maginn was rather under the middle stature, slight in figure, active in motion, and very natural in manners. He was gray at the age of 26, and, during his last ten years, was almost white—exhibiting the peculiarity of bright, keen eyes, and youthful features with the hoary locks of age.—MACKENZIE, R. SHELTON, 1854, *ed., Noctes Ambrosianæ, Memoir of William Maginn, p.* xii.

To him the gossip of the modern world was as familiar as the learning of the ancient. From some organic defect of utterance his speech was occasionally hesitating; yet when his words came forth they were full of meaning—always pleasant, often wise. It cannot, however, be denied he was best of a morning,—the double excitement of the table and the talk was sometimes too much for him.—KNIGHT, CHARLES, 1863, *Passages of a Working Life During Half a Century, p.* 265.

What can be therefore more sad than to survey, however imperfectly, this profitless and broken career; and know that, after all, one so variously and rarely gifted, —of learning so profound and extensive,—who, in philosophy was pronounced by Dr. Moir, "abler than Coleridge," in satire, declared by Macnish "equal to Swift,"—as a political writer, termed by another great authority, "the greatest in the world,"—as a companion, remembered by Charles Knight as "one of the pleasantest and most improving of his visitors,"—whose intellect, as the "Modern Pythagorean" wrote "adorned every theme that it touched,"—who was characterized by his biographer, Kenealy, "as a scholar, perhaps the most universal of his time,—far more various in his learning than Voltaire, far more profound and elegant than Johnson,"—of whose "abilities as a writer and a conversationalist, and excellent nature as a man," Maclise could not find "words powerful enough to convey his opinion,"—whom Richard Oastler, who was his companion in the Fleet, styled "the brightest star of intellectual light,"—to whom the able editor of the "Homeric Ballads" said the "celebrated eulogy of Parr on Fox so perfectly applied that it seemed to have been written for him,"—and who was described to Sir Robert Peel by the friend who wrote to that illustrious statesman on behalf of the dying man, as "an individual of exhalted genius, the most universal scholar, perhaps, of the age, and as good, and kind, and gentle-hearted a being as ever breathed;"—should perish in the very prime and flower of life; and this, as we must infer, from his own imprudences in great measure;—and be indebted to the munificence of a stranger for the support of his last days, and the means of decent burial.—BATES, WILLIAM, 1874-98, *Maclise Portrait Gallery of Illustrious Literary Characters, p.* 41.

A literary Swiss who readily sold himself to any buyer, or to two buyers at the same time—one being Tory, the other Whig. . . . Maginn came to London in 1823-24 with as large a "stock-in-trade" of knowledge as was ever brought by one man from Ireland to England; yet it was profitless and almost fruitless. His profound learning, extensive reading, his familiarity with ancient and modern languages, his ready and brilliant wit, were utterly ineffectual in achieving for him independence or fame. . . . He had an awkward impediment of speech, not quite a stutter; and soon after he achieved repute, his countenance, never very expressive, and certainly not handsome, assumed the terrible character that self-indulgence never fails to give. He is an example of the men who could fight for the shadow, while utterly ignoring the substance of honor, and is one of the shames as well as one of the glories of Literature. No doubt the fertile source of his misery was drink. He was always drunk when he could obtain the means of intoxication; consequently he seldom put pen to paper in a condition of entire sobriety, and sometimes did not know what he wrote.—HALL, SAMUEL CARTER, 1883, *Retrospect of a Long Life, pp.* 68, 69.

"The Adjutant;" "Ensign;" "The Modern Rabelais;" "Odoherty;" "Peter MacGrawler;" "The Prince of Pedagogues;" "The Standard Bearer."—FREY, ALBERT R., 1888, *Sobriquets and Nicknames, p.* 436.

Maginn's biographers, S. C. Hall excepted, have dealt kindly with him, but his character is scarcely a more agreeable spectacle than his life. His dissipation might be forgiven, but it is not so easy to overlook the discredit he brought upon the profession of letters by his systematic want of principle, his insensibility to the courtesies and amenities of life, in a word, by the extreme debasement of his standard in everything but scholarship. Thackeray's portrait of him as "Captain Shandon" in "Pendennis" is probably the best which we possess; the vague encomiums of his other friends, Lockhart's epitaph excepted, seem mainly prompted by good nature.—GARNETT, RICHARD, 1893, *Dictionary of National Biography, vol.* XXXV, *p.* 322.

We are by no means proud of the part Maginn took in the Magazine, nor of himself or the connection so speedily formed, and to place him immediately after the Great Twin Brethren who formed it is too honourable a place. But there was no one of the contributors who had for a number of years so much to do with "Maga," or who wore her colours with more apparent devotion: and his history, never written at any length or deserving to be so, is full of the tragic contrast—so often, alas! to be found in the lives of self-ruined men—of brilliant and careless youth and a maturity miserable and shameful. He was turned, indeed, into Captain Shandon, a picture in some respects too good for him, by Thackeray; and Lockhart for one had a lingering affection for him all through, and wrote him a tragico-jesting epitaph. But he has never had any justice, as who of his kind ever has? He was not a bad man: he was full of generous and friendly impulses, wit, and sometimes wisdom: but so spoilt and hampered by other qualities that every promise ended in the mean and squalid misery of a nature fallen, fallen, fallen from its high estate. Such a man cannot have justice from the world, scarcely even pity. It is almost immoral to be sorry for him, or to remember that once he was young and an emblem of all that was joyous, delightful, and gay.—OLIPHANT, MARGARET O. W., 1897, *William Blackwood and His Sons, vol.* I, *p.*363.

GENERAL

Originality, the distinctive attribute of genius, he possessed in no ordinary degree; and whether we examine his criticisms or his maxims, grave or gay, his translations or his songs, his tales or his humorous compositions, we shall find that to no one preceding writer is he much indebted for his mode of thought and style. He resembles Aristophanes, or Lucian, or Rabelais, more perhaps than any modern author; he has the same keen and delicate raillery, the withering sarcasm, the strange and humorous incident, the quaint learning, the bitter scorn of quackery and imposture, the grave and laughable irony, the profound and condensed philosophy of this illustrious triad; but the grossness and obscenity, the loose and depraved sentiments, the utter defiance of modesty and decorum, which their ordinary imitators substitute for wit and wisdom, he does not possess in the slightest degree. Nothing can be more sly than his satire—nothing, when he wishes it, more terrific or more scathing; but it is always clothed in the robe of decency, and does not ever disgust. Even Swift has not equalled him in sarcasm, though in the power of irony he may be entitled to more praise, as having preceded Maginn.—KENEALY, EDWARD VAUGHAN HYDE, 1844, *William Maginn, Dublin University Magazine, vol.* 23, *p.* 74.

Why are not his essays collected? Who holds them back from an expectant public? He wrote when our periodical literature was in its zenith; yet he bore away the palm; and his clear, firm hand might be discerned amid a host of inferior writers. There was no mistaking that emphatic, pure, and stately English of his. No modern writer in periodicals has ever given to satire a less repulsive form of personality. No private venom seemed to direct the powerful pen which spared not Affectation and lashed Presumption till she bled to death.—THOMSON, KATHERINE, 1854, *Recollections of Literary Characters, vol.* I, *p.* 4.

It is, to be sure, enviable praise to be associated with so brilliant a name as Swift; but, much as we admire the writings of the Dean, we must in justice say that they are far short of those of Maginn, for Swift was morose and cynical and austere, Maginn was kind and gentle and child-like. Swift's whole conversation was irony or sarcasm; Maginn's was entirely genial and anecdotical, and free from bitterness.—TIMBS, JOHN, 1874, *Anecdote Lives of the Later Wits and Humourists, vol.* II, *p.* 153.

One of the most brilliant of the band of magazine writers to whom Blackwood first afforded a medium—younger than the great critics of the reviews, more dashing but less serious, who in one way never reached the level of Jeffrey, but in another surpassed and excelled him. . . . Maginn was, if anything, less scrupulous than the original coterie of Edinburgh, the compilers of the Chaldee Manuscript: and he had not only an excellent style, but an easy and powerful command of classical subjects, than which nothing is more effective and telling in periodical literature. A bit of brilliant translation, an adaptation from Homer, a scrap of Horace, lightly turned into contemporary use, is everything to the light gallop of a slashing article, and confers on the writer a position which the world immediately appreciates, and the less learned envy. Everybody will remember Captain Shandon, in "Pendennis," peppering his sentences with learned extracts from old Burton. Maginn, unfortunately, had many features like those of Shandon, and like him lived a distracted life from luxury to misery, through prisons and disreputable hidings, and every vicissitude that poverty, and levity and bad habits and an unstable mind produce.—OLIPHANT, MARGARET O. W., 1882, *Literary History of England, XVIII-XIXth Century, vol.* III, *pp.* 217, 218.

The man who seldom wrote except in company and generally in the midst of tumult, who in the middle of a sentence would relieve the strain of thought by throwing himself back in his chair and telling a humorous story, and who then would suddenly break off in his talk and resume his pen, could not possibly concentrate his powers for the production of steady continuous work.—MONTAGU, R. W., 1885, *Miscellanies by William Maginn, Memoir, p.* xvi.

Nevertheless it is doubtful whether Maginn can be regarded as a "wasted genius;" for if he had really anything serious to say which would have been of much interest to humanity at large, surely here or there some note of it would have been apparent in his current work. But we look in vain for any such sign. Jokes innumerable and excellent, parodies many and first-rate, paraphrases from Horace of much wit and ingenuity, we find indeed; but all these were humorous reflections in the current with which he and his fame were swept away. His translations show more stability; and if we take his Homeric ballads and put them beside his translation from Vidocq we must admit an unusually wide range of literary sympathy. But the light of these is reflected; and though it is impossible to deny him originality or imagination, both of these required a stimulus from some other mind to set them in action. It was not when alone with his own thoughts, but when he was parodying Coleridge or Shelley, that he was in most danger of "dropping into poetry."—MONKHOUSE, COSMO, 1886, *The Academy, vol.* 29, *p.* 86.

His faculties were undoubtedly extraordinary; they were those of an accomplished scholar grafted on a brilliant improvisatore, the compound constituting a perfectly ideal magazinist. Exuberant to the verge of extravagance, he could provide inexhaustible entertainment on any number of topics; his humour made the most ephemeral trifles interesting for the moment, and his learning and critical discrimination gave weight to his more serious disquisitions. His extreme facility inevitably prejudiced him as an artist. He has left only two works of imagination perfect in their respective styles: "The City of the Demons," and "Bob Burke's Duel with Ensign Brady," perhaps the raciest Irish story ever written. Half a dozen more like it would have won him a high reputation.—GARNETT, RICHARD, 1893, *Dictionary of National Biography, vol.* XXXV, *p.* 322.

All the persons hitherto mentioned in this chapter appear by undoubted right in any history of English Literature: it may cause a little surprise to see that of Maginn figuring with them. Yet his abilities were scarcely inferior to those of any; and he was kept back from sharing their fame only by infirmities of character and by his succumbing to that fatal Bohemianism which, constantly recurring among men of letters, exercised its attractions with special force in the early days of journalism in this century. . . . The collections of Maginn's work are anything but exhaustive, and the work itself suffers from all the drawbacks, probable if not inevitable, of work written in the intervals of carouse, at the last moment, for ephemeral purposes. Yet it is instinct with a perhaps brighter genius than the more accomplished productions of some much more famous men. The Homeric Ballads, though they have been praised by some, are nearly worthless; and the longer attempts in fiction are not happy. But Maginn's shorter stories in Blackwood's, especially the inimitable "Story without a Tail," are charming; his more serious critical work, especially that on Shakespeare, displays a remarkable combination of wide reading, critical acumen, and sound sense; and his miscellanies in prose and verse, especially the latter, are characterised by a mixture of fantastic humour, adaptive wit, and rare but real pathos and melody, which is the best note of the specially Irish mode. It must be said, however, that Maginn is chiefly important to the literary historian as the captain of a band of distinguished persons, and as in a way the link between the journalism of the first and the journalism of the second third of the century.—SAINTSBURY, GEORGE, 1896, *History of Nineteenth Century Literature, pp.* 203, 204.

Thackeray has immortalised him in Captain Shandon; but if he had the weaknesses of that well-known character he had certainly all his cleverness and more than all his accomplishments. For Maginn's more serious articles show no inconsiderable learning; while his best humorous articles are simply excellent.—WALKER, HUGH, 1897, *The Age of Tennyson, p.* 70.

John Banim

1798–1842

Born, at Kilkenny, 3 April 1798. Educated at private schools, 1802–10; at Kilkenny Coll., 1810–13. In 1813 to Dublin, to study drawing in Academy of Royal Dublin Society. Returned to Kilkenny, 1815. To Dublin 1820, to adopt literary career. Contrib. to "Limerick Evening Post" and other periodicals. "Damon and Pythias" produced at Covent Garden, 28 May 1821. Married Ellen Ruth, 27 Feb. 1822. "O'Hara" tales planned with brother Michael, 1822. To London, March 1822. On staff of "Literary Register," July 1822 to May 1823. Ill health began, 1823. Tragedy, "The Prodigal," accepted for Drury Lane, but not performed. Took his wife to France, and returned to London early in 1825. "Tales by the O'Hara Family," written in collaboration with brother, first appeared April 1825. At Eastbourne, 1827; at Sevenoaks, 1827–29. To Blackheath, April 1829; to Boulogne, Aug. 1829, owing to ill-health. Wrote for magazines and theatre. Attacked by cholera, 1832. To Paris, 1833. Lower limbs paralyzed. Moved to London, thence to Dublin, 1835. Benefit performance in Dublin Theatre, 21 July 1835. To Kilkenny in Sept. 1835. Pension of £190 per annum, 1836. Tragedy "Sylla" (written in 1827), produced in Dublin, June 1837. Died, 13 Aug. 1842. *Works:* "The Celt's Paradise," 1821; "Damon and Pythias," 1821; "Letter to the Committee appointed to appropriate a fund for a national testimonial, etc.," 1822; "Revelations of the Dead-Alive" (anon.), 1824; "The Fetches" and collaboration in "John Doe," in "Tales by the O'Hara Family" (anon.), 1825; "The Nowlans" and collaboration in "Peter of the Castle," in "Tales by the O'Hara Family," 2nd series (anon.), 1826; "The Boyne Water" (anon.), 1826; "The Anglo-Irish of the Nineteenth Century" (anon.), 1828; "The Denounced" (anon.), 1830; "Chaunt of the Cholera," (with M. Banim; anon.), 1831; "The Smuggler" (anon.), 1831; "The Bit o' Writin" (with M. Banim; anon.), 1838. *Posthumous:* "London and its Eccentricities in the year 2023" (anon.), 1845. *Life:* by P. J. Murray, 1857.—SHARP, R. FARQUHARSON, 1897, *A Dictionary of English Authors, p.* 15.

PERSONAL

During the twelve months succeeding this day Banim merely existed. The whole system seemed shattered. His head ached so violently, that in his paroxysms of pain his body rocked with an involuntary motion so violently that as his head rested upon his mother's breast it required all the latter's strength to curb the violent swaying of the sufferer. "It seemed," he said, "as if the brain were surging through the skull from rear to front and from front to rear alternately." He lost all anxiety for his profession, or for literature; no occupation could interest him; he could rarely be induced to leave the house; and when he did go abroad he quickly became wearied; he seldom spoke: and thus his first love laid the seeds of that frightful suffering which during the greater part of his existence rendered him one of the most miserable of men. The three nights of suffering and exposure to which at Anne D—'s decease he was subjected broke down the stamina of life, and left him at twenty years of age a victim to spinal disease, which but a few years later reduced him to a crippled body, whilst gifted with a mind active as ever genius possessed; his fate indeed was harder than that of Tantalus. . . . "No day passed without its term of suffering. For at two, or at most three hours after retiring to bed, he might, with the assistance of opiates, forget himself in sleep; he was sure to awake, however, after a short repose, screaming loud from the torture he suffered in his limbs, and along his spine; the attack continuing until exhaustion followed, succeeded by, not sleep, but lethargy of some hours' continuance. This was not an occasional visitation, but was renewed night after night. It was not during the hours of darkness only that he suffered—frequently the pains came on in the day-time, —after he endured them all night long, if the weather lowered, or the atmosphere pressed heavily, they were present in the day: to say nothing of his decrepitude, few of his hours were free from agony."—MURRAY, PATRICK JOSEPH, 1858, *The Life of John Banim.*

GENERAL

The author of the "O'Hara Tales" stands pre-eminent among the delineators of Irish character, and quite distinct from the mere painters of Irish manners. He goes to the very heart and soul of the matter. He is neither the eulogist nor the vilifier, neither the patronizing apologist, nor the caricaturist of his countrymen, but their true dramatic historian. Fiction such as his, is truer than any history because it deals not only in facts and their causes, but with the springs of motive and action. It not only details circumstances, but probes into and discovers the living elements on which circumstances operate. His Irishmen are not strange, unaccountable creatures, but members of the great human family, with a temperament of their own, marking a peculiar race, and his Irish women are in especial drawn with the utmost truth and depth of feeling. He knows well the sources of those bitter waters which have converted the impulsive, generous, simple-minded, humorous, and irascible race with whom he has to deal, into lawless ruffians, or unprincipaled knaves. He loves to paint the national character in its genial state, ardent in love, constant in friendship, with a ready tear for the mourner, and a ready laugh for the reveller, overflowing with gratitude for kindness, with open hand and heart, and unsuspicious as a child; and reversing the picture, to show that same character goaded by oppression and contemptuous injustice, into a cruel mocking demon in human form, or into some reckless, libertine, idle, hopeless, tattered rascal. The likeness cannot be disputed. The description carries internal evidence with it. Whoever has been in Ireland remembers illustrations of it, and begins to discover the how and the why of things which before puzzled him.—HORNE, RICHARD HENRY, 1844, *A New Spirit of the Age, p.* 271.

Of a certainty the tales of Mr. Banim were purely original. They had no precursors either in our language or in any other, and they produced accordingly the sort of impression, more vivid than durable, which highly-colored and deeply-shadowed novelty is sure to make on the public mind. But they are also intensely national. They reflect Irish scenery, Irish character, Irish crime, and Irish virtue, with a general truth which, in spite of their tendency to melo-dramatic effects, will keep them fresh and life-like for many a day after the mere fashion of the novel of the season shall be past and gone. The last of his works, especially, "Father Connell," contains the portrait of a parish priest, so exquisitely simple, natural, and tender, that in the whole range of fiction I know nothing more charming.—MITFORD, MARY RUSSELL, 1851, *Recollections of a Literary Life, p.* 21.

Less imaginative and refined than Griffin, and wholly wanting in his humour, Banim was constituted to see the peasant only on his passionate and tragic side—only as he existed in storm and tumult, or the prostrations of deep distress; and with the special end he had in view—to rouse attention to his rustic subject—it cannot be doubted that his limitation was an enlargement of his power. It was the source of that intensity with which he reproduced the terrible struggles and convulsions of rural life, and lifted their sad realities up to the level of romance.—BERNARD, BAYLE, 1874, *The Life of Samuel Lover, p.* 190.

Banim had little humor, and his descriptions are often too detailed and elaborate; but, on the other hand, he possessed a vivid fancy, patriotic fervor, and great intellectual vigor. . . . They are among the most hearty, direct, and graceful specimens of epistolary correspondence in English literature. There is about them a simplicity, easy dash, and pointed brevity for which we look in vain among the letters of other famous authors.—MURRAY, JOHN O'KANE, 1877–84, *Lessons in English Literature, p.* 363.

Although his poems are few, John Banim is one of the most national and powerful of the Irish poets.—WILLIAMS, ALFRED M., 1881, *ed., The Poets and Poetry of Ireland, p.* 259.

He delineated the national character in a striking manner, and his pictures of the Irish peasantry will doubtless live for many generations. . . . Full justice has been done to the realistic powers of Banim, one English critic acknowledging that he united the truth and circumstantiality of Crabbe with the dark and gloomy power of Godwin; while in knowledge of Irish character, habits, customs, and feeling, he was superior even to Miss Edgeworth or Lady Morgan. Had Banim possessed the hearty humour of a Lover or a Lever, he would have been saved from many of his literary excesses. As a delineator of life in the higher ranks of society, Banim conspicuously failed; his strength lay in his vigorous and characteristic sketches of the Irish peasantry, and these in their light and shade have something of the breadth and the strong effects of Rembrandt.—SMITH, GEORGE BARNETT, 1885, *Dictionary of National Biography, vol.* III, *p.* 116.

Where his songs are at all tolerable, they are full of fire and feeling, and written with a quite natural simplicity and strength. Such are the pieces here quoted. His chief fault is his general disregard of metrical laws. . . . His "Soggarth Aroon" is one of the most popular of Irish poems, and has found a place in many anthologies.—O'DONOGHUE, D. J., 1900, *A Treasury of Irish Poetry, eds. Brooke and Rolleston, p.* 106.

William Hone

1780–1842

A London publisher, and subsequently an Independent minister in Eastcheap, published several curious works. Among these were "The Apocryphal New Testament," and many political pieces. One of the latter, "The Political House that Jack Built," ran through fifty editions. Hone is generally known, however, by his three miscellaneous publications, "The Every-day Book," "The Table Book," and "The Year Book."—HART, JOHN S., 1872, *A Manual of English Literature, p.* 503.

PERSONAL

I went again to the King's Bench, Guildhall. Lord Ellenborough sat to-day. I was curious to see how he would succeed where Abbott had failed, and whether he could gain a verdict on Hone's second trial after a former acquittal. Hone was evidently less master of himself before Ellenborough than before Abbott, and perhaps would have sunk in the conflict, but for the aid he received from the former acquittal. He pursued exactly the same course as before. This charge was for publishing a parody on the Litany, and it was charged both as an anti-religious and a political libel; but the Attorney-General did not press the political count. After a couple of hours' flourishing on irrelevant matter, Hone renewed his perusal of old parodies. On this Lord Ellenborough said he should not suffer the giving them in evidence. This was said in such a way that it at first appeared he would not suffer them to be read. However, Hone said, if he could not proceed in his own way he would sit down, and Lord Ellenborough might send him to prison. He then went on as before. Several times he was stopped by the Chief Justice, but never to any purpose. Hone returned to the offensive topic, and did not quit it till he had effected his purpose, and the judge, baffled and worn out, yielded to the prisoner.—ROBINSON, HENRY CRABB, 1817, *Diary, Dec.* 19; *Diary, Reminiscences and Correspondence, ed. Sadler, vol.* I, *p.* 375.

We went into a little parlor where the funeral party was, and God knows it was miserable enough, for the widow and children were crying bitterly in one corner, and the other mourners (mere people of ceremony, who cared no more for the dead man than the hearse did) were talking quite coolly and carelessly together in another; and the contrast was as painful and distressing as anything I ever saw. There was an independent clergyman present, with his bands on and a Bible under his arm, who, as soon as we were seated, addressed C[ruikshank] thus, in a loud, emphatic voice: "Mr. C., have you seen a paragraph respecting our departed friend, which has gone the round of the morning papers?" "Yes, sir," says C., "I have:" looking very hard at me the while, for he had told me with some pride coming down that it was his composition. "Oh!" said the clergyman. "Then you will agree with me, Mr. C., that it is not only an insult to me, who am the servant of the Almighty, but an insult to the Almighty, whose servant I am." "How is that, sir?" says C. "It is stated, Mr. C., in that paragraph," says the minister, "that when Mr. Hone failed in business as a bookseller, he was persuaded by *me* to try the pulpit; which is false, incorrect, unchristian, in a mannner blasphemous, and in all respects contemptible. Let us pray." With which, and in the same breath, I give you my word, he knelt down, as we all did, and began a very miserable jumble of an extemporary prayer. I was really penetrated with sorrow for the family (he exerted himself zealously for them afterward, as the kind-hearted C. also did), but when C., upon his knees and sobbing for the loss of an old friend, whispered me that "if that wasn't a clergyman, and it wasn't a funeral, he'd have punched his head," I felt as if nothing but convulsions could possibly relieve me. —DICKENS, CHARLES, 1842, *Letter to Prof. Felton.*

I knew him well, and respected him for warmth of heart, kindness of disposition, and strength of head; but he was most improvident and indiscreet in the management of money affairs. Had these been placed in the charge of an honest, good accountant, William Hone might have lived to be a rich man, and died a happy one. —REES, THOMAS, 1853, *Reminiscences of Literary London, p.* 103.

I have bought books from Hone when he kept the book-seller's shop; had coffee from him when he kept the eating-house; and listened to one of his wearisome sermons when he turned preacher. . . . Hone was a small and insignificant-looking man: mild, kindly, conciliatory in manner, the very opposite of the traditional demagogue. He must have read a vast deal; there is evidence of that in his memorable defences as well as in the books he edited and bequeathed as valuable legacies to posterity. These books contain very little indeed to which objection can be urged, either on moral, political, or religious grounds. It is clear that in later life he abjured much, if not all, hostility to those personages and institutions against whom and which in his earlier career he had directed his envenomed attacks. The evil he did was almost atoned for by the good he accomplished; if the one is forgotten let the other be remembered, and the verdict of posterity be recorded as "forgiven" on the stone that covers the dust of a very remarkable, and I believe, conscientious man.—HALL, SAMUEL CARTER, 1883, *Retrospect of a Long Life, pp.* 320, 321.

Hone had twelve children, nine of whom, together with his widow, survived him. The "Quarterly Review" naturally styled Hone "a wretch as contemptible as he is wicked," and "a poor illiterate creature." . . . Hone was a thoroughly honest and conscientious man, and deserves to be remembered for his sacrifices on behalf of the freedom of the press and cheap literature. There is a portrait of him in stipple by Rogers from a drawing by Cruikshank. Towards the end of his life (1833) he is said to have been "rather corpulent, dressed very plainly; and his lofty forehead, keen eye, grey and scanty locks, and very expressive countenance, commanded respect." — TEDDER, H. R., 1891, *Dictionary of National Biography, vol.* XXVII, *p.* 245.

GENERAL

I like you, and your book, ingenuous Hone!
In whose capacious all-embracing leaves
The very marrow of tradition 's shown;
And all that history—much that fiction—weaves.
By every sort of taste your work is graced.
Vast stores of modern anecdote we find,
With good old story quaintly interlaced—
The theme as various as the reader's mind.
Rome's lie-fraught legends you so truly paint—
Yet kindly,—that the half-turn'd Catholic
Scarcely forbears to smile at his own saint,
And cannot curse the candid heretic.
Rags, relics, witches, ghosts, fiends, crowd your page;
Our father's mummeries we well-pleased behold,
And, proudly conscious of a purer age,
Forgive some fopperies in the times of old.
Verse-honouring Phœbus, Father of bright *Days*,
Must needs bestow on you both good and many,
Who, building trophies of his Children's praise,
Run their rich Zodiac through, not missing any.
Dan Phœbus loves your book—trust me, friend Hone—
The title only errs, he bids me say:
For while such art, wit, reading, they are shown,
He swears, 'tis not a work of *every day*.

—LAMB, CHARLES, 1825, *To the Editor of the "Every-Day Book."*

By-the-by, I have brought Hone's "Every-day Book" and his "Table Book," and am sorry I had not seen them before my "Colloquies" were printed, that I might have given him a hearty good word there. I have not seen any miscellaneous books that are so well worth having; brimful of curious matter, and with an abundance of the very best wood-cuts. Poor fellow, he outwent the march of intellect; and I believe his unwearied and almost unparalleled industry has ended in bankruptcy. I shall take the first opportunity of noticing these books; perhaps it will be in Allan Cunningham's periodical.—SOUTHEY, ROBERT, 1830, *Letter to Henry Taylor, Life and Correspondence, ed. Southey, ch.* xxxiii.

His later publications were useful and valuable, as calculated to combine amusing with good historical, topographical, and antiquarian information. They were "The Every-Day Book," "The Year Book," "The Table Book," and "Ancient Mysteries." Never, perhaps, was political and personal satire, irony, ridicule, burlesque, caricature, sarcasm, and unflinching temerity of language and graphic representation carried to such a pitch as in his once-popular pamphlets, which, with the exalted and illustrious personages represented and ridiculed, are now scarcely to be described in the haze of distance. Had there not been gross delinquency and bad conduct in the parties satirized, and also palpable originality and talent in the author and the artist, these publications would not have attained their surprising and unprecedented popularity. — REES, THOMAS, 1853, *Reminiscences of Literary London, p.* 103.

His "Every-Day Book" (1826), "Table Book" (1827–8), and "Year Book" (1829) are full of out-of-the-way information, and are still read with pleasure, more especially when it is remembered that Lamb took part in their preparation. . . . Hone at least deserves admiration for possessing the courage of his opinions, and in the history of Radicalism his name has an honourable place.—SANDERS, LLOYD C., *ed.*, 1887, *Celebrities of the Century, pp.* 571, 572.

Thomas Hamilton

1789-1842

Born at Glasgow, 1789: died at Pisa, Italy, Dec. 7, 1842. A Scottish author, brother of Sir William Hamilton (1788-1856). He wrote "Cyril Thornton" (1827), "Annals of the Peninsular Campaign" (1829), "Men and Manners in America" (1833). —SMITH, BENJAMIN E., *ed.*, 1894-97, *The Century Cyclopedia of Names, p.* 477.

PERSONAL

Mr. Hamilton exhibited a remarkable union of scholarship, high breeding, and amiability of disposition. To the habitual refinement of taste which an early mastery of the classics had produced, his military profession and intercourse with society had added the ease of the man of the world, while they had left unimpaired his warmth of feeling and kindliness of heart. Amidst the active services of the Peninsular and American campaigns, he preserved his literary tastes; and, when the close of the war restored him to his country, he seemed to feel that the peaceful leisure of a soldier's life could not be more appropriately filled up than by the cultivation of literature. The characteristic of his mind was rather a happy union and balance of qualities than the possession of any one in excess; and the result was a peculiar composure and gracefulness, pervading equally his outward deportment and his habits of thought.—MOIR, GEORGE, 1843, *Death of Thomas Hamilton, Blackwood's Magazine, vol.* 53, *p.* 280.

GENERAL

As for Tom Hamilton, the resources of his mind, the brilliancy of his wit, and the play of his fancy, are quite uncommon. "Cyril Thornton" is certainly a work of great ability, though by no means what I should have expected from him.—GRANT, ANNE, 1831, *Letters, Jan* 17; *Memoir and Correspondence, ed. Grant, vol.* III, *p.* 218.

It ["Men and Manners in America"] is undoubtedly as we have said, in point of literary execution, one of the best that have yet appeared upon the United States. The style is not deficient in strength or spirit, and evinces at times a remarkable power of description, as in the passages on the Falls of Niagara and the river Mississippi. On the other hand, it is far from being uniformly so pure and correct as might be wished,—is often unpardonably coarse, and is pervaded throughout by an affected pertness and a silly air of pretension, which are offensive from the beginning, and finally become by repetition completely nauseous. . . . That a spirit of unjust depreciation is the one that predominates in his work, is—as we shall have occasion abundantly to show—very certain. —EVERETT, ALEXANDER HILL, 1834, *North American Review, vol.* 38, *pp.* 211, 213.

The only work of fiction which he has given to the public certainly indicates high powers both of pathetic and graphic delineation; but the qualities which first and most naturally attracted attention, were rather his excelling judgment of character, at once just and generous, his fine perception and command of wit and quiet humour, rarely, if ever, allowed to deviate into satire or sarcasm, and the refinement, taste, and precision with which he clothed his ideas, whether in writing or in conversation. From the boisterous or extravagant he seemed instinctively to recoil, both in society and in taste. . . . The "Annals of the Peninsular Campaign" had the merit of clear narration, united with much of the same felicity of style; but the size of the work excluded that full development and picturesque detail which were requisite to give individuality to its pictures. His last work was "Men and Manners in America," of which two German and one French translations have already appeared; a work eminently characterized by a tone of gentlemanly feeling, sagacious observation, just views of national character and institutions, and their reciprocal influence, and by tolerant criticism; and which, so far from having been superseded by recent works of the same class and on the same subject, has only risen in public estimation by the comparison.—MOIR, GEORGE, 1843, *Death of Thomas Hamilton, Blackwood's Magazine vol.* 53, *p.* 280.

It was at Chiefswood that the greater part of "The Life and Manhood of Cyril Thornton" was written. It appeared in 1827, and was most favourably received. The sketches of college, military, and civic life are drawn with great vividness. The portraiture, in particular, of former

ROBERT SOUTHEY

WILLIAM WORDSWORTH

Engraving by G. J. Stodart, after Lupton's

Glasgow manners, is, whether overdrawn or not, one of the raciest bits of writing in the language.—VEITCH, JOHN, 1869, *Memoir of Sir William Hamilton, p.* 129.

He visited America, and wrote a lively ingenious work on the New World, entitled "Men and Manners in America," 1833. Captain Hamilton was one of the many travellers who disliked the peculiar customs, the democratic government, and social habits of the Americans; and he spoke his mind freely, but apparently in a spirit of truth and candour.—CHAMBERS, ROBERT, 1876, *Cyclopædia of English Literature, ed. Carruthers.*

Hamilton's novel "Cyril Thornton" appeared in 1827. Apart from its considerable merits as a work of fiction, it remains a bright and valuable record of the writer's times, from his early impressions on Scottish university life and Glasgow citizens—when as yet he could call Govan "a pretty and rural village"—on to his varied military experiences. . . . His "Men and Manners in America" appeared in 1833. Here his fund of humour and his genial satire—characteristics that struck Carlyle in his interviews with him in 1832-3—found scope, but his fun, if occasionally extravagant, was never unfair, nor were his criticisms directed by prejudice or charged with ill-nature. The book was popular, and in ten years had been translated once into French and twice into German.—BAYNE, THOMAS, 1890, *Dictionary of National Biography, vol.* XXIV, *p.* 213.

No doubt the novel of "Cyril Thornton" has in time past owed much of its popularity to its varied action and frequently shifting scene, and if we are to judge it now on literary grounds we have no choice but to acknowledge that a great portion of its interest has perished. Still, there remain a few admirable passages, and in this particular instance the lines of cleavage between true and false are marked with peculiar distinctness. For the book may be described as fragments of autobiography embedded in a paste of romance. Now imagination was by no means Hamilton's strong point; his fancy was neither very happy nor very abundant, and when he essays character-painting on an important scale—as in the case of old David Spreull, the conventional eccentric but beneficient uncle of the story, and his faithful servant Girzy, he is as deficient in anything like true insight as he is in lightness of touch. But though his fiction is of this heavy quality, he could present to admiration what he himself had seen and taken part in, and from time to time he has thought fit to do so, with excellent effect.—DOUGLAS, SIR GEORGE, 1897, *The Blackwood Group (Famous Scots), p.* 153.

Robert Southey

1774-1843

1774—Born, August 12th, in Bristol. 1788—A scholar at Westminster. 1792—Expelled from Westminster School, for printing an article upon flogging. 1793—Enters Oxford University. 1794—Studies medicine for a short time. Publishes a volume of poems, the joint work of himself and Robert Lovell. Leaves Oxford. Plans a Pantisocracy, with Coleridge and others. 1795—Marries Miss Edith Fricker, privately. Goes to Lisbon with his uncle. Publishes "Joan of Arc." 1796—Returns to England, and lives with his wife in Bristol. 1797—Resides in London, in order to study law. 1800—Goes to Lisbon with his wife. 1801—Returns to England. Publishes "Thalaba." Becomes private secretary to the Irish Lord Chancellor of the Exchequer. 1802—Resigns his position as Secretary. Lives at Bristol with his wife. 1803—Takes his wife to Greta Hall, at Keswick. 1805—Publishes "Madoc." 1807—Receives a pension of two hundred pounds per annum. 1809—Contributes to the first numbers of "The Quarterly Review." 1810—Publishes the "Curse of Kehama," and the first volume of "The History of Brazil." 1813—Becomes Poet Laureate. Publishes "The Life of Nelson." 1814—Publishes "Roderick." 1817—"Wat Tyler," a revolutionary sketch, written in Southey's youth, is published, without his consent. 1820—Publishes "The Life of Wesley." 1824—Publishes "The Book of the Church." 1826—Elected to Parliament, but declines to serve. 1829—Publishes "Colloquies." 1834—Publishes "The Doctor." 1835—Publishes "The Life of Cowper." Declines a baronetcy, offered to him by Sir Robert Peel. Receives an addition of 300*l.* per annum to his pension. 1837—His wife dies. 1839—Marries Miss Catherine Bowles. 1843—Dies, March 21st.—MASON, EDWARD T., 1885, *Personal Traits of British Authors, Byron-Landor, p.* 214.

PERSONAL

Literature is now Southey's trade; he is a manufacturer, and his workshop is his study,—a very beautiful one certainly, but its beauty and the delightful environs, as well as his own celebrity, subject him to interruptions. His time is his wealth, and I shall therefore scrupulously abstain from stealing any portion of it.—ROBINSON, HENRY CRABB, 1816, *Diary, Sept.* 9; *Diary, Reminiscences and Correspondence, ed. Sadler, vol.* I, *p.* 340.

Bob Southey! You're a poet—Poet-Laureate,
And representative of all the race,
Although 'tis true that you turn'd out a Tory at
Last—yours has lately been a common case,—
And now, my Epic Renegade! what are ye at?
With all the Lakers, in and out of place?
—BYRON, LORD, 1819, *Don Juan, Dedication.*

He is certainly an extraordinary man, one of those whose character I find it difficult to comprehend, because I hardly know how such elements can be brought together, such rapidity of mind with such patient labour and wearisome exactness, so mild a disposition with so much nervous excitability, and a poetical talent so elevated with such an immense mass of minute, dull learning.—TICKNOR, GEORGE, 1819, *Journal; Life, Letters and Journals, vol.* I, *p.* 286.

His figure is rather tall and slim, but apparently muscular, and has altogether an air of gentility about it. He has nothing whatever about him of the stiffness or awkwardness of a great student; but, on the contrary, were he a mere ordinary person, I should describe him as a genteel-looking man, possessing much natural elegance, or even grace. But his head and countenance bespeak the poet. His hair is black, and bushy, and strong, and gives him a bold, free, and even dignified look; his face is sharp; his nose high; and his eyes, without having that piercing look which is often felt to be disagreeable, because too searching, in the eyes of men of genius, are, without any exception, the most acute and intelligent I ever beheld. Yet I believe he is near-sighted; and this seems to have given him a habit of elevating his face when he speaks, as if he were looking up, which brings all his features fully before you, and seemed to me to impart to his whole demeanour a singular charm of sincerity and independence. His voice seemed to me at first to be shrill and weak, and perhaps it is so, but there is in it a kind of musical wildness, which I could not help considering to be characteristic of the author of "Thalaba;" and when he chanced to recite a few lines of poetry it became quite empassioned.—LOCKHART, JOHN GIBSON (PHILIP KEMPFERHAUSEN), 1819, *Letters from the Lakes, Blackwood's Magazine, vol.* 4, *p.* 401.

Sir,—You have done me an unfriendly office, without perhaps much considering what you were doing. You have given an ill name to my poor lucubrations. In a recent paper on Infidelity, you usher in a conditional commendation of them with an exception; which, preceding the encomium, and taking up nearly the same space with it, must impress your readers with the notion, that the objectionable parts in them are at least equal in quantity to the pardonable. The censure is in fact the criticism; the praise—a concession merely. Exceptions usually follow, to qualify praise or blame. But there stands your reproof, in the very front of your notice, in ugly characters, like some bugbear, to frighten all good Christians from purchasing. Through you I become an object of suspicion to preceptors of youth, and fathers of families. "A book which wants only a sounder religious feeling to be as delightful as it is original." With no further explanation, what must your readers conjecture, but that my little volume is some vehicle for heresy or infidelty? . . . You have never ridiculed, I believe, what you thought to be religion, but you are always girding at what some pious, but perhaps mistaken folks, think to be so. For this reason, I am sorry to hear that you are engaged upon a life of George Fox. . . . You pick up pence by showing the hallowed bones, shrine, and crucifix; and you take money a second time by exposing the trick of them afterwards. You carry your verse to Castle Angelo for sale in a morning; and, swifter than a peddler can transmute his pack, you are at Canterbury with your prose ware before night.—LAMB, CHARLES, 1823, *Letter to Southey, The Tombs in the Abbey, Works, ed. Shepherd, pp.* 174, 176, 177.

Mr. Southey, as we formerly remember to have seen him, had a hectic flush upon his cheek, a roving fire in his eye, a falcon glance, a look at once aspiring and dejected—it was the look that had been impressed upon his face by the events that marked the outset of his life, it was the dawn of Liberty that still tinged his cheek, a smile betwixt hope and sadness that still played upon his quivering lip. . . . Mr. Southey is not of the court, courtly. Every thing of him and about him is from the people. He is not classical, he is not legitimate. He is not a man cast in the mould of other men's opinions: he is not shaped on any model: he bows to no authority: he yields only to his own wayward peculiarities. He is wild, irregular, singular, extreme. He is no formalist, not he! All is crude and chaotic, self-opinionated, vain. He wants proportion, keeping, system, standard rules. He is not *teres et rotundus*. Mr. Southey walks with his chin erect through the streets of London, and with an umbrella sticking out under his arm, in the finest weather. He has not sacrificed to the Graces, nor studied decorum. With him everything is projecting, starting from its place, an episode, a digression, a poetic license. He does not move in any given orbit, but like a falling star, shoots from his sphere. He is pragmatical, restless, unfixed, full of experiments, beginning everything a-new, wiser than his betters, judging for himself, dictating to others. He is decidedly revolutionary. He may have given up the reform of the State: but depend upon it, he has some other hobby of the same kind. . . . Mr. Southey's conversation has a little resemblance to a common-place book; his habitual deportment to a piece of clock-work. He is not remarkable either as a reasoner or an observer: but he is quick, unaffected, replete with anecdotes, various and retentive in his reading, and exceedingly happy in his play upon words as most scholars are who give their minds this sportive turn. We have chiefly seen Mr. Southey in company where few people appear to advantage, we mean in that of Mr. Coleridge. He has not certainly the same range of speculation, nor the same flow of sounding words, but he makes up by the detail of knowledge, and by a scrupulous correctness of statement for what he wants in originality of thought, or impetuous declamation.—HAZLITT, WILLIAM, 1825, *The Spirit of the Age.*

He is in person above the middle size, but slender, with something of the stoop and listless air of an habitual student. A retiring forehead, shaded in part by thick curled hair, already gray; strongly marked arching eyebrows; uncommonly full, dark eyes, blue I incline to think; a thin but very prominent nose; a mouth large and eloquent, and a retreating but well-defined chin.—GRIFFIN, EDMUND DORR, 1831, *Remains, Compiled by Francis Griffin.*

Now hurried we home, and while taking our tea
We thought—Mr. Southey at Church we might see!
Next morning, the church how we wished to be reaching!
I'm afraid 'twas as much for the poet as preaching!

. . . .

Howe'er *I* forgave,—'deed I scarcely did know it,
For really we were "cheek-by-jowl" with the poet!
His hair was no colour at all by the way,
But half of't was black, slightly scattered with grey;
His eyes were as black as a coal, but in turning
They flashed, ay, as much as that coal does in burning!
His nose in the midst took a small outward bend,
Rather hooked like an eagle's, and sharp at the end;
But his dark lightning eye made him seem half inspired,
Or like his own Thalaba, vengefully fired.
We looked, and we gazed, and we stared in his face;
Marched out at a slow-stopping, lingering pace;
And as towards Keswick delighted we walked,
Of his face, and his form, and his features we talked.

—RUSKIN, JOHN, 1831, *The Iteriad.*

My first interview with Mr. Southey was at the Queen's Head Inn, in Keswick, where I had arrived, wearied, one evening, on my way to Westmoreland; and not liking to intrude on his family circle that evening, I sent a note up to Greta Hall, requesting him to come down and see me.

He came on the instant, and stayed with me about an hour and a half. But I was aggrieved as well as an astonished man, when I found that he refused all participation in my beverage of rum punch. For a poet to refuse his glass was to me a phenomenon; and I confess I doubted in my own mind, and doubt to this day, if perfect sobriety and transcendant poetical genius can exist together. . . . Before we had been ten minutes together my heart was knit to Southey, and every hour thereafter my esteem for him increased. . . . Southey certainly is as elegant a writer as any in the kingdom. But those who would love Southey as well as admire him, must see him, as I did, in the bosom, not only of one lovely family, but of three, all attached to him as a father, and all elegantly maintained and educated, it is generally said, by his indefatigable pen. The whole of Southey's conversation and economy, both at home and afield, left an impression of veneration on my mind, which no future contingency shall ever either extinguish or injure. Both his figure and countenance are imposing, and deep thought is strongly marked in his dark eye; but there is a defect in his eyelids, for these he has no power of raising, so that when he looks up he turns up his face, being unable to raise his eyes; and when he looks towards the top of one of his romantic mountains, one would think he was looking at the zenith. This peculiarity is what will most strike every stranger in the appearance of the accomplished laureate. He does not at all see well at a distance, which made me several times disposed to get into a passion with him, because he did not admire the scenes which I was pointing out.—HOGG, JAMES, 1832, *Autobiography.*

There was . . . an habitual delicacy in his conversation, evidencing that cheerfulness and wit might exist without ribaldry, grossness, or profanation. He neither violated decorum himself, nor tolerated it in others. I have been present when a trespasser of the looser class has received a rebuke, I might say a castigation, well deserved, and not readily forgotten. His abhorrence also of injustice, or unworthy conduct, in its diversified shapes, had all the decision of a Roman censor; while this apparent austerity was associated, when in the society he liked, with so bland and playful a spirit, that it abolished all constraint, and rendered him one of the most agreeable, as well as the most intelligent of companions.—COTTLE, JOSEPH, 1837–47, *Reminiscences of Coleridge and Southey, p.* 223.

Ye vales and hills whose beauty hither drew
The poet's steps, and fixed him here, on you
His eyes have closed! And ye, loved books, no more
Shall Southey feed upon your precious lore,
To works that ne'er shall forfeit their renown,
Adding immortal labours of his own—
Whether he traced historic truth, with zeal
For the State's guidance, or the Church's weal,
Or Fancy, disciplined by studious art,
Informed his pen, or wisdom of the heart,
Or judgments sanctioned in the Patriot's mind
By reverence for the rights of all mankind.
—WORDSWORTH, WILLIAM, 1843, *Inscription for a Monument in Crosthwaite Church in the Vale of Keswick.*

Southey's house, which lies at a little distance from the town of Keswick, on the way to Bassenthwaite water, is a plain stuccoed tenement, looking as you approach it almost like a chapel, from the apparent absence of chimneys. Standing upon the bridge over the Greta which crosses the high-road here, the view all round of the mountains, those which lie at the back of Southey's house Skiddaw being the chief, and those which lie in front, girdling the lake of Derwentwater, is grand and complete. From this bridge the house lies at the distance of a croft, or of three or four hundred yards, on an agreeable swell. In front, that is, between you and the house, ascends toward it a set of homelike crofts, with their cut hedges and a few scattered trees. When Southey went there, and I suppose for twenty years after, these were occupied as a nursery ground, and injured the effect of the immediate environs of the house extremely. Nothing now can be more green and agreeable. On the brow of the hill, if it can be called so, stand two stuccoed houses; the one nearest to the town, and the largest, being Southey's.—HOWITT, WILLIAM, 1847, *Homes and Haunts of the Most Eminent British Poets, vol.* II, *p.* 269.

His domestic affections were warm; his domestic temper venerable and sweet; his self-denial and benevolence for the sake of the erring and the helpless were a life-long protest against the injurious laxity which enters into our estimate of the morals of genius. He was eminently happy in his life-long toils. He loved labor for itself, and he loved the subjects on which he toiled; and his conscience, nice as it was, could not but be satisfied and gratified at the spectacle of the aid and solace which, by his labors, he was able to give beyond his own family, to some who had no natural claim on him for support. In the spectacle of his social and domestic virtues, all remembrance of a bitter political and religious spirit may well be sunk. He was not a man qualified to have opinions, strictly so called. He could not sympathise in any views but those immediately held by himself; and the views which he most quarreled with were usually those which had been, no long time before, virulently held by himself.—MARTINEAU, HARRIET, 1849, *A History of the Thirty Years' Peace, A. D.* 1815–1846, *vol.* IV, *p.* 428.

His forehead was very broad; his height was five feet eleven inches; his complexion rather dark, the eyebrows large and arched, the eye well shaped and dark brown, the mouth somewhat prominent, muscular, and very variously expressive, the chin small in proportion to the upper features of his face. He always, while in Keswick, wore a cap in his walks and partly from habit, partly from the make of his head and shoulders, we never thought he looked well or like himself in a hat. He was of a very spare frame, but of great activity, and not showing any evidence of a weak constitution. My father's countenance, like his character, seems to have softened down from a certain wildness of expression to a more sober and thoughtful cast; and many thought him a handsomer man in age than in youth; his eye retaining always its brilliancy, and . . . his countenance its play of expression. Though he did not continue to let his hair hang down on his shoulders according to the whim of his youthful days, yet he always wore a greater quantity than is usual; and once, on his arrival in town, Chantrey's first greetings to him were accompanied with an injunction to go and get his hair cut. When I first remember it, it was turning from a rich brown to the steel shade, whence it rapidly became almost snowy white, losing none of its remarkable thickness, and clustering in abundant curls over his massive brow.—SOUTHEY, CHARLES CUTHBERT, 1849–50, *Life of Southey, ch.* xxxii.

Never in the course of my existence have I known a man so excellent on so many points. What he was as a son, is now remembered by few; what he was as a husband and a father, shows it more clearly than the best memory could represent it. The purity of his youth, the integrity of his manhood, the soundness of his judgment, and the tenderness of his heart, they alone who have been blest with the same qualities can appreciate. And who are they? Many with one, some with more than one, nobody with all of them in the like degree. So there are several who possess one quality of his poetry; none who possess the whole variety. . . . Conscience with Southey stood on the other side of Enthusiasm. What he saw, he said; what he found, he laid open.—LANDOR, WALTER SAVAGE, 1850, *To the Rev. C. Cuthbert Southey, Fraser's Magazine, vol.* 42, *pp.* 647, 649.

Some people assert that genius is inconsistent with domestic happiness, and yet Southey was happy at home and made his home happy, he not only loved his wife and children *though* he was a poet, but he loved them better *because* he was a poet. He seems to have been without taint of worldliness. London with its pomps and vanities, learned coteries with their dry pedantry, rather scared than attracted him. He found his prime glory in his genius, and his chief felicity in home affections. I like Southey.—BRONTË, CHARLOTTE, 1850, *Letter to W. S. Williams, April* 12; *Charlotte Brontë and her Circle, ed. Shorter, p.* 399.

How great and how good a man he was! how fine a specimen of the generosity of labor! Giving so largely, so liberally, so unostentatiously, not from the superfluities of an abundant fortune, but from the hard-won earnings of his indefatigable toil! Some people complain of his change of politics; and I, for my own particular part, wish very heartily that he had been content with a very moderate modification of opinion. But does not the violent republicanism of youth often end in the violent toryism of age? Does not the pendulum, very forcibly set in motion, swing as far one way as it has swung the other? Does not the sun rise in the east and set in the west? As to his poetry, I suspect people of liking it better than they say. . . . Never was a man more beloved by all who approached him. Even his peculiarities, if he had any, were genial and pleasant.—MITFORD, MARY RUSSELL, 1851, *Recollections of a Literary Life.*

His long and valuable works advanced slowly, because he always had different tasks on hand, and like a thorough-bred man of business, could at any time turn from one to another; but they advanced unremittingly; they were not scrawled and patched up *invitâ Minervâ*, careless of all but the citizen's only object, to obtain immediate pelf; but they were finished so as to gain the author's approbation in the first place. Among his minor peculiarities I cannot but remember how in his unequalled calligraphy, he revived the accomplishment of monastic scribes in the middle ages, and how in divers instances he completed a long MS., bound it handsomely, and kept it for years on his shelves, before he thought of publication. *Labor ipsa voluptas erat*, even without one particle of pecuniary gain.—GILLIES, ROBERT PEARCE, 1854, *Memoirs of a Literary Veteran.*

His hair [in 1839] was black, and yet his complexion was fair; his eyes I believe to be hazel and large; but I will not vouch for that fact: his nose aquiline; and he has a remarkable habit of looking up into the air, as if looking at abstractions. The expression of his face was that of a very acute and aspiring man. So far, it was even noble, as it conveyed a feeling of a serene and gentle pride, habitually familiar with elevating subjects of contemplation. And yet it was impossible that this pride could have been offensive to anybody, chastened as it was by the most unaffected modesty; and this modesty made evident and prominent by the constant expression of reverence for the great men of the age (when he happened to esteem them such), and for all the great patriarchs of our literature. The point in which Southey's manner failed the most in conciliating regard was in all which related to the external expressions of friendliness. No man could be more sincerely hospitable—no man more essentially disposed to give up even his time (the possession which he most valued) to the service of his friends. But there was an air of reserve and distance about him—the reserve of a lofty, self-respecting mind, but, perhaps, a little too freezing—in his treatment of all persons who were not among the *corps* of his ancient fireside friends. Still, even towards the veriest strangers, it is but justice to notice his extreme courtesy in sacrificing his literary employments for the day, whatever they might be, to the duty (for such he made it) of doing the honours of the lake and the adjacent mountains. . . . Were it to his own instant ruin, I am satisfied that he would do justice and fulfil his duty under any possible difficulties, and through the very strongest temptations to do otherwise. For honour the most delicate, for integrity the firmest, and for generosity within the limits of prudence, Southey cannot well have a superior.—DE QUINCEY, THOMAS, 1854, *Autobiography from* 1803 *to* 1808, *Collected Writings of Thomas De Quincey, vol.* II, *pp.* 317, 327.

In associating with Southey, not only was it necessary to salvation to refrain from touching his books, but various rites, ceremonies, and usages must be rigidly observed. At certain appointed hours only was he open to conversation; at the seasons which had been predestined from all eternity for holding intercourse with his friends. Every hour of the day had its commission—every half-hour was assigned to its own peculiar, undeviating function. The indefatigable student gave a detailed account of his most painstaking life, every moment of which was fully employed and strictly pre-arranged, to a certain literary Quaker lady. "I rise at five throughout the year; from six till eight I read Spanish; then French for one hour; Portuguese next, for half an hour,—my watch lying on the table; I give two hours to poetry; I write prose for two hours; I translate so long; I make extracts so long," and so of the rest until the poor fellow had fairly fagged himself into his bed again. "And, pray, when dost thou think, friend?" she asked, dryly, to the great discomfiture of the future Laureate.—HOGG, THOMAS JEFFERSON, 1858, *The Life of Percy Bysshe Shelley, vol.* II, *p.* 27.

An English worthy, doing his duty for fifty noble years of labour, day by day storing up learning, day by day working for scant wages, most charitable out of his small means, bravely faithful to the calling which he had chosen, refusing to turn from his path for popular praise or princes' favour; I mean *Robert Southey.* We have left his old political landmarks miles and miles behind; we protest against his dogmatism; nay, we begin to forget it and his politics; but I hope his life will not be forgotten, for it is sublime in its simplicity, its energy, its honour, its affection! In the combat between Time and Thalaba, I suspect the former destroyer has conquered; Kehama's curse frightens very few readers now; but Southey's private letters are worth piles of epics, and are sure to last among us as long as kind hearts like to sympathize with goodness and purity and love and upright life.—THACKERAY, WILLIAM MAKEPEACE, 1861, *George the Fourth, The Four Georges.*

Southey was a man well up in the fifties; [1835, was sixty-one] hair gray, not yet hoary, well setting off his fine clear-brown complexion; head and face both smallish; as indeed the figure was *while seated;* features finely cut; eyes, brow, mouth, good in their kind; expressive all, and even vehemently so, but betokening rather keenness than depth either of intellect or character; a serious, human, honest, but sharp almost fierce-looking thin man, with very much of the *militant* in his aspect,—in the eyes especially was legible a mixture of sorrow and of anger, or of angry contempt, as if his indignant fight with the world had not yet ended in victory, but also never should in defeat. . . . Southey at last completely rose from his chair to shake hands: he had only half-risen and nodded on my coming in; and all along I had counted him a lean little man; but now he shot suddenly aloft into a lean tall one; all legs, in shape and stature like a pair of tongs,—which peculiarity my surprise doubtless exaggerated to me, but only made it the more notable and entertaining. . . . Had again more than once to notice the singular readiness of the *blushes,*—amiable *red* blush, beautiful like a young girl's, when you touched genially the pleasant theme; and serpent-like flash of *blue* or black blush (this far, very far the *rarer* kind, though it did recur, too), when you struck upon the opposite. . . . Now blushing, under his gray hairs, rosy like a maiden of fifteen; now *slaty* almost, like a rattle-snake, or fiery serpent. How has he not been torn to pieces long since, under such furious pulling this way and that? He must have somewhere a great deal of methodic virtue in him; I suppose, too, his heart is thoroughly honest, which helps considerably!—CARLYLE, THOMAS, 1867, *Southey, Reminiscences, ed. Norton, vol.* II, *pp.* 279, 281, 284.

A man so lovable, so pure-hearted, sound-hearted, manly, tender, and true.—JACOX, FRANCIS, 1872, *Literary Society, Aspects of Authorship, p.* 159.

I never met any literary man who so thoroughly answered my expectations as Southey. His face is at once shrewd, thoughtful, and quick, if not irritable, in its expression; a singular deficiency of space in its lower portion, but no deficiency of feature or expression; his manner cold, but still; in conversation, bland and gentle, and not nearly so dogmatic as his writings would lead one to imagine.—CHORLEY, HENRY FOTHERGILL, 1873, *Autobiography, Memoirs and Letters, vol.* I, *p.* 277.

He wrought in his place day after day, season after season. He submitted to the good laws of use and wont. He grew stronger, calmer, more full-fraught with stores of knowledge, richer in treasure of the heart. Time laid its hand upon him gently and unfalteringly: the bounding step became less light and swift; the ringing voice lapsed into sadder fits of silence; the raven hair changed to a snowy white; only still the indefatigable eye ran down the long folio columns, and the indefatigable hand still held the pen—until all true life had ceased. . . . What makes the life of Southey eminent and singular, is its unity of purpose, its persistent devotion to a chosen object, its simplicity, purity, loyalty, fortitude, kindliness, truth. —DOWDEN, EDWARD, 1880, *Southey* (*English Men of Letters*), *p.* 80.

I knew Southey only in London, meeting him more than once at the house of Allan Cunningham. I wish I had known more of him, for in my heart and mind he holds a place higher than is held by any other great man with whom I have been acquainted. To me, he is the beau-ideal of the Man of Letters; a glory to his calling to whom all succeeding authors by profession may point back with pride. Not only was his life one of diligent and fruitful labor; it was marked by almost every manly virtue that may combine to crown a king of men. If we look at his public career we find it distinguished throughout by industry, energy, rigid integrity, and noble pride—the pride of a Sidney of the pen, whose aim before all things was to keep his honor stainless. We turn to his private life, and all we learn of it shows to us Southey as a devoted husband, a judicious and affectionate father, a warm and faithful friend. Though he had to struggle, nearly all his own life through with poverty, he was ever ready to hold out a helping hand to those whose struggles for fame were just beginning, or as in the case of Chatterton's sister, to tender generous and effectual aid to the unfortunate relatives they had left. . . . My remembrance of him is that of a form, not tall but stately—a countenance full of power, yet also of gentleness; and eyes whose keen and penetrating glance had justly caused them to be likened to the hawk's, but that on occasion could beam and soften with the kindliest and tenderest emotion. His head was perhaps the noblest and handsomest among English writers of his time.—HALL, SAMUEL CARTER, 1883, *Retrospect of a Long Life, pp.* 321, 322.

His guerdon of praise must be without suspicion of blame where his life and character stand for judgment. His personal purity was indeed the purity of Marcus Cato, who was virtuous by the necessity of a happy nature which could not be otherwise.—CAINE, HALL, 1883, *Cobwebs of Criticism, p.* 52.

In his conversation Southey was perfectly easy and unpretending, never shunning to speak his real sentiments of men, or of principles, either of a public or a private nature. And though very caustic sometimes, and even severe in his remarks, yet generally far more inclining to the good-natured in his opinions and in his discourse.—BRAY, ANNA ELIZA, 1883, *Autobiography, ed. Kempe, p.* 309.

In the autumn of 1823 I went to the Lake country and paid a visit to Southey. He was then about fifty years of age. He was the first of our great men with whom I had come face to face. Afterwards I became acquainted with most of his eminent contemporaries, and of my own—with Wordsworth, Coleridge, Scott, Moore, Campbell, Tennyson, and Browning, among poets; among historians, with Hallam, Macaulay, Froude, Carlyle, and Lecky; among statesmen, with all, I think, that were conspicuous except Canning, Brougham, and Disraeli; and I have found none who combined with intellectual pre-eminence so much of what was personally attractive.—TAYLOR, SIR HENRY, 1885, *Autobiography, vol.* I, *p.* 46.

Southey was probably one of the most representative of literary men. His feelings in his library are those of all book-lovers, although he could express these feelings in language which few of them have at command.—WHEATLEY, HENRY B., 1886, *How to Form a Library, p.* 54.

"The Ballad-Monger," "The Bard of the Bay," "The Blackbird," "My Epic Renegade," "The First Man of Letters in Europe," "Illustrious Conqueror of Common-Sense," "Mouthy," "The Poet of Greta Hall," "Turncoat."—FREY, ALBERT R., 1888, *Sobriquets and Nicknames, p.* 466.

Such was this knightly, this true brotherly and *fatherly* man—this gentleman, head and shoulders above the literati of his day in pure unselfishness, unworldliness, and simple-minded honesty; such this true defender of the sanctities of house and home; this pattern father, husband, and friend; this exemplar of unostentatious piety; this high-souled, pure-hearted, patient man; this genial host. Such was this lofty scholar, this humble, child-like doer of each day's work to the full reach of his power; this encyclopædia of learning; this grave thinker; this poet of his time.—RAWNSLEY, H. D., 1894, *Literary Associations of the English Lakes, vol.* I, *p.* 59.

He did not write very rapidly; and he corrected, both in MS. and in proof, with the utmost sedulity. Of the nearly 14,000 books which he possessed at his death, it is safe to say that all had been methodically read, and most read many times; while his almost mediæval diligence did not hesitate at working through a set of folios to obtain the information or the corrections necessary for a single article. —SAINTSBURY, GEORGE, 1896, *A History of Nineteenth Century Literature, p.* 66.

It is a curious fact that Southey holds no place in the hearts of present lovers of poetry, yet in his lifetime no one was more honoured than he. It may be that his personality, rather than his poems, attracted the admiration of his contemporaries. Now no one knows him. Who in the present generation has read "Thalaba," that "wild and wondrous song," or the "Curse of Kehama," as wild, as strange, as fascinating? Why were these poems the delight of the age which saw their birth, and are yet forgotten now? To me, who in my childhood *lived* upon them, this must ever remain a mystery. Let me try to picture Southey as he sat in my mother's drawing-room. I do not remember that his features were particularly striking, and he was not tall, or of the stately presence which characterised his brother, Dr. H. H. Southey. But his eyes! A dark and liquid brown, so full of love, when he was silent and calm, that you thought perchance nothing but love was there; but when he spoke the liquid brown was fire, yet fire made of roses, and the beam that darted from his eyes seemed to reach far into the room. Again I say, would that I could remember the words he spoke; but I was a child, and a very young one.—AGNEW, MARY COURTENAY, 1896, *Lions in the Twenties, Temple Bar, vol.* 107, *p.* 114.

The change in Southey's political and religious opinions which made the republican of 1793 a tory, the author of "Wat Tyler" a poet laureate, and the independent thinker whom Coleridge had just managed to convert from deism to unitarianism a champion of the established church, inevitably exposed Southey to attack from the advocates of the opinions he had forsaken. There can be no question of Southey's perfect sincerity. The evolution of his views did not differ materially from that traceable in the cases of Wordsworth and Coleridge. But the immediate advantage to the convert was more visible and tangible, and Southey provoked retaliation by the uncharitable tone he habitually adopted in controversy with those whose sentiments had formerly been his own. Every question presented itself to him on the ethical side. But constitutionally he was a bigot; an opinion for him must be either moral or immoral; those which he did not himself share inevitably fell into the latter class, and their propagators appeared to him enemies of society. At the same time his reactionary tendencies were not unqualified. He could occasionally express liberal sentiments.—GARNETT, RICHARD, 1898, *Dictionary of National Biography, vol.* LIII, *p.* 287.

POEMS

I should say that the predominant qualities of his poetry were picturesqueness, sweetness of sentiment, and purity of diction. . . . He is now my favorite. His miscellaneous poems are full of various excellence.—STORY, JOSEPH, 1799, *Life and Letters, vol.* I, *p.* 80.

Southey never treads in the beaten track; his thoughts, while they are those of nature, carry that cast of originality which is the stamp and testimony of genius. . . . To this faculty of bold discrimination I attribute many of Mr. Southey's peculiarities as a poet. He never seems to enquire how other men would treat a subject, or what may happen to be the usage of the times; but, filled with that strong sense of fitness, which is the result of bold and unshackled thought, he fearlessly pursues that course which his own sense of propriety points out.—
—WHITE, HENRY KIRKE, 1806, *Melancholy Hours, Remains, vol.* II, *pp.* 287, 288.

O Southey! Southey! cease thy varied song!
A bard may chant too often and too long:
As thou art strong in verse, in mercy, spare!
A fourth, alas! were more than we could bear.
But if, in spite of all the world can say,
Thou still wilt verseward plod thy weary way;
If still in Berkeley ballads most uncivil,
Thou wilt devote old women to the devil,
The babe unborn thy dread intent may rue;
"God help thee" Southey, and thy readers too.

—BYRON, LORD, 1809, *English Bards and Scotch Reviewers.*

How Southey has fallen! A Pegasus like his turned into a cream-coloured horse for State occasions: it is quite melancholy.—MOORE, THOMAS, 1814, *Correspondence of Leigh Hunt, vol.* I, *p.* 94.

His Laureate odes are utterly and intolerably bad, and, if he had never written anything else, must have ranked him below Colley Cibber in genius, and above him in conceit and presumption.—JEFFREY, FRANCIS LORD, 1816, *The Lay of the Laureate, Edinburgh Review, vol.* 26, *p.* 449.

Of Mr. Southey's larger epics, I have but a faint recollection at this distant time, but all that I remember of them is mechanical and extravagant, heavy and superficial. His affected, disjointed style is well imitated in the Rejected Addresses. The difference between him and Sir Richard Blackmore seems to be that the one is heavy and the other light, the one solemn and the other pragmatical, the one phlegmatic and the other flippant; and that there is no Gay in the present time to give a Catalogue Raisonné of the performances of the living undertaker of epics.—HAZLITT, WILLIAM, 1818, *Lectures on the English Poets, Lecture* viii.

The poetry of Mr. Southey occupies not fewer than 14 volumes in crown octavo; and it embraces subjects of almost every description. "Thalaba" has long been, and will long continue to be, very generally known and admired. It was abundantly popular at the period of its publication. The "Curse of Kehama" is perhaps the greatest effort of the author's genius; but his "Roderic," or the "Last of the Goths," is that which seems to have received his most careful elaboration and finishing. It is a grand poem. "Madoc," though full of wild imagery, and with verse of occasionally uncouth structure, is not destitute of some of the most brilliant touches of the poet.—DIBDIN, THOMAS FROGNALL, 1824, *The Library Companion, p.* 737, *note.*

His poems, taken in the mass, stand far higher than his prose works. The Laureate Odes, indeed, among which the "Vision of Judgment" must be classed, are, for the most part, worse than Pye's and as bad as Cibber's; nor do we think him generally happy in short pieces. But his longer poems, though full of faults, are nevertheless very extraordinary productions. We doubt greatly whether they will be read fifty years hence; but that, if they are read, they will be admired, we have no doubt whatever.—MACAULAY, THOMAS BABINGTON, 1830, *Southey's Colloquies on Society, Edinburgh Review; Critical and Miscellaneous Essays.*

Southey, among our living Poets, stands aloof and "alone in his glory;" for he alone of them all has adventured to illustrate, in Poems of magnitude, the different characters, customs, and manners of nations. "Joan of Arc" is an English and French story; "Thalaba," Arabian; "Kehama," Indian; "Madoc," Welsh and American; and "Roderick," Spanish and Moorish; nor would it be easy to say (setting aside the first, which was a very youthful work) in which of these noble Poems Mr. Southey has most successfully performed an achievement entirely beyond the power of any but the highest genius. . . . Of all his chief Poems the conception and the execution are original; in much faulty and imperfect both; but bearing throughout the impress of original power, and breathing a moral charm, in the midst of the wildest, and some times even extravagant, imaginings, that shall preserve them forever from oblivion, embalming them in the spirit of delight and of love.—WILSON, JOHN, 1831–42, *An Hour's Talk About Poetry, Recreations of Christopher North.*

Rare architect of many a wondrous tale
Which, till Helvellyn's head lie prostrate,
shall remain!
—LANDOR, WALTER SAVAGE, 1833, *To Southey, Works, vol.* VIII.

There is a plain, searching, but not vulgar truth in his eclogues, which places them by the side of Crabbe's most forcible and finished cabinet pictures,—a quaintness, a credulity, and a humour in his ballads, especially in those of witchcraft and monkery, which belong to one steeped in the spirit of ancient tradition. Again, in his more elaborate works, how rich is their diction, and how superior in its richness to the cumbrous and false pomp of some of his predecessors, who have attempted the epic.—CHORLEY, HENRY FOTHERGILL, 1838, *Authors of England, p.* 25.

Southey,—who, with all his rich and varied accomplishments, has comparatively but a small portion of Wordsworth's genius, and whose "wild and wondrous lays" are the very antithesis to Wordsworth's intense musings on humanity and new consecrations of familiar things.—TALFOURD, THOMAS NOON, 1842, *Critical and Miscellaneous Writings.*

Keen as an eagle whose flight towards the dim empyréan
Fearless of toil or fatigue ever royally wends!
Vast in the cloud-coloured robes of the balm-breathing Orient
Lo! the grand Epic advances, unfolding the humanest truth.
—MEREDITH, GEORGE, 1851, *Works, vol.* 31, *p.* 139.

Southey shone in the paths of gentle meditation and philosophic reflection; but his chief strength lay in description, where he had few equals. It was there that he revelled and rioted in the exuberant energy of his spirit,—a devoted worshipper of nature. Akenside describes a landscape as it affects the fancy; Cowper as it impresses the feelings; Southey daguerreotypes the landscape itself. Coleridge descants on the waving of a leaf; Southey, on its colour and configuration. Wordsworth delights in outflowing sentiment; Southey in picturesque outline. His capacious mind may be likened to a variegated continent, one region of which is damp with fogs, rough with rocks, barren and unprofitable; the other bright with glorious sunshine, valleys of rich luxuriance, and forests of perpetual verdure.—MOIR, D. M., 1851–52, *Sketches of the Poetical Literature of the Past Half-Century.*

Southey's "Madoc," "Don Roderick," and the "Curse of Kehama" are splendid metrical histories, but they do not contain the traits which speak at once to all mankind: they are addressed to the learned and studious, and these are a mere fragment of the human race. Admired, accordingly, by the well-informed, they are already comparatively unknown to the great body of readers; and the author's poetical fame rests chiefly on "Thalaba," in which his brilliant imagination revelled without control, save that of high moral feeling, in the waterless deserts and palm-shaded fountains and patriarchal life of the Happy Arabia.—ALISON, SIR ARCHIBALD, 1853–59, *History of Europe*, 1815–1852, *vol.* I, *ch.* V.

He went to it too mechanically, and with too much nonchalance; and the consequence was a vast many words to little matter. Nor had he the least music in him at all. The consequence of which was, that he wrote prose out into lyrical wild shapes, and took the appearance of it for verse. Yet there was otherwise a poetical nature distributed through the mass, idly despising the concentration that would have been the salvation of it.—HUNT, LEIGH, 1855, *Correspondence, vol.* II, *p.* 176.

I am not sure whether it might not be put as a test of the existence or otherwise of a pure love of the art in any man that he should like or dislike these achievements of Southey; and if Ariosto is able to retain his readers, it appears hardly creditable to the public taste of our time that Southey should entirely lose his. It is at least certain that for many subtle and pleasing varieties of rhythm, for splendor of invention, for passion and incident sustained often at the highest level, and for all that raises and satisfies wonder and fancy, there will be found in "Thalaba," "Kehama," and "Roderick" passages of unrivalled excellence ("perfect," even Byron thought); and these may here excuse, if they do not wholly justify, the hopes that once centred in them, and to which exalted expression is given in the correspondence of the friends.—FORSTER, JOHN, 1869, *Walter Savage Landor, p.* 129.

Southey divides with Scott the honor of writing the first long narrative poems in our language which can be read without occasional weariness.—BRYANT, WILLIAM CULLEN, 1870, *A New Library of Poetry and Song, Introduction, vol.* I, *p.* xliii.

Southey, like Drayton, has left little work vividly penetrated with the spirit of poetry, in comparison with his many pages of skilful and industrious manufacture.—PALGRAVE, FRANCIS TURNER, 1875, *ed., The Children's Treasury of English Song, p.* 290, *note.*

Southey never freed himself absolutely from the shackles prescribed for poets of "sense" and "wit." His vital impulse never burst forth unmanageably into spiritual landscapes hitherto untrodden. No ungovernable flash of natural magic ever came uppermost in his soul to pester his genius with dread of trespassing on the realm of arbitrary reason. He was never troubled to weave into the woof of his rational art, the weft of some irrational emotion. All that came to him, came tranquilly; all that he could see he could command; and no unsatisfied yearning after unattainable things ever threatened to drive him beyond limits of sanity. Moreover, his poetry dealt with lofty or obscure, noble, dubious, or distant subjects, not with homely ones.—CAINE, HALL, 1883, *Cobwebs of Criticism, p.* 32.

Southey's patriotic rubbish was no better, and not much worse, than his verse at large.—STEDMAN, EDMUND CLARENCE, 1887, *Twelve Years of British Song, The Century, vol.* 34, *p.* 902.

No one has described the invigorating and soothing power of books more happily than Southey; and, with two or three exceptions, there is, perhaps, no man of letters of this century whose name is worthier of esteem. Yet the reader who acknowledges this allegiance may confess at the same time that a measured feeling of admiration is the utmost he can give to Southey's poetry. His epics are not among the books he reads upon sleepless nights; neither will he take them with him on a voyage. . . . Poetry made Southey happy, and he thought that it would make him immortal. The happiness was enjoyed to the full, but the ten volumes of his verse have not as yet received the recognition which their author anticipated. We are interested in learning that William Taylor, of Norwich, called "Madoc" the best English poem that had left the press since "Paradise Lost;" that Walter Scott read it through four times; that it kept Fox up until after midnight; that Landor said of "Roderick," "there is no poem in existence that I shall read so often;" and that even Byron pronounced it "the first poem of the time." And in our day we hear with curiosity how Dean Stanley upheld against all comers the poetical merits of "Thalaba" and "Kehama." People read these criticisms and opinions, but they do not read the poems; and, as a poet, Southey is chiefly known to the present generation by his fantastic ballads and by a few personal lyrics which, like the "Holly Tree" and the stanzas written in his library, touch all hearts.—DENNIS, JOHN, 1887, *Robert Southey, Introduction, pp.* 9, 10.

Southey's larger poems, "Thalaba," "The Curse of Kehama," and especially "Roderick," seemed to me then the great epics of the age. I am not at all certain that I gave them too high a place in my admiration, and as I write I cannot remember any English epic that I have been able to read through since I read "Roderick," not even "Festus" or "Orion."—JESSOPP, AUGUSTUS, 1888, *Books That Have Helped Me, p.* 62.

His disciple and latest unflinching admirer, Sir Henry Taylor, has told us that Southey "took no pleasure in poetic passion"—a melancholy admission. We could have guessed as much from his voluminous and vigorous writing, from which imagination is conspicuously absent, though eloquence, vehemence, fluency, and even fancy are abundant.—GOSSE, EDMUND, 1897, *A Short History of Modern English Literature, p.* 286.

JOAN OF ARC

1796

With "Joan of Arc" I have been delighted, amazed; I had not presumed to expect anything of such excellence from Southey. Why the poem is alone sufficient to redeem the character of the age we live in from the imputation of degenerating in Poetry.—LAMB, CHARLES, 1796, *Letter to Coleridge, Final Memorials, ed. Talfourd.*

Robert Southey, author of many ingenious pieces of poetry of great promise, if the young gentlemen would recollect what old Chaucer says of poetry,

"'Tis every dêle
A rock of ice and not of steel."

He gave the publick a long quarto volume of epick verses, "Joan of Arc," written, he says in the preface, in *six weeks.* Had he meant to write well, he should have kept it at least six years.—I mention this, for I have been much pleased with many of the young gentleman's little copies of verses. I wish also that he would review *some of his principles.*—MATHIAS, THOMAS JAMES, 1798, *The Pursuits of Literature, Eighth ed. p.* 352.

Mr. Southey's "Joan of Arc," though incorrect, and written with inexcusable rapidity, reflects great credit on his genius and abilities; the sentiments are noble and generous, and burn with an enthusiastic ardour for liberty; the characters, especially that of his Heroine, are well supported, and his visionary scenes are rich with bold and energetic imagery. His fable, however, I can not but consider peculiarly unfortunate, as directly militating against national pride and opinion. . . . The versification of this poem is in many parts very beautiful, and would have been altogether so, had the author condescended to bestow more time on its elaboration.—DRAKE, NATHAN, 1798–1820, *Literary Hours, vol.* II, *p.* 107.

I looked over the first five books of the first quarto edition of "Joan of Arc" yesterday, at Hood's request, in order to mark the lines written by me. I was really astonished, first, at the schoolboy wretched allegoric machinery,—second, at the transmogrification of the fanatic virago, into a modern novel-pawing proselyte of "The Age of Reason," a Tom Paine in Petticoats, but so lovely?—

"On her ruby cheek hung pity's crystal gem,"

third, at the utter want of all rhythm in the verse, the monotony and dead plumb down of the pauses, and of the absence of all bone, muscle, and sinew, in the single lines.—COLERIDGE, SAMUEL TAYLOR, 1814, *Letter, July.*

"Joan of Arc," as it was first in the order of time, so was never to be properly regarded as anything more than a splendid promise, and has not been reared into any thing higher by all the careful emendation of its author in his riper years.—WARE, JR., HENRY, 1839, *Southey's Poetical Works, North American Review, vol.* 48, *p.* 368.

"Joan of Arc" was an achievement of strenuous ambition. Crude and feeble as many of its pages are, the poem has in it the glow and ardor of the time.—DOWDEN, EDWARD, 1897, *The French Revolution and English Literature, p.* 165.

THALABA THE DESTROYER
1801

The first thing that strikes the reader of "Thalaba" is the singular structure of the versification, which is a jumble of all the measures that are known in English poetry (and a few more), without rhyme, and without any sort of regularity in their arrangement. Blank odes have been known in this country about as long as English sapphics and dactylics; and both have been considered, we believe, as a species of monsters, or exotics, that were not very likely to propagate, or thrive, in so unpropitious a climate. Mr. Southey, however, has made a vigorous effort for their naturalization, and generously endangered his own reputation in their behalf. The melancholy fate of his English sapphics, we believe, is but too generally known; and we can scarcely predict a more favourable issue to the present experiment.—JEFFREY, FRANCIS LORD, 1802, *Southey's Thalaba, Edinburgh Review, vol.* I, *p.* 72.

"Thalaba" was the first fruits of one of Southey's earliest ambitions, for he tells us himself that even in his schooldays he had formed the design of writing a great poem on each of the more important mythologies. "Thalaba" is based upon the Mahometan and is written in an irregular form of blank verse. . . . Southey describes it as "the Arabesque ornament of an Arabian tale," and as such it is perhaps the fitting garb of an Oriental fiction—a lawless measure for a lawless song. The poem recounts the adventures and triumphs of an Arabian hero at war with the powers of evil, but though often characterized by beauty of expression and grandeur of scene, lacks the human interest which attaches only to the record of the thoughts, feelings, and actions of men and women moving within the limits of natural law, and the sphere of human sympathy.—MILES, ALFRED H., 1892, *The Poets and the Poetry of the Century, Southey to Shelley, p.* 4.

MADOC
1805

It is well calculated to confirm our admiration of Mr. Southey's genius and capacity, and our dislike of those heresies by which so much of their merit is obscured.—JEFFREY, FRANCIS LORD, 1805, *Southey's Madoc, Edinburgh Review, vol.* 7, *p.* 28.

Tea and chess with Mrs. Barbauld. Read on my way to her house Chapters VIII. to XIV. of Southey's "Madoc." Exceedingly pleased with the touching painting in this poem. It has not the splendid glare of "Kehama," but there is a uniform glow of pure and beautiful morality and interesting description, which renders the work very pleasing. Surely none but a pedant can effect or be seduced to think slightingly of this poem. At all events, the sensibility which feels such beauties is more desirable than the acuteness which could suggest severe cirticism.—ROBINSON, HENRY CRABB, 1811, *Diary, March* 12; *Diary, Reminiscences and Correspondence, ed. Sadler, vol.* I, *p.* 207.

On returning from a vist to the Lakes, I told Porson that Southey had said to me, "My 'Madoc' has brought me in a mere trifle; but that poem will be a valuable possession to my family." Porson answered, "'Madoc' will be read—when Homer and Virgil are forgotten" (a *bon-mot* which reached Lord Byron, and which his lordship spoilt).—MALTBY, WILLIAM, 1854, *Porsoniana.*

"Madoc" stands somewhat away from the line of Southey's other narrative poems. Though, as Scott objected, the personages in "Madoc" are too nearly abstract types, Southey's ethical spirit dominates this poem less than any of the others. The narrative flows on more simply. The New-World portion tells a story full of picturesque incident, with the same skill and grace that belong to Southey's best prose writings. . . . Those, however, who opened the bulky quarto were few: the tale was out of relation with the time; it interpreted no need, no aspiration, no passion of the dawn of the present century. And the mind of the time was not enough disengaged to concern itself deeply with the supposed adventures of a Welsh prince of the twelfth century among the natives of America.—DOWDEN, EDWARD, 1880, *Southey (English Men of Letters), p.* 190.

Southey went to Wales on purpose to make himself sure of the scenery, and accumulated as much learning in his notes as would not have misbecome the most authentic and dignified history. We can but say alas! when all is done. How is it that the effect does not follow? Here there is everything but one thing, the altar laid, the sacrifice extended, the faggots ready as in that famous offering prepared by the priests of Baal; but the divine spark is wanting, and no touch from heaven sets it alight.—OLIPHANT, MARGARET O. W., 1882, *Literary History of England, XVIII-XIX Century, vol.* I, *p.* 302.

THE CURSE OF KEHAMA
1810

The subject you have chosen is magnificent. There is more genius in the conception of this design than in the execution of any recent poem, however perfect. Shall I avow to you that in general I am most delighted with those passages which are in rhyme, and that when I come into the blank verse again my ear *repines?* . . . You have begun a poem which will be coeval with our language. March on: conciliate first, then conquer. The ears of thousands may be captivated,—the mind and imagination of but few.—LANDOR, WALTER SAVAGE, 1808, *Letter to Southey, May* 8; *Life of Landor by Forster, bk.* i.

Spent part of the evening with Charles Lamb (unwell) and his sister. He had just read the "Curse of Kehama," which he said he liked better than any of Southey's long poems. The descriptions he thought beautiful, particularly the finding of Kailyal by Ereenia. He liked the opening, and part of the description of hell; but, after all, he was not made happier by reading the poem. There is too much trick in it. The three statutes and the vacant space for Kehama resemble a pantomime scene; and the love is ill managed. On the whole, however, Charles Lamb thinks the poem infinitely superior to "Thalaba."—ROBINSON, HENRY CRABB, 1811, *Diary, Jan.* 8; *Diary, Reminiscences and Correspondence, ed. Sadler, vol.* I, *p.* 204.

The general diction of the work is admirably strong, and various, and free; and, in going through it, we have repeatedly exulted in the capabilities of the English language. The author seems to have in a great measure grown out of that affected simplicity of expression, of which he has generally been accused. The versification, as to measure and rhyme, is a complete defiance of all rule and all example; the lines are of any length, from four syllables to fourteen; there are sometimes rhymes and sometimes none; and they have no settled order of recurrence. This is objectionable, chiefly, as it allows the poet to riot away in a wild wantonness of amplification, and at the very same time imposes on him the petty care of having the lines so printed as to put the letter-press in the form of a well-adjusted picture.—FOSTER, JOHN, 1811, *Southey's Curse of Kehama, Critical Essays, ed. Ryland, vol.* I, *p.* 494.

"Kehama" is a loose sprawling figure, such as we see cut out of wood or paper, and pulled or jerked with wire or thread, to make sudden and surprising motions, without meaning, grace, or nature in them.—HAZLITT, WILLIAM, 1818, *Lectures on the English Poets, Lecture* viii.

"Kehama," the only great poem in which the poet no longer disdains the almost indispensable aid to poetry in our modern and loosely quantified tongue, is much better than any of the others. The Curse itself is about as good as it can be, and many other passages are not far below it; but to the general taste the piece suffers from the remote character of the subject, which is not generally and humanly interesting, and from the mass of tedious detail.—SAINTSBURY, GEORGE, 1896, *A History of Nineteenth Century Literature, p.* 68.

RODERICK

1814

I have read "Roderick" over and over again, and am more and more convinced that it is the noblest epic poem of the age. I have had some correspondence, and a good deal of conversation, with Mr. Jeffrey about it, though he does not agree with me in every particular. He says, it is too long, and wants *elasticity* and will not, he fears, be generally read, though much may be said in its favor.—HOGG, JAMES, 1814, *Letter to Southey.*

This is the best, we think, and the most powerful of all Mr. Southey's poems. It abounds with lofty sentiments, and magnificent imagery; and contains more rich and comprehensive descriptions—more beautiful pictures of pure affection—and more impressive representations of mental agony and exaltation than we have often met with in the compass of a single volume. . . . The author is a poet undoubtedly; but not of the highest order. There is rather more of rhetoric than of inspiration about him—and we have oftener to admire his taste and industry in borrowing and adorning, than the boldness or felicity of his inventions. He has indisputably a great gift of amplifying and exalting; but uses it, we must say, rather unmercifully. He is never plain, concise, or unaffectedly simple, and is so much bent upon making the most of every thing, that he is perpetually overdoing. . . . This want of relief and variety is sufficiently painful of itself in a work of such length; but its worst effect is, that it gives an air of falsetto and pretension to the whole strain of the composition, and makes us suspect the author of imposture and affectation, even when he has good enough cause for his agonies and raptures.—JEFFREY, FRANCIS LORD, 1815-44, *Southey's Roderick, Contributions to the Edinburgh Review, vol.* III, *p.* 133.

In "Kehama" he has exhibited virtue struggling against the most dreadful inflictions with heavenly fortitude, and made manifest to us the angel-guards who love to wait on innocence and goodness. But in "Roderic" the design has even a higher scope, is more difficult of execution; and, so far as I know, unique. The temptations which beset a single soul have been a frequent subject, and one sure of sympathy if treated with any power. Breathlessly we watch the conflict, with heartfelt anguish mourn defeat, or with heart-expanding triumph hail a conquest. But, where there *has* been defeat, to lead us back with the fallen one through the thorny and desolate paths of repentance to purification, to win not only our pity, but our sympathy, for one crushed and degraded by his own sin; and finally, through his faithful though secret efforts to redeem the past, secure to him, justly blighted and world-forsaken as he is, not only our sorrowing love, but our respect;—*this* Southey alone has done, perhaps alone could do.—OSSOLI, MARGARET FULLER, 1850? *Art, Literature and the Drama, p.* 96.

The hero of this poem is no far-off shadowy creature; he is a man, with a man's passions, and thoughts, and weakness, who treads the common path, and is kin to ourselves by his failures. And in point of technique also, "Roderick" may be taken as representing Southey's maturer powers. His faculty of simple, vivid description is here at its highest, though, like most of his predecessors and contemporaries, he only looked upon Nature from the outside; and the dramatic quality is here more strongly developed than in his other work.—THOMPSON, SIDNEY R., 1888, *ed., Selected Poems of Robert Southey* (*Canterbury Poets*), *Introduction, p.* xli.

The blank verse of Southey's "Roderick, the Last of the Goths" has great merit as narrative verse, and is worthy of careful study. The variations on the theme-metre, and the resultant pause melody, show not only great metrical skill, but a moulding spirit which is quite a law to itself, and beyond mere skill.—CORSON, HIRAM, 1892, *A Primer of English Verse, p.* 222.

"Roderick" was the last of his great poems, and is in many respects the best.—MILES, ALFRED H., 1892, *The Poets and the Poetry of the Century, Southey to Shelley, p.* 5.

WAT TYLER

1817

The poem "Wat Tyler," appeared to him to be the most seditious book that was ever written; its author did not stop short of exhorting to general anarchy; he vilified kings, priests, and nobles, and was for universal suffrage and perfect equality. The Spencean plan could not be compared with it: that miserable and ridiculous performance did not attempt to employ any arguments; but the author of "Wat Tyler" constantly appealed to the passions, and in a style which the author, at that time, he supposed, conceived to be eloquence. Why, then, had not those who thought it necessary to suspend the Habeas Corpus Act taken notice of this poem? Why had not they discovered the author of that seditious publication, and visited him with the penalties of the law? The work was not published secretly, it was not handed about in the darkness of night, but openly and publicly sold in the face of day. It was at this time to be purchased at almost every bookseller's shop in London: it was now exposed for sale in a bookseller's shop in Pall-Mall, who styled himself bookseller to one or two of the royal families. He borrowed the copy from which he had just read the extract from an honourable friend of his, who bought it in the usual way; and, therefore, he supposed there could be no difficulty in finding out the party that wrote it.—SMITH, WILLIAM, 1817, *Speech in the House of Commons; March* 14; *Hansard's Parliamentary Debates, vol.* 35, *p.* 1091.

As to "Wat Tyler." Now, sir, though you are not acquainted with the full history of this notable production, yet you could not have been ignorant that the author whom you attacked at such unfair advantage was the aggrieved, and not the offending, person. You knew that this poem had been written very many years ago, in his early youth. You knew that a copy of it had been surreptitiously obtained and made public by some skulking scoundrel, who had found booksellers not more honorable than himself to undertake the publication. You knew that it was published without the writer's knowledge, for the avowed purpose of insulting him, and with the hope of injuring him, if possible. You knew that the transaction bore upon its face every character of baseness and malignity. You knew that it must have been effected either by robbery or by breach of trust. These things, Mr. William Smith, you knew! and, knowing them as you did, I verily believe, that if it were possible to revoke what is irrevocable, you would at this moment be far more desirous of blotting from remembrance the disgraceful speech, which stands upon record in your name, than I should be of canceling the boyish composition which gave occasion to it. "Wat Tyler" is full of errors, but they are the errors of youth and ignorance; they bear no indication of an ungenerous spirit or of a malevolent heart.—SOUTHEY, ROBERT, 1817, *A Letter to William Smith, M. P.*

It obtained a far greater notoriety, through incidental circumstances, than its intrinsic merit or demerit could warrant; and posterity will wonder at the extreme acrimony exhibited in the writings of the parties, who waged a warfare of petty personal annoyance and spite, on account of so ordinary a performance.—WARE, HENRY, JR., 1839, *Southey's Poetical Works, North American Review, vol.* 48, *p.* 354.

Many years after this was written, and, as Southey fondly hoped, forgotten, he being at the time a pensioned supporter of the Government, he was startled by reading an advertisement of "Wat Tyler," by Robert Southey, "a Dramatic Poem, with a preface suitable to recent circumstances, London, W. Hone," and shortly afterwards he received a copy of the drama, addressed to *Robert Southey, Poet Laureate, and Renegade.* By the advice of his friends, Southey applied for an injunction to restrain the publication; Lord Eldon refused to grant this protection, on the plea that "a person cannot recover damages upon a work which in its nature is calculated to do injury to the public." This decision was not only extremely annoying to Southey, but greatly increased the notoriety of the reprint of the drama, of which no less than 60,000 copies were sold in a very short time, and it is even now much more frequently met with than any of his other poems. Southey's political opponents did not let the matter rest here, for both Lord Brougham and Mr. William Smith, member for Norwich, drew attention in the House to Southey's inconsistent writings, contrasting "Wat Tyler" with his later Conservative articles in "The Quarterly Review," and inquiring why the Government had taken no steps to prosecute the author of that treasonable play. These proceedings reflected little credit on either party.—HAMILTON, WALTER, 1879, *Robert Southey, The Poets Laureate of England, being a History of the Office of Poet Laureate, p.* 224.

A VISION OF JUDGMENT
1821

We are too happy to be done with him, to think of adding a word more.—JEFFREY, FRANCIS LORD, 1821, *Laureate Hexameters, Edinburgh Review, vol.* 35, *p.* 436.

It hath been wisely said, that "One fool makes many," and it hath been poetically observed

"That fools rush in where angels fear to tread."

If Mr. Southey had not rushed in where he had no business, and where he never was before, and never will be again, the following poem would not have been written. It is not impossible that it may be as good as his own, seeing that it cannot, by any species of stupidity, natural or acquired, be *worse*. The gross flattery, the dull impudence, the renegado intolerance, and impious cant, of the poem by the author of "Wat Tyler," are something so stupendous as to form the sublime of himself—containing the quintessence of his own attributes.—BYRON, LORD, 1824, *The Vision of Judgment, Preface.*

Byron's satire has given that poem an immortality which it would never otherwise have gained. But Southey's poem is more profane than even Byron's. Southey really ventured on anticipating the judgment of heaven; Byron only intended to sneer at Southey's gross presumption.—WALPOLE, SPENCER, 1878, *A History of England from the Conclusion of the Great War in* 1815, *vol.* I, *p.* 355.

In this most impious work, he fearlessly condemns or rewards political personages at the day of judgment, according as their opinions coincide or not with his own, in a manner so little short of blasphemy, as to disgust his best friends and create greater activity amongst his foes.—HAMILTON, WALTER, 1879, *The Poets Laureate of England, p.* 227.

It is always to be regretted that in his anxiety to do his whole duty, to fulfill all the obligations of his office, Southey should have written "The Vision of Judgment." The error was also partly due to a wish to strike out a new path in a somewhat dreary field, to write something different from the tiresome odes of his predecessors, to be original at the expense of good taste.—HOWLAND, FRANCES LOUISE (KENYON WEST), 1895, *The Laureates of England, p.* 154.

LIFE OF NELSON
1813

His prose is perfect. Of his poetry there are various opinions. There is, perhaps, too much of it for the present generation; posterity will probably select. He has *passages* equal to any thing. At present he has *a party*, but no *public*,—except for his prose writings. The "Life of Nelson" is beautiful.—BYRON, LORD, 1813, *Journal, Nov.* 22; *Moore's Life of Lord Byron.*

But though in general we prefer Mr. Southey's poetry to his prose, we must make one exception. The "Life of Nelson" is, beyond all doubt, the most perfect and the most delightful of his works. The fact is, as his poems most abundantly prove, that he is by no means so skilful in designing as filling up. It was therefore an advantage to him to be furnished with an outline of characters and events, and to have no other task to perform than that of touching the cold sketch into life. No writer, perhaps, ever lived, whose talents so precisely qualified him to write the history of the great naval warrior.—MACAULAY, THOMAS BABINGTON, 1830, *Southey's Colloquies on Society, Edinburgh Review; Critical and Miscellaneous Essays.*

The little "Life of Nelson," written to furnish young seamen with a simple narrative of the exploits of England's greatest naval hero, has perhaps never been equalled for the perfection of its style.—SHAW, THOMAS B., 1847, *Outlines of English Literature, p.* 342.

The "Life of Nelson" is a model of unaffected, direct narrative, allowing the facts to speak for themselves through the clearest possible medium of expression; and yet this most popular of Southey's books, far from being the offspring of any strong personal sympathy or perception, was so entirely a literary job, that he says it was thrust upon him, and that he moved among the sea-terms like a cat among crockery.—TUCKERMAN, HENRY T., 1857, *Essays, Biographical and Critical, p.* 73.

That Southey should live mainly by a book which was merely a publisher's commission, and not by the works which he and his contemporaries deemed immortal, is one of the ironies of literature —SHORTER, CLEMENT K., 1897, *Victorian Literature, Sixty Years of Books and Bookmen, p.* 6.

LIFE OF JOHN WESLEY
1820

Few persons could have been found, we think, better qualified for the undertaking than Mr. Southey has shown himself to be. —HEBER, REGINALD, 1820, *Southey's Life of Wesley, Quarterly Review, vol.* 24, *p.* 9.

The "Life of Wesley" will probably live. Defective as it is, it contains the only popular account of a most remarkable moral revolution, and of a man whose eloquence and logical acuteness might have rendered him eminent in literature, whose genius for government was not inferior to that of Richelieu, and who, whatever his errors may have been, devoted all his powers, in defiance of obloquy and derision, to what he sincerely considered as the highest good of his species.—MACAULAY, THOMAS BABINGTON, 1830, *Southey's Colloquies on Society, Edinburgh Review; Critical and Miscellaneous Essays.*

To this work, and to the Life of R. Baxter, I was used to resort whenever sickness and langour made me feel the want of an old friend of whose company I could never be tired. How many and many an hour of self-oblivion do I owe to this Life of Wesley! and how often have I argued with it, questioned, remonstrated, been peevish, and asked pardon—then again listened, and cried, Right! Excellent! and in yet heavier hours entreated it, as it were, to continue talking to me,—for that I heard and listened, and was soothed, though I could make no reply! Ah! that Robert Southey had fulfilled his intention of writing a history of the Monastic Orders,—or would become the Biographer at least of Loyola, Xavier, Dominic, and the other remarkable Founders.—COLERIDGE, SAMUEL TAYLOR, 1834? *Southey's Life of John Wesley, vol.* I, *note.*

It is unnecessary to say that Southey's work possesses all the merit, and has attained to all the popularity, which befits an elaborate effort of one of the most brilliant of English prose-writers. If the author had no special qualifications for his task, and no unpublished sources of information at his command, his work may nevertheless claim to rival Boswell's "Johnson" as one of the most entertaining books in the language. Where Southey describes a scene or a person his description may generally be relied on as trustworthy as well as picturesque. Where he ventures to analyse motives or to draw conclusions, his want of fitness for his task becomes very apparent. He diligently compiled for the general reader a "Life of Wesley," as he did a "Life of Nelson." But the founder of a religious system is not so easily portrayed as a victorious admiral. Southey's theory of Methodism was hastily formed, on few and superficial data. Starting with the idea that Wesley, with all his virtues, was an enthusiast, rash, impetuous, credulous, with an ambition to form a great religious sect, Southey allowed this inadequate and erroneous idea to tinge the narrative, and to reduce its permanent value. Thus he laid himself open to the free and friendly rebukes administered by Coleridge, and printed in the notes which appear in the later editions of the book; and he laid himself open to the still sharper criticism of a less distinguished reader, who summed up his opinion of the laureate's fitness for his task in the significant words, "Thou hast nothing to draw with, and the well is deep."—URLIN, R. DENNY, 1869, *John Wesley's Place in Church History, p.* 3.

Few more delightful books exist in the language, and none more honest, than his "Life of Wesley." This "darling book," the favorite of his library, was more often in his hands, Coleridge wrote, than any other, and he added that it would not be uninteresting to the author to know that to this work, and to the "Life of Baxter," he was used to resort whenever sickness or langour made him feel the want of an old friend.—DENNIS, JOHN, 1887, *Robert Southey, Introduction, p.* 18.

HISTORY OF THE PENINSULAR WAR
1823-32

Talked of Southey: the little reliance that is to be placed upon him as a historian; his base persecution of the memory of Sir J. Moore.—MOORE, THOMAS, 1824, *Diary, Nov.* 23; *Memoirs, ed. Russell, vol.* IV, *p.* 255.

It is very good, indeed—honest English principle in every line; but there are many prejudices, and there is a tendency to augment a work already too long, by saying all that can be said of the history of ancient times appertaining to every place mentioned.—SCOTT, SIR WALTER, 1826, *Diary, Oct.* 19; *Lockhart's Life of Scott, ch.* lxxii.

The "History of the Peninsular War" is already dead: indeed the second volume was deadborn. The glory of producing an imperishable record of that great conflict seems to be reserved for Colonel Napier. —MACAULAY, THOMAS BABINGTON, 1830, *Southey's Colloquies on Society, Edinburgh Review; Critical and Miscellaneous Essays.*

It tells an epic story, illustrious with heroic incident and character. From the commencement of the contest, Southey had entertained the hope and intention of recording its events; but he delayed in order to become possessed of the gradually accumulating material. The hero of the epic is Wellington.—DOWDEN, EDWARD, 1897, *The French Revolution and English Literature, p.* 233.

THE DOCTOR
1834–37

The wit and humor of "The Doctor" have seldom been equalled. We cannot think Southey wrote it, but have no idea who did.—POE, EDGAR ALLAN, 1836, *Marginalia, Works, ed. Stedman and Woodberry, vol.* VII, *p.* 270.

"The Doctor," of which the first volume was published anonymously in 1833, and the last some years after his death, the whole pleasantness of Southey's character with his best sense of life breathes through his love of books.—MORLEY, HENRY, 1881, *Of English Literature in the Reign of Victoria with a Glance at the Past, p.* 145.

A book showing vast accumulation of out-of-the-way bits of learning—full of quibs, and conceits, and oddities; there are traces of Sterne in it and of Rabelais; but there is little trenchant humor of its own. It is a literary jungle; and all its wit sparkles like marsh fire-flies that lead no whither. You may wonder at its erudition; wonder at its spurts of meditative wisdom; wonder at its touches of scholastic cleverness, and its want of any effective coherence, but you wonder more at its waste of power.—MITCHELL, DONALD G., 1897, *English Lands Letters and Kings, The Later Georges to Victoria, p.* 20.

LIFE OF COWPER
1836

I have just read Southey's "Life of Cowper;" that is to say, the first volume. It is not a book to be read by every man at the fall of the leaf. It is a fearful book. Have you read it? Southey hits hard at Newton in the dark; which will give offence to many people; but I perfectly agree with him. At the same time I think that Newton was a man of great power. Did you ever read his life by himself? Pray do, if you have not. His journal to his wife, written at sea, contains some of the most beautiful things I ever read: fine feeling in very fine English.—FITZGERALD, EDWARD, 1835, *Letters, vol.* I, *p.* 34.

His sketches of literary history in the "Life of Cowper" are characteristic. The writer's range is wide, his judgment sound, his enjoyment of almost everything literary is lively; as critic he is kindly yet equitable. But the highest criticism is not his. Southey's vision was not sufficiently penetrative; he culls beauties, but he cannot pluck out the heart of a mystery. —DOWDEN, EDWARD, 1880, *Southey (English Men of Letters), p.* 195.

Southey's "Life" is horribly long-winded and stuffed out; still, like Homer's "Iliad," it remains the best.—BIRRELL, AUGUSTINE, 1892, *Res Judicatæ, p.* 91.

One chapter of that work is given up to a sketch of English poetry from the time of Chaucer downward. It is made interesting by its style, its partialities, dislikes, prejudices, and especially by the general wrath exhibited in it towards French authors and France. The criticism contained in it will frequently startle the reader. It is the statements of fact, however, that will confound him. They will not confound him so much because they are erroneous, as that Southey should have been ignorant that they were erroneous. He tells us, quite as a matter of course, that Davenant was a poet of higher grade than Dryden; that alliterative verse became obsolete almost as soon as "Piers Ploughman's Visions" had been composed in it; that Chaucer adopted the seven-lines stanza of "Troilus and Cressida" from the Provençal poets; that in the composition of the ten-syllable couplet he had been shown the way by Richard Rolle, the hermit of Hampole; that Ben Jonson was one of the two authors by whom the so-called metaphysical style of poetry was brought into vogue, Donne being the other; that the well-known line in Dryden's characterization of Settle's poetry, that

"If it rhymed and rattled, all was well,"

was written of Blackmore; and that

"Blair's Grave" was the only poem that had been composed in imitation of Young's "Night Thoughts," both works having been contemporaneous in appearance. These are not all the novel facts that can be found in this one chapter; but these will do. After reading it one feels a certain respect for Southey's courage in censuring Dryden for his carelessness and inaccuracy whenever he touched upon the history of his art. The charge was true; but under the circumstances his were hardly the lips from which it could appropriately come.—LOUNSBURY, THOMAS R., 1892, *Studies in Chaucer, vol.* I, *p* 333.

GENERAL

The story ["Chronicle of the Cid"] is something between a history and a romance; and Mr. Southey has not attempted to distinguish what is true from what is fabulous; the Spanish literature evidently supplied no means for doing this, nor would it have been worth while, had it been practicable, as the fabulous parts are probably quite as amusing as the true, and gives as striking a picture of the times. In this view, the work is very interesting. We are transported into an age and country where the gentlemen go out to work in the morning, with their steeds and lances, as regularly as the farmers with their team and plough, and indeed, a good deal more so. The Cid surpasses all his contemporaries for diligence and success in such laudable occupation. His course of enterprise is so rapid, so uniformly successful, and so much of a piece in other respects, that in some parts of the book the mind is quite tired of following him. In many other parts, however, the narrative is eminently striking, especially in describing some of the single combats, and most of all, in the long account of an extraordinary court of justice, held on two young princes or noblemen, who had abused their wives, the daughters of the Cid. Nothing in the whole library of romantic history can exceed this narrative.—FOSTER, JOHN, 1809, *Southey's Chronicle of the Cid, Critical Essays, ed. Ryland, vol.* I, *p.* 284.

Mr. Southey is a most unblushing character; and his political lucubrations are very notable.—CARLYLE, THOMAS, 1817, *Letter to R. Mitchell, July* 5; *Early Letters, ed. Norton, p.* 53.

Reflect but on the variety and extent of his acquirements! He stands second to no man, either as a historian or as a bibliographer; and when I regard him as a popular essayist (for the articles of his composition in the reviews are, for the greater part, essays on subjects of deep or curious interest rather than criticisms on particular works)—I look in vain for any writer, who has conveyed so much information, from so many and recondite sources, with so many just and original reflections, in a style so lively and poignant, yet so uniformly classical and perspicuous; no one, in short, who has combined so much wisdom with so much wit, so much truth and knowledge with so much life and fancy. His prose is always intelligible, and always entertaining. In poetry he has attempted almost every species of composition known before, and he has added new ones; and if we except the highest lyric—(in which how few, how very few, even of the greatest minds have been fortunate)—he has attempted every species successfully. . . . It is Southey's almost unexampled felicity, to possess the best gifts of talent and genius free from all their characteristic defects. . . . As son, brother, husband, father, master, friend, he moves with firm yet light steps, alike unostentatious and alike exemplary. As a writer, he has uniformly made his talents subservient to the best interests of humanity, of public virtue, and domestic piety; his cause has ever been the cause of pure religion and of liberty, of national independence and of national illumination.—COLERIDGE, SAMUEL TAYLOR, 1817, *Biographia Literaria, ch.* iii.

While he himself is anomalous, incalculable, eccentric, from youth to age (the "Wat Tyler" and the "Vision of Judgment" are the Alpha and Omega of his disjointed career) full of sallies of humour, of ebullitions of spleen, making *jets-d'eaux*, cascades, fountains, and water-works of his idle opinions, he would shut up the wits of others in leaden cisterns, to stagnate and corrupt, or bury them under ground—

"Far from the sun and summer gale!"

He would suppress the freedom of wit and humour, of which he has set the example, and claim a privilege for playing antics. —HAZLITT, WILLIAM, 1825, *The Spirit of the Age, p.* 115.

We find, we confess, so great a charm in Mr. Southey's style, that, even when he writes nonsense, we generally read it with pleasure, except indeed where he tries to be droll. A more insufferable jester never existed. He very often attempts to be humorous, and yet we do not remember a single occasion on which he has succeeded further than to be quaintly and flippantly dull. In one of his works, he tells us that Bishop Sprat was very properly so called, inasmuch as he was a very small poet. And in the book now before us, he cannot quote Francis Bugg without a remark on his unsavory name. A man might talk folly like this by his own fireside; but that any human being, after having made such a joke, should write it down, and copy it out, and transmit it to the printer, and correct the proof-sheets, and send it forth into the world, is enough to make us ashamed of our species.—MACAULAY, THOMAS BABINGTON, 1830, *Southey's Colloquies on Society, Edinburgh Review; Critical and Miscellaneous Essays.*

But the most various, scholastic, and accomplished of such of our literary contemporaries as have written works as well as articles, and prose as well as poetry—is, incontestably, Mr. Southey. The "Life of Nelson" is acknowledged to be the best biography of the day. "The Life of Wesley" and "The Book of the Church," however adulterated by certain prepossessions and prejudices, are, as mere compositions, characterized by an equal simplicity and richness of style,—an equal dignity and an equal ease. No writer blends more happily the academical graces of the style of the last century with the popular vigor of that which distinguishes the present. . . . The great charm of that simple power which is so peculiarly Southeian. . . . Southey's rich taste and antique stateliness of mind.—LYTTON, EDWARD BULWER LORD, 1833, *England and the English.*

In vigour and variety of genius Robert Southey has few equals. He ranks in poetry with the foremost; in criticism none can be named more sensible and accurate; in biography he is without rivals; while in history he occupies the first rank and is on the right hand.—CUNNINGHAM, ALLAN, 1833, *Biographical and Critical History of the Literature of the Last Fifty Years.*

As it stands, it is a piece of mere task-work, executed by a practised and skilful artist, no doubt, but with that economy of labour and thought which may be generally expected to characterise such undertakings. . . . He has evidently contented himself ["Life of Raleigh"] with the materials nearest at hand, and made no attempt whatever either to correct or to amplify the existing stock of information by any researches amongst unpublished documents.—NAPIER, MACVEY, 1840, *Edinburgh Review, vol.* 71, *p.* 5.

A name long dear to the public, as it will be to posterity; an author, the accuracy of whose knowledge does not yield to its extent.—DISRAELI, ISAAC, 1841, *Cædmon and Milton, Amenities of Literature, note.*

He was a dogmatist of the most provoking kind,—cool, calm, bitter, and uncompromising; and he delighted to dogmatize on subjects which his mind was unfitted to treat. Nothing could shake his egotism. . . . As a prose writer Southey was more successful than as a poet. His prose style is of such inimitable grace, clearness and fluency, that it would make nonsense agreeable. His poetry indicates a lack of shaping imagination, and is diffusely elegant in expression. He often gives twenty lines to a comparison, which Shelley or Wordsworth would have compressed into an epithet. In narrative skill, and constructive power, he excels both; and is himself excelled only by Scott. . . . As a poet, he sems to us to fall below Scott, Shelley, Wordsworth, Coleridge, Byron, and to belong to the second class of contemporary poets. In imagination and true poetic feeling, we should hesitate to place him on an equality with Campbell, Barry Cornwall, Tennyson, and Keats, although in general capacity and acquirements, and especially in force of individual character, he is their superior. It requires no prophetic gift to predict that most of his verse is destined to die.—WHIPPLE, EDWIN P., 1845, *English Poets of the Nineteenth Century, American Review, July; Essays and Reviews.*

Perhaps the raciest English writer of his day.—MILLER, HUGH, 1852, *Essays, p.* 457.

The mental habits of Robert Southey, which about a year ago were so extensively praised in the public Journals, are the type of literary existence, just as the praise bestowed on them shows the admiration excited by them among literary people. He wrote poetry (as if anybody could) before breakfast; he read during breakfast. He wrote history until dinner; he corrected proof sheets between dinner and tea; he wrote an essay for the *Quarterly* afterwards; and after supper, by way of relaxation, composed "The Doctor"—a lengthy, and elaborate jest. Now, what can any one think of such a life?—except how clearly it shows that the habits best fitted for communicating information, formed with the best care, and daily regulated by the best motives, are exactly the habits which are likely to afford a man the least information to communicate. Southey had no events, no experiences. His wife kept house and allowed him pocket-money, just as if he had been a German professor devoted to accents, tobacco, and the dates of Horace's amours. And it is pitiable to think that so meritorious a life was only made endurable by a painful delusion. He thought that day by day, and hour by hour, he was accumulating stores for the instruction and entertainment of a long posterity. His epics were to be in the hands of all men, and his history of Brazil the "Herodotus of the South American Republics;" as if his epics were not already dead, and as if the people who now cheat at Valparaiso care a *real* who it was that cheated those before them. Yet it was only by a conviction like this that an industrious and caligraphic man (for such was Robert Southey), who might have earned money as a clerk, worked all his days for half a clerk's wages, at occupation much duller and more laborious. —BAGEHOT, WALTER, 1853, *Shakespeare; Works, ed. Morgan, vol.* I, *p.* 266.

Few better or more blameless men have ever lived; but he seems to lack color, passion, warmth, or something that should enable me to bring him into close relation with myself.—HAWTHORNE, NATHANIEL, 1855, *English Note-Books, vol.* I, *p.* 229.

If we were to name, in a single term, the quality for which Southey is eminent, we should call him a verbal architect. . . . For pure narrative, where the object is to give the reader unalloyed facts, and leave his own reflection and fancy to shape and color them, no English author has surpassed Southey.—TUCKERMAN, HENRY T., 1857, *Essays, Biographical and Critical, p.* 74.

In the first rank, Southey, a clever man, who, after several mistakes in his youth, became the professed defender of aristocracy and cant, an indefatigable reader, an inexhaustible writer, crammed with erudition, gifted in imagination, famed like Victor Hugo for the freshness of his innovations, the combative tone of his prefaces, the splendours of his picturesque curiosity, having spanned the universe and all history with his poetic shows, and embraced, in the endless web of his verse, Joan of Arc, Wat Tyler, Roderick the Goth, Madoc, Thalaba, Kehama, Celtic, and Mexican traditions, Arabic and Indian legends, successively Catholic, Mussulman, Brahman, but only in verse; in fine, a prudent and licensed Protestant.—TAINE, H. A., 1871, *History of English Literature, tr. Van Laun, vol.* II, *bk.* iv, *ch.* I, *p.* 250.

There is not, perhaps, any single work of Southey's the loss of which would be felt by us as a capital misfortune. But the more we consider his total work, its mass, its variety, its high excellence, the more we come to regard it as a memorable, an extraordinary achievement.—DOWDEN, EDWARD, 1880, *Southey (English Men of Letters), p.* 1.

There have been few English men of letters the difference between whose contemporary and posthumous fame is so great as it is in the case of Southey. He was not, indeed, idolized by his time, and his works have not, to be sure, fallen into complete oblivion, though they avoid that fate by the narrowest of margins, we suspect. Macaulay said of them that he had great doubts whether they would be read "fifty years hence," but none at all that, if read, they would be admired; but the truth is that they are not read now because it has been discovered that they are not upon the whole admirable.—BROWNELL, W. C., 1880, *Dowden's Southey, The Nation, vol.* 30, *p.* 158.

There were greater poets in his generation, and there were men of a deeper and more far-reaching philosophic faculty; but take him for all in all,—his ardent and genial piety, his moral strength, the magnitude and variety of his powers, the field which he covered in literature, and the beauty of his life,—it may be said of him, justly, and with no straining of the truth, that of all *his* contemporaries he was the greatest MAN.—TAYLOR, SIR

HENRY, 1880, *The English Poets, ed. Ward, vol.* IV, *p.* 164.

The pure and altogether admirable Southey.—LOWELL, JAMES RUSSELL, 1883, *Fielding; Prose Works, Riverside ed., vol.* VI. *p.* 60.

I love all Southey, and all that he does; and love that Correspondence of his with Caroline Bowles.—FITZGERALD, EDWARD, 1883, *Letters, May; Letters to Fanny Kemble, ed. Wright, p.* 251.

The second to come was a comely man, right manly in his going; and when the true-men were brought to speak of him there was quarrelling in their companies, for he had kinsmen in both their camps, and loath were they to do battle with him. But those that knew him not dealt him many back-handed blows, and for every stroke he received he gave two others, and inch by inch he fought his way upward with his face kept steadfastly to the true-men and his back to the summit. And though the guard cut away both coif and laurel in the strife, yet because his kinsmen fought not against him but against their fellows to his behoof, therefore he prevailed and won the heights.—CAINE, HALL, 1883, *The Fable of the Critics, Cobwebs of Criticism, p.* vii.

His prose style is the most uniformly good of any English writer who has written on anything like the same scale and with anything like the same variety of subject and class of work.—SAINTSBURY, GEORGE, 1886, *Specimens of English Prose Style, p.* 294.

Southey, like Dryden, is one of the manliest of writers. He is totally devoid of affectation; he has no mannerism, and expresses himself simply because he thinks clearly. . . . His prose-writings, no doubt, exhibit the weakness, as well as strength, of his nature. He acknowledges that he could not stand severe thought. There are subjects about which he knew little and wrote feebly; there are opinions scattered through his volumes at which we are forced to smile. When he prophesies he fails, just as Cobden fails, and as Mr. Bright fails; and when he touches on spiritual experiences that arouse no corresponding emotion in his own heart, there is an evident want of sympathy and breadth.—DENNIS, JOHN, 1887, *Robert Southey, Introduction, pp.* 16, 17.

Southey interested, but I cannot say that he in any way influenced me.—FARRAR, FREDERIC WILLIAM, 1887, *Books which Have Influenced Me, p.* 83.

Southey's biographies mark the beginnings, and fix the character, of nineteenth-century prose. Less formal in structure and less rhetorical in vocabulary than the prose of the preceding era, it has gained in simplicity and directness, in artistic compression and reserve. Southey's prose had none of the qualities which impress us in the prose of Gibbon, or which enchant and almost intoxicate us in that of Burke; but we feel, all the same, that neither Burke nor Gibbon could have turned their instrument of language to the purposes of a short biography with such mastery as Southey in the "Life of Nelson" displays in the use of his. Above all, we feel that a race of beings among whom mortal will always be more common than immortal writers have been supplied with an incomparably more useful model for imitation in the prose of Southey than in that of Gibbon or of Burke.—TRAILL, HENRY DUFF, 1896, *Social England, vol.* V, *p.* 588.

Poetical criticism, whether of his own writings or of those of others, was one of Southey's weakest points. But while egregiously deceived as to the absolute worth of his epics, he obeyed a happy instinct in selecting epic as his principal field in poetry. The gifts which he possessed—ornate description, stately diction, invention on a large scale—required an ample canvas for their display. Although the concise humour and simplicity of his lines on "The Battle of Blenheim" ensure it a place among the best known short poems in the language, there are not half a dozen of his lyrical pieces, some of his racy ballads excepted, that have any claim to poetic distinction. The "English Eclogues," however, have an important place in literature as prototypes of Tennyson's more finished performances, but are hardly poetry. As a writer of prose Southey is entitled to very high praise, although, as De Quincey justly points out, the universally commended elegance and perspicuity of his style do not make him a fine writer. But within his own limits he is a model of lucid, masculine English—"sinewy and flexible, easy and melodious."—GARNETT, RICHARD, 1898, *Dictionary of National Biography, vol.* LIII, *p.* 289.

Washington Allston

1779-1843

Washington Allston, A. R. A. Born in South Carolina. Graduated at Harvard College, 1800. Entered the schools of the Royal Academy in London soon after. His first work of importance, "The Dead Man Revived," gained a prize of two hundred guineas from the British Institute, and was purchased by the Philadelphia Academy of Fine Arts. This was followed by "St. Peter liberated by the Angel," "Uril and the Sun," "Jacob's Dream," and several smaller pictures, which are in private galleries in England. They were generally exhibited at the Royal Academy in London, of which he was an associate. In 1818 he opened a studio in Boston, and spent the remainder of his life in his native country. Among the better known of Allston's works are, "Jeremiah," (in Yale College) and "The Witch of Endor;" "Miriam," owned by the late David Sears of Boston; "Rosalie," owned by Nathan Appleton; "Belshazzar's Feast," in the Boston Athenæum; "Madonna;" "Spanish Girl," and "Spalatro's Vision of the Bloody Hand," painted in Cambridge, Mass., in 1832, for H. S. Ball, of Charleston, S. C., and sold in the collection of John Taylor Johnston, in 1876, for $3,900. It has been made familiar and popular by means of the engraving. It was at the Centennial Exhibition of 1876, as was also a landscape of Allston's belonging to the estate of Mrs. S. A. Eliot; "Rosalie;" "Isaac of York" (property of the Boston Athenæum); and "The Head of a Jew." In 1831 he published "The Sylphs of the Season," a poem, and a little later, "The Paint King" and "The Two Painters." His romance of "Monaldi," which followed these, attracted some attention in the literary world, and has been dramatized. Among Allston's portraits are Benjamin West, in the Boston Athenæum, and Coleridge, the poet, in the National Portrait Gallery, of England.—CLEMENT AND HUTTON, 1879-84, *Artists of the Nineteenth Century*, p. 10.

PERSONAL

Allston has a mild manner, a soft voice, and a sentimental air with him,—not at all Yankeeish; but his conversation does not indicate the talent displayed in his paintings. — ROBINSON, HENRY CRABB, 1818, *Diary, Apr.* 30; *Diary, Reminiscences and Correspondence, ed. Sadler, vol.* I, *p.* 385.

Nothing new in Boston, except an *old* painting by Allston, just brought to light and for show. A beautiful fancy-sketch; two girls,—one from Titian, the other his own *dreamerie*. They talk of getting up an exhibition of all his paintings, for his benefit. He needs it. O ye gods! how hard a fate! This old painting, which he loved and cherished as a child of his youth, and valued at fifteen hundred dollars, he has been obliged to part with for five hundred.—LONGFELLOW, HENRY WADSWORTH, 1839, *To Samuel Ward, March* 11; *Life, ed. Samuel Longfellow, vol.* I, *p.* 326.

His MS., notwithstanding an exceedingly simple and boyish air, is one which we particularly admire. It is forcible, picturesque, and legible, without ornament of any description. Each letter is formed with a thorough distinctness and individuality. Such a MS. indicates caution and precision, most unquestionably; but we say of it as we say of Mr. Peabody's (a very different MS.), that no man of original genius ever did or could habitually indite it under any circumstances whatever.—POE, EDGAR ALLAN, 1842, *A Chapter on Autography, Works, ed. Stoddard, vol.* V, *p.* 423.

No picture is more pleasing to my heart and fancy than to see Mr. Allston, seated at his parlor fire in the evening, after a day spent in his studio, his eyes resting meditatively upon the fire, his beautiful countenance marked with taste and thought, the smoke from his cigar going up in little clouds and mingling among the gray curls of his hair, and then rising, to etherealize the whole, with the social glass of wine on the table which he has placed before his visitor,—the whole is painted with warm colors in my mind.—DANA, RICHARD HENRY, 1843, *Journal, April* 22; *Life of Dana, by C. F. Adams, vol.* I, *p.* 71.

As we contemplate the life and works of Allston, we are inexpressibly grateful that he lived. His example is one of our best possessions. And yet, while rejoicing that he has done much, we seem to hear a whisper that he might have done more. His productions suggest a higher genius than they display; and we are disposed sometimes to praise the master rather than the work. Like a beloved character in English literature, Sir James Mackintosh, he finally closed a career of beautiful, but fragmentary labors, leaving much undone which all had hoped he would do. The great painting which haunted so many years of his life, and which his friends and country awaited with anxious interest, remained unfinished at last. His Virgilian sensibility and modesty would doubtless have ordered its destruction, had death arrested him less suddenly. Titian died, leaving incomplete, like Allston, an important picture, on which his hand was busy down to the time of his death. A pious and distinguished pupil, the younger Palma, took up the labor of his master, and, on its completion, placed it in the church for which it was destined, with this inscription: "That which Titian left unfinished Palma reverently completed and dedicated to God." Where is the Palma who can complete what our Titian has left unfinished?—SUMNER, CHARLES, 1846, *The Scholar, The Jurist, The Artist, The Philanthropist; Works, vol.* I, *p.* 283.

Once in a winter, or possibly oftener, his evening hearth was brightened by the presence of Washington Allston. He loved this friend for his lofty purity of character, as much as he admired his grand genius; and the courtesy with which each recognized the other's greatness was most noble. Mr. Allston was prompt to seek his friend's judgment of a new picture, so much did he confide in his simple instincts of beauty and truthfulness of taste. And by the hour would Dr. Channing listen, rapt and silent, with childlike animation on his spiritual countenance, whilst the painter poured forth his golden floods of high idealism, devout sentiment, criticism, anecdote, description. He joyfully made the sacrifice of wasted days following such wakefulness, for the artist's best hour for talk was midnight.—CHANNING, WILLIAM HENRY, 1848, *Memoir of William Ellery Channing, vol.* III, *p.* 468.

He took particular pleasure in works of devout Christian speculation, without, however, neglecting a due proportion of strictly devotional literature. These he varied by a constant recurrence of the great epic and dramatic masters and occasional reading of the earlier and the living novelists, tales of wild romance and lighter fiction, voyage and travels, biographies and letters. Nor was he without a strong interest in the current politics of his own country and of England, as to which his principles were highly conservative.—DANA, RICHARD HENRY, JR., 1850, *ed., Lectures on Art and Poems, Preface, p.* vii.

To the eye of the multitude his life glided away in secluded contentment, yet a prevailing idea was the star of his being —the idea of beauty. For the high, the lovely, the perfect, he strove all his days. He sought them in the scenes of nature, in the masterpieces of literature and art, in habits of life, in social relations, and in love. Without pretense, without elation, in all meekness, his youthful enthusiasm chastened by suffering, he lived above the world. Gentleness he deemed true wisdom, renunciation of all the trappings of life a duty. He was calm, patient, occasionally sad, but for the most part happy in the free exercise and guardianship of his varied powers.—TUCKERMAN, HENRY T., 1852, *A Sketch of American Literature.*

So refined was his whole appearance, so fastidiously neat his apparel,—but with a neatness that seemed less the result of care and plan than a something as proper to the man as whiteness to the lily,—that you would have at once classed him with those individuals, rarer than great captains and almost as rare as great poets, whom Nature sends into the world to fill the arduous office of Gentleman. . . . A *nimbus* of hair, fine as an infant's, and early white, showing refinement of organization and the predominance of the spiritual over the physical, undulated and floated around a face that seemed like pale flame, and over which the flitting shades of expression chased each other, fugitive and gleaming as waves upon a field of rye. It was a countenance that, without any beauty of feature, was very beautiful. I have said that it looked like pale flame, and can find no other words for the impression it gave. Here was a man all soul, his body seeming a lamp of finest clay, whose service was to feed with magic oils, rare and fragrant, that wavering fire which hovered over it. You, who are an adept in such matters, would have detected in the eyes that artist-look which seems to see pictures ever in the air, and which, if it fall on you, makes you feel as if all the world were a gallery, and yourself the rather indifferent Portrait of a Gentleman hung therein.—LOWELL, JAMES RUSSELL, 1854–90, *Cambridge Thirty Years Ago; Prose Works, Riverside ed., vol.* I, *pp.* 72, 73.

I first became acquainted with Washington Allston, early in the spring of 1805. He had just arrived from France, I from Sicily and Naples. I was then not quite twenty-two years of age—he a little older. There was something, to me, inexpressibly engaging in the appearance and manners of Allston. I do not think I have ever been more completely captivated on a first acquaintance. He was of a light and graceful form, with large blue eyes and black silken hair, waving and curling round a pale expressive countenance. Everything about him bespoke the man of intellect and refinement. His conversation was copious, animated, and highly graphic; warmed by a genial sensibility and benevolence, and enlivened at times by a chaste and gentle humor . . . a man whose memory I hold in reverence and affection, as one of the purest, noblest, and most intellectual beings that ever honored me with his friendship.—IRVING, WASHINGTON, 1855, *Letter in Duyckinck's Cyclopædia of American Literature, vol.* II, *pp.* 18, 20.

ART

The admirable works exhibiting now by Allston; whose great picture, with his Hebe, landscape, and sea-piece, would of themselves suffice to elucidate the fundamental doctrines of colour, ideal form, and grouping; assist the reasoner in the same way as the diagrams aid the geometrician, but far more and more vividly.—COLERIDGE, SAMUEL TAYLOR, 1814, *On the Principles of Sound Criticism; Miscellanies, Æsthetic and Literary, ed. Ashe, p.* 9.

What painter (excepting perhaps Raffaelle) ever came near his own conception or that of any other man?—LOWELL, JAMES RUSSELL, 1839, *To G. B. Loring, April* 29; *Letters, ed. Norton, vol.* I, *p.* 38.

The calm and meditative cast of these pictures, the ideal beauty that shone *through* rather than *in* them, and the harmony of colouring were as unlike anything else I saw, as the "Vicar of Wakefield" to Cooper's novels. I seemed to recognise in painting that self-possessed elegance, that transparent depth, which I most admire in literature; I thought with delight that such a man as this had been able to grow up in our bustling, reasonable community, that he had kept his foot upon the ground, yet never lost sight of the rose-clouds of beauty floating above him. I saw, too, that he had not been troubled, but possessed his own soul with the blandest patience; and I hoped, I scarce knew what; probably the *mot d'enigme* for which we are all looking. How the poetical mind can live and work in peace and good faith! how it may unfold to its due perfection in an unpoetical society!—OSSOLI, MARGARET FULLER, 1839, *A Record of Impressions Produced by the Exhibition of Mr. Allston's Pictures; Art, Literature and the Drama, p.* 285.

Our country has the right to claim, then, at least one great name upon the list of living artists. On him descended those nameless influences, which, in all countries and ages, have from time to time fallen upon such as Heaven has chosen to delineate and adorn in various modes the images that fill the worlds of reality and of dreams. In the midst of the trials and fatigues of common life, from which none of us, and least of all the artist, escape, he has been laboring for us and for our children, to combine the scattered beauties of nature, to reproduce in more permanent form the shapes that alternately are moulded and melted away among the clouds of imagination, to call back in renewed existence the creations of the past. And it is not mere natural genius to which we owe our admiration and gratitude, but genius improved by patient study, refined by still seclusion, warmed by good affections, and therefore diffusing itself in images as finished, as pure, as full of gentle feelings; even as one planet is reflected with the same light from the bosom of many waters.—HOLMES, OLIVER WENDELL, 1840, *The Allston Exhibition, North American Review, vol.* 50, *p.* 380.

All the pictures to which I have just referred, and many others, to which I shall presently turn your attention, are examples of that peculiar charm, in art, styled by the critics, repose. There is hardly a work from the hand of Allston which is not, either in the whole, or in some considerable part, an instance in point. The word Repose alone, perhaps, with sufficient accuracy, describes the state of mind, and the outward aspect of nature intended by it.—WARE, WILLIAM, 1842, *Lecture on Allston, p.* 894.

Allston's style was extremely varied, as were the subjects he treated. His was no formal manner, operating with the regularity, fecundity, and swiftness of a machine. Who would assign to the same hand the landscapes at Boston and the "Desert," purchased by Mr. Labouchere? When I reflect upon the character of his works and the immense labor bestowed upon them, I am surprised that this age, so prone to regard art as a handmaid of luxury, should have employed him as it did. When I remember the astonishing rapidity of his execution, the ease with which his hand and eye mirrored the beauty before him, when I remember that his will alone stood between his poverty and the most prolific outpouring of production, with all the renown and emolument that accompany it, then I form a clear idea of the character of his genius. His was truly a great and a noble example. Was such ever thrown away? Surely never. More even than his works do I believe that he will live in the awakened minds of American art, and who shall say where the republic will carry the achievements of painting with him for her first-born poet-painter. —GREENOUGH, HORATIO, 1844, *Letter to R. H. Dana, Jr., June* 11.

It seemed to me that in him America had lost her third great man. What Washington was as a statesman, Channing as a moralist, *that* was Allston as an artist.—JAMESON, ANNA BROWNELL, 1844-46, *Washington Allston, Memoirs and Essays, p.* 126.

It was Allston who first awakened what little sensibility I may possess to the beauties of colour. He first directed my attention to the Venetian school, particularly to the works of Paul Veronese, and taught me to see, through the accumulated dirt of ages, the exquisite charm that lay beneath. Yet, for a long time, I took the merit of the Venetians on trust, and, if left to myself, should have preferred works which I now feel to be comparatively worthless. I remember when the picture of "The Ages," by Titian, was first pointed out to me by Allston as an exquisite work, I thought he was laughing at me. It is but fair to myself, however, to say, that from the first I was delighted with the Raffaelles in the same collection (the Bridgwater).—LESLIE, CHARLES ROBERT, 1860, *Autobiographical Recollections, ed. Taylor, p.* 22.

The method of this artist was to suppress all the coarser beauties which make up the substance of common pictures. He was the least *ad captandum* of workers. He avoided bright eyes, curls, and contours, glancing lights, strong contrasts, and colors too crude for harmony. He reduced his beauty to her elements, so that an inner beauty might play through her features. Like the Catholic discipline which pales the face of the novice with vigils, seclusion, and fasting, and thus makes room and clears the way for the movements of the spirit, so in these figures every vulgar grace is suppressed. No classic contours, no languishing attitudes, no asking for admiration,—but a severe and chaste restraint, a modest sweetness, a slumbering intellectual atmosphere, a graceful self-possession, eyes so sincere and pure that heaven's light shines through them, and, beyond all, a hovering spiritual life that makes each form a presence.—CLARKE, SARAH, 1865, *Our First Great Painter and His Works, Atlantic Monthly, vol.* 15, *p.* 131.

With the name of this great painter, painting reached its acme of excellence among us. In genius, character, life, and feeling, he emulated the Italian masters, partook of their spirit, and caught the mellow richness of their tints. . . . From an Alpine landscape luminous with frosty atmosphere and sky-piercing mountains to moonbeams flickering on a quiet stream, from grand scriptural to delicate fancy figures, from rugged and solemn Jewish heads to the most ideal female conceptions, from "Jeremiah" to "Beatrice," and from "Miriam" to "Rosalie," every phrase of mellow and transparent—almost magnetic color, graceful contours, deep expression, rich contrasts of tints—the mature, satisfying, versatile triumph of pictorial art, as we have known and loved it in the Old World, then and there, justified the name of "American Titian" bestowed on Allston at Rome.—TUCKERMAN, HENRY T., 1867, *Book of the Artists, p.* 9.

The versatility of Allston in painting at will historical compositions, portraits, ideal heads, landscapes, marines, and *genre* pictures was accompanied with a minute and delicate finish bestowed on all alike. It was a matter of wonder, when his pictures were collected in Boston, how so much work could have been crowded into one short life, and that a crippled one. The grand figures of his prophets and kings were not more carefully and minutely painted than the accessories of still-life, —the vases, jewels, and back-grounds. But this versatility was fatal to the master's pre-eminence in American art, for life is not long enough for the noblest mind and deftest hand to attain illustrious excellence in so many departments of endeavor. He should have confined himself to small ideal subjects, with which he had full sympathy. Allston's love for sublimity was hardly less than his devotion to beauty, though it was not so often displayed in his art. . . . In expression, or the power of portraying emotions and dispositions, Allston found another of his noble characteristics, though he withheld a display of this gift in a majority of his pictures, preferring to paint calm and passionless faces, full of tender and thoughtful beauty, and giving free scope to the imagination. Dignity is paramount, a grand abstraction, a passive majesty.—SWEETSER, M. F., 1878, *Allston (Artist-Biographies), pp.* 178, 179.

He is one of our great men. Pure in his life as a child, modest in his character, and of a delicacy and refinement of imagination in his art that entitles him to take rank with the great masters. When I remember the place in which he worked, the difficulties which he had to encounter, the absence of all stimulus save that which he found within himself, his prosaic surroundings, the want of models and means for his art, and in every way the restrictions of his position, the works that he produced were almost marvelous; but genius makes its own place, and time breaks the difficulties of circumstance. . . . He filled my mind with his own enthusiasm and taught me the dignity of art, the sincere devotion it demanded. The earnest study, the consecration of the whole mind and heart it required. And he led me into its precincts as a high-priest leads the trembling neophyte to the altar. I can never be grateful enough to him for the high standard which he set before me, as before all who came into his presence. —STORY, WILLIAM WETMORE, 1880, *Letter to Committee on Allston Celebration, Boston, November* 1.

Some of those who mark in much of Allston's work the gap which divides intentions from accomplishments, and mark also the non-pictorial, "literary" character of these intentions, are led to think that he should not have tried to paint at all—that he was meant to be an artist in words, and not in lines and colours. But the volume of poems he has left does not in the least confirm such theories. Within certain narrow limits he was successful in his pictures, while he never even approched success in verse. His prose writing, however, is very interesting; and if space sufficed I should like to show how fine and keen and sane a critical instinct he possessed. . . . And yet, if a pathetic fact for himself, it was a fortunate fact for us that his ideals and ambitions—these being but the translation of his whole nature—were so much loftier than his gifts and opportunities. If his pictures can have no notable influence upon American art, his life and character had an immense and happy influence upon the reverence for, and appreciation of, art in America. What we needed fifty years ago was not so much great artists as a great prophet and apostle and servant of art. We may wish, if we will, that Allston had left us finer works and more voluminous critical writings; but after all, the best service he could have done us was to work in the spirit he did and to be the man he was. I do not think I underestimate the value of his painting when I say that he was by no means the potent artist our fathers thought him. But I am sure I could not over-estimate the value of his life, of his example, of himself—a strong and needed and gracious influence while he lived, and to-day a helpful, an inspiring tradition.—VAN RENSSELAER, M. G., 1889, *Washington Allston, Magazine of Art, vol.* 12, *p.* 150.

His outline drawings, which have been much admired, are round and unaccented, and show little sense of structure. His composition often seems mechanical rather than organic. The "Dead Man Revived" seems pieced together, and has no unity of arrangement. His costumes are in a curious, hybrid, pseudo-classic taste, and his prettily feminine angels, with their hair dressed in the fashion of Lawrence's portraits, are strangely in contrast with the heavy-muscled prophets and apostles after Michael Angelo and Raphael, which have sometimes an undeniable dignity. "Handling" he avowedly despised, and his technical methods were of the elaborate kind common when artists still believed in "the secret of Titian," and the old art of "painting in oils" had not succumbed in the struggle with modern demands. . . . Allston must, on the whole, be classed, as one of the failures in art.—COX, KENYON, 1893, *Washington Allston, The Nation, vol.* 56, *p.* 33.

GENERAL

Though we have not allowed to Mr. Allston a mastery over the more intense passions, yet he seems filled with the milder feeling and to have nothing pass through the imagination untouched by them. All that the world contains is, with him, a sentiment, and quickens the feelings and thoughts. Indeed, it seems to be peculiarly the character of his, and almost all good modern poetry, to make all that surrounds us within doors, and in our daily affairs abroad, administer good to our hearts and minds, so that, if it does not make poets of us all, it will cause us to be wider and more accurate thinkers, as well as better men. Besides this character, the poems before us, in many parts, run up into the wild, and visionary, and magnificent, and the eye brightens and enlarges, and the spirits are lifted, as we enter into them. All, however, is of the same joyous temperament; for if the scene, viewed alone, would be dark and awing, you find it in the midst of satire and humour, and their lights are observed, playing and sparkling over it, as in "The Paint King," and "The Two Painters."—DANA, RICHARD HENRY, 1817, *Sylphs of the Seasons, North American Review, vol.* 5, *p.* 371.

He who, returning
Rich in praise to his native shores, hath left a remembrance
Long to be honoured and loved on the banks of Thames and of Tiber:
So may America, prizing in time the worth she possesses,
Give to that hand free scope, and boast hereafter of Allston.

—SOUTHEY, ROBERT, 1821, *A Vision of Judgment.*

"The Two Painters," an admirable satire, intended to ridicule the attempts to reach perfection in one excellency in the art of painting, to the neglect of every other, proves equally his descriptive powers. These poems, and the "Paint King," a singularly wild, imaginative story, evidence, also, his *creative* genius. They are all original, in their fable, style, and cast of thought; and all have the purest and most cheerful influences upon the mind.—GRISWOLD, RUFUS W., 1842, *The Poets and Poetry of America, p.* 41.

No man ever possessed a more exquisite appreciation of the Beautiful, than Washington Allston, one of the most gifted of painters, and yet no man ever kept the Beautiful in more severe subordination to the Good and True, in the productions of both his pencil and pen. That appreciation made him shrink from frequent efforts in the higher department of his art, for he felt the impuissance of his hand in the delineations of the glorious visions of his genius.—LOSSING, BENSON J., 1855–86, *Eminent Americans, p.* 262.

His poems, though few in number, are exquisite in finish, and in the fancies and thoughts which they embody. They are delicate, subtle, and philosophical. Thought and feeling are united in them, and the meditative eye

which hath kept watch
o'er man's mortality

broods over all.—DUYCKINCK, EVERT A. AND GEORGE L., 1855–65–75, *Cyclopædia of American Literature, ed. Simons, vol.* II, *p.* 17.

Comparatively little known as a writer to the present generation of Americans, there is yet much in his prose and poetical productions to please the fancy and to elevate and refine the taste.—DESHLER, CHARLES D., 1879, *Afternoons With the Poets, p.* 275.

As a poet, however, he is now but little known. As a prose writer, his lectures on art, and especially his romance of "Monaldi," show that he could paint with the pen as well as with the brush. It is difficult to understand why "Monaldi" has not obtained a permanent place in our literature. There is in one discription of a picture representing the visible struggle of a soul in the toils of sin which in intensity of conception and passion exceeds any picture he ever painted.—WHIPPLE, EDWIN PERCY, 1886, *American Literature and Other Papers, ed. Whittier, p.* 41.

He wrote a romance, "Monaldi," which

had many excellences, but not the quality of impressiveness; unless we except the description of a picture of a soul struggling in the toils of sin, which is more effective than any of Allston's actual pictures. . . . Finally, he produced some sonnets which are placid and pale-hued records of personal feeling, and whose chief merit is the negative one of being free from vulgarity. But though the definite information to be had about Allston arouses a certain intellectual impatience, it would be wrong to dismiss him as a vapid and featureless pretender.—HAWTHORNE, JULIAN, AND LEMMON, LEONARD, 1891, *American Literature, pp.* 116, 117.

His appearance was indeed impressive. No one could see him without feeling something of his character. To those who have seen him, it is not surprising that the genial poet of Boston needed no one to designate Allston. There was in him a remarkable symmetry of endowment. As an artist he seemed to possess every gift requisite to produce the best effects in every department. As a poet he had the same fulness of natural qualities. . . . Allston was not deficient in strength or in the adventuring boldness of genius. Beauty did not check, if we may so express it, the effrontery of his imagination, or smoothe the rugged strength of his thought. Symmetry was ever present, but never to weaken his work. His exquisite adjustment of all elements in the production of effects, his love of symmetry, with harmony, distinguished him to a remarkable degree. The gentle stood not alone, or as over-balancing the grand.—FLAGG, JARED B., 1892, *The Life and Letters of Washington Allston, pp.* 395, 398.

While his poems have many beauties, it is chiefly as an influence that he is remembered in literature. Compared with many of his contemporaries, his production was small indeed, yet it should not be forgotten that, in introducing America to the culture of Europe, Allston did a service to our literature second only to that rendered by Longfellow.—PATTEE, FRED LEWIS, 1896, *A History of American Literature, p.* 167.

John Foster

1770-1843

Born at Wadsworth Lane, near Halifax, 17 Sept. 1770. At Baptist Coll., Bristol, Sept. 1791 to May 1792. Baptist preacher at Newcastle, 1792. In Dublin, 1793-94. Returned to England, 1794. To Dublin again, 1795. Returned to Wadsworth Lane, Feb. 1796. Baptist minister at Chichester, 1797. To Battersea, 1799. Minister at Downend, Bristol, 1800-04; at Sheppard's Barton, near Frome, 1804-06. Contrib. to "Eclectic Review," 1806-39. Married Maria Snooke, May 1808; settled at Bourton, Gloucestershire. Minister at Downend again, 1817-21. Removed to Stapylton, Gloucestershire, 1821. Lectured in Broadmead Chapel, Bristol, 1822-23. Wife died, 1832. Contrib. to "Morning Chronicle," 1834-35. Died, 15 Oct. 1843. Buried in Downend Baptist Chapel burial-ground. *Works:* "Essays," 1805, (2nd end. same year); "Discourse on Missions," 1818; "On the Evils of Popular Ignorance," 1820; "Introductory Observations on Dr. Marshman's Statement," 1828. *Posthumous:* "Contributions . . . to the 'Eclectic Review'" (2 vols.), 1844. He *edited:* Doddridge's "Rise and Progress of Religion," 1825; Hall's "Works," 1832. *Life:* "Life and Correspondence," by J. E. Ryland, 1846.—SHARP, R. FARQUHARSON, 1897, *A Dictionary of English Authors, p.* 102.

PERSONAL

His disposition was unresentful. He felt warmly, and even indignantly, when taking the part which he deemed incumbent upon him in a righteous cause—in defending the injured; in resisting what he deemed unjust; and exposing what to his eye was dishonourable;—but he thus felt and acted for others. In what had relation simply to himself, he felt it beneath him to cherish an unforgiving, revengeful temper. He excited strong attachment, but he encountered little personal enmity, for it was not his habit to indulge it himself. At the same time, he was ready to act as a mediator, and was glad to heal differences, taking sometimes an active part in the exercise of Christian charity.—CRISP, THOMAS S., 1843, *Sermon on the Death of Rev. John Foster, Oct.* 22.

The sermons of Foster were of a cast quite distinct from what is commonly called oratory, and, indeed, from what many seem to account the highest style of eloquence, namely, a flow of facile thoughts through the smooth channels of uniformly elevated polished diction, graced by the utmost appliances of voice and gesture. But they possessed for me, and for not a few hearers, qualities and attractions much preferable to these. The basis of important thoughts was as much original or underived from other minds, as, perhaps, that of any reading man's reflections in our age of books could be; still more so the mode and aspect in which they were presented. That unambitious and homely sort of loftiness, which displayed neither phrase nor speaker, but things,—while the brief word and simple tone brought out the sublime conception "in its clearness;" that fund of varied associations and images by which he really illustrated, not painted or gilded his truths; the graphic master-strokes, the frequent hints of profound suggestion for after-meditation, the cogent though calm expostulations and appeals, the shrewd turns of half-latent irony against irreligion and folly, in which, without any descent from seriousness and even solemnity, the speaker moved a smile by his unconscious approaches to the edge of wit, yet effectually quelled it by the unbroken gravity of his tone and purpose,—all these characteristics had for me an attractive power and value, both by novelty and instructiveness, far above the qualities of an oratory, or eloquence more fashioned on received rules and models.—SHEPPARD, JOHN, 1844, *The Life and Correspondence of John Foster, ed. Ryland, vol.* II, *p.* 306.

At the latest glimpse that we can get of the distinguished author . . . we find him an infirm, retired octogenarian, long, gaunt, and ghastly, careless and slovenly in dress, with a countenance deeply furrowed by a life of intense thought, and indicating great mental vigor and rigid inflexibility of character. He was revered and cherished as the last of a constellation of luminaries, that had for half a century or more shed lustre on the previously obscure and overshadowed denomination of Particular or Calvinistic Baptists.—PEABODY, ANDREW P., 1846, *John Foster's Essays, North American Review, vol.* 62, *p.* 141.

GENERAL

We take our leave of this work with sincere reluctance. For the length to which we have extended our review, the subject must be our apology. It has fared with us as with a traveller who passes through an enchanting country, where he meets with so many beautiful views and so many striking objects which he is loath to quit, that he loiters till the shades of evening insensibly fall upon him. We are far, however, from recommending these volumes as faultless. Mr. F's work is rather an example of the power of genius than a specimen of finished composition: it lies open in many points to the censure of those minor critics, who, by the observation of a few technical rules, may easily avoid its faults, without reaching one of its beauties. The author has paid too little attention to the construction of his sentences. They are for the most part too long, sometimes involved in perplexity, and often loaded with redundances. They have too much of the looseness of an harangue, and too little of the compact elegance of regular composition. An occasional obscurity pervades some parts of the work. The mind of the writer seems at times to struggle with conceptions too mighty for his grasp, and to present confused masses, rather than distinct delineations of thought. This, however, is to be imputed to the originality, not the weakness, of his powers. The scale on which he thinks is so vast, and the excursions of his imagination are so extended, that they frequently carry him into the most unbeaten track, and among objects where a ray of light glances in an angle only, without diffusing itself over the whole.—HALL, ROBERT, 1805, *Review of Foster's Essays, Miscellaneous Works and Remains, p.* 446.

Mr. Foster's "Essays" are full of ingenuity and original remark. The style of them is at once terse and elegant.—DIBDIN, THOMAS FROGNALL, 1824, *Library Companion.*

He has been prevented from preaching by a complaint affecting the throat; but, judging from the quality of his celebrated "Essays," he could never have figured as a truly splendid rhetorician; for the imagery and ornamental parts of his "Essays" have evidently not grown up in the loom, and concurrently with the texture of the thoughts, but have been separately added afterwards, as so much embroidery or fringe.—DE QUINCEY, THOMAS, 1828–59, *Rhetoric, Works, ed. Masson, vol.* X, *p.* 110.

Foster was a Calvinist of the old school as to his theological opinions; and his opinions were all theological. He took cognizance, indeed, of a wide diversity of subjects, but viewed them only in their religious aspects and relations. His general knowledge was great, and his learning accurate and profound; but every thing, ancient and modern, sacred and profane, was tried by the unelastic standard of his own creed. . . . Of course, the moral tone of all his writings is pure and lofty. His ethics are eminently Christian as to their positive side; but they lack the breadth and catholicity of the Christian standard. They omit all the æsthetic aspects of virtue. They give but narrow scope and reluctant tolerance to those innocent amenities of domestic and social life, of literature and art, which grow in the most luxuriant beauty under true Christian culture. His morality would be represented by a rigid code, formed of precise precepts, stated and defined with logical accuracy, and bristling all over with stern penalties, rather than by a pervading, plastic spirit of devotion and humanity, multiform in its manifestations, and blending with all that is graceful and beautiful in nature and in life. —PEABODY, A. P., 1846, *Foster's Essays, North American Review, vol.* 62, *p.* 143.

We have in his works the collected thoughts of a powerful mind that has lived "collaterally or aside" to the world—that never flattered a popular prejudice—that never bent to a popular idol—that never deserted in the darkest hour the cause of liberty—that never swore to the Shibboleth of a party —or, at least, never kept its vow, and conspicuous, a mighty and mysterious fragment, the Stonehenge of modern moralists. Shall we inscribe immortality upon the shapeless yet sublime structure? He who reared it seems, from the elevation he has now reached, to answer No. What is the thing you call immortality to me, who have cleft that deep shadow and entered on this greater and brighter state of being? —GILFILLAN, GEORGE, 1847, *Life and Correspondence of John Foster, Tait's Edinburgh Magazine, vol.* 14, *p.* 10.

Perhaps the most successful essayist of his time was the Rev. John Foster, last of Bristol. His "Essays" passed through eighteen editions during his life; and they are still spreading. There is no great precision in the thoughts; but the tone of morality is pure, and the views are original and broad, while the style is eminently interesting. The volume was one which met the wants of the time; and if some of the matter is vague, and the views narrow, they were a welcome escape from the shallow prosings which they superseded. —MARTINEAU, HARRIET, 1849, *A History of the Thirty Years' Peace, A. D.* 1815–46, *vol.* IV, *p.* 426.

The miscellaneous production of his pen hold high rank among the most brilliant English classics. All his writings are noted for remarkable comprehensiveness, the interest, strength, and great originality and majesty of conception. His eloquence consisted, not in pompous phrases or brilliant explosions, but the pure force of sense, adorned with the sweetest imagery, and an admirable neatness and compactness of style.—FISH, HENRY C., 1856, *History and Repository of Pulpit Eloquence, vol.* I, *p.* 411.

He cultivated originality both in thought and in expression. His command of language and illustration is copious, but his style has a want of flow, an air of labour. He repeats an idea again and again, but the successive repetitions do not, like the varied expression of Chalmers, make the meaning more and more luminous; they often burden rather than illuminate the general reader, and they strike the critic as a laboured exercise in the accumulation of synonyms and similitudes.—MINTO, WILLIAM, 1872–80, *Manual of English Prose Literature, p.* 510.

Mr. Foster's essays are excellent models of vigorous thought and expression, uniting metaphysical nicety and acuteness with practical sagacity and common-sense.—CHAMBERS, ROBERT, 1876, *Cyclopædia of English Literature, ed. Carruthers.*

Foster is a distinct variety among the professors of literature. He is the impersonation of a somewhat gloomy Dissenter, shut up by circumstances in a small circle, sitting among his little group of intellectual persons with a heartfelt sense of aggrieved superiority, and contemplating most things in heaven and earth as subjects to be discussed by letter or by word of mouth. His essays had, at one time a wide reputation, and they have always been of the kind of literature appreciated by persons of thoughtful minds without much education, to whom the gravity of steady intellectual investigations, not of too scientific an order, is new and delightful. An essay "On decision of Character" does not seem likely to be very original, but yet there is the originality of a mind not too much cultivated or too much pervaded by other men's thinkings in the conscientious examination of his subject, which Foster gives.—OLIPHANT, MARGARET O. W., 1882, *Literary History of England, XVIII-XIX Century, vol.* II, *p.* 288.

Noah Webster

1758-1843

Born at Hartford, Conn., Oct. 16, 1758: died at New Haven, Conn., May 28, 1843. An American lexicographer and author. He entered Yale in 1774; served in the Revolutionary War in 1777; graduated at Yale in 1778; and was admitted to the bar in 1781. He taught in various places, and in 1788 settled in New York as a journalist. In 1798 he removed to New Haven, and in 1812 to Amherst, Massachusetts, where he took part in the founding of the college and was the first president of its board of trustees. He returned to New Haven in 1822. He published "A Grammatical Institute of the English Language" (1783-85; comprising spelling-book, grammar, and reader), "Dissertations on the English Language" (1789), "A Compendious Dictionary of the English Language" (1806), and "A Grammar of the English Language" (1807). He is best known from his large "American Dictionary of the English Language" (1828: 2d ed. 1841). Among his other works are "Rights of Neutrals" (1802), "Collection of Papers on Political, Literary, and Moral Subjects" (1843), and a brief history of the United States (1823).—SMITH, BENJAMIN E., *ed.*, 1894-97, *The Century Cyclopedia of Names, p.* 1053.

PERSONAL

Feb. 18,—At evening rode to Wethersfield [from Hartford, where he was then living] with the ladies, who reminded us of the mile-stones and bridges. . . . *Feb.* 19, *P. M.*—Rode to East Windsor; had a clergyman with us, who sang an excellent song. Mile-stones and bridges almost totally neglected. — WEBSTER, NOAH, 1784, *Diary, Life by Scudder, p.* 11.

Webster has returned, and brought with him a pretty wife. I wish him success, but I doubt, in the present decay of business in our profession [the law], whether his profits will enable him to keep up the style he sets out with. I fear he will breakfast upon Institutes, dine upon Dissertations, and go to bed supperless.—TRUMBULL, JOHN, 1789, *Letter to Oliver Wolcott.*

I have never been a hard student, unless a few years may be excepted; but I have been a steady, persevering student. I have rarely used lamp or candle light, except once, when reading law, and then I paid for my imprudence, for I injured my eyes. My practice has usually been to rise about half an hour before the sun, and make use of all the light of that luminary. But I have never or rarely been in a hurry. When I first undertook the business of supporting General Washington's administration, I laboured too hard in writing or translating from the French papers for my paper, or in composing pamphlets. In two instances I was so exhausted that I expected to die, for I could not perceive any pulsation in the radial artery; but I recovered. While engaged in composing my "Dictionary," I was often so much excited by discoveries I made, that my pulse, whose ordinary action is scarcely 60 beats to the minute, was accelerated to 80 or 85. My exercise has not been violent nor regular. While I was in Amherst I cultivated a little land, and used to work at making hay, and formerly I worked in my garden, which I cannot now do. Until within a few years, I used to make my fires in the morning, but I never or rarely walked before breakfast. My exercise is now limited to walking about the city to purchase supplies for my family. . . . I began to use spectacles when fifty years of age, or a little more, and that was the time when I began to study and prepare materials for my "Dictionary." I had had the subject in contemplation some years before, and had made memorandums on the margin of Johnson's "Dictionary," but I did not set myself to the work till I wore spectacles. When I finished my copy I was sitting at my table in Cambridge, England, January, 1825. When I arrived at the last word, I was seized with a tremor that made it difficult to proceed. I, however, summoned up strength to finish the work, and then walking about the room I soon recovered.—WEBSTER, NOAH, 1836, *Letter to Dr. Thomas Miner, Nov.* 21.

To men of the present generation, Dr. Webster is known chiefly as a learned philologist; and the natural inference would be, that he spent his whole life among his books, and chiefly in devotion to a single class of studies. The fact, however, was far otherwise. Though he was always a close student,—reading, thinking, and writing at every period of his life,—he never withdrew himself from the active employments of society. After his first removal to New Haven, he was for a number of years one of the aldermen of the city, and judge of one of the state courts. He also frequently represented that town in the legislature of the state. During his residence at Amherst, he was called, in repeated instances, to discharge similar duties, and spent a part of several winters at Boston as a member of the General Court. . . . In the discharge of his duties, Dr. Webster was watchful, consistent, and firm. Though immersed in study, he kept in his hands the entire control of his family arrangements, down to the minutest particulars. Everything was reduced to exact system; all moved on with perfect regularity and order, for *method* was the presiding principle of his life. In the government of his children there was but one rule, and that was instantaneous and entire obedience. This was insisted upon as *right*,—as, in the nature of things, due by a child to a parent. He did not rest his claim on any explanations, or on showing that the thing required was reasonable or beneficial. . . . In his religious feelings, Dr. Webster was remarkably equable and cheerful. He had a very strong sense of the providence of God, as extending to the minutest concerns of life. In this he found a source of continual support and consolation, under the severe labors and numerous trials which he had to endure. To the same divine hand he habitually referred all his enjoyments; and it was known to his family that he rarely, if ever, took the slightest refreshment, of any kind, even between meals, without a momentary pause, and a silent tribute to God as the giver. He made the Scriptures his daily study.—GOODRICH, CHAUNCEY A., 1847, *Memoir of Noah Webster*.

It is not vanity which upholds a man working silently year after year at a task ridiculed by his neighbors and denounced by his enemies. Webster had something better to sustain him than an idle self-conceit. He had the reserve of a high purpose, and an aim which had been growing more clearly understood by himself, so that he could afford to disregard the judgments of others. There was in the outward circumstance of his life something which testifies to the sincerity and worth of his purpose. He had withdrawn himself into the wilderness that he might free himself from encumbrances in his work, and with his love of society this was no light thing to do. His family went with him reluctantly; but when did not an enthusiast drag with him to his own light sacrifice the unwilling attendants of his life!—SCUDDER, HORACE E., 1881, *Noah Webster (American Men of Letters)*, p. 233.

SPELLING BOOK

Noah Webster, who wrote the earliest American spelling-book, was the first author whose writings I ever read; and what a work it was to my young imagination! In its externals, as well as its internals, it is before me now precisely as it was nearly half a century ago. The narrow yellow-white leathern back, with not quite all the hairs tanned out of it in some copies; the palish-blue cover; the thick, whitish paper, whose smell I inhale as freshly at this moment as when it first pervaded my young nostrils—all are "present with me." And its contents! How palpable are their first impressions upon the mind! —from the pregnant moral inculcations in one syllable, onward to the reading-lessons in wider and taller words, which, in certain parts, sometimes bothered "us boys" not a little: yet not much, either, after encountering the spelling-lessons that preceded them, which enabled me generally to conquer the most formidable of them; especially after I had "gone up to the head" in spelling them in the longest class in the old log school-house. The moral and patriotic inculcations of those one-syllable lessons are familiar to tens of thousands of readers at this moment, who perhaps have not looked into the good old book for the last thirty years; and yet of which more than *one million* of copies have been sold every twelve months!—CLARK, LEWIS GAYLORD, 1870, *Noah Webster, Lippincott's Magazine, vol.* 5, *p.* 448.

The final success of the little book has been quite beyond definite computation, but a few figures will show something of the course it has run. In 1814, 1815, the sales averaged 286,000 copies a year; in 1828 the sales were estimated to be 350,000 copies. In 1847 the statement was made that about twenty-four million copies of the book had been published up to that time, and that the sale was then averaging a million of copies a year. It was also then said, that during the twenty years in which he was employed in compiling his "American Dictionary," the entire support of his family was derived from the profits of this work, at a premium for copyright of five mills a copy. The sales for eight years following the Civil War, namely 1866-1873, aggregated 8,196,028. —SCUDDER, HORACE E., 1881, *Noah Webster (American Men of Letters), p.* 70.

But what pleasant memories remain with those who long ago studied Webster's "Spelling-Book!" The very pages in their precise form are pictured for us on indelible tablets. It was a great triumph when the young student got to "baker," for it was the first step away from monosyllables. But it seemed like a long road to him before he would get to "immateriality" and "incomprehensibility." How or when he was to do it seemed incomprehensible enough then. Those who, in beginning to read, discovered that "She fed the old hen," "Ann can hem my cap," "Fire will burn wood and coal," "A tiger will kill and eat a man," and other similar facts, little thought that in all their after life nothing they might learn would ever seem so touching and significant. On this little book, by whose aid we have since read the historians, novelists, and poets, and been inducted into fields of various learning, there rests now a gleam and fascination that no poet or novelist can give, or ever gave. It seems like that light that never was on sea or land. It is the twilight halo tinting the first far boundary of youth; and restores now a little glimpse, almost, of a pre-existent world.—BENTON, JOEL, 1883, *The Webster Spelling-Book, Magazine of American History, vol.* 10, *p.* 306.

Webster's "Speller" (dating from 1783), which supplanted "The New England Primer," is almost literature by reason of its admirable fables.—BRONSON, WALTER C., 1900, *A Short History of American Literature, p.* 79, *note.*

AMERICAN DICTIONARY
1828–41

Called with Mr. Gibbs on the celebrated Noah Webster, and passed three-quarters of an hour in his study. He is now absorbed in the project of publishing his great "Dictionary,"— showed me his manuscript, and explained his plan. There can be no doubt of Mr. Webster's very profound researches into the origin and structure of the English language, and particularly in tracing the analogy of languages. He is an enthusiast, and so must any man be who will make progress in any pursuit. . . . For the learned I am fully convinced that Mr. Webster's "Dictionary" will have great value, although it may contain objectionable points and peculiarities, which a mind of another cast would not have admitted. The preface will be the most difficult part for him to execute. In all his publications he has manifested a singular want of judgment in estimating the comparative value of his own attainments, and in setting forth what he deems the most important discoveries which he has made. His friends in New Haven are aware of this foible, and they are resolved to counteract it in the present instance as far as the nature of the case will admit. . . . The author does not contemplate publishing it at present, perhaps never, as he says he was assured in Europe that such a work would not pay for the printing. I am glad to have seen Noah Webster, for I respect him for his great attainments, and for the noble, untiring zeal with which he has devoted a whole life to the investigation of an important though neglected subject. The example is worthy of all praise. Let those who condemn, first do as much, and do it better.—SPARKS, JARED, 1826, *Journal of a Southern Tour, June* 29; *Life and Writings, ed. Adams, vol.* I, *pp.* 500, 501, 502.

About thirty-five years ago, I began to

think of attempting the compilation of a Dictionary. I was induced to this undertaking, not more by the suggestion of friends, than by my own experience of the want of such a work while reading modern books of science. In this pursuit I found almost insuperable difficulties, from the want of a dictionary for explaining many new words which recent discoveries in the physical sciences had introduced into use. To remedy this defect in part, I published my "Compendious Dictionary" in 1806, and soon after made preparations for undertaking a larger work. . . . I had not pursued this course more than three or four years before I discovered that I had to unlearn a great deal that I had spent years in learning, and that it was necessary for me to go back to the first rudiments of a branch of erudition which I had before cultivated, as I had supposed, with success. I spent ten years in this comparison of radical words, and in forming a "Synopsis of the principal Words in twenty Languages, arranged in Classes under their primary Elements or Letters." The result has been to open what are to me new views of language, and to unfold what appear to be the genuine principles on which these languages are constructed. After completing this "Synopsis," I proceeded to correct what I had written of the "Dictionary," and to complete the remaining part of the work. But before I had finished it, I determined on a voyage to Europe, with the view of obtaining some books and some assistance which I wanted, of learning the real state of the pronunciation of our language in England, as well as the general state of philology in that country, and of attempting to bring about some agreement or coincidence of opinions in regard to unsettled points in pronunciation and grammatical construction. In some of these objects, I failed; in others, my designs were answered. . . . To that great and benevolent Being, who, during the preparation of this work, has sustained a feeble constitution amidst obstacles and toils, disappointments, infirmities and depression,—who has borne me and my manuscripts in safety across the Atlantic, and given me strength and resolution to bring the work to a close,—I would present the tribute of my most grateful acknowledgments. And if the talent which he intrusted to my care has not been put to most profitable use in his service, I hope that it has not been "kept laid up in a napkin," and that any misapplication of it may be graciously forgiven.—WEBSTER, NOAH, 1828, *American Dictionary of the English Language, Preface, pp.* xv, xvi.

I imagine that Webster's dictionary will never be current. The plan of citing *names,* instead of *passages,* is unsatisfactory and unfair.—ALEXANDER, JAMES W., 1829, *Letter, July* 15; *Forty Years' Familiar Letters, vol.* I, *p.* 132.

The appearance of this dictionary, considering the circumstances under which it was begun, the amount of time and labor bestowed upon its composition, and the value of the improvements actually made, is an event upon which we may well congratulate the public. The proper effect of the author's labors in the cause of the language of his country, will not fail, sooner or later, to be produced. It will be seen in the better understanding of authors, who will ever be the boast of the English tongue; it will be seen in the more correct use of words, in the check which will be put on useless innovations, in the cleared distinction generally marked between new words which are necessary, and those which are merely the offspring of caprice, and we will add, in the increased respect, we hope, with which the author will be viewed, for his talents, learning, and persevering industry. . . . Our criticisms on this work do not affect its substantial merits; these are manifest, and in despite of all attempts to conceal or decry them, they will be ultimately seen and acknowledged in their real number and value. . . . No new English dictionary will hereafter serve, either at home or abroad, for popular use, which does not contain many of the additions and corrections of this.—KINGSLEY, J. L., 1829, *Webster's Dictionary, North American Review, vol.* 28, *p.* 478.

One is ashamed to linger on cases so mild as those,—coming, as one does, in the order of atrocity, to Elphinston, to Noah Webster, a Yankee,—. . . Noah would naturally have reduced us all to an antediluvian simplicity. Shem, Ham and Japhet probably separated in consequence of perverse varieties in spelling,—so that orthographical unity might seem to him one condition for preventing national schisms.—DE QUINCEY, THOMAS, 1847-60, *Orthographic Mutineers, Works, ed. Masson, vol.* XI, *p.* 441.

He was regarded with suspicion, and frequently openly opposed: for his well known views as a reformer of the language laid him particularly open to attack; since speech being common property, every one was bound more or less to question his proceedings. Though the dictionary bearing Webster's name is now in very general use, it has secured this result by the number of its words, and particularly the extent of its scientific terms and the accuracy of their definitions, in spite of the peculiar Websterisms of orthography. His mistake, as the compiler of a dictionary, at the outset was, in seeking to amend the language, while his duty was simply to record the use of words by the best authors. In the attempt to impose new conditions, and with his American innovations, he placed himself beyond the recognition of the highest authorities of the language in the universities of England and the colleges of America.—DUYCKINCK, EVERT A. AND GEORGE L., 1855-65-75, *Cyclopædia of American Literature, ed. Simons.*

His "Dictionary" is rapidly approaching the position of highest authority, especially among men of purest taste and most comprehensive knowledge.—LOSSING, BENSON J., 1855-86, *Eminent Americans, p.* 225.

In the beauty, conciseness, and accuracy of its definitions, and in the department of etymology, it is superior to all other English dictionaries. The learning and ability with which he prosecuted the abstruse and difficult etymological investigations were generally acknowledged, both at home and abroad, and have laid the foundation of a wide-spread and enduring reputation.—CLEVELAND, CHARLES D., 1859, *A Compendium of American Literature, p.* 140.

He worked alone, and his solitariness was not wholly due to his idiosyncrasies. It was in part the penalty paid by a student of the time. The resolution and self-reliance of an American were his, and so was the individuality. That such enterprises are not now conducted single-handed is owing not to a lack of courage but to the greater complexity of life, the more constant sense of interdependence, the existence of greater solidarity in intellectual pursuits. Webster was unable to believe that a company of scholars could ever be formed who should carry forward a revision of the Bible, and therefore, he made the attempt himself. Individual criticism has been abundant ever since, but no one, however learned or popular, has ever been able to impress his work upon the community. The most carefully organized body of scholars submits the results of ten years' conference to the votes of the world. The history of Webster's Dictionary is parallel with the growth of national life out of individualism.—SCUDDER, HORACE E., 1881, *Noah Webster (American Men of Letters), p.* 293.

GENERAL

It may be said that the name of NOAH WEBSTER, from the wide circulation of some of his works, is known familiarly to a greater number of the inhabitants of the United States, than the name, probably of any other individual except the FATHER OF HIS COUNTRY. Whatever influence he thus acquired was used at all times to promote the best interests of his fellowmen. His books, though read by millions, have made no man worse. To multitudes they have been of lasting benefit, not only by the course of early training they have furnished, but by those precepts of wisdom and virtue with which almost every page is stored.—GOODRICH, CHAUNCEY A., 1847, *Memoir of Noah Webster.*

Henry Ware, Jr.

1794-1843

A Unitarian clergyman of Massachusetts, pastor of the Second Church in Boston, 1817-30, and Parkman professor at Harvard University, 1830-42. "The Vision of Liberty," an ode; "Hints on Extemporaneous Speaking;" "Discourses on the Offices and Character of Christ;" "Sermons on Small Sins;" "On the Formation of Christian Character," which has been very widely read; "Life of the Savior;" Lives of Priestley and Noah Worcester.—ADAMS, OSCAR FAY, 1897, *A Dictionary of American Authors, p.* 406.

PERSONAL

Mr. Ware's character is an excellent one, and I doubt not will abide severe scrutiny. He is so modest and unpretending, his talents so respectable and his application so steady, that he must command every one's respect.—SEDGWICK, CATHARINE M., 1823, *To Mrs. Pomeroy, Jan.* 10; *Life and Letters, ed. Dewey, p.* 158.

The most noticeable characteristic of his intellect seems to have been that general equality of the different faculties,—that just proportion and balance of power among them,—which constitutes the most useful and available mind. It was the intellect of this description, sanctified, as it were, by the moral elements of his character, which gave him his strong hold on the love and confidence of men. Perhaps the most important of these elements was a perfect and entire sympathy with, and love of, mankind, under all circumstances and conditions, with all degrees of cultivation, and with every variety of moral character. . . . He could not therefore be called, in the common sense of the words, a hard student or an accomplished scholar, though he studied a great deal and read a great many books, and read them, so far as his objects in life were concerned, to great advantage. . . . He was very happy, during all the earlier portion of his life, in the possession of a certain tranquility of spirit, which prevented him from being disturbed in his occupations by the little, common interruptions, which are so annoying to most students. —WARE, JOHN, 1846, *Memoir of the Life of Henry Ware, Jr., pp.* 462, 466.

It was my good fortune to be in the Theological School two or three years, while it most fully enjoyed his services. I loved him as I have seldom loved a man heretofore, and perhaps shall never love another. He was not always equal—some times was absent, and *seemed* cold. But he drew my heart after him by the very tones of his voice, by his look and his kind way of speaking to a young man. He never flattered. He told truth, and did not wound, even though it was a painful truth. I can't believe any student ever slighted any hint he gave. I treasured up his words as oracles—not Delphic, but Christian. His presence at our religious meetings was the presence of a saint; it was the fragrance of violets in a library; and we felt it. He tuned the most discordant strings. His lectures, I mean those delivered before the whole school, were not professedly religious; but they brought a man step by step to the throne of God, and before he knew it he knelt and prayed. His influence was wholly through his holiness. But that affected all he said and did. . . . Your brother began moderately, with no promise of a great soul-stirring sermon; but gradually he gained greatness of thought, and lovely images, and a sweetness and poetry of devotion and trust in God which charmed your heart away. And then his prayers! I have heard none such. I know nothing to compare them with, public or private, unless it be the music I have heard sometimes in a cathedral, when one little voice begins—like our own thrush in the mornings of May—and softly, gently sings out strains exquisitely tender; then comes another, different but accordant; and then another, and so on till every column, arch, altar-stone seems vibrating with the psalm. His arrow kindled as it rose, and disappeared a flame.—PARKER, THEODORE, 1846, *To John Ware, Jan.* 2; *Life and Correspondence, ed. Weiss, vol.* I, *p.* 262.

His, indeed, was the work of an invalid, yet performed with such practical widsom, such intensity of devotional feeling, such delicate sense of the capacities, needs, and sensibilities of individual students, and such intimacy of friendly relation with them, that they sustained no loss by infirmities which made his life a constant weariness, and brought it to its close in what would else have been its meridian. His appointment bears even date with my entering the Divinity School. . . . The senior and middle classes preached, each member in his turn, on Friday and Saturday evenings. Mr. Ware took our sermons home, and invited the preacher to breakfast on some specified morning shortly afterward. We had thus the privilege of participating in his family worship,—always both edifying and instructive,—and a half-hour with his lovely wife, whose rich endowments of mind were hardly transcended by her unsurpassed beauty of character, and her lifelong, in some instances grandly heroic, philanthrophy. From the table we went into the professor's study, where our sermons were literally taken to pieces and reconstructed.

THOMAS HOOD

THOMAS CAMPBELL

Engraving by J. F. E. Prudhomme. Portrait

. . . We had, also, a great deal of informal intercourse with Mr. Ware. He sometimes called on us at our rooms; we were always welcome, and often invited visitors at his house; and I know not how adequately to express my sense of the educational value of a three-years' intimacy with such a man, in preparation for the Christian ministry.—PEABODY, ANDREW P., 1888, *Harvard Reminiscences, pp.* 98, 99.

GENERAL

As a poet, he seems to have aimed only to prove, by a few masterly attempts, his possession of the "vision and the faculty divine."—GRISWOLD, RUFUS W., 1842, *The Poets and Poetry of America, p.* 122.

Had he done less, or wrought more carelessly, or with a less holy purpose, he would have been called a genius. . . . There are scattered through his works abundant indications that, had his avocations been more early and strictly scholastic, he might have been a subtle and cogent reasoner on metaphysical and moral subjects. Several of his lighter pieces evince the felicities of taste, thought, and style, which would have insured his success in any portion of that large and vague domain entitled general literature. Nor was even the comic vein wanting; for we have among the miscellanies before us two or three perfect gems of native wit and general humor, free from verbal conceit, and manifesting a prompt perception of incongruity and a rare faculty of grotesque combination. We suppose that Dr. Ware's sermons will do less for his reputation, in an intellectual point of view, than his other writings.—PEABODY, ANDREW P., 1847, *Ware's Works, Christian Examiner, vol.* 42, *p.* 409.

These varied compositions are all well sustained in their appropriate sphere. Dr. Ware thought and wrote with energy, tempered by the care and reserve of the scholar.— DUYCKINCK, EVERT A. AND GEORGE L., 1855-65-75, *Cyclopædia of American Literature, ed. Simons, vol.* I, *p.* 890.

Thomas Campbell

1777-1844

Born, in Glasgow, 27 July, 1777. Educated at Glasgow Grammar School, 1784-91; at Glasgow University, Oct. 1791 to Spring, 1796. As private tutor at Downie, 1796-97. Returned to Glasgow. Removed to Edinburgh to study Law. A few weeks later undertook literary work for Messrs. Mundell and Co., publishers. Also gave private tuition. First poems published, April 1799. To Germany, 1800; studied and wrote poems. Returned to London, April 1801. Married Matilda Sinclair, 10 Oct. 1803. Devoted himself to literary work, and lived in London for rest of life. Crown pension of £200 granted him, 1805. Lectured on poetry at Royal Institution, 1810. Visit to Paris, 1814. Royal Institution lectures repeated at Liverpool and Birmingham, 1819. In Germany and Austria, May to Nov. 1820. Edited "New Monthly Magazine," Nov. 1820 to 1830. Scheme of London University conceived, 1824. Visit to Berlin University, Sept. 1825. Lord Rector of Glasgow University, 1826-29. Wife died, 1828. Edited "Metropolitan Magazine," 1831-32. Founded Polish Association, 1832. Visit to Paris and Algiers, 1834. Returned to London, 1835. Settled in Victoria Square, Pimlico, with niece (Mary Campbell) as companion. Edited "The Scenic Annual" for 1838. To Boulogne for health, June 1843. Died there, 15 June 1844. Buried in Westminster Abbey. *Works*. "The Pleasures of Hope," 1799; "Annals of Great Britain" (anon.), 1807; "Gertrude of Wyoming," 1809; "Essay on English Poetry," 1819; "Specimens of the British Poets" (7 vols.), 1819; "Miscellaneous Poems," 1824; "Theodric," 1824 [?] (2nd edn., 1824); "Rectorial Address," 1827; "Poland" 1831 [?] (2nd edn., 1831); "Life of Mrs. Siddons" (2 vols.), 1834; "Letters from the South" (2 vols.), 1837; "Life of Petrarch" (2 vols.), 1841; "The Pilgrim of Glencoe," 1842; "History of Our Own Times" (anon.), 1843. *Posthumous:* "Life and Letters," ed. by W. Beattie, 1849. He *edited:* Byron's Works (with Moore, Scott, etc.), 1835; Shakespeare's Plays, 1838; "Frederick the Great; his Court and Times," 1842-43. *Collected Poems:* in 2 vols., 1810, 1815; in 2 vols., 1828; in 2 vols., 1833, 1837, 1839, 1851 (ed. by W. A. Hill, illustrated by Turner), etc.—SHARP, R. FARQUHARSON, 1897, *A Dictionary of English Authors, p.* 47.

PERSONAL

This morning I returned from a visit to our poet Campbell. He has fixed himself in a small house upon Sydenham Common, where he labours hard, and is perfectly happy with his wife and child. I have seldom seen so strong an argument, from experiment, in favour of matrimony, as the change it has operated on the general tone of his temper and manners. —HORNER, FRANCIS, 1805, *Memoirs and Correspondence, vol.* I, *p.* 323.

I told the little poet, after the proper softenings of wine, dinner, flattery, repeating his verses, etc., etc., that a friend of mine wished to lend him some money, and I begged him to take it. The poet said that he had a very sacred and serious notion of the duties of independence; that he thought he had no right to be burdensome to others from the mere apprehensions of evil, and that he was in no immediate want. If it was necessary, he would ask me hereafter for the money without scruple; and that the knowing he *had* such resources in reserve, was a great comfort to him. This was very sensible, and very honourable to him; nor had he the slightest feeling of affront on the subject, but, on the contrary, of great gratitude to his benefactor, whose name I did not mention, as the money was not received; I therefore cancel your draft, and will call upon you, if he calls upon me. This, I presume, meets your approbation. I had a great deal of conversation with him, and he is a much more sensible man than I had any idea of.—SMITH, SYDNEY, 1808, *To Lady Holland, Letters, ed. Mrs. Austin.*

Mr. Campbell asked me to come out and see him to-day, and make it a long day's visit. So, after the morning service, I drove out, and stayed with him until nearly nine this evening. He lives in a pleasant little box, at Sydenham, nine miles from town, a beautiful village, which looks more like an American village than any I have seen in England. His wife is a bonny little Scotchwoman, with a great deal of natural vivacity; and his only child, a boy of about ten, an intelligent little fellow, but somewhat injured by indulgence, I fear. . . . They seem very happy, and have made me so, for there was no one with them but myself, except an old schoolmate of Campbell's now a barrister of considerable eminence. . . . Campbell had the same good spirits and love of merriment as when I met him before,—the same desire to amuse everybody about him; but still I could see, as I partly saw then, that he labors under the burden of an extraordinary reputation, too easily acquired, and feels too constantly that it is necessary for him to make an exertion to satisfy expectation. The consequence is, that, though he is always amusing, he is not always quite natural.—TICKNOR, GEORGE, 1815, *Journal, June* 25; *Life, Letters and Journals, vol.* I, *p.* 65.

Do you happen to know Mr. Campbell? I dare say not. I do. Oh! he is such a pretty, little, delicate, lady-like, finical gentleman. He would look so well in a mob-cap, hemming a pocket-handkerchief; or in a crape turban, flirting a fan. He is such a doubter, such a hummer and hawer, such a critical Lord Eldon, so heavy and so slow. He was full fifteen years getting up that notable failure, the "Specimens," the whole of his part of which might have been put into an eighteen-penny pamphlet or two sides of the "Times" newspaper—fifteen years was he at that! Think of what will become of the Magazine, which, as Talfourd says, "is like a steamboat, and must come to the hour in spite of wind and tide." Then his reputation is just of that sort (high and tottering) which will make him afraid to praise for fear of setting up a rival, or to blame for fear of being thought envious.—MITFORD, MARY RUSSELL, 1820, *Letter to Sir William Elford, Dec.* 12; *Life, ed. L'Estrange.*

Now, the Minstrel of Gertrude—Compiler of Colburn—
Once the bard of high Scotland—now that of High Holborn;
Whose jinglings the Cockney-lambs lead like a ram-bell,
And, after the toast, strike up, "Ranting Tom Campbell."
—WILSON, JOHN, 1822, *Noctes Ambrosianæ, July.*

He is heartless as a little Edinburgh advocate. There is a smirk on his face which would befit a shopman or an auctioneer. His very eye has the cold vivacity of a conceited worldling. His talk is small, contemptuous and shallow. The blue frock and trousers, the eye-glass, the wig, the very fashion of his brow, proclaim the literary dandy. His wife has black eyes, a fair skin, a symmetrical but vulgar face; and she speaks with that accursed Celtic accent—a twang which I never yet heard associated with any manly or profitable thought or sentiment, which to me is but the symbol of Highland vanity and filth and famine. "Good heavens!" cried I, on coming out, "does literature lead to this? Shall I, too, by my utmost efforts realise nothing but a stupid Gaelic wife, with the pitiful gift of making verses, and affections cold as those of a tinker's cuddie, with nothing to love but my own paltry self and what belongs to it?" . . . Perhaps I am hasty about Campbell. Perhaps I am too severe. He was my earliest favorite. I hoped to have found him different.—CARLYLE, THOMAS, 1824, *Letter to Miss Welsh, Early Life by Froude, vol.* I, *p.* 178.

A little man, with a shrewd eye, and a sort of pedagoguish, *parboiled* voice; plenty to say for himself, especially about other people, and not restrained from saying whatever seemed good to him by any caution.—CHORLEY, HENRY FOTHERGILL, 1837, *Autobiography, Memoirs and Letters, vol.* II, *p.* 76.

Sterling says that Campbell is a man who more than any other has disappointed him in society,—sitting in a corner and saying nothing.—FOX, CAROLINE, 1840, *Journal, Feb.* 23; *Memories of Old Friends, ed. Pym, p.* 67.

He has, considering his advanced age, a full round face, with a dark complexion. His forehead does not appear to be so amply developed as it really is, owing to his brown wig overlapping the upper part of it.—GRANT, JAMES, 1841, *Portraits of Public Characters.*

Campbell resided at Sydenham eighteen years. His house was on Peak-hill, and had a quiet and sweet view towards Forest-hill. The house is one of two tenements under the same roof, consisting of only one room in width, which, London fashion, being divided by folding doors, formed, as was needed, two. The front looked out upon the prospect already mentioned. To the left was a fine mass of trees, amid which showed itself a large house, which, during part of the time, was occupied by Lady Charlotte Campbell. The back looked out upon a small neat garden, inclosed from the field by pales; and beyond it, on a mass of fine wood, at the foot of which ran a canal, and now along its bed, the atmospheric railway from London to Croydon. The house is, as appears, small, and very modest; but its situation is very pleasant indeed, standing on a green and quiet swell, at a distance from the wood, and catching pleasant glimpses of the houses in Sydenham, and of the country round. In the little back parlor he used to sit and write; and to prevent the passage of sound, he had the door which opened into the hall covered with green baize, which still remains.—HOWITT, WILLIAM, 1847, *Homes and Haunts of the Most Eminent British Poets, vol.* II, *p.* 242.

There is but one point connected with these Memoirs which I approach with reluctance. Every friend of the Poet will anticipate what I have to say—and none of his readers will expect me to say more that is due to the veracity of history: they will not pass over many excellent qualities to enlarge upon one failing—a failing common to him with too many great men—a habit which he condemned in others, but could not conquer in himself. But make allowance, kind reader, for the tempting circumstances under which the social cup was often presented to his lips —for the exhilaration which the weary, the sad, and the suffering are too ready to purchase at any price—and then the censure may be allowed to fall lightly.

Narratur et prisci Catonis
Sæpe mero caluisse virtus.

At my own family table, where he dined oftener, perhaps, during the last twelve or fourteen years of his life, than at any other, he was never "merry, even beyond the limits of becoming mirth."—BEATTIE, WILLIAM, 1848, *ed., Life and Letters of Thomas Campbell, vol.* II, *p.* 488.

They who knew Mr. Campbell only as the author of "Gertrude of Wyoming," and the "Pleasures of Hope," would not have suspected him to be a merry companion, overflowing with humor and anecdote, and any thing but fastidious. . . . He was one of the few men whom I could at any time have walked half a dozen miles through snow to spend an evening with; and I could no more do this with a penurious man than I could with a sulky one. I know but of one fault he had, beside an extreme cautiousness in his writings, and that one was national, a matter of words, and amply overpaid by a stream of conversation, lively, piquant, and liberal, not the less interesting for occasionally betraying an intimacy with pain, and for a high and somewhat strained tone of voice, like a man speaking with suspended breath, and in the habit of subduing his feelings. . . . When I first saw this eminent person, he gave me the idea of a French Virgil. Not that he was like a Frenchman, much less the French translator of Virgil. I found him as handsome, as the Abbé Delille is said to have been ugly. But he seemed to me to embody a Frenchman's ideal notion of the Latin poet; something a little more cut and dry than I had looked for; compact and elegant, critical and acute, with a consciousness of authorship upon him; a taste over-anxious not to commit itself and refining and diminishing nature as in a drawing-room mirror. This fancy was strengthened in the course of conversation, by his expatiating on the greatness of Racine. . . . His skull was sharply cut and fine; with plenty, according to the phrenologists, both of the reflective and amative organs: and his poetry will bear them out. . . . His face and person were rather on a small scale; his features regular; his eye lively and penetrating; and when he spoke, dimples played about his mouth; which, nevertheless had something restrained and close in it.—HUNT, LEIGH, 1850, *Autobiography, ch.* X.

Campbell's appearance was more in unison with his writings than is generally the case with authors. He was about thirty-seven years of age; of the middle size, lightly and genteelly made; evidently of a delicate, sensitive organization, with a fine intellectual countenance and a beaming poetic eye. He had now been about twelve years married. Mrs. Campbell still retained much of that personal beauty for which he praises her in his letters written in the early days of matrimony; and her mental qualities seemed equally to justify his eulogies: a rare circumstance, as none are more prone to dupe themselves in affairs of the heart than men of lively imaginations. She was, in fact, a more suitable wife for a poet than poet's wives are apt to be; and for once a son of song had married a reality and not a poetical fiction.—IRVING, WASHINGTON, 1850, *Life and Letters of Thomas Campbell, ed. Beattie, Introduction, vol.* I, *p.* xii.

He had never sufficient control over himself, never sufficient command of his intellectual condition and movements, to be sure he might not be tempted, at a moment's warning, to abandon the wide and populous solitude of his little study at Sydenham, or the sweet society of his own "Gertrude of Wyoming," . . . for the boisterous good-fellowship . . . of Tom Hill's after-dinner table, with its anomalous olla-podrida of "larking" stockbrokers, laughing punsters, roaring [?] farce-writers, and riotous practical jokers. . . . To sum up this speculation in a word, . . . *Tom* Campbell was a very good fellow, and a very pleasant one withal; but he prevented Thomas Campbell from being a great poet, though not from doing great things in poetry.—PATMORE, P. G., 1854, *My Friends and Acquaintance, vol.* I, *pp,* 146, 148.

In the spring of 1832 I introduced Campbell to Lady Blessington. The acquaintance commenced inauspiciously. There was a coolness in it from the beginning, which soon made it very evident to both parties there was no cordiality between them to be expected. The lady, who was disappointed with Byron at her first interview with him, was not very likely to be delighted with Campbell—a most *shivery* person in the presence of strangers—or to have her *beau ideal* of the poetic character and outward appearance of a bard realized by an elderly gentleman in a curly wig, with a blue coat and brass buttons, very like an ancient mariner out of uniform, and his native element, being on shore. Campbell, on the other hand, had a sort of instinctive apprehension of any person who was supposed to be an admirer of Byron, and he could not divest his mind of the idea that Lady Blessington did not duly appreciate his own merits. After dining at Seamore place twice, I believe, and freezing her ladyship with the chilliness of his humor, the acquaintance dropped, and left no pleasing recollections on the minds of either of the parties.—MADDEN, R. R., 1855, *The Literary Life and Correspondence of the Countess of Blessington, vol.* II, *p.* 274.

There was poor Campbell the poet, obtruding his sentimentalities, amidst a quivering apprehension of making himself ridiculous. He darted out of our house, and never came again, because, after warning, he sat down, in a room full of people (all authors, as it happened) on a low chair of my old aunt's which went very easily on castors, and which carried him back to the wall and rebounded, of course making everybody laugh. Off went poor Campbell in a huff; and, well as I had long known, never saw him again: and I was not very sorry, for his sentimentality was too soft, and his craving for praise too morbid to let him be an agreeable companion.—MARTINEAU, HARRIET, 1855-77, *Autobiography, ed. Chapman, vol.* I, *p.* 265.

His mode of life at Sydenham was almost uniformly that which he afterwards followed in London, when he made it a constant residence. He rose not very early, breakfasted, studied for an hour or two, dined at two or three o'clock, and then made a call or two. . . . He would return home to tea, and then retire early to his study, remaining there till a late hour; sometimes even till an early one. His life was strictly domestic; he gave a dinner-party now and then, and at some of them Thomas Moore, Rogers, and other literary friends from town were present. His table was plain, hospitable, and cheered by a hearty welcome.—REDDING, CYRUS, 1858, *Fifty Years' Recollections, Literary and Personal.*

I remember being told by a personage who was both a very popular writer and a very brilliant converser, that the poet Campbell reminded him of Goldsmith—his conversation was so inferior to his fame. I could not deny it; for I had often met Campbell in general society, and his talk had disappointed me. Three days afterwards, Campbell asked me to come up and sup with him *tête-à-tête.* I did so. I went at ten o'clock. I stayed till dawn; and all my recollections of the most sparkling talk I have ever heard in drawing-rooms, affords nothing to equal the riotous affluence of wit, of humour, of fancy, of genius, that the great lyrist poured forth in his wondrous monologue. Monologue it was; he had it all to himself.—LYTTON, EDWARD BULWER LORD, 1863-68, *Caxtoniana, Miscellaneous Prose Works, vol.* III, *p.* 114.

He spoke with a marked Scotch accent, which added a zest, allied to humor, to the amusing anecdotes and stories which he told so well. When in this facetious mood, there was a roguish twinkle in his eye; and you could hardy conceive the touching and impressive poet to be hid behind the mantling smile and genial chuckle.—JERDAN, WILLIAM, 1866, *Men I have Known.*

In ordinary society Campbell did not appear by any means to the same advantage as Jeffrey, though he possessed incomparably more genius and sensibility. The former made no attempt at display in conversation; but the occasional splendid expression, the frequent tear in the eye, bespoke the profound emotion which was felt.—ALISON, SIR ARCHIBALD, 1867? *Some Account of My Life and Writings, vol.* I, *p.* 33.

The remaining glories of Poet's Corner belong to our own time and to the future. It would seem as if, during the opening of this century, the place for once had lost its charm. Of that galaxy of poets which ushered in this epoch, Campbell alone has achieved there both grave and monument, on which is inscribed the lofty hope of immortality from his own poems.—STANLEY, ARTHUR PENRHYN, 1867-96, *Historical Memorials of Westminster Abbey, p.* 318.

Had a cold, Scotch manner, but that was merely the educated habit or manner of his country—cautious, canny. There was sap behind the bark. If the oppression of the Poles or any other flagrant enormity was brought before him, his energy quickly flamed up. And he was also very vivacious, not to say riotous, in his cups.—PROCTER, BRYAN WALLER (BARRY CORNWALL) 1874? *Recollections of Men of Letters.*

Campbell's career was deeply weighted in other ways. His only son, whose childhood had been beautiful beyond expression to the tender father, who felt, as young parents often do, his own child a revelation from heaven, was a life-long grief and disappointment to him, and spent most of his life in a lunatic asylum. His wife died early; and he was left to make up to himself, as far as he could, by a hundred gentle flirtations, chiefly with ladies under the age of ten, for the absence of a woman's society, and the bright faces of children. Some of his innocent adventures in this way are at once amusing and pathetic.—OLIPHANT, MARGARET O. W., 1882, *Literary History of England, XVIII-XIX Century, vol.* II, *p.* 166.

Campbell, when he did himself justice, is known to have been an interesting converser: he rarely left you without having made some observation that was singularly suggestive, and which haunted the memory. Let us remember that it was Campbell who said—

> To live in hearts we leave behind
> Is not to die.

But the graceless Hogan kenned nothing of this; he was only able to tell me that Campbell was a feeble little fellow, that he spoke with a broad Scottish accent, that he wore a wig. Poor Campbell! Poor Hogan! Hogan knew even less about Campbell than Crabbe appeared to Moore to have known about Burke.—LOCKER-LAMPSON, FREDERICK, 1895, *My Confidences*, p. 139.

Though Campbell was a poet, he was a great contrast to my beloved Southey. You could *see* that Southey was a poet, the very embodiment of poetry, while Campbell looked more like a lively and intelligent man who might never have written a line in his life. I think the difference was this: Southey wrote because he could not help it, Campbell because he liked to do it.—AGNEW, MARY COURTENAY, 1896, *Lions in the Twenties, Temple Bar, vol.* 107, *p.* 116.

PLEASURES OF HOPE
1799

I am not sure if Mr. Campbell's "Pleasures of Hope" be not the most poetical production of the age. From the moment of its appearance to the present moment, the reading of it has always filled me with equal admiration of its plan, its melody, and powers of execution. It is full of genius and of noble conceptions—expressed in numbers at once polished and perfect.—DIBDIN, THOMAS FROGNALL, 1824, *The Library Companion*, *p.* 737, *note.*

Is one of the few standard heroic poems in our language. Poetic taste has undergone many remarkable changes since it appeared, but its ardent numbers are constantly resorted to by those who love the fire of the muse as well as her more delicate tracery.—GRISWOLD, RUFUS W., 1844, *The Poets and Poetry of England in the Nineteenth Century*, *p.* 114.

The various and magnificent range of English poetry presents no example of early excellence to equal the "Pleasures of Hope." . . . The laborious polish in the verses of the "Pleasures of Hope" are among the best proofs to what an extent English is capable of being refined, and how far the capabilities of the language will go to attain in the eyes of true taste a classical and healthful longevity —but to make further comment upon the merit of that which has received the plaudit of the world for half a century would be superfluous and out of place, stamped as it is with the impress of permanent endurance.— REDDING, CYRUS, 1846, *Life and Reminiscences of Thomas Campbell, New Monthly Magazine, vol.* 77, *p.* 347.

It is almost impossible to speak of it in terms of exaggerated praise; and whether taking it in parts, or as a whole, I do not think I overrate its merits in preferring it to any didactic poem of equal length in the English language. No poet, at such an age, ever produced such an exquisite specimen of poetical mastery—that is, of fine conception and of high art combined. . . . Sentiments tender, energetic, impassioned, eloquent, and majestic, are conveyed to the reader in the tones of a music forever varied—sinking or swelling like the harmonies of an Æolian lyre—yet ever delightful; and these are illustrated by pictures from romance, history, or domestic life, replete with power and beauty. . . . It is like a long fit of inspiration —a checqered melody of transcendent excellence; passage after passage presenting only an ever-varying and varied tissue of whatever is beautiful and sublime in the soul of men and the aspects of nature.— MOIR, D. M., 1851–52, *Sketches of the Poetical Literature of the Past Half-Century.*

Of the nature of a prize poem, though a brilliant one.—ARNOLD, THOMAS, 1868–75, *Chaucer to Wordsworth, p.* 413.

It is true that marks of juvenility are everywhere apparent; that the diction is often redundant, and sense not always commensurate with sound. Still it is a poem of sustained rhythmical march of sentiments expressive of every note in the gamut of feeling; and of episodes, whether from history, fiction or domestic life, full of beauty, force, pathos and natural truth. . . . Perhaps there is no didactic poem in our language so well known and loved as this, if not as a whole, by its component parts. There is hardly a doubt that it will continue to be so, in spite of new schools of poetry, and poetical criticism; and that it will retain its place, as a classic, in our literature, nobly closing that bright era of which Dryden and Pope heralded the morn, and which closed when the star of Wordsworth's genius appeared above the political horizon, to announce a new day-spring of poetry and beauty.—BATES, WILLIAM, 1874–98, *The Maclise Portrait Gallery of Illustrious Literary Characters*, p. 5.

Campbell's fame is secure in quotation. Many of his lines have become household words.—WELSH, ALFRED H., 1883, *Development of English Literature and Language*, vol. II, p. 274.

In the last year of the last century appeared Campbell's "Pleasures of Hope." The "Pleasures of Memory," published about seven years previously, had already passed through ten editions, and from Rogers the young Scottish poet seems to have caught his inspiration. It made him famous at once; yet it is difficult to say what attraction readers found in a poem full of inaccuracies and platitudes, and in which, as Hazlitt wittily says, "the decomposition of prose is substituted for the composition of poetry." Campbell's youthful success, however, affords a striking illustration of the obvious fact that in "the realms of gold" immediate popularity is no proof of sterling worth. . . . Yet the fact remains that Campbell's extraordinary reputation at the outset of his career was due to a poem that is comparatively worthless.—DENNIS, JOHN, 1887, *Robert Southey, Introduction*, pp. 12, 13.

There are flaws in Campbell's works as there were faults in his life, yet his name is associated with the finest lyrics in the English language, and no higher honour can be coveted by the most ambitious. The rather too rhetorical "Pleasures of Hope" survive, and will endure in single lines only; still it is no mean achievement or slight glory to have added even a few lines to the household speech of a people. —RAE, W. FRASER, 1890, *The Bard of Hope, Temple Bar*, vol. 90, p. 52.

Its success was so sudden that he was astonished, and so great that he was bewildered; for from that day forward he was, as his friend Scott remarked, afraid of the shadow that his own fame cast before him. Young persons of immature taste and abundant leisure may still recall the glittering and turgid lines of this overrated production; but no lover of its writer cares for it now.—STODDARD, RICHARD HENRY, 1891, *A Box of Autographs, Scribner's Magazine*, vol. 9, p. 223.

In "The Pleasures of Hope" these romantic enthusiasms were poured with much skill into the classical mould of Popian verse, suffusing without breaking its delicate contours. The literary public was captivated by a succession of impressive images, conveyed in lines of arrowy swiftness and strength.—HERFORD, C. H., 1897, *The Age of Wordsworth*, p. 198.

Much of the success of the poem was no doubt due to the circumstance that it touched with such sympathy on the burning questions of the hour. If, as Stevenson remarks, the poet is to speak efficaciously, he must say what is already in his hearer's mind. This Campbell did, as perhaps no English poet had done before. The French Revolution, the partition of Poland, the abolition of negro-slavery—these had set the passion for freedom burning in many breasts, and "The Pleasures of Hope" gave at once vigorous and feeling expression to the doctrine of the universal brotherhood of man. . . . It is not easy at this time of day to approach "The Pleasures of Hope" without a want of sympathy, if not an absolute prejudice, resulting from a whole century of poetical development.—HADDEN, J. CUTHBERT, 1899, *Thomas Campbell (Famous Scots Series)*, p. 44.

GERTRUDE OF WYOMING
1809

We rejoice to see once more a polished and pathetic poem in the old style of English pathos and poetry. This is of the pitch of the "Castle of Indolence," and the finer parts of Spenser; with more feeling, in many places, than the first, and more condensation and diligent finishing than the latter. If the true tone of nature be not everywhere maintained, it gives place, at least, to art only, and not to affectation—and, least of all, to affectation of singularity or rudeness. . . . There are but two noble sorts of poetry—the pathetic, and the sublime; and we think he has given very extraordinary proofs of his talents for both.—JEFFREY, FRANCIS LORD, 1809, *Campbell's Gertrude of Wyoming, Edinburgh Review*, vol. 14, pp. 1, 19.

I am very glad that Jeffrey thinks so favourably of Campbell's new poem, for *his* good opinion is very essential to the poet's prosperity. Nobody will deny that it abounds in touches of a true genius; but the obscurity and embarrassment in the narrative, and the many *boutsrimés* which we may charge upon the impatience of his subscribers, prevent me from reading the work yet with that uninterrupted pleasure which poetry must give, or it fails.—HORNER, FRANCIS, 1809, *Memoirs and Correspondence, vol.* I, *p.* 489.

The secret of Tom Campbell's defense of *inaccuracy* in costume and description is, that his "Gertrude," etc., has no more locality in common with Pennsylvania than with Penmanmaur. It is notoriously full of grossly false scenery, as all Americans declare, though they praise parts of the poem. It is thus that self-love forever creeps out, like a snake, to sting anything which happens, even accidentally, to stumble upon it —BYRON, LORD, 1821, *Journal, Jan.* 11.

We conceive that Mr. Campbell excels chiefly in sentiment and imagery. The story moves slow, and is mechanically conducted, and rather resembles a Scotch canal carried over lengthened aqueducts and with a number of *locks* in it, than one of those rivers that sweep in their majestic course, broad and full, over Transatlantic plains and lose themselves in rolling gulfs, or thunder down lofty precipices. But in the center, the inmost recesses of our poet's heart, the pearly dew of sensibility is distilled and collects, like the diamond in the mine, and the structure of his fame rests on the crystal columns of a polished imagination. We prefer the "Gertrude" to the "Pleasures of Hope," because with perhaps less brilliancy, there is more of tenderness and natural imagery in the former.—HAZLITT, WILLIAM, 1825, *The Spirit of the Age, p.* 236.

The greatest effort of Campbell's genius, however, was his "Gertrude of Wyoming," nor is it ever likely to be excelled in its own peculiar style of excellence. It is superior to "The Pleasures of Hope" in the only one thing in which that poem could be surpassed—purity of diction; while in pathos, and in imaginative power, it is no whit inferior.—MOIR, D. M., 1851–52, *Sketches of the Poetical Literature of the Past Half-Century.*

The construction of the entire poem is loose and incoherent. Even the love scenes, which, as Hazlitt says, breathe a balmy voluptuousness of sentiment, are generally broken off in the middle. Then he was unwise in adopting the Spenserian stanza. It was quite alien to his style; even Thomson, living long before the romantic revival, managed it more sympathetically than Campbell. The necessities of the rhyme led Campbell to invert his sentences unduly, to tag his lines for the mere sake of the rhyme, and to use affected archaisms with a quite extraordinary clumsiness. Anything more unlike the sweet, easy, graceful compactness of Spenser could scarcely be imagined. Nor are the characters of the poem altogether successful; indeed, with the single exception of the Indian, they are mere shadows. Gertrude herself makes a pretty portrait; but as Hazlitt has remarked, she cannot for a moment compare with Wordsworth's Ruth, the true infant of the woods and child-nature.— HADDEN, J. CUTHBERT, 1899, *Thomas Campbell (Famous Scots Series), p.* 96.

SPECIMENS OF THE BRITISH POETS
1819

It is the singular goodness of his criticisms that makes us regret their fewness; for nothing, we think, can be more fair, judicious and discriminating, and at the same time more fine, delicate and original, than the greater part of the discussions with which he has here presented us. It is very rare to find so much sensibility to the beauties of poetry, united with so much toleration for its faults; and so exact a perception of the merits of every particular style, interfering so little with a just estimate of all.—JEFFREY, FRANCIS LORD, 1819–44, *Contributions to the Edinburgh Review, vol.* II, *p.* 250.

Read the Poets—English, that is to say —out of Campbell's edition. There is a good deal of taffeta in some of Tom's prefatory phrases, but his work is good as a whole. I like him best, though, in his own poetry. — BYRON, LORD, 1821, *Journal, Jan.* 12.

There are also several incidental critical opinions in Campbell's "Specimens" very elegantly expressed, and of a pure as well as highly cultivated taste; but there are others very careless; and some, I think, not a little prejudiced.—BRYDGES, SIR

SAMUEL EGERTON, 1824, *Recollections of Foreign Travel, July* 23, *vol.* I, *p.* 258.

A mere piece of task-work for the Booksellers and a thing of scissors and paste, save the fine Introduction and a half-a-dozen of the little Memoirs.—GROSART, ALEXANDER B., 1869, *ed., Poems of Phineas Fletcher, Essay, vol.* I. *p.* ccxxvi.

The essays on poetry which precedes the "Specimens" is a notable contribution to criticism, and the lives are succinct, pithy, and fairly accurate, though such a writer is inevitably weak in minor details. He is especially hard on Euphuism, and it is curious that one of his most severe thrusts is made at Vaughan, to whom he probably owes the charming vision of "the world's grey fathers" in his own "Rainbow." The most valuable portions of the essay are those on Milton and Pope, which, together with such concise and lucid writing as the critical sections of the lives of Goldsmith and Cowper, show that Campbell was master of controversial and expository prose. Despite Miss Mitford's merry-making, in one of her letters, over the length of time spent in preparing the "Specimens," students cannot but be grateful for them as they stand. The illustrative extracts are not always fortunate, but this is due to the editor's desire for freshness rather than to any lack of taste or judgment.—BAYNE, THOMAS, 1886, *Dictionary of National Biography, vol.* VIII, *p.* 395.

THEODRIC

1824

It is distinguished accordingly by a fine and tender finish, both of thought and of diction—by a chastened elegance of words and images—a mild dignity and tempered pathos in the sentiments, and a general tone of simplicity and directness in the conduct of the story, which, joined to its great brevity, tends at first perhaps to disguise both the richness and the force of the genius required for its production. But though not calculated to strike at once on the dull palled ear of an idle and occupied world, it is of all others perhaps the kind of poetry best fitted to win on our softer hours, and to sink deep into vacant bosoms—unlocking all the sources of fond recollection, and leading us gently on through the mazes of deep and engrossing meditation—and thus ministering to a deeper enchantment and more lasting delight than can ever be inspired by the more importune strains of more ambitious authors.—JEFFREY, FRANCIS LORD, 1825–44, *Contributions to the Edinburgh Review, vol.* II, *p.* 447.

Campbell wrote one other long story, "Theodric" by name, which he calls "domestic," and in which he resumes the old heroic couplet (why called "heroic" it is hard to understand), stumping along as if with two wooden legs. It is a commonplace tragedy of real life prosaically related, into which a plainness of speech not usually met with in poetry is occasionally introduced, with a view no doubt to give the effect of reality and truth. Such language might have fulfilled its purpose had the story been written in prose; but being in verse of a stiff and pompous form, the effect is that of incongruity combining two affectations, an affectation of poetic elevation with an affectation of simplicity. In short, the poem is altogether unworthy of its author.—TAYLOR, SIR HENRY, 1880, *The English Poets, ed. Ward, vol.* IV, *p.* 231.

GENERAL

To the famed throng now paid the tribute due,
Neglected genius! let me turn to you.
Come forth, O Campbell! give thy talents scope;
Who dares aspire if thou must cease to hope?

—BYRON, LORD, 1809, *English Bards and Scotch Reviewers.*

Campbell, for Hope and fine war-songs renown'd,
With a wail underneath them of tenderer sound.

—HUNT, LEIGH, 1811, *The Feast of the Poets.*

Have you seen Campbell's poem of "O'Connor's Child?" it is beautiful. In many parts I think it is superior to Scott. —EDGEWORTH, MARIA, 1811, *To Miss Ruxton, April, Letters; vol.* I, *p.* 177.

If the rank of poets were to be settled by particular passages, I should place Campbell above Scott; I should predict, with more confidence, that "Lochiel," the "Exile of Erin," and the "Mariner's Song" would endure, than I could venture to do about any other verses since Cowper and Burns—I had almost said, since Gray and Goldsmith. I am sorry to hear that he is engaged on an epic poem;—his genius is lyrical.—MACKINTOSH, SIR JAMES, 1811,

Journal, Jan. 20; *Memoirs of Mackintosh, ed. his Son, vol.* II, *p.* 82.

The exquisite harmony of his versification is elaborated, perhaps, from the "Castle of Indolence" of Thomson, and the serious pieces of Goldsmith;—and it seems to be his misfortune, not to be able to reconcile himself to any thing which he cannot reduce within the limits of this elaborate harmony. This extreme fastidiousness, and the limitation of his efforts to themes of unbroken tenderness or sublimity, distinguish him from the careless, prolific, and miscellaneous authors of our primitive poetry;—while the enchanting softness of his pathetic passages, and the power and originality of his more sublime conceptions, place him at a still greater distance from the wits, as they truly called themselves, of Charles II. and Queen Anne.—JEFFREY, FRANCIS LORD, 1811–44, *Contributions to the Edinburgh Review, vol.* II, *p.* 295.

Byron's and Scott's "Poems" (I have read) and must admire,—though you recollect, *we* used to give Campbell a decided preference, and I still think, with justice. —CARLYLE, THOMAS, 1814, *To Robert Mitchell, Oct.* 18; *Early Letters, ed. Norton, p.* 90.

Mr. Campbell always seems to me to be thinking how his poetry will look when it comes to be hot-pressed on superfine wove paper, to have a disproportionate eye to points and commas, and dread of errors of the press. He is so afraid of doing wrong, of making the smallest mistake, that he does little or nothing. Lest he should wander irretrievably from the right path, he stands still. He writes according to established etiquette. He offers the Muses no violence. If he lights upon a good thought he immediately drops it for fear of spoiling a good thing. When he launches a sentiment that you think will float him triumphantly for once to the bottom of the stanza, he stops short at the end of the first or second line, and stands shivering on the brink of beauty, afraid to trust himself to the fathomless abyss. *Tutus nimium, timidusque procellarum.* His very circumspection betrays him. The poet, as well as the woman, that deliberates, is undone. He is much like a man whose heart fails him just as he is going up in a balloon, and who breaks his neck by flinging himself out of it when it is too late.—HAZLITT, WILLIAM, 1818, *Lectures on the English Poets, Lecture* viii.

I understand that Mr. Thomas Campbell has in some newspaper in a paltry refutation of some paltry charge of plagiarism regarding his paltry poem in the paltry Edinburgh touched the egg of my last man—the gentleman is completely addled.—BEDDOES, THOMAS LOVELL, 1825, *To Thomas Forbes Kelsall, Letters, p.* 55.

I wonder often how Tom Campbell, with so much real genius, has not maintained a greater figure in the public eye than he has done of late. The Magazine seems to have paralyzed him. The author, not only of the "Pleasures of Hope," but of "Hohenlinden," "Lochiel," &c., should have been at the very top of the tree. Somehow he wants audacity, fears the public, and what is worse, fears the shadow of his own reputation. He is a great corrector too, which succeeds as ill in composition as in education. Many a clever boy is flogged into a dunce, and many an original composition corrected into mediocrity. Tom ought to have done a great deal more: his youthful promise was great.—SCOTT, SIR WALTER, 1826, *Journal, June* 29; *Life by Lockhart, ch.* lxxi.

Campbell, whom Freedom's deathless Hope
endears.

—ELLIOTT, EBENEZER, 1829, *The Village Patriarch, Book* iv.

What the devil did you mean by classing Campbell and one Pollok together in your toast at the St. Andrew's dinner? Your wine must have been detestable. No sensible man like yourself could have made such a remark under the influence of champagne or Scottish whiskey. Campbell and Pollok. Hyperion to a satyr! Pray can you repeat without a book six lines of the "Course of Time?" If so, you have a very good memory badly employed. Can you not repeat without book every line which Tom Campbell has published? If not, you have never been as happy a man as you ought to have been.—HALLECK, FITZ-GREENE, 1831, *Letter to James Lawson, Life and Letters, ed. Wilson, p.* 349.

I should not omit this opportunity to mention that the Greenock paper was established by a Mr. John Davidson, a connexion with whom was afterwards formed by Mr. Thomas Campbell, the poet, in his marriage. Mr. Davidson was a very worthy illess bodie, and he has in my opinion the merit of first shewing with how little intellectual ability a newspaper may be conducted. I say not this in malice, but in sober sadness; for when Campbell wrote his "Battle of Hohenlinden," I got an early copy, which I sent to Mr. Davidson to be inserted, but he with a sage face afterwards told me, that it was not worthy of a place in his paper.—GALT, JOHN, 1833, *Autobiography, vol.* I, *p.* 52.

The conversation here turned upon Campbell's poem of "Gertrude of Wyoming," as illustrative of the poetic materials furnished by American scenery. . . . He (Scott) cited several passages of it with great delight. "What pity it is," said he, "that Campbell does not write more, and oftener, and give full sweep to his genius." He has wings that would bear him to the skies; and he does, now and then, spread them grandly, but folds them up again, and resumes his perch, as if he was afraid to launch away. . . . "What a grand idea is that," said he, "about prophetic boding, or, in common parlance, second sight—

'Coming events cast their shadows before.'

. . . .

The fact is," added he, "Campbell is, in a manner, a bugbear to himself. The brightness of his early success is a detriment to all his further efforts. *He is afraid of the shadow that his own fame casts before him.*"—IRVING, WASHINGTON, 1835, *Abbottsford.*

Dinner at Rogers's. Almost over when I arrived. Company: Wordsworth, Landseer, Taylor, and Miss R. A good deal of talk about Campbell's poetry, which they were all much disposed to carp at and depreciate, more particularly Wordsworth. I remarked that Campbell's lesser poems, his sea odes, &c., bid far more fair, I thought, for immortality than almost any of the lyrics of the present day; on which they all began to pick holes in some of the most beautiful of these things.—MOORE, THOMAS, 1837, *Diary, Aug.* 10; *Memoirs, Journal and Correspondence, vol.* VII, *p.* 197.

Do not start if I tell you that in my poor opinion Campbell is a much better poet than Petrarch. I do not say a better; I say a *much* better.—LANDOR, WALTER SAVAGE, 1842, *Some Letters of Walter Savage Landor, The Century, vol.* 35, *p.* 520.

What lauding sepulchre does Campbell want?
'Tis his to give, and not derive renown.
What monumental bronze or adamant,
Like his own deathless lays can hand him down?
—SMITH, HORACE, 1844, *Campbell's Funeral.*

In yon Minster's hallow'd corner, where the bards and sages rest,
Is a silent chamber waiting to receive another guest. . . .
Tears along mine eyes are rushing, but the proudest tears they be,
Which in manly eyes may gather,—tears 'twere never shame to see;
Tears that water lofty purpose; tears of welcome to the fame
Of the bard that hath ennobled Scotland's dear and noble name.
—MARTIN, SIR THEODORE, 1844, *The Interment of Thomas Campbell.*

Campbell's poetry has little need of critical illustration. His chief merit is rhetorical. There is not vagueness of mysticism in his verse. The scenes and feelings he delineates are common to human beings in general, and the impressive style with which these are unfolded, owes its charm to vigor of language and forcible clearness of epithet. Many of his lines ring with a harmonious energy, and seem the offspring of the noblest enthusiasm. This is especially true of his martial lyrics, which in their way are unsurpassed.—GRISWOLD, RUFUS W., 1844, *The Poets and Poetry of England in the Nineteenth Century, p.* 114.

Campbell possessed a noble nature, but its impulses were checked by an incurable laziness. He "dawdled" too much over his long compositions. The curse of his life was a pension of two hundred pounds. The capacity of the man is best displayed in those burning lyrics, which were called forth by the events of his time. When his soul was roused to its utmost, it ever manifested great qualities. His poems, generally, will probably live. . . . Had Campbell written "Childe Harold," it would have cost him ten years more labor than it did the author, and would not have been half as long.—WHIPPLE, EDWIN P., 1845, *English Poets of the Nineteenth Century, American Review, July; Essays and Reviews.*

I looked at the life of Campbell by a foolish Dr. Beattie; a glorious specimen of the book-making of this age. Campbell may have written in all his life three hundred good lines, rather less than more. His letters, his conversation, were mere trash. A life such as Johnson has written of Shenstone, or Akenside, would have been quite long enough for the subject; but here are three mortal volumes. —MACAULAY, THOMAS BABINGTON, 1848, *Journal, Dec.* 12; *Life and Letters, ed. Trevelyan, vol.* II, *p.* 161.

No poet of the nineteenth century has, in my estimation, a higher rank than Thomas Campbell; no one is more universally admired, and no one will be longer remembered. His exquisite harmony of versification, his occasional sublimity, his enthusiasm, his pathetic tenderness, his richness of natural description, together with his elevation and purity of moral sentiment, all combine to make him a classic secure of his immortality—standing upon the same shelf with Goldsmith, Thomson and Gray.—CLEVELAND, CHARLES D., 1853, *English Literature of the Nineteenth Century, p.* 426.

We know of few specimens of English verse comparable to the best of Campbell's for effective rhythm.—TUCKERMAN, HENRY T., 1857, *Essays, Biographical and Critical, p.* 451.

His mind, deficient in manly vigor of thought, had worked itself out in the few first bursts of youthful emotion, but no one has clothed with more of romantic sweetness the feelings and fancies which people the fairy-land of early dreams, or thrown around the enchanted region a purer atmosphere of moral contemplation.—BOTTA, ANNE C. LYNCH, 1860, *Hand-Book of Universal Literature, p.* 512.

With all his classic taste and careful finish, Campbell's writing, especially in his earlier poetry, is rarely altogether free for any considerable number of lines from something hollow and false in expression, into which he was seduced by the conventional habits of the preceding bad school of verse-making in which he had been partly trained, and from which he emerged, or by the gratification of his ear lulling his other faculties asleep for the moment. —CRAIK, GEORGE L., 1861, *A Compendious History of English Literature and of the English Language, vol.* II, *p.* 511.

Campbell was a great artist, but on reading his lyrics we are struck with the fact that they are in a large measure the product of a skilled mind rather than of a real singer.—SMITH, GEORGE BARNETT, 1875, *Elizabeth Barrett Browning, Poets and Novelists, p.* 82.

Campbell described the fall of freedom in some of the most beautiful lines which were ever composed; and the vigour of his descriptions breathed new life into the cause of the popular party, both in England and Europe.—WALPOLE, SPENCER, 1878, *A History of England from the Conclusion of the Great War in* 1815, *vol.* I, *p.* 349.

A mild and moonlike lustre surrounds the name of Campbell. He is like one of those holy personages whom the painter, in the later ages of Italian or Christian art, represents with a faint lumour round the head, in the company of Saints of a more illustrious order who have a full-circleted glory, while the Madonna or other protagonist is endowed with a cruciform nimbus on a complete scale. The question arises in the artist's and the spectator's mind whether it were wiser to define this holy personage by that lowest symptom of sainthood, or rather to merge him in the mass of men to whom no occiptal glimmer appertains. Even to himself, could he answer the question articulately, might it not be more congenial to remain undistinguished than thus to be distinguished by the minimum of outward beatitude? The painter is in half a mind to rub out the lumour round his head: but at last he determines the question on grounds of strict and accurate right. This personage is entitled to his lumour: Simeon, Joachim, Zacharias, or what not, he has a right to the distinctive sign, and must not be despoiled of it. And so with Campbell. Any reader who should deny him the name of poet, and the aureole of poesy, would do an injustice; but one may heedfully discriminate as to which of his various compositions have rightly earned him this eminence, and may demur to rating the eminence, in any instance, higher than its demonstrable value.—ROSSETTI, WILLIAM MICHAEL, 1878, *Lives of Famous Poets, p.* 257.

The English language has nothing finer or more inspiriting in their kind than the patriotic ballads which were perfected at this period. . . . It is one of the mysteries of genius which is least comprehensible, how a youth of the most peaceable sort, trained upon letters, and sea-sick and wretched when fate compelled him to cross the Channel, should have been the person to add to our national literature those boldest and most gallant of sailor-lyrics.—OLIPHANT, MARGARET O. W., 1882, *Literary History of England, XVIII-XIX Century, vol.* II, *p.* 163.

There are poems by Campbell which can be forgotten only with the language in which they are written. There is that weird "Lochiel! Lochiel! beware of thy day!" which no school-book of our time ought to omit, and no collection should be without. It will never be an easy task to banish "Gertrude of Wyoming" from the poetry of love and passion; or those noble lyrics, "The Battle of the Baltic," and "Ye Mariners of England," from the patriot-poetry of the world. One of the most touching pieces in any language is that pathetic story in verse about a parrot, which, by the force of genius, is lifted into an atmosphere of the rarest beauty.—FIELDS, JAMES T., 1885, *Thomas Campbell, Some Noted Princes, Authors and Statesmen of Our Time, ed. Parton, p.* 162.

He was the Tyrtæus of England's song, the laureate of her naval victories, unsurpassed and unsurpassable.—STODDARD, RICHARD HENRY, 1891, *A Box of Autographs, Scribner's Magazine, vol.* 9, *p.* 223.

It is by his shorter pieces that Campbell will retain his hold upon posterity. It is difficult to imagine a time in which human hearts will not thrill with patriotic ardour at the recital of "Hohenlinden," "Ye Mariners of England," and the "Battle of the Baltic" or throb with sympathy at the recital of "The Soldier's Dream," and the story of "Lord Ullin's Daughter." There are a lofty tone and rhythmic movement in these ballads which one would think could never fail to please. "The Last Man" is one of the grander of these shorter pieces, and well-nigh rises to the level of its sublime theme. "O'Connor's Child" is a more sustained effort, full of passion, pathos, and poetic fervour. Campbell was at his best when his heart was stirred by patriotic emotion or sympathy for the suffering and the oppressed. Had he written no more than this small group of poems, with "O'Connor's Child" for his longest effort, he would have written himself deep in human hearts, and therefore high in human estimation.—MILES, ALFRED H., 1892, *The Poets and the Poetry of the Century, Southey to Shelley, p.* 154.

In Campbell's work, which is known to every school-boy and school-girl in lines and extracts, but which nobody reads now as a whole except under some other compulsion than the fascination of the poetry, there were no signs of a disposition to break with the past either in form or in choice of subject. . . . Like Gray, Campbell lacked the courage of his imagination. The incubus of literary tradition lay heavy on him. He had a distrustful critic within, the creation of scholastic training, which clung to the skirts of his imagination and impeded its freedom of movement whenever it tried to burst away from the beaten track. His diffidence about "Hohenlinden" is sometimes quoted as an example of the saw that "genius is unconscious of its own excellence." But against this must be set the fact that late in life Campbell considered the "O'Connor's Child" was his best poem, and that in this he has the support of most people who are familiar with his poetry. It is unlike his popular lyrics, in the fact that it takes more than one reading to appreciate, but it is worth the trouble of reading more than once. Some think that if "Gertrude of Wyoming" had been published before the "Pleasures of Hope" it might have ranked as his chief work, but the subject is too remote to have achieved any great amount of popularity.—MINTO, WILLIAM, 1894, *The Literature of the Georgian Era, ed. Knight, pp.* 217, 223.

The three splendid war-songs . . . the equals, if not the superiors, of anything of the kind in English, and therefore in any language—set him in a position from which he is never likely to be ousted. In a handful of others—"Lochiel," the exquisite lines on "A Deserted Garden in Argyleshire," with, for some flashes at least the rather over-famed "Exile of Erin," "Lord Ullin's Daughter," and a few more—he also displays very high, though rather unequal and by no means unalloyed, poetical faculty; and "The Last Man," which, by the way, is the latest of his good things, is not the least. But his best work will go into a very small compass: a single octavo sheet would very nearly hold it, and it was almost all written before he was thirty. . . . It is to be noted that even in Campbell's greatest things there are distinct blemishes, and that these blemishes are greatest in that which in his best parts reaches the highest level—"The Battle of the Baltic." Many third and some tenth rate poets would never have left in their work such things as "The might of England flushed *To anticipate the scene,*" which is half fustian and half nonsense: no very great poet could possibly have been guilty of it. Yet for all this Campbell holds, as has been said, the place of best singer of war in a race and language which are those of the best singers and not the worst fighters in the history of the world—in the race of Nelson and the language of Shakespeare. Not easily shall a man win higher praise than this.—SAINTSBURY, GEORGE, 1896, *A History of Nineteenth Century Literature, pp.* 93, 94.

He was a born actor—in need (for his best work) of the foot-lights, the on-lookers, the trombone, the bass-drum. He never glided into victories of the pen by natural inevitable movement of brain or heart; he stopped always and everywhere to consider his *pose.*—MITCHELL, DONALD G., 1897, *English Lands Letters and Kings, The Later Georges to Victoria, p.* 57.

What Campbell felt and expressed with singular power was the terrible sublimity of Battle. His battle-pictures have touches of Hebraic imagination, the "hurricane eclipse of the sun," or "Her march is o'er the mountain-waves, her home is on the deep." But Campbell's sublimity hovers near the verge of the melodramatic, and one of these otherwise magnificent songs is marred by false notes like that which tells how the "might of England flush'd to anticipate the scene," or how a kindly mermaid "condoles" with the mourners for the dead. Nor does he quite escape the naivetés incident to agressive patriotism; as when the victors, after hailing their foes as "men and brothers," proceed to demand that they shall surrender fleet and crews "and make submission meet to our King." Little of Campbell but these songs now survives.—HERFORD, C. H., 1897, *The Age of Wordsworth, p.* 199.

He had a remarkable gift for lucid, rapid, and yet truly poetical narrative; his naval odes or descants, the "Battle of the Baltic" and "Ye Mariners of England," are without rivals in their own class, and Campbell deserves recognition as a true romanticist and revolutionary force in poetry, although fighting for his own hand, and never under the flag of Wordsworth and Coleridge. For the time being, however, Campbell did more than they—more, perhaps, than any other writer save one—to break down in popular esteem the didactic convention of the classic school. —GOSSE, EDMUND, 1897, *A Short History of Modern English Literature, p.* 288.

The well-spring of poetry was not vouchsafed to Campbell. He worked from the outside, not from the depths of his own spirit. He spoke of having a poem "on the stocks," of beating out a poem "on the anvil." By these words does he not stand, before the highest tribunal, condemned? We read of him polishing and polishing until what little of original idea there was must have been almost refined away. We never hear of him bringing forth his thoughts with pain and travail. His letters are full of complaints about his vein being dried up, of his mind being too much cumbered with mundane concerns to have leisure for poetry; but we never once get a hint of any real misgiving as to his powers. . . . Time has brought in its revenges for Campbell. His poems enshrine no great thoughts, engender no consummate expression. Felicities, prettinesses, harmonies of a sort one may find; respectabilities, vigour, patriotic and liberal sentiments declaimed with gusto. But these do not raise him above the level of a third-rate poet. His war songs will keep him alive, and that after all is no mean praise.—HADDEN, J. CUTHBERT, 1899, *Thomas Campbell* (*Famous Scots Series*), *p.* 155.

William Beckford

1759-1844

Born, at Fonthill, Wilts, 1 Oct. 1760. Privately educated. At Geneva with tutor, 1777-79. Visit to Netherlands, 1780; to Italy, 1782. Married Lady Margaret Gordon, 5 May 1783; lived partly in Switzerland until her death, 26 May 1786. M. P. for Wells, 1784-90. Visit to Portugal and Spain, 1787. In Paris, 1791-92; at Lausanne,

WILLIAM BECKFORD

Engraving by S. Freeman. From Original by P. Savage.

ISAAC DISRAELI

Engraving by G. Cook. From the Original by Denning.

1792–93. Visit to Portugal, 1794. M. P. for Hindon, 1806–20. Lived in seclusion at Fonthill Giffard, 1796–1822; obliged to sell estate, 1822. Removed to Bath. Died there, 2 May 1844; buried there. *Works:* "Dreams, Waking thoughts and Incidents" (anon.), 1783; "Vathek," *in English* (anon., surreptitiously published in London by S. Henley, who translated from Beckford's MS.), 1786; *in French* (anon.), Paris, 1787 (another edn. same year, published at Lausanne with author's name); "Modern Novel Writing: or, The Elegant Enthusiast" (under pseud. of Lady Harriet Marlow), 1796; "Amezia" (under pseud. of "Jacquetta Agneta Marianna Jenks"), 1797; "Biographical Memoirs of Extraordinary Painters" (anon.), 1824; "Italy, with Sketches of Spain and Portugal," 1834; "Recollections of . . . the Monasteries of Alcobaça and Batalha" (anon.), 1835. He *translated:* "Al Ravni," 1783. *Life:* by Cyrus Redding (anon.), 1859.—SHARP, R. FARQUHARSON, 1897, *A Dictionary of English Authors, p.* 21.

PERSONAL

There thou, too, Vathek! England's wealthiest son,
Once form'd thy Paradise, as not aware
When wanton Wealth her mightiest deeds hath done,
Meek Peace voluptuous lures was ever wont to shun.
Here didst thou dwell, here schemes of pleasure plan,
Beneath yon mountain's ever beauteous brow;
But now, as if a thing unblest by man,
Thy fairy dwelling is as lone as thou!
Here giant weeds a passage scarce allow
To halls deserted, portals gaping wide;
Fresh lessons to the thinking bosom, how
Vain are pleasaunces on the earth supplied;
Swept into wrecks anon by Time's ungentle tide.

—BYRON, LORD, 1812, *Childe Harold, Canto* i.

His mind was vigorous, his spirits were good, and he displayed his wonted activity of body nearly to the last. He declared to the present writer, in his seventy-sixth year, that he never felt a minute's *ennui* in his life. To this the great variety of his mental resources, as well as his bodily temperament, which would never permit him to remain inactive, greatly contributed. He was the most accomplished man of his time; his reading was perhaps the most extensive. Besides the classical languages of antiquity, he spoke five modern European tongues, writing three of them with great elegance. He read the Persian and Arabic, was an excellent designer with the pencil, and a perfect master of the science of music. The last he was taught by Mozart, to whom he was so attached, that when the great musician settled in Vienna, he made a visit to that capital, as he said himself, "that he might once more see his old master." . . . I walked towards the further end of the room, from whence Mr. Beckford, then in his seventy-fourth year, but in appearance some years younger, came to meet me. . . . In person he was scarcely above the middle height, slender, but well formed, with features indicating great intellectual power. His eyes were wonderfully acute, his apprehension exceedingly quick, his enunciation rather more rapid than that of the average of speakers in general. His constitution had not, according to his own account, been strong. In early life he had been unable in consequence to remain in parliament, though he had sat both for Wells and Hindon. By activity, temperance, and care, more than all by spending as much time as possible in the open air, with plenty of exercise, he had rendered himself comparatively hale. He was dressed in a green coat with cloth buttons, a buff striped waistcoat, breeches of the same kind of cloth as the coat, and brown topboots, the fine cotton stockings appearing over them, in the fashion of a gentleman thirty or forty years ago. I never saw him in any other costume when indoors.—REDDING, CYRUS, 1844, *Recollections of the Author of "Vathek," New Monthly Magazine, vol.* 71, *pp.* 143, 148.

We should perhaps hardly prolong this article by an account of the abbey, but for the fact that it avenged the Vandalism that attended its erection by crippling the owner, and that its celebrity is now only historic; for after passing from Beckford to Mr. Farquhar, a wealthy miser, in whose hands the great central tower, its distinctive feature, fell, it passed again out of aristocratic keeping to Mr. Morison, a tradesman, who died in 1858, leaving twenty millions of dollars, thus ending about where Beckford began. . . . The building was in the form of a cross, the arms of which were nearly of the same length, although differing in breadth. The exterior measurement was two hundred and seventy feet from east to west, and from north to south three hundred and twelve. In the aziş of the cross rose the central octagon tower, to the vast height of two hundred and seventy-six feet. The interior was divided into numberless halls, staircases, galleries, saloons, libraries, oratories, drawing-rooms, and cabinets. Everything like convenience was sacrificed to grand effect, to long perspective aisles and arches. One octagonal room, formed by the great tower, was thirty-five feet only in diameter, and one hundred and twenty-eight feet high. In the huge fabric there were but seventeen bed-rooms, thirteen of which were at a most distressing height; and the whole far better merited the satire of Pope on Blenheim, than the sumptuous palace of Marlborough:—

"'Tis very fine;
But where d'ye sleep, or where d'ye dine?
I find, by all you have been telling,
That 'tis a house, but not a dwelling."

—TIFFANY, O., 1860, *William Beckford, North American Review, vol.* 90, *p.* 317.

The life that the youthful Beckford not only dreamed but carried out was exactly that which Tennyson has pictured in his "Palace of Art,"—a life of luxurious self-culture, apart from the cares, loves, and concerns of men. It is only fair to say that Beckford seems to have extracted more happiness from such a life than the poet has conceived possible. But we should remember that before he gave himself up to it he had loved purely and fondly; and probably the death of the wife he adored, after three years of unclouded happiness, had much to do in determining the eccentric recluseness of his later life. —LESLIE, CHARLES ROBERT, AND TAYLOR, TOM, 1865, *Life and Times of Sir Joshua Reynolds, vol.* II, *p.* 350.

Mr. Beckford left two daughters, the eldest of whom, Susan Euphemia, was married to the Marquis of Clydesdale in 1810, and became Duchess of Hamilton. The tomb at Lansdown, with its polished granite, emblazoned shields, and bronzed and gilt embellishments, was not long cared for; since, in 1850, it presented in its neglected state a lamentable object.—TIMBS, JOHN, 1866, *English Eccentrics and Eccentricities, vol.* I, *p.* 21.

VATHEK

"Vathek" is, indeed, without reference to the time of life when the author penned it, a very remarkable performance; but, like most of the works of the great poet who has thus eloquently praised it, it is stained with some poison-spots—its inspiration is too often such as might have been inhaled in the "Hall of Eblis." We do not allude so much to its audacious licentiousness, as to the diabolical levity of its contempt for mankind. The boy-author appears already to have rubbed all the bloom off his heart; and, in the midst of his dazzling genius, one trembles to think that a stripling of years so tender should have attained the cool cynicism of a *Candide*.—LOCKHART, JOHN GIBSON, 1834, *Travels in Italy, Spain and Portugal, Quarterly Review, vol.* 51, *p.* 427.

This romance is very much what Byron would have written in prose—the same splendid, vivid, and ever fresh pictures of the external nature of the most beautiful and interesting region of the world, the same intensity of passion, the same gloomy colouring of unrepenting crime. . . . This is the "Gil Blas" of Oriental life. . . . Perhaps there is no work in the world which gives so vast, so lively, and so accurate a picture of every grade, every phase of Oriental existence. —SHAW, THOMAS B., 1847, *Outlines of English Literature, p.* 397.

His true monument is his novel, "Vathek," though he spent enormous amounts of money in building his wonderful edifice of Fonthill. His great tower, 300 feet high, fell down, was rebuilt, and fell again; but "Vathek" remains.—MARTINEAU, HARRIET, 1849, *A History of the Thirty Years' Peace, A. D.* 1815–1846, *vol.* IV, *p.* 424.

Never was a more homogeneous creation. It bears in every line an impress of audacious and weird imagination, which gives it a place as far apart from all the originals of Eastern romance as from the imitations of them. The wonder is the greater if we remember the time when it was written, the mingled decorousness and flatulence, pomposity and poverty of invention in its many Eastern Tales and Apologues. Compare "Vathek" with the best of these, "Rasselas." It is like comparing a glacier with a lava stream as it comes out of the burning mountain.—LESLIE, CHARLES ROBERT, AND TAYLOR, TOM, 1865, *Life and Times of Sir Joshua Reynolds, vol.* II, *p.* 349.

"Vathek" is, perhaps, the most interesting Oriental story ever written. It abounds in scenes of surpassing beauty and magnificence. Its splendor of description, varied liveliness of humor, gorgeous richness of fancy, and wild and supernatural interest, are perhaps unequalled in the whole range of fictitious literature. It seems as if all the sweets of Asia are poured upon it. It is full of glittering palaces, and temples, and towers; of jeweled halls, tables of agate, and cabinets of ebony and pearl; of crystal fountains, radiant columns, and arcades, and perfumes burning in censers of gold.—GRIFFIN, G. W., 1870, *Studies in Literature*, p. 97.

Many a reader has got through "Vathek" at a sitting, but very few authors indeed could or would emulate Beckford's feat of writing it at one. True the sitting was a long one, for it lasted three days and two nights, and it cost him a severe illness—which, some will think, and perhaps he thought, served him right.—JACOX, FRANCIS, 1872, *Enthralling Books, Aspects of Authorship*, p. 340.

Of all the glories and prodigalities of the English Sardanapalus, his slender romance, the work of three days, is the only durable memorial. . . . There is astonishing force and grandeur in some of these conceptions. The catastrophe possesses a sort of epic sublimity, and the spectacle of the vast multitude incessantly pacing those halls, from which all hope has fled, is worthy the genius of Dante. The numberless graces of description, the piquant allusions, the humour and satire, and the wild yet witty spirit of mockery and derision—like the genius of Voltaire—which is spread over the work, we must leave to the reader. The romance altogether places Beckford among the first of our imaginative writers, independently of the surprise which it is calculated to excite as the work of a youth of twenty-two, who had never been in the countries he describes with so much animation and accuracy.—CHAMBERS, ROBERT, 1876, *Cyclopædia of English Literature, ed. Carruthers.*

Byron considered this tale superior to "Rasselas." . . . "Vathek" gives evidence of a familiarity with oriental customs, and a vividness of imagination which are remarkable in so youthful an author. The descriptions of the Caliph and of the Hall of Eblis are full of power. But in depth of meaning, and in that intrinsic worth which gives endurance to a literary work, it bears no comparison to "Rasselas." The one affords an hour's amusement; the other retains its place among those volumes which are read and re-read with constant pleasure and satisfaction.—TUCKERMAN, BAYARD, 1882, *A History of English Prose Fiction*, p. 247.

Not much need be or can be said about the literary qualities of "Vathek." Alive with undiminished vitality after a century's existence, it has proved its claim to a permanent place in literature by obtaining it; nor, at any period of its history, has it been a book which criticism could greatly help or hinder, or which allowed sound criticism much scope for controversy. Its beauties are by no means of the recondite order; and inability to appreciate them is one of those innate distastes, not for the book but its *genre*, against which expostulation is impotent.—GARNETT, RICHARD, 1893, *ed. Vathek: An Arabian Tale, Introduction*, p. xxv.

A stronger work than Walpole's romance is the "Vathek" of William Beckford. "The History of the Caliph Vathek," as its full title reads, is yet more grotesque and wilder in its freaks of fancy than is "The Castle of Otranto;" but its Oriental setting, its remarkable likeness to some tale among the thousand and one of the "Arabian Nights," above all, its consistency in the fantastic character assumed and the extraordinary imaginative power of its author, have given to this tale a popularity and a length of life shared by no other of the grotesque romances of this period. "Vathek" reappears regularly in edition after edition, delighting lovers of the marvellous in fiction to-day as it did a hundred years ago.—SIMONDS, WILLIAM EDWARD, 1894, *An Introduction to the Study of English Fiction*, p. 58.

Has maintained its position as the finest Oriental tale written by an Englishman. The breath of the Romantic movement stirs in it, and distinguishes it in kind from the exquisitely witty Oriental tales of Count Anthony Hamilton, on which it was modelled. The grotesque extravagance of Eastern supernaturalism only tickled the fancy of Count Hamilton; it held the imagination of Beckford.—RALEIGH, WALTER, 1894; *The English Novel*, p. 250.

Well worth your reading on a spare day,

and which in its English version has made his fame, and keeps his name alive, now that his great houses and moneys are known and reverenced no more.—MITCHELL, DONALD G., 1895, *English Lands Letters and Kings, Queen Anne and the Georges*, *p.* 287.

Although the romantic school of fiction has had its day, the gorgeous, almost Miltonic tale "Vathek," the admiration of Lord Byron, who preferred it to "Rasselas," still survives after more than a hundred years. The statement made by its author to Mr. Redding, that it was produced at the age of twenty-two, in one sitting of three days and two nights, is a piece of imagination of like character with the work itself. The time taken to write it appears to have been about three months, but however long its production may have occupied, it stands, in a fashion, unique in the language, and had the author but been visited with a little pecuniary misfortune, it might have proved the precursor to a delightful series of imaginative stories.—GARNETT, W. J., 1895, *English Prose, ed. Craik, vol.* IV, *p.* 571.

Its debts to the old Oriental tale are more apparent than real; those to the fantastic satirical romance of Voltaire, though larger, do not impair its main originality; and a singular gust is imparted to its picture of unbridled power and unlimited desire by the remembrance that the author himself was, in not such a very small way, the insatiable voluptuary he draws. The picture of the Hall of Eblis at the end has no superior in a certain slightly theatrical, but still real, kind of sombre magnificence, and the heroine Nouronihar is great.—SAINTSBURY, GEORGE, 1898, *A Short History of English Literature, p.* 611.

In his sarcasm, Beckford carried on this humorous treatment of Eastern fable. The kicking of "the stranger" through the apartments, down the steps, through the courts of the Caliph's palace, and then through the streets of Samarah, is a piece of extravagance as delightful as anything in the romances of Voltaire. In his love of grotesque horror, Beckford is brought into line with Walpole. His Caliph, in league with the Intelligences of Darkness, commits to admiration every form of crime simply because he has nothing else to do. His bloated Giaour, "with ebony forehead and huge red eyes" drinks the aristocratic blood of fifty beautiful youths, and still his thirst is not slacked. The tale closes with a cleverly devised punishment for the damned. In the magnificent Hall of Eblis, strewn with gold dust and saffron, amid censers burning ambergris and aloes, they walk a weary round for eternity; their faces corrugated with agony, and their hands pressing upon hearts enveloped in flames.—CROSS, WILBUR L., 1899, *The Development of the English Novel, p.* 103.

GENERAL

Beckford wishes me to go to Fonthill with R; anxious that I should look over his "Travels" (which were printed some years ago, but afterwards suppressed by him), and prepare them for the press. Rogers supposes he would give me something magnificent for it—a thousand pounds, perhaps; but if he were to give me a hundred times that sum I would not have my name coupled with his. To be Beckford's *sub*, not very desirable.—MOORE, THOMAS, 1818, *Diary, Oct.* 18; *Memoirs, Journal and Correspondence, ed. Russell, vol.* II, *p.* 193.

Mr. Beckford's book is entirely unlike any book of travels *in prose* that exists in any European language; and if we could fancy Lord Byron to have written the "Harold" in the measure of "Don Juan," and to have availed himself of the facilities which the *ottava rima* affords for intermingling high poetry with merriment of all sorts, and especially with sarcastic sketches of living manners, we believe the result would have been a work more nearly akin to that now before us than any other in the library. . . . We risk nothing in predicting that Mr. Beckford's "Travels" will henceforth be classed among the most elegant productions of modern literature: they will be forthwith translated into every language of the Continent—and will keep his name alive, centuries after all the brass and marble he ever piled together have ceased to vibrate with the echoes of *Modenhas*.—LOCKHART, JOHN GIBSON, 1834, *Travel in Italy, Spain and Portugal, Quarterly Review, vol.* 51, *pp.* 428, 456.

Beckford's book greatly offends me in all that relates to Holland and Germany, often offends me even in Italy, but for the most part delights me in Portugal and Spain. The vile, sneering, morbid tone that more or less pervades the first volume is detestable to me.—BOWLES, CAROLINE

A., 1834, *To Robert Southey, July* 23; *The Correspondence of Robert Southey with Caroline Bowles, ed. Dowden, p.* 307.

His celebrity as a remarkable personage would have endured had he never written anything; and as an author he achieved a renown which he probably valued more than literary fame of the first order, the distinction of being the most brilliant amateur in English literature. Hardly any other man has produced such masterpieces with so little effort. "Vathek" was written at a sitting, and his letters betray no trace of unusual pains. These works are masterpieces nevertheless. European literature has no Oriental fiction which impresses the imagination so powerfully and permanently as "Vathek." Portions of the story may be tedious or repulsive, but the whole combines two things most difficult of alliance—the fantastic and the sublime. Beckford's letters display a corresponding versatility and union of seemingly incongruous faculties. He is equally objective and subjective; his pictures, while brilliantly clear in outline, are yet steeped in the rich hues of his own peculiar feeling; he approaches every object from its most picturesque side, and the measure of his eloquence is the interest with which it has actually inspired him. His colouring is magical; he paints nature like Salvator, and courts like Watteau. His other works make us bitterly regret the curse of wealth and idleness which converted a true son of the muses into an eccentric dilettante. As a literary figure Beckford occupies a remarkable position, an incarnation of the spirit of the eighteenth century writing in the yet unrecognised dawn of the nineteenth, flushed by emotions which he does not understand, and depicting the old courtly order of Europe on the eve of its dissolution.—GARNETT, RICHARD, 1885, *Dictionary of National Biography, vol.* IV, 84.

John Sterling

1806–1844

Born at Kames Castle, Bute, Scotland, July 20, 1806: died at Ventnor, Isle of Wight, Sept. 18, 1844. An English poet and author, best known as a friend of Carlyle. His father, Edward Sterling (1773–1847) was an editor of the "Times." Sterling studied at Glasgow and Cambridge (but left without a degree); went to London and purchased the "Athenæum" in 1828, but soon gave it up; and in 1834 became curate at Hurstmonceaux, where Julius Hare was vicar. He wrote "Arthur Coningsby" (1833), "Poems" (1839), "Strafford" (1843), "Essays and Tales" edited by Hare (1848), and "The Onyx Ring" reprinted from "Blackwood" in (1856). His life was written by Carlyle (1851).—SMITH, BENJAMIN E., *ed.*, 1894–97, *The Century Cyclopedia of Names, p.* 957.

PERSONAL

One who hated every kind of falsehood with an intense hatred, and whose spirit burnt with a consuming love of truth; not like the fiery bush, which is the type indeed of the very highest minds, such as St. Paul's and Luther's, when the Spirit of God takes possession of them; but with a flame approaching more nearly thereto than is often found in this world of phantoms and interests. . . . The representation of his life is unsatisfactory, because the problem of his life was incomplete. That problem, as has been truly observed to me by one of his chief friends, was the same as the great problem of our age. In fact, it was the same with the great problem of all ages, to reconcile faith with knowledge, philosophy with religion, the subjective world of human speculation with the objective world in which God has manifested Himself by a twofold Revelation, outwardly to our senses, and spiritually to our spirits. —HARE, JULIUS CHARLES, 1847, *ed., Essays and Tales, Memoir, pp.* ccxx, ccxxi.

All my thoughts of Sterling are mingled with shame and self-reproach, which it is better to lay before God, who does understand it, than before the public or even friends who could not. I quite feel with you that until Christ be presented to men as related to themselves—to every one—and not merely as a character in a book, we shall see more and more noble spirits sinking into distrust and despair. The thought is sometimes very overwhelming, yet I wish it pressed upon me more habitually; one would be obliged then to speak in season and out of season, and above all to live as if the truth were no lie.—MAURICE, FREDERICK DENISON, 1848, *To Mr. Erskine, Feb.* 1; *Life, ed. Son, p.* 452.

A lean, tallish, loose-made boy of twelve; strange alacrity, rapidity and joyous eagerness looking out of his eyes, and of all his ways and movements. I have a picture of him at this stage; a little portrait, which carries its verification with it. In manhood too, the chief expression of his eyes and physiognomy was what I might call alacrity, cheerful rapidity. You could see, here looked forth a soul which was winged; which dwelt in hope and action, not in hesitation or fear. . . . As a gifted amiable being, of a certain radiant tenuity and velocity, too thin and rapid and diffusive, in danger of dissipating himself into the vague, or alas into death itself: it was so that, like a spot of bright colours, rather than a portrait with features, he hung occasionally visible in my imagination. . . . A loose, careless-looking, thin figure, in careless dim costume, sat, in a lounging posture, carelessly and copiously talking. I was struck with the kindly but restless swift-glancing eyes, which looked as if the spirits were all out coursing like a pack of merry eager beagles, beating every bush. The brow, rather sloping in form, was not of imposing character, though again the head was longish, which is always the best sign of intellect; the physiognomy in general indicated animation rather than strength. . . . His address, I perceived, was abrupt, unceremonious; probably not at all disinclined to logic, and capable of dashing in upon you like a charge of cossacks, on occasion: but it was also eminently ingenious, social, guileless. . . . Sterling was of rather slim but well-boned wiry figure, perhaps an inch or two from six feet in height; of blonde complexion, without colour, yet not pale or sickly; dark-blonde hair, copious enough, which he usually wore short. The general aspect of him indicated freedom, perfect spontaneity, with a certain careless natural grace. In his apparel, you could notice, he affected dim colours, easy shapes; cleanly always, yet even in this not fastidious or conspicuous: he sat or stood, oftenest, in loose sloping postures; walked with long strides, body carelessly bent, head flung eagerly forward, right hand perhaps grasping a cane, and rather by the middle to swing it, than by the end to use it otherwise. An attitude of frank, cheerful impetuosity, of hopeful speed and alacrity; which indeed his physiognomy, on all sides of it, offered as the chief expression. Alacrity, velocity, joyous ardour, dwelt in his eyes too, which were of brownish gray, full of bright kindly life, rapid and frank rather than deep or strong. A smile, half of kindly impatience, half of real mirth, often sat on his face. The head was long; high over the vertex; in the brow, of fair breadth, but not high for such a man. In the voice, which was of good tenor sort, rapid and strikingly distinct, powerful too, and except in some of the higher notes harmonious, there was a clear-ringing *metallic* tone,—which I often thought was wonderfully physiognomic.—CARLYLE, THOMAS, 1851, *Life of John Sterling.*

John Sterling would have been a far better, happier, and greater man, had he remained a working curate to the last, instead of becoming a sort of petty Prometheus, equally miserable, and nearly as idle, with a big black crow (elegantly mistaken for a vulture) pecking at his morbid liver. —GILFILLAN, GEORGE, 1855, *A Third Gallery of Portraits, p.* 271.

Of all those very remarkable young men, John Sterling was by far the most brilliant and striking in his conversation, and the one of whose future eminence we should all of us have augured most confidently. But though his life was cut off prematurely, it was sufficiently prolonged to disprove this estimate of his powers. The extreme vividness of his look, manner, and speech gave a wonderful expression of latent vitality and power; perhaps some of this lambent, flashing brightness may have been but the result of the morbid physical conditions of his existence, like the flush on his cheek and the fire in his eye; the over stimulated and excited intellectual activity, the offspring of disease, mistaken by us for morning instead of sunset splendor, promise of future light and heat instead of prognostication of approaching darkness and decay. It certainly has always struck me as singular that Sterling, who in his life accomplished so little and left so little of the work by which men are generally pronounced to be gifted with exceptional ability, should have been the subject of two such interesting biographies as those written of him by Julius Hare and Carlyle.

I think he must have been one of those persons in whom genius makes itself felt and acknowledged chiefly through the medium of personal intercourse; a not infrequent thing, I think, with women, and perhaps men, wanting the full vigor of normal health.—KEMBLE, FRANCES ANN, 1879, *Records of a Girlhood, p.* 185.

"Poor Sterling,"—such is the ever recurring burden of Carlyle's tribute to his friend, which he seems to have been pricked into writing largely because Sterling's other loyal friend and biographer, Archdeacon Hare, who had loved and labored with him in the Church of England, deplored overmuch his throwing off its rule and vestments. Though Carlyle has no sympathy for Sterling's knightly efforts to help the exile and the slave, and for his apostolic labors among the poor of England, scouts his verses and makes light of his essays and romance, and ever chafes because this fine courser was not a mighty drag-horse like himself,—yes, sad and soured by physical ailments, he more than half blamed his brave friend for having the cruel and long disease through which he worked, even to his censor's admiration,—yet, in spite of all, Carlyle's "Life of Sterling" shows in every page that this man's short, brave course lifted and illuminated all about him, even that weary and sad-eyed Jeremiah himself as he sat apart and prophesied and lamented.—EMERSON, EDWARD WALDO, 1897, *ed., A Correspondence between John Sterling and Ralph Waldo Emerson, p.* 5.

POETRY

We began to read his volume of poetry with considerable expectations, both from the commendations bestowed upon it by some of our friends, whose judgment we esteemed, and from the ability which his prose had unquestionably displayed, but we confess ourselves to have been somewhat disappointed. It has, it is true, all those good elements to recommend it, which can be drawn from the moral nature and from the affections. It is the work of one, who thinks justly and feels rightly, who fears God and loves his neighbour, but it wants poetic power, originality, and grace. The tone of his mind seems too cold for poetry, and more adapted to philosophy. He reflects and moralizes when he ought to feel and paint. He dwells too long upon particulars and details; his figures want life and his coloring warmth, and we are too often reminded of Hamlet's pithy criticism, "What read you? Words, Words, Words."—HILLARD, GEORGE S., 1842, *Recent English Poetry, North American Review, vol.* 55, *p.* 228.

This work has fairly taken us by surprise. On first reading its announcement we had many misgivings. That it would be a work worthy of serious attention, that it would be a work of unquestionable talent, we felt assured; the author's previous writing, various in form, but all the offspring of the same earnest, thoughtful spirit, were sufficient guarantee: but John Sterling a dramatist! The very advertisement was a paradox; and we will venture to assert that hardly one of his warmest friends and admirers (and among the latter we beg to rank ourselves) took up "Strafford" without an uneasy sense of the author's having chosen a wrong path. We would advise all, therefore, not to be satisfied with a first reading; it was not till our second reading that we fairly estimated it; prejudice and astonishment had marred our judgment, and we had to get accustomed to its excellence before we could believe in it. . . . In conclusion we may say that, although judged by the high and severe standard we are wont to erect as the model of the dramatic poet, the foundations of which are in truth of human passion, "Strafford" is found wanting; yet, judged by the standard of the day, it is an admirable production. It springs from a cultivated, thoughtful mind, and it bears the marks of its parentage in every scene. Of all the works of its author it is the most perfect and mature. The traces of imitation have almost completely vanished. His mind seems more self-sufficing and sustained. The expression does not struggle with the meaning, as in his former writings; there is less struggle and more victory, less artifice and more art. In his next venture we hope to meet him on less formidable, less ungrateful ground than that of the Historical Drama.—LEWES, GEORGE HENRY, 1844, *Strafford and the Historical Drama, The Westminster Review, vol.* 41, *pp.* 119, 128.

Superior to the prose articles:—beautiful and highly wrought as these are—are the author's poetical writings, distinguished alike for purity of thought, delicacy of fancy, and depth and tenderness of feeling.—GRISWOLD, RUFUS W., 1844, *The Poets and Poetry of England in the Nineteenth Century*, p. 371.

Strafford never alters, never is kindled by or kindles the life of any other being, never breathes the breath of the moment. Before us, throughout the play, is the view of his greatness taken by the mind of the author; we are not really made to feel it by those around him; it is echoed from their lips, not from their lives.—OSSOLI, MARGARET FULLER, 1850? *The Modern Drama; Art, Literature and the Drama*, p. 144.

John Sterling has some high qualities of mind, but he was utterly destitute of the self-reliance necessary to constitute a great poet. The finest of all his productions, as a mere poem, is "The Sexton's Daughter," a striking lyrical ballad produced in early youth, ere he sank into poetic misgivings.—MOIR, D. M., 1851-52, *Sketches of the Poetical Literature of the Past Half-Century*, p. 326.

John Sterling, the subject of this short memoir, was a Poem. He had the quick discerning soul in which knowledge passed rapidly into feeling, and feeling flashed back into new knowledge. And while he himself ever remained more poetical than his poetry, he did not "leave out" the poems. Though truth compels the statement that his poetry, diligently as he laboured over it, never secured success or admiration in his own day, even from those who loved and honoured him, and only are read nowadays because he has been immortalised in one of the finest biographies in our language, "The Life of John Sterling," by his friend Thomas Carlyle.—GIBBS, H. J., 1892, *The Poets and the Poetry of the Century, Frederick Tennyson to Arthur Hugh Clough, ed. Miles*, p. 125.

GENERAL

In broken tones and by lapses he obtained utterance. No shapely and complete temple rose beneath the hand whose nerves disease had unstrung; and hints instead of revelations are bequeathed by a mind seldom allowed to work continuously. —TUCKERMAN, HENRY T., 1849, *Characteristics of Literature*, p. 194.

The life of John Sterling, however, has intrinsic interest, even if it be viewed simply as the struggle of a restless aspiring soul, yearning to leave a distinct impress of itself on the spiritual development of humanity, with that fell disease which, with a refinement of torture, heightens the susceptibility and activity of the faculties, while it undermines their creative force. Sterling, moreover, was a man thoroughly in earnest, to whom poetry and philosophy were not merely another form of paper currency or a ladder to fame, but an end in themselves—one of those finer spirits with whom, amid the jar and hubbub of our daily life,

> "The melodies abide
> Of the everlasting chime."

But his intellect was active and rapid, rather than powerful, and in all his writings we feel the want of a stronger electric current to give that vigor of conception and felicity of expression, by which we distinguish the undefinable something called genius; while his moral nature, though refined and elevated, seems to have been subordinate to his intellectual tendencies and social qualities, and to have had itself little determining influence on his life.—ELIOT, GEORGE, 1851, *Carlyle's Life of Sterling*.

Though not an exact scholar, Sterling became well and extensively read, possessing great facilities of assimilation for all kinds of mental diet. His studies were irregular and discursive, but extensive and encyclopedic.—SMILES, SAMUEL, 1860, *Brief Biographies*.

Of John Sterling a few words must suffice. His name cannot be omitted, and yet we cannot dwell on it, nor are we called upon to do so. There must have been an infinite attractiveness in the man to have drawn out as he did such treasures of affection from teachers so different as Hare and Maurice on the one side and Carlyle on the other. . . . It must have been a lovable character which drew around him so much love. There must also have seemed in Sterling a marvellous potency as if, with due maturity, he might have done great things in literature if not in theology. But the brightness of his promise soon spent itself. It may be doubted even whether if he had lived he would have achieved much. "Over-haste," says Carlyle, "was his continual fault. Over-haste and want of due strength." His genius flashed and coruscated like sheet-lightning round a subject rather than went to the heart of it. He lacked depth and capacity of continuous thought. He was moved, if not by "every wind of doctrine," by every breath of speculation that braced his intellectual lungs for a time. It was now Coleridge, and now Edward Irving, and now Schleiermarcher, and now Carlyle that swept the strings of his mind and made them vibrate. . . . Sterling was not destined to be any force of religious thought for his generation. With all his "sleepless intellectual vivacity" he was "not a thinker at all." The words are Carlyle's and not ours. Yet he deserves to be remembered, as he will continue to be associated with the great Teacher who first kindled both his intellectual and religious enthusiasm. Carlyle has embalmed his name and discipleship in beautiful form, and the picture will remain while English literature lasts. But students of religious opinion will always also think of him as a disciple of Coleridge and the friend of Maurice and Hare.—TULLOCH, JOHN, 1885, *Movements of Religious Thought in Britain During the Nineteenth Century, pp.* 29, 30.

His writings were edited in 1848 by Julius Hare ("Essays and Tales by John Sterling," 2 vols. London, 8vo), with a memoir in many respects most admirable, but its inadequacy, inevitable from the writer's point of view, stimulated Carlyle to the composition in 1851 of the biography which has made Sterling almost as widely and intimately known as Carlyle himself. The book is remarkable for its inversion of the usual proportion between biographer and hero. Johnson for once writes upon Boswell. Sterling is a remarkable instance of a man of letters of no ordinary talent and desert who nevertheless owes his reputation to a genius, not for literature, but for friendship.—GARNETT, RICHARD, 1895, *Dictionary of National Biography, vol.* LIV, *p.* 195.

Posterity has not preserved the name of John Sterling as his contemporaries must have believed it was worthy to be preserved. What we know of him now is not by his own writings, but by the curious fact that two biographies of a man who did nothing in his short life of importance, and left nothing behind him to justify such a double record, were given to the world shortly after his death, one of which at least has a high place in permanent literature,—the extraordinary elegy, apology, eulogium of Thomas Carlyle. That there were reasons besides the merits of their subject for the two books—that of Archdeacon Hare on the side of his own benign and moderate churchmanship, and Carlyle's on that of a wilder freedom and negation—no one would deny.—OLIPHANT, MARGARET O. W., 1897, *William Blackwood and His Sons, vol.* II, *p.* 185.

Henry Francis Cary

1772-1844

Born, at Gibraltar, 6 Dec. 1772. Father settled in Staffordshire. Educated first at Uxbridge; at Rugby, 1783-85; at Sutton Coldfield Grammar School, 1785-87; at Birmingham Grammar School, 1787-90. Contrib. to "Gentleman's Magazine," from 1788. To Ch. Ch., Oxford, 29 April 1790; B. A., 14 Jan. 1794; M. A., 23 Nov. 1796. Ordained, Spring of 1796; Vicar of Abbott's Bromley, Staffordshire. Married Jane Ormsby, 19 Sept. 1796. Instituted in living of Kingsbury, Warwickshire, 27 June 1800; removed thither, 12 Nov. 1800. Occupied on Dante translation, 1797-1812. To London, 1807. Reader at Berkeley Chapel, 1810-13. To Chiswick, as Curate and Lecturer, 1814. Curate of Savoy, June 1816. Contrib. to "London Magazine," 1821-24. Assistant-Keeper of printed books in British Museum, June 1826 to July 1837. Crown pension, 23 Aug. 1841. Died, at Willesden, 14 Aug. 1844. Buried in Westminster Abbey. *Works:* "Sonnets and Odes" 1788; "Ode to General Kosciusko," 1797. *Posthumous:* "Lives of English Poets," 1846; "The Early French Poets," 1846. He *translated:* Dante's "Divina Commedia," 1814 ("Inferno," 1805); Aristophanes' "Birds," 1824; Pindar, 1833; and *edited:* Cowper's Poems, 1839; Milton, Thomson, and Young's Poems, 1841. *Life:* by his son, H. Cary, 1847.—SHARP, R. FARQUHARSON, 1897, *A Dictionary of English Authors, p.* 49.

PERSONAL

Cary was one of Coleridge's frequent visitors; I saw him at Highgate; but he was more often seen at the British Museum; where he had a position that gave him congenial occupation. His translation of

Dante retains its place of honor on the book-shelves. Ugo Foscolo, than whom there could be no better authority, told me he considered it not only the best English translation of any foreign poet, but the best in any language. I recall him to memory as very kindly, with a most gracious and sympathizing expression; slow in his movements, as if he were always in thought, living among the books of which he was the custodian, and seeking only the companionship of the lofty spirits who had gone from earth—those who though dead yet speak.—HALL, SAMUEL CARTER, 1883, *Retrospect of a Long Life*, *p.* 318.

GENERAL

To whom Dante owes more than ever poet owed to translator. . . . I will only say that there is no other version in the world, as far as I know, so faithful, yet that there is no other version which so fully proves that the translator is himself a man of poetical genius. Those who are ignorant of the Italian language should read it to become acquainted with the Divine Comedy. Those who are most intimate with Italian literature should read it for its original merits: and I believe that they will find it difficult to determine whether the author deserves most praise for his intimacy with the language of Dante, or for his extraordinary mastery over his own.—MACAULAY, THOMAS BABINGTON, 1824, *Criticisms on the Principal Italian Writers, Critical and Miscellaneous Essays.*

Cary's literary fame is almost wholly identified with one work. There will probably always be two schools of Dante translation in England, the blank verse and the terza rima, and until some great genius shall have arisen capable of thoroughly naturalising the latter metre, Johnson's terse remark on the translators of Virgil will continue to be applicable. "Pitt," he says, "is quoted, and Dryden read." Cary's standard is lower, and his achievement less remarkable, than that of many of his successors, but he, at least, has made Dante an Englishman, and they have left him half an Italian. He has, nevertheless, shown remarkable tact in avoiding the almost inevitable imitation of the Miltonic style, and, renouncing the attempt to clothe Dante with a stateliness which does not belong to him, has in a great measure preserved his transparent simplicity and intense vividness. In many other respects Cary's taste was much in advance of the standard of his day; his criticisms on other poets are judicious, but not penetrating. His original poems and his translation of Pindar scarcely deserve a higher praise than that of elegance.—GARNETT, RICHARD, 1887, *Dictionary of National Biography, vol.* IX, *p.* 244.

His famous translation of the "Divina Commedia," published in 1814, is not only one of the best verse translations in English, but, after the lapse of eighty years, during which the study of Dante has been constantly increasing in England, in which poetic ideas have changed not a little, and in which numerous other translations have appeared, still attracts admiration from all competent scholars for its combination of fidelity and vigour. — SAINTSBURY, GEORGE, 1896, *A History of Nineteenth Century Literature*, *p.* 110.

Basil Hall

1788–1844

Basil Hall, writer of travels, was born in Edinburgh, 31st December 1788. His father, Sir James Hall of Dunglass, baronet (1761–1832), was a chemist and the founder of experimental geology. Basil entered the navy in 1802, and in 1816 commanded a sloop in the naval escort of Lord Amherst's mission to Peking, visiting Corea, as described in "A Voyage of Discovery to Corea," (1818). He also wrote "Journal on the Coast of Chili, Peru, and Mexico in 1820–22;" "Travels in North America in 1827–28;" and "Fragments of Voyages and Travels" (1831–40). "Schloss Hainfeld" (1836) was a semi-romance, and "Patchwork" (1841) a collection of tales and sketches. He died insane in Haslar Hospital, Gosport, 11th Sept. 1844.—PATRICK AND GROOME, *eds.*, 1897, *Chambers's Biographical Dictionary*, *p.* 452.

PERSONAL

I have met with Basil Hall, and was never more surprised; I looked for a bold weather-beaten tar, but I found a gentleman, with a soft voice and soft manners, pouring out small-talk in half whispers to ladies; I believe, however, he is very estimable.—GRANT, ANNE, 1824, *To Mrs. Hook, June* 23; *Memoir and Correspondence, ed. Grant, vol.* III, *p.* 36.

GENERAL

We think the author's style uniformly happy, and peculiarly well suited to this species of composition. He is a discriminating observer, his topics are selected with good judgment and good taste, his language is terse, appropriate, and varied; sometimes perhaps a little too much studied, but never stiff nor ponderous. In short, we could hardly name a better model of journal-writing, than the little volume, whose contents we have just been reviewing; and whoever would read for the double purpose of instruction and amusement, will find themselves richly compensated for the time they may give to its perusal.—SPARKS, JARED, 1828, *Captain Hall's Voyage to the Eastern Seas, North American Review, vol.* 26, *p.* 538.

It is, indeed, with considerable diffidence, that we express the opinion, that the style of Captain Hall errs in the extreme of plainness. It is frequently slovenly, and still more frequently incorrect. His pages contain a good deal of bad grammar, and several words, which are neither English nor American. . . . His work will do considerable mischief, not in America, but in England. It will furnish food to the appetite for detraction, which reigns there toward this country. It will put a word in the mouths of those, who vilify because they hate, and hate because they fear us. Captain Hall is too brave for fear, and too generous for hate; but he has undesignedly played into the hands of those who are neither. This matter deserves his consideration; and as he will probably revise his work for the correction of its numerous faults in a literary point of view, the consequence of the haste in which it was written, we must recommend to him, in the calmness of afterthought, to review his whole system of thought and feeling toward this country. —EVERETT, EDWARD, 1829, *Captain Hall's Travels, North American Review, vol.* 29, *pp.* 534, 574.

Captain Hall's book (and himself too, by the way) has put the Union in a blaze from one end to the other. I never on any occasion heard so general an expression of contempt and detestation as that which follows his name. This hubbub made me very desirous of seeing his book, but I am glad to say I did not succeed till after my first volume was finished, and most of the notes for the second collected. I thus escaped influence of any kind from the perusal. A few days ago, however, I was at Philadelphia, and there I got his very strange work. I had one or two long and interesting conversations with Lee (the publisher), who knew him well, and, from one or two anecdotes he gave me, it appears that the "agreeable captain" was under writing orders as surely as he ever was, or hopes to be again, under sailing orders. He would have done quite enough service to the cause he intends to support if he had painted things exactly as they are, without seeking to give his own eternal orange-tawny color to every object. His blunders are such as clearly to prove he never, or very rarely, listened to the answers he received—for we must not suppose that he knew one thing and printed another. Do not suppose, however, that I am coming home fraught with the Quixotic intention of running a tilt with Captain Hall. My little book will not be of him, but of all I have seen, and of much that he did not.—TROLLOPE, FRANCES, 1830, *Letter to Miss Mitford, July* 28; *Friendships of Mary Russell Mitford, ed. L'Estrange.*

That he has a keen, quick eye, voracious curiosity, restless activity, a gay temperament, and an upright, virtuous mind—no man who has perused his previous lucubrations can doubt. That he is apt to see one side of a thing so vividly as to forget that there is another side at all—that his complete satisfaction with himself and everything about him, though unaccompanied with the slightest shade of cynicism, is too prominent not to move now and then a passing smile—and that his sincerity cannot always excuse his dogmatism, are facts which his warmest admirers seem to admit. That he tells a story with clearness and energy—describes manners and scenery with very considerable skill and effect—seizes the strong points of a moral or political question, in general, with ready shrewdness, and delivers his opinions on all subjects fairly and frankly—writes in a manly, unaffected style, rough but racy—and makes us feel throughout that we are in the hands of a practical man, clever, humorous, kind-hearted, who has read much, seen more, studied and enjoyed life in a hundred spheres and shapes, a staunch and ardent lover of his country, and in all respects a gentleman—these are statements to which we presume the Captain's bitterest political opponent would hardly refuse his *imprimatur.*—LOCKHART, JOHN GIBSON, 1831, *Captain Hall, Quarterly Review, vol.* 45, *p.* 145.

Wit is not to be measured, like broadcloth, by the yard. Easy writing, as the adage says, and as we all know, is apt to be very hard reading. This brings to our recollection a conversation, in the presence of Captain Basil Hall, in which some allusion having been made to the astounding amount of Scott's daily composition, the literary argonaut remarked, "There was nothing astonishing in all that, and that he did as much himself nearly every day before breakfast." Some one of the company unkindly asked "whether he thought the *quality* was the same." It is the quality, undoubtedly, which makes the difference. —PRESCOTT, W. H., 1837, *Lope de Vega, North American Review, vol.* 15, *p.* 11.

Thomas Hood

1799-1845

Born, in London, 23 May 1799. At school in London. In mercantile house, 1813-15. Health failed. At Dundee, 1815-18; contrib. to local Press from 1814. Articled to firm engravers in London, 1818; but owing to ill-health devoted himself to literature. On staff of "London Mag.," 1821-23. Married Jane Reynolds, 5 May 1824. Edited "The Gem," 1829; edited "The Comic Annual," 1830-42. Financial losses, 1834. Lived at Coblentz, 1835-37; at Ostend, 1837-40. Returned to England, April 1840. Joined staff of "New Monthly Mag.," 1840; editor, Aug. 1841 to Jan. 1844. "The Song of the Shirt," published in "Punch," Christmas 1843. Started "Hood's Mag.," Jan. 1844. Crown Pension of £100 granted to his wife, Nov. 1844. Died, at Hampstead, 3 May 1845. Buried in Kensal Green Cemetery. *Works:* "Odes and Addresses to Great People" (anon.), 1825; "Whims and Oddities" (2 ser.), 1826-27; "National Tales" (2 vols.), 1827; "The Plea of the Midsummer Fairies," 1827; "The Epping Hunt," 1829; "The Dream of Eugene Aram," 1831; "Tylney Hall" (3 vols.), 1834; "Hood's Own," 1839; "Up the Rhine," 1840 (2nd edition same year); "Whimsicalities" (2 vols.), 1844. *Posthumous:* "Fairy Land," (with his daughter, Mrs. Broderip), 1861 (1860); "Hood's Own," 2nd series, ed. by his son, 1861. *Collected Works:* "Poems" (2 vols.), 1846; "Works," ed. by his son and daughter (10 vols.), 1869-73. *Life:* "Memorials," by Mrs. Broderip, 1860.—SHARP, R. FARQUHARSON, 1897, *A Dictionary of English Authors, p.* 135.

PERSONAL

I think Hood, perhaps the most taking lion I have seen, perhaps because he does not try to take, and his wit comes out really because it cannot stop in, there is so much behind.—CHORLEY, HENRY F., 1834, *Autobiography, Memoir and Letters, p.* 99.

Take back into thy bosom, earth,
This joyous, May-eyed morrow,
The gentlest child that ever mirth
Gave to be reared by sorrow!
'Tis hard—while rays half green, half gold,
Through vernal bowers are burning,
And streams their diamond mirrors hold
To Summer's face returning—
To say we're thankful that his sleep
Shall nevermore be lighter,
In whose sweet-tongued companionship
Stream, bower, and beam grow brighter!
—SIMMONS, BARTHOLOMEW, 1845, *To the Memory of Thomas Hood.*

Let laurelled marbles weigh on other tombs,
Let anthems peal for other dead,
Rustling the bannered depth of minster glooms
With their exulting spread.
His epitaph shall mock the short-lived stone,
No lichen shall its lines efface,
He needs these few and simple lines alone
To mark his resting place:—
"Here lies a Poet. Stranger, if to thee
His claim to memory be obscure,
If thou wouldst learn how truly great was he,
Go, ask it of the poor."
—LOWELL, JAMES RUSSELL, 1845, *To the Memory of Hood.*

I have the greatest tenderness for the memory of Hood, as I had for himself. But I am not very favourable to posthumous memorials in the monument way, and I should exceedingly regret to see any such appeal as you contemplate made public, remembering another public appeal that was made and responded to after Hood's death. I think that I best discharge my duty to my deceased friend, and best consult the respect and love with which I remember him, by declining to join in any such public endeavours as that which you (in all generosity and singleness of purpose, I am sure) advance. I shall have a melancholy gratification in privately assisting to place a simple and plain record over the remains of a great writer that should be as modest as he was himself, but I regard any other monument in connection with his mortal resting-place as a mistake. —DICKENS, CHARLES, 1852, *To Mr. John Watkins, Oct.* 18; *A Collection of Letters of Dickens, p.* 84.

My father's religious faith was deep and sincere: but it was but little known to a world ever too apt to decide by hearing professions, rather than by scrutinising actions. Those to whom his domestic life was every day revealed, felt how he lived after the divine requirements: for he "did justice," sacrificing comfort, health, and fortune, in the endeavor; he "loved mercy" with a love that was whispering into his ear, even as he was dying, new labours for his unhappy fellows; and he "walked humbly with his God" in a faith too rare to be made a common spectacle. . . . Almost my father's last words were, "Lord—say 'Arise, take up thy cross, and follow me.' " He had borne that cross during his whole life, but the quiet unobtrusive religious faith I have endeavoured to describe, supplied him with exemplary patience under severe sufferings, with cheerfulness under adverse circumstances, with a manly resolution to wrong no one, with an affectionate longing to alleviate the suffering of all classes, and with a charity and love that I will not do more than touch on, for fear I should be thought to be carried away by my feelings.—HOOD, THOMAS, 1860, *Memorials of Thomas Hood, Preface, vol.* I, *pp.* xi, xiii.

He possessed the most refined taste and appreciation for all the little luxuries and comforts that make up so much of the enjoyments of life; and the cares and annoyances that would be scarcely perceptible to a stronger and rougher organisation, fell with a double weight on the mind overtasked by such constant and harassing occupation. He literally fulfilled his own words, and was one of the "master minds at journey-work—moral magistrates greatly underpaid—immortals without a living—menders of the human heart, breaking their own—mighty intellects, without their mite." The income his works now produce to his children, might *then* have prolonged his life for many years; although, when we looked on the calm happy face after death, free at last from the painful expression that had almost become habitual to it, we dared not regret the rest so long prayed for, and hardly won.—BRODERIP, FRANCES FREELING (HOOD), 1860, *Memorials of Thomas Hood, vol.* I, *p.* 2.

He dies in dearest love and peace with his children, wife, friends; to the former especially his whole life had been devoted, and every day showed his fidelity, simplicity, and affection. In going through the record of his pure, modest, honorable life, and living along with him, you come to trust him thoroughly, and feel that here is a most loyal, affectionate, and upright soul, with whom you have been brought into communion. Can we say as much of the lives of all men of letters? Here is one at least without guile, without pretension, without scheming, of a pure life, to his family and little modest circle of friends tenderly devoted.—THACKERAY, WILLIAM MAKEPEACE, 1863, *Roundabout Papers.*

In his moral and social relations in life, Hood's character lives, I believe, untainted, and in his commerce with his own soul he appears to have been imbued with a deep sense of true and rational piety. Throughout the whole of his works that I am acquainted with there will not be found a single expression that shall bring in question the integrity of his character upon this point. And yet he did not escape the arraignment of persons who constituted themselves an authority to question his orthodoxy in such matters, and to denounce him accordingly. — CLARKE, CHARLES COWDEN, 1872, *On the Comic Writers of England, Gentleman's Magazine, n. s., vol.* 8, *p.* 666.

There seemed to be a mint in his mind in which the coining of puns was incessantly and almost unconsciously in process, not with the mere object of raising a laugh, but because his marvellous command of language enabled him to use words in every possible sense in which they could be understood; and he could not help playing upon them, even in his most serious moods. —PLANCHÉ, J. R., 1872, *Recollections and Reflections, vol.* I, *p.* 100.

His labors consisted of writing verse, and his pastime in making puns and shooting sparrows. I have often wondered that he did not make his passerine sport the subject of an ode; for no one was more capable of jesting with his own peculiarities than Thomas Hood. . . . He had a quiet face, the laughter lying hid behind its gravity. Just before his death, when consumption had mastered him, and the caprice of public favor had much diminished his means of living, he bore himself very independently.—PROCTER, BRYAN WALLER, 1874? *Recollections of Men of Letters.*

His was slow wit: it was neither spontaneous nor ready: the offspring of thought rather than an instinctive sparkle; but it was always kindly, gracious, sympathetic; never coarse, never "free," never even caustic, neither tainted with distrust of the goodness of God, nor to rail at the ingratitude of man. His countenance had more of melancholy than of mirth, it was calm even to solemnity. There was seldom any conscious attempt at brilliancy in his talk; and so far from sharing in that weakness with which wits are generally credited, a desire to monopolize the conversation, he seemed ever ready in society to give way to any who would supply talk. No, not a mere jester was Thomas Hood. He made humanity his debtor, to remain so as long as there are men and women with hearts to feel and understand the lesson he taught. He was the poet of the poor, above all, of the poor who are women, and whose sufferings seem perpetual.—HALL, SAMUEL CARTER, 1883, *Retrospect of a Long Life, p.* 341.

In the story of Hood there are no dark places which the friendly biographer must leave unnoticed, or gloss over as best he may; no dubious actions to be accounted for by "temperamental causes;" no vices to be referred to "inherited tendencies." Few men stand less in need of apologies than he does. His character is a most effective protest against the theory that genius exempts its possessor from the obligations which bind ordinary men, giving him license to covet and to appropriate the goods of his neighbor, and to make himself variedly obnoxious to those around him. Here was a man, endowed with gifts of the highest order, delicate, sensitive, keenly alive to every impression of pleasure or of pain, yet living a life of unobtrusive heroism; and, under most trying circumstances, practising the homely, every-day virtues; as faithful in the performance of social and domestic duties as though he had been the most mildly prosaic country gentleman who ever dozed through a life of tranquil prosperity. He was free from egotism. His own pains and troubles were the last things he thought of bringing forward for public or private notice. Under such trials as his, despondency would have seemed only natural, and much complaining would have been excusable; but he showed a brave front to the world, hid his sorrows in his own heart, and uttered no lamentations, no moans of self-commiseration. His fine temper was not easily ruffled; but on just occasion he could prove himself a formidable adversary. Notwithstanding his modesty and his peaceable disposition, he was a dangerous man to trifle with when his self-respect was concerned; and no one ever assailed him on this ground without finding cause for regret. Anything approaching patronage or intrusion upon his private affairs—still more, any meddlesome attempts to pry into his motives, or to impugn his personal character, were sure to be repelled promptly, and in a way not to be forgotten. To see with what spirit he resented and rebuked such offences, read his letter to the fanatical woman, who presumed to sit in judgment upon him for the frivolity of his writings.—MASON, EDWARD T., 1885, *ed., Personal Traits of British Authors, p.* 5.

When they were getting up a subscription in London for his monument, some of the most distinguished names in England were prominent on the list; but, to my thinking, those small sums that came up from the working-people of Manchester and Bristol and Preston, far outweighed the piles of guineas poured out by the great ones. Some of those little packages, that were sent in from the working-districts, were marked, "From a few poor needle-women," "From seven dressmakers," "From twelve poor men in the coal-mines." The rich gave of their abundance to honor the wit; the Englishman of genius, the great author; but the poor women of Britain remembered who it was that sang the "Song of the Shirt," and "The Bridge of Sighs;" and, down there in their dark dens of sorrow and poverty, they resolved to send up their mite, though coined out of heart's blood, for the good man's monument. They had heard all about their dying friend, who had been pleading their cause through so many years. They knew that he had been sending out from his sick-chamber lessons of charity and forbearance, reminding Wealth of Want, Feasting of Fasting, and Society of Solitude and Despair.—FIELDS, JAMES T., 1885, *Thomas Hood, Some Princes, Authors and Statesmen of Our Time, ed. Parton, p.* 154.

The monument to Hood in Kensal Green was erected by public subscription, at the suggestion of Eliza Cook, and was unveiled by Lord Houghton, July 18, 1854. The simple epitaph was of his own selecting: "He sang 'The Song of the Shirt.'"—HUTTON, LAURENCE, 1885, *Literary Landmarks of London, p.* 139.

Hood I saw at his chambers in the Adelphi when I went to fetch his drawings for his "Comic Annual," queer pen-and-ink drawings to be cut in fac-simile, some by myself. I recall him only as a spare man of fair stature, grave but not ungenial. But I most regarded his tools. Beside pencil and pen there lay on his desk an old graver, a reminiscence of his early time as an engraver in copper, a penknife, and a nail, with which it appeared he cut or scraped out any wrong line in his drawing. —LINTON, WILLIAM JAMES, 1894, *Three Score and Ten Years,* 1820 *to* 1890. *Recollections, p.* 11.

GENERAL

North—"That original and inimitable genius in his way, and his way is wider and more various than most people think —Thomas Hood—and the verses by the editor himself, therein quoted, 'Eugene Aram's Dream,' are among the best things I have seen for some years."—WILSON, JOHN, 1828, *Noctes Ambrosianæ, November.*

His "Dream of Eugene Aram" places him high among the bards who deal in dark and fearful things and intimate rather than express deeds which men shudder to hear named. Some other of his poems have much tenderness, and a sense of nature, animate and inanimate.—CUNNINGHAM, ALLAN, 1833, *Biographical and Critical History of the Literature of the Last Fifty Years.*

Mr. Hood possesses an original wealth of humour, invention and an odd sort of wit that should rather be called whimsicality, or a faculty of the "high fantastic." Among comic writers he is one of those who also possess genuine pathos; it is often deep, and of much tenderness, occasional of expression, and full of melancholy memories. The predominating characteristics of his genius are humorous fancies grafted upon melancholy impressions.—HORNE, RICHARD H., 1844, *A New Spirit of the Age.*

We look upon this writer as a quaint masquer—as wearing above a manly and profound nature, a fantastic and deliberate disguise of folly. He reminds us of Brutus, cloaking under pretended idiocy, a stern and serious design, which burns his breast, but which he chooses in this way only to disclose. Or, he is like Hamlet—able to form a magnificent purpose, but, from constitutional weakness, not able to incarnate it in effective action. A deep message has come to him from the heights of his nature, but, like the ancient prophet, he is forced to cry out, "I cannot speak—I am a child!" Certainly there was, at the foundation of Hood's soul, a seriousness, which all his puns and mummeries could but indifferently conceal. Jacquez, in the forest of Arden, mused not with a profounder pathos, or in quainter language, upon the sad pageant of humanity, than does he; and yet, like him, his "lungs" are ever ready to "crow like a chanticleer" at the sight of its grotesquer absurdities. Verily, the goddess of melancholy owes a deep grudge to the mirthful magician, who carried off such a promising votary.—GILFILLAN, GEORGE, 1847, *Thomas Hood, Tait's Edinburgh Magazine, vol.* 14, *p.* 69.

The beautiful stanzas called "The Bridge of Sighs," and the painfully touching "Song of the Shirt," were the means of exciting for an unhappy and neglected class of his countrywomen the pity, the interest, and even the active benevolence of the nation. Such things are not only good *works,* but good *actions;* and the triumph of having made genius a minister to philanthrophy is a glory worthy of the friend of Lamb and the first humorous writer of his age.—SHAW, THOMAS B., 1847, *Outlines of English Literature, p.* 433.

The vigor of this poem ["Bridge of Sighs,"] is no less remarkable than its pathos. The versification, although carrying the fanciful to the very verge of the fantastic, is nevertheless admirably adapted to the wild insanity which is the thesis of the poem.—POE, EDGAR ALLAN, 1850, *The Poetical Principle, Works, ed. Stedman and Woodberry, vol.* VI, *p.* 25.

Hood's verse, whether serious or comic, —whether serene like a cloudless autumn evening, or sparkling with puns like a frosty January midnight with stars,—was very pregnant with materials for thought. . . . Like every author distinguished for true comic humour, there was a deep vein of melancholy pathos running through his mirth; and even when his sun shone brightly, its light seemed often reflected as if only over the rim of a cloud. Well may we say in the words of Tennyson, "Would he could have stayed with us!" for never could it be more truly recorded of any one—in the words of Hamlet characterizing Yorick—that "he was a fellow of infinite jest, of most excellent fancy." —MOIR, D. M., 1851–52, *Sketches of the Poetical Literature of the Past Half-Century.*

Hood's pathos culminates in "The Song of the Shirt," "The Lay of the Laborer," and "The Bridge of Sighs." These are marvellous lyrics. In spirit and in form they are singular and remarkable. We cannot think of any poems which more show the mystic enchantment of genius. How else was a ragged sempstress in a squalid garret made immortal, nay, made universal, made to stand for an entire sisterhood of wretchedness? Here is direst poverty, blear-eyed sorrow, dim and dismal suffering,—nothing of the romantic. A stern picture it is, which even the softer touches render sterner; still there is nought in it that revolts or shocks; it is deeply poetic, calls into passionate action the feelings of reverence and pity, and has all the dignity of tragedy. Even more wonderful is the transformation that a rustic mind undergoes in "The Lay of the Laborer," in which a peasant out of work personifies, with eloquent impressiveness, the claims and calamities of toiling manhood. But an element of the sublime is added in "The Bridge of Sighs." In that we have the truly tragic; for we have in it the union of guilt, grief, despair, and death. An angel from heaven, we think, could not sing a more gentle dirge, or one more pure; yet the ordinary associations suggested by the corpse of the poor, ruined, self-murdered girl are such as to the prudish and fastidious would not allow her to be mentioned, much less bring her into song.—GILES, HENRY, 1860, *Thomas Hood, Atlantic Monthly, vol.* 6, *p.* 522.

Like other men, Hood had his "fixed ideas" in life—permanent thoughts and convictions, in behalf of which he could become pugnacious or even savage, or under the excitement of which every show of humour would fall off from him, and he would appear as a man purely sorrowful and serious. The sentiment of Anti-Pharisaism may be regarded as traditional in all men of popular literary genius; and back from our own days to those of Burns and still farther, British Literature has abounded with expressions of it, each more or less powerful in its time, but not superseding the necessity of another, and still another, in the times following. Almost last in the long list of these poets of Anti-Pharisaism comes the name of Hood. His writings are full of this sentiment, and especially of protests against over-rigid Sabbatarianism. On no subject did he so systematically and resolutely exert his powers of sarcasm and wit; and perhaps the English language does not contain any single poem from which the opponents of extreme Sabbatarianism and of what is called religious formality in general can borrow more pungent quotations, or which is really in its way a more eloquent assertion of personal intellectual freedom, than the "Ode to Rae Wilson, Esquire."—MASSON, DAVID, 1860, *Thomas Hood, Macmillan's Magazine, vol.* 2, *p.* 323.

I look back at the good which of late years the kind English Humourists have done; and if you are pleased to rank the present speaker among that class, I own to an honest pride at thinking what benefits society has derived from men of our calling. That "Song of the Shirt," which Punch first published, and the noble, the suffering, the melancholy, the tender Hood sang, may surely rank as a great act of charity to the world, and call from it its thanks and regard from its teacher and benefactor. That astonishing poem, which you all of you know, of the "Bridge of Sighs," who can read it without tenderness, without reverence to Heaven, charity to man, and thanks to the beneficient genius which sang for us so nobly?—THACKERAY, WILLIAM MAKEPEACE, 1853, *The English Humourists of the Eighteenth Century, p.* 288.

. . . strange glad and sad brain,
Whose mirth, you may notice, turns all upon pain.
His puns are such breeders of puns, in and in,
Our laughter becomes a like manifold din:
Yet a right poet also was Hood, and could vary
His jokes with deep fancies of Centaur and Fairy;
And aye on his fame will a tear be attending,
Who wrote the starv'd song, with its burden unending.
—HUNT, LEIGH, 1859, *The Feast of the Poets, Postscript.*

Pass we now to the serio-comic Hood, —a poet whose memory is "emblazoned with a halo of light-hearted mirth and pleasantry," but whose coruscations of wit and fancy do not more charm us, than do the genial charities and deep human sympathies which characterize his graver productions. If he was the "prince of punsters," he was also pre-eminently the poet of pathos; for, as a portrayer of life in its various phases, his rich and graceful imagery, and vivid descriptions of sorrow and suffering, were no less conspicuous than the kindly spirit with which his sarcasms and satires are tempered, so that while they cauterize, they cure. How much of human suffering has been mitigated, how many a home of sadness consoled, by the pleadings of his powerful pen! The spirit of his playful productions, so chaste, and so glittering with sportive gayety and humour, are yet enriched with the pure gold of wisdom, so that while they charm the imagination, they also benefit the heart.—SAUNDERS, FREDERICK, 1865–74, *Festival of Song, p.* 251.

A genius of a high class cutting capers and making jokes, an author of the humour and deeper calibre of the highest Elizabethan poets, and with the gentle satire of Touchstone, an essayist in his way as subtile as Charles Lamb, a tale-maker with the *drolatique* power and capability of Rabelais, and a poet with much of the sweetness and more than the pathos of Keats;—these together would make up Thomas Hood.—FRISWELL, JAMES HAIN, 1869, *Essays on English Writers, p.* 348.

Hood was not one of those men of commanding intellect who arise but once or twice at most in a nation's history. He did not signalize himself by being the first to climb the slippery steeps of Pisgah, and catch sublime glimpses of the promised land with which to gladden the heart of the world. He is no cold unapproachable idol of the intellect—to be worshipped from afar with awe and trembling. Rather is he enshrined amid the Lares and Penates of our hearts—our household favorites—our Charley Lambs and Sir Philip Sidneys; a kind, genial, honest-hearted man of genius, whom one feels it is good to know and pleasant to remember, whose laugh has a hearty ring wherewith to blow away the cobwebs of sorrow and care, and the shake of whose hand does one's heart good. There have been three or four greater writers in our nation's history, and a few more as great, but there has been no one whose noble efforts on behalf of the poor, the outcast, and the sinning, will serve to embalm his memory and his works in a kindlier affection and regard than Thomas Hood, "the darling of the English heart." —FRASER, J., 1871, *Thomas Hood, The Westminster Review, vol.* 95, *p.* 354.

He was the poet of the heart, and sound at heart himself,—the poet of humane sentiment, clarified by a living spring of humor, which kept it from any taint of sentimentalism. To read his pages is to laugh and weep by turns; to take on human charity; to regard the earth mournfully, yet be thankful, as he was, for what sunshine falls upon it, and to accept manfully, as he did, each one's condition, however toilsome and suffering, under the changeless law that impels and governs all. Even his artistic weakness (and he had no other) were frolicsome and endearing. Much of his verse was the poetry of the beautiful, in a direction opposite to that of the metaphysical kind. His humor—not his jaded humor, the pack-horse of daily task-work, but his humor at its best, which so lightened his pack of ills and sorrows, and made all England know him—was the merriment of hamlets and hostels around the skirts of Parnassus, where not the gods, but Earth's common children, hold their gala-days within the shadow. Lastly, his severer lyrical faculty was musical and sweet: its product is as refined as the most exacting need require, and keeps more uniformly than other modern poetry to the idiomatic measures of English song. . . . There are no strained and affected cadences in his songs. Their diction is so clear that the expression of the thought has no resisting medium,—a high excellence in ballad-verse. With respect to their sentiment, all must admire the absolute health of Hood's poetry written during years of prostration and disease. He warbled cheering and trustful music, either as a foil to personal distress,—which would have been quite too much to bear, had he encountered its echo in his own voice,—or else through a manly resolve that, come what might, he would have nothing to do with the poetry of despair. The man's humor, also, buoyed him up, and thus was its own exceeding great reward.—STEDMAN, EDMUND CLARENCE, 1875-87, *Victorian Poets, pp.* 73, 88.

On the whole, we can pronounce Hood the finest English poet between the generation of Shelley and the generation of Tennyson.—ROSSETTI, WILLIAM MICHAEL, 1878, *Lives of Famous Poets, p.* 381.

Whether, under favourable circumstances, he would have produced more work of a high character is a question that it is scarcely profitable to discuss; but it is manifest that during his life-time the somewhat coarse-palated public welcomed most keenly not so much his best as his second-best. The "Tom Hood" they cared for was not the delicate and fanciful author of the "Plea of the Midsummer Fairies," but the Hood of "Miss Kilmansegg and her Precious Leg,"—the master of broad-grin and equivoque, the delightful parodist, the impressible and irresistible joker and Merry-Andrew. It is not to be denied that much of his work in this way is excellent of its kind, admirable for its genuine drollery and whim, having often at its core, moreover, that subtle sense of the *lacrimæ rerum,* which lends a piquancy of sadness and almost a quality of permanence to much of our modern jesting. But the rest!—the larger part! Nothing except the record of his over-strained, over-burdened life can enable us to understand how the author of the "Ode to Rae Wilson," the "Lament for Chivalry," and the lines "On a distant Prospect of Clapham Academy" could ever have produced such mechanical and melancholy mirth as much of that which has been preserved appears to be. Yet his worst work is seldom without some point; it is better than the best of many others; and, with all its drawbacks, it is at least always pure. It should be remembered too that the fashions of fun pass away like other fashions.—DOBSON, AUSTIN, 1880, *The English Poets, ed. Ward, vol.* IV, *p.* 531.

The sonnets of Hood scarcely appear to have received the recognition that they deserve. They have a strength of thought, and clearness of expression that should insure them a higher rank than they have yet been permitted to take.—WADDINGTON, SAMUEL, 1882, *English Sonnets by Poets of the Past, p.* 235.

Hood was indeed a boom to the literature of this century; for he had, not only the language of genius, but the genius of language as well. He was *facile princeps* in diction as well as in thought. The ground he occupies is an exceptional one, quite as peculiar to himself as that which belongs to Tennyson or Dickens. He is no reproduction of anybody else. He is nobody's echo, nobody's mantle-bearer. He is Hood the Only, just as the Germans claim for Jean Paul that special distinction of individuality.—FIELDS, JAMES T., 1885, *Thomas Hood, Some Noted Princes Authors and Statesmen of our Time, ed. Parton, p.* 155.

To Hood, with his grim imagination and his strange fantastic humour, death was meat and drink. It is as though he saw so much of the "execrable Shape" that at last the pair grew friends, and grinned whenever they foregathered even in thought.—HENLEY, WILLIAM ERNEST, 1890, *Views and Reviews, p.* 168.

Hood produced in twenty-four years an amount of prose and verse of which at least one-half the world might willingly let die. Of the other half, all the serious poetry is remarkable, and a small portion of first-rate excellence. Lyrics such as the "Song of the Shirt," the "Bridge of Sighs," "Eugene Aram," the song beginning "I remember, I remember, the house where I was born," and the "Ode to Melancholy" are of an assured immortality. His humorous verse—and in the best of it, as in "Miss Kilmansegg," are often blended poetry, pathos, and even real tragic power—is of a kind that Hood absolutely created. Not only was he the most prolific and successful punster that ever used that form of wit, but he turned it to purposes of which no one had ever supposed it capable. It became in his hands the most natural and obvious vehicle for all his better gifts. The truth is, he brought to it the transfiguring power of real imagination and, instead of its degrading whatever object touched, in his hands it ministered to the noblest ends.—AINGER, ALFRED, 1890, *Chambers's Encyclopædia, vol.* V, *p.* 768.

In reply to the further question, "What was Thomas Hood?" we answer, Punster, poet, preacher, all combined; a teacher both in life and word on highest Christian principle. Hood's reputation with the general public is undoubtedly only as a joker, and, beyond controversy, he was in act and word, constitutionally, spontaneously, necessarily, always and everywhere, the perpetrator of jests, verbal and practical. The design of this paper is to correct, if possible, this false estimate of a brave knight who went laughingly to battle, but still *went to battle*, against giant falsehoods and follies and giant wrongs and giant misbeliefs, and with his smooth round stones of song did smite them. Its aim is to portray him as poet; in highest, truest sense a poet in life and verse; a maker, creator, who of materials old and familiar doth fashion results startling in their beauty, and in themselves a revelation. And its further aim is to claim for the punster-poet the honor due to the preacher, though unordained and unrecognized, and to show from his sermons how effective was his preaching of that charity "which suffereth long and is kind, which envieth not, vaunteth not itself, is not puffed up, thinketh no evil;" of toleration, that hardest lesson for humanity to learn. —DUDLEY, T. U., 1891, *Thomas Hood, Harper's Magazine, vol.* 82, *p.* 720.

There was little that was didactic or practical in these famous songs of sorrow. Not his was the mission of teaching or the hand to build up reformatory institutions. He fulfilled the true office of poetry in giving vent to that boundless sympathy with suffering and remorseful horror of having any share in the system which makes it possible—which has become in our days the warmest sentiment of the common mind, little as even that has been able to do for the long established evils which mock reformation, or for those human incapacities and weakness which force so many struggling creatures downward to the lowest hopeless depths of worthless labour and starvation. Hood's poems did more perhaps to awaken the national heart than the most appalling statistics could have done, more a hundred times than recent attempts to make capital of vice and feed the impure imagination and gather profit from a vile curiosity, ever could accomplish. That dreadful image of the drowned creature "fashioned so slenderly" taken out of the tragic river with who could tell what piteous past behind her, and no refuge but the dark and awful tides surging between its black banks—has been impressed for ever on the imagination, intolerable yet perfect in the tragedy of its voiceless despair.—OLIPHANT, MARGARET O. W., 1892, *The Victorian Age of English Literature, p.* 236.

Few have taught so forcibly as Hood the truth that the resources of laughter and tears are very near together. Whether we look upon him as a master of frolic, or a master of pathos, his place among English poets is a high one. His hard struggle for existence enriched him with the qualities in which he at first seemed deficient; and the pieces composed under pressure of necessity, and perhaps without direct poetic intention, place him far higher than his deliberate bids for the name and fame of a poet.—GARNETT, RICHARD, 1894, *The Poets and the Poetry of the Century, John Keats to Edward Lord Lytton, ed. Miles, p.* 218.

As a poet he takes a place among contemporary poets and a place peculiarly his own. —MILES, ALFRED H., 1894, *The Poets and the Poetry of the Century, Humour, Society, Parody and Occasional Verse, p.* 250.

I am very fond of Hood, who is strongest on his whimsical side.—LOCKER-LAMPSON, FREDERICK, 1895, *My Confidences, p.* 179.

The fountain of his fun was really inexhaustible, since he drew from it without ceasing for a quarter of a century. But at intervals in later years the waters ran thin and flat, without sparkle or effervescence. Yet no humorist ever wrote so much with so large a remainder of excellence. His puns are not mere verbal sleight of hand, but brilliant verbal wit. Not even Charles Lamb has so mastered the subtlety and the imagery of the pun. Hood goes beyond the analogy of sound and catches the analogy of meaning. But leaving out of the question this inimitable control of words, his drollery is still unrivaled, because it is the whimsical expression, not of the trifler but of the thinker, even of the moralist, and always of the imaginative poet. In the whirl of his absurdities suddenly appears a glimpse of everlasting truth. The merry-Andrew rattles his hoop and grins, but in his jest there is a hint of wholesome tears.—RUNKLE, LUCIA GILBERT, 1897, *Thomas Hood, Library of the World's Best Literature, ed. Warner, vol.* XIII, *p.* 7590.

Hood, it is true, was too great a man to be dismissed as merely a writer of the transition; yet, just because of his greatness, his history shows better than that of any other man how earnestness was discouraged and triviality fostered. Seldom have so great poetic gifts been so squandered—with no dishonour to Hood—on mere puns. The poet, as an early critic pointed out, was a man of essentially serious mind; but he had to earn bread for himself and his children, and as jesting paid, while serious poetry did not, he was compelled to jest. . . . Perhaps the most original fruit of Hood's genius is "Miss Kilmansegg," which conceals under a grotesque exterior deep feeling and effective satire. It has been sometimes ranked as Hood's greatest work; and if comparison be made with his longer pieces only, or if we look principally to the uniqueness of the poem, the judgment will hardly be disputed; but probably the popular instinct which has seized upon "The Song of the Shirt" and "The Bridge of Sighs," and the criticism which exalts "The Haunted House," are in this instance sounder.—WALKER, HUGH, 1897, *The Age of Tennyson, pp.* 54, 55.

Humour and Pathos, a century ago, linked their hands across the cradle of Thomas Hood to vow him for their own. And he was theirs till death. Over the events of his life, or the creations of his brain, that joint-possession never slacked its hold for an hour. If, to visible seeming, Pathos holds supremacy to-day in the sufferings of the poet's body, Humour claims the guidance of his muse; if to-morrow Humour should irradiate his outward life with laughter, we may be sure that Pathos will cast its shadow within. Tears and laughter are never far apart in that strangely-mingled life. Behind the smile there is a thinly-veiled sadness; through the tears there comes a gleam of mirth. It was a dual life he lived, an April day of shine and shadow.—SHELLEY, H. C., 1899, *Thomas Hood's First Centenary, Fortnightly Review, vol.* 71, *p.* 987.

Sydney Smith

1771-1845

Born, at Woodford, Essex, 3 June 1771. At school at Southampton, 1777-82. At Winchester School, July 1782 to 1789. Matric., New Coll., Oxford, 7 Feb. 1789; Fellow, 1790-1800; B. A., 1792; M. A., 1796. Ordained, 1794. Curate of Nether-Avon, Wilts., 1794-97. To Edinburgh, as private tutor to Michael Beach, 1798. Married Catherine Amelia Pybus, 2 July 1800. Founder of "Edinburgh Review," 1803; contributor till March 1827. Removed to London, 1803. Lectured at Royal Institution, 1804, 1805, 1806. Preacher at Foundling Hospital, March 1805 to Oct. 1808. Rector of Foston-le-Clay, Yorkshire, 1806-29. Rector of Londesborough, 1825-32. Visit to Paris, 1826. Canon of Bristol, 1828. Rector of Combe-Florey, Somersetshire, 1829-31. Canon Residentiary of St. Paul's Cathedral, 1831. Visit to Paris, 1835. Died, in London, 22 Feb. 1845. Buried at Kensal Green. *Works:* (exclusive of separate sermons); "Six Sermons," 1800; "Sermons" (2 vols.), 1801, (2nd edn., same year); "Letters on the Subject of the Catholics" (under pseud.: "Peter Plymley") 1807-08; "Sermons" (2 vols.), 1809; "The Judge that smites contrary to the Law" (priv. ptd.), 1824; "Catholic Claims," 1825; "Letters to the Electors on the Catholic Question," 1826 (2nd edn. same year); "Mr. Dyson's Speech to the Freeholders on Reform," 1831; "Three Letters to Archdeacon Singleton," 1837, 1838, 1839; "Letter to Lord John Russell," 1838; "Ballot," 1839 (3rd edn. same year); "Works," (4 vols.), 1839-40; "Letters on American Debts," 1844 (2nd edn. same year).

Posthumous: "A Fragment on the Irish Roman Catholic Church," 1845; (7th edn. same year); "Sermons preached at St. Paul's Cathedral," 1846; "Elementary Sketches of Moral Philosophy," ed. by Lord Jeffrey, 1850 (2nd edn. same year; priv. ptd., 1849); "Essays" (from "Edinburgh Rev.") [1874]. *Collected Works:* in 3 vols., 1854. *Life:* "Life and Letters" by Lady Holland, 1855; "Life," by S. J. Reid, 1884.—SHARP, R. FARQUHARSON, 1897, *A Dictionary of English Authors, p.* 262.

PERSONAL

I never saw a man so formed to float down the stream of conversation, and, without seeming to have any direct influence upon it, to give it his own hue and charm. He is about fifty, corpulent, but not gross, with a great fund of good nature, and would be thought by a person who saw him only once, and transiently, merely a gay, easy gentleman, careless of everything but the pleasure of conversation and society. This would be a great injustice to him, and one that offends him, I am told; for, notwithstanding the easy grace and light playfulness of his wit, which comes forth with unexhausted and inexhaustible facility, and reminded me continually of the phosphoric brilliancy of the ocean, which sparkles more brightly in proportion as the force opposed to it is greater, yet he is a man of much culture, with plain good-sense, a sound, discreet judgment, and remarkably just and accurate habits of reasoning, and values himself upon these, as well as on his admirable humor. This is an union of opposite qualities, such as nature usually delights to hold asunder, and such as makes him, whether in company or alone, an irresistibly amusing companion; for, while his humor gives such grace to his argument that it comes with the charm of wit, and his wit is so appropriate that its sallies are often logic in masquerade, his good-sense and good-nature are so prevalent that he never, or rarely, offends against the proprieties of life or society, and never says anything that he or anybody else need to regret afterwards.—TICKNOR, GEORGE, 1819, *Journal, Jan.; Life, Letters and Journal, vol.* I, *p.* 265.

Dined at Rogers's. A distinguished party. . . . Smith particularly amusing. Have rather held out against him hitherto; but this day he conquered me; and I now am his victim, in the laughing way, for life. His imagination of a duel between two doctors, with oil of croton on the tips of their fingers, trying to touch each other's lips highly ludicrous. What Rogers says of Smith, very true, that whenever the conversation is getting dull, he throws in some touch which makes it rebound, and rise again as light as ever. Ward's artificial efforts, which to me are always painful, made still more so by their contrast to Smith's natural and overflowing exuberance. Luttrel too, considerably extinguished to-day; but there is this difference between Luttrel and Smith—that after the former, you remember what good things he said, and after the latter, you merely remember how much you laughed.—MOORE, THOMAS, 1823, *Diary, April* 10; *Memoirs, Journal and Correspondence, ed. Russell, vol.* IV., *p.* 53.

> The very powerful parson, Peter Pith,
> The loudest wit I e'er was deafen'd with.

BYRON, LORD, 1824, *Don Juan, Canto, XVI,* s. 81.

Tickler. "Yes—Sydney Smith has a rare genius for the grotesque. He is, with his quibs and cranks, a formidable enemy to pomposity and pretension. No man can wear a big wig comfortably in his presence; the absurdity of such enormous frizzle is felt; and the dignitary would fain exchange all that horsehair for a few scattered locks of another animal."—WILSON, JOHN, 1826, *Noctes Ambrosianæ, June.*

I have really taken a great liking to him. He is full of wit, humor, and shrewdness. He is not one of those show-talkers who reserve all their good things for special occasions. It seems to be his greatest luxury to keep his wife and daughters laughing for two or three hours every day. His notions of law, government, and trade are surprisingly clear and just. His misfortune is to have chosen a profession at once above him and below him. Zeal would have made him a prodigy; formality and bigotry would have made him a bishop; but he could neither rise to the duties of his order, nor stoop to its degradations. — MACAULAY, THOMAS BABINGTON, 1826, *To His Father, July* 26; *Life and Letters, ed. Trevelyan.*

Sydney Smith preached a most beautiful, eloquent sermon this morning to a crowded, alas! dining-room. I like him better so than when in society He is, as Mr. Sneyd says, something between Cato and Punch. You must allow that this describes his physique admirably.—GRANVILLE, HARRIET COUNTESS, 1826, *To Lady Carlisle, May*; *Letters ed. Gower, vol.* I, *p.* 384.

I do not know any man whom I should wish more to make my friend: super eminent talents and an excellent heart, which in my opinion almost always go together. —EDGEWORTH, MARIA, 1827, *To Captain Basil Hall, April* 25; *Letters, vol.* II, *p.*154.

Went to St. Paul's yesterday evening, to hear Sydney Smith preach. He is very good; manner impressive, voice sonorous and agreeable, *rather* familiar, but not offensively so, language simple and unadorned, sermon clever and illustrative.—GREVILLE, CHARLES C. F., 1834, *Memoirs, Dec.* 1.

His great delight was to produce a succession of ludicrous images: these followed each other with a rapidity that scarcely left time to laugh; he himself laughing louder and with more enjoyment than any one. This electric contact of mirth came and went with the occasion; it cannot be repeated or reproduced. Any thing would give occasion to it. For instance, having seen in the newspapers that Sir Æneas Mackintosh was come to town, he drew such a ludicrous caricature of Sir Æneas and Lady Dido, for the amusement of their namesake, that Sir James Mackintosh rolled on the floor in fits of laughter, and Sydney Smith, striding across him, exclaimed "Ruat Justitia!"—RUSSELL, LORD JOHN, 1853, *Memoir, Journal and Correspondence of Thomas Moore, Preface.*

He had no philosophic turn, little poetic fancy, and scarce any eloquence, but a prodigious fund of innate sagacity, vast powers of humorous illustration, and a clear perception of the practical bearing of every question. . . . In society he was very much sought after, from the fame of his convivial talents and the real force of his colloquial expressions; but there was a constant straining after effect, and too little interchange of thought to raise his discourse to a very high charm.—ALISON, SIR ARCHIBALD, 1853–59, *History of Europe*, 1815–1852, *ch.* V.

It signified not what the materials were: I never remember a dull dinner in his company. He extracted amusement from every subject, however hopeless. He descended, and adapted himself to the meanest capacity, without seeming to do so; he led without seeking to lead; he never sought to shine—the light appeared because he could not help it. Nobody felt excluded. He had the happy art of always saying the best thing in the best manner to the right person at the right moment; it was a touch-and-go impossible to describe, guided by such tact and attention to the feelings of others, that those he most attacked seemed most to enjoy the attack; never in the same mood for two minutes together, and each mood seemed to be more agreeable than the last.—HOLLAND, LADY, 1855, *A Memoir of the Rev. Sydney Smith.*

He was a giant when roused, and the goad which roused him was Injustice. He was clear from envy, hatred, and all uncharitableness, and incapable of any littleness. He was ever ready to defend the weak. He showed as much zeal in saving a poor village boy, as in aiding a Minister of State. His hatred of every form of cant and affectation was only equalled by his prompt and unerring detection of it. . . . There never was a man in whom they were calculated to excite more disgust than the brave, frank, and high-spirited gentleman whose letters are before us. For in him a passion for truth was enlightened by the utmost perspicacity of mind, and the most acute sense of the ludicrous and unseemly.—AUSTIN, SARAH, 1855, *Letters of Sydney Smith, Preface.*

He came, and sat down, broad and comfortable, in the middle of my sofa, with his hands on his stick, as if to support himself in a vast development of voice; and then he began, like the great bell of St. Paul's, making me start at the first stroke. He looked with shy dislike at my trumpet, for which there was truly no occasion. I was more likely to fly to the furthest corner of the room. It was always his boast that I did not want my trumpet when he talked with me.—MARTINEAU, HARRIET, 1855–77, *Autobiography, ed. Chapman, vol.* I, *p.* 244.

He seems to have been a thoroughly good husband, good father, good master—loving and beloved—caring for the convenience, the feelings, of all round him—free from parsimony, equally free from prodigality—free from the vulgarity which is ashamed of poverty, and the vulgarity which pretends to despise wealth.—KINGSLEY, CHARLES, 1855, *Sydney Smith, Fraser's Magazine, vol.* 52, *p.* 84.

In default of an episcopal palace, Sydney Smith removed, in 1828, to Combe Florey, near Taunton, which he soon converted into one of the most comfortable and delightful of parsonages. . . . On one occasion, when some London visitors were expected, he called in art to aid nature, and caused oranges to be tied to the shrubs in the drive and garden. The stratagem succeeded admirably, and great was his exultation when an unlucky urchin from the village was detected in the act of sucking one through a quill. . . . Another time, on a lady's happening to hint that the pretty paddock would be improved by deer, he fitted his two donkeys with antlers, and placed them with this extraordinary head-gear on a rising ground immediately in front of the windows. The effect, enhanced by the puzzled looks of the animals, was ludicrous in the extreme.—HAYWARD, ABRAHAM, 1855, *Rev. Sydney Smith, Biographical and Critical Essays.*

Like pious and brave old Herbert, he found a kingdom in his mind which he knew how to rule and to enjoy; and this priceless boon was his triumph and comfort in the lowliest struggles and in the highest prosperity. It irradiated the damp walls of his first parsonage with the glow of wit; nerved his heart, as a poor vicar, to plead the cause of reform against the banded conservatives of a realm; hinted a thousand expedients to beguile isolation and indigence of their gloom; invested his presence and speech with self-possession and authority in the peasant's hut and at the bishop's table; made him an architect, a physician, a judge, a schoolmaster, a critic, a reformer, the choicest man of society, the most efficient of domestic economists, the best of correspondents, the most practical of political writers, the most impressive of preachers, the most genial of companions; a good farmer, a patient nurse, and an admirable husband, father, and friend. The integrity, good sense, and moral energy, which gave birth to this versatile exercise of his faculties, constitute the broad and solid foundation of Sydney Smith's character; they were the essential traits of the man, the base to that noble column of which wit formed the capital and wisdom the shaft. In the temple of humanity what support it yielded during his life, and how well-proportioned and complete it now stands to the eye of memory, an unbroken and sky-pointing cenotaph on his honored grave!—TUCKERMAN, HENRY T., 1857, *Essays, Biographical and Critical, p.* 368.

I at this time [1832] became acquainted with Sydney Smith, through my friend Newton. His wit and humour were always unpremeditated, and seemed not so much the result of efforts to amuse, as the overflowing of a mind full of imagery, instantly ready to combine with whatever passed in conversation. His very exaggerations took away the sting of his most personal witticisms, and I suppose no man was ever so amusing with so little offence; for those who were the subjects of his jokes were often the most ready to relate them.—LESLIE, CHARLES ROBERT, 1860 *Autobiographical Recollections, ed. Taylor,* 71.

Such eyes, so noble a brow, with its brown hair thinly scattered; so symmetrical a profile, so expressive a mouth, so fine and glowing a complexion; such a combination of manly dignity and beauty, —were never before seen, nor since, as were combined in the face of that short, slight, active youth, Sydney Smith.—THOMSON, KATHERINE (GRACE WHARTON), 1862, *The Literature of Society, vol.* II, *p.* 304.

While his main delight was in intellectual intercourse, and, during his more active life, in intellectual exertion, he could hardly be called a student of literature. He thought it no more necessary for a man to remember the different books that had made him wise than the different dinners that had made him healthy: he looked for the result of good feeding in a powerful body, and that of good reading in a full strong mind. Thus his pleasure in the acquaintance of authors was rather in the men and women themselves than in the merit of this or that production.—MILNES, RICHARD MONCKTON (LORD HOUGHTON), 1873, *Monographs, Personal and Social, p.* 260.

The only wit, perhaps, on record, whom brilliant social success had done nothing to spoil or harden; a man who heartened himself up to enjoy, and to make others enjoy, by the sound of his own genial laugh; whose tongue was as keen as a Damascus blade when he had to deal with bigotry, or falsehood, or affectation; but whose forbearance and gentleness to those, however obscure, whom he deemed honest, were as healing as his sarcasm could be vitriolic.—CHORLEY, HENRY FOTHERGILL, 1873, *Autobiography, Memoirs and Letters, vol.* I, *p.* 196.

The special and reportable sallies of Sydney Smith have been, of course, often repeated, but the fanciful fun and inexhaustible humorous drollery of his conversation among his intimates can never be adequately rendered or reproduced. He bubbled over with mirth, of which his own enjoyment formed an irresistible element, he shook, and his eyes glistened at his own ludicrous ideas, as they dawned upon his brain; and it would be impossible to convey the faintest ideas of the genial humor of his habitual talk by merely repeating separate witticisms and repartees.—KEMBLE, FRANCES ANN, 1882, *Records of Later Life, p.* 64.

He was buried at Kensal Green Cemetery, on Friday the 28th; the funeral was strictly private, and only a few of his nearest relatives and friends were present; but in spirit at least, there was no section of the nation which was not represented by the sorrow round that grave. There is an official handbook to the vast and silent city of the dead in which he sleeps, and yet so late as the summer of 1883, the name of one of the truest benefactors of the English people who rests within its gates, was not judged of sufficient importance to be included in the pages of that manual. Those who wish to make a pilgrimage to the grave of Sydney Smith, will therefore be glad to know that they can easily find it, by following the north walk until they are opposite the entrance to the catacombs. Turning to the left at that point, they will discover in the fifth row from the walk a raised tomb of Portland stone. . . . With the solitary exception of a small painted window (erected through the efforts of his successor Mr. Sanford) in the church at Combe-Florey, the grave in Kensal Green is the only memorial to Sydney Smith which England has to show. REID, STUART J., 1884, *A Sketch of the Life and the Times of Rev. Sydney Smith, pp.* 390, 392.

He was a very striking looking man, with a countenance indicating great intellectual power; a countenance, indeed, which might have been said to wear a thoughtful, if not rather a stern expression in repose—only that it never was in repose. His strength of mind, firmness of purpose, and great general ability, ought, no doubt, to have earned for him a bishopric from the Whigs, but unluckily his wit lost it him. The chiefs of his party had not courage enough (more shame to them) to place so unquenchable a live firework upon the episcopal bench, though nobody who knew him ever doubted that he would have made an excellent bishop. For he was thoroughly conscientious, knew men, and understood life in all its forms and varieties, and was rendered indulgent, both to high and low, by the softening influence of humour, as well as by the breadth and vigor of his mind. He also distinguished himself as a preacher, but that as a qualification for a bishop, whose business it is to rule, guide, and organise, seems to me to be of secondary importance. DOYLE, SIR FRANCIS HASTINGS, 1886, *Reminiscences and Opinions, p.* 62.

The manner of the preacher remains more vividly present to my mind than his words. He spoke with extreme rapidity, and had the special gift of combining extreme rapidity of utterance with very perfect clearness. His manner, I remember thinking, was unlike any that I had ever witnessed in the pulpit, and appeared to me to resemble rather that of a very earnest speaker at the hustings than the usual pulpit style. His sentences seemed to run down-hill, with continually increasing speed till they came to a full stop at the bottom. It was, I think, the only sermon I ever heard which I wished longer. He carried me with him completely, for the century was in those days, like me, young. —TROLLOPE, THOMAS ADOLPHUS, 1888, *What I Remember, p.* 278.

GENERAL

If no publication ever came with more defective claims, in point of theological quality, than these sermons, we must employ a different language as to what they exhibit of intellectual ability and moral instruction. They display a great deal of acuteness, diversified mental activity, and independent thinking. Whatever else there is, there is no commonplace. The matter is sometimes too bad, sometimes too good, but always too shrewd, to be dull. The author is a sharp observer of mankind, and has a large portion of knowledge of the world. . . . The cast of his language compels an unwilling suspicion, that the purpose is not so much to enforce the subject, as to parade it; and, in doing so, to play off the greatest possible number of quaint pranks of rhetorical manœuvre. We doubt whether we ever saw, within an equal space, so many fantastic quiddities of diction, such a perverse study to twitch our strong, honest, manful, old language into uncouth postures and vain antics.—FOSTER, JOHN, 1809, *Sydney Smith's Sermons, Critical Essays, ed. Ryland, vol.* I, *pp.* 303, 309.

The present publication ["A sermon preached before his Grace the Archbishop of York,"] etc., is by far the worst of all his performances, avowed or imputed. Literary merit it has none; but in arrogance, presumption, and absurdity it far outdoes all his former outdoings.—CROKER, JOHN WILSON, 1810, *Sydney Smith's Visitation Sermon, Quarterly Review, vol.* 3, *p.* 193.

Almost everything he has written is so characteristic, that it would be difficult to attribute it to any other man. The marked individual features, and the rare combination of powers, displayed in his works, give them a fascination unconnected with the subject of which he treats, or the general correctness of his views. He sometimes hits the mark in the white, he sometimes misses it altogether; for he by no means confines his pen to themes to which he is calculated to do justice; but whether he hits or misses, he is always sparkling and delightful. . . . The great peculiarity of his works, apart from the qualities of character they display, is their singular blending of the beautiful with the ludicrous; and this is the source of his refinement. He is keen and personal, almost fierce and merciless, in his attacks on public abuses; he has no check on his humor from authority or conventional forms; and yet he very rarely violates good taste. There is much good nature in him in spite of his severity. His quick perception of what is laughable modifies his sensibility to what is detestable. He cannot be grave for ten minutes, though on the gravest of subjects. His indignation and invective are almost ever followed by some jesting allusion or grotesque conceit. He draws down upon the object of his censure both scorn and laughter; and makes even abuse palatable by clothing it in phrases or images which charm by their beauty or wit. —WHIPPLE, EDWIN P., 1844, *Sydney Smith, North American Review, July; Essays and Reviews.*

His sermons are replete with pure doctrine, toleration, and liberality of sentiment. The Irish Catholics ought to erect a monument to him, with his statue on the top —looking very grave, but with the hands "holding both his sides," and the tablets at the base covered with bas-relief selected from the graphic pages of Peter Plymley. Although wit is the great predominating characteristic of the writings of Sydney Smith, the finest and most original humour is not unfrequently displayed.—HORNE, RICHARD HENGIST, 1844, *A New Spirit of the Age, p.* 165.

A pen which, I think, I may venture to assert was never sullied by private passion or private interest, never degraded by an impure or unworthy motive, and, with all its unexampled powers of sarcasm, never wounding but for the public good. . . . He was a sort of rough-rider of a subject; sometimes originating, but more frequently taking up what others had for years been stating humbly, or timidly, or obscurely, or lengthily, or imperfectly, or dully, to the world; extracting at once its essence, unveiling the motives of his opponents, and placing his case clearly, concisely, simply, eloquently, boldly, brightly, before the public eye. Thus the subject became read, thought of, discussed, and often acted upon by thousands of persons dispersed over various parts of the world. This cannot have been without powerful influence on the opinions and conduct of society.—HOLLAND, LADY, 1855, *A Memoir of the Rev. Sydney Smith.*

Sydney Smith was an after-dinner writer: his words have a flow, a vigor, an expression, which is not given to hungry mortals; you seem to read of good wine, of good cheer, of beaming and buoyant enjoyment. There is little trace of labor in his composition: it is poured forth like an unceasing torrent, rejoicing daily to run its course. And what courage there is in it! There is as much variety of pluck in writing across a sheet as in riding across a country.—BAGEHOT, WALTER, 1855, *The First Edinburgh Reviewers, Works, ed. Morgan.*

Mrs. Austin justly remarks that the reputation of Sydney Smith has risen since his death. It has risen, and it is to rise. Every year lessens the number of those who can remember the marvellous charm of his conversation, that diaphragm-shaking, fancy-chasing, oddity-piling, incongruity-linking, hyperbole-topping, wonder-working faculty of his, which a bookful of Homeric compound adjectives would still leave undescribed. But meanwhile, the true proportions of that large intellect have been growing upon the vision of men. Blinded with tears of laughter, they could not estimate his magnitude. Hands palsied by convulsive cachinnations were too unsteady to hold the measure and fit the colossus with a judgment. Now it is better understood how all that wit was only the efflorescence of his greatness—the waving wild flowers on the surface of a pyramid. Time may take from the edifice of his fame some of its lighter decorations, obliterate quaint carvings, decapitate some grotesque and pendant gargoles, destroy some rich flamboyant word traceries; but that very spoliation will only display more completely the solid foundation, the broad harmonious plan of his life's structure, and exhibit the fine conscientiousness with which those parts of the building most remote from the public eye were finished, even as they most seem. . . . The wit of Sydney Smith was always under the control of good taste and good feeling. It was never mischievous to him by any unseemliness, impertinence, or vulgarity. Throughout his writings, so remarkable for natural flow and freedom of style, so simple and so idiomatic, you search in vain for anything slipshod, for triteness or chit-chat, for a single colloquial solescism. His style, like golden haired Pyrrha, is always *simplex munditiis.*—VAUGHAN, ROBERT ALFRED, 1857? *Essays and Remains, vol.* II.

There are passages in them tinged with the wit which made him so delightful a companion out of the pulpit, but this does not in the least impair their seriousness. He seems to me, in these discourses, to be at all times equally earnest, eloquent, and sound in the view he takes of his subject, and the more I read them the more I find them to contain.—LESLIE, C. R., 1860, *Autobiographical Recollections, p.* 75.

Underneath the almost riotous exuberance of his humour, joyous to himself as to all around him, there ever lay a foundation of strong masculine sense, as well as of wholesome satire upon the foibles or wrongdoings of the world. . . . Swift somewhere speaks of "the Ghost of Wit delighting to walk after the death of the body." Sydney Smith's writings are never haunted by this spirit. His wit comes unsought for, serves its purpose, and he passes at once again into serious argument—serious, but always short and pithy in style. Those who love Dryden—and they ought to be legion—will recognise the charm, belonging to the bold and unexpected phrases of his poetry. Sydney Smith's prose has the same charm. His phrases are never pedantic or pirated, but always fresh from the mint of his own genius. He never looked over again what he had once written, and, as I know, could hardly ever be persuaded to correct the errors of a proof-sheet. He revelled in his own manner of handling a subject, and was comparatively careless of its effect on others.—HOLLAND, SIR HENRY, 1871, *Recollections of Past Life, pp.* 276, 277.

His style has something of the reported character of his conversation; mixed up with the "infinite humour," we have clear statement of pertinent facts and sound arguments. We are not conscious of any awkwardness of transition from the comic to the serious; he usually writes with a serious purpose—with the object of discrediting, both by reason and by ridicule, something that he disapproves of. He is often humorous, purely for the sake of the humour, but his prevailing purposes are serious. What is more, he did not, like the "Spectator," the "Rambler," and the "Citizen of the World," attack ignorance, folly, bigotry, and vice with inoffensive generality, directing his ridicule against imaginary types; but he openly assailed and turned to scorn living men, and laws, parties, and institutions that were in actual existence. He was far from surveying mankind with the artistic impartiality of Goldsmith; he used his wit unmercifully on the side of a party; he was one of the most aggressive of the Edinburgh Reviewers. . . . Although a good-natured man, without a trace of the sourness and fierceness of Swift, and now recognised as having used his powers in the main on the side of good sense and good feeling, he was most provokingly and audaciously personal in his strictures. This point must be especially attended to in an estimate of Sydney Smith as a master of the ludicrous; the mere fact of overt personality distinguishes him from all our great humorists or satirists except Swift, and he is distinguished from Swift by his greater heartiness of nature. He is too complacent, too aboundingly self-satisfied, too buoyantly full of spirits, to hate anybody; but he burlesques them, derides them, and abuses them with the most exasperating effrontery—in a way that is great fun to the reader, but exquisite torture to the victim. —MINTO, WILLIAM, 1872–80, *Manual of English Prose Literature, pp.* 532, 533.

Sydney Smith was one of the most formidable pamphleteers which this country has ever produced. With extraordinary powers of wit, sarcasm, and expression, his writings had an immense effect on the politics of his time. Born in 1771, and producing his most pungent work—"The Letters of Peter Plymley"—in 1807 and 1808, he was at the zenith of his reputation at the close of the great war. Smith's forte lay in unsparing and occasionally indiscriminating attack. His writings were logical; but he rarely relied on his arguments alone for the success of his cause. He did not convert his readers to his own side. He overwhelmed his opponents with ridicule. The process of damning the plaintiff's attorney has been often resorted to; but it has usually been adopted by advocates with a weak cause to rely upon. Sydney Smith thrust home his attack on the person of his adversary, when his adversary might have been beaten with more logical weapons. His exuberant wit shone forth in his most argumentative writings, and dazzled with its brilliancy those who were not convinced by his arguments.—WALPOLE, SPENCER, 1878, *A History of England from the Conclusion of the Great War in* 1815, *vol.* I, *p.* 385.

Sydney Smith would not appear to have encountered many of the griefs of life, and his witticisms are a constant succession of mere *jeux d'esprit;* they are pretty rainbow-tinted foam-bells on the waters of life. And while it is impossible not to admire their brilliancy and their point, it is only the prejudice of friendship that can draw any parallel between him and many of his contemporaries, while to a name like that of Lamb there is not the most remote approach. It is also true that Sydney Smith approached more nearly to a wit than a humorist. He attacked the world's follies rather by satire than by banter; yet let us not be ungrateful, he lived to a purpose, and he employed his great and lively powers to advance the interests and the well-being of humanity.—HOOD, E. PAXTON, 1882, *The Kings of Laughter, Leisure Hour, vol.* 31, *p.* 552.

When one tries to estimate the genius of Sydney Smith, what strikes one most is his humor unaccompanied by melancholy. Most great humorists have been melancholy men, like Molière. Sydney Smith, on the other hand, was not a jester only in his books and in society. His wonderful high spirits were almost constantly with him in the home which they filled with happiness and laughter. The essence of his wit is this volatile and airy spirit, soaring without trammel high above the laboring world, and discovering, from its familiar heights, mirthful resemblances in things where other men only saw incongruities. Boldness, freedom, vivacity, these are the characteristics of his humor. He had an extraordinary audacity in venturing almost on the verge of nonsense. He was daring in humorous exaggeration. This buoyant courage and gayety of fancy sometimes give his good things the character of American humor.—LANG, ANDREW, 1884, *Sydney Smith, Harper's Magazine, vol.* 69, *p.* 899.

In life and in conversation, as well as more rarely in his private letters, he may sometimes have passed from comedy to farce, but he never does this in his regular literary work. There is, as a rule, no verbal horseplay, no literary practical joking allowed in these remarkable productions. Even in the most daring and the most unscrupulous of them, "Peter Plymley," there is little of either. That quality of exact proportion and measure which Thackeray—no lenient judge in that case—rightly assigned to Swift's humour, is in a lower degree and share equally characteristic of Sydney Smith's wit. . . . Intensely amusing as it is, Sydney Smith's pleasantry belongs on the whole to the severer styles and orders of literary architecture. It is Greek rather than Gothic, and Ionic rather than Corinthian.—SAINTSBURY, GEORGE, 1896, *English Prose, ed. Craik, vol.* V, *pp.* 128, 129.

Nor had he, . . . either the imagination or the grasp of large issues, which makes the great satirist. He was English to the core in his overmastering instinct for the matter of fact. His best work was done in promoting definite practical ends, and his wit in its airiest gambols never escaped his control. He did not write to entertain, but because he had strong opinions. Few men of letters of his standing have had less of the foppery of the literary man.—HERFORD, C. H., 1897, *The Age of Wordsworth, p.* 55.

The great success of the review brought a reputation to the chief contributors. Smith's articles are among the best, and are now the most readable. Many of them are mere trifles, but nearly all show his characteristic style. He deserves the credit of vigorously defending doctrines then unpopular, and now generally accepted. Smith was a thorough whig of the more enlightened variety, and his attacks upon various abuses, though not in advance of the liberalism of the day, gave him a bad name among the dispensers of patronage at the time. His honesty and manliness are indisputable. —STEPHEN, LESLIE, 1898, *Dictionary of National Biography, vol.* LIII, *p.* 120.

Richard Harris Barham

1788–1845

Born, at Canterbury, 6 Dec. 1788. Educated at St. Paul's School, London, 1800–07. Matric. Brasenose Coll., Oxford, 13 June 1807, as a Pauline Exhibitioner; B. A. Nov. 1811. Ordained 1813; Curate of Ashford, 1813–14. Married Caroline Smart, 30 Sept. 1814. Curate of Westwell, 1814–17; Vicar of Snargate, Romney Marsh, 1817–24; Minor Canon, St. Paul's Cathedral, April 1821. To London, Aug. 1821. Rector of St. Mary Magdalene and St. Gregory, and Priest in Ordinary to Chapels Royal, 1824–42. Rector of St. Faith, 1824. Assisted J. G. Gorton in compilation of "Biographical Dictionary," 1828. Contrib. to "Blackwood," "John Bull," "Globe," "Literary Gazette," and "London Chronicle." Edited latter for a time. "Ingoldsby Legends" appeared in "Bentley's Miscellany," 1837–43; in "New Monthly Magazine," 1843–44. Divinity Lecturer at St. Paul's 1842. Vicar of St. Faith, 1842. Died in London, 17 June 1845. Buried in vault of St. Mary Magdalene's; on its being burnt down his remains were removed to Kensal Green Cemetery, and memorial tablet transferred to crypt of St. Paul's. *Works:* "Look at the Clock" [1830?]; "Ingoldsby Legends," 1st series, 1840; 2nd series, 1842; "Some Account of my Cousin Nicolas" (under pseud. of Thomas Ingoldsby), 1841. *Posthumous:* 3rd series of "Ingoldsby Legends," edited by R. H. D. Barham, 1847; "Ingoldsby Lyrics" (miscellaneous poems), 1881. "Life and Letters," by R. H. D. Barham, 1870.—SHARP, R. FARQUHARSON, 1897, *A Dictionary of English Authors, p.* 16.

PERSONAL

I am perfectly convinced that the same social influence would have followed Mr. Barham into any other line of life that he might have adopted; that the profits of agitating pettifoggers would have materially lessened in a district where he acted as a magistrate; and that duels would have been nipped in the bud at his regimental mess. It is not always an easy task to do as you would be done by; but to think as you would be thought of and thought for, and to feel as you would be felt for, is perhaps still more difficult, as superior powers of tact and intellect are here required in order to second good intentions. These faculties, backed by an uncompromising love of truth and fair dealing, indefatigable good nature, and a nice sense of what was due to every one in the several relations of life, both gentle and simple, rendered our late friend invaluable, either as an adviser or a peacemaker, in matters of delicate and difficult handling. How he managed to get through his more important duties is a marvel. Certain it is that they were well and punctually performed in every point relating to cathedral matters, as well as his engagements as a parochial incumbent and "Priest of the Household," (which I believe was the nature of his office at the Chapel Royal).—HUGHES, JOHN, 1845, *Sketch of the Late Rev. R. H. Barham, New Monthly Magazine, vol.* 74, *p.* 527.

Independently, indeed, of any admiration Mr. Barham's wit and talent might excite, there was a warmth of heart about him, and an amiability of disposition, which rendered him justly dear to many even beyond the pale of intimacy. His spirits were fresh and buoyant, his constitution vigorous, and his temperament sanguine. His humour never ranged "beyond the limits of becoming mirth," and was in its essence free from gall. Where irony was employed, it was commonly just, and always gentle. On his writings might, in fairness, be inscribed:—

Non ego mordaci distrinxi carmine quenquam,
Nulla venenato est litera mixta joco.

Perhaps his virtues were of a kind especially adapted to win their own reward; certain it is that to him humanity was ever presented under its fairest aspect. He never lost a friend; he never met with coldness or neglect. . . . Those upon whom he was instrumental in conferring benefits were rarely, if ever, wanting in gratitude; and his own claims to consideration were readily and liberally allowed.—BARHAM, R. H. D., 1870, *ed., The Life and Letters of the Rev. Richard Harris Barham, vol.* II, *p.* 225.

The life of Barham was in a certain sense typical of the class to which he belonged. He enjoyed life, loved his friends, was fond of a good dinner and a good story, a right-minded, jovial English parson. Literature was as much his amusement as his employment.—STODDARD, RICHARD HENRY, 1874, *ed., Personal Reminiscences by Barham, Harness and Hodder, Preface, p.* xii.

As a man Barham was exemplary, a pattern Englishman of the most distinctively national type. The associate of men of wit and gaiety, making himself no pretension to any extraordinary strictness of conduct, he passed through life with perfect credit as a clergyman and universal respect as a member of society. He mitigated the prejudices of his education by the innate candour of his disposition, and added to other endowments soundness of judgment and solidity of good sense.—GARNETT, RICHARD, 1885, *Dictionary of National Biography, vol.* III, *p.* 189.

INGOLDSBY LEGENDS
1840–47

All Barham's care and forethought were employed on mere prosaic matters of business, professional and otherwise, and the "Ingoldsby Legends" were the occasional relief of a suppressed plethora of native fun. The same relaxation which men seek in music, pictures, cards, or newspapers, he sought in, as it were, stripping off his coat to have a hearty romp with the laughing part of the public, in the confidence of a bold unsuspicious nature. Many of these effusions were written while waiting for a cup of tea, a railroad train, or an unpunctual acquaintance, on some stray cover of a letter in his pocket-book: one in particular served to relieve the tedium of a hot walk up Richmond Hill. It was rather a piece of luck if he found time to joint together the *disjecti membra poetæ* in a fair copy: and before the favoured few had done laughing at some rhyme which had never entered a man's head before, the zealous Bentley had popped the whole into type.—HUGHES, JOHN, 1845, *Sketch of the Late Rev. R. H. Barham, New Monthly Magazine, vol.* 74, *p.* 530.

The humor of these poems approaches more nearly to that of Hudibras than any other similar poem, and, like that work, they are unsparing in their ridicule of hypocrisy and knavery.—BALDWIN, JAMES, 1882, *English Literature and Literary Criticism, Poetry, p.* 567.

Barham owes his honourable rank among English humourists to his having done one thing supremely well. He has thoroughly naturalised the French metrical *conte* with the adaptations necessary to accommodate it to our national genius. French humour is rather finely malicious than genial: Barham carries geniality to the verge of the exuberant. He riots in fancy and frolic, and his inexhaustible faculty of grotesque rhyming is but the counterpart of his intellectual fertility in the domain of farcical humour. There is, indeed, an element of farce in his fun, an excessive reliance on forced contrasts between the ghastly and the ludicrous, and a not unfrequent straining after cheap effects; nor can the most successful work of the professional jester be compared to the recreation of a great poet, such as Browning's "Pied Piper of Hamelin." It is nevertheless true that no English author, with the exception of Hood, has produced such a body of excellent rhymed mirth as Barham; and that, if his humour is less refined than Hood's, and his gaiety not equally purified and ennobled by being dashed with tears, he excels his rival as a narrative poet. He may, indeed, be said to have prescribed the form in our language for humorous narrative in irregular verse, which can now hardly be composed without seeming to imitate him.—GARNETT, RICHARD, 1885, *Dictionary of National Biography, vol.* III, *p.* 189.

I have been told indeed that "The Ingoldsby Legends" of very late years have shown a certain loss of grip on popular, at least on popular literary estimation. They are not so often quoted; the young man of letters of the day does not appreciate them, but rather disdains and so forth. Even, however, if this were true (and I am rather doubtful of its truth), even if we were to suppose that the very amusing onslaught made upon the "Legends" some ten or a dozen years ago by a person of the æsthetic persuasion, in very nearly the same terms as those which good Roger Ascham applied to the "Morte d'Arthur," had effect, it would remain certain that for at least an entire generation after their first collected appearance in 1840, and probably for an entire generation after their author's death in 1845, they enjoyed an almost unexampled and a certainly unexceeded popularity.—SAINTSBURY, GEORGE, 1893, *Three Humourists, Macmillan's Magazine, vol.* 69, *p.* 110.

His "Ingoldsby Legends" have enjoyed a popularity wider, probably, than that of any other humorous verse of the century. They are clever, rapid in narrative, and resourceful in phrase and in rhyme. Yet a certain want of delicacy in the wit and of melody in the verse is evident when we compare them with the work of Hood and Praed, or that of such later humorists as Calverley, or J. K. Stephen, or Lewis Carroll.—WALKER, HUGH, 1897, *The Age of Tennyson, p.* 58.

GENERAL

The intimate friend of Theodore Hook, Mr. Barham had something of Hook's manner, with a love of punning and pleasantry as irrepressible as that of Hood, though accompanied with less literary power.—CHAMBERS, ROBERT, 1876, *Cyclopædia of English Literature, ed. Carruthers.*

He had a vein of humour both rollicking and grim, and he was an expert in the art of weaving a story into verse. His command of rhyme was almost unsurpassable. The most intractable phrases become plastic and fluent at his touch; words which seem to defy the resources of the language to wed them with rhyme are set dancing down his lines in the most unexpected and comical partnerships. The ingenuity and vigour of the style, the wealth of incident, the gusto with which the best stories are told, the brisk canter and jingle of the verse, the broad drollery of some passages, and the grotesque power of others, account for the immense popularity which "The Legends" at once secured, and which, in a great measure, they retain. And yet, with all their cleverness, have not their merits been somewhat over-rated? When two or three of them are read consecutively, does not the cleverness become a trifle irksome? Does not the dead rattle of the rhyme begin to jar on the ear? Does not one grow weary before long of the gluttonous, bibulous, amorous crew of burlesque monks, and churchmen, and saints, and devils, and frail fair ladies? His transitions from the jocose to the serious are often inartistic, and sometimes even repellent.—WHYTE, WALTER, 1894, *The Poets and the Poetry of the Century, Humour, Society, Parody and Occasional Verse, ed. Miles, p.* 199.

Carolina Oliphant

Baroness Nairne

1766–1845

Song-writer, was born 16th August 1766, at the "auld house" of Gask in Perthshire, third daughter of its Jacobite laird. In 1806 she married her second cousin, Major Nairne (1757–1830), who in 1824, by reversal of attainder, became sixth Lord Nairne, and to whom she bore one son, William (1808–37). They settled at Edinburgh, and after her husband's death she lived for three years in Ireland, then for nine on the Continent. She died at Gask, 27th October 1845. Her eighty-seven songs appeared first in "The Scottish Minstrel" (1821–24), and posthumously as "Lays from Strathearn." Some of them are mere Bowdlerisations of "indelicate" favourites; but four at least live and shall live with the airs to which they are wedded—the "Land o' the Leal" (*c.* 1788), "Caller Herrin'," "The Laird o' Cockpen," and "The Auld House." See Rogers's "Life of Lady Nairne" (1869), and Kington Oliphant's "Jacobite Lairds of Gask" (1870).—PATRICK AND GROOME, *eds.*, 1897, *Chambers's Biographical Dictionary, p.* 683.

PERSONAL

The personal aspects of our Poetess are represented in the portrait with which this volume is adorned. The original was painted by the late Sir John Watson Gordon, in 1816, and is preserved at Gask. In her fiftieth year the "Flower of Strathearn" retains her charms. The countenance is of the aristocratic type; the nose aquiline, a small mouth, dark expressive eyes, and a high and gracefully moulded forehead. She was of middle size; her hands and arms were elegantly shaped; and her very movement betokened the polished gentlewoman. Her manners were such as to evoke respect and reverence. She possessed an abundant vivacity and much enjoyed the tale of humour. By her kindly ways she attracted the young. . . . As a Christian gentlewoman, Lady Nairne was an honor to her country and age. No dispenser of charity ever fulfilled the injunction more literally as to the bestowal of alms in secret. When any of her good deeds became known, she was sensibly pained. "Religion is a walking and not a talking concern" was her favourite maxim: she acted upon it.—ROGERS, CHARLES, 1869, *ed. Life and Songs of the Baroness Nairne, Memoir, pp.* 141, 142.

Carolina Oliphant, in her songs for the people, vindicated nobly the genuine humanity of true nobility, and the strong, sweet sympathies of a patriarchal life. But Carolina Oliphant also was a grand dame. The blue blood in her veins ran very blue. In her stateliness as a bride, she put aside with some impatience and vexation the kiss of her cousin and bridegroom, as being too bold and public an assertion of the rights which she had just given him. She had even a greater horror than Lady Anne Linsday cherished of being reduced to the level of literary publicity, and of being exposed to rude praise and blame along with the common herd of authors. Not only was she a woman,—and authorship was counted unfeminine by these great ladies,—she was also a lady, an Oliphant, a Nairne. Lady Nairne did not so much as confide to Lord Nairne the secret which would have made his heart proud, if he were a match for his wife in genius and feeling. She did not even tell him that she was the author of "The Land o' the Leal," lest his honest gratification should tempt him to betray the truth. —TYTLER, SARAH, AND WATSON, J. L., 1871, *The Songstresses of Scotland, vol.* II, *p.* 112.

In her youth she was so notable for her personal charms that she was known in popular language as the Flower of Strathearn; and the beauty of her mind, manifested in an early occupation with music and lyrical poetry, was not inferior to the fascination of her person. She lived single till she was forty years of age, and then married Captain William Murray Nairne, a military gentleman of noble descent, whose duties as inspector-general of barracks in Scotland forced him to reside in Edinburgh. The house which she occupied, still recognised by the visitor in the letters C. N. above the portal, is pleasantly situated beneath the shadow of the lofty Arthur's Seat, looking eastward towards Portobello and the Forth. In this abode Lady Nairne dwelt for about thirty years, performing her part gracefully in the literary society of the Modern Athens, and at the same time, as a christian woman, signalising herself, in her own modest way, by contributing munificently towards the support of the popular charities, then rising into notice under the intelligent apostleship of Dr. Chalmers.—BLACKIE, JOHN STUART, 1888, *Scottish Song, p.* 228.

She was foremost in all scenes of gayety, and is said to have taken a carriage at midnight and driven several miles to bring one of her young lady friends out of bed for a party where partners were scarce. In the simple social pleasures of the local aristocracy, the country balls and meetings, and the gatherings of the tenantry, "the Flower of Strathearn" was a conspicuous figure, while her keen eyes were taking in the queer figures that appeared later in all the glow of bright humor in "The Laird of Cockpen," "The County Meeting," and "Jamie, the Laird." . . .

She would not allow her son to be taught to dance, and regarded her poetry as the somewhat flagitious exercise of a worldly spirit, and spent her days in the doubt and self-affliction of a harsh creed and in the petty interests of a narrow church. She was deeply interested in the hopeless task of "converting" the Catholics of Ireland and the Jews to Scotch Presbyterianism, and was the mentor of her relatives after the fashion of Mrs. Hannah More, the patroness of bazaars, and at one time with her sister was expelled from an Italian town for distributing Protestant Bibles to the people. But her native nobleness of character shone through the theological clouds. She was regarded with affection as well as reverence by her younger relatives and her servants, and impressed all who came in contact with her by the cordial grace of her manners, and the aristocratic and highly marked contour of her features, which in the bloom of youth had made her "the Flower of Strathearn." Her benevolence was unceasing and self-sacrificing, if not always wisely directed, and at one time she had all her family plate sold and the proceeds sent to Dr. Chalmers for the support of an industrial school for the poor.—WILLIAMS, ALFRED M., 1894, *Studies in Folk-Song and Popular Poetry*, *pp*. 109, 113.

In her later years Lady Nairne was involved in the atmosphere of pietism which began to prevail over Scotland, dating from the pious crusade of the Haldanes. Secular amusements—save painting—were no longer to her mind, the fashions of the world that pass away were no more to the taste of her who had in unregenerate days written the "Laird o' Cockpen." She had always been religious, though the humour would bubble over into fun in her songs. — GRAHAM, HENRY GREY, 1901, *Scottish Men of Letters of the Eighteenth Century*, *p*. 351.

GENERAL

Two great motives may be distinguished in her verse—sympathy with the life of the common people among whom she moved with old-fashioned familiarity as a radiant comforter and joy-bringer, and sympathy with the chivalrous spirit of Jacobitism, which was the air she breathed in her own family. Her songs contain all that is best and highest in the Jacobite poetry of Scotland,—the tender regret that never sinks into wailing, the high-tempered gaiety that bends but will not break, the fiery spirit that reaches forward to victory and never thinks of defeat. It was a misfortune for the Pretender that such a poet-laureate of his cause did not appear till forty years after that cause was hopelessly lost.—MINTO, WILLIAM, 1880, *The English Poets, ed. Ward, vol.* III, *p*. 572.

Lady Nairne, who was a religious person, and yet loved her country's songs, and felt how much they contain, which, if not directly religious, was yet "not far from the kingdom of heaven," desired to remove the barrier; and she sang one strain, "The Land o' the Leal," which, even were there none other such, would remain to prove how little alien to Christianity is the genuine sentiment of Scottish song,—how easily it can rise from true human feeling into the pure air of spiritual religion.—SHAIRP, JOHN CAMPBELL, 1881, *Scottish Song and Burns, Aspects of Poetry*.

It seems to me that by far the finest of this group of writers is the Baroness Nairne, "The Flower of Strathearn," as she was fitly called in her own district. She may not have the strength of Joanna Baillie, or the versatility of Mrs. Hemans, but her songs are full of deep pathos and kindly humour. They are never local nor of an interest purely temporary, as was the case with the poems of many of her compeers, but they are instinct with fine feeling that comes straight from the heart and goes straight to the hearts of all readers.— SHARP, ELIZABETH A., 1890, *Women Poets of the Victorian Era, Preface, p*. XXV.

That this woman had ever written a line of verse was a secret which she all but carried to the grave with her. And yet for fifty years, no less, people all round her had been singing her songs and talking about them with admiration, and phrases from them had become household words throughout Scotland, and some of them were universally spoken of as the finest Scottish songs, the songs of keenest and deepest genius, since those of Burns. . . Then there are love-songs, satirical songs, humorous songs and songs of Scottish character and oddity, nonsense songs and songs of philosophic "pawkiness" and good sense, songs of scenery and places, and songs of the most tearful pathos. A few are of a distinctively religious character.

Passing from matter or subject to quality, one may say that there is a real *moral* worth in them all, and that all have that genuine characteristic of a song which consists of an inner *tune* preceding and inspiring the words, and coiling the words as it were out of the heart along with it. Hence there is not perhaps one of them that, with the advantage they have of being set to known and favourite airs, would not please sufficiently if sung by a good singer. Apart from this general melodiousness or suitability for being sung, the report for *all* of them might not be so favourable; but, tried by the standard of strict poetic merit, about twenty or twenty-five of the whole number, I should say, might rank as good, while eight or ten of these are of supreme quality.—MASSON, DAVID, 1892, *Edinburgh Sketches and Memories, pp.* 130, 134.

Lady Nairne was a true poet. Her "Laird o' Cockpen" is full of a humour that is quite peculiar to herself; while her Jacobite songs, "Wha'll be King but Charlie," and "Charlie is my Darling," are alive with warlike spirit as sincere and earnest as though they had been written in the heat of the struggle, during the pauses of the very battles. In these poems she evidently feels every word she writes, and this quality of sincerity alone, even apart from their other conspicuous merits, causes them to reach a far higher standard of excellence than all the other Jacobite verse which was written in her time. "Caller Herrin" written to a tune representing the chime of the bells of the Tron Kirk at Edinburgh, will always be worthy of study as a fine example of words arranged to musical sounds. Her masterpiece is "The Land o' the Leal." This faultless poem is worthy of the pathetic situation it renders so irresistibly. We seem to hear the very accents of the dying woman as she speaks to the fond husband who was the father of her dead child. Yet "The Land o' the Leal," flawless as it is, seems as spontaneous as her more crude work. Indeed it may be said of this kind of lyric no less than of the Jacobite ballads, that Lady Nairne never wrote a line that she did not feel; and this fact gives to her poems a strength which nothing else could give.—BELL, MACKENZIE, 1892, *The Poets and Poetry of the Century, Joanna Baillie to Mathilde Blind, ed. Miles, p.* 19.

Lady Nairne excels in the humorous ballad, the Jacobite song, and songs of sentiment and domestic pathos. She skilfully utilised the example of Burns in fitting beautiful old tunes with interesting words; her admirable command of lowland Scotch enabled her to write for the Scottish people, and her ease of generalisation gave breadth of significance to special themes. In her "Land o' the Leal," "Laird o' Cockpen," and "Caller Herrin'," she is hardly, if at all, second to Burns himself. "The Land o' the Leal," set to the old tune "Hey tutti taiti," also used by Burns for "Scots wha ha'e," was translated into Greek verse by the Rev. J. Riddell, fellow of Balliol College, Oxford. "Caller Herrin'" was written for the benefit of Nathaniel Gow, son of the famous Perthshire fiddler Neil Gow, whose melody for the song, with its echoes from the peal of church bells, has been a favourite with composers of variations.—BAYNE, THOMAS, 1894, *Dictionary of National Biography, vol.* XL, *p.* 25.

Perhaps the most perfect example of the lyric song, in which the melody is mingled with and sustains and elevates the feeling, and both are conjoined in an effect which melts the heart and possesses the ear, although the strain is not of so high a rapture of love or sorrow as parts of Burns's "Ae Fond Kiss" or Lady Anne Bothwell's "Balow," and is of a peaceful sweetness and resignation rather than passion, is "The Land of the Leal," by Carolina, Lady Nairne. In its original and simplest form, before she had interpolated a verse to express some of her theological ideas, it is the perfect interpretation of a sweet, solemn, and simple thought, the tenderest and purest emotion, breathed in an equally simple, but absolutely perfect melody, that is like the flowing of limpid water, crystal clear and unbroken to the end. The heart of the world has responded, and it has a place like none other in the tongue of song. . . . The fame of the authoress, so far as she can be said to have any of her own individual personality, rests upon this song, and sufficiently, while the English language shall last, but it was not the solitary example of her genius, and her poetical work, although not great in bulk, contains other lyrics of a very high quality, with a wide range from high martial spirit and homely pathos to gay and frolicsome humor, and instinct with the vital and living element of song. —WILLIAMS, ALFRED M., 1894, *Studies in Folk-Song and Popular Poetry, pp.*105, 107.

For the number and beauty of her lyrics of all kinds, among the song-writers of Scotland Lady Nairne is excelled only by Burns and rivalled only by Tannahill. . . . With a genius which was equally at home in the pathetic, the humorous, and the patriotic, Carolina Oliphant remains not only the sweetest and most famous singer of the lost Jacobite cause, but far and away the greatest of all Scottish lyric poets of her sex, and in two of her pieces, the two above mentioned, it does not appear extravagant to say, she is not surpassed even by Burns himself.—EYRE-TODD, GEORGE, 1896, *ed. Scottish Poetry of the Eighteenth Century, vol.* II, *pp.* 293, 295.

Samuel Laman Blanchard

1804-1845

Born at Great Yarmouth, England, May 15, 1804: died at London, Feb. 15, 1845. An English littérateur and journalist. He was acting editor of the "Monthly Magazine" (1831), editor of "The True Sun" (1832), of "The Constitutional" (1836), "The Court Journal" (1837), "The Courier" (1837-39), and other periodicals, and author of "Lyric Offerings," "Sonnets," etc.—SMITH, BENJAMIN E., *ed.*, 1894-97, *The Century Cyclopedia of Names, p.* 161.

PERSONAL

It was impossible to help trusting a man so thoroughly generous and honest, and loving one who was so perfectly gay, gentle, and amiable. . . . On the night of the 14th February, in a gust of delirium, having his little boy in bed by his side, and having said the Lord's Prayer but a short time before, he sprang out of bed in the absence of the nurse (whom he had besought not to leave him) and made away with himself with a razor. He was no more guilty in his death than a man who is murdered by a madman, or who dies of the rupture of a blood-vessel. In his last prayer he asked to be forgiven, as he in his whole heart forgave others; and not to be led into that irresistible temptation under which it pleased Heaven that the poor wandering spirit should succumb. At the very moment of his death his friends were making the kindest and most generous exertions in his behalf. Such a noble, loving, and generous creature, is never without such. — THACKERAY, WILLIAM MAKEPEACE, 1846, *A Brother of the Press, Fraser's Magazine, vol.* 33, *pp.* 332, 339.

In person, Laman Blanchard was small and slight, though sufficiently well knit. His dark features, of rather an oriental cast, were prepossessing in themselves, and made still more so by their expression of intelligence and urbanity. His eyes and hair were beautiful. His manners were more than ordinarily attractive; quiet, but not reserved; and gentle, but never servile. His natural kindness was so great, so visible in the small details of life, that it imparted to him that high and delicate breeding which we are accustomed to consider the peculiar attribute of loftier birth and more tender nurturing. . . . When I asked a friend who saw him more frequently than myself what faults he possessed, as drawbacks to his apparent excellences; shadows that might enable me to show him, to use my own phrase "as flesh and blood;" the answer after a pause was, "Why, I know of no faults, unless it is that he was hardly even of flesh and blood." — LYTTON, EDWARD BULWER LORD, 1846, *Memoir of Laman Blanchard.*

The beautiful mask which his mind almost always wore, and which was reflected in the *set* smile that always illumined his regular and finely moulded, but small and somewhat sharp features, was not a thing put on for the nonce, to serve a purpose; it was a natural endowment. The extreme sweetness, amounting to benignity, of his natural disposition, rendered him that anomaly in social life, a natural courtier —a courtier without knowing or intending it—above all, without thinking or hoping to get anything by it. But if this was one of the great charms of Blanchard's mind and personal bearing, it was also their one besetting sin; for it made him equally beloved and popular with all manner of men; which an honest and delicately-minded man can scarcely permit himself to be.—PATMORE, P. G., 1854, *My Friends and Acquaintance, vol.* III. *p.* 195.

As a poet, essayist, and editor he took prominent and honorable rank. A more estimable man I have rarely known. He died sadly; his mind had become gloomily o'ercast by the death of his admirable wife, to whom he was devotedly attached. He died in a moment of madness, brought on by despondency that had reached despair.—HALL, SAMUEL CARTER, 1883, *Retrospect of a Long Life.*

GENERAL

I question Sir Bulwer Lytton's statement about Blanchard, viz. that he would have been likely to produce with leisure, and under favourable circumstances, a work of the highest class. I think his education and habits, his quick, easy manner, his sparkling, hidden fun, constant tenderness and brilliant good humour, were best employed as they were. At any rate he had a duty, much more imperative upon him than the preparation of questionable great works,—to get his family their dinner. A man must be a very great man, indeed, before he can neglect this precaution. His three volumes of essays, pleasant and often brilliant as they are, give no idea of the powers of the author, or even of his natural manner, which, as I think, was a thousand times more agreeable. He was like the good little child in the fairy tale, his mouth dropped out all sorts of diamonds and rubies. His wit, which was always playing and frisking about the company, had the wonderful knack of never hurting anybody. He had the most singular art of discovering good qualities in people; in discoursing of which the kindly little fellow used to glow and kindle up, and emphasize with the most charming energy.—THACKERAY, WILLIAM MAKEPEACE, 1846, *A Brother of the Press, Fraser's Magazine, vol.* 33, *p.* 335.

His style and his conceptions were not marked by the vigor which comes partly from concentration of intellect, and partly from heat of passion; but they evince, on the other hand, a purity of taste, and propriety of feeling, which preserve him from the caricature and exaggeration that deface many compositions obtaining the praise of broad humor or intense purpose. His fancy did not soar high, but its play was sportive, and it sought its aliment with the grateful instincts of the poet. He certainly never fulfilled the great promise which his "Lyric Offerings" held forth. He never wrote up to the level of its source. . . . Born at an earlier day, Laman Blanchard would probably have known sharper trials of pecuniary circumstance; and instead of the sufficient, though precarious income, which his reputation as a periodical writer afforded him, he might have often slept in the garret, and been fortunate if he had dined often in the cellar. But then he would have been compelled to put forth all that was in him of mind and genius; to have written books, not papers; and books not intended for the week or the month, but for permanent effect upon the public.—LYTTON, EDWARD BULWER LORD, 1846, *Memoir of Laman Blanchard.*

This difference of mere manner between Blanchard and Lamb was perhaps to be accounted for by the habits and incidents of their early lives. . . . The moral and intellectual resemblances of these two men were equally striking, and were equally worn with marked and almost strange differences. There was a benign humanity, a truly *Christian* spirit and temper, about both, which I have never seen equalled or even approached, in any other men—a universal loving-kindness and toleration, which scarcely allowed them to see, and absolutely forbad them to feel, any essential difference, morally and humanly speaking, between the vilest of mankind and the purest, between the wisest and the weakest. And yet this universal and almost divine sympathy and toleration, so far from deadening their sense of superior moral claims and intellectual endowments in individual instances, seemed to act in precisely an opposite direction; and this was especially the case with Blanchard, who felt an almost worshipful and religious admiration for superiority of intellectual or moral pretensions, of whatever kind they might be.—PATMORE, P. G., 1854, *My Friends and Acquaintance, vol.* III, *p.* 199.

Blanchard was in his own day a very popular writer of light literature, but he wrote nothing of lasting merit. His "Sonnets" and his "Lyric Offerings" show the influence of Wordsworth, but are commonplace in sentiment and versification. His *vers de société* run easily, but are less readable now than those of many of his contemporaries. His prose essays take an invariably cheerful view of life, but they are not to be classed in the same category as the "Essays of Elia," which Blanchard clearly took as his model. Bulwer-Lytton warned Blanchard in early life that "periodical writing is the grave of true genius," and Blanchard's literary career proves the wisdom of the warning. —LEE, SIDNEY, 1886, *Dictionary of National Biography, vol.* V, *p.* 194.

He is more forgotten and overlooked than he ought to be, considering the varied kinds of work he did, and that he did all with skill and individuality. . . . Laman Blanchard as a poet is marked at once by great tenderness and freshness of feeling, by flowing metres, and by very felicitous lines and touches. If not a great poet, he is everywhere an attractive and pleasing one. He touches a varied lyre too —always pure, elevated, and inclined to celebrate common incident and the domestic affections. As a humorous poet, he shares with Thomas Hood the power of punning with a kind of natural ease and grace; and sometimes in his case this is more effective than anywhere else we can recall save in the pages of "Hood's Own." Some of his parodies are exceedingly good. In one or two pieces there is a felicity and daintiness of touch to be surpassed only by the happiest efforts of Praed, Locker, or Austin Dobson.—JAPP, ALEXANDER H., 1894, *The Poets and the Poetry of the Century, John Keats to Lord Lytton, ed. Miles, pp.* 547, 549.

He was an agreeable writer, but not, even at his best, a distinguished one.—WALKER, HUGH, 1897, *The Age of Tennyson, p.* 57.

Joseph Story

1779–1845

American jurist, was a native of Massachusetts, and was educated at Harvard College. In 1805 he was elected to the State legislature, and in 1811 was appointed Associate Justice of the Supreme Court of the United States, a post he filled for thirty-four years. Story became law professor at Harvard in 1829. He is chiefly remembered as a writer of legal treatises which are considered of the highest authority. Among them the most important are his "Commentary on the Constitution of the United States" (1833), "Commentaries on the Conflict of Laws" (1837), "Commentaries on Equity Jurisprudence" (1836), "On the Law of Agency" (1839), and "On the Law of Bills of Sale" (1843).—SANDERS, LLOYD C., *ed.*, 1887, *Celebrities of the Century, p.* 957.

PERSONAL

Judge Story's power of conversation among the hills and monuments and deep shady graves of Mount Auburn was incomparable. He lead Ma by the arm all the way, and he was eloquence, and poetry, and pathos, and feeling and tenderness, and anecdote, and boundless benignity, all personified in his identical person. I believe he is the most accomplished and ardent and enlightened intellect extant.—KENT, JAMES, 1836, *To William Kent, July* 4; *Memoirs and Letters, ed. his Great-grandson, p.* 266.

At Cambridge, three miles off, we have Judge Story, of the Supreme Court, eloquent, deeply learned, garrulous, lively, amiable, excellent in all and every way that a mortal can be. He is, decidedly, the gem of this western world.—GRATTAN, T. C., 1841, *Letter to Mrs. Trollope; What I Remember, by T. A. Trollope, p.* 503.

A newspaper from America, directed by Charles Sumner, which I joyfully opened; to be struck down with anguish in reading at the head of a column "*Funeral of Mr. Justice Story.*" That great and good man—that dear and revered and inestimable friend—is taken from us! God's will be done! But how the cords that bind us to life are rapidly loosening—one is here snapped! Wrote to Charles Sumner on dear Judge Story's death—*Vale! Amice dilecte et reverende—vale! vale!*—MACREADY, W. C., 1845, *Diary, Sept.* 29; *Reminiscences, ed. Pollock, p.* 571.

His countenance, familiar in this presence, was always so beaming with goodness and kindness that its withdrawal seems to lessen sensibly the brightness of the scene. We are assembled near the seat of his favorite pursuits, among the neighbors intimate with his private virtues, close by the home hallowed by his domestic altar. These paths he often trod; and all that our eyes here look upon seems to reflect his genial smile. His twofold official relations with the University, his high judicial station, his higher character as Jurist, invest his name with a peculiar interest, while the unconscious kindness which he showed to all, especially the young, touches the heart, making us rise up and call him blessed. How fondly would the youth nurtured in jurisprudence at his feet—were such an offering, Alcestis-like, within the allotments of Providence — have prolonged their beloved master's days at the expense of their own! —SUMNER, CHARLES, 1846, *The Scholar, The Jurist, The Artist, The Philanthropist, Works, vol.* I, *p.* 258.

In his religious tenets, he was a Unitarian. He thought more of a good life than creed, and judged of a man's faith by the fruits it bore. He was wholly free from sectarianism, bigotry, and proselytism. He never sought to shake the belief of any man in his own dogmas, believing them to be the mere metaphysics, not the realities of religion. He was desirous that Christians of all denominations should be represented in the University at Cambridge, and that the question as to their appointment should be in respect to their qualifications, not to their creed. He believed in the inspiration and the doctrines of Christ, in the immortality of the soul, in the unity of God, and he often intimated a design to write a work, in which the rules of legal evidence should be applied to the facts of the Gospel narration, and the question of its authenticity argued as before a court of justice. His religious faith was not a dry and barren belief, but an ever-living principle, animating every act and thought. In his bereavements, he found in it consolation and support. In his happiness, it was never out of sight. He lived a truly religious life. He died in the full faith of a renewed and purified existence beyond the grave.—STORY, WILLIAM WETMORE, 1851, *Life and Letters of Joseph Story, vol.* II, *p.* 612.

In reviewing his life we are not so much struck with his genius as with his simplicity, unselfishness, and laboriousness. He worked not for himself, but for posterity. What he acquired he used not for his own advancement, but freely bestowed it on the world. Free from vanity, arrogance, and self-seeking, he passed his life in seeking the greatest good of mankind. As few men have bestowed so much, so few have labored so hard to acquire. Order, method, and punctuality marked his whole career. . . . Story's fame is the result, not of genius, but of that labor which conquers all things.—BROWNE, IRVING, 1878, *Short Studies of Great Lawyers, p.* 306.

My acquaintance with this distinguished man began when, as an undergraduate, I dined with him in Salem, during a visit to that town. As a boy I was fascinated by the brilliancy of his conversation, and now that I was at the base of the profession which he adorned I regarded him with peculiar reverence. I remember my father's graphic account of the rage of the Federalists when "Joe Story, that country pettifogger, aged thirty-two," was made a judge of our highest court. He was a bitter Democrat in those days, and had written a Fourth of July oration which was as a red rag to the Federal bull. It was understood that years and responsibilities had greatly modified his opinions. —QUINCY, JOSIAH, 1883, *Figures of the Past from the Leaves of Old Journals, p.* 188.

His charges were perfect in point of explicitness, comprehensiveness, and adaptation to the non-legal mind; never deep, though the manifest result of deep thought; never technical, though on subjects that seemed to crave technical treatment; never dry or dull, though in cases that seemed wholly void of interest. I think that it could always be seen in what direction his own opinion turned; but he never failed to do full justice to both sides of the case in hand. His charges might have been too prolix for the eye, but not for the ear.— PEABODY, ANDREW P., 1888, *Harvard Reminiscences, p.* 58.

GENERAL

The work ["Constitutional Law"] properly used, with a diligent and faithful resort to the authorities cited, amounts to a digested course of reading on constitutional law; and the student, well possessed of its contents, would need nothing farther in this great department, than that which the active and discriminating mind must elaborate itself, in order to make any study profitable. It is a question that unavoidably presents itself, now we have the book, How we did without it?—It is evidently such a course on constitutional law, as is indispensable to the enlightened politician, to the accomplished lawyer, to the student of our history, and even the well informed American citizen. . . . Mr. Justice Story relates the history of the formation of the Constitution. A chapter on the objections to it follows. To this succeeds a discussion of the nature of the Constitution,—whether it be a *compact.* This is one of the most able, luminous, and valuable chapters of the work. The whole artillery of constitutional law, on this great topic of present interest, is brought out with masterly skill and power; and the politician, who knows nothing of his calling, but how to inflame popular feeling on topics of local interest, may read this chapter and learn how mean his occupation is. And here begins the great business of this work, not indeed, that the previous chapters are not of close connexion with its main subject, and some of them, in fact, not inferior in present interest and seasonableness. But in this discussion of the question, whether the Constitution is a compact or a government, we enter the great temple of constitutional law.—EVERETT, EDWARD, 1834, *Story's Constitutional Law, North American Review, vol.* 38, *pp.* 63, 81.

Every page and ordinary topic is replete with a copious and accurate display of principles, clothed in a powerful and eloquent style, and illustrated and recommended by striking analogies, and profuse and brilliant illustrations. You handle the topic of the mechanical arts, and the science on which they are founded, enlarged, adorned, and applied, with a mastery, skill, and eloquence, that is unequalled. And as for jurisprudence, you have again and again, and on all occasions, laid bare its foundations, traced its histories, eulogized its noblest masters, and pressed its inestimable importance, with a gravity, zeal, pathos, and beauty, that is altogether irresistible.—KENT, JAMES, 1836, *To Joseph Story; Life and Letters of Joseph Story, ed. Story, vol.* II, *p.* 217.

In regarding the deceased as an author, jurisprudence mourns one of her greatest sons,—one of the greatest not only among those of his own age, but in the long succession of ages, whose fame has become a familiar word in all lands where the law is taught as a science, whose works have been translated and commented on in several of the classical languages of the European Continent, and have been received as authorities throughout the civilized world. It was his lot, while yet alive, to receive as from a distant posterity, the tribute of foreign nations to his exalted merit as a jurist.—WEBSTER, DANIEL, 1845, *Resolutions of the Suffolk Bar.*

The first of these, Contracts, Agency, Bailments, Bills of Exchange, Promissory Notes and Partnership, are made the subjects of as many distinct elementary treatises by that indefatigable, learned and experienced jurist Mr. Justice Story. We have been for some time familiar with them, and can confidently recommend them to the student as better adapted for his purpose, and indeed for those of practitioners, than any others which we are aware of being extant.—WARREN, SAMUEL, 1845, *Law Studies, 2nd ed., p.* 759.

His legal reputation in America rests, perhaps, upon a work little known in this country,—his Commentaries upon the Constitution of the United States. This was followed, within a few months, by his Commentaries on the Conflict of Laws, and preceded by his admirable work on Bailments. These works, followed between 1833 and his death by treatises on the law of Principal and Agent, Bills of Exchange and Promissory Notes, Equity Jurisprudence and Equity Pleading, have, from their fulness, their research, their candor, and the comprehensiveness which characterizes them, placed the name of Professor Story in the very first rank of the legal authors of the age.—JOY, H. H., 1847, *Letters on the Present State of Legal Education.*

The style of Story, both in his Commentaries and in his Miscellanies, is that of the scholar and man of general reading, as well as the thoroughly practised lawyer. It is full, inclined to the rhetorical, but displays everywhere the results of laborious investigation and calm reflection. His law books have fairly brought what in the old volumes was considered a crabbed science to the appreciation and sympathy of the unprofessional reader.—DUYCKINCK, EVERT A. AND GEORGE L., 1855–65–75, *Cyclopædia of American Literature, ed. Simons, vol.* II, *p.* 16.

As an author, Judge Story began his career early in life, by publishing an excellent edition of Abbott on the "Law of

Shipping." Soon after his appointment to the Dane Professorship, he published his "Commentaries on the Constitution of the United States," in three volumes, octavo. These were followed by a succession of treatises on different branches of the law, the extent and excellence of which, with the vast amount of legal learning displayed in them, leave it a matter of astonishment that they could be prepared, within the short space of twelve years, by a man who was all the while discharging, with great assiduity, the onerous duties of a Judge of the Supreme Court of the United States, and a Professor in the Law School of the University. But in his devotion to the science of the law, he did not forget the claims of literature and general scholarship; and his addresses on public occasions, his contributions to the "North American Review," and the other miscellaneous writings, show a mind imbued with sound and varied learning.—CLEVELAND, CHARLES D., 1859, *A Compendium of American Literature, p.* 270.

The style of Judge Story is clear, flowing, and often elegant. His legal knowledge was undoubtedly great, but his opinions are somewhat diffuse, and lack the point that characterizes some less known authors.—UNDERWOOD, FRANCIS H., 1872, *A Hand-book of English Literature, American Authors, p.* 61.

Judge Story's name is among the first that impress themselves upon the attention of the young American student of law, and ranks in importance second only to that of Chancellor Kent. . . . By the breadth of research and the liberality of spirit manifested in these works, especially in the "Treatise on the Conflict of Laws," the author earned for himself a lasting reputation not only among his countrymen but also among the jurists of France, Germany, and England. Judge Story's works, however, all suffer from one defect. They are too diffuse. The materials which they contain are very ample, but they are not sufficiently worked up by the author. The young student especially is bewildered oftentimes in a labyrinth of seemingly contradictory decisions and arguments, and feels the want of a few skilful, trenchant words from the compiler.—HART, JOHN S., 1872, *A Manual of American Literature, pp.* 126, 127.

Like a good many other men who have turned out to be nothing but lawyers, Story early imagined that he was a poet. Not content with an occasional flirtation with the muse, he committed himself to a serious declaration by a volume of verse. . . . So Story, possessing a dangerous facility for rhyming, wrote some unobjectionable didactic sentiments in correct heroic verse, after the manner, but not after the matter, of Pope. No valid cause could be why his verse should not be suppressed; it might just as well have been prose. His maturer judgment told him he was not a poet, and he assiduously endeavored to buy up and suppress the volume, with such success that it has become very scarce. His son has given copious extracts from the "Power of Solitude," which one finds it difficult to read. —BROWNE, IRVING, 1878, *Short Studies of Great Lawyers, pp.* 299, 300.

John Hookham Frere

1769–1846

John Hookham Frere, the translator of Aristophanes, was born in London, 21st May 1769, and educated at Eton and Caius College, Cambridge. He entered the Foreign Office, in 1796 was returned for [West] Looe, supported Pitt's government, and contributed to the *Anti-Jacobin.* His chief piece was "The Loves of the Triangles," a parody on Darwin's "Loves of the Plants," but he had a share with his schoolfellow Canning in "The Needy Knife-grinder." Under-secretary for Foreign Affairs (1799), he was appointed envoy to Lisbon (1800), and twice minister to Spain (1802 and 1808). Recalled after the retreat to Corunna, he retired in 1821 to Malta, where he devoted himself to Greek, Hebrew, and Maltese, and died 7th January 1846. Frere's clever mock-heroic "Specimen of an Intended National Work by William and Robert Whistlecraft" (1817) suggested its *ottava rima* to Byron for his "Beppo;" but his fame rests on his admirable translations of the "Acharnians," "Knights," "Birds," and "Frogs" of Aristophanes.—PATRICK AND GROOME, *eds.*, 1897, *Chambers's Biographical Dictionary, p.* 386.

PERSONAL

Frere is a slovenly fellow. His remarks on Homer, in the "Classical Journal," prove how fine a Greek scholar he is; his "Quarterly Reviews," how well he writes; his "Rovers, or The Double Arrangement," what humor he possesses; and the reputation he has left in Spain and Portugal, how much better he understood their literatures than they do themselves: while, at the same time, his books left in France, in Gallicia, at Lisbon, and two or three places in England; his manuscripts, neglected and lost to himself; his manners, lazy and careless; and his conversation, equally rich and negligent, show how little he cares about all that distinguishes him in the eyes of the world. He studies as a luxury, he writes as an amusement, and conversation is a kind of sensual enjoyment to him. If he had been born in Asia, he would have been the laziest man that ever lived.—TICKNOR, GEORGE, 1819, *Journal; Life, Letters and Journals, vol.* I, *p.* 267.

Those who knew him most intimately soon discovered that the largest tolerance and charity were not incompatible with a thorough contempt for all that was mean and base; among other marks of true nobility of character he possessed the royal art of never humiliating one in any way inferior to himself. Meaner natures near him, while they saw and felt his superiority, tasted the luxury of feeling their own aims elevated, and of discovering a higher standard than that by which they had been accustomed to regulate their own actions. It was this quality which secured for him at one and the same time the affection of the poorest and weakest, and the respect of the best and noblest who knew him well enough to judge of his true character.—FRERE, SIR BARTLE, 1871, *Memoir of John Hookham Frere, p.* 344.

In conversation always animated and pleasant, he yet found his chief happiness in the quiet of old books and whimsical reveries, the "*inertes horæ*" of the poet. His strange absences of mind were the subject of some amusing anecdotes among the few with whom he continued in habits of intercourse. He knew and humorously vindicated his own indolence, in its contrast with the angry and agitated lives of many of his political friends.—HOLLAND, SIR HENRY, 1871, *Recollections of Past Life, p.* 273.

Never could one who contemplated a literary career have been better prepared for it than Frere. The cause of his limited reputation was that he cared nothing for popular applause. He saw no advantage in fighting his way into notoriety, and preferred the appreciation of a limited number of clever men to the noisy acclamations of the many. He did everything so easily that he had not the ordinary ambition which is obliged to toil laboriously to achieve its ends. By taste, culture, and position he entered the ranks of authorship; he was in no sense a rival of the professional author. Such ideas as he had were original in conception, and elegant and refined in execution; but he sometimes exercised his talents on small and inadequate subjects. If he had been thrown upon the world without a friend he would have become a great man. His audience may be small but it is a keenly appreciative one.—SMITH, GEORGE BARNETT, 1888, *John Hookham Frere, Gentleman's Magazine, vol.* 264, *p.* 48.

GENERAL

I saw Frere in London, and he has promised to let me print his translations from the "Poema del Cid." They are admirably done. Indeed, I never saw anything so difficult to do, and done so excellently, except your supplement to Sir Tristrem.—SOUTHEY, ROBERT, 1808, *To Sir Walter Scott, April* 22; *Life and Correspondence, ed. C. C. Southey, ch.* xiv.

Tickler. "Why, whom *do* you call a good versifier, then?" *Odoherty.* "We have not many of them. Frere and Coleridge are, I think, the most perfect, being at once more scientific in their ideas of the matter than any others now alive, and also more easy and delightful in their melody which they themselves produce."—WILSON, JOHN, 1824, *Noctes Ambrosianæ, June.*

I have only met, in my researches into these matters, with one poem, which, if it had been produced as ancient, could not have been detected on internal evidence. It is the War Song upon the Victory at Brunnanburgh, translated from the Anglo-Saxon into Anglo-Norman, by the Right Hon. John Hookham Frere. See Ellis's "Specimens of English Poetry," vol. I, p. 32. The accomplished editor tells us, that this very singular poem was intended as an imitation of the style and language of the fourteenth century, and was written during the controversy occasioned by the poems attributed to Rowley. Mr. Ellis adds—"The reader will probably hear with some surprise that this singular instance of critical ingenuity was the composition of an Eton schoolboy."—SCOTT, SIR WALTER, 1830, *Essay on Imitations of the Ancient Ballad, p.* 19.

One of the most accomplished scholars England has produced, and one whom Sir James Mackintosh has pronounced to be the first of English translators.—TICKNOR, GEORGE, 1849, *History of Spanish Literature, First Period, ch.* i.

Mr. Frere's best-known original production (besides his share in the poetry of the "Anti-Jacobin") is a poem called "The Monks and the Giants," in the Ottava Rima stanza, and, as Southey said of it, "being an adaptation of Pulci, Berni, and Ariosto in his sportive mood." Frere's stanzas contain several very poetical passages, and many of great humour. The characters also of several of the leading men of the time are sketched in it with great skill and poignancy. But it offers little to interest the general reader; and it never obtained extensive popularity. It is chiefly remembered as having furnished the hint and the metrical model, on which Byron avowedly framed his far-better-known "Beppo." It was as a translator that Hookham Frere shone to most advantage. . . . Frere's renderings of passages from the old Spanish epic, the "Chronicles of the Cid," appear to me to be the best specimens of his skill as a translator, and especially of his marvellous ear for rhythm.—CREASY, SIR EDWARD, 1850-75, *Memoirs of Eminent Etonians, pp.* 518, 519.

The translation is far above my praise, but as a woman privileged to avow her want of learning, it may be permitted to express the gratitude which the whole sex owes to the late illustrious scholar, who has enabled us to penetrate to the heart of one of the scholar's deepest mysteries; and to become acquainted with something more than the name of Aristophanes.—MITFORD, MARY RUSSELL, 1851, *Recollections of a Literary Life, p.* 487.

There are few books of its size which contain as much genuine wit, humor, and fancy, or which display greater skill in the management of both light and serious verse, or indicate fuller resources of culture. It is a fresh and unique *jeu d'esprit*, which exhibits a quality of cleverness as rare as it is amusing. The form and method of the poem, the structure of its verse, its swift transitions from sprightly humor to serious description or reflection, its mingling of exaggeration with sober sense, its heroi-comic vein, are all derived from the famous Italian romantic poems, especially from the "Morgante Maggiore" of Pulci, and in a less degree from the "Animali Parlanti" of Casti. It has no moral object, and does not confine itself to a single continuous narrative, but is a simple work of amusement, free in its course, according to the whim and fancy of the writer. It is the overflow of an abundant and lively spirit, restrained only by the limits imposed by a fine sense of the proprieties of humor, and a thorough acquaintance with the rules of art. Its execution displays a command of style so complete in its way that it may be called perfect. . . . It is a misfortune for the lovers of good letters, that all of Mr. Frere's books are so scarce as to be practically inaccessible. No better gift could be made to the best readers than a new edition of them, together with such unpublished works, even if only fragments, as he may have left to his literary executors. Mr. Frere's name is not to be found in the Biographical Dictionaries. If literary genius gave title to a place in their voluminous and crowded columns, few names would stand before his.—NORTON, CHARLES ELIOT, 1868, *John Hookham Frere, North American Review, vol.* 107, *pp.* 143, 166.

The vein of humour in Hookham Frere, like that of his and my friend William Rose, was strongly tinged with the style of the Italian romantic poetry of the fifteenth century, that of Ariosto, Boiardo, Casti, &c. His strange poem of "Whistlecraft," coloured in this serio-comic fashion, put at defiance all common comprehension, and was indeed very little known or read. He counted upon the saying of Lord Shaftesbury, "that it is a dull sort of wit which amuses all alike," and in this spirit rather enjoyed, I think, the failure of his poem. His translations from Simonides, almost in the boyhood of life, show how early his powers as a poet were evoked. But Frere's chief revelry when I knew him was in Aristophanes; and his translations of that great comic writer, though fragmentary, mark the strong hold he had got of the spirit as well as text of his author.—HOLLAND, SIR HENRY, 1871, *Recollections of Past Life*, p. 272.

Whatever differences of opinion may exist as to the capacity of John Hookham Frere as a statesman or diplomatist, there can be no question as to the scholarship and literary calibre of the friend of Canning, the author of "Monks and Giants," the translator *par excellence* of Aristophanes and Theognis. . . . His translations of Aristophanes stand alone above all other classical translations in the English language. . . . There may not be in his published works much evidence of the originality which goes to the making of a first-rate poet, though none will deny to him the gifts of a bright fancy, a correct ear, an abundant flow of lyric power. His classical predilections and the bent of his humour disposed him to content himself with the praise of complete mastery of Aristophanes, and successful efforts in the region of burlesque. Referable indeed to this taste and aim are almost all of his best and happiest literary efforts. The "Monks and Giants" would not entitle him to rank high among original poets, but as an outcome of the same vein of humour which we trace in the *Anti-Jacobin* and in the Aristophanic free translations, they claim a place of honour amid the writings of English humorists. This in fact was his *métier*.—DAVIES, JAMES, 1872, *John Hookham Frere, Contemporary Review, vol.* 19, *pp.* 512, 523, 533.

Frere's versions of the Aristophanic Comedy have an established reputation for spirit of rendering and mastery of metre. His translations from the "Poema del Cid," which were printed in Southey's "Chronicle," have also a fine balladic lilt; but their literal fidelity to the Spanish has been lately challenged. Of his original work, the best examples are to be found in the *Anti-Jacobin* and the *Whistlecraft* fragment. He had a hand in all the great successes of the former, —notably the immortal "Needy Knife-Grinder" and the excellent imitations of Darwin and Schiller in the "Loves of the Triangles" and "The Rovers." . . . Notwithstanding the cleverness and versatility of "The Monks and the Giants," its interest was too remote and its plan too uncertain to command any but an eclectic audience.—DOBSON, AUSTIN, 1880, *The English Poets, ed. Ward, vol.* IV, *p.* 240.

If the poetry of wit and cleverness were equal to the poetry of inspiration, then the right Honourable John Hookham Frere would be one of the greatest of English poets. He is the author of a *jeu d'esprit* which undoubtedly suggested the idea of "Don Juan" to Lord Byron, and while "The Monks and the Giants" of Frere is equal to Byron's satiric masterpiece in brilliancy, force, and versification, it is devoid of the objectionable elements which disfigure the latter. Nor is this the only claim that Frere has to remembrance. He is so saturated with the old Greek writers that we verily breathe the Attic air as we read his pages, while his appreciation and apprehension of the ancient Saxon are nobly manifest in his translation of the Saxon poem on the "Victory of Athelstan at Brunanburgh." Coleridge described him as one able to convince Tieck that there was amongst us a man in whom taste at its maximum had vitalised itself into productive power.—SMITH, GEORGE BARNETT, 1888, *John Hookham Frere, Gentleman's Magazine, vol.* 264, *p.* 30.

As a diplomatist Frere is now almost forgotten, and it is only by the few that he is remembered as a brilliant wit and a sparkling writer of humorous poetry. His translations of Aristophanes cannot fail to be the most lasting memorials of his genius, and the manner in which he has successfully caught the spirit of the original comedies places him in an almost unique place as a translator.—BARKER, G. F. RUSSELL, 1889, *Dictionary of National Biography, vol.* XX, *p.* 269.

It is, however, by his translation of "Aristophanes" that he will retain a place in literature. It is one of the very best translations in any language, and that it will ever be surpassed by another metrical version is improbable in the extreme. The changing, many-coloured style of the incomparable satirist—the wonderful interplaying of lyric fire with lyric laughter, of bird-like song with poignant wit and riotous buffoonery—can never be more than very imperfectly reproduced by even the most consummate master of English.

Nevertheless, Frere's version is infinitely delightful to read; it is scholarly, spirited, racy in diction and richly humorous—a frolic and sparkling "revel of rhymes." A harder task was surely never attempted by a translator of Greek or Latin poetry, and no such translator has left a happier example of difficulties boldly encountered and dexterously overcome. — WHYTE, WALTER, 1894, *The Poets and the Poetry of the Century, Humour, Society, Parody and Occasional Verse, ed. Miles, p.* 26.

Frere stands in far closer relation than Tennant to the Italian burlesque of Pulci. His work travesties an Arthurian legend, as the "Morgante" (1843) had done the legend of Roland, and is quite without the realism of detail. . . . Frere shows rather accomplishment of style than strength in narrative. Many single stanzas are on a level with all but the best in "Beppo," but the poem as a whole is wanting in organic *vis.*—HERFORD, C. H., 1897, *The Age of Wordsworth, p.* 237.

Thomas Chalmers

1780–1847

Born at Anstruther, Fife, 17th March 1780, educated at St. Andrews, and in 1803 ordained minister of Kilmany. He carried on mathematical and chemistry classes at St. Andrews in 1803–4, and in 1808 published an "Inquiry into National Resources." Shortly after this he came under profound religious impressions; in 1815 he was translated to the Tron parish in Glasgow, where his magnificent oratory, partly published as "Astronomical Discourses" (1817) and "Commercial Discourses" (1820), took the city by storm. He laboured hard to abate the apalling ignorance and immorality of his parish by "re-modelling and extending the old parochial economy of Scotland." To the English compulsory assessment for the poor, he preferred the old Scotch method of voluntary church-door contributions, administered by elders; and as minister of St. John's parish (after 1819), by reviving this method, he in four years reduced the pauper expenditure in the parish from £1400 to £280 per annum. Edward Irving was for two years his assistant. In 1823 he accepted the Moral Philosophy chair in St. Andrews, where he wrote his "Use and Abuse of Literary and Ecclesiastical Endowments" (1827). In 1827 he was transferred to the chair of Theology in Edinburgh, and in 1832 published a work on political economy. In 1833 appeared his Bridgewater treatise, "On the Adaptation of External Nature to the Moral and Intellectual Constitution of Man." As convener of the Church-extension Committee (1834), after seven years of enthusiastic labour, he collected £300,000 for building 220 new churches. Meanwhile, the struggles in regard to patronage became keener, until in 1843 Chalmers, followed by 470 ministers, left the church of his fathers, and founded the Free Church, whose swift and successful organisation was greatly owing to his indefatigable exertions. He spent the close of his life as principal of the Free Church College, and in completing his "Institutes of Theology." He died suddenly, May 30, 1847. His works, in 34 vols., deal especially with natural theology, apologetics, and social economy.—PATRICK AND GROOME, *eds.*, 1897, *Chambers's Biographical Dictionary, p.* 196.

PERSONAL

At first sight, no doubt, his face is a coarse one—but a mysterious kind of meaning breathes from every part of it, that such as have eyes to see, cannot be long without discovering. It is very pale, and the large, half-closed eye-lids have a certain drooping, melancholy weight about them, which interested me very much. . . . The lips, too, are singularly pensive in their mode of falling down at the sides, although there is no want of richness and vigour in their central fulness of curve. The upper-lip, from the nose downwards, is separated by a very deep line, which gives a sort of leonine firmness of expression to all the lower part of the face. The cheeks are square and strong, in texture like pieces of marble, with the cheek-bones very broad and prominent. The eyes themselves are light in colour, and have a strange, dreamy heaviness, that conveys any idea rather than that of dulness, but which contracts in a wonderful manner, with the dazzling, watery glare they exhibit when expanded in their sockets, and illuminated into all their flame and fervour, in some moment of high entranced enthusiasm.—LOCKHART, JOHN GIBSON, 1819, *Peter's Letters to his Kinsfolk, Letter* lxxiii.

He is rather inattentive to his dress and person, and has much of the abstractedness which generally goes to the credit of genius. He wears a deep-crowned hat, drawn so much over his eyes, as to disfigure him. He is above all the little arts, by which some men attempt to build greatness upon personal dignity, or gracefulness of manners. . . . I have been told, by one of his friends, that having left his house, at a very early hour, one morning, with a bundle under his arm, to take his departure for some neighboring place, in a steamboat, he was arrested by one of the city watch, who did not know him, and who insisted upon conveying him to the watch-house. Dr. C., impatient to be interrupted, told the man who he was. "Na, na," said the guard of the police, "yure no Dr. Chalmers; he's not such a man as you; and he'd not be seen strolling at this hour." To the watch-house therefore he went, where he was immediately recognized, and set at liberty.—GRISCOM, JOHN, 1823, *A Year in Europe*, 1818–19, *vol.* II, *p.* 399.

He is like the very genius or demon of theological controversy personified. He has neither airs nor graces at command; he thinks nothing of himself: he has nothing theatrical about him (which cannot be said of his successor and rival); but you see a man in mortal throes and agony with doubts and difficulties, seizing stubborn knotty points with his teeth, tearing them with his hands, and straining his eyeballs till they almost start out of their sockets, in pursuit of a train of visionary reasoning, like a Highland-seer with his second sight. The description of Balfour of Burley in his cave, with his Bible in one hand and his sword in the other, contending with the imaginary enemy of mankind, gasping for breath, and with the cold moisture running down his face, gives a lively idea of Dr. Chalmers's prophetic fury in the pulpit. . . . Dr. Chalmers's manner, the determined way in which he gives himself up to his subject, or lays about him and buffets sceptics and gainsayers, arrests attention in spite of every other circumstance, and fixes it on that, and that alone, which excites such interest and such eagerness in his own breast! Besides, he is a logician, has a theory in support of whatever he chooses to advance, and weaves the tissue of his sophistry so close and intricate, that it is difficult not to be entangled in it, or to escape from it.—HAZLITT, WILLIAM, 1825, *The Spirit of the Age, pp.* 59, 60.

A lady who lives very near me, is an invalid, and staid in town for the attendance of physicians, summoned me last evening to meet her confessor, Dr. Chalmers, a person whose genius and whose piety I respect highly, though there are certain points on which I much differ from him. There is a perfect artlessness and originality about his conversation that is very pleasing; he is modest too, and quite unspoilt. He and the great Well-known are the only persons I see whose manners are perfectly simple.—GRANT, ANNE, 1827, *Letter to Mrs. Hook, Sept.* 12; *Memoir and Correspondence, ed. Grant, vol.* III, *p.* 101.

He is of low stature, and square built, with a full, but by no means corpulent person. His head is very large, though not disproportionably so. Features, regular and commanding; a high, uncommonly broad, retreating forehead; even and strongly marked brows; eyes, though dimmed by study, yet mildly intellectual; a straight, though prominent nose; a well defined and proportioned mouth.—GRIFFIN, EDMUND DORR, 1831, *Remains.*

He could reason broadly and powerfully; he could explain and illustrate with exhaustless profusion; he could persuade by all the earnestness of entreaty, all the pathos of affection, and all the terrors of threatening; he could apply, with great skill and knowledge of men's ways, the truth he would inculcate; and he could pour, in a torrent of the most impassioned fervor, the whole molten mass of thought, feeling, description, and appeal, upon the hearts and consciences of his hearers. Thus singularly endowed, and thus wisely using his endowments, he arrived at a place of the highest eminence in the highest walk of popular oratory.—ALEXANDER, WILLIAM LINDSAY, 1846, *A Discourse on the Qualities and Worth of Thomas Chalmers.*

He is of middle height, thick set and brawny, but not corpulent. His face is rather broad, with high cheek-bones, pale, and, as it were, careworn, but well-formed and expressive. His eyes are of a leaden color, rather dull when in a state of repose, but flashing with a half-smothered fire when fairly roused. His nose is broad and lion-like, his mouth, one of the most expressive parts of his countenance, firm, a little compressed and stern, indicating courage and energy, while his forehead is ample and high, . . . covered with straggling grey hair.—TURNBULL, ROBERT, 1847, *The Genius of Scotland.*

By those of his school-fellows, few now in number, who survive, Dr Chalmers is remembered as one of the idlest, strongest, merriest, and most generous-hearted boys in Anstruther school. Little time or attention would have been required from him to prepare his daily lessons, so as to meet the ordinary demands of the schoolroom; for when he did set himself to learn, not one of all his school-fellows could do it at once so quickly and so well. When the time came, however, for saying them, the lessons were often found scarcely half-learned, sometimes not learned at all. . . . Joyous, vigorous, and humorous, he took his part in all the games of the playground, ever ready to lead or to follow, when school-boy expeditions were planned and executed; and wherever, for fun or for frolic, any little group of the merry-hearted was gathered, his full, rich laugh might be heard rising amid their shouts of glee. — HANNA, WILLIAM, 1849, *Memoirs of the Life and Writings of Thomas Chalmers, vol.* I, *ch.* i.

Another of our occasional guests, during the winter of 1806, was a young student from the University of St. Andrews, named Thomas Chalmers, who, I believe, had not then assumed the title of reverend, nor ever dreamed of being dubbed Doctor of Divinity. In truth I think no one could then have rationally predicted in what particular path of life a spirit so energetic and yet so versatile would at last determine to move. . . . Retaining the broadest Scotch accent, he spoke with rapidity and fervor on subjects numberless and completely incongruous. Considering his force and calibre, he might indeed have seemed born to grapple with all pursuits and all sciences; . . . he entered with equal zest into all studies, theological, poetical, political, metaphysical, and mathematical. Apparently there were no obstacles too great for him. Difficulties could not weigh him down, because he was *au dessus de tout cela;* he could look down upon the difficulties, and he trampled on them; yet no one could say that this was the effect of arrogance. On the contrary, the consideration of his subject, or object, whatsoever it might be, was paramount; it absorbed his attention; he was not disturbed by the morbid sensibility and idiosyncrasies of genius, and the consideration of *self* disappeared utterly. —GILLIES, ROBERT PIERCE, 1851, *Memoirs of a Literary Veteran.*

Thomas Chalmers was a Great Man. All the characteristics of genuine greatness marked him as he stood among others. It was not that he surpassed all men around him in pure intelligence, or in any single element of moral excellence; but, taken altogether, mind and heart, and visible bearing—you gave him involuntarily, and he naturally took, the foremost position in almost any assemblage of notable persons with whom he had to do. The unassumingness of a child did not avail to screen him from that homage of which he was the object. The admitted merits and talents of others, on the right hand or the left, did not render that homage ambiguous—did not abate it. There might often be men near him who surpassed him in talent, but they did not dislodge him, in the view of others, from his place. All was harmony in Chalmers's conformation. His figure and attitude very nearly accorded with the Ideal of such a man, after Michael Angelo; and if it showed a rusticity to which that great artist would have applied his chisel, there was beneath the rugged surface a refinement, an intellectuality, to which only the hand of Raphaelle could have given expression.—TAYLOR, ISAAC, 1852, *Memoirs of Dr. Chalmers, North British Review, vol.* 17, *p.* 206.

Dr. Chalmers was a ruler among men: this we know historically; this every man who came within his range felt at once. He was like Agamemnon, a native ἄναξ ἀνδρῶν, and with all his homeliness of feature and deportment, and his perfect simplicity of expression there was about him "that divinity that doth hedge a king." You felt a power, in him, and going from him, drawing you to him in spite of yourself. He was in this respect a *solar* man, he drew after him his own firmament of planets. They, like all free agents, had their centrifugal forces acting ever towards an independent, solitary course, but the centripetal also was there, and they moved with and around their imperial sun,—gracefully or not, willingly or not, as the case might be, but there was no breaking loose: they again, in their own spheres of power, might have their attendant moons, but all were bound to the great massive luminary in the midst. . . . Dr. Chalmers would have made a sorry Balaam; he was made of different stuff, and for other purposes. Your "respectable" men are ever doing their best to keep their status, to maintain their position. He never troubled himself about his status; indeed, we would say *status* was not the word for him. He had a *sedes* on which he sat, and from which he spoke: he had an *imperium*, to and fro which he roamed as he listed: but a *status* was as little in his way as in that of a Mauritanian lion. —BROWN, DR. JOHN, 1858-61, *Horæ Subsecivæ, Second Series, pp.* 117, 130.

He was of middle stature, square built, with light florid complexion and hair partly gray, about sixty years of age. His appearance was prepossessing, and I expected to be much pleased. My chagrin was therefore great when he read the hymn and I found it impossible to understand him. His voice was almost inaudible from hoarseness, his articulation indistinct from loss of teeth, and a broad Fifeshire accent made his language seem like a foreign tongue. The singing of that hymn was delightful. Of the prayer I understood a little, and it was unlike any that I ever before heard. By the time he came to the sermon the power of his voice increased, and I was able to understand most of it.—FARRAR, MRS. JOHN, 1866, *Recollections of Seventy Years, p.* 239.

He was a man of much natural dignity, ingenuity, honesty, and kind affection, as well as sound intellect and imagination. A very eminent vivacity lay in him, which could rise to complete impetuosity (glowing conviction, passionate eloquence, fiery play of heart and head),—all in a kind of *rustic* type, one might say, though wonderfully true and tender. He had a burst of genuine fun too, I have heard; of the same honest, but most plebeian, broadly natural character. . . . He was a man essentially of little culture, of narrow sphere, all his life; such an intellect, professing to be educated, and yet so ill-*read*, so ignorant in all that lay beyond the horizon in place or in time, I have almost nowhere met with. A man capable of much soaking indolence, lazy brooding, and do-nothingism, as the first stage of his life well indicated; a man thought to be timid, almost to the verge of cowardice: yet capable of impetuous activity and blazing audacity, as his latter years showed.—CARLYLE, THOMAS, 1866, *Edward Irving, Reminiscences, ed. Norton, vol.* II.

It has been questioned whether, like so many men of genius, who have been masters of the most delicious harmony in their writings, . . . he was really destitute of what is usually termed an *ear* for music. From all that I can learn, he had only an ear for good marked *tunes*. . . . He was present at an evening party, where a very accomplished lady was discoursing most eloquent music from the fashionable opera of the day. When she was at the overture and the recitative he looked perplexed, as if listening to a medley of madness; but when she struck upon some lively and expressive airs, he turned round with a look of great relief to the gentleman who was next to him, "Do you know, sir, I love these lucid intervals!"—DODDS, JAMES, 1870, *Thomas Chalmers, p.* 303.

It was interesting to observe the never-failing attention of his class. From the commencement to the close of his lecture they maintained a breathless silence; during his more impassioned flights of oratory they eagerly bent forward, and sometimes those that were in the back rows stood up. On one remarkable occasion, when he was powerfully demonstrating the impossibility of order arising out of chaos without the agency of an intelligent Creator, I observed that by degrees, not merely the front rows, but nearly the whole class had risen. I am not sure that I was not myself among those who instinctively gave this evidence of excitement.—SINCLAIR, JOHN, 1875, *Sketches of Old Times and Distant Places, p.* 681.

It would be hard to name an orator of equal fame who had so few of the usual external helps and ornaments of eloquence; and hence the first feeling of almost every hearer whom his fame had attracted, was a shock of disappointment. As he rose to speak, and the hearer contrasted with his ideal of an orator, or with his preconceived notions, the middle-sized, and somewhat strange and uncouth figure before him, with its broad but not lofty forehead, its prominent cheek bones, and its drooping, lack-lustre eyes; as he observed the abrupt and awkward manner, apparently indicating embarrassment or irreverence, or both, and listened to the harsh croaking tones, the broad Fifeshire tongue, while the speaker bent over his manuscript, and following it with his finger, read every word like a schoolboy, —it seemed incredible that this could be the man who had stormed the hearts of his countrymen for more than thirty years, and whose published discourses had rivalled in their sale the productions of the great Wizard of the North. . . . Gradually the great preacher would unveil himself; the ungainly attitude, the constraint and awkwardness, the vacant look, and feebleness of voice and manner, would be cast aside, or if in some degree retained, would be overlooked by the hearer in the deepening interest of the theme; the voice, though still harsh and unmusical, would ring out and thrill like a clarion; the eye, which was so dull and half-closed, would be lighted up with intelligence; the breast would heave, and the body sway to and fro, with the tumult of the thought; voice and face would seem bursting with the fury of excitement, while his person was bathed with perspiration; the words, before so slow, would leap forth with the rapidity and force of a mountain torrent; argument would follow argument, illustration would follow illustration, and appeal would follow appeal, in quick succession, till at last all hearts were subdued, and carried captive by the flood of an overwhelming and resistless eloquence.—MATHEWS, WILLIAM, 1878, *Oratory and Orators*, *pp.* 400, 401.

Not very familiar with the Scotch brogue which Chalmers spoke, of the rudest Glasgow kind, and finding it not only difficult to understand but painful to listen to, I was little disposed, at first, to give much heed to his sermon. His appearance and manner in the pulpit, moreover, were by no means attractive. His face and features were coarse and large; his lank gray hair fell carelessly about a narrow forehead, and he kept his head bent, and his blinking eyes close to his manuscript; while his only action was an up and down or sawing movement with his right arm, from the elbow. In spite of all these personal disadvantages, which, at the beginning, were very repulsive to me, I was soon so interested in his fervid utterances, and absorbed by the quick alternations of emotion with which my feelings responded to his earnest appeals, that I unresistingly yielded to the torrent of his eloquence. The man, in the mean time, seemed transfigured, and my tearful eyes saw, as it were through a sacred halo, the prophet or apostle.—TOMES, ROBERT, 1880, *My College Days*, *p.* 85.

He was one of nature's nobles, and most of the qualities which stamped him with that character were obvious—almost glaring—to all who came across his path. I do not mean merely his rich and glowing eloquence, but his warrior grandeur, his unbounded philanthropy, his strength of purpose, his mental integrity, his absorbed and absorbing earnestness. They might not be so well aware of his singular simplicity and detachment from the world, of which I remember to have been deeply struck on a particular occasion. He sometimes gave me the honor of a walk with him, and one day he said he wished to make an appointment of this kind with me, when during our walk he would explain to me fully his situation with respect to the emoluments of his professorship—the chair of Divinity. If I remember right that chair, when he was appointed to it, was believed to have a large endowment, but a point of law was, I think, subsequently raised which, if affirmed, would have swept away nearly the whole. After forty-five years I may state this inaccurately, but what I remember clearly is that the question was a very grave one, and I think it materially affected his prospects, and even the status of himself and his family. The day came and the walk began, and lasted, I suppose a couple of hours or more. At our starting he opened one of his favorite and engrossing subjects, probably that of evangelizing the country by the means of manageable districts, each with its church and minister. Having begun, he forgot all about his endowment and his status. The conversation held fast by the original theme till we were within a few yards of my father's door. He seemed then to recollect himself, and said: "If you will allow me I will send my man of business to call upon you, and he will acquaint you with all particulars of the question which has been raised." Such was the impotence of lucre to lay hold on his great, stately and heavenly mind.—GLADSTONE, WILLIAM EWART, 1880, *To Lord Moncreiff.*

It was a smart saying of Robert Hall, that the mind of Chalmers seemed to "move on hinges, not on wheels. There is incessant motion, but no progress." Hall was more discursive in thought, and in style far more finished. But Chalmers knew what he was about, and secured the effect at which he aimed. He concentrated his force on one important truth at a time, turned it round and round in every light, and would not leave it till he had made full demonstration of it to those who heard him, and pressed it home upon them with all his energy. Till this was accomplished he would not, and could not, pass on to other matters. In this sense it may be admitted that he moved—he was born to move—on hinges, and not on wheels. And it must also be admitted that this, while it may arrest and convince an audience, may not suit so well the quiet examination of students. . . . Let Thomas Chalmers be remembered. Those who knew him need no such exhortation, those who were his students or his helpers cry with an air of triumph, "We were with Chalmers!" as soldiers who had been in the Peninsular or at Waterloo used to say, "We were with Wellington!"—FRASER, DONALD, 1881, *Thomas Chalmers.*

The end of the life was in exquisite keeping with his saintly and genial character. After a happy Sunday evening spent in the sweet intercourse of his family and of a brother minister, he retired with a beaming countenance and a general "good-night," promising to conduct worship himself the following morning. But long ere it dawned he had entered into his eternal rest. The countenance was so calm and sweet, and the grand head and form were so full of dignity and repose, that it was only the marble chillness and the dread silence which informed the surprised household that it was death, not sleep, they were gazing on. A sorrow such as occurs only when a nation mourns marked the last honours which affection could pay to his remains. More than 100,000 citizens witnessed the burial, and they were but the representatives of multitudes, in all churches and in all lands, who felt that in Thomas Chalmers they had lost a leader and a friend. He rests in the Cemetery of the Grange, beneath the shadow of Arthur's Seat and Salisbury Crags.—MACLEOD, DONALD, 1883, *Scottish Divines (St. Giles Lectures), p.* 315.

The large, benignant simplicity of the man is what first and most deeply impresses one. Not the simplicity of the recluse, a selfish compound of quiescence and indifference; for his nature was broadly social, and his life was spent in ceaseless and widely varied labors for the well-being of others. Chalmers was a peaceful man, but his peace was the assured peace of conscious power, and beneath all his serenity there beat a fiery heart, capable of noble wrath and heroic action.—MASON, EDWARD T., 1885, *ed., Personal Traits of British Authors, p.* 129.

Of Chalmers' oratorical powers, it would be a waste of time to speak. His was a voice that filled the world, the English-speaking world at any rate, from end to end in its day, although if, as they say, he was one of those apt to confound Augustine of Hippo with our first Canterbury Archbishop, rhetoric rather than theological learning must have been his strong point. —DOYLE, SIR FRANCIS HASTINGS, 1886, *Reminiscences and Opinions, p.* 102.

The greatest of Scottish preachers. . . . Other preachers seek to make different impressions in different portions of their sermons, Chalmers was content to make no more than one by the whole sermon, but when he had made that, it was indelible. No man who ever heard him could help seeing what he would be at, or could ever forget the importance which he gave it. His iterations and reiterations and re-reiterations were but like the whirlings of the sling from which at length the stone was sent whizzing to its mark; or like the gyrations of the eagle as it circles round and round in order only the more unerringly to swoop down upon its prey. His style was not meant for the eye, and so one soon tires of reading him; but for the ear it was most effective; and wherever, to this day, you meet with one who was privileged to listen to him from the pulpit, you will be sure to find him repeating to you the essence of the sermon which the great orator had distilled into a phrase that could not be misunderstood, and that would not allow itself to be forgotten.—TAYLOR, WILLIAM M., 1887, *The Scottish Pulpit, pp.* 194, 223.

He was not the model of a mild and benevolent pastor and apostle, nor was the ideal of a dispassionate legislator—occupied above all the tides of sentiment, with a profound study of the best and highest principles upon which men were to be ruled and guided for their own best advantage—his. He was of an imperious nature, born to command, not unready to fight, impatient of interruption and misconception, accustomed to carry through his purpose, whatever it was, with a high hand, to mould everything around him to his will; a natural despot, though a most genial and friendly one. There was not air enough for him to breathe (one would have said) in any limited sphere.—OLIPHANT, MARGARET O. W., 1893, *Thomas Chalmers, p.* 140.

His broad Scotch accent was so marked as to make it difficult to catch some of his utterances; but as he advanced with his subject his manner of delivery—which was the opposite of Irving's, being heavy and dull—then became eloquent in diction and earnest in manner.—SAUNDERS, FREDERICK, 1894, *Character Studies, p.* 12.

The great merit of Chalmers as a professor lay in the enthusiasm with which he inspired his students. It would have been hard indeed for any conscientious youth to be under him and not feel his soul quickened, at least occasionally, to a sublime ardour, and fired with new ambition. So wonderful was his influence, that at the Disruption nine-tenths of those who passed through his classes stood by his side. The present writer, though he spent but one session under him before the Disruption, can bear testimony, not only to the intellectual and spiritual impulse he gave, but to the subtle sympathy which drew his students to share his church views, though he never alluded to them in the class, and to the enthusiasm with which they listened to him in the General Assembly.—BLAIKIE, W. GARDEN, 1896, *Thomas Chalmers (Famous Scots Series), p.* 145.

His grasp of mathematical truths and of applied science was rather vigorous and effective than profound or exact, but he brought to both an ardent imagination, which gave to these pursuits a vividness of interest that absorbed his enthusiastic energy. To his eyes they were coloured with brilliancy and an attractiveness which they assume only for a few. It was to these pursuits that his attention was chiefly devoted, and in them that he hoped to find the best outlet for his ambition. He had early found employment in connection with the teaching of mathematics at St. Andrews University, and he was firmly resolved that his clerical calling should not interfere with his work in this field. But his popularity as a teacher—a popularity due to his marvellous powers of exposition and to the rich vein of imagination which clothed his conception of scientific truths—was resented by the duller but more authorised representatives of the Faculty, and he found himself thrust aside with little ceremony by men to whom his genius was something of a reproach. —CRAIK, SIR HENRY, 1901, *A Century of Scottish History, vol.* II, *p.* 316.

GENERAL

The grand old Christian Giant—the John Knox of the nineteenth century.—GILFILLAN, GEORGE, 1855, *A Third Gallery of Portraits, p.* 96.

When we come to think of English literature at large, and to think of it as influenced or favoured by no special or national feelings, it is quite certain that the "Works" will undergo a severe sifting. Portions—large portions, of the mass, we cannot doubt, must subside, and, at no distant date, will cease to be often asked for, or popularly read. The works of the very best writers (if voluminous) have undergone the same discerptive process. Nor has any human reputation hitherto been of such plenary force as might suffice for immortalizing every paragraph or treatise that a man has written and printed. Assuredly Chalmers will not stand his ground as an exception to this almost universal doom—a doom which has consigned to oblivion a half—a three-fourth—or a nine-tenth of the products of even the brightest minds; especially if they have been, in their day, teeming and industrious minds, and if such writers have mixed themselves at large with the social and political movements of their times.—TAYLOR, ISAAC, 1856, *Dr. Chalmers' Works, North British Review, vol.* 26, *p.* 2.

The "Astronomical Discourses" of Dr. Chalmers ran to nine editions within a year; and, according to Dr. Hanna, never previously, nor ever since, has any volume of sermons met with such immediate and general acceptance. The "Tales of My Landlord" had a month's start in the date of publication, and even with such a competitor it ran an almost equal race. Not a few curious observers are said to have been struck with the novel competition, and watched with lively interest the almost neck to neck course, for a whole year, of Scotland's great preacher and her great novelist.—JACOX, FRANCIS, 1872, *A Run upon a Book, Aspects of Authorship, p.* 330.

As an author, he is distinguished more for his exposition of the views of others than for the excogitation of anything profoundly original. It may with confidence be pronounced that he had a greater genius for style than any other Scotchman of this century except Carlyle. We cannot read a page of Chalmers without feeling ourselves in the hand of a master of luminous and varied exposition. Himself possessing the clearest grasp of his subject, he fully comprehended and kept steadily in view the difficulties of the reader: he sought to unfold his matter in the most luminous sequence, and to make sure that one point was thoroughly expounded before he proceeded to the next.—MINTO, WILLIAM, 1872-80, *Manual of English Prose Literature, p.* 521.

In his philosophical works he unfolds and enforces a number of very important principles, not, it may be, absolutely original, but still fresh and independent in his statement and illustration of them, and setting aside error on the one side or other. His "Sketches of Moral and Mental Philosophy" cannot be said to be a full work on ethics, but it enforces great truths in a very impressive and eloquent way. . . . His views on natural theology appeared first in the "Bridgewater Treatise," on "The Adaptation of External Nature to the Moral and Intellectual Constitution of Man." The feeling of admiration excited was mingled with disappointment. The bulk was too great for the matter, and the work had the appearance of a hasty recooking of his old thoughts which were grand in themselves, but were not formed into a duly proportioned whole. His arguments and his illustrations have a much better form given them in his subsequently published work,—"Natural Theology."—MCCOSH, JAMES, 1874, *The Scottish Philosophy, pp.* 401, 402.

The name of Chalmers is in all the churches honored as one of Christian genius consecrated to the highest services which any man can render to his church and his country. His characteristic work, however, was not in the field of Christian thought. He broke out no new lines in this field. He initiated no new movement. Both he and Andrew Thomson were powerful leaders on the old lines—the latter with inferior, although stanch intellectual weapons.—TULLOCH, JOHN, 1885, *Movements of Religious Thought in Britain During the Nineteenth Century, p.* 103.

It was this time that he delivered his famous "Astronomical Discourses," which, whatever may be said either of the objection which he sought to meet, or of the argument by which he met it, must be pronounced unrivalled for the grandeur and amplitude of their sweep through the depths of space, and for what John Foster called "the brilliant glow of a blazing eloquence" with which they displayed the sublime poetry of the heavens.—TAYLOR, WILLIAM M., 1887, *The Scottish Pulpit, p.* 207.

Looking at the influence of Chalmers on the religious thought and life of Scotland generally, we may say that he let in daylight and fresh air on the evangelical enclosure of the church. He hardly ever opened his lips without uttering something fresh and racy. The evangelical message assumed a new importance at his hands. It came from him sustained by intellect, embellished by imagination, and enforced by eloquence, while new relations, hitherto overlooked, were brought into view—to the science, the culture, the thinking of the age. As Chalmers advanced in life a rare sagacity became conspicuous; with broad, statesmanlike view he was seen to have apprehended the evils of modern society—to have detected the remedy, and girded himself, in all his strength, to apply it. While thus broadening out and acquiring fresh influence, he was at the same time growing in humility and devoutness.—BLAIKIE, W. GARDEN, 1887, *Dictionary of National Biography, vol.* IX, *p.* 454.

My third biography is that of Dr. Chalmers, fruitful of beneficent example in more directions than could be easily specified, but to me of peculiar service in relation to poverty in Glasgow, with its attendant evils and vices. In his modes of averting pauperism, of relieving want in person and in kind, of bringing preventive measures to bear on the potential nurseries of crime, and of enlisting the stronger in the aid and comfort of the feebler members of the community, I found many valuable suggestions for the local charities which came under my direction or influence while I was a parish minister; and in the fewer trusts of that kind which I still retain, and in my present limited intercourse with the poor and suffering, I see his insight and foresight continually verified.—PEABODY, ANDREW P., 1888, *Books That Have Helped Me, p.* 48.

The long and painful struggle for emancipation from theological dogma can hardly be treated in such a paper as this without liability to misunderstanding. Strange as it may seem, the starting-point of the change with me was the reading of the works of Dr. Thomas Chalmers, whose writings were great favorites with me in the early years of my life as a minister. Some of his books I read on horseback, riding from one preaching place to another. I recall particularly the "Astronomical Discourses," the "Bridgewater Treatise," and certain portions of the "Institutes of Theology." Dr. Chalmers believed himself to be a sound Calvinist, but there were certain things, rather in his method than in his conclusions, that changed my way of thinking on these things.—EGGLESTON, EDWARD, 1888, *Books That Have Helped Me, p.* 55.

As literature his works have hardly maintained the reputation which they once had, and even those who revere him, unless they let reverence stifle criticism, are apt to acknowledge that there is more rhetoric than logic in him, and that the rhetoric itself is not of the finest.—SAINTSBURY, GEORGE, 1896, *A History of Nineteenth Century Literature, p.* 375.

Most of his compositions were cast in a rhetorical mould, and betray at times all the faults peculiar to that form of writing. Pomposity, verbiage, bombast, and rodomontade are there to be discovered in abundance. Often, again, he employs a phraseology and a mode of expression which are unintelligible, when they are not repellent, to our generation. The "scowling infidel" and the "pigmy philosopher" play by much too prominent a part in his apologetic writings, while the favourite and well-worn image of the storm-tossed sailor-boy and his weeping mother seems no longer capable of exciting the desired emotion. . . . A straining for effect—a lack of the sense of proportion—are but too manifest in his most admired pieces. . . . He is by no means more satisfactory in handling the principles of ethics than in casuistry; and his contributions to moral philosophy deservedly exercised very little influence on the thought of his own generation, and exercised none on the thought of this. But, when ample allowance has been made for such palpable and serious defects, there remains no inconsiderable mass of truly admirable writing. It is not merely that we find vigour, impetuosity, and earnestness, though these qualities are present in a very high degree. But we find, when he is at his best, a copious, dignified, and aptly employed, if not exactly elegant, vocabulary, a rare felicity of illustration and metaphor, a swelling rotundity of diction, and a complete mastery of a certain species of rhythm and balance. . . . Of his literary, as of his speculative, influence at the present day it is impossible to discover any important traces; but those who are ambitious enough to aspire to a lofty type of the ecclesiastical, or, indeed, of any, sort of eloquence, will find in Chalmers an eminently noble and inspiring, though, at the same time a highly dangerous, model.—MILLAR, J. H., 1896, *English Prose, ed. Craik, vol.* v, *p.* 224, 225.

Chalmers was an orator of undoubted genius, an administrator of great talent, an accomplished scientist, and a second rate thinker. . . . His intellect had a natural grandeur, apprehended things in their largest relations, and ranged congenially among the heights and depths of the universe; it was equally remarkable for mastery of detail, and for clear concrete vision. . . . He popularized the sublimities of science with singular power; the profounder bearing of philosophy and of history upon theology lay beyond his purview.—HERFORD, C. H., 1897, *The Age of Wordsworth, p.* 31.

Sharon Turner

1768-1847

Born in London, Sept. 24, 1768, was educated at a school in Pentonville, and at an early age was articled to an attorney. The first volume of his "History of the Anglo-Saxons" appeared in 1799, and the third in 1805. The three volumes of the "History of England during the Middle Ages, from the Norman Conquest to 1509," appeared in 1814, 1815, and 1823; "The History of the Reign of Henry VIII." in 1826; and "The History of the Reigns of Edward VI., Mary, and Elizabeth," in 1829. Sharon Turner wrote some poems, and "The Sacred History of the World," in three volumes, which appeared in 1832, 1834, and 1837. He died in Red Lion Square, London, Feb. 13, 1847. —TOWNSEND, GEORGE H., 1870, *The Every-Day Book of Modern Literature, vol.* I, *p.*204.

HISTORY OF THE ANGLO-SAXONS
1799–1805

So much new information was probably never laid before the public in any one historical publication.—SOUTHEY, ROBERT, 1805, *Letter to John May, Aug.* 5; *Life and Correspondence, ed. C. C. Southey, ch.* xi.

Among many historical efforts, principally concerning England in different periods, his "History of the Anglo-Saxons" stands out prominently as a great work. He was an eccentric scholar, and an antiquarian, and he found just the place to delve in when he undertook that history. The style is not good—too epigrammatic and broken; but his research is great, his speculations bold, and his information concerning the numbers, manners, arts, learning, and other characters of the Anglo-Saxons, immense. The student of English history must read Turner for a knowledge of the Saxon period.—COPPÉE, HENRY, 1872, *English Literature, p.* 448.

The first edition was published as early as 1805; and though for the edition of 1807 the work was carefully revised, it can hardly be considered a standard authority at the present day. The investigations of Kemble, Palgrave, and others have deprived it of a value it once possessed. It will be found, however, that the volumes contain many minute details of considerable interest. The author was a special student of this period; but, though he accumulated a vast number of interesting facts, his methods were much less philosophical than those of his more distinguished successors in the same field. The literary style is not such as to give additional value to the volumes. Aside from its intrinsic merits, the work is entitled to some respect; for, when it was first published, it was a genuine revelation to the English people. Until that time, no one had taken the trouble to collect the accessible evidence and bring it into a single book. Turner, therefore, performed a very useful work in calling attention to a field which has since been very successfully cultivated.— ADAMS, CHARLES KENDALL, 1882, *A Manual of Historical Literature, p.* 443.

GENERAL

One of the best writers, of the most learned antiquarians and most enlightened scholars of his time.—CUMBERLAND, RICHARD, 1807, *Memoirs, vol.* II, *p.* 324.

We shall not otherwise advert to living historians than to observe, that Mr. Sharon Turner has earned the honourable reputation of indefatigable diligence, of the love of truth and mankind, but has exposed himself more and more in each successive volume to literary criticisms.—ALLEN, JOHN, 1831, *Lingard's History of England, Edinburgh Review, vol.* 53, *p.* 17.

Mr. Turner is often capable of affording his reader valuable topics of reflection; but, though apparently a most patient antiquarian, his imagination is so active, that his style is unexpectedly loaded with metaphors, to a degree that is not only inconsistent with historic composition, but with *all* composition. Very extensive reading is displayed; and on the whole, the work may be consulted with advantage. There is nothing said of the laws of Edward the Confessor, a strange omission! nor of the rise of the English House of Commons, though Mr. Turner evidently conceives that the Commons formed no part of the witenage mote. Mr. Turner has, since I wrote this paragraph, published three quarto volumes on the English History, from William I. to Henry VIII. He is an antiquarian, as I have mentioned, and whatever a man who looks into original records publishes, must be more or less of importance. Mr. Turner often gives his reader the impression of an amiable man, rather than one of a very superior understanding: yet many curious particulars may be collected, and much instruction may be derived from his learned and often amusing work.—SMYTH, WILLIAM, 1839, *Lectures on Modern History, Lecture* v.

Turner's "History of England" down to the lives of the Tudors is replete with Anglo-Saxon and other ancient learning; and it is written with dignity, purity, and eloquence. Turner surpasses Hume in the depth and fulness of his researches, and in the spirit and tenor of his moral reflections.—KENT, JAMES, 1840-53, *Outline of a Course of English Reading, p.* 42.

Is most honourably laborious and trustworthy, though wearisomely heavy and pompous.—SPALDING, WILLIAM, 1852, *A History of English Literature, p.* 392.

Turner's "History of England," though distinguished by the same research and acuteness, [as the "History of the Anglo-Saxons"], is not of equal merit; and, unfortunately, the peculiarities and uncouthness of its style, as well as a strange attempt to introduce novelty in spelling, has hindered the work from acquiring the popularity which it really deserves.—ALISON, SIR ARCHIBALD, 1853-59, *History of Europe,* 1815-1852, *ch.* v.

From an ambitious attempt to rival Gibbon in loftiness of style and diction, Mr. Turner has disfigured his "History" by a pomp of expression and involved intricacy of style, that often border on the ludicrous, and mar the effect of his narrative. This defect is more conspicuous in his latter volumes. The early part of his "History," devoted to the Anglo-Saxons, and the labour as he informs us, of sixteen years, is by far the most valuable.—CHAMBERS, ROBERT, 1876, *Cyclopædia of English Literature, ed. Carruthers.*

His "History of the Anglo-Saxons" contains a mass of valuable matter, handled with a rather too obvious reminiscence of the large evolution of the "Decline and Fall," and in a style which has caught Gibbon's pomp without his splendour. He subsequently carried on the history to the reign of Elizabeth, but this part of his work was soon obscured by Lingard, while his Anglo-Saxon labours retained prestige until superseded by Kemble and Thorpe, who built upon the broader foundation of the school of Grimm.—HERFORD, C. H., 1897, *The Age of Wordsworth, p.* 42.

Henry Francis Lyte

1793-1847

Henry Francis Lyte was born at Ednam, a village situated on the Eden, a tributary of the Tweed near Kelso, Roxburghshire, on the 1st of June, 1793. He was educated at Portora, Inniskillen, and at Trinity College, Dublin, where he distinguished himself in three successive years by taking the English poem prize. Though at first intending to follow the medical profession he entered the Church (1815), and accepted a curacy at Taghmon, near Wexford, afterwards removing to Marazion, Cornwall (1817), where he married. Subsequently he held curacies at Lymington, Hampshire (1819), and Charlton, Devon, and finally took charge of the new parish of Lower Brixham, Devonshire, where he ministered for five-and-twenty years. His "Tales on the Lord's Prayer in Verse," written at Lymington, were published in 1826, his "Poems Chiefly Religious" in 1833, and his "Spirit of the Psalms," a metrical version of the Psalter, in 1834. His "Remains," containing poems, sermons, letters, etc., and a memoir by his daughter, was published in 1850, and a volume of his "Miscellaneous Poems" in 1868. He also published an edition of the poem of Henry Vaughan, with a memoir, in 1847.—MILES, ALFRED H., 1897, *The Poets and the Poetry of the Century, Sacred, Moral, and Religious Verse, p.* 157.

PERSONAL

It was good for a young man to be in the society and under the influence of such a true gentleman, scholar, poet, and saint, to be impressed by the beauty of holiness, and to be so happily assured that the voice of joy and health is in the dwellings of the righteous. He was revered by all who knew him, especially by those whose sympathies he prized the most—the poor. —HOLE, S. REYNOLDS, 1893, *Memories, p.* 67.

GENERAL

Among her purest, choicest, and most gifted lyric poets, the Church of Christ will ever delight to number Henry Francis

Lyte. His contributions to "the service of song in the house of the Lord," and in the domestic sanctuary, have been numerous and excellent.—HATFIELD, EDWIN F., 1884, *The Poets of the Church*, p. 391.

A poet whose singular beauty of nature and true instinct for his art were not always adequately rendered in his verse. —PALGRAVE, FRANCIS T., 1896, *Landscape in Poetry*, p. 249.

"Abide with Me." This was the Swan Song of the Rev H. F. Lyte. He produced it on the evening of the Sunday on which he preached his last sermon. It is generally used as an evening hymn. It was not so intended. It refers to the evening of life, not of the day, and is more of a hymn for the dying than for those about to renew their strength by a night's rest. It was sung at the burial of Professor Maurice, and is in constant use throughout the English-speaking world. Lyte is buried in Nice, and his grave is still sometimes sought out by pilgrims from far across the seas who attribute their conversion to this hymn.—STEAD, W. T., 1897, *Hymns that Have Helped*, p. 207.

Lyte had a tender feeling for nature and a sense of the sublime, but he lacked originality and the creative power of imagination. His general poems have no permanent interest. His lines "On a Naval Officer buried in the Atlantic" have been praised, and have received musical setting at the hands of Sir Arthur Sullivan, but they remind one of Campbell, and suffer by the comparison, while the last verse approaches perilously near to bathos. "The Poet's Plea" is one of the best of his longer poems, but it is too long for quotation. The best of his hymns are wholly admirable, and have become indispensable to the psalmody of the Church.—MILES, ALFRED H., 1897, *The Poets and the Poetry of the Century, Sacred, Moral and Religious Verse*, p. 157.

James Kent

1763-1847

James Kent, LL. D., born at Philippi, N. Y., July 31, 1763, graduated at Yale in 1781; was admitted to the bar in 1787, and settled at Poughkeepsie; was a member of the legislature in 1790 and 1792. In 1793 he removed to New York, and became a master in chancery, a leader among the Federalists, and professor of law in Columbia College. In 1797 he became recorder of New York; in 1798-1804 was a puisne judge of the supreme court of New York, and in 1804-14 chief-justice. In the latter year he was appointed chancellor of New York, which office he held till 1823. He was in 1822 a member of the constitutional convention at Albany; in 1824 resumed his professorship in Columbia College. His principal work is "Commentaries on American Law." Died Dec. 12, 1847.—BARNARD AND GUYOT, *eds.*, 1885, *Johnson's New General Cyclopædia, vol.* I, *p.* 720.

PERSONAL

He is, in his conversation, extremely active, simple, entertaining, and I know not when we have had among us a man so much to my mind in all things. I dined with him five or six times, and he dined with us the last day, and a rare display of fine talk we had at table, between him, Mr. Prescott, Mr. Lowell, and Mr. Webster. . . . Everybody was delighted with him. His whole visit among us was an unbroken triumph, which he enjoyed with the greatest openness. . . . Indeed, the Chancellor seemed to give an uncommon stir and brightness to men's faculties, while he was with us, . . . there seemed to be a happy and healthy excitement of the intellectual powers and social feelings of all with whom he came in contact, that was the evident result of his rich talents and transparent simplicity of character, and which I have never known to be produced among us in the same degree by any other individual.—TICKNOR, GEORGE, 1823, *To C. S. Davies, Sept.* 19; *Life, Letters and Journals, vol.* I, *pp.* 339, 340.

He went to the grave as it is given to few men. Having spent a life of the highest usefulness, acknowledged at home and abroad, of an extent far beyond the common limits of human existence; loved, almost adored, by his family, and cherished with venerating affection by bands of friends; active almost to the very limit of his life,—he was allowed to depart in the arms of his own, leaving a name loved as long as they live, and honored as long as our nation shall exist. Are there many mortals who can compare with him?—LIEBER, FRANCIS, 1847, *Letter to William Kent; Memoirs and Letters of James Kent, ed. Kent, p.* 277.

His industry and learning, his intellectual powers, and his unblemished character were all the capital he possessed, and the only dowry of the bride were her personal charms, her firm principles and excellent judgment, the sweetness of her temper, and the purity of her heart. It is true, then, that they were poor—exceedingly poor; but it is also true that, in their poverty, they were exceedingly rich; for, in addition to the riches I have named, their mutual affection was disinterested and sincere, and their trust in Providence unlimited and unwavering.—DUER, JOHN, 1848, *A Discourse on the Life, Character and Public Service of James Kent.*

In the discharge of his judicial duties there was so much gentleness, modesty and simplicity, united with such depth of learning and compass of mind, that the profession and people loved him quite as much as they admired and respected him. Often, during an argument, he reminded counsel of decision touching the case at bar, that, with all their scrutiny and research, they had overlooked. Few of the thousands, in and out of the profession, who have read and admired the writings of Kent understood the unpretentious character and simple manners of their author. In this respect he resembled Chief Justice Marshall and Judge Peterson, of the United States Supreme Court. In his intercourse with his friends and neighbors, he was *et id genus omne*, one of them, without any reserve, though he never lost that ineffable grace of manner which results from a union with exalted mental endowments. A perpetual sunshine seemed to surround him, lighting up all phases of his life, subordinating them almost to a woman-like affection and sympathy. But on the bench he was one of the most dignified of American Judges.—PROCTOR, L. B., 1888, *The Trials and Triumphs of a Young Lawyer, p.* 4.

As Judge Kent himself notes, he did not possess forensic talent, nor was he ever distinguished in contentions at the bar. He spoke through his pen, and, upon the few occasions on which he made public addresses, he spoke entirely from his notes. He was a graceful, eloquent, and interesting speaker. . . . Throughout the long and busy life of Chancellor Kent there was one unchanging undercurrent of feeling which appears in all his correspondence,—his strong and ardent love for his home, his wife, his family, and the pursuit of learning, of which he never wearied. His highest anticipation was that, at some time, he might retire from the "busy haunts of men," and, gathering about him his family and belongings on some sunny hillside, pass the rest of his days in ideal repose. It was the early cultivation of these peaceful pleasures and pursuits which brought such tranquil happiness to his declining years.—KENT, WILLIAM, 1898, *Memoirs and Letters of James Kent, pp.* 227, 257.

During his judicial career his greatness never seems to have been questioned by his contemporaries. They saw that he was a great judge; we see that he was a legal giant—one of those masters whose stature is above that of ordinary men. But when we read his Life, and perceive his simplicity and modesty, and his unfailing refusal to trust to anything but industry and minute accuracy and research, we feel that, wonderful as his powers were, he earned his fame by labor as unusual, and hence to record of his achievements inspires in us, as it did in his contemporaries, less envy than a sort of affectionate veneration. . . . Simplicity of feeling and expression, sometimes approaching naïveté; shrewdness and capacity for dealing with men; honesty, industry, strong domestic affections, combined with great kindliness, suavity, humility, and modesty, shine out in the reminiscences and letters preserved. Kent's career was the opposite of adventurous—in fact, had few incidents of any sort; his biography cannot be made picturesque. Dramatic in a certain sense it is, for he was the architect of a great and enduring position, which he made himself by sheer native force of mind and character.—SEDGWICK, A. G., 1898, *Chancellor Kent, The Nation, vol.* 67, *pp.* 95, 96.

DECISIONS

In his decisions we can everywhere trace the happy use of that marvellous system of doctrines which Justinian collected with so much care, and which stands unrivalled in the world for its general equity, and nice adaptation to the necessities of mankind. . . . Let those who now doubt the importance of the study of the civil law by common lawyers read diligently the opinions of Mr. Chancellor Kent, and they will find all the objections raised by indolence and ignorance and prejudice practically refuted, and the civil law triumphantly sustained. They will perceive the vivid lights which it casts on the paths of juridical science; and they will be instructed and cheered in the pursuit, though they may not hope to move in the brilliant career of such a judge with equal footsteps. . . . As to the chancery decisions of Mr. Chancellor Kent, they are as full of learning, and pains-taking research, and vivid discrimination, as those of any man that ever sat on the English woolsack.—STORY, JOSEPH, 1820, *Chancery Jurisdiction, North American Review, vol.* 11, *pp.* 141, 142, 165.

His researches on every point were so full as to leave little or nothing to be supplied by those who might afterwards wish to have his decisions re-examined or to test the correctness of his conclusions. . . . His judicial opinions are, therefore, uncommonly interesting and instructive to all, but especially to those who have commenced the study of the law, and aspire to eminence in that profession.—JOHNSON, WILLIAM, 1835, *Life of Chancellor Kent, National Portrait-Gallery of Distinguished Americans, vol.* II.

His decisions must forever remain a monument of judicial wisdom, learning, and eloquence, without superior in those of any country or any age.—HOFFMAN, DAVID, 1836, *A Course of Legal Study, 2nd ed.*

I do not scruple to affirm that they (Decisions), form a series of unequalled excellence, and to the Equity lawyer of inestimable value: they are the most precious treasure his library contains. None who reflect on the nature and amount of instruction that these volumes supply, and on the method and style in which that instruction is conveyed, if able to make the comparison, will refuse to admit that there is no series of Reports in England, or in the United States, that, in these distinctive proofs of a superior and permanent value, resembles or approaches them.—DUER, JOHN, 1848, *A Discourse on the Life, Character and Public Services of James Kent.*

COMMENTARIES UPON AMERICAN LAW
1826–32

They ["Commentaries"] may be recommended to the English law-student of the present day as a substitute for Blackstone. They contain not only a clear statement of the English law, with all the alterations that have taken place since the time of Blackstone, but a full account of the main principles of Equity (a topic on which the English commentator is confessedly deficient); also a review of the modifications engrafted on the English law by the different States of the Union, and on all important questions, an instructive parallel between the English, American, Modern Continental, and Civil Laws.—JOHNES, ARTHUR JAMES, 1834, *Reform of the Court of Chancery.*

They ["Commentaries"] are fine examples of lucid and manly reasoning, and the style in which they are written is perspicuous and forcible. From the nature of the work, Chancellor Kent was only able to devote a small portion of his treatise to the Law of Nations; but their brevity is the only thing that is objectionable in these lectures, for all that the author does give us is valuable.—MANNING, WILLIAM OKE, 1839, *Commentaries on the Laws of Nations, p.* 44.

It is the character of the "Commentaries" as a national work, and their masterly execution as such, that have stamped upon them a peculiar value. It is to these causes that the extent of the influence which they rapidly acquire and now exert on the jurisprudence, not of a single State, but of all, must be ascribed. . . . It is now in the hands of every student and of every practitioner of the law, and it ought to be in the hands of every legislator and statesman, and indeed of every man of cultivated mind and liberal studies.—DUER, JOHN, 1848, *A Discourse on the Life, Character and Public Services of James Kent, pp.* 76, 79.

In 1826 he published the first volume of his Commentaries, at the earnest solicitation of his friends, he himself having little expectation of a favourable reception by the public. He originally contemplated but two volumes, but these expanded as he proceeded, into four, the last of which appeared in 1830. They at once took the high place they have since held in legal literature, and as the universally received text-books of the science throughout the country, as by the plan of stating first the common law on each topic, and afterwards the changes introduced by decisions or statute in each state, it is adapted to the use of every portion of the Union.—DUYCKINCK, EVERT A. AND GEORGE L., 1855–65–75, *Cyclopædia of American Literature, ed. Simons, vol.* I, *p.* 527.

Chancellor Kent is the most eminent personage in the annals of American jurisprudence,—not excepting such men even as Marshall and Story. No one had so large a share as had Chancellor Kent in creating the American system of Equity. . . . Chancellor Kent has been called, in allusion to his Commentaries, the "American Blackstone." The comparison does the Englishman the greater honor, for Kent surpassed his predecessor in almost every feature that goes to constitute a jurist. Chancellor Kent was profoundly versed in Roman law, and from that knowledge derived his wonderful symmetry and breadth of culture, whereas not one in ten of the allusions to the Roman Law in Blackstone's Commentaries is respectably accurate. The style of the English jurist is inflated and conceited, that of Kent is easy, natural, and vigorous.—HART, JOHN S., 1872, *A Manual of American Literature, p.* 126.

Even when one reads such law-books as Chancellor Kent's standard "Commentaries on American Law," he finds matter for literary praise in the author's solid English.—RICHARDSON, CHARLES F., 1885, *American Literature*, 1607–1885, *vol.* I, *p.* 514.

But it is to his Commentaries that Kent owes his wide-spread and enduring fame. The first book placed in the hands of the American law student; the source to which the experienced practitioner, after wearying himself among the crudities of other elementary writers and irreconcilable disagreements of judicial decisions, still resorts with confidence; an authority of the supremest influence in our courts; these Commentaries have thus far been without a rival, and probably can never be displaced so long as our present system of jurisprudence prevails.—BROWNE, IRVING, 1894, *Short Studies of Great Lawyers, p.* 224.

Richard Henry Wilde

1789–1847

Richard Henry Wilde was born in Dublin, Ireland, September 24, 1789. His father, a merchant, emigrated to Baltimore, Md., in 1797, and died bankrupt in 1802. His widow removed to Augusta, Ga., where she kept a small shop and educated her family. Richard was admitted to the bar in 1809, became Attorney-General of Georgia, and in 1815 was elected to Congress. He was in Congress again from 1828 to 1835, and then went to Europe, and passed nearly five years in Italy. In Florence he found documents which threw new light upon the life of Dante, and discovered Giotto's portrait of him on the wall of the Chapel of the Bargello. On his return home, Mr. Wilde published, in 1842, "Conjectures and Researches concerning the Love, Madness, and Imprisonment of Torquato Tasso," with translations of several of Tasso's poems. He also wrote the first volume of a projected life of Dante. In 1844 he removed to New Orleans, where he practised his profession, and occupied the chair of Common Law in the University of Louisiana till his death, which took place, September 10, 1847.—JOHNSON, ROSSITER, 1875, *Little Classics, Authors, p.* 245.

GENERAL

Has acquired much reputation as a poet, and especially as the author of a little piece entitled "My Life is Like the Summer Rose," whose claim to originality has been made the subject of repeated and reiterated attack and defence. Upon the whole it is hardly worth quarrelling about. Far better verses are to be found in every second newspaper we take up.—POE, EDGAR ALLAN, 1841, *A Chapter on Autography, Works, eds. Stedman and Woodberry, vol.* IX, *p.* 230.

The romantic love, the madness, and imprisonment of Tasso had become a subject of curious controversy, and he entered into the investigation "with the enthusiasm of a poet, and the patience and accuracy of a case-hunter," and produced a work, published since his return to the United States, in which the questions concerning Tasso are most ably discussed, and lights are thrown upon them by his letters, and by some of his sonnets, which last are rendered into English with rare felicity.—GRISWOLD, RUFUS W., 1842, *The Poets and Poetry of America, p.* 76.

Besides his investigation in the literature of Dante he made a special study of the vexed question connected with the life of Tasso. The result of this he gave to the public on his return to America in his "Conjectures and Researches concerning the Love, Madness, and Imprisonment of Torquato Tasso," a work of diligent scholarship, in which the elaborate argument is enlivened by the elegance of the frequent original translations of the sonnets. In this he maintains the sanity of Tasso, and traces the progress of the intrigue with the Princess Lenora D'Este as the key of the poet's difficulties.—DUYCKINCK, EVERT A. AND GEORGE L., 1855-65-75, *Cyclopædia of American Literature, ed. Simons, vol.* I, *p.* 806.

I know, however, in the whole range of imitative verse, no line superior, perhaps I should say none equal, to that in Wilde's celebrated nameless poem.

Yet as if grieving to efface
All vestige of the human race,
On that lone shore loud moans the sea.

Here the employment of monosyllables, of long vowels and of liquids, without harsh consonantal sounds, together with the significance of the words themselves, gives to the verse a force of expression seldom if ever surpassed.—MARSH, GEORGE P., 1860, *Lectures on the English Language, Lecture* XXV.

Mr Wilde was [one day] surprised to find in a Georgia newspaper a Greek Ode, purporting to have been written by Alcæus, an early Eolian poet of somewhat obscure fame, and it was claimed that Mr. Wilde's verses were simply a translation of this Ode, the ideas in both being almost identical. As Mr. Wilde had never heard of Alcæus, he was much puzzled to account for this resemblance of the two poems. At the suggestion of a friend, the Greek Ode was sent to Mr. Binney for examination and criticism. He at once, much to the relief of Mr. Wilde, pronounced it a forgery, pointing out wherein its style differed from that of the classical Greek. It turned out afterwards that the Ode in question had been written by an Oxford scholar on a wager that no one in that University was sufficiently familiar with the style of the early Greek poets to detect the counterfeit. To carry out this scheme, he had translated Mr. Wilde's verses into Greek.—STILLÉ, CHARLES J., 1870, *Memoir of Horace Binney, Jr.*

The stanzas beginning "My life is like the summer rose" have a curious history. Mr. Wilde had a brother James, an officer in the United States army, who, on his return from the Seminole war, told numerous entertaining stories of his adventures in Florida. This suggested to Richard the idea of a song supposed to be sung by a European held captive among the savages of the Florida coast; and these stanzas, which were intended as the beginning of a longer poem, were the result. Mr. Anthony Barclay, of Savannah, translated the poem into Greek, and afterward somebody started the story that Wilde had stolen it from the Greek of Alcæus. The Georgia Historical Society has published a little volume to set the matter right.—JOHNSON, ROSSITER, 1875, *Little Classics, Authors, p.* 246.

These "Stanzas" were not the work of a "single-poem-writer," for the author wrote other finished and beautiful short poems that have been undeservedly forgotten.—ONDERDONK, JAMES L., 1900-01, *History of American Verse* (1610-1897), *p.* 164.

Grace Aguilar

1816-1847

Grace Aguilar (born 1816, died 1847), authoress of moral tales and religious tracts, was a Jewess of Spanish extraction. For the shortness of her life, her works are very numerous. They may be divided as follows: Two historic novels, "The Vale of Cedars," a story of the Jews in Spain during the fifteenth century, and "The Days of Bruce," which remains the most popular of her works; they are written in the heroic style fit for the mouths of the knights of bygone days or the heroes of modern melodrama, and, but for the entire absence of humor, would recall "Ivanhoe" and the

"Talisman;" three domestic stories, "Home Influence," "The Mother's Recompense," and "Woman's Friendship;" and a collection of short stories, "Home Scenes and Heart Studies," the general character of which is like Miss Edgeworth's tales, though again the style is for the most part heroic, and humour absent; "The Women of Israel," a series of short sketches of some of the notable women in ancient Jewish history; and a few religious treatises, the most important being "The Spirit of Judaism," in which she defends the purity of her religon against the perversions and persecutions of Christianity. She died at Frankfort.—SANDERS, LLOYD C., *ed.*, 1887, *Celebrities of the Century, p.* 23.

PERSONAL

Grace Aguilar was extremely fond of music; she had been taught the piano from infancy; and, in 1831, commenced the harp. She sang pleasingly, preferred English songs, invariably selecting them for the beauty or sentiment of the words. She was also passionately fond of dancing; and her cheerful, lively manners, in the society of her young friends, would scarcely have led any to imagine how deeply she felt and pondered the serious and solemn subjects which afterwards formed the labour of her life. She enjoyed all that was innocent; but the sacred feeling of duty always regulated her conduct.—HALE, SARAH JOSEPHA, 1852, *Woman's Record, p.* 162.

She was a "woman of Israel," truthful, upright, charitable, just and true. We echo the sentiment we read many years ago on her monument: "Let her own works praise her in the gates."—HALL, SAMUEL CARTER, 1883, *Retrospect of a Long Life, p.* 414.

In person she was not at all the typical Jewess. She had soft but expressive grey eyes, and that brown hair which only wants a touch of gold to make it almost auburn. Above the middle height, she was slender to a degree, imparting an air of fragility—with regular features, and an oval face that easily lighted up. Her voice was clear-toned, though gentle, and her manners were essentially what is understood by ladylike. She was devoted to her parents, and proud of having been entirely educated by them, save for an interval in early childhood, too brief to be worth recording. She was proud, too, of being descended from philosophers, physicians, and statesmen of Spain, although they existed under conditions, difficult to realize or wholly to excuse. . . . Indeed, in remembering Grace Aguilar, I always think more of her moral elevation than of her genius; so tender was her conscience, so charitable were her judgments, and so generous her sympathies.—CROSLAND, MRS. NEWTON (CAMILLA TOULMIN), 1893, *Landmarks of a Literary Life, pp.*171, 175.

GENERAL

All of these works are highly creditable to the literary taste and talents of the writer; and they have a value beyond what the highest genius could give—the stamp of truth, piety, and love, and an earnest desire to do good to her fellow-beings.—HALE, SARAH JOSEPHA, 1852, *Woman's Record, p.* 162.

All her novels are of a highly sentimental character, and mainly deal with the ordinary incidents of domestic life. Like the rest of her writings, they evince an intensely religious temperament, but one free from sectarian prejudice.—LEE, SIDNEY, 1885, *Dictionary of Natural Biography, vol.* I, *p.* 180.

Her "Days of Bruce" is a wonderful production for a girl of little more than twenty; and her romance, "The Martyr," shows how well she was versed in Spanish history.—CROSLAND, MRS. NEWTON (CAMILLA TOULMIN), 1893, *Landmarks of a Literary Life, p.* 173.

In her religious writings Miss Aguilar's attitude was defensive. Despite her almost exclusive intercourse with Christians and her utter lack of prejudice, her purpose, apparently, was to equip English Jewesses with arguments against conversionists. She inveighed against formalism, and laid stress upon knowledge of Jewish history and the Hebrew language. In view of the neglect of the latter by women (to whom she modestly confined her expostulations), she constantly pleaded for the reading of the Scriptures in the English version. Her interest in the reform movement was deep; yet, despite her attitude toward tradition, she observed ritual ordinances punctiliously. Her last work was a sketch of the "History of the Jews in England," written for "Chambers's Miscellany." In point of style it is the most finished of her productions, free from the exuberances and redundancies that disfigure the tales—published, for the most part, posthumously by her mother. The defects of her style are mainly chargeable to youth.—SZOLD, HENRIETTA, 1901, *The Jewish Encyclopedia, vol.* I, *p.* 275.

Thomas Frognall Dibdin

1776-1847

Bibliographer, a nephew of Charles Dibdin, was born at Calcutta in 1776. Having lost both parents when hardly four years of age, he was brought up by a maternal uncle, studied at St. John's College, Oxford, tried law, but took orders in 1804. Librarian to Lord Spencer, he proceeded D. D. in 1825; held the vicarage of Exning near Newmarket and the rectory of St. Mary's, Bryanston Square, London; and died 18th November 1847. Among his works were "Bibliomania" (1809); "The Bibliographical Decameron" (1817); "Bibliotheca Spenceriana" (1814–15); "Bibliographical Tour in France and Germany" (1821); "Reminiscences of a Literary Life" (1836); and "Bibliographical tour in the Northern Counties of England and Scotland" (1838). —PATRICK AND GROOME, *eds.*, 1897, *Chambers's Biographical Dictionary, p.* 297.

PERSONAL

I knew him in his later years, and found him full of literary information, and as eager to communicate as I was to receive it. He was small in stature, with a countenance expressive of much firmness, and a profusion of gray hair.—MACKENZIE, R. SHELTON, 1854, *ed. Noctes Ambrosianæ, vol.* I, *p.* 214, *note.*

At the Roxburghe sale the edition of Boccaccio printed by Valdarfer sold for the enormous sum of 2,260*l.*, and to commemorate this Dibdin proposed that several of the leading bibliophiles should dine together on the day. Eighteen met at the St. Alban's Tavern, in St. Alban's Street (now Waterloo Place), on 17 June 1812, with Lord Spencer as president, and Dibdin as vice-president. This was the beginning of the existence of the Roxburghe Club. The number of members was ultimately increased to thirty-one, and each member was expected to produce a reprint of some rare volume of English literature. In spite of the worthless character of some of the early publications (of which it was said that when they were unique there was already one copy too many in existence), and of the ridicule thrown on the club by the publication of Haslewood's "Roxburghe Revels," this was the parent of the publishing societies established in this country, which have done so much for English history and antiquities, to say nothing of other branches of literature; and Dibdin must be credited with being the originator of the proposal.—LUARD, REV. H. R., 1888, *Dictionary of National Biography, vol.* XV, *p.* 7.

GENERAL

Mr. Dibdin has now been for many years employed in composing and compiling some of the most expensive, thickest, largest and heaviest octavos which have ever issued from the press. The volume which is now before us, not the last we presume, is certainly not the least of the Dibdin family. The "Bibliotheca Spenceriana" beats in breadth—the "Bibliographical Decameron" and "Bibliographical Tour" in height, or, as he would say, in tallness,—but, for thickness and specific gravity, the intellectual, as well as material, pound weight, we will back "The Library Companion" against any of them. In all his long, many and weighty labours, Mr. Dibdin seems to have had but one object in view, and that neither a very good-natured nor in him a very gracious one: his ambition has been to raise a laugh at the expense of a very innocent, but not very wise, body of men,—the collectors of scarce and black-letter books. Under the masque of a more than common zeal in their pursuit, and of affectionate regard for their persons, he has bestowed much complimentary sarcasm upon the one, and placed the other with great gravity in exceedingly ludicrous situations.—DISRAELI, ISAAC, 1825, *Quarterly Review, vol.* 32, *p.* 152.

Was the prince of bibliographers. . . . By his writings and publications in this line he contributed largely to the extensive bibliomania which prevailed in England in the early part of the present century.—HART, JOHN S., 1872, *A Manual of English Literature, p.* 494.

Mary Ann Lamb

1764–1847

The daughter of respectable parents, was born in London about 1766. She was subject to attacks of insanity, and in one of them, in 1796, brought on by over-exertion, and anxiety about her mother, then quite an aged person, she stabbed her mother to the heart, killing her instantly. After recovering from this attack, she resided with her brother Charles, the well-known author of "Essays of Elia," who devoted his whole life to her. They lived in or near London. In connexion with her brother, Miss Lamb wrote two volumes of juvenile poetry; "Stories for Children, or Mrs. Leicester's School;" and "Tales from Shakspeare." Miss Lamb was remarkable for the sweetness of her disposition, the clearness of her understanding, and the gentle wisdom of all her acts and words, notwithstanding the distraction under which she suffered for weeks, and latterly for months, in every year. She survived her brother eleven years, dying May 20th, 1847. She was buried with him in Edmonton churchyard.—HALE, SARAH JOSEPHA, 1852, *Woman's Record, p.* 379.

PERSONAL

Bridget Elia has been my housekeeper for many a long year. I have obligations to Bridget, extending beyond the period of memory. We house together, old bachelor and old maid, in a sort of double singleness. . . . We agree pretty well in our tastes and habits—yet so, as "with a difference." We are generally in harmony, with occasional bickerings,—as it should be among near relations. Our sympathies are rather understood, than expressed; and once, upon my dissembling a tone in my voice more kind than ordinary, my cousin burst into tears, and complained that I was altered. We are both great readers in different directions. While I am hanging over (for the thousandth time) some passage in old Burton, or one of his strange contemporaries, she is abstracted in some modern tale, or adventure, whereof our common reading-table is daily fed with assiduously fresh supplies. . . . We are both of us inclined to be a little too positive; and I have observed the result of our disputes to be almost uniformly this—that in matters of fact, dates, and circumstances, it turns out that I was in the right, and my cousin in the wrong. But where we have differed upon moral points, upon something proper to be done, or let alone; whatever heat of opposition, or steadiness of conviction I set out with, I am sure always in the long run, to be brought over to her way of thinking. I must touch upon the foibles of my kinswoman with a gentle hand, for Bridget does not like to be told of her faults. She hath an awkward trick (to say no worse of it) of reading in company; at which times she will answer *yes* or *no* to a question, without fully understanding its purport—which is provoking, and derogatory in the highest degree to the dignity of the putter of the said question. Her presence of mind is equal to the most pressing trials of life, but will sometimes desert her upon trifling occasions. When the purpose requires it, and is a thing of moment, she can speak to it greatly; but in the matters which are not stuff of the conscience, she hath been known sometimes to let slip a word less seasonably. . . . In a season of distress, she is the truest comforter; but in the teasing accidents, and minor perplexities, which do not call out the *will* to meet them, she sometimes maketh matters worse by an excess of participation. If she does not always divide your trouble, upon the pleasanter occasions of life, she is sure always to treble your satisfaction.—LAMB, CHARLES, 1825, *Mackery End in Hertfordshire, Essays of Elia.*

His sister, whose literary reputation is closely associated with her brother's, and who, as the original of "Bridget Elia," is a kind of object for literary affection, came in after him. She is a small, bent figure, evidently a victim to illness, and hears with difficulty. Her face has been, I should think, a fine and handsome one, and her bright, gray eye is still full of intelligence and fire.—WILLIS, NATHANIEL, PARKER, 1835, *Pencillings by the Way, Letter* cxvii.

Yesterday was a painfully interesting day. I attended the funeral of Mary Lamb. At nine a coach fetched me. We drove to her dwelling at St. John's Wood, from whence two coaches accompanied the body to Edmonton across a pretty country, but the heat of the day rendered the drive oppressive. We took refreshment at the house where dear Charles Lamb died, and were then driven towards our homes. . . . There was no sadness assumed by the attendants, but we all talked together with warm affection of dear Mary Lamb, and that most delightful of creatures, her brother Charles; of all the men of genius I ever knew, the one the most intensely and universally to be loved.—ROBINSON, HENRY CRABB, 1847, *Diary, May* 29.

I see that Mary Lamb is dead. She departed, eighty-two years old, on the 20th of May. She had survived her mind in great measure, but much of the *heart* remained. Miss Lamb had a very fine feeling for literature, and was refined in mind, though homely, almost coarse, in personal habits. Her departure is an escape out of prison, to her sweet, good soul.—COLERIDGE, SARA, 1847, *Letter to Miss Fenwick, July* 6; *Memoir and Letters, ed. her Daughter, p.* 315.

The constant impendency of this giant sorrow saddened to "the Lambs" even their holidays; as the journey which they both regarded as the relief and charm of the year was frequently followed by a seizure. . . . Miss Lamb experienced, and full well understood, the premonitory symptoms of the attack, in restlessness, low fever, and the inability to sleep; and, as gently as possible, prepared her brother for the duty he must soon perform; and thus, unless he could stave off the terrible separation till Sunday, obliged him to ask leave of absence from the office as if for a day's pleasure—a bitter mockery! On one occasion Mr. Charles Lloyd met them, slowly pacing together a little footpath in Hoxton Fields, both weeping bitterly, and found, on joining them, that they were taking their solemn way to the accustomed Asylum. . . . Miss Lamb would have been remarkable for the sweetness of her disposition, the clearness of her understanding, and the gentle wisdom of all her acts and words, even if these qualities had not been presented in marvellous contrast with the distractions under which she suffered for weeks, latterly for months in every year. There was no tinge of insanity discernible in her manner to the most observant eye. . . . Hazlitt used to say that he never met with a woman who could reason and had met with only one thoroughly reasonable—the sole exception being Mary Lamb. She did not wish, however, to be made an exception, to the general disparagement of her sex; for in all her thoughts and feelings she was most womanly—keeping under, ever in due subordination to her notion of a woman's province, an intellect of rare excellence which flashed out when the restraints of gentle habit and humble manner were withdrawn by the terrible force of disease. Though her conversation in sanity was never marked by smartness or repartee; seldom rising beyond that of a sensible, quiet gentlewoman, appreciating and enjoying the talents of her friends, it was otherwise in her madness. . . . Her ramblings often sparkled with brilliant description and shattered beauty.—TALFOURD, THOMAS NOON, 1848, *Final Memorials of Charles Lamb, pp.* 289, 298, 299.

Her relapses were not dependent on the seasons; they came in hot summers and with the freezing winters. The only remedy seems to have been extreme quiet, when any slight symptom of uneasiness was apparent. Charles (poor fellow) had to live, day and night, in the society of a person who was—mad! If any exciting talk occurred he had to dismiss his friend, with a whisper. If any stupor or extraordinary silence was observed, then he had to rouse her instantly.—PROCTER, BRYAN WALLER (BARRY CORNWALL), 1866, *Charles Lamb; A Memoir, p.* 113.

Mary Lamb was altogether worthy of her brother's love. In addition to that bond of affection which bound them together through affliction, she was a woman of great mental attractions. She was a continual reader. When in the asylum, Charles took care to furnish her with plenty of books, for they were like her daily bread. She was a delightful writer. Hazlitt held her to be the only woman he had met who could reason. "Were I to give way to my feelings," says Wordsworth, in the note to his poem on Charles Lamb, "I should dwell not only on her genius and intellectual powers, but upon the delicacy and refinement of manner which she maintained inviolable under most trying circumstances. She was loved and honoured by all her brother's friends."—MASSEY, GERALD, 1867, *Charles Lamb, Fraser's Magazine, vol.* 75, *p.* 662.

She had a speaking-voice, gentle and

persuasive; and her smile was her brother's own—winning in the extreme. There was a certain catch, or emotional breathingness, in her utterance, which gave an inexpressible charm to her reading of poetry, and which lent a captivating earnestness to her mode of speech when addressing those she liked. This slight check, with its yearning, eager effect in her voice, had something softenedly akin to her brother Charles's impediment of articulation: in him it scarcely amounted to a stammer, in her it merely imparted additional stress to the fine-sensed suggestions she made to those whom she counselled or consoled. . . . There was a certain old-world fashion in Mary Lamb's diction which gave it a most natural and quaintly pleasant effect, and which heightened rather than detracted from the more heartfelt or important things she uttered.—CLARKE, CHARLES AND MARY COWDEN, 1878, *Recollections of Writers, pp.* 177, 183.

Seldom is the name of Mary Lamb seen without that of her brother. "The Lambs" still walk hand-in-hand in our mention, as they were wont to walk on pleasant holidays to Enfield, and Potter's Bar, and Waltham; when Mary "used to deposit in the little hand-basket the day's fare of savory cold meat and salad," and Charles "to pry about at noon-tide for some decent house where they might go in and produce their store, only paying for the ale that he must call for." Still they pass linked together through our thoughts, as on that sadder day when Charles Lloyd met them, crossing the fields to Hoxton—hand-in-hand, and weeping. It is an act of severance against which the conscience somewhat protests, to present Mary alone to the consideration of the reader. It is like removing her from the protection of his presence who stood so faithfully and long between her and the world.—CONE, HELEN GRAY, AND GILDER, JEANETTE L., 1887, *Pen-Portraits of Literary Women, vol.* I, *p.* 131.

GENERAL

Mary is just stuck fast in "All's Well that Ends Well." She complains of having to set forth so many female characters in boys' clothes. She begins to think Shakespeare must have wanted—Imagination. I, to encourage her, for she often faints in the prosecution of her great work, flatter her with telling her how well such a play and such a play is done. But she is stuck fast.—LAMB, CHARLES, 1806, *Letter to Wordsworth, Final Memorials by T. N. Talfourd.*

I am in good spirits just at this present time, for Charles has been reading over the *tale* I told you plagued me so much, and he thinks it one of the very best: it is "All's Well that Ends Well." You must not mind the many wretchedly dull letters I have sent you: for, indeed, I cannot help it, my mind is so *dry* always after poring over my work all day. But it will soon be over. I am cooking a shoulder of lamb (Hazlitt dines with us); it will be ready at two o'clock, if you can, pop in and eat a bit with us.—LAMB, MARY, 1806, *Letter to Sarah Stoddart, July; Mary and Charles Lamb by Hazlitt, p.* 61.

It is now several days since I read the book you recommended to me, "Mrs. Leicester's School;" and I feel as if I owed a debt in deferring to thank you for many hours of exquisite delight. Never have I read any thing in prose so many times over, within so short a space of time, as "The Father's Wedding-day." Most people, I understand, prefer the first tale—in truth a very admirable one—but others could have written it. Show me the man or woman, modern or ancient, who could have written this one sentence: "When I was dressed in my new frock, I wished poor mamma was alive to see how fine I was on papa's wedding-day; and I ran to my favorite station at her bedroom door." How natural, in a little girl, is this incongruity, this impossibility! . . . A fresh source of the pathetic bursts out before us, and not a bitter one. . . . The story is admirable throughout—incomparable, inimitable.—LANDOR, WALTER SAVAGE, 1831, *To H. C. Robinson, Apr.; Robinson's Diary, Reminiscences and Correspondence.*

It is not generally known, perhaps, that, previously to their circulation in a collective shape, Godwin, the publisher and proprietor of the copyright, offered them to his juvenile patrons and patronesses at No. 41 Skinner Street, in sixpenny books, with the plates (by Blake) "beautifully coloured."—HAZLITT, W. CAREW, 1874, *Mary and Charles Lamb, p.* 170.

The first edition ["Mrs. Leicester's School"] sold out immediately, and four more were called for in the course of five years. It has continued in fair demand ever since, though there have not been any thing like so many recent reprints as of the "Tales from Shakespeare." It is one of those children's books, which, to reopen in after-life, is like revisiting some sunny old garden, some favorite haunt of childhood, where every nook and cranny seems familiar and calls up a thousand pleasant memories.—GILCHRIST, ANNE, 1883, *Mary Lamb* (*Famous Women*), *p.* 214.

How gently rounded and justly balanced the expressions of thought in these letters of hers are! One could imagine that she had got her brother to write them for her. In this year 1808 Mary brought out her charming stories for children, entitled "Mrs. Leicester's School" (three of the narratives being her brother's), and in this year also she undertook the writing of her "Tales from Shakespeare," a book of which the charm is still fresh, and which no one has been able to better. Charles had to help her through with it, by undertaking to summarise the tragedies. Here, as in the case of the other two volumes which brother and sister wrote together, Charles is vehement in maintaining that all the credit of the fine writing is not his, but Mary's. In the following year the still more lovely volume of "Poetry for Children" was produced.—ROBERTSON, ERIC S., 1883, *English Poetesses*, *p.* 130.

Isaac Disraeli

1766-1848

Born, at Enfield, May 1766. Educated at a school near Enfield. At Amsterdam, 1780–82. Contrib. to "Gentleman's Magazine," Dec. 1786 and July 1789; to "St. James's Chronicle," Nov. 1787. In France, 1787–89. In Devonshire, owing to ill-health, 1795–98. Married Maria Basevi, 10 Feb. 1802. Elected Warden of London Synagogue of Spanish and Portuguese Jews, 3 Oct. 1813, but declined the office. Active literary life. Removed from London to Bradenham House, Bucks, 1829. Hon. D. C. L., Oxford, 4 July 1832. Became blind, 1839. Died, at Bradenham, 19 Jan. 1848. Buried there. *Works:* "A Defence of Poetry," 1790; "Narrative Poems," 1803; "Curiosities of Literature" (anon.) vol. i., 1791; vol. ii., 1793; vol. iii., 1817; vols. iv. and v., 1823; vol. vi., 1834 (various edns. of whole, 1793–1841); 2nd series 1823; "A Dissertation on Anecdotes" (anon.) 1793; "Domestic Anecdotes of the French Nation" (anon.), 1797; "Essay on the Manners and Genius of the Literary Character," 1795 (enlarged edn. under title of "The Literary Character," anon. 1818); "Miscellanies," 1796; "Vaurien" (anon.), 1797; "Flim-Flams" (anon.), 1797; "Mejnoun and Leila," 1797; "Romances," 1799; "Despotism" (anon.), 1811; "Calamities of Authors" (anon.), 1812–13; "Quarrels of Authors" (anon.), 1814; "Inquiry into the Literary and Political Character of James I.," 1816; "Commentaries on the Life and Reign of Charles I.," 1828–31; "Eliot, Hampden, and Pym" (anon.), 1832; "The Genius of Judaism" (anon.), 1833; "The Illustrator Illustrated" (anon.), 1838; "Amenities of Literature," 1840. *Collected Works:* ed. by Benjamin Disraeli, 1858–59. *Life:* by Benjamin Disraeli, in 1849 edn. of "Curiosities of Literature."—SHARP, R. FARQUHARSON, 1897, *A Dictionary of English Authors*, *p.* 81.

PERSONAL

An old gentleman, *strictly*, in his appearance; a countenance which at first glance (owing, perhaps to the mouth, which hangs) I fancied slightly chargeable with stolidity of expression, but which developed strong sense as it talked; a rather *soigné* style of dress for so old a man, and a manner good-humoured, complimentary (to Gebir), discursive and prosy, bespeaking that engrossment and interest in his own pursuits which might be expected to be found in a person so patient in research and collection. But there is a tone of the *philosophe* (or I fancied it), which I did not quite like; and that tone (addressing the instinct rather than the judgment) which is felt or imagined to bespeak (how shall it be?) absence of high principle. No one can be more hardy in his negation than Mr. Fonblanque; in no one a sneer be more triumphantly incarnate—and it is sometimes very withering and painful; but he gives you the impression of considering destruction and denial to be his mission; whereas there is an easy optimism and expediency associated with my idea of Mr. Disraeli, which, while it makes his opinions less salient, increases their offence.—CHORLEY, HENRY FOTHERGILL, 1838, *Autobiography, Letters and Memoirs, vol.* I, *p.* 191.

A pale, pensive child, with large dark brown eyes, and flowing hair, such as may be beheld in one of the portraits annexed to these volumes, had grown up beneath this roof of worldly energy and enjoyment, indicating even in his infancy, by the whole carriage of his life, that he was of a different order from those among whom he lived. Timid, susceptible, lost in reverie, fond of solitude, or seeking no better company than a book, the years had stolen on, till he had arrived at that mournful period of boyhood when eccentricities excite attention and command no sympathy. In the chapter on Pre-disposition, in the most delightful of his works, my father has drawn from his own, though his unacknowledged feelings, immortal truths. Then commenced the age of domestic criticism. His mother, not incapable of deep affections, but so mortified by her social position, that she lived until eighty without indulging in a tender expression, did not recognize in her only offspring a being qualified to control or vanquish his impending fate. His existence only served to swell the aggregate of many humiliating particulars. It was not to her a source of joy, or sympathy, or solace. She foresaw for her child only a future of degradation. Having a strong clear mind, without any imagination, she believed that she beheld an inevitable doom. . . . With a home that ought to have been happy, surrounded with more than comfort, with the most good-natured father in the world, and an agreeable man, and with a mother whose strong intellect, under ordinary circumstances, might have been of great importance to him, my father, though himself of a very sweet disposition, was most unhappy. His parents looked upon him as moonstruck, while he himself, whatever his aspirations, was conscious that he had done nothing to justify the eccentricity of his course, or the violation of all prudential considerations in which he daily indulged. . . . He was himself a complete literary character, a man who really passed his life in his library. Even marriage produced no change in these habits; he rose to enter the chamber where he lived alone with his books, and at night his lamp was ever lit within the same walls. Nothing, indeed, was more remarkable than the isolation of this prolonged existence; and it could only be accounted for by the united influence of three causes: his birth, which brought him no relations or family acquaintances, the bent of his disposition, and the circumstance of his inheriting an independent fortune, which rendered unnecessary those exertions, that would have broken up his self-reliance. He disliked business, and he never required relaxation; he was absorbed in his pursuits. . . . He had not a single passion or prejudice.—DISRAELI, BENJAMIN (LORD BEACONSFIELD), 1848, *Curiosities of Literature, Life and Writings of the Author, pp.* 8, 14, 36.

The late Mr. D'Israeli was one of the few men who lived exclusively for literature. Early placed in a position of independence, which rendered it unnecessary for him to adopt the commercial pursuits of his father, he indulged his taste, or rather his passion, for curious research, and never was satisfied in the investigation of any question until he had examined the original authorities. His writings and example have diffused a taste for historical inquiry and criticism, which has become, to a great extent, the prevalent characteristic of our age. In 1841 he was stricken with blindness, and though he submitted to an operation, his sight was not restored. He, the great American writer, Prescott, and Thierry, the author of the "History of the Conquest of England by the Normans," (who has published several considerable works since his blindness), are probably the only historical authors who have continued their labours in spite of so terrible a calamity. Aided by his daughter, he produced the "Amenities of Literature," and completed the revision of his great work on the Reign of Charles I., which, on its first publication, had procured for him the degree of D. C. L. from the University of Oxford. A cultivated and powerful memory enabled him, in the later years of his life, to pour forth the stores he had accumulated in his long and varied studies with a profusion as delightful as it was surprising. "The blind old man eloquent" was a description as applicable to him as to the bard of Scio.—TAYLOR, W. C., 1848, *The Late Isaac D'Israeli, Esq., Bentley's Miscellany, vol.* 23, *p.* 224.

Whether I regard his long and honourable life, exclusively devoted to the best interests of literature,—the pure and elevating pleasure which his writings have bestowed,—the influence which they have had in diffusing that taste for historical and literary investigation which is a marked characteristic of the age,—the impartiality of his judicial decisions,—the catholicity of his sentiments,—the philosophic tone of his criticism,—or the industry and conscientiousness of his research,—I commence a few notes upon the literary career of Isaac D'Israeli, with feelings of profound respect and gratitude.—BATES, WILLIAM, 1874–98, *The Maclise Portrait Gallery of Illustrious Literary Characters, p.* 102.

The reader at this distance will perhaps imagine, wonderingly, whether that career ever commenced at all. He lived to be a very old man, like so many of the subjects of this history. Great genius may exhaust and wear out, though chiefly when associated with great passions; but a little genius is a wonderfully safe and comfortable possession. It gives interest to life whatever may be its burdens, and cheers the weary years.—OLIPHANT, MARGARET O. W., 1882, *Literary History of England, XVIII-XIX Century, vol.* II, *p.* 315.

GENERAL

If we were to form our opinion of this book ["Calamities of Authors"] from its title page, it would not be very favourable: authors are there introduced as a genus, and their moral and literary characters spoken of as if each had not a moral and literary character of his own. Neither should we think more highly of the writer's precision of style by looking at the end, where a portentous metaphor about "barren fertility" stares the reader in the face. But the middle of the book is much better than the two ends: it is one of those works which are designed for the breakfast table and the sofa, and is so well adapted for its purpose, that he who takes it up will not readily lay it down. The matter is as amusing as any lover of light reading can desire, and of such a desultory kind that a comment might easily be made as extensive as the text. —SOUTHEY, ROBERT, 1812, *D'Israeli's Calamities of Authors, Quarterly Review, vol.* 8, *p.* 93.

Read the "Quarrels of Authors," a new work by that most entertaining and researching writer, Israeli.—BYRON, LORD, 1814, *Journals, March* 17.

I wish I had not sent you this great blubbering numskull D'Israeli: his "Calamities" have sunk upon your spirits, and tinged the whole world of intellect with the hue of mourning and despair. The paths of learning seem, in your present mood of mind, to lead but through regions of woe and lamentation and darkness and dead men's bones. Hang the ass!—it is all false, if you take it up in this light. Do you not see that his observations can apply only to men in whom genius was more the want of common qualities than the possession of uncommon ones; whose life was embittered not so much because they had imagination and sensibility, as because they had not prudence and true moral principles? If one chose to investigate the history of the first twenty tattered blackguards to be found lying on the benches of the watch-house, or stewing in drunkenness and squalor in the Jerusalem Tap-room, it would not be difficult to write a much more moving book on the "calamities of shoemakers" or street-porters, or any other class of handicraftsmen, than this of D'Israeli's on Authors. —CARLYLE, THOMAS, 1823, *To Miss Welsh, June* 20; *Early Letters, ed. Norton, p.* 261.

He is one of the most learned, intelligent, lively, and agreeable authors of our era; he has composed a series of works, which, while they shed abundance of light on the character and condition of literary men, and show us the state of genius in this land, have all the attractions for general readers of the best romances. . . . I see it intimated that Disraeli has the History of British Literature in contemplation; he cannot do a more acceptable service to the republic of letters, than write it.—CUNNINGHAM, ALLAN, 1833, *Biographical and Critical History of the Literature of the Last Fifty Years.*

The poetical temperament was not thrown away upon him, it never is on any one; it was this great gift which prevented his being a mere literary antiquary; it was this which animated his page with picture and his narrative with interesting vivacity; above all, it was this temperament, which invested him with that sympathy with this subject, which made him the most delightful biographer in our language. In a word, it was because he was a poet, that he was a popular writer, and made belles-lettres charming to the multitude.—DISRAELI, BENJAMIN (LORD BEACONSFIELD), 1848, *Curiosities of Literature, Life and Writings of the Author, p.* 29.

The work, however, by which the elder D'Israeli will always be best known, because it is the work which has made the deepest impression on the mind of the age, is the "Curiosities of Literature." It was the first revelation to the English people that they possessed materials for historical and critical investigations hardly inferior in value to the celebrated Memoirs of the French; and it was also one of the earliest attempts to vindicate the memory of the Stuarts, but more especially the first James and the first Charles, from the odium which had been accumulated upon them ever since the revolution. More than one of the Waverley Novels was obviously suggested by the "Curiosities of Literature;" and to that work our modern writers of historical romance have been far more deeply indebted than they have ever yet acknowledged. The "Quarrels of Authors," the "Calamities of Authors," and the "Illustrations of the Literary Character," though more immediately connected with literary history, are everywhere marked with the characteristic feelings and sentiments which rendered the author so earnest an advocate and so zealous a pleader for the hapless house of Stuart. The descendant of a fallen race, which still clung to its theocratic title, was the natural sympathiser with a fallen dynasty, which, in the midst of all its misfortunes, never abandoned its hereditary claims —TAYLOR, W. C., 1848, *The Late Isaac D'Israeli, Esq., Bentley's Miscellany, vol.* 23, *p.* 223.

He was among the first who made literary history a study; and notwithstanding the disadvantages under which he labored, he attained an honorable position among his contemporaries; his books were popular; and he had the reputation of being a well-read scholar. This reputation has somewhat declined; but it will not be denied that he had a very extensive acquaintance with English and Continental literature, and that he neglected no opportunity for self-culture. He was, however, a man of facts and details, rather than a man of principles. He had little power of generalization or of sustained reasoning, and he rarely took a comprehensive view of any subject. Hence his works are, almost without exception, fragmentary in form. They are replete with curious and amusing information, but the facts seldom have an orderly and systematic arrangement, or illustrate any central idea. His books, indeed, must be regarded as collections of materials, rather than as elaborate treatises, and their real value consists in the variety and interest of the details of author-life which they embody. Disraeli, as we have intimated, lacked a judicial habit of mind, and like most antiquaries he was disposed to magnify the importance of his researches, and to regard every circumstance which had escaped the notice of previous writers as a piece of secret intelligence. This weakness subjected him to some undeserved criticism, and it is probably one of the causes which have tended to diminish his reputation. In early life his style was florid and pompous, but as he advanced in years it gained clearness and force, and his later works, the "Genius of Judaism" and the "Amenities of Literature," contain many passages of genuine eloquence.—SMITH, C. C., 1860, *Isaac Disraeli, North American Review, vol.* 90, *p.* 536.

In the writings of the elder Disraeli we meet with occasional touches of the felicity of expression so conspicuous in his more distinguished son.—MINTO, WILLIAM, 1872–80, *Manual of English Prose Literature, p.* 516.

Chance directed him to the quiet byways of literature, in which he achieved a mild but complete success. The "Curiosities of Literature" is more interesting than many a book of higher pretensions, and some of Mr. Disraeli's essays were good and able; but, perhaps, had not his son arisen greater than he, we should have thought less of the father: and granting the interest of his chief publication, there is no sort of greatness in it, nor original power.—OLIPHANT, MARGARET O. W., 1882, *Literary History of England, XVIII-XIX Century, vol.* II, *p.* 315.

As a populariser of literary researches D'Israeli achieved a deserved reputation, but he was not very accurate, and his practice of announcing small literary discoveries as "secret histories," exposed him to merited ridicule.—LEE, SIDNEY L.,

1888, *Dictionary of National Biography*, *vol.* xv, *p.* 119,

His style in some of his earlier works is thoroughly bad—a vile imitation of the whimsical caprices which the genius of a Sterne might make acceptable, but which in the hands of imitators was only ridiculous. A specimen of this may be sought in "Flim-flams: the Life and Errors of my Uncle;" but, for the sake of his reputation, it is better forgotten. In his other works the style has perhaps a little too much of formality, and gives the impression that he is taking himself rather more seriously than is necessary. It is not always very correct, and is sometimes open to the charge of ambiguity. But on the other hand it has the graceful and courteous dignity of a scholar, imbued with a deep and reverent sympathy for literature: and at times there is a boldness and happy fancy in the choice and collocation of epithets, which not only marks the author's Eastern origin, but gives a foretaste of that which was the crowning oratorical glory of his son's transcendent genius. Isaac Disraeli had not the intellectual grasp nor the critical insight required for the literary historian: neither had he the subtle art of the essayist, to whom anecdotes only serve as apt illustrations, and who sustains our interest by combining unity of theme with copiousness of allusion. But at his best he has all the grace, the culture, the well-stored memory, the ready sympathy of the retiring and leisurely scholar—with a formality of manner which is at times a little obtrusive.—CRAIK, HENRY, 1895, *English Prose, vol.* IV, *p.* 607.

Isaac Disraeli was not a good writer; and his original reflections may sometimes make the reader doubt for a moment whether Rogers was not more wrong in granting him half an intellect than in denying him a whole one. But his anecdotage, though, as perhaps such anecdotage is bound to be, not extremely accurate, is almost inexhaustibly amusing, and indicates a real love as well as a wide knowledge of letters.—SAINTSBURY, GEORGE, 1896, *A History of Nineteenth Century Literature, p.* 180.

The "Curiosities of Literature," by Isaac D'Israeli, was not a masterpiece, but its storehouses of anecdote and cultivated reflection must have familiarised with the outlines of literary history thousands who would have been repelled by a more formal work.—GOSSE, EDMUND, 1897, *A Short History of Modern English Literature, p.* 299.

A book ["Curiosities of Literature"] which sixty years since used to be reckoned a necessary part of all well-equipped libraries; but which—to tell the truth—has very little value; being without any method, without fulness, and without much accuracy. It is very rare that so poor a book gets so good a name, and wears it so long.—MITCHELL, DONALD G., 1897, *English Lands Letters and Kings, The Later Georges to Victoria, p.* 181.

John Quincy Adams

1767-1848

Born at Braintree, Mass., July 11, 1767; died at Washington, D. C., Feb. 23, 1848. The sixth President of the United States, 1825-29, son of President John Adams. He was graduated at Harvard in 1787, and was admitted to the bar in 1791. He was United States minister to the Netherlands 1794-1797, and to Prussia 1797-1801; United States senator from Massachusetts 1803-08; professor of rhetoric and belles-lettres at Harvard 1806-09; United States minister to Russia 1809-14; one of the negotiators of the treaty of Ghent, 1814; United States minister to England 1815-17; secretary of state 1817-25; candidate for President, 1824, and, there being no choice by electors, chosen by the House of Representatives. In 1828 Jackson defeated him for the Presidency. He was member of Congress from Massachusetts (Anti-Masonic and Whig), 1831-1848, and unsuccessful candidate for governor of Massachusetts 1834. His diary was edited by C. F. Adams (1874-77).—SMITH, BENJAMIN E., *ed.*, 1894-97, *The Century Cyclopedia of Names, p.* 13.

PERSONAL

Already there is considerable stir and whispering as to who is to be the next President. It is thought here that J. Q. Adams will not be a successful candidate. It seems that the great objection to him is, that he is retiring and unobtrusive, studious, cool, and reflecting; that he does nothing to excite attention, or to gain friendships. He contents himself with doing his duty without seeking any reward. I suspect that he is not calculated for popularity; the old proverb asserts that "God helps them who help themselves."—STORY, JOSEPH, 1818, *To Hon. Ezekiel Bacon, March* 12; *Life and Letters, ed. Story, vol.* I, *p.* 312.

My Dear Son: I have received your letter of the 9th inst. Never did I feel so much solemnity as on this occasion. The multitude of my thoughts and the intensity of my feelings are too much for a mind like mine in its ninetieth year. May the blessing of God Almighty continue to protect you to the end of your life, as it has heretofore protected you in so remarkable a manner from your cradle. I offer the same prayer for your lady and your family, and am your affectionate father.—ADAMS, JOHN, 1825, *Letter to John Quincy Adams, Feb.* 17.

I admire the man for that simple dignity which has marked all his proceedings.—ALEXANDER, JAMES W., 1828, *Letter, July* 18; *Forty Years' Familiar Letters, ed. Hall, vol.* I, *p.* 110.

Hard as a piece of granite and cold as a lump of ice.—GRATTAN, J. C., 1841, *Letter to Mrs. Trollope, What I Remember by T. A. Trollope, p.* 503.

We consider this present active member of Congress as, beyond competition, the most potent spirit in America. "Venerable" he is—and "his hand trembles"—but his venerableness is a cavern of power, and his uplifted forefinger

"trembles as the granite trembles
Lashed by the waves."

We know *there is* a level on the mountain of life, where the air is pure and cold—a height at which impurity can scarce come, more, between the climber and his God—but, *it is above where the lightning comes from*—it is above the dark cloud where sleeps the thunder, collected from below, and charged with inseparable good and harm. This incorrupt level is, at least, *one step* above the cloud in which Mr. Adams has pertinaciously lingered; and if his friends insist that he has been long enough lost to common scrutiny to have reached the upper side of the cloud of dangerous power, we must be excused for pointing our conductor till he is done stirring in the thunder.—WILLIS, NATHANIEL PARKER, 1845, *Ephemera.*

Near this place
Reposes all that could die of
JOHN QUINCY ADAMS,
Son of John and Abigail [Smith] Adams,
Sixth President of the United States.
Born 11 July, 1767,
Amidst the storms of Civil Commotion,
He nursed the vigor
Which nerves a Statesman and a Patriot,
And the Faith
Which inspires a Christian.
For more than half a century,
Whenever his Country called for his Labors,
In either Hemisphere or in any Capacity,
He never spared them in her Cause.
On the Twenty-fourth of December, 1814,
He signed the second Treaty with Great Britain,
Which restored peace within her borders;
On the Twenty-third of February, 1848,
He closed sixteen years of eloquent Defence
Of the Lessons of his Youth,
By dying at his Post,
In her Great National Council.
A son, worthy of his Father,
A citizen, shedding glory on his Country,
A Scholar, ambitious to advance mankind,
This Christian sought to walk humbly
In the sight of his God.

—INSCRIPTION ON TABLET, 1848, *Quincy Church.*

Gentlemen of the House of Representatives of the United States,—It has been thought fit that the Chair should announce officially to the House, an event already known to the members individually, and which has filled all our hearts with sadness. A seat on this floor has been vacated, towards which all eyes have been accustomed to turn with no common interest. A voice has been hushed forever in this Hall, to which all ears have been wont to listen with profound reverence. A venerable form has faded from our sight, around which we have daily clustered with an affectionate regard. A name has been stricken from the roll of the living statesmen of our land, which has been associated, for more than half a century, with the highest civil service, and the loftiest civil renown. On Monday, the 21st instant, John Quincy Adams sunk in his seat, in presence of us all, owing to a sudden illness, from which he never recovered; and he died, in the Speaker's room, at a quarter past seven o'clock last evening, with the officers of the House and the delegation of his own Massachusetts around him. Whatever advanced age, long experience, great ability, vast learning, accumulated public honors, a spotless private character, and a firm religious faith, could do, to render any one an object of interest, respect, and admiration, they had done for this distinguished person; and interest, respect, and admiration are but feeble terms to express the feelings, with which the members of this House and the People of this country have long regarded him. After a life of eighty years, devoted from its earliest maturity to the public service, he has at length gone to his rest. He has been privileged to die at his post; to fall while in the discharge of his duties; to expire beneath the roof of the Capitol; and to have his last scene associated forever, in history, with the birthday of that illustrious Patriot, whose just discernment brought him first into the service of his country. —WINTHROP, ROBERT C., 1848, *The Death of John Quincy Adams, Addresses and Speeches on Various Occasions, p.* 614.

Thus has "a great man fallen in Israel," —in many respects the most wonderful man of the age; certainly the greatest in the United States,—perfect in knowledge, but deficient in practical results. As a statesman, he was pure and incorruptible, but too irascible to lead men's judgment. They admired him, and all voices were hushed when he rose to speak, because they were sure of being instructed by the words he was about to utter; but he made no converts to his opinions, and when President his desire to avoid party influence lost him all the favour of all parties. In matters of history, tradition, statistics, authorities, and practice he was the oracle of the House, of which he was at the time of his decease a member. With an unfailing memory, rendered stronger by cultivation, he was never mistaken; none disputed his authority. Every circumstance of his long life was "Penned down" at the moment of its occurrence; every written communication, even to the minute of a dinner invitation, was carefully preserved, and nothing passed uncopied from his pen. He "talked like a book" on all subjects. Equal to the highest, the planetary system was not above his grasp. Familiar with the lowest, he could explain the mysteries of a mousetrap. . . . Mr. Adams's name will be recorded on the brightest page of American history, as statesman, diplomatist, philosopher, orator, author, and, above all a Christian.—HONE, PHILIP, 1848, *Diary, Feb.* 24, *ed. Tuckerman, vol.* II, *pp.* 342, 343.

He rests with the immortals; his journey has been long:
For him no wail of sorrow, but a pæan full and strong;
So well and bravely has he done the work he found to do,
To justice, freedom, duty, God, and man forever true.
Strong to the end, a man of men, from out the strife he passed;
The grandest hour of all his life was that of earth the last.
Now midst his snowy hills of home to the grave they bear him down,
The glory of his fourscore years resting on him like a crown.

—WHITTIER, ELIZABETH H., 1848, *John Quincy Adams.*

In this long career of public service Mr. Adams was distinguished not only by faithful attention to all the great duties of his stations, but to all their less and minor duties. He was not the Salaminian galley, to be launched only on extraordinary occasions, but he was the ready vessel, always launched when the duties of his station required it, be the occasion great or small. As President, as cabinet Minister, as Minister abroad, he examined all questions that came before him, and examined all in all their parts, in all the minutiæ of their detail, as well as in all the vastness of their comprehension. As Senator, and as a member of the House of Representatives, the obscure committee-room was as much the witness of his laborious application to the drudgery of legislation, as the halls of the two Houses were to the ever ready speech, replete with knowledge, which instructed all hearers, enlightened all subjects, and gave dignity and ornament to debate. In the observance of all the proprieties of life, Mr. Adams was a most noble and impressive example. He cultivated the minor as well as the greater virtues. Wherever his presence could give aid and countenance to what was useful and honorable to man, there he was. In the exercises of the school and of the college—in the meritorious meetings of the agricultural, mechanical, and commerical societies—in attendance upon Divine worship—he gave the punctual attendance rarely seen but in those who are free from the weight of public cares. Punctual to every duty, death found him at the post of duty; and where else could it have found him, at any stage of his career, for the fifty years of his illustrious public life? —BENTON, THOMAS HART, 1848, *Eulogy on John Quincy Adams, United States Senate.*

Few public men in any country have possessed attainments more varied than were those of Mr. Adams. Every department of literature and science received more or less of his attention—every path of human improvement seems to have been explored by him. As a statesman, he was unrivalled in the profundity of his knowledge. His state papers—given to the world while Minister, Secretary of State, President, and Member of Congress—his numerous addresses, orations, and speeches, are astonishing in number, and in the learning they display. No man was more familiar with modern history, with diplomacy and international law, and the politics of America and Europe for the last two or three centuries. In other departments he appeared equally at home. His acquaintance was familiar with the classics, and several modern languages. In oratory, rhetoric, and the various departments of belles-lettres, his attainments were of more than an ordinary character. His commentaries on Desdemona, and others of Shakspeare's characters, show that he was no mean critic, in the highest walks of literature, and in all that pertains to human character.—SEWARD, WILLIAM H., 1849, *Life of John Quincy Adams, p.* 232

The basis of his moral character was the religious principle. His spirit of liberty was fostered and inspired by the writings of Milton, Sydney, and Locke, of which the American Declaration of Independence was an emanation, and the constitution of the United States, with the exception of the clauses conceded to slavery, an embodiment. He was the associate of statesmen and diplomatists at a crisis when war and desolation swept over Europe, when monarchs were perplexed with fear of change, and the welfare of the United States was involved in the common danger. After leading the councils which restored peace to conflicting nations, he returned to support the administration of a veteran statesman, and then wielded the chief powers of the republic with unsurpassed purity and steadiness of purpose, energy, and wisdom. Removed by faction from the helm of state, he re-entered the national councils, and, in his old age, stood panoplied in the principles of Washington and his associates, the ablest and most dreaded champion of freedom, until, from the station assigned him by his country, he departed, happy in a life devoted to duty, in a death crowned with every honor his country could bestow, and blessed with the hope which inspires those who defend the rights, and uphold, when menaced, momentous interests of mankind.—QUINCY, JOSIAH, 1858, *Memoir of John Quincy Adams, p.* 428.

The circumstances connected with the decease of Mr. Adams are so well known as to require little development here. On the 20th of February he seemed as well as he had been, and had attended divine service morning and afternoon. On the 21st he went up to the Capitol as usual and took his customary seat in the House of Representatives, with no appearance whatever of illness. A question had sprung up touching a vote of thanks to certain military officers for services rendered during the Mexican War; and the Speaker was rising to put the motion to the House, when he was arrested by Mr. Washington Hunt, a member from New York, sitting near to Mr. Adams, who perceived him in a state of convulsion, and interposed to stop the proceedings. Not being in a condition for removal to his own house, he was placed in one of the Committee-rooms. No medical service was found to be possible, and he lingered with little apparent consciousness till the evening of the 23d, when he died.—ADAMS, CHARLES FRANCIS, 1877, *Memoirs of John Quincy Adams, vol.* XII, *p.* 282.

After his term in the presidency expired, he made the novel experiment of a retired president serving in the house of representatives, and it was the most successful, although not the most practical part of his life. He was called by the notorious Tom Marshall, the "Old Man Eloquent," and he used his eloquence with a power which few could resist. . . . Mr. Adams' speeches from 1833 to 1842, on the subject of slavery and right of petition, and the annexation of Texas, were the best, the ablest, and the most effective made in the country. For his course in the anti-slavery movement, for his clear views of the constitution, and his defense of human freedom, he will be remembered in after ages. He was never popular with politicians, nor even regarded as a party leader. No man ever questioned his integrity. No man ever doubted his patriotism. Of him, with more truth than of Chatham, it might be said: "The secretary stood alone. Modern degeneracy had not reached him."—MANSFIELD, E. D., 1879, *Personal Memories, p.* 205.

He lies buried "under the portal of the church at Quincy" beside his wife, who survived him four years, his father and his mother. The memorial tablet inside the church bears upon it the words "Alteri Sæculo,"—surely never more justly or appropriately applied to any man than to John Quincy Adams, hardly abused and cruelly misappreciated in his own day but whom subsequent generations already begin to honor as one of the greatest of American statesmen, not only pre-eminent in ability and acquirements, but even more to be honored for profound, immutable honesty of purpose and broad, noble humanity of aims.—MORSE, JOHN T., JR., 1882, *John Quincy Adams* (*American Statesmen*), *p.* 309.

In Congress the commanding voice for freedom was that of the most learned, experienced, and courageous of American statesmen, the voice of a scholar and an old college professor, John Quincy Adams. —CURTIS, GEORGE WILLIAM, 1882, *The Leadership of Educated Men, Orations and Addresses, vol.* I, *p.* 329.

President Adams, although at heart instigated by a Puritan intolerance of those who failed to conform with himself, was a true patriot, and as a public man was moved by the highest moral motives. He was a great statesman in so far as the comprehension of the principles of government and a mastery of a wide field of information were concerned, but he could not practically apply his knowledge. Instead of harmonizing the personal feuds between the friends of those who had been candidates with him, he antagonized each one with his Administration at the earliest possible moment, and before the expiration of his first year in the White House he had wrecked the Republican party left by Monroe, as completely as his father had wrecked the Federal party established by Washington. . . . Mr. Adams used to rise between four and six o'clock, according to the season, and either take a ride on horseback or walk to the Potomac River, where he bathed, remaining in the water for an hour or more in the summer. Returning to the White House, he read two chapters of the Bible and then glanced over the morning papers until nine, when he breakfasted. From ten until four he remained in the Executive Office, presiding over Cabinet meeting, receiving visitors, or considering questions of state. Then, after a long walk, or a short ride on horseback, he would sit down to dine at half-past five, and after dinner resume his public duties.—POORE, BEN: PERLEY, 1886, *Perley's Reminiscences of Sixty Years in the National Metropolis, vol.* I, *pp.* 27, 31.

Mr. Adams's speech upon the right of petition in 1837 was one of the most effective and triumphant speeches ever made in Congress. The great speech of Mr. Webster, in reply to Hayne, was not listened to with more interest. Mr. Adams was one of the most remarkable men that this country has produced, and in no respect was he more remarkable than in the fact that he became a great offhand speaker after he had left the Presidency and had reached the period in life after which there is usually a decline instead of improvement in intellectual vigor. . . . He was a free lance, and hard hitter. With his armor always on, he was never unprepared for a tilt with any one who was bold enough to enter the lists. His great learning and command of language made him a most formidable and dangerous antagonist. Pugnacious by temperament, he loved a fight better than he loved his friends, of whom there were few, and with none was he ever long in perfect accord. Before he commenced his Congressional career, he had alienated from himself his old Federal allies, and he entered into no alliances afterwards. He was hated as few public men have been, but his great ability, perfect independence, and thorough uprightness, commanded the respect even of those who hated him. In the great speech to which I have referred, he achieved the very highest reputation as a debater and orator. It was a speech in which learning and argument and the bitterest satire were so combined as to overwhelm his opponents, and secure for himself the name of the "Old Man Eloquent," which he afterwards retained.—McCULLOCH, HUGH, 1888, *Men and Measures of Half a Century, pp.* 38, 39.

The peculiar features of his father's character were so intensified in him that he may be deemed the typical figure rather than his father.—SMITH, GOLDWIN, 1893, *The United States, An Outline of Political History, p.* 192.

It was what he said, more than the way he said it, which told. His vigorous mind never worked more surely and clearly than when he stood alone in the midst of an angry House, the target of their hatred and abuse. His arguments were strong, and his large knowledge and wide experience supplied him with every weapon for defense and attack. Beneath the lash of his invective and his sarcasm the hottest of the slave-holders cowered away. He set his back against a great principle. He never retreated an inch, he never yielded, he never conciliated, he was always an assailant, and no man and no body of men had the power to turn him. He had his dark hours, he felt bitterly the isolation of his position, but he never swerved. He had good right to set down in his diary, when the gag rule was repealed, "Blessed, forever blessed, be the name of God."—LODGE, HENRY CABOT, 1895, *Hero Tales from American History, p.* 158.

From the time he crawled over the kitchen floor and pushed a chair, learning to walk, or tumbled down the stairs and then made his way bravely up again alone, he knew that he would arrive. Precocious, proud, firm, and with a coldness in his nature that was not a heritage from either his father or mother, he made his way. It was a zigzag course, and the way was strewn with the flotsam and jetsam of wrecked parties and blighted hopes, but out of the wreckage John Quincy Adams always appeared, calm, poised, and serene. When he opposed the purchase of Louisiana it looks as if he allowed his animosity for Jefferson to put his judgment in chancery. He made mistakes, but this was the only blunder of his career.—HUBBARD, ELBERT, 1898, *Little Journeys to the Homes of American Statesmen, p.* 215.

GENERAL

John Quincy Adams belongs to neither of the prominent political parties, fights no partisan battles, and cannot be prevailed upon to sacrifice truth and principle upon the altar of party expediency and interest. Hence neither party is interested in defending his course, or in giving him an opportunity to defend himself. But however systematic may be the efforts of mere partisan presses to suppress and hold back from the public eye the powerful and triumphant vindication of the Right of Petition, the graphic delineation of the slavery spirit in Congress, and the humbling disclosure of Northern cowardice and treachery contained in these letters, they are destined to exert a powerful influence upon the public mind. They will constitute one of the most striking pages in the history of our times. They will be read with avidity in the North and South, and throughout Europe. Apart from the interest excited by the subjects under discussion, and viewed only as literary productions, they may be ranked among the highest intellectual efforts of their author. Their sarcasm is Junius-like,—cold, keen, unsparing. In boldness, directness, and eloquent appeal, they will bear comparison with O'Connell's celebrated "Letters to the Reformers of Great Britain." They are the offspring of an intellect unshorn of its primal strength, and combining the ardor of youth with the experience of age. . . On his "gray, discrowned head" the entire fury of slave-holding arrogance and wrath was expended. He stood alone, beating back, with his aged and single arm, the tide which would have borne down and overwhelmed a less sturdy and determined spirit.—WHITTIER, JOHN GREENLEAF, 1837–89, *The Conflict with Slavery, Writings, Riverside ed., vol.* VII, *pp.* 93, 94.

Not many persons have left behind them a greater variety of papers than John Quincy Adams, all more or less marked by characteristic modes of thought, and illustrating his principles of public and private action. Independently of a diary kept almost continuously for sixty-five years, and of numbers of other productions, official and otherwise, already printed, there is a variety of discussion and criticism on different topics, together with correspondence public and private, which, if it were all to be published, as was that of Voltaire, would be likely quite to equal in quantity the hundred volumes of that expansive writer.—ADAMS, CHARLES FRANCIS, 1874, *Memoirs of John Quincy Adams, Preface, vol.* I, *p.* vi.

Mr. Adams seems, in fact, to have positively loved to use his pen. His habit was to get up at a very early hour, often before sunrise; and this he did even when resident at courts, where he was forced to attend parties kept up inordinately late. His working day was thus much longer than that of most of his associates, and was filled by the pen, which indefatigably committed to paper what appear to have been in most cases his first thoughts on every conceivable subject which presented itself, whether in talk, reading, silent observation in company, or solitude. It was, we believe, rarely his habit to revise; and the resulting mass of manuscript is almost beyond precedent in the lives of even industrious men. But it strongly reminds us of the work achieved by one man, of whose writings Mr. Adams was a constant and devoted student, and whose character, though strongly alien to his in many points, was strongly akin to it in others: that is, Cicero. Nor in any point is this resemblance more curiously marked than in the fondness alike of the Volscian and the Yankee for verse composition, of a kind that both contemporaries and posterity persist in thinking the reverse of poetical. The editor has very properly included a few of his father's pieces in these volumes, justly remarking that no true notion of his character can be acquired without them. He retained the habit of translating and composing in verse. —EVERETT, WILLIAM, 1875, *John Quincy Adams, Atlantic Monthly, vol.* 36, *p.* 197.

The author of a diary conspicuous for its malignity, and father of a son unwise enough to publish it.—BLAINE, JAMES G., 1876, *Speech.*

He undoubtedly kept gall and wormwood in his inkstand for daily use, but he was a charming old man all the same. He fulfilled the character which he gave to Roger Williams,—"that conscientious, contentious man."—WINTHROP, ROBERT C., 1880, *Letter, Apr.* 25; *Memoir, ed. Winthrop, p.* 300.

Adams has a distinct claim to be remembered in literature, though not for the highest work. His numerous occasional discourses, biographical sketches and eulogies, published together as "Lives of Celebrated Statesmen," his translations and forgotten verses, amongst them an epic poem, testify to his aspiration if not his inspiration.— NICHOL, JOHN, 1880-85, *American Literature, p.* 107.

Literature had always possessed strong charms for him, and he had cultivated it after his usual studious and conscientious fashion. But his style was too often prolix, sententious, and turgid—faults which marked nearly all the writing done in this country in those days. The world has probably not lost much by reason of the non-completion of the contemplated volumes. He could have made no other contribution to the history of the country at all approaching in value or interest to the Diary.—MORSE, JOHN T., JR., 1882, *John Quincy Adams (American Statesmen), p.* 222.

Volumes ["Memoirs"] of surpassing interest on the personal and political life of one of the noblest and most accomplished of our public men. The most striking and interesting peculiarity of the diary is the fulness of the author's reflections and comments on the men and on the events among which he lived. It was his constant habit to jot down his thoughts on what was taking place about him. Accordingly, there is scarcely an event of importance during the long years of his public career on which he has not expressed an opinion.—ADAMS, CHARLES KENDALL, 1882, *A Manual of Historical Literature, p.* 589.

A minutely faithful diary, worthy of the Adams name, and surpassing in length (twelve octavo volumes), though certainly not in readableness, those of Pepys and Samuel Sewall. . . . John Quincy Adams, like Washington, John Adams, Jefferson and Madison, was a man of culture, which occasionally clothed itself in literary garb. —RICHARDSON, CHARLES F., 1885, *American Literature,* 1607-1885, *vol.* I, *pp.* 208, 209.

Was far more learned and accomplished than his father, though greatly inferior to him in native ability. Though a constant writer, publishing during his life works on rhetoric, European travel, Shakespearean criticism and biography, besides a book of poems and many political articles, he deserves mention rather as a statesman than an author. Like his father, he kept a full diary, and like him maintained a voluminous and charming correspondence. —PATTEE, FRED LEWIS, 1896, *A History of American Literature, p.* 82.

Emily Brontë

1818-1848

Emily Brontë was born at Hartshead-cum-Clifton, near Leeds, in 1818, and lived at the parsonage at Haworth from 1820 to her death. The monotony of this existence was broken only by a brief attempt to be a governess and by a short stay at Brussels in 1842, all exile from home being excessively painful and hurtful to her. She died of consumption at Haworth on the 19th of December, 1848. She published, in conjunction with her sisters, "Poems by Currer, Ellis, and Acton Bell," in 1846, and, alone, the novel of "Wuthering Heights" in 1847.—WARD, THOMAS HUMPHRY, 1880, *ed., The English Poets, vol.* IV, *p.* 581.

PERSONAL

No coward soul is mine,
  No trembler in the world's storm-troubled
    sphere:
I see Heaven's glories shine,
  And faith shines equal, arming me from
    fear,
—BRONTË, EMILY, 1848, *Last Lines.*

. . . she
(How shall I sing her?) whose soul
Knew no fellow for might,
Passion, vehemence, grief,
Daring, since Byron died,
That world-famed son of fire—she, who sank
Baffled, unknown, self-consumed;
Whose too bold dying song
Stirr'd, like a clarion-blast, my soul.
—ARNOLD, MATTHEW, 1855-85, *Haworth Churchyard, April.*

The feeling which in Charlotte partook of something of the nature of an affection, was, with Emily, more of a passion. Some one speaking of her to me, in a careless kind of strength of expression, said, "she never showed regard to any human creature; all her love was reserved for animals." The helplessness of an animal was its passport to Charlotte's heart; the fierce, wild, intractability of its nature was what often recommended it to Emily. Speaking of her dead sister, the former told me that from her many traits in Shirley's character were taken; her way of sitting on the rug reading, with her arm round her rough bull-dog's neck; her calling to a strange dog, running past, with hanging head and lolling tongue, to give it a merciful draught of water, its maddened snap at her, her nobly stern presence of mind, going right into the kitchen, and taking up one of Tabby's red-hot Italian irons to sear the bitten place, and telling no one, till the danger was well-nigh over, for fear of the terrors that might beset their weaker minds. All this, looked upon as a well-invented fiction in "Shirley," was written by Charlotte with streaming eyes; it was the literal true account of what Emily had done. — GASKELL, ELIZABETH CLEGHORN, 1857, *Life of Charlotte Brontë, ch.* xii.

Emily Brontë had . . . a lithesome, graceful figure. She was the tallest person in the house, except her father. Her hair, which was naturally as beautiful as Charlotte's, was in the same unbecoming tight curl and frizz; and there was the same want of complexion. She had very beautiful eyes—kind, kindling, liquid eyes; but she did not often look at you; she was too reserved. Their color might be said to be dark-gray, at other times dark-blue, they varied so. She talked very little. She and Anne were like twins—inseparable companions, and in the very closest sympathy, which never had any interruption.—NUSSEY, ELLEN, 1871, *Reminiscences of Charlotte Brontë, Scribner's Monthly, vol.* 2, *p.* 26.

Her chief delight was to roam on the moors, followed by her dogs, to whom she would whistle in masculine fashion. Her heart, indeed, was given to these dumb creatures of the earth. She never forgave those who ill-treated them, nor trusted those whom they disliked. One is reminded of Shelley's "Sensitive Plant" by some traits of Emily Brontë; . . . like the lady of the poem, her tenderness and charity could reach even

——the poor banished insects, whose intent,
Although they did ill, was innocent.

—REID, THOMAS WEMYSS, 1877, *Charlotte Brontë, a Monograph, p.* 42.

Not even the unstinted praise of three great and very dissimilar poets has given to Emily Brontë her due rank in popular esteem. Her work is not universally acceptable, even to imaginative readers; her personality is almost repulsive to many who have schooled themselves to endure the vehemence of genius but not its ominous self-restraint. Most people were afraid of Emily Brontë's "whitening face and set mouth" when she was alive, and even now that she is dead her memory seems to inspire more terror than affection. Against an instinctive repugnance it is in vain to reason, and in discussing her poetical quality we must assume that her power has at least been felt and not disliked by the reader, since "you must love her, ere to you she should seem worthy to be loved." Those who have come under the spell of her genius will expect no apology for her intellectual rebellion, her stoic harshness of purpose, her more than manlike strength. She was a native blossom of those dreary and fascinating moorlands of which Charlotte has given, in a few brilliant phrases, so perfect a description, and like the acrid heaths and gentians that flourish in the peat, to transplant her was to kill her. Her actions, like her writings, were strange, but consistent in their strangeness. Even the dreadful incident of her death, which occured as she stood upright in the little parlour at Haworth, refusing to go to bed, but just leaning one hand upon the table, seems to me to be no unfit ending for a life so impatient of constraint from others, so implacable in its slavery to its own principles.—GOSSE, EDMUND, 1880, *The English Poets, ed. Ward, vol.* IV, *p.* 581.

In 1833 Emily was nearly fifteen, a tall, long-armed girl, full grown, elastic of tread; with a slight figure that looked queenly in her best dresses, but loose and boyish when she slouched over the moors whistling to her dogs, and taking long strides over the rough earth. A tall, thin, loose-jointed girl—not ugly, but with irregular features and a pallid, thick complexion. Her dark-brown hair was naturally beautiful, and in later days looked well loosely fastened with a tall comb at the back of her head; but in 1833 she wore it in an unbecoming tight curl and frizz. She had very beautiful eyes of haze color. . . . She had an aquiline nose, a large expressive, prominent mouth. She talked little. No grace or style in dress belonged to Emily, but under her awkward clothes her natural movements had the lithe beauty of the wild creatures that she loved. . . . Never was a soul with a more passionate love of Mother Earth, of every weed and flower, of every bird, beast and insect that lived. She would have peopled the house with pets had not Miss Branwell kept her niece's love of animals in due subjection. Only one dog was allowed, who was admitted into the parlor at stated hours, but out of doors Emily made friends with all the beasts and birds. She would come home carrying in her hands some young bird or rabbit, and softly talking to it as she came. "Ee, Miss Emily," the young servant would say, "one would think the bird could understand you." "I am sure it can," Emily would answer. "Oh, I am sure it can." . . . Two lives went on side by side in her heart, neither ever mingling with or interrupting the other. Practical housewife with capable hands, dreamer of strange horrors: each self was independent of the companion to which it was linked by day and night. People in those days knew her but as she seemed—"t' Vicar's Emily"—a shy awkward girl, never teaching in Sunday-school like her sisters, never talking with the villagers like merry Branwell, but very good and hearty in helping the sick and distressed: not pretty in the village estimation—a "slinky lass," no prim, trim little body like pretty Anne, nor with Charlotte Brontë's taste in dress; just a clever lass with a spirit of her own. So the village judged her. At home they loved her with her strong feelings, untidy frocks, indomitable will and ready contempt for the commonplace; she was appreciated as a dear and necessary member of the household. Of Emily's deeper self, her violent genius, neither friend nor neighbor dreamed in those days.—ROBINSON, A. MARY F., 1883, *Emily Brontë (Famous Women), pp.* 65, 69.

Though Emily Brontë's life was not an eventful one in the usual sense of the word, it may certainly be called a crowded life. That twenty-nine years was not a large demesne, but it was fertile enough, though only with rue and rosemary and nightshade and the poppy that bloomed before the harvest.—NOBLE, JAMES ASHCROFT, 1883, *Emily Brontë, The Academy, vol.* 23, *p.* 340.

Few persons of whom so little has been or can be recorded as Emily Brontë have made so deep an impression upon the popular mind, or are so distinctly present to the imagination. There is nothing to be said except that she was born in August 1818, and died of consumption in December 1848; that she was first a teacher without pupils, and then an authoress without readers; that her life was harrassed by an impracticable father, and infected by a base, profligate brother; and that nevertheless she was visited by such noble inspirations, and was such a piece of her own moorland, that one hardly accounts her unfortunate. She was the laureate of the moors, and no fanciful analogy might be drawn between her and these scenes of her residence, and objects of her affections. Like them she was free, rough, wild; in a certain sense barren and limited; in another sense rich and expansive; from one point of view mournful, from another joyous. In one respect only is she false to the teaching of the nature that environed her; the moor is ever healthy, but it is impossible to acquit the creator of "Heathcliff" of a taint of unsoundness.—GARNETT, RICHARD, 1892, *The Poets and the Poetry of the Century, Joanna Baillie to Mathilde Blind, ed. Miles, p.* 283.

The reticent and sadly straightened genius of Emily Brontë found wings only on the Yorkshire moors. In her dusty laborious life as a teacher, always one vision of delight appeared to her:—

"A little and a lone green lane
That opened on a common wide;
A distant, dreamy, dim, blue chain
Of mountains circling every side.
A heaven so clear, an earth so calm,
So sweet, so soft, so hushed an air;
And deepening still the dream-like charm,
Wild moorsheep feeding everywhere."

You do not think of "calm" and "charm" as a blemish; there is a sob in the singer's voice, and it is in the magic mirror of a teardrop that she sees the "moorsheep feeding everywhere."—DAVIDSON, JOHN, 1895, *Sentences and Paragraphs, p.* 49.

WUTHERING HEIGHTS
1847

I trust you have not, as we have, wasted your time on "that little family in Hell," living and dying at "Wuthering Heights." It is a most signal waste of talent. There is a certain resemblance to Jane Eyre, like a family look; the energy of thought and style, the northern mind as well as air that breathes through it, the intimate and masterly acquaintance with a location and coterie, and exclusion from the world, the remarkable directness of style, are all qualities peculiar, and marvelously like Jane Eyre, so that I think the author must be her brother, the masculine of her masculine mind.—SEDGWICK, CATHARINE M., 1848, *To Mrs. K. S. Minot, May* 27; *Life and Letters, ed. Dewey, p.* 307.

"Wuthering Heights" was hewn in a wild workshop, with simple tools, out of homely materials. The statuary found a granite block on a solitary moor; gazing thereon he saw how from the crag might be elicited a head, savage, swart, sinister: a form moulded with at least one element of grandeur—power. He wrought with a rude chisel, and from no model but the vision of his meditations. With time and labour the crag took human shape; and there it stands, colossal, dark, and frowning, half statue, half rock; in the former sense, terrible and goblin-like; in the latter, almost beautiful, for its colouring is of mellow gray, and moorland moss clothes it; and heath, with its blooming bells and balmy fragrance, grows faithfully close to the giant's foot.—BRONTË, CHARLOTTE, 1851, *Wuthering Heights, Preface.*

I've been greatly interested in "Wuthering Heights," the first novel I've read for an age, and the best (as regards power and sound style) for two ages, except "Sidonia." But it is a fiend of a book—an incredible monster, combining all the stronger female tendencies from Mrs. Browning to Mrs. Brownrigg. The action is laid in hell,—only it seems places and people have English names there.—ROSSETTI, DANTE GABRIEL, 1854, *Letters to William Allingham, p.* 58.

Emily Brontë—for it is now time that we should say something of the two other persons in this remarkable trio—was, in certain respects, the most extraordinary of the three sisters. She has this distinction at any rate, that she has written a book which stands as completely alone in the language as does the "Paradise Lost" or the "Pilgrim's Progress." . . . Its power is absolutely Titanic: from the first page to the last it reads like the intellectual throes of a giant. It is fearful, it is true, and perhaps one of the most unpleasant books ever written: but we stand in amaze at the almost incredible fact that it was written by a slim country girl who would have passed in a crowd as an insignificant person, and who had had little or no experience of the ways of the world. . . . We challenge the world to produce another work in which the whole atmosphere seems so surcharged with suppressed electricity, and bound in with the blackness of tempest and desolation.—SMITH, GEORGE BARNETT, 1875, *The Brontës, Poets and Novelists, pp.* 236, 239, 240.

Twice or thrice especially the details of deliberate or passionate brutality in Heathcliff's treatment of his victims make the reader feel for a moment as though he were reading a police report or even a novel by some French "naturalists" of the latest and brutallest order. But the pervading atmosphere of the book is so high and healthy that the effect even of those "vivid and fearful scenes" which impaired the rest of Charlotte Brontë is almost at once neutralized—we may hardly say softened, but sweetened, dispersed, and transfigured—by the general impression of noble purity and passionate straightforwardness, which removes it at once and forever from any such ugly possibility of association or comparison. The whole work is not more incomparable in the effect of its atmosphere or landscape than in the peculiar note of its wild and bitter pathos; but most of all is it unique in the special and distinctive character of its passion. The love which devours life itself, which devastates the present and desolates the future with unquenchable and raging fire, has nothing less pure in it than flame or sunlight. And this passionate and ardent chastity is utterably and unmistakably spontaneous and unconscious. Not till the story is ended, not till the effect of it has been thoroughly absorbed and digested, does the reader even perceive the simple and natural absence of any grosser element, any hint or suggestion of a baser alloy in the ingredients of its human emotion than in the splendour of lightning or the roll of a gathered wave.—SWINBURNE, ALGERNON CHARLES, 1883-86, *Miscellanies, p.* 269.

As to the capability of Branwell to write "Wuthering Heights," not much need be said here. Those who read this book will see that, despite his weaknesses and his follies, Branwell was, indeed, unfortunate in having to bear the penalty, in ceaseless open discussion, of "une fanfaronnade des vices qu'il n'avait pas," and that, moreover, his memory has been darkened, and his acts misconstrued, by sundry writers, who have endeavoured to find in his character the source of the darkest passages in the works of his sisters. Far from being hopelessly a "miserable fellow," an "unprincipled dreamer," an "unnerved and garrulous prodigal," as we have been told he was, he had, in fact, within him, an abundance of worthy ambition, a modest confidence in his own ability, which he was never known to vaunt, and a just pride in the celebrity of his family, which, it may be trusted, will remove from him, at any rate, the imputation of a lack of moral power to do anything good or forcible at all. Those who have heard fall from the lips of Branwell Brontë—and they are few now—all those weird stories, strange imaginings, and vivid and brilliant disquisitions on the life of the people of the West Riding, will recognize that there was at least no opposition, but rather an affinity, between the tendency of his thoughts and those of the author of "Wuthering Heights."—LEYLAND, FRANCIS A., 1886, *The Brontë Family with Special Reference to Patrick Branwell Brontë, vol.* II, *p.* 191.

Undoubtedly, Emily Brontë's genius was unique and masterful, and her book will always charm individual readers. It has been compared with Shelley's "Cenci" and with Webster's "Duchess of Malfi." All such comparisons, of course, only go to indicate a generic likeness, but they sufficiently explain the tale's little popularity. It might not be altogether a good sign for such works to be popular; they are for a "fit audience, though few,"—not for the many. They would not be wholesome food for all, and might cause a mental indigestion. Not every reader can assimilate such strong food, or turn it to good purpose. Those who can, will find it attract them irresistibly. Faulty as a narrative, "Wuthering Heights" burns with energy and pulses with life-blood. It is a poem without the accompaniment of rhyme.—SALMON, ARTHUR L., 1892, *A Modern Stoic, Poet-Lore, vol.* 4, *p.* 69.

In "Wuthering Heights" we have the first novel of a young woman with little knowledge either of literature or of life, and yet the story is told with compactness and force, scenery is described with marvelous vividness and sympathy, characters are represented with amazing individuality, while, though incidents and characters are at times so appalling that many readers turn from the book in horror, there is such power, both of personality and of treatment, as positively fascinates even while it terrifies. But it should be noted Emily Brontë had no conscious intention of exciting terror. It is true that, as Heathcliff reveals himself in all his savagery, one stands aghast at his wolfish ferocity; yet one can plainly see that the author is not seeking for means of affecting her readers, but, heedless of readers, is working out her altogether astounding conception.—WILLIAMS, A. M., 1893, *Emily Brontë, Temple Bar, vol.* 98, *p.* 435.

She wrote "Wuthering Heights" because she was impelled thereto, and the book, with all its morbid force and fire, will remain, for all time, as a monument of the most striking genius that nineteenth century womanhood has given us. It was partly her life in Yorkshire—the local colour was mainly derived from her brief experience as a governess at Halifax—but it was partly, also, the German fiction which she had devoured during the Brussels period, that inspired "Wuthering Heights."—SHORTER, CLEMENT K., 1896, *Charlotte Brontë and her Circle, p.* 158.

Beyond the madness and terror of "Wuthering Heights," romantic fiction has never gone. Its spiritual counterpart in real life is Emily Brontë, who preserved her inexorable will far into the day on which she died.—CROSS, WILBUR L., 1899, *The Development of the English Novel, p.* 167.

The heroines of Emily Brontë have not the artistic completeness of Charlotte Brontë's. They are blocked out with hysterical force, and in their character there is something elemental, as if, like the man who beat and browbeat them, they too were close to the savagery of nature. The sort of supernaturalism, which appears here and there in their story, wants the refinement of the telepathy and presentiment which play a part in Jane Eyre, but it is still more effectual in the ruder clutch which it lays upon the fancy. In her dealing with the wild passion of Heathcliff for the first Catharine, Emily Brontë does not keep even such slight terms with convention as Charlotte does in the love of Rochester and Jane Eyre; but this fierce longing, stated as it were in its own language, is still farther from anything that corrupts or tempts; it is as wholesome and decent as a thunder-storm, in the consciousness of the witness. The perversities of the mutual attraction of the lovers are rendered without apparent sense on the part of the author that they can seem out of nature, so deeply does she feel them to be in nature, and there is no hint from her that they need any sort of proof. . . . No one can deny the charm of this, the absolute reality, the consummate art, which is still art, however unconscious. Did the dying girl who wrote the strange book, where it is only one of so many scenes of unfaltering truth, know how great it was, with all its defects? In any case criticism must recognize its mastery, and rejoice in its courage.—HOWELLS, WILLIAM DEAN, 1900, *Heroines of Nineteenth Century Fiction, Harper's Bazar, vol.* 33, *pp.* 2224, 2230.

POEMS

The poetry of Emily Brontë is small in extent and conventional in form. Its burning thoughts are concealed for the most part in the tame and ambling measures dedicated to female verse by the practice of Felicia Hemans and Letitia Landon. That she was progressing to the last even in this matter of the form is shown by the little posthumous collection of her verses issued by Charlotte, consisting of early, and very weak pieces, and of two poems written in the last year of her life, which attain, for the first time the majesty of rhythm demanded by such sublime emotions. But it is impossible not to regret that she missed that accomplishment in the art of poetry which gives an added force to the verse of her great French contemporary, Marceline Valmore, the only modern poetess who can fitly be compared with Emily Brontë for power of expressing passion in its simplicity. . . . It is difficult to praise Emily's three or four greatest poems without an air of exaggeration. Finest among them all is that outburst of agnostic faith that was found by Charlotte on her desk when she died, a "last poem" not to be surpassed in dignity and self-reliance by any in the language. —GOSSE, EDMUND, 1880, *The English Poets, ed. Ward, vol.* IV, *p.* 582.

Some of Emily's poems in this book are full of such original and intense—though hardly attractive—writing as gives her quite a unique and lofty position among our poets. The note of these poems comes very near despair, but such is the strength of Emily's character that it is rather a desperate courage. Self-dependent in every act and thought of her life, she will recognise nothing in the universe but the beauty of the external world and the strength of her own intellectual being. She expresses no hope in the future or in a God other than a vague pantheistic hope; she throws abroad small sympathy for her fellow-beings. The history of the world does not entice her to be its prophetess; she breathes into her poetry only her individual self, but expresses that self so nobly that we find in some of her verses the elements of such a character as in different circumstances might have turned her into a Maid of Orleans, or a Madam Roland. The soul of Emily Brontë was ever

"Struggling fierce toward Heaven's free wilderness."

with strong wings, and with the loneliness of wings.—ROBERTSON, ERIC S., 1883, *English Poetesses, p.* 324.

Her poetry, in general less powerful, is more pleasing than her fiction; harsh and forbidding as her view of life seems at first, it gains upon us as we realise her proud superiority to external circumstances, and the passionate affection for those she really loves, which redeems her unamiability towards the rest. . . . Almost all the poetry which Emily Brontë published during her lifetime was of this character, though not always attaining the same careless beauty, graceful in its apparent negligence. Not until nigh to death did she compose a strain of quite another sort, which, if it were just to judge her solely by one supreme inspiration, would place her above every other female lyrist since Sappho. The grandeur and eloquence of her last verses have in our judgment never been rivalled by any English poetess: the question whether she could have maintained herself at such an elevation, were it capable of an answer, would help to elucidate the deeper problem how far poetical inspiration is the result of favourable conditions, and how far it is a visitation from above. It must remain for ever unanswered.—GARNETT, RICHARD, 1892, *The Poets and the Poetry of the Century, Joanna Baillie to Mathilde Blind, ed. Miles, pp.* 284, 285.

Her best verse is perhaps the greatest ever written by a woman. "Last Lines" and "The Old Stoic" will rank with the finest poetry in our literature.—SHORTER, CLEMENT K., 1897, *Victorian Literature, Sixty Years of Books and Bookmen, p.* 47.

GENERAL

Emily had a head for logic and a capability of argument, unusual in a man, and rare indeed in a woman, according to M. Héger. Impairing the force of this gift was a stubborn tenacity of will, which rendered her obtuse to all reasoning where her own wishes or her own sense of right was concerned. "She should have been a man—a great navigator," said M. Héger in speaking of her "Her powerful reason would have deduced new spheres of discovery from the knowledge of the old; and her strong imperious will would never have been daunted by opposition or difficulty—never have given way but with life." And yet, moreover, her faculty of imagination was such that, if she had written a history, her view of scenes and characters would have been so vivid, and so powerfully expressed, and supported by such a show of argument, that it would have dominated over the reader, whatever might have been his previous opinions or his cooler preceptions of its truth.—GASKELL, ELIZABETH CLEGHORN, 1857, *Life of Charlotte Brontë, ch.* xi.

To Emily Brontë's genius justice seems hardly to have been done. Her sister, indeed, recognised, and may be said to have adored it. Emily Brontë's mind was at once dark and luminous, like the eyes of an Indian. Her qualities were each and all splendid, but too massive and masculine for her frail frame, worn and worried by consumption. "Wuthering Heights" is a noble work. Frequent passages haunt one like scenes from "Macbeth" or the "Cenci." In some points her genius seems superior to her sister's.—RUSSELL, WILLIAM CLARK, 1871, *The Book of Authors, p.* 499.

Emily Brontë was a wild, original, and striking creature, but her one book is a kind of prose "Kubla Khan"—a nightmare of the superheated imagination.—HARRISON, FREDERIC, 1895, *Charlotte Brontë's Place in Literature, The Forum, vol.* 19, *p.* 32.

The author of "Wuthering Heights"

still remains, what she has ever been, the sphinx of literature. . . . Her genius may be compared to a mountain peak, whose bold contour compels attention yet forbids approach; bare, steep, affording no foothold to the explorer, and shrouding its summit in clouds which shift but do not lift; a Matterhorn which no Whymper has yet appeared to scale. To this proud isolation of spirit is partly due the strong originality which places her in a rank above her sister, and explains why those who have appreciated her—from Sydney Dobell to Mr. Swinburne—have been fit, if few.—MACKAY, ANGUS M., 1897, *The Brontës, Fact and Fiction*, pp. 21, 22.

Her "Wuthering Heights" is a strange, forbidding tale, and no one can read it without wondering how characters and incidents so coarse and repulsive could ever have occurred to a being so retiring and so ignorant of life as she. We have seen how Dr. Wright in his "Brontës in Ireland" has plausibly suggested that the knowledge of the seamy side of human character and life revealed in the work of these sisters came to them from their familiarity with the legends concerning the older Brontës, with which he supposes their father's memory to have been stored; but until his theory finds for itself a firmer basis of authentic fact, Emily Brontë must remain the Sphinx of Victorian literature. —GRAHAM, RICHARD D., 1897, *The Masters of Victorian Literature*, p. 45.

To me Emily Brontë is chiefly interesting as the double of her sister, exaggerating at once and softening her character and genius as showing those limits of superior sense and judgment which restrained her, and the softer lights which a better developed humanity threw over the landscape common to them both.—OLIPHANT, MARGARET O. W., 1897, *Women Novelists of Queen Victoria's Reign*, p. 28.

In sheer genius Emily Brontë probably surpassed Charlotte, though in art she was certainly the inferior of her elder sister. All that she wrote bears the stamp of her sombre imagination and of the gloomy strength of her character.—WALKER, HUGH, 1897, *The Age of Tennyson*, p. 102.

William Tennant

1784–1848

Poet and Orientalist, was born at East Anstruther, Fife, and educated at a school in the place, and at the University of St. Andrews, whither he went in 1799. In 1801 he became clerk to his brother, who was a corn factor at Glasgow. In 1812 he published his humorous poem, "Anster Fair," which gradually became famous, and was at length favourably noticed by Jeffrey in the *Edinburgh Review*. In 1813 Tennant had accepted the situation of parish schoolmaster at Denino, near St. Andrews, became teacher at Lasswade, near Edinburgh, in 1816, and in 1835 professor of Oriental languages in the University of St. Andrews. In 1840 he published grammars of the Syriac and Chaldee languages. He was also the author of a poem, "The Thane of Fife" (1822), a tragedy, "Cardinal Beaton" (1823), and a drama, "John Balliol" (1825), but their success was indifferent.—SANDERS, LLOYD C., *ed.*, 1887, *Celebrities of the Century*, p. 977.

ANSTER FAIR

1812

The author of "Anster Fair," cannot long remain concealed. It contains, in my opinion, unequivocal marks of strong original genius; a vein of humour of an uncommon cast, united with a talent for natural description of the most vivid and characteristic species, and, above all, a true feeling of the sublime—forming altogether one of the most pleasing and singular combinations of the different powers of poetry that I have ever met with.—WOODHOUSELEE, LORD, 1812, *Letter to William Cockburn, August.*

The great charm of this singular composition consists, no doubt, in the profusion of images and groupes which it thrusts upon the fancy, and the crowd and hurry and animation with which they are all jostled and driven along; but this, though a very rare merit in any modern production, is entitled perhaps to less distinction than the perpetual sallies and outbreakings of a rich and poetical imagination, by which the homely themes on which the author is professedly employed are constantly ennobled or contrasted, and in which the ardour of a mind evidently fitted for higher tasks is somewhat capriciously expanded. It is this frequent kindling of the diviner spirit—this tendency to rise above the trivial subjects among which he has chosen to disport himself, and this power of connecting grand or beautiful conceptions with the representation of vulgar objects or ludicrous occurrences, that first recommended this poem to our notice, and still seem to us to entitle it to more general notoriety. The author is occupied, no doubt, in general, with low matters, and bent upon homely mirth;—but his genius soars up every now and then in spite of him;—and "his delights"—to use a quaint expression of Shakespeare—

"his delights
Are dolphin-like, and show their backs above
The element they move in."

—JEFFREY, FRANCIS LORD, 1814, *Anster Fair, Edinburgh Review, vol.* 24, *p.* 176.

William Tennant, in his very original poem of "Anster Fair," gave Frere and Byron more than a hint for "Whistle-craft" and "Beppo;" nor is it unjust to say that the imitators have not at all equalled the life, the naïveté, the ludicrous dashed with the solemn, and the witty with both, which characterize the poet of Dollar. — CUNNINGHAM, ALLAN, 1833, *Biographical and Critical History of the Literature of the Last Fifty Years.*

Tennant's first was, beyond all comparson, also his best poem.—MOIR, D. M., 1851-52, *Sketches of the Poetical Literature of the Past Half-Century.*

There was classic imagery on familiar subjects—supernatural machinery (as in the "Rape of the Lock") blended with the ordinary details of domestic life, and with lively and fanciful description. An exuberance of animal spirits seemed to carry the author over the most perilous ascents, and his wit and fancy were rarely at fault. Such a pleasant sparkling volume, in a style then unhackneyed, was sure of success. . . . "Anster Fair" is the most diversified and richly humorous of them all, and besides being an animated, witty and agreeable poem, it has the merit of being the first work of the kind in our language.—CHAMBERS, ROBERT, 1876, *Cyclopædia of English Literature, ed. Carruthers.*

The author of "Anster Fair," is an extraordinary instance of a single-poem poet. . . . Whether Tennant's poetic vein was exhausted, or crushed beneath his weight of learning, or simply abandoned as out of keeping with his grave and reverend professorial character, we have no means of knowing. The abundance and freshness of the vein almost negatives the hypothesis of exhaustion. Even when read after "Don Juan," "Anster Fair" must excite admiration by the flexibility and rapid freedom of its verse. There is no trace of poverty in the ornaments embroidered on the fantastically cut garment, the artist runs riot in the wealth of his fantastic imagination, spending prodigally as if from an inexhaustible purse. Tennant had told us himself that it was in laughing over "Peebles to the Play" the humorous extravaganza ascribed to James I. of Scotland, that the first thought of "Anster Fair" occurred to him, and his diction shows that he was a delighted student of Spenser and Shakespeare. It was probably from these native sources and not from the Italian masters that he drew his inspiration. His discipleship to Spenser is proclaimed in the Alexandrine with which he closes his eight-rhyme stanza. But he was no mere imitator and copyist; home-grown popular legends and popular sports supplied him with his materials, and he handled them boldly in his own fashion, transporting them into a many-colored atmosphere of humorous imagination.—MINTO, WILLIAM, 1880, *The English Poets, ed. Ward, vol.* IV, *p.* 304.

There are few poems of equal merit that are less known than "Anster Fair." The earliest and only success of its author, it obtained a ready and hearty recognition benorth the Tweed, but its general reputation has never been at all commensurate with its excellence. . . . It is characterised by a vivacious freshness which nearly a hundred years have failed to destroy; a wealth of fancy that bubbles up with inexhaustible profusion, and sparkles with undimmed lustre still; an exuberance of animal spirits which is yet contagious; and an imagination prismatic in its outlook and kaleidoscopic in its rapidity of change. It is difficult to understand why it should be so little known, and still more difficult to think it can ever fail to interest while the eye loves colour and the heart loves fun.—MILES, ALFRED H., 1892, *The Poets and the Poetry of the Century, Southey to Shelley, pp.* 285, 290.

Sarah Flower Adams
1805–1848

She was born Feb. 22d, 1805; married William Bridges Adams, engineer, in 1834; and died of decline in August, 1848. Her life, so far as known to the world, is summed up in the authorship of her drama "Vivia Perpetua" (1841) and her connection with the congregation of Finsbury Unitarian Chapel, under the pastorate of William Johnson Fox. The musical service was organised, and a large proportion of the hymns set to music, by Mrs. Adams's sister; while she herself enriched the collection with many original and translated pieces. Among them was "Nearer, my God, to Thee," which divides with Cardinal Newman's "Lead, kindly Light," the distinction of being at once the most popular and the most poetical modern hymn. One is reminded of Dryden's famous lines; but the feats of the male and the female minstrel were in this instance reversed; for it is Mrs. Adams who "raises the mortal to the skies," and Cardinal Newman who "draws the angel down."—GARNETT, RICHARD, 1892, *The Poets and the Poetry of the Century, Joanna Baillie to Mathilde Blind, ed. Miles, p.* 141.

PERSONAL

There were women too: among them, Mrs. Adams, author of remembered hymns, and of that forgotten drama of "Vivia Perpetua,"—a creature whose beauty and enthusiasm drew around her the flower of the liberal party; the friend of Hunt and Carlyle and W. J. Fox, and of Browning in his eager youth. Of many such as these, in whom the lyrical aspiration was checked by too profuse admixture with a passion for affairs, for active life, for arts of design, or for some ardent cause to which they became devoted, or who failed, through extreme sensibility, to be calm among the turbid elements about them,—of such it may be asked, where are they and their productions, except in the tender memory and honor of their early comrades and friends?—STEDMAN, EDMUND CLARENCE, 1875–87, *Victorian Poets, p.* 257.

The sisters were two of the most beautiful women of their day, daughters of Benjamin Flower, editor of the *Cambridge Intelligencer*, the earliest of our liberal newspapers. They had been friends of Browning in his young manhood,—the first to recognize and call attention to his genius. To me their friendship, a love as of two elder sisters, too soon to be interrupted by their death (that of Eliza Flower in December, 1846, and of Mrs. Adams in 1848, a year and a half later), was indeed a liberal education. With their love and feeling for music and pictorial art, and their high poetic thought, they were such women in their purity, intelligence, and high-souled enthusiasm, as Shelley might have sung as fitted to redeem a world by their very presence.—LINTON, W. J., 1894, *Threescore and Ten Years, p.* 25.

GENERAL

Her celebrated hymn, "Nearer, my God, to Thee;" founded on Jacob's dream, recorded in Genesis, was contributed in 1841 to a Unitarian collection of "Hymns and Anthems," edited by William J. Fox, preacher and member of Parliament. Few hymns have been so widely popular. It has been adopted by all Christian sects, and translated into various languages, adapted to the tune of "Bethany." Professor Hitchcock relates that as he and his travelling companions rounded their way down the foot-hills of Mount Lebanon in 1870, they came in sight of a group of fifty Syrian students, who were singing in Arabic this beautiful hymn to this familiar tune.—SARGENT, EPES, 1880–81, *Harper's Cyclopædia of British and American Poetry.*

All she wrote displays a very feeling heart, some overstrained enthusiasm, and a taste which would have been much improved by a more extended degree of cultivation; but she was too much surrounded by members of a school which, while it fairly brought out the mental power of all who belonged to it, required, it may be said, great native force of character to prevent its on the whole exerting a narrowing influence, moral or mental, over those who belonged to it. To some degree, it *enchained* those whom it had before set free. Whether Mrs. Adams would have asserted a higher power than any displayed during her lifetime had that life been spared, we do not know; but there was so much of pure and beautiful feeling whenever she escaped from mannerism, that we are permitted to believe it most firmly.—TAYLOR, EMILY, 1884, *Memories of Contemporary Poets, p.* 124.

Her dramatic attempt is essentially lyrical. "Vivia Perpetua" is unsatisfactory as a play, but has deep human interest as an idealised representation of the authoress's mind and heart. In the character of Vivia she has shadowed forth her own moral affections and intellectual convictions, and the intensity of her feelings frequently exalts her diction, else artless and slightly conventional, into genuine eloquence. The moral charm, however, takes precedence of the artistic, as is to be expected in the work of a true woman. Lyrical enthusiasm atones in no small measure for the lack of the constructive faculty, and "Vivia Perpetua" fulfils better than many more ambitious works Milton's demand that poetry should be "simple, sensuous, and passionate." The authoress would probably have left a higher reputation if she had given freer scope to her natural instinct for lyrical poetry, instead of devoting the most strenuous endeavor to the difficult undertaking of reviving the poetical drama.—GARNETT, RICHARD, 1892, *The Poets and the Poetry of the Century, Joanna Baillie to Mathilde Blind, ed. Miles, p* 143.

Dear Mr. Stead,—The Prince of Wales desires me to thank you for your letter, and to say that he fully appreciates the compliment you pay him when you ask him to assist you in your proposed work. His Royal Highness would have gladly lent his aid if it had been in his power, but he fears that an opportunity for doing so will hardly be given him. He directs me to mention that among serious hymns he thinks there is none more touching nor one that goes more truly to the heart than No. 7 on your list: "Nearer, my God, to Thee." —KNOLLYS, FRANCIS, 1895, *To Mr. Stead, Dec.* 29; *Hymns that Have Helped, ed. Stead, p.* 158.

"Nearer, my God, to Thee" was written by a woman, that woman a Unitarian, and that Unitarian the daughter of a couple who first met in Newgate Gaol, where her father had been sent to lie for six months as atonement for the heinous crime of defending the French Revolution and criticising the political conduct of a certain Bishop Watson, now fortunately forgotten. Perhaps the sole permanent result and chief end of this Bishop Watson's life was to contribute remotely and unintentionally to the production of this hymn. He was a not unimportant link in the chain of circumstances of which this hymn, with its far-reaching influence, is but the latest outcome.—STEAD, W. T., 1897, *Hymns that Have Helped, p.* 158.

Sarah Flower Adams is sure of at least a small niche in the temple of the English poets were it but the beautiful hymn, "Nearer, my God, to Thee." Her "Vivia Perpetua" is an ill-constructed drama, partly redeemed by fine passages. — WALKER, HUGH, 1897, *The Age of Tennyson, p.* 256.

Frederick Marryat

1792-1848

Born, in Westminster, 10 July 1792. Educated at private schools. Entered Navy, Sept. 1806. At sea, 1806–15; Lieut., Dec. 1812; Commander, June 1815. Royal Humane Society's Medal for saving life, 1818. Married Catherine Shairp, Jan. 1819. F. R. S., 1819. At sea, 1820–26. Post-Captain, 1826. C. B., 26 Dec. 1826. At sea, 1828–30. Resigned command, 1830. Equerry to Duke of Sussex, 1830. Edited "Metropolitan Mag.," 1832–35. French Legion of Honour, 1833. On Continent, mainly at Brussels, 1836. In America, 1837–38. In London, 1839–43. At Langham, Norfolk, 1843-48. Died there, 9 Aug. 1848. *Works:* "Suggestions for the Abolition of . . . Impressment," 1822; "The Naval Officer" (anon.), 1829; "The King's Own" (anon.), 1830; "Newton Forster" (anon.; from "Met. Mag."), 1832; "Peter Simple" (anon.; from "Met. Mag."), 1834; "Jacob Faithful" (anon.; from "Met. Mag."), 1834; "The Pacha of Many Tales" (anon.), 1835; "Mr. Midshipman Easy" (from "Met. Mag."), 1836; "Japhet in Search of a Father" (anon.; from "Met. Mag."), 1836; "The Pirate and the Three Cutters," 1836; "Snarleyyow," 1837; "The Phantom Ship," 1839; "A Diary in America," (2 series), 1839; "Olla Podrida," 1840; "Poor Jack," 1840; "Joseph Rushbrook," 1841; "Masterman Ready," 1841; "Percival Keene," 1842; "Narrative of the Travels and Adventures of Monsieur Violet," 1843; "The Settlers in Canada," 1844; "The Mission," 1845; "The Privateer's Man," 1846;

"The Children of the New Forest," 1847. *Posthumous:* "The Little Savage" (2 pts.), 1848–49; "Valerie," 1849; "The Floral Telegraph" [1850?]. He *edited:* "Rattlin the Reefer" [by Hon. E. G. C. Howard], 1836. *Collected Novels:* 1896, etc. *Life:* "Life and Letters" by Florence Marryat, 1872; life by D. Hannay, 1889.—SHARP, R. FARQUHARSON, 1897, *A Dictionary of English Authors, p.* 186.

PERSONAL

North.—"A captain in the navy, and an honour to it—an admirable sailor, and an admirable writer—and would that he too were with us on the leads, my lads, for a pleasanter fellow, *to those who know him,* never enlivened the social board."—WILSON, JOHN, 1834, *Noctes Ambrosianæ, Blackwood's Magazine, vol.* 36, *p.* 122.

Although not handsome, Captain Marryat's personal appearance was very prepossessing. In figure he was upright and broad shouldered for his height, which measured 5 ft. 10 in. His hands, without being undersized, were remarkably perfect in form, and modelled by a sculptor at Rome on account of their symmetry. The character of his mind was borne out by his features, the most salient expression of which was the frankness of an open heart. The firm decisive mouth, and massive thoughtful forehead, were redeemed from heaviness by the humorous light that twinkled in his deep-set grey eyes, which, bright as diamonds, positively flashed out their fun, or their reciprocation of the fun of others. As a young man, dark crisp curls covered his head; but later in life, when, having exchanged the sword for the pen and the ploughshare, he affected a soberer and more patriarchal style of dress and manner, he wore his grey hair long, and almost down to his shoulders. His eyebrows were not alike, one being higher up and more arched than the other, which peculiarity gave his face a look of inquiry, even in repose. In the upper lip was a deep cleft and in his chin as deep a dimple —a pitfall for the razor, which, from the ready growth of his dark beard, he was often compelled to use twice a day. Like most warm-hearted people he was quick to take offence, and no one could have decided, after an absence of six months, with whom he was friends and with whom he was not.—MARRYAT, FLORENCE, 1872, *Life and Letters of Captain Marryat, vol.* II, *p.* 120.

GENERAL

I have received a great deal of pleasure from some of the modern novels, especially Captain Marryat's "Peter Simple." That book is nearer Smollett than any I remember.—COLERIDGE, SAMUEL TAYLOR, 1834, *Table Talk, March* 5, *ed. Ashe, p.* 276.

If it were put upon me to define Captain Marryat as an author, and to mark him with an appropriate epithet, I should say that he is a pleasant writer. His leading excellence is the untiring verve of his light, easy, and flowing pen, together with a keen sense of the ridiculous, which, while it rarely leads him into broad and unmeaning farce, effectually preserves him from taking a dull, sententious, or matter of-fact view either of men or things. His productions seem to cost him so little that one thinks he might write on for a life uninterruptedly, "eating, drinking, and sleeping hours excepted," and so probably he will till the *canvas* is totally exhausted. That there is no trace of effort in anything he does is in itself a charm. But after all his great and peculiar excellence is his originality—that he is himself alone; and that as he borrows from nobody, so on the other hand nobody can safely borrow from him. — CAMPBELL, THOMAS, 1834? *New Monthly Magazine.*

Captain Marryat stands second in merit to no living novelist but Miss Edgeworth. His happy delineations and contrasts of character, and easy play of native fun, redeem a thousand faults of verbosity, clumsiness, and coarseness. His strong sense and utter superiority to affectation of all sorts command respect; and in his quiet effectiveness of circumstantial narrative he sometimes approaches old Defoe.—LOCKHART, JOHN GIBSON, 1839, *Travels in North America, Quarterly Review, vol.* 64, *p.* 308.

He has always been a very popular writer in the most rigorous sense of the word. His books are essentially "mediocre." His ideas are the common property of the mob, and have been their common property time out of mind. We look throughout his writings in vain for the slightest indication of originality, for the faintest incentive to thought. His plots, his language, his opinions, are neither adapted nor intended for scrutiny.—POE,

EDGAR ALLAN, 1841, *Literary Criticism, Works, ed. Stedman and Woodberry, vol.* VII, *p.* 79.

Foremost amongst the novelists who really do "draw from life," is Captain Marryat. Were it necessary to seek any excuse for occasional blemishes in his tales, the best that could be found is, that they are, more or less, indigenous of the soil he turns up. The life-like earnestness of his sketches may generally be urged with confidence in vindication of any faults which may be detected in them by prudish or captious readers. Captain Marryat is the antipodes of a fine writer. His English is always rough-cast, and his style frequently crude and slovenly. But this negligence of forms only heightens the substantial interest of the matter. He tells a story like one who has his heart in it, and who is indifferent to everything but his facts. The veracity of his fictions, if we may use the expression, constitutes their permanent charm. Few novelists have ever more distinctly shown, that the secret of success in works of this description is close adherence to nature. There are no dramatic perplexities in his books, no fluent descriptions, no turgid appeals to the imagination: his narratives are simple and progressive; he never uses a word more than he actually wants; and the class from which he generally selects his characters, cannot certainly be considered very attractive to the public at large. Yet his novels are read with breathless curiosity in the most refined circles, as well as in those to whose sympathies they are more directly addressed.—HORNE, RICHARD HENGIST, 1844, *A New Spirit of the Age, p.* 142.

At the head of our marine novelists stands Captain Marryat, one of the most easy, lively, and truly humorous story-tellers we possess. One of the chief elements of his talent is undoubtedly the tone of high, effervescent, irrepressible animal spirits which characterizes everything he has written. He seems as if he sat down to compose without having formed the least idea of what he is going to say, and sentence after sentence seems to flow from his pen without thought, without labour, and without hesitation. He seems half tipsy with the very gaiety of his heart, and never scruples to introduce the most grotesque extravagances of character, language, and event, provided they are likely to excite a laugh. This would produce absurdity and failure as often as laughter, were it not that he has a natural *tact* and judgment in the ludicrous; and this happy audacity—this hit-or-miss boldness—serves him admirably well. . . . Marryat's narratives are exceedingly inartificial, and often grossly improbable; but we read on with gay delight, never thinking of the story, but only solicitous to follow the droll adventures, and laugh at the still droller characters. . . . He is generally faithful to reality, and shows an extensive if not very deep knowledge of what his old waterman calls "human natur."—SHAW, THOMAS B., 1847, *Outlines of English Literature, pp.* 398, 399.

His merits lie upon the surface, and are obvious to every man, woman, and child, who take up one of his works and find themselves unable to lay it down again. He tells plainly and straightforwardly a story, tolerably well constructed, of diversified incidents, alive with uncommon characters, and, as his experience was large and had been acquired over a wide expanse, he had always something to tell which would excite curiosity or rivet attention. He had one quality in common with great men, and in which men of finer genius than himself have been deficient,—a thorough manliness of heart and soul, which, by clearly shewing him what he was able to accomplish, preserved him against the perpetration of that sublime nonsense and drivelling cant which now-a-days often pass for fine writing and fine sentiment.—WHITEHEAD, CHARLES, 1848, *Memoir of Captain Marryat, R. N., Bentley's Miscellany, vol.* 24, *p.* 529.

Captain Marryat turned his leisure to very profitable literary account. He may be said to have created a new kind of novel literature, illustrative of naval life; and in that line, though followed and imitated by many, he has been equaled by none. The excellence of his productions, and the great success they met with, considering the large number of them, is remarkable. —MADDEN, R. R., 1855, *The Literary Life and Correspondence of the Countess of Blessington, vol.* II, *p.* 310.

Captain Marryat did make large sums by his writings—by the most popular of which, alone, he realized a fortune of £20,000. The following figures show what he received on first publishing the manuscripts:

		£
1839	Diary in America	1600
1837	Snarley Yow	1300
1836	Midshipman Easy	1200
1832	Peter Simple	1100
1833	Jacob Faithful	1100
1834	Japhet	1100
1834	Pacha of Many Tales . . .	1100

—MARRYAT, FLORENCE, 1872, *Life and Letters of Captain Marryat, vol.* II, *p.* 238.

Captain Marryat, . . . regarded his art with the eyes of a sea officer. The broad arrow is visible—like a water-mark—on every page of his papers. . . . One of the somewhat melancholy pleasures of middle age is to go deliberately through the novels which turned your head when you were a boy, and to see how you like them. Often the result of the experiment is to make you sorry you undertook it. But Marryat bears the test. To be sure, he no longer gives you a wild longing to breathe the free air of the ocean. You have long since reconciled yourself to the fact that your flag will never be seen flying from any mast-head, nor saluted with fifteen guns from any saluting battery. Perhaps, too, the physical changes of life indispose you to attempt ascending to a top, even by Lubber's Hole, much less by the futtock-shrouds. But you can thoroughly enjoy your *Marryat* without wondering at your old enthusiasm, and above all, without being ashamed of it. This man did you no harm with sensuality disguised as sentimentalism, or philosophy empty and gaudy as toy-bladders. He stirred your blood not by putting drugs into it, but as exercise stirs it, as fresh air stirs it. Patriotism, manliness, firm friendship, good faith, kindliness—these are Marryat's "ideals;" and the scenes on which they appear are bathed in the jolliest humour—the humour of common life, and every-day sympathy, exhilarating as sunshine itself.—HANNAY, JAMES, 1873, *Sea Novels, Captain Marryat, Cornhill Magazine, vol.* 27, *pp.* 176, 179.

In the hasty production of so many volumes, the *quality* could not always be equal. The nautical humour and racy dialogue could not always be produced at will of a new and different stamp at each successive effort. Such, however, was the fertile fancy and active observation of the author, and his lively powers of amusing and describing, that he has fewer repetitions and less tediousness than almost any other writer equally voluminous.—CHAMBERS, ROBERT, 1876, *Cyclopædia of English Literature, ed. Carruthers.*

Is the chronicler *par excellence* of naval exploits.—OLIPHANT, MARGARET O. W., 1892, *The Victorian Age of English Literature, ch.* vi.

As a writer Marryat has been variously judged, but his position as a story-teller is assured. He drew the material of his stories from his professional experience and knowledge; the terrible shipwreck, for instance, in "The King's Own," is a coloured version of the loss of the Droits de l'homme and Mr. Chucks was still known in the flesh to the generation that succeeded Marryat. As a tale of naval adventure, "Frank Mildmay" was avowedly autobiographical, and there can be little doubt that Marryat's contemporaries could have fitted other names to Captain Kearney, or to Captain To, or to Lieutenant Oxbelly. Marryat has made his sailors live, and has given his incidents a real and absolute existence. It is in this, and in the rollicking sense of fun and humour which pervades the whole, that the secret of his success lay; for, with the exception perhaps of "The King's Own," his plots are poor.—LAUGHTON, J. K., 1893, *Dictionary of National Biography, vol.* XXXVI, *p.* 203.

The works of Captain Marryatt and Samuel Lover require at least a reference, for the boys who read with delight the stories of Leatherstocking and Long Tom Coffin contrived somehow to make acquaintance with Peter Simple and Handy Andy and Mr. Midshipman Easy. To the generation of yesterday at least, these personages are almost as classic, if not quite so classical, as their predecessors. Though more careless in language and less discreet of demeanor, they linger nevertheless in affectionate memory along with the heroes of Cooper and Scott.—SIMONDS, WILLIAM EDWARD, 1894, *An Introduction to the Study of English Fiction, p.* 64.

A rather careless and incorrect writer, and liable to fits both of extravagance and dulness. But the spirit and humour of the best of his books throughout, and the best parts of the others, are unmistakable and unsurpassed. Nor should it be forgotten that he had a rough but racy gift of verse, the best, though by no means the only good example of which is the piece beginning, "The Captain stood on the carronade."—SAINTSBURY, GEORGE, 1896, *A History of Nineteenth Century Literature*, p. 157.

Upon the whole, one finds no large or fine literary quality in his books; but the *fun* in them is positive, and catching—as our aunts and uncles used to find it; but it is the fun of the tap-room, and of the for'-castle, rather than of the salon, or the library. For all this, scores and scores of excellent old people were shaking their sides—in the early part of this century over the pages of Captain Marryat.—MITCHELL, DONALD G., 1897, *English Lands Letters and Kings, The Later Georges to Victoria*, p. 283.

There is no affectation, no pretentiousness, in Marryat. Through his breezy style there blows the freshness of an Atlantic gale, rude and boisterous, but invigorating. He is moreover the best painter of the naval life of that day, and the fact that it has passed away for ever, by closing the subject to future writers, or condemning them to write at second-hand, gives to his works a special promise of permanence. . . . His plots are rough but sufficient; his characters show little penetration; but the habit of drawing from the life prevented him from going far wrong.—WALKER, HUGH, 1897, *The Age of Tennyson*, p. 79.

Not only is Marryat the most delightful of writers for boys, but it is interesting to note that both Carlyle and Ruskin during long terms of illness solaced themselves with his wonderful sea-stories.—SHORTER, CLEMENT K., 1897, *Victorian Literature, Sixty Years of Books and Bookmen*, p. 67.

Edgar Allan Poe

1809–1849

January 19, 1809—Born at Boston, Massachusetts. December 8, 1811—His mother died at Richmond, Virginia. 1811—[Edgar Poe adopted by Mr. John Allan]. 1816—Brought to Europe, and placed at school in Stoke Newington. 1821—Returns to the United States. 1822—Placed at school in Richmond, Virginia. February 1, 1826—Enters University of Virginia. [Signs matriculation book, 14th February 1826]. December 15, 1826—Leaves University of Virginia. 1827—"Tamerlane and other Poems" printed at Boston. June? 1827—Departs for Europe. March, 1829—Returns to Richmond, Virginia. 1829—Publishes "Al Aaraaf, Tamerlane, and Minor Poems," at Baltimore. July 1, 1830—Admitted as cadet to West Point Military Academy. March 6, 1831—Dismissed the Military Academy. March, 1831—Publishes "Poems," New York. Autumn, 1833—Gains prize from *Saturday Visitor* (Baltimore). December, 1835—Editor of the *Southern Literary Messenger* (Richmond, Virginia). May 16, 1836—Married to his cousin, Virginia Clemm, at Richmond. [Virginia C. born August 13th, 1822]. January, 1837—Resigns editorship of *Southern Literary Messenger*. 1837-8—Resides in New York. July, 1838—"Arthur Gordon Pym" published, New York and London. Autumn, 1838—Removes to Philadelphia. July, 1839—Editor of the *Gentleman's Magazine*, Philadelphia. 1840—"Tales of the Grotesque and Arabesque" published, Philadelphia. 1840—"The Conchologist's First Book" published, Philadelphia. June, 1840—Resigns editorship of *Gentleman's Magazine*. January, 1841—Editor of *Graham's Magazine*, Philadelphia. April, 1842, Resigns editorship of *Graham's Magazine*. Spring, 1843—Gains $100 prize for "The Gold Bug." Autumn, 1844—Sub-editor of the *Evening Mirror*, New York. January 29, 1845—"The Raven" published in *Evening Mirror*. February 28, 1845—Lectures in New York Historical Society's room. March 8, 1845—Joint-editor of the *Broadway Journal*. July, 1845—"Tales" published, New York and London. July, 1845—Sole-editor of the *Broadway Journal*. November 1, 1845—Proprietor of *Broadway Journal*. November, 1845—"The Raven and Other Poems" published, New York and London. Winter, 1845—Lectures at Boston Lyceum. December, 1845—*Broadway Journal* disposed of. February, 1846—"The Literati" begun in Godey's *Lady's Book*. June 23, 1846—*Evening Mirror* publishes libel. June 28, 1846—"Reply" to libel in Philadelphia *Saturday Gazette*. Summer, 1846—Removes to Fordham. January 30, 1847—His wife dies. February 17, 1847—Gains libel suit against *Evening*

EDGAR ALLAN POE

Engraving by F. Halpin.

SARAH MARGARET FULLER

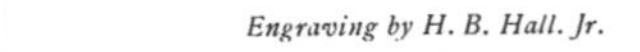

Engraving by H. B. Hall. Jr.

Mirror. February 3, 1848—Lectures in New York Historical Society's room. Summer, 1848—"Eureka" published, New York. Summer, 1848—Richmond, Virginia, revisited. Summer, 1848—Lectures at Lowell, Mass., and Providence, R. I. October, 1848—Betrothed to Mrs. Whitman. December, 1848—Engagement with Mrs. Whitman broken off. June 30, 1849—Departs for the South. Autumn, 1849—In Richmond and neighbourhood. October 7, 1849—Dies at Baltimore, Maryland. November 17, 1875—Monument Inaugurated, Baltimore.—INGRAM, JOHN H., 1880, *Edgar Allan Poe, His Life, Letters and Opinions, vol.* I, *p.* xi.

PERSONAL

Dear Sir—Poe did right in referring to me. He is very clever with his pen—classical and scholarlike. He wants experience and direction, but I have no doubt he can be made very useful to you. And, poor fellow! he is *very* poor. I told him to write something for every number of your magazine, and that you might find it to your advantage to give him some permanent employ. He has a volume of very bizarre tales in the hands of ——, in Philadelphia, who for a year past has been promising to publish them. This young fellow is highly imaginative, and a little given to the *terrific*. He is at work on a tragedy, but I have turned him to drudging upon whatever may make money, and I have no doubt you and he will find your account in each other.—KENNEDY, JOHN PENDLETON, 1835, *Letter to J. W. White, April* 13; *Poe Memorial, ed. Rice, p.* 13.

Edgar A. Poe (you know him by character, no doubt, if not personally), has become one of the strangest of our literati. He and I are old friends,—have known each other since boyhood, and it gives me inexpressible pain to notice the vagaries to which he has lately become subject. Poor fellow! he is not a teetotaller by any means, and I fear he is going headlong to destruction, moral, physical and intellectual.—WILMER, L. A., 1843, *Letter to Mr. Tomlin, May* 20; *Passages from the Correspondence and Other Papers of Rufus W. Griswold, p.* 143.

He really does not possess one tithe of greatness which he seems to regard as an uncomfortable burden. He mistakes coarse abuse for polished invective, and vulgar insinuation for sly satire. He is not alone thoroughly unprincipled, base, and depraved, but silly, vain, and ignorant,—not alone an assassin in morals, but a quack in literature. His frequent quotations from languages of which he is entirely ignorant, and his consequent blunders, expose him to ridicule; while his cool plagiarisms, from known or forgotten writers, excite the public amazement. He is a complete evidence of his own assertion, that "no spectacle can be more pitiable than that of a man without the commonest school education, busying himself in attempts to instruct mankind on topics of polite literature."—ENGLISH, THOMAS DUNN, 1846, *New York Evening Mirror*.

My Dear Heart—My Dear Virginia—Our mother will explain to you why I stay away from you this night. I trust the interview I am promised will result in some *substantial good* for me—for your dear sake and hers—keep up your heart in all hopefulness, and trust yet a little longer. On my last great disappointment I should have lost my courage *but for you*—my little darling wife. You are my *greatest* and *only* stimulus now, to battle with this uncongenial, unsatisfactory, and ungrateful life. I shall be with you to-morrow [illegible] P. M., and be assured until I see you I will keep in *loving remembrance* your *last words*, and your fervent prayer! Sleep well, and may God grant you a peaceful summer with your devoted Edgar.—POE, EDGAR ALLAN, 1846, *Letter to Mrs. Poe, June* 12; *Life, Letters and Opinions, ed. Ingram, vol.* II, *p.* 88.

Edgar Allan Poe is dead. He died in Baltimore on Sunday, October 7th. This announcement will startle many, but few will be grieved by it. . . . His conversation was at times almost supra-mortal in its eloquence. His voice was modulated with astonishing skill, and his large and variably expressive eyes looked repose or shot fiery tumult into theirs who listened, while his own face glowed, or was changeless in pallor, as his imagination quickened his blood or drew it back frozen to his heart. His imagery was from the worlds which no mortals can see but with the vision of genius.—Suddenly starting from a proposition, exactly and sharply defined, in terms of utmost simplicity and clearness, he rejected the forms of customary logic, and by a crystalline process of accretion, built up his acular demonstrations in forms of gloomiest and ghastliest grandeur, or in those of the most airy and delicious beauty—so minutely and distinctly, yet so rapidly, that the attention which was yielded to him was chained till it stood among his wonderful creations—till he himself dissolved the spell, and brought his hearers back to common and base existence, by vulgar fancies or exhibitions of the ignoblest passion. He was at all times a dreamer—dwelling in ideal realms—in heaven or hell—peopled with the creatures and the accidents of his brain. He walked the streets, in madness or melancholy, with lips moving in indistinct curses, or with eyes upturned in passionate prayer (never for himself, for he felt, or professed to feel, that he was already damned, but) for their happiness who at the moment were objects of his idolatry;—or, with his glances introverted to a heart gnawed with anguish, and with a face shrouded in gloom, he would brave the wildest storms; and all night, with drenched garments and arms beating the winds and rains, would speak as if to spirits that at such times only could be evoked by him from the Aidenn, close by whose portals his disturbed soul sought to forget the ills to which his constitution subjected him—close by the Aidenn where were those he loved—the Aidenn which he might never see, but in fitful glimpses, as its gates opened to receive the less fiery and more happy natures whose destiny to sin did not involve the doom of death.—GRISWOLD, RUFUS WILMOT (LUDWIG), 1849, *The Death of Edgar A. Poe, New York Tribune.*

They now appreciate him and will do justice to his beloved memory. They propose to raise a monument to his memory. Some of the papers, indeed, nearly all, do him justice. I enclose this article from a Baltimore paper. But this, my dear Annie, will not restore him. Never, oh, never, will I see those dear lovely eyes. I feel *so desolate, so wretched, friendless, and alone*. . . . I have a beautiful letter from General Morris; he did, indeed, love him. He has many friends, but of what little consequence to him *now*. I have to go out home—to his home to-day, to arrange his papers. Oh, what will I not suffer.—CLEMM, MRS. MARIA, 1849, *Letter to "Annie," Oct.* 13; *Edgar Allan Poe, his Life, Letters and Opinions, ed. Ingram, vol.* II, *p.* 240.

Residing as he did in the country, we never met Mr. Poe in hours of leisure; but he frequently called on us afterwards at our place of business, and we met him often in the street—invariably the same sad-mannered, winning and refined gentleman, such as we had always known him. It was by rumor only, up to the day of his death, that we knew of any other development of manner or character. We heard, from one who knew him well (what should be stated in all mention of his lamentable irregularities) that, with a single glass of wine, his whole nature was reversed, the demon became uppermost, and, though none of the usual signs of intoxication were visible, his *will* was palpably insane. Possessing his reasoning faculties in excited activity, at such times, and seeking his acquaintances with his wonted look and memory, he easily seemed personating only another phase of his natural character, and was accused, accordingly, of insulting arrogance and bad-heartedness. In this reversed character, we repeat, it was never our chance to see him. We know it from hearsay, and we mention it in connection with this sad infirmity of physical constitution; which puts it upon very nearly the ground of a temporary and almost irresponsible insanity.—WILLIS, NATHANIEL PARKER, 1849, *Death of Edgar A. Poe, Home Journal, Oct.* 13; *Poe's Poems and Essays, Memorial, ed., p.* cxii.

I can sincerely say, that although I have frequently *heard* of aberrations on his part from the "straight and narrow path," I have never *seen* him otherwise than gentle, generous, well-bred, and fastidiously refined. To a sensitive and delicately-nurtured woman, there was a peculiar and irresistible charm in the chivalric, graceful, and almost tender reverence with which he invariably approached all women who won his respect. It was this which first commanded and always retained my regard for him. . . . It was in his owr simple yet poetical home, that to me the character of Edgar Poe appeared in its most beautiful light. Playful, affectionate, witty, alternately docile and wayward as a petted child—for his young, gentle, and idolized wife, and for all who came, he had, even in the midst of his most harassing literary duties, a kind word, a pleasant smile, a graceful and courteous attention. At his desk, beneath the romantic picture of his loved and lost Lenore, he would sit, hour after hour, patient, assiduous, and uncomplaining, tracing, in an exquisitely clear chirography, and with almost superhuman swiftness, the lightning thoughts—the "rare and radiant" fancies as they flashed through his wonderful and ever-wakeful brain.—OSGOOD, FRANCES SARGENT, 1850, *Reminiscences of Poe by Griswold, International Magazine, vol.* I.

Literature with him was religion; and he, its high-priest, with a whip of scorpions scourged the money-changers from the temple. In all else he had the docility and kind-heartedness of a child. No man was more quickly touched by a kindness—none more prompt to atone for an injury. For three or four years I knew him intimately, and for eighteen months saw him almost daily; much of the time writing or conversing at the same desk; knowing all his hopes, his fears and little annoyances of life, as well as his high-hearted struggle with adverse fate—yet he was always the same polished gentleman—the quiet, unobtrusive, thoughtful scholar—the devoted husband—frugal in his personal expenses—punctual and unwearied in his industry—*and the soul of honor* in all his transactions.—GRAHAM, GEORGE R., 1850, *To N. P. Willis, Feb.* 2; *Graham's Magazine.*

When first I looked into thy glorious eyes,
And saw, with their unearthly beauty pained,
Heaven deepening within heaven, like the skies
Of autumn nights without a shadow stained,
I stood as one whom some strange dream enthralls;
For, far away, in some lost life divine,
Some land which every glorious dream recalls,
A spirit looked on me with eyes like thine.
E'en now, though death has veiled their starry light,
And closed their lids in his relentless night—
As some strange dream, remembered in a dream,
Again I see, in sleep, their tender beam;
Unfading hopes their cloudless azure fill,
Heaven deepening within heaven, serene and still.

—WHITMAN, SARAH HELEN, 1850, *Poems, p.* 91.

We cannot dismiss this subject without paying our earnest tribute to the womanhood of the poet's chief friend, his wife's mother. To Mrs. Clemm will be awarded in the history of genius the rarest of all crowns, the wreath placed by God's hands—through his noblest creatures—on woman's beautiful and matron brow. Even in her lifetime she will receive the world's acknowledgment of her nobility of soul; and the tongues whom envy or shame froze in the life of her gifted but unhappy son-in-law, will thaw, and like the fable of old utter praises to the perished one, condemning their own wretched selves.—POWELL, THOMAS, 1850, *The Living Authors of America, p.* 122.

A fine, thoughtful face, with lineaments of delicacy, such as belong only to genius or high blood,—the forehead grand and pale; the eye dark, and gleaming with sensibility and soul; a face to inspire men with interest and curiosity.—HANNAY, JAMES, 1853, *Poetical Works of Edgar A. Poe, Life.*

In character he was certainly one of the strangest anomalies in the history of mankind. . . . He was no more a gentleman than he was a saint. His heart was as rotten as his conduct was infamous. He knew not what the terms honor and honorable meant. He had absolutely no virtue or good quality, unless you call remorse a virtue, and despair a grace. Some have called him mad; but we confess we see no evidence of this in his history. He showed himself, in many instances, a cool, calculating, deliberate blackguard. His intellect was of the clearest, sharpest, and most decisive kind. A large heart has often beat in the bosom of a debauchee; but Poe had not one spark of genuine tenderness, unless it were for his wife, whose heart, nevertheless, and constitution, he broke—hurrying her to a premature grave, that he might write "Annabel Lee" and "The Raven!" . . . He died, as he had lived, a raving, cursing, self-condemned, conscious cross between the fiend and the genius, believing nothing, hoping nothing, loving nothing, fearing nothing—himself his own god and his own devil—a solitary wretch, who had cut off every bridge that connected him with the earth around and the heavens above. This, however, let us say in his favor—he has died "alone in his iniquity;" he has never, save by his example (so far as we know his work), sought to shake faith or sap morality. His writings may be morbid, but they are pure. . . . He has gone far away from the misty mid-region of Weir; his dreams of cosmogonies have been tested by the searching light of eternity's truth; his errors have received the reward that was meet; and we cannot but say, ere we close, peace even to the well-nigh putrid dust of Edgar A. Poe.—GILFILLAN, GEORGE, 1855, *A Third Gallery of Portraits*, pp. 327, 330, 338.

A being full of misery, but all beaten out upon his own anvil; a man gifted as few are, but without faith or devotion, and without any earnest purpose in life. . . . What a torn record of a life it is! more sorrowful by far than that of our own Otway or Chatterton. Alternately a seraph and a brute,—an inspired poet and a grovelling sensualist,—a prophet and a drunkard,—his biography unfolds a tale of mingled admiration and horror, such as has been told of very few literary men.—SMILES, SAMUEL, 1860, *Brief Biographies*, pp. 334, 345.

A gushing youth once wrote me to this effect:—"Dear Sir: Among your literary treasures, you have doubtless preserved several autographs of our country's late lamented poet, Edgar A. Poe. If so, and you can spare one, please enclose it to me, and receive the thanks of yours truly." I promptly responded, as follows:—"Dear Sir: Among my literary treasures, there happens to be exactly *one* autograph of our country's late lamented poet, Edgar A. Poe. It is his note of hand for fifty dollars, with my indorsement across the back. It cost me exactly $50.75 (including protest), and you may have it for half that amount. Yours, respectfully." That autograph, I regret to say, remains on my hands, and is still for sale at first cost, despite the lapse of time, and the depreciation of our currency.—GREELEY, HORACE, 1868, *Recollections of a Busy Life*, p. 196

One of the younger poets who received substantial assistance from Mr. Halleck was Edgar A. Poe, to whom he loaned, in answer to an appeal, one hundred dollars, a sum which the gifted but unfortunate young singer, like many others of the rhyming fraternity, who received aid from the generous Halleck, was never able to repay.—WILSON, JAMES GRANT, 1869, *Life and Letters of Fitz-Greene Halleck*, p. 430.

Poe I have known for a whole month closeted in his house, all the time hard at work with his pen, poorly paid, and hard driven to keep the wolf from his slightly-fastened door; intruded on only by a few select friends, who always found him, what they knew him to be, a generous host, an affectionate son-in-law and husband,—in short, a respectable gentleman. . . . In the list of literary men there has been no such spiteful biographer as Rufus Griswold, and never such a victim of posthumous spite as poor Edgar Allan Poe. . . . A lady angelically beautiful in person, and not less beautiful in spirit. No one who remembers that dark-eyed, dark-haired daughter of Virignia,—her own name—her grace, her facial beauty, her demeanour, so modest as to be remarkable; no one who has ever spent an hour in her company, but will endorse what I have said. I remember how we, the friends of the poet, used to talk of her high qualities, and when we talked of her beauty, I well knew that the rose-tint upon her cheek was too bright, too pure to be of earth. It was consumption's colour, that sadly beautiful light that beckons to an early tomb.—REID, CAPTAIN MAYNE, 1869, *A Dead Man Defended, Onward, April.*

Edgar A. Poe I remember seeing on a single occasion. He announced a lecture to be delivered at the Society Library building on Broadway, under the title of the "Universe." It was a stormy night, and there were not more than sixty persons present in the lecture-room. I have seen no portrait of Poe that does justice to his pale, delicate, intellectual face and magnificent eyes. His lecture was a rhapsody of the most intense brilliancy. He appeared inspired, and his inspiration affected the scant audience almost painfully. He wore his coat tightly buttoned across his slender chest; his eyes seemed to glow like those of his own raven, and he kept us entranced for two hours and a half. The late Mr. Putnam, the publisher, told me that the next day the wayward, luckless poet presented himself to him with the manuscript of the "Universe." He told Putnam that in it he solved the whole problem of life; that it would immortalize its publisher as well as its author; and, what was of less consequence, that it would bring to him the fortune which he had so long and so vainly been seeking. Mr. Putnam, while an admirer of genius, was also a cool, calculating man of business. As such, he could not see the matter in exactly the same light as the poet did, and the only result of the interview was that he lent Poe a shilling to take him home to Fordham, where he then resided. —FIELD, MAUNSELL B., 1873, *Memories of Many Men and of Some Women, p.* 224.

Though Edgar Poe is one of the greatest masters of the gruesome who ever lived, there seems to be no reason in that at all for making any kind of assumption as to his character.—HUTTON, RICHARD HOLT, 1874, *Criticisms on Contemporary Thought and Thinkers, vol.* I, *p.* 61.

To
EDGAR ALLAN POE
Author of the Raven
and other Poems,
and of various works of Fiction,
Distinguished alike
for originality in the conception,
skill in word-painting,
and power over the mind of the reader,
THE PUBLIC SCHOOL TEACHERS
of
Baltimore,
admirers of his genius,
have erected this monument.

—BRYANT, WILLIAM CULLEN, 1875, *Inscription on Poe's Monument, Baltimore.*

Edgar Poe might have been, at this time, fifteen or sixteen—he being one of the oldest boys in the school, and I one of the youngest. His power and accomplishments captivated me, and something in me or in him made him take a fancy to me. In the simple school athletics of those days, where a gymnasium had not been heard of, he was *facile princeps.* He was a swift runner, a wonderful leaper, and what was more rare, a boxer, with some slight training. . . . For swimming he was noted, being in many of his athletic proclivities surprisingly like Byron in his youth. There was no one among the schoolboys who would so dare in the midst of the rapids of the James River. . . . In our Latin exercises in school, Poe was among the first—not first without dispute. . . . I remember that Poe was also a very fine French scholar. Yet with all his superiorities, he was not the master-spirit, nor even the favorite of the school. . . . Poe, as I recall my impressions now, was self-willed, capricious, inclined to be imperious, and though of generous impulses, not steadily kind or even amiable; and so what he would exact was refused to him. . . . Of Edgar Poe it was known that his parents were players, and that he was dependent upon the bounty that is bestowed upon an adopted son. All this had the effect of making the boys decline his leadership; and on looking back on it since, I fancy it gave him a fierceness he would otherwise not have had. . . . Not a little of Poe's time, in school and out of it, was occupied with writing verses. —PRESTON, COL. J. T. L., 1875, *Some Reminiscences of Edgar A. Poe as a Schoolboy, Poe Memorial, ed. Rice, pp.* 38, 40, 41.

The next number of the *Saturday Visitor* [1833] contained the "MS. Found in a Bottle," and announced the author. My office, in those days, was in the building still occupied by the Mechanics' Bank, and I was seated at my desk on the Monday following the publication of the tale, when a gentleman entered and introduced himself as the writer, saying that he came to thank me, as one of the committee, for the award in his favor. Of this interview, the only one I ever had with Mr. Poe, my recollection is very distinct indeed, and it requires but a small effort of imagination to place him before me now, as plainly almost as I see any one of my audience. He was, if anything, below the middle size, and yet could not be described as a small man. His figure was remarkably good, and he carried himself erect and well, as one who had been trained to it. He was dressed in black, and his frock-coat was buttoned to the throat, where it met the black stock, then almost universally worn. Not a particle of white was visible. Coat, hat, boots and gloves had very evidently seen their best days, but so far as mending and brushing go, everything had been done, apparently, to make them presentable. On most men his clothes would have looked shabby and seedy, but there was something about this man that prevented one from criticising his garments, and the details I have mentioned were only recalled afterwards. The impression made, however, was that the award in Mr. Poe's favor was not inopportune. *Gentleman* was written all over him. His manner was easy and quiet, and although he came to return thanks for what he regarded as deserving them, there was nothing obsequious in what he said or did. His features I am unable to describe in detail. His forehead was high and remarkable for the great development at the temple. This was the characteristic of his head, which you noticed at once, and which I have never forgotten. The expression of his face was grave, almost sad, except when he was engaged in conversation, when it became animated and changeable. His voice, I remember, was very pleasing in its tone and well modulated, almost rhythmical, and his words were well chosen and unhesitating.—LATROBE, JOHN H. B., 1875, *Reminiscences of Poe, Poe Memorial, ed. Rice, p.* 60.

I have resided and practised my profession of the law in Brooklyn for about thirty years. Shortly after I moved here, in 1845, Mr. Poe and I became personal friends. His last residence, and where I visited him oftenest, was in a beautifully secluded cottage at Fordham, fourteen miles above New York. It was there that I often saw his dear wife during her last illness, and attended her funeral. It was from there that he and his "dear Muddie" (Mrs. Clemm) often visited me at my house, frequently, and at my urgent solicitation, remaining many days. When he finally departed on his last trip south, the kissing and handshaking were at my front-door. He was hopeful; we were sad: and tears gushed in torrents as he kissed his "dear Muddie" and my wife, "good-bye." Alas, it proved, as Mrs. Clemm feared, a final adieu. . . . He was one of the most affectionate, kind-hearted men I ever knew. I never witnessed so much tender affection and devoted love as existed in that family of three persons. His dear Virginia, after her death, was his "lost Lenore." I have spent weeks in the closest intimacy with Mr. Poe, and I never saw him drink a drop of liquor, wine or beer, in my life; and never saw him under the slightest influence of any stimulants whatever. He was, in truth, a most abstemious and exemplary man. But I learned from Mrs. Clemm that if, on the importunity of a convivial friend, he took a single glass, even of wine, it suddenly flashed through his nervous system and excitable brain; and that he was no longer himself or responsible for his acts —LEWIS, S. D., 1875, *Letter to the Poe Memorial, Oct.* 11, *ed. Rice, p.* 86.

Edgar A. Poe was a wonderful man, and he has never had justice done him. Most happy should I be, if in my power, to witness the ceremony of the inauguration of his monument; for after all the abominable calumnies that have been circulated against him, both abroad and at home, he stands higher today in the estimation of kindred poets than he ever did while on earth.—NEAL, JOHN, 1875, *Letter to the Poe Memorial, ed. Rice, Nov.* 3, *p.* 89.

I knocked at the street-door, and was presently shown up to Poe's rooms, on the second or third floor. He received me very kindly. I told my errand, and he promised that my Ode should be printed next week. I was struck with his poetic manner, and the elegance of his appearance. He was slight and pale, I saw, with large luminous eyes, and was dressed in black. When I quitted the room, I could not but see his wife, who was lying on a bed, apparently asleep. She, too, was dressed in black, and was pale and wasted. "Poor lady," I thought, "she is dying of consumption." I was sad on her account, but glad on my own: for had I not seen a real live author, the great Edgar Allan Poe, and was not my Ode to be published at once in his paper? — STODDARD, RICHARD HENRY, 1875-84, *Life of Edgar Allan Poe, Poe's Works, vol.* I, *p.* 128.

Judging from these phenomena, as exhibited in his life and works, he habitually lived in a state bordering upon somnambulism—a disorder that cerebral epilepsy closely resembles. He was a denizen of two worlds and the remark of Dr. Maudsley, that the hereditary madman often gives the idea of a double being, rational and underanged when his consciousness is appealed to, and mastered by his unconscious life when left to his own devices, might have been written after a study of him. He lived and died a riddle to his friends. Those who had never seen him in a paroxysm (among them Mrs. Frances Sargent Osgood) could not believe that he was the perverse and vicious person painted in the circulated tales of his erratic doings. To those who had, he was two men—the one an abnormally wicked and profane reprobate, the other a quiet and dignified gentleman. The special, moral, and mental condition incident to cerebral epilepsy explains these apparent contradictions as felicitously as it elucidates the intellectual and psychical traits of his literature. Its mental phenomena supervene after a stage of incubation more or less prolonged, and the fit generally lasts two or three days. Its supervention is evinced by extreme susceptibility and impulsiveness. Tendency to repeat the same phrase over and over witnesses to the perversion of the will. Distressing delusions and hallucinations prompt to eccentric and impulsive acts. The face is livid, and the eyes have the expression of drunkenness. Monomania may supervene, or dipsomania, or erotomania—as when Poe was expelled from the house of Mr. Allan, his friend and benefactor. Finally, the sufferer falls into a prolonged sleep, easily mistaken for that of drunkenness, and wakes up with re-established sanity.—FAIRFIELD, FRANCIS GERRY, 1875, *A Mad Man of Letters, Scribner's Monthly, vol.* 10, *p.* 696.

There is no necessity for us to touch heavily upon this terrible *trait* in the character of Edgar Poe—this sad, sickening infirmity of his "lonesome latter years:" his error, if such it may be styled—the impulse which blindly impelled him to his destruction—injured no one but himself; but certainly no one before or since has suffered so severely in character as a consequence of such a fault. Other children of genius have erred far worse than Poe ever did, inasmuch as their derelictions have injured others; but with them the world has dealt leniently, accepting *their* genius as a compensation. But for poor Edgar Poe, who wronged no one but himself, the world, misled greatly, it is true, as to his real character, has hitherto had no mercy. The true story of his life has now been told; henceforth let him be judged justly; henceforth let his errors be forgotten, and to his name be assigned that place which is due to it in the glory-roll of fame.—INGRAM, JOHN H., 1876, *A Biographical Sketch, Poe Memorial, ed. Rice, p.* 35.

The Richard Savage of American literature.—CHAMBERS, ROBERT, 1876, *Cyclopædia of English Literature, ed. Carruthers.*

Why, I, the most innocent of divinity students at the time (1847), while walking with Poe, and feeling thirsty, pressed him to take a glass of wine with me. He declined, but finally compromised by taking a glass of ale with me. Almost instantly a great change came over him. Previously engaged in an indescribably eloquent conversation, he became as if paralyzed, and with compressed lips and fixed, glaring eyes, returned, without uttering a word, to the house which we were visiting. For hours, the strange spell hung over him. He seemed a changed being, as if stricken by some peculiar phase of insanity.—CUDWORTH, REV. WARREN H., 1877, *To William Fearing Gill, Life of Poe, p.* 79.

Poe's eyes, indeed, were his most striking feature, and it was to these that his face owed its peculiar attraction. I have never seen other eyes at all resembling them. They were large, with long, jet-black lashes,—the iris dark steel-gray, possessing a crystalline clearness and transparency, through which the jet-black pupil was seen to expand and contract with every shade of thought and emotion, I observed that the lids never contracted, as is so usual in most persons, especially when talking; but his gaze was ever full, open, and unshrinking. His usual expression was dreamy and sad. He had a way of sometimes turning a slightly askance look upon some person who was not observing him, and, with a quiet, steady gaze, appear to be mentally taking the caliber of the unsuspecting subject.—WEISS, MRS. SUSAN A. T., 1878, *Last Days of Edgar A. Poe, Scribner's Magazine, vol.* 15, *p.* 711.

Oh, if his hunted spirit, held at bay
This side of death, has covert found at last,
How restful must the change be, and how sweet!
And if he heeds our censure or our praise,
As once, how glad he must be now to know—
If know he does—that in some generous hearts
The balances are just that measure him,
And that some lips are pitiful and kind,
Saying, "He might have been, and but for this,
And this,—dead weights that circumstance
Threw in the scale—he *would* have been, a man,
A hero, worthy of his poet-soul!"
—MASON, CAROLINE A., 1880, *To Edmund Clarence Stedman after reading his Essay on Poe, Scribner's Monthly, vol.* 20, *p.* 450.

Even as we drive out of mind the popular conceptions of his nature, and look only at the portraits of him in the flesh, we needs must pause and contemplate, thoughtfully and with renewed feeling, one of the marked ideal faces that seem—like those of Byron, DeMusset, Heine—to fulfill all the traditions of genius, of picturesqueness, of literary and romantic effect.—STEDMAN, EDMUND CLARENCE, 1880, *Edgar Allan Poe, p.* 10.

All that makes Poe's career least defensible—his vices, quarrels, desperate straits, attempted suicides, ardent and sometimes simultaneous love-affairs—all these afford great resources for the biographer, who has reason to be grateful for a subject who did not dwell in decencies for ever. It is almost amusing to see how each new memoir of Poe professes to be the first to tell the real story of his life; and how each, while denouncing the obvious malice of Griswold, ends by re-establishing almost all the damaging facts which Griswold left only half-proved. If Poe fared ill at the hands of his enemy, he has fared worse, on the whole, at those of his friends. —HIGGINSON, THOMAS WENTWORTH, 1880, *Recent Works on Edgar Poe, The Nation, vol.* 31, *p.* 360.

In a dream I once had, I saw a vessel on the sea, at midnight, in a storm. It was no great full-rigged ship, nor majestic steamer, steering firmly through the gale, but seemed one of those superb little schooner yachts I had often seen lying anchored, rocking so jauntily, in the waters around New York, or up Long Island Sound; now flying uncontrolled with torn sails and broken spars through the wild sleet and winds and waves of the night. On deck was a slender, slight, beautiful figure, a dim man, apparently enjoying all the terror, the murk, and the dislocation of which he was the centre and the victim. That figure of my lurid dream might stand for Edgar Poe, his spirit, his fortunes, and his poems —themselves all lurid dreams.—WHITMAN, WALT, 1882, *Edgar Poe's Significance, The Critic, vol.* 2, *p.* 147.

I now felt it necessary that I should determine the nature of his disease and make out a correct diagnosis, so as to treat him properly. I did not then know but he might have been drinking, and so to determine the matter, I said, "Mr. Poe, you are extremely weak, pulse very low; I will give you a glass of toddy." He opened wide his eyes, and fixed them so steadily upon me, and with such anguish in them that I had to look from him to the wall beyond the bed. He then said, "Sir, if I thought its potency would transport me to the Elysian bowers of the undiscovered spirit world, I would not take it." "I will then administer an opiate, to give you sleep and rest," I said. Then he rejoined, "Twin sister, spectre to the doomed and crazed mortals of earth and perdition." I was entirely shorn of my strength. Here was a patient supposed to have been drunk, very drunk, and yet refuses to take liquor. The ordinary response is, "Yes, Doctor, give me a little to strengthen my nerves." I found there was no tremor of his person, no unsteadiness of his nerves, no fidgeting with his hands, and not the slightest odor of liquor upon his breath or person. I saw that my first impression had been a mistaken one. He was in a sinking condition, yet perfectly conscious. I had his body sponged with warm water, to which spirits were added, sinapisms applied to his stomach and feet, cold applications to his head, and then administered a stimulating cordial. . . . The appearance of the dead poet had not materially changed; his face was calm and placid; a smile seemed to play around his mouth, and all who gazed upon him remarked how natural he looked; so much so, indeed, that it seemed as though he only slept.—MORAN, DR. JOHN J., 1885, *A Defense of Edgar Allan Poe, Life, Character and Dying Declarations of the Poet, An Official Account of his Death by his Attending Physician, pp.* 65, 82.

The most fantastic of Poe's creations are not the product of the imagination abandoned to the impulses of a dominant mood; the effects are deliberately calculated, as he says they were, step by step and point by point to a prearranged culmination. A man writing on such a system, with the wolf at the door and affections daily on the rack, could hardly have endured the strain if he had had a constitution of iron. It was no wonder that Poe's health became distempered, or that during the last years of his wife's illness and the two remaining years through which he survived her, he had recourse to the dangerous help of stimulants. Not only did he subject his imagination to exhausting conditions, but he wasted his force in doing with superfluous thoroughness what a ready journalist would have dismissed with a few easy sentences of commonplace. . . . Poe failed to make a living by literature, not because he was an irregular profligate in the vulgar sense, but because he did ten times as much work as he was paid to do—a species of profligacy, perhaps, but not quite the same in kind as that with which he was charged by his malignant biographer.—MINTO, WILLIAM, 1885, *Encyclopædia Britannica, Ninth ed., vol.* XIX, *p.* 268.

No doubt many discreditable things were said of him which were not true; but they were growths from the seed which he himself had planted. . . . At the time of Poe's death, and for some years afterward, while his moral lapses were fresh in the minds of numberless contemporaries, few who took public notice of him were so rash as to assert his innocence; and in subsequent years memoirs of him were written, that were satisfactory in every particular, by those who either knew him well or had received their impressions from his associates, and who weighed his character with judicial impartiality. These memoirs are dispassionate and charitable, but they tell the truth. . . . The three headlights to which I have pointed attention—a neglected, dying wife; a seduction deliberately attempted; and a second seduction, with its attendant ruin, as deliberately accomplished—show clearly enough the trend of his character and the range of some of his pursuits. The picture is sufficiently complete. Let the truth prevail. As a writer, Poe's name stands among the very highest on the glory-roll of American authorship. I heartily agree with Prof. Minto that "there is no English author of the present century whose fame is likely to be more enduring." But as a man, he has been weighed in the balance and found wanting. And let his failure to display the triumphs of a pure and noble manhood be set forth in fitting terms side by side with the chronicle of his mental greatness. Let it be presented in sharp contrast with the attractive personal record of his exalted cotemporaries—a Longfellow, a Holmes, a Whittier, and a Bryant,—enforcing the cardinal truth on the minds and hearts of ambitious youth, that one of the most sparkling gems in the coronal of a great author's greatness is the immaculate purity of his daily life.—HARRINGTON, H. F., 1885, *Poe not to be Apotheosized, The Critic, Oct.* 3, *pp.* 157, 158.

Beautiful, gifted, and sensitive, proud, ambitious, and daring, endowed with a subtle charm of manner as well as of person, amiable and generous in his home life, loyal and devoted to his family, a very pleasing picture is presented of the man if we look but on this side. Could he have overcome the fatal fascination of drink, we might never have seen the reverse side of all this. As it is, let us cover his follies with our mantle of charity and dwell only upon his genius and his virtues.—GRISWOLD, HATTIE TYNG, 1886, *Home Life of Great Authors, p.* 320.

"My intimacy with Mr. Poe isolated me a good deal. In fact my girl friends were many of them afraid of him, and forsook me on that account. I knew none of his male friends. He despised ignorant people, and didn't like trifling and small-talk. He didn't like dark-skinned people. When he loved, he loved desperately. Though tender and very affectionate, he had a quick, passionate temper, and was very jealous. His feelings were intense, and he had but little control of them. He was not well balanced: he had too much brain. He scoffed at everything sacred, and never went to church. If he had had religion to guide him, he would have been a better man. He said often that there was a mystery hanging over him he never could fathom. He believed he was born to suffer, and this embittered his whole life. Mrs. Clemm also spoke vaguely of some family mystery, of some disgrace. . . . The only thing I had against him," she continued, "was that he held his head so high. He was proud, and looked down on my uncle, whose business did not suit him. He always liked my father, and talked with him a good deal."—VAN CLEEF, AUGUSTUS, 1889, *Poe's Mary, Harper's Magazine, Vol.* 78, *p.* 636.

It was a positive privilege to hear Poe talk. I have known times when at a dinner party, warmed with wine, and in a genial, glowing mood, he would pour out torrents of learning, and say hundreds of Rochefoucauld-like things apropos of literature and art, which, had they found their way into print, would have delighted cultivated society. It is a pity there was not in his audience a Boswell to take them down. Some of his utterances reminded one of the worldly wise sayings of Tacitus and Seneca. . . . In personal appearance Poe was a slight, small-boned, delicate looking man, with a well developed head, which, at a glance, seemed out of proportion to his slender body. His features were regular, his complexion pale; his nose was Grecian and well molded, his eyes large and luminous, and when excited, peculiarly vivid and penetrating. He dressed with neatness, and there was a suggestion of hauteur in his manner towards strangers. He was impatient of restraint or contradiction, and when his Southern blood was up, as the saying goes, he could be cuttingly rude and bitterly sarcastic.—PAUL, HOWARD, 1892, *Recollections of Edgar Allan Poe, Munsey's Magazine, vol.* 7, *pp.* 555, 557.

Edgar Poe's life was not all dark and desolate. It was his singular good fortune, from his birth to his death, to win and hold the love and friendship of many sweet and sympathetic women. Carlyle says the "story of genius has its bright side as well as its dark." The bright side of Poe's life was, as Washington Irving expresses it, when it "was gladdened by blessed womankind." The poet possessed many of those personal qualities and intellectual gifts which interest and fascinate the gentle sex: he was handsome, polished, richly imaginative, and a perfect master of all the graceful refinements of language. Perhaps there never lived a poet so truly appreciative of the loveliness of woman as Edgar Poe. He was a worshipper of beauty, believing, with a recent poet, that of all beauty a beautiful woman is the supremest. His was the delicate, ethereal, poetical sentiment of the Greek worship of an ideal beauty, so exquisitely personified by Nausicaa in the Odyssey. Poe's female friends, with one or two exceptions, were women who were able to sympathize with his lofty intellectual ambition, able to "point to higher worlds," although, perhaps, not capable of "leading the way" for him to follow. Proud, solitary, and ambitious he found a never-failing congeniality and sympathy in the society of bright and lovely women, some of whom almost realized the creations of his wonderful imagination: Ligeia, Morella, Lenore.—DIDIER, EUGENE L., 1892, *Poe's Female Friends, The Chautauquan, vol.* 15, *p.* 723.

Poe, to be sure, is fantastic and meretricious throughout. In his work as in his life he was haunted by the vices and the falsity of the stage that bred him; but he was really haunted. As one knows him better, one does not love him more. In another way, though, one grows to care for him, or at least to pity him. For with all his falsity, with all his impudence and sham, the man is a man by himself. There is something freakish, not quite earthly, wholly his own in the fancies and the cadences that grow wild amid his work. If it be something to have added a new note to literature, then we Americans must respect the memory of Poe. — WENDELL, BARRETT, 1893, *Stelligeri and other Essays Concerning America, p.* 138.

He spent much of his time with Mrs. Shelton, and finally asked her to marry him, and was, it must be believed from the correspondence, accepted. She was older than he, a plain woman, and wealthy. Poe got the wedding ring, and after his death she wore mourning for him. At the last moment, he still wavered when he thought of "Annie," who was evidently the nearest to him of all, except Mrs. Clemm,—but that was impossible. He was in doubt whether to have Mrs. Clemm come on to Richmond, or to go himself and bring her. He decided on the latter course, and on Sunday, as is conjectured, September 30, or else on the following day, he left his friends in Richmond, and went on the boat sober and cheerful. After reaching Baltimore, it is said that he took the train to Philadelphia, but was brought back, being in the wrong car, from Havre de Grace in a state of stupor. It is also said that he dined with some old military friends, became intoxicated, and was captured by politicians, who kept him stupefied, and made him vote at several booths on Wednesday, election day. All that is known is that, being then partially intoxicated, he called upon his friend, Dr. Brooks, on an afternoon, and, not finding him, went away; and that on Wednesday, October 3, about noon, he was recognised at a rum shop used as a voting-place,—Ryan's Fourth Ward Polls,—and on his saying that he was acquainted with Dr. Snodgrass, word was sent to that gentleman, who had him taken to the Washington Hospital. He was admitted at five o'clock, and word was sent to his relatives, who attended to his needs. He remained, except for a brief interval, in delirium; and on Sunday, Oct. 7, 1849, at about five o'clock in the morning, he died. The funeral was taken charge of by his relatives, and took place the next day. Five persons, including the officiating minister, followed his body to the grave.—WOODBERRY, GEORGE E., 1894, *The Works of Edgar Allan Poe, ed. Stedman and Woodberry, Memoir, vol.* I, *p.* 86.

In the place of moral feeling he had the artistic conscience.—BEERS, HENRY A., 1895, *Initial Studies in American Letters, p.* 168.

Sir:—As you are aware, The New York Shakespeare Society lately secured the passage of an act of the Legislature of the State of New York (now cited as Chapter 537 of the Laws of 1896) appropriating $10,000 to preserve the Edgar Allan Poe cottage, at Fordham, Borough of the Bronx, New York City, by laying out a parcel of land directly opposite the present cite of the cottage, to be called Poe Park: and to remove the cottage thereto, a removal rendered necessary by the widening of the Kingsbridge Road, which takes the original site of the Cottage. It is now proposed to place within Poe Park, and facing the historic Cottage on its new site, a bronze statue of Edgar Allan Poe; and to aid in that design, you are invited to send us your contribution to the expense of such statue, to such extent as the sentiment of the project may appeal to you.—MORGAN, APPLETON, 1896, *Chairman to the Poe Memorial Committee of the Shakespeare Society of New York, Appeal to the Public.*

Near the Boulevard, upon the site of the house No. 206 Eighty-fourth Street and the lot adjoining on the east, stood until a few years ago a large old-fashioned frame dwelling in which Poe wrote that chapter of accumulated horrors, "The Facts in the Case of M. Valdemar,"—one of the best examples of fiction which has the semblance of literal fact. Here, too, according to metropolitan belief, he composed the deathless poem which gave him his highest renown. It is noteworthy that while several localities are now claiming the honor of having been Poe's home when he wrote "The Raven," Dr. Woods is producing specious reasons for his belief that Poe did not write it at all. The house stood high upon the rocks in the midst of a pleasing rural landscape, and was occupied by the parents of Commissioner Brennan, with whom the poet and his family boarded: his room was a large square apartment on the second floor, whose front windows looked across the lordly Hudson to the heights of the Palisades, and here his desk was so placed that his eyes rested upon that inspiring view whenever he lifted them from his page. This chamber was thereafter called the "Raven room," and the belief of the Brennans and their neighbors that the great poem was here composed is alleged to have been founded upon the statements of Poe and Mrs. Clemm.—WOLFE, THEODORE F., 1898, *Some Literary Shrines of Manhattan, Lippincott's Magazine, vol.* 61, *p.* 513.

The winds were bleak on Fordham heights in that winter of 1846–47; visitors speak of that wasting girl-wife wrapped (for warmth) in her husband's cloak, with a "tortoise-shell cat gathered to her bosom" and the mother "chafing the cold feet." Again and again she touches the gates of death, and rallies; even so, Leigeia in that horrific story of the weird lady, with the "black abounding tresses," cheats her lover with ever new, and ever broken promise of life! I don't think the child-wife lamented the approach of death (January, 1847); nor did the mother; but to the "ghoul-haunted" poet, who had lived in regions peopled by shadows, this vanishing of the best he had known of self-sacrificing love, was desolating. He was never the same again. We have hardly a right to regard what he did after this—whether in way of writing, of love-making, or of business projects—as the work of a wholly responsible creature. It were better perhaps if the story of it all had never been told.—MITCHELL, DONALD G., 1899, *American Lands and Letters, Leather-stocking to Poe's "Raven," p.* 391.

He had unquestionably an abnormal sensitiveness to drink—a single glass of the mildest liquor would affect him to the point of stupefaction; but he was in no sense an habitual drinker or a dissolute man, as he has been painted by his detractors for fully half a century—since his untimely death at the hands of the political "repeaters" of Baltimore. Alas, poor Poe! Was not your punishment in life, your poverty, your anguish of privation, a sufficiently terrible expiation for your occasional lapses of will, that your memory should be held up to the execration of posterity by those unfit to loose the lachets of your shoes? To-day we honor Willis, who in life fraternized with Poe as a companion and a gentleman, worthy of the friendship of the ideal Chevalier Bayard of his time. We concede the laurel of genius to the lamented Poe, but we stab him in the back while proffering it, and prelude the study of his matchless genius with materialistic and abhorrent pictures of his personal character.—GILL, WILLIAM FEARING, 1899, *Edgar Allan Poe, After Fifty Years, The Arena, vol.* 22, *p.* 528.

I personally think that Poe was an unfortunate, more sinned against than sinning, who bore his misfortune with resignation, lacking the strength to "fight it out." On the other hand, I think he had more the nature of an artist than of a profound thinker; consequently, he probably was careless in many ways, which his enemies made capital of against him. Be that as it may, it seems to me that the mission in transmitting the image of Poe to posterity, is not to emphasize his shortcomings, if he had any, but his great qualities of a genius. However, I think I ought to preserve a certain sadness in his expression which depicts his unfortunate life. This, in a general way, is my idea of Poe, and I should be under great obligations if you would kindly let me know to what extent my views coincide with your wishes.—ZOLNAY, GEORGE JULIAN, 1899, *Letter to the Poe Memorial Association Executive Committee, Poe Memorial, ed. Kent, p.* 30.

His faults were such
As thousands live and die with, unobserved,
But, being his faults, because of his mind's light,
They loomed like towers upon a sunset hill.
Broken upon the wheel of his misfortunes,
Toiling, alone, where life's dark pathway leads
Close by the steep and treacherous brink of hell,
Haunted by spectres, vexed by easeless griefs,
His soul went down to death, in loneliness,
A death too pitiful for aught save silence,
Too mournful in its wretchedness for tears.
But not with death he dwells. Above his dust
Time's slow impartial hand has made for him
A shaft, memorial, builded of the stones
Which Hate and Envy cast upon his grave.
He dwells not with the shadows.
—WILSON, ROBERT BURNS, 1899, *Memorial Poem, Poe Memorial, ed. Kent, p.* 60.

POETRY

His poems are constructed with wonderful ingenuity, and finished with consummate art. They display a somber and weird imagination, and a taste almost faultless in the apprehension of that sort of beauty which was most agreeable to his temper. But they evince little genuine feeling, and less of that spontaneous ecstasy which gives its freedom, smoothness and naturalness to immortal verse. . . . He was not remarkably original in invention. Indeed some of his plagiarisms are scarcely paralleled for their audacity in all literary history.—GRISWOLD, RUFUS WILMOT, 1850, *Edgar Allan Poe, The International Magazine, vol.* 1, *p.* 340.

So many faculties were brought into play in the expression of Poe's poetical compositions, that readers in whom the critical intellect prevails over the imaginative, often acknowledge the refined art, the tact, the subtlety, the faultless method, while the potent *magnetism* of his genius utterly escapes them. There are persons whom nature has made non-conductors to this sort of electricity. . . . It is not to be questioned that Poe was a consummate master of language; that he had sounded all the secrets of rhythm; that he understood and availed himself of all its resources,—the balance and poise of syllables, the alternations of emphasis and cadence, of vowel-sounds and consonants, and all the metrical sweetness of "phrase and metaphrase." Yet this consummate art was in him united with a rare simplicity. He was the most genuine of enthusiasts, as we think we shall presently show. His genius would follow no leadings but those of his own imperial intellect. With all his vast mental resources, he could never write an occasional poem, or adapt himself to the taste of a popular audience. His graver narratives and fantasies are often related with an earnest simplicity, solemnity, and apparent fidelity, attributable not so much to a deliberate artistic purpose, as to that power of vivid and intense conception that made his dreams realities, and his life a dream.—WHITMAN, SARAH HELEN, 1860–85, *Edgar Poe and his Critics, pp.* 34, 35.

Once as yet, and once only, has there sounded out of it all [America] one pure note of original song—worth singing, and echoed from the singing of no other man; a note of song neither wide nor deep, but utterly true, rich, clear, and native to the singer; the short exquisite music, subtle and simple and sombre and sweet, of Edgar Poe. All the rest that is not of mocking-birds is of corncrakes, varied but at best for an instant by some scant-winded twitter of linnet or of wren.—SWINBURNE, ALGERNON CHARLES, 1872, *Under the Microscope.*

Of Edgar Poe's poems,—except "The Raven," which will always owe a certain popularity to the skill with which rhyme and metre reflect the dreary hopelessness and shudderiness, if I may coin a word, of the mood depicted—it is impossible to speak very highly. His imagination was not high enough for the sphere of poetry, and when he entered it he grew mystical and not a little bombastic.—HUTTON, RICHARD HOLT, 1874, *Criticisms on Contemporary Thought and Thinkers, vol.* I, *p.* 68.

Very different from the poems of Shelley and Keats, and yet burning with the same poetic ardor, and inspired with an imaginative genius scarcely, if at all, inferior, are the poetical productions of our American Shelley, Edgar Allen Poe.—BALDWIN, JAMES, 1882, *English Literature and Literary Criticism, Poetry, p.* 552.

Imagination working on intellectual materials was the one quality which lifted Poe. Experience, a richly-stored memory, a balanced judgment of life, feeling, except in one direction, human sympathy—these play but a very small part in his work. His imagination was powerful for situation and coloring, and the ear had the keenest possible sense of music. But in his attempt to make situations clear and coloring vivid and music pleasing, he everywhere overreaches himself. The strain for musical words made him forget that in verse "more is meant than meets the ear." His repetitions, though often exquisitely timed, create at last a sense of mechanism, and, to the ear only ordinarily nice, suggest the workshop. Again, his straining after lurid accessories, at first indicating a morbid condition, ends with betraying a jaded sensibility. Still, with his deep-lying faults, half-a-dozen poems of Poe's earlier life—and the whole life was a short one—stand out so far above the verse of most of his contemporaries, that we do not hesitate to place him among the most striking of American geniuses—a genius narrow, and, as Mr. Stoddard shows, only meagerly productive, but intense, piercing, original—mad.—MORSE, JAMES HERBERT, 1884, *Edgar Allan Poe, Authors at Home, The Critic, vol.* 5, *p.* 230.

He affects different natures differently, and, unlike many poets, he affects all who are capable of being touched by poetry. To the multitude who enjoy the cheerful optimism of Longfellow and poets of his class, he is gloomy and hateful; to those who are predisposed to melancholy, he is the melodious laureate of dead hopes; to those with whom poetry is an art, and not a feeling, he is at once attractive and repulsive; a gifted creature with a morbid personality, clinging to the weakness which is its wretchedness, and the madness which is its death.—STODDARD, RICHARD HENRY, 1884, *The Genius of Poe, Poe's Works, vol.* I, *p.* x.

"Music is the perfection of the soul or the idea of poetry," so you wrote; "the vagueness of exaltation aroused by a sweet air (which should be indefinite and never too strongly suggestive), is precisely what we should aim at in poetry." You aimed at that mark, and struck it again and again, notably in "Helen, thy beauty is to me," in "The Haunted Palace," "The Valley of Unrest," and "The City in the Sea." But by some Nemesis which might, perhaps, have been foreseen, you are, to the world, the poet of one poem—"The Raven:" a piece in which the music is highly artificial, and the "exaltation" (what there is of it) by no means particularly "vague."—LANG, ANDREW, 1886, *Letters to Dead Authors, p,* 145.

It is not difficult to understand that there were many sides on which Poe was likely to be long distasteful to Boston, Cambridge, and Concord. The intellectual weight of the man, though unduly minimised in New England, was inconsiderable by the side of that of Emerson. But in poetry, as one has to be always insisting, the battle is not to the strong; and apart from all faults, weaknesses, and shortcomings of Poe, we feel more and more clearly, or we ought to feel, the perennial charm of his verses. The posy of his still fresh and fragrant poems is larger than that of any other deceased American writer, although Emerson may have one or two single blossoms to show which are more brilliant than any of his. If the range of the Baltimore poet had been wider, if Poe had not harped so persistently on his one theme of remorseful passion for the irrecoverable dead, if he had employed his extraordinary, his unparalleled gifts of melodious invention, with equal skill, in illustrating a variety of human themes, he must have been with the greatest poets. . . . From Tennyson to Austin Dobson there is hardly one whose verse-music does not show traces of Poe's influence. To impress the stamp of one's personality on a succeeding generation of artists, to be an almost (although not wholly) flawless technical artist one's self, to charm within a narrow circle to a degree that shows no sign, after forty years, of lessening, is this to prove a claim to rank with the Great Poets? No, perhaps not quite; but at all events it is surely to have deserved great honour from the country of one's birthright.—GOSSE, EDMUND, 1888-89, *Has America Produced a Poet? Questions at Issue, pp.* 89, 90.

No singer of old story
Luting accustomed lays,
No harper for new glory,
No mendicant for praise,
He struck high chords and splendid,
Wherein were fiercely blended
Tones that unfinished ended
With his unfinished days.

—BONER, JOHN H., 1889, *Poe's Cottage at Fordham, The Century, vol.* 39, *p.* 85.

Poe's keen sensitiveness to criticism either of himself or of his writings is a noteworthy trait. The melody of his best poems is haunting, but tended ever to degenerate into mere mechanical jingle. His tone is spirituous, never spiritual. Alone among our poets, Poe links us to European literature by his musical despair—so similar to that of Leopardi, Pushkin, Heine, Lenau, Petöfi, and DeMusset (all descendants of Byron).—WHITE, GREENOUGH, 1890, *Sketch of the Philosophy of American Literature, p.* 59.

Poe, like Swinburne, was a verbal poet merely; empty of thought, empty of sympathy, empty of love for any real thing: a graceful and nimble skater up and down over the deeps and shallows of life,—deep or shallow, it was all the same to him. Not one real thing did he make more dear to us by his matchless rhyme; not one throb of the universal heart, not one flash of the universal mind, did he seize and put in endearing form for his fellow men. . . . I am not complaining that Poe was not didactic: didacticism is death to poetry. I am complaining that he was not human and manly, and that he did not touch life in any helpful and liberating way. His poems do not lay hold of real things. I do not find the world a more enjoyable or beautiful place because he lived in it. I find myself turning to his poems, not for mental or spiritual food, as I do to Wordsworth or Emerson or Whitman, or for chivalrous human sentiments as in Tennyson, but to catch a glimpse of the weird, the fantastic, and, as it were, of the nightside or dream-side of things. . . . I would not undervalue Poe. He was a unique genius. But I would account for his failure to deeply impress his own countrymen, outside the professional literary guild. His fund of love and sympathy was small. He was not broadly related to his fellows, as were Longfellow and Whittier and Whitman. His literary equipment was remarkable; his human equipment was not remarkable: hence his failure to reach the general fame of the New England poets.—BURROUGHS, JOHN, 1893, *Mr. Gosse's Puzzle over Poe, The Dial, vol.* 15, *pp.* 214, 215.

To appreciate Poe, the imagination requires either distance of time or independence of attitude. It may, however, be observed that the interest attaching to his poetry is strictly of the personal and private kind. Yet if apart from "The Raven," Poe was the least of the greater American poets, except as to form, in which he was careful exceedingly, who would affirm that in his originality as well as in clearness and execution he was inferior to any particular poet who wrote later?—SIMONDS, ARTHUR B., 1894, *American Song, p.* 50.

Along with "The Raven," other poems by Poe—"Ulalume," "For Annie," "The Haunted Palace," and many another—were a deep well of delight to Rossetti in all these years. He once wrote a parody of "Ulalume." I do not rightly remember it, nor has it left a vestige behind.—ROSSETTI, WILLIAM MICHAEL, 1895, *Dante Gabriel Rossetti, His Family-Letters, with a Memoir, vol.* I, *p.* 107.

And yet in the eyes of foreigners he is the most gifted of all authors of America; he is the one to whom the critics of Europe would most readily accord the full title of genius. At the end of this nineteenth century Poe is the sole man of letters born in the United States whose writings are read eagerly in Great Britain and in France, in Germany, in Italy, and in Spain, where Franklin is now but a name, and where the fame of James Fenimore Cooper, once as widely spread, is now slowly fading away. . . . That his scheme of poetry was highly artificial, that the themes of his poems were vague and insubstantial, and that his stanzas do not stimulate thought—these things may be admitted without disadvantage. What the reader does find in Poe's poetry is the succession of departed but imperishable beauty, and the lingering grace and fascination of haunting melancholy. His verses throb with an inexpressible magic and glow with intangible fantasy. His poems have no other purpose; they convey no moral; they echo no call to duty; they celebrate beauty only—beauty immaterial and evanescent; they are their own excuse for being.—MATTHEWS, BRANDER, 1896, *An Introduction to the Study of American Literature, pp.* 156, 166.

The charm of poetry can be created for us by but few men; but Poe in a few moments was one of those few. His poems, indeed, have been very variously judged; and their merit is of a virtuoso type which needs special defense from those who keenly feel it. Few verse-writers, we must at once admit, have been more barren than Poe of any serious "message;" more unequal to any "criticism of life;" narrower in range of thought, experience, emotion. Few verse-writers whom we can count as poets have left so little verse, and of that little so large a proportion which is indefensibly bad. On some dozen short pieces alone can Poe's warmest admirers rest his poetic repute. And how terribly open to criticism some of even those pieces are! To analyze "Ulalume," for instance, would be like breaking a death's-head moth on the wheel. But nevertheless, a dozen solid British poets of the Southey type would to my mind be well bartered for those few lines of Poe's which after the sternest sifting must needs remain.—MYERS, FREDERIC W. H., 1897, *Library of the World's Best Literature, ed. Warner, vol.* XX, *p.* 11652.

Poe seems to have taken the hint for his characteristic manner, or, at least, borrowed many of his best effects, from Dr. Thomas Holley Chivers, in whose "snatches of sweet unsustained song," Poe confessed to finding "an indefinite charm of sentiment and melody." The themes of death and despair, the sad and resonant refrains, as "nevermore," mellifluous names suggestive of some unearthly grace, as "Israfel" and "Isadore"—this last becoming with Poe "Lenore," subtly interwoven rhythms, sonorous rhymes that beat and beat again upon the ear, the repetitions and parallelisms born of excited feeling, are lyrical devices all to be found in Chivers before they appeared in Poe, but the hand that feebly tuned the strings yielded place to a hand that swept them with the master-touch. — BATES, KATHARINE LEE, 1897, *American Literature, p.* 185.

There seems to be no end of interest in Poe legends and Poeana. Poe is the one American poet—Whitman, perhaps, being a second—whose work has produced a *cult;* and, at the same time, exercises a fascination which is contagious and indescribable. Some might possibly call it hypnotic. He uses what Emerson calls "polarized words;" and, while they haunt the mind, and even the very soul of the reader, they virtually create an atmosphere as distinct as that—though not like that—in one of Corot's landscapes. Poe contributed little to human thought. He had no ethical message whatever to deliver. He could not have written Wordsworth's "Ode on the Intimations of Human Immortality"—which is as pious, though not burdensomely so, as it is poetic. What his poetry is, is not what Matthew Arnold defined poetry to be—"a criticism of life." It is more like a series of musical diversions—fluent, sensuous, weird, sorrowful, and sepulchral, even subterranean almost in passages. But what differentiates it most specifically is, that it is sensuous. It moves no one to do anything; it, on the contrary, makes you feel something. In reading it you mourn for a vanished *Aiden* or a lost *Lenore.* It is a curious fame that rests so much upon so little—at least, upon so small a body of work. For, if you take "The Raven," "Annabel Lee," and "The Bells" from Poe's poems—if you do not consider these at all—what would his poetic fame have been? Could it have been very great?—BENTON, JOEL, 1899, *In the Poe Circle, p.* 54.

THE BELLS

If I were called upon to express my opinon of Poe as a poetic artist, I should say that "The Bells" was the most perfect example of his "power of words," if not, indeed, the most perfect example of that kind of power in all poetic literature. I should also say that "Alexander's Feast," which our ancestors thought so incomparable, was not to be named in the same day with it.—STODDARD, RICHARD HENRY, 1875–84, *The Life of Edgar Allan Poe, Poe's Works, vol.* I, *p.* 172.

The "Bells" is perhaps the rarest instance in the language of the suggestiveness of rhyme and the power of onomatopoetic words.—WELSH, ALFRED H., 1883, *Development of English Literature and Language, vol.* II, *p.* 383.

Poe's doctrine of "rhythm and rhyme" finds its amplest verification in "The Bells." Reason and not "ecstatic intuition," led him to conclude that English versification is exceedingly simple, that "one tenth of it, possibly, may be called ethereal; nine-tenths, however, appertain to the mathematics; and the whole is included within the limits of the commonest common-sense." It must be believed that Poe appropriated, with the finest artistic discernment, the vitalizing power of rhythm and rime, and nowhere with more skill than in "The Bells." It is the climax of his art on its technical side. — FRUIT, JOHN PHELPS, 1899, *The Mind and Art of Poe's Poetry, p.* 136.

ULALUME

Muffled in an unusual number of thicknesses of elaborate rigmarole in rhyme, this is the pith of a ballad, which borrows interest from its position as the last exponent of the perpetual despair that enshrouded Poe's manhood, and the last visit of his tortured soul to the tomb of his lost beautiful, typified by the dead Ulalume. The *geist* of the ballad—that which transfuses it with meaning, and redeems it from the criticism so often passed upon it, that it is mere words—lies solely in the fact of its interpenetration with a kind psychological significance. Thus sang he, then died.—FAIRFIELD, FRANCIS GERRY, 1875, *A Mad Man of Letters, Scribner's Monthly, vol.* 10, *p.* 698.

All things considered, the most singular poem that he ever produced, if not, indeed, the most singular poem that anybody ever produced, in commemoration of a dead woman, which I take to have been Poe's object, or one of his objects, when he sat down to write it. The mood of mind in which it was conceived was no doubt an imaginative one, but it was not, I think, on the hither side of the boundary between sense and madness. I can perceive no touch of grief in it, no intellectual sincerity, but a diseased determination to create the strange, the remote, and the terrible, and to exhaust ingenuity in order to do so. No healthy mind was ever impressed by "Ulalume," and no musical sense was ever gratified with its measure, which is little beyond a jingle, and with its repetitions, which add to its length without increasing its general effect, and which show more conclusively than any thing in the language, the absurdity of the refrain when it is allowed to run riot, as it does here.—STODDARD, RICHARD HENRY, 1875–84, *Life of Edgar Allan Poe, Poe's Works, vol.* I, *p.* 149.

It is so strange, so unlike anything that preceded it, so vague and yet so full of meaning, that of itself it might establish a new method. To me it seems an improvisation, such as a violinist might play upon the instrument which had become his one thing of worth after the death of a companion had left him alone with his own soul.—STEDMAN, EDMUND CLARENCE, 1880, *Edgar Allan Poe, p.* 50.

The ballad of "Ulalume" was written in 1847. The poet, still distraught by the death of his idolized child-wife, shattered in health, and impoverished in fortune, was nearing the borderland of insanity. Though not yet out of his thirties, he lived among the ghosts and shadows of a wasted life, in a world peopled with the horrors of a Dantean Inferno.

"There sighs, complaints, and ululations loud
Resounded through the air without a star."

It was under such circumstances that the poet composed his "Ulalume," pronounced by a competent critic, "the extreme limit of Poe's original genius." The poem will not stand criticism. Many of its lines and rhymes are indefensible. Yet, in spite of its faults, it is an exquisite lyric. It comes like a wail of suffering, wrenched from a tortured, baffled soul, whose very anguish finds expression only in a melodious rhythm. The vagueness of its fantasies is forgotten in the effect of its irresistible music. In spite of the bitter arraignment by Mr. R. H. Stoddard, all classes of minds, healthy and otherwise, have been impressed by the little poem, and if, as that critic asserts, "no musical sense was ever gratified with its measure," it is difficult to explain away its subtle charm.—ONDERDONK, JAMES L., 1899-1901, *History of American Verse, p.* 247.

THE RAVEN

We regard it as the most effective single example of fugitive poetry ever published in this country.—WILLIS, NATHANIEL PARKER, 1845, *The Evening Mirror, Jan.* 29.

Your friend, Mr. Poe, is a speaker of strong words "in both kinds." But I hope you will assure him from me that I am grateful for his reviews, and in no complaining humor at all. As to the "Raven" tell me what you shall say about it. There is certainly a power—but it does not appear to me the natural expression of a sane intellect in whatever mood; and I think that this should be specified in the title of the poem. There is a fantasticalness about the "sir or madam," and things of the sort, which is ludicrous, unless there is a specified insanity to justify the straws. Probably he—the author—intended to be read in the poem, and he ought to have intended it. The rhythm acts excellently upon the imagination, and the "never more" has a solemn chime with it.—BROWNING, ELIZABETH BARRETT, 1845, *Letter to R. H. Horne, May* 12.

It is my design to render it manifest that no one point in its composition is referrable either to accident or intuition—that the work proceeded, step by step, to its completion with the precision and rigid consequence of a mathematical problem. . . . The reader begins now to regard the Raven as emblematical—but it is not until the very last line of the very last stanza that the intention of making him emblematical of *Mournful and Never-ending Remembrance* is permitted distinctly to be seen.—POE, EDGAR ALLAN, 1846, *The Philosophy of Composition, Works, ed., Stedman and Woodberry, vol.* VI, *pp.* 33, 46.

What a dismal tragic, remorseful transcript it is! . . . Perhaps the very finest and most original single poem of its kind that America has yet produced. It indicates a most wayward and subtle genius. It takes you captive by its gloomy, weird power.—SMILES, SAMUEL, 1860, *Brief Biographies.*

"The Raven" is indeed the most original production of American poetry, a strange and original form of the idea that the dark side of nature enters into the existence of man.—SCHERR, J., 1874, *A History of English Literature, tr. M. V., p.* 302.

It would be impossible for the most fastidious workman to alter his poem with advantage.—SMITH, GEORGE BARNETT, 1875, *Robert Buchanan, Poets and Novelists, p.* 333.

Then, to the poet's brain there came
Nought but fierce visions, breathing flame;
Spectres of gibbering horror pale,
All creatures of the house of bale
His fate remorseless urged him o'er
Oceans that stretched without a shore,
Whose swart waves whispered "Nevermore!" . . .
Henceforth, with pinions seldom furled,
His sombre "Raven" roams the world:
All stricken peoples pause to hear
The echo of his burden drear;
For ah! the deathless type is he
Of pangs we may not shun, nor flee,—
And grief's stern immortality.

—HAYNE, PAUL HAMILTON, 1876, *The Poe Memorial, ed. Rice, pp.* 94, 95.

The "Raven" room is little altered since the time Poe occupied it. It has a modern mantlepiece, painted black and most elaborately carved. Poe's name may be found in fine letters cut upon one side of it. His writing-table stood by one of the front windows, and, while seated before it, he could look down upon the rolling waters of the Hudson and over at the Palisades beyond. It was a fitting dwelling for a poet, and though not far from the city's busy hum, the atmosphere of solitude and remoteness was as actual, as if the spot had been in the heart of the Rocky Mountains. The explanations of the composition of "The Raven" given by Poe, even to his most intimate friends, were very conflicting, except that all these agree in stating that the analysis given in the "Philosophy of Composition," was pure fiction,—one of the poet's mischievous caprices to catch the critics, which proved successful beyond his expectation. Mrs. Weiss states that, not only Poe assured her that his published account of the alleged method of the composition of "The Raven" was not genuine, but that he also said that he had never intended it should be seriously received as such.—GILL, WILLIAM FEARING, 1877, *The Life of Edgar Allan Poe, p.* 149.

His reputation rests upon three or four short poems, chiefly remarkable for their melody, and half a dozen tales, distinguished by their weirdness of colouring, their analytic power, and their subtle skill of construction. The best known of his poems is also the most elaborate—"The Raven," and of this it may fairly be said that, in spite of its want of adequate motive, it is unique in conception as in execution, and it occupies a place of its own in our English literature.—ADAMS, W. H. DAVENPORT, 1880, *Wrecked Lives, vol.* II, *p.* 310.

"The Philosophy of Composition," his analysis of "The Raven," is a technical dissection of its method and structure. Neither his avowal of cold-blooded artifice, nor his subsequent avowal to friends that an exposure of this artifice was only another of his intellectual hoaxes, need be wholly credited. If he had designed the complete work in advance, he scarcely would have made so harsh a prelude of rattle-pan rhymes to the delicious melody of the second stanza,—not even upon his theory of the fantastic. Of course an artist, having perfected a work, sees, like the first Artist, that it is good, and sees why it is good. A subsequent analysis, coupled with a disavowal of any sacred fire, readily enough may be made. My belief is that the first conception and rough draft of this poem came as inspiration always comes; that its author then saw how it might be perfected, giving it the final touches described in his chapter on Composition, and that the latter, therefore, is neither wholly false nor wholly true. — STEDMAN, EDMUND CLARENCE, 1884, *The Raven, Illustrated by Gustave Doré, Comment on the Poem, p.* 13.

In the "Evening Mirror," January 29, 1845, "The Raven" was published, with a highly commendatory card from Willis; and a few days later "The American Whig Review" for February, from the advance sheets of which this poem had been copied, was the centre of literary interest and the prey of editorial scissors throughout the length and breadth of the country. In the magazine the author was masked under the pseudonym "Quarles," but in this journal he had been named as E. A. Poe. The popular response was instantaneous and decisive. No great poem ever established itself so immediately, so widely, and so imperishably in men's minds. "The Raven" became, in some sort, a national bird, and the author the most notorious American of the hour.—WOODBERRY, GEORGE E., 1885, *Edgar Allan Poe (American Men of Letters), p.* 221.

Seems to go on in people's minds with a constant crescendo of admiration from one year and generation to another.—BENTON, JOEL, 1897, *Poe's Opinion of "The Raven," The Forum, vol.* 22, *p.* 731.

I remember well with what gusto and unction the poet-editor of that old *Whig Review* read over to me (who had been a younger college friend of his), in his ramshackle Nassau Street office, that poem of the "Raven"—before yet it had gone into type; and as he closed with oratorical effect the last refrain, declared with an emphasis that shook the whole mass of his flaxen locks—"that is amazing—amazing!" It surely proved so; and how little did that clever and ambitious editor (who died only two years later) think that one of his largest titles to remembrance would lie in his purchase and issue of that best known poem of Edgar Poe!—MITCHELL, DONALD G., 1899, *American Lands and Letters, Leather-Stocking to Poe's "Raven," p.* 387.

My brother Dante Gabriel and myself must have been among the earliest readers of Poe's Raven when that classical bird reached the English shore, and how many and many times did we not re-peruse it, and (more especially my brother) recite it!—ROSSETTI, WILLIAM MICHAEL, 1899, *Letter to the Poe Memorial, ed. Kent, p.* 64.

TALES

You are mistaken in supposing that you are not "favorably known to me." On the contrary, all that I have read from your pen has inspired me with a high idea of your power; and I think you are destined to stand among the first romance-writers of the country, if such be your aim.—LONGFELLOW, HENRY WADSWORTH, 1841, *To Edgar A. Poe, May* 19; *Life of Longfellow by Samuel Longfellow, vol.* I, *p.* 377.

In his tales, Mr. Poe has chosen to exhibit his power chiefly in that dim region which stretches from the very utmost limits of the probable into the weird confines of superstition and unreality. He combines in a very remarkable manner two faculties which are seldom found united: a power of influencing the mind of the reader by the impalpable shadows of mystery, and a minuteness of detail which does not leave a pin or a button unnoticed. —LOWELL, JAMES RUSSELL, 1845, *Edgar Allan Poe, Graham's Magazine, Feb.*

I have always found some one remarkable thing in your stories to haunt me long after reading them. The teeth in "Berenice;" the changing eyes of Morella; that red and glaring crack in the "House of Usher;" the pores of the deck in the "MS. Found in a Bottle;" the visible drops falling into the goblet in "Ligeia," etc., etc.,—there is always something of this sort to stick by the mind—by mine at least.—COOKE, PHILIP P., 1846, *Poe in New York, The Century, vol.* 48, *p.* 861.

In his "Tales of the Grotesque and Arabesque," evinces a genius in which a love of the marvelous and an intensity of conception are united with the wildest sympathies, as if the endowments of Mrs. Radcliffe and Coleridge were partially united in one mind.—TUCKERMAN, HENRY T., 1852, *A Sketch of American Literature.*

It is through his tales that Mr. Poe is best known, and in them is displayed the real bent of his genius. Their chief characteristic is a grim horror,—sometimes tangible, but usually shadowy and dim. He revelled in faintly sketching scenes of ghastly gloom, in imagining the most impossible plots, and in making them seem real by minute detail. His wild and weird conceptions have great power; but they affect the fears only, rarely the *heart;* while sometimes his morbid creations are repulsive and shocking; yet, in the path which he has chosen, he is unrivalled.—CLEVELAND, CHARLES D., 1859, *A Compendium of American Literature, p.* 638.

With all the materials at hand, which thirty years of careful observation have supplied, no man living, not subject to the malady it paints, could write a "Fall of the House of Usher;" and if critics are to suppose that Poe elaborated his story without facts upon which to proceed, then they must accept the miracle that, by a simple process of analytic ratiocination, he anticipated all the discoveries and observations of the last quarter of a century. If, on the other hand, he was subject to the malady, the story explains itself and furnishes the clue to the fantastic invention incident to all his tales of monomania, through every one of which, thinly draped and enveloped in impenetrable gloom, stalks his own personality—a madman muttering to himself of his own morbid imaginings.—FAIRFIELD, FRANCIS GERRY, 1875, *A Mad Man of Letters, Scribner's Monthly, vol.* 10, *p.* 697.

Poe's place in purely imaginative prose-writing is as unquestionable as Hawthorne's. —HIGGINSON, THOMAS WENTWORTH, 1879-88, *Short Studies of American Authors, p.* 16.

Poe's most remarkable achievement in the region of the supernatural is "The Fall of the House of Usher," which occupies the same gloomy eminence in prose fiction that Browning's "Childe Roland to the Dark Tower Came" occupies in romantic poetry. It is of imagination all compact, an imagination which reveals the secrets of the heart, the dark places of the soul. —STODDARD, RICHARD HENRY, 1884, *The Genius of Poe, Poe's Works, vol.* I, *p.* xiii.

Although it may be doubted whether the fiery and tumultuous rush of a volcano, which might be taken to typify Poe, is as powerful or impressive in the end as the calm and inevitable progression of a glacier, to which, for the purposes of this comparison only, we may liken Hawthorne, yet the weight and influence of Poe's work are indisputable. One might hazard the assertion that in all Latin countries he is the best known of American authors. Certainly no American writer has been so widely accepted in France. Nothing better of its kind has ever been done than the "Pit and the Pendulum," or than the "Fall of the House of Usher" (which has been compared aptly with Browning's "Childe Roland to the Dark Tower Came" for its power of suggesting intellectual desolation). Nothing better of its kind has ever been done than the "Gold Bug," or than the "Purloined Letter," or than the "Murders in the Rue Morgue." The "Murders in the Rue Morgue" is indeed a story of the most marvellous skill: It was the first of its kind, and to this day it remains a model, not only unsurpassed, but unapproachable. It was the first of detective stories; and it has had thousands of imitations and no rival. The originality, the ingenuity, the verisimilitude of this tale and of its fellows are beyond all praise. Poe had a faculty which one may call imaginative ratiocination to a degree beyond all other writers of fiction.—MATTHEWS, BRANDER, 1885–1901, *The Philosophy of the Short-story*, *p.* 44.

Closely akin to this dryness of treatment is a certain insincerity of tone or flourish of manner, that often interferes with our enjoyment of Poe. We become suddenly aware of the gleaming eye and complacent smile of the concealed manipulator in the writing-automaton. The author is too plainly lying in wait for us; or he is too ostentatiously exhibiting his cleverness and resource, his command of the tricks of the game. One of the worst things that can be said of Poe from this point of view is that he contains the promise and potency of Mr. Robert Hichens, and of other cheap English decadents. Poe himself is never quite a mere acrobat; but he suggests the possible coming of the acrobat, the clever tumbler with the ingenious grimace and the palm itching for coppers.—GATES, LEWIS E., 1900, *Studies and Appreciations*, *p.* 125.

The tales may be said to constitute a distinct addition to the world's literature. From time immemorial there have been tales in prose and in verse, tales legendary, romantic, and humorous, but never any quite like Poe's. How difficult it is to find any derivation for them may be seen from the fact that the writers most commonly mentioned as having given some direction to Poe's genius are Defoe and Bulwer! Godwin and the German Hoffmann would be nearer the mark, yet very distant still. "Bizarre" and "terrific" are the words which Kennedy in his helplessness applied to the tales; and the words represent fairly the first impression which they will always make, for the two qualities of strangeness and power are to be found in nearly all. A few are grotesque only, but they are among the weakest and are seldom read. Perhaps we may venture to divide the important ones, according to their dominant motives, into analytical tales, allegorical or moral tales, and tales of the supernatural.—NEWCOMER, ALPHONSO G., 1901, *American Literature*, *p.* 118.

In the "Tales of Ratiocination" Poe laid the foundation for the modern school of "detective stories." In "The Murders in the Rue Morgue," "The Mystery of Marie Rogêt," "The Gold Bug," and "The Purloined Letter," Poe solved mysteries by the detective's process of analysis. As a result of his success, he received many actual cryptographs to decipher, and still further revealed his powers by publishing in *Graham's Magazine* a careful solution of the intricate plot of Dickens's "Barnaby Rudge," when only the introductory chapters had appeared. Monsieur Dupin, who appears in several of these stories, is the original of Doyle's Sherlock Holmes, while the detective stories of Anna Katherine Green and other moderns have Poe's method without his genius. . . . Poe's detective stories differ from modern imitations not in ingenuity of solution of complex plot, but in artistic selection and handling of material. "The Purloined Letter" is as far from the ordinary "detective story" as Stevenson's "Treasure Island" from the "blood-and-thunder pirate story."—NETTLETON, GEORGE HENRY, 1901, *ed. Specimens of the Short Story*, *pp.* 80, 82.

CRITICISMS

The harshness of his criticisms I have never attributed to anything but the irritation of a sensitive nature, chafed by some indefinite sense of wrong.—LONGFELLOW, HENRY WADSWORTH, 1849, *Southern Literary Messenger*, *November*.

Had he been really in earnest, with what a solid brilliancy his writings might have shone forth to the world. With the moral proportioned to the intellectual faculty he would have been in the first rank of critics. In that large part of the critic's perceptions, he has been unsurpassed by any writer in America; but lacking sincerity, his forced and contradictory critical opinions are of little value as authorities, though much may be gathered from them by any one willing to study the peculiar mood in which they were written.—DUYCKINCK, EVERT A., AND GEORGE L., 1855–65–75, *Cyclopædia of American Literature, ed. Simons, vol.* II, *p.* 404.

As a critic, Poe spent himself upon questions of detail, and, in all cases, belittled his subject. He did not exercise the most engaging faculties of his mind. He is brilliant, caustic, stinging, personal without geniality, expressing an irritated mind.

Reading his criticisms, we think his literary being might be said to resemble a bush that blossoms into a few perfect flowers, but always has its thorns in thickest profusion. Poe was what may be called a *technical critic*. He delighted to involve his reader in the mechanism of poetry, and convict his victim of ignorance, while he used his knowledge as a means to be exquisitely insolent. He was like an art critic stuffed with the jargon of studies, talking an unknown language; careless about the elements of the subject which, properly, are the chief and only concern of the public. That Poe was acute, that he was exact, that he was original, no one can question; but he was not stimulating, and comprehensive, and generous, like the more sympathetic critics, as, for example, Diderot or Carlyle.—BENSON, EUGENE, 1868, *Poe and Hawthorne, The Galaxy, vol.* 6, *p.* 747.

There was but little literary criticism in the United States at the time Hawthorne's earlier works were published; but among the reviewers Edgar Poe perhaps held the scales the highest. He, at any rate, rattled them loudest, and pretended, more than any one else, to conduct the weighing-process on scientific principles. Very remarkable was this process of Edgar Poe's, and very extraordinary were his principles; but he had the advantage of being a man of genius, and his intelligence was frequently great. His collection of critical sketches of the American writers flourishing in what M. Taine would call his *milieu* and *moment*, is very curious and interesting reading, and it has one quality which ought to keep it from ever being completely forgotten. It is probably the most complete and exquisite specimen of *provincialism* ever prepared for the edification of men. Poe's judgments are pretentious, spiteful, vulgar; but they contain a great deal of sense and discrimination as well, and here and there, sometimes at frequent intervals, we find a phrase of happy insight imbedded in a patch of the most fatuous pedantry.—JAMES, HENRY, JR., 1880, *Nathaniel Hawthorne (English Men of Letters), p.* 62.

A keen critic.—DOWDEN, EDWARD, 1880, *Southey (English Men of Letters), p.* 196.

The poor man certainly raked and scraped the field of "American literature" with sufficient assiduity. If the result was not very valuable, certainly it was not alone the critic's mistake. What he said of his illustrious company of incipient celebrities and moribund mediocrities was sometimes bitter, unjust, limited in range, brightened or darkened by personal prejudices, and therefore almost as unread to-day as the books he described. But much in his method and achievement deserves grateful praise. Poe cleared the heated and unwholesome atmosphere which overhung our literature; he exposed many pretentious humbugs, who attitudinized as "men of letters," or "Poetesses;" and, if we except his pseudo-critical praise of the verse of his sympathizing women-friends and his angry screams over his men-enemies the general average of his criticism was both intelligent and wholesome. He showed American authors and scribblers that there existed among them a critic who, though not without favor, could at least write without fear. . . . Poe seems to later critics more often right than wrong; and sometimes his analyses and prophecies were surprisingly accurate. With a mind not unjustly priding itself upon ratiocinative power, this could hardly be otherwise.—RICHARDSON, CHARLES F., 1885, *American Literature*, 1607–1885, *vol.* I, *p.* 406.

In fact, his reputation as a critic would now suffer rather for the mercy he showed than for the vengeance he took. With what hesitancy he suggests that Mrs. Sigourney might profitably forget Mrs. Hemans; with what consideration he hints a fault in Mrs. Ellet, or just notices a blemish in Miss Gould; with what respect he treats Mellen and Gallagher! And if he asserts that Drake had an analogical rather than a creative mind, and insinuates that Halleck's laurel was touched with an artificial green,—these were the names that a lesser man would have let pass unchallenged. The whole mass of this criticism—but a small portion of which deals with imaginative work—is particularly characterized by a minuteness of treatment which springs from a keen, artistic sensibility, and by that constant regard to the orginality of the writer which is so frequently an element in the jealousy of genius. One wearies in reading it now; but one gains thereby the better impression of Poe's patience and of the alertness and compass of his mental curiosity.—WOODBERRY, GEORGE E., 1885, *Edgar Allan Poe (American Men of Letters), p.* 90.

Acute rather than comprehensive, he professed to be a critic, but, apart from the mechanism of authorship, which he called the philosophy of composition, his verdicts were of no value.—STODDARD, RICHARD HENRY, 1891, *A Box of Autographs, Scribner's Magazine, vol.* 9, *p.* 227.

That most exquisite critic Edgar Poe. —SWINBURNE, ALGERNON CHARLES, 1891, *Social Verse, The Forum, vol.* 12, *p.* 181.

I read with no less zest than his poems the bitter, and cruel, and narrow-minded criticisms which mainly filled one of the volumes. As usual, I accepted them implicitly, and it was not till long afterward that I understood how worthless they were.—HOWELLS, WILLIAM DEAN, 1895, *My Literary Passions, p.* 119.

His discriminations with respect to writers of importance have for the most part been confirmed. Sometimes they were affected by gratitude, as in the cases of Kennedy and Willis, the peculiar status of the latter affording Poe a chance to express his conviction that the mere man of letters could not then hold his own in America, but needed the aid of some factitious social position. But he might as well have said this of Bulwer and Disraeli in England. He was not far out in his estimates of Cooper and Bryant; he saw that Hawthorne, Longfellow, and Lowell were to be among the foremost builders of our imaginative literature, and his rally to the defence of young Bayard Taylor was quick and fine. He ranked Lowell high among our poets, on the score of his imagination, but found his ear for rhythm imperfect. Whittier seemed to him distinctly unimaginative, and as a Southerner and artist he was opposed to the poet-reformer's themes; but he recognized his *vivida vis,* his expressional fervor. Poe was among the first to do homage, in an outburst of genuine delight, to the rising genius of Tennyson.—STEDMAN, EDMUND CLARENCE, 1895, *Works of Edgor Allan Poe, ed. Stedman and Woodberry, vol.* vi, *p.* xxii.

His criticism was almost entirely free from that narrow localism which values a writer because he belongs to a section, and not because his work belongs to literature. He brought into the field of criticism large knowledge of the best that had been done in literature, and clear perception of the principles of the art of writing. His touch on his contemporaries who won the easy successes which are always within reach in untrained communities was often caustic, as it had need to be; but the instinct which made him the enemy of inferior work gave him also the power of recognizing the work of the artist, even when it came from unknown hands. He discerned the reality of imagination in Hawthorne and Tennyson as clearly as he saw the vulgarity and crudity of much of the popular writing of his time. By critical intention, therefore, as well as by virtue of the possession of genius, which is never provincial, Poe emancipated himself, and went far to emancipate American literature, from the narrow spirit, the partial judgment, and the inferior standards of a people not yet familiar with the best that has been thought and said in the world. To the claims of local pride he opposed the sovereign claims of art; against the practice of the half-inspired and the wholly untrained he set the practice of the masters. When the intellectual history of the country is written he will appear as one of its foremost liberators.—MABIE, HAMILTON W., 1899, *Poe's Place in American Literature, Poe Memorial, ed. Kent, p.* 58.

GENERAL

There is poetry in the man, though, now and then, seen between the great gaps of bathos. . . . "Politian" will make you laugh—as the "Raven" made *me* laugh, though with something in it which accounts for the hold it took upon such as Mr. N. P. Willis and his peers—it was sent to me from *four* different quarters besides the author himself, before its publication in this form, and when it had only a newspaper life. Some of the other lyrics have power of a less questionable sort. For the author, I do not know him at all—never heard from him nor wrote to him—and in my opinion, there is more faculty shown in the account of that horrible mesmeric experience (mad or not mad) than in his poems. Now do read it from the beginning to the end. That *going out* of the hectic, struck me very much . . . and the writhing *away* of the upper lip. Most horrible! Then I believe so much of mesmerism, as to give room for the full acting of the story on me . . . without absolutely giving full credence to it, understand.—BROWNING, ELIZABETH BARRETT, 1846, *To Robert Browning, Jan.* 26; *The Letters of Robert Browning and Elizabeth Barrett Browning, vol.* I, *p.* 429.

There comes Poe, with his "Raven," like "Barnaby Rudge,"
Three-fifths of him genius and two-fifths sheer fudge,
Who talks like a book of iambs and pentameters,
In a way to make people of common sense damn metres,
Who has written some things quite the best of their kind,
But the heart somehow seems all squeezed out by the mind.

—LOWELL, JAMES RUSSELL, 1848, *A Fable for Critics.*

That the author of the "Raven," &c., was a poet no doubt can exist. Extravagant as our opinion may now appear, we venture to say that in a few years, when the memory of his failings shall have died away, he will be considered one of America's best poets. He was the first who arrested our attention, and conveyed to our mind the fact that a man of great peculiarity was speaking. We use peculiarity out of a sort of insecurity and hesitation we do not often feel, otherwise we have a full and strong inclination to write originality. Had we been in England we should unhesitatingly have done so; but as Mr. Poe is only an American, we forbear to move a second time the indignation of the Press by claiming for a native of this great republic a common share of God's great gift of intellect. The day will, however, come when all the objections of a foreign Press will not prevent justice being done to the native genius of the land of Washington. —POWELL, THOMAS, 1850, *The Living Authors of America, p.* 121.

Just look at the dreadful, the unquenchable, the infernal *life* of Poe's "Lyrics and Tales." No one can read these without shuddering, without pity, and sorrow, and condemnation of the author, without a half-muttered murmur of inquiry at his Maker—"Why this awful anomaly in thy works?" And yet no one can avoid reading them, and reading them again, and hanging over their lurid and lightning-blasted pages, and thinking that this wondrous being wanted only two things to have made him the master of American minds—virtue and happiness.—GILFILLAN, GEORGE, 1855, *A Third Gallery of Portraits, p.* 130.

That exquisite piece of mystery and music, "The Raven;" . . . "Annabel Lee," . . . one of the sweetest lyrics in the language. His prose tales are full of wild and absorbing interest.—COLLIER, WILLIAM FRANCIS, 1861, *A History of English Literature, p.* 531.

Poe is a kind of Hawthorne and *delirium tremens.* What is exquisitely fanciful and airy in the genuine artist is replaced in his rival by an attempt to overpower us by dabblings in the charnel-house and pruient appeals to our fears of the horribly revolting. After reading some of Poe's stories one feels a kind of shock to one's modesty. We require some kind of spiritual ablution to cleanse our minds of his disgusting images.—STEPHEN, LESLIE, 1874, *Hours in a Library, First Series.*

Your desire to honor Poe's genius is in the heart of every man of letters, though perhaps no American author stands so little in need of a monument to perpetuate his memory as the author of the "Raven." His imperishable fame is in all lands.—ALDRICH, THOMAS BAILEY, 1875, *Letter to the Poe Memorial, Oct.* 10, *ed. Rice, p.* 90.

Through many a night of want and woe
His frenzied spirit wandered wild—
Till kind disaster laid him low,
And Heaven reclaimed its wayward child.
Through many a year his fame has grown,—
Like midnight, vast, like starlight sweet,—
Till now his genius fills a throne,
And nations marvel at his feet.

—WINTER, WILLIAM, 1875, *At Poe's Grave, Poe Memorial, ed. Rice, p.* 48.

The hearts of all who reverence the inspiration of genius, who can look tenderly upon the infirmities too often attending it, who can feel for its misfortunes, will sympathize with you as you gather around the resting place of all that was mortal of Edgar Allan Poe, and raise the stone inscribed with one of the few names which will outlive the graven record meant to perpetuate its remembrance.—HOLMES, OLIVER WENDELL, 1875, *Letter to the Poe Memorial, Sept.* 18, *ed. Rice, p.* 80.

The extraordinary genius of Edgar Poe is now acknowledged the world over.—WHITTIER, JOHN GREENLEAF, 1875, *Letter to the Poe Memorial, Sep.* 21, *ed. Rice.*

One whose original genius has done so much to adorn and distinguish American literature.—SAXE, JOHN GODFREY, 1875, *Letter to the Poe Memorial, Oct.* 10, *ed. Rice, p.* 88.

My firm conviction that widely as the fame of Poe has already spread, and deeply as it is already rooted, in Europe, it is even now growing wider and striking deeper as time advances; the surest presage that time, the eternal enemy of small and shallow reputations, will prove in this case also the constant and trusty friend and keeper of a true poet's full-grown fame. —SWINBURNE, ALGERNON CHARLES, 1875, *Letter to the Poe Memorial, Nov.* 9, *ed. Rice.*

No cunning barrister preparing an important brief; no great actor studying a new part; no machinist brooding over the invention of an engine, or a change subversive of the old machinery; no analytic chemist seeking to establish the fact of a murder by the discovery and proof of blood or poison in some unexpected substance; no Dutch painter working for months on the minute finish of all sorts of details in the background as well as foreground of his picture,—ever took more pains than did Edgar Allan Poe in the production of most of his principal works. The more impossible his story, the more perseveringly, learnedly, patiently, and plausibly he labored to prove the facts as he saw them. And, unless you throw the book down, he always succeeds. If you read on steadily, you must go with him.—HORNE, RICHARD HENGIST, 1876, *Letter to the Poe Memorial, Apr.* 8, *ed. Rice, p.* 81.

A literary *Erinaceus*. . . . Professing himself the special apostle of the beautiful in art, he nevertheless forces upon us continually the most loathsome hideousness and the most debasing and unbeautiful horror. This passionate, unhelmed, errant search for beauty was in fact not so much a normal and intelligent desire, as an attempt to escape from interior discord; and it was the discord which found expression, accordingly, instead of the sense of beauty,—except (as has been said) in fragments. Whatever the cause his brain had a rift of ruin in it, from the start, and though his delicate touch often stole a new grace from classic antiquity, it was the frangibility, the quick decay, the fall of all lovely and noble things, that excited and engaged him. . . . Always beauty and grace are with him most poetic in their overthrow, and it is the shadow of ruined grandeur that he receives, instead of the still living light so fair upon them, or the green growth clinging around them.—LATHROP, GEORGE PARSONS, 1876, *A Study of Hawthorne, pp.* 206, 309.

He loved all shadowy spots, all seasons drear;
All ways of darkness lured his ghastly whim;
Strange fellowships he held with goblins grim,
At whose demoniac eyes he felt no fear.
On midnights through dense branches he would peer,
To watch the pale ghoul feed, by tombstones dim,
The appalling forms of phantoms walked with him,
And murder breathed its red guilt in his ear!
By desolate paths of dream, where fancy's owl
Sent long lugubrious hoots through sombre air
Amid thought's gloomiest caves he went to prowl,
And met delirium in her awful lair,
And mingled with cold shapes that writhe or scowl,
Serpents of horror, black bats of despair!
—FAWCETT, EDGAR, 1876-78, *Poe, Fantasy and Passion, p.* 182.

There is not an unchaste suggestion in the whole course of his writings,—a remarkable fact, in view of his acquaintances with the various schools of French literature. His works are almost too spiritual.—STEDMAN, EDMUND CLARENCE, 1880, *Edgar Allen Poe, p.* 93.

One of the most morbid men of genius the modern world has seen; in the regions of the strangely terrible, remotely fantastic, and ghastly, he reigns supreme. With his lyrics we have not here to do. His best prose is no less distinctive and admirable for richness, force, clearness, and the correct choice of phrase, only definable as the literary touch. He, in this field, distances all his competitors, except Balzac, in the mental dissecting-room his only master. But, while the Frenchman deals with anomalous realities, the power of the American consists in making unrealities appear natural. Many of his works, like Hawthorne's, are either pages torn, as it were, from the second or third volumes of a complete romance, or suggestions of what might have been developed into one. This fragmentary manner has its disadvantages; but the writer of real imagination, who confines it within limited bounds, never allows the interest of his readers to flag. Edgar Poe is consequently, save in his acrid criticisms and mistaken attempts at humour, never dull.—NICHOL, JOHN, 1880–85, *American Literature, p.* 163.

I know several striking poems by American poets, but I think that Edgar Poe is (taking his poetry and prose together) the most original American genius.—TENNYSON, ALFRED LORD, 1883, *Criticisms on Poets and Poetry, Memoir by his Son, vol.* II, *p.* 292.

> A certain tyrant, to disgrace
> The more a rebel's resting-place,
> Compelled the people every one
> To hurl, in passing there, a stone,
> Which done, behold, the pile became
> A monument to keep the name.
> And thus it is with Edgar Poe;
> Each passing critic has his throw,
> Nor sees, defeating his intent,
> How lofty grows the monument.

—TABB, JOHN B., 1885, *Poe's Critics, Harper's Magazine, vol.* 70, *p.* 498.

Farewell, Farewell, thou sombre and solitary spirit: a genius tethered to the hack-work of the press, a gentleman among *canaille*, a poet among poetasters, dowered with a scholar's taste without a scholar's training, embittered by his sensitive scorn, and all unsupported by his consolations.—LANG, ANDREW, 1886, *Letters to Dead Authors, p.* 150.

Edgar Allan Poe was fastidious—even morbidly fastidious—in his love of beautiful form; but he had no root of humanity in him, and little passion for actual external nature. He was not an interpreter. He had no mission, save to create dreams. A greater dreamer in prose than in verse, he has yet added to American literature a few poems of the most striking originality; but of deep spirituality he has none. His loftiest flights of imagination in verse, like his boldest efforts in prose fiction, rise into no more empyreal realm than the fantastic. His sense of beauty in language was usually fine. Like Gautier, he loved to work "in" onyx and enamel.—ROBERTSON, ERIC S., 1886, *Life of Henry Wadsworth Longfellow* (*Great Writers*), *p.* 173.

Oblivious of what I may have said, but fully conscious of what I mean to say, Poe was a curious compound of the charlatan and the courtly gentleman; a mixture of Count Cagliostro, of Paracelsus, who was wisely named Bombastes, and of Cornelius Agrippa,—the three beings intermoulded from the dust of Apollonius of Tyana and Elymas the Sorcerer. His first master in verse was Byron, in prose Charles Brockden Brown, and later Hawthorne. Most men are egoists; he was egotistical. His early poems are exquisite, his later ones are simply melodious madness. The parent. of "Annabel Lee" was Mother Goose, who in this instance did *not* drop a golden egg. Always a plagiarist, he was always original. Like Molière, whom he derided, he took his own wherever he found it. Without dramatic instinct, he persuaded himself (but no one else) that he was a dramatist. The proof of this assertion is his drama of "Politian," which was never ended, and which should never have been begun.—STODDARD, RICHARD HENRY, 1889, *Edgar Allan Poe, Lippincott's Magazine, vol.* 43, *p.* 109.

A meteoric genius, a wandering star, a man cursed and ruined by his own follies, and without significance as regards his times.—DAWSON, W. J., 1892, *Quest and Vision, p.* 279.

Turning aside from his own special field of literature, Baudelaire talked and wrote to make the name of Edgar Poe famous; and he was successful, for, as a Frenchman has himself certified, "It was through the labour and genius of Baudelaire that Edgar Poe's tales have become so well known in France, and are now regarded as classical models." Further, it should be noticed that Edgar Poe is the only American writer who has become popular in that land where the literature of the nineteenth century has reached a perfecton which after-ages will certainly record and admire. But we ask ourselves, Is this result due to the exquisite style Baudelaire employed in his translation? and would his magic pen have endowed any foreign author, however unworthy, with fame? Did the strange influence lie in the rich fancy of the American author or in the richer setting given to it by the Frenchman? Baudelaire must evidently have known English well; but did he, whilst reading it, simultaneously clothe the English words in his own French dress, or did English style and New World fancy win his admiration? These questions are difficult to answer. Baudelaire's explanation does not altogether clear up the difficulty. "Believe me or not, as you like," he says, "but I discovered in Edgar Poe's works, poems and stories which had been lying dormant in my own brain, vague, confused, ill-assorted, whilst he had known how to combine, to transcribe, and to bring them to perfection." Here was, according to the French poet, the secret of his success. He had discovered his affinity; he had but to collect his own floating ideas, finding no difficulty in the setting, for all was clear to him. The two authors were of one mind, and the result was this gift of classic work to France, created with alien thought.—STUART, ESMÈ, 1893, *Charles Baudelaire and Edgar Poe, The Nineteenth Century, vol.* 34, *p.* 66.

Hawthorne and Poe stand at the head of American literature in the line of creative ability. The chosen field of both was romance. Hawthorne, as said, had a large sense of humor, in which Poe was somewhat deficient. Hawthorne, though a recluse by nature, had finer touches of human sympathy. Poe had more of that imaginaiton which bodies forth shapes unknown from airy nothingness and clothes them with rarest beauty. In structure of work, in painting with the rich colors of the South, Poe has never been excelled. When we would classify him, we may mention Coleridge and others as similar at a few points, but the author of "The Raven" and "The Fall of the House of Usher" stands alone. His works are unique and original. —LINK, SAMUEL ALBERT, 1898, *Pioneers of Southern Literature, vol.* II, *p.* 331.

It is the first and perhaps the most obvious distinction of Edgar Allan Poe that his creative work baffles all attempts to relate it historically to antecedent conditions; that it detached itself almost completely from the time and place in which it made its appearance, and sprang suddenly and mysteriously from a soil which had never borne its like before. There was nothing in the America of the third decade of the century which seemed to predict "The City in the Sea," "Israfel," and the lines, "To Helen." . . . Poe stood alone among his contemporaries by reason of the fact that, while his imagination was fertilized by the movement of the time, his work was not, in theme or sympathy, representative of the forces behind it. The group of gifted men, with whom he had for most part only casual connections, reflected the age behind them or the time in which they lived; Poe shared with them the creative impulse without sharing the specific interests and devotions of the period. He was primarily and distinctively the artist of his time; the man who cared for his art, not for what he could say through it, but for what it had to say through him. . . . Poe alone, among men of his eminence, could not have been foreseen. This fact suggests his limitations, but it also brings into clear view the unique individuality of his genius and the originality of his work. His contemporaries are explicable; Poe is inexplicable. He remains the most sharply-defined personality in our literary history. His verse and his imaginative prose stand out in bold relief against a background which neither suggests nor interprets them. One may go further, and affirm that both his verse and his prose have a place by themselves in the literature of the world.—MABIE, HAMILTON W., 1899, *Poe's Place in American Literature, Poe Memorial, ed. Kent, pp.*44, 46, 47.

Few, I fancy, will be present at that festival who can recall, as I do, the effect of the first publication of the poem which flamed like a meteor across our literary heavens and made the name of Poe immediately famous. When a boy in the backwoods of Western New York, I saw "The Raven" in one of the hundred of country papers in which it was almost simultaneously copiéd, and recognized at once that a new genius had arisen to divide the homage I paid to Byron, my prime favorite in those early days. Anything connected with the name of Poe interested me intensely from that time; and though I never met him, I felt a shock of personal bereavement when his tragic death occurred, in 1849. Then, it was thought by some, a meteor of a night-time had burned itself out in space. But the genius of Poe was no meteor; it was a star of peculiar brilliancy, from which the mists of doubt and misunderstanding have parted more and more, and which still shows no signs of fading, amidst the brightest luminaries of our sky.—TROWBRIDGE, JOHN TOWNSEND, 1899, *Letter to the Poe Memorial, ed. Kent, p.* 63.

When a boy of seventeen, in Harvard College, I read Poe's "Tales of the Grotesque and Arabesque." It was just after the publication of the book and before it had attracted general attention; but I felt it at once to be the most remarkable production of the imaginative genius of this nation, save the works of Hawthorne alone; nor have I ever varied from that opinion. Later I heard Poe read his "Ligeia," before an audience in Boston, in a voice whose singular music I have never heard equalled. These two early impressions sustained my admiration and gratitude for Poe through all his stormy and sad career. —HIGGINSON, THOMAS WENTWORTH, 1899, *Letter to the Poe Memorial, ed. Kent, p.* 64.

A half century has passed since the death of our poet and romancer, and no man has appeared who is worthy to stand beside him in his chosen field of literature. His maligners make his sky dark, but the stars of his intellect—and they are many—shine all the brighter.—STOCKTON, FRANK R., 1899, *Letter to the Poe Memorial, ed. Kent, p.* 68.

In tales and poems alike he is most characteristic when dealing with mysteries; and though to a certain point these mysteries, often horrible, are genuinely mysterious, they reveal no trace of spiritual insight. They indicate a sense that human perception is inexorably limited, but no vital perception of the eternities which lie beyond it. Excellent in their way, one cannot but feel their way to be melodramatic. The very word, "melodramatic" recalls to us the strolling stage from which Poe almost accidentally sprung in that Boston lodging-house ninety years ago. From beginning to end his temper had the inextricable combination of meretriciousness and sincerity which makes the temperament of typical actors. Theirs is a strange trade, wherein he does best who best shams. At its noblest the stage rises into tragedy or breadthens into comedy; but in our century it has probably appealed most generally to the public when it has assumed its less poetical and more characteristic form of melodrama. Poe, at least temperamentally, seems to have been a melodramatic creature of genius.—WENDELL, BARRETT, 1900, *A Literary History of America, p.* 213.

Maria Edgeworth

1767–1849

Born, at Black Burton, Oxfordshire, Jan. 1, 1767. In Ireland with father, 1773–75. To School in Derby, 1775; in London, 1780. Home to Edgeworthstown 1782. Began to write stories. To Clifton with parents, Dec. 1791; returned to Edgeworthstown, winter of 1793. Visit to France with father, Oct. 1802 to March 1803. Visit to London, spring of 1803; to Bowood, autumn of 1818; to London, 1819; to Paris and Switzerland, 1820 to March 1821. Returned to Edgeworthstown and lived there for rest of life. Occasional visits to London. Visit to Scotland, spring of 1823. Friendship with Sir Walter Scott; he visited her at Edgeworthstown, 1825. Active philanthropy during famine of 1846. Died, at Edgeworthstown, 22 May 1849. *Works:* "Letters to Literary Ladies," 1795; "Parent's Assistant" (anon.), pt. i., 1796; in 6 vols. 1800; "Practical Education," 1798; "Castle Rackrent" (anon.), 1800; Early Lessons," 1801; "Belinda," 1801; "Moral Tales," 1801; "Irish Bulls," 1802; "Popular Tales," 1804; "Modern Griselda," 1804; "Leonora," 1806; "Tales from Fashionable Life," 1809; 2nd series, 1812; "Patronage," 1814; "Continuation of Early Lessons," 1815; "Harington," 1817; "Ormond," 1817; "Comic Dramas," 1817; vol. ii. of R. L. Edgeworth's Memoirs," 1820; "Frank," 1822; "Harry and Lucy, concluded," 1825; "Garry Owen," 1832; "Helen," 1834. *Collected Works:* in 14 vols., 1825; in 18 vols., 1832–33; in 12 vols., 1893. *Life:* by H. Zimmern, 1883 ("Eminent Women" series); "Life and Letters," ed. by Aug. Hare, 1894.—SHARP, R. FARQUHARSON, 1897, *A Dictionary of English Authors, p.* 90.

PERSONAL

I had persuaded myself that the author of the work on Education, and of other productions, useful as well as ornamental, would betray herself by a remarkable exterior. I was mistaken. A small figure, eyes nearly always lowered, a profoundly modest and reserved air, with expression in the features when not speaking: such was the result of my first survey. But when she spoke, which was too rarely for my taste, nothing could have been better thought, and nothing better said, though always timidly expressed.—PICTET, MARC-AUGUSTE, 1802, *Voyage de trois mois en Angleterre, tr. Oliver.*

Mr., Mrs., and Miss Edgeworth are just come over from Ireland, and are the general objects of curiosity and attention. I passed some hours with them yesterday afternoon, under pretence of visiting the new Mint, which was a great object to them, as they are all proficients in mechanics. Miss Edgeworth is a most agreeable person, very natural, clever, and well informed, without the least pretensions of authorship. She had never been in a large society before, and she was followed and courted by all the persons of distinction in London, with an avidity almost without example. The court paid to her gave her an opportunity of showing her excellent understanding and character. She took every advantage of her situation, either for enjoyment or observation; but she remained perfectly unspoiled by the homage of the great.—MACKINTOSH, SIR JAMES, 1813, *Journal, May* 11; *Memoirs of Mackintosh, ed. his Son, vol.* II, *p.* 267.

I went to Lady Davy's in the evening. There were seventy or eighty people there: amongst others Miss Edgeworth, who was my object. She is very small, with a countenance which promises nothing at first sight, or as one sees her in society. She has very winning manners. She received with much warmth what I said of my desire to see the author of her works, and of all the obligations that I felt in common with all our sex towards one of her genius.—BERRY, MARY, 1813, *Extracts of the Journals and Correspondence, ed. Lewis, vol.* II, *p.* 534.

She was a nice little unassuming "Jeanie Deans'-looking bodie" as we Scotch say —and if not handsome certainly not ill-looking. Her conversation was as quiet as herself. One could never have guessed that she could write *her name;* whereas her father talked, *not* as if he could write nothing else, but as if nothing else was worth writing.—BYRON, LORD, 1821, *Journal, Jan.* 19.

We saw, you will readily suppose, a great deal of Miss Edgeworth, and two very nice girls, her younger sisters. It is scarcely possible to say more of this very remarkable person, than that she not only completely answered, but exceeded the expectations which I had formed. I am particularly pleased with the *naïveté* and good-humoured ardour of mind which she unites with such formidable powers of acute observation. In external appearance, she is quite the fairy of our nursery-tale—the Whippity Stourie, if you remember such a sprite, who came flying through the window to work all sorts of marvels. I will never believe but what she has a wand in her pocket, and pulls it out to conjure a little before she begins those very striking pictures of manners.—SCOTT, SIR WALTER, 1823, *Letter to Joanna Baillie, July* 11; *Life by Lockhart, ch.* lix.

Miss Edgeworth, with all her cleverness, anything but agreeable. The moment any one begins to speak, off she starts too, seldom more than a sentence behind them, and in general continues to distance every speaker. Neither does what she says, though of course very sensible, at all make up for this over-activity of tongue. —MOORE, THOMAS, 1831, *Diary, Memoirs, Journal and Correspondence, ed. Russell, vol.* VI, *p.* 187.

As we drove to the door Miss Edgeworth came out to meet us,—a small, short, spare lady of about sixty-seven, with extremely frank and kind manners, and who always looks straight into your face with a pair of mild, deep gray eyes, whenever she speaks to you. . . . Mrs. Edgeworth—who is of the Beaufort family—seems about the age of her more distinguished step-daughter, and is somewhat stout, but very active, intelligent, and accomplished, having apparently the whole care of the household, and adding materially, by her resources in the arts and in literature, to its agreeableness. . . . It is plain they make a harmonious whole, and by those who visited here when the family was much larger, and composed of the children of all the wives of Mr. Edgeworth, with their connections produced by marriage, so as to form the most heterogeneous relationships, I am told there was always the same very striking union and agreeable intercourse among them all, to the number sometimes of fifteen or twenty. . . . What has struck me most today in Miss Edgeworth herself, is her uncommon quickness of perception, her fertility of allusion, and the great resources of fact which a remarkable memory supplies to her, combined into a whole which I can call nothing else but extraordinary vivacity.—TICKNOR, GEORGE, 1835, *Journal, Aug.* 21; *Life, Letters and Journals, vol.* I, *pp.* 426, 427.

The next month—August 1823—was one of the happiest in Scott's life. Never did I see a brighter day at Abbotsford than that on which Miss Edgeworth first arrived there—never can I forget her look and accent when she was received by him at his archway, and exclaimed, "Everything about you is exactly what one ought to have had wit enough to dream!" The weather was beautiful, and the edifice, and its appurtenances, were all but complete; and day after day, so long as she could remain, her host had always some new plan of gayety. One day there was fishing on the Cauldshields Loch, and a dinner on the heathy bank. Another, the whole party feasted by Thomas the Rhymer's waterfall in the glen—and the stone on which Maria that day sat was ever afterwards called *Edgeworth's stone.*—LOCKHART, JOHN GIBSON, 1837–38, *Memoirs of the Life of Sir Walter Scott, ch.* lix.

I am now writing in the Library here: and the great Authoress is as busy as a bee making a catalogue of her books beside me, chattering away. We are great friends. She is as lively, active, and cheerful as if she were but twenty; really a very entertaining person. We talk about Walter Scott whom she adores, and are merry all the day long.—FITZGERALD, EDWARD, 1841, *Letters, vol.* I, *p.* 74.

To have repeatedly met and listened to Miss Edgeworth, seated familiarly with her by the fireside, may seem to her admirers in America a sufficient payment for the hazards of crossing the Atlantic. Her conversation, like her writings, is varied, vivacious, and delightful. Her forgetfulness of self and happiness in making others happy are marked traits in her character. Her person is small and delicately proportioned, and her movements full of animation. The ill-health of the lovely sister, much younger than herself, at whose house in London she was passing the winter, called forth such deep anxiety, untiring attention, and fervent gratitude for every favourable symptom, as seemed to blend features of maternal tenderness with sisterly affection. — SIGOURNEY, LYDIA HUNTLEY, 1842, *Pleasant Memories of Pleasant Lands.*

Miss Edgeworth was delightful — so clever and sensible! She does not say witty things, but there is such a perfume of wit runs through all her conversation as makes it very brilliant.—SMITH, SYDNEY, 1844? *A Memoir of Rev. Sydney Smith, by Lady Holland, ch.* xii.

The fourth wife of Mr. Edgeworth was our hostess, and performed her part charmingly. She must have been very pretty, for, though short, fat, and forty, her appearance was very agreeable. Miss Edgeworth was shorter still, and carried herself very upright, with a dapper figure and quick movements. She was the remains of a blonde, with light eyes and hair; she was now gray, but wore a dark frizette, whilst the gray hair showed through her cap behind. She was so plain that she was never willing to sit for her portrait, and that is the reason why the public has never been made acquainted with her personal appearance. In conversation we found her delightful. She was full of anecdotes about remarkable people, and often spoke from her personal knowledge of them. Her memory, too, was stored with valuable information, and her manner of narrating was so animated, that it was difficult to realize her age.—FARRAR, ELIZA WARE, 1866, *Recollections of Seventy Years.*

I attended with much interest to the conversation of this remarkable woman. She was little and possessed of no personal attractions; it was evident that the usual feminine objects had never interfered with her masculine understanding. Her conversation was chiefly remarkable for its acuteness, good sense and practical sagacity. She had little imagination and scarcely any enthusiasm. Solid sense, practical acquirement—the qualities which will lead to success in the world—were her great endowments, and they appeared at every turn in her conversation, as they do in her writings. This disposition of mind kept her free from the usual littlenesses of authors and raised her far above the ordinary vanity of women. She was simple and unaffected in her manners, entirely free from conceit or effort in her conversation, and kindly and benevolent in her judgment of others, as well as in her views of life and in her intercourse with all around her. But she had neither a profound knowledge of human nature nor the elevated mental qualities which give a lasting ascendency over mankind.—ALISON, SIR ARCHIBALD, 1867–83, *Some Account of My Life and Writings.*

Her face was pale and thin, her features irregular; they may have been considered plain, even in youth; but her expression was so benevolent, her manners were so perfectly well-bred, partaking of English dignity and Irish frankness, that one never thought of her with reference either to beauty or plainness. She ever occupied, without claiming, attention, charming continually by her singularly pleasant voice; while the earnestness and truth that beamed from her bright blue—very blue—eyes increased the value of every word she uttered. . . . She was ever neat and particular in her dress; her feet and hands were so delicate and small as to be almost childlike.—HALL, MRS. SAMUEL CARTER, 1871, *A Book of Memories of Great Men and Women of the Age.*

Maria Edgeworth came frequently to see us when she was in England. She was one of my most intimate friends, warm-hearted and kind, a charming companion, with all the liveliness and originality of an Irishwoman. . . . The cleverness and animation, as well as affection of her letters I cannot express.—SOMERVILLE, MARY, 1872?-3, *Personal Recollections, from Early Life to Old Age, p.* 155.

Her personal appearance was that of a woman plain of dress, sedate in manners, and remarkably small of person. . . . There was a charm in all she looked and said and did. Incessant and yet genial activity was a marked feature of her nature. She seemed to be as nearly ubiquitous as a human creature can be, and always busy; not only as a teacher of her younger brothers and sisters (she was nearly fifty years older than one of them), but as the director and controller of the household. We could but liken her to the benevolent fairy from whose lips were perpetually dropping diamonds; there was so much of kindly wisdom in every sentence she uttered.—HALL, SAMUEL CARTER, 1883, *Retrospect of a Long Life, pp.* 359, 360.

Maria Edgeworth's life did not pass without the romance of love. She received an offer of marriage from a Swedish gentleman, while she was staying in Paris with her family in 1803. She returned his affections, but refused to marry him, sacrificing herself and him to what she believed to be her duty to her father and family. Her third and last step-mother wrote that for years "the unexpected mention of his name, or even that of Sweden, in a book or newspaper, always moved her so much that the words and lines in the page became a mass of confusion before her eyes, and her voice lost all power." Her suitor, M. Edelcrantz, never married. At the altar of filial piety she sacrificed much.—FAWCETT, MILLICENT GARRETT, 1889, *Some Eminent Women of Our Times, p.* 160.

Miss Edgeworth, too, seems to have been lifted from the sphere of matrimony by the unusual strength of her family affections. Her devotion to her father, to her two step-mothers, and to her nineteen brothers and sisters was of such an absorbing nature as to leave her little leisure or inclination for mere matters of sentiment. She was so busy too, so full of pleasant cares, and successful work, and a thousand-and-one delightful interests, above all, she clung so fondly to her home, and country, and the familiar faces she had known from babyhood, that love had no chance to storm her well-defended walls. When that handsome and earnest young Swede, he of the "superior understanding and mild manners," came to woo, he found, alas! that the lady could not tear her heart away from Ireland and her beautiful young step-sisters to give it to his keeping. She acknowledged his merits, both his mildness and his superiority, she liked and admired him in every way; but marry and go to Sweden!—that she would not do, either for M. Edelcrantz or any other man.—REPPLIER, AGNES, 1891, *Three Famous Old Maids, Lippincott's Magazine, vol.* 47, *p.* 691.

Her whole life, of eighty-three years, had been an aspiration after good.—HARE, AUGUSTUS J. C., 1894, *Life and Letters of Maria Edgeworth, vol.* II, *p.* 691.

PRACTICAL EDUCATION
1798

No one who has studied education in theory, or for the purpose of utilizing his information in teaching, should fail to read this book of the Edgeworths. There is a sincerity of purpose, and a direct, clear, and vivacious style, in "Practical Education," which will attract and interest all who are engaged in instruction. Several of the chapters are admirable and brilliant treatises on the subjects they profess to explain.—OLIVER, GRACE A., 1882, *A Study of Maria Edgeworth, p.* 134.

How induced, or why, I know not, I read when I was a boy Miss Edgeworth's treatise on "Practical Education." During many years, while I was officially connected with public schools, I was constantly giving to the teachers under my charge hints and maxims derived from that book, till I found that primary and infant schools in general were adopting as the fresh growth of recent times modes of instructions like those which Miss Edgeworth propounded to a non-receptive public almost a century ago.—PEABODY, ANDREW P., 1888, *Books That Have Helped Me, p.* 43.

CASTLE RACKRENT
1800

The inimitable "Castle Rackrent" I consider as one of the very best productions of genius in the language, in its own way. I only lament that others are not as well qualified as I am to judge of the faithful drawing and vivid colouring of that admirable work. To do this, one must have lived in Ireland, or the West Highlands, which contain much rack-rent; but one must not have lived always there, as, in that case, the force of these odd characters would be lost in their familiarity.—GRANT, ANNE, 1809, *To Mrs. Fletcher, July* 6; *Memoir and Correspondence, ed. Grant, vol.* I, *p.* 214.

Miss Edgeworth's "Castle Rackrent" and "Fashionable Tales" are incomparable in depicting truly several traits of the rather modern Irish character: they are perhaps on one point somewhat overcharged; but, for the most part, may be said to exceed Lady Morgan's Irish novels. The fiction is less perceptible in them: they have a greater air of reality—of what I have myself often and often observed and noted in full progress and actual execution throughout my native country. The landlord, the agent, and the attorney, of "Castle Rackrent" (in fact, every person it describes) are neither fictitious nor even uncommon characters: and the changes of landed property in the country where I was born (where perhaps they have prevailed to the full as widely as in any other united Empire) owed, in nine cases out of ten, their origin, progress, and catastrophe, to incidents in no wise differing from those so accurately painted in Miss Edgeworth's narrative. — BARRINGTON, SIR JONAH, 1830, *Personal Sketches of his Own Times, p.* 375.

One of the most powerful and impressive of her books is devoted to the miserable story of improvidence, recklessness, and folly, by which so many families have been ruined, and which is linked with so much that is attractive in the way of generosity and hospitality and open-handedness, that the hardest critic is mollified unawares, and the sympathetic populace, which is no adept in moral criticism, admires with enthusiasm while he lasts, and pities, when he has fallen, the culprit who is emphatically nobody's enemy but his own.—OLIPHANT, MARGARET O. W., 1882, *Literary History of England, XVIII-XIX Century, vol.* III, *p.* 174.

Miss Edgeworth never surpassed this her first work of note, and in some respects did not again come up to it.—MINTO, WILLIAM, 1894, *The Literature of the Georgian Era, ed. Knight, p.* 277.

A book with little interest of the strictly "novel" kind, but a wonderful picture of the varieties of recklessness and misconduct which in the course of a generation or two ruined or crippled most of the landlords of Ireland.—SAINTSBURY, GEORGE, 1896, *A History of Nineteenth Century Literature, p.* 127.

BELINDA
1801

"Belinda," too, though unequal and in some places absurd, contains more finely drawn and well sustained characters, more conversational wit, more salutary lessons against the abuse of wealth and talents, conveyed with equal facility and vivacity, and a more faithful delineation of modern manners, than any book of the kind that I know.—GRANT, ANNE, 1809, *To Mrs. Fletcher, July* 6; *Memoir and Correspondence, ed. Grant, vol.* I, *p.* 214.

There is no doubt that "Belinda" was much marred by the alterations made by Mr. Edgeworth, in whose wisdom and skill his far cleverer daughter had unlimited and touching confidence.—HARE, AUGUSTUS J. C., 1894, *Life and Letters of Maria Edgeworth, vol.* I, *p.* 73, *note.*

In "Belinda," for example, one of her tales of fashionable life, one of the most brilliantly drawn characters in fiction, Lady Delacour, is converted by the force of circumstances from a gay, heartless, daringly cynical leader of fashion into a model wife, and that, too, after years of outrageous frivolity.—MINTO, WILLIAM, 1894, *The Literature of the Georgian Era, ed. Knight, p.* 278.

TALES OF FASHIONABLE LIFE
1809–12

Despite her doctrines, her genius was too strong for her, and it is thanks to this that sundry of these tales from "Fashionable Life" are among her highest and most successful efforts. They are also as a whole more powerful and varied than any of her previous productions.—ZIMMERN, HELEN, 1883, *Maria Edgeworth (Famous Women), p.* 122.

A second series of "Tales of Fashionable Life" appeared in 1812. Of these "The Absentee" was a masterpiece, and contains one scene which Macaulay declared to be the best thing written of its kind since the opening of the twenty-second book of the "Odyssey." Yet Mrs. Edgeworth tells that the greater part of "The Absentee" was "written under the torture of the toothache; it was only by keeping her mouth full of some strong lotion that Maria could allay the pain, and yet, though in this state of suffering, she never wrote with more spirit and rapidity." Mr. Edgeworth advised the conclusion to be a Letter from Larry, the postillion: he wrote one, and she wrote another; he much preferred hers, which is the admirable finale to "The Absentee." —HARE, AUGUSTUS J. C., 1894, *Life and Letters of Maria Edgeworth, vol.* I, *p.* 190.

HELEN
1834

We know not when we have been more delighted, either as reviewers or as men, with any occurrence in the literary world, than with the opportunity of giving another welcome to Miss Edgeworth, the friend of our earlier years. And yet we must confess that our pleasure was mingled with many fears; for it was possible, that the recollection of the interest her writings used to inspire, might be stronger than the reality; there was a chance too, that during her long silence she might have lost something of her power, or that the public taste, so long used to the excitement of Scott's romances, might be less disposed than formerly to relish that quiet and unassuming excellence, which distinguishes Miss Edgeworth's writings. But whatever sentiments prevailed in our minds,—whether hopes or fears,—we believe that all intelligent readers will agree with us in the acknowledgement, that the fears were uncalled for, and the hopes have been exceeded. We remember her as the morning star, whose radiance was lost for a time in the excessive brightness of the rising sun; now we see her reappearing more beautiful than ever as the planet of evening, after that sun has left the sky.—PEABODY, W. B. O., 1834, *Helen, North American Review, vol.* 39, *p.* 167.

"Helen" shows some defects in the construction of its plot, but none in the execution of the details. There is an ease, lightness of touch, a certain air about it, which makes it as interesting as any of her novels, and far more agreeable than those which are weighted with so much effort to work out a moral. "Helen" is not wanting in a high tone; and the manner in which the untruthfulness of a society life is depicted, and the distress and suffering caused by one who evades or denies a fact, and makes an innocent friend the victim of a mistake of her own, is very interesting, and a valuable study.—OLIVER, GRACE A., 1882, *A Study of Maria Edgeworth, p.* 448.

"Helen," her last novel, which appeared after so long a silence, is in some respects the most charming of her tales—a fact doubtless due in some measure to the time that had elapsed since the cessation of her father's active influence. The old brilliancy, the quick humor, the strong sense of justice and truth which is the moral backbone of her work, are there as before; but through the whole tale there breathes a new spirit of wider tenderness for weak, struggling human nature, and a gentleness towards its foibles, which her earlier writings lacked. Years had taught her a wider toleration, had shown her, too, how large a part quick, unreasoning instincts and impulses play in the lives of men and women, even of those whose constant struggle it is to subdue act and thought to the rule of duty. . . . "Helen" was suggested by Crabbe's tale, "The Confidant," but that feeling which is sinfully gratified and severely punished in Crabbe's story becomes refined and reformed in Miss Edgeworth's crucible. It is, however, interesting to compare her romance with the rapid sketch of the stern original.

Another new feature in "Helen" is a tendency to describe natural objects. . . . Another feature of "Helen" is the lack of a didactic tone. Speaking of Scott's novels, she remarks that his morality is not in purple patches, ostentatiously obtrusive, but woven in through the very texture of the stuff. She knew that her faults lay in the opposite direction, and it is evident she had striven to avoid them. —ZIMMERN, HELEN, 1883, *Maria Edgeworth* (*Famous Women*), *pp.* 260, 265, 266.

GENERAL

As a writer of tales and novels, she has a very marked peculiarity. It is that of venturing to dispense common sense to her readers, and to bring them within the precincts of real life and natural feeling. She presents them with no incredible adventures, or inconceivable sentiments, no hyperbolical representations of uncommon character, or monstrous exhibitions of exaggerated passion. Without excluding love from her pages, she knows how to assign to it, its just limits. She neither degrades the sentiment from its true dignity, nor lifts it to a burlesque elevation. It takes its proper place among the other passions. Her heroes and heroines, if such they may be called, are never miraculously good, nor detestably wicked. They are such men and women as we see and converse with every day of our lives; with the same proportionate mixture in them of what is right and what is wrong, of what is great and what is little.—GIFFORD, WILLIAM, 1809, *Tales of Fashionable Life, Quarterly Review, vol.* 2, *p.* 146.

Thinking as we do, that her writings are, beyond all comparison, the most useful of any that have come before us since the commencement of our critical career, it would be a point of conscience with us to give them all the notoriety that they can derive from our recommendation, even if their execution were in some measure liable to objection. In our opinion, however, they are as entertaining as instructive; and the genius, and wit, and imagination, they display, are at least as remarkable as the justness of the sentiments they so powerfully inculcate.—JEFFREY, FRANCIS LORD, 1809–44, *Miss Edgeworth, Contributions to the Edinburgh Review, vol.* III, *p.* 408.

Where, then, is Miss Edgeworth's merit, her extraordinary merit, both as a moralist and a woman of genius? It consists in her having selected a class of virtues far more difficult to treat as the subject of fiction than others, and which had, therefore, been left by former writers to her. This is the merit both of originality and utility; but it never must be stated otherwise, unless we could doubt that superiority of the benevolent virtues over every other part of morals, which is not a subject of discussion, but an indisputable truth.—MACKINTOSH, SIR JAMES, 1810, *Letter to Mrs. Mackintosh.*

Most of her characters are formed from the most genuine and ordinary materials of human nature,—with very little admixture of anything derived from heaven, or the garden of Eden, or the magnificent part of the regions of poetry. There is rarely anything to awaken for one moment the enthusiasm of an aspiring spirit, delighted to contemplate, and ardent to resemble, a model of ideal excellence. . . . She is very expert at contriving situations for bringing out all the qualities of her personages, for contrasting those personages with one another, for creating excellent amusement by their mutual reaction, and for rewarding or punishing their merits or faults. She appears intimately acquainted with the prevailing notions, prejudices, and habits of the different ranks and classes of society. She can imitate very satirically the peculiar diction and slang of each; and has contrived (but indeed it needed very little contrivance) to make the fashionable dialect of the upper ranks sound exceedingly silly. As far as she has had opportunities for observation, she has caught a very discriminative idea of national characters: that of the Irish is delineated with incomparable accuracy and spirit. It may be added, that our author, possessing a great deal of general knowledge, finds many lucky opportunities for producing it, in short arguments and happy allusions.—FOSTER, JOHN, 1810, *The Morality of Works of Fiction; Critical Essays, ed. Ryland, vol.* I, *p.* 427.

A chat about Miss Edgeworth. Mrs. Aikin willing to find in her every excellence whilst I disputed her power of interesting in a long connected tale, and her possession of poetical imagination. In her numerous works she has certainly conceived and executed a number of forms, which, though not representatives of ideas, are excellent characters. Her sketches and her conceptions of ordinary life are full of good sense; but the tendency of her writings to check enthusiasm of every kind is of very problematical value.—ROBINSON, HENRY CRABB, 1812, *Diary, Sept.* 21; *Diary, Reminiscences and Correspondence, ed. Sadler, vol.* I, *p.* 256.

There are very few who have had the opportunities that have been presented to me, of knowing how very elevated is the admiration entertained by the Author of Waverley for the genius of Miss Edgeworth. From the intercourse that took place betwixt us while the work was going through my press, *I know* that the exquisite truth and power of your characters operated on his mind at once to excite and subdue it. . . . "If I could but hit Miss Edgeworth's wonderful power of vivifying all her persons, and making them alive as *beings* in your mind, I should not be afraid:"—Often has the Author of Waverley used such language to me; and I know that I gratified him most when I could say,—"Positively this *is* equal to Miss Edgeworth."—BALLANTYNE, JAMES, 1814, *Letter to Miss Edgeworth, Nov.* 11; *Lockhart's Life of Scott, ch.* xxxiii.

Miss Edgeworth, with that vigour and originality which are among the principal characteristics of genius, has struck out a line of writing peculiar to herself—a line which it required considerable boldness to adopt, and no common talents to execute with effect. . . . Her pictures are all drawn in the soberest colours. She scarcely makes use of a single tint that is warmer than real life. No writer recurs so rarely, for the purpose of creating an interest, to the stronger and more impetuous feelings of our nature. Even love, the most powerful passion that acts within the sphere of domestic life—the presiding deity of the novel and the drama, is handled by her in a way very different from that in which we have been accustomed to see it treated in works of fiction. . . . Her favourite qualities are prudence, firmness, temper, and that active, vigilant good sense, which, without checking the course of our kindly affections, exercises its influence at every moment, and surveys deliberately the motives and consequences of every action. Utility is her object, reason and experience her means. She makes vastly less allowance than has been usually made for those "amiable weaknesses," "sudden impulses," "uncontrolable emotions," which cut so great a figure in the works of her predecessors. Her heroes and heroines are far more thinking, cautious, philosophizing persons than ever before were produced in that character.—DUDLEY, EARL OF? 1814, *Miss Edgeworth's Patronage, Quarterly Review, vol.* 10, *pp.* 303, 304.

In short, she was a walking calculation,
Miss Edgeworth's novels stepping from their
covers.

—BYRON, LORD, 1819–24, *Don Juan, Canto* i.

She is the author of works not to be forgotten; of works, which can never lose their standard value as "English classics," and deserve that honourable name infinitely more than half the dull and licentious trash bound up in our libraries under that title. . . . Her novels always found an eager reception at a time when the poetry of Scott, of Campbell, and of Crabbe, was issuing in its freshness from the press, when the Edinburgh and Quarterly Reviews, then splendid novelties, were to be duly read and studied, when Madame de Staël was at her zenith, and, in a word, when the competition of the noblest wits was only less keen, than at the present day.—EVERETT, EDWARD, 1823, *Miss Edgeworth, North American Review, vol.* 17, *pp.* 388, 389.

Two circumstances, in particular, recalled my recollection of the mislaid manuscript. The first was the extended and well-merited fame of Miss Edgeworth, whose Irish characters have gone so far to make the English familiar with the character of their gay and kindhearted neighbours of Ireland, that she may be truly said to have done more towards completing the Union than perhaps all the legislative enactments by which it has been followed up. Without being so presumptuous as to hope to emulate the rich humour, pathetic tenderness, and admirable tact which pervade the works of my accomplished friend, I felt that something might be attempted for my own country, of the same kind with that which Miss Edgeworth so fortunately achieved for Ireland—something which might introduce her natives to those of the sister kingdom in a more favourable light than they had been placed hitherto, and tend to procure sympathy for their virtues and indulgence for their foibles.—SCOTT, SIR WALTER, 1829, *General Preface to the Waverley Novels.*

Miss Edgeworth may claim the rare praise of having perfectly succeeded in the great purpose which she proposed, of enlightening and improving the age, by imparting to it new ideas on the subject of education, taken in its most extended sense. Thus, by means of the deep interest attaching to her sagacious and vivid portraiture of character, she has wrought greater results with fiction, than could have been accomplished by the most profound philosophical treatise.—PRESCOTT, WILLIAM HICKLING, 1832, *English Literature of the Nineteenth Century, North American Review, vol.* 35, *p.* 187.

We owe also the popularity of the growing principle to the writings of Miss Edgeworth and of Scott, who sought their characters among the people, and who interested us by a picture of (and not a declamation upon) their life and its humble vicissitudes, their errors and their virtues.—LYTTON, EDWARD BULWER LORD, 1833, *Intellectual Spirit, England and the English, p.* 132.

She excels in reducing a folly, or a false virtue, "ad absurdum;" she is truly Socratic in the manner by which she drives a fallacy to its last defences. She has invariably and perseveringly discountenanced all exaltation and enthusiasm, and this incessant attention to the real and practical, however it may sometimes diminish her glory as a great *artist*, undoubtedly increases her utility as a moral teacher. In one class of characters she is almost unrivalled: no author has, with so much sympathy, penetration and vivacity, exhibited the national peculiarities of the Irish—a nation which she has studied with peculiar interest and love.—SHAW, THOMAS B., 1847, *Outlines of English Literature, p.* 385.

It is from the apex of the pyramid that men calculate its height, and the altitude of genius must be taken where it has attained its culminating point. Let those who wish to appreciate Miss Edgeworth, and derive the greatest amount of refining and elevating enjoyment from her works, pass over the prefaces, short as they are —never think of the moral excellent as it may be—be not over-critical touching the management of the story, but give themselves up to the charm of the dialogue, the scene-painting, the delineation and development of character, the happy blending of pathos and humour with the sobriety of truth. Let them do this, and they will cease to wonder at the proud position conceded to her by the dispassionate judgment of her most eminent contemporaries. —HAYWARD, ABRAHAM, 1867, *Miss Edgeworth, Edinburgh Review, vol.* 126, *p.* 498.

Miss Edgeworth's Irish tales gave the world of readers an interest in the impulsive people among whom the greatest portion of her life was spent. When she turned from Irish scenes to delineate fashionable people in London she did not attain the same degree of excellence. She sketched the Irish faithfully, because she had lived with them all her life and thoroughly understood all their virtues and all their weaknesses. She failed to draw her peers and peeresses with equal accuracy, because she had only a superficial acquaintance with London society. In Ireland she painted portraits, in London caricatures.—WALPOLE, SPENCER, 1878, *A History of England from the Conclusion of the Great War in* 1815, *vol.* I, *p.* 376.

She paints character as it presented itself to her view, sometimes well and sometimes ill, but her men and women have not a life in themselves. Her short tales are excellent, and superior to her novels, for the reason that the things required in a short tale are incident and moral point, not character. In the invention or adaption of incident she is very clever; she also has a large share of the faculty, most conspicuous in Defoe, of giving fiction the air of reality by minute elaboration of detail. She writes decidedly well, and often says witty or sparkling things, of which but few are to be found in Jane Austen.—SMITH, GOLDWIN, 1883, *Miss Edgeworth, The Nation, vol.* 36, *p.* 322.

When the writer looks back upon her own childhood, it seems to her that she lived in company with a delightful host of little playmates, bright busy, clever children, whose cheerful presence remains more vividly in her mind than that of many of the real little boys and girls who used to appear and disappear disconnectedly as children do in childhood, when friendship and companionship depends almost entirely upon the convenience of grown-up people.

Now and again came little cousins or friends to share our games, but day by day, constant and unchanging, ever to be relied upon, smiled our most lovable and friendly companions—simple Susan, lame Jervas, Talbot, the dear Little Merchants, Jem the widow's son with his arms round old Lightfoot's neck, the generous Ben, with his whipcord and his useful proverb of "waste not, want not"—all of these were there in the window corner waiting our pleasure. . . . People justly praised Miss Edgeworth's admirable stories and novels, but from prejudice and early association these beloved childish histories seem unequalled still, and it is chiefly as a writer for children that we venture to consider her here. Some of the stories are indeed little idylls in their way. Walter Scott, who best knew how to write for the young so as to charm grandfathers as well as Hugh Littlejohn, Esq., and all the grandchildren, is said to have wiped his kind eyes as he put down "Simple Susan."—RITCHIE, ANNE ISABELLA THACKERAY, 1883, *A Book of Sibyls*, *pp.* 53, 54.

Her novels have been described as a sort of essence of common sense, and even more happily it has been said that it was her genius to be wise. We must content to take that which she can offer; and since she offers so much, why should we not be content? Miss Edgeworth wrote of ordinary human life, and not of tremendous catastrophes or highly romantic incidents. Hers was no heated fancy. She had no comprehension of those fiery passions, those sensibilities that burn like tinder at contact with the feeblest spark; she does not believe in chance, that favorite of so many novelists; neither does she deal in ruined castles, underground galleries nor spectres, as was the fashion in her day. —ZIMMERN, HELEN, 1883, *Maria Edgeworth (Famous Women)*, *p.* 180.

It was the evil of the religious prejudices in which I was bred that all novels, except those with a ticketed moral, were put into the index. I read nearly all of Miss Edgeworth's tales, but I do not remember one beneficial lesson derived from her common-place minor moralities. To this day, however, I cannot cut the string in unwrapping a parcel without compunction, so strong was the impression made by her "Waste not, Want not." I have saved a few feet of twine, and wasted time much more valuable in picking out knots.—EGGLESTON, EDWARD, 1888, *Books That Have Helped Me*, *p.* 51.

But the great stand-by of our early life, in those days, was in Miss Edgeworth's books. I know perfectly well that it is impossible to make the young people of this generation read them, and I have no tears for their refusal. But I should like, if I could, to say to the authors of this day that they will do well if they study Miss Edgeworth's "Practical Education" first, and make such a critical study as shall show them from what quarters she gained the notions or theories which made her, for more than one generation, the best writer for children. Some things must be changed as a generation goes by, but there is an eternal foundation of good sense and of a knowledge of childhood at the bottom of Miss Edgeworth's success, which any person who is undertaking to write for children of this generation, or of the twentieth century, will be wise if he master. "Harry and Lucy" was, not to say is, an absolute text-book of mine. By this I mean the latter part of "Harry and Lucy," what should have been called the "Sequel to Harry and Lucy," if she had carried out the same nomenclature which she used in the naming the sequel of "Frank." "Harry and Lucy" introduced us to the world of physics. It taught us the mysteries of the still young steam-engine, and inspired us with an enthusiastic desire for invention. It was included in the scanty library of our attic, which served at once as workshop, laboratory, theatre, library, study, and play-room, where it might always be found, among six or seven other books, as a constant resource, whether for amusement or for instruction. At the distance of fifty years, I suppose that if it were necessary (that is, if I found myself standing on a Pacific island with a hundred children who needed "Harry and Lucy"), I could substantially reproduce it on the leaves of any talipat-palm tree which they would furnish for writing.—HALE, EDWARD EVERETT, 1888, *Books That Have Helped Me*, *p.* 6.

The didacticism of the stories for children has not prevented their permanent popularity. Her more ambitious efforts are injured by the same tendency. She has not the delicacy of touch of Miss Austen, more than the imaginative power of Scott.

But the brightness of her style, her keen observation of character, and her shrewd sense and vigour make her novels still readable, in spite of obvious artistic defects. Though her puppets are apt to be wooden, they act their parts with spirit enough to make us forgive the perpetual moral lectures.—STEPHEN, LESLIE, 1888, *Dictionary of National Biography, vol.* XVI.

Maria Edgeworth may be said to have invented the modern novel, which gives the traits, the speech, the manners, and the thoughts of a peasantry instead of moving only among the upper ten thousand. Sir Walter Scott, with his usual frankness and generosity, stated in his preface to the Waverly Novels that what really started him in his career as a novelist was the desire to do for Scotland and the Scottish peasantry what Miss Edgeworth had done for Ireland and the Irish peasantry. . . . Another of the leading writers of this century has acknowledged his indebtedness to Miss Edgeworth. The great Russian novelist, Ivan Tourgenieff, told a friend that when he was quite young he was unacquainted with the English language, but he used to hear his elder brother reading out to his friends translations of Miss Edgeworth's Irish stories, and the hope rose in his mind that one day he would be able to do for Russia and her people what Miss Edgeworth had done for Ireland.—FAWCETT, MILLICENT GARRETT, 1889, *Some Eminent Women of Our Times, p.* 154.

She is sometimes accused of being too common-sensical, not sufficiently romantic and passionate. If this be a fault, she must certainly plead guilty to it. Self-restraint, truth in all things, were the moving principles of her soul. She has been classed with Jane Austen, but no two writers can be less alike. Miss Austen never wrote with a moral purpose, Miss Edgeworth never wrote without one, and her stories are generally made to fit the lessons she wishes to bring out. Miss Austen excels with common-place people, Miss Edgeworth utterly fails with them, but her Irish servants, her wits, and fops, are admirable. Miss Austen has a fine, delicate humour, while her sister authoress deals in broad, racy drollery, in dramatic scenes which are often extravagant and laughable. Miss Austen never seems to think about her plots, Miss Edgeworth takes pains to make hers as ingenious and complicated as possible. Miss Austen was the greater artist, but Miss Edgeworth was a much more useful and practical writer. The fame of Jane Austen rests on six novels, while Maria Edgeworth published forty-seven volumes, dealing with a variety of subjects, and showing an immense amount of reading and observation. She was emphatically the children's friend. As time goes on, even "The Absentee" may rest on the dusty shelves of our libraries, but "Harry and Lucy" and "Simple Susan" will be thumbed in nurseries and schoolrooms as long as the world lasts.—HAMILTON, CATHARINE J., 1892, *Women Writers, First Series, p.* 174.

I suspect it would not be an easy task to bring young people, nowadays, to much enthusiasm about Miss Edgeworth and her books; and yet if I were to tell all that "we fellows" used to think about her when her "Popular Tales," and her delightful "Parent's Assistant," with its stories exactly of the right length—about Lazy Lawrence, and Simple Susan, and the False Key, and Tarlton—were in vogue, I am afraid you would give me very little credit for critical sagacity. A most proper and interesting old lady we reckoned her, and do still.—MITCHELL, DONALD G., 1895, *English Lands Letters and Kings, Queen Anne and the Georges, p.* 277.

Her style is easy, pliant, and vigorous; timid, perhaps, in its avoidance of all eccentricities, and somewhat overburdened by imitation of accredited literary models, but always correct, and free from tawdriness and exaggeration. Like the other attributes of her work, it shows earnestness and thoroughness of care and attention: and we are not surprised, when we watch the result, to read in one of her father's prefaces, that every page of her printed writing represents "twice as many pages as were written;" and yet not the least convincing proof of this care is that she has been able to avoid any obtrusive evidence of toil: and that if she spent much *labor limæ* she has given no sign of it in cumbrousness or pedantry of style. —CRAIK, HENRY, 1895, *English Prose, vol.* IV, *p.* 621.

Those who have made acquaintance with "Castle Rackrent" and other works of Miss Edgeworth will hardly be disposed to assign to these sketches of Irish life and character, vivid, spirited, and amusing as they are, the place which Scott in his generosity claimed for them.—TRAILL, HENRY DUFF, 1897, *Social England, vol.* VI, *p.* 34.

In this effective contrast of manners, Miss Edgeworth is historically midway between Smollett and Henry James.—CROSS, WILBUR L., 1899, *The Development of the English Novel, p.* 97.

In all she wrote a fine eye for character can be detected; but we cannot hold it as fine as Miss Austen's, since not very infrequently we find the black and white laid on with too little care for the nice shades of tone which Miss Austen never neglected. The good people are sometimes *unco guid*, and are for that reason perilously like bores.—POLLOCK, WALTER HERRIES, 1899, *Jane Austen, Her Contemporaries and Herself, p.* 42.

Hartley Coleridge

1796–1849

[Eldest son of Samuel Taylor Coleridge], born, at Clevedon, Somersetshire, 19 Sept. 1796. Educated at Ambleside School. Visit to London, 1807. Matric., New Inn Hall, Oxford, 6 May 1815; B. A. Merton Coll., 11 Feb. 1819. Fellow of Oriel Coll., 1819–20. Deprived of fellowship on ground of intemperance. In London, 1821–23. Returned to Ambleside to engage in tuition. Contrib. occasionally to "Blackwood's Mag.," 1826–31. Tuition abandoned, 1830. Lived in house of Mr. Bingley, a publisher, at Leeds, engaged in literary work, 1831–33. Took up residence at Grasmere. Assistant master at Sedbergh Grammar School for two short periods in 1837 and 1838. Returned to Grasmere. Died there, 6 Jan. 1849. *Works:* "Biographia Borealis," 1833 (another edn. entitled "Lives of Northern Worthies," edited by Derwent Coleridge, 1852; an extract, published spearately as "Lives of Illustrious Worthies of Yorkshire," 1835); "Poems," 1833. *Posthumous:* "Essays and Marginalia" (ed. by Derwent Coleridge), 1851. He *edited:* Massinger and Ford's Dramatic Works, 1840. *Life:* by Derwent Coleridge, in 1851 edn. of Hartley Coleridge's "Poems."—SHARP, R. FARQUHARSON, 1897, *A Dictionary of English Authors, p.* 59.

PERSONAL

When I first saw the child, I did not feel that thrill and overflowing of affection which I expected. I looked on it with a melancholy gaze; my mind was intensely contemplative, and my heart only sad. But when two hours after, I saw it at the bosom of its mother, on her arm, and her eye tearful and watching its little features—then I was thrilled and melted, and gave it the *kiss* of a *father*. . . . The baby seems strong, and the old nurse has over-persuaded my wife to discover a likeness of me in its face, no great compliment to me; for in truth I have seen handsomer babies in my lifetime. Its name is David Hartley Coleridge. I hope that ere he be a man, if God destines him for continuance in this life, his head will be convinced of, and his heart saturated with, the truths so ably supported by that great master of *Christian* Philosophy.—COLERIDGE, SAMUEL TAYLOR, 1796, *Letter to Thomas Poole, Sept.* 24; *Letters, ed. E. H. Coleridge, vol.* I, *p.* 169.

O thou! whose fancies from afar are brought;
Who of thy words dost make a mock apparel,
And fittest to unutterable thought
The breeze-like motion and the self-born carol;
Thou faery voyager! that dost float
In such clear water, that thy boat
May rather seem
To brood on air than on an earthly stream.
. . . .
O blessed vision! happy child!
Thou art so exquisitely wild,
I think of thee with many fears
For what may be thy lot in future years.
. . . .
O too industrious folly!
O vain and causeless melancholy!
Nature will either end thee quite;
Or, lengthening out thy season of delight,
Preserve for thee, by individual right,
A young lamb's heart among the full-grown flocks.

—WORDSWORTH, WILLIAM, 1802, *to H. C., Six Years Old.*

Hartley is from home, visiting Mr. Wordsworth's sisters near Penrith. It is impossible to give you any adequate idea of his oddities; for he is the oddest of all God's creatures, and becomes quainter and quainter every day. It is not easy to conceive what is perfectly true, that he is totally destitute of anything like modesty, yet without the slightest tinge of impudence in his nature. His religion makes one of the most humorous parts of his character. "I'm a boy of a very religious turn," he says; for he always talks of himself, and examines his own character, just as if he was speaking of another person, and as impartially. Every night he makes an extempore prayer aloud; but it is always in bed, and not till he is comfortable there and got into the mood. When he is ready he touches Mrs. Wilson, who sleeps with him, and says "Now listen!" and off he sets like a preacher. If he has been behaving amiss, away he goes for the Bible, and looks out for something appropriate to his case in the Psalms or the Book of Job. The other day, after he had been in a violent passion, he chose out a chapter against wrath. "Ah! that suits me!" . . . I do not know whether I should wish to have such a child or not. There is not the slightest evil in his disposition, but it wants something to make it steadily good; physically and morally there is a defect of courage. He is afraid of receiving pain to such a degree that, if any person begins to read a newspaper, he will leave the room, lest there should be anything shocking in it. This is the explication of his conduct during Mrs. Wilson's illness. He would not see her because it would give him pain, and when he was out of sight he contrived to forget her. I fear that, if he lives, he will dream away life like his father, too much delighted with his own ideas ever to embody them, or suffer them, if he can help it, to be disturbed.—SOUTHEY, ROBERT, 1805, *Letter to C. Danvers, Jan.* 15, *Southey's Life by Dennis, pp.* 172, 174.

Hartley Coleridge is one of the strangest boys I ever saw. He has the features of a foreign Jew, with starch and affected manners. He is a boy pedant, exceedingly formal, and, I should suppose, clever.—ROBINSON, HENRY CRABB, 1816, *Diary, Sept.* 9; *Diary, Reminiscences and Correspondence, ed. Sadler, vol.* I, *p.* 340.

Accounts reached us of the "humble and prayerful" death of Hartley Coleridge. His brother Derwent has been with him three weeks, and had the unspeakable blessing of directing and supporting that weak but humble and loving spirit through its last conflicts with the powers of the world. Much forever gone with this radiant soul, but more radiance and peace clothe the memories he leaves us than those who knew him dared to hope. —FOX, CAROLINE, 1849, *Memories of Old Friends, ed. Pym, Journal, Jan.* 12, *p.* 254.

He lived in a small cottage on the banks of the lake of Grasmere, about a mile from the residence of Wordsworth, in the midst of a region of singular beauty and grandeur, "meet nurse for a poetic child." His life was that of a recluse, mostly divided between solitary walks and solitary studies. He seemed to have no personal relations with the families of the gentlemen resident in the neighborhood, and he rarely crossed the path of the tourists who at certain seasons of the year swarmed like autumnal leaves in that lovely region. This arose from no inherent unsocialness of nature, but more than anything else, from the consciousness of his unfortunate habits, and the sting of self-reproach which they left behind. . . . His head was large and expressive, with dark eyes and white waving locks, and resting upon broad shoulders, with the smallest possible apology for a neck. To a sturdy and ample frame were appended legs and arms of a most disproportioned shortness, and "in his whole aspect, there was something indescribably elfish and grotesque, such as limners do not love to paint, nor ladies to look upon. He reminded you of a spy-glass shut up, and you wanted to take hold of him and pull him out into a man of goodly proportions and average stature. It was difficult to repress a smile at his appearance as he approached, for the elements are so quaintly combined in him that he seemed like one of Cowley's conceits translated into flesh and blood. . . . His manners were like those of men accustomed to live much alone, simple, frank and direct, but not in all respects governed by the rules of conventional politeless. It was difficult for him to sit still. He was constantly leaving his chair, walking about the room and then sitting down again, as if he were haunted by an incurable restlessness. His conversation was very interesting, and marked by a vein of quiet humor, not found in his writings. He spoke with much deliberation and in regularly constructed periods, which might have been printed without any alteration. There was a peculiarity in his voice not easily described. He would begin a sentence in a sort of subdued tone, hardly above a whisper, and end it in something between a bark and a growl.—HILLARD, GEORGE S., 1849, *Hartley Coleridge, Littell's Living Age, vol.* 21, *p.* 161.

My acquaintance with Hartley Coleridge commenced at Oxford, soon after his first examination in the schools, and it continued till the time when he stood for the Oriel fellowship. I then quitted the University, and we never met again. If I had known Hartley later in his career, perhaps something painful might have mingled with my recollections of him; but I remember him only as a young man who possessed an intellect of the highest order, with great simplicity of character, and considerable oddity of manner. His extraordinary powers as a converser (or rather a declaimer) procured for him numerous invitations to what are called at Oxford "wine parties." He knew that he was expected to talk, and talking was his delight. Leaning his head on one shoulder, turning up his dark bright eyes, and swinging backwards and forwards in his chair, he would hold forth by the hour (for no one wished to interrupt him) on whatever subject might have been started —either of literature, politics, or religion —with a originality of thought, a force of illustration, and a facility and beauty of expression, which I question if any man then living, except his father, could have surpassed.—DYCE, ALEXANDER, 1849, *Letter, July* 30; *Memoir of Hartley Coleridge, by his Brother, Poems, vol.* I, *p.* lxix.

He was a most extraordinary child, exhibiting at six years old the most surprising talent for invention. At eight years of age he found a spot upon the globe which he peopled with an imaginary nation, gave them a name, a language, laws, and a senate; where he framed long speeches, which he *translated*, as he said, for my benefit, and for the benefit of my neighbours, who climbed the garden-wall to listen to this surprising child, whom they supposed to be reciting pieces from memory. About this time he wrote a tragedy; and being at a loss in winding up the catastrophe, applied to his father, who excited his indignation by treating the matter too lightly, when he said "he should inform the public that the only bad lines in the tragedy were written by Mr. Coleridge, Senior." He called his nation the "Ejuxrii;" and one day, when walking very pensively, I asked him what ailed him. He said "My people are too fond of war, and I have just made an eloquent speech in the Senate, which has not made any impression on them, and to war they will go." —MONTAGU, MRS. BASIL, 1849, *Letter, April* 4; *Memoir of Hartley Coleridge by his Brother, Poems, vol.* I, *p.* xxxix.

It was, I think, in the summer of the year 1818, that I first saw your brother Hartley, during a visit that I was paying to Mr. Southey at Greta Hall. I cannot easily convey to you the impression of interest which he made on my mind at that time. There was something so wonderfully original in his method of expressing himself, that on me, then a young man, and only cognizant externally of the prose of life, his sayings, all stamped with the impress of poetry, produced an effect analogous to that which the mountains of Cumberland, and the scenery of the North, were working on my southern-born eye and imagination. — TOWNSHEND, CHAUNCEY HARE, 1851, *Letter to Derwent Coleridge, Memoir of Hartley Coleridge by his Brother, Poems, vol.* I, *p.* lxxiii.

Among his friends we must count men, women, and children, of every rank and of every age. While he preserved the tone of his manners (which, though somewhat eccentric, were free from any tincture of vulgarity), and seldom, if ever, failed of being treated with due respect and consideration, he willingly overstepped the conventional distinctions by which society is divided. In the farmhouse or cottage, not alone at times of rustic festivity, at a sheep-sheering, a wedding, or a christening, but by the ingle side with the grandmother or the "bairns," he was made, and felt himself, at home. . . . His manners and appearance were peculiar. Though not dwarfish either in form or expression, his stature was remarkably low, scarcely exceeding five feet, and he early acquired the gait and general appearance of advanced age. His once dark, lustrous hair, was prematurely silvered, and became latterly quite white. His eyes, dark, soft, and brilliant, were remarkably responsive to the movements of his mind, flashing with a light from within. His complexion, originally clear and sanguine, looked weather-beaten, and the contour of his face was rendered less pleasing by the breadth of his nose. His head was very small, the ear delicately formed, and the forehead, which receded slightly, very wide and expansive. His hands and feet were also small and delicate. His countenance, when in repose, or rather in stillness, was stern and thoughtful in the extreme, indicating deep and passionate meditation, so much so as to be at times almost startling. His low bow on entering a room, in which there were ladies or strangers, gave a formality to his address, which wore at first the appearance of constraint; but when he began to talk, these impressions were presently changed,—he threw off the seeming weight of years, his countenance became genial, and his manner free and gracious.—COLERIDGE, DERWENT, 1851, *Memoir of Hartley Coleridge by his Brother, Poems, vol.* I, *pp.* cxxxiv, cxxxvi.

The gentle, humble-hearted, highly gifted man, "Dear Hartley," as my father called him, dreamed through a life of error, loving the good and hating the evil, yet unable to resist it. His companionship was always delightful to the Professor, and many hours of converse they held; his best and happiest moments were those spent at Elleray. My father had a great power over him, and exerted it with kind but firm determination. On one occasion he was kept imprisoned for some weeks under his surveillance, in order that he might finish some literary work he had promised to have ready by a certain time. He completed his task, and when the day of release came, it was not intended that he should leave Elleray. But Hartley's evil demon was at hand; without one word of adieu to the friends in whose presence he stood, off he ran at full speed down the avenue, lost to sight amid the trees, seen again in the open highway still running, until the sound of his far-off footsteps gradually died away in the distance, and he himself was hidden, not in the groves of the valley but in some obscure den, where, drinking among low companions, his mind was soon brought to a level with theirs. Then these clouds would after a time pass away, and he again returned to the society of those who could appreciate him, and who never ceased to love him. Every one loved Hartley Coleridge; there was something in his appearance that evoked kindliness. Extremely boyish in aspect, his juvenile air was aided not a little by his general mode of dress, a dark blue cloth round jacket, white trousers, black silk handkerchief tied loosely round his throat; sometimes a straw hat covered his head, but more frequently it was bare, showing his black, thick, short, curling hair. His eyes were large, dark, and expressive, and a countenance almost sad in expression, was relieved by the beautiful smile which lighted it up from time to time. The tone of his voice was musically soft. He excelled in reading, and very often read aloud to my mother.—GORDON, MRS., 1862, *"Christopher North," A Memoir of John Wilson, ed. Mackenzie, p.* 311.

But for the evil habit that preyed upon him he had been a great man. One of his friends has spoken of him as sometimes like the lofty column which the simoon raises in its mighty breath; the inspiration of great passion ceasing, there remained only the desert sand over which the serpent crawls. Poor Hartley waged unceasing war with his serpent, but never quite conquered it.—CONWAY, MONCURE D., 1880, *The English Lakes and Their Genii, Harper's Magazine, vol.* 62, *p.* 177.

Who is not subdued into thoughtful pity by the legend, "By Thy Cross and Passion," that tells us of the struggle that poor Hartley Coleridge made, as he went from darkness into light? Yes, long as men with poetic susceptibilities to all evil, as well as all good, press on their way of tears to Him who wore the crown of thorns, that tombstone with its double garland of oakleaf and of thorn, and its touching inscription, may do for their souls as much as all the verse he wrote, whose sonnet "On Prayer" is one of the sweetest in our language,—Hartley, the laureate for innocent childhood hereabout, who found "pain was his guest" long before he entered the painlessness of Grasmere churchyard mould.—RAWNSLEY, H. D., 1894, *Literary Associations of the English Lakes, vol.* II, *p.* 171.

While my father was in the Lake Country he fell in with Hartley Coleridge, who discussed Pindar with him, calling Pindar "The Newmarket Poet." "Hartley was wonderfully eloquent," my father said, "and I suspect resembled his father in that respect. I liked Hartley, 'Massa' Hartley. I remember that on one occasion Hartley was asked to dine with the family of a stiff Presbyterian clergyman, residing in the Lake district. The party sat a long time in the drawing-room waiting for dinner. Nobody talked. At last Hartley could stand it no longer, he jumped up from the sofa, kissed the clergyman's daughter, and bolted out of the house. He was very eccentric, a sun-faced little man. He once went on a walking tour with some friends. They suddenly missed him, and could not find him anywhere, and did not see him again for six weeks, when he emerged from some inn. He was a loveable little fellow."—TENNYSON, HALLAM, 1897, *Alfred Lord Tennyson, A Memoir, vol.* I, *p.* 153.

It was a strange thing to see Hartley Coleridge fluctuating about the room, now with one hand on his head, now with both hands expanded like a swimmer's. There was some element wanting in his being. He could do everything but keep his footing, and doubtless in his inner world of thought, it was easier for him to fly than to walk, and to walk than to stand. There seemed to be no gravitating principle in him. One might have thought he needed stones in his pockets to prevent his being blown away.—DEVERE, AUBREY, 1897, *Recollections, p.* 134.

SONNETS

The whole series of sonnets with which the earliest and best work of Hartley began is (with a casual episode on others) mainly and essentially a series on himself. Perhaps there is something in the structure of the sonnet rather adapted to this species of composition. It is too short for narrative, too artificial for the intense passions, too complex for the simple, too elaborate for the domestic; but in an impatient world where there is not a premium on self-describing, who so would speak of himself must be wise and brief, artful and composed—and in these respects he will be aided by the concise dignity of the tranquil sonnet.—BAGEHOT, WALTER, 1852, *Hartley Coleridge, Works, ed. Morgan, vol.* I, *p.* 70.

His Sonnets are very remarkable. They are the most imaginative part of his writings, as well as the most highly finished; and possess that indescribable union of sweetness and subtle pathos for which the sonnets of Shakespeare are so remarkable. —DE VERE, AUBREY, 1858, *Select Specimens of the English Poets.*

Poor Hartley Coleridge, who promised so much and performed so little, produced many sonnets, and is, as a sonnet-writer, as far in front of his father as he is behind his father's friend.—NOBLE, JAMES ASHCROFT, 1880, *The Sonnet in England and other Essays, p.* 43.

There is a grace, a sweetness, a sense of shy, secluded beauty in his sonnets, which separate him from the poets of his time as surely as the odes of Collins separate him from the versifiers of his time, and which have given him an enduring though not a lofty place among the sonneteers of England.—STODDARD, RICHARD HENRY, 1881, *The Sonnet in English Poetry, Scribner's Monthly, vol.* 22, *p.* 921.

Hartley Coleridge now ranks among the foremost sonneteers in our language: as in the case of Charles Tennyson Turner, his reputation rests solely on his sonnet-work. Notwithstanding the reverent admiration he had for his more famous father, Hartley's work betrays much more the influence of Wordsworth than of S. T. Coleridge. In this a wise instinct indutiably guided him. His father was not a sonneteer. There is a firmness of handling, a quiet autumnal tenderness and loveliness about Hartley's sonnets that endows them with an endless charm for all who care for poetic beauty.—SHARP, WILLIAM, 1886, *Sonnets of this Century, p.* 282, *note.*

GENERAL

With strong feeling, a bright fancy, and a facility of versification, there is yet a certain hard resemblance in the poems of the father, which may perhaps be termed an unconscious mechanism of the faculties, acting under the associations of love. His designs want invention, and his rhapsodies abandonment. His wildness does not look quite spontaneous, but as if it blindly followed something erratic. The mirth seems rather forced; but the love and the melancholy are his own. Hartley Coleridge has a sterling vein of thought in him, without a habit and order of thought. It is extremely probable that he keeps his best things to himself. His father talked his best thoughts, so that somebody had the benefit of them; his son for the most part keeps his for his own bosom.—HORNE, RICHARD HENGIST, 1844, *A New Spirit of the Age, p.* 156.

The influence of Wordsworth's peculiar

genius is more discernible in the productions of Hartley Coleridge than that of his father, more especially in the Sonnets, which, I venture to think, may sustain a comparison with those of the elder writer. Their port is indeed less majestic, they have less dignity of purpose, and, particularly in combination, are less weighty in effect; but taken as single compositions, they are not less graceful, or less fraught with meaning; they possess a softer if not a deeper pathos, they have at least as easy a flow and as perfect an arrangement. A tender and imaginative fancy plays about the thought, and as it were lures it forward, raising an expectation which is fully satisfied. Indeed, if I am not wholly mistaken, there will be found among these sonnets, models of composition comparable to those of the greatest masters.—COLERIDGE, DERWENT, 1851, *Memoir of Hartley Coleridge by his Brother, Poems, vol.* I, *p.* clxxv.

Beautiful and touching as these poems are, we are by no means sure that the editor is right in supposing that it is as a poet that his brother will be best remembered. He was a clear, earnest, and original thinker; and he delivered his thoughts in a manner so perspicuous and lively, with the peculiar humour of his own character so shining through, that his essays, which would be worth studying for the sense they contain, though the style were dull, are among the pleasantest things to read in the language. When all are gathered together they will fill, we suppose, several moderate-sized volumes. If so, and if we are not greatly mistaken as to the quality of the volumes which are to come, we may surely (without raising vain questions as to what he might have done if he had not been what he was) say that the last half of his life, though spent in cloud and shadow, has not been spent in vain.—SPEDDING, JAMES, 1851, *Hartley Coleridge, Reviews and Discussions Literary, Political and Historical, Not Relating to Bacon, p.* 315.

In the execution of minor verses, we think we could show that Hartley should have the praise of surpassing his father; but nevertheless it would be absurd, on a general view, to compare the two men, Samuel Taylor was so much bigger. What there was in his son was equally good, perhaps, but then there was not much of it; outwardly and inwardly he was essentially little. In poetry, for example, the father has produced two longish poems which have worked themselves right down to the extreme depths of the popular memory, and stay there very firmly; in part from their strangeness, but in part from their power. Of Hartley, nothing of this kind is to be found. He could not write connectedly: he wanted steadiness of purpose or efficiency of will to write so voluntarily; and his genius did not, involuntarily and out of its unseen workings, present him with continuous creations,—on the contrary, his mind teemed with little fancies, and a new one came before the first had attained any enormous magnitude. As his brother observed, he wanted "back thought." — BAGEHOT, WALTER, 1852, *Hartley Coleridge, Works, ed. Morgan, vol.* I, *p.* 73.

Hartley Coleridge's poetry reminds the reader of Wordsworth in nearly every line, though it is Wordsworth diluted; and at its best, the Lake poetry cannot bear much dilution. Excepting in the sonnets which relate to his own personal unhappiness, the poems sound like the echoes of other poets, rather than welling warm from the writer's own heart. And though, in the personal sonnets referred to, he paints his purposeless life and blighted career in terse and poetic language, it were perhaps better that they had not been written at all. His poems addressed to childhood are perhaps the most charming things in the collection. For poor Hartley loved children, and they returned his love. He loved women, too, but at a distance; and his despondency at his own want of personal attractions for them is a frequent theme of his poetry.—SMILES, SAMUEL, 1860, *Brief Biographies, p.* 149.

Hartley Coleridge always classed himself among "the small poets," and it is true he was not born for great and splendid achievements; but there are some writers for whom our affection would be less if they were stronger, more daring, more successful; and Hartley Coleridge is one of these. . . . A great poet is a toiler, even when his toil is rapturous. Hartley Coleridge did not and perhaps could not toil. Good thoughts came to him as of free grace; gentle pleasures possessed his senses; loving-kindnesses flowed from his heart, and took as they flowed shadows and colours from his imagination; and all these mingled and grew mellow. And so a poet's moods expressed themselves in his verse; but he built no lofty rhyme. The sonnet, in which a thought and a feeling are wedded helpmates suited his genius; and of his many delightful sonnets some of the best are immediate transcripts of the passing mood of joy or pain. . . . All that Hartley Coleridge has written is genuine, full of nature, sweet, fresh, breathing charity and reconciliation. His poems of self-portrayal are many, and of these not a few are pathetic with sense of change and sorrowing self-condemnation; yet his penitence had a silver side of hope, and one whose piety was so unaffected, whose faith though "thinner far than vapour" had yet outlived all frowardness, could not desperately upbraid even his weaker self.—DOWDEN, EDWARD, 1880, *The English Poets, ed. Ward, vol.* IV, *pp.* 518, 519.

His poems are full of graceful beauty, but almost all fall below the level of high poetry. They are not sufficiently powerful for vivid remembrance, and are much too good for oblivion. His striking fragment of "Prometheus" almost seems an exception; but although his brother attributes it to an earlier period, it is plainly composed under the influence of Shelley. The one species of composition in which he is a master is the sonnet, which precisely suited both his strength and his limitations. His sonnets are among the most perfect in the language.—GARNETT, RICHARD, 1887, *Dictionary of National Biography, vol.* XI, *p.* 300.

He saw with his own singular vision, felt with his own peculiar feelings, and spoke as if he were the first medium of expression; but true poet as he was he has made us realise also. He saw nature through rainbows, and he has left us the prisms of his poems. He wrote rapidly, and rarely with a pause, and became such an adept at the sonnet that he could usually complete one—subject to revision—within ten minutes. This is quite in keeping with the remarkable lucidity of his sonnets. From the first word to the last they sing themselves into a natural and gratifying silence. No more was intended by the writer; no more is needed by the reader. Bowles has the sonorous simplicity of Handel; but Hartley Coleridge has the sweet probing subtlety of Mozart.—TIREBUCK, WILLIAM, 1887, *ed., The Poetical Works of Bowles, Lamb and Hartley Coleridge, Introduction, p.* XXX.

The son of a poet, and the son, by adoption, of two other poets, Hartley Coleridge might have proved his relationship to the Triumvirate of the Lakes more surely than he did if his career had not prematurely been blasted. His verse is not much read now, I fancy, but it ought to be, for it is better than the strong lines which are the fashion in this critical age.—STODDARD, RICHARD HENRY, 1892, *Under the Evening Lamp, p.* 199.

His "Prometheus," a dramatic fragment, although regarded by S. T. Coleridge as "full of promise," is poor indeed when compared with such poems as Keats's "Hyperion," or Shelley's "Alastor." And as regards the shorter lyrical poems which he composed, it must be admitted that, with one or two exceptions, they are somewhat thin and vapid. They indicate, it is true, considerable facility in writing, and much genial sympathy and kindness of heart, but they also discover, on the other hand, a feeble intellectual grip, and a defective insight into the facts and realities of the world in which we live. Very different, however, must be our criticism respecting his sonnets. The greatest poets—Dante, Shakespeare, Milton, Keats, and Wordsworth—have, for the most part, written the finest sonnets; Hartley Coleridge was not a great poet, but, as his brother Derwent justly observed, his sonnets will sustain comparison with those by Wordsworth. — WADDINGTON, SAMUEL, 1894, *The Poets and the Poetry of the Century, John Keats to Lord Lytton, ed. Miles, p.* 136.

Many of the miscellaneous poems contain beautiful things. But on the whole the greatest interest of Hartley Coleridge is that he is the first and one of the best examples of a kind of poet who is sometimes contemned, who has been very frequently in this century, but who is dear to the lover of poetry, and productive of delightful things. This kind of poet is wanting, it may be, in what is briefly, if not brutally, called originality. He might not sing much if others had not sung and were not singing around him; he does not sing very much even as it is, and the notes of his song are not extraordinarily piercing or novel. But they are true, they are not copied, and the lover of poetry could not spare them. Hartley Coleridge, if a "sair sicht" to the moralist, is an interesting and far from a wholly painful one to the lover of literature, which he himself loved so much, and practised, with all his disadvantages, so successfully.—SAINTSBURY, GEORGE, 1896, *A History of Nineteenth Century Literature, pp.* 202, 203.

Hartley Coleridge nowhere shows the supreme poetic gift his father possessed; but as in sheer genius the elder Coleridge was probably superior to any contemporary, so Hartley seems to have been the superior by endowment of any poet then writing, Tennyson and Browning alone excepted. Weakness of will, unfortunately, doomed him to excel only in short pieces, and to be far from uniform in these. It would have been wiser to omit the section of "playful and humorous" pieces. But the sonnets are very good, and some of them are excellent. A few of the songs take an equally high rank, especially the well-known "She is not fair to outward view;" and "'Tis sweet to hear the merry lark." There are many suggestions of Wordsworth, but Hartley Coleridge is not an imitative poet. Without any striking originality he is fresh and independent. His verse betrays a gentle and kindly as well as a sensitive character. He evidently felt affection for all living things, and especially for all that was weak, whether from nature, age, or circumstance.—WALKER, HUGH, 1897, *The Age of Tennyson, p.* 60.

Ebenezer Elliott

1781–1849

Ebenezer Elliott, the Corn-Law Rhymer, was born at the New Foundry, Masbro', in Rotherham parish, Yorkshire, on 17th March 1781. A shy and morbid boy, who proved a dull pupil at school, he worked in his father's foundry from his sixteenth to his twenty-third year, and threatened to become a "sad drunken dog," till the picture of a primrose in Sowerby's "Botany" "led him into the fields, and poetry followed." His "Vernal Walk," written at sixteen, was published in 1801; to it succeeded "Night" (1818), "The Village Patriarch" (1829), "Corn-law Rhymes and the Ranter" (3d ed. 1831), and other volumes—collected in 1840 (new ed. 2 vols. 1876). He had married early, and sunk his wife's fortune in his father's business; but in 1821, with a borrowed capital of £100, he started as bar-iron merchant at Sheffield, and throve exceedingly. Though in 1837 he lost one-third of his savings, in 1841 he was able to retire with £300 a year. He died at Great Houghton, 1st December 1849. Elliott the poet is well-nigh forgotten. But Elliott the Corn-Law Rhymer is still remembered as the Tyrtæus of that mighty conflict whose triumph he lived to witness. He had been bred a "Berean" and Jacobin, yet he hated Communists, Socialists, and physical-force Chartists; he lies buried in Darfield churchyard; he left two sons Established clergymen. His whole life long he looked on the Corn-laws as the "cause of all the crime that is committed;" agriculturists, he maintained, "ought not to live by robbing and murdering the manufacturers." On the other hand, "Capital has a right to rule the world," and "competition is the great social law of God." There are two poor memoirs of Elliott, by his son-in-law, John Watkins (1850), and by "January Searle"—*i. e.* George S. Phillips (1850).—PATRICK AND GROOME, *eds.*, 1897, *Chambers's Biographical Dictionary, p.* 336.

PERSONAL

I do not remember the time when I was not dissatisfied with the condition of society. Without ever envying any man his wealth or power, I have always wondered why the strong oppress the weak. —ELLIOTT, EBENEZER, 1840, *Random Thoughts and Reminiscences by the Corn-Law Rhymer.*

In a strange place I should never have recognized Ebenezer Elliott by his portrait. There is no good one of him. He is somewhat above the middle height. He is sixty-five, but not old-looking for his years. His hair is white, and his manner and tone, except when excited by those topics that rouse his indignation against cruelty and oppression, mild, soft, and full of feeling. Perhaps no man's spirit and presence are so entirely the spirit and presence of his poetry. . . . Ebenezer Elliott has conversed too much with nature, and with men in their rough, unsophisticated nature, to have merged one jot of his earnestness into conventionalism of tone or manner. In society or out of it he is one and the same—the poet and the man.—HOWITT, WILLIAM, 1847, *Homes and Haunts of the Most Eminent British Poets, vol.* II, *pp.* 499, 500.

It seems curious to me that this man is not in these days better known. A more singular man has seldom existed,—seldom a more genuine. His first business speculation failed, but when about forty he commenced again, and this time fortune made amends for her former ill-treatment. His warehouse was a small, dingy place, filled with bars of iron, with a bust of Shakespeare looking down on the whole. His country-house contained busts of Achilles, Ajax, and Napoleon. Here is a poet who earned a competence as an iron-merchant; here is a monomaniac on the Corn-laws, who loved nature as intensely as ever did Burns or Wordsworth. Here is a John Bright uttering himself in fiery and melodious verse,—Apollo with iron-dust on his face, wandering among the Sheffield knife-grinders!—SMITH, ALEXANDER, 1863, *Dreamthorp, p.* 206.

No man could be more happy than Elliott in a green lane; though an indefatigable and successful man of business, he devoutly and devotedly loved Nature. If absolutely rabid when he wrote of the "tax-fed aristocracy"—sententious, bitter, sarcastic, loud with his pen in hand and class sympathies and antipathies for his inspiration—all evil thoughts evaporated when communing in the woods and fields with the God by whom the woods and fields were made; among them his spirit was as fresh and gentle as the dew by which they were nourished.—HALL, SAMUEL CARTER, 1883, *Retrospect of a Long Life, p.* 409.

Very shortly before his death his daughter was married to John Watkins, his biographer. Elliott had a family of thirteen children, most of whom, together with his wife, survived him. Elliott was a small, meek-looking man. Though engaged in many almost revolutionary movements, and though once in danger of prosecution, he was really conservative by nature, and brought up two of his sons as clergymen of the established church. It was only under a burning sense of injustice that he acted as he did. . . . As a speaker, Elliott was practical and vigorous, though at times given to extravagant statements. A bronze statue, by Burnard of London, subscribed for by the working men of Sheffield, was erected at a cost of 600*l.* in the market-place of that town, in 1854, to the memory of Elliott. Landor wrote a fine ode on the occasion. The statue was afterwards removed to Weston Park.—WATT, FRANCIS, 1889, *Dictionary of National Biography, vol.* XVII, *p.* 267.

GENERAL

If the whole welkin hang over-cast in dizzly dinginess, the feeblest light-gleam, or speck of blue, cannot pass unheeded. The Works of this Corn-Law Rhymer we might liken rather to some little fraction of a rainbow: hues of joy and harmony, painted out of troublous tears. No round full bow, indeed; gloriously spanning the Heavens; shone on by the full sun; and, with seven-striped, gold-crimson border (as is in some sort the office of Poetry) dividing Black from Brilliant: not such; alas, still far from it! Yet, in very truth, a little prismatic blush, glowing genuine among the wet clouds; which proceeds, if you will, from a sun cloud-hidden, yet indicated that a sun does shine, and above vapours, a whole azure vault and celestian firmament stretch serene. Strange as it may seem, it is nevertheless true, that here we have once more got sight of a Book calling itself Poetry, yet which actually is a kind of Book, and no empty pasteboard Case, and simulacrum or "ghost-defunct" of a Book, such as is too often palmed on the world, and handed over Booskellers' counters, with a demand of real money for it, as if it too were a reality. The speaker here is of that singular class, who have something to say; whereby, though delivering himself in verse, and in these days, he does not deliver himself wholly in jargon, but articulately, and with a certain degree of meaning, that has been *believed*, and therefore is again believable.—CARLYLE, THOMAS, 1832, *Corn-Law Rhymes, Edinburgh Review, vol.* 55, *p.* 339.

Ebenezer Elliott does—not only now and then, but often—ruralize; with the intense passionateness of a fine spirit escaping from smoke and slavery into the fresh air of freedom—with the tenderness of a gentle spirit communing with Nature in Sabbath-rest. Greedily he gulps the dew of morn, like a man who has been long suffering from thirst drinking at a wayside well. He feasts upon the flowers—with his eyes, with his lips; he walks along the grass as if it were cooling to his feet. The slow typhus fever perpetual with townsmen is changed into quick gladsome glow, like the life of life. A strong animal pleasure possesses the limbs and frame of the strong man released from labour, yet finding no leisure to loiter in the lanes—and away with him to the woods and rocks and heaven-kissing hills. But that is not all his pleasure—though it might suffice, one would think, for a slave. Through all his senses it penetrates into his soul—and his soul gets wings and soars.—WILSON, JOHN, 1834, *Poetry of Ebenezer Elliott, Blackwood's Magazine, vol.* 35, *p.* 820.

The time is gone by when the introduction of a reviewer could be of any avail to the Poet of the Poor. Ebenezer Elliott has taken the place to which he is entitled; his name is on the nation's muster-roll of bards; the laurel-crowned have received the unwashed artificer into their fellowship; no future Johnson will edit the works of the British poets without a biography of the man of Hallamshire. Were he never to write another line, this collection of his poems, of which the third volume has just appeared, would be amply sufficient for his credentials. The public know this as well as we do. The verdict of those who are qualified to serve on such a jury is pronounced; the intellectual rank, as a poet, of Ebenezer Elliott is established.—FOX, W. J., 1835, *Ebenezer Elliott, Westminster Review, vol.* 30, *p.* 187.

The man of all the self-educated poets, since the days of Burns, of the most original powers, the finest imagination, and the most copious and animated style.—MITFORD, JOHN, 1836, *The Poetical Works of William Falconer, Life, p.* xxxi.

A man of true genius, "the poor man's poet."—LOWELL, JAMES RUSSELL, 1838, *To G. B. Loring, Nov.* 15; *Letters, ed. Norton, vol.* I. *p.* 34.

One of the most remarkable men of the present age is Ebenezer Elliott, the "Corn-Law-Rhymer," a poet whose productions are distinguished alike for boldness and originality, a singular strength and purity of diction, and a warm sympathy with the oppressed masses. . . . Elliott was for a long time neglected. His subjects, like those of Crabbe, whom in many ways he is like, are of a homely sort, emphatically *human*, such as, for some reason, the popular taste does not readily approve. He gives simple, earnest and true echoes of the affections. His poems, aside from their political character, breathe the spirit of a kind of primitive life, unperverted, unhackneyed, and fresh as the dews on his own hawthorne. Carlyle, Bulwer, and other critics, seeing in him incontestable signs of genius, at length handed him up to fame.—GRISWOLD, RUFUS W., 1844, *The Poets and Poetry of England in the Nineteenth Century, p.* 174.

The great ambition of Elliott is to thunder. He is a brawny man of nature's own make, with more than the usual portion of the ancient Adam stirring within him; and he says, "I do well to be angry." The mere sight of tyranny, bigotry, meanness, prompts his smiting invective. His poetry could hardly have been written by a man who was not physically strong. You can hear the ring of his anvil, and see the sparks fly off from his furnace, as you read his verse. He stoutly wrestles with the difficulties of utterance, and expresses himself by main force. His muscles seem made of iron. He has no fear and little mercy; and not only obeys the hot impulses of his sensibility, but takes a grim pleasure in piling fuel on the flame. He points the artillery of the devil against the devil's own legions. His element is a moral diabolism, compounded of wrath and conscience.—WHIPPLE, EDWIN P., 1845, *English Poets of the Nineteenth Century, Essays and Reviews, vol.* I, *p.* 338.

The Burns of Sheffield did not speak to the dead. The fire which he scattered was electric. It spread rapidly, it kindled in millions of hearts, it became the soul of the sinking multitude. It was slower to seize on the moist and comfortable spirits of the middle classes and master-manufacturers; but the progress of foreign competition soon drove even them into action against the landlord's monopoly. The League arose. The prose-men took up the cry of the poet, and with material and ground prepared by him, went on from year to year advancing, by force of arguments and force of money, the great cause, till at this moment it may be said to be won. The prime minister of England pronounced the doom of the Corn-Law, and fixed the date of its extinction. All honor to every man who fought in the good fight, but what honor should be shown him who began it? To the man who blew, on the fiery trumpet of a contagious zeal, defiance to the hostile power in the pride of its strength, and called the people together to the great contest? In that contest the very name of Ebenezer Elliott has of late ceased to be heard. Others have prolonged the war-cry, and the voice of him who first raised it seems to be forgotten; but not the less did he raise it. Not the less does that cause owe to him its earliest and amplest thanks. Not the less is it he who dared to clear the field.—HOWITT, WILLIAM, 1847, *Homes and Haunts of the Most Eminent British Poets, vol.* II, *p.* 466.

Howsoever he may have been indebted to Burns's example for the notion of writing at all, he has profited very little by Burns's own poems. Instead of the genial loving tone of the great Scotchman, we find in Elliott a tone of deliberate savageness, all the more ugly, because evidently intentional. He tries to curse; "he delights"—may we be forgiven if we misjudge the man—"in cursing"; he makes a science of it; he defiles, of malice prepense, the loveliest and sweetest thoughts and scenes (and he can be most sweet) by giving some sudden, sickening revulsion to his reader's feelings; and he does it generally with a power which makes it at once as painful to the calmer reader as alluring to those who are struggling with the same temptations as the poet. Now and then, his trick drags him down into sheer fustian and bombast; but not always. There is a terrible Dantean vividness of imagination about him, perhaps unequalled in England, in his generation. His poems are like his countenance, coarse and ungoverned, yet with an intensity of eye, a rugged massiveness of feature, which would be grand but for the seeming deficiency of love and of humour—love's twin and inseparable brother.—KINGSLEY, CHARLES, 1848? *Burns and His School, Miscellanies, vol.* I, *p.* 382.

Had he been able to indentify himself with the characters he described, or had he drawn from self, he would have evinced power little lower than Shakspeare—or Byron.— WATKINS, JOHN, 1850, *Life, Poetry and Letters of Ebenezer Elliott, the Corn-Law Rhymer, p.* 417.

On these pale lips, the smothered thought
Which England's millions feel,
A fierce and fearful splendor caught,
As from his forge the steel.
Strong-armed as Thor,—a shower of fire
His smitten anvil flung;
God's curse, Earth's wrong, Dumb Hunger's ire,—
He gave them all a tongue!
—WHITTIER, JOHN GREENLEAF, 1850, *Elliott.*

His sky never shows the calm, clear, unclouded summer blue; some speck on the horizon, although no "bigger than a man's hand," ever predicates a storm; and it is impossible to mistake Elliott's moorlands for the Elysian fields. As a depictor of the phases of humanity, his portraits are almost all of one class; and with that class are identified his entire sympathies. Hence it is that he seems deficient in that genial spirit which characterizes more catholic natures; in those expansive feelings, which embrace society in all its aspects; in those touches which "makes all flesh kin."—MOIR, D. M., 1851–52, *Poetical Literature of the Past Half Century.*

I may not live to hear another voice,
Elliott, of power to penetrate, as thine,
Dense multitudes; another none may see
Leading the Muses from unthrifty shades
To fields where corn gladdens the heart of Man,
And where the trumpet with defiant blast
Blows in the face of War, and yields to Peace.
—LANDOR, WALTER SAVAGE, 1853, *On the Statue of Ebenezer Elliott, The Last Fruit off an Old Tree.*

Any one who reads his poems will not fail to note how closely his soul was knit to universal nature—how his pulse beat in unison with her,—how deeply he read and how truly he interpreted her meanings. With a heart glowing for love of his kind, out of which indeed his poetry first sprung, and with a passionate sense of wrongs inflicted upon the suffering poor, which burst out in words of electric, almost tremendous power, there was combined a tenderness and purity of thought and feeling, and a love for Nature in all her moods, of the most refined and beautiful character. In his scathing denunciations of power misused, how terrible he is; but in his expression of beauty, how sweet! Bitter and fierce though his rhymes are when his subject is "the dirt-kings,—the tax-gorged lords of the land," we see that all his angry spirit is disarmed when he takes himself out beneath the fresh breath of the heavens, in the green lane, on the open heath, or up among the wild mountains. Then he takes Nature to his bosom, —calls her by the sweetest of names, pours his soul out before her, gives her his whole heart, and yields up to her his manly adoration.—SMILES, SAMUEL, 1860, *Brief Biographies, p.* 81.

It is hardly possible, without quotation, to give an idea of the rage and fury which pervade these poems. He curses his political opponents with his whole heart and soul. He pillories them, and pelts them with dead cats and rotten eggs. The earnestness of his mood has a certain terror in it for meek and quiet people. His poems are of the angriest, but their anger is not altogether undivine. His scorn blisters and scalds, his sarcasm flays; but then outside nature is constantly touching him with a summer breeze or a branch of pink and white apple-blossom, and his mood becomes tenderness itself. He is far from being lachrymose; and when he is pathetic, he affects one as when a strong man sobs. His anger is not nearly so frightful as his tears. I cannot understand why Elliott is so little read. Other names not particularly remarkable I meet in the current reviews—his never. His book stands on my shelf, but on no other have I seen it. This I think strange, because, apart from the intrinsic values of his verse *as* verse, it has an historical value. Evil times, and embittered feelings, now happily passed away, are preserved in his books, like Pompeii and Herculaneum in Vesuvian lava.—SMITH, ALEXANDER, 1863, *Dreamthorp, p.* 208.

Elliott's imagination was ambitious, and imperfectly trained: he accordingly dealt with large and passionate themes, entering into them with complete *abandon;* and he was hurried on to passages of genuine inspiration; real heights and depths were within his range; heavenly lights alternate with nether darkness. Few of his longer poems, however, possess imaginative ordonnance; from the sublime he could pass to the turgid; from the pathetic to the pseudo-romantic; and therefore few of these longer poems can be read with satisfaction in each as a whole. Nothing of worth that Elliott wrote was caught out of the air; each poem had its roots in fact; but the colouring in his earlier pieces is sometimes extravagant: as he matured, his imagination gravitated from the romantic to the real. There are not many figures in English poetry drawn from real life worthier of regard than the Ranter, Elliott's pale preacher of reform on Shirecliffe height, and his Village Patriarch, the blind lone father, with wind-blown venerable hair, still unbowed after his hundred years; though seeming coeval with the cliffs around, still a living and heroic pattern of English manhood.—DOWDEN, EDWARD, 1880, *The English Poets, ed. Ward, vol.* IV, *p.* 495.

Anything more gentle, more femininely sweet, than his occasional poetical effusions, I really do not know. One is conscious of having met with a soul capable of the profoundest tenderness; and the loving, heart-stirring tones, are quite irresistible. Excessive, no doubt, he is everywhere; and we become the more convinced of the sincerity and naturalness of his political writings, when we see his habit of investing every character he has to do with, with his own passionate effections.—TAYLOR, EMILY, 1884, *Memories of Some Contemporary Poets, p.* 141.

Does not rank among high sonneteers. He was one of the most convinced opponents of the legitimate or Petrarcan sonnet, and a strong advocate for the Spenserian.—SHARP, WILLIAM, 1886, *Sonnets of this Century, p.* 287, *note.*

His heart was like the sea anemone, that, warmed by the summer sun, unfolds its wealth of colour in the rock-pool by the sea; but touched by the rude hand of man shrinks into unloveliness, and clings with grim fierceness to the rock. And yet even when stung into concentration by the reflection of "what man has made of man," his bitterness is that of a tender heart wrought upon by evils which it cannot ignore, but which it feels itself powerless to overcome.—MILES, ALFRED H., 1892, *The Poets and the Poetry of the Century, Southey to Shelley, ed. Milnes, p.* 234.

He was, however, a very good specimen of the manly, natural representative of the common people, the backbone of the nation —whose local fame is an advantage to his country, and who if he does not escape some of the mistakes natural to limited education and horizon, is far above the tragic folly of those who believe that everything that is wrong can be set right, and prosperity and universal good secured by act of Parliament.—OLIPHANT, MARGARET O. W., 1892, *The Victorian Age of English Literature, vol.* I, *p.* 240.

It is difficult to fix the poetic place of Elliott, for the reason that there is no known definition of poetry which does not suggest and require additions and deductions, and the further reason that he is so different at different times that one cannot but hesitate in the attempt to determine his actual form and pressure. To say that he has written badly is only to say what has been said over and over again of Burns and Byron. But neither Burns nor Byron ever wrote so badly as he, nor with such persistence. Unlike their bad writing, which was accidental, his bad writing seems to have resulted from the system that he pursued, partly, no doubt, through ignorance, but more through obstinacy—the obstinacy which mistakes itself for originality. He was not so much an uneducated poet as a mis-educated poet. He may have read only masterpieces, as he claimed, but if so he read them amiss, since he learned nothing from them. His admiration of Byron, which was life-long, was of Byron at his worst, for Byron taught him to rail and curse, not to reflect and meditate. . . . He has no narrative talent. The movement of his verse, which was uncertain, was perpetually wasting itself in needless digressions—noisy with exclamations, and turbid with the sediments of passion. —STODDARD, RICHARD HENRY, 1892, *Under the Evening Lamp, pp.* 146, 147.

He is a violent and crude thinker, with more smoke than fire in his violence, though not without generosity of feeling now and then, and with a keen admiration of the scenery—still beautiful in parts, and then exquisite—which surrounded the smoky Hades of Sheffield.—SAINTSBURY, GEORGE, 1896, *A History of Nineteenth Century Literature, p.* 111.

Was obviously born with a true delight in Nature and with some power of observation. But his work as a poet was marred —in one way by hasty indifference to finish and concentration, in another by the crude unscrupulous violence with which his political views were rendered: an atmosphere at all times asphyxiating to poetry. —PALGRAVE, FRANCIS TURNER, 1896, *Landscape in Poetry, p.* 209.

Though he probably had more of the "root of the matter" in him than any man living at that time save Tennyson and Browning, it almost necessarily excluded by the self-chosen narrowness of his themes and by their fiercely polemical treatment from any prominent place in such a chronicle as this. One might almost wish that the Corn-Laws had been repealed twenty years earlier, in order to see how it might then have fared with Elliott's poetic development, were it not that in that case he would probably never have sung at all.—TRAILL, HENRY DUFF, 1897, *Social England, vol.* VI, *p.* 155.

Thomas Lovell Beddoes

1803–1849

Born, at Clifton, 20 July 1803. Educated at Bath Grammar School; and at Charterhouse, June 1817–20; Contrib. sonnet to "Morning Post," 1819. Wrote "The Bride's Tragedy," 1819. To Pembroke Coll., Oxford, 1 May 1820; B. A., 25 May 1825; M. A., 16 April 1828. Assisted in publication of Shelley's Posthumous Poems, 1824. To Italy in summer of 1824. Göttingen Univ., studying medicine, July 1825–29. To Würzburg, 1829; degree of M. D. there, 1832. At Zurich, June 1835 to March 1840. To Berlin, 1841. In England, 1842; at various towns in Germany and Switzerland, 1844–46; in England, 1846–47; settled in Frankfort, June 1847. Died, in Basle Hospital, 26 Jan. 1849. Buried in Hospital cemetery. *Works:* "The Improvisatore," 1821; "The Bride's Tragedy," 1822. *Posthumous:* "Death's Jest-Book, or the Fool's Tragedy," 1850; "Poems, Posthumous and Collected," ed. by T. F. Kelsall (2 vols.), 1851; "Poetical Works," ed. by E. Gosse (2 vols.), 1890; "Letters," ed. by E. Gosse, 1894.—SHARP, R. FARQUHARSON, 1897, *A Dictionary of English Authors, p.* 21.

PERSONAL

My Dear Phillips,—I am food for what I am good for—worms. I have made a will here which I desire to be respected, and add the donation of £20 to Dr. Ecklin my physician.

W. Beddoes must have a case (50 bottles) of Champagne Moet 1847 growth to drink my death in.

Thanks for your kindness. Borrow the £200. You are a good & noble man & your children must look sharp to be like you.

Yours,
if my own,
ever,
T. L. B.

Love to Anna, Henry, the Beddoes of Longvill and Zoe and Emmeline King—also to Kelsall whom I beg to look at my MSS. and print or not as he thinks fit. I ought to have been among other things a good poet. Life was too great a bore on one peg and that a bad one. Buy for Dr. Ecklin above mentioned [one of] Reade's best stomach-pumps.—BEDDOES, THOMAS LOVELL, 1849, *Letter to Revell Phillips, Jan.* 26; *Letters, ed. Gosse, p.* 261.

I first knew Thomas Lovell Beddoes at the Charter-house in 1817 or 1818. We were in the same house (Mr. Watkinson's No. 15 in the square). Beddoes was near the top of the school; I was his fag, and in constant attendance upon him. The expression of his face was shrewd and sarcastic, with an assumption of sternness, as he affected the character of a tyrant and bully, though really not much of either; but a persevering and ingenious tormentor, as I knew to my cost. With a great natural turn for humour, and a propensity to mischief; impatient of control, and indisposed to constituted authority over him, he suggested and carried out many acts of insubordination, in the contrivance of which he shewed as much wit, as spirit in their execution; and even when detected in positive rebellion, his invincible assurance and deliberate defiance of the masters, together with the grim composure of his countenance, was so irresistibly comic, that I have seen them unable to speak for laughing when he was brought up for punishment.— BEVAN, CHARLES DACRES, 1851, *Letter to Revell Phillips, The Poems Posthumous and Collected of Thomas Lovell Beddoes, ch.* i, *p.* cxxviii.

Beddoes in person and otherwise was not unlike Keats. Both were short in stature, and independent in manner, and very brief and decided in conversation. Beddoes was too fond of objecting and carping, when the merits of any modern books came into discussion. Not that he was at all vain or envious himself, but he was at all times unwilling to yield homage to any poets, except Shelley and Keats and Wordsworth. Of these Shelley was undoubtedly his favorite. Like that great poet, Beddoes had much love for philosophical questions, although the poetical element was predominant in him.—PROCTER, BRYAN WALLER (BARRY CORNWALL), 1874? *Recollections of Men of Letters.*

His mother was a sister of Maria Edgeworth, and his father a distinguished physician and an intimate friend of Sir Humphry Davy. In the father's character we may trace the principal traits of the son: a strong scientific bent, a fondness for poetic dreams, an invincible independence, were predominant in both. The character of Lovell Beddoes' poetry was the natural outgrowth of his poetry studies. His schoolfellows at the Charterhouse speak of him at the age of fourteen as already thoroughly versed in the best English literature and a close student of the dramatists, from the Elizabethan to those of his own day. He was always ready to invent and carry out any acts of insubordination, which he informed with so much wit and spirit that the very authorities were often subdued by their own irresistible laughter. It was one phase of his dramatic genius, that seemed to be constantly impelling him to get up some striking situation wherein he might pose as a youthful Ajax defying the lightnings. At Oxford his restless independence was continually prompting him to affront his tutors. He was always in opposition to the spirit of the occasion, whatever it might be.—HILLARD, KATE, 1873, *A Strayed Singer, Lippincott's Magazine, vol.* 12, *p.* 551.

In June 1847 he finally quitted England, and settled for twelve months at Frankfort in the house of an actor named Degen, practicing a little as a physician. Here in the early part of 1848 his blood became poisoned from the virus of a dead body entering a slight wound in his hand. This was overcome, but seriously affected his health and spirits. His republican friends had deserted him, and he felt disgusted with life. The circumstances which attended his death were mysterious, and have not been made known to the public. The published account was founded on a letter from Beddoes to his sister, in which he says: "In July I fell with a horse in a precipitous part of the neighbouring hills, and broke my left leg all to pieces." This is the version which he wished to circulate, and this may be accepted in silence. The incident, however, whatever it was, occurred not in July, but in May 1848, in the town of Bâle, where he had arrived the previous night. He was immediately taken to the hospital, where he was placed under the charge of his old friend, Dr. Frey, and of a Dr. Ecklin. . . . In December he walked out of his room twice, and proposed to go to Italy. His recovery was considered certain when, on 26 Jan. 1849, Dr. Ecklin was called to his bedside, and found him insensible. He died at 10 P. M. that night. . . . In person Beddoes was like Keats, short and thick set; in the last year of his life he allowed his beard to grow, and "looked like Shakespeare." His friends in the hospital spoke of his fortitude under suffering, and said that he always showed "the courage of a soldier."—GOSSE, EDMUND, 1885, *Dictionary of National Biography, vol.* IV, *pp.* 96, 97.

THE BRIDE'S TRAGEDY
1822

However, here is Minor Beddoes, born in the very zenith of this mock sun of poetry, while it is culminating in the mid-heaven of our literary hemisphere, shining in watery splendor, the gaze and gape of our foolish-faced, fat-headed nation; here is Minor Beddoes, I say, born amid the very rage and triumph of the Byronian heresy —nay, in a preface more remarkable for good nature than good sense, eulogizing some of the prose-poets—yet what does Minor Beddoes? Why, writing a tragedy himself, with a judgment far different from that exhibited in his own panegyrical preface, he totally rejects, and therewith tactly condemns and abjures, the use of prose-poetry. But it was not the boy's judgment that led him to this; it was his undepraved ear, and his native energy of mind, teaching him to *respue* this effeminate style of versification. "The Bride's Tragedy" transcends, in the quality of its rhythm and metrical harmony, "The Doge of Venice," and "Mirandola," just as much as it does "Fazio," and the other dramas which conform to the rules of genuine English heroic verse in the energy of its language, the power of its sentiments, and the boldness of its imagery—that is incalculably. — DARLEY, GEORGE (JOHN LACY), 1822, *Letters to the Dramatists of the Day, London Magazine.*

DEATH'S JEST BOOK
1850

We must frankly say, in conclusion, that we are not acquainted with any living author who could have written the "Fool's Tragedy."—FORSTER, JOHN, 1850, *The Literary Examiner, July* 20.

Nearly two centuries have elapsed since a work of the same wealth of genius as "Death's Jest Book" hath been given to the world.—LANDOR, SAVAGE WALTER, 1850, *Letter to John Forster, Walter Savage Landor, A Biography, bk.* vii.

Now as to the extracts which might be made: why, you might pick out scenes, passages, lyrics, fine as fine can be: the power of the man is immense and irresistible. — BROWNING, ROBERT, 1872, *To Thomas Forbes Kelsall, Fortnightly Review, vol.* 18, *p.* 52, *note.*

So ends this singular drama,—singular in its plot, its characters, its accessories, and, above all, singular in the felicities and vigour of its composition. It may not be a suitable pillow for the head that would court only placid dreams, but those who turn habitually to poetry as "chief nourisher in life's feast" of some of their noblest faculties, will find such congenial aliment in the imaginative thoughts that crowd this little volume. — KELSALL, THOMAS FORBES, 1872, *Thomas Lovell Beddoes, Fortnightly Review, vol.* 18, *p.* 75.

In . . . 1850 appeared as a posthumous work, a wild play, musical throughout, with grand echoes of Elizabethan thought and passion, the "Death's Jest Book" of Thomas Lovell Beddoes.—MORLEY, HENRY, 1878, *ed., English Plays, p.* 434.

A painful but powerful tragedy, in which the poet endeavoured, as much as a man of the nineteenth century can, to throw himself into the atmosphere of the pre-Shakespearian tragedians. — OLIPHANT, MARGARET O. W., 1892, *The Victorian Age of English Literature, vol.* I, *p.* 243.

"Death's Jest Book" is a nightmare rather than a drama, and should be judged, if one must judge it, for what it is, not for what it might be, or should be. A law unto himself, Beddoes is the most lawless of poets. The scenes of his tragedies are laid in the land of Nowhere, and the actors therein, if not wholly mad, are certainly not sane. They live, move, and have their being in a borderland between the worlds of life and death. The prey of spasmodic emotion and unnatural passion, there is no telling what they will say or do in their fits of delirium, which are as unaccountable as violent. The specialty of the elder Beddoes was the analysis of disease; the specialty of his son was the exhibition of disease in the actors of his gloomy masquerades.—STODDARD, RICHARD HENRY, 1892, *Under the Evening Lamp, p.* 211.

GENERAL

How stately or enduring a monument he may, by the earnest cultivators of English poetic literature, be deemed to have himself erected in his works, this is not perhaps the fitting place in which to venture a prediction. In his life time, he may certainly be said to have strangely missed his fame: the most golden bough of "the everlasting singing-tree,"—the laudarier a laudatis,—as posthumous events have shown, lay already within his reach, would he but have stretched his hands to gather it. But even the full and open requital of these his actual, though hidden, claims of distinction, would still have left, for those who best knew that creative mind in all its undeveloped power, the larger portion of their Hope unsatisfied.—KELSALL, THOMAS FORBES, 1851, *The Poems Posthumous and Collected of Thomas Lovell Beddoes, Memoir, vol.* I, *p.* cxvi.

His later dramatic compositions and fragments, though showing a certain vigorous and passionate thought have an increasing tendency to exaggeration and extravagance, and are hardly amenable to the ordinary rules of criticism.—GRAHAM, J. H., 1871, *An Historical View of Literature and Art in Great Britain, p.* 191.

There is an old saying that the workman may be known by his chips: surely from these chips we may gather a high opinion of that artificer who left such fragments to testify for him. For imaginative power of a very high order, for the true tragic spirit, for exquisitely melodious versification, for that faculty of song which is the flower of the lyric genius, Beddoes was pre-eminently distinguished. Nor for these alone. His style is based upon the rich vocabulary of the old dramatists, and is terse, pregnant and quaint, without any trace of affectation. There was a sturdy genuineness about the man that forbade him to assume, and his phraseology was the natural outgrowth of his mind and his early education. He has not gone to work, like so many of our modern pre-Raphaelite painters, to imitate crudeness of form in the vain hope of acquiring thereby earnestness and innocence of spirit; but he has studied the best tragic models in a reverent spirit, and allowed his muse to work out her own salvation. —HILLARD, KATE, 1873, *A Strayed Singer, Lippincott's Magazine, vol.* 12, *p.* 556.

Beddoes is a poet for poets, and few other readers will enjoy him. He is "of imagination all compact;" his works scarcely contain a single passage of purely subjective feeling. He is, perhaps, the most concrete poet of his day; the most disposed to express sentiment by imagery and material symbolism. In this he resembles Keats, and may be termed a Gothic Keats, the Teutonic counterpart of his more celebrated contemporary's Hellenism. The spirit of Gothic architecture seems to live in his verse, its grandeur and grotesqueness, its mystery and its gloom. His relation to the Elizabethan dramatists, moreover, is nearly the same as that of Keats to the Elizabethan pastoral poets; but the resemblance is one of innate temperament; he borrowed nothing, either from his Elizabethan precursors or the chief objects of his admiration among his contemporaries, Keats and Shelley. The want of constructive power which mars his dramas is even more prejudicial to his lyrics; but some few songs, where the right key note has been struck from the first, rank among the most perfect in our language.—BAYNES, THOMAS SPENCER, *ed.*, 1877, *Encyclopædia Britannica, Ninth ed., vol.* III, *p.* 415.

Beddoes was, so to say, saturated with the spirit of the Elizabethan Dramatists, and cast his poetry for the most part into Elizabethan forms.—EDWARDS, AMELIA B., 1878, *ed., A Poetry-Book, Second Series, The Modern Poets, p.* 322, *note.*

. . . small-craft ride
At anchor, rot while Beddoes breasts the tide!

—BROWNING, ROBERT, 1878, *The Two Poets of Croisic.*

Buffon said, "Show me the style and I'll show you the man" [le style est de l'homme même]. Puttenham (Arte of English Poesie, 1589, p. 161) wrote with equal justice: "his [man's] inward conceits be the metall of his minde, and his manner of utterance the very warp and woofe of his conceits;" or, in other words, "show me the man, and I'll show you his style." Beddoes' Poems and Letters are one more welcome illustration of the truth of Buffon's observation; but, in a far higher sense, of Puttenham's. Here the style is the direct, necessary expression of the writer's inmost nature. Since he was in the highest degree original, the fact has a significance, in matters of English style, far deeper than has been attributed to it. . . . If we class the characteristic works in English literature with reference to the history of style into three periods, the Anglo-Saxon epic style and Shakspeare represent two of them. The third has no complete representative, but among its most significant writers (style being here assumed to have little more to do with constructive power than in the case of the Anglo-Saxon poets) is Thomas Lovell Beddoes. Beddoes' intimate connection with Shakspeare in point, thought and style, is so marked that he has been called an Elizabethan, "a strayed singer," and the like.—WOOD, HENRY, 1883, *T. L. Beddoes, A Survival in Style, American Journal of Philology, vol.* 4, *pp.* 445, 446.

The quality of youth is still more distinctly discernible in some of Thomas Beddoes' dazzling little songs, stolen straight from the heart of the sixteenth century, and lustrous with that golden light which set so long ago. It is not in spirit only, nor in sentiment, that this resemblance exists; the words, the imagery, the swaying music, the teeming fancies of the younger poet, mark him as one strayed from another age, and wandering companionless under alien skies.—REPPLIER, AGNES, 1891, *English Love-Songs, Points of View, p.* 60.

Beddoes is always large, impressive; the greatness of his aim gives him a certain claim on respectful consideration. That his talent achieved itself, or ever could have achieved itself, he himself would have been the last to affirm. But he is a monumental failure, more interesting than many facile triumphs. . . . Beddoes' genius was essentially lyrical: he had imagination, the gift of style, the mastery of rhythm, a strange choiceness and curiosity of phrase. But of really dramatic power he had nothing. He could neither conceive a coherent plot, nor develop a credible situation. He had no grasp on human nature, he had no conception of what character might be in men and women, he had no faculty of expressing emotion convincingly. Constantly you find the most beautiful poetry where it is absolutely inappropriate, but never do you find one of those brief and memorable phrases—words from the heart—for which one would give much beautiful poetry. . . . A beautiful lyrist, a writer of charming, morbid, and magnificent poetry in dramatic form, Beddoes will survive to students not to readers, of English poetry, somewhere in the neighborhood of Ebenezer Jones and Charles Wells.—SYMONS, ARTHUR, 1891, *The Poetical Works of Thomas Lovell Beddoes, The Academy, vol.* 40, *p.* 129.

No nineteenth century English poet with whom I am acquainted, ever promised more and performed less than Thomas Lovell Beddoes, whose verse, like his life, was a wayward fragment. . . . There were the makings of a greater poet in Beddoes than he ever became, except at intervals, and in his most inspired moments; and the poet that he might have been, if fully developed, is of a kind that English poetry has long since outgrown. He belonged to the same guild of dramatists as Marlowe, Tourneur, and Webster, but where they were masters, he was an apprentice. There were the same dark elements in his genius as in theirs, but they were more confused and tumultuous, more chaotic than creative, and more horrible than terrible. — STODDARD, RICHARD HENRY, 1892, *Under the Evening Lamp, pp.* 200, 210.

In all strictly poetical endowments he is most affluent, it is only when he of necessity forsakes the realm of pure poetry that he becomes awkward and ineffectual. He had chosen the drama for his special field—unwisely it might have been said, had his overmastering enthusiasm for the Elizabethan stage allowed him any alternative. . . . He is, however, much more than a writer of exquisite fragments, for his beauties, isolated and disjointed in themselves, are yet inspired with a continuity of feeling, and taken altogether, and especially when read in connection with his letters, form a kind of autobiographic poem, a comment on a character of striking originality and interest. The physiologist and psychologist may learn much from the only English poet whose mind has been deeply tinged by a medical training: but he is especially a poet for poets, readers who can prize the massy ore of poetry, even when it has failed to receive the stamp of artistic finish. Pure ore it is at least: after Shelley and Keats no poet is freer from admixture with inferior matter. Things invariably present themselves to him under their most picturesque and imaginative aspects, and it would be hard to bring him in guilty of a single commonplace. As a lyrical writer he is curiously unequal; some of his pieces are formless and tuneless; while others have placed him among the best lyrists in the language.—GARNETT, RICHARD, 1894, *The Poets and the Poetry of the Century, John Keats to Lord Lytton, ed. Miles, p.* 522.

Except Donne, there is perhaps no English poet more difficult to write about, so as to preserve the due pitch of enthusiasm on the one hand and criticism on the other, than Thomas Lovell Beddoes. . . . Beddoes has sometimes been treated as a mainly bookish poet deriving from the Elizabethans and Shelley. I cannot agree with this. His very earliest work, written when he could not know much either of Shelley or Keats, shows as they do technique perhaps caught from Leigh Hunt. But this is quite dropped later; and his Elizabethanism is not imitation but inspiration. In this inspiration he does not follow but shares with, his greater contemporaries. He is a younger and tragic counterpart to Charles Lamb in the intensity with which he has imbibed the Elizabethan spirit, rather from the nightshade of Webster and Tourneur than from the vine of Shakespeare. As wholes, his works are naught, or naught but nightmares; though "Death's Jest-Book," despite its infinite disadvantages from constant rewriting and uncertainty of final form, has a strong grasp. But they contain passages, especially lyrics, of the most exquisite fancy and music, such as since the seventeenth century none but Blake and Coleridge had given. . . . The author of such things as the "Dirge for Wolfram" ("If thou wilt ease thine heart") in "Death's Jest-Book," and the stanza beginning "Dream-Pedlary," "If there were dreams to sell," with not a few others of the same kind, attains to that small and disputed—but not to those who have thought out the nature of poetry disputable—class of poets who, including Sappho, Catullus, some mediæval hymn-writers, and a few moderns, especially Coleridge, have, by virtue of fragments only, attained a higher position than many authors of large, substantive, and important poems.—SAINTSBURY, GEORGE, 1896, *A History of Nineteenth Century Literature, pp.* 114, 115.

Marguerite, Countess of Blessington

1789-1849

Born at Knockbrit, Tipperary, on the 1st of September, 1789. (The year, however, has been variously stated as 1787 and 1790). She was the daughter of Edmund Power, a country gentleman and magistrate, a man of violent temper and without principle. In 1796 or '97 the Powers removed to Clonmel. In 1804, when she was under fifteen years of age, Marguerite was forced by her father into a marriage with the vicious and half-insane Captain Maurice Farmer. Within a year they agreed to separate. Mrs. Farmer is spoken of as residing in Cahir, Tipperary, in 1807, and in Dublin in 1809. And now occurs that hiatus in the account of her life which has never been satisfactorily filled, and the existence of which the English women of her day refused to overlook. In 1816 she was established in Manchester Square, London; and in 1818, Captain Farmer having died the previous year, she married the Earl of Blessington. Her fashionable life, foreign travels, and literary career now began. In 1823, while at Genoa with her husband, she made the acquaintance of Lord Byron. In 1829 Lord Blessington died in the Hotel Ney, Paris, which had been sumptuously fitted up as his residence. Lady Blessington returned to London in 1830. She lived in Seamore Place,

May Fair, until 1836, when she removed to Gore House, Kensington Gore. . . . In the spring of 1849 "the long-menaced break-up of the establishment at Gore House took place." Lady Blessington left London, accompanied by her nieces, for Paris, where, on the 4th of June, 1849, she died very suddenly of "an apoplectic malady, complicated with disease of the heart." . . . The following are the works of Lady Blessington: "The Magic Lantern; or, Sketches of Scenes in the Metropolis," 1822. "Sketches and Fragments," 1822. "Conversations with Lord Byron," 1832. These articles first appeared in Colburn's *New Monthly Magazine.* "Grace Cassidy; or, The Repealers," 1833. "Meredyth," 1833. "The Follies of Fashion," 1835. "The Two Friends," 1835. "The Victims of Society," 1837. "The Confessions of an Elderly Lady," 1839. "The Governess," 1839. "Desultory Thoughts and Reflections," 1839. "The Idler in Italy," 1839. "The Idler in France," 1841. "The Lottery of Life," 1842. "Strathern; or, Life at Home and Abroad," 1845. "The Memoirs of a Femme de Chambre," 1846. "Lionel Deerhurst," 1847. "Marmaduke Herbert," 1847. "Country Quarters." This were first published in a London Sunday paper, 1848. After Lady Blessington's death it was edited by her neice, Miss Power, and published separately. She also wrote "A Tour Through the Netherlands to Paris," "Confessions of an Elderly Gentleman," "The Belle of a Season," and edited for several years, Heath's "Book of Beauty," "The Keepsake," and another annual entitled, "Gems of Beauty."—CONE, HELEN GRAY, AND GILDER, JEANNETTE L., 1887, *Pen-Portraits of Literary Women, vol.* I, *pp.* 245, 246.

PERSONAL

Irving walked about with me; called together at Lady Blessington's, who is growing very absurd. "I have felt very melancholy and ill all this day," she said. "Why is that," I asked. "Don't you know?" "No." "It is the anniversary of my poor Napoleon's death."—MOORE, THOMAS, 1822, *Diary, May* 5; *Memoirs, Journal and Correspondence, ed. Russell.*

Lady Blessington is much more handsome than Countess Egloffstein, but their countenance, manners, and particularly the tone of voice, belong to the same class. Her dress rich, and her library most splendid. Her book about Lord Byron (now publishing by driblets in the "New Monthly Magazine"), and her other writings, give her in addition the character of a *bel esprit.* Landor, too, says, that she was to Lord Blessington the most devoted wife he ever knew. He says also, that she was by far the most beautiful woman he ever saw, and was so deemed at the Court of George IV. She is now, Landor says, about thirty, but I should have thought her older. She is a great talker, but her talk is rather narrative than declamatory, and very pleasant.—ROBINSON, HENRY CRABB, 1832, *Diary, Sept.* 28; *Reminiscences, ed. Sadler, vol.* II, *p.* 175.

The original is now (she confessed it very frankly) forty. She looks something on the sunny side of thirty. Her person is full, but preserves all the fineness of an admirable shape; her foot is not crowded in a satin slipper for which a Cinderella might long be looked for in vain, and her complexion (an unusually fair skin, with very dark hair and eyebrows) is of even a girlish delicacy and freshness. Her dress of blue satin . . . was cut low, and folded across her bosom, in a way to show to advantage the round and sculpture-like curve and whiteness of a pair of exquisite shoulders, while her hair dressed close to her head, and parted simply over her forehead with a rich *ferronier* of turquoise, enveloped in clear outline a head with which it would be difficult to find a fault. Her features are regular, and her mouth, the most expressive of them, has a ripe fullness and freedom of play peculiar to the Irish physiognomy, and expressive of the most unsuspicious good-humor. Add to all this a voice merry and sad by turns, but always musical, and manners of the most unpretending elegance, yet even more remarkable for their winning kindness, and you have the most prominent traits of one of the most lovely and fascinating women I have ever seen.—WILLIS, NATHANIEL PARKER, 1835–53, *Pencillings by the Way.*

"Lady Blessington!" cried the glad usher aloud,
As she swam through the doorway, like moon from a cloud.
I know not which most her face beam'd with —fine creature!
Enjoyment, or judgment, or wit, or good nature,

Perhaps you have known what it is to feel
longings
To pat buxom shoulders at routs and such
throngings;
Well, think what it was, at a vision like that!
A Grace after dinner!—a Venus grown fat!
—HUNT, LEIGH, 1838, *Feast of the Violets, Monthly Repository.*

In her lifetime she was loved and admired for her many graceful writings, her gentle manners, her kind and generous heart. Men, famous for art and science, in distant lands sought her friendship; and the historians and scholars, the poets and wits, and painters of her own country found an unfailing welcome in her ever-hospitable home. She gave cheerfully, to all who were in need, help and sympathy, and useful counsel; and she died lamented by many friends. Those who loved her best in life, and now lament her most, have reared this tributary marble over the place of her rest.—PROCTER, BRYAN WALLER, (BARRY CORNWALL), 1849, *Epitaph for the Countess of Blessington.*

I have never since beheld so pure and perfect a vision of female loveliness, in what I conceive to be its most perfect phase, that, namely, in which intellect does not predominate over form, feature, complexion, and the other physical attributes of female beauty, but only serves to heighten, purify and irradiate them; and it is this class of beauty which cannot be equalled on canvas. . . . At this time Lady Blessington was about six-and-twenty years of age; but there was about her face, together with that beaming intelligence which rarely shows itself upon the countenance till that period of life, a bloom and freshness which as rarely survive early youth, and a total absence of the undefinable marks which thought and feeling still more rarely fail to leave behind them. Unlike all other beautiful faces that I have seen, hers was, at the time of which I speak, neither a history nor a prophecy; not a book to read and study, a problem to solve, or a mystery to speculate upon, but a star to kneel before and worship.—PATMORE, P. G., 1854, *My Friends and Acquaintance, vol.* I, *pp.* 170, 172.

Beauty, the heritage of the family, was, in her early youth, denied to Marguerite: her eldest brother and sister, Michael and Anne, as well as Ellen and Robert, were singularly handsome and healthy children, while she, pale, weakly and ailing, was for years regarded as little likely ever to grow to womanhood; the precocity of her intellect, the keenness of her perceptions, and her extreme sensitiveness, all of which are so often regarded, more especially among the Irish, as the precursive symptoms of an early death, confirmed this belief, and the poor, pale, reflective child was long looked upon as doomed to a premature grave. The atmosphere in which she lived was but little congenial to such a nature. Her father, a man of violent temper, and little given to study the characters of his children, intimidated and shook the delicate nerves of the sickly child, though there were moments—rare ones, it is true—when the sparkles of her early genius for an instant dazzled and gratified him. Her mother, though she failed not to bestow the tenderest maternal care on the health of the little sufferer, was not capable of appreciating her fine and subtile qualities, and her brothers and sisters, fond as they were of her, were not, in their high health and boisterous gayety, companions suited to such a child.—POWER, MISS, 1854, *A Memoir of the Countess of Blessington, Literary Life and Correspondence, ed. Madden, Introduction, vol.* I, *pp.* 14, 15.

The peculiar character of Lady Blessington's beauty seemed to be the entire, exact, and instantaneous correspondence of every feature, and each separate trait of her countenance, with the emotion of her mind, which any particular subject of conversation or object of attention might excite. The instant a joyous thought took possession of her fancy, you saw it transmitted as if by electrical agency to her glowing features: you read it in her sparkling eyes, her laughing lips, her cheerful looks; you heard it expressed in her ringing laugh, clear and sweet as the gay, joybell sounds of childhood's merriest tones. There was a geniality in the warmth of her Irish feelings, an abandonment of all care, of all apparent consciousness of her powers of attraction, a glowing sunshine of good-humor and of good-nature in the smiles and laughter, and the sallies of wit of this lovely woman in her early and happy days (those of her Italian life, especially from 1823 to 1826), such as have been seldom surpassed. . . . Her voice was sweetly modulated and low. Its tones were always in harmonious concord with the traits of her expressive features. . . . All the beauty of Lady Blessington, without the exquisite sweetness of her voice, and the witchery of its tones in pleasing or expressing pleasure, would have been only a secondary attraction.—MADDEN, R. R., 1854, *Literary Life and Correspondence of the Countess of Blessington, vol.* I, *pp.*51,52.

Virtuous ladies! instead of censuring her faults, attempt to imitate her virtues. Believe that, if any excess may be run into, the excess of tenderness is quite as pardonable as that of malignity and rancour.—LANDOR, WALTER SAVAGE, 1855, *The Landor-Blessington Papers, Literary Anecdotes of the Nineteenth Century, eds. Nicoll and Wise, p.* 233.

Lady Blessington made a very pleasant impression upon me; and in the great circles, when the noble ladies asked me where I had been, I could not abstain from naming Lady Blessington. Then there always was a pause; I asked the reason why I was not to go there, or what was the matter with her, but I always got a short answer that she was not a good woman. One day I spoke of her personal amiability, and of her humour, and related how she was affected when talking of Jenny Lind's representation of La Somnambula and the womanly nobility she manifested; I had seen her shed tears over it! "The creature!" exclaimed an old lady indignantly; "Lady Blessington weeping at the innocence of Jenny Lind!" A few years after I read of Lady Blessington's death at Paris. Count d'Orsay sat at her deathbed.—ANDERSEN, HANS CHRISTIAN, 1871, *The Story of My Life, p.* 302.

A thoughtful little poem written during the past summer for Lady Blessington has been quoted on a previous page: and it may remind me to say here what warmth of regard he [Dickens] had for her, and for all the inmates of Gore-house; how uninterruptedly joyous and pleasurable were his associations with them.—FORSTER, JOHN, 1872, *The Life of Charles Dickens, vol.* II, *ch.* iv.

She said a few kind words in that winning and gracious manner which no woman's welcome can have ever surpassed; and from that moment till the day of her death in Paris, I experienced only a long course of kind constructions and good offices. She was a steady friend, through good report and evil report, for those to whom she professed friendship. Such faults as she had belonged to her position, to her past history, and to the disloyalty of many who paid court to her by paying court to her faults, and who then carried into the outer world depreciating reports of the wit, the banter, the sarcasm, and the epigram, which but for their urgings and incitements would have been always kindly, however mirthful. She must have had originally the most sunny of sunny natures. As it was, I have never seen anything like her vivacity and sweet cheerfulness during the early years when I knew her. She had a singular power of entertaining herself by her own stories; the keenness of an Irishwoman in relishing fun and repartee, strange turns of language, and bright touches of character. A fairer, kinder, more universal recipient of everything that came within the possibilities of her mind, I have never known.—CHORLEY, HENRY FOTHERGILL, 1873, *Autobiography, Memoirs and Letters, vol.* I, *p.* 174.

Of Lady Blessington's tact, kindness, and remarkable beauty Procter always spoke with ardor, and abated nothing from the popular idea of that fascinating person. He thought she had done more in her time to institute good feeling and social intercourse among men of letters than any other lady in England, and he gave her eminent credit for bringing forward the rising talent of the metropolis without waiting to be prompted by a public verdict. —FIELDS, JAMES T., 1875, *"Barry Cornwall" and Some of His Friends, Harper's Magazine, vol.* 51, *p.* 782.

Lady Blessington, fair, florid-complexioned, with sparkling eyes and white, high forehead, above which her bright brown hair was smoothly braided beneath a light and simple blonde cap, in which were a few touches of sky-blue satin ribbon that singularly well became her, setting off her buxom face and its vivid coloring. —CLARKE, MARY COWDEN, 1878, *Recollections of Writers, p.* 42.

With the Countess of Blessington lived Count d'Orsay. As he, too, has often been described, I may dismiss him also with a few words. He had, it is well known, been married to the daughter of the Earl, and the step-daughter of the Countess of Blessington. The match, for some reason or other, proved unhappy. The Count, his wife, and the Countess of Blessington had at one time lived all three together, but after two years of this life the young Countess took leave of her husband and her step-mother, and from that time till their death, in various places and amid various fortunes, Count d'Orsay and the Countess of Blessington lived together. They were perfectly suited the one to the other, and evidently were deeply attached. But as to whether their relations were immoral, as they were equivocal, society had then, as now, strong suspicions, yet no absolute certainty. It is, however, but just to say that, in his last days, when the heavy hand of illness had already fallen on him, and the heavier hand of death was very near, and when already the Countess was dead, Count d'Orsay solemnly declared that he had never borne any love towards her but that of a son to a mother.—O'CONNOR, THOMAS POWER, 1879, *Lord Beaconsfield, A Biography, p.* 11.

Lady Blessington, when I saw her first, was residing at Seamore Place, Park Lane. That was in 1831. . . . Not long afterward she removed to Kensington Gore, and I had a general invitation to her "evenings." At that period she was past her prime no doubt, but she was still remarkably handsome; not so perhaps if tried by the established canons of beauty; but there was a fascination about her look and manner that greatly augmented her personal charms. Her face and features were essentially Irish; and that is the highest compliment I can pay them. Although I knew her history sufficiently well, I attributed to this particular daughter of Erin her share of the "wild sweet briery fence that round the flowers of Erin dwells," and felt conviction that for the unhappy circumstances of Lady Blessington's early life, the sins of others, far more than her own, were responsible, and that she had been to a great extent the victim of circumstances. To that opinion I still hold—some thirty years after her death, and more than fifty since I first saw her. Her "evenings" were very brilliant. Her guests were the leading men of mark of the age, and of all countries. There was certainty of meeting some one who was thenceforward never to be forogtten. The sometime Emperor of the French was seldom absent.—HALL, SAMUEL CARTER, 1883, *Retrospect of a Long Life, p.* 367.

I do not remember the date of the Gore House catastrophe, but I well recollect the sorrow—in a mild form—that I felt when I heard that "The Book of Beauty" was no more, and that the editor, with her friend Count d'Orsay, had exhausted the patience of their creditors at last. Gore House and its contents were thrown open to public inspection previous to the auctioneer's operations, when the female element made up for its enforced absence by crowding each room to suffocation. My first appearance at Gore House was on one of those public days. In a kind of boudoir there was a piece of sculpture which seemed greatly to interest some ladies, who formed a group round it which,—judging from its appearance—was composed of duchesses and marchionesses, and the like. On a cushion lay some marble hands of lovely form, exquisitely sculptured. "Oh, yes," said one of the aristocratic group to the rest; "they are her own hands. I know the man who modelled them. He said he never saw more perfect hands, both in form and color." I have the expression of some of those faces before me at this moment. Curiosity seemed to me the liveliest and the most prevailing, though now and again a haughty dame, after examining some startling evidence of extravagance, would assume an air which, being interpreted, said, "And this is the end of a wicked career. Thank goodness I have lived to see it!"—FRITH, W. P., 1888, *My Autobiography and Reminiscences, vol.* II, *p.* 180.

GENERAL

Her style is always graceful in its total absence of affectation—she excels, too, in the constructiveness which we have some times fancied was peculiar to her sex,—in the power of weaving a plot.—CHORLEY, HENRY F., 1838, *Authors of England, p.* 30.

The fact of her existence as an authoress is an enigma, poor as her pretentions are; for while it is very difficult to write good books, it is not easy to compose even bad ones, and volumes have come forth under her name for which hundreds of pounds have been paid, because (Heaven only can tell how) thousands are found who will read them. Her "Works" have been published in America, in one huge folio, where it seems they meet with peculiar success; and this trash goes down, because it is written by a Countess, in a country where rank is eschewed, and equality is the universal passion. They have (or some of them) been likewise translated into German; and if all this is not proof of literary merit, or at least of success, what is? It would be not uninteresting to trace this current of success to its source, and to lay bare all the springs of the machinery which sustains her artificial character as an authoress. . . . Though I never met with any individual who had read any of her books, except the "Conversations with Byron," which are too good to be hers, they are unquestionably a source of considerable profit, and she takes her place confidently and complacently as one of the literary celebrities of her day.—GREVILLE, CHARLES C. F., 1839, *A Journal of the Reign of Queen Victoria, ed. Reeve, Feb.* 17, *pp.* 146, 147.

If we judge of Lady Blessington's powers by the influence she apparently wielded over men of talent, we shall estimate her intellectual gifts very highly. But this would be a false standard; for none are more impressible than men of genius to the fascinations of the soft voice, the bright eye, the beautiful dress, the rich furniture, which such a woman knows how to employ. If we judge of her by the *descriptions* of her conversation given us by admiring frequenters of her saloons, we shall again place her high on the list of intellectual women. But here, too, the standard would be a false one; for these same accessories lend a delusive charm to words, which, if spoken by an unknown person in a gingham dress, would never have arrested attention a single moment. It is a curious fact, that, of all these brilliant conversations, whose effects are so enthusiastically described, nothing is reported beyond the reach of very commonplace powers of talk. Of her writings, the novels of society, in which we might have supposed she would excel, in tone and style are uniformly flat. The characters are drawn without vigor; the dialogues are carried on without point; the stories display the very poorest invention; the reflections are superficial, and the morality of that shallow and obtrusive kind, which people of doubtful lives are ever ready to furnish in phrases to make up for the short-comings of their conduct. The conversations with Lord Byron, however, are vigorous and instructive; incomparably the best of her ladyship's prose writings. —FELTON, C. C., 1855, *Lady Blessington, North American Review, vol.* 81, *p,* 258.

Also an Irish lady, possessed of a good deal of talent, who worked hard as a journey-woman in the profession of letters, writing novels, editing albums and annuals, a fashion of the day, and turning her hand to any work that was offered.—OLIPHANT, MARGARET O. W., 1892, *The Victorian Age of English Literature, p.* 13.

Despite a certain facility which she possessed, in common with many other women, for scribbling, it was a mistake (one of the many she made) for Lady Blessington to take up the *rôle* of a fashionable novelist. For a woman who spent her life as she did in society (where she was the stimulus of much mental activity), it was morally impossible to make any literary effort worthy of the name. . . . It is no reproach to Lady Blessington to say, that hardly anyone of the present day has ever read, or perhaps heard of, "The Two Friends, or, The Victims of Society," which was one of her best attempts. Sir Walter Besant calls this "a horrid book," and doubtless, according to the standard of to-day, this judgment is correct.—GERARD, FRANCES A., 1897, *Some Fair Hibernians, p.* 161.

Bernard Barton

1784-1849

Bernard Barton, the Quaker poet, was born at Carlisle, 31st January 1784. In 1809 he became clerk to a bank at Woodbridge, a post which he held till within two days of his death, 19th February 1849. His "Metrical Effusions" (1812) brought him into correspondence with Southey; whilst "Poems by an Amateur" (1818), "Poems" (1820), and several more volumes of verse, increased his reputation, and gained him the friendship of Lamb. His devotional poems have an echo of George Herbert, and some of his lyrics are graceful; but he is on the whole less a poet than a versifier, easy and pleasant withal. Lamb's advice to him was sound, "Keep to your bank, and your bank will keep you;" and by Lamb's advice it was that he accepted the sum of £1200, raised by some Quaker friends in 1824. See his "Poems and Letters" (1849), selected by his daughter, with a memoir by her husband, Edward FitzGerald, and E. V. Lucas's "Bernard Barton and his Friends" (1894).—PATRICK AND GROOME, *eds.*, 1897, *Chambers's Biographical Dictionary, p.* 73.

PERSONAL

To those of his own neighbourhood he was known besides as a most amiable, genial, charitable man—of pure, unaffected, unpretending piety—the good neighbour—the cheerful companion—the welcome guest—a hospitable host—tolerant of all men, sincerely attached to many. Few, high or low, but were glad to see him at his customary place in the bank; to exchange some words of kindly greeting with him—few but were glad to have him at their own homes; and there he was the same man and had the same manners to all; always equally frank, genial, and communicative, without distinction of rank. He had all George Fox's "better part"—thorough independence of rank, titles, wealth, and all the distinctions of haberdashery, without making any needless display of such independence. He could dine with Sir Robert Peel one day, and the next day sup off bread and cheese with equal relish at a farmhouse, and relate with equal enjoyment at the one place what he had heard and seen at the other. . . . He was excellent company in all companies; but in none more than in homely parties, in or out of doors, over the winter's fire in the farmhouse, or under the tree in summer. He had a cheery word for all; a challenge to good fellowship with the old—a jest with the young—enjoying all, and making all enjoyable and joyous.—FITZGERALD, EDWARD, 1849, *Death of Bernard Barton, Miscellanies, pp.* 50, 53.

Your father and I visited Woodbridge yesterday. There we saw Bernard Barton's old home, the little quiet house behind the Bank, and the small room where he wrote his poetry and his letters, his bedroom, his kitchen, and that which used to be his drawing-room. We heard many traits of his character, all carefully treasured up in the mind of our informant. We found that his dear friend and housekeeper—the Mary Unwin of his life—has now been dead these five years; and that his daughter Lucy, Mrs. Fitzgerald, lives at Brighton. We were told in their old home, that she was then in Woodbridge, at the house of Mr. Jones, the surgeon, and there we went to call on her. But she was gone. Mr. Jones, however, we saw. He took us into his sumptuous drawing-room, and talked to us about "old Barton," "dear old Barton," "good old Barton," since whose death Woodbridge had never been itself.—HOWITT, MARY, 1864, *Letter to Margaret Howitt, Sept.* 29; *Good Words, vol.* 36, *p.* 243.

I recall him as he walked the streets of London on his visits there, in a broad-brimmed hat and coat of quakerish cut: a tall man, with a complexion telling less of the counting-house than of walks among the fields and lanes that environ Woodbridge in quiet Suffolk.—HALL, SAMUEL CARTER, 1883, *Retrospect of a Long Life, p.* 412.

GENERAL

Some weeks ago my friend Mr. Rogers showed me some of the Stanzas in MS., and I then expressed my opinion of their merit, which a further perusal of the printed volume has given me no reason to revoke. I mention this as it may not be disagreeable to you to learn that I entertained a very favourable opinion of your power before I was aware that such sentiments were reciprocal.—BYRON, LORD, 1812, *Letter to Barton, June* 1.

The volume before us has all the purity, the piety and gentleness, of the Sect to which its author belongs—with something too much perhaps of their sobriety. The style is rather diffuse and wordy, though generally graceful, flowing, and easy; and though it cannot be said to contain many bright thoughts or original images, it is recommended throughout by a truth of feeling and an unstudied earnestness of manner, that wins both upon the heart and the attention. In these qualities, as well as in the copiousness of the diction and the facility of the versification, it frequently reminds us of the smaller pieces of Cowper,—the author, like that eminent and most amiable writer, never disdaining ordinary words and sentiments when they come in his way, and combining, with his most solemn and contemplative strains, a certain air of homeliness and simplicity, which seems to show that the matter was more in his thoughts than the manner, and that the glory of fine writing was less considered than the clear and complete expression of the sentiments, for the sake of which alone he was induced to become a writer.—JEFFREY, FRANCIS LORD, 1820, *Quaker Poetry, Edinburgh Review, vol.* 34, *p.* 350.

As might be expected, he writes with sweetness, simplicity, and good sense; the two latter very rare commodities at present in poetry, when the bards of England go abroad to write, and bring home all the fervid heats of a tropical sun, backed by the scorching sirocco of the desert, to excite us into a proper degree of poetical enthusiasm. Friend Bernard's poetry is tender without exaggeration, and simple without childishness. His Pegasus is neither an elephant, a camel, nor a dromedary, but a horse of good pace and habits. In a better age of poetry he would be more admired. As it is, his Muse wants a few of the buttons of the honourable band of gentlemen pensioners to make her shine, and is, moreover, rather *drab-coloured* for the present flashy taste.—PAULDING, J. K., 1822, *A Sketch of Old England by a New England Man, vol.* II, *p.* 132.

My Dear Sir—Your title of "Poetic Vigils" arrides me much more than a volume of verse, which is no meaning. The motto says nothing, but I cannot suggest a better. I do not like mottoes but where they are singularly felicitous; there is foppery in them. They are unplain and un-Quakerish. They are good only where they flow from the title, and are a kind of justification of it. There is nothing about watchings or lucubrations in the one you suggest; no commentary on vigils. By the way, a wag would recommend you to the line of Pope,

"Sleepless himself—to give his readers sleep."

I by no means wish it; but it may explain what I mean,—that a neat motto is child of the title. I think "Poetic Vigils" as short and sweet as can be desired; only have an eye on the proof, that the printer do not substitute Virgils, which would ill accord with your modesty or meaning.—LAMB, CHARLES, 1824, *To Bernard Barton, Feb.* 25; *Letters of Charles Lamb, ed. Ainger, vol.* II, *p.* 100.

I can hardly tell why I cannot take to him: I have dreamt, I believe, that he is a sort of priggish Quaker, and I hate his straight-haired effigy—a reasonable reason!—BOWLES, CAROLINE, 1829, *To Robert Southey, June* 8; *The Correspondence of Robert Southey and Caroline Bowles, ed. Dowden, p.* 166.

Barton's style is diffuse, but simple and graceful. His poetry is generally descriptive and meditative, tender and devoted, and animated by cheerful views of life.—GRISWOLD, RUFUS W., 1844, *The Poets and Poetry of England in the Nineteenth Century, p.* 192.

The great bulk of Poems is religious; but there are not wanting those of a lighter character, which will be found to be the wholesome relaxation of a pure, good, and essentially religious mind. These may succeed each other as graceful and beneficently as April sunshine and showers over the meadow. So indeed such moods followed in his own mind, and were so revealed in his domestic intercourse.—BARTON, LUCY, 1849, *Memoir, Letters and Poems of Bernard Barton, Preface, p.* vi.

The Poems, if not written off as easily as the Letters, were probably as little elaborated as any that ever were published. Without claiming for them the highest attributes of poetry (which the author never pretended to), we may surely say they abound in genuine feeling and elegant fancy expressed in easy, and often very felicitous, verse. These qualities employed in illustrating the religious and domestic affections, and the pastoral scenery with which such affections are perhaps most generally associated, have made Bernard Barton, as he desired to be, a household poet with a large class of readers—a class, who, as they may be supposed to welcome such poetry as being the articulate voice of those good feelings yearning in their own bosoms, one may hope will continue and increase in England. While in many of these Poems it is the spirit within that redeems an imperfect form—just as it lights up the irregular features of a face into beauty—there are many which will surely abide the test of severer criticism.—FITZGERALD, EDWARD, 1849, *Memoir, Letters and Poems of Bernard Barton, Memoir, p.* 40.

He sang of what he loved—the domestic virtues in man, and the quiet pastoral scenes in nature; and no one can read his poetry without feeling it to be the production of one of a chastened imagination, pure moral feeling, and who sympathized with all that tends to elevate and bless man. His works are full of passages of natural tenderness and his religious poems, while they are animated with a warmth of devotion, are still expressed with that subdued propriety of language which evinces at once a correctness of taste and feeling. —CLEVELAND, CHARLES D., 1853, *English Literature of the Nineteenth Century, p.*494.

"Barton's poetry makes no lofty pretensions, but it is rich in true feeling, and evinces a chaste and cultivated fancy. His verse, which is generally easy and graceful, sometimes conspicuously so, is seldom very faulty; and several of his poems have numerous passages that are affluent of felicities of expression. On the whole, his sonnets, which are quite numerous, are probably the most correct and fervid of his poems, and many of them will compare advantageously with the best by our minor poets."—DESHLER, CHARLES D., 1874, *Afternoons with the Poets, p.* 247.

Bernard Barton is chiefly remembered as the friend of Lamb. His many volumes of verse are quite forgotten. Even the scanty book of selections published by his daughter contains much that might have been omitted. He wrote easily—too easily—and never troubled to correct what he had written. But all his work is unaffected; nor are there wanting occasional touches of deep and genuine pathos. In his devotional verses there is a flavour of old-world quaintness and charm, recalling homely George Herbert's "Temple;" and in other lyrics Edward Fitzgerald found something of the "leisurely grace" that distinguishes the Greek Anthology.—BULLEN, A. H., 1885, *Dictionary of National Biography, vol.* III, *p.* 342.

His verse commended itself both to Southey (who had a kindly but rather disastrous weakness for minor bards) and to Byron, but has little value.—SAINTSBURY, GEORGE, 1896, *A History of Nineteenth Century Literature, p.* 107.

The Quaker poet wrote, in fact, what may be described without disparagement as Quaker poetry, sober, sensible, and modest, if withal formal, homely and drab. . . . He wrote easily and without revision, and aimed at morality rather than poetry, with the result that he produced a large quantity of prosy verse.—MILES, ALFRED H., 1897, *The Poets and the Poetry of the Century, Sacred, Moral and Religious Verse, ed. Miles, p.* 71.

Horace Smith

1779–1849

Horatio Smith, 1779–1849. Born, in London, 1779. Stockbroker by profession. Contrib., with his brother James, to "The Pic-nic," 1802; "The Monthly Mirror," 1807–10; "New Monthly Mag.," etc. Married. In later years of life resided at Brighton. Died, at Tunbridge Wells, 12 July 1849. *Works:* "The Runaway," 1800; "Trevanion," 1801; "Rejected Addresses" (anon.; with his brother James), 1812 (8th edn. same year); "First Impressions," 1813 (2nd edn. same year); "Horace in London," 1813 (4th edn. same year); "Amaranthus the Nympholept" (anon.), 1821; "Gaieties and Gravities" (anon.; 3 vols.), 1825; "Brambletye House" (anon.), 1826; "The Tor Hill" (anon.), 1826; "Reuben Apsley" (anon.), 1827; "Tales of the Great St. Bernard," 1828; "Zillah" (anon.), 1828; "The New Forest" (anon.), 1829; "Walter Colyton" (anon.), 1830; "Midsummer Medley for 1830," 1830; "Festivals, Games and Amusements," 1831; "Tales of the Early Ages" (anon.), 1832; "Gale Middleton" (anon.), 1833; "The Involuntary Prophet" (anon.), 1835; "The Tin Trumpet" (under pseud. "Paul Chatfield, M. D."), 1836; "Jane Lomax" (anon.), 1838; "The Moneyed Man," 1841; "Adam Brown" (anon.), 1843; "Arthur Arundel" (anon.), 1844; "Love and Mesmerism," 1845; "Poetical Works" (2 vols.), 1846. He *edited:* James Smith's "Memoirs," 1840; "Oliver Cromwell," 1840; J. Smith's "Comic Miscellanies," 1841; Dr. Macarthy's "Massaniello," 1842.—SHARP, R. FARQUHARSON, 1897, *A Dictionary of English Authors, p.* 261.

PERSONAL

Mr. Shelley said to me once, "I know not what Horace Smith must take me for sometimes: I am afraid he must think me a strange fellow; but is it not odd, that the only truly generous person I ever knew, who had money to be generous with, should be a stockbroker! and he writes poetry too," continued Mr. Shelley, his voice rising in a fervour of astonishment—"he writes poetry and pastoral dramas, and yet knows how to make money, and does make it, and is still generous."—HUNT, LEIGH, 1828, *Lord Byron and Some of his Contemporaries, vol.* II, *p.* 21.

All contemporary testimony respecting Horace Smith is unanimous as regards the beauty of his character, which was associated not only with wit, but with strong common-sense and justness of perception. His is a remarkable instance of a reputation rescued from undue neglect by the perhaps excessive applause bestowed upon a single lucky hit. Thackeray wrote warmly of Smith's truth and loyalty as a friend and, after his death, he frequently visited his daughters at Brighton; after the youngest of them he named his Laura in "Pendennis." — GARNETT, RICHARD, 1898, *Dictionary of National Biography, vol.* LIII, *p.* 54.

GENERAL

I think the "Rejected Addresses" by far the best thing of the kind since the "Rolliad," and wish *you* had published them. Tell the author "I forgive him, were he twenty times over a satirist;" and think his imitations not at all inferior to the famous ones of Hawkins Browne. He must be a man of very lively wit, and less scurrilous than wits often are: altogether, I very much admire the performance, and wish it all success.—BYRON, LORD, 1812, *Letter to Mr. Murray, Oct.* 19.

Wit and sense,
Virtue and human knowledge, all that might
Make this dull world a business of delight,
Are all combined in Horace Smith.
—SHELLEY, PERCY BYSSHE, 1820, *Letter to Maria Gisborne.*

Horace Smith is a very clever writer in light verse. I do not think we have a better.—SOUTHEY, ROBERT, 1830, *To Caroline Bowles, Feb.* 15; *The Correspondence of Robert Southey with Caroline Bowles, ed. Dowden, p.* 183.

Your goodness about Horace Smith rebukes me, though you do not, for my spitefulness; but really I bore "Zillah" in silence, having my heart full of wrath against that hard measure in the *Quarterly Review*, and would not have breathed one word of my secret thoughts, though he had gone on cockneyfying all antiquity; but when he invaded mine own territory, mine own dear Forest, where he dared get up a lion hunt in one of its quiet glades, which never echoed to any sound more terrible than "Come home, Willy poor Willy" (the beautiful deer call), I could bear it no longer.—BOWLES, CAROLINE, 1830, *To Robert Southey, Feb.* 20; *The Correspondence of Robert Southey with Caroline Bowles, ed. Dowden, p.* 185.

But his imitations in the "Rejected Addresses," his parodies of Horace, and his lyrical contributions to the literary magazines, show him to be not only an admirable versifier, but a possessor of the sense of beauty and a most poetical fancy. His powers are versatile, and he has shown himself able to master any style with which he has chosen to grapple.—GRISWOLD, RUFUS W., 1844, *The Poets and Poetry of England in the Nineteenth Century, p.* 141.

The crowning triumph of his skill, the piece which outweighs all else that he ever wrote, is the surprising "Tale of Drury Lane, by W. S." The verse has the energy, the vividness, the very turn and rhythm of Sir Walter's. The genius of parody could not farther go; Calverley has, indeed, done as well, but no man has done better. Horace, however, was not always successful in his bantering. His lines after the manner of "Childe Harold" lack vigour and point; his attempted reproduction of Johnsonese English is singularly flat; and "Drury's Dirge, by Laura Matilda," provokes a comparison which it cannot sustain with Swift's "Verses by a Lady of Quality." Worst of all is the closing piece, "Punch's Apotheosis," apparently written in imitation of Theodore Hook's rattling and careless rhymes. This essay in doggerel is, indeed, so vulgar and inane, —the words which the author places in the mouths of Othello and Hamlet, and Romeo and Juliet, are such an outrage on good taste, that it is hard to conceive how Horace Smith could have lowered himself to writing it—harder still to understand how, having written it, he allowed it to remain in its present place.—WHYTE, WALTER, 1894, *The Poets and the Poetry of the Century, Humour, Society, Parody and Occasional Verse, ed. Miles, p.* 141.

The familiar volume of "Rejected Addresses" is usually regarded as a storehouse of wit. As a collection, however, it suffers rather from the limitation of its subject-matter, which is strictly dramatic, and of belonging to a particular period. There is perhaps not much in it which can rank as first-rate humorous writing. Most of us know more brilliant lines and classical phrases from the book, than complete poems which we care to quote.—POWELL, G. H., 1894, *ed. Musa Jocosa, p.* 25.

Anne Brontë

1820-1849

Anne Brontë: pseudonym Acton Bell. Born at Thornton, Yorkshire, England, 1820; died at Scarborough, England, May 28, 1849. An English novelist and poet, sister of Charlotte Brontë. She wrote "Agnes Grey" (1847), "The Tenant of Wildfell Hall" (1848), and "Poems" (1846, by "Currer, Ellis, and Acton Bell").—SMITH, BENJAMIN E., *ed.*, 1894-97, *The Century Cyclopedia of Names, p.* 186.

PERSONAL

It is a wind-swept resting-place, well within sight and sound of the sea. St. Mary's is the parish church for Scarborough, and its exact location is at one side of the rocky acclivity that separates the two "bays." It is a hoary old edifice in a hoary old setting. The one atom of "newness" that I could discern—*i. e.*, the obvious fact that the stone marking the tomb of "the gentlest and least assertive of the three sisters" had lately been repainted a startling white—jarred upon me not a little. The black now stands out wonderfully clear and distinct in the awfulness of its simplicity—

HERE LIE THE REMAINS OF
ANNE BRONTË,
Daughter of The Rev. P. Brontë,
Incumbent of Haworth, Yorkshire,
She Died, Aged 28, May 28th, 1849. . . .

In her death as in her life, Anne Brontë was one of the exceptions. She alone of the Brontë daughters was not borne from the Rectory to the churchyard at Haworth by that melancholy doorway which was "reserved for the passage of the dead." Instead, she sleeps by the side of the never resting surge.—STANDING, PERCY CROSS, 1897, *At the Grave of Anne Brontë, The English Illustrated Magazine, vol.* 17, *pp.* 525, 527.

GENERAL

The "Tenant of Wildfell Hall," which deserves perhaps a little more notice and recognition than it has ever received. It is ludicrously weak, palpably unreal, and apparently imitative, whenever it reminds the reader that it was written by a sister of Charlotte and Emily Brontë, but as a study of utterly flaccid and invertebrate immorality it bears signs of more faithful transcription from life than anything in "Jane Eyre" or "Wuthering Heights."—SWINBURNE, ALGERNON CHARLES, 1886, *Miscellanies, p.* 264.

Anne was not in any sense a writer of genius. Her "Agnes Grey" was succeeded by "The Tenant of Wildfell Hall," but neither of these stories exhibits special powers.—CAINE, HALL, 1887, *Celebrities of the Century, ed. Sanders, p.* 175.

It can scarcely be doubted that Anne Brontë's two novels, "Agnes Grey" and "The Tenant of Wildfell Hall," would have long since fallen into oblivion but for the inevitable association with the romances of her two greater sisters. . . . It is not generally known that "The Tenant of Wildfell Hall" went into a second edition the same year; and I should have pronounced it incredible, were not a copy of the later issue in my possession, and Anne Brontë had actually written a preface to this edition. The fact is entirely ignored in the correspondence. The preface in question makes it quite clear, if any evidence of that were necessary, that Anne had her brother in mind in writing the book. "I could not be understood to suppose," she says, "that the proceedings of the unhappy scapegrace, with his few profligate companions I have here introduced, are a specimen of the common practices of society: the case is an extreme one, as I trusted none would fail to perceive; but I knew that such characters do exist, and if I have warned one rash youth from following in their steps, or prevented one thoughtless girl from falling into the very natural error of my heroine, the book has not been written in vain." "One word more and I have done," she continues. "Respecting the author's identity, I would have it to be distinctly understood that Acton Bell is neither Currer nor Ellis Bell, and, therefore, let not his faults be attributed to them. As to whether the name is real or fictitious, it cannot greatly signify to those who know him only by his works."—SHORTER, CLEMENT K., 1896, *Charlotte Brontë and her Circle, pp.* 181, 184.

As for the gentle Anne, she remains—well, just the gentle Anne—pious, patient and trustful. Her talent was of that evangelical, pietistic type which never lacks a certain gracefulness and never rises above a certain intellectual level. Had she lived in our day her novels would have attracted little attention, and her poetry would hardly have found admission into any first-class magazine. It remains clear as ever that her immortality is due to her sisters. Upon those bright twin-stars many telescopes are turned, and then there swims into the beholder's view this third, mild-shining star of the tenth magnitude, which otherwise would have remained invisible. It follows that Anne will always have a place assigned her in the chart of the literary heavens. Nothing, however, is ever likely to occur either to heighten our estimate of her literary ability or to lessen the affection which her character inspires.—MACKAY, ANGUS M., 1897, *The Brontës, Fact and Fiction, p.* 20.

It will be convenient to take the work of the three sisters in the reverse order. That of Anne Brontë may be speedily dismissed. She was a gentle, delicate creature both in mind and body; and but for her greater sisters her writings would now be forgotten. Her pleasing but commonplace tale of "Agnes Grey" was followed by "The Tenant of Wildfell Hall," in which she attempted, without success, to depict a profligate.—WALKER, HUGH, 1897, *The Age of Tennyson, p.* 102.

James Clarence Mangan

1803-1849

James Clarence Mangan was born in Dublin in 1803. His father was a grocer, and became bankrupt. At the age of fifteen James entered a scrivener's office, and seven years later he became a solicitor's clerk, in which occupation he spent three years. Concerning this period he wrote: "I was obliged to work seven years of the ten from five in the morning, winter and summer, to eleven at night; and during the remaining three years nothing but a special providence could have saved me from suicide." The misery of his situation drove him to drink, and he was also an opium-eater. At about the age of twenty-five, just after a grievous disappointment in love, he became connected with the library of Trinity College, Dublin, where he acquired a knowledge of many languages, including several Oriental tongues, and from nearly all of them he made poetical translations, some of which are said to surpass the originals. These translations, together with numerous short original poems, were published in an illustrated weekly in Dublin, and afterward in the penny journals and the famous "Nation," and finally Mangan became a regular contributor to the "Dublin University Magazine." His heart was with the revolutionary movement of 1842-48, and he wrote several ringing ballads to help it on. Broken down by his intemperate habits, he died in a hospital in Dublin, June 20, 1849.—JOHNSON, ROSSITER, 1875, *Little Classics, Authors, p.*169.

PERSONAL

Roll on, my song, and to after ages
Tell how, disdaining all earth can give,
He would have taught men, from wisdom's pages,
The way to live.
And tell how trampled, derided, hated,
And worn by weakness, disease, and wrong,
He fled for shelter to God, who mated
His soul with song—
With song which always, sublime or vapid,
Flowed like a rill in the morning-beam,
Perchance not deep, but intense and rapid—
A mountain stream. . . .
And tell how now, amid wreck and sorrow,
And want, and sickness, and houseless nights,
He bides in calmness the silent morrow,
That no ray lights.
And lives he still, then? Yes! Old and hoary
At thirty-nine, from despair and woe,
He lives, enduring what future story
Will never know.
Him grant a grave to, ye pitying noble,
Deep in your bosoms! There let him dwell!
He, too, had tears for all souls in trouble,
Here and in hell.

—MANGAN, JAMES CLARENCE, 1842, *The Nameless One.*

Behold him passing through our streets with a quick yet shuffling gait, as if some uneasiness hurried him onward, pausing not, looking not to the right or left, until brought suddenly to a full stop before a bookstand. See how eagerly he searches there for some old volume of German black-letter. If it is found, and his finances can secure its purchase, lo! what a flash of joyous feeling lights up those before heavy and lustreless eyes! He passes onward, his pace quickening to a run, until, in the solitude of his lonely chamber, he can commune with his new treasure. Clarence Mangan was about five feet six in height, thin even to emaciation, and slightly stooped in the shoulders, like many men of studious habits and close application. In his dress the eccentricity of his mind was outwardly displayed. His coat, the very little coat, tightly buttoned, was neither a frock coat, dress coat, morning coat, nor shooting coat, and yet seemed to partake of the fashioning of all four. Sometimes, however, it was covered with a blue cloak, the tightest cloak to the form that can be imagined, in which every attempt at the bias cut that gives a free flowing drapery was rigidly eschewed. But it was in the article of hats that poor Clarence's eccentric fancy was especially shown. Such a quaint-shaped crown, such a high, wide-boated leaf as he fancied, has rarely been seen off the stage.—PRICE, JAMES, 1849, *Recollections of Mangan, Dublin Evening Packet.*

In the month of June, 1849, the cholera morbus raged in Dublin; temporary hospitals were erected by the Board of Health for the reception of pauper sufferers from this district, and servants of the Board were despatched with carts to all parts of the city for the purpose of bringing to those hospitals the persons attacked by this dreadful epidemic. While searching for this purpose in an obscure portion of Dublin, the servants of the Board of Health were informed that the tenant of a single room, in one of the most wretched houses of the neighbourhood, had been for some time confined to his bed, and was supposed to be suffering from cholera morbus. They ascended to the lodging thus indicated, and there, stretched on a wretched pallet, and surrounded by proofs of the most squalid misery, they found the wretched form of a man, insensible from exhaustion. Believing that he was reduced to this state by cholera, the servants of the Board of Health placed the sufferer in their cart, and conveyed him to the North Dublin Union cholera sheds. In this miserable wreck of hunger and misery the attendant physician recognised James Clarence Mangan. Upon examination it was found that his disease was not cholera, but absolute starvation. He was immediately transmitted to the Meath Hospital, where everything that skill and kindness could suggest for the purpose of reviving the expiring spark of life was attempted—and attempted in vain. This unfortunate child of genius sank hourly, and died shortly after his admission to the hospital, exhibiting, to the last, his gentle nature, in repeated apologies for the trouble he gave, and constant thanks for the attentions and assistance afforded to him.—ELLIS, HERCULES, 1850, *ed., Romances and Ballads of Ireland*

Mangan was not only an Irishman,—not only an Irish papist,—not only an Irish papist rebel;—but throughout his whole literary life of twenty years, he never deigned to attorn to English criticism, never published a line in any English periodical, or through any English bookseller, never seemed to be aware that there was a British public to please. He was a rebel politically, and a rebel intellectually and spiritually,—a rebel with his whole heart and soul against the whole British spirit of the age. The consequence was sure, and not unexpected. Hardly anybody in England knew the name of such a person. . . . The first time the present biographer saw Clarence Mangan, it was in this wise—Being in the college library, and having occasion for a book in that gloomy apartment of the institution called the "Fagel Library," which is the innermost recess of the stately building, an acquaintance pointed out to me a man perched on the top of a ladder, with the whispered information that the figure was Clarence Mangan. It was an unearthy and ghostly figure, in a brown garment; the same garment (to all appearance) which lasted till the day of his death. The blanched hair was totally unkept; the corpse-like features still as marble; a large book was in his arms, and all his soul was in the book. I had never heard of Clarence Mangan before, and knew not for what he was celebrated; whether as a magician, a poet, or a murderer; yet [I] took a volume and spread it on a table, not to read, but with pretence of reading to gaze on the spectral creature upon the ladder. Here Mangan laboured mechanically, and dreamed, roosting on a ladder, for certain months, perhaps years; carrying the proceeds in money to his mother's poor home, storing in his memory the proceeds which were not in money but in another kind of ore, which might feed the imagination indeed, but was not available for board and lodging. All this time he was the bond-slave of opium. —MITCHEL, JOHN, 1859, *ed., Poems by James Clarence Mangan, Memoir, pp.* 8, 13.

When he emerged into daylight he was dressed in a blue cloak, midsummer or midwinter, and a hat of fantastic shape, under which golden hair as fine and silky as a woman's hung in unkempt tangles, and deep blue eyes lighted a face as colourless as parchment. He looked like a spectre of some German romance, rather than a living creature.—DUFFY, SIR CHARLES GAVAN, 1880, *Young Ireland, p.* 297.

His comrades were strange shadows, the bodyless creations wherein his ecstasy was most cunning. Phantoms trooped to him from the twilight land, lured, as Ulysses lured the ghosts of Hades. . . . We seem to see him hurrying on his life, most melancholy journey, as they saw him gliding through the Dublin streets like the embodiment of the weird fancies of Hoffmann, a new student Anselmus, haunted by the eyes of a visionary Veronica, or buried among books, as Mitchel first found him, his brain, like a pure flame refining all he read and transmuting it to something rich and strange. . . . Of his real life, the existence burning itself fiercely out behind that ghastly mask, few knew anything, but it was not all unhappy. He had loved and been loved; there were moments in his wasted existence, even long intervals, of calm and peace. But Mangan's life is one of unmitigated gloom. . . . Life was to Mangan one long interval. "No one wish of his heart," says Mitchel, "was ever fulfilled; no aspiration satisfied." . . . If he could have faced the denials of destiny with an austere renunciation, if he could have opposed a monastic fortitude to the buffets of the world, his might have been a serener if not a happier story. But a passionate longing after the ideal drove him to those deadly essences which fed for a time the hot flame of his genius at the price of his health, his reason, and his life. Genius and misery have been bed-fellows and board-brothers often enough, but they have seldom indeed been yoked together under conditions as tragic as those which make Mangan's story a record of despair.—MCCARTHY, JUSTIN HUNTLY, *Hours with Great Irishmen.*

From cradle to coffin "Melancholy marked him for her own," and his heart always knew its own bitterness. Infinitely sensitive, of a fragile and tremulous spirit, the harshness of the world was his master, and from the first he succumbed to whatever miseries, real or imagined, came his way. The story of his life is a story of persistent gloom and grayness, peopled by phantoms and phantasies of sorrow: he was a born dreamer of dreams, and passed his days in a kind of *penumbra*. He was gentle and grotesque, eccentric and lovable: but much of a mystery to all and to himself. Fit for nothing but literature, and passionately enamoured of it, he was a desultory, uncertain, capricious writer: always a student with a true love of learning, his knowledge was casual, imperfect, hardly a scholar's. Further, it was a part of his strange nature to be innocently insincere, or inventive, or imaginative, about himself and his: there was "a deal of Ariel, just a streak of Puck" in his composition, and he throws dust in the eyes of his readers, who vainly try to ascertain the precise measure of truth and actuality in his personal or literary statements. With all his devotion to letters and learning, he was incapable of exercising a prolonged and constant energy: it was not in him to concentrate and control his powers. When he wrote without inspiration, but in obedience to some external call or need, he wrote either with a strong and arid rhetoric or with a somewhat ghastly air of mocking merriment and jesting cynicism: and so little could he command his imagination that almost the whole of his greatest and most perfect work owes its inception to the work—often the inferior work — of others.—JOHNSON, LIONEL, 1900, *A Treasury of Irish Poetry, eds. Brooke and Rolleston, p.* 241.

GENERAL

Various and curious are thy strains, O Clarence Mangan!
Rhyming and chiming in a very odd way:
Rhyming and chiming — the like of them no man can
Easily find a long summer's day!
For the true Irish metre is full of tricks and rogueries,
Slipping from your fingers at unawares;
Sometimes full of fun, and frolicing and rollicking,
Sometimes pensive and full of cares.

. . . .

Thou, too, art a Bard—and thy Spirit's River
Is fed by each streamlet from her founts of Song;
Pure thro' her frowning glens it glides in darkness,
It sparkles in her sunshine pure and strong.
—FITZGERALD, WILLIAM, 1847, *Dublin University Magazine.*

I believe there is in these United States quite enough of the Celtic blood and warmth of temperament, enough too of the true Gaelic ear for melody, to recognize in the poems of Mangan that marvellous charm which makes him the household and heart-enshrined darling of many an Irish home. I have never yet met a cultivated Irishman or woman, of genuine Irish nature, who did not prize Clarence Mangan above all the poets that their island of song ever nursed. This one fact, singular as it must needs appear to the Duyckincks, makes it worth while surely to understand with what wand of power, and what musical incantations he wrought so wondrous a magic.—MITCHEL, JOHN, 1859, *ed., Poems by James Clarence Mangan, Memoir, p.* 8.

He is inimitable—the very prince of translators. He is among the few writers of any time or country who have succeeded in transfusing into their own language not merely the literal meaning, graces of style, and musical movement of foreign poems, but also their true spirit and suggestiveness. Often his translation far surpasses the original. He was a most accomplished linguist, and translated from the Irish, French, German, Spanish, Italian, Danish, as well as Turkish and other Asiatic tongues.—MURRAY, JOHN KANE, 1877–84, *Lessons in English Literature, p.* 367.

In many respects, both in life and genius, Mangan bears a resemblance to Edgar A. Poe, and, if he did not achieve a single marked success like "The Raven," his poetical faculty was of the same sombre sort, and his command of original and musical rhythm almost equally great. . . . His original poems are quite few in number, but display the same command of original and powerful rhythm and impressive diction as his translations, while their spirit of hopelessness is beyond any artificial pathos. There is hardly anything more profoundly affecting in English literature than such a poem as "The Nameless One," read with a knowledge of the life of which it was a confession; and it is the more impressive that it has no bitterness nor maudlin arraignment of fortune, such as is apparent in much of the poetry of genius wrecked by its own errors. His political odes were those of a dreamer of noble things for his country, rather than of practical knowledge or faith, notwithstanding their exalted and noble sentiment, and in all things except his personal misery he was not of the actual life of the world.—WILLIAMS, ALFRED M., 1881, *The Poets and Poetry of Ireland, pp.* 325, 328.

He was one of the most artistic and musical of the poets of the present century, yet his verses are but little known.—RYDER, ELIOT, 1881, *The Household Library of Catholic Poets, p.* 46.

Ireland has not yet found a Burns to immortalise her national airs any more than she has a Scott to vivify her ancient story; yet among her sons have been many true singers, the most original, if not the greatest, of whom is Mangan. . . . In 1845, under the title of "Anthologia Germania," he published two volumes of translations from the German, and in them much of his best work is to be found. His renderings from the Irish, on the other hand, which were issued in two posthumous publications, are very disappointing and inferior; generally they are poor in execution and spiritless in tone, while in the mystic and weird minstrelsy of the Teuton, Mangan found a longing for something beyond this life akin to his own vague aspirations. . . . Great as his merits undoubtedly are, Mangan has been so overpraised by his countrymen, who have endeavoured to give a political colouring to his writings, that English critics have been prejudiced against him, and have deemed him a mere provincial poetaster. As an original poet, it is difficult to assign him as high a rank as his countrymen claim, but as a translator his merits are great; no one has transmitted the *spirit* of German ballad lore better than Mangan has, often, indeed, giving it a charm greater than the original possesses.—INGRAM, JOHN H., 1894, *The Poets and the Poetry of the Century, John Keats to Lord Lytton, ed. Miles, pp.* 453, 457, 458.

Is one of those Irishmen with regard to whose work a wide difference of opinion exists between his countrymen and English critics. He had certainly an ear for verse and a gift for making it, and if his equipment of ideas had been porportionate he would have been a great poet. His weakness is that, while he can say things pleasantly, he has but little to say.—WALKER, HUGH, 1897, *The Age of Tennyson, p.* 66.

Several references have already been made to Mangan's incorrigible love of unusual and difficult rhymes and complicated metres, and it has been shown that the concoction of mere rhymes had been a favourite pastime with him from youth. He clearly found the early habit ineradicable, and abandoned it only in his last days when he had themes which moved his very soul. Then the notes of the organ, the trumpet tones of his higher self would roll forth in majesty and power. So much of his poetical work is characterised or, as may be held, defaced by intellectual jugglery, that of his eight hundred and more poems, about three hundred only are worthy of preservation. If he is never prosaic, he is too often eccentric. . . . Mangan's position in Irish poetry is a matter of difference of opinion among Irishmen. Even many of those who admire his work extremely are not altogether disposed to place him above Moore. Yet in lyrical power and range, vigour of expression, variety of treatment, originality of form, mastery of technique, keenness of perception, and in other qualities, Mangan seems to be quite unapproached by any Irish poet. Some of these qualities are possessed in a greater degree by other Irish poets, but in none are they combined in such perfection as in Mangan. Some attributes there are which Mangan lacks, or possesses only in a slender degree, and his perverseness in certain directions has been to no small extent detrimental to his reputation; but, with all deductions, it is perfectly certain that no other Irish poet is his peer in sheer imaginative power or fertility of invention. Those who admire his writings at all must admire them warmly; indifference is impossible in such a case.—O'DONOGHUE, D. J., 1897, *The Life and Writings of James Clarence Mangan, pp.* 199, 232.

Mangan's great work has never been overpraised: not so his less great. He was an Irishman writing English verse during the first half of the century: his wide and genuine if straggling culture, his range of literary interest, his technical mastery of verse, filled his audience with a feeling of novelty. It was a portent, a presage, of an outburst of Irish poetry in English verse such as had not before been heard: and it is not unnatural that Mangan's poetry was received, is often still received, with too lavish an applause, too indiscriminate a welcome. . . . The mass of Mangan's poetry seems less miraculous and immaculate now than it semed half a century ago: then, he had scarce a rival; since then, he has had many and worthy rivals, though none has surpassed him. . . . Words, rhymes, rhythms, were always ready at his call, and he fashioned of them things ingenious, things betraying infinite resource; the ability to create by their means things of the highest beauty, unspoiled by freak or whim, undulled by conventional rhetoric, things poetically pure, was his but once and again. It would be cruel to judge such a man by anything but his supreme achievements; to exalt unduly his lesser achievements is to endanger the just glory of the poet at his loftiest and loveliest height. Mangan wrote much that must always delight lovers of poetry and of Mangan, which is yet but a small part of his title to greatness; he wrote a little which is a possession for evermore of all who "love the highest when they see it." . . . Mangan's flight is highest, his music is noblest, when ancient Ireland speaks to him of her glories, her sorrows, her hopes. He is the poet of much else that is imperishable; but above all he is the poet of a poem foremost among the world's poems of inspired patriotism. It were enough for Mangan's fame that he is the poet of the "Dark Rosaleen."—JOHNSON, LIONEL, 1900, *A Treasury of Irish Poetry, eds. Brooke and Rolleston, pp.* 243, 248, 249.

William Wordsworth

1770-1850

Born, at Cockermouth, Cumberland, 7 April 1770. Early education at Hawkshead Grammar School, 1778-87. Matric. St. John's Coll., Camb., Oct. 1787; B. A., 1791. Travelled on Continent, July to Oct., 1790. Visited Paris, Nov. 1791. Settled with his sister near Crewkerne, Dorsetshire, autumn of 1795. First visit from Coleridge, June 1797. Removed to Alfoxden, Nether Stowey, Somersetshire, July 1797. Friendship with Charles Lamb and Hazlitt begun. In Bristol, 1798. In Germany, Sept. 1798 to July 1799. Settled at Grasmere, Dec. 1799. Visit to France, July to Aug. 1802. Married Mary Hutchinson, 4 Oct. 1802. Friendship with Scott and Southey begun, 1803. Removed to Coleorton, Leicestershire, 1806. Returned to Grasmere, 1808. Contrib. to "The Friend," 1810. Removed to Rydal Mount, spring of 1813. Distributor of stamps for Westmoreland, March 1813 to 1842. Visits to Continent, 1820, 1823, 1828, 1837. Hon. D. C. L., Durham, 1838. Hon. D. C. L., Oxford, 12 June 1839. Crown Pension, 1842. Poet Laureate, 1843. Died, at Rydal Mount, 23 April 1850. Buried in Grasmere Churchyard. *Works:* "An Evening Walk," 1793; "Descriptive Sketches in Verse," 1793; "Lyrical Ballads, with a few other Poems" (2 vols.), 1798—1800; "Poems" (2 vols.), 1807; "On the Relations of Great Britain, Spain, and Portugal to each other," 1809; "The Excursion," 1814; "The White Doe of Rylstone," 1815; "Poems" (3 vols.), 1815-20; "Thanksgiving Ode," 1816; "Letter to a Friend of Robert Burns," 1816; "Peter Bell," 1819; "The Waggoner," 1819; "The River Duddon," 1820; "The Little Maid and the Gentleman; or, We are Seven" (anon.), [1820?]; "Memorials of a Tour on the Continent," 1822; "Ecclesiastical Sketches," 1822; "Description of the Scenery of the Lakes in the North of England," 1822; "Yarrow Revisited," 1835; "Sonnets," 1838; "Poems," 1842; "Poems on the Loss and Rebuilding of St. Mary's Church," by W. Wordsworth, J. Montgomery, and others, 1842; "Ode on the Installation of Prince Albert at Cambridge" [1847]; "The Prelude," 1850. *Collected Works:* "Poetical Works," ed. by E. Dowden (7 vols.), 1892-93; "Prose Works," ed. by W. Knight (2 vols.), 1896. *Life:* by C. Wordsworth, 1851; by E. P. Hood, 1856; by J. M. Sutherland, 2nd edn., 1892.—SHARP, R. FARQUHARSON, 1897, *A Dictionary of English Authors, p.* 304.

PERSONAL

[I visited] Alfoxden, a country seat occupied by a Mr. Wordsworth, of living men one of the greatest—at least, Coleridge, who has seen most of the great men of this country says he is; and I, *who have seen Wordsworth again since*, am inclined very highly to estimate him. He has certainly physiognomical traits of genius. He has a high manly forehead, a full and comprehensive eye, a strong nose to support the superstructure, and altogether a very pleasing and striking countenance.—REYNALL, RICHARD, 1797, *Unpublished Letters of S. T. Coleridge, Illustrated London News, April* 22, 1893.

On Monday, 4th October 1802, my brother William was married to Mary Hutchinson. I slept a good deal of the night, and rose fresh and well in the morning. At a little after eight o'clock, I saw them go down the avenue towards the church. William had parted from me upstairs. When they were absent, my dear little Sara prepared the breakfast. I kept myself as quiet as I could, but when I saw the two men running up the walk, coming to tell us it was over, I could stand it no longer, and threw myself on the bed, where I lay in stillness, neither hearing nor seeing anything till Sara came upstairs to me, and said, "They are coming." This forced me from the bed where I lay, and I moved, I knew not how, straight forward, faster than my strength could carry me, till I met my beloved William, and fell upon his bosom. He and John Hutchinson led me to the house, and there I stayed to welcome my dear Mary. As soon as we had breakfasted, we departed. It rained when we set off.—WORDSWORTH, DOROTHY, 1802, *Journals, vol.* I, *p.* 148.

A visit from Wordsworth. . . . His conversation was long and interesting. He spoke of his own poems with the just feeling of confidence which a sense of his own excellence gives him. He is now convinced that he never can derive emolument from them; but, being independent, he willingly gives up all idea of doing so. He is persuaded that if men are to become better and wiser, the poems will sooner or later make their way.—ROBINSON, HENRY CRABB, 1812, *Diary, May* 8; *Diary, Reminiscences and Correspondence, vol.* I, *p.* 245.

Wordsworth's residence and mine are fifteen miles asunder—a sufficient distance to preclude any frequent interchange of visits. I have known him nearly twenty years, and for about half that time intimately. The strength and the character of his mind you see in "The Excursion;" and his life does not belie his writings, for in every relation of life, and every point of view, he is a truly exemplary and admirable man. In conversation he is powerful beyond any of his cotemporaries; and as a poet—I speak not from the partiality of friendship, nor because we have been so absurdly held up as both writing upon one concerted system of poetry, but with the most deliberate exercise of impartial judgment whereof I am capable, when I declare my full conviction that posterity will rank him with Milton.—SOUTHEY, ROBERT, 1814, *Letter to Bernard Barton, Dec.* 19; *Life and Correspondence, ed. C. C. Southey.*

There seemed to me, in his first appearance, something grave almost to austerity, and the deep tones of his voice added strength to that impression of him. There was not visible about him the same easy and disengaged air that so immediately charmed me in Southey—his mind seemed to require an effort to awaken itself thoroughly from some brooding train of thought, and his manner, as I felt at least, at first reluctantly relaxed into blandness and urbanity. . . . The features of Wordsworth's face are strong and high, almost harsh and severe—and his eyes have, when he is silent, a dim, thoughtful, I had nearly said melancholy expression—so that when a smile takes possession of his countenance, it is indeed the most powerful smile I ever saw. . . . Never saw I a countenance in which Contemplation so reigns. His brow is very lofty—and his dark brown hair seems worn away, as it were, by thought, so thinly is it spread over his temples. The colour of his face is almost sallow; but it is not the sallowness of confinement or ill-health, it speaks rather of the rude and boisterous greeting of the mountain-weather. — LOCKHART, JOHN GIBSON, 1819, *Letters from the Lakes, Blackwood's Magazine. vol.* 4, *pp.* 739, 740.

An extremely pleasant drive of sixteen miles . . . brought me to Wordsworth's door, on a little elevation, commanding a view of Rydal water. . . . It is claimed to be the most beautiful spot and the finest prospect in the lake country, and, even if there be finer, it would be an ungrateful thing to remember them here, where, if anywhere, the eye and the heart ought to be satisfied. Wordsworth knew from Southey that I was coming, and therefore met me at the door and received me heartily. He is about fifty-three or four, with a tall, ample, well-proportioned frame, a grave and tranquil manner, a Roman cast of appearance, and Roman dignity and simplicity. He presented me to his wife, a good, very plain woman, who seems to regard him with reverence and affection, and to his sister, not much younger than himself, with a good deal of spirit and, I should think, more than common talent and knowledge. I was at home with them at once, and we went out like friends together to scramble up the mountains, and enjoy the prospects and scenery. . . . His conversation surprised me by being so different from all I had anticipated. It was exceedingly simple, strictly confined to subjects he understood familiarly, and more marked by plain good-sense than by anything else. When, however, he came upon poetry and reviews, he was the Khan of Tartary again, and talked as metaphysically and extravagantly as ever Coleridge wrote; but excepting this, it was really a consolation to hear him. It was best of all, though, to see how he is loved and respected in his family and neighborhood. . . . The peasantry treated him with marked respect, the children took off their hats to him, and a poor widow in the neighborhood sent to him to come and talk to her son, who had been behaving ill.—TICKNOR, GEORGE, 1819, *Journal, March* 21; *Life, Letters and Journals, vol.* I, *p.* 287.

Coming to a brotherhood of firs, a gate opens into the grounds of the Poet. The house is hung with climbing shrubs, which flower around the windows, and twist themselves together, in a mass upon the roof. We knocked at the glass door, through which I saw the Poet pass, mentioned our name to the servant, and were shown into a parlour by Mrs. Wordsworth,—a lady past the prime of womanhood, dressed in a purple silk pelisse, and straw bonnet. We seated ourselves on a sofa, and expected the appearance of him whose name had been held up to so much ridicule and praise, by the two poetical factions, in the republic of letters. He came loosely carelessly dressed, in white pantaloons and a short coat; his bosom open, a countenance dark and furrowed, a hawk's nose, very similar to Southey's, and drooping eyes, which seemed weak, as a green shade was lying on the table. I apologized for our intrusion, ascribing it to the desire we had of seeing the author of a work, to which we had owed many hours of pleasing and of elevated thought. He set us immediately at ease, entering directly into affable conversation on the Lakes, the birds which frequent them, the plants peculiar to them, the season favourable for visiting them and then on streams, woods, waters, mountains, clouds, fields, torrents, and all that constitute the elements of poetry. He remarked that the lapse of a river seen gleaming at a distance, harmonized with the heaven, which seemed to come down and blend with it in light and colour. . . . Wordsworth, in appearance and conversation, has nothing of that love of puerile simplicity, which is seen in his earlier writings. There is, on the contrary, a manly sense and vigour of conception, joined with much frankness and facility of manner.—WIFFEN, BROTHERS, 1819, *Memoirs and Miscellanies, ed. Samuel Bowles Pattison.*

Wordsworth came at half-past eight, and stopped to breakfast. Talked a good deal. Spoke of Byron's plagiarisms from him; the whole third canto of "Childe Harold" founded on his style and sentiments. The feeling of natural objects which is there expressed, not caught by B. from nature herself, but from him (Wordsworth), and spoiled in the transmission; "Tintern Abbey" the source of it all, from which same poem, too, the celebrated passage about Solitude, in the first canto of "Childe Harold," is (he said) taken, with this difference, that what is naturally expressed by him has been worked by Byron into a laboured and antithetical sort of declamation.—MOORE, THOMAS, 1820, *Journal, Oct.* 27; *Memoirs, Journal and Correspondence, ed. Russell.*

Mr. Wordsworth, in his person, is above the middle size, with marked features, and an air somewhat stately and Quixotic. He reminds one of some of Holbein's heads, grave, saturnine, with a slight indication of sly humour, kept under by the manners of the age or by the pretensions of the person. He has a peculiar sweetness in his smile, and great depth and manliness and a rugged harmony, in the tones of his voice. His manner of reading his own poetry is particularly imposing; and in his favourite passages his eye beams with preternatural lustre, and the meaning labours slowly up from his swelling breast. No one who has seen him at these moments could go away with an impression that he was a "man of no mark or likelihood." Perhaps the comment of his face and voice is necessary to convey a full idea of his poetry. His language may not be intelligible, but his manner is not to be mistaken. It is clear that he is either mad or inspired. —HAZLITT, WILLIAM, 1825, *The Spirit of the Age, p.* 129.

More than all the "Excursion" and the Platonic Ode is developed in his domelike forehead. And his manner and conversation are full of the pleasant playful sincerity and kindness which are so observable in his works. The utter absence of pretension in all he says and looks is very striking. He does not say many things to be remembered; and most of his observations are chiefly noticeable for their delicate taste, strong good sense, and stout healthy diction, rather than for imagery or condensed principles of philosophy. You see in him the repose or the sport, but neither the harlequinade, nor the conflict of genius. I believe he has long turned the corner of life; and yet there is not about him the slightest tendency to be wearied or disgusted with human nature, or to be indifferent toward the common little objects, occurrences, and people round him. All his daily fireside companionable sympathies are as sensitive and good-humoured as ever.—STERLING, JOHN, 1828, *Letters.*

I must say I never saw any manifestation of small jealousy between Coleridge and Wordsworth; which . . . I thought uncommonly to the credit of both. I am sure they entertained a thorough respect for each other's intellectual endowments. . . . Wordsworth was a single-minded man: with less imagination than Coleridge, but with a more harmonious judgment, and better balanced principles. Coleridge, conscious of his transcendent powers, rioted in a licence of tongue which no man could tame. Wordsworth, though he could discourse most eloquent music, was never unwilling to sit still in Coleridge's presence, yet could be as happy in prattling with a child as in communing with a sage. If Wordsworth condescended to converse with me, he spoke to me as if I were his equal in mind, and made me pleased and proud in consequence. If Coleridge held me by the button, for lack of fitter audience, he had a talent for making me feel *his* wisdom and my own stupidity; so that I was miserable and humiliated by the sense of it.—YOUNG, CHARLES MAYNE, 1828, *Journal, July* 6; *Memoir by Julian Charles Young.*

I enjoyed the snatches I was able to have of Wordsworth's conversation, and I think I had quite as much as was good for me. He has a good philosophical bust, a long, thin, gaunt face, much wrinkled and weatherbeaten: of the Curwen style of figure and face, but with a more cheerful and benevolent expression.—EDGEWORTH, MARIA, 1829, *To Mrs. Ruxton, Sept.* 27; *Letters, vol.* II, *p.* 167.

I am just come home from breakfasting with Henry Taylor to meet Wordsworth; the same party as when he had Southey—Mill, Elliot, Charles Villiers. Wordsworth may be bordering on sixty; hard-featured, brown, wrinkled, with prominent teeth and a few scattered gray hairs, but nevertheless not a disagreeable countenance.—GREVILLE, C. F., 1831, *Memoirs, Feb. 25th.*

Well, when word came into the room of the splendid meteor, we all went out to view it; and, on the beautiful platform at Mount Rydale, we were all walking, in twos and threes, arm-in-arm, talking of the phenomenon, and admiring it. Now, be it remembered, that Wordsworth, Professor Wilson, Lloyd, De Quincey, and myself, were present, besides several other literary gentlemen, whose names I am not certain that I remember aright. Miss Wordsworth's arm was in mine, and she was expressing some fears that the splendid stranger might prove ominous, when I, by ill luck, blundered out the following remark, thinking that I was saying a good thing:—"Hout, me'm it is neither mair nor less than joost a treeumphal airch, raised in honour of the meeting of the poets." "That's not amiss—eh? eh?—that's very good," said the Professor, laughing. But Wordsworth, who had De Quincey's arm, gave a grunt, and turned on his heel, and leading the little opium-chewer aside, he addressed him in these disdainful and venomous words:—"Poets? poets? What does the fellow mean? Where are they?" Who could forgive this? For my part I never can, and never will! I admire Wordsworth; as who does not, whatever they may pretend? but for that short sentence I have a lingering ill-will at him which I cannot get rid of. It is surely presumption in any man to circumscribe all human excellence within the narrow sphere of his own capacity. The "*Where are they?*" was too bad! I have always some hopes that De Quincey was *leeing*, for I did not myself hear Wordsworth utter the words.—HOGG, JAMES, 1832, *Autobiography.*

North. How placid and profound the expression of the whole bard! The face is Miltonic—even to the very eyes;—for though, thank Heaven, they are not blind, there is a dimness about the orbs. The temples I remember shaded with thin hair of an indescribable color, that in the sunlight seemed a kind of mild auburn—but now they are bare—and—nothing to break it—the height is majestic. No furrows—no wrinkles on that contemplative forehead—the sky is without a cloud—

"The image of a poet's soul,
How calm! how tranquil! how serene!"

It faintly smiles. There is light and motion round the lips, as if they were about to discourse "most eloquent music."—WILSON, JOHN, 1832, *Noctes Ambrosianæ, Nov.*

After a while he (Professor Wilson) digressed to Wordsworth and Southey, and asked me if I was going to return by the Lakes. I proposed doing so. "I will give you letters to both, if you haven't them. I lived a long time in that neighborhood, and know Wordsworth perhaps as well as any one. Many a day I have walked over the hills with him, and listened to his repetition of his own poetry." . . . "Did Wordsworth repeat any other poetry than his own?" "Never in a single instance to my knowledge. He is remarkable for the manner in which he is wrapped up in his own poetical life." . . . "Was the story true that was told in the papers of his seeing, for the first time, in a large company some new novel of Scott's, in which there was a motto taken from his works; and that he went immediately to the shelf and took down one of his own volumes and read the whole poem to the party, who were waiting for a reading of the new book?" "Perfectly true. It happened in this very house."—WILLIS, NATHANIEL PARKER, 1835, *Pencilings by the Way.*

I went up to Oxford to the Commemoration, for the first time for twenty-one years, to see Wordsworth and Bunsen receive their degrees; and to me, remembering how old Coleridge inoculated a little knot of us with the love of Wordsworth, when his name was in general a byword, it was striking to witness the thunders of applause, repeated over and over again, with which he was greeted in the theatre by Undergraduates and Masters of Arts alike. —ARNOLD, THOMAS, 1839, *To Rev. G. Cornish, July* 6; *Life and Correspondence, ed. Stanley, vol.* II, *p.* 146.

Encouraged by the great inducement of seeing Mr. Bunsen and Mr. Wordsworth receive their honorary degrees at Oxford, my husband was tempted to go from Rugby to the Oxford Commemoration, and Jane and I were delighted to accompany him, though it could only be accomplished by getting up before day, and returning at night after all the excitement and fatigue of the theatre. But it was well worth while. . . . Mr. Bunsen was received exceedingly well, and was I should suppose remarkably well-known for a foreigner; but the thundering applause, from all quarters, when the name of Wordsworth was heard, and his venerable form was seen advancing in the procession, I cannot at all describe. It was really delightful to see such a tribute to such a man. It was the public voice for once harmoniously joining to pay homage to goodness, and to talent, consistently employed in promoting the real happiness of his fellow-creatures. To us who know him so intimately, and the true humility and simplicity of his character, it was very affecting and delightful, and I shall always rejoice that I was there.—ARNOLD, MRS. THOMAS, 1839, *Letter to Miss Trevenen, July.*

He was, upon the whole, not a well made man. His legs were pointedly condemned by all female connoisseurs in legs; not that they were bad in any way which *would* force itself upon your notice—there was no absolute deformity about them; and undoubtedly they had been serviceable legs beyond the average standard of human requisition; for I calculate, upon good data, that with these identical legs Wordsworth must have traversed a distance of 175,000 to 180,000 English miles—a mode of exertion which, to him, stood in the stead of alcohol and all other stimulants whatsoever be the animal spirits; to which, indeed, he was indebted for a life of unclouded happiness, and we for much of what is most excellent in his writings. But, useful as they have proved themselves, the Wordsworthian legs were certainly not ornamental; and it was really a pity, as I agreed with a lady in thinking, that he has not another pair for evening dress parties. . . . I do not conceive that Wordsworth *could* have been an amiable boy; he was austere and unsocial, I have reason to think, in his habits; not generous; and not self-denying. I am pretty certain that no consideration would ever have induced Wordsworth to burden himself with a lady's reticule, parasol, shawl, or anything exacting trouble and attention. Mighty must be the danger which would induce him to lead her horse by the bridle. Nor would he, without some demur, stop to offer his hand over a stile. Freedom—unlimited, careless, insolent freedom—unoccupied possession of his own arms—absolute control over his own legs and motions—these have always been so essential to his comfort, that, in any case where they were likely to become questionable, he would have declined to make one of the party.—DEQUINCEY, THOMAS, 1839–54, *The Lake Poets: William Wordsworth, Works, ed. Masson, vol.* II, *pp.* 242, 262.

Gurney Hoare brought us the good news that William Wordsworth was staying at old Mrs. Hoare's; so thither he took us. He is a man of middle height and not of very striking appearance; the lower part of the face retreating a little; his eye of a somewhat French diplomatic character, with heavy eyelids, and none of the flashing which one connects with poetic genius. When speaking earnestly, his manner and voice become extremely energetic; and the peculiar emphasis, and even accent, he throws into some of his words, add considerably to their force. He evidently loves the monologue style of conversation but shows great candor in giving due consideration to any remarks which others may make. His manner is simple, his general appearance that of the abstract thinker, whom his subject gradually warms into poetry.—FOX, CAROLINE, 1842, *Memories of Old Friends, ed. Pym, Journal, June 4, p.* 173.

Just for a handful of silver he left us,
Just for a riband to stick in his coat—
Found the one gift of which fortune bereft us,
Lost all the others she lets us devote;
They, with gold to give, doled him out silver,
So much was theirs who so little allowed:
How all our copper had gone for his service!
Rags—were they purple, his heart had been proud!
We that had loved him so, followed him, honored him,
Lived in his mild and magnificent eye,
Learned his great language, caught his clear accents,
Made him our pattern to live and to die!
Shakespeare was of us, Milton was for us,
Burns, Shelley, were with us—they watch from their graves!
He alone breaks from the van and the freemen,
—He alone sinks to the rear and the slaves!
—BROWNING, ROBERT, 1842, *The Lost Leader.*

There is, perhaps, no residence in England better known than that of William Wordsworth. Rydal Mount, where he has now lived for more than thirty years, is as perfectly poetical in its location as any poet could possibly conceive in his brightest moment of inspiration. . . . The immediate grounds in which his house stands are worthy of the country and the man. It is, as its name implies, a mount. Before the house opens a considerable platform, and around and beneath lie various terraces and descend various walks, winding on amid a profusion of trees and luxuriant evergreens. Beyond the house, you ascend various terraces, planted with trees now completely overshadowing them; and these terraces conduct you to a level above the house-top, and extent your view of the enchanting scenery on all sides. Above you tower the rocks and precipitous slopes of Nab-scar; and below you, embosomed in its trees, lies the richly ornate villa. . . . The poet's house, itself, is a proper poet's abode. It is at once modest, plain, yet tasteful and elegant. An ordinary dining-room, a breakfast-room in the center, and a library beyond, form the chief apartments. There are a few pictures and busts, especially those of Scott and himself, a good engraving of Burns, and the like, with a good collection of books, few of them very modern.—HOWITT, WILLIAM, 1847, *Homes and Haunts of the Most Eminent British Poets, vol.* II, *pp.* 328, 329.

The sweet songs,
Simple and beautiful as Truth and Nature,
Of him whose whitened locks on Rydal Mount
Are lifted yet by morning breezes blowing
From the green hills, immortal in his lays.
WHITTIER, JOHN GREENLEAF, 1848, *The Bridal of Pennacook.*

Walter Scott said that the eyes of Burns were the finest he ever saw. I cannot say the same of Mr. Wordsworth; that is, not in the sense of the beautiful, or even of the profound. But certainly I never beheld eyes that looked so inspired or supernatural. They were like fires half burning, half smouldering, with a sort of acrid fixture of regard, and seated at the further end of two caverns. One might imagine Ezekiel or Isaiah to have had such eyes.—HUNT, LEIGH, 1850, *Autobiography, ch.* XV.

They (Dr. and Mrs. Davy) were both much struck by the likeness of the countenance, in the deep repose of death, to that of Dante. The expression was much more feminine than it had been in life—very like his sister. She bears this sad loss with unexpected calmness. She is drawn about as usual in her chair. She was heard to say, as she passed the door where the body lay, "O death, where is thy sting? O grave, where is thy victory?" . . . It has . . . been a great privilege to have seen this great and good man so nearly. I think it may be said of him "that he did justly, loved mercy, and walked humbly with his God." The funeral is to be very private—only Dr. Davy invited from this house.—FLETCHER, ELIZA, 1850, *Letter to Lady Richardson, April* 26; *Autobiography, p.* 283.

He reposes, according to his own wish, beneath the green turf, among the dalesmen of Grasmere, under the sycamores and yews of a country churchyard by the side of a beautiful stream, amid the mountains which he loved; and a solemn voice seems to breathe from his grave, which blends its tones in sweet and holy harmony with the accents of his poetry, speaking the language of humility and love, of adoration and faith, and preparing the soul, by a devout contemplation of natural beauty, for translation to a purer, and nobler, and more glorious state of existence, and for a fruition of heavenly felicity. — WORDSWORTH, CHRISTOPHER, 1851, *Memoirs of William Wordsworth, ed. Reed, vol.* II. *p.* 518.

To the Memory of
WILLIAM WORDSWORTH,
a true Philosopher and Poet,
who by special gift and calling of
Almighty God,
whether he discoursed on
Man or Nature,
failed not to lift up the heart to
holy things,
tired not of maintaining the
cause of the Poor and Simple,
and so, in perilous times, was
raised up to be
a chief Minister not only of
the noblest Poesy,
but of high and sacred Truth.

This memorial is placed here by
his friends and neighbors
in testimony of
respect, affection, and gratitude,
Anno 1851.

— KEBLE, JOHN, 1851, *Inscription on the Monument in Grasmere Church.*

Among convivial spirits no one could be more joyous than Wordsworth; no one could enter more heartily and readily into the humors of the passing hour; and among eminent authors no one could ever be found more willing than he was to make allowances for the faults of others, or to afford instruction whenever he met with a pupil whose attachment to literature was not founded on vanity or affectation.— GILLIES, ROBERT P., 1854, *Memoirs of a Literary Veteran.*

At length I reached the head of the lake, and then the church which was my destination. Once more I stood at the grave of Wordsworth, that sacred spot which, as I believe, many generations will visit, and whence a voice, we may hope, will ever speak to men of the beauty of this fair earth and the higher glory of which it is the shadow. The great poet lies by the side of his daughter, Dora Quillinan; next to her lies Dorothy Wordsworth, his sister; then Edward Quillinan and his first wife; and there is space left for Mrs. Wordsworth. Sarah Hutchinson, Mrs. Wordsworth's sister, also lies here: on the stone which marks her grave is the following:

"Near the graves of two young children,
removed from a
family to which through life she was
devoted,
Here lies the body
of
Sarah Hutchinson
the beloved sister and faithful friend
of mourners who have caused this stone to
be erected
with an earnest wish that their own
remains
may be laid by her side, and a humble hope
that through Christ they may together
be made partakers of the same Blessed
Resurrection."

Here follow the dates of her birth and death, and then—

"In fulfillment of the wish above expressed
here repose
the remains of
William Wordsworth,
Dorothy Wordsworth."

—YARNALL, ELLIS, 1855-99, *Walks and Visits in Wordsworth's Country, Wordsworth and the Coleridges, Aug.* 8, *p.* 76.

He told [1845] me I should find visitors a great expense, and that I must promise him,—(and he laid his hand on my arm to enforce what he said) I must promise him to do as he and his sister had done, when, in their early days, they had lived at Grasmere. "When you have a visitor," said he, "you must do as we did;—you must say 'if you like to have a cup of tea with us, you are very welcome: but if you want any meat,—you must pay for your board.' Now promise me that you will do this." Of course, I could promise nothing of the sort. . . . He insisted: I declined promising; and changed the subject. The mixture of odd economies and neighborly generosity was one of the most striking things in the old poet. At tea there, one could hardly get a drop of cream with any ease of mind, while he was giving away all the milk that the household did not want to neighboring cottagers.—MARTINEAU, HARRIET, 1855-77, *Autobiography, ed. Chapman, vol.* I, *p.* 505.

He led me out into his garden, and showed me the gravel walk in which thousands of his lines were composed. . . .

He had just returned from a visit to Staffa, and within three days had made three sonnets on Fingal's Cave, and was composing a fourth, when he was called in to see me. He said, "If you are interested in my verses, perhaps you will like to hear these lines." I gladly assented, and he recollected himself for a few moments, and then stood forth and repeated, one after the other, the three entire sonnets with great animation. . . . This recitation was so unlooked-for and surprising—he, the old Wordsworth, standing apart, and reciting to me in a garden-walk, like a schoolboy declaiming,—that I at first was near to laugh; but recollecting myself, that I had come thus far to see a poet, and he was chanting poems to me, I saw that he was right and I was wrong, and gladly gave myself up to hear.—EMERSON, RALPH WALDO, 1856, *English Traits, ch.* i.

Wordsworth was, if possible, more unlike what he must appear in the fancy of those who have read his poetry and have never seen the author. He was a perfect antithesis to Coleridge—tall, wiry, harsh in features, coarse in figure, inelegant in looks. He was roughly dressed in a long brown *surtout*, striped duck trousers, fustian gaiters, and thick shoes. He more resembled a mountain farmer than a "lake poet." His whole air was unrefined and unprepossessing. This was incontestably the first impression made on others as well as on me. But, on after observation, and a little reflection, I could not help considering that much that seemed unfavourable in Wordsworth might be really placed to his advantage. There was a total absence of affectation, or egotism; not the least effort at display, or assumption of superiority over any of those who were quite prepared to concede it to him. He seemed satisfied to let his friend and fellow-traveller take the lead, with a want of pretension rarely found in men of literary reputation far inferior to his; while there was something unobtrusively amiable in his bearing towards his daughter. There were several gentlemen of the party. Coleridge talked much, and indiscriminately, with those next him, or about him. He did not appear to talk for effect, but purely for talking's sake. He seemed to breathe in words. Wordsworth was at times fluent, but always commonplace; full of remark, but not of observation. He spoke of scenery as far as its aspect was concerned; but he did not enter into its associations with moral beauty. He certainly did not talk well. But in fact he had no encouragement. He had few listeners; and what seemed rather repulsive in him was perhaps chiefly from its grating contrast to the wonderful attraction of Coleridge. His was a mild, enthusiastic flow of language; a broad, deep stream, carrying gently along all that it met with on its course—not a whirlpool that drags into its vortex and engulfs what it seizes on. Almost everything he talked about became the subject of a lecture of great eloquence and precision.—GRATTAN, THOMAS COLLEY, 1862, *Beaten Paths, and those who Trod them.*

In the country he would walk with you, talk with you, and seem gratified with your society; but, somehow or other, it seemed to me as if he were ready to relapse, become wrapt up in speculation, and would rather prefer being left to commune with himself. . . . On his visits to town, the recluse of Rydal Mount was quite a different creature. To me it was demonstrated, by his conduct under every circumstance, that De Quincey . . . had done him gross injustice in the character he loosely threw upon the public, viz., that "he was not generous or self-denying," and farther, that he was "slovenly and regardless in dress." I must protest that there was no warrant for this caricature; but, on the contrary, that it bore no feature of resemblance to the slight degree of eccentricity discoverable in Cumberland, and was utterly contradicted by the life in London. In the mixed society of the great Babylon, Mr. Wordsworth was facile and courteous; dressed like a gentleman, and with his tall, commanding figure—no mean type of the superior order, well trained by education and accustomed to good manners—shall I reveal that he was often sportive, and could even go the length of strong (whatever invidiousness might say, not vulgar) expressions in the off-hand mirth of his observations and criticisms? — JERDAN, WILLIAM, 1866, *Men I have Known.*

Wordsworth was about five feet ten inches in height. His figure was not graceful, but in his countenance there was a fine mixture of poet and philosopher. He resembled the portraits of Locke; his eyes burned with an inward glare, and looked as if they saw things (which they did) in nature not revealed to ordinary vision. His manners were grave and rather austere; but never, even when his poetical fortunes were at their lowest ebb, was he, in the smallest degree, a soured or disappointed man; for nature had given him a sanguine temperament, equable, indeed elastic, spirits; and he had moreover an unshaken faith in the genuineness of his own genius, and a correct appreciation of the value of his own writings, which he was sure would be finally rated at their proper worth, whatever vicissitudes they might meanwhile undergo.—WALLER, J. F., 1866, *Imperial Dictionary of Universal Biography, vol.* IV, *p.* 1389.

For the rest, he talked well in his way; with veracity, easy brevity, and force; as a wise tradesman would of his tools and work-shop,—and as no unwise one could. His voice was good, frank and sonorous, though practically clear, distinct and forcible, rather than melodious; the tone of him business-like, sedately confident, no discourtesy, yet no anxiety about being courteous; a fine wholesome rusticity, fresh as his mountain breezes, sat well on the stalwart veteran, and on all he said and did. You would have said he was a usually taciturn man; glad to unlock himself, to audience sympathetic and intelligent, when such offered itself. His face bore marks of much, not always peaceful, meditation; the look of it not bland nor benevolent, so much as close, impregnable and hard: a man *multa tacere loquive paratus,* in a world where he had experienced no lack of contradictions as he strode along! The eyes were not very brilliant, but they had quite a clearness; there was enough of brow, and well-shaped; rather too much of cheek ("horse-face," I have heard satirists say), face of squarish shape and decidedly longish, as I think the head itself was (*its* "length" going *horizontal*): he was large-boned, lean but still firm-knit, tall, and strong-looking when he stood; a right good old steel-gray figure, with a fine rustic simplicity and dignity about him, and a veracious *strength* looking through him which might have suited one of those old steel-gray *Markgrafs* (Graf=Grau, "Steel-gray") whom Henry the Fowler set up toward the "marches," and to do battle with the intrusive Heathen, in a stalwart and judicious manner.—CARLYLE, THOMAS, 1867, *Wordsworth, Reminiscences, ed. Norton, vol.* II, *p.* 301.

Though they rest by the Lakes they loved so well, Southey's bust looks down upon us from over the shoulder of Shakspeare; and Wordsworth, by the sentiment of a kinsman, is seated in the Baptistry—not unsuited to the innocent presence of childhood at the sacred font—not unworthy to make that angle of the Nave the nucleus of a new Poets' Corner of future years. Beside him, by a like concord of ideas, will be the tablet of Keble, author of the "Christian Year," who himself wrote the reverential epitaph on Wordsworth's monument at Grasmere.—STANLEY, ARTHUR PENRHYN, 1868, *Historical Memorials of Westminster Abbey, p.* 319.

Wordsworth and Dickens did not *take* to each other. Indeed, there was a mutual contempt between them, although they met only once. This was about the year 1843. Some days after, the gentleman whose guest Wordsworth was, in the suburbs of London, asked the Poet, how he liked the great Novelist? Wordsworth had a great contempt for young men, and, after pursing up his lips in a fashion peculiar to him, and swinging one leg over the other, the bare flesh of his ankles appearing over his socks, slowly answered: "Why, I am not much given to turn critic on people I meet; but, as you ask me, I will candidly avow that I thought him a very talkative, vulgar young person,—but I dare say he may be very clever. Mind, I don't want to say a word against him, for I have never read a line he has written." Some time after this, the same querist guardedly asked Dickens how he had liked the Poet Laureate?—"Like him? Not at all. He is a dreadful Old Ass." —MACKENZIE, R. SHELTON, 1870, *Life of Charles Dickens, p.* 243.

I thought there was something prophet-like in the tones of his voice, as well as in his whole appearance, and there was a noble tranquility about him that almost awed one, at first, into silence. As the day was cold and wet, he proposed we should sit down together in the only room in the house where there was a fire, and he led the way to what seemed a common sitting or dinning room. It was a plain apartment, the rafters visible, and no attempt at decoration noticeable. Mrs. Wordsworth sat knitting at the fireside, and she rose with a sweet expression of courtesy and welcome as we entered the apartment. . . . I noticed that Mrs. Wordsworth listened as if she were hearing him speak for the first time in her life, and the work on which she was engaged lay idle in her lap, while she watched intently every movement of her husband's face. I also was absorbed in the man and in his speech. I thought of the long years he had lived in communion with nature in that lonely but lovely region. The story of his life was familiar to me, and I sat as if under the influence of a spell. . . . Now and then I stole a glance at the gentle lady, the poet's wife, as she sat knitting silently by the fireside. This, then, was the Mary whom in 1802 he had brought home to be his loving companion through so many years. I could not help remembering too, as we all sat there together, that when children they had "practiced reading and spelling under the same old dame at Penrith," and that they had always been lovers. There sat the woman, now gray-haired and bent, to whom the poet had addressed those undying poems, "She was a phantom of delight," "Let other bards of angels sing," "Yes, thou art fair," and "O, dearer far than life and light are dear." I recalled, too, the "Lines written after Thirty-six Years of Wedded Life."—FIELDS, JAMES T., 1871, *Yesterdays with Authors, pp.* 254, 255.

Accustomed for many years to unsparing ridicule (which he had learned to endure with philosophical equanimity), the standing target for reviewers (from the formidable Jeffery of the Edinburgh to the anonymous scribbler for the Monthly), and the butt of literary and social circles, he lived long enough to exchange contempt for honours, and excessive depreciation for equally extravagant laudation.—ALLIBONE, S. AUSTIN, 1871, *A Critical Dictionary of English Literature, vol.* III, *p.* 2843.

Mr. Crabb Robinson told me the following story more than once. He was at Charles Lamb's chambers in the Temple when Wordsworth came in, with the new *Edinburgh Review* in his hand, and fume on his countenance. "These reviewers," said he, "put me out of patience. Here is a young man—they say he is a lord—who has written a volume of poetry, and these fellows, just because he is a lord, set upon him, laugh at him, and sneer at his writing. The young man will do something, if he goes on as he has begun. But these reviewers seem to think that nobody may write poetry, unless he lives in a garret." Crabb Robinson told this long after to Lady Byron, who said, "Ah! if Byron had known that, he would never have attacked Wordsworth. He went one day to meet Wordsworth at dinner; when he came home I said, 'Well, how did the young poet get on with the old one?' 'Why, to tell you the truth,' said he, 'I had but one feeling from the beginning of the visit to the end, and that was—*reverence!*' "—DE MORGAN, AUGUSTUS, 1871, *A Budget of Paradoxes, p.* 435.

The latter part of his life was cheered by a redundance of that admiration which before had been confined to a few, and which he certainly did not undervalue. The phrase which Quintilian applies to Ovid, "*nimium amator ingenii sui,*" had its close application to Wordsworth He frequently and fondly referred to his own poems, as if feeling that they had opened a new poetical era to the world.—HOLLAND, SIR HENRY, 1871, *Recollections of Past Life, p.* 206.

Wordsworth was a tall and ungainly man; with a grave and severe face, and a manner that indicated tranquility and independence rather than high breeding. For many years previous to his death he dwelt at Rydal in Westmoreland. His mode of life was favorable to the object that he had in view; doing nothing but what it was a delight for him to do, and doing this only when he was disposed to labor. His "sole ambition and serene employ" was to write verses, to convince the world that his poems were better than all others; and so "finally array his temples with the Muse's diadem." From all accounts that have reached me, Wordsworth entertained small tenderness for persons beyond those who were nearest to him. In that innermost circle his affections were concentrated; and there he dwelt supreme. —PROCTER, BRYAN WALLER (BARRY CORNWALL), 1874? *Recollections of Men of Letters.*

Old "Daddy Wordsworth," as he was sometimes called, I am afraid, from my

Christening, he is now, I suppose, passing under the Eclipse consequent on the Glory which followed his obscure Rise. I remember fifty years ago at our Cambridge, when the Battle was fighting for him by the Few against the Many of us who only laughed at "Louisa in the Shade" &c. His brother was then Master of Trinity College; like all Wordsworths (unless the drowned Sailor) pompous and priggish. He used to drawl out the Chapel responses so that we called him the "Mēēserable Sinner" and his brother the "Mēēserable Poet."—FITZGERALD, EDWARD, 1876, *Letters, vol.* I, *p.* 381.

An excitement which vents itself in bodily exercise carries its own sedative with it. And in comparing Wordsworth's nature with that of other poets whose career has been less placid, we may say that he was perhaps not less excitable than they, but that it was his constant endeavour to avoid all excitement save of the purely poetic kind; and that the outward circumstances of his life—his mediocrity of fortune, happy and early marriage, and absence of striking personal charm—made it easy for him to adhere to a method of life which was, in the truest sense of the term, *stoic*—stoic alike in its practical abstinences and in its calm and grave ideal.—MYERS, F. W. H., 1881, *Wordsworth* (*English Men of Letters*), *p.*177.

Tall, somewhat slender, upright, with a sort of rude grace, his movements suggestive of rustic independence tempered by the delicacy of high intellect—such was Wordsworth to outward seeming when I knew him. I wish it had been among the lovely lakes and quiet dales of Westmoreland; but, as I have said, I only visited them after the poet had been removed by the only power that could have compelled him to quit them—death. He loved every stick and stone in the Lake District: mountain and dale, tarn and ghyll, placid mere and running brook, were all his dear friends: if dumb to the multitude, they had tongues for him, and inspired his own with much of the eloquent music in which he discoursed to the world of the sermons they had taught. Accustomed to gaze with a reverent and discerning eye on the beauties of Nature, he became her great high-priest, the interpreter of a book that is ever open for the whole world to read. He has left millions upon millions his debtors for benefits incalculable conferred on the whole human family. To him, perhaps, more than to any other poet who ever lived, may be applied his own expressive lines, commending those who were of his high calling:

"Blessings be with them and eternal praise,
Who gave us nobler lives and nobler cares,
The poets, who on earth have made us heirs
Of truth and pure delight by heavenly lays."

—HALL, SAMUEL CARTER, 1883, *Retrospect of a Long Life, p.* 325.

Wordsworth's was a face which did not assign itself to any class. It was a hardy, weather-beaten old face, which might have belonged to a nobleman, a yeoman, a mariner, or a philosopher; for there was so much of a man that you lost sight of superadded distinctions. For my own part I should not, judging by his face, have guessed him to be a poet. To my eyes there was more of strength than refinement in the face.—TAYLOR, SIR HENRY, 1885, *Autobiography, vol.* I, *p.* 149.

It was then and there that I was first presented to the illustrious Wordsworth. The great poet sat in state, surrounded by young and enthusiastic admirers. His conversation was very like the "Excursion" turned into vigorous prose. The natural force fitted for new poetical creations was there in abundance, wanting only the "accomplishment of verse." I met him again at a mixed dinner party, where he was less at home. A voluble young woman full of animal spirits, and wanting a good deal more than "the accomplishment of verse," wanting, for instance, reverence and sympathy, talked him down. So that the author of the "Ode to Immortality," and of "Tintern Abbey," gradually became a silent gentleman in a black coat, eating an indifferent dinner like other black-coated gentlemen, to my great disappointment.—DOYLE, SIR FRANCIS HASTINGS, 1886, *Reminiscences and Opinions, p.* 164.

Wordsworth used to come to me when I lived as a young man in the Albany, and my recollections of him are very pleasing. His simplicity, kindness, and freedom from the worldly type, mark their general character.—GLADSTONE, WILLIAM EWART, 1887, *Letter to William Knight, June* 10; *The Life of William Wordsworth, by Knight, vol.* III, *p.* 355.

"The Bard of Rydal Mount," "The

Blockhead," "The Clownish Sycophant," "The Converted Jacobin," "The Cumberland Poet," "The Farmer of a Lay," "The Great God Pan," "The Great Laker," "The Little Boatman," "The Lost Leader," "Old Ponder," "The Poet of Nature," "The Poet of the Excursion," "Poet Wordy," "This Poetical Charlatan," "This Political Parasite," "That Windemere Treasure." —FREY, ALBERT R., 1888, *Sobriquets and Nicknames*, p. 481.

I did listen with much pleasure when Wordsworth recited his own lines descriptive of Little Langdale. He gave them really exquisitely. But his manner in conversation was not impressive. He sat continuously looking down with a green shade over his eyes even though it was twilight; and his mode of speech and delivery suggested to me the epithet "maudering," though I was ashamed of myself for the thought with reference to such a man. As we came away I cross-examined my mother much as to the subject of his talk. She said it had been all about himself and his works, and that she had been interested. But I could not extract from her a word that had passed worth recording. I do not think that he was popular with his neighbors generally. There were stories current, at Lowther among other places, which imputed to him a tendency to outstay his welcome when invited to visit in a house.—TROLLOPE, THOMAS ADOLPHUS, 1888, *What I Remember*, p. 285.

Wordsworth, too, lies amid the scenes he so revered during his long life. At the foot of his own yews in Grasmere churchyard, where his loved Rothay ever whispers its sweet secrets close to his last bed, he lies surrounded by his loved ones: Mary (his wife), Dora, Dorothy, Hartley Coleridge, and all his little circle. Truly he is at home here, at the foot of Nab Scar, in the beautiful Grasmere Vale where he spent so many happy years as Nature's own interpreter. No need of the medallion and tablet graven upon the wall of yonder pretty stone church that was his sanctuary for so many years. The rocks, mountains, and vales of all that beautiful Lake Country are his ineffaceable monuments. He haunts them still. No crag or hidden corner, no group of yews, or tender heather-bed, or rippling water-fall, but belonged to him, and was consecrated by his verse to all humanity.—LORD, ALICE E., 1893, *The Days of Lamb and Coleridge, A Historical Romance*, p. 380.

And here is the impression that Wordsworth made upon the yeomen and peasants in the dales. "Nivver a man of many words ye kna, but quite monstrable wi' his own barns at times; I darsay he wud take em out in a string and nivver say nowt to nin on em at others, but then he was quite a 'object man,' quite a 'ken-speckled,' an as we saay ratherly rough feaced an aw girt big faace wi' out much plesser i' it and vara plaainly drest at best o' times. Nivver a man as laughed not to saay laugh right owt, but a decent quiet man, well spokken on by his sarvants at t' Mount, terble kind to fowlks as was badly and very highly thowt on, paid his way reglar, vara particle an awe about his accounts, and that was Mrs. Wordsworth's doing ye kna, for she was a reglar manasher. Turble fond o' study ont' rwoads, specially at night time, and wi' a girt voice bumming awaay fit to flayte aw the childer to death ameaast, not but what Miss Dorothy did best part o' pitting his potry togidder. He let i fa' and she cam efter and gethered it oop fur him ye kna. Quite yan o' us ye kna, not a bit o' pride in him for o quality thowte ot warld on 'im. But he wasn't a man as was thowte a deal o' for his potry when he was hereabout. It hed no laugh in it same as Lile Hartley's bided a deal o makkin I darsay. It was kept oer long in his head mappen. But then for aw that, he had best eye to mountains and trees, and buildings in the daale, notished ivvry stean o' the fellside, and we nin on us durst bang a bowder stean a bit or cut a bit coppy or raase an old wa' doon when he was astir." —RAWNSLEY, H. D., 1894, *Literary Associations of the English Lakes*, vol. II, p. 136.

Wordsworth, . . . cared little for books; his library was a small one, embracing hardly more than five hundred volumes. He drew his inspiration not from books, but from Nature. From all that I have heard of him I judge him to have been a very dull man. Allibone relates of him that he once remarked that he did not consider himself a witty poet. "Indeed," quoth he, "I don't think I ever was witty but once in my life." His friends urged him to tell them about it. After some hesitation, he said: "Well, I will tell you. I was standing some time ago at the entrance of Rydal Mount. A man accosted me with the question: 'Pray, sir, have you seen my wife pass by?' Whereupon I retorted, 'Why, my good friend, I didn't know till this moment that you had a wife.' " Illustrative of Wordsworth's vanity, it is told that when it was reported that the next Waverley novel was to be "Rob Roy," the poet took down his "Ballads" and read to the company "Rob Roy's Grave." Then he said gravely: "I do not know what more Mr. Scott can have to say on the subject."—FIELD, EUGENE, 1895, *The Love Affairs of a Bibliomaniac, p.* 239.

I did go around next morning—being Sunday—to the little chapel on the heights of Rydal, where he was to worship; and from my seat saw him enter; knowing him on the instant; tall (to my seeming), erect, yet with step somewhat shaky; his coat closely buttoned; his air serious, and self-possessed; his features large, mouth almost coarse; hair white as the driven snow, fringing a dome of baldness; an eye with a dreamy expression in it, and seeming to look—beyond, and still beyond. He carried, too, his serious air into his share of the service, and made his successive responses of "Good Lord deliver us!" and "Amen!" with an emphasis that rung throughout the little chapel.—MITCHELL, DONALD G., 1895, *English Lands Letters and Kings, Queen Anne and the Georges, p.* 329.

Can a man be reckoned a favourite of fortune when he has lost his mother during his eighth year, and his father at sixteen; when he has been arbitrarily deprived of his inheritance, has had to endure a humiliating existence under the roof of stern and narrow-minded grandparents, and for years has been coldly treated by his relations on account of his indolence, his obstinacy, and his refusal to embark upon any of the safe careers suggested to him; when he is kept apart from the sister whom he loves beyond everything else, apparently from fear that she may become contaminated by his disobedience and his subversive opinions; when he entrusts all his dreams of happiness to the French Revolution, only to see them borne under in the tempest, and loses not only his respect and love for his native country, but all hope of progress as well; when, meanwhile, his existence is so straitened, so penurious even, and so utterly without promise for the morrow, that he is compelled to postpone indefinitely his union with his sister's friend, that maiden, chosen long ago, and now beloved, whom he knows not whether he can ever make his wife?—LEGOUIS, ÉMILE, 1896, *The Early Life of William Wordsworth,* 1770–1798, *A Study of "The Prelude," tr. Matthews, p.* 386.

I passed several days under Wordsworth's roof, which I regard as the greatest honour of my life. We rose early, and went to bed early. Each night prayers were read by Mrs. Wordsworth in a voice full of reverence and sweetness. He knelt near her with his face hidden in his hands. That vision is often before me.—DEVERE, AUBREY, 1897, *Recollections, p.* 125.

Some readers of Wordsworth are misled in their judgment of the poet by the vulgar error that he was before all else tranquil, mild, gentle, an amiable pastoral spirit. He sang of the daisy and the celandine, the linnet and the lamb; and therefore he must have been always a serene, tender, benign contemplator of things that make for peace. There can be no greater mistake; at the heart of his peace was passion; his benignity was like the greensward upon a rocky hillside. As a boy, Wordsworth was violent and moody; in his early manhood he was stern, bold, worn by exhausting ardors.—DOWDEN, EDWARD, 1897, *The French Revolution and English Literature, p.* 197.

He could go to the cemetery and look at the tombstones a few hours after his wedding, and that in spite of the fact that the exquisite poem, "She was a Phantom of Delight," was written for his bride. His sister did much to correct this austerity. And though, like Milton, he did not greatly devote himself to his sister or to his wife, he has recognized his debt to Dorothy in his poems.—STRONG, AUGUSTUS HOPKINS, 1897, *The Great Poets and Their Theology, p.* 348.

DESCRIPTIVE SKETCHES IN VERSE
1793

During the last year of my residence at Cambridge, 1794, I became acquainted with Mr. Wordsworth's first publication, entitled "Descriptive Sketches;" and seldom, if ever, was the emergence of an original poetic genius above the literary horizon more evidently announced. In the form, style, and manner of the whole poem, and in the structure of the particular lines and periods, there is a harshness and acerbity connected and combined with words and images all a-glow, which might recall those products of the vegetable world, where gorgeous blossoms rise out of a hard thorny rind and shell, within which the rich fruit is elaborating. The language is not only peculiar and strong, but at times knotty and contorted, as by its own impatient strength; while the novelty and struggling crowd of images, acting in conjunction with the difficulties of the style, demands always a greater closeness of attention than poetry,—at all events, than descriptive poetry—has a right to claim.—COLERIDGE, SAMUEL TAYLOR, 1817, *Biographia Literaria, ch.* iv.

Wordsworth's first poetical ventures, which were published three years before Scott's translations from Bürger, were "An Evening Walk"—an attempt to paint a series of landscape views in his own country, and "Descriptive Sketches," an attempt to paint the scenery of the Alps, among which he had lately made a pedestrian tour with a college friend. The most that can be said of these productions is that they are fairly well written, and that there are touches of natural description in them which could only have been the result of actual observation.—STODDARD, RICHARD HENRY, 1883, *English Verse, Lyrics of the Nineteenth Century, Introduction, p.* xx.

THE BORDERERS
1795-6—1842

I must be allowed to observe that however unjust and however absurd it would be to cite this play of "The Borderers," completed by Wordsworth at the age of twenty-six and published by Wordsworth at the age of seventy-two, as an adequate and important specimen of his work, it is a hundred times more unjust and it is a thousand times more absurd to cite the poem of Queen Mab as an adequate and important specimen of Shelley's. And none but a very rash and very ignorant partisan will venture to deny that if this burlesque experiment in unnatural horror had been attempted by any poet of less orthodox and correct reputation in ethics and theology than Wordsworth's, the general verdict of critical morality would almost certainly have described it and dismissed it as the dream of a probably incurable and possibly a criminal lunatic. I am very far from thinking that this would have been a justifiable or a reasonable verdict: but I have no manner of doubt that it would have been a popular one.—SWINBURNE, ALGERNON CHARLES, 1886, *Wordsworth and Byron, Miscellanies, p.* 119.

The "Borderers" had no success, and it deserved none.—KNIGHT, WILLIAM, 1889, *The Life of William Wordsworth, vol.* I,

Taking the piece upon its own claim to merit as a study in the genesis of sin and in the inequalities of justice, it is not altogether a success. Its characterisation is unclear, and its treatment is unconvincing. With the most amenable disposition to the didactic purpose of the play, the reader is left perplexed. Wordsworth was grappling with a great idea, but the form which he chose was neither suitable to it nor consistent with itself. MAGNUS, LAURIE, 1897, *A Primer of Wordsworth with a Critical Essay, p.* 49.

LYRICAL BALLADS
1798-1800

The principal object, then, which I proposed to myself in these Poems was to chuse incidents and situations from common life, and to relate or describe them, throughout, as far as was possible, in a selection of language really used by men, and, at the same time, to throw over them a certain colouring of imagination, whereby ordinary things should be presented to the mind in an unusual way; and, further, and above all, to make these incidents and situations interesting by tracing in them, truly though not ostentatiously, the primary laws of our nature: chiefly, as far as regards the manner in which we associate ideas in a state of excitement. Low and rustic life was generally chosen, because, in that condition, the essential passions of the heart find a better soil in which they can attain their maturity, are less under restraint, and speak a plainer and more emphatic language; because in that condition of life our elementary feelings co-exist in a state of greater simplicity, and, consequently, may be more accurately contemplated, and more forcibly communicated; because the manners of rural life germinate from these elementary feelings; and from the necessary character of rural occupations, are more easily comprehended, and are more durable; and, lastly, because in that condition the passions of men are incorporated with the beautiful and permanent forms of nature. —WORDSWORTH, WILLIAM, 1800, *Lyrical Ballads, Second Edition, Preface.*

A careful and repeated examination of these confirms me in the belief, that the omission of less than a hundred lines would have precluded nine-tenths of the criticism on this work. I hazard this declaration, however, on the supposition, that the reader has taken it up, as he would have done any other collection of poems purporting to derive their subjects or interests from the incidents of domestic or ordinary life, intermingled with higher strains of meditation which the poet utters in his own person and character; with the proviso, that these poems were perused without knowledge of, or reference to, the author's peculiar opinions, and that the reader had not had his attention previously directed to those peculiarities. . . . In the critical remarks, therefore, prefixed and annexed to the Lyrical Ballads, I believe, we may safely rest, as the true origin of the unexampled opposition which Mr. Wordsworth's writings have been since doomed to encounter.—COLERIDGE, SAMUEL TAYLOR, 1817, *Biographia Literaria, ch.* iv.

His Muse . . . is a levelling one. . . . Fools have laughed at, wise men scarcely understand them. He takes a subject or a story merely as pegs or loops to hang thought and feeling on; the incidents are trifling, in porportion to his contempt for imposing appearances; the reflections are profound, according to the gravity and the aspiring pretensions of his mind.—HAZLITT, WILLIAM, 1825, *The Spirit of the Age, p.* 124.

This volume contained several poems which have been justly blamed for triviality—as "The Thorn," "Goody Blake," "The Idiot Boy;" several in which, as in "Simon Lee," triviality is mingled with much real pathos; and some, as "Expostulation and Reply" and "The Tables Turned," which are of the very essence of Wordsworth's nature. It is hardly too much to say that, if these two last-named poems—to the careless eye so slight and trifling—were all that had remained from Wordsworth's hand, they would have "spoken to the comprehending" of a new individuality, as distinct and unmistakable in its way as that which Sappho has left engraven on the world forever in words even fewer than these. And the volume ended with a poem which Wordsworth composed in 1798, in one day, during a tour with his sister to Tintern and Chepstow. The "Lines written above Tintern Abbey" have become, as it were, the *locus classicus,* or consecrated formulary of the Wordsworthian faith. They say in brief what it is the work of the poet's biographer to say in detail.—MYERS, F. W. H., 1881, *Wordsworth (English Men of Letters), p.* 33.

The tribute which the Poet paid [in "Tintern Abbey"] to his sister is the highest which one soul can pay to another: he was never weary of singing her praise, nor was she ever tired of trying to make herself worthy of his praise. Endowed with faculties capable of gaining distinction in the same sphere of work, she nevertheless chose to let him sing of what she felt and saw. To those familiar with the close of her life these words seem prophetic; for she lingered a few years after her brother'a death, and her chief solace seemed to be the remembrance of days passed in his companionship. More has been written of this poem than of any other of his unless it be the "Platonic Ode."—GEORGE, ANDREW J., 1889, *ed., Selections from Wordsworth, p.* 342, *note.*

There was, indeed, one poem in the volume, the "Lines written above Tintern Abbey," in which a fresh theme was handled with a power that nobody could be insensible to. If all had been like this, the acknowledgment of Wordsworth's greatness would not have been checked and held back by astonishment at the grotesque strangeness of the lyrical ballads, to which the title of the volume challenged special attention. . . . This poem is characteristic of the loftiest side of Wordsworth's genius. In it he struck for the first time the sublime note that has drawn men after him as the prophet of a new delight, a full-voiced speaker of things that all feel dimly and vaguely, but which no poet before him had expressed with such force.—MINTO, WILLIAM, 1894, *The Literature of the Georgian Era, ed. Knight, pp.* 176, 180.

PETER BELL
1798–1819

Lent "Peter Bell" to Charles Lamb. To my surprise, he does not like it. He complains of the slowness of the narrative, as if that were not the *art* of the poet. He says Wordsworth has great thoughts, but has left them out here.—ROBINSON, HENRY CRABB, 1812, *Diary, June* 6; *Diary, Reminiscences and Correspondence, ed. Sadler, vol.* I, *p.* 251.

Wordsworth informs us he was nineteen years
Considering and re-touching Peter Bell;
Watering his laurels with the killing tears
Of slow, dull care, so that their roots to hell
Might pierce, and their wide branches blot the spheres
Of heaven with dewey leaves and flowers; this well
May be, for heaven and earth conspire to foil
The ever-busy gardener's blundering toil.
—SHELLEY, PERCY BYSSHE, 1820, *The Witch of Atlas, Proem.*

None of Wordsworth's productions are better known by name than "Peter Bell," and yet few, probably, are less familiar, even to convinced Wordsworthians. The poet's biographers and critics have commonly shirked the responsibility of discussing this poem, and when the Primrose stanza has been quoted, and the Parlour stanza smiled at, there is usually no more said about "Peter Bell." A puzzling obscurity hangs around its history. We have no positive knowledge why its publication was so long delayed; nor, having been delayed, why it was at length determined upon. Yet a knowledge of this poem is not merely an important, but, to a thoughtful critic, an essential element in the comprehension of Wordsworth's poetry. No one who examines that body of literature with sympathetic attention should be content to overlook the piece in which Wordsworth's theories are pushed to their furthest extremity.—GOSSE, EDMUND, 1891, *Gossip in a Library, p.* 253.

The world, the worldly world, so to speak, has never quite swallowed Peter Bell. A reserve of self-consciousnses has stood in his way. The unheightened simplicity of his story touches the fringe of bathos. Poetry, it is felt, has not been dignified in him, but degraded. The mark of the tract is upon him, and the means of his conversion savour of the revivalist meeting. I cannot but think that such criticism convicts itself. There are indeed inadequacies of expression in the poem, less to-day than when it was first published, but they occur in its business portions, always so difficult to Wordsworth, in its technical setting in the middle of a conversation, and in the narrating of the bare events, as such. . . . It is by his matter that Wordsworth must primarily be judged, and, fortunately, when it was not complicated by technicalities in the telling, his style was always equal to it. The material of Peter Bell's story does not fall below the level of the best of Wordsworth's work. Its theme is true. As knowledge widens, it is recognised more and more that man is not divorced from the rest of nature.—MAGNUS, LAURIE, 1897, *A Primer of Wordsworth with a Critical Essay, pp.* 77, 78.

INTIMATIONS OF IMMORTALITY
1803–6

It is for every one who takes thought of the deep things of his nature, the mysteries of his being, memories of early innocence and yearnings for eternity, that Wordsworth struck his lofty lyric the most sublime ode in this and, perhaps, any language, on the birth—the life—the undying destiny of the soul of man.—REED, HENRY, 1850–55, *Lectures on English Literature, from Chaucer to Tennyson, p.* 33.

His "Ode on Immortality" is the high-water mark which the intellect has reached in this age. New means were employed, and new realms added to the empire of the muse, by his courage.—EMERSON, RALPH WALDO, 1856–84, *English Traits.*

What is valuable in Wordsworth's poetry is very valuable indeed; and I think a true lover of what is highest and best in poetic expression, would rather have written his "Ode on the Intimations of Immortality" than any other existing piece of the same length.—FRISWELL, JAMES HAIN, 1869, *Essays on English Writers, p.* 332.

Produced that noble Ode, in right of which he stands well-nigh supreme even where Milton and Dryden are his rivals. Such inspirations come, indeed, but once in a life, being, as they are, the quintessence of its deepest emotions and its most heavenward thoughts, which in a happy hour run themselves into moulds on immortal beauty.—MARTIN, THEODORE,

1874, *The Life of the Prince Consort, vol.* I, *p.* 320.

That grandest ode that has ever been written. —MACDONALD, GEORGE, 1882, *The Imagination and Other Essays, p.* 256.

That famous, ambitious, and occasionally magnificent poem—which by the way is no more an ode than it is an epic—reveals the partiality and inequality of Wordsworth's inspiration as unmistakably as its purity and its power. Five stanzas or sections—from the opening of the fifth to the close of the ninth—would be utterly above all praise, if the note they are pitched in were sustained throughout: but after its unspeakably beautiful opening the seventh stanza falls suddenly far down beneath the level of those five first lines, so superb in the majesty of their sweetness, the magnificence of their tenderness, that to have written but the two last of them would have added glory to any poet's crown of fame. The details which follow on the close of this opening cadence do but impair its charm with a sense of incongruous realism and triviality, to which the suddenly halting and disjointed metre bears only too direct and significant a correspondence. No poet, surely, ever "changed his hand" with such inharmonious awkwardness, or "checked his pride" with such unreasonable humility, as Wordsworth.—SWINBURNE, ALGERNON CHARLES, 1886, *Wordsworth and Byron, Miscellanies, p.* 135.

In the famous "Ode on Intimations of Immortality," the poet doubtless does point to a set of philosophic ideas, more or less complete; but the thought from which he sets out, that our birth is but a sleep and a forgetting, and that we are less and less able to perceive the visionary gleam, less and less alive to the glory and the dream of external nature, as infancy recedes farther from us, is, with all respects for the declaration of Mr. Ruskin to the contrary, contrary to notorious fact, experience, and truth.—MORLEY, JOHN, 1888, *ed., The Complete Poetical Works of William Wordsworth, Introduction, p.* lxv.

THE WHITE DOE OF RYLSTONE
1807–10–15

The "White Doe" is not in season; venison is not liked in Edinburgh. It wants flavor; a good Ettrick wether is preferable. Wordsworth has more of the poetical character than any living writer, but he is not a man of first-rate intellect; his genius oversets him.—WILSON, JOHN, 1815, *Letter to James Hogg, A Memoir of John Wilson, ed. Mrs. Gordon, p.* 130.

This, we think, has the merit of being the very worst poem we ever saw imprinted in a quarto volume; and though it was scarcely to be expected, we confess, that Mr. Wordsworth, with all his ambition, should so soon have attained to that distinction, the wonder may perhaps be diminished when we state, that it seems to us to consist of a happy union of all the faults, without any of the beauties, which belong to his school of poetry. It is just such work, in short, as some wicked enemy of that school might be supposed to have devised, on purpose to make it ridiculous; and when we first took it up, we could not help suspecting that some ill-natured critic had actually taken this harsh method of instructing Mr. Wordsworth, by example, in the nature of those errors, against which our precepts had been so often directed in vain. We had not gone far, however, till we felt intimately that nothing in the nature of a joke could be so insupportably dull;—and that this must be the work of one who earnestly believed it to be a pattern of pathetic simplicity, and gave it out as such to the admiration of all intelligent readers. In this point of view, the work may be regarded as curious at least, if not in some degree interesting; and, at all events, it must be instructive to be made aware of the excesses into which superior understandings may be betrayed, by long self-indulgence, and the strange extravagances into which they may run, when under the influence of that intoxication which is produced by unrestrained admiration of themselves.—JEFFREY, FRANCIS LORD, 1815–44, *Wordsworth's White Doe, Contributions to the Edinburgh Review, vol.* III, *p.* 269.

We talked of Wordsworth's exceedingly high opinion of himself; and she (Lady Davy) mentioned that one day, in a large party, Wordsworth, without anything having been previously said that could lead to the subject, called out suddenly from the top of the table to the bottom, in his most epic tone, "Davy!" and on Davy's putting forth his head in awful expectation of what was coming, said, "Do you know the reason why I published the 'White Doe' in quarto?" "No, what was it?" "To show the world my own opinion of it."—MOORE, THOMAS, 1820, *Journal, Oct.* 27; *Memoirs, Journal and Correspondence, ed. Russell.*

The poem has no definite end, but passes off, as it were, into the illimitable. It rises out of the perturbations of time and transitory things, and, passing upward itself, takes our thoughts with it, to calm places and eternal sunshine.—SHAIRP, JOHN CAMPBELL, 1881, *The White Doe of Rylstone, Aspects of Poetry, p.* 376.

THE EXCURSION
1814

This will never do! It bears no doubt the stamp of the author's heart and fancy: But unfortunately not half so visibly as that of his peculiar system. His former poems were intended to recommend that system, and to bespeak favour for it by their individual merit;—but this, we suspect, must be recommended by the system—and can only expect to succeed where it has been previously established. It is longer, weaker, and tamer, than any of Mr. Wordsworth's other productions; with less boldness of originality, and less even of that extreme simplicity and lowliness of tone which wavered so prettily, in the "Lyrical Ballads," between silliness and pathos. We have imitations of Cowper, and even of Milton here; engrafted on the natural drawl of the Lakers—and all diluted into harmony by that profuse and irrepressible wordiness which deluges all the blank verse of this school of poetry, and lubricates and weakens the whole structure of their style.—JEFFREY, FRANCIS LORD, 1814–44, *Wordsworth's Excursion, Contributions to the Edinburgh Review, vol.* III, *p.* 233.

Jeffrey, I hear, has written what his admirers call a *crushing* review of "The Excursion." He might as well seat himself upon Skiddaw and fancy that he crushed the mountain.—SOUTHEY, ROBERT, 1814, *Letter to Walter Scott, Dec.* 24; *Life and Correspondence, ed. C. C. Southey, ch.* xix.

The causes which have prevented the poetry of Mr. Wordsworth from attaining its full share of popularity are to be found in the boldness and originality of his genius. The times are past when a poet could securely follow the direction of his own mind into whatever tracts it might lead. . . . If from living among simple mountaineers, from a daily intercourse with them, not upon the footing of a patron, but in the character of an equal, he has detected, or imagines that he has detected, through the cloudy medium of their unlettered discourse, thoughts and apprehensions not vulgar; traits of patience and constancy, love unwearied, and heroic endurance, not unfit (as he may judge) to be made the subject of verse, he will be deemed a man of perverted genius by the philanthropist who, conceiving of the peasantry of his country only as objects of a pecuniary sympathy, starts at finding them elevated to a level of humanity with himself, having their own loves, enmities, cravings, aspirations, &c., as much beyond his faculty to believe, as his beneficence to supply. . . . Those who hate the "Paradise Lost" will not love this poem. The steps of the great master are discernible in it; not in direct imitation or injurious parody, but in the following of the spirit, in free homage and generous subjection.—LAMB, CHARLES, 1814, *Wordsworth's Excursion, Quarterly Review, vol.* 12, *pp.* 110, 111.

This week I finished Wordsworth's poem. It has afforded me less intense pleasure on the whole, perhaps, than I had expected, but it will be a source of frequent gratification. The wisdom and high moral character of the work are beyond anything of the same kind with which I am acquainted, and the spirit of the poetry flags much less frequently than might be expected. There are passages which run heavily, tales which are prolix, and reasonings which are spun out, but in general the narratives are exquisitely tender. That of the courtier parson, who retains in solitude the feelings of high society, whose vigor of mind is unconquerable, and who, even after the death of his wife, appears able for a short time to bear up against desolation and wretchedness, by the powers of his native temperament, is most delightful.—ROBINSON, HENRY CRABB, 1814, *Diary, Nov.* 23; *Diary, Reminiscences and Correspondence, ed. Sadler, vol.* I, *p.* 296.

And Wordsworth, in a rather long "Excursion"
(I think the quarto holds five hundred pages),
Has given a sample from the vasty version
Of his new system to perplex the sages;
'Tis poetry—at least by his assertion,

And may appear so when the dog-star rages—
And he who understands it would be able
To add a story to the Tower of Babel.
—BYRON, LORD, 1819, *Don Juan, Dedication.*

North. Wordsworth—with his eternal—here we go up, up, and up, and here we go down, down, and here we go roundabout, roundabout! Look at the nerveless laxity of his "Excursion!" What interminable prosing! The language is out of condition; fat and fozy, thick winded, purified and plethoric. Can he be compared with Pope? Fie on't! no, no, no!—WILSON, JOHN, 1825, *Noctes Ambrosianæ, March.*

It affects a system without having an intelligible clue to one; and, instead of unfolding a principle in various and striking lights, repeats the same conclusions till they become flat and insipid. . . . The "Excursion," we believe, fell still-born from the press. There was something abortive, and clumsy, and ill-judged in the attempt. It was long and laboured. The personages, for the most part, were low, the fare rustic: the plan raised expectations which were not fulfilled, and the effect was like being ushered into a stately hall and invited to sit down to a splendid banquet in the company of clowns, and with nothing but successive courses of apple-dumpling served up. It was not even *toujours perdrix!*—HAZLITT, WILLIAM, 1825, *The Spirit of the Age, p.* 129.

The views of man, nature, and society, which this truly philosophical poem contains, are the off-spring of deep thought and extensive observation.—CUNNINGHAM, ALLAN, 1833, *Biographical and Critical History of Literature of the Last Fifty Years.*

To show how completely Wordsworth's system is a system of poetical Quakerism, I should be obliged to take his "Excursion," and collate the whole with passages from the writings of the early Friends, Fox, Penn, Barclay, Pennington, and others. The "Excursion" is a very bible of Quakerism. Every page abounds with it. It is, in fact, wholly and fervently permeated by the soul of Quaker theology.—HOWITT, WILLIAM, 1847, *Homes and Haunts of the Most Eminent British Poets, vol.* II, *p.* 320.

The Imagination is a faculty that flouts at foreordination, and Wordsworth seemed to do all he could to cheat his readers of her company by laying out paths with a peremptory *Do not step off the gravel!* at the opening of each, and preparing pitfalls for every conceivable emotion, with guide-boards to tell each when and where it must be caught. But if these things stood in the way of immediate appreciation he had another theory which interferes more seriously with the total and permanent effect of his poems. He was theoretically determined not only to be a philosophic poet, but to be a *great* philosophic poet, and to this end he must produce an epic. . . . In point of fact, the one element of greatness which "The Excursion" possesses indisputably is heaviness. It is only the episodes that are universally read, and the effect of these is diluted by the connecting and accompanying lectures on metaphysics. Wordsworth has his epic mould to fill, and, like Benvenuto Cellini in casting his Perseus, was forced to throw in everything, debasing the metal lest it should run short. Separated from the rest, the episodes are perfect poems in their kind, and without example in the language.—LOWELL, JAMES RUSSELL, 1875, *Wordsworth, Works, Riverside ed., vol.* IV, *pp.* 397, 398.

Although Jeffrey completely failed to recognize Wordsworth's real greatness, he was yet not wrong in saying of the "Excursion" as a work of poetic style, "This will never do."—ARNOLD, MATTHEW, 1879, *ed., Poems of William Wordsworth, Preface, p.* xxii.

Through the "Excursion" Wordsworth dealt with the problem of our common life as it stood after the failure of those who had aimed at a reconstruction of society by Revolution. Wordsworth still maintained the loftiest ideal of a humanized society. He used poetically the characters drawn in the "Excursion" as so many factors in working out his own solution of the problem. The Wanderer represents shrewd, natural sense, strengthened in youth by homely and religious education and in manhood by wide intercourse with men. The Solitary represents one in whom faith seems dead, enthusiasm for the best aims of the Revolution being quelled by the apparent failure of the effort. Talk between Wanderer and Solitary, and all the associated incidents, maintain one flow of thought, until the Pastor, representing culture and religion in acquaintance with the daily lives of men, adds his part to the argument. The full course of reasoning leads to expression of the faith which is at the heart of Wordsworth's poetry. It there first found distinct expression. It is now the faith of all who look for a full civilization.—MORLEY, HENRY, 1881, *Of English Literature in the Reign of Victoria with Glance at the Past, p.* 118.

Judged by ordinary standards the "Excursion" appears an epic without action, and with two heroes, the Pastor and the Wanderer, whose characters are identical. Its form is cumbrous in the extreme, and large tracts of it have little claim to the name of poetry. Wordsworth compares the "Excursion" to a temple of which his smaller poems form subsidiary shrines; but the reader will more often liken the small poems to gems, and the "Excursion" to the rock from which they were extracted. The long poem contains, indeed, magnificent passages, but as a whole it is a diffused description of scenery which the poet has elsewhere caught in brighter glimpses; a diffused statement of hopes and beliefs which have crystallized more exquisitely elsewhere round moments of inspiring emotion. The "Excursion," in short, has the drawbacks of a didactic poem as compared with lyrical poems; but, judged as a didactic poem, it has the advantage of containing teaching of true and permanent value.—MYERS, F. W. H., 1881, *Wordsworth (English Men of Letters).*

Unless a man's imagination is inspired from without, and his design is conceived when the mind is in that excited state, he will do wrong to choose metre as his instrument of expression. Hence it is that so much of Wordsworth's verse seems to be written in violation of the laws of poetical art. In the "Excursion," for instance, though it is full of the most noble incidental passages, evidently written under the influence of direct inspiration, yet, as the design of the whole poem is certainly formed by a process of cool meditation, we are constantly haunted by a sense that we are in an atmosphere unfavourable to the movement of metre.—COURTHOPE, WILLIAM JOHN, 1885, *The Liberal Movement in English Literature, p.* 97.

The performance where we best see the whole poet, and where the poet most absolutely indentifies himself with his subject.—MORLEY, JOHN, 1888, *The Complete Poetical Works of William Wordsworth, Introduction, p.* lxiii.

In reading "The Excursion" after a long interval, I feel so much how good it would have been for Wordsworth to have gone to Oxford. He is a thorough Cantab, has no philosophical vocabulary, and really rather bores one with his constant philosophizing, which is under difficulties and often only half intelligible. Some periods, all involved and crude of phrase, I can't construe. — BROWN, THOMAS EDWARD, 1894, *To S. T. Irwin, Dec.* 15; *Letters, vol.* II, *p.* 76.

Besides these there were standard volumes of poetry, published by Phillips & Sampson, from worn-out plates; for a birthday present my mother got me Wordsworth in this shape, and I am glad to think that I once read the "Excursion" in it, for I do not think I could do so now, and I have a feeling that it is very right and fit to have read the "Excursion." To be honest, it was very hard reading even then, and I could not truthfully pretend that I have ever liked Wordsworth except in parts, though for the matter of that, I do not suppose that any one ever did. I tried hard enough to like everything in him, for I had already learned enough to know that I ought to like him, and that if I did not, it was a proof of intellectual and moral inferiority in me.—HOWELLS, WILLIAM DEAN, 1895, *My Literary Passions, p.* 106.

Natural description of Wordsworth amounted to little. "The Excursion," nominally descriptive, is only diversified by "sunny spots of greenery," curiously few and far between; the poem takes its rank chiefly because of the searching natural metaphysics with which it is permeated and infused from the first line to the last. Nature to Wordsworth has its fascination as revealing an Invisible Power, in whose Presence abides the ultimate grandeur or beauty of man's reverence.—BAYNE, WILLIAM, 1898, *James Thomson (Famous Scots Series), p.* 17.

Wordsworth's "Excursion" was published in 1814, in a two guinea quarto volume, but it took six years to exhaust an edition of five hundred copies.—WHEATLEY, HENRY B., 1898, *Prices of Books, p.* 97.

THE PRELUDE

1850

Friend of the wise! and teacher of the good!
Into my heart have I received that lay
More than historic, that prophetic lay
Wherein (high theme by thee first sung aright)
Of the foundations and the building up
Of a Human Spirit thou has dar'd to tell
What may be told, to the understanding mind
Revealable; and what within the mind
By vital breathings secret as the soul
Of vernal growth, oft quickens in the heart
Thoughts all too deep for words!—
—COLERIDGE, SAMUEL TAYLOR, 1807, *To William Wordsworth, Composed on the night after his recitation of a Poem on the growth of an individual mind.*

We have finished Wordsworth's "Prelude." It has many lofty passages. It soars and sinks, and is by turns sublime and commonplace. It is Wordsworth as he was at the age of thirty-five or forty.—LONGFELLOW, HENRY WADSWORTH, 1850, *Journal, July* 21; *Life by S. Longfellow, vol.* II, *p.* 175.

I brought home, and read, the "Prelude." It is a poorer "Excursion;" the same sort of faults and beauties; but the faults greater, and the beauties fainter, both in themselves, and because faults are always made more offensive, and beauties less pleasing, by repetition. The story is the old story. There are the old raptures about mountains and cataracts; the old flimsy philosophy about the effect of scenery on the mind; the old crazy mystical metaphysics; the endless wilderness of dull, flat, prosaic twaddle; and here and there fine descriptions and energetic declamations interspersed. The story of the French Revolution, and of its influence on the character of a young enthusiast, is told again at greater length, and with less force and pathos, than in the "Excursion." The poem is to the last degree Jacobinical, indeed Socialist. I understand perfectly why Wordsworth did not choose to publish it in his lifetime.—MACAULAY, THOMAS BABINGTON, 1850, *Journal, July* 28; *Life and Letters, ed. Trevelyan, vol.* II, *ch.* xii.

At the time when the "Prelude" was fresh from the press, he [Macaulay] was maintaining against the opinion of a large and mixed society that the poem was unreadable. At last, overborne by the united indignation of so many of Wordsworth's admirers, he agreed that the question should be referred to the test of personal experience: and on inquiry it was discovered that the only individual present who had got through the "Prelude" was Macaulay himself. — TREVELYAN, GEORGE OTTO, 1876, *Life and Letters of Lord Macaulay, vol.* I, *ch.* ii.

There were many who knew Wordsworth's poetry well while he was still alive, who felt its power, and the new light which it threw on the material world. But though they half-guessed they did not fully know the secret of it. They got glimpses of part, but could not grasp the whole of the philosophy on which it was based. But when, after his death, "The Prelude" was published, they were let into the secret, they saw the hidden foundations on which it rests, as they had never seen them before. The smaller poems were more beautiful, more delightful, but "The Prelude" revealed the secret of their beauty. It showed that all Wordsworth's impassioned feeling towards Nature was no mere fantastic dream, but based on sanity, on a most assured and reasonable philosophy. It was as though one who had been long gazing on some building grand and fair, admiring the vast sweep of its walls, and the strength of its battlements, without understanding their principle of coherence, were at length to be admitted inside by the master builder, and given a view of the whole plan from within, the principles of the architecture, and the hidden substructures on which it was built. This is what "The Prelude" does for the rest of Wordsworth's poetry.—SHAIRP, JOHN CAMPBELL, 1877, *On Poetic Interpretation of Nature, p.* 274.

In Wordsworth's case, the posthumous decline may have been owing in part to disappointment occasioned by "The Prelude," which was given to the public a few months after the author's death. For myself, I must confess that I was greatly taken back on first reading that work; it disappointed me sadly: but Coleridge's grand poem in its praise had raised very high expectations in me; which were so far from being met, and indeed so badly dashed, that I did not venture upon a second reading for several years. But I still remembered Coleridge's poem, still had faith in his judgment, and so committed the rather unusual folly of suspecting that the fault, after all, might be in myself. So, at length, I gave it a second perusal, and was then even more disappointed than I had been at first, but disappointed just the other way; and so repented my hasty dislike, that I soon after tried it a third time: this led to a fourth trial, and this to a fifth. Thus its interest kept mounting higher and higher on every fresh perusal; and now for some eighteen years I have not been able to let a year pass without reading it at least twice. And it still keeps its hold on me, still keeps pulling me back to it.—HUDSON, HENRY N., 1884, *Studies in Wordsworth*, p. 96.

The "Prelude," in which Wordsworth gives an account of his own spiritual development, is one of the numerous echoes of the "Confessions" of Rousseau; but it is an echo in which the morbid and unhealthy self-analysis of the "Confessions" has all but disappeared, and in which the interest of the reader is claimed on grounds which are all but independent of the mere individual. Wordsworth seeks to exhibit to us, not so much of his own personal career, as the way in which, amid the difficulties of the time, a human soul might find peace and inward freedom.—CAIRD, EDWARD, 1892, *Wordsworth, Essays on Literature and Philosophy*, vol. I, p. 186.

The system of general spiritual education which is both explicitly and implicitly set forth in "The Prelude," makes this great autobiographical poem one of the most valuable productions in English Literature; and teachers capable of bringing its informing spirit home to their students (capable by virtue of their own assimilation of it), might do great things in the way of a spiritual quickening of their students.—CORSON, HIRAM, 1896, *The Voice and Spiritual Education*, p. 145.

No autobiography, however, is so free from the taint of vanity as "The Prelude." There are no theatrical attitudes, no arrangements of drapery for the sake of effect. The poet takes no pains to give statuesque beauty to his gestures, or dramatic sequence to his actions. Wordsworth had too much pride—if the word may be used to denote justifiable self-confidence—to be vain. He felt, he knew, that he was a great poet, and did not disguise the fact. He was unconscious of any obligation to wrap himself in the detestable cloak of false modesty.—LEGOUIS, ÉMILE, 1896, *The Early Life of William Wordsworth*, 1770–1798, *A Study of "The Prelude," tr. Matthews*, p. 13.

"The Prelude," though long and occasionally prosaic, is an invaluable record. The poet has there disclosed himself more perfectly than Dante or Milton ever did. —STRONG, AUGUSTUS HOPKINS, 1897, *The Great Poets and Their Theology*, p. 339.

SONNETS

The difficulty of the sonnet metre in English is a good excuse for the dull didactic thoughts which naturally incline towards it: fellows know there is no danger of decanting their muddy stuff ever so slowly: they are neither prose nor poetry. I have rather a wish to tie old Wordsworth's volume about his neck and pitch him into one of the deepest holes of his dear Duddon.—FITZGERALD, EDWARD, 1841, *To F. Tennyson, July* 26; *Letters*, vol. I, p. 73.

Wordsworth, in sonnet, is a classick too,
And on that grass-plot sits at Milton's side.
—LANDOR, WALTER SAVAGE, 1853, *To the Author of "Festus", The Last Fruit off an old Tree.*

To Wordsworth has been vouchsafed the last grace of the self-denying artist: you think neither of him nor his style, but you cannot help thinking of—you *must* recall —the exact phrase, the *very* sentiment he wished. Milton's purity is more eager. In the most exciting parts of Wordsworth —and these sonnets are not very exciting —you always feel, you never forget, that what you have before you is the excitement of a recluse. There is nothing of the stir of life; nothing of the brawl of the world.—BAGEHOT, WALTER, 1864, *Wordsworth, Tennyson and Browning; Works, ed. Morgan*, vol. I, p. 218.

Wordsworth, the greatest of modern poets, is perhaps the greatest of English sonnet writers. Not only has he composed a larger number of sonnets than any other of our poets; he has also written more that are of first-rate excellence. There is no intensity of passion in Wordsworth's sonnets; and herein he differs from Shakespeare, and from Mrs. Browning, for whose sonnets the reader may feel an enthusiastic admiration that Wordsworth's thoughtful and calm verse rarely excites; neither has he attained the "dignified simplicity" which marks the sonnets of Milton; but for purity of language, for variety and strength of thought, for the *curiosa felicitas* of poetical diction, for the exquisite skill with which he associates the emotions of the mind and the aspects of nature, we know of no sonnet writer who can take precedence of Wordsworth. In his larger poems his language is sometimes slovenly, and occasionally, as Sir Walter Scott said, he chooses to crawl on all-fours; but this is rarely the case in the sonnets, and though he wrote upwards of four hundred, there are few, save those on the "Punishment of Death" and some of those called *Ecclesiastical* (for neither argument nor dogma find a fitting place in verse) that we could willingly part with. Wordsworth's belief that the language of the common people may be used as the language of poetry was totally inoperative when he composed a sonnet. He wrote at such times in the best diction he could command, and the language like the thought is that of a great master.—DENNIS, JOHN, 1873–80, *English Sonnets: A Selection, note.*

Wordsworth's predilection for the sonnet, and the success wherewith he has cultivated a kind which might seem somewhat artificial for a poet of nature and of the fields, are things to be observed, and important to take account of in the final estimate. He has really excelled in it, and many of his sonnets approach perfection. Although English literature is singularly rich in poetical jewels of this kind, Wordsworth, to my taste, has in this respect rivals, but no superiors. The piece on the sonnet itself, that composed on Westminster Bridge, that addressed to Milton, and half a hundred others (he wrote four hundred), show that combination of ingenious turn and victorious final touch which is the triumph of the kind.—SCHERER, EDMOND, 1880–91, *Wordsworth and Modern Poetry in England, Essays on English Literature, tr. Saintsbury, p.* 196.

He had a right to think highly of his sonnets; for when they are good they surpass those of his contemporaries; but, unfortunately, the number of his good sonnets is small. He has written hundreds (say five hundred in round figures), of which it would be difficult to name twenty that substantiate his poetic greatness. He wrote upon all occasions, and many of his occasions, it must be confessed, are of the slightest. To stub his toe was to set his poetic feet in motion, and to evolve a train of philosophical musings upon toes in particular and things in general. His prime defect (*me judice*) is his stupendous egotism, which dwarfed that of Milton, great as it was, and which led him to worship himself, morning, noon, and night. Sacred in his own eye, he could not be otherwise in the eyes of others. That he was, or could be tedious, never entered into his calculation. I honor his memory this side of idolatry, as Ben Jonson wrote of Shakspere, but when I read his sonnets I am constrained to say, with the wicked Jeffrey, "This will never do."—STODDARD, RICHARD HENRY, 1881, *The Sonnet in English Poetry, Scribner's Monthly, vol.* 22, *p.* 918.

Wordsworth's sonnets are among his most perfect productions, from the artistic point of view. He brought the sonnet into fashion after it had been neglected since Milton's death. He had the feeling for rhetorical expression as well as the rhyming power requisite to bring this form to its finish and perfection. Many of his sonnets, like the one beginning, "The world is too much with us," and, "Scorn not the sonnet, critic," have a permanent lodgment in the general memory.—JOHNSON, CHARLES F., 1885, *Three Americans and Three Englishmen, p.* 37.

Every good sonnet of Wordsworth's is like a mirror wherein we see his poetic nature reflected; and is there another man who would so well stand the test of such a multitude of mirrors? His fatal habit of rhyming upon everything resulted, in his sonnet work, in the many more or less indifferent productions to be found in the "Duddon," and more especially in the Ecclesiastical Series: but speaking generally, his sonnets are freer from his besetting sins than one would naturally expect. He is, and must always be, considered one of the greatest of English sonneteers. At his very best he is *the* greatest. His sonnets are mostly as beautiful and limpid as an amber tinted stream, and the thoughts which are their motives as clear as the large pebbly stones in the shallows thereof. In a word, he, at his best, knew what he wanted to say, and could say it in his own manner supremely well.—SHARP, WILLIAM, 1886, *Sonnets of this Century, p.* 325, *note.*

Nowhere, except in a very few of Milton's, in a very few of Shakespeare's, does that crystallization of thought, the sonnet, carry such largeness and illumination as in Wordsworth's sonnets. — SPOFFORD, HARRIET PRESCOTT, 1890, *A Selection of Wordsworth's Sonnets, The Book Buyer, vol.* 7, *p.* 497.

The greatest of English Sonneteers.—CORSON, HIRAM, 1892, *A Primer of English Verse, p.* 143.

On the response of the common conscience of men Wordsworth's sonnets may rely for their perpetual justification.—QUILLER-COUCH, A. T., 1897, *English Sonnets, Introduction, p.* xix.

In the sonnets, on the other hand, we find much of Wordsworth's finest work, alike in substance and in form. "The sonnet's scanty plot of ground" suited him so well because it forced him to be at once concise and dignified, and yet allowed him to say straight out the particular message or emotion which was possessing him. . . . Taking them at their best you will find that nowhere in his work has he put so much of his finest self into so narrow a compass. Nowhere are there so many splendid single lines, lines of such weight, such imaginative ardour. And these lines have nothing to lose by their context, as almost all the fine lines which we find in the blank verse poems have to lose.—SYMONS, ARTHUR, 1902, *Wordsworth, Fortnightly Review, vol.* 77, *p.* 42.

GENERAL

Wordsworth will . . . leave behind him a name unique in his way. He will rank among the very first poets, and probably possesses a mass of merits superior to all, except only Shakspeare. This is doing much, yet would he be a happier man if he did more.—SOUTHEY, ROBERT, 1804, *To John Rickman, Life and Correspondence, ed. C. C. Southey, ch.* x.

Southey's "Madoc" is in the press, I understand, and will make its appearance the beginning of winter. Wordsworth's Poems, for he has two great ones, that is, long ones, will not be published so soon. One of these is to be called the "Recluse," and the other is to be a history of himself and his thoughts; this philosophy of egotism and shadowy refinements really spoils a great genius for poetry. We shall have a few exquisite gleams of natural feeling, sunk in a dull ugly ground of trash and affectation. I cannot forgive your expression, "Wordsworth & Co.;" he merits criticism, but surely not contempt; to class him with his imitators is the greatest of all contempt. I thought our perusal of the "Lyrical Ballads" in the Temple would have prevented this; we found much to admire, but you will not admire. Sharp, however, is in the other extreme, I admit; but I insist it is the better of the two: he has been living at the Lakes, with these crazed poets; Wordsworth read him some thousand lines, and he repeated to me a few of these one day, which I could not worship as he wished me.—HORNER, FRANCIS, 1804, *Letter to Francis Jeffrey, Aug.* 13; *Memoirs and Correspondence, vol.* I, *p.* 272.

Trouble not yourself about their present reception; of what moment is that compared with what I trust is their destiny? To console the afflicted; to add sunshine to daylight, by making the happy happier; to teach the young, and the gracious of every age, to see, to think, and feel, and therefore to become more actively and securely virtuous—this is their office, which I trust they will faithfully perform, long after we (that is, all that is mortal of us) are mouldered in our graves.—WORDSWORTH, WILLIAM, 1807, *Letter to Lady Beaumont, May* 21; *Knight's Life of Wordsworth, vol.* II, *p.* 88.

I have just got, by a most lucky chance, Wordsworth's new Poems. I owe them some most delightful hours of abstraction from the petty vexations of the little world where I live, and the horrible dangers of the great world, to which my feelings are attached. I applied to him his own verses:—

Blessings be with them, and eternal praise,
Who gave us nobler loves and nobler cares—
the Poëts.

The Sonnets on Switzerland and on Milton are sublime. Some of the others are in a style of severe simplicity, sometimes bordering on the hardness and dryness of some of Milton's Sonnets. Perhaps it might please him to know, that his poetry has given these feelings to one at so vast a distance: it is not worth adding, to one who formerly had foolish prejudices against him.—MACKINTOSH, SIR JAMES, 1808, *Journal, July* 6; *Memoirs of Mackintosh, ed. his Son, vol.* I, *p.* 409.

Next comes the dull disciple of thy school,
That mild apostate from poetic rule,
The simple Wordsworth, framer of a lay
As soft as evening in his favourite May,
Who warns his friend "to shake off toil and trouble,
And quit his books, for fear of growing double;"
Who, both by precept and example, shows
That prose is verse, and verse is merely prose:
Convincing all, by demonstration plain,
Poetic souls delight in prose inane;
And Christmas stories, tortured into rhyme,
Contain the essence of the true sublime.

—BYRON, LORD 1809, *English Bards and Scotch Reviewers.*

Wordsworth, whose porcelain was taken for delf.

—HUNT, LEIGH, 1811, *The Feast of the Poets.*

We do not want Mr. Wordsworth to write like Pope or Prior, nor to dedicate his muse to subjects which he does not himself think interesting. We are prepared, on the contrary, to listen with a far deeper delight to the songs of his mountain solitude, and to gaze on his mellow pictures of simple happiness and affection, and his lofty sketches of human worth and energy; and we only beg, that we may have these noble elements of his poetry, without the debasement of childish language, mean incidents, and incongruous images.—JEFFREY, FRANCIS LORD, 1812, *Wilson's Poems, Edinburgh Review, vol.* 19, *p.* 375.

My Dear Jeffrey,—I am much obliged to you for the Review, and shall exercise the privilege of an old friend in making some observations upon it. I have not read the review of Wordsworth, because the subject is to me so very uninteresting; but, may I ask, do not such repeated attacks upon a man wear in some little degree the shape of persecution?—SMITH, SYDNEY, 1814, *To Jeffrey, A Selection from the Letters of the Rev. Sydney Smith, ed. Mrs. Austin.*

Great being, who will hereafter be ranked as one who had a portion of the spirit of the mighty ones, especially Milton; but who did not possess the power of using that spirit otherwise than with reference to himself, and so as to excite a reflex action only.—HAYDON, BENJAMIN ROBERT, 1815, *Journal.*

He of the cloud, the cataract, the lake,
Who on Helvellyn's summit, wide awake,
Catches his freshness from Archangel's wing.

—KEATS, JOHN, 1817, *Sonnet, addressed to Haydon.*

First; an austere purity of language, both grammatically and logically; in short, a perfect appropriateness of the words to the meaning. . . . The second characteristic excellence of Mr. Wordsworth's work is: a correspondent weight and sanity of the Thoughts and Sentiments,—won, not from books; but—from the poet's own meditative observation. They are *fresh* and have the dew upon them. . . . Even throughout his smaller poems there is scarcely one, which is not rendered valuable by some just and original reflection. . . . Third; . . . the sinewy strength and originality of single lines and paragraphs; the frequent *curiosa felicitas* of his diction. . . . Fourth; the perfect truth of nature in his images and descriptions, as taken immediately from nature, and proving a long and genial intimacy with the very spirit which gives the physiognomic expression to all the works of nature. . . . Fifth; a meditative pathos, a union of deep and subtle thought with sensibility; a sympathy with man as man,—the sympathy of a contemplator, rather than a fellow-sufferer or co-mate (*spectator, haud particeps*), but of a contemplator, from whose views no difference of rank conceals the sameness of nature; no injuries of wind or weather, or toil, or even of ignorance, wholly disguise the human face divine. . . . Here the man and Poet find themselves in each other . . . Last, and pre-eminently, I challenge for this poet the gift of Imagination in the highest and strictest sense of the word. In the play of *fancy*, Wordsworth, to my feelings, is not always graceful, and sometimes recondite. The *likeness* is occasionally too strange, or demands too peculiar a point of view, or is such as appears the creature of predetermined research, rather than spontaneous presentation. Indeed, his fancy seldom displays itself, as mere and unmodified fancy. But in imaginative power he stands nearest of all modern writers to Shakspeare and Milton; and yet in a kind perfectly unborrowed and his own. To employ his own words, which are at once an instance and an illustration, he does indeed to all thoughts and to all objects—

Add the gleam,
The light that never was, on sea or land,
The consecration, and the poet's dream.

—COLERIDGE, SAMUEL TAYLOR, 1817, *Biographia Literaria, ch.* xxii.

Mr. Wordsworth is the most original poet now living. He is the reverse of Walter Scott in all his defects and excellences. He has nearly all that the other wants, and wants all that the other possesses. His poetry is not external, but internal; it does not depend upon tradition, or story, or old song; he furnishes it from his own mind and is his own subject. He is the poet of mere sentiment. . . . He has produced a deeper impression, and on a smaller circle, than any other of his contemporaries. His powers have been mistaken by the age, nor does he exactly understand them himself. He cannot form a whole. He has not the constructive faculty. He can give only the fine tones of thought, drawn from his mind by accident or nature, like the sounds drawn from the Æolian harp by the wandering gale. He is totally deficient in all the machinery of poetry.—HAZLITT, WILLIAM, 1818, *Lectures on the English Poets, Lecture* viii.

He had a mind which was somehow
At once circumference and centre
Of all he might or feel or know;
Nothing went ever out, although
Something did ever enter.
He had as much imagination
As a pint-pot;—he never could
Fancy another situation,
From which to dart his contemplation,
Than that wherein he stood.
Yet his was individual mind,
And new-created all he saw
In a new manner, and refined
Those new creations, and combined
Them by a master-spirit's law.
Thus—although imaginative—
An apprehension clear, intense,
Of his mind's work, had made alive
The things it wrought on; I believe
Wakening a sort of thought in sense.
—SHELLY, PERCY BYSSHE, 1819, *Peter Bell the Third.*

And first—in the great walk of poesy—is Wordsworth, who, if he stood alone, would vindicate the immortality of his art. He has, in his works, built up a rock of defense for his species, which will resist the mightiest tides of demoralizing luxury. Setting aside the varied and majestic harmony of his verse—the freshness and the grandeur of his descriptions—the exquisite softness of his delineations of character—and the high and rapturous spirit of his choral songs—we may pronounce his "divine philosophy" as unequaled by any preceding bard. And surely it is no small proof of the infinity of the resources of genius, that, in this late age of the world, the first of all philosophic poets should have arisen, to open a new vein of sentiment and thought, deeper and richer than yet had been laid bare to mortal eyes. —TALFOURD, THOMAS NOON, 1820, *London Retrospective Review, Critical and Miscellaneous Writings, p.* 212.

The descriptive poetry of the present day has been called by its cultivators a return to nature. Nothing is more impertinent than this pretension. Poetry cannot travel out of the regions of its birth, the uncultivated lands of semi-civilised men. Mr. Wordsworth, the great leader of the returners to nature, cannot describe a scene under his own eyes without putting into it the shadow of a Danish boy or the living ghost of Lucy Gray, or some similar phantastical parturition of the moods of his own mind.—PEACOCK, THOMAS LOVE, 1820, *The Four Ages of Poetry, Calidore and Miscellanea, p.* 64.

I do not know a man more to be venerated for uprightness of heart and loftiness of genius. Why he will sometimes choose to crawl upon all fours, when God has given him so noble a countenance to lift to heaven, I am as little able to account for, as for his quarrelling (as you tell me) with the wrinkles which time and meditation have stamped his brow withal.—SCOTT, SIR WALTER, 1820, *To Allan Cunningham, Nov.; Life of Scott by Lockhart, ch.* l.

The Muse of this poet is of a singular cast and temperament. Objects the most simple, and themes the most familiar, are treated by her in a style peculiarly her own: but if these objects and these themes have been such, as, with a great number of readers, to excite surprise and provoke ridicule, this must have arisen rather in compliance with the tone of what is called fashionable criticism, than from an impartial perusal of the poems themselves. The purest moral strain, and the loftiest feelings of humanity, pervade the productions of Mr. Wordsworth: and these, at times, are united with so much sweetness of diction, and with such just and powerful views of religion that *that* bosom must be taxed with insensibility which is impervious to their impression.—DIBDIN, THOMAS FROGNALL, 1824, *The Library Companion, p.* 738, *note.*

The highest quality of art is to conceal itself: these peasants of Schiller's are what every one imagines he could imitate successfully; yet in the hands of any but a true and strong-minded poet they dwindle into repulsive coarseness or mawkish insipidity. Among our own writers, who have tried such subjects, we remember none that has succeeded equally with Schiller. One potent but ill-fated genius has, in far different circumstances and with far other means, shown that he could have equalled him: the "Cotter's Saturday Night" of Burns is, in its own humble way, as quietly beautiful, as *simplix munditiis*, as the scenes of *Tell*. No other has even approached them; though some gifted persons have attempted it. Mr. Wordsworth is no ordinary man; nor are his pedlars, and leech-gatherers, and dalesmen, without their attractions and their moral; but they sink into whining drivellers beside "Rösselmann the Priest," "Ulric the Smith," "Hans of the Wall," and the other sturdy confederates of Rütli.—CARLYLE, THOMAS, 1825–45, *Life of Friedrich Schiller, pt.* iii, *p.* 205.

Next to Byron, there is no poet whose writings have had so much influence on the taste of the age as Wordsworth. Byron drove on through the upper air till the thunder of his wheels died on the ear. Wordsworth drove to Parnassus by the lower road, got sometims lost in bushes and lowland fogs, and was much molested by mosquito critics. — LONGFELLOW, HENRY WADSWORTH, 1829, *Note Book, Life by S. Longfellow, vol.* I, *p.* 172.

Wordsworth, whose thoughts acquaint us
with our own.
—ELLIOTT, EBENEZER, 1829, *The Village Patriarch, Book* iv.

In spite of the reverence which we feel for the genius of Mr. Wordsworth, we cannot but think that the minuteness of his descriptions often diminishes their effect. He has accustomed himself to gaze on nature with the eye of a lover—to dwell on every feature, and to mark every change of aspect. Those beauties which strike the most negligent observer, and those which only a close attention discovers, are equally familiar to him, and are equally prominent in his poetry.—MACAULAY, THOMAS BABINGTON, 1831, *Moore's Life of Lord Byron, Edinburgh Review; Critical and Miscellaneous Essays.*

In describing external nature as she is, no poet perhaps has excelled Wordsworth —not even Thomson; in imbuing her and making her pregnant with spiritualities, till the mighty mother teems with "beauty far more beauteous" than she had ever rejoiced in till he held communion with her —therein lies his own especial glory, and therein the immortal evidences of the might of his creative imagination. All men at times "muse on nature with a poet's eye,"—but Wordsworth ever—and his soul has grown religious from worship. Every rock is an altar—every grove a shrine. We fear that there will be sectarians even in this Natural Religion till the end of time. But he is the High Priest of Nature—or, to use his own words, or nearly so, he is the High Priest "in the metropolitan temple built by Nature in the heart of mighty poets."—WILSON, JOHN, 1831, *An Hour's Talk About Poetry, Recreations of Christopher North; Blackwood's Magazine, vol.* 30.

I have only a single remark to make on the poetry of Wordsworth, and I do it because I never saw the remark made before. It relates to the richness of his works for quotations. For these they are a mine that is altogether inexhaustible. There is nothing in nature that you may not get a quotation out of Wordsworth to suit, and a quotation too that breathes the very soul of poetry. There are only three books in the world that are worth the opening in search of mottos and quotations, and all of them are alike rich. These are, the Old Testament, Shakspeare, and the poetical works of Wordsworth, and, strange to say, the "Excursion" abounds most in them.—HOGG, JAMES, 1832, *Autobiography.*

Although by his position standing aloof, as it were, from man, he had nothing in him foreign to humanity. His contemplative habits led him to scrutinize his species with a philosophic eye, and by levelling in his own mind the artificial distinctions of society, extended his sympathies to the humblest of his fellow-creatures. A holy calm is shed over his writings, whose general purpose seems to be to reconcile man with himself and his destiny, by furnishing him with a key to the mysteries of his present condition. Wordsworth's soul is instinct with such a pure love of nature, so much simplicity, or as the French call it, loyalty of purpose, that had he not entangled himself in an unlucky theory, he might have shared the popularity of Cowper, whom he must be admitted to surpass in the general elevation, as well as the benevolence of his sentiments. As it is, there are few who read, and fewer still who relish him.—PRESCOTT, WILLIAM HICKLING, 1832, *English Literature of the Nineteenth Century, North American Review, vol.* 35, *p.* 174.

'Tis thine to celebrate the thoughts that make
The life of souls, the truths for whose sweet sake
We to ourselves and to our God are dear.
Of nature's inner shrine thou art the priest,
Where most she works when we perceive her least.
—COLERIDGE, HARTLEY, 1833, *To Wordsworth.*

Among living authors, not one has shown greater command of diction than Mr. Wordsworth; suiting his style to his subjects with consummate address, though sometimes with unhappy effect, from the difficulty, not to say the impossibility, of making general readers partakers, by direct sympathy, with his peculiar experiences and imaginings,—that is, see with his eyes, hear with his ears, feel with his heart, and think with his mind,—possess them wholly with his own spirit, or for the time being absorb each of them into himself. In an age of poetical innovations, Mr. Wordsworth has undoubtedly been one of the boldest and most successful adventurers.—MONTGOMERY, JAMES, 1833, *Lectures on General Literature, Poetry, etc., p.* 118.

I shall never forget with what feeling my friend Bryant, some years ago, described to me the effect produced upon him by his meeting for the first time with Wordsworth's Ballads. He lived, when quite young, where but a few works of poetry were to be had; at a period, too, when Pope was still the great idol in the Temple of Art. He said that, upon opening Wordsworth, a thousand springs seemed to gush up at once in his heart, and the face of Nature, of a sudden, to change into a strange freshness and life. He had felt the sympathetic touch from an according mind; and you see how instantly his powers and affections shot over the Earth and through his kind.—DANA, RICHARD HENRY, 1833, *The Idle Man, Preface.*

Wordsworth is the poet of nature and man,—not of humble life, as some have said, but of noble emotions, lofty feelings, and whatever tends to exalt man and elevate him on the table-land of honor, morality and religion. His style is worthy of his topics,—simple, unaffected and vigorous: he occasionally becomes too minute in his delineations, and some of the subjects which he treats are too homely for inspiration. His poetry is making its way, as true feeling and impassioned thought ever will.—CUNNINGHAM, ALLAN, 1833, *Biographical and Critical History of the Literature of the Last Fifty Years.*

. . . that reverend Priest of Poesy,
Whose presence shines upon these twilight times,
Hath, in "The Churchyard in the Mountains," done
One sacrifice whose scent shall fill the world.
—ALFORD, HENRY, 1835, *The School of the Heart.*

I have been so self-indulgent as to possess myself of Wordsworth at full length, and I thoroughly like much of the contents of the first three volumes, which I fancy are only the low vestibule of the three remaining ones. I never before met with so many of my own feelings expressed just as I could like them.—ELIOT, GEORGE (MARY ANN CROSS), 1839, *To Miss Lewis, Nov,* 22; *George Eliot's Life as Related in her Letters and Journals, ed. Cross, vol.* I, *p.* 44.

Genius is not a creator, in the sense of fancying or feigning what does not exist. Its distinction is, to discern more of truth than common minds. It sees under disguises and humble forms everlasting beauty. This it is the prerogative of Wordsworth to discern and reveal in the walks of life, in the common human heart. He has revealed the loveliness of the primitive feelings, of the universal affections, of the human soul. The grand truth which pervades his poetry is that the beautiful is not confined—the rare, the new, the distant,—to scenery and modes of life open only to the few; but that it is poured forth profusely on the common earth and sky, that it gleams from the loneliest flower, that it lights up the humblest sphere, that the sweetest affections lodge in lowly hearts, that there is sacredness, dignity, and loveliness in lives which few eyes rest on,—that, even in the absence of all intellectual culture, the domestic relations can quietly nourish that disinterestedness which is the element of all greatness, and without which intellectual power is a splendid deformity. Wordsworth is the poet of humanity; he teaches reverence for our universal nature; he breaks down the fictitious barriers between human hearts.—CHANNING, WILLIAM ELLERY, 1841, *The Present Age, Addresses.*

As the chief of the movement, the Xenophon of the return, we are bound to acknowledge this great Wordsworth, and to admire how, in a bravery bravest of all because born of love, in a passionate unreservedness sprung of genius, and to the actual scandal of the world which stared at the filial familiarity, he threw himself not at the feet of Nature, but straightway and right tenderly upon her bosom. And so, trustfully as child before mother, self-renouncingly as child after sin, absorbed away from the consideration of publics and critics as child at play-hours, with a simplicity startling to the *blasé* critical ear as inventiveness, with an innocent utterance felt by the competent thinker to be wisdom, and with a faithfulness to natural impressions acknowledged since by all to be the highest art,—this William Wordsworth did sing his "Lyrical Ballads" where the "Art of criticism" had been sung before, and "the world would not let them die."—BROWNING, ELIZABETH BARRETT, 1843–63, *The Book of the Poets.*

Thro' clouds and darkness to meridian height
Of glory, thou hast upward climbed, and now
In empyrean blue, with cloudless brow
Look'st o'er a prospect clear and infinite—
Rejoicing, by rejoicing in, thy light!
The vapours, which at first would not allow
Full view of thee, are gone, we know not how;
Absorbed into thy splendor, and thy might!
And now, great spirit, thou unto thy close
Art hastening, and trails of glory make
The heavens gorgeous for thy repose—
Thou hast made day for all men to partake,
And having thought of others and their woes,
Shalt be remembered now for thy own sake.
—ELLISON, HENRY, 1844, *To Wordsworth, The Poetry of Real Life.*

When Mr. Wordsworth first stood before the world as a poet, he might as well, for the sorriness of his reception, have stood before the world as a prophet. In some such position, perhaps, it may be said he actually did stand; and he had a prophet's fare in a shower of stones. . . . Mr. Wordsworth began his day with a dignity and determination of purpose, which might well have startled the public and all its small poets and critics, his natural enemies. He laid down fixed principles in his prefaces, and carried them out with rigid boldness, in his poems; and when the world laughed, he bore it well, for his logic apprized him of what should follow: nor was he without the sympathy of Coleridge and a few other first-rate intellects. —HORNE, RICHARD HENGIST, 1844, *A New Spirit of the Age, pp.* 177, 179.

To estimate the degree of longevity which will attach to Wordsworth's poetry might be difficult; but as he has built upon the enduring rock as well as the shifting sand, we cannot tolerate the idea that he will be swept away with things forgotten. As we pause thoughtfully before some of the majestic fabrics of his genius, they seem to wear the look of eternity. And when we consider the vast debt of delight we owe to him, the new inspiration he poured into poetry, and his delivery of it from the bondage of a hundred and fifty years,—the many teasing persecutions he has endured for humanity and literature; —when we think of the consecrations he has shed upon our present existence, and the splendor of the vistas he has opened beyond the grave,—his desire to bring the harsh domain of the actual into closer vicinity to the sunny land of the ideal,—his kindling strains for freedom and right, —his warm sympathy with all that elevates and ennobles our being, and the sway he has displayed over its holiest and tenderest affections,—and the many images of beauty and grace with which he has brightened our daily life;—when we consider these, his faults and errors seem to dwindle into insignificance; reverence and love leap to our lips, and warm from the heart and brain springs our benison.

"Blessings be on him, and eternal praise,
Who gave us nobler loves and nobler cares."
—WHIPPLE, EDWIN P., 1844, *Wordsworth, North American Review, Oct.; Essays and Reviews.*

Subsequently to Shakspere, these notices, as of all phenomena whatsoever that demanded a familiarity with nature in the spirit of love, became rarer and rarer. At length, as the eighteenth century was winding up its accounts, forth stepped William Wordsworth; of whom, as a reader of all pages in nature, it may be said that, if we except Dampier, the admirable buccaneer, the gentle *flibustier*, and some few professional naturalists, he first and he last looked at natural objects with the eye that neither will be dazzled from without nor cheated by preconceptions from within. Most men look at nature in the hurry of a confusion that distinguishes nothing; *their* error is from without. Pope, again, and many who live in towns, make such blunders as that of supposing the moon to tip with silver the hills *behind* which she is rising, not by erroneous use of their eyes (for they use them not at all), but by inveterate preconceptions. Scarcely has there been a poet with what could be called a learned eye, or an eye *extensively* learned, before Wordsworth. Much affectation there has been of that sort since *his* rise, and at all times much counterfeit enthusiasm; but the sum of the matter is this,—that Wordsworth had his passion for nature fixed in his blood; it was a necessity, like that of the mulberry-leaf to the silkworm; and through his commerce with nature did he live and breathe. Hence it was—viz. from the *truth* of his love—that his knowledge grew; whilst most others, being merely hypocrites in their love, have turned out merely sciolists in their knowledge. This chapter, therefore, of *sky*-scenery may be said to have been revivified amongst the resources of poetry by Wordsworth—rekindled, if not absolutely kindled.—DE QUINCEY, THOMAS, 1845-57, *On Wordsworth's Poetry, Works, ed. Masson. vol.* XI, *p.* 318.

My admiration of Wordsworth is composed of two different elements, namely, my admiration of what is peculiar to his genius, and my admiration of what he has in common with other first-class poets; I must therefore adjust the balance between these two admirations; and therefore I cannot agree with those who admire even the inferior poems of his earlier and most characteristic manner more than the best poems written in his later style. . . . Without what is absolutely peculiar to his genius, and to it alone, Wordsworth would not have been a very great, that is, an original poet; but if this, his special merit, had been his only merit, he would have lacked several of those perfections which, in their aggregate alone, make up a first-class poet, as well as an original poet.—COLERIDGE, SARA, 1845, *Letter to Aubrey De Vere, Recollections, pp.* 203, 204.

Others, perchance, as keenly felt,
As musically sang as he;
To Nature as devoutly knelt,
Or toil'd to serve humanity:
But none with those ethereal notes,
That star-like sweep of self-control;
The insight into worlds unseen,
The lucid sanity of soul.
The fever of our fretful life,
The autumn poison of the air,
The soul with its own self at strife,
He saw and felt, but could not share:
With eye made clear by pureness, pierced
The life of Man and Nature through;
And read the heart of common things,
Till new seem'd old, and old was new.

—PALGRAVE, FRANCIS TURNER, 1845, *William Wordsworth.*

Wordsworth, I am told, does not care for music! And it is very likely, for music (to judge from his verses) does not seem to care for him. I was astonished the other day, on looking in his works for the first time after a long interval, to find how deficient he was in all that may be called the musical side of a poet's nature,—the genial, the animal-spirited or bird-like,—the happily accordant. Indeed he does not appear to me, now, more than half the man I once took him for, when I was among those who came to the "rescue" for him, and exaggerated his works in the heat of "reaction." . . . Wordsworth is indeed "cold and diffuse," notwithstanding "all the fine things" which, you justly add, he contains. He seems to like nothing heartily, except the talking about it; and is in danger of being taken by posterity (who will certainly never read two-thirds of him) for a kind of puritan retainer of the Establishment, melancholy in his recommendations of mirth, and perplexed between prudence and pragmaticalness, subserviency and ascendency, retrospection and innovation. I should infallibly (or far as lay in my power) have deposed the god I helped to set up, and put Coleridge in his stead (I mean in the last edition of the "Feast of the Poets"), but I did not like to hurt his feelings in his old age.—HUNT, LEIGH, 1848, *Correspondence, vol.* II, *pp.* 92, 93.

He is not a Shakspeare, but he is the

greatest poet of the day; and this is more remarkable, as he is, par excellence, a didactic poet.—OSSOLI, MARGARET FULLER, 1850? *Modern British Poets; Art, Literature and the Drama, p.* 101.

He, too, upon a wintry clime
Had fallen—on this iron time
Of doubts, disputes, distractions, fears.
He found us when the age had bound
Our souls in its benumbing round;
He spoke, and loosed our heart in tears,
He laid us as we lay at birth
On the cool flowery lap of earth;
Smiles broke from us and we had ease.
The hills were round us, and the breeze
Went o'er the sun-lit fields again;
Our foreheads felt the wind and rain.

. . . .

Others will teach us how to dare,
And against fear our breast to steel;
Others will strengthen us to bear—
But who, ah who, will make us feel?
The cloud of mortal destiny,
Others will front it fearlessly—
But who, like him, will put it by?

—ARNOLD, MATTHEW, 1850, *Memorial Verses.*

That we would assign to Wordsworth a high place among the poets of England the whole tenor of our observations hitherto will have made clear. At the same time, that he falls short of the very highest rank, that he does not stand on the very top of our English Parnassus, where Chaucer, Milton, and Spenser keep reverent company with Shakespeare, but rather on that upper slope of the mountain whence these greatest are visible, and where various other poets hold perhaps as just, if not so fixed, a footing: this also we have sought to convey as part of our general impression. We do not think, for example, that Wordsworth was so great a poet as Burns; and, if it is only in respect of general mental vigour and capacity, and not in respect of poetic genius *per se*, that Dryden, Pope, and Coleridge, could be justly put in comparison with Wordsworth, and, being so put in comparison, preferred to him on the whole, yet there are others in our list of poets for whom, even after the ground of competition has been thus restricted, we believe it would be possible to take up the quarrel. With all the faults of Byron, both moral and literary, the poetic efflux in *him* came from greater constitutional depths, and brought, if less pure, at least more fervent, matter with it than the poetry of Wordsworth: had Keats and Shelley lived longer, even those that sneer at the Byronic might have seen poets comparable, in their estimation, to the Patriarch of the Lakes; and, should our noble Tennyson survive as a constant writer till his black locks have grown grey, one sees qualities in him that predict for him more than a Wordsworth's fame.—MASSON, DAVID, 1850–74, *Wordsworth, Shelley, Keats and Other Essays, p.* 62.

This laurel greener from the brows
Of him that utter'd nothing base.

—TENNYSON, LORD, 1851, *Dedication to the Queen.*

Tennyson says of the laureate wreath which he so deservedly wears, that it is

"Greener from the brows
Of him who uttered nothing base."

And this, which seems at first sight negative praise, is, in reality, a proof of exquisite discernment; for it is just that which constitutes the marked distinction between Wordsworth and the other really original poets who are likely to share with him the honour of representing poetically to posterity the early part of the nineteenth century. In their crowns there is alloy, both moral and intellectual. His may not be of so imperial a fashion; the gems that stud it may be less dazzling, but the gold is of a ethereal temper, and there is no taint upon his robe. Weakness, incompleteness, imperfection, he had, for he was a mortal man of limited faculties, but spotless purity is not to be denied him—he uttered nothing base.—BRIMLEY, GEORGE, 1851–58, *Essays, ed. Clark, p.* 102.

A breath of the mountains, fresh born in the regions majestic,
That look with their eye-daring summits deep into the sky.
The voice of great Nature; sublime with her lofty conceptions,
Yet earnest and simple as any sweet child of the green lowly vale.

—MEREDITH, GEORGE, 1851, *Works, vol.* XXXI, *p,* 140.

Never, perhaps, in the whole range of literary history, from Homer downwards, did any individual, throughout the course of a long life, dedicate himself to poetry with a devotion so pure, so perfect, and so uninterrupted, as he did. It was not his amusement, his recreation, his mere pleasure—it was the main, the serious, the solemn business of his being. . . . It was his morning, noon, and evening thought, the object of his out-of-door rambles; the subject of his in-door reflections; and, as an art, he studied it as severely as ever Canova did sculpture, or Michael Angelo painting.—MOIR, D. M., 1851–52, *Sketches of the Poetical Literature of the Past Half-Century*, p. 66.

> How welcome to our ears, long pained
> By strife of sect and party noise,
> The book-like murmur of his song
> Of nature's simple joys!
> The violet by its mossy stone,
> The primrose by the river's brim,
> And chance-sown daffodil, have found
> Immortal life through him.
> The sunrise on his breezy lake,
> The rosy tints his sunset brought,
> World-seen, are gladdening all the vales
> And mountain-peaks of thought.

—WHITTIER, JOHN GREENLEAF, 1852, *Wordsworth.*

Little attended to as works of that stamp generally are in the outset, they gradually, but unceasingly, rose in public estimation; they took a lasting hold of the highly educated youth of the next generation; and he now numbers among his devout worshippers many of the ablest men, profound thinkers, and most accomplished and discriminating women, of the age. Indeed, great numbers of persons whose mental powers, cultivated taste, and extensive acquirements entitle their opinion to the very highest consideration, yield him an admiration approaching to idolatry, and assign him a place second only to Milton in English poetry. He is regarded by them in much the same light that Goethe is by the admiring and impassioned multitudes of the Fatherland.—ALISON, SIR ARCHIBALD, 1853–59, *History of Europe*, 1815–1852, *vol.* I, *ch.* v.

> We know a poet rich in thought, profuse
> In bounty; but his grain wants winnowing;
> There hangs much chaff about, barndoor dust,
> Cobwebs, small insects: it might make a loaf,
> A good large loaf of household bread; but flour
> Must be well-bolted for a dainty roll.

—LANDOR, WALTER SAVAGE, 1853, *The Last Fruit off an Old Tree.*

Wordsworth is more like Scott, and understands how to be happy, but yet cannot altogether rid himself of the sense that he is a philosopher, and ought always to be saying something wise. He has also a vague notion that Nature would not be able to get on well without Wordsworth; and finds a considerable part of his pleasure in looking at himself as well as at her.—RUSKIN, JOHN, 1856, *Modern Painters, vol.* III, *pt.* iv.

The exceptional fact of the period is the genius of Wordsworth. He had no master but nature and solitude. "He wrote a poem," says Landor, "without the aid of war." His verse is the voice of sanity in a worldly and ambitious age. One regrets that his temperament was not more liquid and musical. He has written longer than he was inspired. But for the rest, he has no competitor.—EMERSON, RALPH WALDO, 1856–90, *English Traits, p.* 243.

He's good, you know, but unbearable.—ROSSETTI, DANTE GABRIEL, 1859, *Letters to William Allingham, p.* 218.

Byron's merits are on the surface This is not the case with Wordsworth. You must love Wordsworth ere he will seem worthy of your love.—TENNYSON, ALFRED LORD, 1869, *Life by his Son, vol.* II, *p.* 69.

His fame has slowly climbed from stage to stage until now his influence is perceived in all the English poetry of the day. If this were the place to criticise his poetry, I should say, of his more stately poems in blank verse, that they often lack compression,—that the thought suffers by too great expansion. Wordsworth was unnecessarily afraid of being epigrammatic. He abhorred what is called a point as much as Dennis is said to have abhorred a pun. Yet I must own that even his most diffuse amplifications have in them a certain grandeur that fills the mind.—BRYANT, WILLIAM CULLEN, 1870, *A New Library of Poetry and Song, Introduction, vol.* I, *p.* 42.

Does it not sometimes come over one (just the least in the world) that one would give anything for a bit of nature pure and simple, without quite so strong a flavor of W. W.? W. W. is, of course, sublime and all that—but! For my part, I will make a clean breast of it, and confess that I can't look at a mountain without fancying the late laureate's gigantic Roman nose thrust between me and it, and thinking of Dean Swift's profane version of *Romanos rerum dominos* into *Roman nose! a rare un! dom your nose!*—LOWELL, JAMES RUSSELL, 1871, *A Good Word for Winter, My Study Windows, p.* 37.

A new Cowper, with less talent and more ideas than the other, was essentially an interior man, that is, engrossed by the concerns of the soul. . . . He saw a grandeur, a beauty, lessons in the trivial events which weave the woof of our most common-place days. He needed not for the sake of emotion, either splendid sights or unusual actions. The dazzling glare of the lamps, the pomp of the theatre, would have shocked him; his eyes are too delicate, accustomed to sweet and uniform tints. He was a poet of the twilight. Moral existence in common-place existence, such was his object—the object of his preference. His paintings are cameos with a grey ground, which have a meaning: designedly he suppresses all which ought to please the senses, in order to speak solely to the heart. . . . Half of his pieces are childish, almost foolish; dull events described in a dull style, one nullity after another, and that on principle.—TAINE, H. A., 1871, *History of English Literature, tr. Van Laun, vol.* II, *bk.* iv, *ch.* i, *pp.* 260, 261, 262.

What made Wordsworth's poems a medicine for my state of mind, was that they expressed, not mere outward beauty, but states of feeling, under the excitement of beauty. They seemed to be the very culture of the feelings which I was in quest of. In them I seemed to draw from a source of inward joy, of sympathetic and imaginative pleasure, which could be shared in all by human beings, which had no connexion with struggle or imperfection, but would be made richer by every improvement in the physical or social condititon of mankind. From them I seemed to learn what would be the perennial sources of happiness, when all the greater evils of life shall have been removed. And I felt myself at once better and happier as I came under their influence.—MILL, JOHN STUART, 1873, *Autobiography, p.* 148.

Wordsworth, it is true, is probably now, by most cultivated and intellectual men, admitted to be a great and original writer; a writer whose compositions it is right to be acquainted with as a part of literary history and literary education. Few men would now venture to deny him genius or to treat his poetry with contempt. No one probably would dare to echo or even to defend the ribald abuse of the *Edinburgh Review*. But he is not generally appreciated even now; he is far too little read; and, as I think, for the idlest and weakest of all reasons. He suffers still from the impression produced by attacks made upon him by men who, I should suppose, if they had tried, were incapable of feeling. his beauty and his grandeur, but who seem to me never to have had the common honesty to try. Fastening upon a few obvious defects, seizing upon a few poems (poems admitting of complete defence, and, viewed rightly, full of beauty, yet capable no doubt of being presented in a ridiculous aspect), the critics of the *Edinburgh Review* poured out on Wordsworth abuse, invective, malignant personality, which deterred the unreflecting mass of men from reading for themselves and finding out, as they must have found out, the worthlessness of the criticism. They destroyed his popularity and blighted his reputation, though they have had no power whatever over his fame.—COLERIDGE, SIR JOHN DUKE, 1873, *Wordsworth, Macmillan's Magazine, vol.* 28, *p.* 290.

Wordsworth has dug out of nature the stones and moss and crumbling matters which common men tread upon, and contemplated them through his intellectual microscope, until they have yielded up all their beauty and meaning, and shown on what their motion and vitality depend. And all this knowledge he has kneaded and intermingled with such human matter as is allied to the earthy materials of his themes. The peasant, the beggar, the wagoner, the idiot and his mother, become the actors in his dramas, and we are moved by them and the common objects around them, instead of by those fierce internal throes and terrible disasters which make up the stature and grandeur of antique tragedy.—PROCTER, BRYAN WALLER (BARRY CORNWALL), 1874? *Recollections of Men of Letters, p.* 140.

Those who wish to understand his influence, and experience his peculiar savour, must bear with patience the presence of an alien element in Wordsworth's work, which never coalesced with what is really delightful in it, nor underwent his special power. Who that values his writings most has not felt the intrusion there, from time to time, of something tedious and prosaic? . . . And this duality there—the fitfulness with which the higher qualities manifest themselves in it, gives the effect in his poetry of a power not altogether his own, or under his control, which comes and goes when it will, lifting or lowering a matter, poor in itself; so that that old fancy which made the poet's art an enthusiasm, a form of divine possession, seems almost literally true of him. . . . He meets us with the promise that he has much, and something very peculiar, to give us, if we will follow a certain difficult way, and seems to have the secret of a special and privileged state of mind. And those who have undergone his influence, and followed this difficult way, are like people who have passed through some initiation, a *disciplina arcani*, by submitting to which they become able constantly to distinguish in art, speech, feeling, manners, that which is organic, animated, expressive, from that which is only conventional, derivative, inexpressive.—PATER, WALTER, 1874, *Appreciations, pp.* 38, 39, 40.

He sings of God, of Man, of Nature, and, as the result of these three, of Human Life, and they are all linked by thought, and, through feeling, one to another; so that the result is a complete whole which we can study as if it were a world of his own. —BROOKE, STOPFORD A., 1874, *Theology in the English Poets, p.* 93.

Some of Wordsworth's poetry is, as his person was, too gaunt; it wants a fuller clothing of flesh.—CALVERT, GEORGE H., 1874, *Brief Essays and Brevities, p.* 210.

I gladly take for granted—what is generally acknowledged—that Wordsworth in his best moods reaches a greater height than any other modern Englishman. The word "inspiration" is less forced when applied to his loftiest poetry than when used of any of his contemporaries. With defects too obvious to be mentioned, he can yet pierce furthest behind the veil; and embody most efficiently the thoughts and emotions which come to us in our most solemn and reflective moods. Other poetry becomes trifling when we are making our inevitable passages through the Valley of the Shadow of Death. Wordsworth's alone retains its power. We love him the more as we grow older and become more deeply impressed with the sadness and seriousness of life; we are apt to grow weary of his rivals when we have finally quitted the regions of youthful enchantment. And I take the explanation to be that he is not merely a melodious writer, or a powerful utterer of deep emotion, but a true philosopher. His poetry wears well because it has solid substance. He is a prophet and a moralist as well as a mere singer. His ethical system, in particular, is as distinctive and capable of systematic exposition as that of Butler. By endeavoring to state it in plain prose, we shall see how the poetical power implies a sensitiveness to ideas which, when extracted from the symbolical embodiment, fall spontaneously into a scientific system of thought.—STEPHEN, LESLIE, 1874–79, *Wordsworth's Ethics, Hours in a Library, Second Series, p.* 276.

You have, I think, a more religious regard for him than we on this side of the water: he is not so much honoured in his own country, I mean, his Poetry. I, for one, feel all his lofty aspiration, and occasional Inspiration, but I cannot say that, on the whole, he makes much of it; his little pastoral pieces seem to me to be his best: less than a Quarter of him.—FITZGERALD, EDWARD, 1876, *Letters, vol.* I, *p.* 384.

There *is* the select circle of lovers of Wordsworth—yearly widening—and there are the far-off multitudes of the future to whom WILLIAM WORDSWORTH will be the grand name of the 18th–19th century, and all that SHAKESPEARE and MILTON are now; and consequently the letters of one so chary in letter-writing ought to be put beyond the risks of loss, and given to Literature in entirety and trueness. WORDSWORTH had a morbid dislike of writing letters, his weak eyes throughout rendering all penmanship painful; but the present Editor, while conceding that his letters lack the charm of style of COWPER'S and the vividness and passion of BYRON'S, finds in them, even the hastiest, matter of rarest biographic and interpretative value. He was not a great sentence-maker; in a way prided himself that his letters were so (intentionally) poor as sure to be counted unworthy of publication; and altogether had the prejudices of an earlier day against the giving of letters to the world; but none the less are his letters informed with his intellect and meditative thoughtfulness and exquisiteness of feeling.—GROSART, ALEXANDER B., 1876, *ed., The Prose Works of William Wordsworth, Preface, vol.* I, *p.* xxxi.

The Prodigal Son said to his Father, "Make me as one of thy hired servants." If we transfer this conception from the region of morals or religion to that of poetry, and imagine the poetic son of Father Apollo, overwhelmed with the privileges and heights of sonship, petitioning his parent to be "as one of his hired servants," and, taken at his word, we have a tolerable image of Wordsworth. He *is* a son of Apollo; he works with exquisite humility, and at the same time with a lofty filial feeling, and a self-respect all the more vital through its outward abnegation: yet the work which he produces is not absolutely son's work, but partly servant's work, and would look wholly so at times, but that other portions of it keep us better informed.—ROSSETTI, WILLIAM MICHAEL, 1878, *Lives of Famous Poets, p.* 218.

Confined himself almost exclusively to the confection of primrose pudding and flint soup, flavored with the lesser celandine, and only now and then a beggar-boy boiled down in it to give it a color. The robins and drowned lambs which he was wont to use, when an additional piquancy was needed, were employed so sparingly that they did not destroy in the least the general vegetable tone of his productions; and these form in consequence an unimpeachable Lenten diet.—MALLOCK, W. H., 1878, *Every Man his own Poet, or the Inspired Singer's Recipe Book, p.* 10.

There is no possibility of exhausting Wordsworth, any more than of exhausting Plato. When the time comes for the world to believe that the last word has been said about the great idealist of antiquity, men may perhaps think that Wordsworth also is exhausted. Plato, indeed, moves in a sphere, and speaks in a dialect, that is philosophically more profound; but he never soars into a more ethereal region. He does not interpret Nature or human Life more adequately, nor does the student of his works breathe a more untroubled air, than that in which Wordsworth lived and had his being. . . . I claim for Wordsworth a clear knowledge of the profoundest problems, with which the human mind has grappled, from Heraclitus to Immanuel Kant. He seems to have penetrated to the very core of philosophical ideas, not by laboured argumentation, but by intuitive discernment—both intellectual and moral—which began early and developed rapidly, keeping pace with the growth of his imagination. By that consummate vision, which is superior to all processes of reasoning, he reached the ultimate data of speculative Philosophy and Theology. . . . There is no poet after Shakespeare more worthy of prolonged, careful, and even reverential study, and especially of study by women. There is none whose influence on character is more ennobling, and from contact with whose spirit you can draw a serener inspiration.—KNIGHT, WILLIAM, 1879, *Studies in Philosophy and Literature, pp.* 283, 313, 316.

I firmly believe that the poetical performance of Wordsworth is, after that of Shakspeare and Milton, of which all the world now recognises the worth, undoubtedly the most considerable in our language from the Elizabethan age to the present time. . . . If it is a just claim, if Wordsworth's place among the poets who have appeared in the last two or three centuries is after Shakspeare, Molière, Milton, Goethe, indeed, but before all the rest, then in time Wordsworth will have his due. We shall recognise him in his place, as we recognise Shakspeare and Milton; and not only we ourselves shall recognise him, but he will be recognised by Europe also. . . . His best work is in his shorter pieces, and many indeed are there of these which are of first-rate excellence. But in his seven volumes the pieces of high merit are mingled with a mass of pieces very inferior to them; so inferior to them that it seems wonderful how the same poet should have produced both.—ARNOLD, MATTHEW, 1879, *ed., Poems of Wordsworth, Preface, pp.* x, xi.

Wordsworth was, and felt himself to be, a discoverer, and like other great discoverers, his victory was in seeing by faith things which were not yet seen, but which were obvious, or soon became so, when once shown. He opened a new world of thought and enjoyment to Englishmen; his work formed an epoch in the intellectual and moral history of the race. But for that very reason he had, as Coleridge said, like all great artists, to create the taste by which he was to be relished, to teach the art by which he was to be seen and judged. And people were so little prepared for the thorough and systematic way in which he searched out what is deepest or highest or subtlest in human feeling under the homeliest realities, that not being able to understand him they laughed at him. Nor was he altogether without fault in the misconceptions which occasioned so much ridicule and scorn.—CHURCH, RICHARD WILLIAM, 1879, *Wordsworth, Dante and Other Essays, p.* 202.

Taking him where he is pure and without blemish—that is to say, somewhere half-way between his deliberate simplicity, between his propensities of a somewhat didactic kind, and between the lyrism, also too conscious and slightly declamatory, of the great odes—you find something of altogether superior quality. Wordsworth is a very great poet, and at the same time one of those who lend themselves best to everyday intercourse—a puissant and beneficent writer who elevates us and makes us happy. We must not be astonished if his renown has passed through vicissitudes of admiration and disdain, for his work is certainly unequaled. But we must also not be astonished if, after these vicissitudes, he is in the way of taking rank among the classics of his country; for his beauties are of those which time consecrates instead of aging them. I should not be surprised if the selection of his poems published by Mr. Matthew Arnold, and the attention thus recalled to him, serve to fix his place definitely in the heaven of British glories. If Shakespeare, as I hold, remains absolutely and forever peerless, Wordsworth seems to me to come after Milton; decidedly, I think, below him, but still first after him. He is of the stuff whereof the immortals are made.—SCHERER, EDMOND, 1880–91, *Wordsworth and Modern Poetry in England, Essays on English Literature, tr. Saintsbury, p.* 225.

Of sluggish or unmusical rhythm there are abundant specimens, especially in his earlier works. In reading Wordsworth, I often feel about his rhythm as if I were wading against a stream instead of floating along with it. This would never be so were the feeling of form in the poet's soul as sensitive as his thought. We could dispense with much profundity of thought, were we only borne along by a musical motion which wedded itself spontaneously to the idea. A perfect poem demands a fine accord between the body and the soul of thought. We are often moved by the *soul* of Wordsworth's thought; not often, I think, by the soul in intimate conjunction of form with his thought.—CRANCH, CHRISTOPHER P., 1880, *Wordsworth, Atlantic Monthly, vol.* 45, *p.* 248.

In the first place, we may say that his happiness was as wholly free from vulgar or transitory elements as a man's can be. It lay in a life which most men would have found austere and blank indeed; a life from which not Crœsus only but Solon would have turned in scorn; a life of poverty and retirement, of long apparent failure, and honour that came tardily at the close; it was a happiness nourished on no sacrifice of other men, on no eager appropriation of the goods of earth, but springing from a single eye and a loving spirit, and wrought from those primary emotions which are the innocent birthright of all.—MYERS, F. W. H., 1881, *Wordsworth (English Men of Letters), p.*73.

I should suppose that any ordinary educated man could, if asked, describe Wordsworth as a poet of nature, and he has with the utmost emphasis described himself as a "worshipper of nature;" nevertheless it would seem that Wordsworth is essentially the poet of *Man*. He is in fact less of a poet than of a Seer. It is *man* whom he chiefly busies himself about. It is the emotions and thoughts of *men* which fill his thoughts. Nature is the type of permanence and reality, man is transient and ever changing; nevertheless nature is ever subservient to man. Seen by man's intellect inanimate nature becomes "an ebbing and a flowing mind." It is intellect projected upon the bleak side of some tall peak "familiar with forgotten years," that gave to it its "visionary character." It was the transitory nature of the being that stood upon its bank that gave to the flowing stream its lesson of "life continuous—being unimpair'd."—SHORTHOUSE, J. H., 1881–89, *The Platonism of Wordsworth, Wordsworthiana, p.* 5.

Is acknowledged to be one of the chief glories of English poetry, and to have exercised a greater, purer, healthier, and more elevating influence upon the thought-currents and literature of the age, than any poet who has appeared in the world since the days of Shakspere and Milton. Goethe, among European moderns, has by some been deemed "a larger and more splendid luminary;" but, from his want of spirituality and deficiency in clear moral perception, he belongs to a lower circle. Goethe knew more than Wordsworth of the world, as developed in the various phases of artificial society—more, unfortunately, than was for his own higher good. As an all-sided artist, he occupied a wider surface of earth; but, with greater spontaneity and naturalness, although more circumscribed in such directions, our great poet was, otherwise, both higher and deeper than Goethe, and from his habitual height, actually commanded wider horizons of time space; while, for absolute purity of aim and moral worth, the two men are not, for one instant, to be named together.—SYMINGTON, ANDREW JAMES, 1881, *William Wordsworth, vol.* I, *p.* 13.

Turn to "Yarrow Revisited," which was written twenty-eight years later, in 1831. The rhythm is the same, but how different the movement; how much sweeter and slower, how many more the syllables on which you must dwell, sometimes with what the ear admits to be an over-emphasis; how much richer the music, when it is music; how much more hesitating, not to say vacillating, the reflection; and how the versification itself renders all this, with its sedate pauses,—pauses, to use another poet's fine expression, "as if memory had wept,"—its amplitude of tender feeling, its lingerings over sweet colours, its anxious desire to find compensations for the buoyancy of youth in wise reflection!—HUTTON, RICHARD HOLT, 1882, *On Wordsworth's Two Styles, Wordsworthiana, p.* 72.

And to this consecration—"the silent influences of the morning poured upon his head by the Invisible Hand"—he remained faithful as few priests have ever been to their calling, a priest of nature, a priest of God.—FARRAR, F. W., 1883, *With the Poets, Preface, p.* xxi.

It was the vast number of these "harmonious apposites" united in Wordsworth, and the closeness with which they were interfused, which imparted to his poetry those characteristics of magnanimity, of large-hearted humanity, and of vastness in unity, which, taken together, constitute what is felt as the personal character of Wordsworth's poetry.—DEVERE, AUBREY, 1883, *Remarks on the Personal Character of Wordsworth's Poetry, Wordsworthiana, p.* 154.

No other English poet has touched me quite so closely as Wordsworth. All classes of men delight in Shakspere; he is the universal genius; but Wordsworth's poetry has more the character of a message, and a message special and personal to a few readers. He stands for a particular phase of human thought and experience, and his service to certain minds is like an initiation into a new order of mysteries. His limitations make him all the more private and precious, like the seclusion of one of his mountain dales. He is not and can never be the world's poet, but the poet of those who love solitude and solitary communion with nature.—BURROUGHS, JOHN, 1884, *In Wordsworth's Country, The Century, vol.* 27, *p.* 418.

He is the most spiritual, and the most spiritualizing of all the English poets, not Shakespeare, no, nor even Milton, excepted: indeed, so far as I know or believe, the world has no poetry outside the Bible that can stand a comparison with his in this respect. And, with all his surpassing spirituality of thought, he carries a genius so powerful and so penetrating, his poetry breathes a music so deep and so sweet, that even the hardest-headed science is constrained to recognize it, to feel and own its power, and to draw refreshment from it; or, to speak more fairly, the two seem drawn, at length, to a recognition of each other; and both are now working apparently, to a mutual interchange of services. . . . A considerable portion of Wordsworth's matter, a fourth at least, perhaps a third, may well be set down as little better than worthless; mere slag, for the most part, with a few grains, here and there, and sometimes a small nugget, of pure gold.—HUDSON, HENRY N., 1884, *Studies in Wordsworth, pp.* 8, 14.

The vague pantheism of the "Excursion" implies rather a lack of distinctive dogma than any fresh insight into religious problems or capacity of co-ordinating them in a new manner. And so soon as the need of definite religious conceptions came to the poet, the Church in her customary theology became his satisfactory refuge. The "Ecclesiastical Sonnets" mark this definite stage in his spiritual development. Wordsworth did for the religious thought of his time something more and better, perhaps, than giving it any definite impulse. While leaving it in the old channels he gave it a richer and deeper volume. He showed with what vital affinity religion cleaves to humanity in all its true and simple phases when uncontaminated by conceit or frivolity. Nature and man alike were to him essentially religious, or only conceivable as the outcome of a Spirit of Life, "The Soul of all the worlds." Wordsworth in short remained, as he began, a poet. He did not enter into the sphere of religious thought or busy himself with its issues.—TULLOCH, JOHN, 1885, *Movements of Religious Thought in Britain During the Nineteenth Century*, p. 9.

There is no pathos profounder than his. . . . It is a kind of inarticulate, still-life pathos. That of the episode of Margaret in the "Excursion" would be crushing but for the old narrator's own calm faith. . . . Certainly Wordsworth is one of the very great poets, for he can both soar with dignity, and stoop with grace. His good and enduring work is not only ample in quantity, but varied in scope. . . . One may be sorry indeed, but one ought hardly to be surprised that Mr. Rossetti should have told his biographer that he grudged Wordsworth "every vote he got." For, although he himself has done some very fine work, yet he was the head of a school which is the natural enemy of Wordsworth.—NOEL, RODEN, 1886, *Wordsworth, Essays on Poetry and Poets*, p. 133.

Neither in the presence of his fellowmen, whatever their myriad march, nor of Nature, how countless soever her worlds, can the indestructible personality of Wordsworth forget itself. His spirit, like that of Shelley, is divine; but it is no mere fragment of a vast divinity; backwards into the illimitable past, forwards into the illimitable future, now and for ever in the face of man and Nature, it dwells, has dwelt, shall dwell like a star apart in an individuality unmade, unmakable, unchangeable. Before this profound sense of personality, partially Platonic, partially Christian, but most of all awakened by the physical and social conditions of the poet's age, Nature assumes a depth of meaning which only beings of Wordsworthian mould may feel. Byron's descriptive powers, Shelley's musical communion with the sounds of Nature, give place to a realisation of Nature's being all the more terribly significant because the observer refuses to reconcile its conflict with his own personality either by material or immaterial unity; and while the associations of his childhood, youth, and age become consecrated as the earthly dress of an eternal being—not the melancholy entirety of one made of such stuff as dreams are made of —Wordsworth fears not to be materialised by the companionship of Nature, because he has neither deified her being at the expense of his own, nor denied her divinity in order to make himself eternal.—POSNETT, HUTCHESON MACAULAY, 1886, *Comparative Literature*, p. 387.

What was it, first and foremost, and most important, which one learned from Wordsworth? One learned, I say, more about Man, and more about Nature, and more about the union of the two, than is to be learned anywhere else. That was the lesson which I learned. The sympathy, the intelligence with which man is regarded and portrayed and put before his fellow-men throughout the works of Wordsworth is, I think, something unique in all literature.—SELBORNE, LORD, 1886, *President's Address to the Wordsworth Society, Wordsworthiana*, p. 279.

Devotion to Wordsworth, if it has a tendency to exalt, has also a tendency to infatuate the judicial sense and spirit of his disciples: to make them, even as compared with other devotees, unusually prone to indulgence in such large assertions and assumptions on their master's behalf as seem at least to imply claims which it may be presumed that their apparent advocates would not seriously advance or deliberately maintain. It would in some instances be as unreasonable to suppose that they would do so as to imagine that Mr. Arnold really considers the dissonant doggerel of Wordsworth's halting lines to a skylark equal or superior to Shelley's incomparable transfusion from notes into words of the spirit of a skylark's song. Such an instance is afforded us by the most illustrious —with a single exception—of all Wordsworth's panegyrists. . . . If Wordsworth's claims as a poet can only be justified on grounds which would prove him a deeper student of nature, a saner critic of life, a wiser man and a greater poet than Shakespeare, the inference is no less obvious than inevitable: Wordsworth's claims as a poet must in that case go by the board altogether, and at once, and for ever. . . . Meditation and sympathy, not action and passion, were the two main strings of his serene and stormless lyre. On these no hand ever held more gentle yet more soverign rule than Wordsworth's. His command of all qualities and powers that are proper to the natural scope and adequate to the just application of his genius was as perfect as the command of those greater than he—of the greatest among all great poets—over the worlds of passion and of action.—SWINBURNE, ALGERNON CHARLES, 1886, *Wordsworth and Byron, Miscellanies, pp.* 113, 115, 117.

Of great English writers, the one that held the most powerful sway over my early years was Wordsworth. He, in fact, along with Goethe and my other German gods, held out an effective arm to redeem me from that "whirling gulf of fantasy and flame" into which the violent sweep of Lord Byron's indignant muse had a tendency to plunge his admirers. From the day that I became acquainted with Wordsworth, I regarded Byron only as a very sublime avatar of the devil, and would have nothing to do with him. What influenced me in Wordsworth was the kindly spirit with which he tried to bind the highest and the lowest in one bond of reverential sympathy, the truly evangelical as well as profoundly philosophical insight with which he set forth in so many attractive forms the superiority of a wise humility to a wilful pride, and his habitual subjection of delicate fancy and purified passion to the legitimate sway of reason.—BLACKIE, JOHN STUART, 1887, *Books which Have Influenced Me, p.* 74.

On reaching the age of twenty-one, I published a book of verse, and was considered to be a pupil of Wordsworth. In fact, however, I did not possess a copy of Wordsworth's poems, and had read very little of him, admiring only short pieces here and there. I afterwards bought a complete edition of the poems and read them, with the same result. The love of nature that Wordsworth expressed, laboriously and at great length, was in harmony with my own feelings, but there was something in the poet that I found repellent, perhaps his belief in his own moral and intellectual excellence.—HAMERTON, PHILIP GILBERT, 1887, *Books which Have Influenced Me, p.* 54.

Every one has been influenced by Wordsworth, and it is hard to tell precisely how. A certain innocence, a rugged austerity of joy, a sight of the stars, "the silence that there is among the hills," something of the cold thrill of dawn, cling to his work and give it a particular address to what is best in us. I do not know that you learn a lesson; you need not—Mill did not agree with any one of his beliefs; and yet the spell is cast.—STEVENSON, ROBERT LOUIS, 1887, *Books which Have Influenced Me, p.* 11.

Wordsworth has exercised more influence over English poetry than any other man of this century. He has done so mainly by virtue of his originality, for he is pre-eminently original. It is, of course, true that we find among his predecessors, and especially in Burns, anticipations of his style, and, at times, of his mode of thought. It is also true that the spirit of Wordsworth is simply the spirit of his time poetically expressed. Wordsworth gives a poetic exposition of the cry of Rousseau for a return to nature, and in making it less a theory makes it much more profoundly true. But it is just in this that his originality consists. He gives a clear expression to tendencies which before his day had been vague and undefined. To do so he breaks boldly with the past, and enters upon a path of his own, a path which had been missed just because it is so very obvious. Wordsworth's great principle is to be in all things natural, natural in thought, natural in language; to avoid far-fetched ingenuities of fancy and expression, and to trust for success to the force of simple truth.—WALKER, HUGH, 1887, *Celebrities of the Century, ed. Sanders, p.* 1069.

Wordsworth, though he rarely attains that bold, easy execution which is so habitual with Shelley, always evinces a health and integrity of feeling which make our sympathy complete. Actuality, fact—a sufficient rendering united to inner validity of thought—are of far more moment with him. When, therefore, we are satisfied, we are abundantly satisfied, and rest on intellectual soundness as well as on emotional tenderness. While, then, I should put Shelley and Wordsworth together as giving habitually the higher pleasures of spiritual art, taking but one of them, I should take Wordsworth without hesitation.—BASCOM, JOHN, 1888, *Books that Have Helped Me, p.* 31.

We are not called upon to place great men of his stamp as if they were collegians in a class-list. It is best to take with thankfulness and admiration from each man what he has to give. What Wordsworth does is to assuage, to reconcile, to fortify. He has not Shakespeare's richness and vast compass, nor Milton's sublime and unflagging strength, nor Dante's severe, vivid, ardent force of vision. Probably he is too deficient in clear beauty of form and in concentrated power to be classed by the ages among these great giants. We cannot be sure. We may leave it to the ages to decide. But Wordsworth, at any rate, by his secret of bringing the infinite into common life, as he evokes it out of common life, has the skill to lead us, so long as we yield ourselves to his influence, into inner moods of settled peace, to touch "the depth and not the tumult of the soul," to give us quietness, strength, steadfastness, and purpose, whether to do or to endure. All art of poetry that has the effect of breathing into men's hearts, even if it be only for a space, these moods of settled peace, and strongly confirming their judgment and their will for good,—whatever limitations may be found besides, however prosaic may be some or much of the details,—is great art and noble poetry, and the creator of it will always hold, as Wordsworth holds, a sovereign title to the reverence and gratitude of mankind.—MORLEY, JOHN, 1888, *The Complete Poetical Works of William Wordsworth, Introduction.*

If I were to seek to express the main characteristic of the poetic mood of Wordsworth at its highest reach, I should say that his mind was open equally to the world of sense—the infinite, and to the sphere of the infinite which borders and surrounds this world of ours. . . . The Transcendent Power which held Wordsworth through life was not discovered by him, or got through a process of dialectical exercise; it was revealed to him as a Being external to himself, which laid its hand upon him absolutely, overpoweringly. The light which shone and the voice which called from heaven on Saul of Tarsus were not more distinctly influences which unconditionally seized and swayed the apostle than was the Power in the outward world which surrounded, revealed itself, and made the poet-seer its own, its daily vassal and its impassioned voice.—VEITCH, JOHN, 1888, *The Theism of Wordsworth, Wordsworthiana, pp.* 291, 316.

From Shelley's dazzling glow or thunderous haze,
From Byron's tempest-anger, tempest-mirth,
Men turned to thee and found—not blast and blaze,
Tumult of tottering heavens, but peace on earth.
Nor peace that grows by Lethe, scentless flower,
There in white langours to decline and cease;
But peace whose names are also rapture, power,
Clear sight, and love: for these are parts of peace.
—WATSON, WILLIAM, 1890, *Wordsworth's Grave.*

Wordsworth, working apart from his contemporaries, expressed man's affinity to nature and man's dependence on the cosmic order with greater reserve. Still, it is difficult to go farther in nature-worship than Wordsworth did in those sublimely pathetic lines written above Tintern Abbey; and nothing indicates the difference between the Victorian and the Elizabethan touch on the world better than his blank verse fragment describing a pedestrian journey through the Simplon Pass.—SYMONDS, JOHN ADDINGTON, 1890, *Essays Speculative and Suggestive, vol.* II, *p.* 271.

The forty years which have elapsed since his death have not brought to light one disgraceful action, one single utterance or incident that need shrink from day. Words with him were as sacred as things; his life was an absolutely consistent whole, the poet was the man. And it is this veracity and uprightness of moral character which makes us derive such invigoration from his poetry. The vision in the temple is made real to our minds by the fact that the prophet has shown his sincerity and trustworthiness in matters of which we ourselves can judge. In like manner also Wordsworth's spiritual insight, his strong and unchanging moral convictions, come to us with imperative force because his eye for outward nature is so true, and his readiness to contemplate even her lowliest aspects is so unfailing. He stands out, with his steadfast countenance, his unshrinking gaze, his unfaltering utterance, his noble directness and singleness of purpose, in the midst of a perplexed and vacillating crowd; his voice gives no uncertain sound, his purpose is fixed, his faith is clear, he has looked Truth in the face, he has vowed himself to the service of Duty.—WORDSWORTH, ELIZABETH, 1891, *William Wordsworth, Preface, p.* ix.

The influence of Wordsworth upon his time has been the influence of the Gulf-stream; it has flowed silently and surely, and has conquered. . . . We shall forgive him that his poetry has so little of passion in it, and upon the whole we shall be thankful for it. There are many other poets who can give us passion; but who else can give us peace? . . . If poetry is, as some one has beautifully described it, the Sabbath influence of literature, Wordsworth breaths upon us the very Sabbath of poetry—its rest, its devotion, and its healing calm. . . . The gift, then, that Wordsworth brings to us is serenity, and the message he delivers is simplicity. We do not go to him to be excited but to be strengthened. He, in his turn, does not pose before us in a dramatic attitude, as a suppliant for sentimental pity; he stands before us as a wise teacher, on whose lips are the words of everlasting life. Those who do not love him must revere him; but, for my part, I find it easy to do both. If poetry be something more than a pool of chaotic sentiment, that gives forth iridescent vapors, brilliant films and bubbles; if it be a healing stream, flowing clear as crystal from the throne of God and bordered by the trees of life; if it be an inspired voice, "a vision and a faculty divine," then in Wordsworth I recognize the noblest poet of our century. —DAWSON, W. J., 1892, *Quest and Vision, pp.* 43, 67, 68, 70.

Wordsworth, with his narrow intellect and wide emotions,—he had patrons; the cloth took him up, and the public followed suit, an act they could only have performed for a third-rate poet, the first and second-rate being much above their comprehension.—HAKE, GORDON, 1892, *Memoirs of Eighty Years, p.* 77.

Wordsworth tried the moral lesson, and spoiled some of his best work with botany and the Bible. A good many smaller men than he have tried the same thing since, and have failed. Perhaps "Cain," and "Manfred" have taught the human heart more wisdom than "Matthew" or the unfortunate "idiot boy" over whom Byron was so mercilessly merry. And yet Byron probably never meant to teach any one anything in particular, and Wordsworth meant to teach everybody, including and beginning with himself.—CRAWFORD, F. MARION, 1893, *The Novel, What it Is, p.* 19.

The zealous fault-hunter, to be sure, is not a critic; no more is the fault-dodger. I like to read Sainte-Beuve; but I lay at his door and Wordsworth's much of the insignificance of literary art at this moment. The conception of art in the body of Wordsworth's poetry and the notion of criticism in Sainte-Beuve's essays have easily formed the whey of commonplace and the curd of "appreciation."—THOMPSON, MAURICE, 1893, *The Ethics of Literary Art, p.* 25.

> In the hottest crowd, when grace
> Seems to hide her maiden face,
> Here you'll find a mystic voice
> Full of heaven's supernal noise,
> And a breath of mountain wind
> Rustling in the leaves you'll find:
> In the world's seducing clan
> It shall be your talisman.

—RHYS, ERNEST, 1894? *Written in a Copy of Wordsworth.*

There was nobody to revolt against when Wordsworth appeared; the throne was vacant, open to any comer powerful enough to establish his right by poetic might.—MINTO, WILLIAM, 1894, *The Literature of the Georgian Era, ed. Knight, p.* 131.

Probably few men have ever lived more loyally with their minds than Wordsworth. Fame found him a recluse and left him solitary; crowds had no charms for him, and at dinner-tables he had no gifts. He was at his best pacing his garden walk and carrying on that long colloquy with his mind which was his one consuming passion. The critics speak of him as an isolated, often as a cold, nature; but no man of his time, not even Byron, put more passion into his work: only his passion was not for persons, it was for ideas.—MABIE, HAMILTON WRIGHT, 1894, *My Study Fire, Second Series, p.* 25.

Blessed be William Wordsworth among teachers, and rectifiers of the human spirit. —CORSON, HIRAM, 1894, *The Aims of Literary Study, p.* 12.

It is Wordsworth's meditative rapture, spiritual passion, sane imagination and serenity, his power of bringing the infinite into everyday life, that enthrall me; but, for myself, all Wordsworth's best could be collected into a thin volume. I care little for his "Laodamia."—LOCKER-LAMPSON, FREDERICK, 1895, *My Confidences, p.* 177.

Wordsworth's place is a very high one; some things he has done are incomparable; some altitudes of thought he has reached range among the Miltonic heights. But he has printed—as so many people have—too much. . . . If Wordsworth had possessed Browning's sense of humor, he would have withdrawn an eighth of his published works; if he had possessed Hood's sense of humor, I think he would have withdrawn a third.—MITCHELL, DONALD G., 1895, *English Lands Letters and Kings, Queen Anne and the Georges, pp.* 331, 332.

Take him for all in all, in his spiritual history as well as his poetic achievement, Wordsworth is probably a better exponent than Shelley of the democratic ideal in all its length and breadth. In spite of "The Warning," his conservatism was pure matter of surface opinion. He grew despondent over the political tendencies of the day; but his very despondency, however misguided, had its deep source in the love of the common people. The radiance of his democratic faith did indeed as he grew older fade into the light of common day; yet those first affections, those shadowy recollections of a divine glory once shed on human life, remained to the end the master-light of all his seeing, a power to cherish and to uphold. His poetry made incursions into stupid regions as he grew older, and we miss the old concentrated intensity of phrase. But through mistaken dissertation on politics, as through his glorified contemplation of human life, pulses the same unwavering interest and faith in men and women as they are.—SCUDDER, VIDA D., 1895, *The Life of the Spirit in the Modern English Poets, p.* 58.

On the merits of this famous writer the world has long ago made up its mind, and Coleridge, more than any other man, has helped the world to truly appreciate his gifted friend. No poet ever had a nobler purpose in his work than Wordsworth. He was a good man as well as a wise one. Those who read seriously his work must love and venerate the memory of a man whose purpose was so pure and whose life so consistently fulfilled it.—WARREN, INA RUSSELLE, 1895, *William Wordsworth, The Magazine of Poetry, vol.* 7, *p.* 165.

Wordsworth's example redeemed his thories, and Coleridge had no theories to redeem. The latter's influence was therefore the earlier in its operation, while that of the former has been perhaps the greater in the long run. Yet, by a somewhat ironical fate, it has turned out that Coleridge, who concerned himself rather with the matter than the mechanism of poetry, has taken rank as one of the greatest English masters of poetic form, while Wordsworth, who believed himself to be the inventor of a new, or at any rate the restorer of the true, language of poetry, owes his place in our literature to a force and depth of poetic feeling which even his many defects of form have proved unable to outweigh. The matchless music of the one singer has enriched the note, as the inspired vision of the other has enlarged the outlook, of all English poetry since their day.—TRAILL, HENRY DUFF, 1896, *Social England, vol.* V, *p.* 582.

The noblest products in the field of pure literature which the Napoleonic wars have left us are Wordsworth's political sonnets, his poem "The Happy Warrior," and his pamphlet on the "Convention of Cintra." The sonnets are records of the most impassioned moments in the history of Wordsworth's imagination, as it dealt with public events from 1802 to the battle of Waterloo.—DOWDEN, EDWARD, 1897, *The French Revolution and English Literature, p.* 213.

According to Mr. Hall Caine, as quoted by Mr. W. M. Rossetti, "Rossetti thought Wordsworth was too much the high priest of Nature to be her lover." Mr. Caine speaks also of "Rossetti's grudging Wordsworth every vote he gets." His indifference to the beautiful poet was perhaps due to his having spent all his childhood and youth, and most of his manhood, in London.—HILL, GEORGE BIRKBECK, 1897, *ed. Letters of Dante Gabriel Rossetti to William Allingham, p.* 220.

Wordsworth is the master of moral beauty. He is never swayed by a licentious passion for the beautiful for its own sake. He does not long to pass into a Nirvana of sensuous and imaginative delight, to be lapped in soft Lydian airs; but he elevates his soul to high and ennobling activity. Nor does he, like Goethe, speak experience for Art's sake. Wordsworth valued Art only as strengthening and

FRANCIS JEFFREY

Engraving by Sartain. From the Original by G. Hayter.

JOHN WILSON

Engraving by F. Halpin.

elevating Life; Goethe sought experience merely as a stimulant to art expression. Wordsworth cultivated Art for Life, Goethe Life for Art; and this antipodal relation explains the invincible repugnance which Wordsworth always manifested to Goethe and his works. With Wordsworth it was not Art for Art's sake, but Art for Life's sake, and he had neither understanding of nor sympathy with pure Art or pure Science. He sought the Beautiful and the True only as a means of purifying, ennobling, and sanctifying character. He was early convinced that a mine of moral beauty, unheeded and unsuspected by literary artists, lay hid in the commonest and humblest objects, and he devoted himself to disclosing and exhibiting this treasure with a strenuousness and perseverance perhaps unparalleled in the history of poetry. He elicits a wealth of spiritual beauty from the most unlikely things, and reveals the heaven which lies beneath our feet.—STANLEY, HIRAM M., 1897, *Essays on Literary Art*, p. 32.

It is his power of interpreting the elementary feelings common to all mortals that has made Wordsworth the poet of humanity; and he is destined to live as a poet because he is natural, pure, and true to his ideal of nature and humanity,—an ideal based upon a sympathetic knowledge of the visible outward world and of man. We find no artificiality in Wordsworth.—PEABODY, ANDREW P., 1897, *William Wordsworth, The Forum, vol.* 23, *p.* 626.

He shuts off his light and heat, and leaves us chilly and stumbling among common-place perhaps for pages, when suddenly we meet again the light that never was on land or sea.—WINCHESTER, C. T., 1899, *Some Principles of Literary Criticism, p.* 94.

He felt instinctively, and his feeling was nature's. But thought, coming to him thus immediately as it did, and representing the thinking part of himself with unparalleled fidelity, spoke out of an intellect by no means so responsive to the finer promptings of that supreme intellectual energy of which we are a part. It is thus often when he is most solemnly satisfied with himself that he is really showing us his weakness most ingenuously: he would listen to no external criticism, and there was no inherent critical faculty to stand at his mind's elbow and remind him when he was prophesying in the divine language and when he was babbling like the village idiot. . . . When one has said that he wrote instinctively, without which there could be no poetry, one must add that he wrote mechanically, and that he wrote always.—SYMONS, ARTHUR, 1902, *Wordsworth, Fortnightly Review, vol.* 77, *pp.* 39, 40.

Francis Lord Jeffrey

1773-1850

Born, in Edinburgh, 23 Oct. 1773. At Edinburgh High School, Oct. 1781 to 1787, at Glasgow Univ., 1787-89. Studied Law in Edinburgh, 1789-91. Matric. Queen's Coll., Oxford, 17 Oct. 1791. Left Oxford, 5 July, 1792. Studied Law in Edinburgh, 1792-93. Called to Scotch Bar, 16 Dec. 1794. Visit to London, 1798. Married Catherine Wilson, 1 Nov. 1801; settled in Edinburgh. Contrib. to "Monthly Rev.," 1802. Started "Edinburgh Review," with Sydney Smith and others; first number appeared, 10 Oct. 1802; he edited it till June 1829; contrib. to it, Oct. 1802 to Jan. 1848. Joined Volunteer regiment, 1803. One of founders of "Friday Club," 1803. Visit to London, 1804. Wife died, 8 Aug. 1805. Visit to London, 1806. Duel with Moore (followed by reconciliation), Chalk Farm, 11 Aug. 1806. Legal practice in Scotland increasing. Fell in love with Charlotte Wilkes, 1810; followed her to America, 1813; married her in New York, Nov. 1813. Tour with her in America. Returned to England, Feb. 1814. Settled at Craigcrook, near Edinburgh, 1815. Visit to Continent same year. Joined Bannatyne Club, 1826. Dean of Faculty of Advocates, Edinburgh, 2 July 1829; Lord Advocate, 1830. M. P. for Forfarshire Burghs, 1830; unseated owing to irregularity in election. M. P. for Malton, April and June 1831. Ill-health, in London, 1831. M. P. for Edinburgh, Dec. 1832 to 1834. Judge of Court of Sessions, as Lord Jeffrey, June 1834. Ill-health, 1841. Died, in Edinburgh, 26 Jan. 1850. Buried in Dean Cemetery. *Works:* "A Summary View of the rights and claims of the Roman Catholics of Ireland" (anon.), 1808; "A Short

Vindication of the late Major A. Campbell" (anon.), 1810; "Contributions to the Edinburgh Review" (4 vols.), 1844. He *edited:* J. Playfair's Works, 1822; Byron's Poems, 1845. *Life:* (with selected Correspondence) by Lord Cockburn, 1852 — SHARP, R. FARQUHARSON, 1897, *A Dictionary of English Authors, p.* 149.

PERSONAL

His manner is not at first pleasing; what is worse, it is of that cast, which almost irresistibly impresses upon strangers the idea of levity and superficial talents. Yet there is not any man, whose real character is so much the reverse; he has indeed a very sportive and playful fancy, but it is accompanied with very extensive and varied information, with a readiness of apprehension almost intuitive, with judicious and calm discernment, with a profound and penetrating understanding. Indeed, both in point of candour and of vigour in the reasoning powers, I have never personally known a finer intellect than Jeffrey's, unless I were to except Allen's.—HORNER, FRANCIS, 1802, *Memoirs and Correspondence, vol.* I, *p.* 212.

The chaise being in readiness, we set off for Chalk Farm. . . . On reaching the ground we found Jeffrey and his party already arrived. . . . And then it was that, for the first time, my excellent friend Jeffrey and I met face to face. He was standing with the bag, which contained the pistols, in his hand, while Horner was looking anxiously around. It was agreed that the spot where we found them, which was screened on one side by large trees, would be as good for our purpose as any we could select; and Horner, after expressing some anxiety respecting some men whom he had seen suspiciously hovering about, but who now appeared to have departed, retired with Hume behind the trees, for the purpose of loading the pistols, leaving Jeffrey and myself together. . . . They then retired to a little distance; the pistols were on both sides raised; and we waited but the signal to fire, when some police officers, whose approach none of us had noticed, and who were within a second of being too late, rushed out from a hedge behind Jeffrey; and one of them, striking at Jeffrey's pistol with his staff, knocked it to some distance into the field, while another running over to me, took possession also of mine. We were then replaced in our respective carriages, and conveyed, crestfallen, to Bow Street. — MOORE, THOMAS, 1806, *Journal; Memoirs, Journal and Correspondence, ed. Russell.*

It is a face which any man would pass without observation in a crowd, because it is small and swarthy, and entirely devoid of lofty or commanding outlines—and besides, his stature is so low, that he might walk close under your chin or mine without ever catching the eye even for a moment. Mr. Jeffrey . . . is a very short and very active-looking man, with an appearance of extraordinary vivacity in all his motions and gestures. His face is one which cannot be understood at a single look—perhaps it requires, as it certainly invites, a long and anxious scrutiny before it lays itself open to the gazer. The features are neither handsome, nor even very defined in their outlines: and yet the effect of the whole is as striking as any arrangement either of more noble or more marked features, which ever came under my view. The forehead is very singularly shaped, describing in its bend from side to side a larger segment of a circle than is at all common; compressed below the temples almost as much as Sterne's; and throwing out sinuses above the eyes, of an extremely bold and compact structure. The hair is very black and wiry, standing in ragged, bristly clumps out from the upper part of his head, but lying close and firm lower down, especially about the ears. Altogether, it is picturesque, and adds to the effect of the visage. The mouth is the most expressive part of his face. . . . The lips are very firm, but they tremble and vibrate, even when brought close together, in such a way as to give the idea of an intense, never-ceasing play of mind. There is a delicate kind of sneer almost always upon them, which has not the least appearance of ill-temper about it, but seems to belong entirely to the speculative understanding of the man. . . . A sharp, but at the same time, very deep-toned and impressive voice—a very bad pronunciation, but accompanied with very little of the Scotch accent—a light and careless manner, exchanged now and then for an infinite variety of more earnest expression and address—this is as much as I could carry away from my first visit.—LOCKHART, JOHN GIBSON, 1819, *Peter's Letters to His Kinsfolk, Letter* vi.

I dined with Walter Scott, and was delighted with the unaffected simplicity of his family. Jeffrey has a singular expression, poignant, bitter, piercing—as if his countenance never lighted up but at the perception of some weakness in human nature. Whatever you praise to Jeffrey, he directly chuckles out some error you did not perceive. Whatever you praise to Scott, he joins heartily with yourself, and directs your attention to some additional beauty. Scott throws a light on life by the beaming geniality of his soul, and so dazzles you that you have no time or perception for anything but its beauties: while Jeffrey seems to revel in holding up his hand before the light in order that he may spy out its deformities. The face of Scott is the expression of a man whose great pleasure has been to shake Nature by the hand, while to point at her with his finger has certainly, from the expression of his face, been the chief enjoyment of Jeffrey. —HAYDON, BENJAMIN ROBERT, 1820, *Letter to Miss Mitford, Dec.* 5; *Life, Letters and Table Talk, ed. Stoddard, p.* 203.

My dear Jeffrey—We are much obliged by your letter, but should be still more so were it legible. I have tried to read it from left to right, and Mrs. Sydney from right to left, and we neither of us can decipher a single word of it.—SMITH, SYDNEY, 1822, *Letter to Francis Jeffrey, Memoir of Rev. Sydney Smith by Lady Holland, ch.* viii.

There is no subject on which he is not *au fait:* no company in which he is not ready to scatter his pearls for sport. . . . His only difficulty seems to be, not to speak, but to be silent. . . . . He is never absurd, nor has he any favorite points which he is always bringing forward. It cannot be denied that there is something bordering on petulance of manner, but it is of that least offensive kind which may be accounted for from merit and from success, and implies no exclusive pretensions nor the least particle of ill-will to others. On the contrary Mr. Jeffrey is profuse of his encomiums and admiration of others, but still with a certain reservation of a right to differ or to blame. He cannot rest on one side of a question: he is obliged, by a mercurial habit and disposition, to vary his point of view. If he is ever tedious it is from an excess of liveliness: he oppresses from a sense of airy lightness. He is always setting out on a fresh scent: there are always *relays* of topics. New causes are called; he holds a brief in his hand for every possible question. This is a fault. Mr. Jeffrey is not obtrusive, is not impatient of opposition, is not unwilling to be interrupted; but what is said by another, seems to make no impression on him; he is bound to dispute, to answer it, as if he was in Court, or as if he were in a paltry Debating Society, where young beginners were trying their hands. . . . He cannot help cross-examining a witness, or stating the adverse view of the question. He listens not to judge, but to reply. In consequence of this, you can as little tell the impression your observations make on him as what weight to assign to his.—HAZLITT, WILLIAM, 1825, *Spirit of the Age, pp.* 188, 189.

I never was more surprised than when, having heard at Bellamy's that he was on his legs, I ran down and became witness, ocular and auricular, of the style and methods in which he had thought fit to present himself to the House. I have not frequented the Jury Court of late years, it is true—but I certainly should hardly have recognised any thing whatever of my old acquaintance. First of all, he looked smaller and grayer than I could have anticipated—then his surtout and black stock did in no wise set him—then his attitude was at once jaunty and awkward, spruce and feckless. Instead of the quick, voluble, fiery declaimer of other days or scenes, I heard a cold thin voice doling out little, quaint, metaphysical sentences, with the air of a provincial lecturer on logic and belles letters. The House was confounded—they listened for half an hour with great attention, waiting always for the real burst that should reveal the redoubtable Jeffrey—but it came not—he took out his orange, sucked it coolly and composedly—smelt to a bottle of something—and sucked again—and back to his freezing jargon with the same nonchalance. At last he took to proving to an assembly of six hundred gentlemen, of whom I take it at least five hundred were squires, that property is really a thing deserving of protection. "This will never do," passed around in a whisper. Old Maule tipped the wink to a few good Whigs of the old school, and they adjourned up stairs —the Tories began to converse *de omnibus rebus et quibusdam aliis*—the Radicals were either snoring or grinning—and the great gun of the north ceased firing amidst such a hubbub of inattention, that even I was not aware of the fact for several minutes. —WILSON, JOHN, 1831, *Noctes Ambrosianæ, Aug., ed. Mackenzie, vol.* IV, *p.* 354.

In person, Mr. Jeffrey is below the middle size, and slenderly made. There is something of a thoughtful expression in his countenance. His face is small and compact, rather, if anything, inclining to the angular form. His eyelashes are prominent. His forehead is remarkably low, considering the intellectual character of the man. His complexion is dark, and his hair black.—GRANT, JAMES, 1835, *Random Recollections of the House of Commons from the Year* 1830 *to the Close of* 1835, *p.* 187.

Is almost a lecturer in society; so much so, that there was no room for any one to put in a word.—FOX, CAROLINE, 1839, *Memories of Old Friends, ed. Pym, Journal, Dec.* 15, *p.* 29.

Poor dear Jeffrey! I bought a *Times* at the station yesterday morning, and was so stunned by the announcemment, that I felt it in that wounded part of me, almost directly; and the bad symptoms (modified) returned within a few hours. I had a letter from him in extraordinary good spirits within this week or two—he was better, he said, than he had been for a long time—and I sent him proof-sheets of the number only last Wednesday. I say nothing of his wonderful abilities and great career, but he was a most affectionate and devoted friend to me; and though no man could wish to live and die more happily, so old in years and yet so young in faculties and sympathies, I am very, very deeply grieved for his loss.—DICKENS, CHARLES, 1850, *Letter to John Forster, Jan.* 29; *Life of Dickens, ed. Forster, vol.* II, *p.* 483.

Jeffrey is gone. . Dear fellow! I loved him as much as it is easy to love a man who belongs to an older generation. And how good, and kind, and generous he was to me! His goodness, too, was the more precious because his perspicacity was so great. He saw through and through you. He marked every fault of taste, every weakness, every ridicule; and yet he loved you as if he had been the dullest fellow in England. He had a much better heart than Sydney Smith. I do not mean that Sydney was in that respect below par. In ability I should say that Jeffrey was higher, but Sydney rarer. I would rather have been Jeffrey; but there will be several Jeffreys, before there is a Sydney. After all, dear Jeffrey's death is hardly matter for mourning. God grant that I may die so! Full of years; full of honors; faculties bright, and affections warm, to the last; lamented by the public, and by many valuable private friends.—MACAULAY, THOMAS BABINGTON, 1850, *Journal, Jan.* 28; *Life and Letters, ed. Trevelyan, vol.* I, *p.* 178.

Francis Jeffrey died on the afternoon of Saturday the 26th January 1850. Four days before, he occupied his accustomed place on the Bench, as vigorous, clear, and discursive under the weight of seventy-seven years, as in the most brilliant period of his manhood. Time had not pressed more heavily on the elasticity of his step, than on his cheerful and playful spirit; and he trod the streets of our city, which his name has contributed to make famous, on that last fatal day, with a strength which seemed to promise a still prolonged evening to his bright, though declining sun. But the triumph of an insidious disease, with which he had wrestled at intervals for more than twenty years, was at last at hand. On the morning of the 26th, it was rumoured that he was sinking under an attack of bronchitis. In the evening, it was told that he was dead. . . . He has gone down to his grave laden with all under which a man would wish to die—honour, love, obedience—troops of friends—everything which should accompany the old age of such a man—the gratitude of a nation in whose service his life was spent, and the unfeigned tears of all who were ever privileged to come within the reach of his influence.—MONCRIEFF, J., 1850, *Lord Jeffrey, North British Review, vol.* 13, *pp.* 273, 284.

Notwithstanding one questionable habit, the judicial duties have rarely been better performed than they were by him. His ability need not be mentioned—nor the sensitiveness of his candour—nor his general aptitude for the law. Surpassed, perhaps, by one or two in some of the more mystical depths of the law of real property, his general legal learning was more than sufficient to enable him, after ordinary argument, to form sound views, and to defend them, even on these subjects. The industry that had turned the vivacity of his youth to account, and had marked all his progress, followed him to the bench. His opinions were always given fully, and with great liveliness, and great felicity of illustration. His patience, for so quick a person, was nearly incredible. He literally never tired of argument. . . . This was partly the result of a benevolent anxiety to make parties certain that they had at least been fully heard; but it also proceeded from his own pleasure in the game. . . . The questionable thing in his judicial manner consisted in an adherence to the same tendency that had sometimes impaired his force at the bar—speaking too often and too long. He had no idea of sitting, like an oracle, silent, and looking wise; and then, having got it all in, announcing the result in as many calm words as were necessary, and in no more. Delighted with the play, instead of waiting passively till the truth should emerge, he put himself, from the very first, into the position of an inquirer, whose duty it was to extract it by active processes. His error lay in not perceiving that it would be much better extracted for him by counsel than it generally can be by a judge. But disbelieving this, or disregarding it, his way was to carry on a running margin of questions, and suppositions, and comments, through the whole length of the argument. — COCKBURN, HENRY LORD, 1852, *Life of Lord Jeffrey, vol.* I.

How susceptible he was to the beauty of nature—to the clouds, the sky, the birds, the flowers; how loving to children; how warm and generous in his friendships; how affectionate to women; how every thing that a man should be!—SEDGWICK, CATHARINE M., 1853, *To Dr. Dewey, April, Life and Letters, p.* 349.

No artist could paint Jeffrey. His expression was so variable, that in different moods he seemed a different man. At the Bar, in Parliament, on the Bench, or in the romantic scenery of his own Craig-Crook, there was a different man—and yet there were not half-a-dozen Jeffreys, but one! To hear him talk, in that sharp shrill voice, whose lowest whisper floated through the air, and was heard by all, was indeed a pleasure and delight. Above all, he had the gentlest courtesy towards women, irrespective of their age. And, to crown all, he was fond, really and truly, of children. (I never knew a bad man who was. I am, and the inference is inevitable!) It was at home, that Jeffrey was ever seen to full advantage.—MACKENZIE, R. SHELTON, 1854, *ed., Noctes Ambrosianæ, vol.* III, *p.* 429, *note.*

Jeffrey, whom flattery, success, and himself cannot spoil, or taint that sweet, generous nature—keen, instant, unsparing, all true as a rapier; the most painstaking and honest-working of all clever men.—BROWN, DR. JOHN, 1858–61, *Horæ Subsecivæ.*

A delicate, attractive, dainty little figure, as he merely walked about, much more if he were speaking: uncommonly bright, black eyes, instinct with vivacity, intelligence and kindly fire; roundish brow, delicate oval face, full, rapid expression; figure light, nimble, pretty, though so small, perhaps hardly five feet four in height: he had his gown, almost never any wig, wore his black hair rather closely cropt,—I have seen the back part of it jerk suddenly out in some of the rapid expressions of his face, and knew, even if behind him, that his brow was then puckered, and his eyes looking archly, half-contemptuously out, in conformity to some conclusive little cut his tongue was giving. His voice, clear, harmonious, and sonorous, had something of metallic in it, something almost plangent; never rose into alt, into any dissonance or shrillness, nor carried much the character of humour, though a fine feeling of the ludicrous always dwelt in him,—as you would notice best, when he got into Scotch dialect, and gave you, with admirable truth of mimicry, old Edinburgh incidents and experiences of his. . . . His accent was indeed singular, but it was by no means Scotch: at his first going to Oxford (where he did not stay long) he had peremptorily crushed down his Scotch (which he privately had in store, in excellent condition, to the very end of his life, producible with highly ludicrous effect on occasion), and adopted instead a strange swift, sharp-sounding, fitful modulation, part of it pungent, quasi-latrant, other parts of it cooing, bantery, lovingly quizzical; which no charm of his fine ringing voice (*metallic* tenor, of sweet tone), and of his vivacious rapid looks and pretty little attitudes and gestures, could altogether reconcile you to; but in which he persisted through good report and bad. . . . There was something of Voltaire in him; something even in bodily features: those bright-beaming swift and piercing hazel-eyes, with their accompaniment of rapid keen expressions in the other lineaments of face, resembled one's notion of Voltaire; and in the voice too, there was a fine, half-plangent, kind of a metallic ringing tone, which used to remind me of what I fancied Voltaire's voice might have been: "*voix sombre et majestueuse,*" Duvernet calls it. —CARLYLE, THOMAS, 1867, *Lord Jeffrey, Reminiscences, ed. Norton.*

He never took up his pen till the candles were lit, . . . he did most of his work in those fatal hours of inspiration from ten at night till two or three o'clock in the morning. . . . His manuscript was inexpressibly vile; for he wrote with great haste, . . . generally used a wretched pen, . . . and altered, erased, and interlined without the slightest thought either of the printer or his correspondent. . . . The explanation is, of course, the usual one with men of Jeffrey's temperament and genius. He had a horror and hatred of the work of the desk. . . . His favourite hours of reading were in the morning and in bed, unless he had to deal with a subject of peculiar difficulty, and in that case he read it up . . . at night; for he had a notion that hints and suggestions, facts and thoughts, illustrations and authorities, picked up promiscuously over-night, assorted themselves in sleep round their proper centres, and thus reappeared in the morning in logical order.—PEBODY, CHARLES, 1870, *The Edinburgh Reviewers, Gentleman's Magazine, n. s., vol.* 5, *p.* 42.

He was represented as the quintessence of meanness and malevolence, when in truth he was not only a most high-minded and honorable man, but united to manly independence and firmness the sensibilities of a woman. A true and considerate friend, he sympathized with the struggles of unknown and friendless authors, to many of whom he was in private a liberal benefactor.—CONSTABLE, A. G., 1874, *Archibald Constable and his Friends, Harper's Magazine, vol.* 48, *p.* 505.

I often peeped through the green curtain which hung before his contracted judicial stall, and watched the wondrous little man unravelling, in his quick, impatient way, the tangle of Scotch Law. His restless person was in a state of perpetual movement; his eyes turning here, there, and everywhere; his features in constant play; his forehead rippling in quick successive wrinkles, as if striving to throw off his close-fitting judicial wig, which seemed to grasp his diminutive head painfully, almost down to his eyebrows, and with its great stiff curls of white horse-hair heavily to oppress him with its weight. His arms, too, he was ever moving with an uneasy action, thrusting them out, and shaking them, as if he would rid himself of the incumbrance of his official robe of scarlet, which covered his shoulders, and hung in loose folds from his neck to his wrists.—TOMES, ROBERT, 1880, *My College Days, p.* 83.

Jeffrey was a Benthamite on the surface, and underneath an Epicurean, with a good-humoured contempt for enthusiasm and high aspirations. Between him and a man so "dreadfully in earnest" as Carlyle, there could be little effective communion. —FROUDE, JAMES ANTHONY, 1882, *Thomas Carlyle, A History of the First Forty Years of his Life, vol.* I, *p.* 321.

In 1806 Tom Moore, the charming poet, got into a great rage with Francis Jeffrey (since Lord Advocate of Scotland), who had written an article for the *Edinburgh Review* attacking Moore's poems with some severity, and wrote the latter a letter, calling him a liar and demanding a meeting. Jeffrey accepted, of course. On the day of the "encounter," on which it had been arranged to have the Bow Street officers rush upon the combatants just as they were about to fire (which was carried out with precision), and while the seconds were loading their pistols with paper pellets instead of bullets, the two principals approached each other, and Jeffrey exclaimed, "What a very beautiful morning this is, ain't it?" Moore replied calmly, with a smile, "It is, indeed, a very beautiful morning—much too beautiful for such purposes as we have met for." They were then permitted to chat together until the minions of the law put in their appearance. Moore and Jeffrey became great friends afterward, but the former alienated himself from his second for thirty years for "giving the thing away." —TRUMAN, BEN C., 1884, *The Field of Honor, p.* 555.

Jeffrey was a man of extraordinary

sprightliness and untiring zeal. He had keen literary interests, and, within a very limited range, much acuteness of critical insight. He saw very clearly what was assailable in the existing state of things, although his political ideas were rather those of the versatile lawyer than of a statesman, and were, as those of the lawyer are apt to be, confined in their range. . . . We are bound to admit his deftness and his versatility; no one could deny his political sincerity; it would be rash even to belittle his literary gifts. But to him the wider range of imagination was a closed region. As a lawyer he made no claim to professional erudition. Even as a forensic orator he never attempted to appeal to the feelings, or to rise to the highest flights. But he poured forth arguments with a rapidity and a versatility that at once astonished, amused, and flattered his hearers, and made him eminently successful in appealing to the not very high standards of the juryman's intelligence. . . . His estimates of men and books were quick, confident, and lucidly expressed, but singularly narrow in range. —CRAIK, SIR HENRY, 1901, *A Century of Scottish History, vol.* II, *pp.* 250, 251.

GENERAL

Health to immortal Jeffrey! once, in name,
England could boast a judge almost the same;
In soul so like, so merciful, yet just,
Some think that Satan has resign'd his trust,
And given the spirit to the world again
To sentence letters, as he sentenced men.
—BYRON, LORD, 1809, *English Bards and Scotch Reviewers.*

Our very ideas of what is poetry, differ so widely, that we rarely talk upon these subjects. There is something in his mode of reasoning that leads me greatly to doubt whether, notwithstanding the vivacity of his imagination, he really has any *feeling* of poetical genius, or whether he has worn it all off by perpetually sharpening his wit on the grindstone of criticism.—SCOTT, SIR WALTER, 1812, *Letter to Joanna Baillie, Jan.* 17; *Lockhart's Life of Scott, ch.* xxiv.

You little know me, if you imagine that any thoughts of fear or favour would make me abstain from speaking publicly of Jeffrey as I think, and as he deserves. I despise his commendation, and I defy his malice.—SOUTHEY, ROBERT, 1814, *Letter to James Hogg, Dec.* 24.

Alas for Jeffrey!—if my fancy dreams,
Let not that dream's delusion pass away,—
For still 'midst all his poverty it seems
As if a spark of some ethereal ray,
Some fragment of the true Promethean beams,
Had been commingled with his infant clay;
As if for better things he had been born
Than transient flatteries and eternal scorn.
Alas for Jeffrey! for he might have clombe
To some high niche in glory's marble fane;
But he, vain man, preferred a lowlier home,
An easier triumph and a paltrier reign;
Therefore his name is blotted from the Tome
Of Fame's enduring record, and his gain
Hath in his life been given him, and the wreath
That his youth won scarce waits the wintry breath
Of the Destroyer, to shed all its bloom
And dissipate its fragrance in the air.
—LOCKHART, JOHN GIBSON, 1819, *The Mad Banker of Amsterdam, Blackwood's Magazine, vol.* 4, *p.* 565.

Taste in him is exalted into Imagination. —Ingenuity brightens into genius. He hath also Wisdom. But *nemo omnibus horis sapit;* and he made an unfortunate stumble over the Lyrical Ballads. He has had the magnanimity, however, I am told, to repent that great mistake, which to his fame was a misfortune—and, knowing the error of his ways, has returned to the broad path of Nature and Truth. How nobly has he written of Crabbe and Campbell, and Scott and Byron! Incomprehensible contradiction—the worst critic of the age is also the best—but the weeds of his mind are dead—the flowers are immortal. He is no orator, they say, in St. Stephen's; but that mouth, even on the silent paper, gives them the lie; and I have heard him a hundred times the most eloquent of speakers. His is a brilliant name in the literature of Scotland.—WILSON, JOHN, 1832, *Noctes Ambrosianæ, Nov.*

The *maximus minimus.*—SMITH, SYDNEY, 1843, *Letter to John Murray, June* 4; *A Memoir of Sydney Smith by Lady Holland, ch.* x.

When I compare him with Sydney and myself, I feel, with humility perfectly sincere, that his range is immeasurably wider than ours. And this is only as a writer. But he is not only a writer; he has been a great advocate, and he is a great judge. Take him all in all, I think him more nearly an universal genius than any man of our time.—MACAULAY, THOMAS

BABINGTON, 1843, *Letter to Macvey Napier, Dec.* 13; *Correspondence, ed. Son.*

I wrote the first article in the first Number of the Review, in October 1802, and sent my last contribution to it in October 1840! It is a long period to have persevered in well—or in ill doing! But I was by no means equally alert in the service during all the intermediate time. I was sole Editor, from 1803 till late in 1829; and during that period was no doubt a large and regular contributor. In that last year, however, I received the great honour of being elected, by my brethren of the Bar, to the office of Dean of the Faculty of Advocates; when it immediately occurred to me that it was not quite fitting that the official head of a great Law Corporation should continue to be the conductor of what might be fairly enough represented as, in many respects, a Party Journal; and I consequently withdrew at once and altogether from the management. . . . I wrote nothing for it, accordingly, for a considerable time subsequent to 1829; and during the whole fourteen years that have since elapsed, have sent in all but four papers to that work, none of them on political subjects. I ceased in reality to be a contributor in 1829.—JEFFREY, FRANCIS LORD, 1843, *Contributions to the Edinburgh Review, Preface, vol.* I.

A prominent defect of Jeffrey's literary criticism arose from his lack of earnestness,—that earnestness which comes, not merely from the assent of the understanding to a proposition, but from the deep convictions of a man's whole nature. He is consequently ingenious and plausible, rather than profound,—a man of expedients, rather than of ideas and principles. In too many of his articles, he appears like an advocate, careless of the truth, or skeptical as to its existence or possibility of being reached, and only desirous to make out as good a case for his own assumed position as will puzzle or unsettle the understandings of his hearers. His logical capacity is shown in acute special pleading, in sophistical glosses, more than in fair argument.—WHIPPLE, EDWIN P., 1845, *North American Review, Essays and Reviews, vol.* II, *p.* 128.

Take him all in all, where, we ask, is the critic of the present century who is to be placed in the scale against Francis Jeffrey? His peculiar fitness for his task resulted mainly from the exquisiteness of his taste, his fearless honesty, and the integrity of his judgment. His few mistakes arose chiefly from certain partial defects in faculty. These, however, were important enough to prevent him, if not from taking his place as the first of contemporary critics, from at least entering those highest walks of British criticism in which a very few of the master minds of the past were qualified to expatiate, and but few exclusively.—MILLER, HUGH, 1850, *Essays, p.* 84.

The great coryphæus of English critics.—CLEVELAND, CHARLES D., 1853, *English Literature of the Nineteenth Century p.* 509.

Jeffrey, who took the lead in this great revolution in literature, was a very remarkable man, but more so from the light, airy turn of his mind, and the felicity of illustration which he possessed, than from either originality of thought or nervous force of expression. His information was far from extensive: he shared in the deficiency of his country at that period in classical knowledge; he was ignorant of Italian and German; and his acquaintance with French literature was chiefly confined to the gossiping memoirs of the day, and, with that of his own country, to the writings of the Scotch metaphysicians or the old English dramatists. But these subjects he knew thoroughly; within these limits he was thoroughly master. He was fitted by nature to be a great critic. A passionate admirer of poetry, alive to all the beauties and influences of nature, with a feeling mind and a sensitive heart, he possessed at the same time the calm judgment which enabled him to form an impartial opinion on the works submitted to his examination, and the correct taste which, in general, discovered genius and detected imperfections in them.—ALISON, SIR ARCHIBALD, 1853–59, *History of Europe,* 1815–52, *ch.* V.

You must not criticize papers like these, rapidly written in the hurry of life, as you would the painful words of an elaborate sage, slowly and with anxious awfulness instructing mankind. Some things, a few things, are for eternity; some, and a good many, are for time. We do not expect the everlastingness of the Pyramids from the vibratory grandeur of a Tyburnian mansion. . . . He invented the trade of editorship: before him an editor was a bookseller's drudge, he is now a distinguished functionary. If Jeffrey was not a great critic, he had what very great critics have wanted,—the art of writing what most people would think good criticism. He might not know his subject, but he knew his readers: people like to read ideas which they can imagine to have been their own. "Why does Scarlett always persuade the jury?" asked a rustic gentleman. "Because there are twelve Scarletts in the Jury-box," replied an envious advocate. What Scarlett was in law, Jeffrey was in criticism: he could become that which his readers could not avoid being. He was neither a pathetic writer nor a profound writer; but he was a quick-eyed, bustling, black-haired, sagacious, agreeable man of the world. He had his day, and was entitled to his day; but a gentle oblivion must now cover his already subsiding reputation.—BAGEHOT, WALTER, 1855, *The First Edinburgh Reviewers, Works, ed. Morgan, vol.* I, *pp.* 29, 33.

There was a pertness about his general manner of writing. Amazingly clever, adroit, subtle—he always gave you the impression of smallness. — GILFILLAN, GEORGE, 1855, *A Third Gallery of Portraits, p.* 193.

By nature, education, and habits of thought, was a special pleader. He used words and ideas for an immediate purpose; his object, when most in earnest, is to gain a point; his liberality and depth of feeling were in reverse proportion to his cleverness and information. His great moral defect was want of modesty. He does not appear to have known, by experience, the feeling of self-distrust, but thought himself quite competent to dictate to the world, not only on legal, but on literary and social topics. This reliance upon his own reason gives force and point to those disquisitions the scope of which come within his legitimate range, but makes him offensive, with all his agreeability of style, the moment he transcends his proper sphere. He manifests, in an extraordinary degree, the Scotch idiosyncrasy which refers everything exclusively to the understanding. He was essentially literal. . . . The order of his mind is within the sphere of the familiar; only in aptness, in constant exercise and skill, was it above the average. —TUCKERMAN, HENRY T., 1857, *Essays, Biographical and Critical, pp.* 166, 168.

Jeffrey's labors as editor were unceasing, and I will venture to say, if we had searched all Europe, a better man, *in every respect*, could not have been found. As a critic he was unequalled; and, take them as a whole, I consider his articles were the best we had.—BROUGHAM, HENRY LORD, 1871, *Life and Times, Written by Himself, ch.* iv.

In his criticisms of Wordsworth we see vividly at once his own character and his failure to appreciate a character very different from his own. He was an affectionate man, intensely attached to his friends, and uncontrollably fond of their society; and the passages that he admires in Wordsworth are chiefly passages of tenderness. He loved natural scenery, too, in a way, and does justice to Wordsworth's more striking word-pictures; but he was too much attracted to "the busy haunts of men" to follow the raptures of a genuine nature-worshipper, and he found Wordsworth's minute descriptions intolerably tedious. But what he chiefly failed to understand, and what chiefly offended him, were the meditations natural to a recluse, and the glorification of children and of country personages to a degree altogether out of keeping with their conventional place in the social scale. He was constantly accusing Wordsworth of clothing the commonest commonplaces with unintelligible verbiage, and of debasing tenderness with vulgarity. A similar narrowness, the same tendency to lay down the law without a suspicion that other people were differently constituted from himself, appears in his essay on "Beauty." Himself defective in the feeling for colour, he denies that colour possesses any intrinsic beauty, and is utterly sceptical regarding the statements of artists and connoisseurs, suspecting them of pedantry and jargon. His style is forcible and copious, without any pretence to finished or elegant structure. His diction is perhaps too overflowing; his powers of amplification and illustration sometimes ran away with him; "his memory," says Lockhart, "appeared to range the dictionary from A to Z, and he had not the self-denial to spare his readers the redundance which delighted himself." His collected works give but a feeble idea of the cleverness of his ridicule; he refused to republish the most striking specimens of his satirical skill. —MINTO, WILLIAM, 1872–80, *Manual of English Prose Literature, p.* 530.

Jeffrey had neither the exuberance of wit nor the lightness of expression which characterised Sidney Smith. But he was on the whole a greater writer, just as he was undoubtedly a greater critic and a better editor. His criticisms are strict; they are occasionally unfair, but are always able; and, though many of his conclusions have been reversed by the judgment of posterity, his opinions are still uniformly quoted with deference, and usually accepted as authoritative.—WALPOLE, SPENCER, 1878, *A History of England from the Conclusion of the Great War in* 1815, *vol.* I, *p.* 386.

Had an adequate share of his attention been concentrated on some special branch of literature, had his fluency been held in check by a more thorough acquaintance with the subjects which engaged his interest, his regard for immediate impressiveness not been exaggerated by the influence of his professional duties, his artistic sense, which was keen and true so far as it went, not been mutilated and deteriorated by untoward circumstances, he would undoubtedly have earned for himself a high place among the writers of his epoch. As it is, his reputation is now unsubstantial and shadowy, and he is remembered chiefly from his accidental and not always gratifying and desirable relation to others who have gained an independent fame.—HENDERSON, T. F., 1881, *Encyclopædia Britannica, Ninth ed., vol.* XIII, *p.* 628.

The peculiar value of Jeffrey is not, as that of Coleridge, of Hazlitt, or of Lamb, in his very subtle, very profound, or very original views of his subjects. He is neither a critical Columbus nor a critical Socrates: he neither opens up undiscovered countries, nor provokes and stimulates to the discovery of them. His strength lies in the combination of a fairly wide range of sympathy with an extraordinary shrewdness and good sense in applying that sympathy. Tested for range alone, or for subtlety alone, he will frequently be found wanting; but he almost invariably catches up those who have thus outstripped him when the subject of the trial is shifted to soundness of estimate, intelligent connection of view, and absence of eccentricity. And it must be again and again repeated that Jeffrey is by no means justly chargeable with the Dryasdust failings so often attributed to academic criticism. They said that on the actual Bench he worried counsel a little too much, but that his decisions were on the whole invariably sound. Not quite so much perhaps can be said for his other exercise of the judicial function. But however much he may sometimes seem to carp and complain, however much we may sometimes wish for a little more equity and a little less law, it is astonishing how weighty Jeffrey's critical judgments are after three quarters of a century which has seen so many seeming heavy things grow light. There may be much that he does not see: there may be some things which he is physically unable to see; but what he does see, he sees with a clearness, and co-ordinates in its bearings on other things seen with a precision which are hardly to be matched among the fluctuating and diverse race of critics. — SAINTSBURY, GEORGE, 1887, *Francis Jeffrey, Macmillan's Magazine, vol.* 56, *p.* 267.

Jeffrey, the "arch-critic," as he was sometimes called, was universally looked upon as the soul of the "Edinburgh Review." His work was marked by great ability, and, we think, by a spirit of justice, or at least a desire for justice. That he made violent and bitter attacks upon authors who did not deserve his censure cannot be denied, but it is equally incontestable that he was saying what he thought was right. . . . The fault that we have nowadays to find with Jeffrey is that of his extreme minuteness, the anxiety not to miss any detail, which seems to us to make him often miss the effect of the whole, and to find faults instead of beauties by his persistent habit of looking down, rather than up.—OLIPHANT, MARGARET O. W., 1892, *The Victorian Age of English Literature, pp.* 44, 46.

In conversation and in criticism his influence was always on the side of a pure morality. He had a keen and vivacious rather than an original or profound mind. —ROBERTSON, J. LOGIE, 1894, *A History of English Literature, p.* 363.

That amazing person, Lord Jeffrey, in one of his too numerous contributions to the *Edinburgh Review*, wrote of the poverty of Swift's style. Lord Jeffrey was, we hope, a professional critic, not an amateur. —BIRRELL, AUGUSTINE, 1894, *Essays about Men, Women and Books, p.* 14.

In spite of its undeniable verboseness, Jeffrey's style was considered brilliant and sprightly. How such a verdict could be passed on a style whose average sentence is fifty words, with only 6 per cent. of very short sentences to vary the monotony, is hard for a modern reader to see. The secret lies in the comparative absence of periodicity. Jeffrey's huge sentences are mere groups of clauses. Many clauses are oppositional; these are often set off by dashes. Jeffrey went as far in the direction of aggregating loose clauses as Macaulay went in the direction of segregating them. Otherwise, in the case of these two men, one style is almost as modern as the other. Jeffrey's length of paragraph is not far from Macaulay's. As a structural unit Jeffrey's lacks emphasis, from neglect of the short period: Macaulay's lacks gradation of emphasis, from his neglect of the moderately long period. Jeffrey makes clauses out of periods; Macaulay makes periods out of clauses. Jeffrey's usual paragraph order is loose. His subject is often delayed, however, by verbose introductions. He has no sense of the importance of the first sentence and the last. His coherence is good but not graceful. There is occasional abuse of coördinate conjunctions.—LEWIS, EDWIN HERBERT, 1894, *The History of the English Paragraph, p.* 129.

Though his works no longer delight the general public, Lord Jeffrey will always occupy a respectable position in English letters as the founder, to all intents and purposes, of reviewing. His intellect was nimble rather than penetrating, and his knowledge miscellaneous rather than profound; while his sensibility at times was too strong for his sense. Indeed, his characteristic admission to Macvey Napier that he had read Macaulay's essay on Bacon "not only with delight but with emotion, with throbbings of the heart and tears in the eye," seems to afford a hint at once of the measure of his attainments in philosophy and of his extreme susceptibility to any form of excitation. Yet his brisk and dapper habit of mind was no bad qualification for the literary work of his life; and perhaps the best proof of his success is the long existence which his convention has enjoyed. Every sentence of Macaulay attests his statement that he had read and re-read Jeffrey's old articles till he knew them by heart; and for close upon a hundred years critic after critic, consciously or unconsciously, has copied his methods, has imitated his tone and bearing, has aped his omniscience, and has endeavoured to assume his awful air of authority.—MILLAR, J. H., 1896, *English Prose, ed. Craik, vol.* V, *p.* 143.

Was a critic of no mean ability, as many an acute and impartial appreciation of contemporary literature under his hand exists to prove.—TRAILL, HENRY DUFF, 1896, *Social England, vol.* V, *p.* 591.

Jeffrey was before all things a literary critic, and, within the limits of his discernment, one of the acutest and liveliest of his time. His point of view was that of refined but positive common-sense, qualified by a rooted distrust of innovation. To the simple and obvious poetry of Rogers, Campbell, Crabbe, he brought a keen if somewhat excessive appreciation; mawkish sentiment and pseudo-mediævalism he exposed with signal effect. We cannot now wholly disapprove of the stricture upon "Marmion" which angered Scott, nor share his effusive penitence for those upon Byron's "Hours of Idleness." But he was, unfortunately, as proof against the true Romantics as against the false, and comprehended the mysticism of imaginative poetry in the same anathema with the crude supernaturalism of the school of horrors. The manifesto against the "Lake school" with which he opened the review is one of the most striking examples in literature of the fatuous efforts of a clever man to interpret a larger world than his own. The naked simplicity of Wordsworth, the tumultuous energy of Coleridge, the irregular metres of Southey were equally offensive to him, and he classed them together, as if innovators formed one brotherhood.—HERFORD, C. H., 1897, *The Age of Wordsworth, p.* 52.

Those two hundred papers which he wrote in the *Edinburgh Review* are of the widest range—charmingly and piquantly written. Yet they do not hold place among great and popular essays; not with Macaulay, or Mackintosh, or Carlyle, or even Hazlitt.—MITCHELL, DONALD G., 1897, *English Lands Letters and Kings, The Later Georges to Victoria, p.* 95.

William Lisle Bowles

1762–1850

Born 24th September 1762, at King's Sutton vicarage, Northamptonshire. Educated at Winchester and Trinity College, Oxford; in 1804 he became a prebendary of Salisbury and rector of Bremhill, in Wiltshire. Here he spent in easy circumstances the rest of his long life, dying at Salisbury, 7th April 1850. His "Fourteen Sonnets, written chiefly on Picturesque Spots during a Journey" (1789), had Coleridge, Wordsworth, and Southey among their enthusiastic admirers; and through his influence over them Bowles may be looked on as the founder of a school of English poetry in which his own name was soon eclipsed by theirs. Of his subsequent poetical works (14 vols. 1789–1837), the longest is "The Spirit of Discovery," and the best, perhaps, the "Missionary of the Andes." In 1806 he published an edition of Pope, and an opinion which he expressed on Pope's poetical merits led to a rather memorable controversy (1809–25), in which Campbell and Byron were his antagonists. Of his prose writings may be mentioned a rather dry "Life of Bishop Ken" (2 vols. 1830). See the Memoir by Gilfillan prefixed to his collected poems (Edin. 1855).—PATRICK AND GROOME, *eds.*, 1897, *Chambers's Biographical Dictionary*, p. 124.

PERSONAL

My Sheridan task . . . interrupted by Bowles, who never comes amiss; the mixture of talent and simplicity in him are delightful. His parsonage house at Bremhill is beautifully situated, but he has a good deal frittered away its beauty with grottos, hermitages, and Shenstonian inscriptions: When company is coming he cries, "Here, John, run with the crucifix and missal to the hermitage, and set the fountain going." His sheep-bells are tuned in thirds and fifths; but he is an excellent fellow notwithstanding; and if the waters of his inspiration be not those of Helicon, they are at least very *sweet* waters, and to my taste pleasanter than some that are more strongly impregnated.—MOORE, THOMAS, 1818, *Diary; Memoirs, Journal and Correspondence, ed. Russell.*

Madame de Staël had a great wish to see Mr. Bowles, the poet, or as Lord Byron calls him, the sonneteer; she admired his sonnets, and his "Spirit of Maritime Discovery," and ranked him high as an English genius. In riding to Bowood he fell, and sprained his shoulder, but still came on. Lord Lansdowne alluded to this in presenting him to Madame de Staël before dinner in the midst of the listening circle. She began to compliment him and herself upon the exertion he had made to come and see her: "O ma'am, say no more, for I would have done a great deal more to see so great a *curiosity!*" Lord Lansdowne says it is impossible to describe the *shock* in Madame de Staël's face—the breathless astonishment and the total change produced in her opinion of the man. She afterwards said to Lord Lansdowne, who had told her he was a simple country clergyman, "Je vois bien que ce n'est qu' un simple curé qui n'a pas le sens commun, quoique grand poéte."—EDGEWORTH, MARIA, 1818, *To Mrs. Edgeworth, Letters, vol.* I, *p.* 250.

Mr. Bowles was very pleasant and sociable, talked a great deal of Lord Byron and the Pope question, in which we exactly agree, and in which, from not having read the prosy pamphlet in which he has so marred his own good cause, I was able to agree with him most conscientiously. Pray do you like his wife? Is not she a coarse, cold, hard woman, and rather vulgarish? All this she seemed to me. He is very unaffected and agreeable. — MITFORD, MARY RUSSELL, 1821, *To Sir William Elford, July* 1; *Life of Mary Russell Mitford, ed. L'Estrange, vol.* I, *p.* 363.

He appeared to me an amiable, well-informed, and extremely able man. I am willing to believe him a good man, almost as good a man as Pope, but no better.—BYRON, LORD, 1821, *On Bowles's Strictures on Pope.*

Lisle Bowles is another name to be marked with a white stone. A delightful spot was Bremhill—indeed, is still—with the quaint garden, and the swans, Snowdrop and Lily, sailing up to the parlour window to inquire after their dinner, and Peter the hawk, and the Vicar holding his watch to his ear, to make sure that he had not grown deaf since breakfast. Southey visited the Parsonage when the lovable old man was in his seventy-third year, and presented to the eye of his friend the most entertaining mixture that could be of untidiness, simplicity, benevolence, timidity, and good nature; but nobody smiled at his oddities more heartily than the owner.—WILLMOTT, ROBERT ARIS, 1856, *The Poets of the Nineteenth Century, Preface, p.* vii.

Mr. Bowles had a blunt, almost a rough manner, which did not quite answer my preconceived (immature) idea of a poet. I had imagined that I should see a melancholy man, pressed down by love disappointed, and solemn with internal trouble; I found a cheerful married man, with no sympton of weakness or sentiment about him. He had a pretty garden at his Bremhill parsonage, where he erected a hermitage, and was unwise enough to endow it with a multitude of inscriptions; at which his neighbors were fond of laughing, as instances of affectation. For myself, I never saw anything affected or fantastic in this gentleman. His wife was a lady, tall, and of good manners; not ill adapted to a poet who had previously exhausted all his sorrows in song.—PROCTER, BRYAN WALLER (BARRY CORNWALL), 1874? *Recollections of Men of Letters, p.* 131.

All the anecdotes told of his eccentricities are pleasant, simple, and harmless; and Bowles the man was the faithful counterpart of Bowles the poet—pure in spirit, sweet in nature, and tender of heart—good rather than great.—HALL, SAMUEL CARTER, 1883, *Retrospect of a Long Life, p.* 315.

Latterly Bowles became very deaf, but he kept up the habit of going about as long as he could. Once on the occasion of the archdeacon's visitation to Chippenham, Mr. Julian Young, as the last instituted incumbent in the district, had to preach the sermon. This gentleman, the son of Young the actor, was a very popular preacher, but full of gesticulations and display in the pulpit—a manner by no means approved by all his hearers. After church the assembled parsons always had a luncheon at the Angel Hotel. My informant, Sir Gabriel Goldney tells me that "It was the duty of Canon Bowles, as the oldest incumbent, to thank the new incumbent for his sermon." In the somewhat droning but still emphatic way that Bowles had in speaking, he said—"Excellent sermon, Mr. Young—wonderful sermon. I never heard a word of it, but the acting was admirable."—CROSSE, MRS. ANDREW, 1894, *Poet, Parson and Pamphleteer, Temple Bar, vol.* 103, *p.* 45.

SONNETS

Let sonneteering Bowles his strains refine,
And whine and whimper to the fourteenth line.

—BYRON, LORD, 1809, *English Bards and Scotch Reviewers.*

I had just entered on my seventeenth year, when the sonnets of Mr. Bowles, twenty in number, and just then published in a quarto pamphlet, were first made known and presented to me. . . . It was a double pleasure to me, and still remains a tender recollection, that I should have received from a friend so revered the first knowledge of a poet, by whose works, year after year, I was so enthusiastically delighted and inspired. My earliest acquaintances will not have forgotten the undisciplined eagerness and impetuous zeal, with which I labored to make proselytes, not only of my companions, but of all with whom I conversed, of whatever rank, and in whatever place. As my school finances did not permit me to purchase copies, I made, within less than a year and a half, more than forty transcriptions, as the best presents I could offer to those, who had in any way won my regard. And with almost equal delight did I receive the three or four following publications of the same author. . . . My obligations to Mr. Bowles were indeed important, and for radical good.—COLERIDGE, SAMUEL TAYLOR, 1817, *Biographia Literaria, ch.* i.

"The further development of the uses of the sonnet and the enlargement of its scope and influence are largely due to a poet upon whom the example of those who rejected the canon of the intellectual school of Addison and Pope had not been lost. The poet to whom I refer has not been accorded, nor indeed did he deserve to be accorded, the highest, or even a high poetical rank; but yet, unquestionably, he exerted a powerful plastic influence, especially as regards the powers and scope of the sonnet, upon two modern poets of acknowledged genius, whose writings have exercised a subtler, more widely diffused, and more permanent impression on English poetry than those of any other authors of modern times."—DESHLER, CHARLES D., 1879, *Afternoons with the Poets, p.* 180.

The sonnet work of William Lisle Bowles has a certain literary interest on account of the influence—a somewhat inexplicable one, it must be owned—which it exercised in the formation of the poetic taste of Coleridge. — NOBLE, JAMES ASHCROFT, 1880, *The Sonnet in England and other Essays*, p. 38.

It is the fashion in the present day to speak slightingly of Bowles, but his sonnets have unquestionable merit. Their language is melodious to a degree which perhaps only Collins in that century had surpassed, and it expressed a tender melancholy, which may have been inspired also by the study of the same poet.—AINGER, ALFRED, 1882, *Charles Lamb (English Men of Letters)*, p. 13.

Cowper, who died as may be remembered in the last year of the eighteenth century, wrote one fine poem of this class to Mary Unwin. Gradually the sonnet began to awake from its poetic hibernation, and though one or two women writers not altogether unworthily handled it, and though William Roscoe and Egerton Brydges even used it with moderate success, the first real breath of spring came in the mild advent of William Lisle Bowles. His sonnets move us now hardly at all, but when we remember the season of their production we may well regard them with more kindly liberality.—SHARP, WILLIAM, 1886, *Sonnets of this Century, Introduction.*

His sonnets are simple, graceful, but withal tame productions, about which no enthusiasm is possible now; and yet Coleridge could say of them that they had done his heart more good than all the other books he ever read, excepting his Bible. —MILES, ALFRED H., 1897, *The Poets and the Poetry of the Century, Sacred, Moral and Religious Verse, Appendix*, p. ii.

The event which, strange to say, had the greatest influence upon Coleridge at this time, was the chance reading of Bowles's "Sonnets;" these had been sent to him by his friend Middleton, who had entered Cambridge a year before. In this slight volume of twenty sonnets he met "nature unsophisticated by classic tradition," and was captivated by their freshness, originality, and simplicity. He copied them again and again, in order that his friends might enjoy them with him. In writing to one of these, he says, "They have done my heart more good than all the other books I ever read excepting the Bible." It is difficult for us in these days to conceive of a time when such influences could be produced by a little quarto. But Coleridge was not the only one over whom it cast its spell, for Wordsworth was not long after captivated by it. He first met the volume as he was leaving London with friends for a walk; he seated himself in a recess on Westminster Bridge, and kept them waiting until he read the twenty sonnets. We may call these incidents and their results chance if we please, but "it chanced—eternal God that chance did guide." If we wish to see what was the character of that spark which thus kindled two natures, we have but to read a few of Bowles's "Sonnets." Although they may seem somewhat tame to us now, yet we must admit that they have what was needed to revive sick poetry,—directness of expression, genuine sensibility, and wholesome love of nature and man.—GEORGE, ANDREW J., 1897, *ed. Coleridge's The Ancient Mariner, Preface*, p. x.

POPE CONTROVERSY

Pope's works have been twice given to the world by editors who cannot be taxed with the slightest editorial partiality towards his fame. The last of these is the Rev. Mr. Bowles, in speaking of whom I beg leave most distinctly to disclaim the slightest intention of undervaluing his acknowledged merit as a poet, however freely and fully I may dissent from his critical estimate of the genius of Pope.—CAMPBELL, THOMAS, 1819, *Essay on English Poetry.*

It had been more honourable in this gentleman, with his known prejudices against the class of poetry in which Pope will always remain unrivalled, to have declined the office of editor, than to attempt to spread among new generations of readers the most unfavourable and the most unjust impressions of the poet, and of the man. — CROKER, JOHN WILSON, 1820, *Spence's Anecdotes of Books and Men, Quarterly Review*, vol. 23, p. 407.

Bowles's edition is not without its faults, it is indeed not without its vices, for it displays an *animus* against Pope which makes the editor unfair to his judgment of biographical details, as well as ungenerous in the picture which he draws of his author as a man. Yet Bowles has been justly termed the most poetical editor of Pope; and it was he who, under the influences of a new current in English literature with which Byron had more in common than he cared to know, first succeeded in establishing those defects in his author which no candid criticism can since pretend to overlook.—WARD, ADOLPHUS, WILLIAM, 1869, *ed., Poetical Works of Alexander Pope, Introductory Memoir, p.* xlvii.

His poetic sensibility was exquisite, and he was well-read, shrewd, and candid. His failing was a hurry of mind which disqualified him for a painstaking commentator. He was content to jot down in a careless, colloquial style the off-hand thoughts of his quick cultivated intellect, and he did not add much to the scanty explanations of Warton and Warburton. The chief merit of his edition is his excellent literary criticism, which is truer, deeper, and more refined than that of his old Winchester master. The estimate Bowles formed of the poetry and character of Pope was allowed to pass unchallenged for thirteen years, when some remarks of Campbell, in his "Specimens of British Poets," commenced a controversy which lasted from 1819 to 1826. In the series of pamphlets he published to vindicate his opinions, Bowles exhibited his wonted acuteness, courage, and negligence. With all his slips in minor points the fresh facts which have come to light have more than confirmed his view of Pope's moral obliquities, and in the discussion on the principles of poetry he reduced the whole of his adversaries to silence. He and Hazlitt were the only persons among the disputants, eminent or obscure, who showed any real comprehension of the subject.—ELWIN, WHITWELL, 1871, *ed., The Works of Alexander Pope, Introduction, vol.* I, *pp.* xxiii, xxiv.

Mr. Bowles wrote a book upon Pope. Mr. Campbell abused Mr. Bowles's book upon Pope. Mr. Bowles wrote an answer to Mr. Campbell's abuse of Mr. Bowles's book on Pope. Lord Byron wrote a letter to certain stars in Albemarle street in answer to Mr. Bowles's answer to Mr. Campbell's abuse of Mr. Bowles's book on Pope. Jeremy Bentham, Esq., wrote a letter to Lord Byron about Lord Byron's letter to certain stars in Albemarle street, in answer to Mr. Bowles's answer to Mr. Campbell's abuse of Mr. Bowles's book on Pope. Mr. Bowles wrote an answer, not to Jeremy Bantham, but to Lord Byron's letter to certain stars in Albermarle street, in answer to Mr. Bowles's answer to Mr. Campbell's abuse of Mr. Bowles's book on Pope. Here the controversy ended, leaving each disputant more thoroughly satisfied with his own judgment.—RUSSELL, WILLIAM CLARK, 1871, *ed., The Book of Authors, p.* 359, *note.*

Bowles was without an ear for the versification, and without knowledge of the history of the eighteenth century, and contributed nothing to the elucidation of the confessed obscurities of Pope's allusions. —PATTISON, MARK, 1872–89, *Pope and his Editors, Essays, ed. Nettleship, vol.* II, *p.* 374.

Though he was often wrong, and though his general view of the poet is too much coloured with animosity, Bowles may fairly lay claim to having exposed certain features in Pope's real character, which had been altogether disguised in the pompous panegyrics of Warburton.—COURTHOPE, WILLIAM JOHN, 1881, *Introduction to the Moral Essays and Satires, Pope's Works, vol.* III, *p.* 16.

GENERAL

My heart has thank'd thee, *Bowles!* for those soft strains
Whose sadness soothes me, like the murmuring
Of wild-bees in the sunny showers of spring!
For hence not callous to the mourner's pains.
Through Youth's gay prime and thornless paths I went:
And when the *darker* day of life began,
And I did roam, a thought-bewildered man,
Their mild and manliest melancholy lent
A mingled charm, such as the pang consign'd
To slumber, though the big tear it renew'd;
Bidding a strange mysterious *Pleasure* brood
Over the wavy and tumultuous mind,
As the great *Spirit* erst with plastic sweep
Mov'd on the darkness of the unform'd deep.
—COLERIDGE, SAMUEL TAYLOR, 1794–96, *Sonnet to the Rev. W. L. Bowles.*

Breathes not the man with a more poetical temperament than Bowles. No wonder that his eyes "love all they look on," for they possess the sacred gift of beautifying creation, by shedding over it the charm of melancholy. . . . No vain repinings, no idle regrets, does his spirit ever breathe over the still receding Past. But time-sanctified are all the shews that arise before his pensive imagination; and the common light of day, once gone, in his poetry seems to shine as if it had all been dying sunset or moonlight, or the new-born dawn. His human sensibilities are so fine as to be in themselves poetical; and his poetical aspirations so delicate as to be felt always human. Hence his Sonnets have been dear to poets—having in them "more than meets the ear"—spiritual breathings that hang around the words like light around fair flowers; and hence, too, have they been beloved by all natural hearts who, having not the "faculty divine," have yet the "vision"—that is, the power of seeing and of hearing the sights and the sounds which genius alone can awaken, bringing them from afar, out of the dust and dimness of vanishment.—WILSON, JOHN, 1831, *An Hour's Talk About Poetry, Recreations of Christopher North; Blackwood's Magazine, vol.* 30, *p.* 475.

This morning I received your "St. John in Patmos." I have just read the poem through, and with much pleasure. Yours I should have known it to have been by the sweet and unsophisticated style upon which I endeavoured, now almost forty years ago, to form my own.—SOUTHEY, ROBERT, 1832, *Letter to Rev. W. Lisle Bowles, July* 30; *Life and Correspondence, ed. C. C. Southey.*

Bowles was an inferior artist to Rogers, although taste and elegance are also the chief features of his poetry. . . . The latter and more ambitious efforts of Lisle Bowles—for he wrote at least four long poems—could not be said to have been thoroughly, that is, eminently, successful. In all, passages of tender sentiment and fine description abound; but, on the whole, they were more the pumpings up, than the pourings out, of genius. His mind possessed more elegance than vigour; was rather reflective than imaginative. He is deficient in variety; and he ventured not, like Crabbe, to paint things exactly as he saw them; hence there is a sameness about his outlines that savours of mannerism. His familiar walk was amid the gentler affections of our nature; but his tenderness seldom rises into passion; or it is merely the anger of the dove,

"Pecking the hand that hovers o'er its mate."

The Attic taste of his scholarship seemed to trammel that enthusiasm, essential for the creation of high lyric poetry; and in this he resembles Thomas Warton—to whom, in his descriptive sketches, as well as in his chivalresque tendencies, he bore a greater resemblance than to any other.—MOIR, D. M., 1851–52, *Sketches of the Poetical Literature of the Past Half-Century, pp.* 54, 55.

His diction at the beginning of his career, both in verse and prose, was cumbrous and awkard; but he gradually acquired ease, directness, and elegance. His ear was always correct, and inclined to melodious composition. Yet in his greater blank-verse poems he shows himself acquainted with the intricacies and elaborate subtleties that enter into the production of harmony, and encounters and subdues difficulties with the courage and confidence that imply conscious skill and practised power. To the right-hearted and earnest student of poetry they will always be welcome, and not only be carefully perused, but sedulously studied, as examples of the art in which he would excel.—HERAUD, JOHN A., 1863, *William Lisle Bowles, Temple Bar, vol.* 8, *p.* 446.

Those who to-day turn to the much-praised verses will scarcely find in their pensive amenity that enduring charm which they presented to the hungry and restless soul of Coleridge, seeking its fitting food in unpropitious places. They exhibit a grace of expression, a delicate sensibility, and above all a "musical sweet melancholy" that is especially grateful in certain moods of mind; but with lapse of time and change of fashion they have grown a little thin and faint and colourless. Of Bowles's remaining works it is not necessary to speak. He was over-matched in his controversy with Byron as to Pope, and the blunt

"Stick to thy sonnets, Bowles,—at least they pay"

of the former must be accepted as the final word upon the poetical efforts of the cultivated and amiable Canon of Salisbury.—DOBSON, AUSTIN, 1880, *The English Poets, ed. Ward, vol.* IV, *p.* 99.

His was the first significant note of conscious transition from the formalism and the affected classicism of the epoch of Johnson and Pope to the lyric freedom of

Wordsworth, Shelley, and Keats. Even Bowles was rather an indication than a fulfilment. Though he revolved freely on his own individuality, he was not absolutely free from the conventionalities of poetry of his time. Nor did he fully indicate the breadth of the change that was to arise in his own later days. There were depths deeper and flights higher than his to follow; nevertheless, the significant fact is that he had the impulse and the courage to advance according to his light. Compared with his brilliant successors his light was doubtless dim, but on that very account is his case the more interesting, his attitude the more touching. . . . Bowles' was an experiment, and he survived to witness his experiment become demonstrations of success in others.—TIREBUCK, WILLIAM, 1887, *ed., The Poetical Works of Bowles, Lamb and Hartley Coleridge, Introduction, pp.* vii, ix.

As the English romantic poets went forth both to combat the classic school with its super-sense and pride of strict rules, and to endow the poetry of the fairy tale with new life, their first halt was under the shadow of Bowles. Compared with such a poet of the intellect as Pope, who had maintained that, with a clear head and dexterous style, nothing was too prosaic to be converted into poetry, such an elegist as Bowles, who aimed at all effect through the heart, was a most refreshing contrast.—BRANDL, ALOIS, 1887, *Samuel Taylor Coleridge and the English Romantic School, tr. Lady Eastlake, p.* 37.

One cannot help regretting that the inspiration did not come more directly from Cowper or Burns, or from both; but I confess my inability to join in the expression of amused wonder which has so often greeted Coleridge's acknowledgments of his obligation to Bowles. . . . The first breath of Nature unsophisticated by classical tradition came to Coleridge from Bowles's sonnets; and he recognised it at once. Nor was he alone in this experience. Four years, later, the same sonnets captivated Wordsworth.—CAMPBELL, JAMES DYKES, 1894, *Samuel Taylor Coleridge, p.* 17.

A country clergyman of leisure and means, he continued at long intervals to lift up his little light in the midst of the glory he had helped to kindle, sang sympathetically of the battle of the Nile, and the sorrows of Switzerland, and showed how little he comprehended the poetic revolution by galvanizing the defunct didactic poem into such semblance of vitality as belongs to his "Spirit of Discovery by Sea."—HERFORD, C. H., 1897, *The Age of Wordsworth, p.* 183.

Sarah Margaret Fuller

Marchioness Ossoli

1810–1850

Educator and philosopher, born in Cambridge, Mass., 23d May, 1810, lost at sea 15th July, 1850. She received a broad education and early felt a deep interest in social questions. She learned French, German and the classics, and her associates in Cambridge were persons of culture, experience and advanced ideas. In 1833 the family removed to Groton, Mass., where she gave lessons to private classes in languages and other studies. Her father, Timothy Fuller, died of cholera, 26th September, 1835, and his death threw the family upon Margaret for support, and her plans for a trip to Europe were abandoned. In 1836 she went to Boston, where she taught Latin and French in A. Bronson Alcott's school, and taught private classes of girls in French, German and Italian. In 1837 she became a teacher in a private school in Providence, R. I., which was organized on Mr. Alcott's plan. She translated many works from the German and other languages. In 1839 she removed to Jamaica Plain, Mass., and took a house on her own responsibility, to make a home for the family. The next year they returned to Cambridge. In 1839 she instituted in Boston her conversational class, which was continued for several years. She did much writing on subjects connected with her educational work. In 1840 she became the editor of "The Dial," which she managed for two years. Her contributions to that journal were numerous. Several volumes of translations from the German were brought out by her. In 1843 she went on a western tour with James Freeman Clarke and his artist-sister, and her first original work, "Summer on the Lakes," was the result of that trip. In 1844 she removed to New York City, where for two years she furnished literary criticisms for the "Tribune." In 1846 she published her volume, "Papers on Literature and Art." After twenty months of life in New York she went to Europe. She met in Italy, in 1847, Giovani Angelo, Marquis Ossoli, a man younger than she and of less intellectual culture, but a simple and noble man, who had given up his rank and station in the cause of the Roman Republic. They were married in 1847. Their son, Angelo Philip Eugene Ossoli, was born in Rieti, 5th September, 1848. After the fall of the republic it was necessary for them to leave Rome, and Madame Ossoli, desiring to print in America her history of the Italian struggle, suggested their return to the United States. They sailed on the barque "Elizabeth" from Leghorn, 17th May, 1850. The trip was a disastrous one. Capt. Hasty died of the small-pox and was buried off Gibraltar. Mme. Ossoli's infant son was attacked by the disease on 11th June, but recovered. On 15th July the "Elizabeth" made the New Jersey coast at noon, and during a fog the vessel ran upon Fire Island and was wrecked. Madame Ossoli refused to be separated from her husband, and all three were drowned. The body of their child was found on the beach and was buried in the sand by the sailors, to be afterwards removed to Mount Auburn Cemetery, near Boston. The bodies of Marquis and Madame Ossoli were never found.—MOULTON, CHARLES WELLS, 1893, *A Woman of the Century, eds. Willard and Livermore, p.* 551.

PERSONAL

She is of the medium height; nothing remarkable about the figure; a profusion of lustrous light hair; eyes a bluish gray, full of fire; capacious forehead; the mouth when in repose indicates profound sensibility, capacity for affection, for love—when moved by a slight smile, it becomes even beautiful in the intensity of this expression; but the upper lip, as if impelled by the action of involuntary muscles, habitually uplifts itself, conveying the impression of a sneer. Imagine, now, a person of this description looking you at one moment earnestly in the face, at the next seeming to look only within her own spirit or at the wall; moving nervously every now and then in her chair; speaking in a high key, but musically, deliberately (not hurriedly or loudly), with a delicious distinctness of enunciation.—POE, EDGAR ALLAN, 1846, *The Literati, Works, ed. Stedman and Woodberry, vol.* VIII, *p.* 84.

Yesternight there came a bevy of Americans from Emerson, one Margaret Fuller, the chief figure of them, a strange, lilting, lean old maid, not nearly such a bore as I expected.—CARLYLE, THOMAS, 1846, *Letter, Oct.* 8; *Thomas Carlyle: A History of his Life in London, ed. Froude, vol.* I, *p.* 342.

Here Miranda came up, and said, Phœbus! you know
That the infinite soul has its infinite woe,
As I ought to know, having lived cheek by jowl,
Since the day I was born, with the Infinite Soul;
I myself introduced, I myself, I alone,
To my Land's better life authors solely my own,
Who the sad heart of earth on their shoulders have taken,
Whose works sound a depth by Life's quiet unshaken,
Such as Shakespeare, for instance, the Bible, and Bacon,
Not to mention my own works; Time's nadir is fleet,
And, as for myself, I'm quite out of conceit—
"Quite out of conceit! I'm enchanted to hear it,"
Cried Apollo aside. "Who'd have thought she was near it?
To be sure, one is apt to exhaust those commodities
One uses too fast, yet in this case as odd it is
As if Neptune should say to his turbots and whitings,
'I'm as much out of salt as Miranda's own writings'
(Which, as she in her own happy manner has said,
Sound a depth, for 't is one of the functions of lead.)
She often has asked me if I could not find
A place somewhere near me that suited her mind;
I know but a single one vacant, which she
With her rare talent that way, would fit to a T.
And it would not imply any pause or cessation
In the work she esteems her peculiar vocation,—
She may enter on duty to-day, if she chooses,
And remain Tiring-woman for life to the Muses."

—LOWELL, JAMES RUSSELL, 1848, *A Fable for Critics.*

I still remember the first half hour of Margaret's conversation. She was then twenty-six years old. She had a face and frame that would indicate fullness and tenacity of life. She was rather under the middle height; her complexion was fair, with strong, fair hair. She was then, as always, carefully and becomingly dressed, and of lady-like self-possession. For the rest, her appearance had nothing prepossessing. Her extreme plainness—a trick of incessantly opening and shutting her eyelids—the nasal tone of her voice—all repelled; and I said to myself, we shall never get far. It is to be said that Margaret made a disagreeable first impression on most persons, including those who became afterwards her best friends, to such an extreme that they did not wish to be in the same room with her. This was partly the effect of her manners, which expressed an overweening sense of power, and slight ésteem of others, and partly the prejudice of her fame. She had a dangerous reputation for satire, in addition to her great scholarship. The men thought she carried too many guns, and the women did not like one who despised them. I believe I fancied her too much interested in personal history; and her talk was a comedy in which dramatic justice was done to everybody's foibles. I remember that she made me laugh more than I liked. . . . She had an incredible variety of ancedotes, and the readiest wit to give an absurd turn to whatever passed; and the eyes, which were so plain at first, soon swam with fun and drolleries, and the very tides of joy and superabundant life. This rumor was much spread abroad, that she was sneering, scoffing, critical, disdainful of humble people, and of all but the intellectual. . . . It was a superficial judgment. Her satire was only the pastime and necessity of her salient, the play of superabundant animal spirits. . . . Her mind presently disclosed many moods and powers, in successive platforms or terraces, each above each, that quite effaced this first impression, in the opulence of the following pictures.—EMERSON, RALPH WALDO, 1851, *Memoirs of Margaret Fuller Ossoli, vol.* I, *pp.* 202, 203.

She was the centre of a group very different from each other, and whose only affinity consisted in their all being polarized by the strong attraction of her mind—all drawn toward herself. Some of her friends were young, gay, and beautiful; some old, sick, or studious. Some were children of the world, others pale scholars. Some were witty, others slightly dull. But all in order to be Margaret's friends, must be capable of seeking something—capable of some aspiration for the better. And how did she glorify life to all! All that was tame and common vanishing away in the picturesque light thrown over the most familiar things by her rapid fancy, her brilliant wit, her sharp insight, her creative imagination, by the inexhaustible resources of her knowledge, and the copious rhetoric which found words and images always apt and always ready. Even then she displayed almost the same marvelous gift of conversation, which afterwards dazzled all who knew her—with more, perhaps, of freedom, since she floated on the flood of our warm sympathies. Those who know Margaret only by her published writings, know her least; her notes and letters contain more of her mind; but it was only in conversation that she was perfectly free and at home.—CLARKE, JAMES FREEMAN, 1851, *Memoirs of Margaret Fuller Ossoli, vol.* I, *p.* 78.

Her temperament was predominantly what the physiologists would call nervous-sanguine; and the gray eye, rich brown hair, and light complexion, with the muscular and well-developed frame, bespoke delicacy balanced by vigor. Here was a sensitive, yet powerful being, fit at once for rapture or sustained effort, intensely active, prompt for adventure, firm for trial. She certainly had not beauty; yet the high arched dome of the head, the changeful expressiveness of every feature, and her whole air of mingled dignity and impulse, gave her a commanding charm. Especially characteristic were two physical traits. The first was a contraction of the eyelids almost to a point—a trick caught from near-sightedness—and then a sudden dilatation, till the iris seemed to emit flashes; an effect, no doubt, dependent on her highly-magnetized condition. The second was a singular pliancy of the vertebræ and muscles of the neck, enabling her by a mere movement to denote each varying emotion; in moments of tenderness, or pensive feeling, its curves were swan-like in grace, but when she was scornful or indignant, it contracted, and made swift turns like that of a bird of prey. Finally, in the animation yet *abandon* of Margaret's attitude and look, were rarely blended the fiery force of northern, and the soft langour of southern races.—CHANNING, WILLIAM HENRY, 1851, *Memoirs of Margaret Fuller Ossoli, vol.* II, *p.* 35.

Though we were members of the same household, we scarcely met save at breakfast; and my time and thoughts were absorbed in duties and cares, which left me little leisure or inclination for the amenities of social intercourse. Fortune seemed to delight in placing us two in relations of friendly antagonism, or rather, to develop all possible contrasts in our ideas and social habits. She was naturally inclined to luxury and a good appearance before the world. My pride, if I had any, delighted in bare walls and rugged fare. She was addicted to strong tea and coffee, both which I rejected and contemned, even the most homœopathic dilutions; while, my general health being sound, and hers sadly impaired, I could not fail to find in her dietetic habits the causes of her almost habitual illness; and once, while we were still barely acquainted, when she came to the breakfast-table with a very severe headache, I was tempted to attribute it to her strong potations of the Chinese leaf the night before. She told me quite frankly that she "declined being lectured on the food or beverage she saw fit to take," which was but reasonable in one who had arrived at her maturity of intellect and fixedness of habits. So the subject was henceforth tactly avoided between us; but, though words were suppressed, looks and involuntary gestures could not so well be; and an utter divergency of views on this and kindred themes created a perceptible distance between us. —GREELEY, HORACE, 1851, *Memoirs of Margaret Fuller Ossoli, vol.* II, *p.* 153.

From first to last she was a woman of noble aims, and, with all her egotism, unselfish in action. The longer I live, the more presumptuous and futile it seems to me to attempt judgment of character, and Miss Fuller's was exceptional. Her self-esteem was so inordinate as to be almost insane, but it appears (and it is, I think, so stated) to have been a constitutional and inherited defect, and certainly without moral taint. Her truth was exemplary, and all her conduct after she had left off theorizing and began the action of life in the accustomed channels was admirable, her Italian life beautiful. The close had the solemnity of a fulfilled prophecy, and, with all its apparent horrors, was it not merciful? Had she come safely to our shores, she must have encountered harassing struggles for the mere means of existence, anxiety, and all the petty cares that perplex and obstruct a noble nature, and, worse than all, disappointment!—SEDGEWICK, CATHARINE M., 1852, *To Mrs. Channing, Life and Letters, p.* 340.

Over his millions Death has lawful power,
But over thee, brave D'Ossoli! none, none.
After a longer struggle, in a fight
Worthy of Italy to youth restored,
Thou, far from home, art sunk beneath the surge
Of the Atlantick; on its shore; in reach
Of help; in trust of refuge; sunk with all
Precious on earth to thee . . . a child, a wife!
Proud as thou wert of her, America
Is prouder, showing to her sons how high
Swells woman's courage in a virtuous breast.
She would not leave behind her those she loved:
Such solitary safety might become
Others; not her; not her who stood beside
The pallet of the wounded, when the worst
Of France and Perfidy assail'd the walls
Of unsuspicious Rome. Rest, glorious soul,
Renown'd for strength of genius, Margaret!
Rest with the twain too dear! My words are few,
And shortly none will hear my failing voice,
But the same language with more full appeal
Shall hail thee. Many are the sons of song
Whom thou hast heard upon thy native plains
Worthy to sing of thee: the hour is come;
Take we our seats and let the dirge begin.

—LANDOR, WALTER SAVAGE, 1853, *On the Death of M. D'Ossoli and his Wife Margaret Fuller, The Last Fruit off an Old Tree.*

While she was living and moving in an ideal world, talking in private and discoursing in public about the most fanciful and shallow conceits which the transcendentalists of Boston took for philosophy, she looked down upon persons who acted instead of talking finely, and devoted their fortunes, their peace, their repose, and their very lives to the preservation of the principles of the republic. While Margaret Fuller and her adult pupils sat "gorgeously dressed," talking about Mars and Venus, Plato and Göethe, and fancying themselves the elect of the earth in intellect and refinement, the liberties of the republic were running out as fast as they could go, at a breach which another sort of elect persons were devoting themselves to repair: and my complaint against the "gorgeous" pedants was that they regarded their preservers as hewers of wood and drawers of water, and their work as a less vital one than the pedantic orations which were spoiling a set of well-meaning women in a pitiable way.—MARTINEAU, HARRIET, 1855–77, *Autobiography, ed. Chapman, vol.* I, *p.* 381.

She was a person anxious to try all things, and fill up her experience in all directions; she had a strong and coarse nature, which she had done her utmost to refine, with infinite pains; but of course it could only be superficially changed. The solution of the riddle lies in this direction, nor does one's conscience revolt at the idea of thus solving it, for (at least, this is my own experience) Margaret has not left in the hearts and minds of those who knew her any deep witness of her integrity and purity. She was a great humbug—of course, with much talent and much moral reality, or else she could never have been so great a humbug. But she had stuck herself full of borrowed qualities, which she chose to provide herself with, but which had no root in her. . . . There never was such a tragedy as her whole story, the sadder and sterner, because so much of the ridiculous was mixed up with it, and because she could bear anything better than to be ridiculous. It was such an awful joke, that she should have resolved—in all sincerity, no doubt—to make herself the greatest, wisest, best woman of the age. And to that end she set to work on her strong, heavy, unpliable, and, in many respects, defective and evil nature, and adorned it with a mosaic of admirable qualities, such as she chose to possess; putting in here a splendid talent and there a moral excellence, and polishing each separate piece, and the whole together, till it seemed to shine afar and dazzle all who saw it. She took credit to herself for having been her own Redeemer, if not her own Creator; and, indeed, she is far more a work of art than any of Mozier's statues. But she was not working on an inanimate substance, like marble or clay; there was something within her that she could not possibly come at, to re-create or refine it; and, by and by, this rude old potency bestirred itself, and undid all her labor in the twinkling of an eye. On the whole, I do not know but I like her the better for it; because she proved herself a very woman after all.—HAWTHORNE. NATHANIEL, 1857–59, *Extract from Roman Journal, Nathaniel Hawthorne and his Wife, by Julian Hawthorne, vol.* I, *pp.* 260, 261.

Like John Sterling, Charles Pemberton, and others of kindred gifts, the wonder to many who never came within the reach of her personal influence is how to account for the literary reputation she had achieved, upon a basement of writings so slender and so incomplete. It was the individual influence, the magnetic attraction, which she exercised over the minds within her reach, which accounts for the whole. —SMILES, SAMUEL, 1860, *Brief Biographies, p.* 196.

Her sweet persuasive voice we still can hear,
Ruling her charmèd circle like a queen;
While wit and fancy sparkled ever clear
Her graver moods between.
The pure perennial heat
Of youth's ideal love forever glowed
Through all her thoughts and words, and overflowed
The listeners round her seat.
So, like some fine-strung golden harp,
Tuned by many a twist and warp
Of discipline and patient toil,
And oft disheartening recoil,—
Attuned to highest and to humblest use,—
All her large heroic nature
Grew to its harmonious stature,
Nor any allotted service did refuse;
While those around her but half understood
How wise she was, how good,
How nobly self-denying, as she tasked
Heart, mind, and strength for truth, nor nobler office asked.

—CRANCH, CHRISTOPHER P., 1870, *Ode, Read at the Festival celebrating the birthday of Margaret Fuller Ossoli, held by the New England Women's Club, Boston, May* 23; *Atlantic Monthly, vol.* 26, *p.* 232.

It was a strange history and a strange destiny, that of this brilliant, restless, and unhappy woman—this ardent New Englander, this impassioned Yankee, who occupied so large a place in the thoughts, the lives, the affections, of an intelligent and appreciative society, and yet left behind her nothing but the memory of a memory. Her function, her reputation, were singular, and not altogether reassuring:

she was a talker; she was *the* talker; she was the genius of talk.—JAMES, HENRY, JR., 1880, *Nathaniel Hawthorne (English Men of Letters), p.* 76.

Those who think of this accomplished woman as a mere *bas bleu*, a pedant, a solemn Minerva, should have heard the peals of laughter which her profuse and racy humor drew from old and young. The Easy Chair remembers stepping into Noah Gerrish's West Roxbury omnibus one afternoon in Cornhill, in Boston, to drive out the nine miles to Brook Farm. The only other passenger was Miss Fuller, then freshly returned from her "summer on the lakes," and never was a long, jolting journey more lightened and shortened than by her witty and vivid sketches of life and character. Her quick and shrewd observation is shown in the book, but the book has none of the comedy of the *croquis* of persons which her sparkling humor threw off, and which she too enjoyed with the utmost hilarity, joining heartily in the laughter, which was only increased by her sympathy with the amusement of her auditor.—CURTIS, GEORGE WILLIAM, 1882, *Easy Chair, Harper's Magazine, vol.* 64, *p.* 627.

Thou, Sibyl rapt! whose sympathetic soul
Infused the myst'ries thy tongue failed to tell;
Though from thy lips the marvellous accents fell,
And weird wise meanings o'er the senses stole,
Through those rare cadences, with winsome spell;
Yet, even in such refrainings of thy voice,
There struggled up a wailing undertone,
That spoke thee victim of the Sisters' choice,—
Charming all others, dwelling still alone.
They left thee thus disconsolate to roam,
And scorned thy dear, devoted life to spare.
Around the storm-tost vessel sinking there
The wild waves chant thy dirge and welcome home;
Survives alone thy sex's valiant plea,
And the great heart that loved the brave and free.

—ALCOTT, A. BRONSON, 1882, *Sonnets and Canzonets, p.* 113.

An Oriental priestess sent by some mischance into a prim Puritan abode, where her wild fervor, idealism, imagination, passion, were curbed by an iron hand, and classics and ancient history crammed into an already over-excited brain. A sybil in a straight jacket! Was it a wonder that she raved? Smiles or sneers follow her statement that she was a queen. But queen she proved herself, though uncrowned; more truly fitted to reign than many a woman born to the purple. Her conceit was half frankness, and conceit seems a frequent fault with the truly great. —SANBORN, KATE, 1883, *Our Famous Women, p.* 297.

On Thursday, July 18th, the "Elizabeth" was off the Jersey coast, in thick weather, the wind blowing east of south. . . . Here, on Fire Island beach, she struck, at four o'clock on the morning of July 19th. . . . From their new position, through the spray and rain they could see the shore, some hundreds of yards off. Men were seen on the beach, but there was nothing to indicate that an attempt would be made to save them. At nine o'clock it was thought that some one of the crew might possibly reach the shore by swimming, and, once there, make some effort to send them aid. Two of the sailors succeeded in doing this. Horace Sumner sprang after them, but sank, unable to struggle with the waves. A last device was that a plank, with handles of rope attached, upon which the passengers in turn might seat themselves, while a sailor, swimming behind, should guide their course. Mrs. Hasty, young and resolute, led the way in this experiment, the stout mate helping her, and landing her out of the very jaws of death. . . . Oh that Margaret had been willing that the same means should be employed to bring her and her's to land! Again and again, to the very last moment, she was urged to try this way of escape, uncertain, but the only one. It was all in vain. Margaret would not be separated from her dear ones. Doubtless she continued for a time to hope that some assistance would reach them from the shore. The life-boat was even brought to the beach; but no one was willing to man her, and the delusive hope aroused by her appearance was soon extinguished. The day wore on; the tide turned. The wreck would not outlast its return. The commanding officer made one last appeal to Margaret before leaving his post. To stay, he told her, was certain and speedy death, as the ship must soon break up. He promised to take her child with him, and to give Celeste, Ossoli, and herself each the aid of an able seaman. Margaret still refused to be parted from her child or husband. The crew were then told to "save themselves," and all but four jumped overboard.—HOWE, JULIA WARD, 1883, *Margaret Fuller (Famous Women), pp.* 270, 271, 274.

Her life seems to me, on the whole, a triumphant rather than a sad one, in spite of the prolonged struggle with illness, with poverty, with the shortcomings of others and with her own. In later years she had the fulfillment of her dreams; she had what Elizabeth Barrett, writing at the time of her marriage to Robert Browning, named as the three great desiderata of existence, "life and love and Italy." She shared great deeds, she was the counselor of great men, she had a husband who was a lover, and she had a child. They loved each other in their lives, and in death they were not divided. Was not that enough?—HIGGINSON, THOMAS WENTWORTH, 1884, *Margaret Fuller Ossoli (American Men of Letters), p.* 314.

I had never heard her personal appearance described, and it rather took me by surprise. When I entered the drawing-room, several, but not all, of the expected guests had arrived. The party was not planned to be a large one, and I saw at a glance who was the cynosure of the evening. A lady of medium height and size, and of graceful figure, was leaning back in an easy-chair, and alternately listening with interest, or talking with animation to the group around her, the American twang in her voice betraying her nationality. Her light hair was simply arranged, and her cheeks showed the fading, so often noticed in her country-women when the thirtieth year is passed, yet without exactly ageing the face. The outline of her head was fine, and her blue eyes beamed with candour and intelligence. She wore a dress of lilac silk, enriched with a good deal of black lace drapery. In a few minutes I found myself seated by her side, and very soon any prejudice which I might have entertained against the "strong-minded" woman ebbed away. Though egotistic, certainly, she was wise, genial, and womanly, and when I shook hands with her at parting it was with the hope of seeing her again.—CROSLAND, MRS. NEWTON, 1893, *Landmarks of a Literary Life, p.* 224.

Opposing forces were constantly at war within her—the intellect and the emotions, the large, unasking sympathies, and the close, hungry, human affections. "Her brain was all heart," as Frederick Robertson said about her; and so her point of view was always confused and colored with personality. Despite her Puritan conscience and discipline, she, was perhaps, a bacchante, with something lawless, chaotic, and unregulated, over which she herself never had perfect control. For so complex a nature as hers, what was needed was some large, unifying principle that could coördinate all the facts of life, and bring them into harmony and accord; in other words, some deep spiritual conviction, that inner vision and touch of the divine which opens out horizons always luminous, and deeps where there is forever peace. Lacking this, her ideals were always human, her kindom was of the earth, and she never gained that full mastery and knowledge of the truth which alone can make us free—free of self and the limitations of sense. Nevertheless, her destiny, though incomplete, was a high one, and worthy to be crowned with martydom.—LAZARUS, JOSEPHINE, 1893, *Margaret Fuller, The Century, vol.* 45, *p.* 932.

Margaret Fuller, who had always struck me as a very plain woman, was the oracle.* She had a very long neck, which Dr. Holmes described "as either being swan-like or suggesting the great ophidian who betrayed our Mother Eve." She had a habit of craning her head forward as if her hearing were defective; but she had a set of woman-worshippers who said that the flowers faded when she did not appear. She was the Aspasia of this great council. She seemed to have a special relationship to each of the intellectual men about her, discerning and reading them better than they did themselves. Some one said of her that she was a kind of spiritual fortune-teller, and that her eyes were at times visible in the dark. Their devotion to her was akin to fanaticism, and they would talk of the magic play of her voice as the singing of a fountain. She had a very kind way to the colored stage-driver, who was the Mr. Weller of Concord, and he distinguished her by his respect. The "chambermaid would confide to her her homely romance." The better class of

*In Brook Farm, 1847.

young Cambridge students believed in her as though she had been a learned professor. Her all-seeing eye could shoot through the problems which engaged them. Many distinguished men kept this opinion of her to their deaths.—SHERWOOD, M. E. W., 1897, *An Epistle to Posterity, p.* 37.

WOMAN IN THE NINETEENTH CENTURY

"Woman of the Nineteenth Century" is a book which few women in the country could have written, and no woman in the country would have published, with the exception of Miss Fuller. In the way of independence, of unmitigated radicalism, it is one of the "Curiosities of American Literature," and Doctor Griswold should include it in his book.—POE, EDGAR ALLAN, 1846, *The Literati, Works, ed. Stedman and Woodberry, vol.* VIII, *p.* 76.

Every page is loaded—we had almost said overloaded—with thought, and the subject is one which the writer had so near her heart that it commanded her best powers and warmest sympathies, and cannot fail to instruct and interest the reader even when there is not perfect agreement with the views advanced.—HALE, EDWARD EVERETT, 1855, *Woman in the Nineteenth Century, North American Review, vol.* 81, *p.* 558.

Was perhaps framed on two large a scale for one who had so little constructive power. It was noble in tone, enlightened in its statements, and full of suggestion; yet after all it was crude and disconnected in its execution.—HIGGINSON, THOMAS WENTWORTH, 1868, *Eminent Women of the Age, p.* 193.

In 1840, Margaret Fuller published an essay in the *Dial*, entitled "The Great Lawsuit, or Man *vs.* Woman: Woman *vs.* Man." In this essay she demanded perfect equality for woman, in education, industry, and politics. It attracted great attention and was afterwards expanded into a work entitled "Woman in the Nineteenth Century." This, with her parlor conversations, on art, science, religion, politics, philosophy, and social life, gave a new impulse to woman's education as a thinker. —STANTON, ANTHONY AND GAGE, *eds.*, 1881–87, *History of Woman Suffrage, vol,* I, *p.* 40.

Before Margaret Fuller's day the agitation regarding woman's career and work in the world was practically unknown here; and all the ideas which have now become incorporated into the platform of the woman's party found in her their first and perhaps their best exponent. Very little that is new has since been urged upon this question. Her powerful mind seemed to have grasped the whole subject, and to have given it the best expression of which it was capable. She embodied her ideas after a time in her book, "Woman in the Nineteenth Century," and although the literature of the subject is now voluminous, that book is still read and referred to.—GRISWOLD, HATTIE TYNG, 1886, *Home Life of Great Authors, p.* 305.

GENERAL

It is for dear New England that I want this review, [*The Dial*] for my self, if I had wished to write a few pages now and then, there were ways and means enough of disposing of them. But in truth I have not much to say; for since I have had leisure to look at myself, I find that, so far from being an original genius, I have not yet learned to think to any depth, and that the utmost I have done in life has been to form my character to a certain consistency, cultivate my tastes, and learn to tell the truth with a little better grace than I did at first. For this the world will not care much, so I shall hazard a few critical remarks only, or an unpretending chalk sketch now and then, till I have learned to do something.—OSSOLI, MARGARET FULLER, 1840, *Memoirs of Margaret Fuller Ossoli, vol.* II, *p.* 26.

In spite of these things, however, and of her frequent unjustifiable Carlyleisms (such as that of writing sentences which are no sentences, since, to be parsed, reference must be had to sentences preceding), the style of Miss Fuller is one of the very best with which I am acquainted. In general effect, I know no style which surpasses it. It is singularly piquant, vivid, terse, bold, luminous; leaving details out of sight, it is everything that a style need be.—POE, EDGAR ALLAN, 1846, *The Literati, Works, ed. Stedman and Woodberry, vol.* VIII, *p.* 81.

Margaret is an excellent soul: in real regard with both of us here. Since she went, I have been reading some of her Papers in a new Book we have got; greatly superior to all I knew before; in fact the undeniable utterances (now first undeniable to me) of a true heroic mind;—altogether unique, so far as I know, among the Writing Women of this generation; rare enough, too, God knows, among the Writing Men. She is very narrow, sometimes; but she is truly high.—CARLYLE, THOMAS, 1847, *Letter to Emerson, 2d March; Correspondence of Carlyle and Emerson, ed. Norton, vol.* II. *p.* 155.

Few can boast so wide a range of literary culture; perhaps none write so well with as much facility; and there is marked individuality in all her productions. As a poet, we have few illustrations of her abilities; but what we have are equal to her reputation.—GRISWOLD, RUFUS WILMOT, 1848, *The Female Poets of America, p.* 251.

An American author of great eminence, some time since, denominated Margaret Fuller the George Sand of America; and, much as we disliked that hackneyed fashion of making the great intellect of one nation a kind of duplicate of another, yet there is more justness in this comparison than generally falls to the lot of that absurd method of getting at facts, or something like them. . . . She is one of those few authors who have written too little. We hope to read more of her prose, so thoughtful and vigorous; and of her poetry, at once so graceful, yet so strong and simple.—POWELL, THOMAS, 1850, *The Living Authors of America, pp.* 287, 318.

Those who knew her in early youth, who witnessed her extraordinary intellectual developments, who experienced her wonderful power in conversation, and who cast the horoscope of the woman from the brilliant promise of the girl, predicted for her a distinguished literary career. They saw in her a future D'Arblay or De Staël. . . . For ourselves, we incline to the belief that in no circumstances, by no favor of fortune, would Margaret have produced a work which should have worthily expressed her genius. With all her mental wealth and race faculty, we doubt whether she possessed the organic power, the concentration and singleness of purpose, necessary for such an undertaking. Her mind was critical, not constructive; impulsive, not laborious. Her strength lay rather in oracular judgments, in felicitous statements and improvisations, than in patient elaboration. True, she has written much and well. Her critical essays, and especially her papers on Goethe, in the *Dial*, are unsurpassed in their kind. But all that she has written is fragmentary; nothing epic, nothing that possesses formal excellence, no one complete work.—HEDGE, FREDERICK HENRY, 1856, *Madame Ossoli's At Home and Abroad, North American Review, vol.* 83, *p.* 261.

She was often misled ["Art, Literature and the Drama"] in her first judgment, as in one well-known instance, by the strength of her affection and her sympathy; but let the merit be real, and of a kind which she was glad to recognize, and no one ever did more exquisite justice to thought and to its form. Every word which she ever wrote of Goethe was admirable, and yet what we possess was only *her preparation* for better work. Nothing was ever more tender and true than her sketch of "The Two Herberts" in this volume. Let the reader dwell also on what she has to say of "American Literature," and the "Lives of the Great Composers."—DALL, CAROLINE H., 1860, *Margaret Fuller Ossoli, North American Review, vol.* 91, *p.* 127.

In her published works there are passages of great power and beauty. Her descriptions of scenery—that of Niagara, for instance—are given with a few bold strokes, that suggest much more than at first meets the eye. She paints, in fact, our inward emotion in presence of the scene, and so gives us the ideal of nature. Her critical articles often show insight, and the power of clear statement; but either she was warped by personal dislikes or she took pleasure in demolishing popular idols. In her view there were but half a dozen people with brains in America. In her way of writing, the editorial we had a royal sound, that would have been offensive if it had not been so often absurd. . . . It was some time before it was discovered that philosophic diction did not always clothe philosophic thought. Perhaps Margaret Fuller had passed through her *destructive* stage, and was ready to build. Perhaps if she had lived, she would have justified the opinions of her admirers by the creation of some artistic work. If this were so, the calamity of the shipwreck is the more to be lamented. As in the case of great orators, actors, and singers, who, after charming a generation, die and leave only a tradition of their powers, this extraordinary woman will be a mere name in our literary history. Something of her influence survives. The advocates for the elevation of woman hold her in high regard as a pioneer in their cause. In this, as in everything else in which she took part, she put her own intense personality forward, and did much to win for her sex the right of discussion and the privilege of being heard.—UNDERWOOD, FRANCIS H., 1872, *A Hand-Book of English Literature, American Authors.*

After all that has been said of Miss Fuller by her many earnest friends, after the zealous and sometimes unseemly criticisms and defences of which she has been the subject, and after the fullest recognition of her merits, faults, and foibles, her personality and the memory of her influence are the things that interest us, not the present value of her printed pages. Her learned girlhood, her solitary ways, and her burning zeal, remind us of Mrs. Browning. As Mrs. Browning's name is first among women who have contributed to English literature, so the name of Margaret Fuller is practically the first to show the position woman has already begun to take, and must make more and more conspicuous, in the literature of America. — RICHARDSON, CHARLES F., 1885, *American Literature, 1607–1885, vol.* I, *p.* 433.

Margaret Fuller never appeared as a candidate for popular favor. On the polishing of furniture she was absolutely silent; nor, though she professed "high respect for those who 'cook something good,' and create and preserve fair order in houses," did she ever fulfill the understood duty of woman by publishing a cookery book. On the education of daughters she had, however, a vital word to say; demanding for them "a far wider and more generous culture." Her own education had been of an exceptional character; she was fortunate in its depth and solidity, though unfortunate in the forcing process that had made her a hard student at six years old. Her equipment was superior to that of any American woman who had previously entered the field of literature; and hers was a powerful genius, but, by the irony of fate, a genius not prompt to clothe itself in the written word. As to the inspiration of her speech, all seem to agree; but one who knew her well has spoken of the "singular embarrassment and hesitation induced by the attempt to commit her thoughts to paper." The reader of the Sibylline leaves she scattered about her in her strange career receives the constant impression of hampered power, of force that has never found its proper outlet. . . . She accomplished comparatively little that can be shown or reckoned. Her mission was "to free, arouse, dilate." Those who immediately responded were few; and as the circle of her influence has widened through their lives, the source of the original impulse has been unnamed and forgotten. But if we are disposed to rank a fragmentary greatness above a narrow perfection, to value loftiness of aim more than the complete attainment of an inferior object, we must set Margaret Fuller, despite all errors of judgment, all faults of style very high among the "Writing Women" of America. It is time that, ceasing to discuss her personal traits, we dwelt only upon the permanent and essential, in her whose mind was fixed upon the permanent, the essential. Her place in our literature is her own; it has not been filled, nor does it seem likely to be. The particular kind of force which she exhibited—in so far as it was not individual—stands a chance in our own day of being drawn into the educational field, now that the "wider and more generous culture" which she claimed has been accorded to women. — CONE, HELEN GRAY, 1890, *Woman in American Literature, The Century, vol.* 40, *p.* 924.

Few women, in so short a life, have done so much as she; and the tragic close of her career invests it with a pathetic dignity.—HAWTHORNE, JULIAN, AND LEMMON, L., 1891, *American Literature, p.* 153.

In many respects Margaret Fuller stands, like Poe, solitary in our literature. Her strong, masculine personality which placed her alone among American women, and her keen, peculiar intellect which made her a powerful influence on the intellectual men of her generation, defy classification. If judged alone by her actual literary product, she would deserve but a passing notice, yet she is ranked with the great builders of American literature. Concerning few American writers, save Poe and Whitman, can one find such extremes of opinion. Some of her contemporaries characterized her as superficially learned, disagreeable, warped by intense personal likes and dislikes, domineering, oracular, inordinately fond of monologue; while others, like Emerson, Carlyle, Channing, and Higginson, declared her a rare genius, a profound thinker and scholar. . . . She is almost the only American author who, like a great singer or actor, keeps a place in our memories chiefly through the testimony of contemporaries. . . . The place which Margaret Fuller will ultimately occupy in the history of American letters can only be conjectured. "Her genius was not quick to clothe itself in the written word," and it seems but fair to judge that any literary fame that rests largely upon tradition must ultimately be lost. . . . She held frequent "Conversations," during which her admirers listened with bated breath as to a goddess. She drew about her with scarcely an effort a circle of the purest and most spiritual men and women of New England and she ruled it with singular power. And after her death the noblest and best minds of both hemispheres united to do honor to her memory.—PATTEE, FRED LEWIS, 1896, *A History of American Literature with a View to the Fundamental Principles Underlying its Development*, pp. 231, 234.

Margaret Fuller's literary significance does not chiefly depend upon the actual writings that her busy hand turned off. As the underpaid, overworked editor of the "aëriform" *Dial* and, later, as stated contributor of critical articles of the *New York Tribune*, whose famous chief, Horace Greeley, found her "a most fearless and unselfish champion of truth and human good at all hazards," she accomplished a fair amount of creditable work, suggestive rather than symmetrical, but her inspiring personality counted for more than her best paragraphs.—BATES, KATHARINE LEE, 1897, *American Literature*, p. 222.

Jane Porter

1776–1850

Born, at Durham, 1776. Educated at Edinburgh. Part editor (with her sister and T. F. Dibdin) of "The Quiz," 1797. Created "Lady of Chapter of St. Joachim" by the King of Würtemberg after the success of her novel, "Thaddeus of Warsaw." Tragedy "Switzerland" performed at Drury Lane, 5 Feb. 1819; "Owen, Prince of Powys," Drury Lane, 28 Jan. 1822. Lived for some time with her mother and sister at Esher. Returned to London with her sister, 1831. Visit to her brother at St. Petersburg, 1842. Grant from Literary Fund, Nov., 1842. Contrib. to "Gentleman's Mag.," "Amulet," and other periodicals. Died, at Bristol, 24 May, 1850. *Works*: "Thaddeus of Warsaw," 1803; "A Sketch of the Campaigns of Count A. Suwarrow Rymnikski," (anon.), 1804; "The Scottish Chiefs," 1810; "The Pastor's Fireside," 1815; "Duke Christian of Luneburg," 1824; "Tales Round a Winter Hearth" (with A. M. Porter), 1826; "The Field of the Forty Footsteps" (with A. M. Porter's "Coming Out"), 1828; "Sir Edward Seaward's Narrative of his Shipwreck," 1831. She *edited:* "Young Hearts. By a Recluse," 1834.—SHARP, R. FARQUHARSON, 1897, *A Dictionary of English Authors*, p. 231.

PERSONAL

Her stately figure and graceful manners made an impression on me. Few ladies have been so gifted with personal attractions, and at the same time been so respectable as authors.—ROBINSON, HENRY CRABB, 1812, *Diary, May* 11; *Diary, Reminiscences and Correspondence, ed. Sadler, vol.* I, *p.* 246.

GENERAL

Miss Porter has no wit, she invariably bungles a picture of the conversation of ordinary persons whenever she attempts it. Why does she delight in unfolding the forward weaknesses of the *female* heart, and making even Mary Beaufort love first? Yet with all her deficiencies she is interesting: never failing to excite our sympathy, though she cannot rank with our Fieldings or Smolletts. She infinitely surpasses the insipid froth of

"The mob of Gentlemen, who write with ease."

—CARLYLE, THOMAS, 1815, *To R. Mitchell, March* 25; *Early Letters, ed. Norton, p.* 16.

"Thaddeus of Warsaw" and the "Scottish Chiefs" are as widely known as any books of their class in the language. They are read by every school-boy and school-girl in the sentimental period of life, and call forth a perennial outburst of tears or enthusiasm. Neither work is distinguished for historical accuracy or profound insight into human nature. Yet the two are unique, and will be read and enjoyed by each successive generation of youth by reason of their sweet style and sentiment. —HART, JOHN S., 1872, *A Manual of English Literature*, p. 537.

Abound in striking scenes, and are written in an animated style, but display little knowledge of life, or discrimination of character.—DAVIES, JAMES, 1873, *English Literature from the Accession of George III. to the Battle of Waterloo*, p. 144.

The first successful attempt at this kind of writing was made by Miss Jane Porter in 1810. "The Scottish Chiefs" is the story of the heroic William Wallace related with some animation and many pleasing details. But the style is artificial and declamatory, and, as a picture of Scotch manners in the fourteenth century, the work is by no means trustworthy. The many picturesque descriptions, and the interest which the story awakens regarding the fate of the hero, has made the book a favorite, especially among the younger class of romance readers, and has, despite its many faults, placed it among the classics of our language.—BALDWIN, JAMES, 1883, *English Literature and Literary Criticism, Prose*, p. 177.

Jane, although writing less than her sister, and beginning her literary work later in life, is much better known and loved by us, because her works accord with the spirit of the times in which she lived. —RUTHERFORD, M., 1890, *English Authors*, p. 317.

It was "The Scottish Chiefs," by Miss Porter, a work that was destined to create within me a new want, and to turn my thoughts to the reading and study of history. . . . Its influence is still with me. I read the book by stealth, concealing it under my text book during school hours, when my quiet attitude led my teacher and others to suppose I was absorbed in study. —LAMB, MARTHA J., 1891, *Formative Influences, The Forum, vol.* 11, p. 54.

The success of the book was immense. Kosciusko sent his portrait and a medal to the author; she was made a member of foreign societies, received gold crosses of honor; and oddly enough, even from America there came, under the guiding providence of Mr. John Harper, then I believe Mayor of the City of New York, an elegant carved armchair, trimmed with crimson plush, to testify "the admiring gratitude of the American people" to the author of "Thaddeus of Warsaw." The book, by its amazing popularity, and by the entertaining way in which it marshals its romantic effulgencies in favor of a great cause, may very naturally suggest that other, later and larger enlistment of all the forces of good story-telling, which—fifty years thereafter—in the hands of an American lady (Mrs. Stowe) contributed to a larger cause, and with more abiding results. "The Scottish Chiefs" has less of gusto than the Polish novel—and as I took occasion to say when we were at that date of Scottish history—is full of bad anachronisms, and of historical untruths. Yet there is a good bracing air of the Highlands in parts of it, and an ebullient martial din of broadswords and of gathering clans which go far to redeem its maudlin sentiment.—MITCHELL, DONALD G., 1895, *English Lands Letters and Kings, Queen Anne and the Georges*, p. 283.

"Thaddeus of Warsaw," long cherished by our great-grandfathers, and not entirely unknown to our fathers, had some faint merit.—GOSSE, EDMUND, 1897, *A Short History of Modern English Literature*, p. 299.

Jane Porter sent to school to Joseph Strutt would have been a rival to Sir Walter Scott.—CROSS, WILBUR L., 1899, *The Development of the English Novel*, p. 114.

John Caldwell Calhoun

1782–1850

John Caldwell Calhoun, a statesman of Irish Presbyterian descent, was born in Abbeville County, South Carolina, March 18, 1782; studied at Yale, and became a successful lawyer. In congress he supported the measures which led to the war of 1812–15 with Great Britain, and promoted the protective tariff. In 1817 he joined Monroe's cabinet as Secretary of War, and did good work in reorganising the war department. He was vice-president under John Q. Adams (1825–29), and then under Jackson. In 1829 he declared that a state can nullify unconstitutional laws; and his "Address to the People of South Carolina" (1831), set forth his theory of state rights. On the passing by South Carolina in 1832 of the nullification ordinance he resigned the vice-presidency, and entered the senate, becoming a leader of the states-rights movement, and a champion of the interests of the slave-holding states. In 1844, as Secretary of State, he signed a treaty annexing Texas; but once more in the senate, he strenuously opposed the war of 1846-47 with Mexico. He died at Washington, March 31, 1850. He, Henry Clay, and Daniel Webster were "the great triumvirate" of American political orators. See the Life by R. S. Jenkins (1851); his collected works (6 vols. 1853-54), with a Life by Crallé; and H. von Holst's "John C. Calhoun" (1882).—PATRICK AND GROOME, *eds.*, 1897, *Chambers's Biographical Dictionary, p.* 168.

PERSONAL

His character was marked and decided, not prematurely exhibiting its peculiarities, yet formed and perfected at an early age. He was firm and prompt, manly and independent. His sentiments were noble and elevated, and everything mean or grovelling was foreign to his nature. He was easy in his manners, and affable and dignified. His attachments were warm and enduring; he did not manifest his affection with enthusiastic fervor, but with deep earnestness and sincerity. . . . As a citizen, he was without blemish; he wronged no one; and there were no ugly spots on his character to dim the brilliancy of his public career. His social qualities were endearing, and his conversational powers fascinating in the extreme. He loved to talk with the young; he was especially animated and instructive when engaged in conversation with them, and scarcely ever failed to inspire a sincere attachment in the breast of those who listened to him.—JENKINS, JOHN S., 1851, *The Life of John Caldwell Calhoun, pp.* 446, 447.

Even we, who knew him only in his gaunt and sad decline, can easily imagine that at twenty-six he must have been an engaging, attractive man. Like most of his race, he was rather slender, but very erect, with a good deal of dignity and some grace in his carriage and demeanor. His eyes were always remarkably fine and brilliant. He had a well-developed and strongly set nose, cheek-bones high, and cheeks rather sunken. His mouth was large, and could never have been a comely feature. His early portraits show his hair erect on his forehead, as we all remember it, unlike Jackson, whose hair at forty still fell low over his forehead. His voice could never have been melodious, but it was always powerful. At every period of his life, his manners, when in company with his inferiors in age or standing, were extremely agreeable, even fascinating.—PARTON, JAMES, 1865, *John C. Calhoun, North American Review, vol.* 101, *p.* 388.

Life is not only "stranger than fiction," but frequently also more tragical than any tragedy ever conceived by the most fervid imagination. Often in these tragedies of life there is not one drop of blood to make us shudder, nor a single event to compel the tears into the eye. A man endowed with an intellect far above the average, impelled by a high-soaring ambition, untainted by any petty or ignoble passion, and guided by a character of sterling firmness and more than common purity, yet, with fatal illusion, devoting all his mental powers, all his moral energy and the whole force of his iron will to the service of a doomed and unholy cause, and at last sinking into the grave in the very moment when, under the weight of the top-stone, the towering pillars of the temple of his impure idol are rent to their very base,—can anything more tragical be conceived?—HOLST, DR. H. VON, 1882, *John C. Calhoun* (*American Statesmen*), *p.* 1.

Mr. Calhoun was to me the guiding star in the political firmament and I was honored by him with such confidence as made our intercourse not only instructive, but of enduring love.—DAVIS, JEFFERSON, 1887, *Letter to the Calhoun Monument Association, p.* 117.

During a long and active life; amid fierce differences of thought on questions of grave and of burning interest, his strong views were never withheld, nor were the honesty and sincerity of his convictions ever questioned, and the widest dissent from his opinions was ever attended with the knowledge of the sincerity and the purity in which they were entertained, and with an appreciation of the force, with which they were maintained.—FISH, HAMILTON,

1888, *Letter to the Calhoun Monument Association, p.* 122.

He was a man of bold temper, of intense earnestness, and of deep convictions,—convictions so strong as to have "all the force of passions." Such a man must needs antagonize where he could not convince. But in the retirement of home and among friends and neighbors other and more attractive elements appear. . . . He seldom quoted books or the opinions of others. A rapid reader, he would absorb the congenial thoughts of an author and reject whatever did not assimilate with his own mental habits. His mind always seemed to work from within, by spontaneous impulse, not by external influences, either educational, social, or political. It drove on its rapid way like some mighty automatic engine, without friction, without noise, apparently without ever stopping for fuel or water. Its own ardor generated heat enough to sustain the rapid motion. No other mind has ever appeared to me so original, so full, so self-reliant. Others I have since met of more culture and more learning; but the streams that flowed from their lips, however copious, always suggested a well-filled reservoir.—PINCKNEY, CHARLES COTESWORTH, 1898, *John C. Calhoun, Lippincott's Magazine, vol.* 62, *pp.* 81, 87.

ORATORY

The eloquence of Mr. Calhoun, or the manner in which he exhibited his sentiments in public bodies, was part of his intellectual character. It grew out of the qualities of his mind. It was plain, strong, terse, condensed, concise; sometimes impassioned, still always severe. Rejecting ornament, not often seeking far for illustrations, his power consisted in the plainness of his propositions, in the closeness of his logic, and in the earnestness and energy of his manner.—WEBSTER, DANIEL, 1850, *Speech in the Senate of the United States, on the day when the death of Mr. Calhoun was announced.*

Speaking with aggressive aspect, flashing eye, rapid action and enunciation, unadorned argument, eccentricity of judgment, unbounded love of rule; impatient, precipitate in ambition, kind in temper; with conception, perception, and demonstration, quick and clear; with logical precision arguing paradoxes, and carrying home conviction beyond rhetorical illustration; his own impressions so intense, as to discredit, scarcely to listen to any other suggestions.—INGERSOLL, CHARLES JARED, 1853, *History of the Second War between Great Britain and the United States.*

Although Calhoun was an orator who cannot be overlooked in any account of American oratory his mind was of the order that belongs prëeminently to statecraft. He made great speeches, but they were great in the closeness of their reasoning and the plainness of their propositions, coupled at times with an impassioned delivery, oftener with a severity and dignity of manner which men respected, but over which they did not go wild with enthusiasm nor drift far from their well-formed judgments. Accepting his premises it was difficult to escape from the conclusions of his rigid logic. Whatever the sense of the speaker's profound sincerity and earnestness could accomplish was secured by the unfaltering devotion to his convictions and his unwavering persistence in imparting them to those who could not help listening with respect, though they might be far from accepting the legitimate results of his processes.—SEARS, LORENZO, 1895, *The History of Oratory, p.* 333.

GENERAL

Few men have exerted a more powerful and controlling sway over the opinions of vast masses of men, than Mr. Calhoun, for his views on several topics coincided with those of the great majority of the Southern people; and he was known to be inflexibly honest and true, and eminently reliable. No man of his faith ever doubted that leader any more than his creed. As a statesman, he was full of forecast, acute in judgment, and comprehensive in his general views. He was eminently conservative in many things, and by precept and example, recommended "masterly inactivity" as preferable to mere impulsive and effervescent movements.—LOSSING, BENSON J., 1855–86, *Eminent Americans, p.* 327.

The style of John C. Calhoun was terse and condensed, and his eloquence, though sometimes impassioned, was always severe. He had great skill as a dialectician and remarkable power of analysis, and his works will have permanent place in American literature.—BOTTA, ANNE C. LYNCH, 1860, *Hand-Book of Universal Literature.*

Mr. Calhoun was a debater of signal power, none being his equal upon the floor of the Senate, except Webster and Clay. It was his lot to take part in the affairs of the country for many years, and it was always a prominent part. He was earnestly devoted to what he believed to be for the prosperity of his State and section. His love for the Union, and fealty to it, was subordinate to his allegiance to his State. Much might be written concerning the influence of his teachings upon the subsequent history of the country, but it would extend this brief sketch beyond its intended limits, and would be, even then, unsatisfactory to those who might desire to make a careful study of the subject.—WHITMAN, C. M., 1883, *American Orators and Oratory, p.* 213.

Calhoun, from his mistaken point of view, was as loyal to the idea of Right as was Webster; his private character was higher, and his public career less open to charges of selfish ambition. In ability he was undoubtedly inferior to the great Massachusetts statesman, but among all the politicians and orators of the Southern States he was easily the leader.—RICHARDSON, CHARLES F., 1885, *American Literature,* 1607-1885, *vol.* I, *p.* 227.

He had known that his end was near, and, as a dying bequest to the Union that he loved, had spent a few months that other men would have devoted to rest, in composing his "Disquisition on Government," and his "Discourse on the Constitution and Government of the United States." Of these two treatises it will be sufficient to say, that they are in many respects the most remarkable political documents the student of American history is called upon to read. He must read them if he wishes to get a full and well rounded view of Calhoun's constitutional theories, although it is at once plain that all their important points are covered in the better known speeches. It is to the "Disquisition" that we must go for the famous praise of the Constitution of Poland, as well as for the fullest explanation of the doctrine of the concurrent majority. The reader must, however, be warned that it is not safe to approach these books unless he has thoroughly disabused his mind of the notion that sovereignty can really be divided and a government founded on compact. If one start with these notions in one's head, the sure grip of Calhoun's logic will end by making one a nullifier or a lunatic.—TRENT, WILLIAM P., 1897, *Southern Statesmen of the Old Régime, p.* 190.

Francis Sargent Osgood

1811-1850

Born at Boston, June 18, 1811: died at Hingham, Mass., May 12, 1850. An American poet. Among her works is "A Wreath of Wild Flowers from New England" (1838). She contributed to a number of English and American periodicals, and was editor of "The Ladies' Companion" for some time. She also wrote a play, "The Happy Release, or the Triumphs of Love."—SMITH, BENJAMIN E., *ed.*, 1894-97, *The Century Cyclopedia of Names, p.* 765.

PERSONAL

In character she is ardent, sensitive, impulsive—the very soul of truth and honor; a worshipper of the beautiful, with a heart so radically artless as to seem abundant in art; universally admired, respected, and beloved. In person, she is about the medium height, slender even to fragility, graceful whether in action or repose; complexion usually pale; hair black and glossy; eyes a clear, luminous gray, large, and with singular capacity for expression.—POE, EDGAR ALLAN, 1846, *The Literati, Works, ed. Stedman and Woodberry, vol.* VIII, *p.* 112.

The delicacy of her organization was such that she had always the quick sensibility of childhood. The magnetism of life was round about her, and her astonishingly impressible faculties were vital in every part, with a polarity toward beauty, all the various and changing rays of which entered into her consciousness, and were refracted in her conversation and action. . . . Probably there was never a woman of whom it might be said more truly that to her own sex she was an object almost of worship. She was looked upon for her simplicity, purity, and childlike want of worldly tact or feeling, with involuntary affection; listened to, for her freshness, grace, and brilliancy, with admiration; and remembered, for her unselfishness, quick sympathy, devotedness, capacity of suffering, and high aspirations, with a sentiment approaching reverence.—GRISWOLD, RUFUS WILMOT, 1850, *Frances Sargent Osgood, The Memorial, ed. Mrs. Hewitt.*

Of a rare gracefulness and delicacy, Mrs. Osgood lived a truly poetic life. Her unaffected and lively manners, with her ready tact in conversation, combined with an unusual facility in writing verses, charmed a large circle of friends, as her winning lines in the periodicals of the day engaged the attention of the public.—DUYCKINCK, EVERT A. AND GEORGE L., 1855–65–75, *Cyclopædia of American Literature, ed. Simons, vol.* II, *p.* 457.

No human face was ever more perfectly chiseled than hers—due regard having been had, meanwhile, to the fact that a woman, and not a statue, was being formed. That calm, pleasant face, those soft and kindly brown eyes, and that wealth of waved dark hair drawn low over her fair, white forehead, in the fashion of the time (since called the "Agnes Robertson"), won many hearts, the homage of which was kept by the always kindly and tender words flowing from the faultless lips seldom opened but to emit a sparkle.—MORFORD, HENRY, 1880, *John Keese, his Intimates; Morford's Magazine, June.*

GENERAL

There is scarcely a form of poetical composition in which she has not made experiment; and there is none in which she has not very happily succeeded. Her defects are chiefly negative and by no means numerous. Her versification is sometimes exceedingly good, but more frequently feeble through the use of harsh consonants, and such words as "thou'dst" for "thou wouldst," with other unnecessary contractions, inversions, and obsolete expressions. Her imagery is often mixed;—indeed, it is rarely otherwise. The epigrammatism of her conclusions gives to her poems, as wholes, the air of being more skilfully constructed than they really are. On the other hand, we look in vain throughout her works for an offence against the finer taste, or against decorum—for a low thought or a platitude. A happy refinement—an instinct of the pure and delicate—is one of her most noticeable excellences. She may be properly commended, too, for originality of poetic invention, whether in the conception of a theme or in the manner of treating it. Consequences of this trait are her point and piquancy. Fancy and *naïveté* appear in all she writes. Regarding the loftier merits, I am forced to speak of her in more measured terms.—POE, EDGAR ALLAN, 1846, *The Literati, Works, ed. Stedman and Woodberry, vol.* VIII, *p.* 111.

She has done much in prose; but all her compositions of this class are instinct with the poetical spirit. She is at times forcible and original, and is frequently picturesque; but throughout all appears the poet, and the affectionate and enthusiastic woman. Of none of our writers has the excellence been more steadily progressive. Every month her powers have seemed to expand and her sympathies to deepen. With an ear delicately susceptible to the harmonies of language, and a light and pleasing fancy, she always wrote musically and often with elegance; but her later poems are marked by freedom of style, a tenderness of feeling, and a wisdom of apprehension, and are informed with a grace, so undefinable, but so pervading and attractive, that the consideration to which she is entitled is altogether different in kind, as well as in degree, from that which was awarded to the playful, piquant, and capricious improvisatrice of former years. —GRISWOLD, RUFUS WILMOT, 1848, *The Female Poets of America, p.* 272.

It is very seldom that a woman of any real genius has so great a facility of throwing her fancies into shape as Mrs. Osgood. Had her utterance been more difficult she would have written better. . . . Mrs. Osgood is somewhat too profuse of her "ah's" and "oh's;" they mar the harmony and repose of some of her finest verses. . . . She has a lively fancy, but little imagination; and her fancy is sometimes displayed so artificially as to induce the reader to put it down altogether to the score of mere prettiness of thought and conceit of expression. Still, there are a feminine power, pathos, and tenderness about the writings of Mrs. Osgood, which will always render her one of ths most pleasing poets of the New World.—POWELL, THOMAS, 1850, *The Living Authors of America, pp.* 276, 285, 286.

Her poetical faculty was an endowment of nature, not an acquired art; nor in our

JAMES FENIMORE COOPER

Engraved by J. C. Buttre.

FREDERICK MARRYAT

Engraving by C. Cook. Drawing by William Behnes.

research through the annals of female genius have we found another instance, among the Anglo-Saxon race, of the true improvisatrice.—HALE, SARAH JOSEPHA, 1852, *Woman's Record, p.* 458.

The feminine counterpart of N. P. Willis.—FORD, EMILY ELLSWORTH, 1893, *Early Prose and Verse, p.* 129.

Frances Sargent Osgood was the first woman to write good poetry in this country. . . . She is especially successful with short poems of a character ardent, arch, and dreamy, such as "A Dancing Girl," "Calumny," and "He may go—if he can."—SIMONDS, ARTHUR B., 1894, *American Song, p.* 166.

James Fenimore Cooper

1789-1851

Born at Burlington, N. J., Sept. 15, 1789. Father, of Quaker descent and a congressman; mother, of Swedish descent. Family settled in Cooperstown, N. Y., 1790, where Mr. Cooper owned much land. Attended the village school; then became the private pupil of an Albany rector; entered Yale, 1802; dismissed for participation in a frolic, 1805. Served before the mast in a merchant vessel, 1806-1807; served as midshipman in the navy, part of the time on Lakes Ontario and Champlain, 1807-11. Married Miss DeLancey, 1811; five daughters and two sons were born to him. Resided at Mamaroneck, 1811-1814; Cooperstown, 1814-1817; Scarsdale, 1817-1822; New York, 1822-1826. Lived in Europe, chiefly in France and Italy, 1826-1833; consul at Lyons, 1826-1829. Returned to America, 1833; lived by turns at New York and at Cooperstown. Died at Cooperstown, Sept. 14, 1851; wife died four months later. An Episcopalian. *Works:* "Precaution," 1820. "The Spy," 1821. "The Pioneers," 1823. "The Pilot," 1824 (imprint, 1823). "Lionel Lincoln," 1825. "The Last of the Mohicans," 1826. "The Prairie," 1827. "The Red Rover," 1828. "The Wept of Wish-ton-Wish" (="The Borderers"), 1829. "The Water-Witch," 1830. "The Bravo," 1831. "The Heidenmauer," 1832. "The Headsman," 1833. "The Monikins," 1835. "Homeward Bound," 1838. "Home as Found" (="Eve Effingham"), 1838. "The History of the Navy of the United States of America," 1839; abridged edition, 1841. "The Pathfinder," 1840. "Mercedes of Castile," 1840. "The Deerslayer," 1841. "The Two Admirals," 1842. "The Wing-and-Wing" (="The Jack o' Lantern"), 1842. "Wyandotte," 1843. "Ned Myers" [the life of one of Cooper's shipmates], 1843. "Afloat and Ashore," 1844. "Miles Wallingford" (="Lucy Hardinge") [sequel to "Afloat and Ashore"], 1844. "Satanstoe," 1845. "The Chainbearer," 1846. "Lives of Distinguished American Naval Officers," 1846. "The Redskins" (="Ravensnest"), 1846. "The Islets of the Gulf," 1846-1848 in *Graham's Magazine;* 1848 in book form, as "Jack Tier" (="Captain Spike"). "The Crater" (="Mark's Reef"), 1847. "The Oak Openings" (="The Bee Hunter"), 1848. "The Sea Lions," 1849. "The Ways of the Hour," 1850. The titles of the English editions, when they differed from the American are given in parentheses. Cooper also wrote several tales for *Graham's Magazine*, ten volumes of travels, and a good deal of controversial matter.—BRONSON, WALTER C., 1900, *A Short History of American Literature, p.* 126, *note.*

PERSONAL

Visited Princess Galitzin, and also Cooper, the American novelist. This man, who has shown so much genius, has a good deal of the manners, or want of manners, peculiar to his countrymen.—SCOTT, SIR WALTER, 1826, *Journal, Nov.* 3; *Life by Lockhart, ch.* lxxii.

I met this evening (for the first time) with Cooper, the American writer. He is the author of the "Pioneers," the "Spy," etc. He has a dogged, discontented look, and seems ready to affront or to be affronted. His eye is rather deep-set, dull, and with little motion. One might imagine that he had lost his life in gazing at seas and woods and rivers, and that he would gaze—gaze on for ever. His conversation is rough, abrupt, and unamusing; yet I am told that he can recount an adventure well, and I can easily believe it. There was something peculiar in his physiognomy, but I could not make out what it was. . . . He resembles very much a caricature that I remember to have seen indicative of "Damme, who cares?"—PROCTER, BRYAN WALLER (BARRY CORNWALL), 1828, *Autobiographical Fragments, May* 17, *pp.* 74, 76.

Mr. Cooper's manuscript is very bad—*unformed*, with little of distinctive character about it, and varying greatly in different epistles. In most of those before us a steel pen has been employed, the lines are crooked, and the whole chirography has a constrained and school-boyish air.—POE, EDGAR ALLAN, 1841, *A Chapter on Autography, Works, ed. Stedman and Woodberry, vol.* IX, *p.* 212.

Anne A. and I went a few evenings since to take a sociable dish of tea with Mrs. Banyer, and Fenimore Cooper dropped in. I rather think the light by which we see the world emanates from ourselves. He moves in a belligerent spirit, waging war with classes and masses, boarding and broadsiding his fellow-creatures. He maintained that his own country was below France, Italy, and even England in civilization, intellectual development, *morals*, and manners; that we were going in every thing backward; that in common honesty we were below any other nation. Being in the presence of Mrs. Banyer and Miss Jay, who sanctify the very names of Christian and saint, he attacked the whole class with man-of-the-world slang, and wound up with promising me a pamphlet of his, just coming out, which is to grind M'Kenzie to powder. With all this, he was good-humored, and talked strongly and amusingly. He is a perfect John Bull in shape, dimensions, action, even to the growl.—SEDGWICK, CATHARINE M., 1843, *To Mrs. K. S. Minot, June* 6; *Life and Letters, p.* 285.

We are among those who regard Mr. Cooper as a wronged and persecuted man. We conceive that his countrymen have done him gross injustice—that they have not only shown themselves ungenerous but ungrateful, and that, in lending a greedy ear to the numerous malicious aspersions which have assailed his person and his reputation, they have only given confirmation and strength to the proverbial reproach, of irreverence and ingratitude, to which countries, distinguished by popular governments, have usually been thought obnoxious. We do not mean to regard him as wholly faultless—on the contrary, we look upon Mr. Cooper as a very imprudent person; one whose determined will, impetuous temperament, and great self-esteem, continually hurry forward into acts and expressions of error and impatience. We propose to compare sides in this question:—to put the case fairly between himself and countrymen, and show where the balance of justice lies.—SIMMS, WILLIAM GILMORE, 1845, *Views and Reviews in American Literature, History and Fiction, p.* 210.

Of his failings I have said little; such as he had were obvious to all the world; they lay on the surface of his character; those who knew him least made the most account of them. With a character so made up of positive qualities—a character so independent and uncompromising, and with a sensitiveness far more acute than he was willing to acknowledge, it is not surprising that occasions frequently arose to bring him, sometimes into friendly collision, and sometimes into graver disagreements and misunderstandings with his fellow-men. For his infirmities, his friends found an ample counterpoise in the generous sincerity of his nature. He never thought of disguising his opinions, and he abhorred all disguise in others; he did not even deign to use that show of regard towards those of whom he did not think well, which the world tolerates, and almost demands. A manly expression of opinion, however different from his own, commanded his respect. . . . His character was like the bark of the cinnamon, a rough and astringent rind without, and an intense sweetness within. Those who penetrated below the surface found a genial temper, warm affections, and a heart with ample place for his friends, their pursuits, their good name, their welfare. They found him a philanthropist, though not precisely after the fashion of the day; a religious man, most devout where devotion is most apt to be a feeling rather than a custom, in the household circle; hospitable, and to the extent of his means liberal-handed in acts of charity.—BRYANT, WILLIAM CULLEN, 1852, *Orations and Addresses, p.* 85.

Mr. Cooper was in person solid, robust, athletic; in voice, manly; in manner, earnest, emphatic, almost dictatorial,—with something of self-assertion, bordering on egotism. The first effect was unpleasant, indeed repulsive, but there shone through all this a heartiness, frankness, which excited confidence, respect, and at last affection.—GOODRICH, SAMUEL GRISWOLD, 1856, *Recollections of a Lifetime, Letter* xxxvi.

A man of unquestioned talent,—almost genius,—he was aristocratic in feeling and arrogant in bearing, altogether combining in his manners what a Yankee once characterized as "winning ways to make people hate him." Retiring to his parental acres near Cooperstown, N. Y., he was soon involved in a difficulty with the neighboring villagers, who had long been accustomed, in their boating excursions on the Lake (Otsego), to land and make themselves at home for an hour or two on a long, narrow promontory or "point," that ran down from his grounds into the lake, and whom he had now dissuaded from so doing by legal force. The Whig newspaper of the village took up the case for the villagers, urging that their exclusion from "The Point," though legal, was churlish, and impelled by the spirit of the dog in the manger; whereupon Cooper sued the editor for libel, recovered a verdict, and collected it by taking the money—through a sheriff's officer—from the editor's trunk.—GREELEY, HORACE, 1868, *Recollections of a Busy Life*, p. 261.

I had known Mr. Cooper during the later years of his life, and used to see him occasionally when he visited New York. He was an amazingly fluent talker as well as speaker and writer; and he affected an intense bitterness against the institutions of his native country in his conversation as well as in his writings. I can see him now, in my mind's eye, standing with his back to the fire-place in my office, with his legs apart and his coat-tails under his arms, pouring out diatribes which did not seem half in earnest —FIELD, MAUNSELL B., 1873, *Memories of Many Men and of Some Women*, p. 178.

Of the group around there was one who left an impression on my memory—Fenimore Cooper. He "stalked" around the *salon*—a tall, stalwart man, with the unmistakable air of self-confidence I have noticed in many Americans; as if it were a prime thought that independence was to be maintained by a seeming indifference to the opinions of on-lookers—a sensation that vanishes, however, when the demeanor that has given rise to it is found but the rough shell of a sweet kernel; for Americans are among the most socially generous of humankind. I had other and better opportunities of seeing Fenimore Cooper afterward; but in that *salon*, jostled by *petits maîtres*, he was out of place—as much so as an Indian cross-bow would have been among a collection of Minié rifles. Proctor, in 1828, wrote of him: "He has a dogged, discontented look, and seems ready to affront or be affronted. His eye is rather deep-set, dull, and with little motion." He describes Cooper as rude even to coarseness in English society. That is not my experience of the author of the "Spy"—the originator of the class of sea-fictions—to whom the reading world owes a large debt. He was certainly the opposite of genial, and seemed to think it good taste and sound judgment to be condescending to his equals.—HALL, SAMUEL CARTER, 1883, *Retrospect of a Long Life*, p. 227.

The distinguished author died at his residence, Cooperstown, September 14, 1851, being then in his sixty-second year, and since that time his beautiful home, known as Otsego Hall, has been destroyed by fire and the property passed into other hands. He was buried among his kindred, in the family enclosure in the Episcopal churchyard of Christ Church, and beneath the shadows of a fine fir-tree, planted by himself, and several graceful elms and maples. The marble above his grave bears these simple lines:

JAMES FENIMORE COOPER,
Born September 15, 1789.
Died September 14, 1851.

—WILSON, JAMES GRANT, 1885, *Bryant and his Friends*, p. 242.

THE SPY
1821

Quite new scenes and characters, humour and pathos, a picture of America in Washington's time; a surgeon worthy of Smollett or Moore, and quite different from any of their various surgeons; and an Irishwoman, Betty Flanagan, incomparable.—EDGEWORTH, MARIA, 1821, *To Mrs. Ruxton, July* 8; *Letters, vol.* II, *p.* 29.

"The Spy" was an event. It was the boldest and best attempt at the historical romance which had ever been made in America. It is somewhat the practice, at this day, to disparage that story. This is in very bad taste. The book is a good one,—full of faults, perhaps, and blunders; but full also of decided merits, and marked by a boldness of conception, and a courage in progress, which clearly showed the confidence of genius in its own resources. The conception of the Spy, as a character, was a very noble one.—SIMMS, WILLIAM GILMORE, 1845, *Views and Reviews in American Literature, History and Fiction, p.* 211.

It is said that if you cast a pebble into the ocean, at the mouth of our harbor, the vibration made in the water passes gradually on till it strikes the icy barriers of the deep at the south pole. The spread of Cooper's reputation is not confined within narrower limits. The "Spy" is read in all the written dialects of Europe, and in some of those of Asia. The French, immediately after its first appearance, gave it to the multitudes who read their far-diffused language, and placed it among the first works of its class. It was rendered into Castilian, and passed into the hands of those who dwell under the beams of the Southern Cross. At length it crossed the eastern frontier of Europe, and the latest record I have seen of its progress towards absolute universality, is contained in a statement of the *International Magazine*, derived, I presume, from its author, that in 1847 it was published in a Persian translation at Ispahan. Before this time, I doubt not, they are reading it in some of the languages of Hindostan, and, if the Chinese ever translated anything, it would be in the hands of the many millions who inhabit the far Cathay.—BRYANT, WILLIAM CULLEN, 1852, *Orations and Addresses, p.* 52.

That "Spy" made the groundwork of Cooper's fame in this country, in England, and on the Continent. There were men who modelled their lives on lines traceable in the career of Harvey Birch, and were proud to do it. His devotion, his trueness to the cause he loved and served—his modesty, his strength of purpose, his self-effacement made up the preaching of a good moral sermon; none the less effective because his story was founded upon actual occurrences detailed to Mr. Cooper by his host, upon the occasion of some visit to the Jay homestead in Westchester. —MITCHELL, DONALD G., 1897, *American Lands and Letters, The Mayflower to Rip-Van-Winkle, p.* 234.

The success of "The Spy" was not altogether due to the novelty of its subject. With many of Cooper's characteristic faults, it has also his characteristic merits. It is full of scenes that show the vigor and dash of his narrative power; and its central character, the humble peddler Harvey Birch, cool, brave, incorruptible, quick in resource in times of peril, is a noble example of that homely heroism in the portrayal of which Cooper excelled. —PANCOAST, HENRY S., 1898, *An Introduction to American Literature, p.* 133.

THE PILOT
1824

In regard to the style of execution, the work has one fault which was mentioned in our notice of the "Spy;" it is in some instances, and more especially where the author speaks in his own person, overloaded with epithets, and the detail of particular circumstances. The author leaves too little to his readers, and from his solicitude to omit nothing of the quality, degree, and manner of everything related or described, he impairs the vivacity and force of the expression. . . . The choice of incidents and actors, and the frequent allusions to our history, manners, and habits, make the story strike deep into the feelings of American readers; and by implicating the tale with our naval history, the author possesses himself of one of the few positions from which our national enthusiasm is accessible.—PHILLIP, W., 1824, *The Pilot, North American Review, vol.* 18, *p.* 328.

All who have since written romances of the sea have been but travelers in a country of which he was the great discoverer; and none of them all seemed to have loved a ship as Cooper loved it, or have been able so strongly to interest all classes of readers in its fortunes.—BRYANT, WILLIAM CULLEN, 1852, *Orations and Addresses, p.* 57.

"Pilot," the first salt-water novel ever written, and to this day one of the very best. Its nameless and mysterious hero was a marine, Harvey Birch; obviously he had been modeled upon the Paul Jones whose name is held in terror to this day on the British coasts he harassed. In Long Tom Coffin, the Nantucket whaler, Cooper created the only one of his other characters worthy to take place beside Leatherstocking; and Tom, like Natty, is simple, homely, and strong. In writing the "Pilot," Cooper evidently had in mind the friends who thought it impossible to interest the general reader in a tale of the ocean, and he laid some of his scenes on land; but it is these very passages which are tedious to-day, while the scenes at sea keep their freshness and have still unfailing interest. — MATTHEWS, BRANDER. 1896, *An Introduction to the Study of American Literature, p.* 64.

"The Pilot" is very uneven. The plot is conventionally trivial; and most of the characters are more so still. But Long Tom Coffin is a living Yankee sailor; and when we come to the sea, with its endless variety of weather, and to sea-fights, such as that between the "Ariel" and the "Alacrity," it is hardly excessive to say that there is little better in print. If the plot and the characters had been half so good as the wonderful marine background in which they are set, the book would have been a masterpiece.—WENDELL, BARRETT, 1900, *A Literary History of America, p.* 185.

GENERAL

Has the almost singular merit of writing American novels which everybody reads, and which we are of course bound to review now and then. For these last five or six years he has supplied the reading public annually with a repast of five or six hundred pages of such matter; so that we have a right to consider him as publicly professing this department of elegant literature. It is too late to say, that he does not excel in it; or at least, that he has not some considerable merit; for, however far he may fall short of our ideal standards, or wherever we may rank him among living writers, the public voice has long since confirmed to him the apellation of the American novelist, a title which was but sparingly and timidly suggested for the author of the "Spy." No one has yet appeared among us who has been wholly able to cope with him in his proper walk; and we see no good reason why he should not be allowed, for the present at least, to maintain the distinction.—GARDINER, W. H., 1826, *Cooper's Novels, North American Review, vol.* 23, *p.* 150.

Mr. Cooper is admitted by very general consent to have distanced every other competitor in the route struck out by the author of Waverley. We would not be understood by this language, to imply any thing like a servile imitation, in the detracting spirit of some English journals; for Cooper is no more an imitator of Scott, than Milton is of Shakspeare, because they both wrote in blank verse, or than Scott himself is of this latter, whom he resembles in the *fond*, though not the form of his writings. If this be imitation, it is more glorious than most originality. . . . Cooper's great defect is his incapacity to seize the tone of good society; we say incapacity, for his repeated failures, we think, put it beyond a doubt. Nothing can be more lamentable than the compound of affectation, primness, and pedantry, a sort of backwoods gentility, which makes up with him the greater part of its dialogue and its manners. Defects like these would seem to be the natural result of an imperfect education, as well as a want of familiarity with well-bred society. But this last can scarcely be imputed to Mr. Cooper, and his experience of late years must have abundantly enlarged the sphere of his social observation, for all practical purposes. Has he shown a corresponding improvement?—PRESCOTT, WILLIAM HICKLING, 1832, *English Literature of the Nineteenth Century, North American Review. vol.* 35, *p.* 190.

Do not hasten to write; you cannot be too slow about it. Give no ear to any man's praise or censure; know that that is *not* it: on the one side is as Heaven if you have strength to keep silent, and climb unseen; yet on the other side, yawning always at one's right-hand and at one's left, is the frightfulest Abyss and Pandemonium! See Fenimore Cooper;—poor Cooper, he is *down in it;* and had a climbing faculty too. — CARLYLE, THOMAS, 1837, *To Ralph Waldo Emerson, Dec.* 8; *Correspondence, ed. Norton, vol.* I, *p.* 142.

Mr. Cooper's works, for the last three or four years, seem to have been written under no higher inspiration than that of spleen. They abound in uncalled-for political disquisitions, filled up with expressions of the bitterest scorn and hatred. They are deformed by perpetual out-breaks of a spirit, which might be expected to show itself in the pages of a ruthless partisan, careless of truth in aiming at the reputation of an opponent whom he wishes to ruin; but from which the writings of the poet and the man of letters, sitting apart, "in the still air of delightful studies," ought to be wholly exempt. He has added nothing to the range of characters in fiction, which amuse and occupy our hours of leisure, and to which the mind returns, as to old familiar scenes, or the faces of friends; he has told no new tale of human passions, for our instruction or warning; but he has given us, both in his books of travels, and his last novel, a few brilliant descriptions of natural scenery, both by land and sea.—BOWEN, FRANCIS, 1838, *Cooper's Homeward Bound, North American Review, vol.* 47, *p.* 488.

He has drawn you one character, though, that is new,
One wildflower he's plucked that is wet with the dew
Of this fresh Western world, and, the thing not to mince,
He has done naught but copy it ill ever since;
His Indians, with proper respect be it said,
Are just Natty Bumpo, daubed over with red,
And his very Long Toms are the same useful Nat,
Rigged up in duck pants and a sou'-wester hat
(Though once in a Coffin, a good chance was found
To have slipped the old fellow away underground).
And his other men-figures are clothes upon sticks,
The *dernière chemise* of a man in a fix
(As a captain besieged, when his garrison's small,
Sets up caps upon poles to be seen o'er the wall);
And the women he draws from one model don't vary,
All sappy as maples and flat as a prairie.
When a character's wanted, he goes to the task
As a cooper would do in composing a cask;
He picks out the staves, of their qualities heedful,
Just hoops them together as tight as is needful,
And, if the best fortune should crown the attempt, he
Has made at the most something wooden and empty.

—LOWELL, JAMES RUSSELL, 1848, *A Fable for Critics.*

The first enthusiasm about Cooper having subsided, we remember more his faults than his merits. His ready resentment and way of showing it in cases which it is the wont of gentlemen to pass by in silence, or meet with a good humoured smile, have caused unpleasant associations with his name, and his fellow citizens, in danger of being tormented by suits for libel, if they spoke freely of him, have ceased to speak of him at all. But neither these causes, nor the baldness of his plots, shallowness of thought, and poverty in the presentation of character, should make us forget the grandeur and originality of his sea-sketches, nor the redemption from oblivion of our forest-scenery, and the noble romance of the hunter-pioneer's life. Already, but for him, this fine page of life's romance would be almost forgotten. He has done much to redeem these irrevocable beauties from the corrosive acid of a semi-civilized invasion. — OSSOLI, MARGARET FULLER, 1850? *Modern British Poets; Art, Literature and the Drama, p.* 305.

The greatest charm about Cooper's novels is the perfect truthfulness of their forest scenery; there is nothing artificial in a single word—the very trees seem to grow around you; it is not scene painting, it is nature. . . . Even in the very worst of his novels, there are glimpses of nature so exquisitely painted as to justify the highest praise it is possible to bestow. It is just probable that the very success of this description of writing has led Mr. Cooper to persevere in a course which has exposed him to the charge of being considered a writer of limited range.—POWELL, THOMAS, 1850, *The Living Authors of America, pp.* 12, 13.

Remarkable ["Pathfinder"], even among its companions, for the force and distinctness of its pictures. For ourselves—though we diligently perused the despatches—the battle of Palo Alto and the storming of Monterey are not more real and present to our mind than some of the scenes and characters of "The Pathfinder," though we have not read it for nine years; —the little fort on the margin of Lake Ontario, the surrounding woods and waters, the veteran major in command, the treacherous Scotchman, the dogmatic old sailor, and the Pathfinder himself. . . . "The Prairie," the last of the Leather-stocking Tales, is a novel of far inferior merit. The story is very improbable, and not very interesting. The pictures of scenery are less true to nature than in the previous volumes, and seem to indicate that Cooper had little or no personal acquaintance with the remoter parts of the West.—PARKMAN, FRANCIS, 1852, *James Fenimore Cooper, North American Review, vol.* 74, *pp.* 153, 157.

Thought Leatherstocking a creation. No one would care to meddle with that class of character after Cooper.—IRVING,

WASHINGTON, 1859, *Journal, Oct.* 7; *Life and Letters, ed. Irving, vol.* IV, *p.* 313.

He is colonel of the literary regiment; Irving, lieutenant-colonel; Bryant, the major; while Longfellow, Whittier, Holmes, Dana, and myself may be considered captains. . . . Two or three of Cooper's characters I consider the first in American fiction. Which are they? Why, Leatherstocking, Long Tom Coffin, and Uncas. Why this noble creation has been so neglected by painters and sculptors I am at a loss to understand. Certainly there is no nobler Indian character depicted in our literature. Thackeray calls the first of these immortal creations—and he was certainly a competent judge—one of "the great prize-men" of fiction, better perhaps than any of Scott's men, and ranks dear old "Natty Bumppo" with Uncle Toby, Sir Roger de Coverley, and Falstaff—heroic figures all. — HALLECK, FITZ-GREENE, 1867? *Bryant and his Friends, by Wilson, p.* 238.

When he began writing he stood almost alone where now an innumerable crowd are contesting every inch of vantage-ground; and although his style has its defects, his novels are powerful and interesting in themselves, besides presenting valuable pictures of the infancy of our country, the life of the pioneer, the characteristics of the Indians, and the struggle for national liberty both on land and sea. All public libraries are obliged to provide themselves with numerous copies of his works, and no private library is considered complete without a costly edition. As an evidence of his popularity abroad, it may be mentioned that in Holland alone there are three different translations of his novels into three different dialects of the country.—WOOLSON, CONSTANCE FENIMORE, 1871, *The Haunted Lake, Harper's Magazine, vol.* 44, *p.* 26.

An English critic can hardly know which are held in the greatest esteem among his own countrymen; but among English readers "The Last of the Mohicans" is considered his masterpiece. — YONGE, CHARLES DUKE, 1872, *Three Centuries of English Literature, p.* 619.

We pass to brief consideration of a less gentle, but on the whole a greater, power. Irving's fame has, for some time, been unduly eclipsed; that of the greatest, with one exception, of American novelists, J. Fenimore Cooper, has seldom been sufficiently recognised. In their portraits you can read the differences of their characters: they had genius in common, industry and honesty, and good descent, but little more. That Irving made no enemies seems to me his weak point: that Cooper made too many was, if not his fault, at least his misfortune. . . . It is impossible in the case of Cooper, as of Irving, to do him any justice by quotations, for his genius is panoramic rather than dioramic: we must sit out a whole scene, or even act, to realise the power of the dramatist. There is, moreover, a certain severity in his style, which restricts the range of his readers. He often wastes words on circumstance, is exhaustive where he might have been suggestive; and his plots—a remark that does not apply to the "Red Rover," where from first to last there is not a dull page—are apt to drag; and he has carried too far the practice of trotting out a single character, and making us accompany him—as Trollope and even Thackeray are apt to do—through the lives of his men and women, from the cradle to the grave. . . . An American to the core: he needs no slang or affectation to establish his originality, but moves in his own path, with something like disdain of comment.—NICHOL, JOHN, 1880–85, *American Literature, pp.* 175, 176, 177.

Characteristics there are of Cooper's writings which would and do repel many. Defects exist both in manner and matter. Part of the unfavorable judgment he has received is due to the prevalence of minor faults, disagreeable rather than positively bad. These, in many cases, sprang from the quantity of what he did and the rapidity with which he did it. . . . In the matter of language this rapidity and carelessness often degenerated into downwright slovenliness. . . . He too often passed the bounds that divide liberty from license. It scarcely needs to be asserted that in most of these cases the violation of idiom arose from haste or carelessness. But there were some blunders which can only be imputed to pure unadulterated ignorance. He occasionally used words in senses, unknown to past or present use. He sometimes employed grammatical forms that belong to no period in the history of the English language. . . . All this is, in itself, of slight importance when set off against positive merits. . . . There are imperfections far more serious than these mistakes in language. He rarely attained to beauty of style. The rapidity with which he wrote forbids the idea that he ever strove earnestly for it. Even the essential but minor grace of clearness is sometimes denied him. . . . These are imperfections that have led to the undue depreciation of Cooper among highly cultivated men. Taken by themselves they might seem enough to ruin his reputation beyond redemption. It is a proof of his real greatness that he triumphs over defects which would utterly destroy the fame of a writer of inferior power. . . . The more uniform excellence of Cooper, however, lies in the pictures he gives of the life of nature.—LOUNSBURY, THOMAS R., 1882, *James Fenimore Cooper (American Men of Letters), pp.* 271, 272, 273, 274, 275, 281, 283.

We are not without peculiar types; not without characters, not without incidents, stories, heroisms, inequalities; not without the charms of nature in infinite variety; and human nature is the same here that it is in Spain, France, and England. Out of these materials Cooper wrote romances, narratives stamped with the distinct characteristics of American life and scenery, that were and are eagerly read by all civilized peoples, and which secured the universal verdict which only breadth of treatment commands.—WARNER, CHARLES DUDLEY, 1883–96, *The Relation of Literature to Life, p.* 165.

He has had few rivals in this power of breathing into phantoms of the brain the breath of life. His fame in the description of natural scenery under new and striking aspects is world-wide. His portraiture, without warm and varied coloring, is remarkable for fidelity and strength. —WELSH, ALFRED H., 1883, *Development of English Literature and Language, vol.* II, *p.* 308.

Though he could draw very well a sailor's sweetheart, like Mary Pratt, or a soldier's daughter, like Mabel Dunham, yet of *fine* women he had only a chivalrous notion, and painted them from a respectful distance. They were delicate creatures, to be handled like porcelain. Dressed out and beautified, they were to be protected and worshiped. They walk through the halls of his heroes, and take seats at the upper end to distribute the prizes after the tournament.—MORSE, JAMES HERBERT, 1883, *The Native Element in American Fiction, The Century, vol.* 26, *p.* 290.

With all his foibles, Cooper was inspired by an intense patriotism, and he had a bold, vigorous, aggressive nature. He freed his talents at a stroke, and giving them full play attained at once a world-wide reputation, which no man of colonial mind could ever have dreamed of reaching. Yet his countrymen, long before his days of strife and unpopularity, seem to have taken singularly little patriotic pride in his achievements, and the well bred and well educated shuddered to hear him called the "American Scott;" not because they thought the epithet inappropriate and misapplied, but because it was a piece of irreverent audacity toward a great light of English literature. Cooper was the first, after the close of the war of 1812, to cast off the colonial spirit and take up his position as a representative of genuine American literature. — LODGE, HENRY CABOT, 1884, *Studies in History, p.* 353.

James Fenimore Cooper, whose writings are instinct with the spirit of nationality, stands at the head of American novelists. —WILSON, JAMES GRANT, 1885, *Bryant and his Friends, p.* 230.

No Hamlets or Werthers or Renés or Childe Harolds were allowed to tenant his woods or appear on his quarter-decks. Will, and the trained sagacity and experience directing will, were the invigorating elements of character which he selected for romantic treatment. Whether the scene be laid in the primitive forest or on the ocean, his men are always struggling with each other or with the forces of nature. This primal quality of robust manhood all men understand, and it shines triumphantly through the interposing fogs of French, German, Italian, and Russian translations. A physician of the mind could hardly prescribe a more efficient tonic for weak and sentimental natures than a daily diet made up of the most bracing passages in the novels of Cooper. Another characteristic of Cooper, which makes him universally acceptable, is his closeness to nature. He agrees with Wordsworth in this, that in all his descriptions of natural objects he indicates that he and nature are familiar acquaintances, and, as Dana says, have "talked together." —WHIPPLE, EDWIN PERCY, 1886, *American Literature and other Papers, ed. Whittier, p.* 46.

But the reader always feels that within the mountain of solid flesh and bone that Cooper offers to the eye, there is a love of beauty, goodness and pure ideals. The things this author most loves and reverences are revered and loved by all men: he never strikes an unsympathetic note of emotion or principle. And when he is afloat on his quarter-deck, or immersed in the untrodden wilderness of the Western Continent, he gives us an enjoyment new in kind, as well as of compelling interest. To plunge into one of his great books brings a refreshment only to be likened to that of the sea and forest which they describe. We proceed majestically from one stirring event to another; and though we never move faster than a contemplative walk, we know, like the man on his way to the scaffold, that nothing can happen till we get there. It is one of Cooper's most remarkable feats that, in spite of his weakness in dialogue, he should have created a number of characters as solid and recognizable as any in American fiction. Indeed, it would be difficult to find anywhere in the literature of the century creatures of imagination having a firmer hold on popular sympathy and belief than Natty Bumppo, Long Tom Coffin, and many of their associates. We know them, as we see them and we can even hear them between the lines, as it were, that the author gives them to speak. He has fashioned them so well that they cease to appear as puppets, and seem to come to independent life. As soon as Cooper left the realm of his imagination, his genius deserted him. The moment he began to wrangle, to exhort or to instruct, he failed. —HAWTHORNE, JULIAN, AND LEMMON, LEONARD, 1891, *American Literature, p.* 51.

One of the very greatest characters in fiction, the old woodsman, Natty Bumppo. . . . The five tales vary in value, no doubt, but taken altogether they reveal a marvelous gift of narration, and an extraordinary fullness of invention. . . . Time may be trusted safely to make a final selection from any author's works, however voluminous they may be, or however unequal. Cooper died almost exactly in the middle of the nineteenth century; and already it is the "Spy" and the "Leather-stocking Tales" and four or five of the "Sea Tales" which survive, because they deserve to survive, because they were at once new and true when they were written, because they remain to-day the best of their kind. Cooper's men of the sea, and his men of the forest and the plain, are alive now though other fashions in fiction have come and gone. Other novelists have a more finished art nowadays, but no one of them all succeeds more completely in doing what he tried to do than did Cooper at his best. And he did a great service to American literature by showing how fit for fiction were the scenes, the characters, and the history of his native land.—MATTHEWS, BRANDER, 1896, *An Introduction to the Study of American Literature, pp.* 62, 63, 67.

When the "Red Rover" appeared, I succeeded, on a Saturday evening, in obtaining a copy at the circulating library I patronized, and when the church bells on the following morning rang for nine o'clock, as they did at that time, I had just finished the last volume. — HASWELL, CHARLES H., 1896, *Reminiscences of an Octogenarian, p.* 130.

The strength of a creative artist is unlike that of a chain; it lies in the strongest, not in the weakest link. . . . Men forget his failures, as they have forgotten his altercations; but he still speaks that universal language which the young and the people of all lands comprehend, and the boyhood of American literature bids fair, in Cooper's tales, to preserve a long-enduring youth.—HOWE, M. A. DEWOLFE, 1897–98, *American Bookmen, p.* 50.

It seems to me that it was far from right for the Professor of English Literature in Yale, the Professor of English Literature in Columbia, and Wilkie Collins to deliver opinions on Cooper's literature without having read some of it. It would have been much more decorous to keep silent and let persons talk who have read Cooper. Cooper's art has some defects. In one place in "Deerslayer," and in the restricted space of two-thirds of a page, Cooper has scored 114 offences against literary art out of a possible 115. It breaks the record. There are nineteen rules governing literary art in the domain of romantic fiction—some say twenty-two.

In "Deerslayer" Cooper violated eighteen of them. . . . Cooper's gift in the way of invention was not a rich endowment; but such as it was he liked to work it, he was pleased with the effects, and indeed he did some quite sweet things with it. In his little box of stage properties he kept six or eight cunning devices, tricks, artifices for his savages and woodsmen to deceive and circumvent each other with, and he was never so happy as when he was working these innocent things and seeing them go. A favorite one was to make a moccasined person tread in the tracks of the moccasined enemy, and thus hide his own trail. Cooper wore out barrels and barrels of moccasins in working that trick. Another stage-property that he pulled out of his box pretty frequently was his broken twig. He prized his broken twig above all the rest of his effects, and worked it the hardest. It is a restful chapter in any book of his when somebody doesn't step on a dry twig and alarm all the reds and whites for two hundred yards around. Every time a Cooper person is in peril, and absolute silence is worth four dollars a minute, he is sure to step on a dry twig. There may be a hundred handier things to step on, but that wouldn't satisfy Cooper. Cooper requires him to turn out and find a dry twig; and if he can't do it, go and borrow one. In fact, the Leather Stocking Series ought to have been called the Broken Twig Series.—CLEMENS, SAMUEL LANGHORNE (MARK TWAIN), 1897, *Fenimore Cooper's Literary Offences, How to Tell a Story and other Essays, pp.* 93, 97.

His long introductions he shared with the other novelists of the day, or at least with Scott, for both Miss Austen and Miss Edgeworth are more modern in this respect and strike more promptly into the tale. His loose-jointed plots are also shared with Scott, but he knows as surely as Scott how to hold the reader's attention when once grasped. Like Scott's, too, is his fearlessness in giving details, instead of the vague generalizations which were then in fashion, and to which his academical critics would have confined him. . . . Balzac, who risked the details of buttons and tobacco pipes as fearlessly as Cooper, said of "The Pathfinder," "Never did the art of writing tread closer upon the art of the pencil. This is the school of study for literary landscape painters." He says elsewhere: "If Cooper had succeeded in the painting of character to the same extent that he did in the painting of the phenomena of nature, he would have uttered the last word of our art." Upon such praise as this the reputation of James Fenimore Cooper may well rest.—HIGGINSON, THOMAS WENTWORTH, 1898, *American Prose, ed. Carpenter, p.* 151.

As a master of healthy and manly fiction, deserves to be better remembered than he seems to be at the present day, especially as the novel of romantic adventure has, for the time at least, regained its vogue. . . . On reading over the Leather-Stocking Series afresh, I have sometimes been struck with the absence of all wild animal-life in the forests, especially bird-life, in which, according to Audubon and Wilson, the western woodlands were particularly rich. . . . Cooper was true to nature in not representing Leather-Stocking as taking that interest in zoology which belongs rather to a state of advanced civilisation. He might however, one would think, have made some use of materials which would have greatly enhanced the effect of many of his scenes. The gloomy croak of the raven, supposed by so many races of mankind to be an omen of evil, and the hideous wail of the horned owl heard in the forest solitude, must often have startled the watchers during those nights of terror so graphically described in these novels. But we see no trace in Cooper of any of those tastes or sympathies which would have led him to seek fresh elements of interests in the sources here indicated. The want of them is more apparent now than it would have been eighty years ago; but perhaps even now such accessories will be little missed by the great majority of his readers.—KEBBEL, T. E., 1899, *Leather-Stocking, Macmillan's Magazine, vol.*79, *pp.*191, 200, 201.

The gist of the matter is that Cooper was not a verbal artist, and that his endowment of what we are pleased to call literary conscience was scant. With no special training as a writer, when, at thirty or thereabout, it accidentally came into his head to try his hand at a novel, he struck boldly out, not particularly considering whither. Some of his early books, written for his own pleasure, brought him popularity which surprised no one more than himself. The art of writing engaged his attention far less than the panorama and the story. Robust and impetuous, he disdained details of style and academic standards. To apply to him academic standards is as if one should inquire whether Hard-Heart's horsemanship conforms to the rules of the riding-school; for nobody cares. It is to miss the point that, heaven knows how or why, he struck—Heaven be praised!—a new trail which, admitting all the shortcomings in style that any one may choose to allege, the world is not yet weary of following. The indisputable, the essential fact is that, entering unheralded and possessing the land, he founded a realm, and became by divine right king of American fiction.—CLYMER, W. B. SHUBRICK, 1900, *James Fenimore Cooper* (*Beacon Biographies*), *p.* 59.

Great as was his success at home and in England, indeed, it is sometimes said to have been exceeded by that which he has enjoyed throughout continental Europe. For this there is a reason which has been little remarked. The mere number and bulk of Cooper's works bear evidence to the fact that he must have written with careless haste. He had small literary training and little more tact in the matter of style than he displayed in his personal relations with people who did not enjoy his respect. Cooper's English, then, is often ponderous and generally clumsy. An odd result follows. His style is frequently such as could hardly be altered except for the better. A translator into whatever language can often say what Cooper said in a form more readable and agreeable than Cooper's own. Many of the minor passages in his writings seem more felicitous in French translation than in his own words. Yet his own words, though even in his best work impaired by clumsiness and prolixity, are well worth reading.—WENDELL, BARRETT, 1900, *A Literary History of America*, *p.* 183.

Joanna Baillie

1762–1851

Joanna Baillie, the daughter of a Scotch clergyman, was born at Bothwell, in Lanarkshire, in 1762. When she was about six years old, her father exchanged the Bothwell Kirk for that of Hamilton. At ten she was sent to boarding-school in Glasgow; and, her father having been appointed to a professorship in Glasgow University, when Joanna was fifteen the family removed to that city. Two years later her father died, and the Baillies left Glasgow for Long Calderwood, in the Middle Ward of Lanarkshire. In 1784, Joanna's brother, Dr. Matthew Baillie, took his mother and sisters to live in London. In 1790, Joanna published anonymously a volume of miscellaneous poems; and in 1798, also anonymously, the first volume of "Plays on the Passions." In 1802, a second, and in 1812, a third volume appeared. Meanwhile Miss Baillie had published, in 1804, a volume of "Miscellaneous Dramas;" and in 1810 a tragedy, "The Family Legend," was brought out at the Edinburgh Theatre. It was played fourteen nights; and in 1814 was again acted in London. In 1826 appeared "The Martyr," a tragedy, and in 1836 three more volumes of plays. In 1831 Miss Baillie published "A View of the General Tenor of the New Testament regarding the Nature and Dignity of Jesus Christ." She was also the author of "Metrical Legends of Exalted Characters." In 1801, Joanna, her mother, and her sister, Agnes, had established themselves at Hampstead, where Mrs. Baillie died in 1806. The sisters more than once revisited Scotland. Joanna "passed away without suffering" on the 23rd of February, 1851.—CONE, HELEN GRAY, AND GILDER, JEANNETTE L., 1887, *Pen-Portraits of Literary Women, vol.* I, *p.* 223.

PERSONAL

We met Miss Joanna Baillie, and accompanied her home. She is small in figure, and her gait is mean and shuffling, but her manners are those of a well-bred woman. She has none of the unpleasant airs too common to literary ladies. Her conversation is sensible. She possesses apparently considerable information, is prompt without being forward, and has a fixed judgment of her own, without any disposition to force it on others. Wordsworth said of her with warmth: "If I had to present anyone to a foreigner as a model of an English gentlewoman, it would be Joanna Baillie."—ROBINSON, HENRY CRABB, 1812, *Diary, May* 24; *Diary, Reminiscences and Correspondence, ed. Sadler, vol.* I, *p.* 248.

Here's to Shakespeare in petticoats, noble Jŏanna.
—WILSON, JOHN, 1822, *Noctes Ambrosianæ, July*.

She wore a delicate lavender satin bonnet; and Mrs. J— says she is fond of dress, and knows what every one has on. Her taste is certainly exquisite in dress. . . . I more than ever admired the harmony of expression and tint, the silver hair and silvery gray eye, the pale skin, and the look which speaks of a mind that has had much communing with high imagination, though such intercourse is only perceptible now by the absence of everything which that lofty spirit would not set his seal upon. . . . Age has slackened the active part of genius, and yet is in some sort a substitute for it. There is a declining of mental exercitation. She has had enough of that; and now for a calm decline, and thoughts of Heaven.—COLERIDGE, SARA, 1834, *Letter to her Husband, Memoir and Letters, ed. her Daughter, p.*88.

We made a most delightful visit to Miss Joanna Baillie. . . . She talked of Scott with a tender enthusiasm that was contagious, and of Lockhart with a kindness that is uncommon when coupled with his name, and which seemed only characteristic of her benevolence. It is very rare that old age, or, indeed, any age, is found so winning or agreeable. I do not wonder that Scott, in his letters, treats her with more deference, and writes to her with more care and beauty, than to any other of his correspondents, however high or titled.—TICKNOR, GEORGE, 1838, *Journal, April* 7: *Life, Letters and Journals, vol.* II, *p.*153.

She had enjoyed a fame almost without parallel, and had outlived it. She had been told every day for years, through every possible channel, that she was second only to Shakspere,—if second; and then she had seen her works drop out of notice so that, of the generation who grew up before her eyes, not one in a thousand had read a line of her plays:—yet was her serenity never disturbed, nor her merry humour in the least dimmed. I have never lost the impression of the trying circumstances of my first interview with her, nor of the grace, simplicity and sweeetness with which she bore them. She was old; and she declined dinner-parties; but she wished to meet me, . . . and therefore she came to Miss Berry's to tea, one day when I was dining there. Miss Berry, her contemporary, put her feelings, it seemed to me, to a most unwarrantable trial, by describing to me, as we three sat together, the celebrity of the "Plays on the Passions" in their day. She told me how she found on her table, on her return from a ball, a volume of plays; and how she kneeled on a chair to look at it, and how she read on till the servant opened the shutters, and let in the daylight of a winter morning. She told me how all the world raved about the plays; and she held on so long that I was in pain for the noble creature to whom it must have been irksome on the one hand to hear her own praises and fame so dwelt upon, and, on the other, to feel that we all knew how long that had been quite over. But, when I looked up at her sweet face, with its composed smile amidst the becoming mob cap, I saw that she was above pain of either kind.—MARTINEAU, HARRIET, 1855–77, *Autobiography, ed. Chapman, vol*, I, *pp.* 270, 271.

She was past fifty when I first saw her, and appeared like an old lady to me, then in my teens. She dressed like an aged person, and with scrupulous neatness. She lived with a sister who looked older still, because she had not the vivacity of Joanna, and was only distinguished for the amiability with which she bore being outshone by her more gifted relative. Miss Baillie, according to the English custom, took the title of Mrs. Joanna Baillie, on passing her fiftieth birthday. She gave the prettiest and the pleasantest dinners, and presided at them with peculiar grace and tact, always attentive to the wants of her guests. . . . She took such pleasure in writing poetry, and especially in her "Plays on the Passions," that she said, "If no one ever read them, I should find my happiness in writing them." Though she was young when she left her native land, she never lost her Scotch accent. I thought it made her conversation only the more piquant. She was full of anecdotes and curious facts about remarkable people. I only recollect her telling one of Lord Byron being obliged, by politeness, to escort her and her sister to the opera, and her perceiving that he was provoked beyond measure at being there with them, and that he made faces as he sat behind them.—FARRAR, ELIZA, 1866, *Recollections of Seventy Years, p.* 74.

Joanna Baillie lived many years at Hampstead, in Bolton House, on Windmill Hill, a little below the Clock House. Perhaps no person of literary distinction ever led a more secluded and unambitious life so near the metropolis. In the society of her sister, Miss Agnes Baillie, she seemed to care but little whether the world forgot her or not. But of this forgetfulness there was no danger. Every man of pre-eminent genius delighted to do her honor. The last time I saw the poet Rogers he was returning from a call on Joanna Baillie.—HOWITT, WILLIAM, 1869, *The Northern Heights of London, Hampstead.*

Of Joanna Baillie too I saw much both as a friend and patient. Her gentle simplicity, with a Scotch tinge colouring it to the end of life, won the admiration even of those who knew nothing of her power of dramatic poetry. It was pleasant to visit her in the quiet house at Hampstead, in which she lived with her sister Agnes. She reached, I think, her ninety-second year. Agnes lived to a hundred.—HOLLAND, SIR HENRY, 1871, *Recollections of Past Life, p.* 246.

She was the most sensible of wilful geniuses; the most retiring of "wise" women; the most maidenly of experienced elderly ladies; the most tenderly attached of daughters and sisters; one of the meekest and most modest of Christians. Joanna Baillie's was a noble soul. She had a great man's grand guilelessness, rather than a woman's minute and subtle powers of sympathy; a man's shy but unstinted kindness and forbearance, rather than a woman's eager but measured cordiality and softness; a man's modesty in full combination with a woman's delicacy; and, as if to prove her sex beyond mistake, she had, after all, more than the usual share of a woman's tenacity and headstrongness, when the fit was upon her. . . . Joanna appeared to her companions a capable young woman, with much decision of character, like her mother. She was shy amongst strangers, but sufficiently frank to her friends; and in the midst of her seriousness, she was the merriest soul when the fit took her. She had quietly written some clever Scotch songs, most of them adaptations from old ditties. These were already sung with glee around many a rustic hearth and at many a homely supper-table. . . . Joanna was not handsome. . . . Joanna was below the middle height, and had the large, statuesque features which suit better with a stately figure. Years lent these features dignity rather than robbed them of grace. There is no word of her youthful bloom. She wore her hair for many years simply divided and braided across her forehead; but the hair must have grown low on it from the first, and, whether in a crop, or in braids, must have nearly concealed the expansive brow, which thus lent no relief to the dark gauntness of the face. . . . The brows were firmly arched. Her mouth was wide, and expressed benevolence. Her chin was clearly moulded, and slightly projecting. —TYTLER, SARAH, AND WATSON, J. L., 1871, *Songstresses of Scotland, vol.* II, *pp.* 181, 199, 200.

Her gentle and lovely life had no incident in it. She was one of those maiden princesses about whom there always breathes a soft and exquisite perfume, too delicate for common appreciation, of that reserved and high virginity, which, never reaching to any second chapter of life, involves an endless youth.—OLIPHANT, MARGARET O. W., 1882, *Literary History of England, XVIII-XIX Century, vol.* II, *p.* 272.

Not handsome, below the middle height, with large square features; her hair grew low down on her capacious forehead, her grey eyes were large and thoughtful, though sometimes humorous, her mouth was wide, and her chin slightly projecting. Altogether, though her face had little beauty, it was frank and sensible.—HAMILTON, CATHARINE J., 1892, *Women Writers, First Series, p.* 115.

GENERAL

Do you remember my speaking to you in high terms of a series of plays upon the passions of the human mind, which had been sent to me last winter by the author? I talked to everybody else in the same terms of them at the time, anxiously enquiring for the author; but nobody knew them, nobody cared for them, nobody would listen to me; and at last I unwillingly held my tongue, for fear it should be supposed that I thought highly of them only because they had been sent to me. This winter the first question upon everybody's lips is, "Have you read the series of plays?" Everybody talks in the raptures (I always thought they deserved) of the tragedies and of the introduction as of a new and admirable piece of criticism. Sir G. Beaumont, who was with us yesterday morning, says he never expected to see such tragedies in his days; and C. Fox, to whom he had sent them, is in such raptures with them, that he has written a critique of 5 pages upon the subject to Sir George.—BERRY, MARY, 1799, *Letter, March* 12; *Extracts of the Journals and Correspondence of Miss Berry, vol.* II, *p.*88.

Upon the whole, then, we are pretty decidedly of opinion, that Miss Baillie's plan of composing separate plays upon the passions, is, in so far as it is at all new or original, in all respects extremely injudicious; and we have been induced to express this opinion more fully and strongly, from the anxiety that we feel to deliver her pleasing and powerful genius from the trammels that have been imposed upon it by this unfortunate system. It is paying no great compliment, perhaps, to her talents, to say, that they are superior to those of any of her contemporaries among the English writers of tragedy; and that, with proper management, they bid fair to produce something that posterity will not allow to be forgotten. . . . We think there is no want of genius in this book, although there are many errors of judgment; and are persuaded, that if Miss Baillie will relinquish her plan of producing twin dramas on each of the passions, and consent to write tragedies, without any deeper design than that of interesting her readers, we shall soon have the satisfaction of addressing her with more unqualified praise, than we have yet bestowed upon any poetical adventurer.—JEFFREY, FRANCIS LORD, 1803, *Miss Baillie's Plays on the Passions, Edinburgh Review, vol.* 2.

. . . if to touch such chord be thine,
Restore the ancient tragic line,
And emulate the notes that rung
From the wild harp, which silent hung
By silver Avon's holy shore
Till twice an hundred years roll'd o'er;
When she, the bold Enchantress, came,
With fearless hand and heart on flame,
From the pale willow snatch'd the treasure,
And swept it with a kindred measure,
Till Avon's swans, while rung the grove
With Montfort's hate and Basil's love,
Awakening at the inspired strain,
Deem'd their own Shakespeare lived again!
—SCOTT, SIR WALTER, 1808, *Marmion, Introduction to Canto* iii.

I hope Miss Baillie's thistle will flourish longer than those perishable wreaths which have hitherto bound the brows of female genius. Will you think me extremely national when I remark that, though the Scottish muse never wore the tragic stole until after the Union, no tragedy written since that period has kept possession of the stage but those of Caledonian origin,—Home's "Douglas," Thomson's "Sigismunda," and Miss Baillie's Tragedies, which do not seem born to die.—GRANT, ANNE, 1815, *To Miss C. M. Fanshawe, Aug.* 30; *Memoir and Correspondence, vol.* II, *p.* 83.

Her tragedies and comedies, one of each to illustrate each of the passions, separately, from the rest, are heresies in the dramatic art. She is a Unitarian in poetry. With her the passions are, like the French republic, one and indivisible: they are not so in nature, or in Shakspeare. Mr. Southey has, I believe, somewhere expressed an opinion that the Basil of Miss Baillie is superior to Romeo and Juliet. I shall not stay to contradict him. On the other hand, I prefer her De Montfort, which was condemned on the stage, to some later tragedies, which have been more fortunate—to the Remorse, Bertram, and lastly, Fazio.—HAZLITT, WILLIAM, 1818, *Lectures on the English Poets, Lecture* viii.

I well remember when her plays upon the "Passions" first came out, with a metaphysical preface. All the world wondered and stared at me, who pronounced them the work of a woman, although the remark was made everyday and everywhere that it was a masculine performance. No sooner, however, did an unknown girl own the work, than the value so fell, her booksellers complained they could not get themselves paid for what they did, nor did their merits ever again swell the throat of public applause.—PIOZZI, HESTER LYNCH, 1819, *Letter to Sir James Fellowes, March* 28; *Autobiography, Letters and Literary Remains, ed. Hayward, p.* 436.

. . . tragic Baillie stole from Nature's side
The mantle left by Shakspeare, when he died.
—ELLIOTT, EBENEZER, 1823, *Love, bk.* i.

She has created tragedies which Sophocles—or Euripides—nay, even Æschylus himself, might have feared, in competition for the crown. She is our Tragic Queen;

but she belongs to all places as to all times; and Sir Walter truly said—let them who dare deny it—that he saw her Genius in a sister shape sailing by the side of the Swan of Avon. Yet Joanna loves to pace the pastoral mead; and then we are made to think of the tender dawn, the clear noon, and the bright meridian of her life, passed among the tall cliffs of the silver Calder, and in the lonesome heart of the dark Strathaven Muirs.—WILSON, JOHN, 1831–42, *An Hour's Talk About Poetry, Recreations of Christopher North.*

She has unfortunately written on a theory; for everybody works on a theory in this philosophic age. The principal purpose of her's, was to make each play subservient to the development of some one particular passion. In this way, she excluded herself from the legitimate range of character, which belongs to the drama; nor, indeed, was it possible, with any degree of skill, to adhere to her plan, since the *rôles* of the subordinate agents must often be at variance, and obviously require a different play of passion from that of the principal character. — PRESCOTT, WILLIAM HICKLING, 1832, *English Literature of the Nineteenth Century, North American Review, vol.* 35, *p.* 179.

If Joanna Baillie had known the stage practically, she would never have attached the importance she does to the development of single passions in single tragedies; and she would have invented more stirring incidents to justify the passion of her characters, and to give them that air of fatality which, though peculiarly predominant in the Greek drama, will also be found, to a certain extent, in all successful tragedies. Instead of this, she contrives to make all the passions of her main characters proceed from the wilful natures of the beings themselves. Their feelings are not precipitated by circumstances, like a stream down a declivity, that leaps from rock to rock; but, for want of incident, they seem often like water on a level, without a propelling impulse.—CAMPBELL, THOMAS, 1834, *Life of Mrs. Siddons, p.*208.

Read Joanna Baillie's play of "Basil," which I think can scarcely be made pathetic enough for representation; there is a stiffness in her style, a want of appropriateness and peculiarity of expression distinguishing each person, that I cannot overcome in reading her plays; it is a sort of brocaded style, a thick kind of silk that has no fall or play—it is not the flexibility of nature.—MACREADY, W. C., 1836, *Diary, Feb.* 16; *Reminiscences, ed. Pollock, p.* 369.

Joanna Baillie is, as you say, "a glorious old lady." She has a glorious mind. It is impossible for you to admire her more than I do; but one thing I must remark, you will see now the whole world of criticism exalt her to the skies, and not on the strength of her own noble intellect, but at the expense of every other woman who has written tragedy. It is the fashion of modern criticism: the idol of the day must be the head of a pyramid, erected on other men's fame. . . . I never deny the wonderful excellence of Joanna Baillie, but no one shall persuade me that "Rienzi" is not as good as any drama by her.—HOWITT, MARY, 1836, *Letter to Miss Mitford, Feb.* 4; *The Friendships of Mary Russell Mitford.*

The most remarkable of her works are her "Plays of the Passions," a series in which each passion is made the subject of a tragedy and a comedy. In the comedies she failed completely; they are pointless tales in dialogue. Her tragedies, however, have great merit, though possessing a singular quality for works of such an aim, in being without the earnestness and abruptness of actual and powerful feeling. By refinement and elaboration she makes the passions sentiments. She fears to distract attention by multiplying incidents; her catastrophes are approached by the most gentle gradations; her dramas are therefore slow in action and deficient in interest. Her characters possess little individuality; they are mere generalizations of intellectual attributes, theories personified. —GRISWOLD, RUFUS W., 1844, *The Poets and Poetry of England in the Nineteenth Century, p.* 40.

The powerful dramatic writer, the graceful and witty lyrist.—HOWITT, WILLIAM, 1847, *Homes and Haunts of the Most Eminent British Poets, vol.* II, *p.* 285.

Lady revered, our Island's Tragic Queen.
—COLERIDGE, HARTLEY, 1850? *To Joanna Baillie, Sonnet.*

The first woman who won high and undisputed honors in the highest class of English poetry. . . . Her tragedies have a boldness and grasp of mind, a firmness of hand, and a resonance of cadence, that scarcely seem within the reach of a female writer; while the tenderness and sweetness of her heroines—the grace of the love-scenes—and the trembling outgushings of sensibility, as in "Orra," for instance, in the fine tragedy on Fear—would seem exclusively feminine, if we did not know that a true dramatist—as Shakspeare or Fletcher—has the wonderful power of throwing himself, mind and body, into the character that he portrays. That Mrs. Joanna *is* a true dramatist, as well as a great poet, I, for one, can never doubt, although it has been the fashion to say that her plays do not act.—MITFORD, MARY RUSSELL, 1851, *Recollections of a Literary Life, p.* 152.

Her knowledge of the human heart, of its wide range for good or evil, of its multifarious, changeful, and wayward nature, was great, and her power of portraying character has rarely been excelled. Her female portraits are especially beautiful, and possess an unusual degree of elevation and purity. But though distinguished chiefly for her dramatic writings, her lyric and miscellaneous poetry takes a very high rank among similar productions of the present century. To great simplicity and womanly tenderness of feeling, she unites at times a conciseness and vigor of expression which are not often surpassed.—CLEVELAND, CHARLES D., 1853, *English Literature of the Nineteenth Century, p.* 546.

Unquestionably she was a great writer, as strong as a man, but with all the delicate purity and sweetness, the instinctive quickness and fine sensibility, of a woman.—SMILES, SAMUEL, 1860, *Brief Biographies, p.* 449.

Among the works of the numerous minor poets, the tragedies of Joanna Baillie, with all their faults as plays, are noble additions to the literature, and the closest approach made in recent times to the merit of the old English drama.—BOTTA, ANNE C. LYNCH, 1860, *Hand-Book of Universal Literature.*

Miss Joanna Baillie was a great friend of Mrs. Siddons's, and wrote expressly for her the part of Jane de Montfort, in her play of "De Montfort." . . . The peculiar plan upon which she wrote her fine plays, making each of them illustrate a single passion, was in a great measure the cause of their unfitness for the stage. "De Montfort," which has always been considered the most dramatic of them, had only a very partial success, in spite of its very great poetical merit and considerable power of passion, and the favorable circumstance that the two principal characters in it were represented by the eminent actors for whom the authoress originally designed them. In fact, though Joanna Baillie selected and preferred the dramatic form for her poetical compositions, they are wanting in the real dramatic element, resemblance to life and human nature, and are infinitely finer as poems than plays.—KEMBLE, FRANCES ANN, 1879, *Records of a Girlhood, p.* 349.

Joanna Baillie's dramas are "nice" and rather dull; now and then she can write a song with the ease and sweetness that suggest Shakespearian echoes. But Scott's judgment was obviously blinded by his just and warm regard for Joanna Baillie herself.—HUTTON, RICHARD HOLT, 1879, *Sir Walter Scott (English Men of Letters), p.* 91.

In reading Joanna Baillie's poetry we find her to possess a quickness of observation that nearly supplies the place of insight; a strongly moralised temperament delighting in natural things; a vigorous, simple style. These are not especially dramatic qualities, and although she won her reputation through her plays, the poetry by which she is remembered is chiefly of a pastoral kind. . . . Few women possess the faculty of construction, and Joanna Baillie was not one of these; nor had she qualities rare enough to cover the sins of a wandering story. Even in the revelation of a passion she is more occupied with the moral to be inferred than with the feeling itself, and few of her *dramatis personæ* are more than the means to bring the moral to its conclusion. . . . Her country songs, written in the language of her early home, have the best qualities of Scottish national poetry; their simplicity, their cautious humour, endeared them at once to the national heart; they have the shrewdness and the freshness of the morning airs, the homeliness of unsophisticated feeling. Such songs as "Woo'd and Married and a'," "The weary pund o' Tow," "My Nanny O," and the lovely trysting song beginning "The gowan glitters on the sward," are among the treasures of Scottish minstrelsy.—ROBINSON, A. MARY F., 1880, *The English Poets, ed. Ward, vol.* IV.

That she was superior to many men of her time is no reason for claiming for her an approach to the circle of the greatest: and to name her with Wordsworth or with Coleridge would be folly, although there is now and then a Shakspearian melody in her blank verse which pleased the general ear more than the stronger strain of the "Excursion," and stood no unfavorable comparison with the diction of Coleridge's dramas.—OLIPHANT, MARGARET O. W., 1882, *Literary History of England, XVIII-XIX Century, vol.* II, *p.* 271.

As a song-writer, Joanna Baillie is rarely impassioned, but she is always hearty and sympathetic. Her humour is full-flavoured, and her pathos is natural if it is not deep.—ROBERTSON, ERIC S., 1883, *English Poetesses, p.* 174.

It will always be a delightful contemplation to the student of literary history, that the Scottish lady who made her ideal figures tread the stage with all the grace of a Sophocles and the majesty of a Corneille, could at the same time give utterance to the kindliest and gentlest of human feelings, with all the sly humour and shrewd merriment that belong to a masterpiece of Scottish song. In this double form of presentation she, like Burns and Scott, was bilingual in the noblest sense: while she held converse on an equal platform with the first masters of the noble English tongue, she could at the same time address the meanest peasant of her native land in the musical and expressive speech which they had imbibed with their mother's milk; and verily she has had her reward. Her plays will win the admiration of the few; her songs warm the hearts of the many.—BLACKIE, JOHN STUART, 1889, *Scottish Song, p.* 97.

She out-distances Hannah More inasmuch as her works, if somewhat ponderous, are yet interesting and full of dramatic feeling, and their occasional harshness is refreshing after the frequent mawkish commonplaces of her predecessors.—SHARP, ELIZABETH A., 1890, *Women Poets of the Victorian Era, Preface, p.* xxiv.

Heartiness is one of the gifts most essential to a song-writer. Joanna Baillie had the gift. Of all English women-poets, she speaks in accents least easily distinguishable from a man's. The songs "Woo'd and Married an' a," and "Saw ye Johnny comin' " (the best of them all), and "Fy let us a' to the Wedding," were, in her own phrase, "Auld Songs new Buskit." But she made them her own—even as Burns made so many an old ditty his own—by skilful verbal changes, by refining their tone without lessening their spontaneity and pith. Her fame has suffered a sad eclipse since Sir Walter deemed her "the immortal Joanna," and paid high tribute to her in the introduction to the third canto of "Marmion." But while her dramas are never to be revived and seldom, very seldom to be read, her vigorous, bracing, hearty lyrical work endures, and will endure.—WHYTE, WALTER, 1892, *The Poets and the Poetry of the Century, Joanna Baillie to Mathilde Blind, ed. Miles, p.* 4.

Her "natural" language is often as insipid as Wordsworth's, but not so crude, her passion has an air of being rather forced upon her characters in compliance with her program than elicited from their circumstances. She had talent, grace, eloquence; and generous fellow-countrymen, like Scott and Wilson, hailed a new Shakespeare in "our Joanna," while more cautious ones, like Jeffrey and Campbell, pointed out her lack of the fundamental nerve and sinew of tragedy.—HERFORD, C. H., 1897, *The Age of Wordsworth.*

She had some poetic faculty; but her "Plays on the Passions" (1768 and later) and others, though admired at the time, and somtimes acted, are neither great dramas nor great literature, the author never seeming quite to know whether she is writing for the theatre or the study, and not producing the best things for either.—SAINTSBURY, GEORGE, 1898, *A Short History of English Literature, p.* 641.

John James Audubon

1780-1851

Born near New Orleans, May 4, 1780: died at New York, Jan. 27, 1851. A noted American ornithologist, of French descent, chiefly celebrated for his drawings of birds. He was educated in France, where he was pupil of the painter David, and on his return to the United States made various unsuccessful attempts to establish himself in business in New York, Louisville, and New Orleans. His time was chiefly devoted to his favorite study, in the pursuit of which he made long excursions on foot through the United States. His chief work, the "Birds of America," was published, 1827–30, by subscription, the price of each copy being $1,000. In 1831–39 he published "Ornithological Biography" (5 volumes). His "Quadrupeds of America" (chiefly by John Bachman and Audubon's sons) appeared 1846–54.—SMITH, BENJAMIN E., *ed.*, 1894–97, *The Century Cyclopedia of Names, p.* 94.

PERSONAL

I cannot help thinking Mr. Audubon a dishonest man. Why did he make you believe that he was a man of property? How is it his circumstances have altered so suddenly? In truth I do not believe you fit to deal with the world, or at least the American world.—KEATS, JOHN, 1819, *Letter to George Keats, Sept.* 17; *The Poetical Works and other Writings of John Keats, ed. Forman, vol.* IV, *p.* 5.

He is the greatest artist in his own walk that ever lived, and cannot fail to reap the reward of his genius and perseverance and adventurous zeal in his own beautiful branch of natural history, both in fame and fortune. The man himself—whom I have had the pleasure of frequently meeting—is just what you would expect from his works,—full of fine enthusiasm and intelligence—most interesting in looks and manners—a perfect gentleman—and esteemed by all who know him for the simplicity and frankness of his nature.—WILSON, JOHN, 1827, *Noctes Ambrosianæ, Jan.*

At the Academy of Natural Sciences today Dr. Morton introduced me to the justly-celebrated Audubon, so well known by his great work on ornithology. He is a man of fifty, with the countenance of a bird, having a projecting forehead, a sunken black eye, a parrot nose, and a long protruding chin, combined with an expression bold and eagle-like.—BRECK, SAMUEL, 1839, *Note-Book, Nov.* 16; *Recollections, ed. Scudder, p.* 260.

With gun, knapsack, and drawing materials, he traversed the dark forests and pestiferous fens, sleeping beneath the broad canopy of heaven, procuring food with his rifle, and cooking it when hunger demanded appeasement, and undergoing, day after day, the greatest fatigues and privations. For months and years he thus wandered, from the shores of the Gulf of Mexico to the rocky coasts of Labrador, studying and preserving, with no other motive than the gratification of a great controlling passion.—LOSSING, BENSON J., 1855–86, *Eminent Americans, p.* 272.

His love of nature was not philosophic, like that of Wordsworth, nor scientific, like that of Humboldt, nor adventurous, like that of Boone; but special and artistic—circumstances, rather than native idiosyncrasy, made him a naturalist; and his knowledge was by no means so extensive in this regard as that of others less known to fame. But few men have indulged so genuine a love of nature for her own sake, and found such enjoyment in delineating one of the most poetical and least explored departments of her boundless kingdom. To the last his special ability, as an artistic naturalist, was unapproached; and, while one of his sons drew the outline, and another painted the landscape, or the foreground, it was his faithful hand that, with a steel-pen, made the hairy coat of the deer, or, with a fine pencil, added the exquisite plumage to the sea-fowl's breast. . . . His high-arched brow, dark-gray eye, and vivacious temperament, marked him as fitted by nature to excel in action as well as thought—a destiny which his pursuits singularly realized. There was something bird-like in the very physiognomy of Audubon, in the shape and keenness of his eye, the aquline form of the nose, and a certain piercing and vivid expression when animated. He was thoroughly himself only amid the freedom and exuberance of nature; the breath of the woods exhilarated and inspired him; he was more at ease under a canopy of boughs than beneath gilded cornices, and felt a necessity to be within sight either of the horizon or the sea. Indeed, so prevailing was this appetite for nature, if we may so call it, that from the moment the idea of his last-projected expedition was abandoned,—in accordance with the urgent remonstrances of his family, mindful of his advanced age,—he began to droop, and the force and concentration of his intellect visibly declined.—TUCKERMAN, HENRY T., 1857, *Essays, Biographical and Critical, pp.* 305, 309.

The interval of about three years which passed between the time of Audubon's return from the West and the period when his mind began to fail, was a short and sweet twilight to his adventurous career. His habits were simple. Rising almost with the sun, he proceeded to the woods to view his feathered favorites till the hour at which the family usually breakfasted, except when he had drawing to do, when he sat closely to his work. After breakfast he drew till noon and then took a long walk. At nine in the evening he generally retired. He was now an old man, and the fire which had burned so steadily in his heart was going out gradually. Yet there are but few things in his life more interesting and beautiful than the tranquil happiness he enjoyed in the bosom of his family, with his two sons and their children under the same roof, in the short interval between his return from his last earthly expedition, and the time when his sight and mind began to grow dim, until mental gloaming settled on him, before the night of death came. . . . His loss of sight was quite peculiar in its character. His glasses enabled him to see objects and to read, long after his eye was unable to find a focus on the canvas. The first day he found that he could not adjust his glasses so as to enable him to work at the accustomed distance from the object before him, he drooped. Silent, patient sorrow filled his broken heart. From that time his wife never left him; she read to him, walked with him, and toward the last she fed him.—AUDUBON, MRS. JOHN J., 1869, *The Life of John James Audubon, pp.* 435, 436.

Surrounded by his large family, including his devoted wife, his two sons with their wives, and quite a troop of grandchildren, his enjoyment of life seemed to leave to him little to desire. He was very fond of the rising generation, and they were as devoted in their affectionate regards for him. He seemed to enjoy to the utmost each moment of time, content at last to submit to an inevitable and well-earned leisure, and to throw upon his gifted sons his uncompleted tasks. A pleasanter scene or a more interesting household it has never been the writer's good fortune to witness. Five years afterward the spirit of its great master had taken its final flight. The "American Woodsman," the unequalled painter, the gifted historian of nature, had died as he had lived, surrounded by all that

"Should accompany old age,
As honor, love, obedience, troops of friends."

—BREWER, THOMAS M., 1880, *Reminiscences of John James Audubon, Harper's Magazine, vol.* 61, *p.* 675.

He was a very simple man, a little rough in appearance, with long shaggy black hair, and the most piercing eyes I ever saw,—real eagle eyes.—HEALY, GEORGE P. A., 1894, *Reminiscences of a Portrait Painter, p.* 204.

GENERAL

That work, while it reflects such great credit on our country, and contributes so largely to the advancement of one of the most delightful departments of science, is likely, from the extreme expense attendant upon it, to repay but poorly the indefatigable labor of a lifetime. The high price necessarily put on the copies of Mr. Audubon's magnificent work places it beyond the means of the generality of private individuals. It is entitled therefore to the especial countenance of our libraries and various other public institutions. It appears to me, that the different departments in Washington ought each to have a copy deposited in their libraries or archives.—IRVING, WASHINGTON, 1836, *Letter to Martin Van Buren, Oct.* 19; *Life of John James Audubon, ed. his Widow, p.* 395.

It is the kingdom of birds, an unknown world, which lives in these beautiful engravings. The text is worthy of the plates; it is not a cold analysis nor a pompous description, but the romance of this winged people which the author has studied in their retreats. He communicates the love of birds to the reader. Audubon mingles his own history, with that of his favorites; he associates you in his adventures; he gives gratefully the names of all who helped him in his work. You cross with him those vast American landscapes. You follow the course of those gigantic streams, whose immense floods gather on their way the brooks of the same continent, and roll the mingled waters to the main. Sometimes Audubon travels alone; sometimes his wife and children accompany him. Let us hear him; or rather, travel with him. . . . We will not insult the reader by any comments upon these beautiful pages; they are animated by a true sentiment; this pure and vivid coloring, this simple and ardent tone; this inimitable conviction show the happiest genius. Audubon writes as he sees, under the dictates of his personal impressions. . . . Audubon has not only understood this harmony, in the midst of which he has lived, and whereof the music has re-echoed in the very deeps of his soul; but he has reproduced it in a style admirable for its simplicity, full of savor, of sap, of eloquence, and of sobriety. It is his glory! More varied than Irving; more brilliant and pure than Fenimore Cooper, with him ceases what we may call the first literary epoch of the United States.—CHASLES, PHILARÈTE, 1852, *Anglo-American Literature and Manners, pp.* 67, 73, 93.

The great naturalist of America, John James Audubon, left behind him, in his "Birds of America" and "Ornithological Biography," a magnificent monument of his labors, which through life were devoted to the illustration of the natural history of his native country. His grand work on the Biography of Birds is quite unequaled for the close observation of the habits of birds and animals which it displays, its glowing pictures of American scenery, and the enthusiastic love of nature which breathes throughout its pages. The sunshine and the open air, the dense shade of the forest, and the boundless undulations of the prairies, the roar of the sea beating against the rock-ribbed shore, the solitary wilderness of the Upper Arkansas, the savannas of the South, the beautiful Ohio, the vast Mississippi, and the green steeps of the Alleghanies,—all were as familiar to Audubon as his own home. The love of birds, of flowers, of animals,—the desire to study their habits in their native retreats, —haunted him like a passion from his earliest years, and he devoted almost his entire life to the pursuit. . . . While you read Audubon's books, you feel that you are in the society of no ordinary naturalist. Everything he notes down is the result of his own observation. Nature, not books, has been his teacher. You feel the fresh air blowing in your face, scent the odor of the prairie-flowers and the autumn-woods, and hear the roar of the surf along the sea-shore.—SMILES, SAMUEL, 1860, *Brief Biographies, pp.* 98, 100.

With those whose privilege it was to know the Naturalist, so full of fine enthusiasm and intelligence; with so much simplicity of character, frankness and genius, he will continue to live in their memories, though "with the buried gone;" while to the artistic, literary, and scientific world, he has left an imperishable name that is not in the keeping of history alone. Long after the bronze statue of the naturalist that we hope soon to see erected in the Central Park, shall have been wasted and worn beyond recognition, by the winds and rains of Heaven; while the towering and snow-covered peak of the Rocky Mountains known as Mount Audubon, shall rear its lofty head among the clouds; while the little wren chirps about our homes, and the robin and reed-bird sing in the green meadows; while the melody of the mocking-bird is heard in the cypress swamps of Louisiana, or the shrill scream of the eagle on the frozen shores of the Northern seas, the name of John James Audubon, the gifted Artist, the ardent lover of Nature, and the admirable writer will live in the hearts of his grateful countrymen.—WILSON, JAMES GRANT, 1869, *The Life of John James Audubon, Introduction, p.* v.

Audubon's work not only won for himself universal renown but gave to the study of ornithology a new impulse, under which it has since made prodigious advances. It is difficult to say which is most fascinating, his pictures of the birds, which were manifestly drawn with a loving hand, or his description of their habits and of his solitary rambles in studying them.—HART, JOHN S., 1872, *A Manual of American Literature, p.* 121.

His "Birds of America" is a monument of genius and industry; the designs are exquisite, every bird appearing with its native surroundings. Nor are they merely correct in form and color; on the contrary, they are shown in characteristic attitudes or in natural motion, and every figure is instinct with life. The letter-press descriptions mostly concern us. They are simply perfect, equally removed from the insipidity of a so-called "popular" style and from the scientific dryness that usually marks the mere naturalist. His own personal adventures are modestly told, and give a rare charm to the work. It will readily be imagined that it is very difficult to make selections that will do justice to such an author. Scattered through his volumes are many touches of nature and hints of scenery that are inimitable—especially because they are the unconscious utterances of a soul highly susceptible to beauty, and without the least vain desire of parading its emotions. —UNDERWOOD, FRANCIS H., 1872, *A Hand-Book of English Literature, American Authors*, p. 68.

If he had not the tongue or pen of the poet, certainly had the eye and ear and heart—"the fluid and attaching character—" and the singleness of purpose, the enthusiasm, the unworldliness, the love, that characterizes the true and divine race of bards.—BURROUGHS, JOHN, 1873, *The Birds of the Poets, Scribner's Monthly, vol.* 6, *p.* 555.

I use "great" advisedly. He *was* great —a great dilettante—impostor,—a mere easy-chair Naturalist compared with Alexander Wilson.—GROSART, ALEXANDER B., 1876, *ed., The Poems and Literary Prose of Alexander Wilson, Essay, vol.* II, *p.* xxxvii.

In reading Audubon's books you feel the fresh air blowing in your face, scent the odour of the prairie flowers and autumn woods, or hear the surging of the sea. He takes you into the squatter's hut, in the lowly swamp, where he tells the story of the woodcutter's pioneer life; or he sallies out into the night to hunt the conger, and when daylight returns he invokes the fairy singers of the woods to your listening ear. —SAUNDERS, FREDERICK, 1887, *The Story of Some Famous Books, p.* 143.

With extraordinary enthusiasm, he carried out his great enterprise of describing the habits and executing colored portraits of the birds of America. Most of these portraits are of life size, and are accurate in every detail. The letter-press of the gigantic volumes is not only scientifically valuable, but is written in a glowing and attractive style. — HAWTHORNE, JULIAN, AND LEMMON, LEONARD, 1891, *American Literature, p.* 300.

For more than half a century he followed with almost religious devotion a beautiful and elevated pursuit, enlarging its boundaries by his discoveries, and illustrating its objects by his art. In all climates and in all weathers, scorched by tropic suns and frozen by arctic colds; now diving fearlessly into the densest forests and now wandering alone over desolate prairies, far beyond the haunts of civilization, and frequented only by savage beasts or more savage men; in perils, in difficulties and in doubt; listening only to the music of the birds and the lofty inspirations of his own thoughts, he kept for a lifetime on an original path, which to some seemed chimerical and to others utterly useless, until in the later years and fading twilight of his days his efforts were crowned with success. The records of man's endeavor contain few nobler examples of strength of purpose and indefatigable zeal. . . . It was impossible, in turning over the leaves of his large book, or in looking at the collection which he exhibited at the Lyceum Hall, not to imbibe some of his own enthusiasm for birds. One was made to feel that they were in some way nearer to our affections than any of the other animal tribes. . . . This recognition of Audubon was late, but all the more honorable in that it bears witness of the fact that Time, which rapidly obliterates the highest and the fairest fames, has yet a corner on its tablets which it does not always touch with its winnowing wings, or touches only to waft away the gathered dust, and render the record more bright and clear.—GODWIN, PARKE, 1894, *Commemorative Addresses, pp.* 150, 185, 191.

His style in writing is pure, vivid, and so clear as to place before us the very thing or event described. The accounts of his travels and of the adventures he met with in his search for his birds and animals are very natural and picturesque; and they show also his own fine nature and attractive character.—MANLY, LOUISE, 1895, *Southern Literature, p.* 155.

The journals of this trip are of surpassing interest. To the historian and student of Americana they furnish glimpses of early frontier life, and notes, interspersed with prophetic visions, of commerce and conditions along the Missouri River; to the ethnologist they give truthful pictures of the appearance, dress, and character of the Indians; to the naturalist they offer entertaining accounts of the discovery and habits of new or little known species, of the abundance and manner of hunting wolves, buffaloes, and other big game, and observations concerning the former ranges of animals no longer found in the region. —MERRIAM, C. H., 1898, *Audubon, The Nation, vol.* 66, *p.* 152.

Mary Wollstonecraft Shelley

1797-1851

[Daughter of William Godwin]. Born, in London, 30 Aug. 1797. Met Shelley, 1814. Eloped to Continent with him, 28 July 1814; returned, Sept. 1814. Married to Shelley, after his wife's suicide, 30 Dec. 1816. Lived at Marlow, 1817-18. To Italy, on account of Shelley's health, March 1818; he was drowned there, 8 July 1822. She returned to London, 1823; devoted herself to literature. Travelled on Continent, 1840, 1842-43. Died, in London, 21 Feb. 1851. Buried in Bournemouth Churchyard. *Works:* "History of a Six Weeks' Tour through a Part of France, etc." (with her husband; anon.), 1817; "Frankenstein" (anon.), 1818; "Valperga" (anon.), 1823; "The Last Man" (anon.), 1826; "The Fortunes of Perkin Warbeck" (anon.), 1830; "Lodore" (anon.), 1835; "Falkner" (anon.), 1837; "Lives of the most Eminent, Literary, and Scientific Men of France" (anon.; 2 vols.), 1838-39; "Rambles in Germany and Italy" (2 vols.), 1844. *Posthumous:* "The Choice," ed. by H. B. Forman (priv. ptd.), 1876. She *edited:* Shelley's "Posthumous Poems" [1824]; "Poetical Works," 1839; "Essays, etc.," 1840. *Collected Works:* "Tales and Stories," ed. by R. Garnett, 1891. *Life:* "Life and Letters," by F. A. Marshall, 1889.—SHARP, R. FARQUHARSON, 1897, *A Dictionary of English Authors, p.* 254.

PERSONAL

And what art thou? I know, but dare not speak:
Time may interpret to his silent years.
Yet in the paleness of thy thoughtful cheek,
And in the light thine ample forehead wears,
And in thy sweetest smiles, and in thy tears,
And in thy gentle speech, a prophecy
Is whispered, to subdue my fondest fears:
And, through thine eyes, even in thy soul I see
A lamp of festal fire burning internally.
They say that thou wert lovely from thy birth,
Of glorious parents thou aspiring child.
I wonder not—for One then left this earth
Whose life was like a setting planet mild,
Which clothed thee in the radiance undefiled
Of its departing glory; still her fame
Shines on thee, through the tempests dark and wild
Which shake these latter days; and thou canst claim
The shelter, from thy sire, of an immortal name.

—SHELLEY, PERCY BYSSHE, 1817, *The Revolt of Islam, Dedication.*

Mrs. Shelley was, I have been told, the intimate friend of my son in the lifetime of his first wife, and to the time of her death, and in no small degree, as I suspect, estranged my son's mind from his family, and all his first duties in life; with that impression on my mind, I cannot agree with your Lordship that, though my son was unfortunate, Mrs. Shelley is innocent; on the contrary, I think that her conduct was the very reverse of what it ought to have been, and I must, therefore, decline all interference in matters in which Mrs. Shelley is interested.—SHELLEY, SIR TIMOTHY, 1823, *Letter to Lord Byron, Feb.* 6; *The Life and Letters of Mary Wollstonecraft Shelley, ed. Marshall, vol.* II, *p.* 66.

At the time I am speaking of Mrs. Shelley was twenty-four. Such a rare pedigree of genius was enough to interest me in her, irrespective of her own merits as an authoress. The most striking feature in her face was her calm, grey eyes; she was rather under the English standard of woman's height, very fair and light-haired, witty, social and animated in the society of friends, though mournful in solitude; like Shelley, though in a minor degree, she had the power of expressing her thoughts in varied and appropriate words, derived from familiarity with the works of our vigorous old writers. Neither of them used obsolete or foreign words. This command of our language struck me the more as contrasted with the scanty vocabulary used by ladies in society, in which a score of poor hackneyed phrases suffice to express all that is felt or considered proper to reveal.—TRELAWNY, EDWARD JOHN, 1858-78, *Records of Shelley, Byron and the Author, p.* 15.

Genial, gentle, sympathetic, thoughtful and matured in opinion beyond her years, for she was then but twenty-nine; essentially liberal in politics, ethics, and theology, indeed, yet devoid alike of stiff prejudice against the old or ill-considered prepossession in favor of the new; and, above all, womanly, in the best sense, in every sentiment and instinct; she impressed me also as a person with warm social feelings, dependent for happiness on loving encouragement; needing a guiding and sustaining hand. . . . In person, she was of middle height and graceful figure. Her face, though not regularly beautiful, was comely and spiritual, of winning expression, and with a look of inborn refinement as well as culture. It had a touch of sadness when at rest; yet when it woke up in animated conversation, one could see that underneath there was a bright, cheerful, even playful nature, at variance, I thought, with depressing circumstances and isolated position.—OWEN, ROBERT DALE, 1874, *Threading My Way, p.* 322.

Her well-shaped, golden-haired head, almost always a little bent and drooping; her marble-white shoulders and arms statuesquely visible in the perfectly plain black velvet dress, which the customs of that time [1824] allowed to be cut low, and which her own taste adopted (for neither she nor her sister-in-sorrow ever wore the conventional "widow's weeds" and "widow's cap"); her thoughtful, earnest eyes; her short upper lip and intellectually curved mouth, with a certain close-compressed and decisive expression while she listened, and a relaxation into fuller redness and mobility when speaking; her exquisitely formed, white, dimpled, small hands, with rosy palms, and plumply commencing fingers, that tapered into tips as slender and delicate as those in a Vandyke portrait.—CLARKE, MARY COWDEN, 1878, *Recollections of Writers.*

A spirit akin to that of Greek tragedy informs the double story of mother and daughter. Mary Godwin inherited her fate. The peculiar reverence in which she must necessarily have held the mother who had died to give her life, the implicit confidence with which she must have received that mother's doctrines, and set forth in her life and preserved in her books,—this was the strongest determining influence in the life of the girl, Mary Godwin. When, at the age of seventeen, she unhesitatingly plighted her faith to a man already bound by the laws of society to another, there is significance in the fact that their hands were clasped over her mother's grave—the spot which a woman of opposite traditions must have shunned with shame at such a moment. That sacred place seemed fittest for the strange betrothal of Mary Godwin, who had no doubt that the mother who there slept would have smiled upon the lovers. Censure of this step has properly no place in a sketch of Mary Godwin Shelley; the entire responsibility rests with Shelley and her parents; her action was simply an inevitable result.—CONE, HELEN GRAY, AND GILDER, JEANNETTE L., 1887, *Pen-Portraits of Literary Women, vol.* I, *p.* 109.

From the time of her union with him [Shelley] Mary had been his consoler, his cherished love, all the dearer to him for the thought that she was dependent on him and only on him for comfort and support, and enlightenment of mind; but yet she was a child,—a clever child,—sedate and thoughtful beyond her years, and full of true womanly devotion,—but still one whose first and only acquaintance with the world had been made by coming violently into collision with it, a dangerous experience, and hardening, especially if prolonged. From the time of her marriage a maturer, mellower tone is perceptible throughout her letters and writings, as though, the unnatural strain removed, and, above all, intercourse with her father restored, she glided naturally and imperceptibly into the place Nature intended her to fill, as responsible woman and wife, with social as well as domestic duties to fulfill.—MARSHALL, MRS. JULIAN, 1889, *The Life and Letters of Mary Wollstonecraft Shelley, vol.* I, *p.* 184.

Who, in truth, can remember without profound sympathy, I had almost said, without tears, that sorrowful letter which Mary Shelley, the desolate widow, wrote on the 15th of August, 1822, to Mrs. Gisborne telling the story of those days of agony? The terrible drama of which those two women, Mrs. Shelley, and Mrs. Williams foresaw the end, is narrated with so true, so natural a *crescendo* of horror and of pathos as might move even the author of "The Real Shelley," if certain critics condescended to possess hearts. If no more were known of Shelley's beloved companion, this letter would be enough to prove how worthy she was to be invoked as "Mine own heart's home," as he calls her in the dedication of the "Revolt of Islam," in which he says: "Through thine eyes, even in thy soul I see, a lamp of vestal fire burning internally." "The days pass," she writes after the terrible event, "pass one after another, and we still live. 'Adonais' is not Keats' elegy but his very own." Who knows how often she read, and re-read it in those twenty-nine long years during which she outlived him, widowed vestal of her one and only love? The proof is found in a copy of the Pisan edition of this poem, that she possessed, where after her death a tiny silken sack was found among the pages, containing ashes, taken by her from his funeral urn.—BIAGI, GUIDO, 1891–98, *The Last Days of Percy Bysshe Shelley, p.* 2.

It was Mary Wollstonecraft Godwin who awoke in Shelley such a burst of song that men yet listen to its cadence. It was she who gave his soul wings: her gentle spirit blending with his made music that has enriched the world. Without her he was fast beating out his life against the bars of unkind condition, but together they worked and sang. All of his best lines were recited to her, all were weighed in the critical balances of her woman's judgment. She it was who first wrote it out, and then gave it back. Together they revised; and after he had passed on, she it was who collected the scattered leaves, added the final word, and gave us the book we call "Shelley's Poems."—HUBBARD, ELBERT, 1897, *Little Journeys to Homes of Famous Women, p.* 401.

FRANKENSTEIN
1818

When we have thus admitted that "Frankenstein" has passages which appall the mind and make the flesh creep, we have given it all the praise (if praise it can be called) which we dare to bestow. Our taste and our judgment alike revolt at this kind of writing, and the greater the ability with which it may be executed the worse it is.—SCOTT, SIR WALTER, 1818, *Frankenstein, Quarterly Review, vol.* 13, *p.* 385.

How changed is the taste of verse, prose, and painting, since *le bon vieux temps*, dear madam! Nothing attracts us but what terrifies, and is within—*if* within—a hair's breadth of positive disgust. Some of the strange things they write remind me of Squoire Richard's visit to the Tower Menagerie, when he says: "Odd, they are *pure* grim devils,"—particularly a wild and hideous tale called "Frankenstein."—PIOZZI, HESTER LYNCH (THRALE), 1818, *Letter to Mme. D'Arblay, Diary and Letters of Mme. D'Arblay, ed. Woolsey.*

Your talents are truly extraordinary. "Frankenstein" is universally known, and though it can never be a book for vulgar reading, is everywhere respected. It is the most wonderful work to have been written at twenty years of age that I ever heard of. You are now five and twenty, and, most fortunately, you have pursued a course of reading, and cultivated your mind in a manner the most admirably adapted to make you a great and successful author. If you cannot be independent, who should be?—GODWIN, WILLIAM, 1823, *Letter to Mrs. Shelley, Feb.* 18; *Life and Letters of Mary Wollstonecraft Shelley, ed. Marshall, vol.* II, *p.* 68.

He made some amends for his indifference to Shelley, by his admiration of Mrs. Shelley's "Frankenstein," which he thought the most extraordinary realisation of the idea of a being out of nature which had ever been effected.—TALFOURD, THOMAS NOON, 1837, *The Life and Letters of Charles Lamb, p.* 404.

That a young creature of this age should have produced anything at once so horrible and so original as the hideous romance of "Frankenstein," is one of the most extraordinary accidents in literature; and that she should never, having made such a beginning, have done anything more, is almost equally wonderful. . . . Mary Shelley's individual appearances afterwards are only those of a romantically-desolate widow, pouring out her grief and fondness in sentimental gushes, which look somewhat overstrained and ridiculous in print, whatever they may have done in fact; but to hear her read, with her girlish lips, this most extraordinary and terrible of imaginations, must have been a sensation unparalleled. It is one of the books adopted into the universal memory, which everybody alludes to, and thousands who can never have read it understand the main incidents of—which is a wonderful instance of actual fame. That this should be merely stated as a fact in the history, and no one pause to wonder at it, is another odd instance of the insensibility of contemporaries.—OLIPHANT, MARGARET O. W., 1882, *Literary History of England, XVIII-XIX Century, vol.* III, *p.* 58.

Her literary productions were few and disproportionate to her intellectual force; disappointing when viewed side by side with her peculiar gift of evoking the most artistic literary work in others. . . . Of Mrs. Shelley's writings, "Frankenstein" is without question the most noteworthy. From the day of its first appearance in print down to the present, it has had accorded to it a position as a unique and remarkable production. . . . It is one of the few books that can be called *sui generis*. . . . The world, by its acknowledgment of the coercive quality of "Frankenstein," has given silent acceptance of its genius. The other works, novels, critiques, biographies, while they have had literary merit, feeling, even power, have not shown genius. "Frankenstein" alone was personal, it alone reflected Mrs. Shelley's true self. Her other books contain simply what she wrote in them: this alone contains what was written in her. Being, as she was, stronger in her personality than as a literary artist, the book that alone partook of that personality would alone partake of her peculiar genius. This, considered in its fullest light, "Frankenstein" does.—MOORE, HELEN, 1886, *Mary Woolstonecraft Shelley, pp.* 244, 245, 257.

That a work by a girl of nineteen should have held its place in romantic literature so long is no small tribute to its merit; this work, wrought under the influence of Byron and Shelley, and conceived after drinking in their enthralling conversation, is not unworthy of its origin. A more fantastically horrible story could scarcely be conceived; in fact, the vivid imagination, piling impossible horror upon horror, seems to claim for the book a place in the company of a Poe or a Hoffmann. Its weakness appears to be that of placing such an idea in the annals of modern life; such a process invariably weakens these powerful imaginative ideas, and takes away from, instead of adding to, the apparent truth, and cannot fail to give an affectation to the work. True, it might add to the difficulty to imagine a different state of society, past or future, but this seems a *sine quâ non.*—ROSSETTI, LUCY MADOX, 1890, *Mrs. Shelley* (*Eminent Women Series*), *p.* 101.

GENERAL

Mrs. Shelley has published, besides a "Frankenstein," a romance entitled "Valperga," which is less known than the former, but is of high merit. She exhibits in her hero, a brave and successful warrior, arriving at the height of his ambition, endowed with uncommon beauty and strength, and with many good qualities, yet causes him to excite emotions of reprobation and pity, because he is cruel and a tyrant, and because in the truth of things he is unhappy. This is doing a good work, taking the false glory from the eyes and showing things as they are. There are two female characters of wonderful power and beauty. The heroine is a lovely and noble creation. The work taken as a whole, if below "Frankenstein" in genius, is yet worthy of its author and of her high rank in the aristocracy of genius, as the daughter of Godwin and Mary Wollstonecraft, and the widow of Shelley.—HORNE, RICHARD HENGIST, 1844, *A New Spirit of the Age, p.* 321.

Mrs. Shelley found Italy for the first time, real Italy, at Sorrento, she says. Oh that book—does one wake or sleep? The "Mary dear" with the brown eyes, and Godwin's daughter and Shelley's wife, and who surely was something better once upon a time—and to go through Rome and Florence and the rest, after what I suppose to be Lady Londonderry's fashion: the intrepidity of the commonplace quite astounds me.—BROWNING, ROBERT, 1845, *To Elizabeth Browning, Sept.* 11; *Letters of Robert Browning and Elizabeth Barrett Barrett, vol.* I, *p.* 196.

Her command of history and her imaginative power are shown in such books as "Valperga" and "Castruccio;" but the daring originality of her mind comes out most distinctly in her earliest published work, "Frankenstein."—HUNT, THORNTON, 1863, *Shelley Atlantic Monthly, vol.* 11, *p.* 198.

It ["Lodore"] differs from the others in being a novel of society, and has been stigmatised, rather unjustly, as weak and colourless, although at the time of its publication it had a great success. It is written in a style which is now out of date, and undoubtedly fails to fulfill the promise of power held out by "Frankenstein" and to some extent by "Valperga," but it bears on every page the impress of the refinement and sensibility of the author, and has, moreover, a special interest of its own, due to the fact that some of the incidents are taken from actual occurrences in her early life, and some of the characters sketched from people she had known.—MARSHALL, MRS. JULIAN, 1889, *The Life and Letters of Mary Wollstonecraft Shelley, vol.* II, *p.* 264.

Mary undoubtedly received more than she gave. Nothing but an absolute magnetising of her brain by Shelley's can account for her having risen so far above her usual self as in "Frankenstein." The phenomenon might have been repeated but for the crushing blow of the death of her boy William in 1819.—GARNETT, RICHARD, 1897, *Dictionary of National Biography, vol.* LII, *p.* 29.

In spite of much descriptive and analytic talent she shared the inaptitude for history which marked the Godwinian and Radcliffian schools alike. "The Last Man" . . . has a pathetic significance as shadowing her own tragic loneliness,—the "Loneliness of Crusoe"—as she herself long afterwards declared it to have been. —HERFORD, C. H., 1897, *The Age of Wordsworth, p.* 98.

David Macbeth Moir

1798-1851

Born at Musselburgh, 1798; died 1851; a modern poet and prose writer, who was educated for and practiced the medical profession. He made his first appearance as an author in 1812, by publishing a small volume of poems. He next wrote for some local magazines and journals, and at the commencement of "Blackwood's Magazine," he became a contributor to its pages and remained so until his death. For the same magazine he also wrote the "Autobiography of Mansie Wauch." In 1831 he published the "Outlines of the Ancient History of Medicine," and, in the same year, exerted himself energetically while the cholera raged in Musselburgh, where he practiced his profession, and subsequently he published a pamphlet entitled "Practical Observations on Malignant Cholera." In 1851 he delivered a course of lectures upon the "Poetical Literature of the Past Half Century," at the Edinburgh Philosophical Institution. As a poet, he was tender and pathetic rather than forcible and original. His poetic works were collected in 1852 and to them was prefixed his life. Dr. Moir was a graceful essayist, and competent man of science, and was moreover a kind and excellent man. —BEETON, SAMUEL ORCHART, 1862, *Dictionary of Universal Biography.*

PERSONAL

Although we never met him in private, we can testify with perfect certainty, that a better man, or a lovelier specimen of the literary character, did not exist: he had many of its merits, and none of its defects; he used literature as a "staff, not a crutch" —it was the elegant evening pastime of one vigorously occupied through the day in the work of soothing human anguish, and going about doing good. Hence he preserved to the last his child-like love of letters; hence he died without a single enemy; hence his personal friends—and they were the *elite* of Scotland—admired and loved him with emulous enthusiasm.—GILFILLAN, GEORGE, 1851, *A Third Gallery of Portraits, p.* 217.

Professional reputation is a desirable thing, and literary honor is not to be despised; but all distinctions fade away as comparatively cheap to those who had the privilege of knowing Mr. Moir in the "mild majesty of private life." Constituted and composed of so many harmonious excellencies, the Christian gentleman, in the bosom of his beautiful family, was the consummation of them all.—AIRD, THOMAS, 1852, *ed., The Poetical Works of David Macbeth Moir, Memoir.*

In person Moir was tall, well-formed and erect, of sanguine complexion and with hair tending to the "sandy" hue, his keen sense of humour, during friendly intercourse, being particularly manifest in his countenance. In private life, he was amiable and exemplary, and much beloved by many friends.—DOUGLAS, SIR GEORGE, 1897, *The Blackwood Group (Famous Scots Series), p.* 104.

GENERAL

I consider him the most monotonous and the least original of all poets, barring his harmony of numbers, which is delightful. —HOGG, JAMES, 1817, *Letter to Blackwood, William Blackwood and his Sons, ed. Oliphant, vol.* I, *p.* 356.

Of Moir, our own "delightful Delta," as we love to call him—and the epithet now by right appertains to his name—we shall now say simply this, that he has produced many original pieces which will possess a permanent place in the poetry of Scotland. Delicacy and grace characterize his happiest compositions; some of them are beautiful in a cheerful spirit that has only to look on nature to be happy; and others breathe the simplest and purest pathos. His scenery, whether sea-coast or inland, is always truly Scottish; and at times his pen drops touches of light on minute objects, that till then had slumbered in the shade, but now "shine well where they stand" or lie, as component and characteristic parts of our lowland landscapes. Let others labour away at long poems, and for their pains get neglect or oblivion; Moir is seen as he is in many short ones, which the Scottish Muses may "not willingly let die."—WILSON, JOHN, 1831–42, *An Hour's Talk about Poetry, Recreations of Christopher North.*

His book ["Poetical Literature"] is not only worthy of his reputation, but is really one of the heartiest, sincerest, and most delightful works of criticism we have read for many a long year. — GILFILLAN, GEORGE, 1851, *A Third Gallery of Portraits, p.* 216.

In Delta's earlier strains there are general fancy, and feeling, and musical rhythm, but not much thought. His love of poetry, however, never suffered abatement, and as "a maker," he was improving to the very last. To unfaded freshness of heart he was adding riper thought; such was one of the prime blessings of his pure nature and life. Reserve and patience were what he wanted, in order to be a greater name in song than he is.—AIRD, THOMAS, 1852, *ed., The Poetical Works of David Macbeth Moir, Memoir.*

In 1851, he delivered a course of "Six Lectures at the Edinburgh Philosophical Institution on the Poetical Literature of the Past Half Century," which were soon after published. It would be difficult to speak of these in terms of too high praise, for I know not where, in so small a compass, may be found so much sound criticism and judicious reflections upon the Poets of Great Britain of the Nineteenth Century. —CLEVELAND, CHARLES D., 1853, *English Literature of the Nineteenth Century, p.* 553.

A gentle melancholy is the ruling spirit of his works; but from his novel of "Mansie Wauch," a mellow Scottish humor shines softly out.—COLLIER, WILLIAM FRANCIS, 1861, *A History of English Literature, p.* 501.

The eulogies of "Delta" by the "Blackwood" coterie will probably not be accepted by present-day critics. His verse will be commended for its study of nature and its pleasant rhythm. His humorous pieces, though sprightly, have, for the most part, a solely contemporary interest. His reputation now rests on his novel, "Mansie Wauch," written in the manner of Galt.—SMITH, G. GREGORY, 1894, *Dictionary of National Biography, vol.* XXXVIII, *p.* 114.

It is as an elegiac poet—if as a poet at all—that the author is now remembered, and one of these elegies—called by the self-conferred name of one of the babes, "Casa Wappy"—has enjoyed great popularity and is still included in anthologies, though in my own opinion a less meritorious composition than the second of the three poems on the same subject, entitled "Casa's Dirge."—DOUGLAS, SIR GEORGE, 1897, *The Blackwood Group (Famous Scots Series), p.* 100.

Thomas Moore

1779-1852

Born, in Dublin, 28 May 1779. At school in Dublin. Contrib. verses to "Anthologia Hibernica," 1793. To Trin. Coll., Dublin, 1794; B. A., 1798 [or 1799?]. Student at Middle Temple, 1799. Admirality Registrar at Bermuda, Aug. 1803. Left deputy in office and removed to New York, 1804; travelled in U. S. A. Returned to London, Nov. 1804. Contrib. to "Edinburgh Rev." from 1806. Married Bessie Dyke, 25 March 1811. Settled near Ashbourne. Friendship with Byron begun, 1811. Visit to Paris, 1817. His deputy at Bermuda proved defaulter for £6,000, 1818. In Paris and Italy, 1819–22. Returned to England, April 1822; debt to Admiralty reduced to

£1,000, and paid by Lord Landsdowne's help. Settled in Wiltshire again, Nov. 1822. Literary Fund Pension, 1835; Civil List Pension, 1850. Died, 25 Feb. 1852. Buried at Bromham. *Works:* "The Poetical Works of the late Thomas Little" (pseud.), 1801; "Epistles, Odes, and other poems," 1806; "Irish Melodies" (10 nos.), 1807–34; "Corruption and Intolerance" (anon.), 1808; "The Sceptic" (anon.), 1809; "Letter to the Roman Catholics of Dublin," 1810 (2nd edn. same year); "M. P.," 1811; "Intercepted Letters; or, the Twopenny Post-Bag" (under pseud. "Thomas Brown the Younger"), 1813 (11th edn. same year); "National Airs," 1815; "Lines on the Death of——[*i. e.*, Sheridan"], (anon.), 1816; "The World at Westminster" (anon.), 1816; "Sacred Songs," 1816; "Lalla Rookh," 1817 (6th edn. same year); "The Fudge Family in Paris" (by "Thomas Brown the Younger"), 1818 (8th edn. same year); "Tom Crib's Memorial" (anon.), 1819 (4th edn. same year); "Rhymes on the Road" (by "Thomas Brown the Younger"), 1823; "The Loves of the Angels," 1823 (5th edn. same year); "Fables for the Holy Alliance" (by "Thomas Brown the Younger"), 1823; "Evenings in Greece" [1825?]; "The Fudges in England" (by "Thomas Brown the Younger"), 1825; "Memoirs of Captain Rock" (anon.), 1824; "Memoirs of the Life of Sheridan," 1825 (3rd edn. same year); "The Epicurean," 1827 (with addition of "Alciphron," 1839); "Rhymes of the Times" (anon.), 1827; "Odes upon Cash, Corn, Catholics and other matters" (anon.), 1828; "Legendary Ballads" [1830?]; "The Life and Death of Lord Edward Fitzgerald" (2 vols.), 1831; "The Summer Fête" [1831]; "Travels of an Irish Gentleman in Search of a Religion" (anon.), 1833; "History of Ireland" (in Lardner's "Cabinet Cyclopædia," 4 vols.), 1835-46; "Poetical Works," 1840; "Songs, Ballads and Sacred Songs," 1809. *Posthumous:* "Memoirs, Journals and Correspondence," ed. by Earl Russell (8 vols.), 1853-56. He *translated:* "Odes of Anacreon," 1800; and *edited:* Byron's "Letters and Journals," 1830; Sheridan's Works, 1833; Byron's Works, 1835.—SHARP, R. FARQUHARSON, 1897, *A Dictionary of English Authors, p.* 201.

PERSONAL

When Anacreon would fight, as the poets have said,
  A reverse he display'd in his vapour,
For while all his poems were loaded with lead,
  His pistols were loaded with paper.
For excuses, Anacreon old custom may thank,
  Such a salvo he should not abuse,
For the cartridge, by rule, is always made blank,
  That is fired away at *Reviews.*

—HOOK, THEODORE EDWARD, 1806, *On Moore's Duel with Lord Jeffrey.*

Moore has a peculiarity of talent, or rather talents,—poetry, music, voice, all his own; and an expression in each which never was, nor will be, possessed by another. . . . There is nothing Moore may not do, if he will but seriously set about it. In society, he is gentlemanly, gentle, and altogether more pleasing than any individual with whom I am acquainted.——BYRON, LORD, 1813, *Journals, Nov.* 22.

I saw Moore (for the first time I may say) this season. We had indeed met in public twenty years ago. There is a manly frankness, with perfect ease and good breeding about him which is delightful. Not the least touch of the poet or pedant. A little—very little man. Less, I think, than Lewis, and something like him in person; God knows not in conversation, for Matt, though a clever fellow, was a bore of the first description. Moreover, he always looked like a schoolboy. Now Moore has none of this insignificance. His countenance is plain, but the expression so animated, especially in speaking or singing, that it is far more interesting than the finest features could have rendered it.—SCOTT, SIR WALTER, 1825, *Journal, Nov.* 22; *Life by Lockhart, ch.* lxv.

His forehead is bony and full of character, with "bumps" of wit, large and radiant enough to transport a phrenologist. His eyes are as dark and fine, as you would wish to see under a set of vine-leaves; his mouth generous and good-humored, with dimples; his nose sensual, prominent and at the same time the reverse of acquiline. There is a very peculiar character in it, as if it were looking forward, and scenting a feast or an orchard. The face, upon the whole, is Irish, not unruffled with care and passion, but festivity is the prominent expression.—HUNT, LEIGH, 1828, *Lord Byron and some of his Contemporaries, vol.* I, *p.* 282.

"I never spent an hour with Moore,"

said Byron, "without being ready to apply to him the expression attributed to Aristophanes, 'You have spoken roses;' his thoughts and expressions have all the beauty and freshness of those flowers, but the piquancy of his wit, and the readiness of his repartees, prevent one's ear being cloyed by too much sweets, and one cannot 'die of a rose in aromatic pain' with Moore; though he does speak roses, there is such an endless variety in his conversation. Moore is the only poet I know," continued Byron, "whose conversation equals his writings; he comes into society with a mind as fresh and buoyant as if he had not expended such a multiplicity of thoughts on paper; and leaves behind him an impression that he possesses an inexhaustible mine equally brilliant as the specimens he has given us. . . . Moore is a delightful companion," continued Byron, "gay without being boisterous, witty without effort, comic without coarseness, and sentimental without being lachrymose. . . . My *tête-à-tête* suppers with Moore are among the most agreeable impressions I retain of the hours passed in London. . . . I have known a dull man live on a *bon mot* of Moore's for a week." —BLESSINGTON, COUNTESS, 1832, *Conversations with Lord Byron, ch.* x.

To see him only at table, you would think him not a small man. His principal length is in his body, and his head and shoulders are those of a much larger person. Consqeuently he *sits tall*, and with the peculiar erectness of head and neck, his diminutiveness disappears. . . . Moore's head is distinctly before me while I write, but I shall find it difficult to describe. His hair, which curled once over it in long tendrils, unlike anybody else's in the world, and which probably suggested his *sobriquet* of "Bacchus," is diminished now to a few curls sprinkled with grey, and scattered in a single ring above his ears. His forehead is wrinkled, with the exception of a most prominent development of the organ of gaiety, which, singularly enough, shines with the lustre and smooth polish of a pearl, and is surrounded by a semicircle of lines drawn close about it, like entrenchments against Time. His eyes still sparkle like a champagne bubble, though the invader had drawn his pencillings about the corners; and there is a kind of wintry red, of the tinge of an October leaf, that seems enamelled on his cheek, the eloquent record of the claret his wit has brightened. His mouth is the most characteristic feature of all. The lips are delicately cut, slight and changeable as an aspen; but there is a set-up look about the lower lip, a determination of the muscle to a particular expression, and you fancy that you can almost see wit astride upon it. It is written legibly with the imprint of habitual success. It is arch, confident, and half diffident, as if he were disguising his pleasure at applause, while another bright gleam of fancy was breaking on him. The slightly tossed nose confirms the fun of the expression, and altogether it is a face that sparkles, beams, radiates,—everything but *feels*. Fascinating beyond all men as he is, Moore looks like a worldling.—WILLIS, NATHANIEL PARKER, 1834, *Pencillings by the Way.*

We saw Tom Moore in all his glory, looking, as Barclay said, "like a little Cupid with a quizzing-glass in constant motion." He seemed as gay and happy as a lark, and it was pleasant to spend a whole evening in his immediate presence. —FOX, CAROLINE, 1836, *Memories of Old Friends, ed. Pym, Journal, Aug.* 22, *p.* 5.

It is Sloperton cottage which hereafter will be regarded with the chief interest as the residence of the poet. It stands in the midst of a delightful country, and though itself buried, as it were, in an ordinary thickly wooded lane, branching off to the left from the high-road, about two miles from Devizes, on the way to Chippenham, yet from its upper windows, as well as from its garden, enjoys peeps through the trees into lovely scenes. Down southward from the far end of the house opens the broad and noble vale toward Trowbridge; in front to the right, across a little valley, stands on a fine mount, amid nobly grown trees, the village of Bromham, with a gentleman's house standing, boldly backed and flanked by the masses of wood, and the church spire peering above it. More to the left, in front, you look across some miles of country, and see the historical foreland of Roundaway hill, the termination of the chalk-hills of the Whitehouse-vale, proudly overlooking Devizes. —HOWITT, WILLIAM, 1847, *Homes and Haunts of the Most Eminent British Poets, vol.* II, *p.* 458.

Poor Mr. Moore! I knew him well, and,

rating him as a poet much lower than you do, delighted in him as a companion and wit—the most perfectly graceful, genial, and kindly of all wits. As a family man, he was, I believe, more than usually amiable. My acquaintance with him was in town, but a dear friend of mine was his near neighbor and Mrs. Moore's intimate friend at Sloperton and she says that she never knew a more exemplary husband and father.—MITFORD, MARY RUSSELL, 1852, *Letters to Mr. Starkey, March* 16; *The Friendships of Mary Russell Mitford, ed. L'Estrange.*

But let us linger not, my soul beside
The poet's bier, or his neglected grave;
Nor burn to think of those to whom he gave
A portion of his immortal fame,
Who, when the last sad moment came—
The hour that claimed the funeral rite august
For the poor portion of him that had died—
Sullenly shunned the poet's sacred dust,
Heedless of what was due to generous lays,
And all the friendly fire of former days.
—MCCARTHY, DENIS FLORENCE, 1852, *A Lament for Thomas Moore, Dublin University Magazine, vol.* 39, *p.* 495.

With a keen sense of enjoyment, he loved music and poety, the world and the playhouse, the large circle of society, and the narrow precincts of his home. His heart was thrilled by deep feelings of devotion, and his mind expatiated over the wide field of philosophy. In all that he did, and wrote, and spoke, there was a freedom and a frankness which alarmed and delighted:—frightened old men of the world, and charmed young men and young women who were something better than the world. . . . Mrs. Moore brought him no fortune; indeed it was intended that she should earn her living by the stage, and Moore, afraid that so unworldly a match might displease his parents, at first concealed from them the fact of his marriage. But the excellence of his wife's moral character; her energy and courage; her abhorrence of all meanness; her disinterested abstinence from amusement; her persevering economy; made her a better, and even a richer partner to Moore, than an heiress of ten thousand a year would have been with less devotion to her duty, and less steadiness of conduct.—RUSSELL, LORD JOHN, 1853, *ed., Memoirs, Journal and Correspondence of Thomas Moore, Preface, vol.* VI, *pp.* v, xviii.

I was very much struck by his conversation. It was brilliant and sparkling in the highest degree, abounding in those Eastern images and poetical thoughts which appear with such lustre in his "Lalla Rookh" and "Irish Melodies," mingled with the quick repartee and rapid interchange of ideas acquired in the highest and most intellectual London society. It was easy to see that he was thoroughly a poet; perhaps a little spoilt by the adulation he had met with from the most intoxicating of all quarters, that of elegant young women of fashion. Delightful and sociable, when he continued, as he generally was, the idol of the circle, he was apt to be pettish if another shared its attention, and in an especial manner to be jealous of the admiration of young ladies.—ALISON, SIR ARCHIBALD, 1867?–83, *Some Account of My Life and Writings, an Autobiography, ed. Lady Alison, vol.* I, *p.* 198.

Moore's democracy did not prevent his being remarkably fond of the society of aristocrats. In his journal, he duly chronicles with what untiring perseverance he went to the mansions of noble lords and lovely or fashionable ladies; and how constantly he was inventing excuses for going to London, that he might mingle in their society,—they, to do justice to both, being as happy to receive him as he was to visit them. The compliment, in his case, was as much *bestowed* as *received*, if he only would have thought so. It was mean for Byron to say of Moore, as reported by Leigh Hunt on his return from Italy, "Tommy dearly loves a lord;" but it was meaner still, besides being spiteful, for Hunt to repeat it. Nevertheless, it was true. Moore was, I will not say happiest,—for he was a domestic man in his way,—but very happy, in the society of the peerage.—MACKENZIE, R. SHELTON, 1871, *Sir Walter Scott: The Story of His Life, p.* 374.

His "Journals" curiously indicate what I repeatedly witnessed in my own house and elsewhere, his morbid sensitiveness when singing his Irish Ballads, to the effect they produced on those around him. In the most touching passages his eye was wandering around the room scrutinising jealously the influence of his song.—HOLLAND, SIR HENRY, 1871, *Recollections of Past Life, p.* 208.

He was a very little round-faced man, and had an easily worn but not unpleasant assurance. His estimates of persons seemed to depend much on their position or rank; he did not trouble himself to discuss persons who had no rank at all.—PROCTER, BRYAN WALLER (BARRY CORNWALL), 1874? *Recollections of Men of Letters, p.* 152.

Thomas Moore (or Tom Moore, as he was usually called) was small in stature and almost girlish in appearance when he came to the United States in 1804. He had been a "show child"—attractive and noteworthy almost from babyhood. He was a clever rhymer at the age of fourteen years, and at twenty he had earned fame as a poet, and was "patronized" and flattered by the Prince of Wales, afterward King George the Fourth. His face was small and intellectual in expression, sweet and gentle. His eyes were dark and brilliant; his mouth was delicately cut and full-lipped; his nose was slightly upturned, giving an expression of fun to his face; his complexion was fair and somewhat ruddy; his hair was a rich dark brown, and curled all over his head; his forehead was broad and strongly marked; and his voice, not powerful, was exquisitely sweet, especially when he was singing. Such is a description of Moore's personal appearance at the time of his visit here, which was given me by Mrs. M—r, an elderly lady at Fredericksburg, Virginia, almost thirty years ago.—LOSSING, BENSON J., 1877, *Tom Moore in America, Harper's Magazine, vol.* 55, *p.* 537.

Moore clung to Ireland with an intense and unchanging affection, which is testified by every act of his life and every page of his writings; and all who, now or hereafter, may cherish true attachment to her, whatever may be their honest varieties of sentiment, will find in him—when they have eliminated all they can disapprove in his dealings with temporary struggles and the passions they aroused—an Irishman with whose love for Ireland and constant desire to promote her welfare they can have cordial sympathy. According to his conception of her interests and his own duty, he was staunch to her, in periods of the worst discouragement as in those of the highest hope; and he refused for her sake, to falsify his convictions, when he might have gained place and power by giving even silent countenance to public action of which he disapproved. For these things, he should command the respect of men of every creed and party.—O'HAGAN, LORD, 1879, *Address at Moore's Centenary, Dublin, May* 28; *Life of Moore by Symington, p.* 238.

I recall him at this moment—his small form and intellectual face rich in expression, and that expression the sweetest, the most gentle, and the kindliest. He had still in age the same bright and clear eye, the same gracious smile, the same suave and winning manner I had noticed as the attributes of what might in comparison be styled his youth (I have stated I knew him as long ago as 1821), a forehead not remarkably broad or high, but singularly impressive, firm and full, with the organs of music and gayety large, and those of benevolence and veneration greatly preponderíng. The nose, as observed in all his portraits, was somewhat upturned. Standing, or sitting, his head was invariably upraised, owing, perhaps, mainly to his shortness of stature. He had so much bodily activity as to give him the attribute of restlessness, and no doubt that usual accompaniment of genius was eminently a characteristic of his. His hair was, at the time I speak of, thin and very gray, and he wore his hat with the jaunty air that has been often remarked as a peculiarity of the Irish. In dress, although far from slovenly, he was by no means precise. He had but little voice, yet he sang with a depth of sweetness that charmed all hearers; it was true melody, and told upon the heart as well as the ear. No doubt much of this charm was derived from association, for it was only his own melodies he sang. . . . I repeat I never knew a better man than Moore in *all* the relations of life; the best of God's creatures may take him as a model without going wrong; and those who adopt literature as a profession can accept him as an example, in proof that genius may pass unscathed through seductions so perilous as to seem irresistible.—HALL, SAMUEL CARTER, 1883, *Retrospect of a Long Life, pp.* 353, 354.

"Anacreon Moore," "The Bard of Erin," "Jove's Poet," "The Lansdowne Laureate," "The Pander of Venus," "That Piperly Poet of Green Erin," "Poor Little," "Sweet, Melodious Bard," "Trumpet Moore," "The Young Catullus of His Day."—FREY, ALBERT R., 1888, *Sobriquets and Nicknames, p.* 442.

That Moore suffered no serious deterioration under the blandishments of society was very much owing to the influence of his high-minded wife. We get glimpses of this admirable woman in tne fact that Rogers, who knew her well, was aware that he could give her no more acceptable present than five or ten sovereigns for her sick poor. She was once met at some festive gathering, when the hostess remarked, "You may be quite sure there is no one desperately ill or dying in the neighborhood, or we should not see Mrs. Moore here." We must remember that there was no professional nurses in those days, and the aid of this kind, capable lady was often needed at the Hall as well as in the cottage.—CROSSE, MRS. ANDREW, 1894, *Poet, Parson and Pamphleteer, Temple Bar, vol.* 103, *p.* 42.

ODES OF ANACREON
1800

Oh! mourn not for Anacreon dead,
Oh! weep not for Anacreon fled;
The lyre still breathes he touch'd before,
For we have one Anacreon Moore.
—ERSKINE, THOMAS LORD, 1800, *On Moore's Translation from Anacreon.*

Moore's early fancy luxuriated among the classics, and his elegant, spirited, and congenial translation—say rather paraphrase—of Anacreon was the first-fruits. —MOIR, D. M., 1851–52, *Sketches of the Poetical Literature of the Past Half-Century.*

If we open a collection of his poems now, and read his "Odes of Anacreon," to which the Prince of Wales and other notabilities of rank subscribed, we desist after a time with something of the disgust we should feel at a profuse display of pretty, sham jewelry. The ample, brimming bowls and goblets of wine, the wreaths and garlands of roses, the rich perfumes, the sparkling eyes, and the golden tresses, and the snowy necks, are well enough in moderation, but some eighty odes of such materials pall for lack of variety. Any variety that there is lies within the narrowest limits: now it is a bowl and now it is a goblet, now we drink and now we quaff, now it is a bud and now it is a full-blown rose, now a garland and now a cluster, now ringlets and now tresses; but it is always wine and flower, with little variation of phrase. We are soon surfeited with such sentiment, and disposed to laugh at its artificiality. Moore's prettinesses, always expressed in soft and melodious verse, were probably a pleasant surprise to a generation weary of didactic poems; but if we have a liking for such things now, we can find more genuine articles of the same kind, compounded with much higher art, in the poetry of the seventeenth century, the volumes of Queen Henrietta's poets, Lovelace, and Carew, and Suckling, and above all, Herrick.—MINTO, WILLIAM, 1894, *The Literature of the Georgian Era, ed. Knight.*

IRISH MELODIES
1807–1834

Now, of all the song-writers that ever warbled, or chanted, or sung, the best, in our estimation, is verily none other than Thomas Moore.—WILSON, JOHN, 1831, *An Hour's Talk About Poetry, Recreations of Christopher North, Blackwood's Magazine, vol.* 30, *p.* 477.

There is a liquid ease, a dance of words, and a lyrical grace and brevity in them all; but there is, likewise, an epigrammatic point and smartness, a courtly and a knowing air, so to speak, alien to the simplicity of the music and to the nature of song. . . . In one word, there is not a little affectation in them, put-on graces, and artificial raptures. These faults are nearly balanced by beauties. — CUNNINGHAM, ALLAN, 1833, *Biographical and Critical History of the Literature of the Last Fifty Years.*

By these his name will be known, so long as there are voices to sing and hearts to feel.—CHORLEY, HENRY F., 1838, *Authors of England, p.* 54.

The "Irish Melodies," as songs, have never been surpassed in their particular kind. The versification is so exquisite, and executed with such delicacy of rhythm, that, on hearing them well read, we involuntarily and certainly conceive the tune, even though we may never have heard it.—SHAW, THOMAS B., 1847, *Outlines of English Literature, p.* 346.

His Irish and national melodies will be immortal: and they will be so for this reason,—that they express the feelings which spring up in the breast of every successive generation at the most important and imaginative period of life. They have the delicacy of refined life without its fastidiousness, the warmth of natural feeling without its rudeness.—ALISON, SIR ARCHIBALD, 1853–59, *History of Europe,* 1815–52, *ch.* v.

In one only of his writings Moore attained a positive perfection of style. Those homely and sentimental lyrics which have endeared themselves to thousands of hearts under the name of the "Irish Melodies," form a part and parcel of our literature, the extinction of which would leave a sad blank behind it.—GOSSE, EDMUND, 1880, *The English Poets, ed. Ward, vol.* IV, *p.* 311.

It provided him with a solid basis for his reputation of making him the national lyrist of Ireland, a character which, notwithstanding the numerous charges which may justly be brought against his "Irish Melodies," on the ground both of false poetry and false patriotism, he must retain until some one arises to deprive him of it. Better isolated pieces have no doubt been written by some of his successors, but he, and he alone, has produced an imposing body of national song; nor have his fancy, melody, and pathos, on the whole, been yet equalled by any competitor.—GARNETT, RICHARD, 1894, *Dictionary of National Biography, vol.* XXXVIII, *p.* 381.

No such distinguished success was ever before, or has ever since, been achieved in the not very distinguished art of "writing up to" music. The "Irish Melodies," it is true, show many marks of their conventional origin; they are in a certain sense artificial products, altogether wanting in the freshness and *naïveté*, the epic force and simplicity of the genuine folksong; but they were the work of a man in whom the melancholy charm of his country and of his country's music inspired a feeling so genuine and, indeed, so intense as continually to lift, if it could not consistently maintain, his expression above the level of the commonplace. It is the lack of this emotional sincerity which leaves his more ambitious efforts comparatively cold and lifeless, and has consigned "Lalla Rookh" to an oblivion which the "Irish Melodies" and a few other lyrics of Moore's have escaped.—TRAILL, HENRY DUFF, 1896, *Social England, vol.* V, *p.* 587.

The chief characteristic of Moore's Irish melodies, that is to say the lyrics, is their lack of Irish characteristics. To be candid, though here and there an Irish town, or vale, or waterfall, or lake is mentioned, all the Irish songs are absolutely English in form, metre and sentiment. Erin comes in nowhere; and Hibernia is only scantily and half shamefully referred to as a sort of apology for the music which is so essentially Irish. Again the words are not always wedded to the music, they are only joined to it, fitted and fixed to it—the music plays the second part and not the first. Though Thomas Moore, "who dearly loved a lord," as his friend Lord Byron said, was a poet of Ireland, he was in nowise an Irish poet in sentiment, sympathy or sensibility. Still we are not ungrateful to him for his labour in saving to us these classic pieces.—FITZ-GERALD, S. J. ADAIR, 1897, *Stories of Famous Songs, p.* 151.

LALLA ROOKH
1817

I have read two pages of "Lalla Rookh," or whatever it is called. Merciful Heaven! I dare read no more, that I may be able to answer at once to any questions, "I have but just looked at the work." O Robinson! if I could, or if I dared, act and feel as Moore and his set do, what havoc could I not make amongst their crockery-ware! Why, there are not three lines together without some adulteration of common English, and the ever-recurring blunder of using the possessive case, "*compassion's* tears," &c., for the preposition "of,"—a blunder of which I have found no instances earlier than Dryden's slovenly verses written for the trade.—COLERIDGE, SAMUEL TAYLOR, 1817, *Letter to H. C. Robinson, June; Robinson's Diary, Reminiscences and Correspondence, ed. Sadler, vol.* I, *p.* 363,

There is something very extraordinary, we think, in the work before us—and something which indicates in the author, not only a great exuberance of talent, but a very singular constitution of genius. While it is more splendid in imagery—(and for the most part in very good taste)—more rich in sparkling thoughts and original conceptions, and more full indeed of exquisite pictures, both of all sorts of beauties and virtues, and all sorts of sufferings and crimes, than any other poem that has yet come before us; we rather think we speak the sense of most readers when we add, that the effect of the whole is to mingle a certain feeling of disappointment with that of admiration! to excite admiration rather than any warmer sentiment of delight—to dazzle, more than to enchant—and, in the end, more frequently to startle the fancy, and fatigue the attention, by the constant succession of glittering images and high-strained emotions, than to maintain a rising interest, or win a growing sympathy, by a less profuse or more systematic display of attractions. The style is, on the whole, rather diffuse, and too unvaried in its character. But its greatest fault, in our eyes, is the uniformity of its brilliancy—the want of plainness, simplicity and repose.—JEFFREY, FRANCIS LORD, 1817–44, *Moore's Lalla Rookh, Contributions to the Edinburgh Review, vol.* III, *p.* 200.

Mr. Moore ought not to have written "Lalla Rookh," even for three thousand guineas. His fame is worth more than that. He should have minded the advice of Fadladeen. It is not, however, a failure, so much as an evasion and a consequent disappointment of public expectation. He should have left it to others to break conventions with nations, and faith with the world. He should, at any rate, have kept his with the public. "Lalla Rookh" is not what people wanted to see whether Mr. Moore could do—namely, whether he could write a long epic poem. It is four tales. The interest, however, is often high wrought and tragic, but the execution still turns to the effeminate and voluptuous side. — HAZLITT, WILLIAM, 1818, *Lectures on the English Poets, Lecture* viii.

Moore is but a sort of refined Mahometan, and (with immense deference) I think that his character in a late "Edinburgh Review" is somewhat too high. His imagination seldom quits material, even sexual objects—he describes them admirably,—and intermingles here and there some beautiful traits of natural pathos; but he seems to have failed (excepting partially in the Fire-Worshippers) in his attempts to portray the fierce or lofty features of human character. Mokannah in particular, insensible to pain or pity or any earthly feeling, might as well, at least for all practical purposes, have been made of clockwork as of flesh and blood. I grieve to say that the catastrophe excited laughter rather than horror. The poisoned believers sitting round the table, with their black swollen jobber-nowls reclining on their breasts, and saucy-eyes fixed upon the ill-favoured prophet—appeared so like the concluding scene of an election-dinner, when all are dead-drunk but the Provost, a man of five bottles, with a carbuncled face and an amorphous nose, that I was forced to exclaim, *Du sublime au ridicule il n'y a qu'un pas.*—CARLYLE, THOMAS, 1818, *To R. Mitchell, May* 25; *Early Letters, ed. Norton, p.* 73.

He has shewn in the poetry selected for the "Irish Melodies," and more so in his celebrated "Lalla Rookh," how beautifully the feelings of a delicate passion can be conveyed in language of the most brilliant and powerful description. —DIBDIN, THOMAS FROGNALL, 1824, *The Library Companion, p.* 741, *note.*

When Moore is termed "a fanciful poet," the epithet is applied with precision. He *is.* He is fanciful in "Lalla Rookh," and had he written the "Inferno," in the "Inferno" he would have contrived to be still fanciful and nothing beyond.—POE, EDGAR ALLAN, 1849, *A Chapter of Suggestions, Works, ed. Stedman and Woodberry, vol.* VIII, *p.* 344.

Its great charm consists in the romance of its situations and characters, the splendour of its diction and style, and the prodigal copiousness of its imagery. Indeed, its principal fault is want of repose: it is overloaded with ornament; you cannot see the green turf for roses; you cannot see the blue heavens for stars; and the narrative is thus clogged, while its interest is marred.—MOIR, D. M., 1851–52, *Sketches of the Poetical Literature of the Past Half-Century.*

It is still possible to read "Lalla Rookh" with pleasure, and even with a sort of indulgent enthusiasm. Rococo prettiness could hardly reach a higher point of accomplishment, and the sham-oriental is perhaps not more hopelessly antiquated than our own sham-mediæval will be sixty years hence. The brilliance of Moore's voluptuous scenes has faded; he gilded them too much with the gold of Mrs. Tighe's "Psyche," a preparation that was expressly made to tarnish. But underneath the smooth and faded surface lie much tenderness and pathos in the story of the Peri, much genuine patriotism in the fate of the Fire Worshippers, much tropical sweetness in the adventures of the "Light of the Haram." These narratives possess more worth, for instance, than all but the very best of Byron's tales, and would be read with more pleasure than those were they not overburdened by a sensuous richness of style. This quality, which Moore considered his chief claim to immortality, was in point of fact a great snare to him.—GOSSE, EDMUND, 1880, *The English Poets, ed. Ward, vol.* IV, *p.* 310.

A dainty confection of Eastern romance. —MORLEY, HENRY, 1881, *Of English Literature in the Reign of Victoria with a Glance at the Past, p.* 201.

It still seems to me a very respectable poem indeed of the second rank. Of course it is artificial. The parade of second, or third or twentieth-hand learning in the notes makes one smile, and the whole reminds one (as I dare say, it has reminded many others before) of a harp of the period with the gilt a little tarnished, the ribbons more than a little faded, and the silk stool on which the young woman in ringlets used to sit much worn. All this is easy metaphorical criticism, if it is criticism at all. For I am not sure that, when the last age has got a little further off from our descendants, they will see anything more ludicrous in such a harp than we see in the faded spinnets of a generation earlier still. But much remains to Lalla if not to Feramorz. The prose interludes have lost none of their airy grace. Even Mr. Bernard has not been able to make Mokanna ridiculous, nor have the recent accounts of the actual waste of desert and felt huts banished at least the poetical beauty of "Merou's bright palaces and groves." — SAINTSBURY, GEORGE, 1888, *Thomas Moore, Macmillan's Magazine, vol.* 57, *p.* 343.

"Lalla Rookh" may be little read nowadays; but not many years have passed since this poem and others of the author's used to get into the finest of bindings, and have great currency for bridal and birthday gifts. Indeed, there is a witching melody in Moore's Eastern tales, and a delightful shimmer and glitter of language, which none but the most cunning of our present craftmasters in verse could reach. —MITCHELL, DONALD G., 1897, *English Lands Letters and Kings, The Later Georges to Victoria, p.* 153.

LIFE OF LORD BYRON
1830

Moore will have a ticklish task to perform all through, and if he brings me in, which he can hardly help doing, I may, perhaps, make him cry *O*, if he does not take care of his *p's* and *q's*.—SOUTHEY, ROBERT, 1828, *The Correspondence of Robert Southey with Caroline Bowles, p.* 140.

We have read this book with the greatest pleasure. Considered merely as a composition, it deserves to be classed among the best specimens of English prose which our age has produced. It contains, indeed, no single passage equal to two or three which we could select from the "Life of Sheridan"; but, as a whole, it is immeasurably superior to that work. The style is agreeable, clear, and manly; and when it rises into eloquence, rises without effort or ostentation. Nor is the matter inferior to the manner. It would be difficult to name a book which exhibits more kindness, fairness, and modesty. It has evidently been written, not for the purpose of showing, what, however, it often shows, how well its author can write; but for the purpose of vindicating, as far as truth will permit, the memory of a celebrated man. —MACAULAY, THOMAS BABINGTON, 1830, *Moore's Life of Lord Byron, Edinburgh Review, Critical and Miscellaneous Essays.*

The poet could not forecast that Moore would get the money and not publish the book; that his bibliopolist's compilation —all puff and laudation to sell his stock —would be substituted—a lifeless life, giving no notion of the author, nothing told as Byron told it, and, excepting the letters it contains, unreadable and unread. Byron could not escape the poet's fate— his true life suppressed, and a bookish, elaborate eulogy of his poetry to sell his works substituted.—TRELAWNY, EDWARD JOHN, 1858–78, *Records of Shelley, Byron and the Author, p.* 38.

Moore's vice is cautious, soft, seductive, slippery, and covered at times with a thin, tremulous veil of religious sentimentalism. In regard to Byron, he was an unscrupulous, committed partisan: he was as much bewitched by him as ever man has been by woman; and therefore to him, at last, the task of editing Byron's Memoirs was given. This Byron, whom they all knew to be obscene beyond what even their most drunken tolerance could at first endure; this man, whose foul license *spoke out* what most men conceal from mere respect to the decent instincts of humanity; whose "honor was lost,"—was submitted to this careful manipulator, to be turned out a perfected idol for a world longing for one, as the Israelites longed for the calf in Horeb.—STOWE, HARRIET BEECHER, 1870, *Lady Byron Vindicated, p.* 99.

Murray eventually gave £4,200 for one of the most delightful and entertaining biographies in our literature—a companion volume, in every way, to Boswell's "Johnson" and Lockhart's "Scott."—CURWEN, HENRY, 1873, *A History of Booksellers, p.* 187.

It was exactly the biography which that age required: by no means complete or entirely authentic, nor claiming to be so, but presenting Byron in the light in which contemporaries desired to regard him, and in every respect a model of tact and propriety. The fearless criticism and the deep insight which are certainly missing were not at that time required, and until they are supplied elsewhere the work will rank as a classic, even though its interest be less due to the efforts of Moore's own pen than to the charm of the letters which he was the first to give to the world.—GARNETT, RICHARD, 1894, *Dictionary of National Biography, vol.* XXXVIII, *p.* 383.

HISTORY OF IRELAND
1835–46

See also the first volume of Moore's "History of Ireland," where the claims of his country are stated favourably and with much learning and industry, but not with extravagant partiality.—HALLAM, HENRY, 1837-39, *Introduction to the Literature of Europe, vol.* I, *ch.* i, *par.* 7, *note.*

Moore wasted much time on uncongenial tasks, such as his "History of Ireland." He bestowed great pains upon it, but the result proved that he had spent his strength in vain. His great and lasting achievement is to have set forth and lamented in exquisite verse the sorrows and wrongs of his native land. Moore's admirers can forgive his shortcomings as the historian of Erin when they regard him as its bard. —RAE, W. FRASER, 1885, *"The Bard of Erin," Temple Bar, vol.* 75, *p.* 45.

The last years of his life were spent in writing a "History of Ireland," now quite unknown. He persisted in this work, and this gives us a higher idea of his character. With all his apparent affectation he was a genuine patriot, an industrious worker, and a most exemplary son and husband, and there is no doubt that it was these qualities that helped to make him the darling of the London drawing-rooms.—MINTO, WILLIAM, 1894, *The Literature of the Georgian Era, ed. Knight, p.* 234.

GENERAL

Moore's poems and his translations will, I think, have more influence on the female society of this kingdom, than the stage has had in its *worst period*, the reign of Charles II. Ladies are not ashamed of having the delectable Mr. Little on their toilet, which is a pretty good proof that his voluptuousness is considered as quite veiled by the sentimental garb in which it is clad. But voluptuousness is not the less dangerous for having some slight resemblance of the veil of modesty. On the contrary, her fascinations are infinitely more powerful in this retiring habit than when she boldly protrudes herself on the gazer's eye, and openly solicits his attention. The broad indecency of Wycherley, and his contemporaries, was not half so dangerous as this insinuating and *half-covered mock*-delicacy, which makes use of the blush of modesty in order to heighten the charms of vice. —WHITE, HENRY KIRKE, 1806, *Letter to P. Thompson, April* 8; *Remains, ed. Southey, vol.* I, *p.* 237.

He . . . may boast, if the boast can please him, of being the most licentious of modern versifiers, and the most poetical of those who, in our times, have devoted their talents to the propagation of immorality. We regard his book, indeed, as a public nuisance, and would willingly trample it down by one short movement of contempt and indignation, had we not reason to apprehend that it was abetted by patrons who are entitled to a more respectful remonstrance and by admirers who may require a more extended exposition of their dangers. . . . It seems to be his aim to impose corruption upon his readers by concealing it under the mask of refinement; to reconcile them imperceptibly to the most vile and vulgar sensuality by blending its language with that of exalted feeling and tender emotion; and to steal impurity into their hearts, by gently perverting the most simple and generous of their affections. In the execution of this unworthy task he labours with a perseverance at once ludicrous and detestable. . . . A publication which we would wish to see consigned to universal reprobation.—JEFFREY, FRANCIS LORD, 1806, *Moore's Poems, Edinburgh Review, vol.* 8, *pp.* 456, 457, 465.

Who in soft guise, surrounded by a choir,
Of virgins melting, not to Vesta's fire,
With sparkling eyes, and cheek by passion flush'd,
Strikes his wild lyre, while listening dames are hush'd?
'Tis Little! young Catullus of his day,
As sweet, but as immortal, in his lay!
Grieved to condemn, the muse must still be just,
Nor spare melodious advocates of lust.
Pure is the flame which o'er her altar burns;
From grosser incense with disgust she turns:
Yet kind to youth, this expiation o'er,
She bids thee "mend thy line and sin no more."

—BYRON, LORD, 1809, *English Bards and Scotch Reviewers.*

Mr. Moore's Muse is another Ariel, as light, as tricksy, as indefatigable, and as humane a spirit. His fancy is forever on the wing, flutters in the gale, glitters in the sun. Every thing lives, moves, and sparkles in his poetry, while over all love waves his purple light. . . . The fault of Mr. Moore is an exuberance of involuntary power. His facility of production lessens the effect of, and hangs as a dead weight upon, what he produces. His levity at last oppresses. The infinite delight he takes in such an infinite number of things, creates indifference in minds less susceptible of pleasure than his own. He exhausts attention by being inexhaustible. His variety cloys; his rapidity dazzles and distracts the sight. The graceful ease with which he lends himself to every subject, the genial spirit with which he indulges in every sentiment, prevents him from giving their full force to the masses of things, from connecting them into a whole. He wants intensity, strength, and grandeur. His mind does not brood over the great and permanent: it glances over the surfaces, the first impressions of things, instead of grappling with the deep-rooted prejudices of the mind, its inveterate habits, and that "perilous stuff that weighs upon the heart." His pen, as it is rapid and fanciful, wants momentum and passion. It requires the same principle to make us thoroughly like poetry, that makes us like ourselves so well, the feeling of continued identity.—HAZLITT, WILLIAM, 1818, *Lectures on the English Poets, Lecture* viii.

To whom the lyre and laurels have been given,
With all the trophies of triumphant song—
He won them well, and may he wear them long!

—BYRON, LORD, 1819, *Don Juan, Canto,* i, *st.* civ.

From her wilds Irene sent
The sweetest lyrist of her saddest wrong,
And love taught grief to fall like music from his tongue.

—SHELLEY, PERCY BYSSHE, 1821, *Adonais; An Elegy on the Death of John Keats, st.* xxx.

Come, fill high for Tom Moore! would this bumper could gain us
A truce with the sweet *little* Pander of Venus.
'Tis diamond cut diamond when he and we quarrel,
But we value his wrath as the dregs of that barrel.
Then Tommy, agra! if you fall out with Blackwood,
For dying luxuriously, purchase a Packwood—
Frank Jeffrey, *and all that,* was nothing for certain,
To us; but that's all in my eye, Betty Martin.
Then, here's to poor Tom, and his verses so sunny,
That made all our maids and young widows so funny;
Which sent all the *spalpeens* of Munster dragooning,
And sent all the punks in the kingdom *slooning.*

—WILSON, JOHN, 1822, *Noctes Ambrosianæ, July.*

Anacreon Moore, too, has been nearly put out by the ascending star of his Lordship's genius; and his sprightly, luxurious levity, has yielded to the more energetic force of heroic debaucheries. The laughing lyrics of the one have given precedence to the passionate heroics of the other, seasoned as they both were with about the same proportion of the salt of sensuality. Moore's epigrammatic license is fast fading before the tragic profligacy of Childe Harold's abstraction, aided by the comical wickedness of Don Juan, who reduces to practice the theory of the Childe. Certain it is, that Moore has either degenerated in fancy and sprightliness, or the world has become tired of the tinkling of his pretty little fingers. I think he will scarcely last out another fashionable age.—PAULDING, J. K., 1822, *A Sketch of Old England, by a New-England Man, vol.* II, *p.* 128.

I take it for granted that you have seen

Cupid's "Loves of the Angels." What beautiful air-grown bubbles! Was ever such a string of pearly words so delightfully and so absurdly congregated before? —GALT, JOHN, 1823, *To the Countess of Blessington, Jan.* 6; *The Literary Life and Correspondence of the Countess of Blessington, ed. Madden, vol.* II, *p.* 327.

While in the parlour I delayed,
Till they their persons had array'd,
A dapper volume caught my eye,
That on the window chanc'd to lie;
A book's a friend—I always choose
To turn its pages and peruse:—
It prov'd those poems known to fame
For praising every cyprian dame;
The bantlings of a dapper youth,
Renown'd for gratitude and truth;
A little pest, hight Tommy Moore,
Who hopp'd and skipp'd our country o'er;
Who sipp'd our tea and lived on sops,
Revell'd on syllabubs and slops,
And when his brain, of cobweb fine,
Was fuddled with five drops of wine,
Would all his puny loves rehearse,
And many a maid debauch—in verse.

—IRVING, WASHINGTON, 1824, *Salamagundi.*

Yes, I have read Moore's "Sheridan," and was deeply interested. But, my dear friend, it is more the excuse of an admirer than the impartial memoir of a biographer. —HAYDON, BENJAMIN ROBERT, 1825, *Letter to Miss Mitford, Dec.* 10; *Life, Letters and Table Talk of Haydon, ed. Stoddard, p.* 225.

In Moore's style, the ornament continually outstrips the sense.—NEWMAN, JOHN HENRY, 1829–71, *Poetry with Reference to Aristotle's Poetics; Essays Critical and Historical, vol.* I, *p.* 26.

"The Loves of the Angels" is an invaluable gem, which will rank, not with the "Elegy in a Country Churchyard," but with the "Rape of the Lock." Sometimes, indeed, we cannot help thinking that the author might have periwigged his angles with advantage. But I beg pardon—it is no longer fashionable for young coxcombs to wear wigs.—ELLIOTT, EBENEZER, 1833, *Spirits and Men, Preface, p.* 214.

His radiance, not always as bright as some flashes from other pens, is yet a radiance of equable glow, whose total amount of light exceeds by very much, we think, that total amount in the case of any cotemporary writer whatsoever. A vivid fancy, an epigrammatic spirit, a fine taste, vivacity, dexterity, and a musical ear have made him very easily what he is, the most popular poet now living, if not the most popular that ever lived; and, perhaps, a slight modification at birth of that which phrenologists have agreed to term *temperament*, might have made him the truest and noblest votary of the Muse of any age or clime. As it is, we have only casual glimpses of that *mens divinior* which is assuredly enshrined within him.—POE, EDGAR ALLAN, 1840, *Moore's "Alciphron," Works, ed. Stedman and Woodberry, vol.* VI, *p.* 260.

His notion of Paradise comes from the Koran, not the New Testament. His works are pictorial representations of Epicurianism. Pathos, passion, sentiment, fancy, wit, are poured melodiously forth in seemingly inexhaustible abundance, and glitter along his page as though written down with sunbeams; but they are still more or less referable to sensation, and the "trail of the serpent is over them all." He is the most superficial and empirical of all the prominent poets of his day. With all his acknowledged fertility of mind, with all his artistical skill and brilliancy, with all his popularity, he never makes a profound impression on the soul, and few ever think of calling him a great poet, even in the sense in which Byron is great. He is the most magnificent trifler that ever versified. Nothing can be finer than his sarcasm, nothing more brilliant than his fancy, nothing more softly voluptuous than his sentiment. But he possesses no depth of imagination, no grandeur of thought, no clear vision of purity and holiness. He has neither loftiness nor comprehension. Those who claim for him a place among the immortals, are most generally girls who thrum pianos, and who are conquered by the "dazzling fence" of his rhetoric, and the lightning-like rapidity with which he scatters fancies one upon another. He blinds the eye with diamond dust, and lulls the ear with the singing sweetness of his versification. Much of his sentiment, which fair throats warble so melodiously, is merely idealized lust. The pitch of his thought and feeling is not high. The impression gained from his works is most assuredly that of a man variously gifted by nature, adroit, ingenious, subtle, versatile, "forgetive"—a most remarkable man, but not a great poet. Nothing about

his works "wears the aspect of eternity."
—WHIPPLE, EDWIN P., 1845, *English Poets of the Nineteenth Century, American Review, July; Essays and Reviews.*

Idol of youths and virgins, Moore!
Thy days, the bright, the calm, are o'er!
No gentler mortal ever prest
His parent Earth's benignant breast.
What of the powerful can be said
They did for thee? They *edited.*
What of that royal gourd? Thy verse
Excites our scorn and spares our curse.
Each truant wife, each trusting maid,
All loves, all friendships, he betrayed.
Despised in life by those he fed,
By his last misstress left ere dead,
Hearing her only wrench the locks
Of every latent jewel-box.
There spouse and husband strove alike,
Fearing lest Death too soon should strike,
But fixt no Plunder to forego
Till the gross spirit sank below.

—LANDOR, WALTER SAVAGE, 1853, *On Moore's Death, The Last Fruit off an Old Tree.*

As a poet Moore must always hold a high place. Of English lyrical poets he is surely the first.—RUSSELL, LORD JOHN, 1853, *Memoirs, Journal and Correspondence of Thomas Moore, Preface, vol.* I, *p.* xxii.

Moore had in his time many imitators, but all his gayety, his brilliant fancy, his somewhat feminine graces, and the elaborate music of his numbers, have not saved him from the fate of being imitated no more.—BRYANT, WILLIAM CULLEN, 1870, *A New Library of Poetry and Song, Introduction, vol.* I, *p.* 43.

In this multitude of travellers and historians, disguised as poets, how shall we select? They abound like swarms of insects hatched on a summer's day amidst the rank of vegetation; they buzz and glitter, and the mind is lost in their sparkle and hum. Which shall I quote? Thomas Moore, the gayest and most French of all, a witty railer, too graceful and *recherché*, writing descriptive odes on the Bermudas, sentimental Irish melodies, a poetic Egyptian romance, a romantic poem on Persia and India.—TAINE, H. A., 1871, *History of English Literature, tr. Van Laun, vol.* II, *bk.* iv, *ch.* i, *p.* 250.

Moore is nothing in my opinion, and never would have been anything but for the lovely music he is identified with.—OLIPHANT, MARGARET O. W., 1872, *To Mr. Blackwood, Autobiography and Letters.*

As to the songs and other poems one can seldom imagine that they were written in the open air, in the woods or fields, or in the face of nature. There is (so to speak) always a boudoir or indoor air about them: the very flowers seem to be artificial. Mr. Moore's verses are also too saccharine: they want substance and relief. One may be smoothered even with roses; and if the roses want their natual dew and freshness, the suffocation becomes unpleasant.—PROCTER, BRYAN WALLER, 1874? *Recollections of Men of Letters, p.* 153.

In *Satire*, it must be admitted that Moore is entitled to a distinguished place. Not, indeed, that he wielded the massive and ruthless weapon of the great Roman, the cutting lash of Ariosto and Dryden, the delicate scalpel of Boileau and Pope, or the poisoned dagger of Junius. The edge of his sarcasm seems turned by its wit, and the smile of the archer to blunt his arrow's point.—BATES, WILLIAM, 1874–98, *The Maclise Portrait Gallery, p.* 25.

In the cosmical diapason and august orchestra of poetry, Tom Moore's little Pan's-pipe can at odd moments be heard, and interjects an appreciable and rightly-combined twiddle or two. To be gratified with these at the instant is no more than the instrument justifies, and the executant claims: to think much about them when the organ is pealing or the violin playing (with a Shelley performing on the first, or a Mrs. Browning on the second) or to be on the watch for their recurrences, would be equally superfluous and weak-minded.
—ROSSETTI, WILLIAM MICHAEL, 1878, *Lives of Famous Poets, p.* 284.

He not only produced the most exquisite songs in the language, but he concurrently composed some of the best satires that were ever written. Birth had made Moore an advocate for rebellion. Society had stripped his advocacy of it of every shadow of bitterness.—WALPOLE, SPENCER, 1878, *A History of England from the Conclusion of the Great War in* 1815, *vol.* I, *p.* 361.

The land where the staff of Saint Patrick was planted,
Where the shamrock grows green from the cliffs to the shore,
The land of fair maidens and heroes undaunted,
Shall wreath her bright harp with the garlands of Moore!

—HOLMES, OLIVER WENDELL, 1879, *For the Moore Centennial Celebration.*

Perhaps he was not hero born,
Like those he sung—Heaven only knows;
He had the rose without the thorn,
But he deserved the rose!
For underneath its odorous light
His heart was warm, his soul was strong;
He kept his love of country bright,
And sung her sweetest song!
—STODDARD, RICHARD HENRY, 1879, *Thomas Moore, Scribner's Monthly, vol.* 18, *p.* 404.

Ah, "Lalla Rookh!" O charmèd book!
First love, in manhood slighted!
Today we rarely turn the page
In which our youth delighted.

. . . .

The centuries roll; but he has left,
Beside the ceaseless river,
Some flowers of rhyme untouched by Time,
And songs that sing forever.
—TROWBRIDGE, JOHN TOWNSEND, 1879-81. *Recollections of Lalla Rookh, A Home Idyl and other Poems, p.* 92.

No one would go to Moore expecting to find the robust vigour, condensed wisdom, and epigrammatic point of a Shakspere or a Burns; but sentiment, though less deep and more diffuse, may still be true and touch our hearts.—SYMINGTON, ANDREW JAMES, 1880, *Thomas Moore, p.* 134.

He shone as a morning star in the awakening eye of the nineteenth (century); and though he was apt to disfigure his songs by what he meant for a crowning ornament—a metaphor artificially set forth, and too much like "the posy of a ring,"—yet in his more genuine poetic moods, whether plaintive or festive, or, as he could sometimes contrive it, a graceful combination of the two, he could not but charm an audience who had forgotten the songsters of Elizabeth and James, and, so far as the poetry of song was concerned, had had nothing better to listen to in their own times than what was called "the Della Cruscan school," or "the school of Laura Matilda."—TAYLOR, SIR HENRY, 1885, *Autobiography, vol.* I, *p.* 155.

Nearly every line he wrote is pregnant with platitude and literary affectations; nearly every song he sang is either playfully, or forlornly, or affectedly, genteel; and though he had a musical ear, he was deficient in every lofty grace, every word-compelling power, of the divine poetic gift. Above all, he lacked simplicity—that one unmistakable gift of all great national poets, form Homer downwards. And the cardinal defect of the verse was the true clue to the thoroughly artificial character of the man. . . . I have granted the merit of Moore's verses and the amusing nature of his personality; but I must protest in the name of justice against his acceptance as the national poet of Ireland. If Irishmen accept him and honour him as such, so much the worse for Irishmen, since his falsehood of poetic touch must respond to something false and unpoetic in their own natures.—BUCHANAN, ROBERT, 1886, *The Irish "National" Poet, A Look Round Literature, pp.* 205, 206.

His prose, less known than his poetry, is facile, elegant, and, on the whole, correct. —SAINTSBURY, GEORGE, 1886, *Specimens of English Prose Style, p.* 318.

"Surely you must have been born with a rose in your lips, and a nightingale singing on the top of your bed," said Samuel Rogers to Moore; and there is much significance in the conceit. Moore's poems are full of colour, while their melody is almost faultless. His verse is sensuous and sweet. It seldom reached passion or heroic aspiration. There is no profound depth of thought, no far insight of human nature or character. But it is full of airy fancies which are wrought into musical numbers characterised by exquisite finish which at its best shows no signs of elaboration. The flow and modulation of his lines give them an immediate affinity to music, and it seems but in the natural order of things that they should have been sung in a tender, sympathetic voice by the poet himself. Moore's songs still live in popular appreciation now that "Lalla Rookh" is seldom read, and its splendors—astonishing as they are—have to a great extent ceased to hold the fancy of a younger generation. Even his Irish patriotic songs are remembered with something of the thrill which they have caused when they were sung in fashionable drawing-rooms more than half a century ago. — ARCHER, THOMAS, 1892, *The Poets and the Poetry of the Century, Southey to Shelley, ed. Miles, p.* 187.

It was a society which loved bric-à-brac, and Moore gave it bric-à-brac poetry of the best kind. Never was it better done; and the verse had a melodious movement, as of high-bred and ignorant ladies dancing on enamelled meadows, which pleased the ear and almost seemed to please the

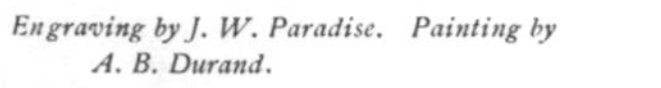

JOHN QUINCY ADAMS.

Engraving by J. W. Paradise. Painting by A. B. Durand.

DANIEL WEBSTER

From a Portrait by Healy.

eye. He was quite, then, in harmony with the society for which he wrote, and it would be rather surly of us if we judged him altogether from our standard of poetry and abused him for complying with the taste of his time. No one dreams of comparing him with the greater men, or of giving his poetry too important a place in the history of English song. But the man whose work Byron frankly admired; whom Scott did not dispraise; who received letters of thanks and appreciation from readers in America, Europe, and Asia; who fulfilled Mathew Arnold's somewhat foolish criterion of a poet's greatness by being known and accepted on the Continent; whom the Italians, French, Germans, Russians, Swedes, and Dutch translated; whose "Lalla Rookh" was partly put into Persian, and became the companion of Persians, on their travels and in the streets of Ispahan; to whom publishers like Longmans gave 3,000*l.* for a poem before they had even seen it, "as a tribute to reputation already acquired"—can scarcely be treated with the indifferent contempt which some have lavished upon him. He pleased, and he pleased a very great number. Time has altered that contemporary verdict, and rightly—but when it is almost universal, not merely the verdict of a clique, it counts.—BROOKE, STOPFORD A., 1900, *A Treasury of Irish Poetry, ed. Brooke and Rolleston, p.* 36.

Daniel Webster

1782–1852

Born at Salisbury (Franklin), N. H., Jan. 18, 1782: died at Marshfield, Mass., Oct. 24, 1852. A famous American statesman, orator, and lawyer. He studied at Exeter Academy and Boscawen, New Hampshire; graduated at Dartmouth College in 1801; was admitted to the bar at Boston in 1805; practised law at Boscawen and Portsmouth; was Federalist member of Congress from New Hampshire 1813-1817; and removed to Boston in 1816. He acquired a national reputation as a lawyer in the Dartmouth College case in 1818; was member of Congress from Massachusetts 1823–27; was Whig United States senator from Massachusetts 1827–41; became famous for his constitutional speeches in reply to Hayne in 1830, and in opposition to Calhoun in 1833; opposed Jackson on the United States Bank question; received several electoral votes for President in 1836; and was an unsuccessful candidate for the Whig nomination in later years. In 1839 he visited Europe. He was secretary of State 1841–43; negotiated the Ashburton treaty with Great Britain 1842; was United States senator from Massachusetts 1845–50; opposed the Mexican war and the annexation of Texas; supported Clay's compromise measures in his "7th of March speech" in 1850; was secretary of state 1850–52; and was again candidate for the Whig nomination for President in 1852. His chief public speeches (aside from those made in Congress and at the bar) are addresses delivered on the anniversary at Plymouth in 1820, on the laying of the corner-stone of Bunker Hill monument in 1825, on the deaths of Jefferson and Adams in 1826, on the dedication of Bunker Hill monument in 1843, and on the laying of the corner-stone of the addition to the Capitol in 1851.—SMITH, BENJAMIN E., 1894–97, *ed., The Century Cyclopedia of Names, p.* 1053.

PERSONAL

He is a magnificent specimen; you might say to all the world, This is your Yankee Englishman, such Limbs *we* make in Yankeeland! As a Logic-fencer, Advocate, or Parlimentary Hercules, one would incline to back him at first sight against all the extant world. The tanned complexion, that amorphous crag-like face; the dull black eyes under their precipice of brows, like dull anthracite furnaces, needing only to be *blown;* the mastiff-mouth, accurately closed:—I have not traced as much of silent *Berserkir-rage,* that I remember of, in any other man. "I guess I should not like to be *your* nigger!"—Webster is not loquacious, but he is pertinent, conclusive; a dignified, perfectly bred man, though not English in breeding; a man worthy of the best reception from us; and meeting such, I understand.—CARLYLE, THOMAS, 1839, *To Ralph Waldo Emerson, June* 24; *Correspondence of Thomas Carlyle and Ralph Waldo Emerson, ed. Norton, vol.* I, *p.* 260.

Now those thirsty eyes, those portrait-eating, portrait-painting eyes of thine, those fatal perceptions, have fallen full on the great forehead which I followed about all my young days, from court-house to senate-chamber, from caucus to street. He has his own sins no doubt, is no saint, is a prodigal. He has drunk his rum of Party too so long, that his strong head is soaked, sometimes even like the soft sponges, but the "man's a man for a' that." Better, he is a great boy,—as wilful, as nonchalant and good-humored. But you must hear him speak, not a show speech which he never does well, but *with cause* he can strike a stroke like a smith. I owe to him a hundred fine hours and two or three moments of Eloquence. His voice in a great house is admirable. I am sorry if you decided not to visit him. He loves a *man*, too. I do not know him, but my brother Edward read law with him, and loved him, and afterwards in sick and unfortunate days received the steadiest kindness from him.—EMERSON, RALPH WALDO, 1839, *To Thomas Carlyle, Aug.* 8; *Correspondence of Thomas Carlyle with Ralph Waldo Emerson, ed. Norton, vol.* I, *p.* 268.

Daniel Webster dined with me on his own invitation. He was on his way to Morristown and to Sussex County to meet a gathering of the Whigs. Dr. Condit, of Morristown, dined with me. Mr. Collins dined here. It was a very interesting party, and Mr. Webster charmed the party. He is 57 years old, and looks worn and furrowed; his belly becomes protuberant, and his eyes deep in his head. I sympathize with his condition. He has been too free a liver. He ate but little and drank wine freely.—KENT, JAMES, 1840, *Diary, Aug.* 22; *Memoirs and Letters, ed. Kent, p.* 261.

A column indeed, stately and graceful with its Corinthian capital, gives no bad idea of Mr. Webster; of his tall and muscular person, his massive features, noble head, and the general expression of placid strength by which he is distinguished. This is a mere fanciful comparison; but Sir Augustus Callcott's fine figure of Columbus has been reckoned very like him; a resemblance that must have been fortuitous, since the picture was painted before the artist had even seen the celebrated orator. When in England some ten or twelve years ago, Mr. Webster's calm manner of speaking excited much admiration and perhaps a little surprise, as contrasted with the astounding and somewhat rough rapidity of progress which is the chief characteristic of his native land. And yet that calmness of manner was just what might be expected from a countryman of Washington, earnest, thoughtful, weighty, wise. No visitor to London ever left behind him pleasanter recollections, and I hope that the good impression was reciprocal. Everybody was delighted with his geniality and taste; and he could hardly fail to like the people who so heartily liked him.—MITFORD, MARY RUSSELL, 1851, *Recollections of a Literary Life, p.* 228.

Dipped here and there into "Faust" (Anna Swanwick's translation), and am admitted more intimately than by Hayward's or Anster's version into the subtleties of the modern Satan, the world-spirit of the nineteenth century. Our devil has partaken of the cosmopolitan culture; he, too, is a scholar and a gentleman, scarcely distinguishable in a crowd from any mortal else,—his complexion sallower by a shade, perhaps, and, if surveyed closely, some show of hoofs in his boots. . . . Faust's dealings with him are infinitely suggestive and profitable, and inclusive of the whole range of guile. "The demon sat gladly,"—the portrait is sketched by a master, and is exhaustive of the subject. Goethe knew too much to paint well anything else; and this, his masterpiece, remains as the last likeness, finished up to the latest dates. Yet he lived too early to sketch this Western democratic shape, some fifty or more years later. Apropos of him, just now and here in this Western hemisphere everybody is putting down the dark Webster as the latest and best devil, concrete and astir in space perhaps,—certainly in these American parts,—clearly responsible for the sins of cities, North and South,—a Satan of national type and symmetry. 'Tis a great pity that Goethe should have come too soon. Head, shoulders, all, all of Webster should have gone into the picture, and this legal, logical, constitutional Mephistopheles of the States had justice done him by his master. —ALCOTT, A. BRONSON, 1851, *Diary.*

In his personal appearance Mr. Webster was an extraordinary man, and at the age of forty was considered the handsomest man in Congress. He was above the ordinary size, and stoutly formed, but with small hands and feet, had a large head, very high forehead, a dark complexion, large black, deeply sunken, and solemn-looking eyes, black hair (originally), very heavy eyebrows, and fine teeth. To strangers his countenance appeared stern, but when lighted up by conversation, it was bland and agreeable. He was slow and stately in his movements, and his dress was invariably neat and elegant; his favorite suit for many years having been a blue or brown coat, a buff vest, and black pantaloons. His manner of speaking, both in conversation and debate, was slow and methodical, and his voice generally low and musical, but when excited, it rang like a clarion.—LANMAN, CHARLES, 1852, *The Private Life of Daniel Webster, p.* 179.

We called him giant, for in every part
He seemed colossal; in his port and speech,
In his large brain and in his larger heart.
And when his name upon the roll we saw
Of those who govern, then we felt secure,
Because we knew his reverence for the law.
So the young master of the Roman realm
Discreetly thought, we cannot wander far
From the true course, with Ulpian at the helm.
. . . .
We have no high cathedral for his rest,
Dim with proud banners and the dust of years;
All we can give him is New England's breast
To lay his head on—and his country's tears.
—PARSONS, THOMAS WILLIAM, 1852, *On the Death of Daniel Webster, Poems, pp.* 62, 64.

Consider that from the day he went upon the Committee of Foreign Relations, in 1813, in time of war, and more and more, the longer he lived and the higher he rose, he was a man whose great talents and devotion to public duty placed and kept him in a position of associated or sole command; command in the political connexion to which he belonged, command in opposition, command in power; and appreciate the responsibilities which that implies, what care, what prudence, what mastery of the whole ground—exacting for the conduct of a party, as Gibbon says of Fox, abilities and civil discretion equal to the conduct of an empire. Consider the work he did in that life of forty years—the range of subjects investigated and discussed; composing the whole theory and practice of our organic and administrative politics, foreign and domestic. . . . How much then, when rising to the measure of a true, and difficult, and rare greatness, remembering that he had a country to save as well as a local constituency to gratify, laying all the wealth, all the hopes, of an illustrious life on the altar of a hazardous patriotism, he sought and won the more exceeding glory which now attends—which in the next age shall more conspicuously attend—his name who composes an agitated and saves a sinking land—recall this series of conduct and influences, study them carefully in their facts and results—the reading of years—and you attain to a true appreciation of this aspect of his greatness—his public character and life. —CHOATE, RUFUS, 1853, *Address on Daniel Webster before Dartmouth College.*

No gloom that stately shape can hide,
No change uncrown his brow; behold!
Dark, calm, large-fronted, lightning-eyed,
Earth has no double from its mould.
—HOLMES, OLIVER WENDELL, 1856, *Birthday of Daniel Webster, Jan.* 18.

I have looked on many mighty men,—King George, the "first gentleman in England;" Sir Astley Cooper, the Apollo of his generation; Peel, O'Connell, Palmerston, Lyndhurst,—all nature's noblemen; I have seen Cuvier, Guizot, Arago, Lamartine, marked in their persons by the genius which has carried their names over the world; I have seen Clay, and Calhoun and Pinckney, and King, and Dwight, and Daggett, who stand as high examples of personal endowment in our annals; and yet not one of these approached Mr. Webster in the commanding power of their personal presence. There was a grandeur in his form, an intelligence in his deep, dark eye, a loftiness in his expansive brow, a significance in his arched lip, altogether beyond those of any other human being I ever saw. —GOODRICH, SAMUEL GRISWOLD, 1856, *Recollections of a Lifetime, Letter* lv.

Accordingly, at noon on Friday, the 29th day of October, 1852, the gates of his late residence were thrown wide, that all who wished might come to look for the last time upon that majestic form. The coffin was placed upon the lawn, in front of the mansion-house, and a rich autumn sun poured down upon it the full light of day. A concourse of more than ten thousand filled the grounds, and passed slowly around the bier, each one pausing for an instant, to take the last look of that gracious figure, which was arrayed for burial in the same well-known dress that he had always worn. The great multitude present represented or comprehended all classes, all ages, all stations, the rich and the poor, the educated and the uneducated, from far and near. But, in that crowd, there came one unknown man, in a plain and rustic garb, who truly and fitly, because in homeliest words, interpreted the thoughts that silently oppressed them all, when, looking down upon the face of the dead, he said, as if for himself alone: "Daniel Webster, the world, without you, will seem lonesome."—CURTIS, GEORGE TICKNOR, 1870, *Life of Daniel Webster, vol.* II, *p.* 703.

I was intimate and in frequent correspondence with another American of still higher eminence, Daniel Webster; a man whom Sydney Smith aptly described as a "steam-engine in trousers." His massive forehead indeed strikingly betokened the massive intellect that lay within. He belonged to the higher and earlier class of American Statesmen; though falling upon times when political partisanship and election trading had usurped so largely on the original institutions of the Republic, that he, as well as his contemporaries Clay and Calhoun, were excluded from its highest office because they signally deserved it. I am half inclined to believe that the civil war might have been averted, had Webster's genius and masculine eloquence, as they at one time existed, placed him in a position where they could be of national avail.—HOLLAND, SIR HENRY, 1871, *Recollections of Past Life, p.* 189.

He did not "let himself out," and display his lighter, frolicsome, and humorous moods, except in presence of those whom he had known long and well, and between whom and himself there existed strong mutual attachment. Those who did know him as he was, however, were aware that not only was he simple in manners, and often boyish in spirits; not only was he hearty, hospitable, and affectionate, steadfast in his love of his family and his attachment to his friends, kind of heart towards men and towards animals, courteous to his adversaries, courageous, benevolent,—but that he was also fond of fun, and had a very keen zest for, and sense of, the humorous.—HARVEY, PETER, 1877, *Reminiscences and Anecdotes of Daniel Webster, p.* 316.

I was very fond of Mr. Webster, with his sweet and tender smile, his very white teeth, and his dark complexion and heavy brows. He was fond of children, and was very kind to me.—OAKEY, S. W., 1881, *Recollections of American Society, Scribner's Monthly, vol.* 21, *p.* 417.

He was the "godlike Daniel" to his countrymen in general, who thus called him by a phrase which, with a certain semi-conscious humor in it racy of the national character, redeemed its own excess of veneration by a corrective dash of associated familiarity. But no less the educated men among his fellows were accustomed to employ in their own more scholarly way a similar language. To them he was "Jove," a "descended god," a "demi-god," "the Olympian." If he went abroad, some Englishmen said he "looked like a cathedral," or Sydney Smith, with irreverent homage to his Titan might, said he "was a steam-engine in breeches." This imposing effect of Webster's personal presence was partly due to the remarkable physical mold in which he was cast. He was not gigantic in proportions, was not even greatly above the medium height; but somehow the beholder took from him an instantaneous and overwhelming impression of immense mass, weight, momentum,—in one word, of power. He was always one of the sights of Boston, where his presence in the streets made the neighboring buildings look smaller. Men from the country, that did not know who it was, would stand to gaze at him.—WILKINSON, WILLIAM CLEAVER, 1882, *Daniel Webster, Century, vol.* 23, *p.* 538.

A congenial marriage seems to be essential to the best development of a man of genius, and this blessing rested upon that household. It was like organ-music to hear Webster speak to or of the being upon whom his affections reposed, and whom, alas! he was so soon to lose. I am sure that those who knew the man only when this tenderest relation had been terminated by death, never knew him in his perfect symmetry. Whatever evil-speakers might choose to say about the subsequent career of Daniel Webster, he was at that time [1826], "whole as the marble, founded as the rock." He was on the happiest terms with the world, which had crowned him with its choicest blessing, and stood forth in all respects as an example and a hero among men. . . . Without asking the reason, men once subjected to his spell were compelled to love, to honor, and (so some cynics would wish to add) to forgive him. No man of mark ever satisfied the imagination so completely. The young men of to-day who go to Washington find a city of luxurious appointments and noble buildings, very different from the capital of muddy streets and scattered houses with which I was familiar. But where is the living figure, cast in heroic mould, to represent the ideal of American manhood? Can the capital of to-day show anything so majestic and inspiring as was Daniel Webster in the Washington of 1826?—QUINCY, JOSIAH, 1883, *Figures of the Past from the Leaves of Old Journals, pp.* 256, 267.

When Mr. Webster failed it was a moral failure. His moral character was not equal to his intellectual force. All the errors he ever committed, whether in public or in private life, in political action or in regard to money obligations, came from moral weakness. He was deficient in that intensity of conviction which carries men beyond and above all triumphs of statesmanship, and makes them the embodiment of the great moral forces which move the world. If Mr. Webster's moral power had equalled his intellectual greatness, he would have had no rival in our history. . . . He stands to-day as the pre-eminent champion and exponent of nationality. He said once, "there are no Alleghanies in my politics," and he spoke the exact truth. Mr. Webster was thoroughly national. There is no taint of sectionalism or narrow local prejudice about him. He towers up as an American, a citizen of the United States in the fullest sense of the word. He did not invent the Union, or discover the doctrine of nationality. But he found the great fact and the great principle ready to his hand, and he lifted them up, and preached the gospel of nationality throughout the length and breadth of the land. In his fidelity to this cause he never wavered nor faltered.—LODGE, HENRY CABOT, 1883, *Daniel Webster (American Statesmen), pp.* 360, 361.

Huge and solemn as were his eyeballs, vast and capacious as was his skull, massive as were his shoulders, and sonorous as was his voice, there was yet occasionally something deprecating in his manners and apologetic in his discourse. These deficiencies for championship were due to the influence of Puritanism, which had done its work upon him in his youth.—KEYES, GEN. E. D., 1884, *Fifty Years' Observations, p.* 148.

As an infant he is described as a crying baby who worried his parents considerably. He grew up to boyhood pale, weak, and sickly; as he himself often told me, he was the slimest in the family. And yet, by doing a boy's work on his father's farm, by indulging a propensity for outdoor sports, by leading a temperate and frugal life, he succeeded in building up a robust constitution. On arriving at manhood he had a physical frame which seemed made to last a hundred years. It was an iron frame, large and stately, with a great mountain of a head upon it. When Thorwaldsen, the Danish sculptor, saw his head in Powers's studio in Rome, he exclaimed: "Ah! a design for Jupiter, I see." He would not believe that it was a living American. Parker describes him as "a man of large mold, a great body, and a great brain. . . . Since Socrates there has seldom been a head so massive, huge. Its cubic capacity surpassed all former measurements of mind. A large man, decorous in dress, dignified in deportment, he walked as if he felt himself a king. Men from the country who knew him not stared at him as he passed through our streets. The coal-heavers and porters of London looked on him as one of the great forces of the globe. They recognized in him a native king." Carlyle called him "a magnificent specimen whom, as a logic fencer or parliamentary Hercules, one would incline to back at sight against all the world." And Sydney Smith said he was "a living lie, because no man on earth could be as great as he looked."—ALLEN, STEPHEN M., 1885, *Reminiscences of Daniel Webster, The Century, vol.* 29, *p.* 724.

The fame of Whitfield rests entirely on his oratorical genius; his published sermons show a mind below mediocrity. But Webster's speeches read with a clearness, an argumentative force, a grasp of thought, a magnificence of style, that indicate unusual intellectual powers. In his time Webster stood at the head of the American Bar; as a lawyer he was the peer of Jeremiah Mason. The cases he argued and won are among the most remarkable of the century. In his legal arguments he exhibited a power to deal with details, and to search out and win on the essential points of a case, while displaying great fairness in considering both sides of the argument. His fame was secure both as an orator and a lawyer when Destiny summoned him to display yet another phase of his many-sided genius in the councils of the nation. We have had many orators, many great lawyers and jurists, but very few statesmen of the first order, or for that matter of any degree of merit; politicians in abundance, but rarely statesmen. Among those characters who have achieved that high eminence, Daniel Webster occupies no second place.—BENJAMIN, S. G. W., 1887, *Daniel Webster, Magazine of American History, vol.* 18, *p.* 324.

There is hardly a scrap of self-applause to be found in Webster's career,—not even in the Boswellian "Reminiscences" of Peter Harvey. Of course Webster knew that all the world never estimated him at any less than the equal of the greatest men of his day, whether at the Bar or in the Senate, but he seems to have been absolutely clear of all vanity.—MORRILL, JUSTIN S., 1887, *Self-Consciousness of Noted Persons, p.* 31.

Mr. Webster was the only man I ever knew or heard of who united in himself the highest qualities of an advocate, orator and debater. He has never been excelled, if equalled, in making difficult and intricate questions intelligible to jurors. Seeing clearly the real points at issue, and using language that anybody could understand, his statements of the points at issue were arguments. He never permitted the minds of jurors to be diverted from the real question upon which a case turned. Brushing aside everything that was not essential, the strong points only were presented by him, and those with exceeding clearness.—MCCULLOCH, HUGH, 1888, *Men and Measures of half a Century, p.* 18.

A friend of mine once gave the proprietor of the Astor House, for courtesies extended to him, a dozen of his finest Maderia. He had the curiosity years after to ask his host of the Astor what became of this wine. He replied, "Daniel Webster came to my house, and I opened a bottle of it for him, and he remained in the house until he had drunk up every drop of it." This was the famous "Butler 16."—MCALLISTER, WARD, 1890, *Society as I have Found it, p.* 270.

Looking back upon the time in which he lived, it [we] beholds the statuesque form towering with strange grandeur among its contemporaries, huge in his strength, and huge also in its weakness and faults; not indeed an originator of policies or measures, but a marvelous expounder of principles, laws, and facts, who illumined every topic of public concern he touched, with the light of a sovereign intelligence and vast knowledge; who, by overpowering argument, riveted around the Union unbreakable bonds of constitutional doctrine; who awakened to new life and animated with invincible vigor and national spirit; who left to his countrymen and to the world invaluable lessons of statesmanship, right, and patriotism, in language of grand simplicity and prodigiously forceful clearness; and who might stand as its greatest mind in the political history of America, had he been a master character as he was a master mind.—SCHURZ, CARL, 1897, *Library of the World's Best Literature, ed. Warner, vol.* XXVII, *p.* 15735.

He of all men next to Napoleon deserved the title of magnetic. His powerful face, so often described, so characterized by Carlyle, Macaulay, and Sydney Smith, was capable of the most lustrous and winning and beautiful smile I can remember. Had Mr. Webster been, like Charles James Fox, a professional lady-killer, he would have won every woman in the land. But I never heard that he went into the business of flirtation at all.—SHERWOOD, M. E. W., 1897, *An Epistle to Posterity, p.* 20.

ORATIONS

It is the effort of a great mind, richly stored with every species of information. If there be an American who can read it without tears, I am not that American. Mr. Burke is no longer entitled to the praise—the most consummate orator of modern times. What can I say of what regards myself? To my humble name "*Exegisti monumentum œre perennius.*" The oration ought to be read at the end of every century.—ADAMS JOHN, 1820, *On the "First Settlement of New England."*

Considered merely as literary productions, we think the three volumes of "Speeches and Forensic Arguments," quoted at the head of this article, take the highest rank among the best productions of the American intellect.—WHIPPLE, EDWIN P., 1844, *Daniel Webster, North American Review, July; Essays and Reviews.*

I admire your style of address. It is stringent and terse, simple and strong. It is the severe simplicity and strength of Demosthenes, and not the art and elegance and *Copia* verborum of Cicero. The latter was the characteristic of the speeches and writings of our friend Story. But yours is the better model for a great political speaker.—KENT, JAMES, 1845, *Letter to Daniel Webster, Nov.* 11; *Private Correspondence of Daniel Webster, vol.* II, *p.* 212.

Notwithstanding our admiration of Mr. Webster's talents, we do not precisely place him at the head of the list of American orators. He wants the pathos of Preston, the electric rapidity of Calhoun, and the versatile graces and manifold excellences of Clay. But in massive volume of thought, in depth and closeness of reasoning, and in the eloquence of the *head*, he is scarcely equalled, certainly not surpassed, by any. This is his *forte*, and it manifests itself on all occasions, whether he is called on to defend the Union and the Constitution, or to vindicate his own State of Massachusetts. With him the flowers of rhetoric and appeals to feeling are but secondary things; he uses them with considerable effect, when they come in his way, but he would not move one step from his path to cull all the flowers of a whole *parteere*.—SPALDING, MARTIN JOHN, 1855, *Miscellanea.*

The best speeches of Webster are among the very best that I am acquainted with in the wide range of oratory, ancient or modern. They have always appeared to me to belong to that simple and manly class which may be properly headed by the name of Demosthenes. Webster's speeches sometimes brings before my mind the image of the Cyclopean walls,—stone upon stone, compact, firm, and grand. After I had perused, and aloud, too, the last speech which you sent me, I was desirous of testing my own appreciation, and took down Demosthenes, reading him aloud too. It did not lessen my appreciation of Webster's speech. You know that I insist upon the necessity of entire countries for high, modern citizenship; and all my intercourse with Webster made me feel that the same idea or feeling lived in him, although he never expressed it. Webster had a big heart,—and for that very reason was a poor party leader in our modern sense. Everything in Webster was capacious, large; he was a statesman of Chatham's type, I think. I believe he thought he was strong in political economy, but I think this was his weak point. I do not recollect that he was ever profound in that branch of statesmanship; and he may have become occasionally in this branch a special pleader, which he never was on other questions, and which many others have almost always been in their public career. —LIEBER, FRANCIS, 1860, *Letter to S. Austin Allibone, Jan.* 16; *Critical Dictionary of English Literature, vol.* III, *p.* 2624.

He was the Chatham of the New World. —CHAMBERS, ROBERT, 1876, *Cyclopædia of English Literature, ed. Carruthers.*

In debate Webster was quick at retort. If it was a personal insult that aroused the slumbering lion, his roar of rage was appalling, and the spring and death blow that followed, were like lightning in their suddenness. But it was on momentous occasions, when great public interests were at stake, that the full might of his intellect was visible. When feeble men, awed by the darkness of the political sky, fled for shelter from the tempest, he rushed forth exultingly to the elemental war, with all his faculties stimulated to their utmost. When the thunders of Nullification muttered in the distance, he coolly watched the coming storm; and when they burst, he bared his head to the bolts, like the mammoth of tradition, shaking them off as they fell. No man ever spoke, in whose utterances, even the simplest, the power of great personality was more deeply felt. —MATHEWS, WILLIAM, 1878, *Oratory and Orators, p.* 327.

In the Senate and in occasional speeches he was at his best, and above any other American of whom we have sufficient means of judging. . . . Webster has passed into history as one of the handful of men whom the world acknowledges as the great masters of eloquence.—LODGE,

HENRY CABOT, 1884, *Studies in History*, *pp.* 312, 313.

Upon the exterior of the Sanders Theatre of Harvard University—the oratorical centre of the oldest American college—are seven sculptured heads of the greatest orators of the world, who, according to this selection, are Demosthenes the Greek, Cicero the Roman, St. Chrysostom the Syrian, Bossuet the Frenchman, Chatham and Burke the Englishmen, and Daniel Webster the American. The choice is a fit one. Whatever the claims of other leading American orators, Webster, all in all, is their chief. So he was regarded during his lifetime, and the years since his death have not diminished their renown. Indeed, now that Webster's intense ambitions and bitter disappointments have been quenched in ashes, the solidity of his renown as an orator has become more apparent. — RICHARDSON, CHARLES F., 1885, *American Literature*, 1607–1885, *vol.* I, *p.* 221.

He trod no deck; he rode no horse; he bore
No truncheon and no sword. He only sate
A simple Senator within the gate;
But when he spoke, men listened: from every door.
Surged round him like a sea without a shore—
This man of the majestic mien who, late
On his own shoulders had borne up the State;
Hearts beat, eyes glistened. He would speak once more.
The thunders gathered on his awful brow:
He spoke. We know the story. He who shone
On all the summits of occasion, now
Shone upon this; and made the day his own:
He did but speak within the Senate Hall
Some pregnant hours, yet in that time saved all.

—BLOOD, HENRY AMES, 1886, *Webster*, 1830-1886.

Americans claim for Daniel Webster the highest place among modern orators. The verifications of such a claim would be a complicated process. But there can be no doubt that Webster was a magnificent speaker, or that his speeches, like those of Bright and unlike those of Clay, have a literary value of the highest and most lasting kind. In political oratory it would be hard to find anything superior to the reply to Hayne; in forensic oratory it would be hard to find anything superior to the speech on the murder of White; among show speeches it would be hard to find anything superior to the Plymouth oration. The economical and financial speeches have also the highest merits of speeches of that class. . . . Webster had not much imagination, and he seldom appealed to feeling. He reasons with irresistible force and in language plain but well-chosen, terse, and thoroughly effective. His sentences have been compared to the strokes of a trip hammer. Like the strokes of a trip hammer they are in sureness of aim and in the force with which they shatter the arguments on the other side, but not in monotony, for their construction and connection are sufficiently varied. — SMITH, GOLDWIN, 1888, *American Statesman, The Nineteenth Century, vol.* 24, *p.* 262.

Great as the Plymouth Oration was acknowledged by all to be, the Bunker Hill Address was a distinct advance upon it, both in the scope of the ideas and in the skill with which they are wrought into an organic whole. It is more compact, more picturesque, more vigorous, more finished. In this field of oratory he probably has never had any equal in the English-speaking world. . . . Probably no speech in history has had so many readers as the Reply to Hayne.—GEORGE, ANDREW J., 1892, *ed., Select Speeches of Daniel Webster*, *pp.* 375, 381.

I have said that Webster was called on to make this speech [Reply to Hayne], at short notice. A single night was, if I remember right, all that he had for immediate preparation for the first day's effort, and one other night for that of the second day. He could have made but few notes, and the Brief which has been published—a very short one—may have been all that he committed to writing. Before going to the Senate Chamber on the morning of the first day he told Mr. Everett that as to the defence of the Constitution he had no misgivings, that he was always ready for that; and that his only anxiety was in regard to the personal and sectional parts of Colonel Hayne's attack. As he entered the Senate Chamber, John M. Clayton, the senator from Delaware, said to him, "Webster, are you primed and loaded?" "Seven fingers," was his only reply, with a gesture as if pointing to a gunbarrel. He spoke under great excitement, and with almost an air of inspiration. Of his emotions he said himself, not long afterward, "I felt as if everything I had ever seen or read or heard was floating before me in one grand panorama, and I had little else to do than to reach up and cull a thunderbolt and hurl it at him."—WINTHROP, ROBERT C., 1894, *Webster's Reply to Hayne, Scribner's Magazine, vol.* XV, *p.* 120.

The greatest of American forensic orators, if, indeed, he be not the greatest of all orators who have used the English tongue. Webster's speeches are of the kind that have power to move after the voice of the speaker is still. The thought and the passion in them lay hold on feelings of patriotism more lasting than the issues of the moment.—BEERS, HENRY A., 1895, *The Era of National Expansion, Initial Studies in American Letters, p.* 89.

Webster's very cravat, blue coat, and buff waistcoat seemed invested with an intellectual majesty. Even now, it is only needful to read over one of his grand speeches, as the second reply to Hayne, accounted his masterpiece, equally wonderful for its steady tramp of arguments and tremendous floods of feeling, to realize that overwhelming power. Webster's earnestness and force of mind impressed themselves like sheer weight. Much as his regal presence and organ-range of voice enhanced the first effect of his oratory, it remains in print colossal eloquence. —BATES, KATHARINE LEE, 1897, *American Literature, p.* 255.

James Lowell and I were very angry with Webster for staying in old Tyler's cabinet, and as he was to speak in Faneuil Hall on the evening of the 30th of September, 1842, we determined to go in and hoot at him and to show him that he had incurred our displeasure. There were three thousand people there, and we felt sure they would hoot with us, young as we were. But we reckoned without our host. Mr. Webster, beautifully dressed, stepped calmly forward. His great eyes looked, as I shall always think, straight at me. I pulled off my hat; James pulled off his. We both became cold as ice and respectful as Indian coolies. I saw James turn pale; he said I was livid. And when the great creature began that most beautiful exordium our scorn turned to deepest admiration, from abject contempt to belief and approbation.—STORY, WILLIAM WETMORE, 1897, *M. E. W. Sherwood's Epistle to Posterity, p.* 47.

GENERAL

Earnestness, solidity of judgment, elevation of sentiment, broad and generous views of national policy, and a massive strength of expression, characterize all his works. We feel, in reading them, that he is a man of principles, not a man of expedients; that he never adopts opinions without subjecting them to stern tests; and that he recedes from them only at the bidding of reason and experience. He never seems to be playing a part, but always acting a life. . . . His patriotism has become part of his being. Deny him that, and you deny the authorship of his works. It has prompted the most majestic flights of his eloquence. It has given intensity to his purposes, and lent the richest glow to his genius. It has made his eloquence a language of the heart, felt and understood over every portion of the land it consecrates.—WHIPPLE, EDWIN P., 1844, *Daniel Webster, North American Review, July; Essays and Reviews.*

Whoever, in after-times, shall write the history of the United States for the last forty years, will write the life of Daniel Webster; and whoever writes the life of Daniel Webster, as it ought to be written, will write the history of the Union from the time he took a leading part in its concerns. — EVERETT, EDWARD, 1852, *Speech in Fanueil Hall, Oct.* 27.

His style is remarkable for great clearness of statement. It is singularly emphatic. Clearness of statement, vigor of reasoning, and a faculty of making a question plain to the understanding by the mere terms in which it is presented, are the traits which uniformly distinguish his writings, evident alike in a diplomatic note, a legislative debate, and an historical discourse. His dignity of expression, breadth of view, and force of thought, realize the ideal of a republican statesman, in regard, at least, to natural endowments; and his presence and manner, in the prime of his life were analogous.—TUCKERMAN, HENRY T., 1852, *A Sketch of American Literature.*

He found his fertile nourishment in the books of the Bible, the simple energy of Homer, and the vivid grandeur of Milton. He has left traces of these studies on many a page. There was about Webster a constant air of nobility of soul. Whatever subject he touched lost nothing of its dignity with him. The occasion rose in his hand, as he connected it with interests beyond those of the present moment or the passing object.—DUYCKINCK, EVERT A. AND GEORGE L., 1855-65-75, *Cyclopædia of American Literature, ed. Simons, vol.* I, *p.* 720.

And he put his own crown-stamp on almost everything he uttered. There was no mistaking one of Webster's great efforts. There is no mistaking them now. They will be distinguished, in all time to come, like pieces of old gold or silver plate, by an unmistakable mint-mark. He knew, like the casters or forgers of yonder Statue, not only how to pour forth burning words and blazing thoughts, but so to blend and fuse and weld together his facts and figures, his illustrations and arguments, his metaphors and subject matter, as to bring them all out at last into one massive and enduring image of his own great mind!—WINTHROP, ROBERT C., 1876, *Oration at the Unveiling of the Statue of Daniel Webster, Central Park, New York, Nov.* 25.

In the sphere of literature to be held as one of the greatest authors and writers of our mother tongue that America has produced. We all recognize the great distinction in this regard of Burke and of Macaulay. In the flow of their eloquence as writers, and in the splendors of their diction, Mr. Webster did not approach them, nor would he have desired to imitate them. But I propose to the most competent critics of the Nation, that they can find nowhere six octavo volumes of printed literary production of an American, that contains as much noble and as much beautiful imagery, as much warmth of rhetoric, and of magnetic impression upon the reader, as are to be found in the collected writings and speeches of Daniel Webster. —EVARTS, WILLIAM M., 1876, *Oration at the Unveiling of the Statue of Daniel Webster, Central Park, New York, Nov.* 25.

It is more than twenty years since we stood in the presence of Daniel Webster. We may now look at the great American with a steady gaze, and see him in his true proportions. He stands out against the sky of the past like Mont Blanc among the Alps. Not comprehended, not appreciated by the country in his time, we can observe him now through the serene light of intervening years, and study the elements that constituted his greatness. His fame will never be less than it is today. It must endure as long as the government which he upheld while he lived.—HILLIARD, HENRY W., 1877, *Webster and the Constitution, Harper's Magazine, vol.* 54, *p.* 595.

To the Memory
of
DANIEL WEBSTER,
Our greatest Orator, Statesman, Author, the
Saver of
our National Union, the Crown and Consumation of
American Intellect and Manhood, this
edition
of his fovourite Poet is, with reverential
affection, inscribed by the
Editor.

—HUDSON, HENRY N., 1880, *Complete Works of William Shakespeare, Harvard ed., Dedication, vol.* I.

I have dwelt on the career of the grandest post-Revolution figure of the New World, because his work is less known in England than that of any other great American. In a country whose intellectual *forte* is oratory he surpasses all other orators.

"Quantum lenta solent inter viburna cupressi."

More than this, his place among English-speaking orators is in the front rank. True, his style has traces of the exaggeration characteristic of almost all young countries, and the haste, to which we have referred as one of the attributes of his own. It superabounds in classical allusions (a fashion common to the closing years of the last and early years of this century in Great Britain, France, and Germany); its imagery is profuse, here and there florid. In Webster's pages, as in those of most orators, we have platitudes side by side with passages of real power, and we are made alive to his want of true humour by his lack of reticence. But beneath all the verbiage there is constantly present to us a man of realities, of pith and power and catholic sympathies enough to make us forget the cavils of superfine critics, with no more energy than mantlepiece ornaments, whose one idea is to make pedestals to themselves by smoothing sentences. Under the "barbaric pearl and gold" there is a buff jerkin;

the flowers make summer over a block of Puritan granite. Webster, fed on strong meat—the Bible, Homer and Milton—is always strong, always clear. His six volumes can be read with little fatigue, and relished for instruction as well as heat; though superfluent, he never brings in bombast to plaster lack of knowledge or impotence of thought.—NICHOL, JOHN, 1880–85, *American Literature, p.* 127.

We watch the feats of some superb athlete, and all that he does is impossible to us, far beyond our reach; but we understand how everything is done, and what muscles are needed. We observe the performances of an Eastern juggler; we see the results, we appreciate the skill, but the secret of the trick escapes us. This is true also of mental operations; it is the difference between the mind of Shakespeare and that of Pitt, a difference, not of degree, but of kind. Webster belongs to the athletes.—LODGE, HENRY CABOT, 1882–84, *Daniel Webster, Studies in History, p.* 327.

A careful study of his speeches cannot fail to be of interest and benefit to the student of English prose literature and English style.—BALDWIN, JAMES, 1883, *English Literature and Literary Criticism, Prose, p.* 402.

He understood the character and genius of the American people, and the principles upon which their national organization was founded. No one more fully appreciated the importance of abiding consistently by those great principles, as their successful operation in this country was of vast importance in the progress of humanity, in bringing it to a proper understanding of individual responsibility and governmental authority.—WHITMAN, C. M., 1883, *American Orators and Oratory, p.* 113.

We can not imagine a time nor a condition of society when Webster's morning drum-beat passage will lose its charm. His description of a superior human intellect in his eulogy on Adams and Jefferson is so true, so graphic, and so grand, that it must always command the admiration of the reader. Without exaggeration he has painted the scene of the murder of Captain White, and given voice to the thoughts and sentiments of the assassin, in manner and form so truthful and attractive that his words must find a place in the living literature of future times.—BOUTWELL, GEORGE S., 1887, *The Lawyer, the Statesman, and the Soldier, p.* 62.

Daniel Webster is not likely to be forgotten, nor will his words cease to be read. For he wasted no time on party politics, or on small questions, or on issues now dead; but always in the courts, or in the Senate, or before the people, applied his matchless powers to subjects of great moment and popular interest, sure to remain vital, and, like the seasons, ever returning. In these respects he stands alone among the statesmen of his day; and therefore, if they would, the people can never forget him. Nor can statesmen, jurists, or scholars; because, about government, laws, and public policy he said the most authoritative word, save John Marshall's, and said it in a way not easily bettered.—CHAMBERLAIN, MELLEN, 1893, *A Glance at Daniel Webster, The Century, vol.* 46, *p.* 709.

As the master of a pure and vigorous English prose style, Webster has had few equals. His best orations may be studied as models of correct diction and rhetorical finish. His style may be characterized as majestic. It abounds in sonorous and elaborate word pictures. He was a clear thinker, and his sentences are as clear as his thought. His combinations are accurate and logical, and his illustrations are forceful. The orations of Clay and Calhoun seem dull and spiritless as we read them now; the magnetism of the orator, the tones of his voice, the flash of his eye, and the thrill of the occasion gave the words a life and power which vanished as soon as they passed into print. But Webster's orations lose nothing with time. They are full of their original force and fire. They hold the reader as the orator held his audience, and we feel the thrill and excitement of the original occasion. It is this that brings the work of Webster into the realm of pure literature.—PATTEE, FRED LEWIS, 1896, *A History of American Literature, p.* 187.

Of the generation of American statesmen that followed those of the Revolutionary period, few will live as long in the memory of the people, and none as long in the literature of the country, as Daniel Webster.—SCHURZ, CARL, 1897, *Library of the World's Best Literature, ed. Warner, vol.* XXVII, *p.* 15725.

Henry Clay

1777–1852

Born in Hanover County, near Richmond, Va., April 12, 1777: died at Washington, D. C., June 29, 1852. A celebrated American statesman and orator. He was United States senator from Kentucky 1806–07 and 1810–11; was member of Congress from Kentucky 1811–21 and 1823–25 (serving as speaker 1811–14, 1815–20, and 1823–25); was peace commissioner at Ghent in 1814; was candidate for the Presidency in 1824; was secretary of state 1825–29; was United States senator 1831–42 and 1849–52; was Whig candidate for the Presidency in 1832 and 1844; was the chief designer of the "Missouri Compromise" of 1820, and of the compromise of 1850; and was the author of the compromise tariff of 1833. Complete works, with biography, edited by Colton (1857).—SMITH, BENJAMIN E., *ed.*, 1894–97, *The Century Cyclopedia of Names, p.* 257.

PERSONAL

The object of his exertions was, at once, worthy of his power, and adapted to their noblest manifestations. He has been deservedly called "The great commoner." It is in the defence of popular rights, and the indignant denunciation of aristocratical tyranny, that his eloquence has been most frequently exerted.—PRENTICE, GEORGE DENISON, 1831, *Life of Henry Clay, p.* 23.

Mr. Clay is particularly remarkable, as a politician, for a large and comprehensive scope of mind. He looks at his subject from an elevated point,—takes in at one view all the various considerations that bear upon it, and is thus enabled to give to each its proper relative importance. This faculty is in him the more commendable, inasmuch as it is not the natural result of the professional pursuits to which a large part of his life has been devoted. —EVERETT, ALEXANDER HILL, 1831, *Life of Henry Clay, North American Review, vol.* 33, *p.* 395.

Whatever may be Mr. Clay's defects, we are happy to be able to state, that they do not grow out of principle, but they are referable to the sanguineous nature of his constitution, rendering him easily excitable and irritable; in other words, his errors are those of feeling, and venial ones, if any are. Our surprise is, not that he occasionally suffered its impetuous tide to control his judgment, momentarily, but our astonishment, on the other hand, is, that this was not borne entirely away by it, and stranded among the quicksands of folly and violence, set upon, as he was, at every stage of his career, by political harpies and vampyres, and bayed by the furious mastiffs of unprincipled and licentious faction, as if he had been a beast of prey, prowling through the land to devour its substance. Fatigued, exhausted, and lacerated, with such a temperament as he possessed, it must have required, if possible, more than the "patience of Job," to bear in silence the most painful inflictions which the ingenuity of his legion of tormentors could devise.—MALLORY, DANIEL, 1844, *Life of Henry Clay, vol.* I, *p.* 193.

Mr. Clay is now (1848) in his seventy-first year, and, notwithstanding his varied and arduous labors, tasking his mental and physical powers to an extraordinary degree, and the several periods of dangerous illness to which he has been subject, he bears in his personal appearance the promise of a vigorous, healthful, and protracted old age. In stature, he is tall, sinewy, erect, and commanding, with finely-formed limbs, and a frame capable of much endurance. From his features, you might at first infer that he was a hardy backwoodsman, who had been accustomed rather to the privations and trials of a frontier life, than to the arena of debate and the diplomatic table. But when you meet his full, clear gray eye, you see in its flashes the conscious power of a well-trained and panoplied intellect, as well as the glance of an intrepid soul. Its lustre gives animation to the whole countenance, and its varying expression faithfully interprets the emotions and sentiments of the orator. Much of the charm in his speaking lies in his clear, rotund, and indescribably melodious voice, which is of wide compass, and as distinct in its low as in its high tones.—SARGENT, EPES, 1848–52, *Life of Henry Clay, ed. Greeley, p.* 315.

He was indeed eloquent—all the world knows that. He held the keys to the hearts of his countrymen, and he turned the wards within them with a skill attained by no other master. But eloquence was nevertheless only an instrument, and one of many that he used. His conversation, his gestures, his very look, was magisterial, persuasive, seductive, irresistible. And his appliance of all these was courteous, patient, and indefatigable. Defeat only inspired him with new resolution. He divided opposition by his assiduity of address, while he rallied and strengthened his own bands of supporters by the confidence of success which, feeling himself, he easily inspired among his followers. His affections were high, and pure, and generous, and the chiefest among them was that one which the great Italian poet designated as the charity of native land. In him that charity was an enduring and overpowering enthusiasm, and it influenced all his sentiments and conduct, rendering him more impartial between conflicting interests and sections, than any other statesman who has lived since the Revolution. —SEWARD, WILLIAM H., 1852, *Remarks on the Death of Mr. Clay, United States Senate.*

Mr. Clay, born in poverty and obscurity, had not even a common-school education, and had only a few months' clerkship in a store, with a somewhat longer training in a lawyer's office, as preparation for his great career. Tall in person, though plain in features, graceful in manner, and at once dignified and affable in bearing, I think his fervid patriotism and thrilling eloquence combined with decided natural abilities and a wide and varied experience to render him the American more fitted to win and enjoy popularity than any other who has lived. . . . The careless reader of our history in future centuries will scarcely realize the force of his personal magnetism, nor conceive how millions of hearts glowed with sanguine hopes of his election to the Presidency, and bitterly lamented his and their discomfiture. —GREELEY, HORACE, 1868, *Recollections of a Busy Life, p.* 168.

Mr. Clay's complexion was very fair; so fair, indeed, that I had supposed that his hair, when a young man, must have been of a sandy or yellowish tint; and on expressing that opinion to Mrs. Clay several years after his death, I was greatly surprised by her prompt reply, "You were never more mistaken; he had when a young man the whitest head of hair I ever saw." His eyes were gray, and when excited were full of fire; his forehead high and capacious, with a tendency to baldness; his nose prominent, very slightly arched, and finely formed. His mouth was unusually large without being disfiguring. It, however, was so large as to attract immediate notice; so large, indeed, that, as he said, "he never learned how to spit," he had learned to snuff and smoke tobacco, and but for his unmanageable mouth he would have learned to chew also. His chief physical peculiarity, however, was in the structure of his nervous system; it was so delicately strung that a word, a touch, a memory would set it in motion. But though his nervous system was thus sensitive, yet his emotions, however greatly excited, were of themselves never strong enough to disturb the self-poise of his deliberate judgment.—HARRISON, J. O., 1886, *Henry Clay, Century Magazine, vol.* 33, *p.* 179.

"The Apostle of Liberty," "The Gallant Harry of the West," "The Great Commoner," "The Great Pacificator," "Harry of the West," "The Judas of the West," "The Mill-Boy of the Slashes," "Old Chief," "The Savior of His Country."—FREY, ALBERT R., 1888, *Sobriquets and Nicknames, p.* 392.

I am fully conscious that critical readers, who are familiar with our parliamentary literature but never heard Clay speak, are ready to ask: "If Henry Clay's speeches were so very wonderful and captivating, why is it that nobody ever reads any of them now?" The answer to that question is that Henry Clay's speeches derived their irresistible power from his irresistible personality. It was *that*—his personality which took people captive. He spoke to an audience very much as an ardent lover speaks to his sweetheart when pleading for her hand. Everybody knows that the more successful a lover's speech is on such an occasion, the less readable it is when it gets into cold print. The lover speaks for the purpose of carrying his point and winning his cause just then and there, and is content with immediate success. It was the same with Henry Clay. He spoke to win his cause right there and then and gain a favorable verdict on the spot; and no lover was ever more ardent, more vehement, more impassioned, or more successful in his appeal than Clay; and he was content with his immediate success.—DYER, OLIVER, 1889,

Great Senators of the United States Forty Years Ago, p. 230.

About this time, Henry Clay, the great Kentucky orator, paid a visit to Rochester. I went to hear him speak at the Court House, the only place of public meeting, besides the church, Rochester could boast of in those days. Such oratory I had never heard before; nor have I met anything to equal it since. His voice had the peculiarly musical tone, at once sweet and sonorous, which proved so effective in the large assembly room in which we were gathered to hear him. That speech of Henry Clay affected me to a singular extent. It may sound a strange statement, but I don't think I should be talking extravagantly, if I declare that the orator Clay was the direct cause of my taking to the composition of descriptive songs. Certainly, it was his speech . . . that first put the idea into my head. While reading in my room, at the "Eagle" Hotel that night, I asked myself: Why, if Henry Clay could create such an impression by his distinct enunciation of every word, should it not be possible for me to make music the vehicle of grand thoughts and noble sentiments, to speak to the world through the power of poetry and song! The idea gained upon me. I became more and more fascinated with the thought, not only of trying my fortune as a vocalist, but also of composing my own songs. With me at that time to devise was to act. I commenced there and then to set to music Mackay's beautiful poem, "Wind of the Winter Night, Whence comest Thou?" All the night through I paced up and down my room arranging the music for the poem, and I remember that the notion uppermost in my mind was to infuse into my music, as it were, the subtle charm of the voice of Henry Clay. It was a quaint idea, but it took entire possession of my mind, and I hope my readers will not laugh at me for saying that I believe it inspired me. A few days later I had my musical rendering of Mackay's fine verses all ready, and I took the first opportunity of playing it over to some friends. They applauded it, and their praise was emphatic enough to be sincere. This success decided me. From that day, song composing became the serious object of my life.—RUSSELL, HENRY, 1895, *Cheer! Boys, Cheer! p.* 60.

ORATORY

In the entire roll of distinguished orators, British and American, there is hardly one whose printed speeches give so inadequate an idea of his powers as do those of Henry Clay. His eloquence was generally of a warm and popular rather than of a strictly argumentative cast, and abound in just those excellencies which lose their interest when divorced from the orator's manner and from the occasion that produced them, and in those faults that escape censure, only when it can be pleaded for them that they are the inevitable overflow of a mind too vividly at work to restrain the abundance of its current. . . . Probably no orator ever lived who, when speaking on a great occasion, was more completely absorbed in his theme.—MATHEWS, WILLIAM, 1878, *Oratory and Orators, pp.* 315, 319.

Clay was perhaps the first consummate party leader of the Congressional and platform type, Jefferson having worked, not on the platform, but in the closet and through the press. He was a paragon of the personal fascination now styled magnetism. Magnetic, indeed, his manner and voice must have been if they could make the speeches that he has left us pass for the most cogent reasoning and the highest eloquence. Yet multitudes came from distances, in those days immense, to hear him. A cynical critic said that Clay could get more people to listen to him and fewer people to vote for him than any other man in the Union. He however did get many votes though never quite enough. His power of winning the hearts of men was unique. When at last he missed his prize by losing the election for the Presidency his partisans wept like children; one of them is said to have died of grief. He was as ardently patriotic, after the warhawk fashion, but the Presidency was always in his thoughts and its attraction accounts for the perturbations of his political orbit. He said that he would rather be right than be President; but it has been too truly remarked that even at the moment of that memorable utterance he was thinking more of being President than of being right. His policy and sentiments were intensely American, and by the cosmopolitans would now be designated as jingo. He was a protectionist on what he deemed patriotic grounds, and the chief author of a system to which Hamilton had only moderately inclined.—SMITH, GOLDWIN, 1893, *The United States, An Outline of Political History*, 1492–1871, *p.* 179.

His honest convictions underlay his best eloquence. To express these was always the purpose of his speaking. Grand as was his utterance the thought behind it was broader and deeper than his expression of it, and his sincerity added weight to both. Bold and frank in his nature he had no inclination to palter in a double sense, and no wavering in his opinions and purposes. He could not be eloquent off the line of his strong convictions. On that line he was ardent, fearless and full of hope, with the rare power of inspiring others with his own sentiments and his own expectations And those who could not be swayed from their personal beliefs and interests paid tribute to the honesty and sincerity of his straightforward words. . . . He was an eloquent man in an age of eloquence and a statesman in an age of statesmanship. If he had not been more than a mere orator he would not have been an eminent one in such an age. If he had not had *êthos* which the ancients counted so highly, a devotion to that which is right and honorable; in a word if he had not been a greater man he could not in the judgment of his own time have been so great an orator.—SEARS, LORENZO, 1896, *The History of Oratory*.

GENERAL

In the speeches of Henry Clay there is a chivalric freshness which readily explains his great popularity as a man; not so profound as Webster, he is far more rhetorical and equally patriotic.—TUCKERMAN, HENRY T., 1852, *A Sketch of American Literature*.

His speeches are sincere and impassioned, qualities which distinguished the man, and which are among the chief causes of the great personal popularity which he enjoyed. Full, flowing, sensuous, his style of oratory was modulated by a voice of sustained power and sweetness, and a heart of chivalrous courtesy. — DUYCKINCK, EVERT A. AND GEORGE L., 1855–65–75, *Cyclopædia of American Literature, ed. Simons, vol.* I, *p.* 682.

The rare brightness of his intellect and his fertile fancy served, indeed, to make himself and others forget his lack of accurate knowledge and studious thought; but these brilliant qualities could not compensate for his deficiency in that prudence and forecast which are required for the successful direction of political forces. His impulses were vehement and his mind not well fitted for the patient analysis of complicted problems and of difficult political situations. His imagination frequently ran away with his understanding. His statesmanship had occasionally something of the oratorical character. Now and then he appeared to consider it as important whether a conception or a measure would sound well, as whether, if put into practice, it would work well.—SCHURZ, CARL, 1887, *Life of Henry Clay* (*American Statesmen*), *vol.* II, *p.* 409.

Sara Coleridge

1802–1852

The only daughter of the poet, was born at Keswick, and lived for many years with her uncle, Robert Southey. In 1829 she married her cousin, Henry Nelson Coleridge, who was the chief editor of the poet's "Table Talk" and "Literary Remains" (1836). She herself gave much assistance to this task, and was sole editor of the "Aids to Reflection." In 1837 she published her only original work, "Phantasmion," a long, romantic fairy story, that met with little appreciation at the time, but has since (in 1847) been re-issued by Lord Coleridge.—SANDERS, LLOYD C., *ed.*, 1887, *Celebrities of the Century*, *p.* 272.

PERSONAL

Last of the Three, though eldest-born,
Reveal thyself, like pensive morn,
Touched by the skylark's earliest note,
Ere humbler gladness be afloat.

. . . .

Her brow hath opened on me—see it there,
Brightening the umbrage of her hair;
So gleams the crescent moon, that loves
To be descried through shady groves.
Tenderest bloom is on her cheek;
Wish not for a richer streak;
Nor dread the depth of meditative eye;
But let thy love upon that azure field
Of thoughtfulness and beauty, yield
Its homage, offered up in purity.
— WORDSWORTH, WILLIAM, 1828, *The Triad*.

She was one of those whose thoughts are growing while they are in the act of speaking, and who never speak to surprise. Her intellectual fervour was not that which runs over in excitement; a quietude belonged to it, and it was ever modulated by a womanly instinct of reserve and dignity. She never thought for effect, as many do. She never found it difficult to conceive how others should differ from her in their conclusions. She was more a woman than those who had not a tenth part of her intellectual energy. The seriousness and softness of her nature raised her far above vanity, its coldness and its contortions. Her mind could move at once and be at rest.—DE VERE, AUBREY, 1873, *Letters, Recollections, p.* 198.

Of his [Hartley] sister Sara, it has been said that "her father looked down into her eyes, and left in them the light of his own." Her beauty and grace were as remarkable as her talents, her learning, and her accomplishments; but her chief characteristic was "the radiant spirituality of her intellectual and imaginative being." This, with other rare qualities of mind and spirit, is indicated in Wordsworth's affectionate appreciation in "The Triad," and conspicuous in her fairy-tale "Phantasmion," and in the letters which compose the bulk of her "Memoirs."—CAMPBELL, JAMES DYKES, 1894, *Samuel Taylor Coleridge, p.* 283.

GENERAL

Sterling remarked that she shows the limited nature of a woman's mind in her "Phantasmion;" she does not make Ariel an element, but the whole thing is Ariel, and therefore very wearisome and unsubstantial.—FOX, CAROLINE, 1843, *Memories of Old Friends, ed. Pym, Journal, Oct.* 30, *p.* 204.

With an imagination like a prism shedding rainbow changes on her thoughts, she shows study without the affectation of it, and a Greek-like closeness of expression.—BETHUNE, GEORGE WASHINGTON, 1848, *The British Female Poets, p.* 430.

Sara Coleridge's chief claim to remembrance in connection with literature lies in the essays and notes, mainly on controverted topics of theology and metaphysics, with which she illustrated the editions of her father's works that she superintended. They display learning rare in a woman, as well as a considerable power of speculation and of skill in dealing with the terms and propositions of metaphysics. But she had inherited from her father the tendency to over-refinement and subtlety rather than clearness of thought, and she had adopted from him his mode of speculation, in which baseless assumptions are often made to do the duty of sound arguments, and to serve as substructure for the most lofty but unsubstantial edifices of fancy. . . . The chief impression left by the letters is that Sara Coleridge's existence was far too much intellectualized. The sweet feminine soul was starved by the claims of the restless and dissatisfied intelligence. Her letters, even those to her husband, take the form of essays; they want the grace of easy friendly communication. She is always a little conscious of being seated in a lecturer's chair, and what she has to say must, to our regret, turn out at times, if not tedious, at least commonplace.—NORTON, CHARLES ELIOT, 1873, *Sara Coleridge, The Nation, vol.* 17, *p.* 426.

Great and various as were your mother's talents, it was not from them that she derived what was special to her. It was from the degree in which she had inherited the feminine portion of genius. She had a keener appreciation of what was highest and most original in thought than of subjects nearer the range of ordinary intellects. She moved with the lightest step when she moved over the loftiest ground. Her "feet were beautiful on the mountain tops" of ideal thought. . . . In this respect, I should suppose she must have differed from almost all women whom we associate with literature. I remember hearing her say that she hardly considered herself to be a woman "of letters." She felt herself more at ease when musing on the mysteries of the soul, or discussing the most arduous speculations of philosophy and theology, than when dealing with the humbler topics of literature.—DEVERE, AUBREY, 1873, *Memoirs and Letters of Sara Coleridge, ed. her Daughter, p.* 65.

The helpful, loving, and unselfish spirit which made her a willing and affectionate partner in her husband's labors, after his death took a more commanding form, and led her to dedicate the whole of her intellectual existence to the great object of carrying out a husband's wishes, of doing justice to a father's name. In the fulfillment of this sacred trust she found occasion to illustrate and adorn the works which fell under her editorship with several compositions of no inconsiderable extent, and displaying powers of critical analysis, and of doctrinal, political, and historical research and discussion, of no common order.—CONANT, S. S., 1873, *The Last of the Three, Harper's Magazize, vol.* 47, *p.* 898.

Sara Coleridge had not less genius than her brother Hartley, but she had nothing like the same gift of expression. She resembled her famous father in her tendency to lyric music, while Hartley's genius was distinctly inclined to express itself in more monumental forms.—SHARP, WILLIAM, 1886, *Sonnets of this Century, p.* 284, *note.*

After George Eliot's, we should pronounce Sara Coleridge's the most powerful female mind which has yet addressed itself to English literature. While deficient in no feminine grace, she is intellectually distinguished by a quality for which we can find no better name than manliness. She displays the strongest, massiest common sense, goes direct to the root of a matter, sweeps antagonism from her path in a twinkling, and exhibits a refreshing liberality, despite a burden of hereditary and conventional prejudice. Circumstances forced her learning and her reasoning faculty into prominence, her pious labours as her father's editor and annotator leaving her but little opportunity for the exercise of the imaginative gift which she had equally inherited from him. "Phantasmion," though too unsubstantial a work to create a permanent impression, shows that she possessed this endowment in rich measure, and the little lyrics scattered through its pages confer upon her a secure though a modest place among English poetesses.—GARNETT, RICHARD, 1892, *The Poets and the Poetry of the Century, Joanna Baillie to Mathilde Blind, ed. Miles, p.* 127.

His sister Sara likewise inherited intellectual and imaginative gifts probably little if at all inferior to his; but circumstances prevented her from making a great name. . . . Her only book is "Phantasmion," a fairy tale, whose lyric snatches prove her worthy of remembrance among English poetesses.—WALKER, HUGH, 1897, *The Age of Tennyson, p.* 61.

John Howard Payne

1792-1852

Born at New York, June 9, 1792: died at Tunis, April 10, 1852. An American dramatist, actor, and song-writer. He first appeared on the stage at New York in 1809, and fulfilled a number of engagements in other cities as "The American Juvenile Wonder," etc. He played also in England and Ireland, part of the time with Miss O'Neill. He retired from the stage in 1832, and was in Tunis as American consul 1843-45 and 1851-52. He is famous as the author of "Home, Sweet Home" (originally in the opera of "Clari"), and was author and translator and adapter of more than 60 plays.—SMITH, BENJAMIN E., *ed.*, 1894-97, *The Century Cyclopedia of Names, p.* 788.

PERSONAL

(Paris). Mary Lamb has begged me to give her a day or two. She comes to Paris this evening, and stays here a week. Her only male friend is a Mr. Payne, whom she praises exceedingly for his kindness and attentions to Charles. He is the author of "Brutus," and has a good face.—ROBINSON, HENRY CRABBE, 1822, *Diary, Aug.* 20; *Diary, Reminiscences and Correspondence, ed. Sadler, vol.* I, *p.* 477.

I hope it will bring you here. I should be most glad of that. I have a room for you, and you shall order your own dinner three days in the week. I must retain my own authority for the rest.—LAMB, CHARLES, 1822, *Letter to Payne, Nov; Letters, ed. Ainger, vol.* II, *p,* 49.

My Dear Sir:—It affords me great pleasure to comply with your request for the words of "Home, Sweet Home." Surely there is something strange in the fact that it should have been my lot to cause so many people in the world to boast of the delights of my home, when I never had a home of my own, and never expect to have one, now—especially since those here at Washington who possess the power, seem so reluctant to allow me the means of earning one!—PAYNE, JOHN HOWARD, 1851, *Letter to C. E. Clark.*

I became acquainted with him as the

editor of the *Thespian Mirror*, when he was about thirteen years of age. A more engaging youth could not be imagined; he won all hearts by the beauty of his person and his captivating address, the premature richness of his mind and his chaste and flowing utterance. — FRANCIS, JOHN W., 1857, *Old New York, p.* 213.

The banishment was overlong,
But it will soon be past;
The man who wrote home's sweetest song
Shall have a home at last!
And he shall rest where laurels wave
And fragrant grasses twine;
His sweetly kept and honored grave
Shall be a sacred shrine.
And pilgrims with glad eyes grown dim
Will fondly bend above
The man who sung the triumph hymn
Of earth's divinest love.

—CARLETON, WILL, 1883, *Coming Home at Last,* Harper's Weekly, Feb.* 10.

How much of Payne's success on the stage was due to his absolute merits as an actor, and how much to the curiosity he excited as a precocious lad, doing or attempting to do, work that only the most finished and mature tragedians had ever undertaken before in America, it is, of course, difficult now to determine. He certainly was associated, and in equal parts, with some of the most distinguished men and women in his profession, and with them he shared the honors and the applause. It must be confessed, however, that he did not grow in popularity as he grew in years, and that his later engagements were less successful, in a pecuniary way, than those of his youth. He seems to have become careless and indifferent, to have devoted less time to study and preparation, and it is believed that he was dissatisfied with the profession, and with his position in it, even before he went abroad in 1813.—HUTTON, LAWRENCE, 1883, *John Howard Payne the Actor, Magazine of American History, vol.* 9, *p.* 337.

And here, for the benefit of those who can appreciate an incident which seems almost unique in its pathos, I submit the following: One winter night in London, Payne was without money or credit, had not where to lay his head. He tried to quiet the pangs of hunger and homelessness by looking in at the windows, and from the areas scenting good cheer. It was Christmas eve, the snow fell fast, the wind was sharp and keen. At one luxurious house the hungry man stopped and watched the lighting of the Christmas tree. Its candles streamed brightly on the pavement, and among the evergreens he could see the red berries of holly, the toys and garlands, and the pretty heads of children. They danced and clapped their hands while the presents were being distributed and the air rang with shouts of laughter and screams of delight. When the merriment had spent itself a little, one young girl went to the piano and warbled "Sweet Home," while the family joined in the rousing chorus. And what a story! John Howard Payne—"Home, Sweet Home"—not a penny in the world—a lonely grave overlooking the ruins of Carthage—a death journey of several thousand miles—and a monument in the metropolis of his native land.—LANMAN, CHARLES, 1885, *Haphazard Personalities, p.* 236.

*On the proposed removal of the remains of John Howard Payne to this country.

To write the life of such a man as John Howard Payne is a task that requires much forbearance and a good judgment of human character. His varied talents, and his constantly changing disposition to follow this object and the other, causes the writer some difficulty in finding a climax to any of the many vocations which Mr. Payne attempted throughout his life. Yet with all the perplexities of his kaleidoscopic sort of mind, that at the least touch or turn of thought would lead him off to another form as unlasting as the one that had gone before, we cannot fail to see something to admire, and to make his life highly interesting to the reader.—HARRISON, GABRIEL, 1885, *Life and Writings of John Howard Payne, p.* 11.

GENERAL

Thirty-six consecutive performances of "Brutus," each attended by crowded and brilliant audiences, may be cited as a proof of the deep impression created by Kean in the character of the Roman patriot. The tragedy, or rather compilation, of "Brutus" exhibits no particular originality or skill on the part of Howard Payne, but when efficiently acted it is highly effective, and will never go in want of an intellectual and appreciative audience.—HAWKINS, F. W., 1869, *The Life of Edmund Kean, vol.* II, *p.* 66.

"Brutus, or the Fall of Tarquin," a

historical tragedy, by John Howard Payne. There is no originality or genius displayed in this drama, but, when well acted, it is highly effective on the stage.—CHAMBERS, ROBERT, 1876, *Cyclopædia of English Literature, ed. Carruthers.*

The acknowledged difficulty of writing a really great song brings to mind the fact that of all the songs endeared to us by early and familiar association there is not one that Americans can claim exclusively except this. Tender old ballads by the score we borrow from the Irish, Scotch, English and German, but of our own there is but one. The wonderful influence of "Home, Sweet Home" is not easily explained. Its spell is one of feeling, subtle as a perfume, which eludes the scalpel of the critic and defies analysis. Simple as the utterance of a child, it has the pathos of a strong man's yearning. It touches the heart by its suggestion of sympathy with all other hearts, and its soft tones bring to the dullest ear some echo of what Wordsworth calls

"The still, sad music of humanity."

—FAUST, A. J., 1883, *John Howard Payne, Catholic World, vol.* 37, *p.* 90.

Payne seems to have been a little inclined to the hearsay that the world owed him a living. The success of the beautiful music which has floated his commonplace words across the sea of time seems to have deceived him into the idea that he was an unappreciated genius, which was hardly true. We are told that it made him sad to hear the music boxes of foreign cities pour forth his immortal song when he had not a shilling in his pocket or a place to lay his head. But it was not his song which the hand-organs played; it was the unknown Italian's glorious melody; and if there are statues to be raised today, that unknown should have as high as the best of them. —CARPENTER, FRANK D. Y., 1883, *The Literary World, vol.* 14, *p.* 193.

Frederick William Robertson

1816–1853

Born in London, 3d February 1816, the son of an artillery captain, and was educated for the army at Beverley, Tours, and Edinburgh Academy and University. Resolving, however, to take orders, he studied at Brasenose, Oxford, 1837–40, and for nearly a year held a curacy at Winchester. His health broke down; but a walking tour on the Continent cured it, and at Geneva he married. In 1842 he became the curate of Christ Church, Cheltenham. His faith in Evangelicalism was shaken by the intolerance of its partisans. After holding for a time the curacy in Oxford, in 1847 he became incumbent of Trinity Chapel, Brighton, where his earnestness, originality, and wide sympathy arrested public attention. But the comprehensiveness of his Christian ideal exposed him to not a little odium—he was suspected alike by Evangelicals and High Churchmen. During his last years he suffered from disease of the brain. He resigned in June 1853 because his vicar had refused to confirm his nomination of a curate, and died 15th August 1853. He published but one sermon—the four series (1855, 1857, 1859–63) so well known over the English-speaking world are really recollections, sometimes dictated and sometimes written out. Yet another volume, "The Human Race, &c.," was issued in 1880. Other works are "Expository Lectures on St. Paul's Epistles to the Corinthians" (1859), "Lectures and Addresses (1858), "An Analysis of 'In Memoriam'" (1862), and "Notes on Genesis" (1877). See his "Life and Letters," by the Rev. Stopford A. Brooke (1865).—PATRICK AND GROOME, *ed.*, 1897, *Chambers's Biographical Dictionary, p.* 794.

PERSONAL

So lived and so died, leaving behind him a great legacy of thought, a noble gentleman, a Christian minister. To the tenderness of a true woman he joined the strong will and the undaunted courage of a true man. With an intellect at home in all the intricacies of modern thought, he combined the simple spirit of a faithful follower of Christ. To daring speculation he united severe and practical labour among men. Living above the world, he did his work in the world. Ardently pursuing after liberty of thought he never forgot the wise reticence of English conservatism. He preserved, amid a fashionable town, the old virtues of chivalry. In a very lonely and much-tried life he was never false or fearful. Dowered with great gifts of intellect, he was always humble; dowered with those gifts of the heart which are peculiarly perilous to their possessor, he never became their slave. He lived troubled on every side, yet not distressed; perplexed, but not in despair; persecuted, but not forsaken; cast down, but not destroyed; always bearing about in the body the dying of the Lord Jesus, that the life also of Jesus might be made manifest in his body. He died, giving up his spirit with his last words, in faith and resignation to his Father. He lies in a hollow of the Downs he loved so well. The sound of the waves may be heard there in the distance; and standing by his grave, it seems a fair and fitting requiem; for if the inquietude of the sea was the image of his outward life, its central calm is the image of his deep peace of activity in God.—BROOKE, STOPFORD A., 1865–66, *ed., Life and Letters of Frederick W. Robertson, vol.* II, *p.* 238.

We cannot think, and few besides his own friends will think, that he had laid his hand with so sure an accuracy and with so much promise upon the clue which others had lost or bungled over. But there is much to learn in his thoughts and words, and there is not less to learn from his life. It is the life of a man who did not spare himself in fulfilling what he received as his task, who sacrificed much in order to speak his message, as he thought, more worthily and to do his office more effectually, and whose career touches us the more from the shadow of suffering and early death that hangs over its aspirations and activity.—CHURCH, R. W., 1865–97, *Life of Frederick Robertson, Occasional Papers, vol.* II, *p.* 255.

The incidents in Robertson's life are few and unimportant; its dramatic interest lies in the inward conflict, which was incessantly renewed. However keenly wounded in his deepest affections, he made no sign of suffering; his soul was too proud, too noble to betray its secret anguish. His sermons give scarcely any indication of the conflicts within; few could guess how deeply agitated was the soul that could express itself with such quiet strength. Yet every word was perfectly sincere; the calmness was no mere mask, it was a manly self-conquest. He was like the young Spartan who kept a quiet face while the wild beast was gnawing at his vitals, and would have deemed it dishonour to betray his agony. The publication of Robertson's life was, therefore, a revelation to the readers of his sermons. It showed how much every sermon had cost him.—PRESSENSÉ, E. DE, 1880, *Contemporary Portraits, p.* 346.

I have been greatly impressed by the extraordinary influence which Robertson almost unconsciously exercised upon those who were brought within the range of his personal influence. I know many persons who have been brought into close personal relationship with celebrated men. But I have known no case in which the influence has been more profound and lasting than in the case of Robertson. His, indeed, was one of the most rare and radiant natures that, with all its errors and imperfections, has ever adorned humanity. He has left hardly anything which he distinctly designed for publication, but the letters, lectures, and sermons which he threw off, and which have been mainly preserved through the devotion of his friends, make up some eight volumes, which increasingly invite and repay analysis and criticism. But the man himself is infinitely greater than his utterances, and affords a study of the utmost pathos and interest.—ARNOLD, FREDERICK, 1885, *Robertson of Brighton, p.* 1.

Robertson, whose character, in all points that were comprehended within the region of morality, was not only stainless but exalted, nevertheless suffered from some minor defects disastrous in his public position—fiery vehemence, exaggerated sensitiveness, and an entire lack of humour. He went into fits of passion over his detractors' iniquity without any countervailing perception of their absurdity, and every petty annoyance still further impaired the nervous energy which, apart from all merely external causes, was continually preying upon itself.—GARNETT, RICHARD, 1896, *Dictionary of National Biography, vol.* XLVIII, *p.* 405.

In the portrait, a water-colour drawing executed by Basebé in 1853, . . . even casual students of physiognomy may read the soul and genius of Robertson. It is a superbly intellectual brow and forehead. The lines of close and constant thought are scored in every lineament of the face. But the expression is not merely that of a thinker: it is also that of a born leader of men, of one fitted equally for the task whether the leadership were moral or physical, an attack upon a redoubt, bristling with cannon and steel, or a resistance to the forces of social and religious corruption, banded in a corrupt age against gravity and truth. The scorn of the mean, of the false, of the low, lighting up the whole countenance, is that which so often illuminated in pulpit, on platform, and in private talk, the features of Arthur Penrhyn Stanley. The serenity of soul; betokened by the quiet eye, recalls in his happiest moments the tranquility that Jowett always seemed to have at his command.—ESCOTT, T. H. S., 1899, *Robertson of Brighton, Fortnightly Review, vol.* 72, *p.* 1002.

GENERAL

The publication of Mr. Robertson's "Letters" was considered to be of great importance. They seemed to add a personal interest to his "Sermons," to explain fully his mode of thought, to indicate the source of progress of many of his views, and to supplement his general teaching. They are full of tender human thought, of subtle and delicate feeling, and of much tried and suggestive experience. They possess also, in common with his "Sermons," a peculiar literary interest. This interest lies not so much in the originality of their ideas as in the mode in which these ideas are represented. The choice of words in them is remarkable. There is sometimes a happy indefiniteness which belongs to and which suggests the infinite nature of the things discussed. A spirit pervades them which influences unconsciously their reader, and renders him receptive of their truths, by inducing in him a kindred tone of heart. Even Robertson's slight sketches of an idea, traced perhaps in a single sentence, contain the materials for a finished composition. If he is not a Creator he is eminently a lucid Interpreter of thought. It is in this power of apt, logical, and striking expression that the chief *literary* interest of his writings consists.—BROOKE, STOPFORD A., 1865, *ed., Life and Letters of Frederick W. Robertson, vol.* I, *p.* xii.

I had once seen him, heard him preach, but he did not please me, and I did him no justice. Now I shall read his sermons which, from the impression I took, I had abstained from reading, and, very likely, I shall make him the subject of a lecture at Oxford.—ARNOLD MATTHEW, 1865, *Letters, ed. Russell, vol.* I, *p.* 362.

Robertson's "Sermons" have the merit of being very thoughtful and suggestive, but appear to me, both as to form and substance, to have been given to the world too much in the state of raw material. Perhaps you see more of the process of thought, which is no doubt interesting, but you miss the finished results.—THIRLWALL, CONNOP, 1866, *Letters to a Friend, ed. Stanley, Jan.* 5, *p.* 54.

Everything with him was done with a view to edifying. Wherever he quarried he was in search of spiritual ideas. Literature, science, history, art, furnished him material for sermons. He found moral significance in everything. The dryest text was juicy to him. He turned stones into bread. He was a brave man, too; he faced doubt; he did justice to skepticism and unbelief and denial; he dealt honestly with Romanist and with atheist, with Greek and Jew, as well as he could; and the ground of this honest dealing was his faith that truth was identical with itself under all the varieties of its symbolism. He poured the old wine into the new bottles and the new wine into the old bottles, in perfect confidence that no bottle would burst under the pressure of fermentation, and that no wine would be spilled in the hasty decanting from one vessel into another. He can find a great truth anywhere, and he can find an antique vase for every truth he discovers. . . . The reader is fascinated by the ingenuity, the brilliancy, the beauty, the swift legerdemain which shuffles meanings so deftly in and out; the boldness, the candor, the keenness, the charity, the seeming insight, are charming; but before long comes a sense of illusion and mystification; thoughtfulness pauses to ask if all this can be true; if the candor is quite candid or the fairness quite fair. The critical mind asks if there are then no distinctions; if there is not some trick about either the bottles or the wine; if everything is true, and everything is new, and everything is old, and where we are to stop in the process of legitimizing old credences and myths and superstition. Why should we not all be Romanists at once? Nay, for the matter of that, why should we not all be pagans? The glamour becomes so painfully bewildering to some persons that they lay down the volume in a sort of despair.—FROTHINGHAM, O. B., 1869, *Robertson's Sermons The Nation, vol.* 9, *p.* 413.

Men there are with such fullness of the higher life in their brains that they overflow procreatively upon their fellows. Of this chosen few was Robertson, one of those deep, pure, abundant human springs that, at far intervals along our track, gush up strong and clear, where all may drink and be slaked, the laborer and the lord, the scholar and the artisan, man and woman. The depth and beauty and limpidity and, I will add, the practicality, of Robertson's teaching all come from its spirituality. Few are as intelligent as he; and so spiritually-minded I know, in our generation, of no man who has been in the public eye. He was a many-sided man, morally and intellectually. Had he not been what he became,—a light such as shone from no other pulpit within the British realm,—he might have made himself an influential parliamentary orator, or a far-eyed military leader, foremost in the advance, or a brilliant scientific expounder.—CALVERT, GEORGE H., 1874, *Brief Essays and Brevities, p.* 115.

The influence of Robertson increases every day; he stands acknowledged as one of the greatest minds of the age, and as the happy exponent of its best aspirations. His theology is not exempt from the imperfections of a transition period. It should rather be regarded as representing in its noblest phase an era of deep religious agitation.—PRESSENSÉ, E. DE, 1880, *Contemporary Portraits, p.* 318.

The name of Frederick Robertson is on many accounts remarkable. There is probably no one of our time whose writings have had such an extended influence after his death, and who yet was during his lifetime so little known except to the immediate circle to whom he ministered. His extraordinary merits as a preacher were acknowledged in that limited range, but beyond this, although from time to time his fame reached the outer world, yet his manner, his voice, his appearance, were entirely unknown. . . . How remarkable is the contrast of this obscurity with his widespread popularity in after years! It is not too much to say that he has become, beyond question, the greatest preacher of the nineteenth century, the most widely admired, and with the most powerful reasons for this wide-spread judgment.—STANLEY, ARTHUR PENRHYN, 1882, *Frederick W. Robertson, Century, vol.* 23, *p.* 559.

It was in all the nobler qualities of thought, insight, and feeling that he excelled; as it is these qualities that still live in his sermons and have made them such a marvellous power. He was characteristically a Thinker in the Pulpit. He went straight to the heart of every subject that he touched, and with a rare combination of imaginative and dialectic power brought out all its meaning. He felt a truth before he expressed it; but when once he felt it, and by patient study had made it its [his] own, he wrought it with the most admirable logic—a logic closely linked, yet living in every link—into the minds of his hearers. This live glowing concatenated sequence of thought is seen in all his greater sermons. It could only have been forged in a brain stirred to its depths—on fire with the ideas which possessed him for the time—yet never mastered by, always mastering, his subject. This impress of creative force as he proceeded in his sermons gives them their wonderful perfection of form amidst all their hurrying energy. They are many of them great as literary compositions, with a living movement rare even in the higher literature. The truth is, they were literally the creation of moments of inspired utterance. We cannot imagine them written in cold blood. Their organization shows a heated yet controlled enthusiasm.—TULLOCH, JOHN, 1885, *Movements of Religious Thought in Britain During the Nineteenth Century, p.* 192.

Robertson was not merely fervent with the impassioned energy of youth (he died at thirty-seven) and eloquent with the earnestness of deep conviction, but he was the most quickening and suggestive of thinkers. He denied creeds and formulas only to affirm more grandly the truths at their heart.—PITMAN, ROBERT C., 1888, *Books that Have Helped Me, The Forum, vol.* 4, *p.* 609.

Robertson had a vein of reflective sentiment, an almost feminine softness, sadness, and the wistful reflectiveness about him, which had a sympathetic attraction beyond that of any of his contemporaries.—OLIPHANT, MARGARET O. W., 1892, *The Victorian Age of English Literature, p.* 339.

Open the sermons of Robertson where

you will, take him on any subject, you will find him teaching plain, simple, common sense. He is never hampered by tradition, yet never violent. He is never daring you to follow him. He simply unfolds the truth and makes it luminous with the choicest words. He treats old faiths with the utmost respect. He brings out what truths there are in them, and with a magic touch transforms them into life and beauty. With him the atonement loses its harsh and vindictive character, the doctrine of the trinity becomes natural and plausible, prophecy is changed from petty prediction to the grandest statement of universal truths, regeneration becomes a plain necessity to ever true nature, and Christ is the fulfillment of the longing desire of imperfect man.—BISBEE, R. E., 1896, *An Inspired Preacher, The Arena, vol.* 15, *p.* 191.

Robertson's preaching is not very easy to judge, because the published sermons are admittedly not what was actually delivered, but after-reminiscences or summaries, and the judgment is not rendered easier by the injudicious and gushing laudation of which he has been made the subject. He certainly possessed a happy gift of phrase now and then, and remarkable earnestness.—SAINTSBURY, GEORGE, 1896, *A History of Nineteenth Century Literature, p.* 377.

Owes his position entirely to the celebrated sermons which he preached at Brighton during the last six years of his life. They are not great in scholarship, nor even in eloquence, but they exhibit a character of many-sided attractiveness which was the real secret of Robertson's power.—WALKER, HUGH, 1897, *The Age of Tennyson, p.* 157.

Amelia Opie

1769-1853

Amelia Opie (*b.* 1769, *d.* 1853), daughter of Dr. Alderson of Norwich, was well known as a writer of tales and novels, and as a leader in the literary and artistic society of the first half of this century. Her first story was "Father and Daughter" (1801), and it was followed by "Adeline Mowbray" (1804). Both enjoyed high reputation and wide popularity. She also published a collection of "Poems" (1802), "Simple Tales" (1806), and "Tales of Real Life" (1813). Her "Memorials," containing passages from her diaries and letters, edited by Cecilia Brightwell (1854), have considerable historic interest.—SANDERS, LLOYD C., *ed.*, 1887, *Celebrities of the Century, p.* 798.

PERSONAL

Mrs. Opie's habits are very singular. At Norwich she lives in seclusion, attends at the Quaker meeting-house, and visits nobody. When she comes to town, her house is the scene of an eternal levée, and who is so busily gay as Mrs. Opie?—BOWRING, SIR JOHN, 1822-77, *Autobiographical Recollections, p.* 351.

I owed Mrs. Opie a grudge for having made me in my youth cry my eyes out over her stories; but her fair, cheerful face forced me to forget it. She long ago forswore the world and its vanities, and adopted the Quaker faith and costume; but I fancied that her elaborate simplicity, and the fashionable little train to her pretty satin gown, indicated how much easier it is to adopt a theory than to change one's habits.—SEDGWICK, CATHERINE, 1841, *Letters from Abroad.*

Dined with Amelia Opie; she was in great force and really jolly. Exhibited her gallery, containing, some fine portraits by her husband, one being of her old French master, which she insisted on Opie painting before she would accept him. She is enthusiastic about Father Mathew; reads Dickens voraciously; takes to Carlyle, but thinks his appearance against him; talks much and with great spirit of people, but never ill-naturedly.—FOX, CAROLINE, 1843, *Memories of Old Friends, ed. Pym, Journal, Oct.* 22, *p.* 203.

During Mr. Opie's life, excitements abounded. After his death and when her mourning was over, she wrote little novels, read them to admiring friends in Norwich, who cried their eyes out at the pathetic scenes, read in her dramatic manner, and then she carried them to London, got considerable sums by them, enjoyed the homage they brought to her feet, sang at supper-tables, dressed splendidly, did not scruple being present at Lady Cork's and others' Sunday concerts, and was very nearly marrying a younger brother of Lord Bute. Lord Herbert Stewart's carriage appeared, and made a great clatter in the narrow streets of Norwich; and the old gentleman was watched into Dr. Alderson's house; and the hours were counted which he spent, it was supposed, at Mrs. Opie's feet. But it came to nothing. For a while she continued her London visits; and her proud father went about reading her letters about her honors. But she suddenly discovered that all is vanity: she took to gray silks and muslin, and the "thee" and "thou," quoted Habakkuk and Micah with gusto, and set her heart upon preaching. That, however, was not allowed.—MARTINEAU, HARRIET, 1853, *Biographical Sketches, p.* 17.

I knew her as a Quakeress, and as the gayest and pleasantest member of the pleasantest and most intelligent society in London. Unluckily, as a Norwich woman, she was thrown among the Gurneys, and took a fancy to Joseph John, who, after she had very literally set her Quaker cap at him, married a pretty girl of seventeen. She had been previously engaged to Lord Herbert Stewart—a match which had gone off, because in that age, when broughams and pages were not, they could not muster money enough for such an establishment as their wants required in married people, so she remained the artist's widow, yearning ever after the Quakerly proselytism for her old pleasant society, and certainly attending the May meetings that she might creep into more parties under their cover. —MITFORD, MARY RUSSELL, 1853, *Letter to Miss Jephson, Oct.* 6; *The Friendships of Mary Russell Mitford, ed. L'Estrange.*

Her countenance was animated, bright and beaming; her eyes soft and expressive, yet full of ardour; her hair was abundant and beautiful, of auburn hue, and waving in long tresses. Her figure was well formed, her carriage fine, her hands, arms, and feet well shaped—and all around and about her was the spirit of youth and joy and love. —BRIGHTWELL, CECILIA LUCY, 1854, *Memorials of the Life of Amelia Opie, p.* 35.

She joined the Society of Friends conscientiously, she adhered to it with perfect fidelity, and she never repented. But it was the work of the influence of zealous friends, and it changed little in her life. . . . It was a sacrifice, no doubt, but it was not made in the fervent and productive years; hence it never worked any of those radical changes which gives so much significance to renunciation.—KAVANAGH, JULIA, 1862, *English Women of Letters, p.* 288.

When Mrs. Opie became a gay widow, we often met her at the house of a mutual friend, where her eccentric conduct amused some, and disgusted others. I have seen her astonish a grave circle of elderly people by jumping up and dancing a shawl-dance then in vogue on the stage, flourishing away to a tune of her own singing, apparently unconscious of the effect she was producing. She used to carry about with her in all her visits a pretty little stringed instrument, in the classic form of a lyre, and sing her own songs, with great expression, to that accompaniment. She said she could always find out the secrets of a young girl's heart, if she could sing to her alone. She tried her experiment on me and proved right.—FARRAR, MRS. JOHN, 1866, *Recollections of Seventy Years, p.* 25.

A bird-of-paradise suddenly descending to pick up crumbs in an English farmyard could scarcely have created more astonishment among Dame Partlet's brood than did this pea-hen among the supberbly dressed and jeweled dames of the Parisian *salon.* The good General seemed to know her well, rose and greeted her with the grace of the days he had so largely helped to spoil —when a French gentleman was known to be the gentleman *par excellence.* Dear Mrs. Opie: she seemed utterly indifferent to the murmurs of inquiry and surprise that would have confounded any one less self-possessed and turned to us with that sweet *navieté* which was at all periods of her life her especial charm. — HALL, SAMUEL CARTER, 1883, *Retrospect of a Long Life, p.* 228.

She had a temperament both excitable and indolent, and essentially pleasure-loving. With a sufficient income, absolute independence and leisure, many flatterers, and no close home ties or duties, she might easily have drifted into aimless self-indulgence in the world *où l'on s'amuse,* had she been without the restraints of deepened religious feeling, and a creed which especially enjoined temperance, moderation and quietness.—MAYER, GERTRUDE TOWNSHEND, 1894, *Women of Letters, vol.* II, *p.* 113.

GENERAL

Mrs. Opie has pathetic scenes, but the object is not attained; for the distress is not made to arise from the unnuptial union itself, but from the opinions of the world against it; so that it may as well be taken to be a satire on our prejudices in favour of marriage as on the paradoxes of sophists against it.—MACKINTOSH, SIR JAMES, 1805, *Life, ed. Mackintosh, vol.* I, *ch.* V.

We cannot place Mrs. Opie so high in the scale of intellect as Miss Edgeworth; nor are her Tales, though perfectly unobjectionable on the score of morality, calculated to do so much good. They are too fine for common use, and do not aim at the correction of errors, and follies of so extensive and fundamental a nature. She does not reason so powerfully; and she is not sufficiently cheerful: indeed, she is too pathetic to be read with much advantage to practical morality. Her writings, however, are very amiable and very beautiful, and exhibit virtuous emotions under a very graceful aspect. They would do very well to form a women that a gentleman should fall in love with, but can be of no great use in training ordinary mortals to ordinary duties.—JEFFREY, FRANCIS LORD, 1806, *Mrs. Opie's Simple Tales, Edinburgh Review, vol.* 8, *p.* 470.

Mrs. Opie's "Lays for the Dead" is a book of truest beauty: and, although the perusal of it resembles (from the mournfulness of its subjects) a visit to a churchyard, the effect it produces upon us is of a most pleasing character. It hushes all unquiet emotion; bids the cares of earth far into the distance; and awakens a calm, sweet pensiveness of feeling, which nothing could make us wish to change. We seem to converse with the Past and the Departed, and to stand on the very shore of the great ocean of Eternity.—ROWTON, FREDERIC, 1848, *The Female Poets of Great Britain, p.* 283.

Her stories, "Father and Daughter," "Tales of the Heart," "Temper," etc., as their titles show, were tales of real life, written with a rather too obvious moral, and hardly vigor enough to keep them alive.—RICHARDSON, ABBY SAGE, 1881, *Familiar Talks on English Literature, p.* 334.

It would be impossible to attempt a serious critique of Mrs. Opie's stories. They are artless, graceful, written with an innocent good faith which disarms criticism. That Southey, Sydney Smith, and Mackintosh should also have read them and praised them may, as I have said, prove as much for the personal charm of the writer, and her warm sunshine of pleasant companionship, as for the books themselves. They seem to have run through many editions and to have received no little encouragement. Morality and sensation alternate in her pages. Monsters abound there. They hire young men to act base parts, to hold villainous conversations which the husbands are intended to overhear. They plot and scheme to ruin the fair fame and domestic happiness of the charming heroines, but they are justly punished, and their plots are defeated.—RITCHIE, ANNE ISABELLA THACKERAY, 1883, *A Book of Sibyls, p.* 184.

As a novelist Mrs. Opie is a woman of first-rate genius; all she does flows from the heart, and where she depicts the heart in its delicate and morbid feelings she has scarcely any equal, and never a superior. But in painting character in general (except some few admirable instances), in devising incident, or in weaving the plot of a tale, she is very defective, and sins so frequently against probability, that one wonders how she could manage so badly or devise such absurdities. The truth is she has nothing of mere cleverness and very little tact. All she does well, she does *exceedingly well;* there is no mediocrity either in her faults or her beauties; such is the force of her *genius,* that when she pours forth her own feelings she takes yours by storm, and you can praise her only by your emotions and your tears; she leaves you no power to discuss her merits. —BRAY, ANNA ELIZA, 1883, *Autobiography, ed. Kempe, p.* 140.

Mrs. Opie's poems still retain some hold upon public attention. Judged by our own canons of taste, she cannot be refused credit for real poetical feeling.—ROBERTSON, ERIC S., 1883, *English Poetesses, p.* 104.

It is recorded of Mrs. Inchbald, that on making Mrs. Opie's acquaintance, she (Mrs. Inchbald) exclaimed after a short conversation, "You're cleverer than your books!" It was most true. Mrs. Opie was rapid, careless, often superficial: and, if we were to judge her by her novels and tales, we might say that any present reading of them would leave a poor impression of their author's power. Yet she sometimes constructed and developed a plot extremely well; and there were some social points upon which she was really strong. She was a good observer; and her remarks on matters of conduct and principle were sometimes delivered with wisdom and even with weight.—TAYLOR, EMILY, 1884, *Memories of Some Contemporary Poets, p.* 87.

Mrs. Opie's poems are simple in diction. Two or three of them are deservedly found in every anthology, and one, "There seems a voice in every gale," is well known as a hymn. Her novels, which were among the first to treat exclusively of domestic life, possess pathos and some gracefulness of style, but belong essentially to the lachrymose type of fiction, and are all written to point a moral.—LEE, ELIZABETH, 1895, *Dictionary of National Biography, vol.* XLII, *p.* 229.

John Wilson

Christopher North

1785–1854

Born, at Paisley, 18 May 1785. Studied at Glasgow Univ., 1797–1803. Matric. Magdalen Coll., Oxford, 26 May 1803; Newdigate Prize Poem, 1806; B. A., 1807; M. A., 1810. Student of Lincoln's Inn, 1806. Settled at Ellerlay, Windermere, 1807. Married Jane Penny, 11 May 1811; she died, 1837. Contrib. to "Annual Register," 1812. Called to Scottish Bar, 1815. In Edinburgh, 1815–17. Contrib. to "Edinburgh Monthly Mag.," 1817; to "Edinburgh Review," 1817. Literary editor, and contributor (under pseud. "Christopher North"), to "Blackwood's Mag.," Oct. 1817 to Sept. 1852. Prof. of Moral Philosophy, Edinburgh Univ., 1820–51. Pres. of Edinburgh Philosophical Institution, 1847–54. Crown Pension, 1851. Died in Edinburgh, 3 April 1854. Buried in Dean Cemetery, Edinburgh. *Works:* "The Isle of Palms," 1812; "The Magic Mirror," 1812; "The City of the Plague," 1816; "Lights and Shadows of Scottish Life" (under pseud. "Arthur Austin"), 1822; "The Trials of Margaret Lindsay" (anon.), 1823; "The Foresters" (anon.), 1825; "Poetical and Dramatic Works" (2 vols.), 1825; "The Land of Burns" (with R. Chambers; 2 vols.), 1840; "Blind Allan" (anon.) [1840?]; "On the Genius and Character of Burns," 1841; "Recreations of Christopher North" (from "Blackwood"; 3 vols.), 1842; "Noctes Ambrosianæ" (from "Blackwood"; anon.), 1843; Letter-press to "Scotland Illustrated," 1845; "Specimens of the British Critics" (from "Blackwood"; pubd. in Philadelphia), 1846. *Collected Works:* ed. by Prof. Ferrier (12 vols.), 1855–58. *Life:* by Mrs. Gordon, new edn., 1879.—SHARP, R. FARQUHARSON, 1897, *A Dictionary of English Authors, p.* 301.

PERSONAL

He is an eccentric genius, and has fixed himself upon the banks of Windermere, but occasionally resides in Edinburgh, where he now is. . . . He seems an excellent, warm-hearted, and enthusiastic young man; something too much, perhaps, of the latter quality, places him among the list of originals.—SCOTT, SIR WALTER, 1812, *Letter to Joanna Baillie, Jan.* 17; *Lockhart's Life of Scott, ch.* xxiv.

A very robust, athletic man, broad across the back—firm-set upon his limbs—and having altogether very much of that sort of air which is inseparable from the consciousness of great bodily energies. I suppose in leaping, wrestling, or boxing, he might easily beat any of the poets, his contemporaries. . . . In complexion, he is tne best specimen I have ever seen of the genuine or ideal *Goth.* His hair is of the true Sicambrian yellow; his eyes are of the lightest, and at the same time of the clearest blue. . . . I had never suspected, before I saw him, that such extreme fairness and freshness of complexion could be compatible with so much variety and tenderness, but, above all, with so much depth of expression. . . . I have never seen a physiognomy which could pass with so much rapidity from the serious to the most ludicrous of effects. It is more eloquent, both in its gravity and in its levity, than almost any countenance I am acquainted with is in any one cast of expression.—LOCKHART, JOHN GIBSON, 1819, *Peter's Letters to his Kinsfolk, Letter* xii.

Last night I supped with John Wilson,

Professor of Moral Philosophy here, author of the "Isle of Palms," &c., a man of the most fervid temperament, fond of all stimulating things, from tragic poetry down to whisky punch. He snuffed and smoked cigars and drank liquors, and talked in the most indescribable style. It was at the lodging of one John Gordon, a young very good man from Kirkcudbright, who sometimes comes here. Daylight came on us before we parted; indeed, it was towards three o'clock as the Professor and I walked home, smoking as we went. I had scarcely either eaten or drunk, being a privileged person, but merely enjoyed the strange volcanic eruptions of our poet's convivial genius. He is a broad sincere man of six feet, with long dishevelled flax-coloured hair, and two blue eyes keen as an eagle's. Now and then he sank into a brown study, and seemed dead in the eye of law.—CARLYLE, THOMAS, 1827, *Letter to John Carlyle; Thomas Carlyle, A History of the First Forty Years of his Life, ed. Froude, vol.* I. *p.* 324.

I went to hear a lecture on "Moral Philosophy" from Professor Wilson, the celebrated editor of *Blackwood's Magazine.* He is what some people would think a fine-looking man; but to my eye there appeared to be something excessively low and gross in his countenance. His lecture was, in parts, pretty good. His appearance was that of a man who had been spending the whole night at the shrine of Bacchus, and had just got himself gathered together to discharge what appeared to him a very irksome duty. His papers were all to regulate when he came to his chair; and four times he had to stop in the lecture till he found the right piece of paper, to enable him to go on with his remarks.—BLAKEY, ROBERT, 1838, *Memoirs, p.* 113.

Cock-fighting, wrestling, pugilistic contests, boat-racing, horse-racing, all enjoyed Mr. Wilson's patronage; all were occasionally honored by his personal participation. I mention this in no unfriendly spirit toward Professor Wilson; on the contrary, these propensities grew out of his ardent temperament and his constitutional endowments—his strength, speed, and agility: and, being confined to the period of youth—for I am speaking of a period removed by five-and-twenty—can do him no dishonour amongst the candid and the judicious. . . . And, though a man of prudence cannot altogether approve of his throwing himself into the convivial society of gipsies, tinkers, potters, strolling players, &c., nevertheless it tells altogether in favour of Professor Wilson's generosity of mind, that he was ever ready to forego his advantage of station and birth, and to throw himself fearlessly upon his own native powers, as man opposed to man. Even at Oxford he fought an aspiring shoemaker repeatedly—which is creditable to both sides; for the very *prestige* of the gown is already overpowering to the artisan from the beginning, and he is half beaten by terror at his own presumption. Elsewhere he sought out, or, at least, did not avoid the most dreaded of the local heroes; and fought his way through his "most verdant years," taking or giving defiances to the right and to the left in perfect carelessness, as chance or occasion offered. No man could well show more generosity in these struggles, nor more magnanimity in reporting their issue, which naturally went many times against him.—DE QUINCEY, THOMAS, 1840–89, *Lake Reminiscences, Works, ed. Masson, vol.* II, *pp.* 432, 433.

Walking up and down the hall of the courts of law . . . was a tall, burly, handsome man of eight-and-fifty, with a gait like O'Connell's, the bluest eye you can imagine, and long hair—longer than mine—falling down in a wild way under the broad brim of his hat. He had on a surtout coat, a blue checked shirt; the collar standing up, and kept in its place with a wisp of black neckerchief; no waistcoat; and a large pocket-handkerchief thrust into his breast, which was all broad and open. At his heels followed a wiry, sharp-eyed, shaggy devil of a terrier, dogging his steps as he went slashing up and down, now with one man beside him, now with another, and now quite alone, but always at a fast, rolling pace, with his head in the air, and his eyes as wide open as he could get them. I guessed it was Wilson, and it was. A bright, clear-complexioned, mountain-looking fellow, he looks as if he had just come down from the Highlands, and had never in his life taken pen in hand.—DICKENS, CHARLES, 1841, *Letter, Life by Forster, vol.* I, *p.* 253.

The cottage of Wilson at Elleray is a simple, but elegant little villa, standing on high ground overlooking Windermere, but at the distance of some miles. As you approach Ambleside from Kendal, you pass, as you begin to descend the hill toward Lowood, a gate leading into a gentleman's grounds. The gateway is, on either side, hung with masses of the Ayrshire rose. There is a poetical look about the place; and that place is the country retreat of John Wilson. A carriage-road, winding almost in a perfect circle, soon introduces you to a fine lawn, surrounded by plantations, and before you, on a swelling knoll, you discern the cottage. It is hung with ivy and Ayrshire roses; and commands a splendid view over the lake, and all the mountains round. At the back a plantation of larches ascends the hill, screening it from the north. At the foot of these plantations, and sheltered in their friendly bosom, lie the gardens, with bees, and the pleasant nooks for reading or talk.—HOWITT, WILLIAM, 1847, *Homes and Haunts of the Most Eminent British Poets, vol.* II, *p.* 505.

In the multiform nature of Wilson his mastery over the hearts of ingenuous youth is one of his finest characteristics. It was often won in this peculiar way: An essay is submitted to him as professor, editor, or friend, by some worthy young man. Mr. Wilson does not like it, and says so in general terms. The youth is not satisfied, and, in the tone of one rather injured, begs to know specific faults. The generous Aristarch, never dealing haughtily with a young worth, instantly sits down, and begins by conveying, in the most fearless terms of praise, his sense of that worth; but, this done, woe be to the luckless piece of prose or "numerous verse!" Down goes the scalpel with the most minute savagery of dissection, and the whole tissues and ramifications of fault are laid bare. The young man is astonished; but his nature is of the right sort; he never forgets the lesson; and with bands of filial affection stronger than hooks of steel he is knit for life to the man who has dealt with him thus.—AIRD, THOMAS, 1852, *Memoir of D. M. Moir.*

On a bright frosty day in December, 1827, as I was quitting the mathematical class in the University of Edinburgh, of which I had been a member about two months, one of my class fellows said suddenly: "If you want to see Christopher North, he's yonder!" . . . A faded, tattered gown, put on carelessly, fluttered in the keen wind, and seemed a ludicrous appendage to as fine, tall, manly a figure, and free, fearless bearing, as I have ever looked upon. As he came nearer, his limbs and their motions gave the idea of combined strength, agility, and grace; and there was a certain sort of frank, buoyant unaffectedness about his demeanour that seemed to indicate light-hearted consciousness of great mental and physical endowments. When he came near enough for his face to be seen with distinctness, in it I forgot everything else about him; and I shall never forget the impression it produced. . What a magnificent head! How finely chiselled his features! What compression of the thin but beautifully formed lips! What a bright blue flashing "Eye, like Mars, to threaten or command!" Add to all this the fair transparent complexion, flowing auburn hair, and the erect commanding *set* of his head upon his shoulders, and surely no Grecian sculptor could have desired anything beyond it. As for his eye it lightened on me as he passed, and suddenly disappeared. — WARREN, SAMUEL, 1854, *A Few Personal Recollections of Christopher North, Blackwood's Magazine, vol.* 76, *p.* 731.

Such a presence is rarely seen; and more than one person has said that he reminded them of the first man, Adam; so full was that large frame of vitality, force, and sentience. His tread seemed almost to shake the streets, his eye almost saw through stone walls; and as for his voice, there was no heart that could stand before it. He swept away all hearts, whithersoever he would.—MARTINEAU, HARRIET, 1854, *Biographical Sketches, p.* 23.

He was well known in the houses of the poor. No humble friend was ever cast aside if honest and upright. During the summer, an old servant of my mother's, who had formerly lived many years in her service, had fallen into bad health, and was ordered change of air. She was at once invited to Roslin, . . . but the change was of little service. . . . That she was considerately tended and soothed . . . was only what was to have been expected, but it was an infrequent sight to see my father, as early dawn streaked the sky, sitting by the bedside of the dying woman, arranging with gentle but awkward hand the pillow beneath her head, or cheering her with encouraging words, and reading, when she desired it, those portions of the Bible most suitable to her need.—GORDON, MRS. MARY, 1862, *"Christopher North," A Memoir of John Wilson, ed. Mackenzie, pp.* 385, 386.

His handwriting, curiously enough, reflected the change which occurred in his intellectual temperament when he forsook verse for prose. The manuscript of the "Isles of Palms," that dreamy and paradisaical tale of the sea, is singularly elegant and clear; but as he advanced in years, and threw himself impetuously into that poetic prose which proved so congenial to him, his manuscript broke the fetters of neatness and precision, and became bounding and leaping, hurrying along in almost illegible haste, and evidently tasked to the uttermost to keep pace with the rapid outpourings of the mental fountains.—PATTERSON, R. H., 1862, *Essays in History and Art, p.* 515.

Wilson's eloquence was of a very brilliant kind, but it had not the condensation necessary for the highest flights of oratory. He was enthusiastic, poetical, diffuse, but not weighty. With an unbounded command of language and romantic imagery, he wanted those brief expressions and burning thoughts which strike home to the human heart. Hence his speeches sounded better at the time than they appeared on reflection; and while they delighted all present, left little that could be carried away or stored in the memory.—ALISON, SIR ARCHIBALD, 1867, *Autobiography, ed. Alison, vol.* I. *p.* 195.

Christopher North was himself a kind of Thor and Baldur in one, with a touch of the frost-giant in him to boot. Now we find him daring dangerous Windermere in a snow-storm, in darkness too, vainly trying for hours to recover shore, and nearly dying of cold. "Master was well-nigh frozen to death," reported his man Billy, "and had icicles a finger long hanging from his hair and beard." Next evening, like as not, he is at Charles Lloyd's fine mansion dancing with the belle of the Lakes —gracefulest dancer he in the district! And when the first breath of spring has called out the wild flowers, lo! he is amid them, perhaps calling the Greek Meleager to his aid to tell them how lovely they are, and then how perfect must she be who is lovelier—that aforesaid Belle of Brathay! —CONWAY, MONCURE D., 1880, *The English Lakes and their Genii, Harper's Magazine, vol.* 62, *p.* 17.

Mr. Fields was present at some one of his lectures, however, and he always said in after life that Professor Wilson's method and manner with his students was his ideal of what the relation of a teacher to his scholars should be. The eager way in which he talked to them, his whole heart being in his work, made it impossible for their thoughts to wander. They were fascinated by his living interest in their behalf. "Ah, that is what lecturing to students can be made," he was accustomed to say.—FIELDS, ANNE, 1889, *A Second Shelf of Old Books, Scribner's Magazine, vol.* 5, *p.* 465.

John Wilson was one of the most interesting figures of a time when learning was at a premium; he was a big man amongst big men, and even in this irreverential time genius uncovers at the mention of his name. His versatility was astounding; with equal facility and felicity he could conduct a literary symposium and a cock-fight, a theological discussion and an angling expedition, a historical or a political inquiry and a fisticuffs. Nature had provided him with a mighty brain in a powerful body; he had a physique equal to the performance of what suggestion so ever his splendid intellectuals made. To him the incredible feat of walking seventy miles within the compass of a day was mere child's play; then, when the printer became clamorous, he would immure himself in his wonderful den and reel off copy until that printer cried "Hold; enough!" It was no unusual thing for him to write for thirteen hours at a stretch; when he worked he worked, and when he played he played—that is perhaps the reason why he was never a dull boy.—FIELD, EUGENE, 1895, *The Love Affairs of a Bibliomaniac, p.* 176.

In 1837 he sustained the supreme bereavement by losing his beloved and devoted wife. His grief on this occasion was profound and lasting, and a touching picture of its uncontrollable outbursts in the presence of his class has been preserved. There, if anything occurred to renew the memory of his sorrow, he would pause for a moment or two in his lecture, "fling himself forward on the desk, bury his face in his hands, and while his whole frame heaved with visible emotion, would weep and sob like a very child." So, in his work and his play, his joy and his sorrow, the whole man was cast in an heroic mould.—DOUGLAS, SIR GEORGE, 1897, *The Blackwood Group* (*Famous Scots Series*), *p.* 35.

He lived to be an old man—one of the landmarks of the faithful city which has a knack of turning its favourites into demigods. A Norse demigod, not a Greek, was Wilson, with his yellow locks hanging about his great shoulders. It is one of the recollections of my early days to have been taken to see him—a young writer, much abashed with so novel a character—when he was near the end of his life. My companion and patron was Dr. Moir, the gentle "Delta" of *Blackwood*, the well-beloved physician, whom everybody delighted to honour. Professor Wilson came to us, large and loosely clad, with noiseless large footsteps such as some big men have the gift of: his hair thin, which had been so abundant, and dimmed out of its fine colour, but still picturesquely falling about his ears, making a background for his still ruddy countenance.—OLIPHANT, MARGARET O. W., 1897, *William Blackwood and his Sons, vol.* I, *p.* 315.

Wilson was a turbulent personality, with a whimsical strain of romance and poetry, a few stray notions of literary criticism, and an overflowing torrent of animal spirits which he himself and many of his contemporaries accepted as genius. But of any power of concentrated or systematic thought he was absolutely destitute. He might carry on the traditions which made literary criticism one of the subjects of philosophical disquisition, but it was in a method and with aims far different from those of his predecessors. He was open to literary impressions by which they were unstirred, and he caught something of the spirit of a school of poetry which had not arisen in their day; but for philosophical speculation he was incapable either by nature or by training.—CRAIK, SIR HENRY, 1901, *A Century of Scottish History, vol.* II, *p.* 226.

NOCTES AMBROSIANÆ

There is not so curious and original a work in the Englinsh or Scotch languages. It is a most singular and delightful outpouring of criticism, politics, and descriptions of feeling, character, and scenery, of verse and prose, and maudlin eloquence, and especially of wild fun. It breathes the very essence of the Bacchanalian revel of clever men. And its Scotch is the best Scotch that has been written in modern times.—COCKBURN, HENRY LORD, 1830–54, *Memorials of His Time, ch.* v.

The Ettrick Shepherd of the "Noctes Ambrosianæ" is one of the finest and most finished creations which dramatic genius ever called into existence. . . . In wisdom the shepherd equals the Socrates of Plato; in humor he surpasses the Falstaff of Shakspeare.—FERRIER, JAMES, 1855, *ed., Noctes Ambrosianæ.*

Verily, they are Walpurgis Nights, these "Noctes Ambrosianæ." The English language contains nothing so grotesque as some of their ludicrous descriptions, nothing so graphic, so intense, so terrible, as some of their serious pictures; no dialogue more elastic, no criticism more subtle, no gossip more delightful, no such fine diffusion, like the broad eagle wing, and no such vigorous compression, like the keen eagle talon; but when we remember, besides, that the "Noctes" contain *all* these merits combined into a wild and wondrous whole, our admiration of the powers displayed in them is intensified to astonishment, and, if not to the pitch of saying, "Surely a greater than Shakspeare is here," certainly to that of admitting a mind of cognate and scarce inferior genius.—GILFILLAN, GEORGE, 1855, *A Third Gallery of Portraits, p.* 375.

It must be confessed that the "Noctes Ambrosianæ" are not easy things to commend to the modern reader, if I may use the word commend in its proper sense and with no air of patronage. Even Scotchmen (perhaps, indeed, Scotchmen most of all) are wont nowadays to praise them rather apologetically, as may be seen in the case of their editor and abridger Mr. Skelton. Like most other very original things they drew after them a flock of imbecile imitations; and up to the present day those who have lived in the remoter parts of Scotland must know or recently remember dreary compositions in corrupt following of the "Noctes" with exaggerated attempts at Christopher's worst mannerisms, and invariably including a ghastly caricature of the Shepherd.—SAINTSBURY, GEORGE, 1886, *Christopher North, Macmillan's Magazine, vol.* 54, *p.* 174.

There is imperishable stuff in the "Noctes." That famous series has not the even excellence—the close grain—of Holmes's "Breakfast-Table" papers. There is too much of it, and it should be read with judicious skipping. A large part of the dialogue is concerned with matters of temporary interest. The bacchanalian note in it becomes at time rather forced, and the reader wearies of the incessant consumption of powldoodies, porter, and Welsh rabbits.—BEERS, HENRY A., 1893, *"Crusty Christopher" (John Wilson), The Century, vol.* 45, *p.* 362.

Poetry, sport, and revelry were three fountains of inexhaustible inspiration; and it was from an intimate blending of the most vivid joys of all three that his most original and lasting work proceeded. Tavern meetings with good cheer and good society, long tramps among the heathery glens—"glorious guffawing," as the Wilsonian Hogg put it, "all night, and immeasurable murder all day,"—were the elements which, flung across the rich refracting medium of his imagination, envolved those unique compounds of poetry, wit, humour, drama, high spirits, and balderdash—the "Noctes Ambrosianæ." —HERFORD, C. H., 1897, *The Age of Wordsworth, p.* 73.

It would not seem that these Symposia were under any regular system at first or subjected to any editorship. When they began it was frequently Lockhart who was the author, sometimes Maginn (after the advent of that still more unruly contributor): occasionally Hogg had, or was allowed to suppose that he had, a large share in them. Finally they fell into the hands of Wilson, and it is chiefly his portion of these admirable exchanges of literary criticism and comment which have been preserved and collected. To produce them required many gifts beyond these of the moralist or critic. A certain amount of creative skill and dramatic instinct, in addition to the flow of wit and power of analysis and analogy, was necessary to one who had to keep up a keen argument single-handed, like a Japanese juggler with his balls, especially when every man who was supposed to speak was a notable man, whose thoughts and diction could both be easily indentified; or to carry out all the quibs of a prolonged jest, in which the tempers of some of the interlocutors were naturally roused, and free speaking was the rule; while, on the other hand, the number of subjects which had to be touched upon in a monthly commentary upon the doings of the world was very great.—OLIPHANT, MARGARET O. W., 1897, *William Blackwood and his Sons, vol.* I, *p.* 201.

A poet of little mark, but an essayist and *causeur* of commanding and singularly varied powers, whose "Noctes Ambrosianæ," though always somewhat of a stumbling-block to the Southron reader, still preserves for those who have attained the proper "point of view" the original charm of its gaiety, wit, and dramatic humour, its criticism, and its occasional passages of admirably eloquent prose.—TRAILL, HENRY DUFF, 1897, *Social England, vol.* VI, *p.* 31.

NOVELS

It ["Margaret Lindsay"] is very beautiful and tender; but something cloying, perhaps, in the uniformity of its beauty, and exceedingly oppressive in the unremitting weight of the pity with which it presses on our souls. Nothing was ever imagined more lovely than the beauty, the innocence, and the sweetness of Margaret Lindsay, in the earlier part of her trials; and nothing, we believe, is more true, than the comfortable lesson which her tale is meant to inculcate,—that a gentle and affectionate nature is never inconsolable nor permanently unhappy, but easily proceeds from submission to new enjoyment. —JEFFREY, FRANCIS LORD, 1823–44, *Secondary Scotch Novels, Contributions to the Edinburgh Review, vol.* III, *p.* 530.

Professor Wilson's great strength as a prose writer lies in his power of pathetic description; and here he has never been surpassed. As a delineator of Scottish pastoral life—his "Lights and Shadows," his "Trials of Margaret Lindsay," and his "Foresters" seem destined to remain unapproached in their peculiar excellencies, and have as fair a chance of becoming immortal as any thing of a similar character in the English language.—CLEVELAND, CHARLES D., 1853, *English Literature of the Nineteenth Century, p.* 607.

Wilson is too Ossianic in his style of narration and description; and had he attempted a novel in three or four volumes, it had been absolutely illegible. Even "Margaret Lindsay," his longest tale, rather tires before the close, through its sameness of eloquence and monotony of pathos; only very short letters should be *all* written in tears and blood.—GILFILLAN, GEORGE, 1855, *A Third Gallery of Portraits, p.* 385.

POETRY

Almost the only passions with which his poetry is conversant are the gentler sympathies of our nature,—tender compassion, confiding affection, and guiltless sorrow. From all this there results, along with a most touching and tranquilizing sweetness, a certain monotony and languor, which, to those who read poetry for amusement merely, will be apt to appear like dullness, and must be felt as a defect by all who have been used to the variety, rapidity, and energy of the more popular poetry of the day. The poetry before us, on the other hand, is almost entirely contemplative or descriptive. — JEFFREY, FRANCIS LORD, 1816, *Wilson's City of the Plague, Edinburgh Review, vol.* 26, *p.* 461.

His poetical powers are very varied,—that is, he can handle any subject in its own peculiar spirit. His "Edith and Nora" is one of those fairy fictions of which he once promised a volume; there is a wondrous beauty shed over the landscape on which he brings out his spiritual folk to sport and play and do good things to men; nor has he wasted all his sweetness on the not-insensible earth; he has endowed his fairies with charms from a hundred traditions, assigned them poetic and moral tasks, and poured inspiration into their speech. Another fine poem of his is "An Address to a Wild Deer;" for bounding elasticity of language, hurrying thoughts, and crowding imagery, it is without a parallel. Indeed, throughout all his smaller poems there is a deep feeling for nature; an intimate knowledge of the workings of the heart; and a liquid fluency of language almost lyrical.—CUNNINGHAM, ALLAN, 1833, *Biographical and Critical History of the Literature of the Last Fifty Years.*

Wilson is most successful as a descriptive poet. His fancy is somewhat too exuberant, his metaphors too profuse: but they are from life and nature, and not from the elder bards. He has great delicacy of sentiment, and some of his delineations of character are not surpassed in English poetry. His morality is never hesitating or questionable. In all his works there is no sentiment of doubtful application.—GRISWOLD, RUFUS W., 1844, *The Poets and Poetry of England in the Nineteenth Century, p.* 245.

The grand characteristics of the poetry of Wilson are delicacy of sentiment and ethereal elegance of description. He refines and elevates whatever he touches, and if in his hands common things lose their vulgar attributes, they are exchanged by him for something better. . . . Wilson makes nearer approach, in tone of thought, to the Lake School than to any other great class of writers; nor do his ideas of the philosophical principles of composition seem widely different from theirs; but he never offends, like them, by endeavouring to extract sentiment from incongruous subjects. . . . The great defect in the earlier poetry of Professor Wilson will be found to result from "the fatal facility" with which he found expression for his exuberant riches of thought and imagery.—MOIR, D. M., 1851–52, *Sketches of the Poetical Literature of the Past Half-Century.*

As to his poetry, I cannot say that it has been underrated,—I only say that it has been eclipsed by his splendid prose. But in the "Isle of Palms" and "The City of the Plague," to say nothing of his smaller poems, there is much which "the world will not willingly let die." Scott, Southey, and Wilson are men who, had they never written prose, would have stood higher among Poets than they do. . . . As for Professor Wilson, his poetry has been almost traditional, full of beauty though it be, since it became overshadowed by the multifarious brilliancy and fecundity of Kit North. — MACKENZIE, R. SHELTON, 1854, *Life of Professor Wilson, Noctes Ambrosianæ, vol.* II, *pp.* xxiv, xxv.

His poetry is the Sabbath of his soul. And there are moods of mind—quiet, peaceful, autumnal moments—in which you enjoy it better than the poetry of any one else.—GILFILLAN, GEORGE, 1855, *A Third Gallery of Portraits, p.* 388.

Wilson's poetry was not such as we would have looked for from one who was a "varra bad un to lick" at a wrestling bout, and who made the splinters fly when his bludgeon went thwacking into a page of controversial prose. His verse is tender; it is graceful; it is delicate; it is full of langours too; and it is tiresome—a gentle girlish treble of sound it has, that you can hardly associate with this brawny mass of manhood.—MITCHELL, DONALD G., 1897, *English Lands Letters and Kings, The Later Georges to Victoria, p.* 45.

CRITICISM

You did late review my lays,
Crusty Christopher;
You did mingle blame and praise
Rusty Christopher.
When I learnt from whom it came,
I forgave you all the blame,
Musty Christopher;
I could not forgive the praise
Fusty Christopher.
—TENNYSON, ALFRED LORD, 1833, *To Christopher North, Poems.*

Though the *Edinburgh*, the *Quarterly*, and the *Westminster* are the chief of our critical periodicals, we are by no means disposed to consider them as alone influencing our literature. In truth, some of the best disquisitions on poetry ever penned in the island belong not to them, but to *Blackwood's Magazine*, and are by a true poet, John Wilson. The imagination which Jeffrey wants, he has to overflowing; the mercury of his genius stands as high as that of any one. He has fancy for the highest and humour for the lowest; and in no flight or vagary can any genius indulge in which he cannot sympathize. Such a singular combination of qualities was perhaps never before known. He will dream with the proudest poet that ever sat on Parnassus, and then leave a heavenly superstructure, worthy of the imagination of Martin, to snickle hares and rabbits with some poacher at its base. —CUNNINGHAM, ALLAN, 1833, *Biographical and Critical History of the Literature of the Last Fifty Years.*

A living writer of the most ardent and enthusiastic genius, whose eloquence is as the rush of mighty waters.—HALLAM, HENRY, 1837-39, *Introduction to the Literature of Europe, vol.* II, *pt.* ii, *ch.* v.

His contributions to "Blackwood's Magazine" raised the whole tone and character of periodical literature. The keenest wit, the most playful fancy, the most genial criticism, the deepest pathos, were lavished, year after year, with a profusion almost miraculous.—KNIGHT, CHARLES, 1847-48, *Half-Hours with the Best Authors.*

The whole literature of England does not contain a more brilliant series of critical essays than those with which he has enriched the pages of *Blackwood's Magazine;* and, which is rarer still, the generosity of feeling by which they are distinguished equals their critical acuteness and delicacy of taste. . . . If his criticisms have any imperfections, it is that they are too indulgent. He is justly alive to faults, and, when obliged to notice, signalizes them with critical justice; but the generosity of his nature leads him rather to seek for excellences, and, when he finds them, none bestows the meed of praise with more heartfelt fervor.—ALISON, SIR A., 1853-59, *History of Europe,* 1815-52, *ch.* v.

His critical papers on Homer and Spenser have a magnificent breadth and eloquence, rarely, if ever before, found in disquisitions of that class, and his essays on our modern poets—on Thomson, Burns, Wordsworth, Coleridge, and Crabbe—exhibit profound sympathy with the creations and temperaments of genius and insight into the sources of emotion and passion. A "frater feeling strong" impelled his teeming fancy and his fluent pen. . . . The collective works of Professor Wilson have not been generally popular. When seen in a mass, they had a character of sameness and repetition. Much of the original freshness was gone; both bloom and odour had perished in the using.—CARUTHERS, ROBERT, 1860, *Encyclopædia Britannica, Eighth ed., vol.* XXI, *p.* 878.

His literary criticism, though interesting as the utterance of a rich personality, is seldom wise or sure.—BEERS, HENRY A., 1893, *"Crusty Christopher" (John Wilson), The Century, vol.* 45, *p.* 362.

GENERAL

Wilson's papers, though not perfect have a masterly cast about them: a little custom would make him the best periodical writer of the age,—keep hold of him.—HOGG, JAMES, 1817, *Letter to Blackwood, William Blackwood and his Sons, ed. Oliphant, vol.* I, *p.* 324.

A man of great power and acquirements, well known to the public as the author of the "City of the Plague," "Isle of Palms," and other productions.—BYRON, LORD, 1820, *Observations upon an Article in Blackwood's Magazine.*

Wilson had much nobleness of heart, and many traits of noble genius, but the central *tie-beam* seemed always wanting; very long ago I perceived in him the most irreconcilable contradictions; Toryism with *sansculottism;* Methodism of a sort with total incredulity; a noble, loyal and religious nature, not *strong* enough to vanquish the perverse element it is born into. Hence a being all split into precipitous chasms and the wildest volcanic tumults; rocks overgrown indeed with tropical luxuriance of leaf and flower, but knit together at the bottom—that was my old figure of speech —only by an ocean of whisky punch. On these terms nothing can be done. Wilson seemed to me always by far the most *gifted* of all our literary men either then or still; and yet intrinsically he has written nothing that can endure. The central gift was wanting.—CARLYLE, THOMAS, 1854, *Journal, April* 29; *Thomas Carlyle, A History of His Life in London, ed. Froude, vol.* II.

In Wilson's "Lights and Shadows of Scottish Life," and in his other Scottish stories, we have, unless my impression of them deceives me, a spirit of lyrical pathos, and of poetical Arcadianism, which tinges, without obscuring, the real Scottish colour, and reminds us of the Lake poet and disciple of Wordsworth, as well as of the follower of Scott; while in his "Noctes Ambrosianæ," he burst away in a riot of Scotticism of which Scott had never ventured—a Scotticism not only real and humorous, but daringly imaginative and poetic, to the verge of Lakism and beyond —displaying withal an originality of manner natural to a new cast of genius, and a command of resources in the Scottish idiom and dialect unfathomed even by Scott.—MASSON, DAVID, 1859, *British Novelists and Their Styles, p.* 216.

Was he not a man?—Oh, large, brave heart, yet tender as a child! *But no letter-writer!* What a pity that the bulk of the work should have been so increased by letters which are little else than so much dead weight,—scarce half a dozen of them worth the paper. Aside from these, there is a fresh air blowing upon us from out the spirit of the man, which seems to breathe over and through us something of his rejoicing health and strength.—DANA, RICHARD HENRY, 1863, *Letter to James T. Fields, Nov.* 24; *Biographical Notes and Personal Sketches, p.* 148.

As regards Wilson's style, it has been said by Mr. Hallam that "his eloquence is like the rush of mighty waters." He greatly admired Jeremy Taylor; and while, from temperament, he does not display the same habitual breathless eagerness in the accumulation of words but pours out his full eloquence with less appearance of excitement, he often reminds us of Taylor's manner in his way of following out picturesque similitudes. Comparing them upon one point only, and disregarding other characteristics, we should say that of the two Taylor is more rhetorical, and Wilson the more eloquent: Taylor rather accumulates his wealth of expression upon given themes; Wilson flows out spontaneously and often somewhat irrelevantly to the subject in hand, concerning what strongly interested him in real life: Taylor can flexibly bring his powers to bear upon any subject; Wilson, although from the width of his interests the distinction is not glaringly obtrusive, is copious only when he happens to strike a plentiful spring in his own nature. With all Wilson's Nimrod force and abounding animal spirits, perhaps his richest and most original vein of expression is connected with his love of peaceful beauties in natural scenery.—MINTO, WILLIAM, 1872-80, *Manual of English Prose Literature, p.* 543.

Notwithstanding the exuberance of his imaginative faculty the ornateness of his English, the purity of his language is well preserved in the easy, clear flowing periods which mark the "Essays;" the style in which he wrote was more specially characteristic of that period in literature than ours.—LEE, RUDOLPH, 1891, *"Christopher North," The Westminster Review, vol.* 136, *p.* 320.

On the poetic imagination, then, he looms as one heroically proportioned; whilst more practical thinkers will cherish his memory as that of a most brilliant contributor to the periodical literature of his day, a great inspirer of youth, and a standard and pattern to his countrymen of physical and intellectual manhood.—DOUGLAS, SIR GEORGE, 1897, *The Blackwood Group* (*Famous Scots Series*), *p.* 46.

He cannot help his delightfully wanton play with language and sentiment; and into whatever sea of topics he plunged—early or late in life—he always came up glittering with the beads and sparkles of a highly charged rhetoric.—MITCHELL, DONALD G., 1897, *English Lands Letters and Kings, The Later Georges to Victoria*, p. 43.

Wilson covers some even pages of quarto in discussing the matter [Thomson's treatment of Burns]. He goes into it in great detail, and with that tiresome redundancy of diction and "blather" (to use a favourite term of his own) for which he was famous.—HADDEN, J. CUTHBERT, 1898, *George Thomson the Friend of Burns*, p. 139.

It happened the other day, in the library of a remote house, that I lighted upon a shelf of old *Blackwoods*, from fifty to sixty years old, and, being confined to the house by wet weather, read largely in them. Christopher North was at his glory then, with his flagrant egotism and stupid bellowings.—BENSON, ARTHUR CHRISTOPHER, 1894, *Essays*, p. 292.

For rapid, daring, vehement, electrifying bursts of straightforward rushing eloquence, as a matter of course defective in the very best kinds of chiselled or intricate beauty, but full of splendour, he is, where really inspired, unrivalled in his own generation; and the last impressions of him left on a reader's mind are those of amazing energy and fire. — HILLIER, ARTHUR CECIL, 1899, "*Christopher North*," *Temple Bar*, vol. 116, p. 75.

John Gibson Lockhart

1794-1854

Born, at Cambusnethan, Lanarkshire, 14 July 1794. At school in Glasgow. At Glasgow Univ., 1805–09. Matric. Balliol Coll., Oxford, as Exhibitioner, 16 Oct. 1809; B. C. L., 1817. Studied Law in Edinburgh, 1813–16; Advocate, 1816. Travelled in Germany, 1816–17; visited Goethe at Weimar. Contrib. to "Blackwood's Mag." from Oct. 1817. Friendship with Sir Walter Scott begun, May 1818. Married Sophia Scott, 29 April 1820. Lived at Chiefswood, near Abbotsford. Active literary life. Removed to London, 1825. Edited "Quarterly Review," 1825–53. Called to Bar at Lincoln's-Inn, 22 Nov. 1831. D. C. L., Oxford, 13 June 1834. Auditor of the Duchy of Lancaster, 1843. Withdrew from society in later years. In Italy, winter 1853–54. Died, at Abbotsford, 25 Nov. 1854. Buried in Dryburgh Abbey. *Works:* "Peter's Letters to his Kinsfolk" (under pseud. "Peter Morris"), 1819; "Valerius" (anon.), 1821; "Some passages in the life of Mr. Adam Blair" (anon.), 1822; "Reginald Dalton" (anon.), 1823; "The History of Matthew Wald" (anon.), 1824; "Life of Robert Burns," 1828; "History of Napoleon Buonaparte" (anon.), 1829; "History of the late War," 1832; "Memoirs of the Life of Sir Walter Scott" (7 vols.), 1836-38; "Songs of the Edinburgh Squadron" (anon.), 1839; "The Ballantyne Humbug Handled," 1839; "Theodore Hook" (anon.), 1852. He *edited:* Motteux's translation of "Don Quixote," 1822; Sir W. Scott's "Poetical Works" (under initials J. G. L.), 1833–34; Byron's Works (with Sir W. Scott), 1835; and *translated:* "Ancient Spanish Ballads," 1823. *Life:* "Life and Letters," by A. Lang, 1897.—SHARP, R. FARQUHARSON, 1897, *Dictionary of English Authors*, p. 171.

PERSONAL

To Moore, Lockhart offers a strong and singular contrast. Tall, and slightly, but elegantly formed, his head possesses the noble contour, the precision and harmony of outline, which distinguish classic sculpture. It possesses, too, a striking effect of color, in a complexion pale yet pure, and hair as black as the raven's wing. Though his countenance is youthful (he seems scarce more than thirty), yet I should designate reflection as the prominent, combined expression of that broad, white forehead; those arched and pencilled brows; those retired, yet full, dark eyes; the accurately chiselled nose; and compressed, though curved lips. His face is too thin, perhaps, for mere beauty; but this defect heightens its intellectual character. —GRIFFIN, EDMUND D., 1829, *Pencillings*.

When it is considered what literary celebrity Lockhart has gained so early in life, and how warm and disinterested a friend he has been to me, it argues but little for my sagacity that I scarcely recollect anything of our first encounters. He was a mischievous Oxford puppy, for whom I was terrified, dancing after the young ladies, and drawing caricatures of every one who came in contact with him.

But then I found him constantly in company with all the better rank of people with whom I associated, and consequently it was impossible for me not to meet with him. I dreaded his eye terribly; and it was not without reason, for he was very fond of playing tricks on me, but always in such a way that it was impossible to lose temper with him. I never parted company with him that my judgment was not entirely jumbled with regard to characters, books and literary articles of every description. Even his household economy seemed clouded in mystery; and if I got any explanation, it was sure not to be the right thing.—HOGG, JAMES, 1832, *Autobiography, p.* 469.

A precise, brief, active person of considerable faculty, which, however, had shaped itself *gigmanically* only. Fond of quizzing, yet not *very* maliciously. Has a broad black brow, indicating force and penetration, but the lower half of face diminishing into the character at best of distinctness, almost of triviality. Rather liked the man, and shall like to meet him again.—CARLYLE, THOMAS, 1832, *Journal, Jan.* 21: *Early Life of Thomas Carlyle, ed. Froude, vol.* II, *p.* 188.

Among some other places I went to afterwards was John Murray's,—the publisher's,—where I fell in with Lockhart, with whom I have exchanged cards this week, but whom I had not seen. He is the same man he always was and always will be, with the coldest and most disagreeable manners I have ever seen. I wanted to talk with him about Prescott's "Ferdinand and Isabella," and by a sort of violence done to myself, as well as to him, I did so. He said he had seen it, but had heard no opinion about it. I gave one with little ceremony, which I dare say he thought was not worth a button; but I did it in a sort of tone of defiance, to which Lockhart's manner irresistibly impelled me, and which I dare say was as judicious with him as any other tone, though I am sure it quite astonished Murray, who looked . . . as if he did not quite comprehend what I was saying.—TICKNOR, GEORGE, 1838, *Journal, March* 29; *Life, Letters and Journals, vol.* II, *p.* 147.

Those who best know him have spoken cordially and gratefully of his kindly nature—among these were Hogg, Moore, Sterling, and Haydon. A certain *hauteur* of manner, which sometimes was even supercilious, has contributed to strengthen the opinion that he was cold, proud, and distant. But he has been afflicted with deafness for many years,—an ailment which naturally checks the geniality of one's nature, by preventing familiar companionship.— MACKENZIE, R. SHELTON, 1854, *ed., Noctes Ambrosianæ, Memoir of John Gibson Lockhart, vol.* III, *p.* xv.

Lockhart lived in an age of literary animosities. He played an active, a manly, and sometimes a mischievous part in the intellectual life of his day. He had a clear "complication-proof" head, a quick temper, a pitiless pen, and a dangerous sense of humor. He was loyal and loving to his friends, and not particularly forgiving to his foes. He failed to understand the valuable art of hedging, and prudence and amiability were by no means his characteristic virtues. When we add to these natural qualifications of making enemies, the ill-will aroused by the acrimonious warfare of political creeds, and the curious fact that personal abuse of the Whigs by the Tories has always been accounted a graver crime than personal abuse of the Tories by the Whigs, we comprehend why Lockhart has carried on his shoulders for half a century the weight of other people's sins, just as Claverhouse bears the blame of all the brutality committed by the royalists in Scotland, and Sidney Smith is held responsible for every witticism uttered in his day.—REPPLIER, AGNES, 1896, *In the World of Art and Letters, The Cosmopolitan, vol.* 22, *p.* 222.

He has been spoken of as cold, heartless, incapable of friendship. We have written in vain, and his own letters are vainly displayed, if it be not now recognised that the intensity of his affections rivalled, and partly caused, the intensity of his reserve. Garrulous lax affections and emotions are recognised and praised: ready tears, voluble sorrows, win sympathy,—and may have forsaken the heart they tenanted almost in the hour of their expression. Lockhart felt too strongly for words, and his griefs were "too great for tears," as the Greek says. His silence was not so much the result of a stoical philosophy, as of that constitutional and ineradicable play of nature which, when he was a child, left his cheeks dry while others wept, and ended in a malady of voiceless grief. He was born to be so, and to be misconstrued. . . . Unfortunate in so much, Lockhart was most happy in a wife and daughter who inherited the sweetness of spirit of their father and their grandfather. To their influence, in part, we may trace the admirable qualities which, in his later years, contrasted with the acerbity of his early manhood. To adapt the noble phrase of the Greek historian, "Being a man, he bore manfully such things as mortals must endure."—LANG, ANDREW, 1896, *ed., The Life and Letters of John Gibson Lockhart, vol.* II, *pp.* 408, 412.

A man of many gifts and accomplishments, a good scholar, a keen satirist and critic, a powerful novelist, an excellent translator. He was accomplished with the pencil as well as with the pen, and some of his caricatures are at once irresistibly amusing and profoundly true. His "Scotch judge" and "Scotch minister" would make the reputation of a number of *Punch*. His biting wit won for him the *sobriquet* of "the Scorpion;" but notwithstanding his sting he won and retained through life many warm friends.—WALKER, HUGH, 1897, *The Age of Tennyson, p.* 136.

He was slim and straight and self-contained, a man of elegance and refinement—words dear to the time—in mind as in person, dark of hair and fine of feature, more like a Spaniard than a Saxon, a perfect contrast to the Berserker hero by his side. They were both of that class which we flatter ourselves in Scotland produces many of the finest flowers of humanity, the mingled product of the double nation—pure Scot by birth and early training, with the additional polish and breadth of the highest English education: Glasgow College, as it was then usual to call that abode of learning, with Oxford University to complete and elaborate the strain. . . . All energy and darting wit on one side, all kindness and tender domestic feeling on the other; fastidious, keen, refined, yet quite capable of picking up the coarsest missile, and flinging it with a sudden impulse hotter and swifter than anything the ruddy Berserker was capable of. Men like Wilson are to be found everywhere in Scotland, if seldom with his endowment of genius. Men like Lockhart are very rare anywhere.—OLIPHANT, MARGARET O. W., 1897, *William Blackwood and his Sons.*

PETER'S LETTERS TO HIS KINSFOLK
1819

What an acquisition it would have been to our general information to have had such a work written, I do not say fifty, but even five-and-twenty years ago! and how much of grave and gay might then have been preserved, as it were in amber, which have now mouldered away. When I think that, at an age not much younger than yours, I knew Black, Ferguson, Robertson, Erskine, Adam Smith, John Home, &c., and at least saw Burns, I can appreciate better than any one the value of a work which, like this, would have handed them down to posterity in their living colours.—SCOTT, SIR WALTER, 1819, *Letter to Lockhart, July* 19; *Scott's Life by Lockhart, ch.* xlv.

A worthless book, will give you some idea of the state of literature in Edinburgh at this time: it was in great vogue three years ago, but is now dead as mutton.—CARLYLE, THOMAS, 1823, *Early Letters, ed. Norton, p.* 294.

It gives us the pictures, mental and bodily, of some of the leading men of Scotland with great truth and effect. It is a singular hotch-potch, and full of wit and humour.—CUNNINGHAM, ALLAN, 1833, *Biographical and Critical History of the Literature of the Last Fifty Years.*

Nobody but a very young and a very thoughtless person could have dreamed of putting forth such a book. . . . Since I have alluded to "Peter's Letters" at all, I may as well take the opportunity of adding that they were not wholly the work of one hand.—LOCKHART, JOHN GIBSON, 1836–38, *Life of Sir Walter Scott, ch.* xlv.

A prying criticism may discern a few of those contraband epithets and slipshod sentences, more excusable in *young* "Peter's Letters to his Kinsfolk," where, indeed, they were thickly sown, than in the production of a grave Aristarch of British criticism.—PRESCOTT, WILLIAM HICKLING, 1838, *Sir Walter Scott, Biographical and Critical Miscellanies.*

VALERIUS
1821

It is an attempt, in short, which, though creditable to the spirit and talents of the author, we think he has done wisely in not seeking to repeat, and which, though it has not failed through any deficiency of his, has been prevented, we think, from succeeding by the very nature of the subject.—JEFFREY, FRANCIS LORD, 1823, *Secondary Scotch Novels, Edinburgh Review, vol.* 39, *p.* 180.

Though the skeleton was dug out of the grave, he has clothed it so dexterously with flesh and muscle, and breathed into it so strongly the breath of life, that it seems the work of nature.—CUNNINGHAM, ALLAN, 1833, *Biographical and Critical History of Literature of the Last Fifty Years.*

Seems to me one of the most remarkable works of fiction ever composed.— —BRYANT, WILLIAM CULLEN, 1852, *Orations and Addresses, p.* 55.

The most successful attempt which has ever yet been made to engraft the interest of modern romance on ancient story: its extreme difficulty may be judged by the brilliant genius of Bulwer having alone rivaled him in the undertaking. —ALISON, SIR ARCHIBALD, 1853,-59, *History of Europe,* 1815–52, *ch.* v.

Immediately took its place among the secondary Scottish novels, as those were called which would have been first but for Scott's series. That book was full of interest, and of promise of moral beauty which was not fulfilled.—MARTINEAU, HARRIET, 1854, *Biographical Sketches, p.* 30.

A highly accomplished attempt to resuscitate domestic society under Trajan. —GOSSE, EDMUND, 1897, *A Short History of Modern English Literature, p.* 327.

ADAM BLAIR
1822

It is a story of great power and interest, though neither very pleasing, nor very moral, nor very intelligible. . . . There is no great merit in the design of this story, and there are many things both absurd and revolting in its details; but there is no ordinary power in the execution; and there is a spirit and richness in the writing, of which no notion can be formed from our little abstract of its substance.—JEFFREY, FRANCIS LORD, 1823–44, *Secondary Scotch Novels, Contributions to the Edinburgh Review, vol.* III, *pp.* 526, 527.

Amid scenes of dramatic talent and passages impressed with the finest sensibilities, there is evidence now and then of the distempered feeling of the German school. — CUNNINGHAM, ALLAN, 1833, *Biographical and Critical History of the Literature of the Last Fifty Years.*

His novel is not of the first rank (I should call it an excellent second-rate one), but it borrows a charm from the fact that his vigorous, but not strongly imaginative, mind was impregnated with the reality of his subject. He did not always succeed in rendering this reality; the expression is sometimes awkward and poor. But the reader feels that his vision was clear, and his feeling about the matter very strong and rich.—JAMES, HENRY, JR., 1880, *Nathaniel Hawthorne, (English Men of Letters), p.* 112.

"Adam Blair" is almost a masterpiece in concentrated power and passion.— SAINTSBURY, GEORGE, 1896, *English Prose, ed. Craik, vol.* V, *p.* 316.

There are scenes in that unevenly written Lockhart story of "Adam Blair" —hardly known now—which for thrilling passion, blazing out of clear sufficiencies of occasion, would compare well with kindred scenes of Scott's own, and which score deeper colorings of human woe and loves and remorse than belong to most modern stories; not lighted, indeed, with humor; not entertaining with anecdote; not embroidered with archæologic knowledge; not rattling with coruscating social fireworks, but subtle, psychologic, touching the very marrow of our common manhood with a pen both sharp and fine.— MITCHELL, DONALD G., 1897, *English Lands Letters and Kings, The Later Georges to Victoria, p.* 47.

ANCIENT SPANISH BALLADS
1828

All other translations fade away before them.—CUNNINGHAM, ALLAN, 1833, *Biographical and Critical History of the Literature of the Last Fifty Years.*

These Spanish ballads are known to our public, but generally with inconceivable advantage, by the very fine and animated translations of Mr. Lockhart.—HALLAM, HENRY, 1837–39, *Introduction to the Literature of Europe, pt.* ii, *ch.* v, *par.* 46.

Mr. Lockhart's picturesque version of the Moorish ballads.—PRESCOTT, WILLIAM HICKLING, 1838, *Ferdinand and Isabella.*

A work of genius beyond any of the sort known to me in any language. . . . The admirably spirited but very free translations by Mr. Lockhart.—TICKNOR, GEORGE, 1849–54, *History of Spanish Literature, vol.* I, *p.* 115, *note, vol.* III, *p.* 413.

Long esteemed for the spirit and elegance with which the poet has exhibited the peculiar beauties of this literature in our English dress.—SCRYMGEOUR, DANIEL, 1850, *Poetry and Poets of Great Britain.*

These translations derive, as I have said, not a little of their excellence from Mr. Lockhart's being himself a poet of fine genius, clear in his conceptions and masculine in execution. . . . What was tame he inspired; what was lofty gained additional grandeur; and even the tender —as in the lay of "Count Alarcos"—grew still more pathetic beneath his touch.—MOIR, D. M., 1851-52, *Sketches of the Poetical Literature of the Past Half-Century.*

Mr. Lockhart's spirited volume of Spanish ballads, to which the art of the modern translator has given the charm of the vigorous old poets.—MITFORD, MARY RUSSELL, 1851, *Recollections of a Literary Life, ch.* xvi.

LIFE OF SIR WALTER SCOTT
1836-38

Fortunate as Sir Walter Scott was in his life, it is not the least of his good fortunes that he left the task of recording it to one so competent as Mr. Lockhart, who to a familiarity with the person and habits of his illustrious subject unites such entire sympathy with his pursuits, and such fine tact and discrimination in arranging the materials for publication.—PRESCOTT, WILLIAM HICKLING, 1838, *Biographical and Critical Miscellanies.*

Executed with so much skill, and in so admirable a manner, that, next to Boswell's "Life of Johnson," it will probably always be considered as the most interesting work of biography in the English language.—ALISON, SIR ARCHIBALD, 1853-59, *History of Europe*, 1815-52, *ch.* v.

The defect of Lockhart's book is that he devotes too much space to a discussion of the connection between Scott and the Ballantynes. The tone and temper of this discussion are equally out of keeping with the biography and its author's intention of exhibiting Scott in a favorable light. The executors of James Ballantyne replied, in a voluminous pamphlet, the object of which was to show that Ballantyne was more sinned against than sinning. Lockhart retorted, in a bitter publication called "The Ballantyne Humbug Handled." It was contemptuous and personal. Then followed a rejoinder, going closely into detail, in which they showed how constantly Scott used to draw on Ballantyne for money, and how improvident he was. To this there was no reply, but the discussion, which was provoked by Lockhart's aspersions, did not tend to exalt Scott in public estimation.—MACKENZIE, R. SHELTON, 1854, *ed. Noctes Ambrosianæ, Memoir of John Gibson Lockhart, vol.* III, *p.* xiv.

It seems as if, in that darkly-guessed-at-Wisdom which governs our world, Lockhart had been born to love Scott, and, beyond even that regard which Scott's works awaken in every gentle heart, to make him by all men yet more beloved. Lockhart has given to us a friend, the object of his own intense and undemonstrative devotion; and we, who find that even his death before our day cannot sever from our living affection the man whom, "not having seen, we love," owe this great debt to Lockhart, and for very gratitude, must forgive all that in him which is less noble than himself—*quia multum amavit.* —LANG, ANDREW, 1896, *ed., The Life and Letters of John Gibson Lockhart, vol.* II, *p.* 72.

As a man of letters, Lockhart is a fascinating, if not a prominent, figure in the history of the earlier half of our century; but to the majority he will never be more than the biographer of Scott.—HUTCHINSON, T., 1896, *The Academy, vol.* 50, *p.* 344.

It is by his "Life of Scott" that Lockhart will live in literature.—WALKER, HUGH, 1897, *The Age of Tennyson, p.* 137.

GENERAL

Has been universally accepted ["Life of Burns"] as a graceful treatment of the subject; kind, without being partial, towards Burns, and informed with a fine spirit of criticism. It adds, however, little to the details previously known, and certainly any effort made by the author to attain correctness in the statement and arrangement of facts, was far from what would appear to have been necessary in the case.—CHAMBERS, ROBERT, 1850, *The Life and Works of Robert Burns, Preface, vol.* I, *p.* vi.

Its present accomplished editor [of the *Quarterly Review*] Lockhart, who at a short interval succeeded Gifford in its direction, brought to his arduous task qualities which eminently fitted him for its duties.

He is not political in his disposition, at least so far as engaging in the great strife of public questions is concerned: he is one of the light, not the heavy armed, infantry, and prefers exchanging thrusts with a court rapier to wielding the massy club of Hercules. But in the lighter branches of literatuure he has deservedly attained the very highest eminence. As a novelist, a critic, and a biographer, he has taken a lasting place in English literature.—ALISON, SIR ARCHIBALD, 1853-59, *History of Europe*, 1815-52, *ch.* v.

It was his own callousness which made the sensitiveness of others so highly amusing to him.—MARTINEAU, HARRIET, 1854, *Biographical Sketches*, *p.* 34.

No student of biography can afford to overlook Lockhart. Apart from his skill in choosing significant circumstances, he is peculiarly distinguished by his faithful adherence to reality: his biographies are remarkably free from the distortions of romance and hero-worship. He objected on several grounds to the writing of the lives of persons recently deceased; but he held that if "contemporaneous biography," as he called it, is to be permitted the biographers should be peculiarly careful not to make in favour of the hero suppressions that might do injustice to other persons concerned. It was probably in pursuance of this principle that he made revelations concerning Scott which extreme admirers of the poet would rather he had left unsaid. Lockhart's is not a studied, finished style, but he had a great mastery of language, and is exceedingly fresh and varied in his diction. His characteristic qualities are keen incisive force, and sarcastic exuberant wit.—MINTO, WILLIAM, 1872-80, *Manual of English Prose Literature*, *p.* 544.

Only a word on his novels,—"Valerius, a Roman Story," coldly and sternly classical as a romance of Apuleius or Barclay; "Adam Blair," with its burning passion and guilt, which startled the kirk like a bombshell; "Reginald Dalton," light, easy and superficial, in which the author sought to depict, with a difference, —as "Tom Brown" has done for us in later days,—undergraduate life at Oxford, as it was during the earlier period of his own academical career; and lastly, not the least remarkable, "Matthew Wald" forcibly portraying a character, which, though redeemed by some better impulses, gradually sinks downward, by reason of its innate selfishness, to degradation and madness. These storys are, one and all, powerfully written; they exhibit force of narrative, passages of surpassing beauty and pathos, and elegance of style; but they have failed to gain for their writer an exhalted or permanent place among the great masters of fiction.—BATES, WILLIAM, 1874-98, *The Maclise Portrait-Gallery of Illustrious Literary Characters*, *p.* 9.

The truth is, that Lockhart, in his own line, was as narrow as the Shepherd was in his.—VEITCH, JOHN, 1885, *Memorials of James Hogg, ed. Mrs. Garden, Preface*, *p.* xiii.

He was very much more than a satirist and a snarler. From the first he seems to have had the command of a really excellent style—a style in which a few slight oversights may be noted here and there, but which in the main is one of the very best examples of a class too generally undervalued—the class showing the latest phase of the "classical" style of the eighteenth century, free from over-classicism, slightly suppled and modernised by foreign and vernacular influences, but as yet untouched by the tendencies to lawlessness, to extreme ornament, and to other excesses which were successively illustrated in Landor, in DeQuincey, in Carlyle, and in Mr. Ruskin. And he put this style, in his avowed and substantive work, to most excellent use, assisting its operation by the display of good reading, of sound, if sometimes slightly grudging criticism, and above all of a manly and judicial sense with which few have shown themselves better provided.—SAINTSBURY, GEORGE, 1896, *English Prose, ed. Craik, vol.* v, *p.* 315.

Lockhart, though an acute critic, and a very clever translator, was a supreme worshipper of "conditions," rather than of qualities.—MITCHELL, DONALD G., 1897, *English Lands Letters and Kings, The Later Georges to Victoria*, *p.* 280.

He was not a swashbuckler like Wilson, making his sword whistle round his head, and cutting men down on every side. His satire was mischievous, virulent, not so much from hate as from nature. It was as if he had a physical necessity for discharging that point of venom, which he emitted suddenly without warning, without passion or excitement, proceeding on his way gaily with perfect unconcern when the dart was flung. It is impossible to imagine anything more unlike the roaring choruses of conviviality which were supposed to distinguish Ambrose's than this reticent, sensitive, attractive, yet dangerous youth, by whose charm such a giant as Scott was immediately subjugated, and who slew his victims mostly by the midnight oil, not by any blaze of gaiety, or in the accumulative fervour of social sarcasm. From him came the most of those sharp things which the victims could not forget. Wilson hacked about him, distributing blows right and left, delivered sometimes for fun, though sometimes with the most extraordinary impulse of perversity, in the impetus of his career. Lockhart put in his sting in a moment, inveterate, instantaneous, with the effect of a barbed dart—yet almost, as it seemed, with the mere intention of giving point to his sentences, and no particular feeling at all.—OLIPHANT, MARGARET O. W., 1897, *William Blackwood and His Sons, vol.* I, *p.* 194.

Sir Thomas Noon Talfourd

1795–1854

Born, at Doxey, near Stafford, 26 Jan. 1795. Educated at a school at Mill Hill, and at Reading Grammar School. To London, to study Law, 1813. On staff of "London Mag." Contrib. to "Edinburgh Review," "Quarterly Review," "New Monthly Mag.," etc. Called to Bar at Middle Temple, Feb. 1821. Married Miss Rutt, 1821. Sergeant-at-Law, 1835. M. P. for Reading, 1835–41, 1847–49. Play, "Ion," produced at Covent Garden, 26 May 1836; "The Athenian Captive," Haymarket, 1838; "Glencoe," Haymarket, 23 May 1840. Hon. D. C. L., Oxford, 20 June 1844. Recorder of Banbury, Queen's Sergeant, 1846. Judge of Court of Common Pleas, 1849–54. Knighted, 30 Jan. 1850. Died, suddenly, at Stafford, 13 March 1854. *Works:* "Poems on Various Subjects" (anon.), 1811; "An Attempt to estimate the Poetical Talent of the Present Age," 1815; "Ion" (priv. ptd.), 1835; "The Athenian Captive," 1838; "Observations on the Law of Copyright," 1838. "Glencoe" (priv. ptd.), 1839; "Three Speeches . . . in favour of an Extension of Copyright," 1840; "Speech for the Defendant in the Prosecution, the Queen *v.* Moxon," 1841; "Recollections of a first visit to the Alps" (priv. ptd.), 1841; "Dramatic Works," 1843; "Vacation Rambles and Thoughts" (2 vols.), 1845; "The Castilian" (anon.; priv. ptd.), 1853; "Supplement to 'Vacation Rambles,'" 1854. *Posthumous:* "Memoirs of Charles Lamb," edited (from memoirs by Talfourd in his edns. of Lamb's "Letters" and "Final Memorials") by P. Fitzgerald, 1892. He *edited:* W. D. Dickinson's "Practical Guide to the Quarter Sessions," 3rd edn., 1829; Charles Lamb's "Letters," 1837; and "Final Memorials," 1848; W. F. Deacon's "Annette," 1852.—SHARP, R. FARQUHARSON, 1897, *A Dictionary of English Authors, p.* 274.

PERSONAL

I heard the late Lord Chief-Justice Tindal praise him highly for judgment and skill in the management of business. He said he was altogether a successful advocate. No man got more verdicts, and no man deserved more to get them. Talfourd is a generous and kind-hearted man. To men of letters and artists in distress, such as Leigh Hunt, Haydon, &c., he was always very liberal. He did not forget his early friends, and at the large parties he has hitherto delighted to give, poets, players, authors of every kind were to be seen, together with barristers and now and then judges.—ROBINSON, HENRY CRABB, 1847, *Diary for* 1813, *note; Diary, Reminiscences and Correspondence, ed. Sadler, vol.* I, *p.* 264.

Talfourd I was glad to see but he disappointed me. He is no doubt a poet of genius, within certain limits, and a very hard-working successful lawyer, but he is a little too fat, red-faced, and coarse in his appearance. . . . He talks strikably rather than soundly, defending "Cato," for instance as an admirable poetical tragedy; and was a little too artificial and too brilliant, both in the structure and phraseology of his sentences and in the general tone of his thoughts.—TICKNOR, GEORGE, 1838, *Journal, June* 2; *Life, Letters and Journals, vol.* II, *p.* 181.

Of all the men whom I have known,

after long intercourse with the business of the world, the Sergeant is the one whom most preserves, to all outward appearance, the freshness and integrity of his youthful spirits.—DE QUINCEY, THOMAS, 1840? *Literary Reminiscences, ch.* XX.

He was much more than a merely distinguished leader, an eminent judge, or a great ornament of our literature. He had one ruling purpose of his life,—the doing good to his fellow creatures in his generation. He was eminently courteous and kind, generous, simple-hearted, of great modesty, of the strictest honour, and of spotless integrity.—COLERIDGE, J.T., 1854, *Charge to the Grand Jury on the day after Talfourd's Sudden Decease.*

The career of this eminent and good man, from his onset in life to the recent close of it on the bench, was in keeping—uniformly entitled to the admiration of all thinking and good men. Talfourd, seeking eminence in his profession, distinction in literature, renown in his judicial capacity, was always true to the interests of humanity and of literature. He had strong sympathies with his fellow-men—with poverty and suffering. He had a sound taste in matters appertaining to art and letters, and kindly feeling toward those who cultivated those pursuits.—MADDEN, R. R., 1855, *The Literary Life and Correspondence of the Countess of Blessington, vol.* II, *p.* 532.

Retaining, no doubt, to the last the peculiar ideas of the school in literature to which he belonged, consistent in all actions, just in feeling, and in morals correct, it is still impossible to recall him as he was more than forty years ago, and to follow up his career to the last, and not to pronounce an eulogy upon a most virtuous and excellent man of talent, of undoubted integrity, by whose loss there seemed a gap made in a class of the social body, which time, to those who knew him, can never fill up. My only purpose here is to record a few fleeting recollections of men and their doings, which I either knew of at the time, or with which I was in some degree connected.—REDDING, CYRUS, 1867, *Personal Reminiscences of Eminent Men, vol.* II, *p.* 165.

Those who knew him will never forget his kindly, genial face, the happiness radiating from it when imparting pleasure to others, and his generous hospitality extended in no niggard spirit.—BALLANTINE, WILLIAM, 1882, *Some Experiences of a Barrister's Life, vol.* I, *p.* 140.

ION

1835

I do not much like Talfourd's "Ion;" but I mean to read it again. It contains pretty lines; but, to my thinking, it is neither fish nor flesh. There is too much, and too little, of the antique about it. Nothing but the most strictly classical costume can reconcile me to a mythological plot; and Ion is a modern philanthropist whose politics and morals have been learned from the publications of the Society for the Diffusion of Useful Knowledge.—MACAULAY, THOMAS BABINGTON, 1836, *To Ellis, July* 25; *Life and Letters, ed. Trevelyan.*

This remarkable poem has justly called to itself more attention than any other work of the times. . . . "Ion" is evidently the work of many years. It is constructed on the principles of the Grecian drama, and is, on the whole, the most successful reproduction of the antique spirit with which we are acquainted. . . . Mr. Talfourd has been remarkably successful in two respects. His tragedy is at once true to the antique models, and deeply interesting to the mere modern reader. The classical scholar, as he reads its exquisite pages, can hardly escape the delusive impression that he has found a long-lost work of Sophocles. Its harmonious lines, to his ear, sound like the old Greek iambics, into which they fall so readily that at times he hardly knows whether he is reading Greek or English. The reader, whose knowledge is bounded by the literature of his mother tongue, finds in it such clear conceptions of character, such a polished and melodious versification, such rich and enchanting imagery, that he yields his spirit to the master's spell. "He knows not why, and cares not wherefore." He rises from its perusal with a pervading sense of beauty, which no other late poem can give him. It is all high thought, nobly expressed. It is heroic sentiment and sublime action, tempered and subdued with the softest and most delicate humanity.—FELTON, CORNELIUS C., 1837, *Talfourd's "Ion," North American Review, vol.* 44, *pp.* 485, 486.

Of the concentration and passion of the

Shaksperean drama, Mr. Talfourd's first dramatic production does not, as we have assumed, partake. The appeal of this tragedy is to the *conscientiousness* of its audience; and it purifies less by pity and terror, than by admiration and exultation. Its power is less an intellectual and poetical than a moral power; and the peculiarity of its sublime lies significantly in the excellence of its virtue. . . . The mixture of the pure Christian principle of faith and love with the Greek principle of inexorable fate, produces an incongruity in the tragedy which raises a conflict in the mind. . . . To the language may be attributed appropriateness and eloquence, with some occasional redundance, and a certain deficiency in strength: the images are rather elegant than bold or original; and the versification flows gracefully and copiously within the limits of the school. The effect of the whole is such as would be created were it possible to restore the ground-plan of an Athenian temple in its majestic and simple proportions, and decorated it with the elegant statues of Canova. —HORNE, RICHARD HENGIST, 1844, *A New Spirit of the Age, pp.* 149, 150.

When Talfourd's "Ion" was published, it appeared to myself (as it still appears) to be the most noble, highly-finished, and picturesque modern classical tragedy existing on the English stage.—CHORLEY, HENRY FOTHERGILL, 1873, *Autobiography, Memoirs and Letters, vol.* I, *p.* 113.

GENERAL

Whose criticism I think masterly.—LAMB, CHARLES, 1832, *The Death of Munden.*

His style is richly laden with ornament, and almost monotonously musical in its flow. His thoughts are more often seen in the imperial robes of rhetoric than in its suit of "homely russet brown." The rich flush of imagination colors his whole diction. At times, he is fastidiously nice in his choice of language, and a fondness for dainty and delicate epithets too often gives to his style an appearance of prettiness and enfeebling affectation. He luxuriates too much in the "nectared sweets" of language and imagery, and is apt to impair the manliness and vigor of his diction by redundant fancies and sugared words. When his own stores of sweetness fail him, he avails himself of those belonging to others. His diction is studded with apt quotations, teeming with richness of sentiment and style. But still he shares in all the essential characteristics of the school of Wordsworth, and gives evidences on every page of that "quiet eye, which sleeps and broods on his own heart." . . . In kindly feeling, in genial sympathy with his race, in that running over of the heart in the worship of all that is great and good in character and life, in all those qualities which mark the musing and imaginative poet, he is perhaps not excelled by any contemporary.—WHIPPLE, EDWIN P., 1843, *Talfourd, North American Review, Oct. Essays and Reviews.*

"Talfourd's greatest literary efforts were in the line of the drama; and if his plays seldom reached to the heights of sublimity, they never descended to the level of the commonplace, and have been uniformly successful upon the stage. His tragedy is a mild-complexioned muse, impressing us more by its gentleness, sweetness, and free play of the affections than by those grand or sublime, or terrible situations and doings, or those violent and startling mutations which make tragedy tragical: while they often draw tears of pity or compassion, they rarely vehemently move the sterner feelings or stir the passions. His friend Macready correctly described 'Ion,' his dramatic masterpiece, when he styled it a 'sweet tragic poem;' and the characterization is not an inapt one for all his dramatic performances. His sonnets are fair exponents of the average style of the most of those by recent writers—clever, correct, dignified, garrulous rather than full, and temperately cold."—DESHLER, CHARLES D., 1879, *Afternoons with the Poets, p.* 251.

Of his dramatic works "Ion" was the most, and "The Massacre of Glencoe" the least, successful. It was in the treatment of classical subjects that he produced his best results. "Ion" is characterised by the simplicity and dignity belonging to its Greek theme.—MILES, ALFRED H., 1894, *The Poets and the Poetry of the Century, Keats to Lytton, p.* 108.

The cold dignity of Talfourd's style hardly atones for the commonplace character of his thought.—WALKER, HUGH, 1897, *The Age of Tennyson, p.* 47.

Caroline Anne Bowles Southey

1787-1854

Born in Hampshire, England, in 1787. She was the daughter of a retired officer, and both of her parents died when she was very young. She remained in the retirement at the country home which had been her father's, and published, "Ellen Fitz-Arthur," a poem, 1820; "The Widow's Tale, and other Poems," 1822; "Solitary Hours, Prose and Verse," 1826; and "Chapters on Churchyards," a series of tales and sketches originally contributed to "Blackwood," 1829. On June 5th, 1839, she married Robert Southey, the Poet Laureate (1774-1843), whose first wife had died two years before. Miss Bowles and he had long been warm personal friends, and had talked of writing books together. After his death she published two or three fragmentary volumes of poetry with both his initials and her own on the title page. She died in 1854.—JOHNSON, ROSSITER, 1875, *Little Classics, Authors*, p. 227.

PERSONAL

Neither in prose nor in verse is Caroline Southey strong enough to maintain a high place. She will probably be best remembered by her connection with Southey and by her share in the volume of his correspondence edited by Professor Dowden. His part is the more important, but Caroline's letters prove that she possessed more liveliness and satiric talent than might have been expected from the authoress of "Chapters on Churchyards." She was diminutive, and had suffered from smallpox; the portrait prefixed to Professor Dowden's edition of her correspondence is, however, by no means unprepossessing.—GARNETT, RICHARD, 1898, *Dictionary of National Biography, vol.* LIII, *p.* 283.

GENERAL

Her productions are distinguished for correctness, simplicity and tenderness. She has little imagination, but she has a kindly disposition and an unusual depth of sentiment. Occasionally she is playful, but the genius of her poetry is religious. The range of her subjects is limited, but her writings evince a nice observation, a sympathy with the suffering, and a pious trustfulness. — GRISWOLD, RUFUS W., 1844, *The Poets and Poetry of England in the Nineteenth Century, p.* 255.

It would be difficult, I think, to find among our Female Poets one who in vigour of mind, intensity of feeling, and gracefulness of expression, excels Mrs. Southey. Her poems have a simplicity, a naturalness, which is as pleasing as it is rare. Her verses are the very perfection of direct and inartificial thought. In terse force of style I do not know her superior: whilst at the same time she has the quickness of vision and the sensitiveness of sympathy which characterise her sex.—ROWTON, FREDERIC, 1848, *The Female Poets of Great Britain, p.* 374.

No man, could have written such poetry—at least no man has ever yet done so; it breathes of "a purer ether, a diviner air" than that respired by the *soi-disant* lords of the creation; and in its freedom from all moral blemish and blot—from all harshness and austerity of sentiment—from all the polluting taints which are apt to cleave to the human thought, and its expansive sympathy with all that is holy, just, and of good report—it elevates the heart even more than it delights the fancy. We doubt if the English language possess any thing more profoundly pathetic than Mrs. Southey's four tales, "The Young Grey Head," "The Murder Glen," "Walter and William," and "The Evening Walk;" and I envy not the heart-construction of that family group, of which the father could read these compositions aloud to his children either himself with an unfaltering voice, or without exciting their tears.—MOIR, D. M., 1851-52, *Sketches of the Poetical Literature of the Past Half-Century.*

No English poetess has written sweeter, or has touched more tenderly the chords of the heart, or has gone down deeper into its well-springs, than Caroline Anne, Bowles now Mrs. Southey.—CLEVELAND, CHARLES D., 1853, *English Literature of the Nineteenth Century, p.* 765.

It is sufficiently astonishing to most of us, in this generation, that Robert Southey's contemporaries took him for a great poet; but it is still more astonishing that they took Miss Bowles, who became his second wife, for a great poetess. "Delta" represented the opinions of many when he declared that she equalled Mrs. Hemans; and the *Quarterly Review* calls her "the Cowper of Poetesses." She was no poetess at all. Certainly it cannot be said of her, as it was said of Shadwell, that she "never deviates into sense." Her verse is full of sense, but it never deviates into poetry. —ROBERTSON, ERIC S., 1883, *English Poetesses, p.* 248.

She was the author of various stories, poems, and essays — the latter of which, in the form of series of "Chapters on Churchyards," published in *Blackwood's Magazine*, are almost the only relics of her that have a faint survival.—OLIPHANT, MARGARET O. W., 1883, *Literary History of England, XVIII-XIXth Century, vol.* I, *p.* 327.

Mrs. Southey's verse had a greater charm for her own generation than it can ever have again. There is a natural simplicity about it which gives it a certain affinity with the so-called "Lake school," and which was much newer in her day than it is in ours. And yet, after the lapse of so many years, like flowers that have been preserved, her work still emits a sweet mild fragrance, and recalls a tender, sympathetic personalty. One can scarcely read her general poems without feeling that they came from a true, loving heart, nor peruse the poems which with an almost morbid recurrence she wrote upon the subject of death, without feeling that she had a true sense of the sublime. Faulty in form, she possessed a spontaneity which some masters of form never show, besides in some degree that magic touch which invests a subject with the nameless environment which for want of a better term we call atmosphere.—MILES, ALFRED H., 1892, *The Poets and the Poetry of the Century, Joanna Baillie to Mathilde Blind, p.* 41.

The decent worth of Caroline Bowles.—SAINTSBURY, GEORGE, 1896, *A History of Nineteenth Century Literature, p.* 124.

Susan Edmonstone Ferrier

1782–1854

Born in Edinburgh, 7th September 1782. Her first work, "Marriage" (1818), was followed by "The Inheritance" (1824) and "Destiny" (1831); for the three she received £150, £1,000, and £1,700. Miss Ferrier enjoyed the esteem and friendship of Sir Walter Scott, who was by some for a time credited with the authorship of her tales. Her "Recollections of Visits to Ashiestiel and Abbotsford" were published, along with a Memoir, in Bentley's edition of her works (1881). She died at Edinburgh, 5th November 1854.—PATRICK AND GROOME, *ed.*, 1897, *Chambers's Biographical Dictionary, p.* 362.

PERSONAL

This gifted personage, besides having great talents, has conversation the least *exigeante* of any author, female at least, whom I have ever seen among the long list I have encountered with; simple, full of humour, and exceedingly ready at repartee; and all this without the least affectation of the blue stocking.—SCOTT, SIR WALTER, 1831, *Journal, May* 12; *Life by Lockhart, ch.* lxxx.

MARRIAGE
1818

I am almost sorry when I ought to be glad, now that I send you the end. I have had more enjoyment and pleasure in the progress of your work for the last twelve months than I have ever had in any that have passed through my hands. I am now as impatient to have it fairly afloat as I was to have it concluded, being confident that there will only be one opinion of its merits.—BLACKWOOD, WILLIAM, 1818, *William Blackwood and his Sons, ed. Oliphant, vol.* I, *p.* 39.

INHERITANCE
1824

On Wednesday I dined in company with Sir Walter Scott, and he spoke of the work in the very highest terms. I don't always set the highest value on the Baronet's favourable opinion of a book, because he has so much kindness of feeling towards every one; but in this case he spoke so much *con amore*, and entered so completely and at such length into the spirit of the book, and of the characters, as showed me at once the impression it had made on him. Every one I have seen who has read the book gives the same praise to it.—BLACKWOOD, WILLIAM, 1824, *William Blackwood and his Sons, ed. Oliphant, vol.* I, *p.* 43.

Is a model of its kind, whilst from first to last the conduct of the narrative is perfect. Indeed the *form* of the story could not be improved—a rare merit even in a masterpiece of British fiction; and though the book is a long one, it contains not a superfluous page.—DOUGLAS, SIR GEORGE, 1897, *The Blackwood Group, (Famous Scots Series), p.* 124.

DESTINY
1831

Miss Ferrier was a very careful craftswoman—a fact to which much of her success has been attributed—and it was not until 1831 that her next book, "Destiny," appeared. Much of it was written at Stirling Castle, while she was on a visit to the wife of the Governor of the garrison. The new novel was dedicated to Sir Walter Scott, to whom the authoress had good reason to feel obliged, for it was largely in consequence of his skilful bargaining that she had received for it the large sum of £1,700 from Cadell. The prices paid to her by Blackwood for her two previous books had been £150 and £1,000 respectively.—DOUGLAS, SIR GEORGE, 1897, *The Blackwood Group (Famous Scots Series), p.* 128.

GENERAL

There is a lady here whom I think you must know,—Miss Ferrier; her father is a very old man, and she, who is not very young, and has indifferent health, secludes herself almost entirely with him. The fruits of this seclusion appeared three or four years since in the form of a novel called "Marriage:" it was evidently the production of a clever, caustic mind, with much good painting of character in it, that could not be produced without talent and considerable knowledge of men and books. I have just finished a hasty perusal of a new work by the same author, called "The Inheritance," and join the general voice in pronouncing it clever, though there is, perhaps, too much caricature throughout. Pray read it; there is strong sense in it, and it keeps attention awake even when it does not entirely please. There are some here who praise this work beyond measure, and even hold it up as excelling the invisible charmer.—GRANT, ANNE, 1824, *Letter to Mrs. Hook, June* 23; *Memoir and Correspondence, ed. Grant, vol.* III, *p.* 35.

To a warm heart, a lively fancy, and great powers of discrimination, Miss Ferrier has added variety of knowledge, and a graphic art of describing all she sees and all she feels, which give her a distinguished place among the novelists of the day.—CUNNINGHAM, ALLAN, 1833, *Biographical and Critical History of the Literature of the Last Fifty Years.*

This lady was a Scottish Miss Edgeworth—of a lively, practical, penetrating cast of mind; skilful in depicting character and seizing upon national peculiarities; caustic in her wit and humour, with a quick sense of the ludicrous; and desirous of inculcating sound morality and attention to the courtesies and charities of life. In some passages, indeed, she evinces a deep religious feeling, approaching to the evangelical views of Hannah More; but the general strain of her writing relates to the foibles and oddities of mankind, and no one has drawn them with greater breadth of comic humour or effect. Her scenes often resemble the style of our best old comedies, and she may boast, like Foote, of adding many new and original characters to the stock of our comic literature.—CHAMBERS, ROBERT, 1876, *Cyclopædia of English Literature, ed. Carruthers.*

Of the four requisites of the novelist, plot, character, description, and dialogue, she is only weak in the first. The lapse of an entire half-century and a complete change of manners have put her books to the hardest test they are ever likely to have to endure, and they come through it triumphantly.—SAINTSBURY, GEORGE, 1882, *Miss Ferrier's Novels, The Fortnightly Review, vol.* 37, *p.* 331.

Miss Ferrier was, in point of natural ability, far above the average novel-writer of to-day. We doubt whether at the present moment there exists in England any living authoress (unless it be Mrs. Oliphant or Mrs. Thackeray Ritchie) who stands, in acuteness, in humor, in insight into character, much above the writer of "Inheritance." We shall not do Miss Ferrier injustice if we place her only a little below Miss Austen in point of humor, and Miss Edgeworth in point of wit and sterling sense. But high as we are inclined to put Miss Ferrier among the female novelists of England, we admit at once that she exhibits a want of literary skill which would hardly be betrayed by any one among the number of authors whose works are to be read in every month's magazine, and are forgotten before the month is out.—DICEY, A. V., 1883, *Miss Ferrier's Novels, The Nation, vol.* 37, *p.* 231.

Miss Ferrier's novels show keen powers of observation, and are brightly and clearly written. They are chiefly satirical sketches of character in the upper classes of Scottish society. They belong to the same school as Miss Edgeworth's stories, and are marked by the same rather stiff didacticism. . . . In spite of their old-fashioned character they still have attraction due to genuine wit and vivacity. —STEPHEN, LESLIE, 1889, *Dictionary of National Biography, vol.* XVIII, *p.* 392.

She was a keen satirist, but showed up the follies and vices of society more from an overpowering sense of humour than from any intention to be a reformer. Her pictures of contemporary Scottish life and character are most amusing.—KIRKLAND, E. S., 1892, *A Short History of English Literature, p.* 308.

Miss Ferrier lived to old age, and became, we are told, so completely occupied with religious questions as to dislike and disapprove of the delightful works of her earlier days, which is an unfortunate circumstance. She has retained a high and quite individual place in fiction, one of a band of three women who form a sort of representative group in their way of the three countries, which, it is to be hoped, no unpropitious fate will ever sunder or make to be other than one.—OLIPHANT, MARGARET O. W., 1897, *William Blackwood and his Sons, vol.* I, *p.* 45.

It is more than eighty years since "Marriage" was published, and you can buy it to-day in any book-shop for fourpence halfpenny. That shows at least a singularly robust power of survival, and immortality is freely claimed for authors who have very much less to show for it than a lady who has amused four generations of readers. If she had been content to do that, her fame might rest secure; but unhappily she was possessed with the desire to convey moral instruction, and that has overlaid her humour and her genuine faculty of creation with a dead weight of platitudes under which they must inevitably sink.—GWYNN, STEPHEN, 1899, *Miss Ferrier, Macmillan's Magazine, vol.* 79, *p.* 419.

James Montgomery

1771–1854

Born, at Irvine, Ayrshire, 4 Nov. 1771. To Moravian school at Fulneck, near Leeds, 1777–87. Worked as shop-assistant, 1787–92. Clerk in office of "Sheffield Register" (afterwards "Sheffield Iris"), April 1792; editor, 1794; proprietor, 1795–1825. Imprisoned in York Castle for libel, Jan. to April 1795, and Jan. to July 1796. Contrib. to "Eclectic Rev.," and other periodicals. Prolific writer of poetry. Lectured on Poetry at Royal Institution, 1830 and 1831. Crown Pension, 1835. Unmarried. Died, in Sheffield, 30 April 1854. Buried in Sheffield Cemetery. *Works:* "Prison Amusements" (under initials: J. M.), 1797; "The Whisperer" (under pseud. "Gabriel Silvertongue"), 1798; "The Ocean," 1805; "The Wanderer of Switzerland," 1806; "Poems on the abolition of the Slave Trade" (with J. Grahame and E. Benger), 1809; "The West Indies," 1810; "The World before the Flood," 1813; "Verses to the Memory of the late Richard Reynolds," 1817; "Greenland," 1819; "Songs of Zion," 1822; "The Chimney-Sweeper's Friend," 1824; "Prose by a Poet" (anon.), 1824; "The Christian Psalmist," 1825; "The Pelican Island," 1826; "The Christian Poet," 1827 (2nd edn. same year); "An African Valley," 1828; "An Essay on the Phrenology of the Hindoos and Negroes," 1829; "Verses in commemoration of . . . J. Hervey," 1833; "Lectures on Poetry," 1833; "A Poet's Portfolio," 1835; "Hymns for the opening of Christ Church, Newark on Trent," 1837; "Our Saviour's Miracles," 1840; "Poetical Works," 1841; "Original Hymns," 1853. He *edited:* Cowper's "Poems," 1824; "Journal of Voyages and Travels, by the Rev. D. Tyerman and G. Bennet," 1831; "The Christian Correspondent," 1837; Milton's "Poetical Works," 1843; "Gleanings from Pious Authors," 1850. *Life:* "Memoirs," by J. Holland and J. Everett (7 vols.), 1854–56.—SHARP, R. FARQUHARSON, 1897, *A Dictionary of English Authors, p.* 201.

PERSONAL

His appearance speaks of antiquity and not of decay. His hair has assumed a snowy whiteness, and the lofty and full-arched coronal regions exhibit what a brother poet has well termed the "clear, bald polish of the honored head;" but the expression of the countenance is that of middle life. It is a thin, clear, speaking countenance; the features are high, the complexion fresh, though not ruddy, and age has failed to pucker either cheek or forehead with a single wrinkle. . . . The figure is quite as little touched by age as the face. It is well, but not strongly made, and of the middle size; and yet there is a touch of antiquity about it, too, derived, however, rather from the dress than from any peculiarity of the person itself. To a plain suit of black Mr. Montgomery adds the voluminous breast-ruffles of the last age, exactly such things as, in Scotland, at least, the fathers of the present generation wore on their wedding-days.—MILLER, HUGH, 1841, *The Witness.*

As a model of the Christian citizen, he stands pre-eminent. Steadfastly promoting public improvements, and patiently fostering every charitable enterprise, catholic in spirit and loyal to conscience, unselfish in his aims and rich in practical wisdom, prudent in counsel and warm in his affections, he identified himself with all the best interests of Sheffield, and took a high place in the confidence and respect of his towns-fellows. Nor were his labors of love bounded by Sheffield. Welcoming all the new-born activities, which mark the Church of Christ during the present century, he engaged in their furtherance with singular devotedness. And even when age and infirmities might justly have pleaded exemption from duty, a scrupulous fidelity to its claims kept him to his post even to the end.—KNIGHT, HELEN C., 1857, *Life of James Montgomery, Preface, p.* iv.

Ireland, Scotland, Wales, and England may be proud of a man who did so much that was good and so little that was bad; in whose long life, indeed, we find nothing that was not designed, and calculated to advance the temporal and spiritual welfare of humanity. . . . Few poets ever suffered more severely at the hands of critics; and, acting on a naturally sensitive nature, the attacks of Jeffrey in the *Edinburgh* and of lesser Zoiluses in other reviews, probably had the effect they are designed to produce. In a letter I received from him in 1837, Montgomery thus alludes to himself: "The disappointment of my premature poetical hopes brought a blight with it, from which my mind has never recovered. For many years, I was as mute as a molting-bird; and when the power of song returned, it was without the energy, self-confidence, and freedom which happier minstrels among my contemporaries manifested."—HALL, SAMUEL CARTER, 1883, *Retrospect of a Long Life, p.* 413.

GENERAL

We took compassion upon Mr. Montgomery on his first appearance; conceiving him to be some slender youth of seventeen, intoxicated with weak tea, and the praises of sentimental Ensigns and other provincial literati, and tempted, in that situation, to commit a feeble outrage on the public, of which the recollection would be a sufficient punishment. A third edition, however, is too alarming to be passed over in silence; and, though we are perfectly persuaded, that in less than three years nobody will know the name of the "Wanderer of Switzerland," or any of the other poems in this collection, still we think ourselves called on to interfere, to prevent, as far as in us lies, the mischief that may arise from the intermediate prevalence of so distressing an epidemic. It is hard to say what numbers of ingenious youth may be lead to expose themselves in public by the success of this performance, or what addition may be made in a few months to that great sinking-fund of bad taste, which is daily wearing down the debt which we have so long owed to the classical writers of antiquity. . . . When every day is bringing forth some new work from the pen of Scott, Campbell, Rogers, Baillie, Sotheby, Wordsworth, or Southey, it is natural to feel some disgust at the undistinguishing voracity which can swallow down three editions of songs to convivial societies and verses to a pillow. —JEFFREY, FRANCIS LORD, 1807, *Montgomery's Poems, Edinburgh Review, vol.* 9, *pp.* 347, 354.

With broken lyre and cheek serenely pale,
Lo! sad Alcæus wanders down the vale;
Though fair they rose, and might have
bloom'd at last,

His hopes have perish'd by the northern
blast.
Nipp'd in the bud by Caledonian gales,
His blossoms wither as the blast prevails!
O'er his lost works let *classic* Sheffield weep:
May no rude hand disturb their early sleep.
—BYRON, LORD, 1809, *English Bards and Scotch Reviewers*.

Never did any volume more truly deserve the reception which it found. Faults there were in it; for where is the volume without them? The longest of the poems ["The Wanderer of Switzerland"] is an experiment, treating an heroic subject in lyric measure and upon a dramatic plan. . . . Notwithstanding the inherent and irremediable defect of the poem, no person capable of appreciating poetry could read it without perceiving that it was the production of a rich and powerful mind. . . . There stands upon record only one piece of formal criticism as mischievous as this; [Jeffrey's review of "The Wanderer"] and that is the criticism upon Kirke White in a Monthly Journal, of which the notorious folly and injustice have been reprobated by the thousands who regret and admire that extraordinary and excellent youth. . . . Twice three years have elapsed; the poems are still heard of, still read and admired, and purchased, and re-edited; and, what must be still more alarming to the careful guardian of the public taste, a second volume ["The West Indies, and other Poems"] has been published.—SOUTHEY, ROBERT, 1811, *Montgomery's Poems, Quarterly Review, vol.* 6, *pp.* 408, 413.

Delicacy, tenderness, and a sacred feeling of the highest order, mark the effusions of Montgomery's highly-cultivated muse. —DIBDIN, THOMAS FROGNALL, 1824, *Library Companion, p.* 747, *note.*

His bursts of sacred poetry, compared with his "Greenland," remind us of a person singing enchantingly by ear, but becoming languid and powerless the moment he sits down to a note-book.—KEBLE, JOHN, 1825, *Sacred Poetry, Quarterly Review, vol.* 32, *p.* 217.

It was said by the *Edinburgh Review*, that none but maudlin milliners and sentimental ensigns supposed that James Montgomery was a poet. Then is Maga a maudlin milliner—and Christopher North a sentimental ensign. We once called Montgomery a Moravian; and though he assures us that we were mistaken, yet having made an assertion, we always stick to it, and therefore he must remain a Moravian, if not in his own belief, yet in our imagination. Of all religious sects, the Moravians are the most simple-minded, pure-hearted, and high-souled—and these qualities shine serenely in "The Pelican Island." In earnestness and fervour, that poem is by few or none excelled; it is embalmed in sincerity, and therefore shall fade not away, neither shall it moulder—not even although exposed to the air, and blow the air ever so rudely through time's mutations.—WILSON, JOHN, 1831, *An Hour's Talk About Poetry, Recreations of Christopher North; Blackwood's Magazine, vol.* 30, *p.* 476.

A new controversial pamphlet in verse ["The West Indies"] on this exhausted subject, containing all the old commonplaces of bleeding negroes and bloodthirsty planters, clanking chains and echoing whips,—even though embodied in vigorous and harmonious versification and relieved by sketches of natural scenery of singular freshness and beauty,—was but ill-calculated to afford pleasure to the lovers of genuine poetry. . . . Few, we suppose, have read the poem twice through, though many may often have turned back to such passages as those which describes the charm with which love of country invests alike the bleakest as well as the richest shore.—MOIR, GEORGE, 1835, *Montgomery's Poems, Edinburgh Review, vol.* 61, *pp.* 474, 475.

James Montgomery is the most popular of the religious poets who have written in England since the time of Cowper, and he is more exclusively the poet of devotion than even the bard of Olney. Probably no writer is less indebted to a felicitous selection of subjects, since the themes of nearly all his longer productions are unpleasing and unpoetical; but for half a century he has been slowly and constantly increasing in reputation, and he has now a name which will not be forgotten, while taste and the religious sentiment exist together. . . . The minor poems of Mr. Montgomery, his little songs and cabinet pieces, will be the most frequently read, and the most generally admired. They have the antique simplicity of pious George Withers, a natural unaffected earnestness, joined to a pure and poetical diction, which will secure to them a permanent place in English literature. The character of his genius is essentially lyrical; he has no dramatic power, and but little skill in narrative. His longest and most elaborate works, though they contain beautiful and touching reflections, and descriptions equally distinguished for minuteness, fidelity, and beauty, are without incident or method; but his shorter pieces are full of devotion to the Creator, sympathy with the suffering, and a cheerful, hopeful philosophy.—GRISWOLD, RUFUS W., 1844, *The Poets and Poetry of England in the Nineteenth Century, p.* 73.

The most genuinely religious poet of the age. With a wisdom, founded not on calculation, but on a sacred sense of duty, he had made even his ambition subservient to his aspirations as a Christian, and he has thus reared for himself a pedestal in the poetic Walhalla of England peculiarly his own. The longer his fame endures, and the wider it spreads, the better it will be for virtue and for man.—HOWITT, WILLIAM, 1847, *Homes and Haunts of the Most Eminent British Poets, vol.* II, *p.* 368.

With the exception, perhaps, of Moore, Campbell, and Hemans, I doubt indeed if an equal number of the lyrics of any other modern poet have so completely found their way to the national heart, there to be enshrined in hallowed remembrance. . . . One great merit which may be claimed for James Montgomery is, that he has encroached on no man's property as a poet; he has staked off a portion of the great common of literature for himself, and cultivated it according to his own taste and fancy.—MOIR, D. M., 1851–52, *Sketches of the Poetical Literature of the Past Half-Century.*

Of all dull, stagnant, unedifying *entourages*, that of middle-class Dissent, which environed Montgomery, seems to me the stupidest.—ARNOLD, MATTHEW, 1855, *Letters, ed. Russell, vol.* I, *p.* 49.

The beautiful sacred lyrics of Montgomery live not only in our church-books of psalmody, but some are also embalmed in the common heart of Christendom. Who does not remember his fine poem, "Oh, where shall rest be found?" And where shall we find a nobler burst of elevated sentiment in song than is to be found in his Advent hymn, "Angels, from the realms of glory?"—SAUNDERS, FREDERICK, 1885, *Evenings with the Sacred Poets, p.* 369.

A mild and gentle poet, the author of many verses dear to pious souls.—OLIPHANT, MARGARET O. W., 1892, *The Victorian Age of English Literature, p* 12.

As a poet he is only eminent in descriptive passages, for which he is usually indebted to books rather than his own observation of nature. There are some indications of creative power in "The World before the Flood," and the character of Javan is well drawn; but, as Mrs. Hofland remarked, he drew from himself. The minor pieces which have obtained a wide circulation usually deserve it, but they are buried in his works among masses of commonplace which should never have been printed. He is largely indebted for his fame to the approbation of religious circles, better judges of his sentiments than of his poetry: this has, on the other hand, occasioned unreasonable prejudice against him in other quarters. On the whole he may be characterised as something less than a genius and something more than a mediocrity.—GARNETT, RICHARD, 1894, *Dictionary of National Biography, vol.* XXXVIII, *p.* 319.

Was a rather copious and fairly pleasing minor bard, no bad hand at hymns and short occasional pieces, and the author of longer things.—SAINTSBURY, GEORGE, 1896, *A History of Nineteenth Century Literature, p.* 107.

It is not however by these longer poems that the name of James Montgomery will be perpetuated. It is as a religious poet, and as a writer of sacred lyrics which give expression to the aspirations and reflections of devout hearts, that he will be longest remembered; and it is not too much to say that in this department of poetic work his permanence seems fairly secure. Over a hundred of his hymns are said to be still in use. . . . His Christian songs are vigorous in thought and feeling, simple, and direct in diction, broad in Christian charity, lofty in spiritual aspiration, and entirely free from cant. As such they form a not unworthy opening section for a volume devoted to the sacred poetry of the century.—MILES, ALFRED H., 1897, *The Poets and the Poetry of the Century, Sacred, Moral and Religious Verse, pp.* 3, 4.

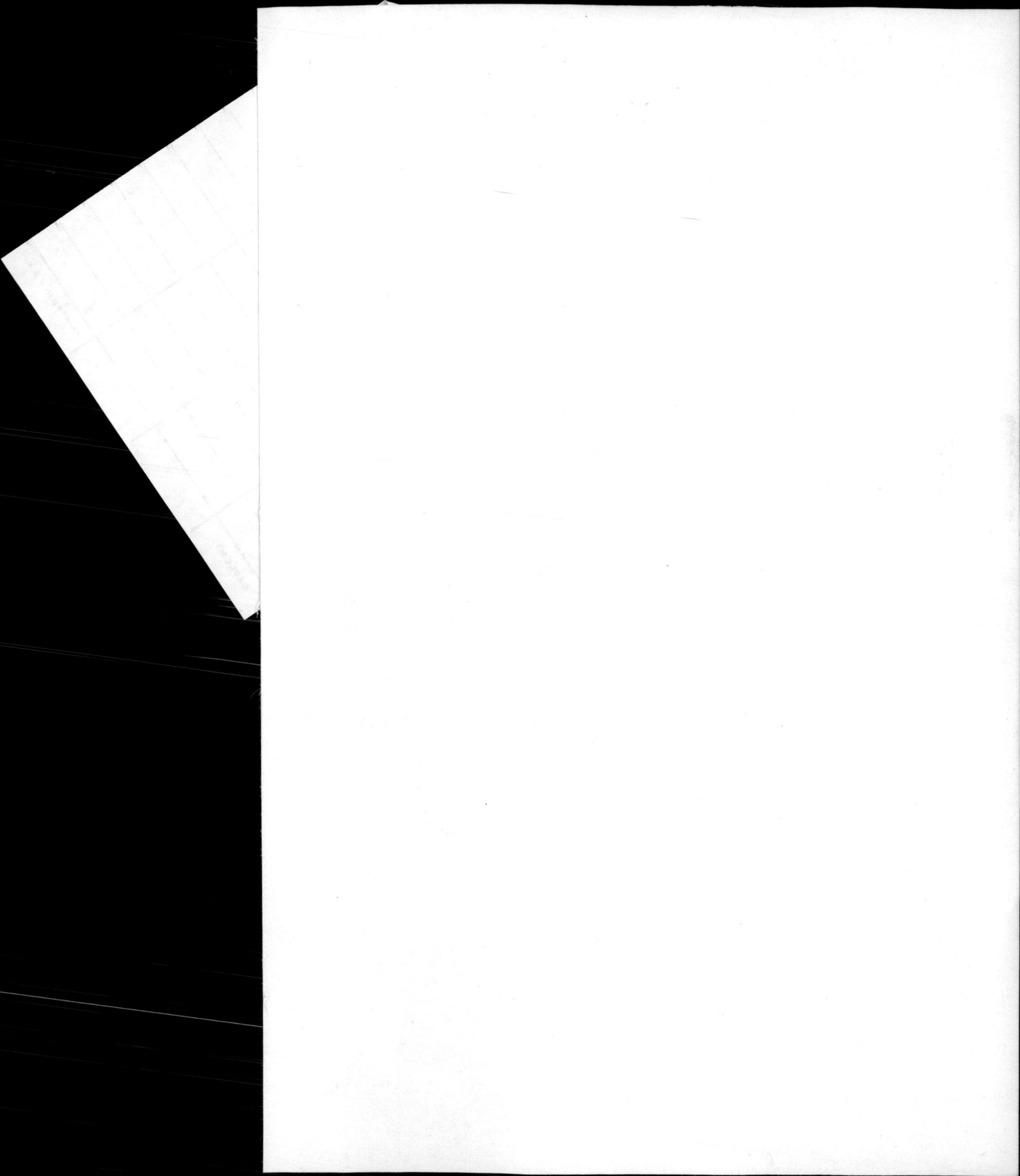

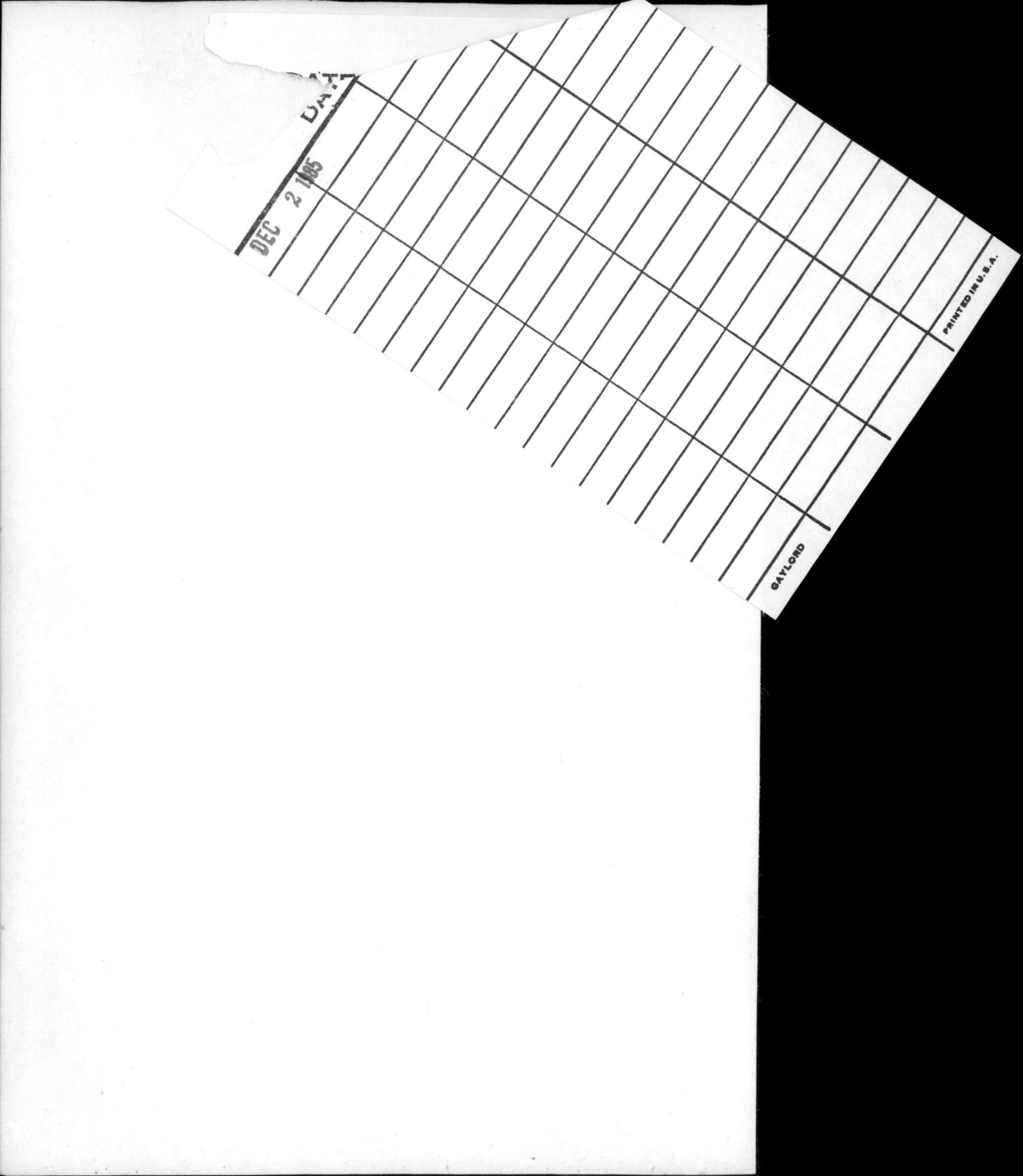
DEC 2 1985
GAYLORD
PRINTED IN U.S.A.